T0189811

Communications
in Computer and Information Science 1424

More information about this series at http://www.springer.com/series/7899

Xingming Sun · Xiaorui Zhang ·
Zhihua Xia · Elisa Bertino (Eds.)

Advances in Artificial Intelligence and Security

7th International Conference, ICAIS 2021
Dublin, Ireland, July 19–23, 2021
Proceedings, Part III

 Springer

Editors
Xingming Sun 🄭
Nanjing University of Information Science
and Technology
Nanjing, China

Xiaorui Zhang 🄭
Nanjing University of Information Science
and Technology
Nanjing, China

Zhihua Xia 🄭
Jinan University
Guangzhou, China

Elisa Bertino 🄭
Purdue University
West Lafayette, IN, USA

ISSN 1865-0929   ISSN 1865-0937 (electronic)
Communications in Computer and Information Science
ISBN 978-3-030-78620-5   ISBN 978-3-030-78621-2   (eBook)
https://doi.org/10.1007/978-3-030-78621-2

This Springer imprint is published by the registered company Springer Nature Switzerland AG
The registered company address is: Gewerbestrasse 11, 6330 Cham, Switzerland

Preface

The 7th International Conference on Artificial Intelligence and Security (ICAIS 2021), formerly called the International Conference on Cloud Computing and Security (ICCCS), was held during July 19–23, 2021, in Dublin, Ireland. Over the past six years, ICAIS has become a leading conference for researchers and engineers to share their latest results of research, development, and applications in the fields of artificial intelligence and information security.

We used the Microsoft Conference Management Toolkits (CMT) system to manage the submission and review processes of ICAIS 2021. We received 1013 submissions from authors in 20 countries and regions, including the USA, Canada, the UK, Italy, Ireland, Japan, Russia, France, Australia, South Korea, South Africa, Iraq, Kazakhstan, Indonesia, Vietnam, Ghana, China, Taiwan, and Macao, etc. The submissions covered the areas of artificial intelligence, big data, cloud computing and security, information hiding, IoT security, multimedia forensics, encryption and cybersecurity, and so on. We thank our Technical Program Committee (TPC) members and external reviewers for their efforts in reviewing the papers and providing valuable comments to the authors. From the total of 1013 submissions, and based on at least three reviews per submission, the Program Chairs decided to accept 183 papers to be published in three Communications in Computer and Information Science (CCIS) volumes and 122 papers to be published in two Lecture Notes in Computer Science (LNCS) volumes, yielding an acceptance rate of 30%. This volume of the conference proceedings contains all the regular, poster, and workshop papers.

The conference program was enriched by a series of keynote presentations, and the keynote speakers included Michael Scott, MIRACL Labs, Ireland, and Sakir Sezer, Queen's University of Belfast, UK. We enjoyed their wonderful speeches.

There were 49 workshops organized as part of ICAIS 2021 which covered all the hot topics in artificial intelligence and security. We would like to take this moment to express our sincere appreciation for the contribution of all the workshop chairs and their participants. We would like to extend our sincere thanks to all authors who submitted papers to ICAIS 2021 and to all TPC members. It was a truly great experience to work with such talented and hard-working researchers. We also appreciate the external reviewers for assisting the TPC members in their particular areas of expertise. Moreover, we want to thank our sponsors: Association for Computing Machinery; Nanjing University of Information Science and Technology; Dublin City University; New York University; Michigan State University; University of Central Arkansas; Université Bretagne Sud; National Nature Science Foundation of China; Tech Science Press; Nanjing Normal University; Northeastern State University; Engineering

Research Center of Digital Forensics, Ministry of Education, China; and ACM SIGWEB China.

April 2021   Xingming Sun
Xiaorui Zhang
Zhihua Xia
Elisa Bertino

Organization

General Chairs

Martin Collier   Dublin City University, Ireland
Xingming Sun   Nanjing University of Information Science
     and Technology, China
Yun Q. Shi   New Jersey Institute of Technology, USA
Mauro Barni   University of Siena, Italy
Elisa Bertino   Purdue University, USA

Technical Program Chairs

Noel Murphy   Dublin City University, Ireland
Aniello Castiglione   University of Salerno, Italy
Yunbiao Guo   China Information Technology Security Evaluation
     Center, China
Suzanne K. McIntosh   New York University, USA
Xiaorui Zhang   Engineering Research Center of Digital Forensics,
     Ministry of Education, China
Q. M. Jonathan Wu   University of Windsor, Canada

Publication Chairs

Zhihua Xia   Nanjing University of Information Science
     and Technology, China
Zhaoqing Pan   Nanjing University of Information Science
     and Technology, China

Workshop Chair

Baowei Wang   Nanjing University of Information Science
     and Technology, China

Organization Chairs

Xiaojun Wang   Dublin City University, Ireland
Genlin Ji   Nanjing Normal University, China
Zhangjie Fu   Nanjing University of Information Science
     and Technology, China

Technical Program Committee Members

Saeed Arif	University of Algeria, Algeria
Anthony Ayodele	University of Maryland, USA
Zhifeng Bao	Royal Melbourne Institute of Technology, Australia
Zhiping Cai	National University of Defense Technology, China
Ning Cao	Qingdao Binhai University, China
Paolina Centonze	Iona College, USA
Chin-chen Chang	Feng Chia University, Taiwan, China
Han-Chieh Chao	Taiwan Dong Hwa University, Taiwan, China
Bing Chen	Nanjing University of Aeronautics and Astronautics, China
Hanhua Chen	Huazhong University of Science and Technology, China
Xiaofeng Chen	Xidian University, China
Jieren Cheng	Hainan University, China
Lianhua Chi	IBM Research Center, Australia
Kim-Kwang Raymond Choo	University of Texas at San Antonio, USA
Ilyong Chung	Chosun University, South Korea
Robert H. Deng	Singapore Management University, Singapore
Jintai Ding	University of Cincinnati, USA
Xinwen Fu	University of Central Florida, USA
Zhangjie Fu	Nanjing University of Information Science and Technology, China
Moncef Gabbouj	Tampere University of Technology, Finland
Ruili Geng	Spectral MD, USA
Song Guo	Hong Kong Polytechnic University, Hong Kong
Mohammad Mehedi Hassan	King Saud University, Saudi Arabia
Russell Higgs	University College Dublin, Ireland
Dinh Thai Hoang	University of Technology Sydney, Australia
Wien Hong	Nanfang College of Sun Yat-sen University, China
Chih-Hsien Hsia	National Ilan University, Taiwan, China
Robert Hsu	Chung Hua University, Taiwan, China
Xinyi Huang	Fujian Normal University, China
Yongfeng Huang	Tsinghua University, China
Zhiqiu Huang	Nanjing University of Aeronautics and Astronautics, China
Patrick C. K. Hung	University of Ontario Institute of Technology, Canada
Farookh Hussain	University of Technology Sydney, Australia
Genlin Ji	Nanjing Normal University, China
Hai Jin	Huazhong University of Science and Technology, China
Sam Tak Wu Kwong	City University of Hong Kong, China
Chin-Feng Lai	Taiwan Cheng Kung University, Taiwan, China
Loukas Lazos	University of Arizona, USA

Sungyoung Lee	Kyung Hee University, South Korea
Chengcheng Li	University of Cincinnati, USA
Feifei Li	Utah State University, USA
Jin Li	Guangzhou University, China
Jing Li	Rutgers University, USA
Kuan-Ching Li	Providence University, Taiwan, China
Peng Li	University of Aizu, Japan
Yangming Li	University of Washington, USA
Luming Liang	Uber Technology, USA
Haixiang Lin	Leiden University, Netherlands
Xiaodong Lin	University of Ontario Institute of Technology, Canada
Zhenyi Lin	Verizon Wireless, USA
Alex Liu	Michigan State University, USA
Guangchi Liu	Stratifyd Inc., USA
Guohua Liu	Donghua University, China
Joseph Liu	Monash University, Australia
Quansheng Liu	University of South Brittany, France
Xiaodong Liu	Edinburgh Napier University, UK
Yuling Liu	Hunan University, China
Zhe Liu	University of Waterloo, Canada
Daniel Xiapu Luo	Hong Kong Polytechnic University, Hong Kong
Xiangyang Luo	Zhengzhou Science and Technology Institute, China
Tom Masino	TradeWeb LLC, USA
Suzanne K. McIntosh	New York University, USA
Nasir Memon	New York University, USA
Sangman Moh	Chosun University, South Korea
Yi Mu	University of Wollongong, Australia
Elie Naufal	Applied Deep Learning LLC, USA
Jiangqun Ni	Sun Yat-sen University, China
Rafal Niemiec	University of Information Technology and Management, Poland
Zemin Ning	Wellcome Trust Sanger Institute, UK
Shaozhang Niu	Beijing University of Posts and Telecommunications, China
Srikant Ojha	Sharda University, India
Jeff Z. Pan	University of Aberdeen, UK
Wei Pang	University of Aberdeen, UK
Chen Qian	University of California, Santa Cruz, USA
Zhenxing Qian	Fudan University, China
Chuan Qin	University of Shanghai for Science and Technology, China
Jiaohua Qin	Central South University of Forestry and Technology, China
Yanzhen Qu	Colorado Technical University, USA
Zhiguo Qu	Nanjing University of Information Science and Technology, China

Yongjun Ren	Nanjing University of Information Science and Technology, China
Arun Kumar Sangaiah	VIT University, India
Di Shang	Long Island University, USA
Victor S. Sheng	University of Central Arkansas, USA
Zheng-guo Sheng	University of Sussex, UK
Robert Simon Sherratt	University of Reading, UK
Yun Q. Shi	New Jersey Institute of Technology, USA
Frank Y. Shih	New Jersey Institute of Technology, USA
Biao Song	King Saud University, Saudi Arabia
Guang Sun	Hunan University of Finance and Economics, China
Jianguo Sun	Harbin University of Engineering, China
Krzysztof Szczypiorski	Warsaw University of Technology, Poland
Tsuyoshi Takagi	Kyushu University, Japan
Shanyu Tang	University of West London, UK
Jing Tian	National University of Singapore, Singapore
Yoshito Tobe	Aoyang University, Japan
Cezhong Tong	Washington University in St. Louis, USA
Pengjun Wan	Illinois Institute of Technology, USA
Cai-Zhuang Wang	Ames Laboratory, USA
Ding Wang	Peking University, China
Guiling Wang	New Jersey Institute of Technology, USA
Honggang Wang	University of Massachusetts Dartmouth, USA
Jian Wang	Nanjing University of Aeronautics and Astronautics, China
Jie Wang	University of Massachusetts Lowell, USA
Jin Wang	Changsha University of Science and Technology, China
Liangmin Wang	Jiangsu University, China
Ruili Wang	Massey University, New Zealand
Xiaojun Wang	Dublin City University, Ireland
Xiaokang Wang	St. Francis Xavier University, Canada
Zhaoxia Wang	A-Star, Singapore
Sheng Wen	Swinburne University of Technology, Australia
Jian Weng	Jinan University, China
Edward Wong	New York University, USA
Eric Wong	University of Texas at Dallas, USA
Shaoen Wu	Ball State University, USA
Shuangkui Xia	Beijing Institute of Electronics Technology and Application, China
Lingyun Xiang	Changsha University of Science and Technology, China
Yang Xiang	Deakin University, Australia
Yang Xiao	University of Alabama, USA
Haoran Xie	The Education University of Hong Kong, China
Naixue Xiong	Northeastern State University, USA

Wei Qi Yan	Auckland University of Technology, New Zealand
Aimin Yang	Guangdong University of Foreign Studies, China
Ching-Nung Yang	Taiwan Dong Hwa University, Taiwan, China
Chunfang Yang	Zhengzhou Science and Technology Institute, China
Fan Yang	University of Maryland, USA
Guomin Yang	University of Wollongong, Australia
Qing Yang	University of North Texas, USA
Yimin Yang	Lakehead University, Canada
Ming Yin	Purdue University, USA
Shaodi You	Australian National University, Australia
Kun-Ming Yu	Chung Hua University, Taiwan, China
Weiming Zhang	University of Science and Technology of China, China
Xinpeng Zhang	Fudan University, China
Yan Zhang	Simula Research Laboratory, Norway
Yanchun Zhang	Victoria University, Australia
Yao Zhao	Beijing Jiaotong University, China

Organization Committee Members

Xianyi Chen	Nanjing University of Information Science and Technology, China
Zilong Jin	Nanjing University of Information Science and Technology, China
Yiwei Li	Columbia University, USA
Yuling Liu	Hunan University, China
Zhiguo Qu	Nanjing University of Information Science and Technology, China
Huiyu Sun	New York University, USA
Le Sun	Nanjing University of Information Science and Technology, China
Jian Su	Nanjing University of Information Science and Technology, China
Qing Tian	Nanjing University of Information Science and Technology, China
Yuan Tian	King Saud University, Saudi Arabia
Qi Wang	Nanjing University of Information Science and Technology, China
Lingyun Xiang	Changsha University of Science and Technology, China
Zhihua Xia	Nanjing University of Information Science and Technology, China
Lizhi Xiong	Nanjing University of Information Science and Technology, China

Leiming Yan   Nanjing University of Information Science
                           and Technology, China
Li Yu   Nanjing University of Information Science
                           and Technology, China
Zhili Zhou   Nanjing University of Information Science
                           and Technology, China

Contents – Part III

Information Hiding

IoT Security

Cloud Computing and Security

Design and Implementation of Information Detection System Based on Privacy Sensitive Data

Jiazhen Che[1], Chong Zhang[2], Xiao Xing[2], and Xiangzhan Yu[1(✉)]

[1] School of Cyberspace Science, Harbin Institute of Technology, Harbin 150001, China
yxz@hit.edu.cn
[2] National Computer Network Emergency Response Technical Team/Coordination Center of China, Beijing 100032, China

Abstract. In recent years, with the development of network technology, network applications and network transmission protocols emerge one after another. Although a growing awareness for the protection of private data, network applications and transmission protocol is to protect user privacy data by using various methods, but there are still a part of the application or web access to user data is not to make any protective measures, its may cause the user's private data during transmission cause leaks, have serious consequences. This paper mainly studies the detection of private data by collecting data traffic in the network, analyzing the content, and determining whether the data is encrypted during the transmission process. A private data detection system including traffic capture, data processing, protocol analysis and regular matching is implemented. At the same time, some technical methods are used to optimize and innovate all parts of the system.

This paper will briefly introduce the current development trend of network information security, and briefly describe the implementation of each part of the whole system, each part will be described from the functional introduction, specific implementation, and finally through some test samples and the results of the system function test analysis.

Keywords: Privacy data · Traffic capture · Transport protocol · Winpcap · Regular expressions

1 Introduction

In the rapid development of network security technology today, from the technical level, the current network security technology and products are facing the main aspect of the problem is that we should pay more attention to the application level of security protection. Today, the network information security research has experienced the communication security, data protection two stages, and is entering the network information security research stage, such as the development of firewall, security gateway, intrusion detection system, etc., and the current security agreement, modern cryptography theory, and other research will form a organic whole, become the key to the development of

© Springer Nature Switzerland AG 2021
X. Sun et al. (Eds.): ICAIS 2021, CCIS 1424, pp. 3–16, 2021.
https://doi.org/10.1007/978-3-030-78621-2_1

information network technology. The relatively rapid development is for the network structure of the network layer, application layer protocol, for example, early HTTP, TCP, IP, etc., to prevent data breaches, gradually produced a variety of security protocols such as HTTPS, SSL, IPSec protocol family, etc., its implementation mainly through encryption and authentication data protection, effectively avoid the information leak, tampering with such attacks.

But nowadays there are still many problems, most mainstream browser Google browser, for example, if a user query, given the browser page order has certain differences, namely, such as using the HTTPS protocol would be preferred, although this part of information security, but did not effectively prompt the user some requires users to enter information website whether or not to use the security protocols in the transport. For this problem, we will implement a detection system for private data. If it is found that some types of private data are not encrypted during transmission, it will prompt the user. For the traffic capture part, we will use a passive packet catcher program to achieve the capture of network packets. For the protocol analysis part, we will extract the protocol type field, quaternion (source IP address, destination IP address, source port number, destination port number), load part of the content and store it. The data matching part matches the payload part of the packet based on the constructed regular expression, detects the existence of several private data listed and is encrypted, and prompts the user for risks in the transmission process.

At present, the Internet environment is undergoing a series of changes, mainly reflected in the wireless network, mobile phones become a new attack area; spam is more serious; system vulnerabilities, network vulnerabilities, software vulnerabilities are found and exploited by attackers for a shorter time; DoS attacks are more frequent and covert, and it is difficult to trace the attackers. At present, network security technology mainly includes network firewall technology: it is set between networks, as a security barrier between networks, to ensure the security of local network resources, through the screening of data flow through the firewall to audit and control the service and access to the internal network, and strengthen the internal security; IDS: intrusion detection system provides Real time protection of internal attack, external attack and misoperation, alarm, intercept and respond before or during computer network and system intrusion; encryption technology: encryption technology can effectively solve network file theft or tampering attacks, for the network layer, transport layer, application layer have corresponding different encryption methods, such as SSL, HTTPS, IPSec protocol Access control technology: access control refers to the different authorized access of the subject to the object itself or resources according to some control policies or permissions. At the same time, security technology and safety management are inseparable, and they need to coordinate, promote and promote each other. Even with a complete security equipment and system, if there is no complete system of security management measures and implementation, it can not guarantee the existence of a good security network environment. Therefore, the improvement of the legal system of network information security and the use of privacy data norms is the focus of future development.

2 Related Work

The research content of this paper is to capture network data packets by passive packet capture program, extract data through protocol analysis, and analyze and combine the data to determine whether these information will leak the user's privacy sensitive information in the process of transmission. Because HTTP protocol is plaintext transmission in the process of transmission, users may be stolen and used when entering their own identity information or password in the web page when they are transmitted to the server. However, there is no systematic software or plug-in to verify the security of information transmission in the process of network transmission. Therefore, in addition to security protocols, the development of information detection system has extremely important practical significance.

The WinPcap tool is used to achieve multithreading packet capture, and four tuples are obtained by analyzing the packet, namely: source port number, destination port number, source IP address, destination IP address and its text load part. In order to determine whether to disclose user privacy sensitive data, it is necessary to list different types of privacy data formats and forms. Different types of privacy data are matched by matching methods such as regular syntax rules, and multiple rules are matched simultaneously by constructing matching rules, and combination discrimination is made to judge that some privacy data can be associated.

At present, most web pages are transmitted by HTTPS, the security protocol. Even if the data is intercepted during transmission, encryption and other methods can prevent the data obtained by attackers from being directly used or read. On the basis of some research web site source code, learn about the part of the page, contains the part of the login screen, registration screen, etc., which requires the user to type in information of web pages, still choose HTTP transport in transmission application layer protocol, while using the HTTP protocol to transmit information in the form of plaintext, so it is easy to cause the leak of information, the user privacy data is extremely irresponsible. The purpose of this paper is to design and implement a detection system. If the data is not encrypted or transmitted without security protocol, it will prompt the user of the risk, enhance the user's vigilance, and reduce the possibility of privacy disclosure.

In the past, much of the work has been focused on one layer, but the method described in this paper will simultaneously detect multiple layers of different protocol data, such as application layer and transport layer. In terms of network protocol parsing, we will propose a new protocol parsing and data processing process by improving the original method. The new processing method will improve the efficiency of protocol solution and data processing, and avoid the leakage of private data, that is, the working efficiency of the whole process will not be reduced when working in the encrypted traffic.

In data recognition, because the method USES the regular grammar rules to identify different types of data, so can't identify the encrypted data in the data identification, this module will work in clear text, although this will enhance the accuracy in data recognition, but there will be data reveal that risk, so the work will be in protecting data confidentiality and integrity to make improvements.

In the network traffic identification method, in Yi Can's paper proposes a time-enhanced traffic identification method based on Bayesian model. Firstly, the original traffic data is preprocessed to obtain the training subset of the data flow, and then a classifier is established, through which the traffic objects are identified.

In 2019, Yuan's paper combining the two scenarios of abnormal traffic identification and application traffic identification, the key technologies of encrypted network traffic analysis are studied. In this paper, LightTGBM algorithm is applied for the first time and good results are achieved.

In 2016, Wu's paper the deep learning technology is used to study the identification of P2P traffic, and an improved model that can accurately identify the normal P2P traffic and P2P botnet traffic is designed and implemented.

In 2014, Wang's paper on the basis of the traditional port classification method, the popular self-adaptive deep learning mechanism is introduced, and the self-organizing mapping network algorithm is used to achieve reasonable network traffic classification.

3 Packet Capture

The high-speed data packet capture module sends the received data packets uniformly to the independent receiving queue through the network card driver. Each queue corresponds to an independent data cache area in the upper layer, and each data cache area is processed directly by a separate CPU core to realize the parallel receiving and processing of data packets.

3.1 Passive Trap Program

This article uses the Winpcap tool to capture network raw packets. Winpcap, derived from Berkeley Packet capture, intercepts and filters the underlying packets on the Windows operating platform. It is divided into three parts: the first module, NPF, is a virtual device driver file. Its function is to filter packets and send them to the user mode module intact, including some operating system-specific code. The second module, Packet.dll, provides a common interface for win32. Different versions of Windows have their own kernel module and user layer module. Packet.dll is used to address these differences. Programs that invoke Packet. dll can run on different versions of Windows without recompiling. The third module, WPCap.dll, is OS independent. It provides higher-level, abstract functions.

The specific capture process can be roughly divided into the following steps:

(a) Open the network card of the device and set it to hybrid mode. Pcap_findalldevs () was called to get the list of devices. Pcap_open_live () selected the network card device and opened it. The parameter was set to 1, which was hybrid mode, and all frames flowing through the network card were captured.
(b) After the callback function Network Tap obtains the listening command, it collects the data packets from the Network device driver and transfers the monitored data packets to the filter program. Call the Pcap_loop () loop trap.
(c) Packet filter listening to a Packet arrives, the NDIS intermediate driver first call Packet driver, pass the data to the program each participate in the process of Packet filtering process, the Packet filter filtration process determines which packets should

be discarded, which Packet should receive, will need to receive the data copied to the corresponding application, namely call pcap_compile (), pcap_setfilter () function filter filter conditions were set up and compile code and set into the system.

(d) After passing the packet filter, submit the data packet that has not been filtered out to the core buffer, wait for the system buffer to be full, and then copy the data packet to the user buffer. The listener can directly read the captured data packet from the user buffer.

(e) After the capture and read process is completed, close the network card and the program is finished.

3.2 Thread Pooling and Multithreading

In order to improve the efficiency of packet capture, processing and parsing protocol and throughput rate, this paper adopts thread pool technology to implement packet capture. Thread pool that create a thread and thread management of containers, and multithreading technology mainly solve the problem of multiple threads executing within the processor unit, can significantly reduce the idle time processor unit, the reuse of existing threads, reduce the overhead of thread creation and destruction, effectively control the maximum number of concurrent threads, improve the utilization of system resource and the capacity of processor unit. Where, the processing flow of the packet is:

(a) Receive packets from the network card and parse them one by one to obtain load and header information, quad information (i.e., source IP address, destination IP address, source port number, destination port number), etc.

(b) In order to balance the load, a queue index table is assigned to each receiving processing core during initialization, and the quaternion information is hashed and numbered.

(c) According to the queue number, find the corresponding distribution queue to send packets to the queue and process them.

3.3 Zero-Copy Technology and DPDK

Traditional standard I/O interface of the operating system is based on the data copy operations, including I/O operations can lead to data in the operating system kernel address space buffer and the application of the definition of address space buffer between transmission, but in the process of data transmission data copy operation caused great CPU overhead, limiting the ability of the operating system is effective for data transfer operation. Zero-copy technology improves data transfer performance by preventing the CPU from copying data from one storage to another. Zero-copy technologies for device drivers, file systems, and network protocol stacks in operating systems have greatly improved the performance of specific applications, enabling them to utilize system resources more efficiently. In addition, zero-copy technology can reduce the number of data copy and Shared bus operation, eliminate the unnecessary number of intermediate copies of data transmission between storage, and improve the efficiency of data transmission.

Zero-copy technology focus on and reduce data back and forth in the user mode and kernel mode copy, one way is to call mmap () instead of the read (), the application calls the mmap (), the data on the disk will be copied into the kernel through the DMA buffer, then the operating system will this period of kernel and application sharing, don't need to copy the contents of the kernel buffer to the user space. The application then copies the contents of the kernel buffer into the socket buffer through a call to Write (), all in kernel state. When the amount of copied data is large, the efficiency is greatly improved.

DPDK, or data plane development suite, is mainly run on Linux system, mainly used for fast data packet processing function library and driver collection, which greatly improves data processing performance and throughput and the work efficiency of data plane applications. DPDK USES polling to process data packets. When the data packets are received, the NETWORK card driver overloaded by DPDK will not notify THE CPU through the terminal, but directly store the data packets into memory, and deliver the application layer software to process the data packets directly through the interface provided by DPDK, so as to save the CPU interrupt time and memory copy time, thus improving the work efficiency.

4 Protocol Parsing

4.1 TCP Protocol Parsing

TCP, or Transmission Control Protocol, is a connection-oriented, reliable, byte stream based transport protocol located at the transport layer. TCP is a hierarchical protocol hierarchy that ADAPTS to and supports multi-network applications. It is connected to the paired processes of the main computer in different interconnected computer communication networks and relies on TCP to provide reliable communication services. The TCP protocol encapsulates the data in THE TCP datagram, including THE TCP header information and payload, as well as the content format and length of the header information. The payload part encapsulates the upper-layer protocol data, such as HTTP message, SMTP protocol message, and so on. The header information contains address information, that is, the source port number and the destination port number, respectively marking the specific process. In the underlying PROTOCOL IP protocol, the source IP address and the destination IP address mark the two hosts respectively. When parsing A TCP message, it is necessary to extract the quad in the header information and its load.

The header structure of TCP protocol is shown in the Fig. 1 below.

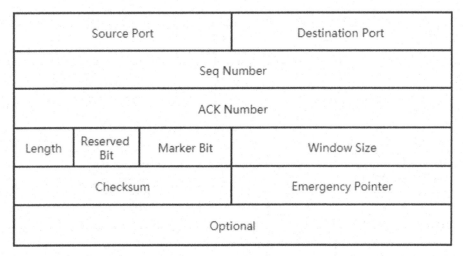

Source Port				Destination Port
Seq Number				
ACK Number				
Length	Reserved Bit	Marker Bit		Window Size
Checksum				Emergency Pointer
Optional				

Fig. 1. The header structure of a TCP packet

4.2 HTTP Protocol Parsing

The HTTP protocol, or hypertext Transfer Protocol, is a transport protocol used to transfer text from the server to the local browser. It is located in the application layer and consists of request messages and response messages. The model is the client server model. The main processes for handling HTTP flows are as follows:

(a) After the TCP flow is determined, the identification information of HTTP, such as the protocol type field in the packet header information, shall be used to determine whether it is an HTTP protocol. If it is HTTP, the TCP stream is retained and the packet is analyzed or dropped.

(b) If it is determined that the flow is the HTTP protocol, then continue to analyze the HTTP header information. For response and request data packets, the information of request line and response line is analyzed respectively, and the URL and response code are extracted. For the response packet, each header field of the header is judged separately and the corresponding value is extracted. Records are saved for fields related to content analysis and their values such as content-type, content-length, etc.

(c) Extract the HTTP content according to the header field information after stripping the HTTP header. The hyperlink content can be extracted directly; For the content of special format or special code such as DOC, PPT, PNG, etc., it may be processed later or discarded directly.

Its flow chart is shown in the Fig. 2

For the blocking mode of HTTP protocol, all HTTP protocol flows that are not visiting the whitelist are reset, packet loss or jump are blocked in an emergency state, and the access whitelist traffic is accurately released.

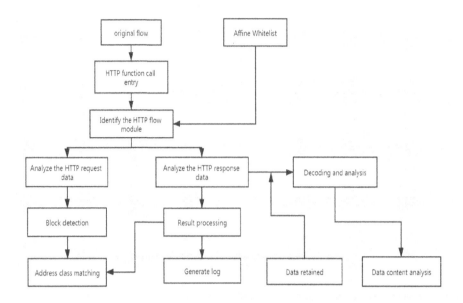

Fig. 2. The process of processing and analyzing HTTP packets

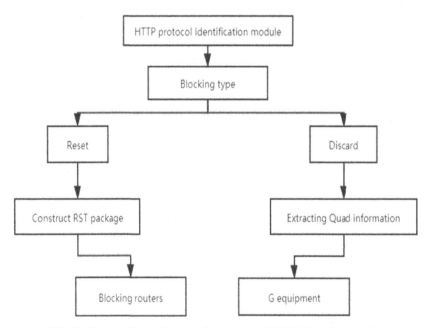

Fig. 3. The specific implementation process of HTTP blocking module

The HTTP protocol blocking module is called by the HTTP protocol identification module, and the HTTP protocol identification module calls the blocking module according to the returned results of content matching. The important role of the HTTP protocol blocking module is to interrupt or pollute the non whitelist transmitted in the HTTP protocol and the related hyperlink content of the white list. HTTP blocking can be divided into three situations, as shown in the following Fig. 3:

(1) Reset: according to the four tuples identified by the HTTP protocol and the serial number, the RST packet is constructed and sent to the blocking router.
(2) Jump: construct a fake HTTP jump response package according to the incoming four tuple and sequence number information, in which the HTTP header response code is set to 301, and the URL information to jump is added after the location header field. The packet is sent by the blocking router.
(3) Packet loss: the quad information is given to the special device, which directly discards the data packets between the quads within a period of time.

5 Identification of Private Data

5.1 Private Data Type

Under the GDPR, the General Data Protection Ordinance, the following personal data are considered as sensitive data: race or ethnic origin, political views, religious beliefs, data relating to health, genetic data, and identifiable data that can be processed to identify specific individuals. This paper mainly focuses on the identification data of specific individuals. Based on the investigation and statistics of most web sites that obtain user information, this paper summarizes the types and formats of privacy data that are frequently transmitted in the network.

(a) Chinese mainland citizen ID number: According to the Citizen Id Number issued by the State Administration of Quality and Technical Supervision, the id standard is 18 digits, consisting of 17 digits and a 1-digit check code, that is, 6-digit address code, 8-digit birth date code, 3-digit sequence code and 1-digit check code.
(b) Mobile phone Numbers in mainland China: The standard for mobile phone Numbers is to consist of 11 digits from 0 to 9, some of which need to be preceded by the character "086" to represent mainland China, and the rest of which need to be preceded by the number 1 as the first digit in the string.
(c) Postal code: The provincial and municipal address information can be obtained from the postal code. It adopts a four-digit code structure, with the first two digits representing the province, the first three digits representing the postal area, and the first four digits representing the city or county. The complete zip code information consists of six Arabic digits.
(d) Email address: This paper lists several commonly used email address formats, such as QQ email, 163 email, sina email, etc., which are composed of strings such as Numbers, letters, underscore, and flags such as "@qq.com", "@163.com", "@sina.com", etc.

5.2 Constructing Regular Expressions

Match Pattern. The matching module is divided into pattern string set and text string input, which correspond to each configuration file in the configuration management module, and text string input pairs the formatting information of various user privacy data that should be resolved in real time from the traffic. In particular, configuration processing is to complete the loading of local configuration files and notify the matching module to have configuration updates. The data inputs for configuration management are configuration files and configuration update signals, and the input data comes from the messaging network distribution subsystem. Configuration management is also responsible for listening to the local loopback interface and constructing new automata with new configuration files if they are updated. The corresponding functional requirements of configuration management module are scattered in various protocols of communication record class and communication interrupt class, as well as providing real-time matching functions for various user privacy data rules. The specific process of configuration is roughly as follows:

(a) Update the configuration file.
(b) Integrity checking of configuration files.
(c) Load the configuration file.
(d) Construct an automaton from a configuration file.

Construction Pattern String. A regular expression, that is, a predefined string of specific characters or combinations of specific characters that are formed to express filtering logic for the string to be matched. Since the regular rules provided by different kinds of programming languages vary, this article USES the regular syntax rules provided by the Java language to construct regular expressions.

(a) According to Sect. 4.1, the pattern string of the ID card number and other information can be obtained by the second generation id card number encoding method as follows:

$$regular\ expression = ([0-9]\{17\})([0-9]|X) \tag{1}$$

(b) According to the coding method of mobile phone Numbers in mainland China, the corresponding regular pattern string can be identified as follows:

$$regular\ expression = \begin{cases} (086-)(1)([0-9]\{10\}) & Begin\ with\ 086 \\ (1)([0-9]\{10\}) & Not\ beginning\ with\ 086 \end{cases} \tag{2}$$

(c) Error-prone because the post code is relatively simple, recognition, therefore in the process of identification need to add a special string prefix, namely according to special information load of transmission usually add logo, such as content contains the post code, post code before the identity of the generally contains the content, such as post or post match pattern string form of the post code is:

$$regular\ expression = [0-9]\{6\} \tag{3}$$

(d) The pattern string for identifying a mailbox address is:

$$regular\ expression =$$
$$^\wedge([a-zA-Z0-9])^*(@)(qq|126|sina|163)(.com|.cn) \qquad (4)$$

Multidomain Combination Matching. Multi-domain combinatorial matching, that is, through the construction of a more complex regular expression to identify the multiple listed privacy data types carried in the response message. In addition, by using a quad information, namely the source IP address, destination IP address, source port, the port USES Hash way quad mapping into a fixed string as a unique identifier of the data packets, each packet all have their own identity by comparing the logo can judge whether different packets from the same host, whether connect the same server, if the quad shows have the same identity of packets from the same user input, if the user input many times of different types of data privacy, privacy is likely to occur.

6 Evaluation

6.1 Module Test

The system test will be carried out under Windows 7 system by selecting some web pages that require users to enter information, such as account application page of some platforms, login page, etc. The test is divided into several parts:

(a) Packet capture test: The text selects the account application page of Amazon website, and the information to be filled in includes account name, mobile phone number, email address and password. At the end of the whole process, the data packets were filtered to obtain a total of 32 HTTP packets, and the data was written into the specified file for matching recognition by the matching module.

(b) Privacy data matching test: through reading load information in the file, through multi-domain combination matching and identification detection of quaternion mapping, it can be obtained that multiple data packets are response packets sent by the same host to the same server, so it can be judged as multiple data packets; The data information from the same user is combined with all the collected information to generate the combination of mobile phone number and E-mail address information, and prompt the user that the web page has security risks.

The test also selects the login interface of Super Star Erya and QQ mailbox, and the results are similar to the above test cases, which will not be repeated.

These data are summarized in the following tables.

Table 1 shows the number of HTTP and TCP packets collected by different sites, these sites include the Amazon, Super Star Erya, QQ mailbox and so on. As we can see in Table 1, the majority of TCP packets are collected.

Table 2 shows the number of useful package, that is to say the number of package which contains the following information such as name, phone number, ID card number,

Table 1. The number of packets captured by different websites

Website Name	HTTP Package	TCP Package
Amazon	32	179
Super Star Erya	48	89
QQ mailbox	19	112

Table 2. Target data packets and recognition accuracy of different websites

Website Name	Uesful Package	Accuracy Rate
Amazon	10	82.4%
Super Star Erya	19	91.2%
QQ mailbox	38	79.6%

post number and so on. The accuracy rate of the last column refers to the correct identification and classification of the mentioned packets containing private information. From the accuracy of the last column, it can be seen that the system can identify data packets containing privacy information and their websites with high accuracy, and remind users of the risks.

6.2 Performance Comparison

In packet capture module, through the way of using thread pool scheduling, improved memory utilization, and reasonable arrangement of packet capture and processing of the data, this test will show who did not use the thread pool scheduling under 50 packets capture time and use a thread pool used by scheduling after the capture of 50 packets as well as the data processing time.

(a) Unused thread pool: The run time is recorded through the currentTimeMillis() provided by Java, and the packet processing time is 17 ms without scheduling.
(b) Use of thread pool scheduling: Running the program with multithreading results in a packet processing time of 5.4 ms, with an efficiency increase of approximately 3.1 times.

7 Conclusion

In this paper, a detection system based on privacy data is designed and implemented in Windows system. By capturing and analyzing network data traffic, the identification of user privacy data type is realized and multi-domain combination matching is achieved through regular expression, which prompts users to realize the function that some web pages may leak user privacy. In the process of implementing the system, it is divided into three parts: packet capture, protocol parsing and private data matching. Each part is separately implemented and three modules are merged to complete the preset functions.

Funding Statement. Supported by National Key R&D Program of China (2017YFC1201204).

Conflicts of Interest. The authors declare that they have no conflicts of interest to report regarding the present study.

References

1. Choi, J., Oh, H., Ullah, S.: IPsec for high speed network links: performance analysis and enhancements. Future Gener. Comput. Syst. (2020)
2. Zhao, J., Hu, Z.: Modeling and optimization of packet forwarding performance processing in software-defined WAN. Netw. Weekly News **3** (2020)
3. Sakharov, A.: Annotated regular expressions and input-driven languages. Inf. Process. Lett. (2020)
4. Vaithyasubramanian, S., Christy, A.: ATM PIN generation - a formal mathematical model to generate PIN using regular grammar, context free grammar and recognition through finite state machine, pushdown automata. Int. J. Internet Protocol Technol. (2019)
5. Sui, J., Xie, P., Lin, Z., Javanmard, M.: Electronic classification of barcoded particles for multiplexed detection using supervised machine learning analysis. Talanta **215**, 120791 (2020). https://doi.org/10.1016/j.talanta.2020.120791
6. Mathew, S.E., Pauline, A.: HTTP botnet defense mechanism using system dynamics based genetic algorithm. Indian J. Sci. Technol. (2016)
7. Zeng, P., Tan, Q., Meng, X., Shao, Z., Xie, Q.: A multi-pattern hash-binary hybrid algorithm for URL matching in the HTTP protocol. PLOS ONE (2017)
8. Luthfi, F., Juanda, E.A., Kustiawan, I.: Optimization of data communication on air control device based on internet of things with application of HTTP and MQTT protocols. In: IOP Conference Series: Materials Science and Engineering (2018)
9. Idhammad, M., Afdel, K., Belouch, M., Li, H.: Detection system of HTTP DDoS attacks in a cloud environment based on information theoretic entropy and random forest. Secur. Commun. Netw. (2018)
10. Hubballi, N., Santini, J.: Detecting TCP ACK storm attack: a state transition modelling approach. IET Netw. (2018)
11. Bhattacharjya, A., Zhong, X., Wang, J.: An end-to-end user two-way authenticated double encrypted messaging scheme based on hybrid RSA for the future internet architectures. Int. J. Inf. Comput. Secur. (2018)
12. Huang, K., Wang, K., Zheng, D., Zhang, X., Yan, X.: Access adaptive and thread-aware cache partitioning in multicore systems. Electronics (2018)
13. Li, J., Peng, D., Wei, Y.: Networked robot identification technology for multi objects based on RFID-ZigBee. In: IOP Conference Series: Materials Science and Engineering (2018)

14. Zheng, W., Xia, F., Yang, C., Zhang, M., Chen, L.Y.: Implementation and applications of a new real-time framework for plasma control system in HL-2A. Fusion Eng. Des. (2018)
15. Ghafoor, M., Iqbal, S., Tariq, S.A., Taj, I.A., Jafri, N.M.: Efficient fingerprint matching using GPU. IET Image Process. (2018)
16. Tahir, M., Sardaraz, M., Ikram, A.A.: EPMA: efficient pattern matching algorithm for DNA sequences. Expert Syst. Appl. (2017)
17. Cong, T.D., Yong, C., Myon, K.J., Hong, K.C.: A novel cooperative warp and thread block scheduling technique for improving the GPGPU resource utilization. KIPS Trans. Comput. Commun. Syst. (2017)
18. Xie, C., Tan, J., Chen, M., Yi, Y., Peng, L.: Emerging technology enabled energy-efficient GPGPUs register file. Microprocess. Microsyst. (2017)
19. Pan, L., Cheng, C., Haberkorn, U., Dimitrakopoulou-Strauss, A.: Machine learning-based kinetic modeling: a robust and reproducible solution for quantitative analysis of dynamic PET data. Phys. Med. Biol. (2017)
20. Gummadidala, K.R., Jeya, R.: Creating web server in Android mobile and easy serving of information to clients. Indian J. Sci. Technol. (2016)
21. Zhu, L., Huang, L., Fu, P., Gao, G., He, S.: Upgrade of the synchronous data management system of the EAST poloidal field power supply. Fusion Eng. Des. (2016)
22. Hu, Z., Shi, T.: The design and implementation of motor control system monitoring software based on WPF. Hans J. Wirel. Commun. (2016)
23. Chen, H., Yang, Y.: Program transmission method of PLC equipments' remote monitoring software based on virtual serial port. Comput. Sci. Appl. (2016)
24. Jabal, S., Ung-arunyawee, R.: Performance improvement of developed program by using multi-thread technique. KKU Eng. J. (2015)
25. Cui, X.M., Zheng, K., Liu, C.R., Zheng, Q.: Multi-threaded technology apply in real time measurement system of dual-camera. Appl. Mech. Mater. (2015)
26. Goik, D., Sieniek, M., Gurgul, P., Paszyński, M.: Modeling of the absorption of the electromagnetic wave energy in the human head induced by cell phone. J. Appl. Math. Phys. (2015)

Performance Modeling of OpenMP Program Based on LLVM Compilation Platform

Chen Yang, Xiangzhan Yu$^{(\boxtimes)}$, and Yue Zhao

School of Cyberspace Science, Harbin Institute of Technology, Harbin 150001, China
yxz@hit.edu.cn

Abstract. With the rapid development of computers and their technologies, high-performance computers (HPC) have gradually become one of the indispensable research methods in the field of basic science. However, with the development of HPC, its scale and complexity have also increased by orders of magnitude, which lead to problems such as high execution efficiency and energy consumption of parallel applications in the HPC system. So it brings many challenges to parallel programming. In order to solve the above situation, the mechanism needs to be proposed, which can predict the performance characteristics of parallel programs before they are executed. Therefore, parallel program performance prediction is the key to solving the above problems. OpenMP program is the most common shared memory parallel program, so it is an important part of the research of parallel program performance evaluation. This article uses the LLVM compilation platform to convert the OpenMP source code into LLVM intermediate code (IR) through Clang, statically and dynamically analyzes the IR, and then obtains the OpenMP performance model to predict the OpenMP execution time and optimal execution time. Based on the modeling of OpenMP parallel applications, we can get the performance model of the OpenMP program. Based on this model, we can predict the performance and scalability of OpenMP-related applications in HPC systems, find program and system bottlenecks, and guide program performance optimization.

Keywords: HPC · OpenMP parallel program · LLVM compilation platform · Static analysis · Dynamic analysis · Performance modeling · Scalability prediction

1 Introduction

Since the beginning of the 21st century, the scale of computing has grown exponentially and computer technology has developed rapidly, so high-performance computers (HPC) have become one of the powerful and effective auxiliary research methods in many basic sciences. In order to cater to various fields with super-large-scale computing strength, the performance of HPC is gradually improving, and its computing speed is developing from P-level to E-level. The HPC system mainly provides storage and computing services for actual applications, so its actual performance indicators are not only related to the HPC hardware architecture, but also affected by the degree of adaptation of the application to

© Springer Nature Switzerland AG 2021
X. Sun et al. (Eds.): ICAIS 2021, CCIS 1424, pp. 17–30, 2021.
https://doi.org/10.1007/978-3-030-78621-2_2

the HPC. However, as HPC systems develop towards E-level computers, the complexity and scale of HPC will certainly increase by orders of magnitude, such as the number of HPC nodes, the internet speed and storage systems. These changes will bring many changes and challenges to the programming of parallel programs.

The current reality is that the execution efficiency and acceleration of many parallel programs in HPC are relatively low, which This also shows that most parallel programs are not well adapted to HPC and do not make full use of HPC's hardware computing resources. This is a waste of resources for both users and HPC. Users will spend too much application resource fees. HPC will also cause waste of system resources and energy consumption.

In the face of the above problems, we need a method to estimate the execution time of parallel programs on HPC and how to make parallel programs have the best execution efficiency on HPC. Therefore, performance evaluation of parallel applications is the key to solving the above problems. OpenMP parallel programs are very commonly used parallel programs with shared memory as the mechanism, so the prediction of OpenMP parallel programs is an important direction for parallel application performance evaluation.

Based on the OpenMP parallel application, the performance model of the OpenMP program can be performed to obtain the performance model of the OpenMP program, which can predict the execution time of the OpenMP program. It is unrealistic to put any OpenMP program on a large-scale HPC system, so the approach in this article is to use an existing small-scale HPC subsystem with a consistent architecture with the HPC system. We run the OpenMP program on this subsystem for performance prediction, that is, scalability prediction.

When the performance model of the program is built, the scalability analysis of the model is performed so that we can Predict the best execution efficiency of the program on the HPC system. In this way, the degree of adaptation of the OpenMP program and HPC can be obtained, and the execution disadvantage of the program can be found.

In summary, OpenMP parallel application modeling and scalability analysis plays an important role in HPC system design and evaluation, performance optimization of parallel applications, and reasonable allocation of system resources. It can effectively promote the development and application of HPC systems.

The paper is organized as follows: Sect. 2 presents the related work. Section 3 introduces LLVM compilation platform. In Sect. 4, the OpenMP program modeling method based on LLVM is proposed and also introduce the key technologies. Some experimental data will be given in Sect. 5. Finally, we summarize the research in Sect. 6 with a discussion of the future.

2   Related Work

The work of this paper is to perform performance modeling and prediction of OpenMP programs. The performance modeling of the OpenMP program can be inspired by the performance analysis of the OpenMP program. At present, there are mainly two methods of instrumentation and measurement for the performance analysis of OpenMP programs. The first method is instrumentation, instrumentation means inserting additional instructions or probes into the source program. It can be instrumented in different compilation periods so that it can allow the program to perform additional functions. Its purpose is to be able to observe various types of performance events during program execution. The instrumentation interface is PAPI [2]. Typical tools are RIOT [3], Pablo [4], Vampir [5], Valgrind [6]. Another method is measurement. Measurement is to calculate various performance data from statistics to solve performance problems. In the implementation process, the additional cost of measurement to the program should be considered. Measurement methods are mainly divided into two categories: profiling and tracing. The main tools are TAU [7], VTune [8], HPCTooklkit [9], Gprof [10], Scalasca [11], etc.

Performance modeling of OpenMP is to establish appropriate models for applications and high- performance computer (HPC) systems; performance prediction is to use models of programs and systems to predict the performance of applications in the target system. From the results of related research papers retrieved, as the number of computing cores in a single node in the HPC system increases, the OpenMP program so that the shared memory programming model, has received more and more attention. However, there is still a lack of research on the performance and scalability of parallel applications such as OpenMP program. P Popov [12] implemented the OpenMP scalability evaluation tool PCERE based on Codelet, but the source program needs to be executed once, and then the execution context of each parallel domain in the program is saved. This greatly increases the overhead of the system and only supports strong scalability predictions for parallel programs. Shudler [13] proposed a method to automatically obtain the equivalent function of a task-based application. It expresses the execution efficiency, the number of cores, and the input scale in the form of an analytical expression, but this method is only a scalable program performance analysis, and cannot predict program performance.

In summary, there are still some shortcomings and challenges in the performance modeling of existing shared memory programming model (OpenMP) applications. How to efficiently implement the performance modeling of OpenMP applications is a problem that needs further research.

3   LLVM Compilation Platform

The realization of the whole framework of this article is carried out on the basis of LLVM IR. Next, let's briefly introduce LLVM.

LLVM is a compiler infrastructure that can provide compilation support for many languages. As shown in Fig. 1, the LLVM architecture is mainly composed of three parts: the front-end, obtain the source code and then convert it into an intermediate representation, we can choose different compilers as the front- end of LLVM, such as GCC, Clang; Common Optimizer is the process of compilation, use Pass to analyze and optimize LLVM; back-end, that is, generate actual machine code.

When the source program is converted to LLVM IR, the whole program is a module (Module), which is composed of multiple functions (Function), and each function contains multiple basic blocks (Basic Block), the basic block consists of multiple instructions (Instruction). Among them, the control flow can only consist of one input and one output in any basic block, which means that the last instruction of the basic block is always a termination or branch statement. We can use LLVM tools to view the control

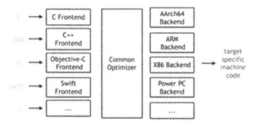

Fig. 1. LLVM compilation platform

flow graph (CFG) of the program. Each node of the control flow graph represents a basic block, and the basic block does not exist in isolation.

4 Performance Modeling of OpenMP Program Based on LLVM Compilation Platform

In this section, the article focus on the performance modeling methods and overall design of OpenMP parallel programs. The performance modeling is to predict the execution time of the OpenMP program. The execution time of a program is related to two parts, one is the program itself, and the other is related to different machines.

Therefore, in performance modeling, we must find the characteristics of the program on the one hand, and the characteristics of the machine on the other. For the characteristics of the program, what needs to know is two points: one is the type of instruction, and the other is the number of instructions; and for the characteristics of the machine, the job is to get the execution time of different instructions. After obtaining the above two points, different instructions can be accumulated, and then multiplied by the execution time of different instructions to obtain the execution time of the program, which is the performance model of the program.

The main idea of performance modeling is to convert OpenMP source code into LLVM intermediate code (IR) through Clang, perform static analysis and dynamic analysis on IR, and then obtain the machine instruction characteristics, and finally obtain the OpenMP performance model.

Abstractly, the calculation time of the OpenMP program can be expressed in the following form:

$$I_i = \sum_{k=0}^{bb_{num}} Ins_k * B_k \tag{1}$$

$$T = \sum_{i=0}^{ins_{num}} I_i * InsTime_i \tag{2}$$

In the above formula: I_i is the number of different instructions. The basic block frequency and the number of instructions corresponding to the basic block are used for accumulation, bb_{num} represents how many basic blocks there are, and ins_{num} represents how many key instructions there are. $InsTime_i$ is the execution time of different instructions. Multiply the number of each instruction and its corresponding time to accumulate, and finally it is the time predicted by the performance model.

This means that we need to obtain different instructions and their number that is program characteristics; and also obtain the time required for the machine to execute different instructions that is the machine characteristics.

4.1   The Method of Obtaining Machine Characteristics

In order to obtain the machine characteristics, we can run an instruction repeatedly at a frequency specified by a CPU. For example, we run base N (1000) load instructions and get a time Time, so we can use Time/N to get InsTime, as shown below:

$$InsTime = \frac{Time}{N} \tag{3}$$

4.2   The Method of Obtaining Program Characteristics

The program features are divided into static features and dynamic features.

The static feature is to obtain the number of basic blocks, the types of instructions in the basic blocks and the number of instructions corresponding to the program by traversing the intermediate code IR corresponding to the source code of the OpenMP program. The dynamic feature is to run the program dynamically to obtain the execution frequency of different basic blocks when the program is executed. The extraction process of static features is static analysis, and the extraction of dynamic features is the process of dynamic analysis. The basic block information (IR instruction and its number) contained in the streamlined program slice obtained by static analysis is available. The dynamic analysis obtains the execution times of each basic block in the program slice. After the above operations, the required parameters in the performance modeling formula can be obtained, and finally the performance modeling of the program is performed using the formula to obtain the performance model.

However, errors need to be considered in performance modeling. Because the CPU cannot execute at a specified frequency when the program is executed, coupled with the influence of related factors such as the instruction set. So it is necessary to consider the error of the performance model for the calculated result, and calculate this part of the error into the prediction time. The calculation of machine characteristics is calculated by the CPU working at full frequency F, so it is necessary to obtain the actual frequency F_{actual} when the program is executed. And then the calculation is shown in the following formula (4).

$$T_{acutal} = \frac{T * F}{F_{actual}} \tag{4}$$

4.3 The Overall Process of Performance Model Construction

From the above content, we can see that the OpenMP performance modeling is divided into the following processes, as shown in the Fig. 2.

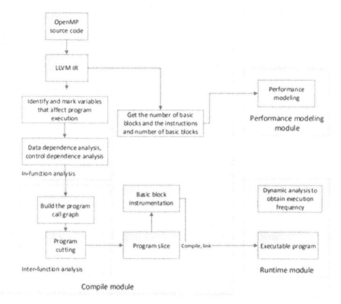

Fig. 2. Overall flow chart of performance modeling

Compile Module

(1) OpenMP source code can be converted to LLVM IR by using Clang;
(2) Some of them directly use LLVM to perform static analysis on IR, which can get the number of basic blocks and the number of instructions in each basic block;
(3) Another part of the intermediate code (IR) performs data dependency analysis and control dependency analysis, identifies and marks key variables that affect the execution of the program, and uses LLVM to construct a call graph of the program to guide the program slicing in the next step;
(4) Compare the source code, intermediate code (IR) and the call graph of the program, further analyze the intermediate code, and cut the program on the basis of the analysis to obtain a greatly simplified program slice. Then performing basic block insertion operations on this slice.

Runtime Module

(1) Compile the program slice generated by the compilation module into an executable program;
(2) Run the executable program and use the code inserted in the slice to obtain the dynamic information of the source program;

(3) Save the dynamic information in the form of a binary file in the disk to facilitate subsequent modeling;
(4) Run the test program to obtain the execution time of the machine instruction, that is, the machine characteristics.

Model Building Module

(1) Read static data, dynamic data and machine characteristics;
(2) Use formulas (1), (2), (3) to calculate I_i, InsTime and T;
(3) Use formula (4) to calculate T_{acutal}.

4.4 The Realization of Key Technologies

The Process of Program Slice Generation: Program Deletion and Slice Processing.
There are a lot of codes in a program that do not affect the execution of the program, so these codes can be deleted in the static analysis, that is, slicing. The code in the IR is reserved that affects the execution of the program (for example: branch, loop, function call, etc.), and the code will be deleted that do not affect program execution (for example: unnecessary calculation instructions, output instructions), finally get the corresponding program slice. Compared with the source program, the content contained in the program slice can meet the requirements of the source program, and some unnecessary processing is deleted, which can greatly speed up the execution time of the program.

The main idea of program reduction and slicing is: the concept of Live set is proposed. This Live set only retains the instructions in IR that affect program execution (for example: branch, loop, function call and other related instructions), and then according to Live set, delete the instructions in the original IR that are not in the Live set, and finally get the program slice. In this process, it is necessary to determine whether the instruction should be added to the Live set according to the relationship between the functions and the characteristics of the LLVM intermediate code.

The Prediction of OpenMP Program Execution Time. For OpenMP programs, the execution method is serial-parallel-serial-parallel-serial. After the OpenMP source code is converted into LLVM intermediate code IR, execute as shown in the Fig. 3.

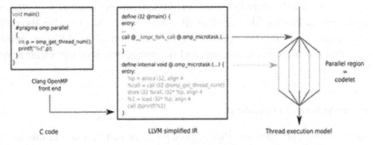

Fig. 3. OpenMP program execution logic under LLVM platform

Only after the function headed by "kmp_fork_call" is executed will it start to the parallel region, and for this basic block, it is divided into two parts, the upper part is the serial part, the middle fork is the parallel region, and the following is another serial part. Due to the allocation of thread resources, the execution of the upper serial part and the lower serial part may not be on the same thread, even if they are in a basic block. Therefore, we need to divide the upper serial part and the lower part into two basic blocks.

In order to correctly evaluate the execution time of a basic block, the following design is adopted. First, traverse the basic block statically to find the serial domain, parallel domain 1, 2, 3... Then, in the dynamic analysis, only the maximum execution time of different threads in each parallel domain is retained, so you only need to add the time of the serial domain to the time sum of the parallel domain. The specific formula is shown in formula (5):

$$time = serialTime + \sum_{k=0}^{n} parallelTime_k \tag{5}$$

Among them:

$$parallelTime_k = max\{threadTime_{0...m}\} \tag{6}$$

that is, the maximum time of different threads in the parallel domain.

In judging the parallel domain, the idea of deep traversal of the graph, the basic block dependency provided by LLVM and some corresponding OpenMP function flags are used to distinguish and judge, finally the execution time of the serial domain and the parallel domain can be counted.

5   Experimental Results

This section is an experiment on the above work. This experiment is run under an HPC-like sub-cluster, using the matrix multiplication program and the prime number calculation program as the test program.

The experiment is mainly to judge the following aspects of this work: (1) Whether the program after the slice processing returns the same value as the original program, that is, the correctness of the slice processing; (2) What is the deviation between the predicted time and the actual time, that is, prediction accuracy. The correctness of the slice processing is mainly to judge whether the execution frequency of the original program and the basic block of the program after the slice are the same. For the prediction accuracy, the actual time and the predicted time are obtained by different numbers of threads, and then calculate the error rate and determine whether the value is within a threshold.

5.1   Slice Correctness Verification

The programs before and after the slicing process were run in a single thread, and the txt file of the basic block execution frequency was obtained after dynamic analsis.

Table 1. The comparison of execution frequency before and after slicing

Before slicing	After slicing
Basic Blocks' label Frequency	Basic Blocks' label Frequency
Basic Block 1 104875	Basic Block 1 104875
Basic Block 2 1074790400	Basic Block 2 1074790400
Basic Block 3 1073741824	Basic Block 3 1073741824
Basic Block 4 1073741824	Basic Block 4 1073741824
Basic Block 5 1048576	Basic Block 5 1048576
Basic Block 6 1	Basic Block 6 1
Basic Block 7 1	Basic Block 7 1
Basic Block 8 1	Basic Block 8 1
Basic Block 9 0	Basic Block 9 0
Basic Block 10 1	Basic Block 10 1
Basic Block 11 1	Basic Block 11 1
Basic Block 12 1025	Basic Block 12 1025
Basic Block 13 1024	Basic Block 13 1024
Basic Block 14 1049600	Basic Block 14 1049600
Basic Block 15 1048576	Basic Block 15 1048576
Basic Block 16 1024	Basic Block 16 1024
Basic Block 17 1024	Basic Block 17 1024
Basic Block 18 1024	Basic Block 18 1024
Basic Block 19 1	Basic Block 19 1
Basic Block 20 1	Basic Block 20 1
Basic Block 21 1	Basic Block 21 1
Basic Block 22 1	Basic Block 22 1
Basic Block 23 1	Basic Block 23 1
Basic Block 24 0	Basic Block 24 0
Basic Block 25 1	Basic Block 25 1
Basic Block 26 1	Basic Block 26 1
Basic Block 27 1025	Basic Block 27 1025
Basic Block 28 1024	Basic Block 28 1024
Basic Block 29 1049600	Basic Block 29 1049600
Basic Block 30 1048576	Basic Block 30 1048576
Basic Block 31 1048576	Basic Block 31 1048576
Basic Block 32 1024	Basic Block 32 1024
Basic Block 33 1024	Basic Block 33 1024
Basic Block 34 1024	Basic Block 34 1024
Basic Block 35 1	Basic Block 35 1
Basic Block 36 1	Basic Block 36 1
Basic Block 37 1	Basic Block 37 1

It can be seen in the Table 1 that the basic block execution frequency was found to be the same in the matrix multiplication test program.

And as shown in Fig. 4, due to the reduction in the number of intermediate codes, the program after the slicing process can shorten the running time of the program, which can increase the utilization rate of HPC.

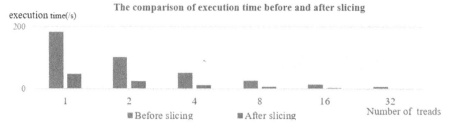

Fig. 4. The comparison of execution time before and after slicing

5.2 Prediction Accuracy Verification

It can be seen from the Table 2 and Table 3, the model, that is, the predicted time has a small difference between the actual time. For these two test programs, as the number of threads increases, the error rate is controlled within 15%, which can explain: Our performance model is predictive for the program. According to these two tables, we

Table 2. Matrix multiplication test program performance modeling error rate table

Threads	Predicted time(/s)	Actual time(/s)	Error rate
1	161.141	185.949	13.34%
2	73.495	102.9	28.58%
4	42.781	51.304	16.61%
6	30.214	34.94	13.53%
8	23.642	26.2112	9.81%
10	18.22	21.356	14.68%
12	16.128	18.244	11.60%
14	13.84	16.023	13.63%
16	12.579	14.251	11.73%
18	11.564	12.689	8.87%
20	10.359	11.568	10.45%
22	9.461	10.667	11.31%
24	8.633	9.732	11.30%
26	8.218	9.155	10.23%
28	7.458	8.818	15.41%
30	6.941	8.67	19.95%
32	6.56	7.623	13.95%
34	6.147	5.793	18.89%
36	6.132	7.513	18.38%

can also find the corresponding relationship between the optimal execution time of the program and the number of threads under the sub-HPC.

Then we can predict the execution time and the optimal number of threads of the OpenMP program under the actual HPC in a scalable manner, according to the machine characteristics of the sub-HCP and the actual HPC, which can reduce the resource consumption of HPC and users.

Table 3. Prime number calculation test program performance modeling error rate table

Threads	Predicted time(/s)	Actual time(/s)	Error rate
1	46.008	50.623	9.12%
2	33.821	37.28	9.28%
4	19.536	21.62	9.64%
6	14.964	15.384	5.77%
8	11.34	12.044	5.85%
10	9.491	10.053	5.59%
12	8.098	8.725	7.18%
14	7.389	7.697	4.01%
16	6.703	6.839	1.99%
18	6.197	6.198	0.02%
20	5.592	5.742	2.62%
22	5.089	5.261	3.27%
24	4.67	4.574	2.11%
26	4.316	4.607	6.33%
28	4.013	4.298	6.64%
30	3.748	4.062	7.73%
32	3.512	3.872	9.30%
34	3.35	3.77	11.15%
36	3.191	3.635	12.20%

6 Conclusions

After testing several sample programs, we can find that our work is useful for performance modeling and scalability prediction of OpenMP programs.

First of all, we delete and slice the program. The main function of this part is to reduce the time required for subsequent performance modeling. After we delete and slice the OpenMP source program, integrate it with the instrumentation program and run it to get the information about the execution frequency of the basic block: data.txt. After testing, our deletion did not change the execution logic of the program, and naturally it did not change the execution time of the program.

Then use the basic block execution frequency and instruction execution time information to model the performance of the source program. Compared with the actual time, the error rate of the predicted time we obtained after modeling the source program performance is basically controlled within 15%, which also shows that our performance model can basically simulate the actual time. However, in the process of performance modeling, there are many influencing factors, such as the state of the server, and the parallelism of the instruction set. We can't achieve the same. This is where we will strive to overcome it in the future.

In terms of scalability prediction, we can perform specific analysis of specific problems for different machines and different programs. On a given machine and program, we can analyze the number of threads for the program on the machine to achieve optimal performance, which can solve serious problems such as the waste of HPC resources.

To sum up: We have done performance modeling and scalability prediction for OpenMP programs, predicting the execution time of the program during the performance modeling process, and discovering the optimal execution efficiency on HPC on the scalability prediction. Combining the above two aspects, it can help users judge how much resources they need to apply for when applying for HPC, and can also maximize the efficiency of each node when HPC is working, so as to prevent the emergence of related problems such as unlimited work on a single node and resource competition on multiple nodes.

In the future, we will strive to reduce the error rate of performance modeling, strive to control all error rates within 10%, and develop a more general scalability prediction method. We can continue to improve in the following aspects:

1. In the judgment of instruction time, we will strive to obtain the instruction execution time at the CPU frequency while the program is running at the same time when the program is running, so as to reduce the error caused by the performance model.
2. And we will try our best to control the problems caused by the hardware resources of the HPC system, aiming at the OpenMP shared memory characteristics and the more powerful functions of the LLVM internal platform, reducing the hardware problems caused by the HPC system mistake.
3. In the follow-up, we will also work hard to study the performance deviation factors of the HPC system under the same architecture, and reduce the impact of performance deviation on the prediction time in the prediction.

References

1. Dagum, L., Menon, R.: OpenMP: an industry standard API for shared-memory programming. IEEE Comput. Sci. Eng. **5**(1), 46–55 (1998). https://doi.org/10.1109/99.660313
2. Browne, S., Dongarra, J., Garner, N., et al.: A portable programming interface for performance evaluation on modern processors. Int. J. High Perform. Comput. Appl. **14**(3), 189–204 (2000). https://doi.org/10.1177/109434200001400303

3. Wright, S.A., Pennycook, S.J., Hammond, S.D., et al.: ROIT – a parallel input/output tracer. Bryologist (2), 86–87 (2011)
4. Reed, D., Roth, P.C., Aydt, R., et al.: Scalable performance analysis: the Pablo performance analysis environment. In: Proceedings of the Scalable Parallel Libraries Conference, pp. 104–113. IEEE (1993)
5. Nagel, W.E., Arnold, A., Weber, M., et al.: VAMPIR: visualization and analysis of MPI resources. Supercomputer 12(1), 69–80 (2010)
6. Nethercote, N., Seward, J.: Valgrind: a framework for heavyweight dynamic binary instrumentation. ACM SIGPLAN Not. 42(6), 89–100 (2007). https://doi.org/10.1145/1273442.125 0746
7. Shende, S., Malony, A.: The tau parallel performance system. Int. J. High Perform. Comput. Appl. 20(2), 287–311 (2006). https://doi.org/10.1177/1094342006064482
8. Adhianto, L., Banerjee, S., Fagan, M.W., et al.: HPCTOOLKIT: tools for performance analysis of optimized parallel programs. Concurr. Comput. Pract. Exp. 22(6), 685–701 (2009)
9. Graham, S.L., Kessler, P.B., Mckusick, M.K., et al.: Gprof: a call graph execution profiler. Compiler Constr. 39(4), 120–126 (1982)
10. Geimer, M., Wolf, F., Wylie, B.J., et al.: The Scalasca performance toolset architecture. Concurr. Comput. Pract. Exp. 22(6), 120–126 (2010)
11. Popov, M., Akel, C., Conti, F., et al.: PCERE: fine-grained parallel benchmark decomposition for scalability prediction. In: Parallel and Distributed Processing Symposium, pp. 1151–1160. IEEE (2015)
12. Shudler, S., Calotoiu, A., Hoefler, T., et al.: Isoefficiency in practice: configuring and understanding the performance of task-based applications. In: The ACM SIGPLAN Symposium, pp. 131–143. ACM (2017)
13. Chen, W.G., Zhai, J.D., Zhang, J., et al.: LogGPO: an accurate communication model for performance prediction of MPI programs. Sci. China Ser. F: Inf. Sci. 52(10), 1785–1791 (2009)
14. Lin, Y., Yang, X., Xu, X., et al.: VACED-SIM: a simulator for scalability prediction in large-scale parallel computing. IEICE Trans. Inf. Syst. 96(7), 1430–1442 (2013)
15. Zhang, W., Cheng, A.M.K., Subhlok, J.: DwarfCode: a performance prediction tool for parallel applications. IEEE Trans. Comput. 65(2), 495–507 (2016). https://doi.org/10.1109/TC.2015.2417526
16. Lattner, C., Adve, V.: LLVM: a compilation framework for lifelong program analysis & transformation. In: International Symposium on Code Generation and Optimization, CGO 2004, pp. 75–86 (2004)
17. Smith, L., Bull, M.: Development of mixed mode MPI/OpenMP applications. Sci. Program. 9(2–3), 83–98 (2001). https://doi.org/10.1155/2001/450503
18. Bertolli, C., Antao, S.F., Eichenberger, A.E., et al.: Coordinating GPU threads for OpenMP 4.0 in LLVM. In: 2014 LLVM Compiler Infrastructure in HPC, pp. 12–21. IEEE (2014)
19. Viswanathan, V.: Discovery of semantic associations in an RDF graph using bi-directional BFS on massively parallel hardware. Int. J. Big Data Intell. 3(3), 176–181 (2016)
20. Hoisie, A., Lubeck, O., Wasserman, H.: Performance and scalability analysis of teraflop-scale parallel architectures using multidimensional wavefront applications. Int. J. High Perform. Comput. Appl. 14(4), 330–346 (2000)
21. Wu, C.C., Ke, J.Y., Lin, H., et al.: Adjusting thread parallelism dynamically to accelerate dynamic programming with irregular workload distribution on GPGPUs. Int. J. Grid High Perform. Comput. (IJGHPC) 6(1), 1–20 (2014)
22. Malyshkin, V.E.: Peculiarities of numerical algorithms parallel implementation for exa-flops multicomputers. Int. J. Big Data Intell. 1(1–2), 65–73 (2014)

23. Pješivac-Grbović, J., Angskun, T., Bosilca, G., et al.: Performance analysis of MPI collective operations. Clust. Comput. **10**(2), 127–143 (2007)
24. Kambadur, M., Tang, K., Kim, M.A.: Harmony: collection and analysis of parallel block vectors. In: 2012 39th Annual International Symposium on Computer Architecture (ISCA), pp. 452–463. IEEE (2012)

A Method of Network Attack Recognition Based on CNN+LSTM Model

Changliang Zheng[1], Xiaodong Zhan[1], Jing Yu[1(✉)], and Wei Song[2]

[1] School of Telecommunication Engineering, Beijing Polytechnic, Beijing 100176, China
yujing@bpi.edu.cn
[2] Media Computing Laboratory, School of Information Engineering,
Minzu University of China, Beijing 100081, China

Abstract. Accurate identification of network attacks has become an important topic in the field of network security, and the use of machine learning methods to identify network attacks has been one of the research hotspots in the field of network security protection in recent years. But they have some limitations, such as model parameters are difficult to optimize, and the prediction accuracy rate is low. Also, the characteristics of time series uncertainty and nonlinearity in network traffic messages increase the difficulty of forecasting. This article proposes a prediction model using the CNN+LSTM network and uses feature engineering methods to preprocess traffic sample data, and then select effective features through information gain and determining feature weights. Use the NSL-KDD data set to conduct empirical research on the prediction algorithm based on feature engineering and long-short-term memory artificial neural network proposed in this paper. The results show that the prediction model based on CNN+LSTM is compared with only LSTM algorithm or only classification algorithm. It can improve prediction accuracy, reduce model training time, and is easier to apply in the actual work of network attack identification and security prevention.

Keywords: Identification of network attacks · CNN · LSTM · Feature engineering

1 Introduction

Facing the complex and changeable cyberspace environment and the three-dimensional network attacks and violations covering each layer of L2–L7, to further control the network security situation effectively, as an important part of the network security protecting technology, identification and early warning of network intrusions and attacks have attracted more and more attention from all parties. Identifying network attacks refers to collecting various security data including data packets and logs from the network including network transmission and security equipment based on relevant experience and knowledge, and then analyzing and modeling the collected data, and according to the corresponding Standards conduct state judgments to obtain current network vulnerabilities and risks faced, and provide support for network security emergency response and network security management.

© Springer Nature Switzerland AG 2021
X. Sun et al. (Eds.): ICAIS 2021, CCIS 1424, pp. 31–41, 2021.
https://doi.org/10.1007/978-3-030-78621-2_3

The research on the identification and analysis of network security attacks started from abroad. Gorodetsky [1] used multiple limited periods and asynchronous data streams as input to detect and identify network attacks and carried out empirical research based on network attack identification characteristics. Convolutional neural network (CNN) [2] is often used to obtain data features of the image. In recent years, it has achieved great success in image data modeling in the field of computer vision and image processing. When processing the image, the convolutional network extracts features from the two-dimensional matrix and obtains the convolution output. And use the pooling layer to retain the important features of the convolution output. Then send the output of the pooling layer to the fully connected layer to get the result. In this article, we use CNN to extract features from sequential sequence data and use them as input to LSTM. ALTHUBITI [3] used Long-Short-Term Memory (LSTM) to train and test on the CIDDS-001 data set. Although the experimental results achieved high accuracy, the test set selected in the article is the training part of the set, so it does not show the generalization of the model. JAVAIDA [4] combined self-taught learning (STL) with a sparse autoencoder (Sparse Autoencoder, SAE), which greatly improved the detection accuracy of the NSL-KDD data set. However, this method inhibits the propagation of certain neurons during the training process and is prone to the imbalance in the detection results of different numbers of samples.

In recent years, with the continuous in-depth research on increasingly complex and rapid network attack patterns, emerging network security vendors such as VENUSTECH, TOPSEC, NSFOCUS, and other companies have developed a series of products, laid a foundation for the practical application of network attack identification. Also, in the field of academic research, research on the detection and recognition of network attack patterns is making continuous progress. At the same time, research on network security involving big data and artificial intelligence technologies is gradually deepening. Based on cluster analysis, Chen [5] discussed the problems of inaccurate acquisition of evaluation parameters, long time, and low accuracy in the case of heterogeneous attack information sources and uneven temporal and spatial distribution of existing network attack evaluation techniques. Zhao [6] selected multi-source data in a big data environment and proposed a parallel reduction algorithm based on the attribute importance matrix to reduce the attributes of data source data. To calculate the situation, the traditional wavelet neural network learning method is easy to fall into the local minimum, the particle swarm algorithm is used to optimize the wavelet neural network parameters, and then the wavelet neural network based on particle swarm optimization is used for calculation. Tian [7] proposed an evaluation method that combines threat propagation and graph theory, quantified the trend of network attacks, and drew a graph of the overall network security trend. Xi [8] based on the previous observation sequence acquisition method is relatively single, and the state transition matrix is highly subjective. Based on the statistical characteristics of the alarm, the concept of alarm quality is proposed to improve the effectiveness of the data source; secondly, based on security in the game process of events and protective measures, a method to determine the state transition matrix is proposed, and the probability of a successful attack is modified to improve the effectiveness of the state transition matrix. Liu [9] proposed a cognitive perception control model that uses long- and short-term memory artificial neural networks for security attack recognition, and proposed a new method of combined normalization to make the input vector of the neural network more suitable for its structure, which can speed up the learning speed of the network and improve the classification accuracy. In 2011, Wu et al. carried out "Research on Network Attack Recognition Algorithm Based on Cluster Analysis" [10] and proposed a network attack recognition method based on a clustering model. Zou [11] proposed a modulation recognition algorithm based on deep long and short-term memory artificial neural network. The algorithm reduces the steps of manual preprocessing and feature extraction, and directly learns the features of the input signal through the deep long and short-term memory artificial neural network, and then performs Softmax classification output. Yuan [12] proposed a network security attack identification and situation prediction method based on PSO-LSTM. LSTM can effectively learn the information contained in sequence data.

Aiming at the shortcomings of the above methods, this paper proposes a combined model based on CNN+LSTM to determine network security attacks. First, the important features are screened among all data attributes and verified on the traditional classification method model, and 15 features that contribute higher to the accuracy and calculation efficiency are screened and selected. Second, use the CNN network to learn the features of the data set independently. Next, based on the timing characteristics of network security attack information, the LSTM network combined with the Softmax network is used to classify the network attack forms. The results show that compared with the traditional single LSTM algorithm, this method can improve the accuracy of the model and reduce the calculation time of the model. The accuracy of the model is up to 99.2%, which is closer to practical applications.

2 Processing Data Set

2.1 Select the NSL-KDD Dataset as the Model Evaluation Data Source

This article chooses the relatively authoritative intrusion detection data set NSL-KDD in the field of network security as the data source for evaluation. The NSL-KDD data set is an improvement over the KDD99 data set. It removes duplicate network traffic data records, which helps the classifier to produce unbiased results. The NSL-KDD data set contains 41 characteristics and 5 main attack types. Table 1 shows the data set information used in this article.

Table 1. KDD-NSL data set information

Data set	Normal	Dos	Total
KDDTrain-set	67343	45927	113322
KDDTest-set	9710	7456	17368

2.2 Data Preprocessing

In order to train the network model more conveniently and accurately, it is necessary to convert the classification features in the data set into digital features and perform numerical normalization.

Feature Digitization. The NSL-KDD data set has 3 classification features "protocol_type", "service" and "flag", including 3, 64, and 10 categories respectively. Through ONEHOT coding technology, these three classification features are transformed into data that only represent 0 and 1.

Numerical Normalization. There are significant differences between the minimum and maximum values of some features in the data set. In order to improve accuracy and computational efficiency, these features are normalized. The process of numerical normalization can be expressed as (1):

$$x_{norm} = (x - x_{min})/(x_{max} - x_{min}) \tag{1}$$

Among them, x represents the original value of the feature, and x_{max} and x_{min} are the maximum and minimum values obtained by the feature.

Data Labeling of Network Attacks. The NSL-KDD data set includes 5 types of network data: Normal, DoS, U2R, R2L, and Probe (Table 2).

Table 2. The basic situation of the 5 types of attacks

Attack type	Description
Denial of service (Dos)	Stop the computer or network service so that the target user cannot access it. DoS attacks achieve this by sending large amounts of traffic or information to the target
Get permission (U2R)	Attempt to obtain root account permissions through illegal means
Remote intrusion (R2L)	Allow the intruder who does not have an account to access a local computer
Detection attack (Probe)	Collect network information necessary before launching other attacks
Normal Traffic (Normal)	Normal network traffic

Among them, this paper selects DoS as the targets for model identification, so the remote intrusion and detection attack data in the NSL-KDD data set is deleted, and the compiled information is encoded using ONEHOT as shown in Table 3.

Table 3. Filtered label type and code

Attack type	Label	ONEHOT code
Denial of service	DoS	100
Normal Traffic	Normal	001

2.3 Feature Selection

To improve the accuracy and efficiency of the detection algorithm, it is necessary to effectively select key features. The data set contains many irrelevant and redundant features. Therefore, removing all irrelevant and redundant features can play a great role in improving performance.

The information gain is considered when selecting the features, that is, the relevant features of the data that have a major influence on the result are selected according to the Shannon formula. The information gain value of a particular attribute is the highest, indicating the best relevant feature, and this attribute becomes the first choice for decision-making. Recursively calculate again the entropy of the remaining attributes and the target attribute to determine the remaining features.

In addition to considering the information gain of the feature, this paper also uses the feature weighting algorithm ReliefF algorithm, the purpose is to calculate the importance of the feature by identifying the feature value difference between the nearest neighbors. First, randomly select an observation point S from the training set, then find the nearest neighbor test point of S with the same attack type label, called NearHit, and then select the nearest neighbor test point of S with different attack type labels, called NearMiss. Then update the weight of each feature according to the following rules: If the distance between the test point S and NearHit is greater than the distance from NearMiss in a certain variable, the weight of the feature will increase, because the feature helps distinguish the target label in the nearest neighbor situation. On the contrary, if the distance between the test point S and NearHit on a certain variable is less than the distance from NearMiss, it means that the feature has little effect on distinguishing labels, and the weight of the variable will be reduced. Repeat the above process m times, and finally, we will get the average weight of each feature variable. The greater the weight of the feature variable, the stronger the classification ability of the feature, and the more it should be left in the final feature subset. Since this method is linear, the weights of all features can be confirmed faster.

After obtaining the feature subsets of the above two methods, because the feature selection method in this paper only involves two subsets, formulas (2) and (3) can be used to simplify the calculation of weights, and obtain the feature subsets with greater contribution to classification as shown in Table 4:

$$Uc = Ug \cap Ur \tag{2}$$

$$Zic = (Zig + Zir)/2 \tag{3}$$

Table 4. Feature subset selected by Information Gain (IG) and ReliefF

IG	25	44	38	37	3	11	29	28	10	4	21	5	33	2	34
Relief	28	33	32	24	25	37	1	23	38	3	15	13	18	17	16
Sum up	24	25	28	37	38	33	3	32	10	13	4	29	5	1	17
IG	32	22	13	36	7	31	9	8	30	17	16	12	0	35	1
Relief	14	12	6	10	8	5	4	0	36	29	9	34	39	21	7
Sum up	21	16	34	8	36	12	9	7	0						

3   Model building

Use CNN for Feature Extraction

In this article, we use the CNN+LSTM network, where the CNN part regards the data record as a CNN input vector sequence, and this article uses a 1-dimensional filter to scan the vector to obtain key features. In the experiment, we used 8 filters to detect the characteristics of the input data. And use the ReLu activation function to get the key feature map.

In the pooling layer of CNN, the Max Pooling method with prominent features is used. This is more conducive to extracting important features and reducing calculations in the convolutional layer. After the Max-pooling layer, the CNN network uses dropout technology to overcome the problem of overfitting. In this process, we set the dropout-rate to 0.3.

Use LSTM Network to Obtain Sequence Features

The long short-term memory network (LSTM) is an upgraded network of RNN. It solves the problem of "gradient disappearance" that occurs as the time series increases when the gradient descent method is used for model optimization. In the LSTM long short-term memory network, the LSTM unit replaces the neuron in RNN, its structure consists of four parts: forget gate, input gate, output gate, and cell unit. Its internal structure diagram is shown in Fig. 1.

The Input Gate, Output Gate, and Forget Gate at time t are expressed as i_t, o_t, f_t, then the update method of LSTM is:

$$i_t = \sigma \left(w_i \, x_t + u_i \, h_{t-1} + b_i \right) \tag{4}$$

$$o_t = \sigma \left(w_o \, x_t + u_o \, h_{t-1} + b_o \right) \tag{5}$$

$$f_t = \sigma \left(w_f \, x_t + u_f \, h_{t-1} + b_f \right) \tag{6}$$

$$c_t = f_t * c_{t-1} + i_t * tanh(W_t \, x_t + U_t \, h_{t-1} + b_t) \tag{7}$$

$$h_t = o_t * tanh(c_t) \tag{8}$$

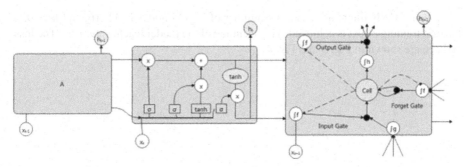

Fig. 1. LSTM unit structure and network composition

At this moment, the cell state is c_t and the output of LSTM is h_t. The sigmoid function is used as the activation function in the network, w represents the output gate weight matrix, and b represents the output gate bias vector.

LSTM causes the output signal to inversely affect each gate in the input stage. Therefore, the network contains sequence-dependent sequence features. For long sequence data such as network traffic, LSTM can effectively identify sequence features that are dependent on before and after.

After LSTM, a fully connected layer is used, and the attack type is determined through the Softmax network. The overall network contains a total of 7 layers. The first layer is composed of CNN units, the next two layers are LSTM networks, and the third layer is composed of fully connected layers, and finally through one Softmax layer classification output, as shown in Fig. 2. The activation function in the network is the ReLu function, and the dropout value is 0.5.

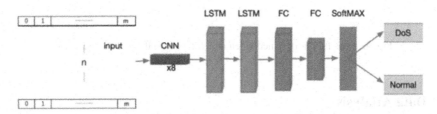

Fig. 2. CNN+LSTM network structure

The experiment is implemented based on open source libraries such as Keras, TensorFlow2.0, and sklearn. The hardware environment is Xeon2.6 GHz CPU, 32GB RAM, GTX2080GPU (16.0 GB RAM). The data set uses the NSL-KDD data set. The training and testing experiments are carried out on CentOs 7.8.2003 (64-bit) operating system, and GPU acceleration is used for model training.

During training, 11.2×10^4 pieces of training data and 2.2×10^4 pieces of test data are used. Cross entropy is used as the loss function during optimization. lr set [0.05, 0.1, 0.15, 0.2], adam = 0.005.

When 8 CNN filters are used, the number of LSTM nodes is 32, 16, and $lr = 0.1$, the best training effect is achieved. The accuracy of the model reaches 99.01%. The loss and acc are shown in Fig. 3 and Fig. 4:

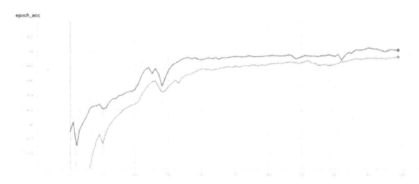

Fig. 3. Training accuracy rate when cnn_filters $= 8$, lh1 $= 128$, lh2 $= 64$

Fig. 4. Loss function trained when cnn_filters $= 8$, lh1 $= 128$, lh2 $= 64$

4   Data Analysis

Use Confusion Matrix to Test Algorithm Performance. First use FP, FN, TP, TN confusion matrix to test the recall rate (Recall) and accuracy rate (Accuracy). Among them, True Positive (TP): Indicates the count of attack samples predicted by the model as attack samples. False Positive (FP): Indicates the count of samples predicted by the model as normal but actually attacked. True Negative (TN): Indicates the count of normal samples predicted by the model but normal samples. False Negative (FN): Indicates the count of normal samples predicted by the model as attacking samples. In the following formulas, PT, PF, NT, and NF represent TP, FP, TN, and FN respectively.

Accuracy (Precision, P): Indicates the frequency of attack samples that the model predicts correctly. It can be expressed as:

$$P = (TP)/(TP + FP) \qquad (9)$$

Recall rate (Recall, R): represents the percentage of attack samples correctly classified by the model to the actual attack samples. It can be expressed as:

$$R = (TP)/(TP + FN) \tag{10}$$

Therefore, the confusion matrix of this experiment can be calculated as shown in Fig. 5. It can be seen that the accuracy rate and recall rate have reached a good level.

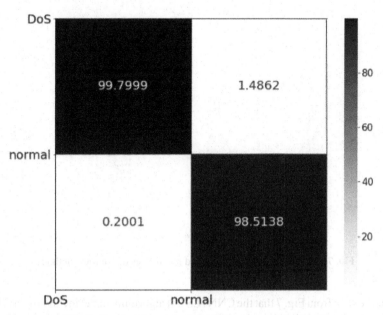

Fig. 5. Confusion matrix for this experimental method

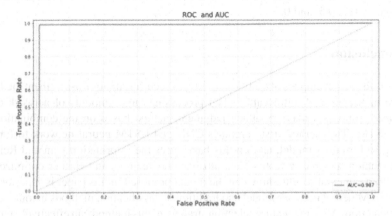

Fig. 6. ROC and AUC of this experimental method

The AUC of the experimental result is 0.987, which also shows the effectiveness of the method introduced in this article. As shown in Fig. 6.

Use the NSL-KDD data set to test the four models as the following: the method in this article, the CNN+LSTM network without feature engineering, the two-layer LSTM network (LSTM-2), and the SVM algorithm, and select the accuracy and recall rates as evaluation indicators. Compare and analyze various models. The index scores of different models are shown in Fig. 7.

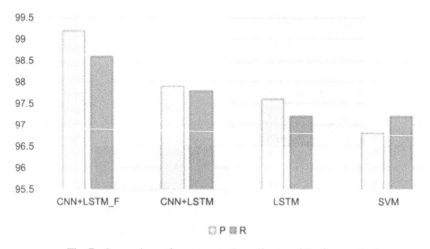

Fig. 7. Comparison of accuracy and recall rates of the four methods

It can be seen from Fig. 7 that the CNN+LSTM algorithm model in this article is better than the other four models in terms of accuracy and recall. Experimental results show that the CNN+LSTM algorithm improves the recall and accuracy of predicting attack types. Compared with the LSTM-2 and SVM models, the Precision of the CNN+LSTM algorithm has increased by 1.3%, 1.6%, and 2.4%, respectively, and the Recall has also increased by 0.2, 0.5, and 0.5.

5   Conclusion

Aiming at the disadvantages of traditional network security situation assessment methods that are inefficient and untraceable when processing large amounts of network data, this paper proposes a network attack judgment method based on the combination of CNN+LSTM. The method first combines CNN and LSTM neural network to form a learning and training model, and on this basis, uses the information gain and ReliefF hybrid method to select effective data attributes as features and further optimize the model. Experimental results show that the model proposed in this paper is superior to a single LSTM neural network model and traditional classification methods in multi-class attack detection. Also, the feature selection strategy in this method can effectively reduce the calculation scale while improving the accuracy of the model, thereby reducing the model training time, which is more conducive to the application of attack prediction algorithms in practice. The work of the next step is to further optimize the detection model by changing the feature construction method of categorical variables.

References

1. Gorodetsky, V., Karsaev, O., Samoilov, V.: On-line update of situation assessment based on asynchronous data streams. In: Negoita, M.G., Howlett, R.J., Jain, L.C. (eds.) KES 2004. LNCS (LNAI), vol. 3213, pp. 1136–1142. Springer, Heidelberg (2004). https://doi.org/10.1007/978-3-540-30132-5_154
2. Cho, K., Merrienboer, B.V., Bahdanau, D., Yoshua, B.: On the properties of neural machine translation: encoder–decoder approaches. arXiv:1409.1259 (2014)
3. Althubiti, S.A., Jones, E.M., Roy, K.: LSTM for anomaly-based network intrusion detection. In: 2018 28th International Telecommunication Networks and Applications Conference, ITNAC, pp. 1–3 (2018)
4. Javaid, A., Niyaz, Q., Sun, W., et al.: A deep learning approach for network intrusion detection system. In: 9th EAI International Conference on Bio-inspired Information and Communications Technologies (formerly BIONETICS), pp. 21–26 (2016)
5. Gang, C.: RF-SVM based awareness algorithm in intelligent network security situation awareness system. In: Proceedings of 2017 3rd Workshop on Advanced Research and Technology in Industry Applications. Institute of Management Science and Industrial Engineering, p. 5 (2017)
6. Zhao, D.M., Liu, J.: Research on network security situation based on particle swarm optimization algorithm. Comput. Ind. Eng.
7. https://www.sci-encedirect.com/science/article/abs/pi/S036083521830007X
8. Tian, J., et al.: Quantitative assessment method of multi-node network security situation based on threat propagation. Comput. Res. Dev. **54**(04), 731–741 (2017)
9. Xi, R.R., Yun, X., Zhang, Y., et al.: An improved quantitative evaluation method for network security. Chin. J. Comput. **38**(4), 749–758 (2015)
10. Liu, X.: Study on data normalization in the input layer of BP neural network. Mech. Eng. Autom. **10**(3), 122–123 (2010)
11. Wu, L.: Research on Intrusion Detection Algorithm Based on Cluster Analysis. Northeastern University, Shenyang (2011)
12. Zou, H.: Communication signal modulation recognition algorithm based on Deep-LSTM. Mod. Comput. **16**, 3–7 (2020)
13. Yuan, Y.: Network security situation awareness prediction method based on PSO-LSTM. Comput. Sci. Appl. **10**(10), 1863–1869 (2020)

Encryption and Cybersecurity

Recognition Method of Abnormal Data in Local Area Network Common Channel Based on Convolutional Neural Network

Weiwei Lin[1,2(✉)] [iD], Sisheng Chen[1], Xingsi Xue[3], and Reiko Haga[4]

[1] School of Electronic and Information Engineering, Fujian Polytechnic Normal University, Fuqing 350300, China
[2] Engineering Research Center for ICH Digitalization and Multi-source Information Fusion, Fujian Province University, Fuqing 350300, China
[3] School of Computer Science and Mathematics, Fujian University of Technology, Fuzhou 350118, China
[4] CommScope Japan KK, Nagatacho 100-0014, Tokyo, Japan

Abstract. In order to strengthen the accuracy of the recognition of abnormal data in the local area network common channel and improve the recognition efficiency, the convolutional network method is applied to data recognition, and the recognition method of the abnormal data in the local area network common channel based on the convolutional neural network is studied. First, the convolutional neural network structure is analyzed and the three main parts of the convolutional neural network are outlined. Second, the optimization algorithm flow of the abnormal data recognition of the common channel of the local area network is designed, and the specific calculation steps of the data recognition are obtained. Finally, a comparative experiment is designed to compare the traditional recognition method of abnormal data based on data stream and the recognition method of abnormal data based on log analysis with the recognition method of abnormal data in local area network common channel based on convolutional neural network designed in this paper. In this way, the loss value and recognition accuracy data are obtained, and the optimal abnormal data recognition method is judged through the data.

Keywords: Convolutional neural network · Local area network · Common channel · Abnormal data · Recognition method

1 Introduction

A local area network usually refers to the interconnection of computer hardware equipment and software facilities within a limited geographic area to form a limited computer network [1, 2]. This computer network can realize almost all the functions of the Internet. The difference is that the local area network can only communicate data within the geographic area, while the Internet can communicate data in any area with a network [3]. After the local area network has become popular, its common channel has become the focus of abnormal data intrusion. Therefore, the recognition method of abnormal data

© Springer Nature Switzerland AG 2021
X. Sun et al. (Eds.): ICAIS 2021, CCIS 1424, pp. 45–52, 2021.
https://doi.org/10.1007/978-3-030-78621-2_4

in the local area network common channel has become the focus of public attention. In the previous methods for identifying abnormal data in common channels of local area networks, the intrusion data monitoring method based on data flow mainly used the initial clustering method to construct a data set, and judged whether the access data is legal or not. If the access data change, the clustered data set can be reconstructed and the access data can be re-judged. Although this method has certain real-time performance, its detection efficiency is not high [4, 5]. Another method for identifying abnormal data in local area network common channels based on log analysis, discovers abnormal data by constructing a suspicious attack pattern graph. This method has high accuracy in identifying abnormal data, but it cannot remove irrelevant data in the common channel of the local area network. In the long run, it will lead to excessive redundant data and low recognition rate [6, 7]. Based on the above two identification methods, this paper designs a method for identifying abnormal data in local area network common channels based on convolutional neural networks.

2   Research on Abnormal Data Recognition Method Based on Convolutional Neural Network

The main idea of convolutional neural network is to simulate the connection structure of human brain neurons, gradually extract the input signal of the hidden layer, and construct basic neurons through the network model [8, 9]. As long as the neurons are built in advance, the convolutional neural network can greatly enhance the recognition ability of the network model, so the structure of the convolutional neural network is optimized first.

2.1   Analysis of Convolutional Neural Network Structure

The convolutional neural network applied to the recognition of abnormal data in the common channel of local area network can generally be divided into three parts: input layer, convolution layer, and pooling layer. In the identification of abnormal data in the common channel of the local area network, the main function of the convolutional layer is to extract the data characteristics of the input data. When the input data is a one-dimensional signal, suppose the data is $X = [X_1, X_2, X_3, \cdots, X_N]$, and N represents the length of the group of data. At this time, the convolutional layer operation expression is:

$$y_j^i = \sum_{i,j} x_i * W_j^i + b \tag{1}$$

Where, W represents the convolution kernel; $*$ represents the convolution operation; W_j^i represents the i-th weight value on the j-th convolution kernel; b represents the offset value of the convolutional nerve; y_j^i represents the data feature that can be obtained after the weight value of W_j^i is calculated. The function of the pooling layer is mainly to filter the input information data, greatly reducing the data features extracted in the convolutional layer, reducing the amount of parameters, and reducing the computing cost [10–12]. The calculation method of the maximum pooling is shown in formula (2) and formula (3):

$$P_i = \left[P_i^1, P_i^2, P_i^3, \cdots, P_i^n \right] \tag{2}$$

$$P_i^k = max(\alpha_i^{(h-1)g+1}, \alpha_i^{(h-1)g+2}, \alpha_i^{(h-1)g+3}, \cdots, \alpha_i^{hg}) \tag{3}$$

Where, P_i represents the calculation result of the pooling layer in the data model; n represents the output dimension of the convolutional neural network, and dimension $h = (1, 2, 3, \cdots, n)$; g represents the pooling size of the convolutional neural network [13–15]. In the activation layer, the activation function mainly converts the features accumulated in the convolutional layer into nonlinear data, and obtains the expression of the hyperbolic tangent function as shown in formula (4).

$$\alpha_j^i = tan(y_j^i) = \frac{e^{y_j^i} - e^{-y_j^i}}{e^{y_j^i} + e^{-y_j^i}} \tag{4}$$

Where, α_j^i represents the activation value obtained by the activation function of the abnormal data in the common channel of the local area network in the activation layer. y_j^i represents the i-th value obtained by the j-th convolution kernel through the convolutional neural network operation [5]. The mapping interval of the hyperbolic tangent function is between $(-1, 1)$. When the hyperbola is saturated, the gradient weight will infinitely approach 0, causing the weight update to stop [16, 17]. The structure diagram is shown below (Fig. 1).

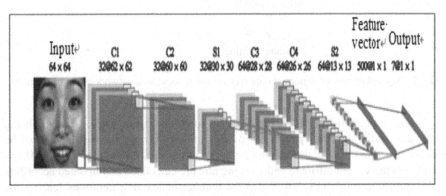

Fig. 1. Convolutional neural network structure

2.2   Abnormal Data Recognition Algorithm Optimization Process

Based on the above three-layer convolutional neural network structure, the specific process of designing an optimization algorithm for identifying abnormal data in local area network common channels is shown in the following figure (Fig. 2).

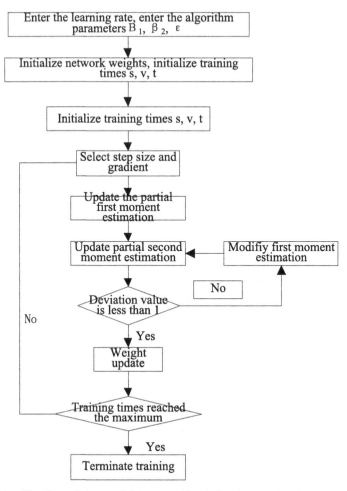

Fig. 2. Algorithm flow of abnormal data recognition in local area network common channel

As shown in the figure above, first, it needs to set the learning rate, generally being 0.001, second, the algorithm parameters β1, β2, ε, are set. Finally, the weight value of the network structure data and the training times are initialized, assigning s = 0, v = 0, t = 0, and then the weight attribute and learning rate are calculated and updated according to the specific formula [18–20]. When the number of learning iterations reaches the maximum, the training is terminated.

3 Experimental Design

3.1 Experiment Preparation

First, a data set of abnormal data on the common channel of the local area network is established. 10,000 original data with accurate labels on the Internet are collected to form the data set V, of which about 200 data are set as abnormal data. The above 10,000 pieces of data are organized into 10 groups, and the data attached to each group is randomly assigned, and the numbers are V1, V2, ..., V10. Then the experimental environment is set up, the main configuration required for this experiment is shown in the following table (Table 1).

Table 1. Experimental environment parameters

	Name	Parameters
Hardware	Processor	Intel 2nd Generation Core i7-2600 @ 3.40 GHz Quad Core
	Hard disk	Seagate ST1000DM003-9YN162
	Motherboard	Asus P8Z68-V LX
	Running memory	16 GB
Software	Operating system	Windows 10 64bit
	Code writing	Notepad++
	Deep learning framework	Tensorflow 1.23

After constructing the network model training platform shown in the above table, the method of identifying abnormal data in the local area network common channel based on the convolutional neural network can be experimentally analyzed. Set algorithm parameters $\beta1 = 0.8$, $\beta2 = 0.865$, $\varepsilon = 10$–8; Initialize the network weight value $\theta = 0$; Initialize the number of training, let $s = 0$, $v = 0$, $t = 0$; Set the maximum number of iterations to 200 and the learning rate to 0.001. Using the convolutional neural network-based abnormal data recognition method of local area network common channel proposed in this paper to calculate the loss value and recognition accuracy. Then, according to the above data set, the traditional data stream-based abnormal data identification method and the log analysis-based abnormal data identification method are used to calculate the loss value and the recognition accuracy rate. Analysis are carried out through the comparison data obtained.

3.2 Analysis of Results

By comparing the three methods for identifying abnormal data in the common channel of the local area network, the data obtained is shown in the following table (Table 2), Fig. 3 and Fig. 4.

The loss value and recognition accuracy of the three methods for identifying abnormal data in the local area network common channel are shown in the table and the figure above. The smaller the loss value, the better the function model used to calculate the loss value. Since the data types and numbers contained in the data sets V1 to V10 are not the same, the loss value of each diversity is different under the same method. However, it can be seen from the horizontal comparison that the loss value of the abnormal data recognition method of the local area network common channel based on the

Table 2. Experimental results

Data set	Based on convolutional neural network		Based on data stream		Based on log analysis	
	Loss value	Recognition accuracy rate	Loss value	Recognition accuracy rate	Loss value	Recognition accuracy rate
V1	0.294	100%	0.985	95.44%	0.563	99.23%
V2	0.265	100%	1.236	90.23%	0.456	100%
V3	0.246	100%	1.342	89.74%	0.741	96.57%
V4	0.365	100%	1.124	88.58%	0.535	99.48%
V5	0.391	100%	1.924	70.23%	0.746	96.74%
V6	0.428	100%	0.463	100%	0.886	91.23%
V7	0.681	98.54%	1.236	86.39%	1.214	84.58%
V8	1.005	95.12%	1.665	80.46%	1.336	85.24%
V9	0.674	98.74%	1.002	86.51%	0.986	90.71%
V10	0.746	96.15%	0.974	87.24%	1.548	80.46%

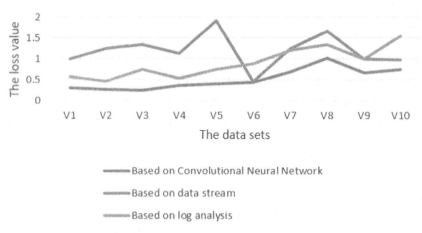

Fig. 3. Experimental results of the loss value

convolutional neural network designed in this paper is generally smaller than the other two methods. The recognition accuracy rate indicates the ability of the function model to recognize abnormal data. The larger the percentage, the higher the accuracy of the method in identifying abnormal data in this experiment. In the above table and the above figure, the abnormal data recognition method of local area network common channel

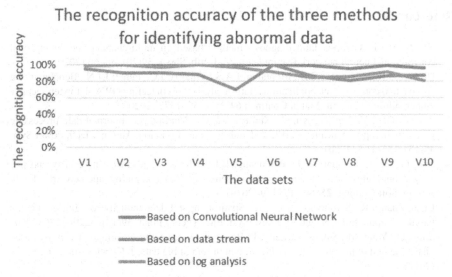

Fig. 4. Experimental results of the recognition accuracy

based on convolutional neural network has the probability of identifying abnormal data in data sets V1 to V10 generally greater than 95%. Compared with the abnormal data recognition method designed in this paper, the accuracy of the other two methods is relatively low. Therefore, it can be judged that the abnormal data recognition method of local area network common channel based on the convolutional neural network designed in this paper is superior to the traditional method and has more practical value.

4 Conclusion

The two commonly used methods for identifying abnormal data in the common channels of local area networks have different limitations. In the experiment, after applying the abnormal data recognition method of the local area network common channel based on the convolutional neural network studied in this paper, the experimental data clearly shows the superiority of the method proposed in this paper. Therefore, in the future research on the abnormal data recognition of the local area network common channel, the method proposed in this article can be used to improve the efficiency of the identification of abnormal data.

Funding Statement. This work was supported by the Natural Science Foundation of Fujian Province, China; Research on network risk assessment method based on dynamic attack behavior (Grant No. 2019J01889), the "Tiancheng Huizhi" Innovation and Education Promotion Fund, China; Construction of Network Risk Assessment Platform Based on Dynamic Attack Behavior(Grant No. 2018A02005), the Education-Scientific research Project for Middle-aged and Young of Fujian Province, China; Research on analysis system of malicious code based on API relevance (Grant No. JT180626).

References

1. Ye, Z., Yu, J.: Gearbox fault diagnosis method based on multi-channel one-dimensional convolutional neural network feature learning. J. Vib. Shock **39**(20), 55–66 (2020)
2. Higuera, J.R.B., Higuera, J.B., Montalvo, J.A.S., Villalba, J.C., Pérez, J.J.N.: Benchmarking approach to compare web applications static analysis tools detecting OWASP top ten security vulnerabilities. Comput. Mater. Continua **64**(3), 1555–1577 (2020)
3. Zou, T., Gao, Y., Yin, H., Xu, C., Xia, R., Wu, C.: Wind power abnormal data processing based on thompson tau-interquartile and multipoint interpolation. Autom. Electr. Power Syst. **44**(15), 156–165 (2020)
4. You, C., Choi, V., Sharma, I., Woungang, B.K.: Bhargava: advances in security and privacy technologies for forthcoming smart systems, services, computing, and networks. Intell. Autom. Soft Comput. **25**(1), 117–119 (2019)
5. Li, J., Zhang, R., Safonov, P., Tong, R.: Spatio-temporal data anomaly recognition method based on copula function and M-K test. Syst. Eng. Theory Pract. **39**(12), 3229–3236 (2019)
6. Yang, G., Yang, M., Salam, S., Zeng, J.: Research on protecting information security based on the method of hierarchical classification in the era of big data. J. Cyber Secur. **1**(1), 19–28 (2019)
7. Wang, L., He, J., Zhang, Z., Zhao, P., Zhang, X.: Research on the method of identifying hydrochemical anomalies of the main component of groundwater based on information screening and laida criterion. Acta Sci. Circum. **38**(03), 919–929 (2018)
8. Fang, W., Zhang, F., Ding, Y., Sheng, J.: A new sequential image prediction method based on LSTM and DCGAN. Comput. Mater. Continua **64**(1), 217–231 (2020)
9. Cai, P., Yang, L., Luo, J.: A fabric defect detection method based on convolutional neural network model fusion. J. Beijing Inst. Fashion Technol. **40**(107(01)), 59–66 (2020)
10. Fang, W., Pang, L., Yi, W.N.: Survey on the application of deep reinforcement learning in image processing. J. Artif. Intell. **2**(1), 39–58 (2020)
11. Hu, X., Chen, Q., Yang, L., et al.: Detection and location of abnormal crowd behavior based on deep spatiotemporal convolutional neural network. Appl. Res. Comput. **037**(003), 891–895 (2020)
12. Liu, C., Wang, Q., Bi, X.: Single image rain removal method based on multi-channel multi-scale convolutional neural network. J. Electron. Inf. Technol. **42**(9), 2285–2292 (2020)
13. Liu, J.: Small sample bark image recognition method based on convolutional neural network. J. Northwest Forestry Univ. **034**(004), 230–235 (2019)
14. Li, J., Chen, G., An, Y.: Image recognition of corn borer pests based on optimized convolutional neural network. J. South China Agric. Univ. **041**(003), 110–116 (2020)
15. Li, Y., Xie, Q., Huang, H., et al: Surface defect detection based on fast region calibration of convolutional neural network. Comput. Integr. Manuf. Syst. (8), 1897–1907 (2019)
16. Long, T., Wan, L., Deng, X.: JavaScript malicious code detection method based on convolutional neural network. Comput. Eng. Appl. **055**(018), 89–94 (2019)
17. Wu, L., Chang, C., Wang, X., et al.: Image recognition method based on locally adjusted convolutional neural network. Comput. Eng. **044**(012), 240–246 (2018)
18. Xue, X., Chen, J.: Optimizing sensor ontology alignment through compact co-firefly algorithm. Sensors **20**(7), 1–15 (2020)
19. Zhang, X., Li, C., Sun, L., et al.: Behavior recognition based on improved 3D convolutional neural network. Comput. Integr. Manuf. Syst. **025**(008), 2000–2006 (2019)
20. Xie, W., Ding, Y., Wang, F., et al.: Camellia seed integrity recognition method based on convolutional neural network. Trans. Chin. Soc. Agric. Mach. (7), 13–21 (2020)

MCF-CSA: A Multi-level Collaboration Framework for Cyber Situation Awareness and Information Sharing

Daochao Huang[1]([⊠]) and Lidong Wang[2]

[1] CNCERT/CC, Beijing 10029, China
huangdc@cert.org.cn
[2] CNNIC, Beijing 10029, China

Abstract. Cyberspace defense has evolved to more than just a single/simple approach to keeping information and infrastructure safe from harm's way. This new trend requires cybersecurity services to be collaboratively provisioned by integrating existing data, capabilities and strategies together, which brings severe challenges as follows: 1) Existing massive, diverse, and heterogeneous data cannot be obtained on demand. 2) Network security-related systems are of various types, complex structures, and diverse models. 3) Due to geographically isolated from each other during operation, these systems are hard to efficiently co-work together. To address these problems, in this paper we propose MCF-CSA, a multi-level collaboration framework for cyber situation awareness and information sharing model against such national broader class of cyber defense. We describe the concept and architecture of MCF-CSA, as well as the initial design of the key components, namely, data collaboration, system collaboration, and operation collaboration. MCF-CSA leverages data collaboration to achieve cybersecurity data convergence, integration and sharing on demand among key industries, enterprises and research institutions. MCF-CSA then leverages system collaboration to realize the interaction between threat recognition, event discovery, and situation awareness. Finally, MCF-CSA leverages operation collaboration to realize interaction of early warning, emergency response and disposal processes based on business needs. In addition, we present convergence, integration and sharing models of data, capabilities and strategies based on data map, threat map and strategy map.

Keywords: Situation awareness · Information sharing · Systematic collaboration · Data collaboration · System collaboration · Operational collaboration

1 Introduction

Today, cyberspace has become the "fifth space" for human activities beyond land, sea, air, and sky. With information technology revolution, infrastructures in the important areas such as politics, economy, military, and culture of the whole society are increasingly connected to cyberspace, and the threats and losses posed by viruses, DoS/DDoS,

© Springer Nature Switzerland AG 2021
X. Sun et al. (Eds.): ICAIS 2021, CCIS 1424, pp. 53–72, 2021.
https://doi.org/10.1007/978-3-030-78621-2_5

Advanced Persistent Threat (APT) attacks, unknown attacks are increasing dramatically. Cyber security threats and security risks in key industries at the national level are also increasing sharply. Therefore, how to make the control of the cyberspace has become a new strategic commanding point, and the problems of cyberspace security have also received more attention in a wider range both in the academic studies [1–3] and industrialization. To enhance the ability of network overall defense at the national level to attack risk, many national information security strategies [4–8] were proposed. Recent trends in the cyberspace security are as follows:

The first is the "new trends of cyberspace". Major countries in the world are increasingly paying attention to research cybersecurity situational awareness technologies and propose new cybersecurity strategies at a national level to meet the challenges of complicated cyberspace. In this field, the United States is preeminent among nations which have invested a lot of resources to form the reasonable rational strategic distribution and mature development work flow. These countries are gradually grasping the current overall security situation and have achieved strategic advantages in cyberspace. According to public information, all countries have elevated cybersecurity to a national strategic level.

The second is "new trends of attack". The attackers are now increasingly focusing on new techniques to keep up with the advances such as cloud computing, big data, machine learning, threat intelligence computing etc. Over the past a few years, there has been a dramatic increase in the scale and diversity of attacks which aims at invalidating critical infrastructure related to the national economy and people's livelihood. These attacks are also evolving quickly, leveraging new or mixed attack vectors, which brings severe challenges beyond traditional defenses. For example, APT always attacks on specific attack targets, through bypassing traditional security protection methods based on signature detection, and can be lurking in the target information system for a long time. Therefore, the traditional defense system built with anti-virus software, firewall, IPS, IDS and other security devices as the main defense methods is difficult to catch up new attacks' evolution.

The third is "new trends of information technology". With the continuously expanding of the Internet scale, an increasing number of vulnerable devices, such as Internet of Things (IoT) devices, cloud platforms and big data platforms are connected online. The risks of these new technologies grow with each passing day, especially with the diverse architectures, the emerging open source components and the geographically dispersed deployment patterns of cloud platforms and big data platforms. More and more security vulnerabilities in these systems are posing a serious threat to users, organizations, and nations at large. How to obtain the overall security situation of these systems has become the major jobs both in the research field and industry field.

The fourth is the "new trends of security situation". With the increasing challenges of new attack situation, attack methods, and attack motives, the stat-of-the-art detection capabilities of existing security products are limited, because they cannot catch up with the unknown attacks such as polymorphic malicious code, APT and 0-day attacks. The existing security defense measures cannot effectively solve the security protection problem, and it is urgent to introduce novel network situation awareness technology to realize security monitoring, early warning and dynamic protection.

Under these newly emerged trends, the cyberspace security situation awareness is also experiencing a new evolution that advocates cooperation among key industries, enterprises and research institutions, and requires cybersecurity services to be collaboratively provisioned by integrating existing data, capabilities and strategies together. However, existing cybersecurity data, capabilities and strategies are provisioned by different providers in a Geo-distributed manner, which brings severe challenges in systematic collaboration. How will we meet these challenges is still an open question.

Key issues of data collaboration: More and more big data platforms involved in cyberspace security situation awareness are proposed to address the data convergence, integration and sharing problems, issues like limited acquisition environment, incomplete data, and cross-domain distribution of data sources are solved partially. However, these platforms typically require a high consumption of bandwidth resources due to the low value dense of the cybersecurity data. On the other hand, current data integration and fusion technologies are conducted in a closed and centralized way, the cybersecurity data runs in a proprietary manner and lacks the mechanism to solve the massive, heterogeneous, complementary, redundant data dispersedly. Besides, there is no guarantee of correctness for data accounting and billing, which may lead to concerns of data sharing to measure and exchange.

Key issues of system collaboration: Most of the existing attack defense solutions focused on how to address new or mixed attacks using one or several systems independently, the recent trends in cyberspace defense, however, need multiple systems to work together to realize capabilities convergence, integration and sharing. This brings new challenges in several aspects. First, a typical threat data integration architecture involves threat data from various source systems being extracted, transformed, and loaded (ETL) into data warehouses, marts, and cubes, where these threat data has characteristics such as wide sources, multiple levels, large differences, and complex internal relationships that are difficult to mine and understand. Second, today's defenses against existing known attacks often fall short for unknown network attacks that are always hidden deeply and difficult to find. Third, for the current network security situation awareness system or platform, they are not comprehensive and enough both from the macro prospective and the micro prospective.

Key issues of operation collaboration: Although existing approaches have delivered certain level of cooperation cross multiple security systems to realize linkage of early warning, emergency response and disposal processes, such solutions require the infrastructure to be managed by a single entity and the services are provisioned by a centralized controller. No feasible solution is proposed to interconnect heterogeneous security infrastructure of multiple entities, which leads to three challenges here. First, the lack of collaboration among different security systems incurs high tracing cost due to the complexity and diversity of the network attacks. Second, the limitations of detection methods and deployment nodes make it difficult to fully track the process of network attacks. Third, how to effectively eliminate event clues from the massive security data is still an open question.

To address these problems described above, this paper introduces MCF-CSA, a cross-system cooperation architecture for integrated cyberspace data, capabilities and strategies based on systematic collaboration. MCF-CSA is composed by three key components, namely, data collaboration, system collaboration, and operation collaboration, which is the first coordinated cyberspace security situation awareness and trust information sharing model against such national broader class of cyber defense.

In the rest of this paper, we survey the related work in Section 2 and present the necessary concepts as well as the envisioned overall architecture of MCF-CSA in Section 3. We will finally conclude this paper in Section 4.

2 Related Work

In this section we introduce the relate work of the collaboration in data, system and operation in cyberspace.

2.1 Data Collaboration

Today, the amount of information on the Internet is continually expanding, and massive data is natively provided by different online platforms. Thus, data processing technology is playing a more and more critical and central role in the development of cyberspace. Data collaboration between platforms in cyberspace, a newly emerging field that encompasses a number of activities, such as data aggregation, integration, fusion and sharing, has become an integral part of situation awareness.

For data collaboration, data acquisition or aggregation is the basis of cyberspace security situation awareness. Most existing approaches now focus on how to ensure that the collected information is a complete set for the fusion analysis in next step and on standardizing the collected datasets. Literature [9] divided the categories of sensors into three categories: activity, configuration, and topology. In addition, in the specific field such as sensor network, IoT, edge computing and smart grid, the scope or type of collected information may be different [10–16].

The fusion analysis ability on the related information is the advantage of cyberspace security situation awareness. The core method is to derive the hidden knowledge from the data from different sources. The related literatures are divided into three parts: one is the instantiation of data fusion model in traditional situation awareness [17, 18]; one is to propose a specific fusion technology or idea based on the characteristics of network security data. For example, Mathews et al. [19] designed data models or coordinate working systems to integrate data from different network sensors. Other literatures attempt to deal with multi-source heterogeneous data [20–27] combined machine learning or deep learning methods. These methods are used in different scenarios, such as truth discovery [20], topic discovery [21], topic mining [22], data fusion [23–25], knowledge fusion [26, 27] respectively.

While the above approaches have provided an important starting point to bridge the heterogeneity among massive data, they often require the infrastructure to be managed by a single entity. No feasible solution is proposed to interconnect heterogeneous data infrastructure of multiple entities. Besides, current data consolidation is conducted in a closed and centralized way, the sharing of data run in a proprietary manner and lacks the mechanism to exchange data across different providers.

2.2 System Collaboration

Some advanced situation awareness algorithms and models have been proposed to address the requirement of cross-system capability integration, high availability and high-performance of attack defense. For common methods in situation awareness, Literature [28] divides the current algorithms into five categories: Bayesian approach, knowledge-based approach, artificial neural systems approach, fuzzy logic approach, and genetic algorithm approach. For the behavior analysis of attackers or defenders, hidden Markov chains are used to predict internal attack threats in literature [29], combined with game theory [30], machine learning method [31], and honeypot technology [32]. For algorithms efficiency in large scale networks, real-time decision analysis method [33] and fast calculation method for static statistical data [34] were approached.

Typically, the attack models contain three components, namely, model definition, model solving algorithm, and solution result. The definition of the model is generally combined with other disciplines, such as game theory [35], and Bayesian network [36], and some articles also focus on the improvement of model description ability [37]. Depending on the definition of the model, the solution algorithm is generally shown together with the solution result. Numinous approaches [38, 39] try to improve on this point, such as the reachable path analysis based on attack graph [40, 41], defense strategy analysis [38], and survivability analysis [37].

As to the systematic evaluation after quantifying, there are three main parts: systematization of evaluation index, index quantification, and quantified results and its application. The research on the systematization of evaluation index and the quantification of corresponding indicators mainly can be divided into two types: security attribute and attack behavior. According to the quantification of the 3 elements (attack severity, attack occurrence/success probability, and attack income), we can form a certain standard and then develop risk assessment algorithm to get the perception or evaluation result on the basis of index system and index quantification.

Although the above approaches actively developed certain level of cooperation between different types of security systems, most of them focused only on one or several mixed known attacks, for the unknown attacks, these situation awareness platforms lack the mechanisms to standardize indicators both from the micro or macro perspective and levels of the security incidents, forcing all security service vendors using a single abstraction would have a long way. In addition, there is no practical deep integration at the level of model and algorithm. Fusion perception must be a process of multiple cycles between information and decision-making. Most of the existing models are unidirectional, and the level of feedback effect should be effectively embodied in the model after perception decision.

2.3 Operation Collaboration

Consideration for the overall logic rather than a certain segment is key challenges in the operation collaboration, in view of the fact that the overall logic means that it should be designed from the perspective of software engineering. For the security incident processing, literature [42] gives a task flow chart according to processes, goals, and concerns. For the practical application of prediction results in specific fields, the present statistical results mainly concentrate on the following field: one is the application of industrial control networks [14, 16, 37]; one is for the emergency management of the key equipment, such as the shared situation awareness; and another is in the military field, such as the practice application of nautical training [12].

Most of the existing approaches are still facing the challenges include the overload of raw data, low speed of reaction, and a lack of context and unified view on cyberspace due to the continuous explosion of technologies such as IoT, edge computing and machine learning. There are a variety of attack techniques, defense solutions target certain techniques do not work for others. Cyberspace security situation awareness is a more advanced stage of network security research. It is not a model or a method. It should be a more valuable framework from all the existing network security concepts or means. There is a long way to go now, and the design and realization of network security situation awareness can be done from the perspective of instrumental software, which integrates the characteristics of all kinds of users and systems in the network.

3   MCF-CSA Architecture

The multi-level collaboration system includes three levels: data collaboration, system collaboration, and operation collaboration, as shown in the figure below. Among them, data collaboration is oriented to the convergence, fusion and sharing of data; system collaboration is oriented to the convergence, fusion and sharing of threat information; operation collaboration is oriented to the convergence, fusion and sharing of strategy (Fig. 1).

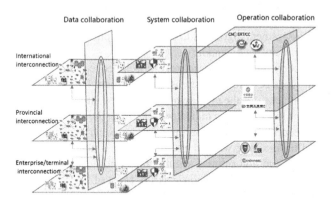

Fig. 1. MCF-CSA architecture

4   Data Collaboration

4.1   Multi-source Discrete Data Description

According to the data source, the cyber security data is divided into five categories: The first type of security data is raw data, including system logs or network communication data. Here, system logs are usually generated by the host system, such as operating system logs, system software logs, application software logs, etc.; Communication data includes network packet records, network flow records, domain name access logs, etc. This type of data is inherently security-independent, and is a record that reflects the attributes of the objective activities of the network and the systems on it, including time attributes, space attributes, creator attributes, content attributes, etc. The meaning of the raw data is given by a specific interpretation act, which can be used for security purposes or for other purposes, such as troubleshooting and billing.

The second type of security data is resource data, which is the attribute data of the key resources of the network, such as domain name resource data.

The third type of security data is event data, for example, the logs generated by the security systems, which is the data obtained after further processing, analysis and distillation of the raw data for network security purposes, such as detected malicious IP addresses, malicious domain names, and phishing email sending addresses, malicious code characteristics, etc. This type of data is directly related to security.

The fourth type of security data is knowledge data, which is systematic and regular data obtained after experience or value refinement and precipitation of long-term cyber threat intelligence data. It is usually called knowledge base, such as virus database, malicious code characteristics, malicious domain name databases and other knowledge bases. Knowledge data forms a knowledge graph through analysis and mining, association mapping, organization and management, and expresses knowledge in a way closer to human understanding.

The fifth type of security data is summary data, which is summary description of the target data set, that is, metadata.

For the multiple heterogeneous data described above, the existing formal description specifications can be summarized as follows:

1) Host system format specification: Syslog protocol
2) Network data packet format specification: Pcap file format
3) Network flow data format specification: Netflow Version 5
4) The indication standard of the failure index: CybOX
5) Threat intelligence representation specification: STIX
6) Network vulnerability description specification: CNVD

4.2 Data Acquisition System

Data aggregation is oriented to the acquisition of multiple heterogeneous data in cyberspace, forming a data acquisition system that combines passive monitoring, active crawling, customized interfaces and international data exchange protocols.

Passive Capture. The physical interface usually uses the optical split mode, and the data objects obtained are generally network original packets (IPv4, IPv6). To improve the acquisition performance, the package catching equipment generally adopts zero copy or DPDK method. Due to the involvement of other device configuration lines, the port mirroring method is classified as a custom protocol acquisition method.

Active Crawling. Active crawling methods are generally oriented to open network service, and the acquired data objects include any publicly accessible service content, such as web content, open source intelligence, etc. Web crawlers follow the crawling mechanism recognized by the industry, and key indicators include collection period of objects, general collection objects, the number of collection targets, the number of supported protocols/services, etc.

Customized Acquisition. Customized acquisition is based on protocol exchange, and the communication method can adopt physical dedicated lines, Internet channels or VPNs, and inter-system interfaces. The acquired data objects are various types of data, including network original message sets, routing data sets, stream data sets, domain name data sets, web log data sets, threat intelligence data sets, APP log data sets, etc. The protocol processing of data needs to be based on the exchange data representation format.

Data Aggregation. Data aggregation includes physical aggregation and logical aggregation. Within the same autonomous domain, data can be physically converged to a centralized or distributed data center, and the data catalog and the data map can be automatically created while converging. Relevant standards and specifications include physical convergence reference models (such as the forwarding island model used by central network security data convergence, which defines fan-in and fan-out indicators for single-node data exchange). Logic convergence can be in the same autonomous domain or among different autonomous domains. Generally, they converge to a distributed data center. The data resource information is synchronized based on the data map, and the data sharing based on the data map can be also considered.

To address the data aggregation problems in cyberspace, we introduce a flexible expansion of high, middle and low levels of data aggregation standards:

1) Passive data catching interface specifications: such as "zero-copy-based network traffic processing platform specifications", "DPDK-based network traffic processing platform specifications". According to these specifications, we made a data catching device, which can handle the maximum network traffic at no less than 15Gbps without packet loss.
2) Standard specifications and mechanisms for customized acquisition: such as "Technical specifications for traction and acquisition of high-value target traffic data".
3) We introduced a novel model that is called "forwarding island model", in which data is gathered from different autonomous domains. Here, this model provided a data hub for data extracting, transform and loading.

To facilitate the data aggregation, we summarized existing data collection specifications as follows:

1) Threat intelligence exchange format specification: TAXII 2.0.
2) NIEM (National Information Exchange Model): this is a reference model developed by the United States to promote efficient information exchange, including core data model and domain data model.

4.3 Multiple Heterogeneous Data Fusion Framework

Based on the representation model and description specification that facilitates data processing and exchange, data fusion meets the needs of multiple heterogeneous data processing and sharing in cyberspace and realizes the convergence of heterogeneous data at the data level of messages, streams, and domain names.

Data fusion includes explicit fusion and mining fusion. Explicit fusion is based on data mapping tables and rule sets. Mining fusion is based on various algorithms to mine implicit association relationships among multi-source data.

Typically, data fusion needs to process a large amount of data. In practice, the characteristics of the data set can be screened to reduce the amount of data processing, that is, the data dimensionality reduction method is employed to find a meaningful low-dimensional structure hidden in high-dimensional observation data by mapping the data samples from the high-dimensional space to the low-dimensional space. Here, the problem of dimensionality disaster in processing high-dimensional data is avoided. Typical data dimensionality reduction methods include principal component analysis, auto-encoding neural network, etc. Some existing research proposes a data dimensionality reduction model based on deep residual coding neural network and a fuzzy rough set-based feature selection method to reduce the data dimensionality, in which the selected feature subset is highly correlated with the classification result, but has little dependence on other features.

To solve these problems, we proposed a multi-view systematic and fine-grained data fusion specification, which support following specifications:

1) The standard of indication of failure index: CybOX
2) Threat intelligence representation specification: STIX
3) Network vulnerability description specification: CNVD
4) A data dimensionality reduction model based on deep residual coding neural network
5) A feature selection based on fuzzy rough set.

4.4 Information Sharing Model Based on Fair Exchange of Multi-party Discrete Data

Data sharing forms a long-term mechanism for network security-related data exchange and sharing at high, middle and low levels respectively, including data sharing models, privacy protection methods, data and service quality evaluation, data pricing models, and information sharing models based on the fair exchange of multi-party discrete data.

Data Sharing Model. To realize rapid positioning of data resources in multi-party data sharing and exchange, we introduce a novel concept called "data map", which is a shared data resource map drew by using data geographic location information. Based on data map, we proposed a data sharing model, that is, a publish-subscribe model to establish real-time interaction of sharing information between supply and demand parties to ensure the timely spread and dissemination of data sharing and multi-party data information.

Privacy Data Protection. According to our design, the data sharing platform does not store the data of all parties, because privacy and data protection standards in different countries and enterprises are incompatible. Based on the feature that the "data sharing platform" does not store the data of all parties, research is conducted to protect privacy during the data transmission phase. A data privacy protection method based on data desensitization is adopted to adaptively realize shared data deactivation according to the own attributes of shared data and different application scenarios, realize privacy data protection in data sharing, and prevent sensitive information from leaking.

Data and Service Quality Evaluation. Based on historical and feedback information of the supplier and the demander, we provide a data and service quality evaluation model to realize the exchange of data quality and service capability evaluation. Our method is the long-term development of data sharing mechanisms and ensures the rights and interests of both the supplier and the demander. We considered three types of evaluation mechanisms, including data quality evaluation, service quality evaluation and service incentive mechanism. Among them, data quality evaluation is an evaluation mechanism for the value of the data provider's information availability and information scarcity; service quality evaluation is an evaluation mechanism for the data provider's service capabilities in the process of sharing information, including interactive response time, ability to provide effective information, etc.; the service incentive mechanism is to provide information sharing parties with their contributions to data quality, service quality (including reputation), etc., and promote all parties reward and punishment mechanism for information sharing enthusiasm.

Data Pricing Model. Data sharing can also be called data transaction. According to different transaction content, different pricing (price) models are required. Considering the actual big data transaction situation, one-to-one, one-to-many and many-to-one models, and many-to-many models are considered.

Information Sharing Model Based on the Fair Exchange of Multi-party Discrete Data. Typically, the information sharing model framework based on the fair exchange of multi-party discrete data includes four parts: identity authentication, authority management, information sharing, and evaluation and incentives among them:

Identity authentication provides an access control mechanism for information exchange and sharing of identity authentication and credit verification of all parties involved.

Authority management provides authority control for information exchange and sharing information access, including: information access authority, information use authority, information operation authority, etc.

Information sharing provides a mechanism for information sharing and exchange to ensure the dissemination and exchange of information among all parties involved. Specifically it includes information pre-processing, data map, demand map, data pricing, data copyright and data exchange, etc.

Evaluation and incentives provide an overall evaluation and service incentive mechanism to ensure the enthusiasm and fairness of services of all parties involved in information sharing, and promote the long-term development of information sharing systems and mechanisms. Specifically it includes information quality evaluation, service quality evaluation and service incentive mechanism.

4.5   Data Collaboration System

As shown in Fig. 2, to achieve better data aggregation, acquisition methods such as passive capture, active crawling, and customized acquisition are used both from high- and low levels. Here, data aggregation can be further divided into two types: one is the intra domain physical aggregation, in which storage resources are deployed and managed by a single owner, it does not provide support to the heterogeneous requirements of different users and the system policy is enforced by a single provider; the other is cross domain logical aggregation, in which all data from different sources has to be stored and shared.

Typically, how to integrate information from multi-source data is critical for finding out the key information about an attack. There are two main challenges here, the dimensionality reduction and the redundant information elimination, the former will slow down the aggregation model response time, while the latter will affect the accuracy of the model. Attribute similarity methods are usually used to remove multi-source data redundancy, which involve in how to determine the feature weight based on rough set theory and knowledge granularity.

Next, the multi-source heterogeneous data set after data aggregation is fused into a new data set so that new knowledge and valuable information can be drawn out from the data, which is convenient for unified query and processing. In the process of data fusion, data conflicts and inconsistencies will inevitably occur. To address this problem, the D-S evidence theory is typically used to calculate the distance gap between the various evidence sources, that is, the larger the gap between the evidence sources, then the lower the confidence level. As an example, explicit or mining data fusion technologies, combined with CHR model or CFM model, are considered to solve the conflicts for fusion of multi-source data.

Finally, multi-party fair exchange mechanism is employed to complete data sharing process. There are two key issues here: one is how to effectively measure and accurately evaluate the data value; the other is how to protect data privacy against external security risks. In a multi-source integration scenario, according to range requirements (such as single row, single table, multiple rows and historical range), data characteristics (such as reversibility, consistency, completeness, relevance, completeness), original data attributes (such as data volume, redundancy), data desensitization methods are approached to preserve the data privacy.

Based on the above aggregation, fusion and integration stages, we form a data map with which subscription and publishing mechanism is used to sharing data among key industries, enterprises and research institutions. Specifications like NIEM are further used to define information exchange specification and information exchange packet format. Besides, data map specification, privacy protection standards are introduced in our model to provide privacy protection and quality evaluation.

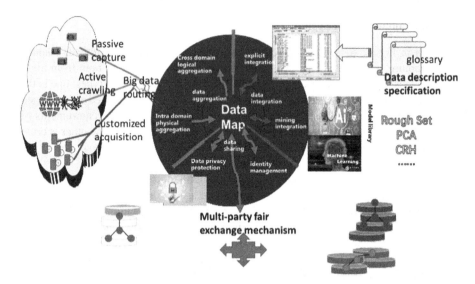

Fig. 2. Data collaboration model based on data map

5   System Collaboration

Network security system collaboration, in the final analysis, is the collaboration of the network security system's capabilities of acquiring, processing, and analyzing cyber security threat intelligence. That is, system collaboration mainly focuses on the convergence, fusion and sharing of network security system capabilities. By designing collaboration models and indicator systems that proposed the formal description of cybersecurity incidents and threat elements, the formal description of cyber environments and abnormal behaviors, cybersecurity quantify index system and situation awareness index are achieved.

5.1   System Capability Convergence and Collaboration

Generally, there are six different types of security systems in the system collaboration model: supply system, investigation system, monitoring system, control system, analysis system and management system. The functions of these systems are as follows:

Supply System. It provides external network security-related raw data, intelligence data, knowledge data or smart data, which can be implemented as an interface module for data collaboration.

Reconnaissance System. It uses active detection methods to obtain information of the target host, system or network, and perceives the specific threat status of specific targets. These systems include but not limited to: IP/domain name attribute detection, service detection, asset modeling, network mapping, website hanging horse detection, webpage tampering detection, webpage counterfeiting detection, threat intelligence crawling, etc.

Monitoring System. There are two types of monitoring system. The first is to passively monitor network traffic (messages, flows, domain names, routes, etc.), including but not limited to protocol identification, anomaly perception, vulnerability exploitation, sample capture, propagation monitoring, zombie worm monitoring, phishing website monitoring, malicious code detection, malicious domain name monitoring, DDoS attack monitoring, 0-day attack monitoring, specific APT attack monitoring, data loss monitoring, dark web monitoring, etc. By matching the content characteristics or behavior characteristics of the traffic data, it recognizes the threat information carried or hidden in the traffic data and identifies network threats. The second is to monitor and detect the terminal system to recognize the potential threat information in the terminal system, including but not limited to: anomaly perception, vulnerability exploitation, etc.

Control System. It uses session reset, redirection, relay and other means to block, bypass, and take over specific sessions, including but not limited to: traffic cleaning, attack blocking, man-in-the-middle, etc.

Analysis System. By deeply mining of log data of various network security systems, information such as threat situation, threat characteristics, and attacker characteristics can be obtained. These analysis systems include but not limited to: attack behavior analysis, attack feature extraction, homologous mutation analysis, unknown threat discovery, network security situational awareness, network actors profile, threat tracing, etc.

Management System. It manages all kinds of data, including but not limited to: unified threat management, incident management, vulnerability management, etc.

The capability of the network security system is manifested in the collection, processing, analysis and mining of security elements (security indicators, status information and event information) in the regional network. Systems with different functions provide different sets of security elements and necessary calculation indicators for situation awareness calculation. The key to jointly complete threat convergence based on security systems described above is the acquisition of threat information generated by multiple heterogeneous cybersecurity systems in cyberspace, forming a combination of specific target detection and perception, traffic feature recognition and monitoring, system feature capture and matching, and further in-depth analysis.

5.2 System Capability Integration and Collaboration

In order to achieve the integration of network security system capabilities, it is necessary to standardize the representation of system capabilities. By standardizing the formal description of network security events and threat elements, the formal description of network environment and behavior abnormalities, we establish a network security threat calculation model, and realize the integration of threat intelligence in the large-scale network security systems.

Specification of Formal Description of Cyber Security Incidents and Threat Elements. In terms of the formal description and sharing of threat intelligence information, there is currently no universal threat intelligence standard in the world. The typical models include TAXII, MAEC, OVAL, CAPEC, X-Force Exchange, OpenIoC, IoCBucker, MISP etc. In view of the fact that most existing systems currently support CybOX, STIX and TAXII specifications, and there are corresponding national standards for threat intelligence and security event descriptions, our indicator system adopts directly these specification for threat intelligence fusion.

Network Security Quantitative Index System. For the situational awareness of a single domain z, we select the basic resources (routing system, domain name system, etc.), important applications (e-commerce services, social services, life services, etc.), key targets (key assets, key departments, and key points) in the domain Users, etc.) to construct a single domain network entity set V_{net_z} and netizen user set U_cA_z. The calculation of the situation index of domain z comprehensively considers the network survivability, the security awareness of netizens, and the overall threat of network security, that is: the better the network survivability, the higher the security awareness of netizens, the safer the network and the higher the situation index; The greater the overall threat to network security, the higher the risk the network faces, and the situation index value is set to be lower. For this reason, the situation index of domain z is defined as (where ρ is the expansion coefficient):

$$Cyber\,Sec\,A_z = \rho \times Netizen\,Sec\,A_{U_cA_z} \times S_{V_{net_z}} / Threat_{V_{net_z}}$$

Where $Threat_{V_{net_j}}$ is the network threat. Based on the integration of threat intelligence, all entities V_{net_z} are facing a series of network attacks $N_cA_{V_{net}} = \{N_cA_1, N_cA_2, ..., N_cA_{cnt}\}$, for attacks $N_cA_j \in N_cA_{V_{net}}$, the set of network entities are defined as V_{net_j}, which is part of V_{net}. For $\forall v_x \in V_{net}$, if we set the importance weight as w_{v_x}, then for the attack N_cA_j, we can the definition of the network threat as follows:

$$Threat_{V_{net}} = \sum_{v_x \in V_{net_j}} w_{v_x}$$

For all current network attacks $N_cA_{V_{net}}$, the overall threat faced by the network V_{net} is defined as:

$$Threat_{V_{net}} = \sum_{V_j \in V_{net}} Threat_{V_j}$$

Next, we further give the definition of the security awareness of netizens, which is manifested in the security risks and threats faced by netizens' terminals. Suppose the sample user terminal set is $U_cA = \{ua_1, ua_2, ..., ua_y\}$. For $ua_i \in U_cA$, suppose that the security risk of its terminal is represented by the weighted sum of the scores of the set of possible weaknesses in the terminal system Vul_{ua_i}, and the security threats it receives are represented by threat intelligence-related networks The network threat index $N_cA_{ua_i}$ brought by the attack set $Threat_{ua_i}$, then its security awareness is defined as:

$$Netizen\,Sec\,A_{ua_i} = 1/\left(w_{nsa_ivul} \times Vul_{ua_i} + w_{nsa_ithreat} \times Threat_{ua_i}\right)$$

The overall security awareness of netizens is quantified as:

$$Netizen\,Sec_c\,A_{U_cA} = \sum_{ua_i \in U_cA} Netizen\,Sec_c\,A_{ua_i}/y$$

For a multi-domain z composed of multiple single domains Z the overall ZZ network situation index is defined as the weighted sum of the network situation indexes of each single domain z:

$$Cyber\,Sec_c\,A_Z = \sum_{z \in Z} w_z Cyber\,Sec_c\,A_z$$

The situational awareness index described above can comprehensively consider intelligence acquisition capabilities, disposal capabilities of different departments and industry networks at high, medium, and low levels, improving the existing methods. It is not only suitable for single-domain situational awareness in a controllable single domain, but also suitable for real cyberspace with dynamic confrontation.

5.3 System Coordination System

To facilitate the cooperation among these systems, a novel model based on threat map is introduced to realize system collaboration. The model mainly focuses on how to aggregate, integration and sharing the threat intelligence according to the threat intelligence fusion specification. In view of the fact that most existing systems already support CybOX, STIX and TAXII specifications, and some other national standards for threat intelligence and security incident descriptions, our indicator system is directly comparably support these existing specifications and standards (Fig. 3).

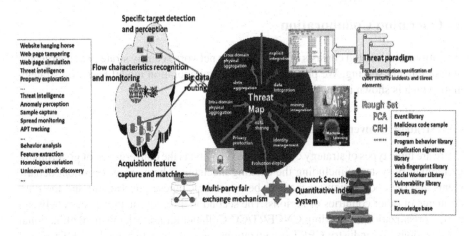

Fig. 3. System collaboration model based on threat map

In our model, basic network operation security, Internet environment security, security risks and netizens' perceptions, etc., are considered together to achieve quantitative evaluation of network security indicators. Besides, we design the formal description of network security events and threat elements, network environment and behavior abnormalities. Based on the indicator and specification designs, a model combined with situational factors that internal and external threat factors, changes in the network environment, the situation and influence of emerging applications/equipment, are introduced to achieve a situational awareness index that integrates multiple states.

A situational factor combination model based on the internal factors (weaknesses) of cybersecurity threats, external factors (cyber-attacks) of cybersecurity threats, changes in the network environment, the situation and influence of emerging applications/equipment (multi-domain) are defined in our model to achieve a situational awareness index that integrates multiple states. We divide the establishment of the model into two steps, the network vulnerability index evaluation and the network threat index calculation.

The network vulnerability index evaluation model adopts the principle of hierarchical and hierarchical calculation. According to the scale of the network topology, the network vulnerability index of the basic network is calculated first, and then the higher-level network vulnerability index is calculated through the basic network index. The network vulnerabilities are classified according to certain classification standards, and the attributes of the vulnerabilities and related network vulnerabilities are evaluated according to the attributes of the classes. In this process, the software quality and the direct losses caused by the exploitation of the vulnerabilities are mainly considered.

Establish a network threat index calculation method based on the characteristics of network threat events. The model adopts the principle of hierarchical and hierarchical calculation. According to the scale of the network topology, the network threat index of the basic network is calculated first, and then the higher-level network threat index is calculated through the basic network threat index.

6   Operation Collaboration

Operation coordination consists of three aspects: network security strategy convergence, integration and sharing. We provided a running collaboration model based on strategy map, which is shown in the Fig. 4.

6.1   Strategy Convergence and Collaboration

There are three types of strategy convergence. The first is the convergence of governmental regulatory systems, including the existing mechanism between government departments and the cooperation mechanism between the Chinese government and the governments of other countries or regions. The second is the coordination system between CERT organizations, including CNCERT/CC Collaboration mechanisms with national organizations and industry CERT organizations, as well as between CNCERT/CC and CERTs in other countries or regions abroad. The third is the support system of cybersecurity enterprises to government departments and CNCERT/CC or other CERTs, including the support system for government departments, the support system for the organization CERT, and the support system for important customers. Through these three

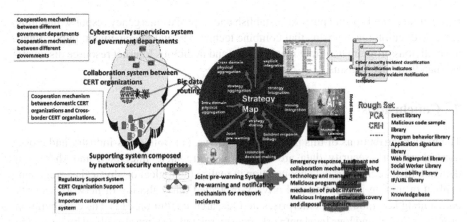

Fig. 4. Operation collaboration model based on strategy map

types of mechanisms, various handling strategies for coordinating specific cybersecurity incidents are brought together.

6.2 Strategic Integration and Coordination

In terms of strategy integration and coordination, by formulating the classification and classification indicators of network security incidents, and network security incident notification templates, the strategies converged by the strategy convergence and coordination system are integrated and excavated to meet the requirements of linkage processing. Then, the classification indicators of cybersecurity incidents, cybersecurity incident information and early warning information are defined separately. For example, incident information is divided into four levels: particularly major, major, large, and general; early warning information is divided into first, second, third and fourth level. Finally, network security incident notification template are designed, which includes incident classification, early warning notification scope, current handling status, situation evolution assessment, emergency response level recommendations, etc.

6.3 Strategy Sharing and Collaboration

To satisfy the cybersecurity needs of early warning and notification of routine, emergency, and special cyber security incidents and cyber security situation, build a joint early warning system, with a three-level early warning notification system of high, medium and low levels, corresponding to countries, provinces, and cities, and establish high, medium and low levels of cyber security incidents Joint early warning and linkage mechanism. Focus on meeting the needs of regular cybersecurity incidents and cybersecurity situation early warning notifications, establishing and improving cybersecurity event early warning notification mechanisms, and proposing early warning notification organizational structure systems, early warning notification methods, models, scopes, procedures, and early warning notifications that are adapted to my country's cybersecurity regulatory system Contents, etc., on this basis, to further share and coordinate needs for emergency and special purpose, establish and improve emergency response handling and coordination mechanisms that combine technology and management, public Internet malicious program handling mechanisms, and malicious Internet resource discovery and handling mechanisms.

7 Conclusions

The main contributions of this paper are as follows. (1) Both cross-industry and cross-domain network security data are efficiently aggregated, integrated and shared on demand. MCF-CSA uses data cooperation to realize the logical or physical aggregation, explicit or mining integration and privacy-protected fairly sharing of network security data among key industries, enterprises and research institutions. (2) The collaboration problem of high- and low-level network security related systems are solved by designing three levels of system collaboration to realize the on-demand aggregation of the capabilities, threat elements, security incidents belonging to different systems. (3) Operational collaboration provides the solution of network security event monitoring, early warning, emergency response and disposal processes for key targets. The key point of operational collaboration is how to use business requirements as a traction to efficiently implement continuous monitoring during the entire life cycle of cybersecurity incidents.

Acknowledgement. This work is supported by The National Key Research and Development Program of China (2017YFB0803001).

References

1. Endsley, M.R.: Design and evaluation for situation awareness enhancement. In: Proceeding of the 32nd Human Factors Society Annual Meeting, pp. 97–101 (1988)
2. Gong, Z.H., Ying, Z.: Research on cyberspace situational awareness. J. Softw. **21**(7), 1605–1619 (2010)
3. Ning, H., Ye, X., Bouras, M., Wei, D., Daneshmand, M.: General cyberspace: cyberspace and cyber-enabled spaces. IEEE Internet of Things J. **5**(3), 1843–1856 (2018). https://doi.org/10.1109/JIOT.2018.2815535
4. Canada's Cyber Security Strategy. https://www.publicsafety.gc.ca/cnt/rsrcs/pblctns/ntnl-cbr-scrt-strtg/ntnl-cbr-scrt-strtg-en.pdf
5. Cyber Security Strategy for Germany Report. http://www.bmi.bund.de
6. New Zealand's Cyber Security Strategy (2019). https://dpmc.govt.nz/sites/default/files/2019-07/Cyber%20Security%20Strategy.pdf
7. UK's Cyber Security Strategy. https://www.gov.uk/government/publications/national-cyber-security-strategy-2016-to-2021
8. Australia's Cyber Security Strategy. https://cybersecuritystrategy.homeaffairs.gov.au/AssetLibrary/dist/assets/images/PMC-Cyber-Strategy.pdf
9. Lenders, V., Tanner, A., Blarer, A.: Gaining an edge in cyberspace with advanced situational awareness. IEEE Secur. Priv. **13**(2), 65–74 (2015)
10. Schreiber-Ehle, S., Koch, W.: The JDL model of data fusion applied to cyber-defence—a review paper. In: 2012 Workshop on Sensor Data Fusion: Trends, Solutions, Applications (SDF), pp. 116–119. IEEE (2012)

11. Ralston, P.A.S., Graham, J.H., Hieb, J.L.: Cyber security risk assessment for SCADA and DCS networks. ISA Trans. **46**(4), 583–594 (2007)
12. Sanfilippo, F.: A multi-sensor fusion framework for improving situational awareness in demanding maritime training. Reliab. Eng. Syst. Saf. **161**, 12–24 (2017)
13. Adhikari, U., Morris, T.H., Dahal, N., et al.: Development of power system test bed for data mining of synchrophasors data, cyber-attack and relay testing in RTDS. In: 2012 IEEE Power and Energy Society General Meeting, pp. 1–7. IEEE (2012)
14. Wu, J., Ota, K., Dong, M., et al.: Big data analysis-based security situational awareness for smart grid. IEEE Trans. Big Data **4**(3), 408–417 (2016)
15. Rapuzzi, R., Repetto, M.: Building situational awareness for network threats in fog/edge computing: emerging paradigms beyond the security perimeter model. Futur. Gener. Comput. Syst. **85**, 235–249 (2018)
16. Mozzaquatro, B.A., Jardim-Goncalves, R., Agostinho, C.: Situation awareness in the Internet of Things. In: 2017 International Conference on Engineering, Technology and Innovation (ICE/ITMC), pp. 982–990. IEEE (2017)
17. Endsley, M.R.: Design and evaluation for situation awareness enhancement. In: Proceedings of the Human Factors Society Annual Meeting, vol. 32, no. 2, pp. 97–101. SAGE Publications, Sage (1988)
18. Endsley, M.R.: Toward a theory of situation awareness in dynamic systems. Hum. Factors **37**(1), 32–64 (1995)
19. Mathews, M.L., Halvorsen, P., Joshi, A., et al.: A collaborative approach to situational awareness for cybersecurity. In: 8th International Conference on Collaborative Computing: Networking, Applications and Worksharing (CollaborateCom), pp. 216–222. IEEE (2012)
20. Chang, C., Cao, J., Zheng, Q., et al.: An unsupervised approach of truth discovery from multi-sourced text data. IEEE Access **7**, 143479–143489 (2019)
21. Wang, X., Wu, X., Xie, X., et al.: Hybrid text topic discovery method for multi-source information. In: 2019 IEEE Fourth International Conference on Data Science in Cyberspace (DSC), pp. 445–452. IEEE (2019)
22. Cai, Y., Wu, X., Xie, X., et al.: A topic mining method for multi-source network public opinion based on improved hierarchical clustering. In: 2019 IEEE Fourth International Conference on Data Science in Cyberspace (DSC), pp. 439–444. IEEE (2019)
23. Zhang, L., Xie, Y., Xidao, L., et al.: Multi-source heterogeneous data fusion. In: 2018 International Conference on Artificial Intelligence and Big Data (ICAIBD), pp. 47–51. IEEE (2018)
24. Mixia, L., Qiuyu, Z., Hong, Z., et al.: Network security situation assessment based on data fusion. In: First International Workshop on Knowledge Discovery and Data Mining (WKDD 2008), pp. 542–545. IEEE (2008)
25. Zheng, Y.: Methodologies for cross-domain data fusion: an overview. IEEE Trans. Big Data **1**(1), 16–34 (2015)
26. Song, Y., Li, A., Jia, Y., et al.: Knowledge fusion: introduction of concepts and techniques. In: 2019 IEEE Fourth International Conference on Data Science in Cyberspace (DSC), pp. 112–118. IEEE (2019)
27. Zhao, X., Jia, Y., Li, A., et al.: Multi-source knowledge fusion: a survey. World Wide Web **23**(4), 2567–2592 (2020)
28. Hinman, M.L.: Some computational approaches for situation assessment and impact assessment. In: Proceedings of the Fifth International Conference on Information Fusion. FUSION 2002 (IEEE Cat. No. 02EX5997), vol. 1, pp. 687–693. IEEE (2002)
29. Tang, K., Zhou, M.T., Wang, W.Y.: Insider cyber threat situational awareness framwork using dynamic Bayesian networks. In: 2009 4th International Conference on Computer Science & Education, pp. 1146–1150. IEEE (2009)

30. Cai, J.Y., Yegneswaran, V., Alfeld, C., et al.: Honeynet games: a game theoretic approach to defending network monitors. J. Comb. Optim. **22**(3), 305–324 (2011)
31. Dietterich, T., Bao, X., Keiser, V., Shen, J.: Machine learning methods for high level cyber situation awareness. In: Jajodia, S., Liu, P., Swarup, V., Wang, C. (eds.) Cyber Situational Awareness, pp. 227–247. Springer, Boston (2010). https://doi.org/10.1007/978-1-4419-0140-8_11
32. Barford, P., Chen, Y., Goyal, A., Li, Z., Paxson, V., Yegneswaran, V.: Employing honeynets for network situational awareness. In: Jajodia, S., Liu, P., Swarup, V., Wang, C. (eds.) Cyber Situational Awareness, pp. 71–102. Springer, Boston (2010). https://doi.org/10.1007/978-1-4419-0140-8_5
33. Stotz, A., Sudit, M.: Information fusion engine for real-time decision-making (INFERD): a perceptual system for cyber attack tracking. In: 2007 10th International Conference on Information Fusion, pp. 1–8. IEEE (2007)
34. Dapoigny, R., Barlatier, P.: Formal foundations for situation awareness based on dependent type theory. Inf. Fusion **14**(1), 87–107 (2013)
35. Zhu, J., Song, B., Huang, Q.: Evolution game model of offense-defense for network security based on system dynamics. J. Commun. **35**(1), 54–61 (2014)
36. Gao, N., Gao, L., He, Y.Y., et al.: Dynamic security risk assessment model based on Bayesian attack graph. J. Sichuan Univ. **48**, 111–118 (2016)
37. Tianfield, H.: Cyber security situational awareness. In: 2016 IEEE International Conference on Internet of Things (iThings) and IEEE Green Computing and Communications (Green-Com) and IEEE Cyber, Physical and Social Computing (CPSCom) and IEEE Smart Data (SmartData), pp. 782–787. IEEE (2016)
38. Yu, Y., Xia, C., Hu, X.: Defense scheme generation method using mixed path attack graph. J. ZheJiang Univ. (Eng. Sci.) **51**(9), 1745–1759 (2017)
39. Chunguang, M., Chenghong, W., Donghong, Z., et al.: A dynamic network risk assessment model based on attacker's inclination. J. Comput. Res. Dev. **52**(9), 2056–2068 (2015)
40. Chen, X.J., Fang, B.X., Tan, Q.F., et al.: Inferring attack intent of malicious insider based on probabilistic attack graph model. Chin. J. Comput. **37**(1), 62–72 (2014)
41. Wang, Q., et al.: You are what you do: hunting stealthy malware via data provenance analysis. In: Symposium on Network and Distributed System Security (NDSS) (2020)
42. Erbacher, R.F., Frincke, D.A., Wong, P.C., et al.: A multi-phase network situational awareness cognitive task analysis. Inf. Vis. **9**(3), 204–219 (2010)

VABox: A Virtualization-Based Analysis Framework of Virtualization-Obfuscated Packed Executables

Zhifeng Liu, Desheng Zheng[✉], Xinlong Wu, Jixin Chen, Xiaolan Tang,
and Ziyong Ran

School of Computer Science, Research Center for Cyber Security, Southwest Petroleum
University, Chengdu 610500, China

Abstract. In the process of malware analysis, information such as the API call
sequences and opcodes of malwares is extremely valuable feature, but a large number of malware writers abuse various anti-reverse technologies to hide malware
information. In order to protect these malwares, they usually use virtualization,
obfuscation, packing, and anti-debugging techniques. These protections hinder
the acquisition of malware information, making the reverse analysis and detection
of malware more difficult. In this paper, we propose VABox: an executable software analysis framework based on virtualization technology. It monitor the packed
and virtualization-obfuscated applications and kernel modules, and is difficult to
be discovered by malware. 1) Compared with the emulator, its execution speed
is faster and it can also provide the detailed virus running information, including the running opcode, completing the API call information and the shellcode
information. 2) Compared with traditional sandbox, it can supply a more realistic operating environment for malware, greatly reducing the possibility of being
detected by malware. 3) Compared with previous work, it can obtain cleaner and
more accurate sample data. 4) In addition, VABox also provides developers with
opportunities to dump memory, obtain and modify contextual information. We
verified the effectiveness of VABox by testing kernel Rootkit and UPX packed
applications protected by VMProtect 3.4 on Windows platform. Experimental
results show that our tool can accurately and completely capture information such
as the API call sequences and parameters of executable files.

Keywords: Virtualization · Obfuscation techniques · Software security ·
Reverse engineering · API monitor

1 Introduction

For the analysis of malicious samples, there are two types of analysis methods in terms
of data acquisition. One is static analysis and the other is dynamic analysis. Both of the
two methods are to obtain more malware sample data for training classifiers or models to
distinguish sample types [1]. Among these data, information such as API call sequences
and opcodes has been used in a lot of research, so it is particularly important [1–3, 24]. At

© Springer Nature Switzerland AG 2021
X. Sun et al. (Eds.): ICAIS 2021, CCIS 1424, pp. 73–84, 2021.
https://doi.org/10.1007/978-3-030-78621-2_6

present, although virus analysis method has achieved remarkable success, the technology for malicious software to hide its own information is also constantly developing, which seriously hinders our reverse analysis and information acquisition of malicious software.

According to previous works, the proportion of packed malwares usually reaches more than 80% [4]. Although the number of malwares in this part is large, due to the application of some anti-reverse technologies to malicious samples, some malicious sample research works have to abandon the analysis of these samples [2, 5]. According to researches, malware widely uses protection tools such as VMProtect, Themida and UPX [6]. Among them, UPX is a typical packer protection tool [7], and VMProtect and Themida are known for the code virtualization protection [8, 9]. In addition, most of the sandbox technologies used in current dynamic analysis are easily detected by malicious samples, which will cause the malwares to change its operation behavior and avoid illegal behavior detected by the virus analysis system [10]. In order to deal with the new anti-reverse engineering technology in this paper, we propose VABox: an executable program analysis framework based on virtualization technology. It is designed to provide a transparent and scalable environment for analysis of malwares. Currently, VABox can run in a 64-bit Windows environment to monitor between user-mode and kernel-mode malwares. In summary, this paper has the following contributions:

1. Compared with the dynamic analysis tool implemented by the emulator, VABox has a faster execution speed [11] and it can also provide fine-grained analysis, including information such as sample opcodes, API call sequences and parameters.
2. Compared with existing works [12, 19], we can obtain cleaner and more detailed datas without filtering noise, and support the analysis of user-mode and kernel-mode malwares at the same time.
3. Compared with tools such as sandbox and APIMonitor [10], our tool can provide malware with a more realistic running environment, and it is difficult to be detected by malwares.
4. The experimental results show that VABox is able to provide opcode and API call analysis results of kernel driver protected by VMProtect 3.4.

The remainder of this paper is organized as follows. In Sect. 2, we briefly introduce some backgound related to virtualization technologies and virtualization-obfuscated protection. In Sect. 3, we review the methods of obtaining binary opcodes and API call sequence in the previous works. In Sect. 4, we introduce the approaches of monitoring malware opcodes and other behaviors proposed in this paper. In Sect. 5, we introduce the implementation of the VABox prototype. In Sect. 6, we use VABox to analyze the packed and virtualization-obfuscated test cases to prove its effectiveness. In addition, we also analyze some malicious samples collected and summarize their behavioral data. Finally, we summarize the whole work and sort out the ideas for future work.

2 Background

2.1 Virtualization Technology

Virtualization technology is mainly divided into two directions: hardware virtualization and software virtualization. Hardware virtualization provides support for interception and redirection of special instructions through physical hardware, thereby realizing the virtualization of hardware resources. Software virtualization is the use of software technology to emulate physical hardware on existing physical hardware, thereby realizing the virtualization of different hardware resources [25].

The advantage of hardware virtualization is that it is safe and reliable and it has low performance loss [13], but it relies heavily on existing physical hardware. Currently, devices that support hardware virtualization are Intel Virtualization Technology (VT-x) and AMD Virtualization (AMD-V).

The advantage of software virtualization is that it can realize the virtualization of different hardware in the same physical device, but the running speed is slow [11]. Currently, the software that realizes software virtualization includes QEMU, Bochs, etc.

2.2 Virtualization-Obfuscated Protection

Obfuscation is to the original application codeby adding excessive instructions, making the original instructions bloated and illegible, while ensuring the correctness and completeness of the original code function [8].

Virtualization transforms the source code to the bytecode executed by a special interpreter that imitates a virtual machine with a specific set of commands. Therefore, virtualization leads to a high and irreducible level of complexity of the resulting code, and if it applied properly, the code protected with such a method does not contain methods to restore the original code explicitly. For example, a specific block of Intel x86 instructions can be converted into different instruction set for each machine, preventing an attacker from recognizing any generated virtual opcode after the transformation from x86 instructions [8, 14].

3 Related Works

3.1 Static Analysis

Renjie Lu [5] used the disassembly tool IDA Pro to obtain opcode sequence of malware. JongCheon Choi et al. [15] obtained the numbers and names of the used DLLs and APIs from the Import Address Table (IAT), which is part of the PE files. Daniel Plohmann et al. [16] crawled through a given memory dump of a process and matched all possible DWORDs and QWORDs against their database yielding as API reference candidates. Vadim Kotow et al. [2] utilized symbolic execution and hides Markov models to predict API names from the arguments passed to the API functions.

3.2 Hook-Based Analysis

Brittany Byrd et al. [17] collected and investigated the sequential component of API calls native to the Windows 32-bit host operating system using API Monitor v2 and general sandboxing techniques. According to the research [10], Cuckoo sandbox has a huge influence on the dynamic analysis of malwares, and the sandbox obtains API call information by hook.

3.3 Emulation-Based Analysis

Monirul Sharif et al. [18] implemented a prototype called Rotalume that uses a QEMU based on component to perform dynamic analysis. The analysis generated both an instruction traced in an intermediate representation (IR) and a dynamic control flow graph (CFG) for offline analysis. Seokwoo Choi et al. [11] developed Bochs emulation-based x64Unpack to monitor major API function calls or conduct fine-grained analysis at the instruction-level.

3.4 Virtualization-Based Analysis

Tamas K. Lengyel et al. [19] located the address of kernel functions by extracting information from the debug data provided by Microsoft. And DRAKVUF monitor all kernel function by #BP injection at the head of the function. Donghai Tian et al. [12] divided the original kernel address space into two separate address space by setting the different memory to access permissions in the EPT. When the kernel module tries to access the kernel code or data, it will trigger an EPT violation that will cause a VM Exit. So, VKRD has a chance to log and analyze this event.

4 Approach

The goal of the tool is to provide a basic platform for automated analysis of malware behavior. The platform can provide macroscopic and malicious sample behavior data, such as logs of operating files, processes, threads, and registries. More importantly, it can also provide cleaner and more detailed information about the internal operation of the program. For example, the opcodes for the program to run in real time, the API information, etc. The architecture designed in this paper is shown in the Fig. 1.

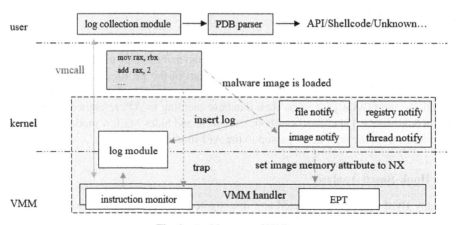

Fig. 1. Architecture of VABox

4.1 General Behavior Monitoring

In the kernel mode of the Windows system, we register the notification callback functions of the process, registry and other operations with the Windows. The methods for setting and canceling these notification callbacks are shown in the Table 1. When a specified behavior occurs in the system, we can obtain the related behavior information in the callback function we set. We collect and store this information in our log cache until the user-level log collection system has obtained log information from the VMM layer through the VMCALL instruction. Finally, the user-level system stores itself as the required log format.

4.2 Opcode-Level Monitoring

We utilize Intel's Extended Page Table (EPT) technology to control physical memory access attributes and set non-executable (NX) attributes for memory blocks that need to be monitored. When the monitored code block is executed, it will cause an EPT violation and VM exit. When falling into VMM mode, we gain full control of the monitored program. At this point, we replace the physical page where the code block is being executed with a new page which filled with the special instruction, int 3 (0xCC), and set the page attribute to executable-only (XO). Therefore, the execution of all executed instructions on this page will be interrupted again into the VMM mode due to the breakpoint (#BP) exception, which will be monitored by us. We can restore the instructions that are not of interest to the original instructions and only keep the instructions that need to be monitored. In this process, we have the opportunity to record any information we need. At the same time, for the read and write access of the page, we replace the corresponding original physical page back, so the read and write access will not be affected in any way.

Table 1. API for setting and canceling behavior notification.

Behavior	API for setting	API for canceling
Process notify	PsSetCreateProcessNotifyRoutine	PsSetCreateProcessNotifyRoutine
Image load	PsSetLoadImageNotifyRoutine	PsRemoveLoadImageNotifyRoutine
Registry operate	CmRegisterCallback	CmUnRegisterCallback
File operate	FltRegisterFilter	FltUnregisterFilter

4.3 Improvements to Existing Work

Hook's Detected. The dynamic analysis technology based on hook is easy to be detected by malware, so it may cause the real malicious behavior can not to be obtained unably [10]. The hardware virtualization technology we used has the highest privilege level, so it is difficult to detect by malware. In addition, we use EPT to isolate executable memory from readable and writable memory so that malicious samples cannot detect hidden hooked instructions. At the same time, on the Windows 8 and above, we do not need to consider the problems caused by Patch Guard when monitoring kernel function [20].

By the way, we use privileged instruction, VMCALL, to communicate directly with the VMM layer at the user level, which should avoid the malware detection of pipe [10].

Noisy Data. In the past API call information acquisition work [12], it was often necessary to filter out a large amount of call from non-malware software, which was not what we expected. In our method, we judge the external function information it calls by monitoring the instructions running by the malware itself, instead of paying attention to the use of known system functions to filter whether it is a call from the malware [12, 19]. Therefore, the datas we get will be less noise and cleaner.

Executive Efficiency. The method of using the emulator to obtain the opcodes is less efficient [11], so we choose to use more efficient hardware virtualization technology to implement instruction-level malware monitoring [26, 27]. At the same time, we use a lot of optimization algorithms to improve our efficiency (see Sect. 5.2).

5 Implementation

We use Visual Studio 2017 and WDK for Windows 10, version 1809 for development. Regarding the monitoring of general behavior, we will not go into details, the following focuses on the implementation of API monitoring and its performance optimization.

5.1 API Monitoring

In order to realize the monitoring of external function calls, we keep branch instructions (such as, JMP, CALL and RET, etc.) as instructions that need to be monitored on the basis of instruction-level monitoring. In this way, all executable codes are divided into code block units with branch instructions. Whenever a branch instruction needs to be executed, we firstly restore the jump instruction, and execute the instruction with the monitor trap flag (MTF) of VT-x. At this point, the executed instruction will jump to the destination address and trigger VM exit with basic exit code 37. We can judge the instruction pointer (RIP) of guest where the current instruction is located to determine whether it has jumped out of our monitoring range. If it is not within our monitoring range, it means that this is an external jump. Therefore, we record the address and context as an external API call log.

Our user-level log collection module continuously polls and collects call logs through VMCALL. Then, through the program database (PDB) symbol analysis function address information, from which we can get the name of the function and its parameter information. If the address does not appear in any known module, then the address is recognized as a shellcode address. We describe the entire monitoring process as Fig. 2.

5.2 Performance Optimization

Reduce the Number of Instructions to be Monitored. By modifying the lightweight instruction parsing library, ldasm [21], we build a fast table of branch instructions to speed up the judgment of instruction type. At the same time, pruning optimization is performed for certain internal branch instruction, which improves the efficiency of API monitoring by reducing a large number of meaningless traps.

Optimize Query Efficiency. In VMM, a balanced binary tree manager is established to improve the efficiency of query instruction address range and reduce query consumption.

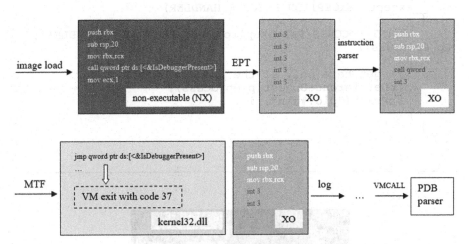

Fig. 2. API monitoring process

6 Experiment and Results

In order to verify the effectiveness of our tools, we have done the following experiments. The experiments are performed on an Intel Core(TM) i5-8300H CPU running at 2.30 GHz. The samples and the test case are executed on a Windows 10 x64 analysis platform.

6.1 Experiment 1

We develop a test case to test the accuracy and correctness of the tools. The test case code is shown in Table 2, and the test result is shown in Fig. 3.

It can be seen from the experimental results that we can obtain the API call status completely and accurately in real time. Through this experiment, we can also see that our tools are more compatible with using exception to detect anti-reverse engineering techniques [22].

Table 2. Codes of the test case

```
void test_enum_all_process()
{
  PEPROCESS p_eprocess = NULL;
  for (int i = 0; i <= 0x1000; i += 4)
  {
    __try
    {
      DbgBreakPoint();     // trigger #BP exception
      KebugCheck(0x1234); // unreachable in right case
    }
    __except (EXCEPTION_EXECUTE_HANDLER)
    {
      if (NT_SUCCESS(PsLookupProcessByProcessId((HANDLE)i,
&p_eprocess)))
      {
        /* get here only if the process exists */
        ObDereferenceObject(p_eprocess);
        DbPrint("pid:%d\n", i);
      }
    }
  }
}
```

Fig. 3. API sequences of the test case

6.2 Experiment 2

In this experiment, we protect the function of the test case by VMProtect 3.4. We unfortunately find that VMProtect's handling of kernel exceptions is not perfect. Therefore, we delete the exception handling part of the test case, and only retain functions. Our protection option is shown in Fig. 5, and the result of the test is shown in Fig. 4.

Fig. 4. API sequences of the protected test case

Experimental results show that our tools can also completely and accurately monitor virtualization-obfuscated software. At the same time, we can see that some other functions (shown in Table 3) have been added to the protected software by VMProtect.

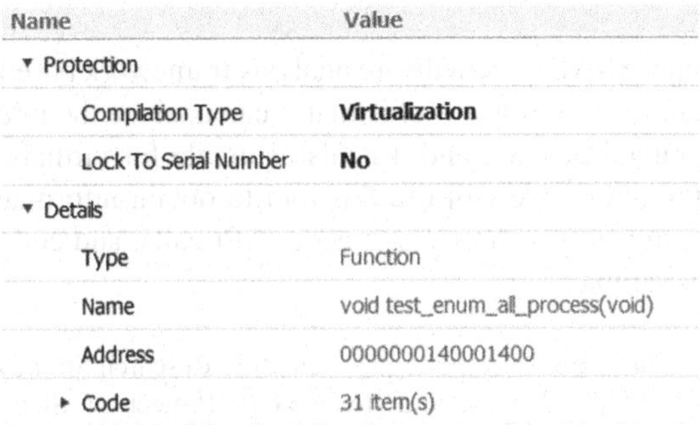

Name	Value
▼ Protection	
Compilation Type	**Virtualization**
Lock To Serial Number	**No**
▼ Details	
Type	Function
Name	void test_enum_all_process(void)
Address	0000000140001400
▸ Code	31 item(s)

Fig. 5. VMProtect 3.4 options of test case

Table 3. Some functions added by VMProtect

ExAllocatePool/ ExFreePoolWithTag
NtQuerySystemInformation
MmProbeAndLockPages/MmUnlockPages
KeQueryActiveProcessors
KeSetSystemAffinityThread
KeRevertToUserAffinityThread

6.3 Experiment 3

In the experiment, we download a compressed package containing 997 samples from the Torrents channel of VirusShare [23]. We randomly sampled some malicious samples (see Table 4) that can work normally for data collection and testing. And the probability of our tools working normally is 100%.

Table 4. Sum of sample

01db10a317194fe7c94a58fae14f787c
1a5d3021db16ee2670c8e3d3b9a0771f
1a985147e4ab082a3f4da52a27525aa4
1a6031959d62cc35e0c9d95a8eadfa38
1abae8bece6b2aa93173df4b08b65ada
1ae1f009df1679433057d09b7a4e1c4f

7 Conclusion

In this paper, we propose VABox, a malware analysis framework based on virtualization technology. The main feature of this tool is that it can analyze the internal operation of malware in a fine-grained manner, and it is also suitable for virtualization-obfuscated software. In the future work, we will use this tool to obtain information about a large number of samples, and start with machine code, API calls, and code block semantics to classify malicious samples.

Funding Statement. This work is supported by Scientific Research Starting Project of SWPU [No. 0202002131604]; Major Science and Technology Project of Sichuan Province [No. 8ZDZX0143, 2019YFG0424]; Ministry of Education Collaborative Education Project of China [No. 952]; Fundamental Research Project [Nos. 549, 550].

References

1. Sahay, S., Sharma, A.: A survey on the detection of windows desktops malware. In: Yu-Chen, H., Tiwari, S., Mishra, K.K., Trivedi, M.C. (eds.) Ambient Communications and Computer Systems. AISC, vol. 904, pp. 149–159. Springer, Singapore (2019). https://doi.org/10.1007/978-981-13-5934-7_14
2. Kotov, V., Wojnowicz, M.: Towards generic deobfuscation of windows API calls. arXiv preprint arXiv:1802.04466 (2018)
3. Xi, Q., Zhou, T., Wang, Q., Zeng, Y.: An API deobfuscation method combining dynamic and static techniques. In: Proceedings 2013 International Conference on Mechatronic Sciences, Electric Engineering and Computer (MEC), pp. 2133–2138. IEEE, December 2013
4. Osaghae, E.O.: Classifying packed programs as malicious software detected. Int. J. Inf. Technol. Electr. Eng. **5**, 22–25 (2016)

5. Lu, R.: Malware Detection with LSTM using Opcode Language. arXiv preprint arXiv:1906. 04593 (2019)
6. Assis, C.R., Miani, R.S., Carneiro, M.G., Park, K.J.: A comparative analysis of classifiers in the recognition of packed executables. In: 2019 IEEE 31st International Conference on Tools with Artificial Intelligence (ICTAI), pp. 1356–1360. IEEE, November 2019
7. UPX: the Ultimate Packer for eXecutables. https://upx.github.io/. Accessed 05 Nov 2020
8. Analysis, cracking and protection of software. http://vmpsoft.com/support/user-manual/int roduction/analysis-cracking-and-protection-of-software/. Accessed 05 Nov 2020
9. Themida. https://www.oreans.com/Themida.php. Accessed 05 Nov 2020
10. Ferrand, O.: How to detect the cuckoo sandbox and to strengthen it? J. Comput. Virol. Hacking Tech. **11**(1), 51–58 (2015)
11. Choi, S., Chang, T., Kim, C., Park, Y.: x64Unpack: hybrid emulation unpacker for 64-bit windows environments and detailed analysis results on VMProtect 3.4. IEEE Access **8**, 127939–127953 (2020). https://doi.org/10.1109/ACCESS.2020.3008900
12. Tian, D., Ma, R., Jia, X., Hu, C.: A kernel rootkit detection approach based on virtualization and machine learning. IEEE Access **7**, 91657–91666 (2019)
13. Intel64 and IA-32 Architectures Software Developer's Manual. https://software.intel.com/con tent/dam/develop/public/us/en/documents/325462-sdm-vol-1-2abcd-3abcd.pdf. Accessed 05 Nov 2020
14. Rolles, R.: Unpacking virtualization obfuscators. In: 3rd USENIX Workshop on Offensive Technologies (WOOT), August 2009
15. Choi, J., et al.: A static birthmark for MS windows applications using import address table. In: 2013 Seventh International Conference on Innovative Mobile and Internet Services in Ubiquitous Computing, pp. 129–134. IEEE, July 2013
16. Plohmann, D., Enders, S., Padilla, E.: ApiScout: Robust Windows API Usage Recovery for Malware Characterization and Similarity Analysis
17. Byrd, B., Malik, R., Kandalam, V., Liu, Q.: Malware detection with computational intelligence. In: Proceedings on the International Conference on Artificial Intelligence (ICAI), p. 1. The Steering Committee of the World Congress in Computer Science, Computer Engineering and Applied Computing (WorldComp) (2014)
18. Sharif, M., Lanzi, A., Giffin, J., Lee, W.: Automatic reverse engineering of malware emulators. In: 2009 30th IEEE Symposium on Security and Privacy, pp. 94–109. IEEE, May 2009
19. Lengyel, T.K., Maresca, S., Payne, B.D., Webster, G.D., Vogl, S., Kiayias, A.: Scalability, fidelity and stealth in the DRAKVUF dynamic malware analysis system. In: Proceedings of the 30th Annual Computer Security Applications Conference, pp. 386–395, December 2014
20. Ermolov, M., Shishkin, A.: Microsoft Windows 8.1 Kernel Patch Protection Analysis
21. Isasm64. https://github.com/leeqwind/ldasm64. Accessed 15 July 2020
22. Chenke, L., Feng, Y., Qiyuan, G., Jiateng, Y., Jian, X.: Anti-reverse-engineering tool of executable files on the windows platform. In: 2017 IEEE International Conference on Computational Science and Engineering (CSE) and IEEE International Conference on Embedded and Ubiquitous Computing (EUC), vol. 1, pp. 797–800. IEEE, July 2017
23. VirusShare_x86–64_WinEXE_20130711. https://virusshare.com/torrents. Accessed 15 Sept 2020
24. Kuang, K., et al.: Exploit dynamic data flows to protect software against semantic attacks. In: 2017 IEEE SmartWorld, Ubiquitous Intelligence & Computing, Advanced & Trusted Computed, Scalable Computing & Communications, Cloud & Big Data Computing, Internet of People and Smart City Innovation (SmartWorld/SCALCOM/UIC/ATC/CBDCom/IOP/SCI). IEEE (2017)

25. Kuang, K., et al.: Exploit dynamic data flows to protect software against semantic attacks. In: 2017 IEEE SmartWorld, Ubiquitous Intelligence & Computing, Advanced & Trusted Computed, Scalable Computing & Communications, Cloud & Big Data Computing, Internet of People and Smart City Innovation (SmartWorld/SCALCOM/UIC/ATC/CBDCom/IOP/SCI), pp. 1–6. IEEE, August 2017
26. Zhao, C., Wang, T., Yang, A.: A heterogeneous virtual machines resource allocation scheme in slices architecture of 5G edge datacenter. Comput. Mater. Continua **61**(1), 423–437 (2019)
27. Ran, Z., Zheng, D., Lai, Y., Tian, L.: Applying stack bidirectional LSTM model to intrusion detection. CMC-Comput. Mater. Continua **65**(1), 309–320 (2020)

Imbalance Malware Classification by Decoupling Representation and Classifier

Jiayin Liu[1,2,3(✉)], Chengchen Zhuge[1,2,3], Qun Wang[1,2,3], Xiangmin Guo[1,2,3], and Ziyuan Li[1]

[1] Department of Computer Information and Cyber Security, Jiangsu Police Institute, Nanjing 210031, China
[2] Jiangsu Electronic Data Forensics and Analysis Engineering Research Center, Jiangsu Police Institute, Nanjing 210031, China
[3] Jiangsu Provincial Public Security Department Key Laboratory of Digital Forensics, Jiangsu Police Institute, Nanjing 210031, China

Abstract. In recent years, with the widespread utilization of automatic and semi-automatic malicious code generation tools, malware has been increased dramatically. Due to the growing malware variants, automatic detection and classification of malware samples is inevitable. A long-tailed distribution is one of the most common problems in malware dataset. However, existing general deep learning model is difficult to identify few-shot classes in the case of frequent classes. To address this challenge, we propose a new training scheme to classify unbalanced malware by decoupling representation learning from classifier learning. Specifically, in representation learning, the model is trained without balancing or oversampling the tail classes in order to learn the best representation. In classifier learning, we fine-tune the classifier under the class-balance sampling scheme. In addition, at this stage, we optimize the classifier with a fixed feature extractor during training to suppress the re-balancing effect on the backbone learned in the first stage. To assess the performance of the proposed approach, experiments are conducted on the BIG 2015 dataset. The experimental results demonstrate that our approach provides far higher classification performance, particularly in few-shot malware families than those proposed in existing literature.

Keywords: Malware classification · Malware visualization · Imbalanced data

1 Introduction

Along with the rapid development of the information industry and related technologies, cybersecurity threats are growing exponentially, among which malware has become one of the major security threats and is incredibly destructive. A total of more than 100 million malicious codes were found in 2018, involving more than 510,000 malicious code families, according to a report released by

© Springer Nature Switzerland AG 2021
X. Sun et al. (Eds.): ICAIS 2021, CCIS 1424, pp. 85–98, 2021.
https://doi.org/10.1007/978-3-030-78621-2_7

CNCERT/CC [1]. Furthermore, with the widespread use of automatic and semi-automatic malicious code generation tools that enhance or generate malware variants by reusing the underlying malware module, malware has been increasing more and more quickly. According to the data released by Symantec, the number of malicious code variants has risen sharply from 5:1 per family in 2011 to 38:1 in 2012 and has leaped to more than 1000:1 in recent years. The increasing malware variants are a challenging task for antivirus vendors.

At present, a lot of techniques have been proposed to detect and classify malware including static analysis method and dynamic analysis method. Static analysis methods are used to examine executable files without running them and thus are very safe. However, most static analysis methods are susceptible to code obfuscation and morphing techniques. Dynamic analysis methods overcome the challenges caused by code obfuscation and polymorphic techniques, Dynamic analysis methods overcome the challenges of code obfuscation and polymorphism, but they are time consuming and subject to the execution environment. Recently, some researchers propose visualization-based methods for classifying malicious software. The motivation for these works is that most malware is generated by reusing existing malware models. Although these variants generate different hash signatures by applying polymorphic and metamorphic methods, the general structure of the image is still retained. Thus, visualization-based methods are more resilient to general code obfuscation faced by traditional static analysis methods.

Despite the recent success of machine learning, the negative effect of data imbalance is still unavoidable. Furthermore, the frequency of objects in the malware domain often exhibits a long-tailed distribution, with some families of malware having significantly more instances than others. To cope with the negative effects of long-tailed distribution, previous works mainly follow two directions: re-sampling and re-weighting learning [2]. Re-sampling might lead to over-fitting on minority classes with duplicated samples or impair feature learning capacity by missing a number of valuable instances. Re-weighting-based methods are highly sensitive to the selection of super parameters and might have gradient issues during optimization. In addition, when learning classifiers for recognition combined with data representations on unbalanced datasets, performance degrades because re-weighting or re-sampling may affect the quality of the features.

As mentioned in literature [3], the best representation is learned when the model is trained without re-sampling, while the best classifier is learned when training on class-balance data. Given that the different stages require different training conditions, it is best to learn them separately rather than jointly. Inspired by the work in [4], we present a novel method for the imbalanced malware classification that decoupling representation from classification. The training of this model is divided into two stages: First, each sample has the same weight, which means that there is no class weight or equilibrium. It is at this stage that the best representation is learned. In the second stage, the representation learned from the first stage is frozen, and the classifier learned in the first stage is reinitialized from scratch. The sampling strategy is also modified to ensure that each class is sampled with an equal probability. Then the model is trained for an additional number of epochs to optimize the classifier for long-tailed recognition.

2 Related Work

Various techniques have been proposed to automatically detect and classify malware, and are generally divided into two categories: dynamic analysis and static analysis. In dynamic analysis, the behavior of malware, such as the sequence of API calls or instruction sequences, is analyzed while running in a controlled environment (e.g., virtual machine, simulator, emulator, or sandbox). Egele et al. [5] proposed a method using tainting techniques to track the behavior associated with the flow of information processed by any Browser Helper object (BHO). Fujino et al. [6] applied unsupervised clustering analysis to extract API call topics from a large corpus of API calls to identify similar malware samples. Lim et al. [7] used network traffic activity feature clustering and sequence alignment algorithm to analyze malware traffic behavior. Tobiyama et al. [8] proposed a malware classification system that extracted features from 5-minute API calls and then passed on to CNN for classification. The major problem with the existing dynamic analysis methods is that they are time-consuming because of the large amount of computational overhead. In addition, as malware is mostly triggered under specific circumstances, some malicious codes and calls cannot be displayed in a virtual environment, which will affect the identification for malware.

In static analysis, malware is analyzed based on the static feature including string signature, byte-sequence n-grams, syntactic library call, control flow graph (CFG), op-code (operational code) frequency distribution, etc. [9]. Santos et al. [10] generated the n-gram instructions feature vectors for each n-instruction sequence to detect variants of known malware families. Liu et al. [11] extracted the opcode features by combining CFG with 3-gram and then passed them on to a decision-making system composed of several classifiers to detect and classify malware. Raff et al. [12] proposed a malware classification scheme that employed a classical fully connected network and recurrent neural network (RNN) model to detect malware with 300 bytes of information from the PE header file. Dai et al. [13] combined software features such as the API call sequence and low-level hardware features such as anti-avoidance of memory dump gray-scale and used an ensemble learning algorithm consisting of multiple classification algorithms to detect malware. Li et al. [14]proposed a method that extracted static and dynamic features information and combined them into a new multi-dimensional hybrid features, which was proved to have better performance than the methods using static methods alone.

In recent years, static analysis based on visualization techniques has been proposed, which combines visualization technology and machine learning to detect malware variants. These methods map the malware to the image field and make it more intuitive to observe the features such as malware fragment information.

Early researches in this area are based on traditional machine learning algorithms, such as KNN, RF, SVM, etc. Natraj et al. [15] used the GIST algorithm to extract the features of malware images, and then utilized K-nearest neighbor to classify malware images. Han et al. [16] partitioned the gray-scale image into blocks and extracted gray-scale co-occurrence matrix feature for each block to detect and classify new malware and malware variants. Gupta et al. [17] used a uniform local binary pattern with a circular neighborhood strategy to extract features from the malware images and then used RF to determine whether a binary executable is malware.

Given that traditional MLA-based methods require a great deal of effort and domain expertise in the field of manual feature engineering, end-to-end malware detection methods that do not require domain knowledge have received more and more attention in recent years. Zhao et al. [18] proposed a malware analysis method against malware variants named "MalDeep", which converted the disassembled malware codes into gray images and then identified their families by the CNN. Yakura et al. [19] proposed a malware classification method that used CNN with the attention mechanism for static malware analysis. CHEN et al. [20] studied adversarial examples for CNN-based malware detectors including black-box attacks and white-box attacks, and then tried to enhance the MalConv using adversarial examples.

3   Imbalance Malware Detection Model

The overall methodology implemented for this project is detailed in Fig. 1. First, malwares are disassembled and converted to grayscale images. Second, the converted images are resized to be the inputs of the ResNeXt network. Finally, we train the long-tailed malware recognition in two stages by decoupling the representation learning from the balanced classifier learning. In the first stage, the entire model is trained under the instance-balance scheme to learn a better representation. In the second stage, we fine-tune the classifier under the class-balance sampling scheme. In addition, to prevent the re-balancing process from affecting the learned representations of the backbone, the representation learned from stage one is frozen, and the classifier is reinitialized from scratch.

3.1   Visualization of Malware

An executable file that is visualized into a two-dimensional gray-scale image is shown in Fig. 2. First, the executable file is disassembled by the IDA disassembly software and saved as an ASM file. Second, the assembly code generated in the previous step is converted to machine code that consisting of hexadecimal values corresponding to the raw binary instructions executed by the processor. Then the binary bit string of machine code is split into multiple 8-bit long sub-strings, each of which can be considered a pixel since an 8-bit binary string can be interpreted as an unsigned integer within the range of [0,255] (0: black, 255: white). Then the machine code sub-strings can be organized into a one-dimensional pixel vector.

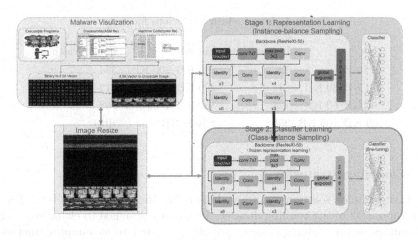

Fig. 1. Overview of the proposed method.

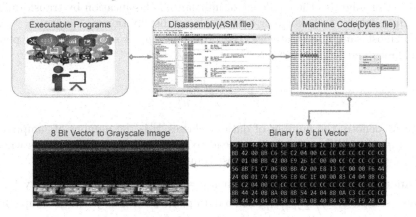

Fig. 2. Malware visualization.

Finally, we transform the one-dimensional vector into a two-dimensional gray-scale image. Since the malware samples varies significantly in size, from a few dozen kilobytes to several megabytes, it is ultimately the most computationally conservative to simply convert the pixel vector into a gray-scale image by rearranging them to a specified length. For simplicity, the width of the image is determined based on the size of the file. Table 1 gives some recommended image widths for different file sizes based on empirical observations, with the height of the image depending on the size of the file.

Table 1. Image width for various file sizes.

File	Image width	File size	Image width
<10 KB	32	100 KB–200 KB	384
10 KB–30 KB	64	200 KB–500 KB	512
30 KB–60 KB	128	500 KB–1000 KB	768
60 KB–100 KB	256	>1000 KB	1024

3.2 Sampling Strategies

The most common solution to an imbalanced classification problem is to change the composition of the training dataset. Techniques designed to change the class distribution in the training dataset are often referred to as sampling methods or re-sampling methods, as we sample an existing data sample. Data sampling addresses or migrates the challenge of imbalanced classification by transforming a training dataset to balance or better balance distribution.

For most sampling strategies, the probability p_j of sampling a data point from class j can be presented as:

$$p_j = \frac{n_j^q}{\sum_{i=1}^{M} n_i^q} \tag{1}$$

where M denotes the number of dataset classes, n_i is the number of sample for class i, $q \in [0, 1]$ different values of q lead to different sampling strategies where $q = 0, q = 1$ correspond to the two most common sampling strategies:

Instance-Balanced Sampling. When $q = 1$, the sampling probability for a training sample is $n_j \big/ \sum_{i=1}^{M} n_i^q$, i.e., a data point from class j will be sampled in proportion to the cardinality n_j of the class. In other words, the probability of each training sample being selected is equal. Therefore, this sampling strategy is called instance-balanced sampling and denoted as p_j^{IB}.

Class-Balanced Sampling. When $q = 0$ the sampling probability for a training sample is $1/M$, i.e., the sampling probability is a constant, a data point from class j will be sampled in proportion to the number of classes and has nothing to do with the cardinality n_j of the class. In other words, each class has an equal chance of being selected. Therefore, we call this sampling strategy class-balanced sampling and denote it as p_j^{CB}. In fact, class-balanced sampling can be regarded as a two-stage sampling strategy. First, a class is selected uniformly from all classes, and then an instance from that class is uniformly sampled.

The two sampling methods mentioned earlier can be clearly distinguished. Instance-balanced sampling can make full use of each sample to learn the best representation shown in literature [21]. But the learned classification model learned based on the instance-balanced sampling tends to be under-fit for few-shot classes. Compare with instance-balanced sampling, class-balanced sampling can alleviate under-fit, but performs poorly on extracting representative features due to the under-sampling of majority class. Both of the above two sampling methods will be applied according to their characteristics which will be presented in the following section.

3.3 ResNeXt Architecture

ResNeXt was proposed by Xie et al. [22], which can be considerd as a combination of ResNet and Inception. As shown in Fig. 3, the major difference of the basic block is that ResNeXt splits the path in ResNet into many small transformations and then recombines them. As mentioned in literature [4], the size of the entire transformation (called cardinality in [4]) proved more effective than going deeper or wider to increase the capacity of the model, especially when increasing depth and width results in diminishing returns. As shown in Fig. 3(b) and Fig. 3(c), unlike Inception or Inception-ResNet modules, ResNeXt shares the same topology among the multiple paths, thus ResNeXt module requires minimal extra effort to design each path.

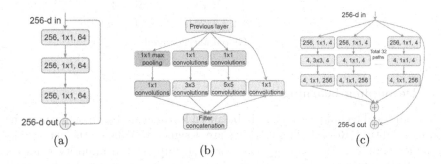

Fig. 3. Basic block unit of three CNN network architectures. (a): The block of ResNet. (b): The block of Inception. (c): The block of ResNeXt with cardinality= 32.

ResNeXt presented the aggregated transformations as

$$\Gamma(x) = \sum_{i=1}^{C} \gamma_i(x) \tag{2}$$

where $\gamma_i(x)$ is an arbitrary function. Similar to a simple neuron, here γ_i projects x into an (optionally low-dimensional) embedding and then transforms it. C is the size of the set of transformations to be aggregated. The aggregated transformations in Eq. 2 serves as the residual function:

$$y = x + \sum_{i=1}^{C} \gamma_i(x) \tag{3}$$

where y is the output of the ResNeXt basic block.

ResNeXt-50 is used for a feature extraction (backbone) in this paper, and its detailed network structure is shown in Table 2.

Table 2. ResNeXt-50 template.

Stage	Output	ResNeXt-50
cov1	112×112	7×7, 64, stride 2
cov2	56×56	3×3, 64, stride 2
		$\begin{bmatrix} 1 \times 1, 128 \\ 3 \times 3, 128, C = 32 \\ 1 \times 1, 256 \end{bmatrix} \times 3$
cov3	28×28	$\begin{bmatrix} 1 \times 1, 256 \\ 3 \times 3, 256, C = 32 \\ 1 \times 1, 512 \end{bmatrix} \times 4$
cov4	14×14	$\begin{bmatrix} 1 \times 1, 512 \\ 3 \times 3, 512, C = 32 \\ 1 \times 1, 1024 \end{bmatrix} \times 6$
cov5	7×7	$\begin{bmatrix} 1 \times 1, 1024 \\ 3 \times 3, 1024, C = 32 \\ 1 \times 1, 2048 \end{bmatrix} \times 3$
	1×1	Global average pool

3.4 Decoupling Learning

Two traditional techniques of class-imbalanced learning are based on re-sampling and re-weighting. Re-sampling methods are designed to balance the class priors by under-sampling the majority class or oversampling the minority class (or both). Re-weighting methods assign higher misclassification costs to the minority class than to the majority class. Furthermore, in most existing methods, when learning a classification model, the classifier weights W and b are usually jointly trained with the model parameters θ to extract the representation $f(x_i, \theta)$ by minimizinbg the cross-entropy loss between the ground truth y_i and prediction $W^T f(x_i, \theta) + b$. However, the joint learning scheme that minimizes the empirical risk maybe decrease in performance on imbalanced datasets because of re-weighting and re-sampling might compromise the feature quality.

To cope with the negative effects of joint learning scheme, we adopt a two-stage training scheme proposed in literature [3], which decouples the representation from the classification in long-tailed recognition and proves be superior to jointly learning the representation and classifier.

Stage1: Representation Learning
As stated in the literature [3], the best representation is learned when the model is trained without balancing or oversampling the tail classes. In this way, the model is trained under the instance-balance sampling scheme in the first stage. To ensure the quality of representation learning, we keep the network structure, super parameter, learning rate, batch size, etc. consistent with that of regular classification in the learning process.

Stage 2: Classifier Learning
In the second stage, we fine-tune the classifier under the class-balance sampling scheme so that each class has the same probability of being sampled. But rebalancing might affect the learn representations of backbone, therefore, in the second stage, the feature extractor (backbone) is fixed and only the classifier (regression layer) is optimized during training, and the classifier in the first stage is reinitialized from scratch. Then the model is trained for an additional number of epochs.

4   Experiments

4.1   Dataset and General Settings

The experimental dataset in this paper is the Microsoft Malware Classification Challenge (BIG 2015) [23], which is used as the learning and verification data for machine learning-based malware detection system. In this dataset with binaries and disassembles, there were 10,868 labeled malware samples from nine families. The distribution of malware samples in the experimental dataset was highly imbalanced, as shown in Table 3. We divided the data as follows: the first 60% of samples in each class were used for training, the second 20% for validation, and the last 20% for testing.

Table 3. Malware families in the dataset.

Class index	Malware name	Number of samples	Type
1	Ramnit	1541	Worm
2	Lollipop	2478	Adware
3	Kelihos ver 3	2942	Backdoor
4	Vundo	475	Trojan
5	Simda	42	Backdoor
6	Tracur	751	Trojan Downloader
7	Kelihos ver 1	398	Backdoor
8	Obfuscator.ACY	1228	Any kind of obfuscator malware
9	Gatak	1013	Backdoor

Experiments were run on a graphics workstation with the hardware environment using an Intel Xeon (R) processor with 48 core, the frequency was 2.30 GHz, the graphics card was NVIDIA Tesla V100 with 32 GB of video memory. The proposed approach was implemented through the python language and PyTorch framework. The experiments were run till 90 epochs with batch size 128, the gradient was optimized using SGD, the learning rate was $lr = 0.2$, momentum was $momentum = 0.9$, and weight decay was $weight_{decay} = 0.0005$.

4.2   Evaluation Criterion

The macro mean treats all classes equally. Hence, the measurement was calculated independently for each class and the calculation results were averaged:

$$Macro_P = \frac{1}{M} \sum_{i=1}^{n} P_i \tag{4}$$

$$Macro_R = \frac{1}{M} \sum_{i=1}^{n} R_i \tag{5}$$

$$Macro_F 1 = \frac{2 \times Macro_P \times Macro_R}{Macro_P + Macro_R} \tag{6}$$

where $P_i, R_i, F1_i$ are accuracy, recall and F1-Score respectively which are the most common indicators to measure the effectiveness of malware classification.

The weighted average is a calculation that takes into account the varying importance of numbers in a dataset. It can be more accurate than the simple average where all samples in a dataset are assigned an equal weight. Typically, all numbers are treated equally and assigned equal weight, so the weighted average is defined as:

$$Weighted_P = \frac{\sum_{i=1}^{n} n_i \times P_i}{\sum_{i=1}^{n} n_i} \tag{7}$$

$$Weighted_R = \frac{\sum_{i=1}^{n} n_i \times R_i}{\sum_{i=1}^{n} n_i} \tag{8}$$

$$Weighted_F 1 = \frac{\sum_{i=1}^{n} n_i \times F1_i}{\sum_{i=1}^{n} n_i} \tag{9}$$

4.3   Experimental Results

Decouple Learning Evaluation. We compare compared the proposed decoupled learning approach with general deep learning models which jointly learn the representation and classifier in order to verify its effectiveness. The confusion matrix obtained from test dataset is shown in Fig. 4. It can be seed from the figure that the joint learning scheme was slightly better than decoupled learning approach alone when classifying Kelihos ver 1 family, and the difference between the two was only one sample. Nevertheless, when classifying other malicious code families, the decoupled learning approach proposed in this paper demonstrated higher classification accuracy than the joint learning scheme. Especially in the classification of the Simba family which is a typical few-shot class, the accuracy, recall and f1-score performance of the proposed approach were 99.13%, 93.06% and 96% respectively, while those of the joint learning scheme were 50%, 50%, 50%, respectively.

Furthermore, the overall performance of decoupled learning and jointly learning was compared, as presented in Table 4. It can be seen from the table that the

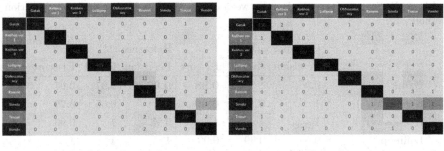

(a) Decouple Learning   (b) Joint Learning

Fig. 4. Confusion matrix of different learning scheme.

decoupled learning approach outperformed jointly learning method by a weighted average of about 1%. But the macro average performance of decoupled learning approach marginally outperformed that of the jointly learning algorithm, with a gap of about 5%–8%.

Table 4. Performance comparison between decoupled learning and jointly learning

	Macro average			Weighted average		
	Percision	Recall	F1-core	Percision	Recall	F1-score
Joint learning	0.039	0.9153	0.9093	0.9711	0.9705	0.9706
Decoule learning	**0.98**	**0.9662**	**0.9724**	**0.9830**	**0.9825**	**0.9835**

From the above experimental analysis, it can be found that the proposed algorithm, which decouples representation learning from classifier learning, could achieve better performance in identifying long-tailed malware.

Experimental Comparison. To validate the effectiveness and efficiency of the proposed approach, we compared our method with the other malware detection method based on deep learning methods. Table 5 shows the results of our approach and malware detection method presented in literature [18].

As can be seen from the table, the proposed approach was much more accurate than those proposed in literature [18] in most malware families. Especially in term of few-shot class such as Simba family, Kelihos ver 1 family, the recall and f1-score, the performance of the proposed approach was much better than those proposed in literature [18]. In addition, the overall performance of our method, either macro average or weighted average, is significantly better than those of literature [18].

Table 5. Performance comparison between our method and other malware detection method.

	Our approach			Reference [18]		
	Percision	Recall	F1-core	Percision	Recall	F1-score
Gatak	0.96	1	**0.98**	**0.98**	0.97	0.97
Kelihos ver 1	1	**0.97**	**0.99**	1	0.65	0.79
Kelihos ver 3	1	1	1	0.93	1	0.96
Lollipop	0.99	0.99	0.99	1	1	1
Obfuscator.acy	**0.99**	0.93	0.96	0.97	**0.98**	**0.98**
Ramnit	**0.95**	**0.99**	**0.97**	0.93	0.95	0.94
Simda	1	**0.88**	**0.93**	1	0.25	0.4
Tracur	**0.99**	**0.97**	**0.98**	0.95	0.93	0.94
Vundo	0.94	**0.98**	0.96	1	0.93	**0.97**
Macro Average	**0.98**	**0.9662**	**0.9724**	0.9733	0.8511	0.8833
Weighted Average	**0.983**	**0.9825**	**0.9825**	0.9635	0.9631	0.96

5 Conclusion

As described herein, to address the challenge that classifiers trained with long-tailed data preforms poorly on minor malware classes, we proposed a novel method for imbalance malware classification that decouples the representation from the classifier, which means that the model is trained in two stages. In the first stage, the model is trained under instance-balance sampling to learn the best representation. In the second stage, the representation learned in the first is frozen, and then the model is trained under class-balance sampling for an additional number of epochs so as to optimize the classifier for long-tailed recognition. Experimental results show that the proposed approach is more accurate than the joint learning method and other malware detection methods in classifying malware.

Acknowledgement. This work is supported in part by the Natural Science Foundation of the Jiangsu Higher Education Institutions of China under Grant No. 19KJB510022, the Research Startup Funds for the Introduction of High-level Talents at Jiangsu Police Institute under Grant No. JSPIGKZ. We also express our thanks to the Jiangsu Electronic Data Forensics Analysis and Research Center (No. 2019SJPT002) and the Key Laboratory of Digital Forensics of Jiangsu Public Security Department. Conflicts of Interest: The authors declare that they have no conflicts of interest to report regarding the present study.

References

1. China Internet Security Report in 2018. https://www.cert.org.cn/publish/main/upload/File/2018annual.pdf. Accessed 17 July 2019
2. Luo, M., Wang, K., Cai, Z., et al.: Using imbalanced triangle synthetic data for machine learning anomaly detection. Comput. Mater. Continua **58**(1), 15–26 (2019)
3. Ye, H.J., Ye, H.Y., Chen, D.C., et al.: Identifying and compensating for feature deviation in imbalanced deep learning (2020). arXiv preprint arXiv:2001.01385
4. Kang, B., Kang, S., Xie, M., et al.: Decoupling representation and classifier for long-tailed recognition. arXiv preprint arXiv:1910.09217 (2019)
5. Egele, M., Kruegel, C., Kirda, E., et al.: Dynamic spyware analysis. In: Proceedings of the Usenix Annual Technical Conference, pp. 233–246. ACM (2007)
6. Fujin, A., Murakami, J., Mori, T.: Discovering similar malware samples using API call topics. In: The 12th Annual IEEE Consumer Communications and Networking Conference (CCNC), pp. 1–8. IEEE (2015)
7. Lim, H., Yamaguchi, Y., Shimada, H., et al.: Malware classification method based on sequence of traffic flow. In: International Conference on Information Systems Security and Privacy (ICISSP), pp. 1–8. IEEE (2015)
8. Tobiyama, S., Yamaguchi, Y., Shimada, H., et al.: Malware detection with deep neural network using process behavior. In: IEEE 40th Annual Computer Software and Applications Conference (COMPSAC), pp. 577–582. IEEE (2016)
9. Kim, D., Shin, G., Han, M.: Analysis of feature importance and interpretation for malware classification. Comput. Mater. Continua **65**(3), 1891–904 (2020)
10. Santos, I., Brezo, F., Nieves, J., Penya, Y.K., Sanz, B., Laorden, C., Bringas, P.G.: Idea: opcode-sequence-based malware detection. In: Massacci, F., Wallach, D., Zannone, N. (eds.) ESSoS 2010. LNCS, vol. 5965, pp. 35–43. Springer, Heidelberg (2010). https://doi.org/10.1007/978-3-642-11747-3_3
11. Liu, L., Wang, B.S., Yu, B., et al.: Automatic malware classification and new malware detection using machine learning. Front. Inf. Technol. Electron. Eng. **18**(9), 1336–1347 (2016). https://doi.org/10.1631/FITEE.1601325
12. Raff, E., Sylvester, J., Nicholas, C.: Learning the PE header, malware detection with minimal domain knowledge. In: Proceedings of the 10th ACM Workshop on Artificial Intelligence and Security (AISec 2017), pp. 121–132. ACM (2017)
13. Dai, Y., Li, H., Qian, Y., et al.: SMASH: a malware detection method based on multi-feature ensemble learning. IEEE Access **7**, 112588–112597 (2019)
14. Li, Y., Xu, H., Xian, L., et al.: Novel android malware detection method based on multi-dimensional hybrid features extraction and analysis. Intell. Autom. Soft Comput. **25**(3), 637–647 (2019)
15. Nataraj, L., Karthikeyan, S., Jacob, G., et al.: Malware images: visualization and automatic classification. In: Proceedings of the 8th International Symposium on Visualization for Cyber Security (VizSec 2011), pp. 1–7. ACM (2011)
16. Han, X.G., Qu, W., Yao, X.X., et al.: Research on malicious code variants detection based on texture fingerprint. J. Commun. **35**(8), 125–136 (2014)
17. Gupta, S., Bansal, P., Kumar. S.: ULBP-RF: a hybrid approach for malware image classification. In: 2018 Fifth International Conference on Parallel, Distributed and Grid Computing (PDGC), pp. 115–119. IEEE (2018)
18. Zhao, Y., Xu, C., Bo, B., et al.: Maldeep: a deep learning classification framework against malware variants based on texture visualization. Secur. Commun. Netw. **2019**, 1–12 (2019)

19. Yakura, H., Shinozaki, S., Nishimura, R., et al.: Malware analysis of imaged binary samples by convolutional neural network with attention mechanism. In: Proceedings of the Eighth ACM Conference on Data and Application Security and Privacy, pp. 127–134. ACM (2018)
20. Chen, B., Ren, Z., Yu, C., et al.: Adversarial examples for CNN-based malware detectors. IEEE Access **7**, 54360–54371 (2019)
21. Wang, Y.X., Girshick, R., Hebert, M., et al.: Low-shot learning from imaginary data. In: Proceedings of the IEEE Conference on Computer Vision and Pattern Recognition, pp. 7278–7286. IEEE (2018)
22. Xie, S., Girshick, R., Dollár, P., et al.: Aggregated residual transformations for deep neural networks. In: Proceedings of the IEEE Conference on Computer Vision and Pattern Recognition, pp. 1492–1500. IEEE (2017)
23. Ronen, R., Radu, M., Feuerstein, M., et al.: Microsoft malware classification challenge. arXiv preprint arXiv:1802.10135 (2018)

The Promotion of Online Communication Ability of Mainstream Media

Xiaoxuan Yang[✉], Zhou Fang, Rui Bai, Xue Song, and Rui Li

Heilongjiang Province Cyberspace Research Center, Harbin 150090, Heilongjiang, China

Abstract. With the rapid development of mobile Internet, public access to information channels have undergone disruptive changes. This article novel coronavirus pneumonia epidemic situation and other public emergencies, analyzed the current public access to information channel characteristics, discussed the new situation of traditional media information dissemination challenges, and put forward some measures to enhance the transmission power, aimed at improving the effectiveness of journalism.

Keywords: Information access channel · Traditional media · Communication power

1 Introduction

On February 23, General Secretary Xi Jinping emphasized at a meeting to coordinate epidemic prevention and control and economic and social development work to improve the effectiveness of news and public opinion work, to adapt to changes in the public's access to information, and to accelerate the improvement of mainstream media's online communication capabilities. Since the outbreak of the new crown pneumonia epidemic, the public has paid great attention to information related to the epidemic. Various emerging media have brought many channels for the public to obtain information, and the media form and public opinion environment have changed. This has brought challenges to traditional mainstream media news and public opinion dissemination guidance.

Under the new situation, traditional mainstream media with strong influence, guidance and authority represented by television, radio, newspapers, magazines, etc., act as public opinion ballasts, social glues, and value vanes, and need to actively comply with public information acquisition channels Diversification, acquisition habits, mobile, fragmentation, and video trends. Under the new situation, it is constrained by traditional thinking, insufficient content form attracts, submerged by distribution algorithms, and weakened inherent advantages. Follow the trend and follow the trend, accelerate the improvement of online communication capabilities by strengthening online and offline benign interactions, accelerating the pace of content innovation, scientifically guiding online public opinion, and reshaping its own advantages, so that the main theme report can release strong positive energy.

X. Sun et al. (Eds.): ICAIS 2021, CCIS 1424, pp. 99–111, 2021.
https://doi.org/10.1007/978-3-030-78621-2_8

2   Changes in Public Access to Information

Traditional media such as television, radio, newspapers, and magazines are traditional channels for the public to obtain news and information. They have the advantages of extensiveness, popularity, easy access, and low cost. The disadvantages of passive access to information have limited its development. With the rapid development of a new generation of information technology based on the Internet, the public's access to information has gradually shifted from traditional channels to Internet channels [1]. The traditional way of getting news is limited by time and space, but the way to get news on the Internet has the following characteristics. The first is to break the limitation of traditional media information dissemination. The second is that the information acquisition channels are scattered, the communication subjects are diversified, and the algorithm recommendation is customized. Third, the habit of information acquisition is fragmented, fast reading and mobile. Finally, the information content is rich and sinking, strong interaction and video.

Since the outbreak of the new crown pneumonia, data from the "Survey Report on Public Understanding of Knowledge Related to New Crown Pneumonia" shows that Internet channels have assumed the responsibility of dissemination. The ranking of novel coronavirus pneumonia information was shown in Fig. 1. In addition to television, the top five are all new Internet channels, including 71.13% via wechat public platform and 57.74% via microblog. Microblog, wechat, client and other we media are regarded as the best way to understand coronavirus pneumonia because of its simplicity, quickness and convenience.

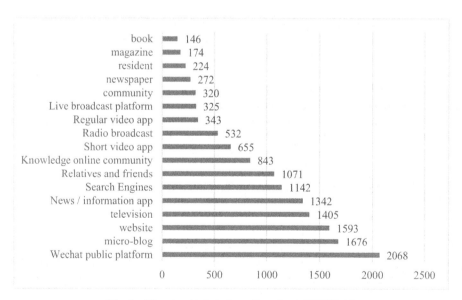

Fig. 1. Ways to obtain information about COVID-19

According to CNNIC's 44th "Statistical Report on Internet Development in China", as of June 2019, the number of Internet users in my country was 854 million, and the Internet penetration rate was 61.2%. Among them, 686 million Internet news users accounted for 80.3% of the total number of Internet users. My country's mobile phone netizens have 660 million news users, accounting for 78% of mobile netizens, and data shows that aggregate news clients occupy almost the entire news client market in my country, and mobile terminals have become the main way for the public to obtain news information.

It can be seen that whether in daily life or in public emergencies like the new crown pneumonia epidemic, new Internet channels represented by social media and aggregated news clients have become the main way for the public to obtain news information.

3 Characteristics of New Channels for the Public to Obtain Information

3.1 Self-media Channels Make Information Generation and Dissemination Diversified

With the development of new Internet technologies and new applications, the public can immediately use the Internet platform to edit and disseminate the information they have or interest in, and become the main body of self-media. The emergence of self-media has provided new channels for the public to obtain information, and has also led to disruptive changes in all aspects of information dissemination.

On the one hand, information disseminators have changed from an authoritative organization to everyone, and information dissemination has become personalized and autonomous. The knowledge or feelings shared by individuals have strong creative initiative and distinct main characteristics, covering subdivisions that cannot be touched by traditional media. Field, and is often not affected by factors such as approval and verification, breaking through the constraints of traditional news releases.

On the other hand, the information dissemination method is more interactive, fast, and covers a wide range. Compared with the traditional media-centric communication method, self-media is a decentralized communication method. The public can obtain the information they want at any time and any place according to their preferences without restriction. At the same time, the audience is allowed to interact with the information obtained. News information is disseminated and expanded quickly in the self-media, and the dissemination is targeted and layered, which is more likely to trigger a chain reaction and strengthen the dissemination effect. For example, during the "hard core road closure" incident during the new crown pneumonia epidemic, people have announced road closure measures on We-media platforms. Of all information dissemination channels, We-media channels represented by Weibo and WeChat accounted for nearly 95%. The measures to block roads were widely spread online, and received "one-sided" praise, triggering a chain reaction.

3.2 WeChat Public Account, Making Information Reading Fragmented

The emergence of fragmented information has enabled the convergence of fragmented needs. Through cloud computing of big data, it has promoted the realization of personalized information customization and accurate push [2]. WeChat official account is an important way for the public to perform fragmented reading. According to the data of "WeChat Data Report 2019" and "WeChat Public Account Crowd Insight Report", in 2019, WeChat has 1.15 billion monthly activities, and 80% of WeChat users use it. After the official account, people use the scattered time on the road, before and after meals to read the newly released content on the official account, which is gradually becoming a new reading habit of the public. According to the monitoring of the Qingbo Big Data website, from the onset of the new crown pneumonia to March 18, the official account of the new crown pneumonia has pushed 1.184 million articles, with a total reading of 2.23 billion.

Different from other social platforms, the core feature of WeChat is a circle of friends formed by a network of acquaintances. The spread of information in this circle shows a higher degree of trust and reach. According to the data in the "WeChat Public Account Crowd Insight Report", the vast majority of users will choose the recommended methods of other people's recommendations, such as the recommendation of the following official account, acquaintance/friend recommendation, friend circle sharing, and sharing from friends/groups. Pay attention to a certain official account, so the WeChat official account users are obviously affected by others. At the same time, as a social platform, WeChat is highly interactive. WeChat official account users can interact with the official account at any time.

3.3   Lack of Interaction with the Audience

With the continuous development of the Internet industry, the way of obtaining information has undergone tremendous changes. The active search method for people seeking information has become a passive algorithm distribution method for information seeking people. Relying on big data and artificial intelligence technology, a recommendation algorithm is formed based on user portraits, historical behavior characteristics, etc., to achieve accurate information push, cultivate new media habits of the public, and make it easier for the public to obtain the information they want.

3.4   Short Video Format Makes Information Display Video

With the advent of the mobile network era, short video as a way of content bearing has become an important development direction of information dissemination [3]. Short videos are widely used in news reports due to their vivid, interactive, and on-site characteristics. On the one hand, short videos are combined with the use of sound and pictures. The information and forms that can be expressed by graphics and text are simply covered by short videos. Things that cannot be expressed by graphics and text can also be presented in short videos. The information is richer and more intuitive and easier to understand by the public. And accept, as of December 2019, the number of active short video users reached 807 million. On the other hand, short video platforms gather a large number of original content producers. When news events, especially breaking news events occur, without the presence of professional reporters and cameras, a mobile phone can realize news reports and make news. The source becomes more extensive.

During the new crown pneumonia epidemic, short video platforms such as Douyin, Kuaishou, and Weishi have also become important channels for public information acquisition. Only the "new coronavirus" Douyin has played more than 18.25 billion times. Moreover, many mainstream media use short video platforms such as Douyin as important channels for publicizing the knowledge of new crown epidemic prevention and dispelling rumors. For example, the video of "Academician Zhong Nanshan's Suggestions" published by People's Daily and CCTV news accounts has more than 140 million views.

4 Problems Faced by Traditional Media Information Dissemination Under the New Situation

The mainstream media's accumulated experience, authoritative information sources, and professional teams in the long-term development process are unmatched by new media. However, in the mobile Internet era, the communication power of traditional mainstream media has suffered from the impact and challenges of new media. The reasons for this are the following problems that restrict mainstream media's communication in the new situation.

4.1 Traditional Media Thinking to Do Online Media

Content Production Lacks User Thinking. The core feature of the mobile Internet era is user-centered and user-oriented. In this era, the ability to disseminate news information is inseparable from meeting user needs. However, confined by traditional news production methods and thinking, the current mainstream media has not completely reversed the inherent thinking mode in the process of news dissemination, and has not paid enough attention to user needs and experience, and did not regard user needs as news production. The starting point is that the demand-oriented status of users is not improved enough. The traditional news dissemination method and the user's habits of receiving news under the new situation are not integrated enough. The traditional media-centered news production method is still used. If user needs are not met for a long time, it is bound to be Causes a drop in transmission.

Lack of Differentiation in Information Release. Some traditional media still follow the habit of publishing the same content in different media at the same time, instead of combining the traditional distribution method with the differentiated content and communication characteristics of each new media platform on the Internet, and simply achieve the same content on different platforms On the one hand, transplantation will cause serious content homogeneity, and on the other hand, it will highlight the disadvantages of traditional media such as poor timeliness and poor portability. Compared with self-media with social attributes, it is difficult to achieve the ideal communication effect.

The Topic Selection Mechanism Needs to be More Scientific. Traditional media has a group of experienced editors, and manuscripts need to go through a strict and standardized review process from topic selection to publication. This reflects the authority and fairness of traditional media, but it will inevitably affect the speed of publication.

However, in an era where everyone is self-media, any social hot news will be forwarded thousands of times within a minute as long as it is exposed. In this situation, traditional mainstream media is affected by factors such as efficiency and misses the best time to choose public opinion hotspots for supervision and reporting, which will weaken the leading position of public opinion.

4.2   The Form and Content of Communication Are not Sufficiently Attractive

In the era of full-staff, holographic, full-process, and full-efficiency dissemination where the boundaries between information disseminators and receivers, producers and consumers are becoming increasingly blurred, the content of news event reports is not innovative enough, does not meet the characteristics of mobile communication, and is not able to speak online If the language and disagreement with netizens are on the same frequency, the spread of news and public opinion will definitely be affected.

Insufficient Innovation of Content Form. The lack of innovation in content forms is especially reflected in short video news event reports. The mobile dissemination of short video news is not only the mobilization of video forms, but also requires new features of content production suitable for mobile dissemination. However, browsing the short video news in the news client and Douyin found that some of the videos are compressed versions of TV news. The key screens of news content published on traditional channels are intercepted, and subtitles and sound effects are added to the audience. It is simple the news and information carried over lacks novelty [4]. There are also some short video productions that do not match the needs of mobile communication in terms of duration control, content presentation, external form, and audience interaction. CSM's survey data shows that users have a high degree of positive and authoritative recognition of TV media short video works, but they have a low evaluation of short video innovation, as shown in Fig. 2. Short video works produced using the traditional TV news model have achieved good communication effects in the short term, but in the long run, audiences will not be satisfied with the freshness of watching short videos, which may cause visual fatigue and weaken attention and communication effects.

News Narrative is Too Grand. When mainstream media reports on major topics, there are insufficient emphasis on grand narratives, templated news organization planning, and rigidity. The news content produced by the traditional model has ungrounded content and low compatibility with public life. The content is clearly formulated and homogenized. It brings the same experience to the public and is not attractive to users, so it cannot reach delivery. The effect of positive energy. At the same time, it is an inevitable phenomenon to report on the same topic for some relatively important news events or with high attention. The content is the same. Many parties quote the same paragraph and the same shot, resulting in intensive coverage of a topic. It is easy to cause fatigue and disgust from the audience.

Lack of Interaction with the Audience. In the traditional media news dissemination, the information dissemination channel is one-way. The media conveys news information through newspapers, radio, television and other media. The big-horn dissemination

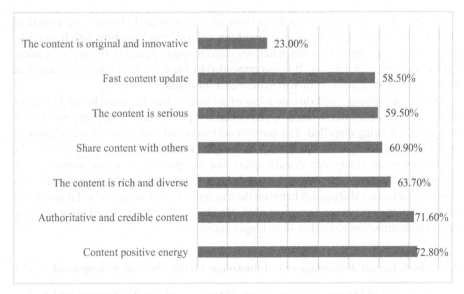

Fig. 2. Evaluation of short video users on TV media (user ratio)

makes the public only accept information unilaterally, and cannot give feedback or interact with it., The public's personality issues and interactive needs are difficult to meet. As passive information receivers, audiences can neither participate in the production of news information content, nor control the flow of information, in addition to the two choices of watching or not watching. Compared with the interactive self-media, it lacks user stickiness.

4.3   Algorithm Distribution Overwhelms Mainstream Media Information

Information distribution that relies on the combination of big data algorithms and artificial intelligence has a great effect on satisfying user interests, improving the efficiency of information distribution, and also fostering new media usage habits for audiences. However, blindly pursuing personalized news recommendations will bring the following potential risks.

First, the commonly used news intelligent recommendation algorithm is to perform keyword analysis and matching in the content resource pool according to the user's personal historical reading preferences to achieve personalized recommendation. The content that is not matched by the algorithm is not very similar to the user's historical preferences. Instead of being recommended by algorithms, the audience's reading horizons will be restricted in the long run, and it is easy for the public to gradually lose their ability to think and fall into the "information cocoon", making the audience only look at the content they identify with and cannot see the content disseminated by mainstream media. It may strengthen audience bias and cause group polarization [5].

Second, in order to increase the activity of the client and attract more people to click, the algorithm-led news aggregation form will make information with high click-through rates get more recommendations, causing some conflicts of public opinion, fake news, rumors and rumors It is recommended by the algorithm, causing widespread dissemination, which is contrary to mainstream information.

Third, the opinions and diverse ideas of all parties will be overwhelmed by algorithms, reducing the effectiveness of diversified and public news. The publicity of news is in danger of being dispelled. The mainstream media's due value to ordinary audiences and even disadvantaged groups Caring will also be weakened.

Fourth, in an emergency disaster event like an epidemic, because users have no historical preferences, the algorithm cannot identify the user's real thoughts and actual concerns, nor can it distinguish between the true and false information, and it is difficult to deal with the emergency in a short time. Matching valuable information for accurate push, the distribution algorithm is no longer smart.

4.4   The Inherent Advantages of Mainstream Media Have Been Impacted

Timeliness is Not Strong.   In an era when everyone is self-media, netizens will publish all kinds of news events happening around them in social media at the first time, but traditional media usually cannot grasp the information in the first time, resulting in limited spreading [6]. This is mainly because the traditional mainstream media cannot reach the first scene of the news in the first time, which limits the timeliness of information release. For example, in the early stage of the new crown pneumonia epidemic, the local mainstream media in Wuhan collectively lost their voices, making the epidemic failed to attract enough public attention Leading to large-scale dissemination is a typical event that indirectly triggered a painful lesson due to the lack of timeliness of the mainstream media in reporting on emergencies. On the other hand, the information release of mainstream media requires professional processes such as collection, editing, and review, and it is impossible to disseminate it anytime and anywhere like we media. Therefore, the mainstream media cannot release authentic and authoritative information in the first time, and the speed of dissemination is also lagging behind the self-media, which will inevitably lead to the phenomenon that "the lies have spread all over the world, and the truth is still wearing shoes", which is bound to affect the mainstream media Credibility. At the beginning of the new crown pneumonia epidemic, various gossips were once popular, which was related to the slow response of some media and the delay of information disclosure.

Decline in the Guidance of Public Opinion.   Public opinion information can quickly find consensus on social media platforms and form a group influence, which to a certain extent affects the public opinion guiding power of traditional mainstream media [7].

On the one hand, what the public sees under the new situation depends entirely on the public's own concern, and the agenda is no longer entirely set by the media. The mainstream media has become an "ordinary user" in the client, and it has become a member of the user's many followed friends, and the information pushed becomes a part of the public browsing information flow. Mainstream media organizations are also unable to sort the entire layout that users see, which weakens the ability of media agenda setting, and the content posted and forwarded by friends will gain more exposure and trust.

On the other hand, the collective voice of the public has changed the previous discourse system of government setting agendas, traditional mainstream media follow-up, and passive acceptance by the public. Instead, there has been a "public opinion fall" in which the public sets agendas, traditional mainstream media follow up, and the government responds. "Force" phenomenon. For example, the incidents of "family being quarantined and children with cerebral palsy died at home alone for 6 days" during the new crown pneumonia epidemic, and "government staff who have "registered" and took away a box of masks" are typical incidents that force public opinion. All kinds of panic and dissatisfaction have spread in the field of public opinion, affecting the orderly progress of epidemic prevention and control.

5 Suggestions for Improving the Online Communication Capabilities of Traditional Media

In the Internet age, the public has more diversified information channels, changes in audience information reception habits, and the reality that everyone is a receiver and disseminator of information. All require traditional media to make full use of their own advantages, and to fully study adapting to the Differentiate the all-media communication environment, accelerate the pace of integration and innovation, and rapidly improve online communication capabilities. In the face of the new situation of development, China's mainstream media can only highlight the mainstream value, amplify the mainstream voice and expand the mainstream position by promoting cultural confidence, giving full play to its unique advantages and exploring integration and innovation [8].

5.1 Using the Internet to Combine Online and Offline Punches

Strengthen Audience-Oriented News Communication Thinking. Traditional media needs to change the traditional media-centric thinking, use Internet big data technology to analyze and mine user psychology, and take user needs and user experience as the core orientation. At the same time, it is necessary to change generalized information transmission thinking, use algorithm recommendation technology under the control of mainstream value, use big data to analyze the audience's use environment and behavior preferences, comprehensively analyze user portraits, and provide content that meets user needs. Accurately push personalized content products.

Strengthen Online Interaction and Communication. Traditional media need to abandon the traditional way of one-way information transmission, strengthen online interactive communication with the audience, gradually establish an equal dialogue relationship with the public, provide a communication platform for the public to participate in the discussion of news content, and earnestly understand and grasp public demands and concerns about the public Respond promptly to form a two-way intercommunication model with good information. In this process, the public will naturally become participants in news events and secondary disseminators of information, which indirectly enhances the online dissemination of news information.

Offline Benign Interaction. In addition to strengthening online communication, traditional media can also set up offline physical activities that require public participation to further enhance positive interactions with the public. According to the characteristics of different groups of the public, through various targeted innovative methods, interesting activities, and attraction The public integrates with public life, attracts public attention, and realizes the simultaneous use of online and offline combination punches on the Internet, and the two ends resonate at the same frequency to amplify the effectiveness of publicity.

5.2 Continuous Optimization of Innovative Content

Create High-Quality Content with the Help of New Technologies and New Platforms. The core advantage of traditional media is that the quality of its published content is guaranteed. Although the development of information technology has broadened the public's access to information, in-depth and high-quality original content is relatively scarce. Under the new situation, traditional media should still insist on in-depth report creation. High-quality content, attract audiences with high-quality content.

First of all, news dissemination should abandon the phenomenon of content homogeneity, and produce different types of news products according to the characteristics of different communication channels to meet the needs of users on different platforms.

Secondly, it is necessary to expand the depth of the report, make a fuss about the deepening and refinement of the content, and give the information a new form and content without changing the original intent of the information, so that the information received by the audience is more comprehensive, objective, and objective than the original information. More credible.

Finally, with the advent of the 5G era and the rapid development of technologies such as big data, artificial intelligence, and machine learning, it is necessary to make good use of the advantages of traditional media in the application of the latest technology. Relying on new technology, scientifically reconstruct the news production process, timely use bionic simulation, immersive communication and other technologies in the production of short video and live content, and appropriately use VR, AR, AI and other new technologies in the form of display, and bring it to the public Various forms of experience achieve the purpose of enhancing news dissemination.

Multi-Perspective Three-Dimensional Presentation, Telling Short Stories Under the Big Background. Whether it is the language style of news reports or the processing of visual products, traditional media pay attention to macro-narratives while also improving the seriousness and process of traditional current affairs news reports. You can switch between different reporting perspectives, start from a small perspective, see the big from the small, select the key points, enlarge the highlights, and interesting points in the use of news materials to adapt to the perspective of mobile communication, combine the popular elements of the Internet, and use the accessible and life-oriented In this way, serious political topics are reconstructed from multiple perspectives, and the story and content of the report are enhanced, and the grand narrative under the general background is subtly transformed into a small-cut narrative that is more likely to arouse public interest, and enhance the acceptability and dissemination effect of news.

Use younger Online Voices to Promote Grounded News Reports. Traditional media need to change the traditional preaching style of propaganda and express it in a language that is more understandable and acceptable to the public, so that the description of news reports is closer to life [9]. On the one hand, keeping up with the new trends and habits of language expression in the Internet era, combining the content of mainstream ideology with younger online voices and expressions familiar to the public, making mainstream news reports more grounded. On the other hand, when disseminating mainstream ideas, go deep into the lives of the masses, choose typical positive cases that are close to real life, and use everyday language to make mainstream ideas more acceptable to the public.

5.3 Unity Network Opinion Leader

With the deepening of the circle formed by the communication power of social media platforms such as Weibo and WeChat, Internet opinion leaders with the right to speak play an important role in the development, climax and decline of public opinion. They usually lead the Internet Pay attention to change the trend of news and public opinion. Therefore, it is necessary to strengthen unity and correctly guide opinion leaders, and use their advantages in information dissemination and opinion guidance to achieve the purpose of mainstream public opinion guidance.

On the one hand, we must pay special attention to and keep abreast of the opinions of opinion leaders in a timely manner, and strengthen positive communication with them through regular offline contact with Internet opinion leaders. Traditional media should absorb and accept the constructive and different opinions put forward by opinion leaders, promptly publicize and introduce the true situation of the incident to them, promptly correct and positively guide the erroneous views and utterances represented by them, and promptly resolve conflicts and negative emotions. The positive online words and deeds of opinion leaders influence the correct value orientation of netizens.

On the other hand, the government's own self-media opinion leaders who lead news and public opinion can be properly cultivated, and a team of opinion leaders with strong political and professional qualities can be cultivated, so that they can assume the responsibility of guiding online public opinion and use their professional operations, High-quality content and extensive influence will seize the commanding heights of public opinion [10].

5.4 Reshape the Advantages of Traditional Media

Comprehensive and In-Depth Reports to Enhance the Depth of Content. The high efficiency of self-media cannot be achieved by traditional media. Traditional media cannot match the depth of the report content, in-depth investigation and in-depth comments. Therefore, traditional media should insist on comprehensive and in-depth reporting, and always maintain their own advantages such as the depth of reporting, the height of comments, and the authority of content. At the same time, with the advantages of UGC (user production information) and PGC (professional production information), rational use of the first-hand information uploaded by the public on the Internet to strengthen the combination of the two, with UGC responsible for the breadth of content, PGC maintains the content Depth, which integrates the level of information interaction and the level of information generation, and enhances user stickiness.

Fully Prepare to Express Carefully and Enhance Credibility. Traditional media should pay attention to enhancing credibility, treat the actual situation of the incident and the authenticity of the information carefully, and try to prevent the occurrence of reversal of news reports. In the era of mobile internet, netizens have a strong ability to delve into the ground and a strong judgment. When traditional mainstream media releases information on new media platforms to clarify their views, they must prepare sufficient evidence, clearly explain the facts, and logically express their opinions, and report what they think. Solve the confusion of the people.

Strengthen the Setting of Issues and Grasp the Initiative of Discourse. As the public's access to information has become diversified, traditional media must continue to strengthen the setting of issues, especially in major emergencies, to actively set up issues to seize opportunities for public opinion and increase influence. On the one hand, it is necessary to seize the opportunity to react quickly and publish in a concentrated manner during major incidents, so as to convey an authoritative voice to the public. On the other hand, it is necessary to skillfully use tags to set issues. Tags can clearly present the main content of tweets and increase the likelihood of audiences retrieving tweets. Under the new situation, traditional media should strengthen the sense of responsibility of leading mainstream public opinion, take the initiative to voice authoritative voices in a timely manner, and stick to mainstream public opinion positions.

6   Conclusion

Public access to information has developed from traditional media channels to internet channels, great changes have taken place in the production, dissemination and acquisition of information. In this context, the traditional media only have a full understanding of their difficult position, use internet thinking, with the help of new technology to continue to create in depth quality content. At the same time, we should strengthen good communication with opinion leaders, dispelling the worries and difficulties of the people. Only in this way, making best use of the advantages and bypass the disadvantages, the advantages of traditional media can be reshaped.

References

1. Zhu, H., Chen X.: The choice of public government information access channels—Based on the comparative analysis of network channels and traditional channels. Intell. Inf. Work (2015)
2. Wu, B.: Information fragmentation. China Inf. Technol. Educ. **8**, 72 (2016)
3. Yin, L., Gao, H.: Development status and communication trend of news short video in traditional media. Contemp. Commun. **203**(06), 47–50 + 55–56 (2018)
4. Meng, X., Mu, J.: Advantages and disadvantages of traditional media content aggregation platform. Young Report. **664**(08), 54–55 (2020)

5. Liu, S.: New "News Production" based on machine algorithms and theoretical exploration of gatekeepers—Taking "Today's Toutiao" as an example. Hubei University, (2017)
6. Zhong, Y.: The dilemma and Countermeasures of traditional media transformation under the epidemic situation. J. News Res. 11, 189(09), 151–152 (2020)
7. Yang, J.: The dilemma and outlet of traditional media public opinion guidance under the new normal of media convergence. China Media Sci. Technol. **000**(004), 26–27 (2019)
8. Hu, Z., Chen, Y.: New environment, new situation and new task for Chinese mainstream media. Journalist, (4) (2020)
9. Cao, S., Miao, F.L.: The development path of new mainstream media in the context of Internet plus. Search News Windows, **000**(006), 56–59 (2016)
10. Guan, Z., Guo, M.: Research on the interactive behavior of opinion leaders in internet public opinion under social media. Media Forum, (22) (2019)

HNN-Based Prediction Method Supporting Discovery of Production Abnormal

Xue Song[1][✉], Zhou Fang[1], Rui Li[1], Xiaoxuan Yang[1], Rui Bai[1], and Chao Ma[2]

[1] Heilongjiang Province Cyberspace Research Center, Harbin 150090, Heilongjiang, China
[2] Harbin University of Science and Technology, Harbin 150040, Heilongjiang, China

Abstract. In order to effectively solve the issue of that the workshop production abnormal is difficult to effectively control in discrete manufacturing enterprise, this paper explored the associative entity that is related to influence factors of production abnormal. And the influence indicators are identified from the three aspects of the space-time characteristics, the static characteristics and dynamic characteristics, then the comprehensive and reasonable influence indicator system is established; secondly, this paper gives the data source and the quantitative methods of the influence index from the technical point of view; thirdly, a prediction model based on hybrid neural networks (HNN) over time series is given.

Keywords: Production abnormal · Hybrid neural networks · Prediction model

1 Introduction

In the workshop production process of manufacturing enterprises, because of the influence of many uncertain factors, there will inevitably be various abnormal situations. Particularly in the workshop production process of discrete manufacturing enterprises, the abnormal situation is more complicated in response to more kinds of production lines and greater differentiation, and there are more kinds of influencing factors related to the abnormal situation. In this scenario, if the effects of these factors cannot be analyzed in time, and the abnormal conditions that they may lead to can be accurately predicted, so as to deal with them in time, the whole workshop production process will become uncontrolled and even result huge direct economic losses. Therefore, it will be helpful to deal with and avoid production anomalies by effectively predicting the abnormal situation of the influencing factors in the production process of discrete manufacturing enterprises. The lack of efficient intelligent workshop production anomaly prediction method has become one of the important problems that need to be solved in the management field of discrete manufacturing enterprises.

At present, in view of the problem of abnormal production prediction in manufacturing workshop, some studies focus on how to establish a high quality prediction system and provide solutions to production abnormal prediction problems from the system implementation level. Different studies have different understanding of production anomalies and different concerns about workshop production process, resulting in different prediction methods. It can be said that in the field of abnormal prediction of

X. Sun et al. (Eds.): ICAIS 2021, CCIS 1424, pp. 112–125, 2021.
https://doi.org/10.1007/978-3-030-78621-2_9

workshop production, there is no uniform standard in present. The research group based on the preliminary explorations on the complete process of monitoring, discovering and handling production abnormalities, a cloud MES architecture for solving problems is given. Further, through the in-depth study of the workshop production management of discrete manufacturing enterprises, it is found that after the end of the whole production process, the workshop production managers pay more attention to the abnormal product quality and abnormal delivery period, because they directly affect the economic benefits of enterprises. Therefore, the literature defined them as production anomaly events, after analysis of the abnormal influencing factors related to them and using the decision tree method to modeling the production anomaly prediction model.

However, as the study progressed, we found that the influence index system established by literature can not fully describe the complexity of the workshop production process of discrete manufacturing enterprises, and the established influence index system is not comprehensive and reasonable enough. To this end, this paper based on the research of literature, in-depth study on the intelligent prediction of two abnormal events in product quality and delivery period, by fully analyzing the abnormal influencing factors in the workshop production process of discrete manufacturing enterprises, we comprehensively analyze the associated entities of abnormal influencing factors (i.e., in-process, material, equipment, operator and process documents), and identify the influence indicators from three different dimensions, then we establish a comprehensive and reasonable influence index system. Based on this, we propose a time sequential multiple HNN anomaly prediction model to ensure the effectiveness and accuracy of abnormal event prediction.

2 Abnormal Factors Analysis

2.1 Classification of Impact Indicators

In the workshop production process of discrete manufacturing enterprises, due to the existence of a large number of abnormal factors, lead to the workshop production situation is changeable, the workshop production anomalies are difficult to be effectively controlled. At present, there is no uniform standard in the field of definition and classification of workshop production anomalies and their influencing factors. This paper fully analyzes the associated entities that lead to abnormal production in the workshop during the production process, that is, the associated entities of abnormal influencing factors, including: WIP, materials, equipment, operators and process documents. Based on this, this paper divides the abnormal influence factors from three dimensions: space-time characteristic, static characteristic and dynamic characteristic, built a workshop production abnormal evaluation system which involved three types of impact indicators: space-time category, static category and dynamic category. Each category contains four impact indicators, as shown in Table 1.

Table 1. Classification of impact indicators

Space-Time category *STuf*	Static category *SSuf*	Dynamic category *DCuf*
Delay in arrival materials $STuf_1$	Degree of Process Update $SSuf_1$	Degree of Process Deviation from Plan $DCuf_1$
Delay in arrival of products $STuf_2$	Skilled workers $SSuf_2$	Degree of Equipment Failures $DCuf_2$
Departure time $STuf_3$	Satisfaction degree of Material Specifications $SSuf_3$	Degree of Order Change $DCuf_3$
Equipment waiting time $STuf_4$	Accuracy of machining equipment $SSuf_4$	Degree of Process Route Change $DCuf_4$

1. Space-time influence factors: uncertainty related to time and space in workshop production.

   - Whether the material is deployed to the planning station at the planning time;
   - Whether the WIP appears on the planning equipment at the planning time;
   - Whether the worker has worked at the planned station for the required time;
   - Whether the equipment on the corresponding station can work at the needed time.

2. Static state influence factors: factors that have been determined before workshop production and may affect the production process.

   - Process changes caused by a process updated before processing;
   - The average technical level of workers assigned to each post prior to processing;
   - The gap between the material specification and standard material assigned to each station before processing;
   - Machining accuracy of equipment assigned before processing.

3. Dynamic condition influence factors: uncertainty factors in workshop production.

   - The deviation between the start time and end time of the process and the expected start time and end time;
   - Equipment failure during processing;
   - Changes in process tasks generated during processing;
   - Temporary change of process route during processing to produce process changes.

2.2   Quantification Methods of Impact Index

Because of keep the high utilization rate of key equipment in workshop production, the processing tasks from different orders will be merged into unified production tasks, which often have a large time span, if use real-time sampling data for analysis, it may lead to the incidence relation too complex between data features and final results, resulting in low prediction accuracy.

Therefore, in order to better reflect the characteristics of uncertainty factors, the data sampling area is designed as a time period, by using the data in a period of time for data analysis, which could better reflect the data characteristics and improve the accuracy of prediction than using the time data from a single sampling point. In the problem of sampling interval span value, according to experimental data, it is found that in the same group of processing data, using different sampling interval spans will also have different effects on the prediction results, the longer the sampling interval, the higher the prediction accuracy, but the lower the prediction frequency.

$$Prediction\,frequency = \frac{Total\,processing\,time}{Sampling\,interval\,spans} \tag{1}$$

$$Prediction\,accuracy = \alpha \times Sampling\,interval\,spans | (\alpha > 1) \tag{2}$$

The α in announcement is forecast accuracy coefficient, the value will be greater than 1 when the span of the sampling interval is reasonable, so the correct sampling interval span should not be fixed, but change with the focus of the producer and the duration of different tasks. At the same time, we should try to ensure that the value of variables in a sampling interval is effective, so the sampling interval should contain complete procedures as far as possible. As shown in Fig. 1, there will be multiple factors in a sampling interval, the principle of sampling interval span is that the variables produced by these factors can be calculated effectively. For example, the material, worker, work in process and start time of a process should all appear in a sampling interval.

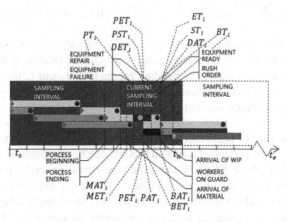

Fig. 1. Sampling interval schematic diagram

Space-Time Influence Index

1) $STuf_1$

Delay in materials arrival $STuf_1$ refers to the difference between the actual arrival time and the planned arrival time of a material. In actual production, there are usually multiple processes at the same time in the same time period, each process may require a variety of materials. At a certain time due to the lack of some material, resulting in multiple processes can not be carried out, this scenario can be used $STuf_1$ measures. The effect of this delay and its occurrence time and duration show a positive correlation trend, the specific calculation formula is as follows:

$$STuf_1 = \sum_{l=1}^{l=P} (MAX\,(e_l^{(MAT_i-MET_i)})) \cdot \frac{t_c - t_s}{t_e - t_s} |(MAT_i > MET_i, i = 1, \ldots, n)$$

(3)

In formula (3), P stands for the number of processes affected in a certain sampling time period, MAT_i represents the actual arrival time of a delayed material i, MET_i represents the expected arrival time of the material, and t_c represents the end time of the current sampling period, t_s represents the processing start time and t_e represents the processing end time. According to the actual situation, when $MAT_i \leq MET_i$, the material is out of the range of calculation without delay, and draw the material with the longest delay time in the time period is obtained by function $MAX()$, and the total delay is obtained by adding the values of multiple processes, draw the $STuf_1$ is obtained by multiplying the value with the time coefficient in the end.

2) $STuf_2$

Pending product delay in arrival of a product refers to the difference between the actual time of arrival and the expected time of a pending product. In the same time period, there are generally multiple processes processing at the same time. The sum of the delay in arrival of each process is $STuf_2$. This value is also positively related to the location and duration of the occurrence time. The formula is as follows:

$$STuf_2 = \sum_{l=1}^{l=P} (e_l^{(BAT_i-BET_i)}) \cdot \frac{t_c - t_s}{t_e - t_s} |(BAT_i > BET_i, i = 1, \ldots, n)$$

(4)

In formula (4), P stands for the number of processes affected in a sampling period, BAT_i represents the actual arrival time of a pending product i, BET_i represents the expected arrival time of the pending product, t_c, t_s and t_e the same as above. According to the actual situation, when $BAT_i \leq BET_i$, the pending product is out of the range of calculation without delay.

3) $STuf_3$

The departure time of personnel refers to the waiting time that cannot be carried out normally in the processing of a certain process due to the absence of corresponding personnel, similarly to $STuf_3$, in the same time period generally contains multiple processes, the sum of the time delay comes from the departure of personnel in each process is $STuf_3$. This variable only calculates the most direct delays generated by personnel, such as leaving the post while operating the equipment. Others requiring personnel participate, such as material supply, equipment maintenance, pending product transfer and so on, but the results are not directly controlled by the personnel in the situation is not reflected in this value. The value is also proportional to the location and duration of the occurrence time. The formula is as follows:

$$STuf_3 = \sum_{l=1}^{l=P} (e_l^{(PAT_i-PET_i)}) \cdot \frac{t_c - t_s}{t_e - t_s} |(PAT_i > PET_i, i = 1, \ldots, n)$$

(5)

In formula (5), P represents the number of processes affected in a sampling time period, PAT_i represents the actual arrival time of a person i, PET_i represents the expected arrival time of the person, t_c, t_s and t_e the same as above. According to the actual situation, when $PAT_i \le PET_i$, the person is undelayed and out of the range of calculations.

4) STuf$_4$

Equipment waiting time refers to the difference between the actual processing start time and the expected time of a certain process on the corresponding equipment, which is the same as above, because usually there are multiple processes processed at the same time in the same time period, the sum of the waiting time for equipment in each process is $STuf_4$, which is also proportional to the position and duration of the occurrence time. The formula is as follows:

$$STuf4 = \sum_{l=1}^{l=P}(e_l^{(DAT_i-DET_i)}) \cdot \frac{t_c - t_s}{t_e - t_s}|(DAT_i > DET_i, i = 1, \ldots, n) \quad (6)$$

In formula (6), P represents the number of processes affected in a sampling time period, DAT_i represents the actual processing start time of a certain equipment i, $DETi$ represents the expected processing start time of the equipment, t_c, t_s and t_e the same as above. According to the actual situation, when $DAT_i \le DET_i$, the equipment is no delay and out of the range of calculation.

Static State Influence Index

1) SSuf$_1$

The degree of technology renewal is the proportion of new processes designed in a technology, according to the actual processing situation, there may be many technologies in the same time period, and the sum of the proportion of new processes contained in each technology in this period of time is $SSuf_1$. The formula is as follows:

$$SSuf1 = \sum_{l=1}^{l=L}(\frac{NP_l}{SP_l}) \quad (7)$$

In formula (7), L is the sum of technologies which process updates within the sampling time period. NP_l express the number of processes updated in a technology l, SP_l express the total number of processes in a time period, sum of these values is the $SSuf_1$.

2) SSuf$_2$

The technical proficiency of workers has a great impact on whether or not occurs the abnormal events. And this value may be affected by a variety of environmental factors, this paper uses the "the average of a worker's skill level and number over time within a time period" to measure the $SSuf_2$ of a certain period of time. The formula is as follows:

$$SSuf2 = \frac{\sum_{i=1}^{i=N}LE_i}{N} \quad (8)$$

In formula (8), N is the total number of workers in a sampling time period, LE_i represents the skill proficiency level of worker i.

3) SSuf₃

Material specification satisfaction refers to the degree of difference between the current material and the standard material. Because the required value of some materials in production is in the range such as granularity (30 μmø–50 μmø), and the most ideal standard material is 40 μmø, the difference between actual material and standard material is specification satisfaction. This value mainly affects the product quality, when the deviation is large, indirect effects such as equipment damage may also occur, the concrete calculation formula is as follows:

$$SSuf3 = \sum_{j=1}^{j=P} \frac{\sum_{i=1}^{i=M_j} \left| MAS_i^j - MES_i^j \right|}{M_j} \tag{9}$$

In formula (9), P is the total number of technologies included in a sampling time period, M_j represents the amount of materials involved in the j process, MAS_i^j represents the actual specification of the i material involved in the j process, and the MES_i^j represents the standard value specification of the i material involved in the j process.

4) SSuf₄

The precision of machining equipment refers to the degree of conformity between the actual geometric parameters after machining and the ideal values specified in the drawing of parts. In the field of machining, the machining accuracy of the equipment affects the processing quality of the WIP, thus ultimately affecting the product quality. The specific formulas are as follows:

$$Suf4 = \sum_{i=1}^{i=D} (DAS_i - DES_i) \tag{10}$$

In formula (10), D is the amount of equipment contained in a certain sampling time period, DAS_i represents the actual machining accuracy of the i equipment, and the DES_i represents the specified machining accuracy of the i equipment. When $DAS_i \leq DES_i$, it is not within the range of calculation.

Dynamic Condition Influence Index

1) DCuf₁

The degree of process deviation directly affects the occurrence of abnormal events. In this paper, "the deviation degree between the actual execution of the process and the planned execution of the process within a time period" is used to measure the deviation degree of the process from the plan. The value has an increasing relationship with the time position and size of its occurrence, that is, the closer to the end of process, the greater the impact, the specific formula is as follows:

$$DCuf1 = \sum_{i=1}^{i=Q} \frac{|ST_i(P) - PST_i(P)| + |ET_i(P) - PET_i(P)|}{PET_i(P) - PST_i(P)} \cdot \frac{t_c - t_s}{t_e - t_s} \tag{11}$$

In formula (11), Q is the total number of processes in the workshop processing task during the p sampling time period, $ST_i(P)$ represents the actual processing start time of the i process during the p time period, $PST_i(P)$ represents the planned processing start time of the i process, $ET_i(P)$ and $PET_i(P)$ respectively the actual processing end time and the planned processing end time of the i process within the time period p, t_c, t_s and t_e the same as above.

2) $DCuf_2$

The degree of equipment failure directly affects the occurrence of abnormal events. In this paper, "the ratio of the total duration of equipment failure to the total number of equipment processing tasks during a period of time" is used to measure the degree of equipment failure. The value has an increasing relationship with the time position and size of its occurrence. The specific formulas are as follows:

$$DCuf2 = \frac{\sum_{i=1}^{i=M} BT_i(P)}{\sum_{i=1}^{i=M} PT_i(P)} \cdot \frac{t_c - t_s}{t_e - t_s} \qquad (12)$$

In formula (12), M is the total number of equipment in the workshop processing task during the sampling time period P, $PT_i(P)$ represents the planned processing time of the i equipment during the time period P, $BT_i(P)$ represents the duration of the failure of the i equipment during the time period P, the actual value can be collected by sensor technology, t_c, t_s and t_e the same as above.

3) $DCuf_3$

The degree of order change refers to the change of order in the process of processing and production. These changes include various factors and have a great impact on the whole processing, such as rush order, temporary increment and so on. Compare the number of ethical processes involved in order changes with the total number of processes, calculate the change rate of the order, and sum up all the order changes in the same time period to get the $DCuf_3$. The formula is as follows:

$$DCuf3 = \sum_{i=1}^{i=N} \frac{|TB_i|}{TC_i} \cdot \frac{t_c - t_s}{t_e - t_s} \qquad (13)$$

In formula (13), N is the number of orders changed during the sampling time period, TB_i represents the number of changing processes involved in the changed order i, TC_i represents the total number of processes in the order, t_c, t_s and t_e the same as above, which used to reflect the relationship between the value and the processing stage.

4) $DCuf_4$

Technology line change refers to the degree of change caused by the influence of order, processing environment and other factors in the production process. This value has a great influence on the processing time, it also has a great influence on the quality of the product in special cases. By calculating the ratio of the number of processes changed and the number of total work order in changed technologies during a certain period of time, the value can be obtained. The formula is as follows:

$$DCuf4 = \sum_{i=1}^{i=N} \frac{PE_i}{PC_i} \cdot \frac{t_c - t_s}{t_e - t_s} \qquad (14)$$

In formula (14), N is the total number of changed technologies involved in the sampling time period, PE_i represents the number of processes changed in the technology

i, PC_i represents the total number of processes in the technology i, t_c, t_s and t_e the same as above, which used to reflect the relationship between the value and the processing stage.

2.3 Analysis of Abnormal Prediction Results

In order to describe the possible effects of the above abnormal factors on product quality and delivery period, this paper defines the product quality outliers and delivery period outliers to measure the product quality anomalies and delivery period anomalies. Abnormal product quality refers to the additional economic cost caused by the quality of some products not up to the planned standard after the end of a certain processing task, and even caused the order can not be delivered as planned. Therefore, QL is the abnormal value of product quality, the formula is as follows:

$$QL = \frac{IPN}{PN} \tag{15}$$

In formula (15), IPN is the number of defective products produced by the processing task, and PN is the total number of products planned for processing by the processing task.

The abnormal delivery period refers to the additional economic cost after the end of a processing task caused by the actual completion time of the task deviates from the planned completion time. For example, if completed ahead of schedule, it will lead to additional inventory costs, and if completed out of schedule, it will result in additional default compensation costs. Therefore, the formula for calculating the value of the delivery period anomaly DP is as follows:

$$DP = |DPA - DPE| \tag{16}$$

In formula (16), DPA is the actual completion time of the processing task, and DPE is the planned completion time.

In the subsequent construction of workshop production anomaly prediction model, considering the business needs of workshop production managers, this paper actually predicts the degree of possible impact of abnormal factors on product quality and delivery period. Table 2 classifies product quality outliers and delivery period outliers according to alarm levels of the impact degree.

Threshold vectors *(ql1, ql2, ql3, ql4)* of the product quality outliers QL, and the threshold vectors *(dp₁, dp₂, dp₃, dp₄)* of the delivery period outliers DP in Table 2 needs to be developed jointly by relevant field experts and workshop production managers according to specific processing task types. The alarm level prediction output of product quality outliers QL and delivery period outliers DP will be provided to workshop production administrators, to assist them in management decisions.

3   Construction HNN-Based Anomaly Prediction Model

An anomaly prediction model based on HNN is implemented by a combination of multiple isomorphic hybrid neural networks. Among them, each hybrid neural network is

Table 2. Alarm levels of the impact degree

Impact level Alarm Level k	Normal (k = 1)	Mild alarm (k = 2)	Alarm (k = 3)	Severe alarm (k = 4)	Serious alarm (k = 5)
Classification criteria QL product quality outliers	$0 \leq QL \leq ql_1$	$ql_1 < QL \leq ql_2$	$ql_2 < QL \leq ql_3$	$ql_3 < QL \leq ql_4$	$ql_4 < QL$
Classification criteria for outlier DP during delivery	$0 \leq DP \leq dp_1$	$dp_1 < DP \leq dp_2$	$dp_2 < DP \leq dp_3$	$dp_3 < DP \leq dp_4$	$dp_4 < DP$
Output code	0	101	202	303	404

cascaded by sparse autoencoder and Softmax classifier. Sparse autoencoder can extract potential features from raw data (i.e., historical data of abnormal influencing factors) by unsupervised learning, which helps to improve the efficiency of subsequent classification models in hybrid neural networks. Softmax classifiers can obtain the nonlinear mapping relationship (i.e., quantitative mapping relationship between abnormal influencing factors and outliers) in sample data sets through supervised learning, which could support the prediction of workshop production anomalies.

In this paper, the data collection of the related calculation indexes of abnormal influencing factors is completed by the method of time period collection. The sampling interval span varies with different requirements and processing tasks, and the principle of value is detailed in Sect. 2.2. By analyzing and processing the data in the sampling interval, the quantitative method in Sect. 2.2 is used to obtain the variable value of the influencing factors that can reflect the situation of the workshop. Because the data of different tasks of the same type may contain similar data features during different sampling time periods, the historical data results associated with these data features may be different. If a single neural network is trained by these data samples with one-to-many relationships, the network model may cause polarization phenomenon, that may result in network overfitting and also may result in inaccurate prediction.

In order to solve this problem, this paper segments according to the sampling interval, and establishes the corresponding hybrid neural network in each interval, trains it with the historical data during the corresponding time period, which is based to construct a number of hybrid neural networks on the time axis. The structure and training process of multiple hybrid neural networks in the anomaly prediction model are shown in Fig. 2. A sparse autoencoder is shared by multiple hybrid neural networks in the anomaly prediction model, and each hybrid neural network contains its own Softmax classifier to predict the quality outliers and delivery period outliers in each time period. Every hybrid neural network has the same structure and similar training process. The following part takes one of the hybrid neural networks as an example to give its training process.

Data sets required during training process:

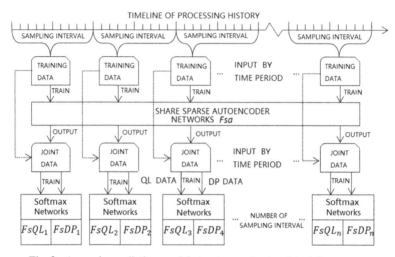

Fig. 2. Anomaly prediction model structure and network training process

A time period in a historical processing task: $TP_i^j = \{STuf \cup SSuf \cup DCuf\}$

Historical processing data for a task: $PE_i = \{TP_i^1, TP_i^2, \ldots, TP_i^m\}$

Historical processing data set for the same type of project: $PAE = \{PE_1, PE_2, \ldots PE_n\}$.

Historical processing result data for a task: $PR_i = \{QL, DP\}$.

Historical processing result data set for the same type of project: $PAR = \{PR_1, PR_2, \ldots PR_n\}$.

Historical processing result data set for the same type of project within the same sampling time: $LTP_j = \{TP_1^j, , TP_2^j, \ldots, TP_n^j\}$ (Table 3).

Table 3. Training sample set

Historical data for the same type of processing task *PAE*					Task outcomes *PAR*
Task	Time period				
	Sampling interval 1 LTP_1	Sampling interval 2 LTP_2	Sampling interval 3 LTP_3	... Sampling interval m LTP_m	
PE_1	TP_1^1	TP_1^2	TP_1^3	... TP_1^m	PR_1
PE_2	TP_2^1	TP_2^2	TP_2^3	... TP_n^m	PR_2
...	...	...	...	... ...	...
PE_n	TP_n^1	TP_n^2	TP_n^3	... TP_n^m	PR_n

3.1 Construction Sparse Autoencoder

The peculiarity of sparse autoencoder model is learning better potential features than the original data from unlabeled data. This feature makes the sparse autoencoder model often used as a molecular network in hybrid neural network or deep neural network to improve the learning efficiency of the whole network. A training algorithm *TA_Fsa* for sparse autoencoder is given below. The *Relu* function is closer to the activation model of neurons than the activation function *sigmod* and hyperbolic tangent commonly used in neural networks, and it is more suitable for processing large-scale and complex data. Therefore, the *TA_Fsa* algorithm in this paper selects the *Relu* function as the activation function of neurons in sparse autoencoder *Fsa*.

3.2 Construction Multi Softmax Classifiers

Softmax classifier model is often used to solve multi-classification problems. In this section, by taking the data sets of multiple time periods in the processing process as training samples, this paper constructs multiple Softmax classifier subnetworks, which can predict the outlier of product quality and the outlier of delivery period in their corresponding time periods. Specifically, in order to learn the data characteristics of different time periods in the processing more accurately, this paper constructs two corresponding Softmax classifier subnetworks for each sampling interval: the *FsQL* subnetwork is used to predict the outlier of product quality and the *FsDP* subnetwork is used to predict the outlier of delivery period.

The input of Softmax classifier subnetwork is the sample data set which is labeled and processed by sparse autoencoder subnetworks *Fsa*. When constructing multiple Softmax classifier subnetworks for different sampling intervals, it is necessary to determine the network structure of Softmax classifier subnetworks. Specifically, the number of layers of the network and the number of neurons in each layer. For more convenient and efficient construction of multiple Softmax classifier subnetworks, this paper designs them as isomorphic subnetworks. For the well-designed Softmax classifier subnetwork, using different model parameters can fully reflect the data characteristics of different sampling intervals. Therefore, we can design a unified training algorithm to construct multiple Softmax classifier subnetworks.

3.3 Construction Time Series Multi HNN Anomaly Prediction Mode

The $FsQL_j$ and $FsDP_j$ hybrid neural network model from multi time periods can be obtained by performing training algorithm *TA_Fsa and TA_FsQLDP*. The essence of training HNN model is to determine their model parameters, specifically to determine the weights and thresholds of each neuron in them. The parameters of these HNN models are different according to the time period, storage of these HNN model parameters is to store multiple HNN models. In the actual use process, according to the different time period of the current workshop processing, selective loading of different HNN model parameters can achieve to use of the corresponding HNN model for abnormal prediction, which fully reflects the data characteristics of different time periods.

However, considering that workshop processing and production are continuous, the events at the previous time will have an impact on subsequent processing, but with the passage of time, the impact of old events will weaken. Therefore, when prediction at current time, the different effects of a series of events on the final result should be considered. For this reason, this paper inspired by the genetic curve model, proposes a time series multi HNN anomaly prediction model. The output of the prediction model is the result which is based on the time variables to time weighting of the actual output of the HNN model at the current time point and many previous time points. The formula of the time weighting function, which reflects the influence of the actual output of the HNN model corresponding to the j sampling time period on the final prediction results, is as follows:

$$f(t) = e^{\lambda * t} | \lambda = \frac{\ln 0.5}{T_0} \tag{17}$$

The value of the function is kept in the range of (0~ 1], T_0 is the half-life of the predicted result, represents the time required to reduce the influence of the actual output of the model to the actual output of the model to half, that is, the influence of the actual output of the model is halved after T_0 time period, λ is decay factor. Among them, $t = t_c - t_j$, t_c represents the end time of the current sampling time period, t_j represents the end time of the j sampling time period.

Suppose the total processing time is T, the sampling interval span is L, the sampling frequency is $F = T/L$. c is the serial number of current sampling time period, $FsQLDP_c$ is the final prediction result of the current sampling period, $FsQLDP_j$ is the actual output of $FsQLDP$ hybrid neural network model during j sampling time period, and $1 \leq j \leq c$, $1 \leq c \leq F$.

$$FsQLDP_c = \sum_{j=1}^{c} FsQLDP_j * \left[f(t_c - t_j) / \sum_{j=1}^{c} f(t_c - t_j) \right] \tag{18}$$

From the above formula, it can be seen that the final prediction result of the time series multi HNN anomaly prediction model is obtained by time-weighted calculation of the actual output of the HNN model in multiple sampling time periods. Therefore, the actual output of the HNN model in different time periods needs to be stored, which could be used for subsequent final prediction results. The final prediction results of the abnormal prediction model in each current time period are the synthetical value which is weighted by the actual output of the current HNN model and the actual output of the previous HNN models. This reflects the influence of a series of events on the current processing. Which could make the anomaly prediction model more reasonable, and the predictions will be more accurate.

3.4 Complimentary Close

In this paper, based on the analysis of correlative entities of abnormal influencing factors such as work-in-process, materials and equipment in workshops of discrete manufacturing enterprises, the influence index system with nonlinear mapping relationship between quality anomaly and delivery time anomaly is established from three aspects of space-time characteristic, static characteristic and dynamic characteristic. Based on this, this paper presents a time series multi HNN anomaly prediction model, which reasonable combination the potential feature extraction capability of sparse autoencoder and the strong learning ability of Softmax classifier to nonlinear mapping relationship, the model ensures the real-time and accurate prediction of workshop production anomalies. Finally, through the case experiment in the production workshop, the validity and accuracy of the abnormal prediction model for the quality anomaly and delivery period anomaly prediction in the workshop production process are verified.

References

1. Li, B., Zhang, L., Ren, L., et al.: Typical characteristics, technologies and applications of cloud manufacturing. Comput. Integr. Manuf. Syst. **18**(7), 1345–1356 (2012)
2. Zhang, F., Du, P., Yang, Y.: Practice of product data collecting of MES for discrete manufacturing enterprise. Mach. Design Manuf. **3**, 245–247 (2011)
3. Wu, B., Shi, G., Ding, Y., et al.: Quantitative evaluation research on uncertainty factors in production scheduling of manufacturing enterprises. In: The 1st International Symposium on Digital Manufacture, pp. 484–489 (2006)
4. Yin, C., Ma, C., Liu, F., et al.: Real-time management system for abnormal production-events in workshop. Comput. Integr. Manuf. Syst. **15**(4), 719–725 (2009)
5. Qiuming, W., Kecheng, L., Huiying, G.: Research of procedure quality forecast based on the grey theory and BP neural networks. Trans. Beijing Inst. Technol. **31**(2), 249–252 (2011)
6. Li, Y., He, W., Dong, R., et al.: Man-hour forecasting and evolution based on MES data collection. Comput. Integr. Manuf. Syst. **19**(11), 2810–2817 (2013)
7. Yin, C., Gan, D., Liang, Z.: Evaluation and early warning method of key assembly process materials quality loss for complex electromechanical products . Comput. Integr. Manuf. Syst. **20**(6), 1432–1441 (2014)
8. Yin, C., Guo, C., Zhao, X.: Evaluation and early warning method of abnormal production loss for minicar rear axle key process. Comput. Integr. Manuf. Syst. **20**(10), 2532–2540 (2014)
9. Shan, S., Mao, Z., Xin, T.: Prediction technology of abnormal events in aircraft assembly workshop based on BP neural network. Assem. Technol. **8**, 42–47 (2014)
10. Xu, D., Liu, S., Ma, C., et al.: A cloud servitization method for job shop scheduling capability of MES in big data environment. Comput. Eng. Sci. 7 (2016, accepted for publication)
11. Ma, C., Xu, D., Zhang, S., Liu, S.: Abnormal event discovery method of discrete manufacture workshop in big data. Comput. Appl. Softw. **34**(09), 288–293 (2017)
12. Zhu, C.: A study on the reduction of uncertain information and knowledge discovery in workshop. Huazhong University of Science and Technology (2006)
13. Shan, S., Mao, Z., Xin, T.: Prediction technology of abnormal events in aircraft assembly workshop based on BP neural network. Aeronaut. Manuf. Technol. **08**, 42–47 (2014)

Efficient Forward and Backward Private Searchable Symmetric Encryption for Multiple Data Sources

Lin Mei, Chungen Xu$^{(\boxtimes)}$, and Lin Li

School of Science, Nanjing University of Science and Technology,
Nanjing 210094, China
xuchung@njust.edu.cn

Abstract. Searchable symmetric encryption (SSE) has been widely applied in the encrypted database for keyword queries. Although SSE is powerful and feature-rich, it is always plagued by information leaks. Some recent researches have pointed out that forward and backward privacy which disallows leakage from update operations should be the basic requirement for a secure SSE scheme. However, most existing forward and backward private SSE schemes only consider the single data source model which is not practical in the IoT scenario (e.g., data are often separately distributed over multiple devices). Considering the above issues, this paper proposes an efficient forward and backward private SSE scheme for multiple data sources (FBSSE-MDS). As far as we know, FBSSE-MDS is the first efficient SSE scheme which supports both forward privacy and backward privacy BP-II (the second level of backward privacy) in the scene of multiple data sources. Finally, we implement our scheme and compare its performance with two other related schemes. The experiment results show that our scheme is highly efficient.

Keywords: Internet of Things · Searchable symmetric encryption · Forward privacy · Backward privacy · Multiple data sources

1 Introduction

Internet of Things (IoT) enables different devices to achieve convenient and efficient connections, during which tremendous data are collected and transferred via the internet. With the sharp increase of the massive data, outsourcing data to the IoT cloud has recently become prevalent. Despite the benefits of cloud storage, such as low cost and ubiquitous access, data privacy is a major concern. To dispel user's concern, encrypting data before uploading it to the untrusted cloud server is a straightforward solution. However, encryption hinders the usability

The authors would like to thank the support from the National Natural Science Foundation of China (No: 62072240), the National Key Research and Development Program of China (No. 2020YFB1804604).

X. Sun et al. (Eds.): ICAIS 2021, CCIS 1424, pp. 126–139, 2021.
https://doi.org/10.1007/978-3-030-78621-2_10

of data, which results in common retrieval methods such as the keyword search fails to be directly executed over ciphertexts. To solve this problem, searchable symmetric encryption (SSE) was introduced in 2000 [16]. It allows a client to retrieve the outsourced encrypted files containing a certain keyword by submitting a cryptographically generated token. The original SSE schemes only provided secure search over static database, which seriously restrict the applicability due to the lack of update functionality. Dynamic searchable symmetric encryption (DSSE) was formally proposed by Kamara et al. [12] to allow users to perform update operations on the outsourced database.

At the core of designing SSE schemes is to improve efficiency while ensuring the security at the same time. The researches of the former goal is focused on storage requirements, bandwidth or latency. The latter faces more challenged issues since tremendous works have uncovered devastating and fairly generic attacks against many SSE schemes. For example, deterministic encryption used in SSE makes it easy for the malicious server to observe repeated queries and other information. These leakages typically include the search pattern that reveals which search queries refer to the same keyword as well as the access pattern that reveals which files are returned for a query. Generally, these leakages could be eliminated by using oblivious RAM (ORAM) [7]. However, applying ORAM brings heavy computational overhead and bandwidth cost. To gain a more practical counter measure, Islam et al. [9] proposed the first database padding approach and be further improved by Xu et al. [22].

Compared with SSE, DSSE introduces two additional privacy concerns, owing to the added functionality. The first is that newly updated files can be related to previous search results. The second is that search queries can leak matching files after they have been deleted. In 2016, Zhang [23] gave a more powerful attack named file injection attack, which shows how the leakages in DSSE can be exploited to reveal a considerable amount of information in practice. In this attack, an adversary can inject files containing some special keywords into the server's database. Then the adversary can use old search queries to search those injected files and then easily recover the keyword of a query.

The work in [23] underlines the importance of forward privacy (FP) when constructing DSSE schemes, which requires that the update (addition and deletion) operations cannot be linked to previous search queries and further ensures that the scheme can resist file injection attacks. The initial work that achieve FP is proposed by Chang and Mitzenmacher, which is designed by utilizing pseudo-random functions [4]. However, in their scheme the size of search query grows linearly in the number of updates, which means there exists a threshold for update, and the communication cost for the search operation will become unacceptably high once the threshold is exceeded. In 2016, Bost [1] creatively proposed an efficient forward secure SSE scheme named $\sum o\varphi o\varsigma$, which only relies on trapdoor permutations. Since then, several schemes have been proposed to achieve FP using different cryptographic primitives [6,13,17,18].

Regarding data deletion, most past schemes cannot resist the server from learning that the new document has a keyword user searched for in the past

[1,6,13,17,18]. To hide the relationship between the deleted files and the query, Bost [2] introduced a formal definition of backward privacy (BP) with three different types of leakage ordered from most to least secure (from BP-I to BP-III). Besides, Bost [2] provided four backward-private constructions that achieve different privacy/efficiency trade-offs. Later, Chamani et al. [3] proposed an enhanced forward and backward secure scheme named MITRA, which offers backward-privacy Type-II.

As far as we know, most existing forward and backward private SSE schemes only consider the single data source model, that is to say, suppose that the searchable index can be directly built by the single data source. This assumption only makes sense when data files are extremely lightweight and stored centrally, which is not realistic in IoT. For example, industry IoT, as a specific application scenario of IoT, always involves multiple data sources (e.g., interconnected sensors, instruments and other devices networked together with computers' industrial applications). It is not rational for a company to centralize all the data and then build a searchable index for secure query. In order to address the mentioned issues, Liu et al. [15] proposed the notion of Multi-Data-Source (MDS) SSE, which allows each data source to build a local index individually and enables the storage provider to merge all local indexes into a global index afterwards.

Contributions. We propose an efficient and secure scheme FBSSE-MDS, which achieves both forward privacy and BP-II (the second level of backward privacy) in the scenario of multiple data sources. To the best of our knowledge, FBSSE-MDS is the first scheme which achieve all above properties. Also, we give the strict security proof of our scheme to show that our scheme is forward private and BP-II private. Through theoretical analysis, our scheme is demonstrated to own rich functionalities and high security while maintaining high efficiency. We implement our scheme and other related schemes using the Java programming language. The experimental results show that our scheme achieves better balance between security and efficiency.

Related Works: SSE was first introduced by Song et al. [16], with a scheme whose search time is linear in the number of documents. To improve efficiency, Curtmola et al. [5] gave the first index-based SSE constructions to achieve sublinear search time. Since then, many works has been done to enrich the functionality [12,14] and improve the security [1–3,6,13,17,18]. Among others, Kamara et al. [12] proposed the first dynamic SSE to support sublinear search with update operations, but it leaks the hashes of the unique keywords contained in the updated documents. Kamara and Papamanthou [11] later improved their construction by increasing the space complexity. Recently, a series of DSSE schemes have been proposed to offer varieties of functionalities [10] and improve efficiency [17] and security [18].

In 2014, Stefanov et al. Stefanov2014 first formalized the notion of FP for DSSE scheme. In 2016, Zhang et al. [23] gave a formalized definition of a very strong attack, named file injection attack. This attack can easily recover the keyword of a query by injecting only a small number of files in a DSSE scheme. Since then, several schemes have been proposed to achieve forward privacy using different cryptographic primitives, including Sophos [1] (uses trapdoor permutation (TDP)), Diana [2] (uses Constrained Pseudorandom Function (CPRF)), Dual [6] (uses keyed hash function), FSSE [21] (uses keyed-block chains), SGX-SE [20] (uses intel SGX) and VFSSE [8] (uses blockchain).

Very recently, Bost et al. [2] introduced a formal definition for backward privacy with three different types of leakage ordered from most to least secure (from BP-I to BP-III). Bost et al. [2] provided four backward private (and forward private) constructions that achieve different privacy/efficiency trade-offs. They first described a simple and generic method to transform a forward private SSE scheme to a backward private SSE scheme at the cost of an extra roundtrip per search query. Moneta and Fides are two instantiations of this method, while the security level of the latter is BP-II. Then they proposed two BP-III schemes named Dianadel and Janus that rely on puncturable cryptographic primitives to achieve better results, but increasing the amount of information leaked. Sun et al. [19] proposed a backward-secure SSE scheme from symmetric puncturable encryption. Compared to Janus (the first non-interactive backward-secure SSE scheme), the proposed construction in [19] is proved to be more practical through implementation.

1.1 Organization

The remainder of this paper is organized as follows. In Sect. 2, we state the system model, threat model and design goals of our scheme. In Sect. 3, we describe the cryptographic background for our construction. In Sect. 4, we introduce the details of our proposed scheme FBSSE-MDS. Then we carry out the security analysis and performance evaluation in Sect. 5 and Sect. 6, respectively. Finally, we conclude the paper in Sect. 7.

2 Problem Statement

2.1 System Model

As shown in Fig. 1, there are four roles in a FBSSE-MDS system: (1) data sources, denoted as DS, who own various collections of data files. (2) data user, denoted as DU, who issues search queries for interested keywords. (3) trusted authority, denoted as TA, who stores some valuable information to help DU and DS perform search or update operation. (4) cloud server, who stores encrypted data files and responses DU's search queries and DS's update operations. Note that the roles of DU and DS are interchangeable, which means an authorized DU who shares the secret key with DS is assumed to be a DS as well or any DS can be called DU when he performs a search query.

Figure 1 illustrates the architecture of our proposed FBSSE-MDS system. Firstly, DS encrypt data files and build searchable indexes before data outsourcing. Upon receiving all indexes from DS, server merges them into one searchable index. Then DU can query the encrypted data by generating a search token, which will later be submitted to the server. Finally, the server searches the index and returns the identities of data files containing searched keywords.

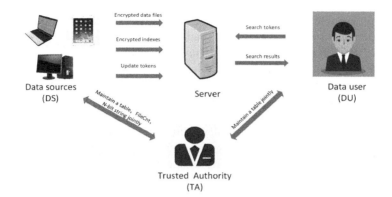

Fig. 1. System model

2.2   Threat Model

We treat the server as the adversary, who behaves "honest-but-curious". As its name implies, the server will follow all the operations defined in the FBSSE-MDS system model, while trying to deduce private information about the original data or searched keywords. Meanwhile, we suppose that DS, DU and TA are fully trusted, that is to say, there is no collusion among DS, Du and TA. Following most of the existing settings, the key is assumed to be transferred via a secure channel between DS and DU.

2.3   Design Goals

The proposed model should accomplish the following goals:

- **Providing forward privacy.** The server cannot violate the privacy of newly updated files by utilizing previously received search tokens. Each search token is associated with a state that is renewed every time files are updated. Therefore, the disclosure of the old token will not pose a threat to the updated files.
- **Providing BP-II backward privacy.** As for the deletion operation, the server cannot learn which deletion cancels which addition. In particular, the identity of files will be hidden by XOR operation. It ensures that FBSSE-MDS achieves BP-II backward privacy.
- **Supporting multiple data sources.** The server can merges indexes built by different DS that are indistinguishable into one index before performing search operations. Afterwards, the server can search over only one index rather than k indexes, which greatly enhances the efficiency.

3   Preliminaries

Forward privacy and backward privacy are two SSE properties that aim to control what information is leaked by dynamic schemes in relation to updates. Informally, a scheme is forward private if it is not possible to relate an update to previous search operations. This is particularly essential in practice, e.g., to hide whether an addition is about a new keyword or a pre-existing one (which may have been previously searched for).

Definition 1 (Forward Privacy). An $\mathcal{L}$-adaptively-secure SSE scheme that supports addition/deletion of a single keyword is forward private iff the update leakage function $\mathcal{L}^{Update}$ can be written as:

$$\mathcal{L}^{Update}(op, w, ind) = \mathcal{L}'(op, ind),$$

where $\mathcal{L}'$ is a stateless function, op is insertion or deletion, and ind is a file identifier.

An SSE scheme satisfies backward privacy if after deleting a document ind matching keyword w, the server cannot reveal the deleted document ind from the subsequent search of keyword w. In 2017, Bost et al. [2] have defined backward privacy at three levels: BP-I, BP-II and BP-III. The definitions of them can be described as follows.

Definition 2 (BP-I). A $\mathcal{L}$-adaptively-secure SSE scheme is insertion pattern revealing backward-private iff leakage functions $\mathcal{L}$ can be written as:

$$\mathcal{L}^{Update}(op, w, ind) = \mathcal{L}'(op),$$

$$\mathcal{L}^{Search}(w) = \mathcal{L}''(TimeDB(w)),$$

where $\mathcal{L}'$ and $\mathcal{L}''$ are stateless and $|TimeDB(w)| = a_w$ for a_w is a constant.

Definition 3 (BP-II). A $\mathcal{L}$-adaptively-secure SSE scheme is update pattern revealing backward-private iff leakage functions $\mathcal{L}$ can be written as:

$$\mathcal{L}^{Update}(op, w, ind) = \mathcal{L}'(op, w), \mathcal{L}^{Search}(w) = \mathcal{L}''(TimeDB(w), Updates(w)),$$

where $\mathcal{L}'$ and $\mathcal{L}''$ are stateless and $|TimeDB(w)| = a_w$ for a_w is a constant.

Definition 4 (BP-III). A $\mathcal{L}$-adaptively-secure SSE scheme is weakly backward-private iff leakage functions $\mathcal{L}$ can be written as:

$$\mathcal{L}^{Update}(op, w, ind) = \mathcal{L}'(op, w),$$

$$\mathcal{L}^{Search}(w) = \mathcal{L}''(TimeDB(w), DelHist(w)),$$

where $\mathcal{L}'$ and $\mathcal{L}''$ are stateless and $|TimeDB(w)| = a_w$ for a_w is a constant.

4   Our Construction

This section mainly introduces the specific structure of FBSSE-MDS scheme, which includes three protocols: setup, update and search. Among them, setup and update are the protocols running between multiple DS, TA and servers,

$DS_p(1 \le p \le k)$:

1: Randomly select $\mathcal{K}$ from $\{0,1\}^\lambda$
2: Initialize an empty collection $\mathcal{L}_p$
3: Initalize an empty list O
4: $FileCnt \leftarrow$ online $FileCnt$
5: **for** $i = FileCnt + 1$ **to do**
6:    $FileCnt + |\mathcal{D}_p|$
7:    $c_i \leftarrow ENC(\mathcal{K}, f_i)$
8:    $ID(f_i) \leftarrow PRP'(\mathcal{K}, i)$
9:    $O[i - FileCnt] \leftarrow ID(f_i)$
10:    $\mathcal{L}_p \leftarrow \mathcal{L}_p \cup \{(c_i, ID(f_i))\}$
11: **end for**
12: Send $\mathcal{L}_p$ to the server via anonymous communication
13: $FileCnt \leftarrow FileCnt + |\mathcal{D}_p|$
14: Initialize an array A of length $|\mathcal{W}|$
15: Initialize a counter $ctr \leftarrow 1$
16: $K_{permute} \leftarrow PRF(\mathcal{K}, 0)$
17: **for** $w \in \mathcal{W}$ **do**
18:    Initialize a counter $j \leftarrow 1$
19:    Initialize an N-bit zero string γ
20:    **for** $f \in \mathcal{D}_i$ **do**
21:      **if** $w \in f$ **then**
22:        $\gamma[\mathcal{F}[j]] \leftarrow 1$

23:      **end if**
24:      $j \leftarrow j + 1$
25:    **end for**
26:    $t_w \leftarrow PRF(\mathcal{K}, w), \alpha \leftarrow H_1(t_w || 0)$
27:    $\beta \leftarrow PRF(\mathcal{K}, w||0), s_{id} \leftarrow PRF'(\beta, id)$
28:    $\gamma \leftarrow \gamma \oplus s_{id}, \delta \leftarrow H_2(t_w||0) \oplus \bot$
29:    $A[PRP(K_{permute}, ctr)] \leftarrow (\alpha, \gamma, \delta)$
30:    $ctr \leftarrow ctr + 1$
31: **end for**
32: Send A to the server.

Server:

1: Initialize an empty dictionary $\mathcal{I}$.
2: **for** $i = 1$ **to** k **do**
3:    Parse $A[i]$ as $(\alpha_{i,1}, \gamma_{i,1}, \delta_{i,1})$,
4:    $(\alpha_{i,2}, \gamma_{i,2}, \delta_{i,2}), ... (\alpha_{i,|\mathcal{W}|}, \gamma_{i,|\mathcal{W}|}, \delta_{i,|\mathcal{W}|})$
5: **end for**
6: **for** $j = 1$ **to** $|\mathcal{W}|$ **do**
7:    $\alpha \leftarrow \alpha_{1,j}$ (note that $\alpha_{1,j} = ... = \alpha_{k,j}$)
8:    $\delta \leftarrow \delta_{1,j}$ (note that $\delta_{1,j} = ... = \delta_{k,j}$)
9:    $\gamma \leftarrow \overset{k}{\underset{i=1}{\oplus}} \gamma_{i,j}$
10: **end for**
11: $\mathcal{I}[\alpha] \leftarrow (\gamma, \delta)$
12: $Z \leftarrow Z \cup \mathcal{L}_p$

Fig. 2. Setup protocol

while search is the protocol running between DU, TA and server. Now we give the detailed descriptions of three protocols as follows.

Setup. During the Setup protocol, each data source DS_p encrypts his data files and builds searchable indexes. The server receives encrypted data files and indexes from each DS_p and merges all indexes.

– DS_p: Take the security parameter λ and an empty collection $\mathcal{L}_p$, an empty list O, the total number of data files currently stored on the server $FileCnt$ as inputs. Let $PRP' : \{0,1\}^\lambda \times \{1, ..., N\} \to \{1, ..., N\}$ be a pseudo-random permutation, and $H_1 : \{0,1\}^* \to \{0,1\}^\lambda$, $H_2 : \{0,1\}^* \to \{0,1\}^N$ be two hash functions, and $PRF : \{0,1\}^\lambda \times \{0,1\}^* \to \{0,1\}^\lambda$, $PRF' : \{0,1\}^\lambda \times \{0,1\}^* \to \{0,1\}^N$ be two pseudo-random functions. Run the first part of Setup protocol (as shown in Fig. 2) to compute the indexes.
– Server: Run the second part of Setup protocol (as shown in Fig. 2) to merge the received indexes into one index and store it.

Update. During the Update protocol, DS_p needs to submit encrypted data files and update tokens to the server, then the server updates index and stores encrypted data files in cipher collection.

– DS_p: Assuming the DS_p wants to update the files in set ID_{add} and ID_{del}, he runs line 1 to 16 of the first part in Update protocol to generate the ciphertexts and identity set (as shown in Fig. 3). Furthermore, in order to

$\underline{DS_p(1 \leq p \leq k)}$:

1: Initialize an empty array ID_{up} whose size is $|ID_{add}| + |ID_{del}|$
2: if $ID_{add} = \emptyset$ then
3:   Padding $Cipher$ with random elements
4: else
5:   for $j = 1$ to $|ID_{add}|$ do
6:     $c_j \leftarrow ENC(\mathcal{K}, f_j)$
7:     $ID(f_j) \leftarrow PRF'(\mathcal{K}, FileCnt + j)$
8:     $Cipher \leftarrow Cipher \cup (c_j, ID(f_j))$
9:     $ID_{up}[j] \leftarrow ID(f_j)$
10:   end for
11: end if
12: if $ID_{del} \neq \emptyset$ then
13:   for $i = |ID_{add}| + 1$ to $|ID_{add}| + |ID_{del}|$ do
14:     $ID_{up}[j] \leftarrow ID_{del}[i - |ID_{add}|]$
15:   end for
16: end if
17: Initialize a empty array F whose size is $|\mathcal{W}_{up}|$
18: Initialize an empty collection $\mathcal{UT}_{\mathcal{W}_{up}}$
19: for $i = 1$ to $|\mathcal{W}_{up}|$ do
20:   $(UpdCnt, st_c) \leftarrow \mathcal{T}(\mathcal{W}_{up}[i])$
21:   $st_{c+1} \xleftarrow{\$} \{0,1\}^\lambda$, $t_w \leftarrow PRF(\mathcal{K}, w)$

22:   $\alpha \leftarrow H_1(t_w || st_{c+1})$
23:   $\delta \leftarrow H_2(t_w || st_{c+1}) \oplus st_c$
24:   Initialize a N-bit string γ_{up} to 0
25:   for $j = 1$ to $|ID_{up}|$ do
26:     if the data file corresponding to $ID_{up}[j]$ contains keyword $\mathcal{W}_{up}[i]$ then
27:       set the $ID_{up}[j]$-th bit of γ_{up} to 1
28:     end if
29:   end for
30:   $UpdCnt \leftarrow UpdCnt + 1$
31:   $\gamma \leftarrow \gamma_{up} \oplus PRF(\mathcal{K}, \mathcal{W}_{up}[i] || UpdCnt)$
32:   $\mathcal{UT}_{\mathcal{W}_{up}} \leftarrow \mathcal{UT}_{\mathcal{W}_{up}} \cup \{(\alpha, \gamma, \delta)\}$
33:   $\mathcal{T}(\mathcal{W}_{up}[i]) \leftarrow (UpdCnt, st_{c+1})$
34:   $FileCnt \leftarrow FileCnt + |D_{add}|$
35: end for
36: Send $(Cipher, \mathcal{UT}_{\mathcal{W}_{up}})$ to the server

server:
1: for $i = 1$ to $|\mathcal{W}_{up}|$ do
2:   $ID_{up}[j] \leftarrow ID_{del}[i - |D_{add}|]$
3:   Parse $\mathcal{UT}_{\mathcal{W}_{up}}$ as $(\alpha_1, \gamma_1, \delta_1), ...,$
4:     $(\alpha_{|\mathcal{W}_{up}|}, \gamma_{|\mathcal{W}_{up}|}, \delta_{|\mathcal{W}_{up}|})$
5:     $\mathcal{I}[\alpha_i] \leftarrow (\gamma_i, \delta_i)$
6:     $Z \leftarrow Z \cup Cipher$
7: end for

Fig. 3. Update protocol

ensure the searchability of the updated files, he computes the update tokens as line 17 to 35 of the first part in Update protocol. Finally, he sends them to the server.
- Server: Run the second part of Update protocol (as shown in Fig. 3) to update the ciphertexts and update tokens.

Search. During the Search protocol, DU issues the search token and then the server returns search results.

- *DU*: Assuming the *DU* wants to search the files containing keyword w, he runs line 1 to 9 of the first part in Search protocol to generate the search token (as shown in Fig. 4). Then, he sends it to the server.
- Server: After receiving the search token, the server runs the second part of Search protocol (as shown in Fig. 4) to obtain the result set and returns it to the DU.

5 Security Analysis

In this section, we analyze the security of our FBSSE-MDS scheme. Our scheme can achieve forward privacy and backward privacy BP-II. We first define the leakage functions in our scheme as follows:

DU:
1: Initialize an empty collection $\mathcal{ST}_w$
2: $(UpdCnt, st_c) \leftarrow \mathcal{T}[w]$
3: $t_w \leftarrow PRF(\mathcal{K}, w)$
4: $\beta_0 \leftarrow PRF(\mathcal{K}, w||0)$,
5: $s \leftarrow \overset{k}{\underset{id=1}{\bigoplus}} PRF'(\beta_0, id)$
6: for $i = 1$ to $UpdCnt$ do
7:    $\beta_i \leftarrow PRF(\mathcal{K}, w||i)$
8:    $s \leftarrow s \oplus \beta_i$
9: end for
10: Send $\mathcal{ST}_w = (t_w, st_c, s)$ to the server
server:
1: Initial an empty collection $ID(w)$, a N-bit string γ' whose all bits are 0

2: Parse $\mathcal{ST}_w$ as (t_w, st_c, s)
3: while $st_c \neq \bot$ do
4:    $\alpha \leftarrow H_1(t_w || st_c)$
5:    $(\gamma, \delta) \leftarrow \mathcal{I}[\alpha]$
6:    $\gamma' \leftarrow \gamma' \oplus \gamma$
7:    $st_{c-1} \leftarrow H_2(t_w || st_c) \oplus \delta$
8:    $st_c \leftarrow st_{c-1}$
9: end while
10: $\gamma' \leftarrow \gamma' \oplus s$
11: for $i = 1$ to N do
12:    if $\gamma'[i] = 1$ then
13:        $ID(w) \leftarrow ID(w) \cup \{i\}$
14:    end if
15: end for
16: Send $ID(w)$ to DU

Fig. 4. Search protocol

$$\mathcal{L}^{Setup}(\{\mathcal{D}_j\}_{1 \leq j \leq k}, \mathcal{W}) = (k, n, N, \mathcal{W}), \mathcal{L}^{Update}(op, w, ind) = \bot$$

$$\mathcal{L}^{Search}(w) = \mathcal{L}'(\mathbf{TimeDB}(w), \mathbf{Updates}(w))$$

where $k, n, N, \mathcal{W}$ stands for the number of data sources, the total number of data files for initialization, the maximum number of update operations and the keyword universe respectively.

We are now ready to state the following theorem regarding the security of FBSSE-MDS.

Theorem 1. *If $H_1, H_2, PRF, PRF', PRP, PRP', SKE$ are secure cryptographic primitives, then our scheme FBSSE-MDS is an adaptively-secure SSE scheme with $\mathcal{L} = (\mathcal{L}^{Setup}, \mathcal{L}^{Update}, \mathcal{L}^{Search})$.*

Proof. For the adversary $\mathcal{A}$, challenger C and simulator S, we define the following two experiments: $\mathbf{Real}_{\mathcal{A},C}(\lambda)$ and $\mathbf{Ideal}_{\mathcal{A},S}(\lambda)$.

$\mathbf{Real}_{\mathcal{A},C}(\lambda)$: the challenger C generates a secret key $\mathcal{K} = KeyGen(1^\lambda)$. $\mathcal{A}$ chooses k collections of data files $D_1, ..., D_k$ containing n data files in total and a keyword universe $\mathcal{W}$. $\mathcal{A}$ receives $\{c_j\}_{1 \leq j \leq n}, \{ID_j\}_{1 \leq j \leq n}, \{\mathcal{I}_j\}_{1 \leq j \leq k}$ such that c_j is an encrypted data file, ID_j is the identity of file c_j and $\mathcal{I}_j$ is the local index built by DS_j. Then $\mathcal{A}$ merges all indexes $\{\mathcal{I}_j\}_{1 \leq j \leq k}$. Afterwards, $\mathcal{A}$ makes a polynomial number of adaptive queries. For each queried keyword w, $\mathcal{A}$ receives a search token $\mathcal{ST}_w$ or update token $\mathcal{UT}_w$ from the challenger C. Finally, $\mathcal{A}$ returns a bit b that is output by the experiment.

$\mathbf{Ideal}_{\mathcal{A},S}(\lambda)$: $\mathcal{A}$ chooses k collections of data files $D_1, ..., D_k$ containing n data files in total and a keyword universe $\mathcal{W}$. Given $\mathcal{L}^{Setup}(\{\mathcal{D}_j\}_{1 \leq j \leq k}, \mathcal{W})$, S simulates and sends $\{c'_j\}_{1 \leq j \leq n}, \{ID'_j\}_{1 \leq j \leq n}, \{\mathcal{I}'_j\}_{1 \leq j \leq k}$ to $\mathcal{A}$ and then $\mathcal{A}$ merge them. Afterwards, $\mathcal{A}$ makes a polynomial number of adaptive queries. For each queried keyword w, S receives $\mathcal{L}^{Query}(w)$ or $\mathcal{L}^{Update}(op, w, ind)$. Meanwhile, S

simulates and sends a search token ST'_w or update token $UT'_{W_{up}}$ to $\mathcal{A}$. Finally, $\mathcal{A}$ returns a bit b that is output by the experiment.

Then we prove that $\mathcal{A}$ cannot distinguish between the experiments $\mathbf{Real}_{\mathcal{A}}(\lambda)$ and $\mathbf{Ideal}_{\mathcal{A},S}(\lambda)$. In other words, $\mathcal{A}$ cannot distinguish between $\{c_j\}_{1 \leq j \leq n}$, $\{ID_j\}_{1 \leq j \leq n}, \{\mathcal{I}_j\}_{1 \leq j \leq k}$, ST_w, UT_w and $\{c'_j\}_{1 \leq j \leq n}$, $\{ID'_j\}_{1 \leq j \leq n}$,$\{\mathcal{I}'_j\}_{1 \leq j \leq k}$, ST'_w, UT'_w. In the following proof, when we say "indistinguishable" or "cannot distinguish" we mean the advantage in distinguishing two variables is limited by $negl(\lambda)$.

Simulating $\{c'_j\}_{1 \leq j \leq n}$: For $1 \leq j \leq n$, S randomly selects a bit string c'_j of length $|c_j|$. As SKE is a secure cryptographic primitive, $\{c_j\}_{1 \leq j \leq n}$ and $\{c'_j\}_{1 \leq j \leq n}$ are indistinguishable to $\mathcal{A}$.

Simulating $\{ID'_j\}_{1 \leq j \leq n}$: For $1 \leq j \leq n$, S simply set $ID'_j = ID_j$.

Simulating $\{\mathcal{I}'_j\}_{1 \leq j \leq k}$: S initializes k arrays $\{\mathcal{I}'_j\}_{1 \leq j \leq k}$ of size $|\mathcal{W}|$. For each $\{\mathcal{I}'_j\}_{1 \leq j \leq k}$, S randomly selects $|\mathcal{W}|$ strings $\{\alpha_j\}_{1 \leq j \leq |\mathcal{W}|}$ of length λ, $|\mathcal{W}|$ bit strings $\{\gamma'_{c,j}\}_{1 \leq c \leq k, 1 \leq j \leq |\mathcal{W}|}$ of length N and $|\mathcal{W}|$ strings $\{\delta_j\}_{1 \leq j \leq |\mathcal{W}|}$ of length λ. S sets $\mathcal{I}'_c[i] = (\alpha'_i, \gamma'_{c,i}, \delta'_i)$ for $1 \leq c \leq k, 1 \leq i \leq |\mathcal{W}|$. As H_1 is a secure hash function, $\{\mathcal{I}_j\}_{1 \leq j \leq k}$ and $\{\mathcal{I}'_j\}_{1 \leq j \leq k}$ are indistinguishable to $\mathcal{A}$.

Simulating $UT'_{W_{up}}$: We model two hash functions H_1 and H_2 as random oracles. During an update query, for update keyword w, S gets the state (t_w, st_c) from TA, chooses string st_{c+1} randomly from $\{0,1\}^\lambda$ and then updates state (t_w, st_{c+1}). Afterwards, S gets string str_1 by sampling at random from $\{0,1\}^\lambda$ and stores $(t_w || st_{c+1}, str_1)$ in H_1. Similarly, S gets string str_2 by sampling at random from $\{0,1\}^N$, stores $(t_w || st_{c+1}, str_2)$ in H_2 and computes $\delta = str_2 \oplus st_c$. Then S chooses string γ randomly from $\{0,1\}^N$. Let i be the timestamp of the update. S stores entry $I(i) = (str_1, \gamma, \delta)$. Then S sends $UT'_{W_{up}} = \{(str_{1,j}, \gamma_j, \delta_j)\}_{1 \leq j \leq |W_{up}|}$ to $\mathcal{A}$.

Simulating ST'_w: During a search, S receives leakage functions $\mathbf{TimeDB}(w)$ and $\mathbf{Updates}(w)$. He/she then infers from $\mathbf{Updates}(w)$ the timestamps of previous updates related to the searched keyword w, denoted by $J = (i_1, ..., i_{up})$. Afterwards, he/she infers from $\mathbf{TimeDB}(w)$ the set of file-identities that currently contain the searched keyword w and generates an N-bit string γ corresponding to the set(for each ID in the set, S sets ID-th bit to 1). Then he/she computes the XOR result s among γ and all strings that stored in $I(i_j)$ for $j = 1, ..., upd$. At last, S gets local state (t_w, st_{c+1}) and sends search token $ST'_w = (t_w, st_{c+1}, s)$ to $\mathcal{A}$. In such a way, S simulates correct search/update tokens which have the same search/update results as in the experiment $\mathbf{Real}_{\mathcal{A},\mathcal{C}}(\lambda)$. Therefore, $\mathcal{A}$ cannot distinguish between $ST_w, UT_{W_{up}}$ and $ST'_w, UT'_{W_{up}}$.

In summary, S cannot distinguish between the view in $\mathbf{Real}_{\mathcal{A},\mathcal{C}}(\lambda)$ and the view in $\mathbf{Ideal}_{\mathcal{A},S}(\lambda)$. Thus we have $|Pr[\mathbf{Real}_{\mathcal{A},\mathcal{C}}(\lambda) = 1] - Pr[\mathbf{Ideal}_{\mathcal{A},S}(\lambda) = 1]| \leq negl(\lambda)$.

6   Performance Evaluation

In this section we implemented our scheme, MITRA [3] and MDS-SSE [15] using
Java 11. All test programs were performed on an Intel(R) Core(TM) i7-9750H
2.60 GHz computer with 8GB RAM running Windows 10. Each data point in the
figures is an average of 50 executions. In all tests, we used a keyword universe of
5000 common English words and set N of FBSSE-MDS and MDS-SSE to 100000.
We are interested in measuring execution time for search and update operations
in MITRA, MDS-SSE and our FBEES-MDS scheme.

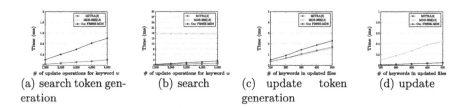

(a) search token gen-   (b) search   (c) update   token   (d) update
eration   generation

Fig. 5. Experiment results

Figure 5(a) and Fig. 5(b) reports the execution time for search token generation and search operation for different numbers of update operations in three
schemes. In two tests, we vary the number of update operations from 1000 to
5000. As can be seen from Fig. 5(a), for MDS-SSE, the execution time of search
token generation is independent of search results. The reason is that the result
extraction is merely to scan a bit string and find all positions where the bit is
1. Such operations are extremely efficient. For MITRA and FBSSE-MDS, the
execution time of search token generation increases when more search results are
returned. This is because they need to perform a_w times hash computation while
FBSSE-MDS needs to perform $(a_w + k)$ times XOR operation in addition. We
can see from Fig. 5(a) that when the number of update times for w is 5000, the
execution time of FBSSE-MDS is below 1.2 ms. It is efficient in the application.

In terms of execution time in search, as we can see from Fig. 5(b), for MDS-
SSE, it is independent of the number of update operations for w, and related
to N which is the maximum number for update operations. In this test, as we
have explained before, we set N to 100000 and the execution time of MDS-SSE
is 17.25 ms. As for MITRA and FBSSE-MDS, the time is linear with the number
of update operations for w. The reason is that for each update operation, there
is a tuple inserted to index. When 5000 results are returned, the time is about
1.5 ms in MITRA and about 2.4 ms in FBSSE-MDS. There is much difference in
search time between MDS-SSE and our FBSSE-MDS.

Figure 5(c) and Fig. 5(d) presents the execution time for update token generation and update operation for different numbers of keywords contained in the
updated file. In the test, we removed the file encryption time from the execution time for update token generation. Obviously, the execution time for update
token generation in three schemes is linear with keywords contained in update
files. For MDS-SSE, $|W_{up}|$ times XOR operation are performed in the update

token generation. While for MITRA, $|W_{up}|$ times hash computation and $|W_{up}|$ times XOR operation are performed. As for our FBSSE-MDS, it needs to perform $2|W_{up}|$ times hash computation and generates $|W_{up}|$ strings of length λ in addition. As can be seen from Fig. 5(c), when the number of keywords in updated files is 500, the time is below 2.5 ms and there is little difference between three schemes.

In terms of execution time in update, as we can see from Fig. 5(d), for all three schemes, the time is linear with $|W_{up}|$ which is the number of keywords in updated files. But there is a difference between three schemes. For MITRA and FBSSE-MDS, the update operation is just inserting tuples (α, γ, δ) into the index. While for MDS-SSE, $|W_{up}|$ times connection operation for strings is performed. As can be seen from Fig. 5(d), when the number of keywords in updated files is 500, the time is about 0.05 ms in MITRA and FBSSE-MDS while the time is about 0.45 ms in MDS-SSE.

7 Conclusion

Motivated by the universal phenomenon in data outsourcing that user's data is often separately distributed, we propose a FBSSE-MDS scheme in the scenario of multiple data sources which also provides both forward privacy and BP-II backward privacy to limit the leakage to the server when data sources perform update operation. Compared to MITRA which is the fastest existing scheme achieving both forward privacy and backward privacy, our FBSSE-MDS scheme supports multiple data sources and reduces one round of interaction while maintains the high efficiency, forward privacy and backward privacy. Compared to MDS-SSE which is an efficient SSE scheme for multiple data sources, our FBSSE-MDS scheme achieves both forward and BP-II backward privacy in addition. Experimental results show that FBSSE-MDS is highly efficient and practical.

References

1. Bost, R.: $\sum o\varphi o\varsigma$: forward secure searchable encryption. In: Weippl, E.R., Katzenbeisser, S., Kruegel, C., Myers, A.C., Halevi, S. (eds.) Proceedings of the 2016 ACM SIGSAC Conference on Computer and Communications Security, Vienna, Austria, pp. 1143–1154. ACM (2016)
2. Bost, R., Minaud, B., Ohrimenko, O.: Forward and backward private searchable encryption from constrained cryptographic primitives. In: Proceedings of the 2017 ACM SIGSAC Conference on Computer and Communications Security, CCS 2017, Dallas, TX, USA, pp. 1465–1482. ACM (2017)
3. Chamani, J.G., Papadopoulos, D., Papamanthou, C., Jalili, R.: New constructions for forward and backward private symmetric searchable encryption. In: Proceedings of the 2018 ACM SIGSAC Conference on Computer and Communications Security, CCS 2018, Toronto, ON, Canada, pp. 1038–1055. ACM (2018)
4. Chang, Y.-C., Mitzenmacher, M.: Privacy preserving keyword searches on remote encrypted data. In: Ioannidis, J., Keromytis, A., Yung, M. (eds.) ACNS 2005. LNCS, vol. 3531, pp. 442–455. Springer, Heidelberg (2005). https://doi.org/10.1007/11496137_30

5. Curtmola, R., Garay, J.A., Kamara, S., Ostrovsky, R.: Searchable symmetric encryption: improved definitions and efficient constructions. In: Proceedings of the 13th ACM Conference on Computer and Communications Security, CCS 2006, Alexandria, VA, USA, pp. 79–88. ACM (2006)
6. Etemad, M., Küpçü, A., Papamanthou, C., Evans, D.: Efficient dynamic searchable encryption with forward privacy. PoPETs **2018**(1), 5–20 (2018)
7. Garg, S., Mohassel, P., Papamanthou, C.: TWORAM: efficient oblivious RAM in two rounds with applications to searchable encryption. In: Robshaw, M., Katz, J. (eds.) CRYPTO 2016. LNCS, vol. 9816, pp. 563–592. Springer, Heidelberg (2016). https://doi.org/10.1007/978-3-662-53015-3_20
8. Guo, Y., Zhang, C., Jia, X.: Verifiable and forward-secure encrypted search using blockchain techniques. In: 2020 IEEE International Conference on Communications, ICC 2020, Dublin, Ireland, pp. 1–7. IEEE (2020)
9. Islam, M.S., Kuzu, M., Kantarcioglu, M.: Access pattern disclosure on searchable encryption: ramification, attack and mitigation. In: 19th Annual Network and Distributed System Security Symposium, NDSS 2012, San Diego, California, USA. The Internet Society (2012)
10. Kamara, S., Moataz, T.: Boolean searchable symmetric encryption with worst-case sub-linear complexity. In: Coron, J.-S., Nielsen, J.B. (eds.) EUROCRYPT 2017. LNCS, vol. 10212, pp. 94–124. Springer, Cham (2017). https://doi.org/10.1007/978-3-319-56617-7_4
11. Kamara, S., Papamanthou, C.: Parallel and dynamic searchable symmetric encryption. In: Sadeghi, A.-R. (ed.) FC 2013. LNCS, vol. 7859, pp. 258–274. Springer, Heidelberg (2013). https://doi.org/10.1007/978-3-642-39884-1_22
12. Kamara, S., Papamanthou, C., Roeder, T.: Dynamic searchable symmetric encryption. In: The ACM Conference on Computer and Communications Security, CCS 2012, Raleigh, NC, USA, pp. 965–976. ACM (2012)
13. Kim, K.S., Kim, M., Lee, D., Park, J.H., Kim, W.: Forward secure dynamic searchable symmetric encryption with efficient updates. In: Proceedings of the 2017 ACM SIGSAC Conference on Computer and Communications Security, CCS 2017, Dallas, TX, USA, pp. 1449–1463. ACM (2017)
14. Li, L., Xu, C., Yu, X., Dou, B., Zuo, C.: Searchable encryption with access control on keywords in multi-user setting. J. Cyber Secur. **2**(1), 9–23 (2020)
15. Liu, C., Zhu, L., Chen, J.: Efficient searchable symmetric encryption for storing multiple source dynamic social data on cloud. J. Netw. Comput. Appl. **86**, 3–14 (2017)
16. Song, D.X., Wagner, D.A., Perrig, A.: Practical techniques for searches on encrypted data. In: 2000 IEEE Symposium on Security and Privacy, Berkeley, California, USA, 14–17 May 2000, pp. 44–55. IEEE Computer Society (2000)
17. Song, X., Dong, C., Yuan, D., Xu, Q., Zhao, M.: Forward private searchable symmetric encryption with optimized I/O efficiency. IEEE Trans. Dependable Secur. Comput. **17**(5), 912–927 (2020)
18. Stefanov, E., Papamanthou, C., Shi, E.: Practical dynamic searchable encryption with small leakage. In: 21st Annual Network and Distributed System Security Symposium, NDSS 2014, San Diego, California, USA. The Internet Society (2014)
19. Sun, S., et al.: Practical backward-secure searchable encryption from symmetric puncturable encryption. In: Proceedings of the 2018 ACM SIGSAC Conference on Computer and Communications Security, CCS 2018, Toronto, ON, Canada, pp. 763–780. ACM (2018)

20. Vo, V., Lai, S., Yuan, X., Sun, S., Nepal, S., Liu, J.K.: Accelerating forward and backward private searchable encryption using trusted execution. CoRR abs/2001.03743 (2020)
21. Wei, Y., Lv, S., Guo, X., Liu, Z., Huang, Y., Li, B.: FSSE: forward secure searchable encryption with keyed-block chains. Inf. Sci. **500**, 113–126 (2019)
22. Xu, L., Yuan, X., Wang, C., Wang, Q., Xu, C.: Hardening database padding for searchable encryption. In: 2019 IEEE Conference on Computer Communications, INFOCOM 2019, Paris, France, pp. 2503–2511. IEEE (2019)
23. Zhang, Y., Katz, J., Papamanthou, C.: All your queries are belong to us: the power of file-injection attacks on searchable encryption. In: 25th USENIX Security Symposium, Austin, TX, USA, pp. 707–720. USENIX Association (2016)

A Feature Extracting and Matching System Based on Magic-Number and AC-Algorithm

Xiankui Wei[1], Chong Zhang[2], Xiangzhan Yu[1], and Zihan Zhuo[2(✉)]

[1] School of Cyberspace Science, Harbin Institute of Technology, Harbin 150001, China
[2] National Computer Network Emergency Response Technical Team/Coordination Center of China, Beijing 100032, China
zzh@cert.org.cn

Abstract. With the rapid development of the Internet in recent years, different types of files could be found in the process of analyzing traffic. Sometimes, the transferred files are in a non-public format. To know the type of the transferred file, we need to analyze and extract the features of this file first, and then we can match the file in the traffic through the extracted feature. In the past, when we want to extract the features of a certain type of file for later matching, it is mostly based on manual analysis, which requires a lot of manpower and material resources, and the efficiency is low. In this paper, a system of feature analysis, extraction, and matching based on magic-number and the Aho–Corasick algorithm is designed and implemented. In the feature extraction module, this paper designs an algorithm to extract magic-number from files. Based on the Aho–Corasick algorithm, an algorithm for extracting string fetures is designed. The extracted features are used to identify the file type in the feature matching module. Through the experiments of four common types of files, it is found that the designed method can effectively identify the types of files based on the extracted features, and the recognition accuracy is generally higher than 90%. Through the analysis of the file features proposed in this paper, a lot of repetitive work can be reduced and the efficiency of traffic analysis can be improved.

Keywords: Feature extraction · Feature matching · N-gram · Aho–Corasick algorithm

1 Introduction

In the process of analyzing the traffic of transferring files, to obtain as much information as possible, it is usually necessary to identify the type of transmitted file, and then we can obtain the information encoded in the file according to the format of this type of file, rather than a simple bitstream. Some file types are in a public format, such as zip, elf, rar, and so on. Many tools can be used to identify and parse these files. However, the format of some file types is not public. It is unacceptable to rudely classify all such files into unknown-type files. When encounter files in this format that are not public, It is important to find a way to analyze and extract the features of this kind of documents. And then we can use the features to identify these types of files.

X. Sun et al. (Eds.): ICAIS 2021, CCIS 1424, pp. 140–151, 2021.
https://doi.org/10.1007/978-3-030-78621-2_11

2   Related Work

There are two common methods for automatic extraction of file features, one is to obtain the statistical features of the file using statistical word frequency, and the other is to obtain the string features of the file by mining frequent patterns and association rules of these patterns in the file.

Research on the extraction of statistical features of documents could be found as early as 2003 [1]. This paper proposes a method to judge the file type by analyzing the content of the file. This method is based on a group of input files of the same type and uses three algorithms to generate the "fingerprint" of this type of file. The features of the file are analyzed and extracted from the point of view of byte frequency analysis, byte frequency cross-correlation analysis, and file header/trailer analysis.

In 2005, a paper [2] also generate "fingerprint" based on file content to identify file types, but compared with the paper in 2003, the algorithm for generating "fingerprint" was optimized, and the algorithm based on 1-g model was used to extract the features that can identify files more effectively.

In 2007, a paper [3] by Zheng Jie and others proposed a method to identify file types based on statistical features. The feature used in this paper is the frequency of 256ASCII characters in the file. After calculating the character frequency, the recognition of the file type is realized by calculating the distance under the sphere model based on Euclidean distance and the k-sphere model.

In his 2011 paper [4], Wang Junbo proposed an improved pattern matching algorithm and a file feature extraction algorithm. The author proposes a new algorithm based on the longest common subsequence algorithm (LCS) and the transfer list. Compared with the LCS algorithm, the advantage of this algorithm is that it can extract multiple common subsequences instead of just one longest common subsequence. Considering that the features of files do not necessarily exist in the longest common subsequence, the proposed algorithm is more universal.

Lei Dong in their 2016 paper [5] mentioned a variety of schemes to identify unknown protocols based on frequent pattern mining and association rule mining. Although the algorithm proposed in this paper is used to identify the features of network communication protocols, considering that there is a certain similarity between extracting the features of unknown protocols and extracting files, so the method proposed in this paper is of the reference value.

It is worth noting that in a 2017 paper [6] Kennedy et al. designed a system based on machine learning to automatically extract file features and use them to identify malware. Feature extraction based on machine learning may be a new direction in the future. Also in a 2017 paper [7]. The authors proposed a method to identify altered file types with high accuracy by employing computational intelligence techniques. The method is composed of feature extraction (Byte Frequency Distribution), feature selection (genetic algorithm) and classification (neural network).

In a 2020 paper [6]. The authors proposed a method based on machine learning to detect file types with the understood of file's context.

3   Methods

3.1   Multi-pattern Matching

A multi-pattern matching algorithm [8] is needed in the process of string feature extraction and matching. The commonly used multi-pattern matching algorithms are the WM algorithm [9], BM algorithm [10], and Aho–Corasick algorithm [11]. After comparison, the Aho–Corasick algorithm is selected to be used in this paper.

Aho–Corasick algorithm was proposed by Aho and Corasick in 1975. Based on finite state automata, the algorithm matches the pattern strings in the target string through the jump between states.

3.2   Usual Methods to Infer File Types

There are two common ways to determine the type of a file which are using suffixes and using magic number. There are also some papers put forward the method of judging the file type based on the statistical features of the file content.

Suffix of the Filename. Under windows, file suffixes are generally used to determine the file type. However, the file suffix is easy to be tampered with, and it is more likely to be lost in the process of transmission over the network. Therefore, the method of judging the file type by using the file suffix name is not reliable in the scenario of traffic analysis for this project.

Magic Number. Unlike windows. It is generally through magic number to determine the type of file under Linux.

Under Linux, there is a commonly used command file that can be used to get the type of file. The concrete realization principle is to judge the type of the file by looking for the magic number in the file. As magic number belongs to the file content, so it is generally not lost in the process of transmission over the network. Therefore, it is feasible to use the magic number as a feature for matching in traffic analysis.

A magic number of nearly 200 different files have been collected in the List of file signatures entry on Wikipedia [12]. Many common file types such as zip, pdf, doc, and elf can be found in the list.

In this paper, we will design an algorithm to extract magic number from input files, and an algorithm to use the extracted magic number to infer the type of file.

Statistical Feature. In a paper in 2003 [1]. This paper puts forward a method to judge the file type by analyzing the content of the file. This method is based on a group of input files of the same type and uses three algorithms to generate the "fingerprint" of this kind of file. the features of the file are analyzed and extracted from the point of view of byte frequency analysis, byte frequency cross-correlation analysis, and file header/trailer analysis. The features extracted by the three algorithms here can be classified as statistical features. In this paper, experiments show that the accuracy of the three algorithms varies from 23% to 96% for different file types, depending on the algorithm used. The theoretical basis of this kind of method is that the statistical features of different types of files are often quite different. For example, the frequency of all invisible characters in text files is 0;

for bioinformatics files that store base pairs, the frequency of ATCG four characters is significantly higher than that of other characters. Of course, there is also the possibility that the character frequency distribution of the two types of files is very similar, in this case, it is impossible to effectively distinguish the file only through the character frequency distribution, and new features need to be introduced.

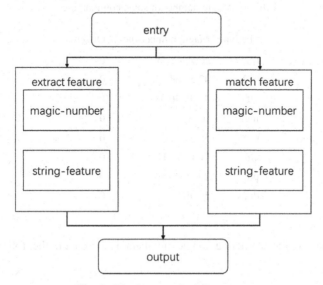

Fig. 1. The framework of the system

4   Our Framework

Our system consists of two modules: the feature extraction module and feature matching module. The feature extraction module is responsible for extracting features from the input file and saving the extracted features into the database. The feature matching module uses the features in the database to match the input file to determine the type of the file.

The system framework is in Fig. 1.

4.1   Extract Feature

The feature extraction module includes the following sub-modules.

1. extract the magic number information of the file. Based on the assumption that there is a magic number in the input file, an algorithm for extracting the magic number is designed.
2. extract the string features of the file. Based on the N-gram segmentation algorithm and the modified Aho-Corasick algorithm, the string features in the file are extracted.

Extract Magic Number. This module is based on the assumption that the input file has a magic number. Based on the analysis of the magic number listed in the List of file signatures [12], this paper designs an algorithm to extract magic number from input files. See Table 1 for the magic-number of some common files.

Table 1. Magic-number of some common files

File type	Magic-number (hex)	Offset
rpm	ed ab ee db	0
bz2	42 5a 68	0
gif	47 49 46 38	0
jpg	ff d8	0
exe	5a 4d	0
elf	7f 45 4c 46	0
pdf	25 50 44 46	0
docx	50 4b	0

The algorithm for extracting magic numbers is based on the following three assumptions:

1. magic numbers exist at the same offset and have the same value in each file.
2. The magic number of each file exists in the header of the file.
3. The size of the magic number is greater than one byte.

The algorithm is mainly divided into two parts:

1. extracts all offset-bytes pairs that satisfy assumptions 1 and 2.
2. returns the merged offset-bytes pair that satisfies assumption 1.

See Algorithm 1 for the algorithm pseudocode for the first part., and Algorithm 2 for the algorithm pseudocode for the second part.

Algorithm 1:   magic-number extraction part-1

Input: inputFiles, maxOffset
Output: list of (offset, value)

```
dics = []
for i = 0 to maxOffset do
dics.append(dict())
end
for file in inputFiles do
data = file.read(maxOffset)
for i=0 to maxOffset do
    dic = dics[i]
    ch = data[i]
    if ch in dic.keys then
        dic[ch] += 1
    end
    else
        dic[ch] = 1
    end
end
end
res = []
for i = 0 to maxOffset do
dic = dics[i]
if len(dic) == 1 then
    res.append(i, dic.value)
end
end
return res
```

Algorithm1 has two parameters, one of which is the content of each file from which features need to be extracted. The second parameter, *maxOffsest*, is a heuristic parameter, which is used to limit the maximum offset of the magic-number of this type of file. The specific value can be adjusted through experiments until a value that makes the extracted feature have a better effect on identifying the file type is obtained.

First, we declare a dictionary array *dics* to store some extracted intermediate variables. Then we initialize the array *dics*. push into *maxOffset* dictionaries.

At this point, we begin to deal with the contents of the file. We deal with each document in turn. For each file, we read the first *maxOffset* bytes of the file and get a byte stream (let's call it *data*). Then we iterate through every byte in the *data*. When processing the i byte data (let's call it *ch*). We use *ch* as a key, to set the I *dics[i]* (*dic*). in dics. Add one to its corresponding value.

After processing each file, we get a dictionary array *dics*. which stores some intermediate variables. The I dictionary *dic[i]* contains the distribution of the i byte of all input files. If the *i-th* byte is part of a magic number, then the *i-th* byte of all input files should be the same. It can be considered that the *i-th* byte of all input files keeps the same is a necessary condition that the *i-th* byte belongs to this type of file magic number.

So Algorithm 1 finally traverses the *dics*. Judge the uniqueness of *dics*[*i*]. If unique, the *i-th* byte may be part of the magic number. Then we can use a (key, value) pair to represent the *i* and *i-th* byte of the record. And finally return the array of (key, value) pairs.

Algorithm 2:   magic-number extraction part-2

Input: list of (offset, value) kvList
Output: list of magics magicList

```
sortedKvList = kvList.keys sorted by offset (ascend)
for i in range(1, kvList.size() - 1) do
    if sortedKvList[i-1] + 1!=sortedKvList[i+1] then
        if sortedKvList[i]+1!=sortedKvList[i+1] then
            kvList.remove(sortedKvList[i])
        end
    end
end
res = []
tmpStr = ""
tmpOffset = -1
for i in range(1, kvList.size()) do
    if sortedKvList[i-1]+1 == sortedKvList[i] then
        tmpStr += kvList[i]
        if tmpOffset == -1 then
            tmpOffset = i
        end
    end
    else
        res.append((tmpOffset, tmpStr))
        tmpStr = ""
        tmpOffset = -1
    end
end
return res
```

Algorithm 2 mainly does two parts of work based on the results of the algorithm, and finally, generate a possible magic number.

The output of Algorithm 1 is an array of (key, value) pairs (*kvList*). The key of each item represents the offset in the file, and the value represents the contents of the file at that offset. Algorithm 2 first performs an ascending sort operation based on key on *kvList*. Then iterate through the sorted array to remove the isolated item. This operation is based on the assumption1 (magic number is greater than 1 byte.)

For example, the input *kvList* is:

$$[(0,'a'), (1,'b'), (3,'c'), (5,'d'), (6,'e')]$$

then the 3rd item (5, 'd') will be filtered out, and the remaining array is

$$[(0,'a'), (1). \text{ 'b'}), (5,'d'), (6,'e')]$$

After filtering, Algorithm 2 merges the remaining arrays. Merge adjacent (key, value) pairs into a longer magic-number. For example, before merging the kvList have these items:

$$[(0,'a'), (1,'b'), (5,'d'), (6,'e')]$$

when merging, the first and second items will be merged into one longer item 'ab'. third item and the fourth item will also be merged into a longer item 'de'.

$$[(0, 'ab'), (5, 'de')]$$

Now the array will be returned by the Algorithm 2.

Extract String Feature. The process of extracting string features can be divided into three steps.

1. Use the N-gram slicing algorithm to slice the input file.
2. Merge the frequent items in the slice result.
3. Filter the merged results using Aho–Corasick algorithm.

Data Slice Scheme Based on N-gram. N-gram is a concept in natural language processing.

which refers to the continuous occurrence of n characters in a text. Considering the balance between performance and efficiency, the value of N is usually 3 or 4. Based on the N-gram algorithm, file data can be divided into several 4-byte size byte blocks. Get a collection of 4-byte blocks.

The algorithm divides each input file in turn and gets a set of slices for each file. Then take the intersection of all sets and get a new set A.

All the slices in set A appear in all files. However, considering such a situation, assuming that a certain type of file has a feature string of "ABCDE", then if the input files are of this type, the set A will contain two slices which are "ABCD" and "BCDE", at this time, we can merge the two blocks into a longer feature string "ABCDE".

Merge Frequent Items in Slice Results. The idea of merging is simple: find all the blocks with the same prefixes and suffixes, and then merge them into a longer slice. But the resulting block may not be a feature string. Suppose that a certain type of file has a feature string which is "AAAA", then if all the input files are of this type. After the N-gram procedure, the set A will contain slice "AAAA". because the prefix and suffix of "AAAA" are the same which are both "AAA", so the merge algorithm will merge them to a longer slice "AAAAA". However, "AAAAA" is not the feature string of this type of file. So a filter is needed for the merged feature strings.

The Filtering Scheme Based on Aho–Corasick Algorithm. To filter out wrong slices from merged slices. Aho–Corasick algorithm is applied to the merged slices.

The set of merged slices is regarded as the pattern set of the Aho–Corasick algorithm. the Aho–Corasick automaton is constructed based on the pattern set, and then each file is matched across the automation as the target string in turn. By modifying the Aho–Corasick algorithm, we can know which slice does not appear in the target string, and these slices can be removed. Finally, the remaining slices are the merged and filtered feature string. Let call the set of these slices set B. Considering that there may be some blocks in set A that have not been merged, it is necessary to remove the blocks that have been contained in set B, and finally, return set A ∪ B as the set of feature strings.

4.2 Match Feature

The main content of this section is the design of the feature matching module. The feature matching module includes the following two modules:

1. identify file types based on the extracted magic number
2. identify file types based on extracted string feature

Match Magic Number. The magic number information extracted by the feature extraction module is in the form of a collection of (offset, bytes) pairs, such as (0, "\x7fELF"), which means this type of file all have 4byte "\x7fELF" at the start of the file. The idea of magic number matching is to compare all the (offset, bytes) pairs in the local database which are from former feature extracting procedure to see if they are consistent. To know whether it is a uniform type of file. The magic number features of all file types stored in the local feature database will also be traversed here and compared with them in turn.

Match String Feature. The form of the string extracted by the feature extraction module is a set of strings. The idea of identifying files based on string features is to find the appearance of string features in the target file. The specific implementation is based on the Aho-Corasick algorithm taking the feature string set as the pattern set to construct an Aho-Corasick automaton and then matching the content of the object file as the feature string, thus we can know the occurrence of each feature string in the target file. Considering that the longer the length of the feature string is, the feature should have a better effect on representing the corresponding type of file. So we can return the sum of the length of all matched pattern strings (match_sum) based on a modified version of the Aho-Corasick algorithm.

The similarity between the target file and some file type is obtained by dividing the match_sum by the sum of the length of all feature strings of this type of file(file_sum).

$$simlarity = match\_sum/file\_sum * 100\% \qquad (1)$$

After calculating the similarities between the input file and all file types in the local database. We can infer the input file type.

4.3 Workflow of System

The overall work flow chart of the system is shown in Fig. 2. After extracting the file from the traffic, we first use the feature matching module of the system for recognition operation. If it is found that there is no file in the local database that matches the characteristics of the input file, the feature extracting module of the system is executed to extract the features from the input file and store them in the local database for later feature matching operations.

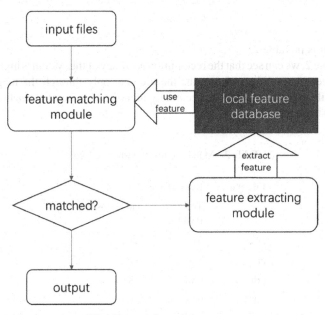

Fig. 2. Workflow of the system

5 Evaluation

We choose Python to implement the whole system, and select 4 types of multiple files to test the system.

Python 3.8 is selected to implement the whole system, and the operating system is ubuntu 16.04LTS. The processor is core i7 9750 h. The memory is 16 GB. The specific testing process is as follows.

Four types of file; zip, elf, pdf, and rar, are selected to test the effect feature extraction and matching effect of the system. The specific testing process is as follows:

Firstly, 20 different files are used for each of the four file formats: zip, elf, pdf, and rar are used to extract features and save them in the local feature database.

Then, 10 different files of each type (not among the 20 files in the first step) are selected to test the feature matching effect. The accuracy of matching is observed.

Table 2. Matching result with extracted features

File types	Magic-number		String-feature	
	True Positive	False Positive	True Positive	False Positive
zip	100%	0%	100%	22.68%
elf	100%	19.50%	83.33%	30.77%
pdf	100%	12.50%	94.44%	0%
rar	86.36%	10.52%	80.00%	0%

The result is in Table 2.

From Table 2, we can see that the recognition accuracy of the system is high. Although it is sometimes impossible to determine the file type only through the magic number feature, the file type can usually be accurately identified by the combination of magic number and string features.

Table 3. Matching result with byte freq

File types	Byte frequency	
	True Positive	False Positive
zip	91%	64%
elf	13%	54%
pdf	66%	23%
rar	93%	64%

From Table 3, we can ses that the recognition accuracy is high for some file types, but unacceptable for some other file types, and the false positive ratio is also to high to be used.

6 Conclusion

Based on previous research, this paper designs and implements a feature analysis, extraction, and matching system for files. We study the common file type recognition methods, including suffix, the magic number, and so on, and proposes a magic number extraction algorithm for files based on some features of the magic number. We also study some common multi-pattern matching algorithms, including the WM algorithm and Aho-Corasick algorithm, and designs and implements a file string feature extraction module based on Aho–Corasick algorithm and a string feature matching module based on the Aho-Corasick algorithm.

Through the experiment, we can see that the effect of the system is very well, and the workload of analyzing file features can be greatly reduced when it is applied to practical work.

With more and more private protocols appears on the network, some of the methods used in this paper can also be applied to the problem of protocol feature extraction.

Funding Statement. Supported by National Key R&D Program of China (2017YFC1201202), National Key R&D Program of China (2017YFC1201204).

Conflicts of Interest. The authors declare that they have no conflicts of interest to report regarding the present study.

References

1. McDaniel, M., Heydari, M.: Content-based file type detection algorithms. In: 36th Annual Hawaii International Conference on System Sciences, Proceedings (2003)
2. Li, W.-J., Wang, K., Stolfo, S., et al.: Fileprints: identifying file types by n-gram analysis. In: Proceedings from the Sixth Annual IEEE SMC Information Assurance Workshop (2005)
3. Zheng, Luo, Lu: File type recognition algorithm based on statistical eigenvalues. Comput. Eng. (01), 142–144 (2007)
4. Wang, J.: Research on file type recognition technology based on pattern matching algorithm. Information Engineering University (2011)
5. Lei, Wang, Zhao, et al.: Overview of unknown protocol identification and analysis techniques for bitstream. Comput. Appl. Res. **33**(11), 3206–3210–3250 (2016)
6. Kennedy, M., Coleman, K.: Automatic generation of generic file signatures: U.S. Patent 9,762,593, 2017-9-12
7. Venkata, S.K., Young, P., Green, A.: Using machine learning for text file format identification. EasyChair (2020).
8. Cao, W., Ge, M.: Research and optimization of the multi-pattern matching algorithm. Intell. Comput. Appl. **8**(02), 129–133 (2018)
9. Wu, S., Manber, U., et al.: A fast algorithm for multi-pattern searching. University of Arizona. Department of Computer Science (1994)
10. Boyer, R.S., Moore, J.S.: A fast string searching algorithm. Commun. ACM **20**(10), 762–772 (1977)
11. Aho, A.V., Corasick, M.J.: Efficient string matching: an aid to bibliographic search. Commun. ACM **18**(6), 333–340 (1975)
12. List of file signatures, Short Name: WOODSTOCK 18 Conference, El Paso, Texas USA ISBN 978-1-4503-0000-0/18/06 (2018). Wikipedia. https://www.wikiwand.com/en/List_of_file_signaturesConference

A Review: How to Detect Malicious Domains

Kang Li, Xiangzhan Yu$^{(\boxtimes)}$, and Jiujin Wang

School of Cyberspace Science, Harbin Institute of Technology, Harbin 150001, China
yxz@hit.edu.cn

Abstract. Malicious domains are one of the critical manifestations of cyber security attacks, severely posing threats to people's privacy and property by providing malicious services (such as spam servers, phishing websites, and C&C servers) to Internet users. Therefore, researches on technology of malicious domains detection have also attracted much attention. Existing methods show significant differences in data sources and method implementations. In this paper, we conduct a retrospective analysis on them, and divide data into two types namely DNS data and DGA data. Different data sources correspond to different data forms and loaded information, so that researchers need to adopt appropriate methods to detect malicious domains by using such information. The detection methods are divided into four types. We describe general detection framework for each type of approach, and make an outlook for future research directions.

Keywords: Malicious domains detection · DGA · Domain Name System

1 Introduction

With the rapid development of the Internet and information technology, the security threat from network has been gradually highlighted, and various malicious cyber attacks are emerging in endlessly. As an essential part of the Internet infrastructure, the Domain Name System (DNS) has been widely abused by cyber attackers. Malicious domains, including spam servers, phishing websites, and command and control (C&C) servers, are the main reasons of many cyber attacks nowadays.

The Domain Name System (DNS) is the core of current Internet, whose function is mapping tough-to-remember Internet Protocol (IP) addresses to easy memorable domain names [1, 2]. Domain names are organized as a suffix tree structure called domain namespace. The root of this tree is the domain called root represented with a zero length label. The domain namespace information in the form of resources records is stored in the hierarchical distributed database. Given the hierarchical structure, it is possible to divide it into separate zones and delegate the control under them to different authorities, which maintain this information in zone files. The Internet Corporation for Assigned Names and Numbers (ICANN) [3], a non-profit organization, is responsible for the creation of TLDs and delegation of their control to companies called registries. These companies are in charge for all the domains ending with that particular TLD. Due to the lack of sufficient security verification mechanism, DNS is abused as an important operational infrastructure for cyber attacks.

© Springer Nature Switzerland AG 2021
X. Sun et al. (Eds.): ICAIS 2021, CCIS 1424, pp. 152–162, 2021.
https://doi.org/10.1007/978-3-030-78621-2_12

The command and control server is the core of DNS-based cyber attacks. Initially, cyber attackers hard-coded the IP address in the malware to establish a connection with the C&C server. Since hard-coded IP addresses have many disadvantages in terms of flexibility, network security administrators can block the IP address to prevent the connection between malware and the server, when a suspicious IP of malware is discovered. In order to resist IP blocking, malware uses DNS resolution to obtain the IP address of the C&C server. This method cannot copes with the defense mechanism based on blacklisting. To avoid early detection of C&C servers, the Domain Generation Algorithm (DGA) is used to generate a large number of pseudo-random domain names, through which malware can connect to the server. The ability to detect malicious domains is critical to ensure Internet security, and for protection against privacy leakage and property loss. In the past, a widely adopted strategy of malicious domains detection was to analyze network traffic by capturing communications with C&C servers. In addition, technologies such as Web content inspection and URL inspection are also used to detect such malicious activities. Today, one of the most promising research directions is to detect malicious domains by analyzing DNS-related or DGA-related data.

To systematically introduce the approaches that have been used by various kinds work in the past, this paper chooses to present them from two different perspectives:

Data Sources: What types of experimental data are used?
Detection Approaches: What technology is the detection method based on?

In Sect. 2, we discuss the data sources used in previous schemes of malicious domains detection. Section 3 presents four types of detection approaches. Finally, we conclude this paper.

2   Data Sources

In this section, we classify the different types of data used in the schemes proposed in the literature. The type of data has an great influence on the selection of malicious domain detection scheme.

A) *DNS-related data*
   DNS-related data plays an import role in detecting and predicting malicious activities. According to the difference of collection methods, it can be divided into active DNS data and passive DNS data.
   To obtain active DNS data, the researcher would deliberately send DNS queries and record the corresponding DNS responses. These data packets are captured at the network entrance. Since the queries are actively sent by the researcher, such data cannot reflect the behavior of actual users. The main purpose of them is to obtain DNS records of the domains. Active DNS data cannot be used in technologies of malicious domains detection which are based on user-level features, because they are not linked to user behavior. In addition, this kind of data is convenient for public sharing due to the same reason, not involving user privacy. Depend on an in-depth analysis of active DNS data, Khalil [4] built high-quality associations

between domains to identify domains controlled by the same entity. Segugio [5] constructed a "host-domain" binary graph to represent host request behavior by monitoring DNS traffic. Antonakakis et al. [6] proposed to extract a large number of NXDomain response packets in the network space by extracting DGA generated by DNS monitoring traffic, and extracted 33 features for analysis and discrimination of DGA domain names and C&Cs.

Passive DNS data comes from real DNS server logs, storing the mapping relationship between domains and IP addresses in the past, which are more representative in sense of various features and statistics. Since passive DNS data are associated with the behavior of actual users, some essential user-level statistical features can be derived to identify malicious activities, which cannot be obtained from DNS data collecting actively. However, for potentially malicious domains, there is no way to discover them through passive collection before registration. Zdrnja et al. [7] were the first to use passive DNS data in malicious DNS detection, but it did not implement the reputation calculation of domains. Notos [8] calculated a dynamic reputation for each unknown domain by extracting the characteristics of the domains. Considering the personal privacy, Kopis [9] detected malicious domains by passively monitoring DNS data at a higher DNS level, instead of local DNS traffic. According to the access characteristics and character characteristics of domain name, Bao et al. [10] designed a complete feature analysis scheme, using passive DNS as the analytical data.

Many external data are used to enrich DNS information, which can be used as an important basis for identifying malicious domains. Zhauniarovich et al. [19] summarized six types of external information namely geo-location, autonomous system number (ASN), registration records, IP/domain blacklists/whitelists, and associated resource records (RRs), and network data. In Wang's research [29], the data collector combined active DNS traffic data with DNS-related external data to enrich the datasets, such as the registration records of domains, the WHOIS information, the public IP blacklists information and other information from the associated resource records. In addition, every method to detect malicious domains requires high-quality ground truth for training and validation, which also can be considered as external data.

B) *DGA-related data*

The Domain Generate Algorithm (DGA) is used to generate a series of pseudo-random strings [13], that is a list of domain names, using an encryption algorithm (such as MD5, XOR operation, etc.). The cyber attacker would obtain an approximate list of domain names by sharing the same random seed of DGA with malware, and then made use of these domain names to connect with C&C server until success. Researchers usually use a binary classification method to distinguish a set of representative clean domain names from malicious domain names generated by algorithms. Clean domain names are associated to legitimate Internet services. In most related studies, the top lists provided by the well-known Internet portal Alexa [14], are used to build a dataset of clean domain names. Alexa provides various top rankings which are classified under different criteria, such as per country and so on. For algorithmically generated domain names, it is more difficult for researchers to collect a large number of negative samples in actual environment. Therefore, Some public datasets (such as DGArchive [15], which contains 62 different DGA families) are usually used for experiments. Selvi et al. [16] used the freely available repository of Bader, which contains thousands of DGA domain names, provided by 26 implementations of DGAs. Ren et al. [17] collected the DGA domain names from two complementary sources, namely Bambenek Footnote 2 and 360 netlab Footnote 3. The data of DGA domain names released by 360 network lab was also used in Mao's work [18], including 40 DGA families.

3 Detection Approaches

In this section, we review the malicious domain detection schemes in recent years, and divide these methods into four categories: heuristic approaches, machine learning based approaches, deep learning based approaches, and graph based approaches.

3.1 Heuristic Approaches

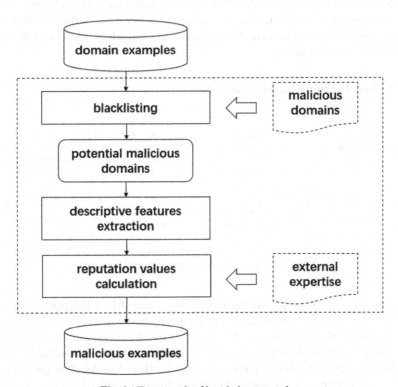

Fig. 1. Framework of heuristic approaches

Heuristic approaches benefit from some external expertise to discriminate between malicious domains and benign domains. Researchers need to find the most descriptive features that can identify malicious domains from the original data. This type of method can also be called knowledge-based method [19]. Figure 1 shows the framework of heuristic approaches.

McGrath [20] found a big difference between the domain name of a phishing website and other normal domain names. They determined that the features of URL itself can be used as information to identify phishing activities, such as the length of URL and the composition of characters. Sandeep [21] developed a method to figure out the distribution of alphanumeric characters and two-tuples in all domains mapped to the same set of IP addresses, and finally calculated a score to judge whether a domain is good or bad. However, the features of domain name itself have limitations and cannot be fully effectively applied to malicious domains detection in all situations. User behavior always reflects whether a domain is good to a certain extent. Tan and Dong [22] proposed a novel lightweight method named Domain Observer to detect malicious domains, by studying the access pattern between Internet users and domains based on passive traffic measurements. In addition, the blacklist [23] is also effective, which can provide the initial protection against malware. A two-phase detection mechanism is proposed by Zhao et al. [24] to achieve efficient and accurate detection. The first phase checks the observed domain name against a blacklist of known malicious URLs, adopting the edit distance to quickly filter malicious domain names to reduce time overhead. OMDD [25] is a multi-engine architecture that also relies on black and white list filtering to largely reduce the amount of real data.

3.2 Machine Learning Based Approaches

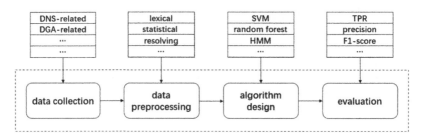

Fig. 2. Framework of machine learning based approaches

Most methods for detecting malicious domains are data-driven with machine learning algorithms at their core, automatically distinguishing between malicious domains and benign domains. Machine learning algorithms are usually divided into two categories: Supervised learning and Unsupervised learning. Supervised learning is suitable for the a large dataset with target labels. On the contrary, when there is no label for given dataset, unsupervised learning is more useful. Machine learning algorithms require researchers to complete the feature engineering, so how to select appropriate features is the focus of machine learning-based technologies. As shown in Fig. 2, the machine learning based approaches consists of four steps: data collection, data preprocessing, algorithm design and evaluation.

It is found in past researches that static lexical features are suitable for more lightweight machine learning based methods. Kidmose et al. [26] divided the domain features into three sets, where the first is general, and the two others are lexical features namely simple lexical features and advanced lexical features. Then they chose to use the Random Forest Classifier with the evaluation performed using the 10-fold cross validation scheme. The results demonstrated that using lexical features can improve the detection performance of malicious domains in many cases. Ghalati [27] proposed a static lexical feature based Random Forest Classification model to classify malicious vs benign URLs. There were three different features extracted from the URLs: blacklist features, lexical features and host-based features. Since researchers need to face many problems occurred in malicious domains detection based on the original machine learning models. Various modified versions of classifier could show more robust and effective performance. Zhu and Zou [28] found that simple SVM model has a detection fall as the detection process goes on while a modified SVM algorithm (F-SVM) proposed by them is capable to keep a high precision rate through whole detection process. F-SVM draws lessons from the idea of feedback learning to solve the problem of high cost of updating models. Its high efficiency makes it suitable for online detection. Tang and Dong [22] achieved an effective detection of malicious domains by using Baum-Welch algorithm and Viterbi algorithm in Hidden Markov Model (BVHMM). Such method based on improved HMM is good at dealing with massive data. The KSDom designed by Wang et al. [29] collects a large number of DNS traffic data and rich external DNS-related data, then employs K-means and SMOTE method to handle the imbalanced data, finally uses Categorical Boosting (CatBoost) algorithm to identify malicious domains. The results show that representative features can also be extracted from active DNS data to effectively identify malicious domains.

3.3 Deep Learning Based Approaches

The deep learning is a complex model derived from the traditional machine learning mechanism. It has made significant achievements in the field of speech and image recognition, and also provides a new idea for malicious domain detection technology. Such approaches can adopt different mechanisms for different application scenarios, effectively improving the accuracy of malicious domain recognition. Researchers only need to input the original domain names to the deep learning architecture, which can automatically and implicitly extracts the best representation of features. Figure 3 displays the framework of deep learning based approaches.

Vinayakumar et al. [30] evaluated the effectiveness of various deep learning based approaches such as recurrent neural network (RNN), long short-term memory (LSTM) and other traditional machine learning classifiers, and the data came from local DNS logs. LSTM obtained highest malicious detection rate in comparison to the other deep learning methods. However, it is difficult for LSTM to learning a reasonable expression when the domain is very long. This paper [31] proposed an LSTM model incorporating with attention mechanism, in which attention will focus on more important substrings in domains and improve the expression of domains. Deep convolutional neural network (CNN) have a robust capability in processing information with translation-invariant properties. Sun et al. [32] used the variational autoencoder (VAE) to extract hidden information from features, then adopted CNN for the classification between the malicious and benign. Xu et al. [33] combined n-gram and CNN, then proposed a novel n-gram combined character based domain classification (n-CBDC) model running in an end-to-end way. This model significantly performed in detecting pronounceable and wordlist-based DGA domain names.

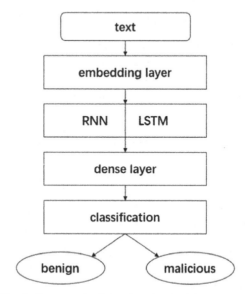

Fig. 3. Framework of deep learning based approaches

3.4 Graph Based Approaches

The graph based approaches uses network and graph theory to study the behavior of individuals, organizations, and the relationships between domains. These methods do not use machine learning classifiers, but relies on domain-IP relationships to calculate the reputation scores of domains to identify malicious domains. Figure 4 shows an example of domain-IP graph, which contains three types of nodes: clients, domains and IP addresses.

The problem of the classification detection technology based on the local characteristics of domain names is that the attackers can construct DNS packets deliberately to avoid detection. The detection method based on domain-IP relationships can make up for this deficiency effectively. Existing path-based inference algorithms in graph theory are specifically designed for DNS data analysis. The key idea of inference techniques is to first define associations between domains based on features extracted from DNS data. Khalil et al. [4] have built high-quality associations between domains by an in-depth analysis of active DNS data to facilitate inference-based malicious domains detection. In addition, deep learning can also be used to analyze graphs. DeepWalk is a representative graph embedding algorithm to build robust representations that are suitable for statistical modeling. He et al. [34] constructed a meaningful domain association graph and used modified DeepWalk to extract local structure features. It is a remarkable fact that the way to construct a graph is very important for graph analysis. HinDom [11] is a robust domain detection system. It obtains a global view by constructing a hetero-geneous information network (HIN) of clients, domains, IP addresses and their diverse relationships. In HGDom [12], graph convolutional network (GCN) was applied to han-dle node features and the graph structure in HIN as the same time, with a meta-path-based attention mechanism.

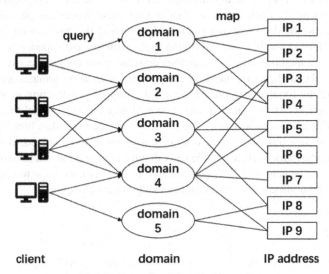

Fig. 4. Example of domain-IP graph

4 Conclusion

Malicious domains are important resources for many illegal activities and pose a huge risk to the security of cyberspace. This paper reviews the previous research results from two perspectives: (1) data resources and (2) detection approaches. DNS-related data and DGA-related data are the main data sources discussed in this paper. DNS-related data can be divided into active DNS and passive DNS according to difference collection methods. Active DNS data does not reflect real user behavior, but it is easy to be shared because it does not involve user privacy. Passive DNS data comes from real DNS server logs. Some important user-level statistical features derived from them can be used to detect malicious domains. The DGA data includes a range of DGA domain names, which are closely related to malicious activities such as botnets, and often comes from publicly available data sets. Each type of data has unique information as well as its limitations. How to use existing data to improve the detection accuracy and efficiency is a challenging task. We divide previous schemes of malicious domain detection into four categories, namely heuristic approaches, machine learning based approaches, deep learning approaches and graph based approaches. The heuristic approaches play an important role in the field of malicious domains detection and rely on external expertise to find potential malicious domains. However, the accuracy of such methods is not high, and the process consumes more labor costs. Machine learning is widely used in many fields. Since malicious domains detection is a classification problem, machine learning methods based on feature extraction have also achieved certain achievements in this field, but they cannot meet the needs of real-time detection and prevention. Many machine learning methods rely on hand-selected features, which face the problem of high False-Negative Rate (FNR) and low overall detection accuracy. The deep learning based methods do not need to perform feature extraction. Researchers just pass the original domain names to the deep learning framework, avoiding the time-consuming process of manual feature extraction, and exhibiting high accuracy and superior performance. The graph based methods identify malicious domains from the perspective of domain relationship. Like the heuristic methods, the potential malicious domains are identified by calculating the reputation score. However, the way of constructing graphs is very important for graph analysis. In the future, how to design an efficient real-time detection system is a difficult point. Secondly, due to the imbalanced samples, how to deal with the problem of data imbalance is also an urgent problem to be solved. Based on the existing detection framework, a suitable and effective combination can be carried out, or better results can be achieved. Through research in this field, we hope to inspire future research to combat illegal network activities using malicious domains.

References

1. Mockapetris, P.V.: Domain names: concepts and facilities. Technical report. Internet Engineering Task Force (1983). https://tools.ietf.org/html/rfc882
2. Mockapetris, P.V.: Domain names: implementation and specification. Technical report. Internet Engineering Task Force (1983). https://tools.ietf.org/html/rfc883
3. The Internet Corporation for Assigned Names and Numbers (ICANN). https://www.icann.org/
4. Khalil, I.M., Guan, B., Nabeel, M., et al.: A domain is only as good as its buddies: Detecting stealthy malicious domains via graph inference. In: Proceedings of the Eighth ACM Conference on Data and Application Security and Privacy, pp. 330–341 (2018)
5. Rahbarinia, B., Perdisci, R., Antonakakis, M.: Segugio: efficient behavior-based tracking of malware-control domains in large ISP networks. In: 2015 45th Annual IEEE/IFIP International Conference on Dependable Systems and Networks, pp. 403–414. IEEE (2015)
6. Antonakakis, M., Perdisci, R., Nadji Y., et al.: From throw-away traffic to bots: detecting the rise of DGA-based malware. Presented as part of the 21st {USENIX} Security Symposium ({USENIX} Security 2012), pp. 491–506 (2012)
7. Zdrnja, B., Brownlee, N., Wessels, D.: Passive monitoring of DNS anomalies. In: Hämmerli, B., Sommer, R. (eds.) DIMVA 2007. LNCS, vol. 4579, pp. 129–139. Springer, Heidelberg (2007). https://doi.org/10.1007/978-3-540-73614-1_8
8. Antonakakis, M., Perdisci, R., Dagon, D., Lee, W., Feamster, N.: Building a dynamic reputation system for DNS. In: Proceedings of USENIX Security Symposium, pp. 273–290 (2010)
9. Antonakakis, M., Perdisci, R., Lee, W., et al.: Detecting malware domains at the upper DNS hierarchy. In: USENIX Security Symposium, vol. 11, pp. 1–16 (2011)

10. Bao, Z., Wang, W., Lan, Y.: Using passive DNS to detect malicious domain name. In: Proceedings of the 3rd International Conference on Vision, Image and Signal Processing, pp. 1–8 (2019)
11. Sun, X., Tong, M., Yang, J., et al.: Hindom: a robust malicious domain detection system based on heterogeneous information network with transductive classification. In: 22nd International Symposium on Research in Attacks, Intrusions and Defenses ({RAID} 2019), pp. 399–412 (2019)
12. Sun, X., Yang, J., Wang, Z., et al.: HGDom: heterogeneous graph convolutional networks for malicious domain detection. In: NOMS 2020–2020 IEEE/IFIP Network Operations and Management Symposium, pp. 1–9. IEEE (2020)
13. Stone-Gross, B., Cova, M., Cavallaro, L., et al.: Your botnet is my botnet: analysis of a botnet takeover. In: Proceedings of the 16th ACM Conference on Computer and Communications Security, pp. 635–647 (2009)
14. Alexa. https://www.alexa.com
15. Fkie, F.: Dgarchive. https://dgarchive.caad.fkie.fraunhofer.de
16. Selvi, J., Rodríguez, R.J., Soria-Olivas, E.: Detection of algorithmically generated malicious domain names using masked N-grams. Expert Syst. Appl. **124**, 156–163 (2019)
17. Ren, F., Jiang, Z., Wang, X., et al.: A DGA domain names detection modeling method based on integrating an attention mechanism and deep neural network. Cybersecurity **3**(1), 1–13 (2020)
18. Mao, J., Zhang, J., Tang, Z., et al.: DNS anti-attack machine learning model for DGA domain name detection. Phys. Commun. **40**, 101069 (2020)
19. Zhauniarovich, Y., Khalil, I., Yu, T., et al.: A survey on malicious domains detection through DNS data analysis. ACM Comput. Surv. (CSUR) **51**(4), 1–36 (2018)
20. McGrath, D.K., Gupta, M.: behind phishing: an examination of phisher modi operandi. LEET **8**, 4 (2008)
21. Yadav, S., Reddy, A.K.K., Reddy, A.L.N., et al.: Detecting algorithmically generated malicious domain names. In: Proceedings of the 10th ACM SIGCOMM conference on Internet measurement, pp. 48–61 (2010)
22. Tang, H., Dong, C.: Detection of malicious domain names based on an improved hidden Markov model. Int. J. Wirel. Mobile Comput. **16**(1), 58–65 (2019)
23. Kührer, M., Rossow, C., Holz, T.: Paint it black: evaluating the effectiveness of malware blacklists. In: Stavrou, A., Bos, H., Portokalidis, G. (eds.) Research in Attacks, Intrusions and Defenses, pp. 1–21. Springer, Cham (2014). https://doi.org/10.1007/978-3-319-11379-1_1
24. Zhao, H., Chang, Z., Wang, W., et al.: malicious domain names detection algorithm based on lexical analysis and feature quantification. IEEE Access **7**, 128990–128999 (2019)
25. Cui, J., Zhang, L., Liu, Z., et al.: An efficient framework for online malicious domain detection. In: 2018 11th International Congress on Image and Signal Processing, BioMedical Engineering and Informatics (CISP-BMEI), pp. 1–6. IEEE (2018)
26. Kidmose, E., Stevanovic, M., Pedersen, J.M.: Detection of malicious domains through lexical analysis. In: 2018 International Conference on Cyber Security and Protection of Digital Services (Cyber Security), pp. 1–5. IEEE (2018)
27. Ghalati, N.F., Ghalaty, N.F., Barata, J.: Towards the detection of malicious URL and domain names using machine learning. In: Camarinha-Matos, L.M., Farhadi, N., Lopes, F., Pereira, H. (eds.) DoCEIS 2020. IAICT, vol. 577, pp. 109–117. Springer, Cham (2020). https://doi.org/10.1007/978-3-030-45124-0_10
28. Zhu, J., Zou, F.: Detecting malicious domains using modified SVM model. In: 2019 IEEE 21st International Conference on High Performance Computing and Communications, IEEE 17th International Conference on Smart City, IEEE 5th International Conference on Data Science and Systems (HPCC/SmartCity/DSS), pp. 492–499. IEEE (2019)

29. Wang, Q., Li, L., Jiang, B., Zhigang, L., Liu, J., Jian, S.: Malicious domain detection based on k-means and smote. In: Krzhizhanovskaya, V.V., et al. (eds.) Computational Science – ICCS 2020: 20th International Conference, Amsterdam, The Netherlands, June 3–5, 2020, Proceedings, Part II, pp. 468–481. Springer, Cham (2020). https://doi.org/10.1007/978-3-030-50417-5_35

30. Vinayakumar, R., Soman, K.P., Poornachandran, P.: Detecting malicious domain names using deep learning approaches at scale. J. Intell. Fuzzy Syst. **34**(3), 1355–1367 (2018)

31. Chen, Y., Zhang, S., Liu, J., et al.: Towards a deep learning approach for detecting malicious domains. In: 2018 IEEE International Conference on Smart Cloud (SmartCloud), pp. 190–195. IEEE (2018)

32. Sun, Y., Chong, N.S.T., Ochiai, H.: Text-based malicious domain names detection based on variational autoencoder and supervised learning. In: 2020 54th Annual Conference on Information Sciences and Systems (CISS), pp. 1–5. IEEE (2020)

33. Xu, C., Shen, J., Du, X.: Detection method of domain names generated by DGAs based on semantic representation and deep neural network. Comput. Secur. **85**, 77–88 (2019)

34. He, W., Gou, G., Kang, C., et al.: Malicious domain detection via domain relationship and graph models. In: 2019 IEEE 38th International Performance Computing and Communications Conference (IPCCC), pp. 1–8. IEEE (2019)

A Homomorphic Encryption Method for Power Data Based on Improved Paillier Algorithm

Weimin He[1], Lei Zhao[1], and Luofei Cheng[2(✉)]

[1] State Grid Jiangsu Electric Power Co., Ltd. Marketing Service Center, Nanjing, China
[2] Nanjing University of Information Science and Technology, Nanjing, China
Luofei_cheng@nuist.edu.cn

Abstract. In the context of wide application of power big data, data security is not only related to user privacy and enterprise development, but also related to national financial security. In recent years, many scholars have proposed various encryption algorithms for the application of power data, trying to find a reliable encryption algorithm to meet the increasingly high security requirements of power data. However, excessively high data security requirements make it difficult for enterprises to share data, which also leads to the frequent occurrence of "data island" phenomenon, which becomes an obstacle for further in-depth analysis of power data. Given this phenomenon, this paper proposes an improved Paillier homomorphic encryption algorithm (I-Paillier) to make the power data available but not visible between different enterprises or institute, which provides technical support for the cooperation of data between different enterprises to get more economic returns. The I-Paillier algorithm proposed in this paper improves the power mode operation of the original Paillier algorithm without changing its security, reduces the number of operations, and improves the efficiency of power data encryption and decryption. A large number of simulation experiments show that the efficiency of I-Paillier algorithm in power data encryption and decryption is higher than that of the original Paillier algorithm.

Keywords: Homomorphic encryption · Privacy protection · Power big data

1 Introduction

As a basic energy facility in China, the power industry is the key to the healthy and sustainable development of China's economy. At the same time, China is largest energy producer and consumer in the world, and the power industry is related to the country's energy security, social development and social stability [1]. The development of power big data is of great practical significance to realize the safer, more economical and more harmonious development of Chinese power industry and the common development of the whole industry.

With the continuous development of power enterprises, it has accumulated tremendous power data about institutions, enterprises and residents, including power marketing data, power equipment operation data and monitoring data and management data of power enterprises. These data can be correlated with many other data, such as energy data, weather data, etc., so that the power data can play a greater potential value.

The current power data analysis has encountered various obstacles. The main problem is data security.

However, data privacy issues will inevitably be involved in the analysis of power big data. Applying Federal Learning to power data, although to a certain extent, it realizes the protection of power data. Meanwhile, there are many privacy protection schemes in Federated Learning, not each privacy protection scheme can protect data privacy well.

The academia has put forward Differential Private [3] technology, Security Multi-parts Compute [4] technology, Homomorphic Encryption [5–9] technology to solute its data security problem. The assumption that Differential Private is too strong for background knowledge leads to a sharp decline in data availability. There are also some problems in Security Multi-parts Compute. When the number of users participating in computing increases, there will be efficiency problems in the interaction between them. Homomorphic encryption is an effective encryption method. Its feature is that it does not need direct access to the plaintext, and the decryption of the cipher text operation is equal to the result of the plaintext operation. Using homomorphic encryption method, the central server can only calculate ciphertext and does not involve the decryption of ciphertext. Sometimes a single addition homomorphism or a multiplicative homomorphism cannot meet the requirements. The full Homomorphic algorithm will provide a complete scheme for data encryption. However, the full homomorphic encryption algorithm has only demonstrated its feasibility on the theoretical level, and its core algorithm and performance problems have not yet been broken through. There are difficulties such as long key and lower efficiency in generating key.

The Paillier homomorphic algorithm only meets the addition homomorphism, and its operation efficiency is higher than that of the Full Homomorphic encryption algorithm, and which meets the practical encryption needs in business situations. Compared with other semihomomorphic encryption algorithms, Paillier algorithm has certain advantages in both security and efficiency. As the length of the key increases, although the security increases, the computational efficiency also decreases. Therefore, it is of great significance to solve the problem of computational efficiency. The I-Paillier algorithm proposed in this paper decomposes the g^m in the encryption equation $c = g^m r^n mod\ n^2$ in the Paillier algorithm into the form of polynomial, so as to reduce the mathematical operation without changing the security. In addition, the I-Paillier decryption equation also reduces the times of Exponential mode operations due to the change of the public key. Therefore, on the basis of not changing the security of the traditional Paillier algorithm, compared with the traditional Paillier algorithm, it improves the efficiency of encryption and decryption, and provides theoretical support for the practical application of power data encryption.

2   Related Work

This section mainly introduces the research progress of homomorphic encryption and the application status of encryption algorithm in power data.

2.1 Research Progress of Homomorphic Encryption

After Rivest et al. first proposed the concept of homomorphic encryption in reference [10], Diffie et al. [11] successively proposed the public key encryption system. The proposal of public key encryption lays the foundation of homomorphic encryption research.

The first public key cryptography algorithm RSA was proposed by Rivest et al., RSA only has the property of multiplicative homomorphism, and encryption does not have randomness. Subsequently, they also made improvements to RSA to make RSA meet the homomorphism characteristics, but the experiment proved that the improved RSA security is not high. ElGamal proposed a public key encryption system based on discrete logarithm difficulty, which has the property of multiplicative homomorphism [12]. The first additive homomorphic encryption scheme GM algorithm based on the quadratic residue problem was proposed by Goldwasse and Micali, and then Benaloh [13] introduced the probabilistic homomorphic encryption scheme on the basis of GM, which has been applied in practice nowadays. Okamoto, Naccache et al. proposed OU and NS systems [14, 15] based on additive homomorphism respectively, both of which can achieve addition homomorphism operations. The first additive homomorphism cryptographic system based on the determination of composite residual class was proposed in 1999, which supports multiple addition homomorphism operations. Damgard [17] et al. promoted Paillier system and proposed DJ system [16]. One of the closest things to a homomorphic encryption scheme is the first BGN system proposed by Boneh et al. [18] in 2005 that supports both arbitrary multiple addition homomorphisms and a single multiplication homomorphism.

In recent years, in the process of exploring homomorphic encryption, domestic scholars have also applied homomorphic encryption technology to cloud computing, multiparty computing, anonymous access, e-commerce and other fields, and have made extensive achievements. For example, Li et al. [19] compared DGHV and CAFED schemes and proposed an improved homomorphic encryption algorithm. Meanwhile, this algorithm was used to realize data uploading, downloading, updating, deleting and retrieving in the cloud storage environment. Peng Changgen et al. [20] proposed a general transitive signature scheme based on homomorphic encryption scheme on the basis of large integer decomposition, discrete logarithm and bilinear equivalence mathematical problem. The scheme supports the characteristics of ciphertext operation and realizes the general model of transitive signature and verification. Yang Yulong et al. [21] proposed a homomorphic encryption scheme to prevent SQL injection attacks, and achieved the requirement information under the condition of important information confidentiality. In the more than 30 years since the concept of homomorphic encryption was proposed, various encryption schemes have been proposed continuously, but most of them are based on semi-homomorphic encryption, and a few of them have not been applied in practice due to security problems. After the semisomorphism encryption scheme gradually mature, many scholars began to study the full homomorphism encryption scheme.

2.2 Application Status of Encryption Algorithm on Power Data

In an open wireless Internet network, there is a Two-way alternating communication between residents' smart electricity meters and the power system. Before the electricity data of users are transmitted to the power system, the state secret algorithm is used to encrypt the data. When the power enterprises acquire the power data of users in the power system, the state secret algorithm is used to decrypt the data. The national secret algorithm SM [22] is a symmetric encryption algorithm. Because the application speed of symmetric encryption technology is relatively fast, a large number of data can be encrypted in the specific application process. The symmetric approach is basically that both sides of the encryption have to encrypt it in the same way. The key is mainly used to effectively control the encryption process, so the security of encryption not only depends on the algorithm itself, but also needs to strengthen management, which can only guarantee the data security in the case that the key is not disclosed [23].

In reality, power operators usually only acquire the aggregation of users' electricity data, which is used to calculate the regional electricity consumption, rather than obtain the electricity data of individual users. Therefore, many scholars have proposed the method of homomorphic encryption to encrypt the user's power data. Even if the key is leaked, the specific electricity data of the user cannot be obtained, which increases the password strength of the electricity acquisition system and enhances the reliability of the system.

3   Paillier Algorithm

3.1   An Overview of Homomorphic Encryption

Homomorphic encryption originates from the concept of isomorphism in modern algebra, which has also developed into a new cryptographic technology.

Definition 1. Let $< A, +>$ and $<B,*>$ be two algebraic systems, $+$ and $*$ are binary (n-ary) operations on A and B, respectively, and let f be a mapping from A to B, such that for any $a1, a2 \in A, f(a1 + a2) = f(a1)*f(a2)$, then f is called a homomorphism mapping from $<A, +>$ to $<B,*>$ (homomorphism mapping), said $<A, +>$ is homomorphic to $<B,*>$, denoted as A ~ B.

Definition 2. Let f be a homomorphism from $<A, +>$ to $<B,*>$, if f is a surjective from A to B, then f is called a full homomorphism; if f is a double from A to B,then f is called an isomorphism mapping, and $<A, +>$ and $<B,*>$ are said to be isomorphism, denoted as $A \cong B$.

Definition 1 and Definition 2 are applied in homomorphic encryption, that is, ciphertext and plaintext are bijective [24], and the result of plaintext operation is equal to the result of decryption after ciphertext operation. The concept of homomorphic encryption was first proposed by Rivest et al. [25] in 1978. Users can directly calculate the ciphertext without knowing the plaintext. In 1979, after the public key cryptosystem was proposed by Diffie et al., various excellent homomorphic encryption algorithms emerged successively, such as Rivest et al., who proposed the first RSA encryption algorithm that met the homomorphic encryption, and ElGamal, who proposed the first ElGamal encryption algorithm based on the assumption of discrete logarithm problem in 1984. These two algorithms are still widely used today.

3.2 Paillier Encryption Algorithm

Paillier encryption scheme was invented by Pascal Paillier [26] in 1999 and named after him. It is a random public key algorithm with features of resisting CCA2 [27] attacks. The Paillier algorithm is based on computing nth residue classes, that is, for a given $z \in Z_{n^2}^*$, judge whether there is $y \in Z_n^*$, so that $z = y^n mod \ n^2$ puzzles.

The key generation process of Paillier algorithm is as follows:

Randomly select two large prime numbers p and q, and ensure that the lengths of p and q are equal, that is, satisfy

$$gcd(pq, (p - 1)(q - 1)) = 1 \tag{1}$$

$gcd()$ is used to find the greatest common divisor of two integers. Calculate the product of p and q, $n = pq$, and the least common multiple of $p - 1$ and $q - 1$, $\lambda = lcm$ $(p - 1, q - 1)$.

Randomly select a g and r, and $g \in Z_{n^2}^*$, $r \in Z_n^*$, to ensure the existence of μ in the following equation,

$$\mu = (L(g^\lambda \ mod \ n^2))^{-1} \ mod \ n^2 \tag{2}$$

The L function is defined as

$$L(x) = \frac{x - 1}{n}$$

The public key of Paillier algorithm is (n, g), and the private key is λ.

Paillier encryption algorithm: for a $m \in Z_n$ in any plaintext space, get the ciphertext

$$c = g^m r^n \ mod \ n^2 \tag{3}$$

It is easy to know that $c \in Z_{n^2}^*$. Its randomness is manifested in that for certain plaintext m_1 and (n, g), due to the introduction of random number r, the same plaintext is encrypted to correspond to different ciphertexts. It is easy to prove that for the same plaintext m_1 and m_2, the same random number r_1 and r_2, the same ciphertext $c1$ and $c2$ can be obtained after encrypted by Paillier encryption algorithm.

Paillier decryption equation as follow:

$$c = g^m r^n \ mod \ n^2 \tag{4}$$

It is easy to know that $c \in Z_{n^2}^*$. Its randomness is manifested in that for certain plaintext m_1 and (n, g), due to the introduction of random number r, the same plaintext is encrypted to correspond to different ciphertexts. It is easy to prove that for the same plaintext m_1 and m_2, the same random number r_1 and r_2, the same ciphertext $c1$ and $c2$ can be obtained after encrypted by Paillier encryption algorithm.

Paillier decryption equation as follow:

$$m = L(c^\lambda mod n^2)\mu mod \ n \tag{5}$$

3.3 Homomorphism of Paillier Algorithm

See Eq., using the same public key (n, g) to encrypt m_1, the ciphertext is $E(m_1) = g^{m_1} r_1{}^n mod\ n^2$, and the ciphertext is $E(m_2) = g^{m_2} r_2{}^n mod\ n^2$ obtained by encrypting m_2.

Additive homomorphism:

The product of the two ciphertexts is decrypted to get the sum of the two plaintexts,

$$D(E(m_1) \cdot E(m_2))) = m_1 + m_2 \tag{6}$$

Because, the result of Eq. 5 and 6 can be calculated from the decryption equation, namely

$$D(E(m_1) \cdot E(m_2)) = D(E(m_1 + m_2)) = m_1 + m_2 \tag{7}$$

Multiplication homomorphism:

The kth power of the ciphertext is equal to the result of k times the encryption of the plaintext, $k \in Z_n$, which is

$$D(E(m)^k) = km \tag{8}$$

Because $E(m)^k = g^{km} r^{nk} \ mod\ n^2$, from the encryption Eq. 5, the result of Eq. 6, it can be calculated, namely

$$D(E(m)^k) = D(E(km)) = km \tag{9}$$

3.4 Security Analysis of Paillier Algorithm

The Paillier algorithm described in the previous section generates the multiplicative subgroup $Z_{n^2}^*$ in the process of encrypting the plaintext m, namely $Z_n \times Z_n^* \to Z_{n^2}^*, (m, r) \to g^m r^n mod\ n^2 = c$. Due to this property, for any, it can be written in a more general form. By this property, for any $g \in Z_{n^2}^*$, it can be written in a more general form.

$$g = (1 + n)^\partial \beta^n \tag{10}$$

$\alpha, \beta \in Z_n^*$.

According to the binomial theorem, $(1 + n)^x mod\ n^2 = (1 + nx) mod n^2$, Euler's function $\varphi(n) = (p - 1)(q - 1)$. From the previous section, $\lambda = lcm(p-1, q-1)$. According to Carmichael's theorem [28], for any $w \in Z_{n^2}^*$, we can get $w^\lambda = 1 mod\ n, w^{n\lambda} = 1 mod\ n^2$. It is easy to prove that for any $g \in Z_{n^2}^*$, there is

$$g^{m\lambda} = (1 + n)^{\lambda \partial m} \cdot \beta^{\lambda mn} \ mod\ n^2 = (1 + \partial \lambda mn)\ mod\ n^2 \tag{11}$$

According to formula and Carmichael's theorem, the ciphertext c of the Paillier encryption system can be written as

$$c = (1 + n)^{\partial m} \beta^{nm} r^n \ mod\ n^2 \tag{12}$$

If there is no guarantee that for all $\alpha \in Z_n^*$, $\beta \in Z_n^*$, the possibility that the attacker can recover α from $g = (1 + n)^{\partial}\beta^n$, there is no guarantee that the attacker will recover from the equation. The difficulty of restoring αm and vice versa. If the Paillier encryption system is secure, it is hard to recover $\alpha \in Z_n^*$ and αm in $c = (1 + \text{n})^{\partial m}\beta^{nm}r^n mod\ n^2$.

For a given $z \in Z_{n^2}^*$, it is hard to judge whether there is $y \in Z_n^*$, so that $z = y^n mod\ n^2$. From the discrete logarithm problem, it is known that for $g \in Z_{n^2}^*$, it is difficult to find $m\ mod\ n$ according to $g^m mod\ n^2$. From this we know that when the discrete logarithm problem on $Z_{n^2}^*$ is difficult, the Paillier encryption system is safe.

Due to the homomorphic nature of Paillier's algorithm, there is a possibility of choosing a ciphertext to attack (IND-CCA2) [29].

4   I-Paillier Algorithm

Under the original conditions without reducing security, changing the rules of operation, thereby enhancing the operational efficiency of encryption and decryption algorithms.

According to Eq. 11, if any $g \in Z_{n^2}^*$ can be converted into a polynomial form, then the large exponential power modulus can be converted into a polynomial modulus form, thereby reducing the amount of calculation the goal of. According to the references [30], if a g_0 is randomly generated, and $g_0 \in Z_n$, when g_1 satisfies $g_1 \bullet \lambda mod = g_0$ then $g = g_1 n + 1$, So Eq. 10 can be expressed as $c = (1 + g_1 n)^m r^n\ mod\ n^2$.

According to the binomial theorem, then

$$(1 + \partial n)^m = \sum_{k=0}^{m} \binom{m}{k} (\partial n)^k\ mod\ n^2 = (1 + \partial mn)\ mod\ n^2 \tag{13}$$

In view of the above description, the following I-Paillier encryption and decryption algorithm is designed:

Public key: (n, α), $\alpha \in Z_n^*$.
Private key: λ

For any $m \in Z_n$ in the plaintext space, the encryption is

$$c = (1 + \partial mn)r^n\ mod\ n^2 \tag{14}$$

Decrypt the ciphertext c as

$$m = L(c^\lambda\ mod\ n^2)b\ mod\ n \tag{15}$$

$b = (\lambda \alpha)^{-1} mod\ n$.

Because $c^\lambda = (1 + \partial mn)^\lambda r^\lambda = (1 + \partial \lambda mn)\ mod\ n^2$, so $m = L(1 + \partial \lambda mn)\ b = (\alpha \lambda m)(\partial \lambda)^{-1} = m\ mod\ n$.

4.1 Improved Paillier Algorithm Security Analysis

The plaintext $m \in Z_n$, it is easy to know the improved ciphertext according to the binomial theorem,

$$c = (1 + \partial mn)r^n \bmod n^2 = (1 + \partial n)^m r^n \bmod n^2$$

Then if g in Eq. 4 is decomposed into $1 + \partial n$, according to the analysis in the previous section, we can see that g can be decomposed in this way, then the (degree of) difficulty of recovering the plaintext from Eq. 4 and Eq. 16 is equal. Both the Paillier algorithm and the I-Paillier algorithm are based on the difficulty of judging n-residue modulo n^2, so that the improved algorithm and the Paillier algorithm are consistent in security.

4.2 Homomorphism of I-Paillier Algorithm

Use encryption Eq. 14 and the same public key to encrypt m_1 to $E(m_1) = (1 + \partial m_1 n)r_1{}^n \bmod n^2$, and encrypt m_2 to $E(m_2) = (1 + \partial m_2 n)r_2{}^n \bmod n^2$.

Additive homomorphism:

The product of the two ciphertexts is decrypted to get the sum of the two plaintexts, because $E(m_1) \cdot E(m_2) = (1 + \partial(m_1 + m_2))(r_1 r_2)^n \bmod n^2$. From the decryption Eq. 15, there is.

$$D(E(m_1) \cdot E(m_2)) = D(E(m_1 + m_2)) = m_1 + m_2$$

Multiplication homomorphism:

The k-th power of the ciphertext is encrypted k times the plaintext, $k \epsilon Z_n$, because $E(m)^k = (1 + \alpha mn)^k r^{kn} \bmod n^2 = (1 + \alpha kmn)r^{kn} \bmod n^2$.

From the decryption Eq. 15, $D(E(m)^k) = D(E(km)) = km$.

4.3 Comparison of I-Paillier Algorithm and Paillier Algorithm in Arithmetic Operation

Paillier encryption and decryption algorithm and improved Paillier algorithm encryption and decryption times are listed in Table 1. It can be seen from the table that the encryption and decryption process of Paillier algorithm requires multiple large exponential modular multiplication operations, which results in low execution efficiency and is not suitable for the encryption of power data. It can be seen from the encryption and decryption process of the improved algorithm that in the encryption stage, since several $r^n \bmod n^2$ are pre-calculated, the encryption process only needs to perform basic operations of addition and multiplication once. In the decryption stage, b is calculated first, a modular multiplication operation is required, and finally the plaintext m is calculated by decryption, which requires a large exponential modular multiplication operation and a modular multiplication operation.

5 Experiments and Results

This section discusses the efficiency of the I-Paillier algorithm in a simulation environment.

Table 1. Comparison of calculation times

Arithmetic operation type	Paillier algorithm	I- Paillier algorithm (excluding pre-calculation)
Encryption process exponentiation modulo large prime multiplication	2	0
Modular multiplication during encryption ($\mathrm{mod}\, n^2$)	1	0
Large prime number power modulus multiplication in the decryption process	2	1
Modular multiplication during decryption ($\mathrm{mod}\, n^2$ and $\mathrm{mod}\, n$)	3	2

5.1 Experimental Setup

The data in the experiment is the power consumption data of the enterprise in the simulation power system. Through the analysis and observation of these data, it is found that these data are integer and decimals with decimal length from 2 bits to 8 bits (the most decimal part is 3 bits), the power consumption is an integer, the cost of electricity is a decimals. In this experiment, we preprocess the experimental data, multiply each decimals by 1000 to meet the encryption algorithm for the encryption of data requirements. In order to achieve better experimental results, it is necessary to simulate the power data and classify these decimal digits by the number of digits, statistics Paillier algorithm and I-Paillier algorithm for each class of decimal number encryption and decryption of the average time, that is, statistical average encryption time and average decryption time. In order to make the average encryption time and average decryption time more accurate, we expanded the number of data to 1000 as simulation data, so the average time it takes to encrypt and decrypt each type of data is the total time it takes to encrypt and decrypt 1,000 of these data divided by 1000.

We installed JDK 8 virtual machine on Intel(R) Core(TM) I7-3537u CPU and 6.00 GB RAM host, and implemented Paillier algorithm and I-Paillier algorithm using Java programming language. In Paillier encryption scheme, it is generally believed that the encrypted data can only be fully guaranteed by selecting 2048 bits at least for the key. In order to be more close to the practical situation, in this experiment, the key length selected by Paillier algorithm and the I-Paillier algorithm is 2048 bits, and the random variable length selected in the encryption system is 1024 bits.

5.2 Encryption Time Efficiency

Both the original algorithm and the I-Paillier algorithm have two-dimensional public keys (n, g) and (n, α) respectively. In the experiment of statistical encryption time, we set g in Paillier's public key as the minimum prime number 2, and 1 in the I-Paillier's public key as the minimum positive integer. The purpose of this setting is to compare the two algorithms when the other variables are the same, by setting the value of the second dimension public key, the computational complexity of the two algorithms is reduced to the minimum, which is convenient for the experiment to be carried out in the limited time.

Before the experiment, the public key and private key, as well as the random number r in the encryption algorithm are generated by the program. As mentioned in Sect. 4, in practical applications, numerical value of $r^n mod\ n^2$ can be precalculated without the need for repeated large-exponential modular operations during the encryption process. So, in this experiment, the I-Paillier algorithm uses the strategy of pre-computation, and the original algorithm does not ues the strategy of pre-computation.

We calculate the average encryption time of Paillier algorithm and the I-Paillier algorithm for 2 digit, 3 digit, 4 digit, 5 digit, 6 digit, 7 digit, 8 digit encryption with sufficient security.

As shown in the algorithm simulation interface diagram in Fig. 1, the I-Paillier algorithm encrypts one data in much less time than the original Algorithm encrypts one data. And as you can see in Fig. 1, the Paillier algorithm shows a slow increase in the average encryption time as the number of decimal digits increases. But the I-Paillier algorithm encrypts a data the average time not to have the obvious difference.

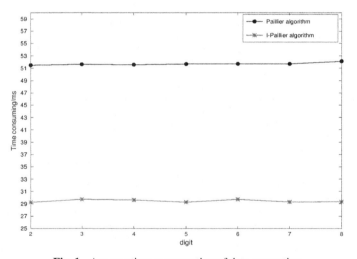

Fig. 1. Average time consumption of data encryption

Figure 1 shows the average time to encrypt each type of data when both the Paillier algorithm and the second dimensional public key of the I-Paillier algorithm take the smallest positive integer. In reality, in order to make the length of ciphertext longer and more secure, it is often required to select the second-dimension public key length. As shown in the simulation experiment in Fig. 2, the second dimension public key length of the I-Paillier algorithm is set to 1 bit, 8 bit, 16 bit, 32 bit and 64 bit, respectively, then statistic the effect of different lengths on the time required to encrypt each type of data. Comparing the polylines in Fig. 2, we can see that the average encryption time increases slightly as the length increases, but it is still much smaller than the average encryption time of Paillier algorithm.

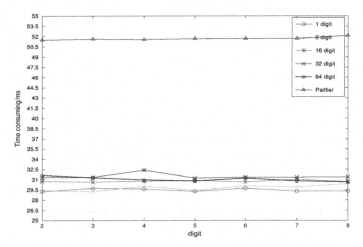

Fig. 2. Effect of public key length of ∂ on encryption time of I-Paillier algorithm

5.3 Decryption Time Efficiency

In the case that the key length and random variable are the same and we set g in Paillier's public key to be the smallest integer 2, and 1 in the I-Paillier's public key. We count the average decryption time between the Paillier algorithm and the I-Paillier algorithm for decrypting 1 000 ciphertext of each type of data with a key length of 2048 bit.

As shown in the algorithm simulation interface diagram in Fig. 3, the average decryption time of the I-Paillier algorithm is much less than the average decryption time of the original algorithm between 2 digit and 8 digit. There is no obvious effect on the decryption efficiency of the cipher text with different digit data in the decryption experiment.

It can be seen from the comparison results of calculation times of encryption and decryption listed in Table 1 that the large prime number power modulus multiplication and modulus multiplication in the decryption process of Paillier algorithm are two and three times respectively, while the I-Paillier algorithm is one and two times respectively.

The experiment results are consistent with the theory.

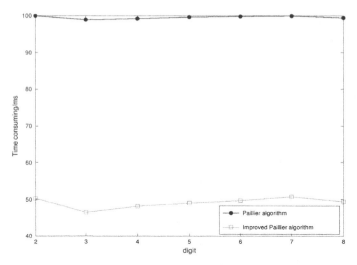

Fig. 3. The average time it takes to decrypt a piece of data

6 Conclusion

In this paper, an I-Paillier algorithm is proposed to protect the privacy of power data, and the data types involved in the power data are experimented to test the average time of encryption and decryption, so as to draw the conclusion that the I-Paillier algorithm is much higher in the time efficiency of encryption and decryption than the original algorithm. It is also found that the encryption time efficiency of Paillier algorithm decreases with the increase of data bits. In this experiment, the second dimensional parameter g of Paillier algorithm is set as 2. If g is a large number in $Z_{n^2}^*$, according to the time complexity of exponential operation, its encryption and decryption efficiency is lower. At present, many scholars have mentioned the use of Paillier encryption technology in the power industry, such as the privacy protection of user data of smart electricity meters. The power system uses homomorphic encryption technology to aggregate the electricity consumption data of a certain area, and then statistics the electricity consumption situation of this area. As for the analysis of the economic value of power data, some technology companies also put forward the scheme of using Federated Learning technology to drive the economic value of power data, so that the power data can be associated with other enterprise data for analysis. While federated learning can solve the power data islands problem, it still requires privacy protection. In Federated Learning, the participant's model parameters can be encrypted, and the central server only involves aggregation of the encrypted model parameters. Paillier homomorphic encryption scheme is used in the existing Federated Learning framework FATE, which has been implemented in projects such as credit risk control and auto insurance pricing [31]. If the data encryption module of the I-Paillier algorithm for Federated Learning can reduce the time of encryption and decryption without changing the original security, then it has great significance for Federated Learning. Faced with huge amounts of power data, the learning will continuously update model parameters, the model parameters was also a huge number of encryption, and homomorphic encryption on the time consumption is much higher than other encryption algorithm, so, if the time can reduce the encryption model parameters, there will be fewer time consumption taked by Federated Learning, it also makes the I-Paillier encryption algorithm based on Federaed Learning of power data on application of effective and efficient as possible.

References

1. Guan, Y., Cui, X.T.: Study on new concept, new strategy and new model of power marketing under deepening power market reform. Agric. Econ. **9**, 143–144 (2020)
2. Yang, Q.: Federated learning: last mile of AI. J. Intell. Syst. **15**(1), 183–186 (2020)
3. Dwork, C.: Differential privacy: a survey of results. In: Agrawal, M., Dingzhu, D., Duan, Z., Li, A. (eds.) theory and applications of models of computation, pp. 1–19. Springer, Heidelberg (2008). https://doi.org/10.1007/978-3-540-79228-4_1
4. Ma, Y.M.: Secure multi-party computation. China New Telecommun. **22**(18), 114–115 (2020)
5. Gentry, C.: Fully homomorphic encryption using ideal lattices. In: Proceedings of the Forty-First Annual ACM Symposium on Theory of Computing, pp. 169–178 (2009)
6. Brakerski, Z.: Fully homomorphic encryption without modulus switching from classical GapSVP. In: Safavi-Naini, R., Canetti, R. (eds.) Advances in Cryptology – CRYPTO 2012, pp. 868–886. Springer, Heidelberg (2012). https://doi.org/10.1007/978-3-642-32009-5_50
7. Fan, J.F., Vercauteren, F.: Somewhat practical fully homomorphic encryption. In: IACRCryptology ePrint Archive, no. 2012, p. 144 (2012)
8. Brakerski, Z., Gentry, C., Vaikuntanathan, V.: (leveled) fully homomorphic encryptionwithout bootstrapping. In: ITCS, pp. 309–325. ACM (2012)
9. Coron, Jean-Sébastien., Lepoint, T., Tibouchi, M.: Scale-invariant fully homomorphic encryption over the integers. In: Krawczyk, H. (ed.) Public-Key Cryptography – PKC 2014: 17th International Conference on Practice and Theory in Public-Key Cryptography, Buenos Aires, Argentina, March 26-28, 2014. Proceedings, pp. 311–328. Springer, Heidelberg (2014). https://doi.org/10.1007/978-3-642-54631-0_18
10. Rivest, R.L., et al.: On data banks and privacy homomorphisms. Found. Secure Comput. **4**(11), 169–180 (1978)
11. Diffie, W., Hellman, M.: New directions in cryptography. IEEE Trans. Inf. Theory **22**(6), 644–654 (2020)
12. Taher, E.: A public key cryptosystem and a signature scheme based on discrete logarithms. IEEE Trans. Inf. Theory **31**(4), 469–472 (1985)
13. Josh, B.: Dense probabilistic encryption. In: Proceedings of Workshop on Selected areas of Cryptography, pp. 120–128 (1994)
14. Okamoto, T., Uchiyama, S.: A new public-key cryptosystem as secure as factoring. In: Nyberg, K. (ed.) EUROCRYPT 1998. LNCS, vol. 1403, pp. 308–318. Springer, Heidelberg (1998). https://doi.org/10.1007/BFb0054135
15. Naccache, D., Stern, J.: A new public key cryptosystem based on higher residues. In: Proceedings of the 5th ACM Conference on Computer and Communications Security, pp. 59–66 (1998)
16. Paillier, P.: Public-key cryptosystems based on composite degree residuosity classes. In: Stern, Jacques (ed.) Advances in Cryptology — EUROCRYPT '99, pp. 223–238. Springer, Heidelberg (1999). https://doi.org/10.1007/3-540-48910-X_16
17. Damgård, I., Jurik, M.: A generalisation, a simplification and some applications of Paillier's probabilistic public-key system. In: Kim, K. (ed.) Public Key Cryptography: 4th International Workshop on Practice and Theory in Public Key Cryptosystems, PKC 2001 Cheju Island, Korea, February 13–15, 2001 Proceedings, pp. 119–136. Springer, Heidelberg (2001). https://doi.org/10.1007/3-540-44586-2_9

18. Boneh, D., Goh, Eu-Jin., Nissim, K.: Evaluating 2-DNF formulas on ciphertexts. In: Kilian, J. (ed.) Theory of cryptography, pp. 325–341. Springer, Heidelberg (2005). https://doi.org/10.1007/978-3-540-30576-7_18

19. Li, J., Chen, S.C., Song, D.J.: Security structure of cloud storagebased on homomorphic encryption scheme. In: Proceedings of the 2nd Inter-National Conference on Cloud Computing and Intelligent Systems, pp. 224–227. IEEE Computer Society, Washington DC (2012)

20. Peng, C.G., et al.: General transitive signature scheme based on homomorphic encryption. J. Commun. **11**, 18–25 (2013)

21. Yang, Y.L., Peng, C.G., Zhou, Z.: A solution of preventing SQL injection attacks based on homomorphic Encryption. Netinfo Secur. **1**, 30–33 (2014)

22. Wang, M.D., et al.: Optimal design of R-ate pair in SM9 algorithm. Commun. Technol. **53**(9), 2241–2244 (2020)

23. Zhang, X., Chen, X.H., Liu, X.: Construction of information security baseline standardization system for power systems. Electric Power Inf. Commun. Technol. **11**(11), 110–114 (2013)

24. Xiang, S., Yang, L.: Robust and reversible image watermarking algorithm in homomorphic encrypted domain. J. Softw. **29**(4), 957–972 (2018)

25. Li, L., et al.: Review of homomorphic encryption. Appl. Res. Comput. **11**, 3209–3214 (2015)

26. Paillier, P., Yung, M.: Public-key cryptosystems based on composite degree residuosity classes. In: Computer Science, vol. 1592, no. 223, pp. 223–238 (2004)

27. Kurosawa, K., Nojima, R., Phong, L.T.: New leakage-resilient CCA-secure public key encryption. J. Math. Cryptol. **7**(4), 297–312 (2013)

28. Carmichael, R.D.: On composite numbers P which satisfy the Fermat congruence a p-1≡1 mod P. Am. Math. Mon. **19**(2), 22–27 (1912)

29. Zeng, P., Chen, S., Choo, K.-K.: An IND-CCA2 secure post-quantum encryption scheme and a secure cloud storage use case. Human-centric Comput. Inf. Sci. **9**(1), 1–15 (2019). https://doi.org/10.1186/s13673-019-0193-6

30. Zhou, Q.T.: Research on point product protocol based on Paillier cryptosystem. M.S. dissertation, Yunnan University, Yunnan (2012)

31. WeBank et al.: Federated learning white paper v2.0 (2020). https://aisp-1251170195.cos.ap-hongkong.myqcloud.com/wpcontent/uploads/pdf/%E8%81%94%E9%82%A6%E5%AD%A6%E4%B9%A0%E7%99%BD%E7%9A%AE%E4%B9%A6_v2.0.pdf

The Vulnerabilities in Smart Contracts: A Survey

Xiangyan Tang[1,2], Ke Zhou[1,2(✉)], Jieren Cheng[1,2], Hui Li[3], and Yuming Yuan[3]

[1] School of Computer Science and Cyberspace Security, Hainan University, Haikou 570228, China
[2] Hainan Blockchain Technology Engineering Research Center, Haikou 570228, China
[3] Hainan Huochain Tech Company Limited, Haikou 570100, China

Abstract. Blockchain has attracted widespread attention since its inception and one of the special technologies is smart contracts. Smart contracts are programs on blockchain that act as trusted intermediary between the users and are widely used in variety of industry (e.g., IoT, supply chain management). Smart contracts can store or manipulate valuable assets which may cause huge economic losses. Unlike traditional computer programs, the code of a smart contract cannot be modified after it is deployed on the blockchain. Hence, the security analysis and vulnerability detection of the smart contract must be performed before its deployment. In this survey, we considered 15 security vulnerabilities in smart contracts and introduced the vulnerable areas and the causes of vulnerabilities. According to the methods used, we introduced the existing smart contract analysis methods and vulnerability detection tools from three aspects of static analysis, dynamic analysis and formal verification. Finally, by considering the analysis tools and security vulnerabilities, we found that a new attack cannot be detected by existing detection tools if the vulnerability without pre-defined. We recommend using machine learning methods to analyze smart contracts in combination with traditional program vulnerabilities, and find vulnerabilities that have not yet been discovered in smart contracts. In addition, many detection tools require too much resources or are too complex, so it is necessary to introduce new detection methods.

Keywords: Ethereum · Smart contracts · Analysis tools · Vulnerability detection

1 Introduction

Bitcoin, A new type of decentralized cryptocurrency [1], has successfully attracted wide attention from industry in academia since its appearance in 2009. Its underlying technology blockchain is a public electronic ledger equivalent to a distributed database, which uses distributed ledger technology (DLT) to achieve valuable assets digital and decentralized public transaction information ledger [2–4]. In recent years, with the development of blockchain technology, it has now entered the blockchain 2.0 era represented by smart contracts. The smart contract based on blockchain is trying to be applied to a wide variety of industry, such as internet of thing (IoT) [5, 6], health care [7, 8], government services [9, 10], supply chain management [11, 12], finance [13, 14] and energy [15, 16].

© Springer Nature Switzerland AG 2021
X. Sun et al. (Eds.): ICAIS 2021, CCIS 1424, pp. 177–190, 2021.
https://doi.org/10.1007/978-3-030-78621-2_14

The smart contract is a program on the blockchain. Therefore, the smart contract has the following three characteristics: (1) The smart contract is immutable; (2) Many smart contracts store or manipulate valuable asset; (3)The smart contract is open to all users and anyone can access it. The code which has already been deployed on the blockchain cannot be patched, even though there are security vulnerabilities. In other words, the correctness execution of the Ethereum smart contract is a necessary condition for the effectiveness of its results. But the correctness alone is not enough to prove the security of the smart contract, which makes the blockchain smart contract have natural mechanism vulnerabilities and it's easy to cause economic loss.

Although people are optimistic about the development of smart contracts, the frequent outbreaks of smart contract security vulnerabilities and privacy issues still cause people's concern. In June 2016, The Dao security vulnerability resulted in an economic loss of $50 million [17]. In July 2017, the security vulnerability of parity multi signature wallet caused by smart contract led to more than US $150 million of ether was lost [18]. In April 2018, hackers used the overflow vulnerability of Batch OverFlow of ERC-20 standard token contract to attack the Beauty chain, which produced a large number of tokens out of thin air, and then sold them in the trading market, resulting in a sharp drop of nearly 94% in its market value [19]. It is necessary to perform security analysis and vulnerability detection before deploying smart contracts. For smart contracts, Ethereum is the most widely used platform in the world now. Therefore, this article mainly considers the vulnerabilities of smart contracts on the Ethereum blockchain.

The rest of this article is organized as follows: in Sect. 2, we introduce the basic theories of blockchain, smart contracts and Ethereum; in Sect. 3, we show the main vulnerabilities of smart contracts; in Sect. 4, we show the detection methods and tools of smart contract vulnerabilities; finally, we conclude the survey in Sect. 5.

2 Theoretical Background

Blockchain is the underlying technology of the Bitcoin system. It was first proposed by Satoshi Nakamoto in "Bitcoin: A peer-to-peer electronic cash system". With respect to data, the blockchain is a block+chain data structure, and all nodes store data in a distributed ledger [20]; with respect to technology, the blockchain is a combination of multiple existing technologies, not a new technology [21]. It has entered the blockchain 2.0 era represented by smart contracts now.

In 1996, Nick Szabo described a smart contract as "a set of promises, specified in digital form, including protocols within which the parties perform on these promises" [22].The smart contract on Ethereum is a program embedded in the Ethereum blockchain which can represent the commitment of both parties in the form of digital rules. It contains a set of predefined states and can make state transition driven by transactions.

The smart contract is stored in the distributed consensus environment and inherits the characteristics of three aspects of blockchain: open and transparent, immutable and permanent operation [23]. For smart contracts, Ethereum is the most widely used platform in the world now.

Ethereum [24] is an open software platform based on blockchain technology. It provides users with a smart contract development framework and numerous application programming interfaces (APIs) in which users can compile, test, deploy and execute various distributed applications.

3 The Vulnerabilities in Smart Contracts

In this section, we will introduce the key vulnerabilities which would cause serious problems in Ethereum smart contracts applications.

In the analysis of the attack on the smart contract in Ethereum, according to the level where the vulnerabilities are introduced, they can be divided into 3 types (Solidity, EVM bytecode, and Blockchain) [25].

3.1 Solidity Level

The main vulnerabilities are in the solidity level, so according to whether it causes serious attack accident and economic loss, the vulnerability in solidity level can be divided into heavy harm and light harm.

Heavy Harm Vulnerabilities

Integer Over/Under Flow. Integer overflow includes three types: addition overflow, subtraction overflow and multiplication overflow. In EVM, the solidity language supports 8–256 bits integer data. For uint256 bits variables, its value range is 0–2^{256}–1. If there is a variable of uint256 called X, and it's value greater than 2^{256}–1 by calculation, an integer overflow will occur and the X will also change from a very large value to 0. If it's value less than 0 by calculation, an integer underflow will occur and the X will also change from a very small value to 2^{256}–1. In smart contracts, integer calculations are usually related to the transfer of digital assets. Attackers often use this vulnerability [26] to cause problems. Ethereum provides the SafeMath [27] digital computing library with security check function to solve this problem.

Re-Entrancy Problem. When a smart contract calls another smart contract, the called smart contract can modify the control flow and state of the original smart contract. By repeatedly calling the original smart contract many times, operations such as malicious repeated transfers can be realized. An attacker can design a malicious smart contract and add malicious code to the callback function, including callbacks to Re-entrancy the contract. When writing a smart contract, you can modify the internal restriction state to ensure the exception will be triggered when Re-entrancy problem occur.

Greedy Contract. These smart contract lock funds by being unable to send Ether. The contracts which call the external library functions will become greedy contract when the library contracts are terminated or destructed by an attacker [28].

Light Harm Vulnerabilities

Denial of Service. There are three types of DOS attacks in Ethereum: 1. When the state transfer of a smart contract depends on the result of the execution of an external function, if the execution of the external function fails many times, the contract may cause DOS attack. 2. DOS attacks caused by gas limit. If the transaction fails due to gas limit many times in a short period of time, the contract may cause DOS attack. 3. DOS vulnerabilities introduced by smart contract writers due to their programming mistakes.

Gas Overspent. In the process of writing smart contract, it is easy to introduce a lot of unnecessary code, which will cause a waste of gas when deploying smart contracts on the Ethereum blockchain.

Transaction Ordering. When a user initiates a transaction to call a smart contract in the Ethereum blockchain, the actual state of the smart contract cannot be predicted [29, 30]. When a transaction calls a smart contract, the user expects the smart contract to run under initialization; however, in reality, if two transactions call the same smart contract at the same time, the user cannot determine the state of the smart contract when they are called. It is also impossible to determine which transaction will be executed first, the order of transaction execution which is determined by the block mining order.

Prodigal Contract. Ethereum smart contract can automatically refund the owners after an attack. But in some cases, The smart contract will transfer funds to someone unrelated to the contract.

Exception Handling. In Ethereum, a smart contract may not be able to complete the transaction, so it needs to call other contracts to achieve the required functionalities. In the called smart contract, an abnormal situation may raised. At this time, the called smart contract will roll back the operation and restore the initial state. Operation failure caused an error value to be returned to the caller, causing the exception to be passed from the caller to the caller, causing the problem of exception propagation. An attacker can invoke a caller contract and cause its send function fail.

Destroyable/Suicidal Contract. The owner of the smart contract can choose to return it when Ethereum fails. But this instruction can also be executed by others to cause the transaction fail. A destroyable contract may be terminated or killed by an anonymous suicide instruction by any external user account or another smart contract.

3.2 EVM Level

Call Stack Depth Limitation. EVM uses a stack-based architecture and its maximum depth is 1024, when one smart contract calls another smart contract, the depth of the call stack will increase by one. Attackers can use this feature to call themselves 1023 times before calling another smart contract, deliberately exceeding the stack length to complete the attack.

Unchecked and Failed Send. When using send instruction to send ether to another user or smart contract, it may fail because the gas limit is exceeded or the balance is insufficient. But it will not return to the smart contract exception or error message, which will make the balance be updated as if it has been sent.

Short Address. The short address attack is mainly for token forwarding based on ERC-20 type. In EVM, transaction information is a string of bytecodes, part of which is a 32-byte target Ethereum address and 32-byte token amount. If the last bit of the target address is 0, the attacker deliberately does not enter this bit. When the EVM analyzes the bytecode of the transaction information, it will take the highest digit of the token amount to make the last digit of the target address. If the highest digit of the token amount is 0, the target address will remain unchanged. The EVM will add 0 to the end of the token amount which lacks the highest digit to make the number of coding digits normal. It will make the amount shift one bit to the left, so that the transfer exceeds the actual number of tokens that should be transferred.

Authentication Through tx.origin. There is a global variable called tx.origin in the smart contract, which traverses the entire call stack and returns the address of the account that originally sent the call (or transaction). Using this variable for authentication in the smart contract will make the contract vulnerable to phishing attacks. Attacker can use this vulnerability to create a contract similar to a trap to attack the user who calls the smart contract.

3.3 Blockchain Level

Block Timestamp Dependency. The execution of some smart contracts will depend on the timestamp of the current block. Usually the timestamp is set to the system time of the local computer or server, but the specific value is determined by the packing node when the block is generated. The node decides that the time stamp value can be adjusted within an error range of about 900s [31].Attackers or malicious miners can set their own timestamps according to the flexibility of timestamps to manipulate the results of smart contracts related to timestamps.

Unsecured Balance. If the ether balance of a smart contract is exposed to attackers, then the smart contract is vulnerable to the attack of unsecured balance.

4   Smart Contract Analysis Methods and Tools

The smart contract is stored in the distributed consensus environment and inherits the characteristics of three aspects of blockchain: open and transparent, immutable and permanent operation. Although smart contracts facilitate the development of distributed applications, they are tamper proof and cannot be upgraded or patched.

The mainly security analysis methods of smart contracts is static analysis, dynamic analysis, and formal verification methods.

4.1 Static Analysis

Static Analysis refers to scanning the program code through lexical analysis, syntax analysis, control flow, data flow analysis and other technologies without executing the program. It is a code analysis technology to verify whether the code meets the specification, security, reliability, maintainability and other indicators. In this section, we will introduce some mainstream static analysis tools.

Slither. Slither [32] is a static analysis framework designed to provide granular information about smart contract code and the flexibility necessary to support many applications.

Slither analyzes smart contracts using static analysis in a multistage procedure. It takes the Solidity Abstract Syntax Tree (AST) generated by the Solidity compiler from the contract source code as input. There are three stages during Slither analyzing smart contracts. In the first stage, Slither will recover important information about smart contracts such as the contract's inheritance graph, the CFG, and the list of expressions. Then, Slither transforms the entire code of the contract to SlithIR, and SlithIR can use static single assessment (SSA) to facilitate the computation of a variety of code analyses. The Final stage is the actual code analysis, Slither will compute a set of predefined analyses which provide enhanced information to the other modules. The Slither overview is shown in Fig. 1.

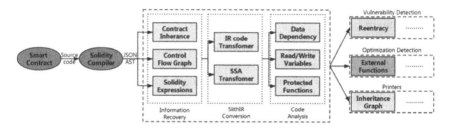

Fig. 1. Slither overview

OYENTE. Luu et al. [28] focus on transaction ordering dependency, re-entrancy, timestamp dependence, and unhandled exceptions, has designed the OYENTE tool based on symbolic execution technology. It takes the bytecode of smart contracts and the state of the Ethereum blockchain as input. OYENTE consists of four main components: control flow graph (CFG) Builder, Explorer, CoreAnalysis and Validator. The architecture of the OYENTE tool is shown in Fig. 2.

Gasper. Chen et al. [33] developed a static analysis tool called Gasper, which does not detect smart contract vulnerabilities, but mainly focuses on the gas cost patterns in smart contracts.

Osiris. Osiris [34] combines symbolic execution and taints analysis to detect integer problems in Solidity smart contracts. It consists of three components: symbolic analysis, taint analysis, and integer error detection. The symbolic analysis can construct a CFG and executes the different paths of the contract. Taint analysis [35] is a technique which can distinguish between benign and malicious overflows. The architecture of Osiris is shown in Fig. 3.

Securify. Securify [23] is an Ethereum smart contract static security analyzer with Ethereum EVM bytecode and vulnerability specifications as input. It will check the smart contract behavior related to the input vulnerability specifications and give the check result.

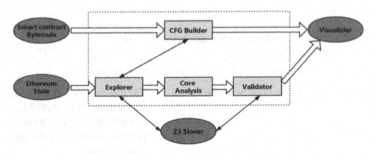

Fig. 2. The architecture of the OYENTE tool

Vandal. Vandal [36] is a security analysis framework consist two parts for identifying the vulnerabilities in Ethereum smart contracts. The first part uses an analysis pipeline for converting the EVM bytecode to the logic relations. The second part is a set of logic specifications for security analysis problems.

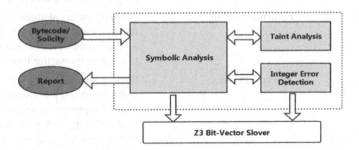

Fig. 3. The architecture of Osiris

Ethir. Ethir [37] is not a standalone tool, it analyzes the smart contracts statically based on the the rule-based representations of the CFG produced by the OYENTE. It will examine the conditional and unconditional jump instructions in smart contract.

SmartCheck. SmartCheck [38] analyzes the solidity source code of the smart contract to find vulnerabilities using static analysis. It uses the Extensible Markup Language (XML) syntax tree to convert the smart contract in an intermediate representation (IR). The vulnerabilities will be specified as XQuery path expressions which are used to search the vulnerability patterns in the Extensible Markup Language tree by using XPath queries on the intermediate representation. But the complex rules cannot be precisely described with XPath, which will lead to false positives.

4.2 Dynamic Analysis

Dynamic analysis is a method which checks a programming application while it is executing or in the run-time. It detects whether there are security vulnerabilities by observing the behavior of the program running under different data.

Table 1. Formal verification tools

Tool/Framework	Formal verification technique	Description
FSolidM [42]	Finite State Machine	The tool is built for designing smart contracts as Finite State Machines on a graphical interface. It can also generate automated Ethereum smart contract code
Hydra [53]	Formal Modelling	The Hydra framework is built to provide bug bounties for honest vulnerability disclosures
F* frame work [44]	F* for program and bytecode verification	The framework analyzes and verifies both functional correctness and runtime safety of Solidity smart contracts with a functional programming language (F*)
Hawk [45]	Formal Modelling	A smart contract platform which does not make financial transactions available publicly on the blockchain to maintain transactional privacy
Raziel [46]	Theorem Proving	Raziel combines secure multi-party computation and proof-carrying code to provide privacy, correctness and verifiability guarantees for smart contracts on blockchains
Town Crier [47]	Theorem Proving	Town Crier acts as a link between existing trusted non-blockchain based websites and smart contracts to provide authenticated data to smart contracts
ZEUS [48]	Theorem Proving	ZEUS is a smart contract safety verifier that utilizes both symbolic model checking and abstract interpretation
KEVM [49]	Theorem Proving	Formal semantics of EVM in K
ContractLarva [50]	Finite State Machine	Runtime safety and verification tool for Solidity smart contracts on Ethereum

ContractFuzzer. ContractFuzzer [39] is a smart contract analysis tool based on fuzz testing. At first, it analyzes all functions in the smart contract and analyzes all external functions of the smart contract which does not provide ABI. Then it generates input data by using the ABI of the smart contract. Finally, the running track recorded by EVM is used for vulnerability analysis. Seven test primitives are defined in ContractFuzzer to support the detection of multiple security vulnerabilities.

MAIAN. Nikolic et al. [40] built a dynamic tool called MAIAN to analyze smart contracts, which extends OYENTE's approach. It can find directly vulnerabilities in the bytecode of the Ethereum smart contract without accessing the source code. It has two major components: symbolic analysis and concrete validation. The symbolic analysis component takes the contract bytecode and analysis specifications as input. The specifications include the vulnerability category to search for and depth of the search space, and there is a custom EVM was implemented to facilitate symbolic execution of smart contract bytecode. Every execution trace takes a set of symbolic variables as its input. The EVM runs for all possible execution traces symbolically for each smart contract candidate until it reaches a problematic trace with a set of predetermined vulnerability properties.

EasyFlow. EasyFlow [41] is a tool to detect whether there is an integer over/under flow vulnerability in the Ethereum smart contract based on dynamic taint analysis. By modifying the EVM, each input parameter is tracked as a taint. Observing the operand during numerical calculation, if the operands are not tainted and the calculation does not overflow, the operation is proved to be safe; if the operand is tainted, a transaction is attempted to cause the operation to overflow. If the overflow is triggered successfully, the overflow vulnerability is reported; if the overflow is not triggered, the potential overflow vulnerability is reported. In addition, EasyFlow can recognize SafeMath and its possible variants which effectively reducing the false alarm rate.

4.3 Formal Verification Method

Based on the formal methods, the formal verification of smart contracts can prove the specific properties in a programming code such as functional correctness, run-time safety, soundness, reliability, and so on. Some formal verification tools is shown in Table 1.

ZEUS. ZEUS takes as input the smart contracts written in high-level languages and leverages user assistance to help generate the correctness and/or fairness criteria in an eXtensible Access Control Markup Language (XACML) styled template [51]. It translates these contracts and the policy specification into a low-level intermediate representation (IR), such as Low-Level Virtual Machine(LLVM) bitcode [52], encoding the execution semantics to correctly reason about the contract behavior. It then performs static analysis atop the IR to determine the points at which the verification predicates (as specified in the policy) must be asserted. Finally, ZEUS feeds the modified IR to a verification engine that leverages constrained horn clauses (CHCs) [53] to quickly ascertain the safety of the smart contract.

F* Frame Work. Smart contracts are generally written in Solidity and compiled down to bytecode by the EVM. Microsoft Research and Harvard University develop a framework to analyze and formally verify Ethereum smart contracts using F* functional programming language [44].

The F* framework contains two tools, Solidity* and EVM*. Solidity* compiles the smart contract source code into F* language, and EVM* compiles EVM bytecode into F* language. After both are converted to F* language, the equivalence is verified using relational reasoning. The architecture of the F* Framework is shown in Fig. 4.

4.4 Comparison Between the Three Analysis Methods

Although there is currently no such a tool that can detect all known smart contract vulnerabilities, a combination of multiple tools can detect the currently defined mainstream smart contract vulnerabilities. Static analysis and dynamic analysis can automatically detect predefined vulnerabilities, while the formal method is to conduct security analysis of smart contracts through formal modeling, theorem proving, language conversion and other methods.

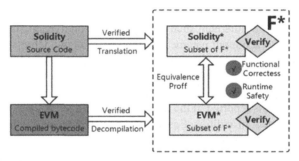

Fig. 4. The architecture of the F* Framework

5 Conclusion

In this survey on the security vulnerabilities of smart contracts, we showed 15 major vulnerabilities, and from Sect. 4 we can know the Re-entrancy problem which caused significant losses in The DAO attack can be detected by 6 tools. Based on this survey, we can conclude that many existing smart contract vulnerabilities can be detected by multiple tools, but there are still some vulnerabilities with a few detection tools, and a new attack cannot be detected by existing detection tools if the vulnerability without predefined. We recommend using machine learning methods to analyze smart contracts in combination with traditional program vulnerabilities, and find vulnerabilities that have not yet been discovered in smart contracts. It is necessary to carry out more work in the verification of smart contracts, or to introduce new detection methods.

Acknowledgements. This work was supported by the Hainan Provincial Natural Science Foundation of China (Grant No. 2019RC041 and 2019RC098), Research and Application Project of Key Technologies for Blockchain Cross-chain Collaborative Monitoring and Traceability for Large-scale Distributed Denial of Service Attacks, National Natural Science Foundation of China (Grant No. 61762033), Opening Project of Shanghai Trusted Industrial Control Platform (Grant No. TICPSH202003005-ZC), and Education and Teaching Reform Research Project of Hainan University (Grant No. hdjy1970).

References

1. Nakamoto S.: Bitcoin: a peer-to-peer electronic cash system (2008). https://bitcoin.org/bit coin.pdf
2. Ahram, T., Sargolzaei, A., Sargolzaei, S., Daniels, J., Amaba, B.: Blockchain technology innovations. In: 2017 Conference Proceedings Technology and Engineering Management Conference (TEMSCON), pp. 137–141. IEEE (2017)
3. Xu, X., et al.: A taxonomy of blockchain-based systems for architecture design. In: 2017 IEEE International Conference on Software Architecture (ICSA), pp. 243–252. IEEE (2017)
4. Peters, G., Panayi, E.: Understanding modern banking ledgers through blockchain technologies: Future of transaction processing and smart contracts on the internet of money. In: Tasca, P., Aste, T., Pelizzon, L., Perony, N. (eds.) Banking beyond banks and money, pp. 239–278. Springer, Cham (2016). https://doi.org/10.1007/978-3-319-42448-4_13
5. Christidis, K., Devetsikiotis, M.: Blockchains and smart contracts for the internet of things. IEEE Access **4**, 2292–2303 (2016)
6. Bahga, A., Madisetti, V.K.: Blockchain platform for industrial internet of things. J. Softw. Eng. Appl. **9**(10), 533 (2016)
7. Azaria, A., Ekblaw, A., Vieira, T., Lippman, A.: Medrec: using blockchain for medical data access and permission management. In: 2016 2nd International Conference on Open and Big Data (OBD), pp. 25–30. IEEE (2016)
8. Mettler, M.: Blockchain technology in healthcare: the revolution starts here. In: 2016 IEEE 18th International Conference on e-Health Networking, Applications and Services (Healthcom), pp.1–3. IEEE (2016)
9. Ølnes, S., Ubacht, J., Janssen, M.: Blockchain in government: benefits and implications of distributed ledger technology for information sharing. Gov. Inf. Q. **34**(3), 355–364 (2017)
10. Staples, M., et al.: Risks and opportunities for systems using blockchain and smart contracts. data61 (2017)
11. Abeyratne, S.A., Monfared, R.P.: Blockchain ready manufacturing supply chain using distributed ledger. Int. J. Res. Eng. Technol. **5**, 1–10 (2016)
12. Chen, S., Shi, R., Ren, Z., Yan, J., Shi, Y., Zhang, J.: A blockchain based supply chain quality management framework. In: 2017 IEEE 14th International Conference on e-Business Engineering (ICEBE), pp. 172–176. IEEE (2017)
13. Bussmann, O.: The future of finance: fintech, tech disruption, and orchestrating innovation. In: Francioni, R., Schwartz, R.A. (eds.) Equity Markets in Transition, pp. 473–486. Springer, Cham (2017). https://doi.org/10.1007/978-3-319-45848-9_19
14. Eyal, I.: Blockchain technology: transforming libertarian cryptocurrency dreams to finance and banking realities. Computer **50**(9), 38–49 (2017)
15. Knirsch, F., Unterweger, A., Eibl, G., Engel, D.: Privacy-preserving smart grid tariff decisions with blockchain-based smart contracts. In: Rivera, Wilson (ed.) Sustainable Cloud and Energy Services, pp. 85–116. Springer, Cham (2018). https://doi.org/10.1007/978-3-319-62238-5_4

16. Mylrea, M., Gourisetti, S.N.G.: Blockchain for smart grid resilience: exchanging distributed energy at speed, scale and security. In: 2017 Resilience Week (RWS), pp. 18–23. IEEE (2017)
17. Sergey, I., Hobor, A.: A concurrent perspective on smart contracts. In: Brenner, M., et al. (eds.) Financial Cryptography and Data Security, pp. 478–493. Springer International Publishing, Cham (2017). https://doi.org/10.1007/978-3-319-70278-0_30
18. Bocek, T., Stiller, B.: Smart contracts – blockchains in the wings. In: Linnhoff-Popien, C., Schneider, R., Zaddach, M. (eds.) Digital Marketplaces Unleashed, pp. 169–184. Springer, Heidelberg (2018). https://doi.org/10.1007/978-3-662-49275-8_19
19. Michaell, Y.: Building a safer crypto token (2018). https://medium.com/cybermiles/building-a-safer-crypto-token-27c96a7e78fd
20. Marc, P.: Blockchain technology: principles and applications (2016, Post-Print)
21. Tapscott, D., Tapscott, A.: Blockchain Revolution: How the technology Behind Bitcoin is Changing Money, Business, and the World. Penguin, New York (2016)
22. Smart Contracts Alliance—In collaboration with Deloitte. Smart Contracts: 12 Use Cases for Business & Beyond (2016). http://upyun-assets.ethfans.org/uploads/doc/file/1428a9bb8 6a140598ec7cb38424de632.pdf?_upd=Smart-contracts-12-use-cases-for-business-and-bey ond.pdf
23. Tsankov, P., Dan, A., Drachsler-Cohen, D., et al.: Securify: practical security analysis of smart contracts. In: Proceedings of the 2018 ACM SIGSAC Conference on Computer and Communications Security (CCS), pp. 67–82. Association for Computing Machinery, USA (2018)
24. Wood, G.: Ethereum: a secure decentralised generalised transaction ledger. Ethereum Project Yellow Paper **151**, 1–32 (2014)
25. Atzei, N., Bartoletti, M., Cimoli, T.: A survey of attacks on ethereum smart contracts (SoK). In: Maffei, M., Ryan, M. (eds.) POST 2017. LNCS, vol. 10204, pp. 164–186. Springer, Heidelberg (2017). https://doi.org/10.1007/978-3-662-54455-6_8
26. Min, T., Cai, W.: A security case study for blockchain games. arXiv preprint arXiv:1906. 05538 (2019)
27. Arias, L., Spagnuolo, F., Giordano, F., et al.: OpenZeppeli (2016). https://github.com/Ope nZeppelin/openzeppelin-contracts
28. Nikolic, I., Kolluri, A., Sergey, I., Saxena, P., Hobor, A.: Finding ´the greedy, prodigal, and suicidal contracts at scale. arXiv preprint arXiv:1802.06038 (2018)
29. Luu, L., Chu, D.-H., Olickel, H., Saxena, P., Hobor, A.: Making smart contracts smarter. In: Proceedings of the 2016 ACM SIGSAC Conference on Computer and Communications Security, Conference Proceedings, pp. 254–269. ACM (2016)
30. Li, X., Jiang, P., Chen, T., Luo, X., Wen, Q.: A survey on the security of blockchain systems. Future Gener. Comput. Syst. **107**, 841–853 (2017)
31. Ethereum Foundation. Block validation algorithm. https://github.com/ethereum/wiki/wiki# block-validation-algorithm
32. Feist, J., Grieco, G., Groce, A.: Slither: a static analysis framework for smart contracts. In: Proceedings of the 2nd International Workshop on Emerging Trends in Software Engineering for Blockchain, WETSEB@ICSE 2019, Montreal, QC, Canada, 27 May 2019, pp. 8–15 (2019)
33. Chen, T., Li, X., Luo, X., Zhang, X.: Under-optimized smart contracts devour your money. In: 2017 IEEE 24th International Conference on Software Analysis, Evolution and Reengineering (SANER), Conference Proceedings, pp. 442–446. IEEE (2017)
34. Torres, C.F., Schütte, J., State, R.: Osiris: hunting for integer bugs in ethereum smart contracts. In: Proceedings of the 34th Annual Computer Security Applications Conference, pp. 664–676 (2018)

35. Pomonis, M., Petsios, T., Jee, K., Polychronakis, M., Keromytis, A.D.: IntFlow: improving the accuracy of arithmetic error detection using information flow tracking. In: Proceedings of the 30th Annual Computer Security Applications Conference, pp. 416–425 (2014)

36. Brent, L., et al.: Vandal: a scalable security analysis framework for smart contracts. arXiv preprint arXiv:1809.03981 (2018)

37. Albert, E., Gordillo, P., Livshits, B., Rubio, A., Sergey, I.: Ethir: a framework for high-level analysis of ethereum bytecode. In: Lahiri, S.K., Wang, C. (eds.) Automated Technology for Verification and Analysis: 16th International Symposium, ATVA 2018, Los Angeles, CA, USA, October 7-10, 2018, Proceedings, pp. 513–520. Springer, Cham (2018). https://doi.org/10.1007/978-3-030-01090-4_30

38. Tikhomirov, S., Voskresenskaya, E., Ivanitskiy, I., Takhaviev, R., Marchenko, E., Alexandrov, Y.: Smartcheck: static analysis of ethereum smart contracts. In: 1st IEEE/ACM International Workshop on Emerging Trends in Software Engineering for Blockchain, WETSEB@ICSE 2018, Gothenburg, Sweden, May 27–June 3, 2018, pp. 9–16 (2018)

39. Jiang, B., Liu, Y., Chan, W.: Contractfuzzer: fuzzing smart contracts for vulnerability detection. In: Proceedings of the 33rd ACM/IEEE International Conference on Automated Software Engineering, pp. 259–269 (2018)

40. Nikolic, I., Kolluri, A., Sergey, I., Saxena, P., Hobor, A.: Finding the greedy, prodigal, and suicidal contracts at scale. In: Proceedings of the 34th Annual Computer Security Applications Conference, ACSAC 2018, San Juan, PR, USA, 03–07 December 2018, pp. 653–663 (2018)

41. Gao, J., Liu, H., Liu, C., et al.: Easyflow: keep ethereum away from overflow. In: Proceedings of the 41st International Conference on Software Engineering: Companion Proceedings, pp. 23–26. IEEE Press (2019)

42. Mavridou, A., Laszka, A.: Tool demonstration: fSolidM for designing secure ethereum smart contracts. In: Bauer, L., Küsters, R. (eds.) Principles of Security and Trust, pp. 270–277. Springer, Cham (2018). https://doi.org/10.1007/978-3-319-89722-6_11

43. Breidenbach, L., Daian, P., Er, F., Juels, A.: Enter the hydra: towards principled bug bounties and exploit-resistant smart contracts. In: The Initiative for Cryptocurrencies and Contracts (IC3), vol. 2017 (2017)

44. Bhargavan, K., et al.: Formal verification of smart contracts: short paper. In: Proceedings of the 2016 ACM Workshop on Programming Languages and Analysis for Security, pp. 91–96 (2016)

45. Kosba, A., Miller, A., Shi, E., Wen, Z., Papamanthou, C.: Hawk: the blockchain model of cryptography and privacy-preserving smart contracts. In: 2016 IEEE Symposium on Security and Privacy (SP), pp. 839–858 (2016)

46. Cerezo Sánchez, D.: Raziel: private and verifiable smart contracts on blockchains. IACR Cryptol. ePrint Arch, pp. 1–56 (2017)

47. Zhang, F., Cecchetti, E., Croman, K., Juels, A., Shi, E.: Town crier: an authenticated data feed for smart contracts. In: Proceedings of the 2016 ACM SIGSAC Conference on Computer and Communications Security, pp. 270–282 (2016)

48. Kalra, S., Goel, S., Dhawan, M., Sharma, S.: ZEUS: analyzing safety of smart contracts. In: 25th Annual Network and Distributed System Security Symposium, NDSS 2018, San Diego, California, USA, 18–21 February 2018

49. Hildenbrandt, E., et al.: KEVM: a complete formal semantics of the ethereum virtual machine. In: 2018 IEEE 31st Computer Security Foundations Symposium (CSF), pp. 204–217 (2018)

50. Ellul, J., Pace, G.J.: Runtime verification of ethereum smart contracts. In: 2018 14th European Dependable Computing Conference (EDCC), pp. 158–163 (2018)

51. Sinnema, R., Wilde, E.: Extensible access control markup language (XACML) XML media type, Internet Eng. Task Force (IETF), pp. 1–8 ((2013))

52. Lattner, C., Adve, V.: LLVM: a compilation framework for lifelong program analysis & transformation. In: International Symposium on Code Generation and Optimization, CGO 2004, pp. 75–86. IEEE (2004)
53. Gurfinkel, A., Kahsai, T., Komuravelli, A., Navas, J.: The seahorn verification framework. In: Kroening, D., Păsăreanu, C.S. (eds.) Computer Aided Verification: 27th International Conference, CAV 2015, San Francisco, CA, USA, July 18-24, 2015, Proceedings, Part I, pp. 343–361. Springer, Cham (2015). https://doi.org/10.1007/978-3-319-21690-4_20

Detection of False Data Injection Attacks in Smart Grid Based on Machine Learning

Li Xu, Xiaoyi Li, and Yanbin Sun$^{(\boxtimes)}$

Guangzhou University, Guangzhou, China
sunyanbin@gzhu.edu.cn

Abstract. The false injection attack on the internal state estimation module of the smart grid energy management system enables the attackers to forge false power, voltage and topology information, which make the false data successfully bypass the residual check module. And they can be upload it to the control center to affect the control decision-making and endanger the normal operation of the power system. Firstly, this paper introduces the principle, attack conditions and impact of false injection attack, and introduces in detail an AC model which is more widely used than DC model. The AC model can generate false data injection attacks against different power system topologies. On this basis, in order to detect the false data injection attack with high robustness and effectively, we propose an attack detection method based on machine learning. The random forest classifier in the integrated learning algorithm is used to detect and classify the false data injection attack, and the state information of the attacked power system is identified by integrating multiple decision trees. A large number of experiments show that the method has good recognition performance in different IEEE node systems.

Keywords: Smart grid · False data injection attack · AC attack model · Attack detection · Random forest classifier

1 Introduction

In recent years, with the continuous integration and development of computer technology and control system, industrial control system is gradually moving towards networking. As one of the typical industrial control systems, the power system has gradually transformed from the traditional physical grid to the smart grid through the continuous integration of a variety of advanced communication technologies [1]. As a new type of cyber physical system, smart grid can achieve efficient and intelligent management and of the power grid, which effectively ensure social stability and promote the rapid and healthy development of the national economy. At the same time, a large number of applications of network technology in the power system is facing with a variety of network attacks, such as data eavesdropping, denial of service attacks and false data injection attacks.

The false data injection attack was first proposed by reference [2]. This attack mainly makes use of the loophole that the state estimation module in the power grid only uses

© Springer Nature Switzerland AG 2021
X. Sun et al. (Eds.): ICAIS 2021, CCIS 1424, pp. 191–203, 2021.
https://doi.org/10.1007/978-3-030-78621-2_15

the residual check mechanism for the important power data uploaded to the control center. By injecting false data into the measured data, the attackers can successfully upload it to the control system. The false data can bypass the bad data detection module, thus interfer with or even destroy the normal operation of the control system. Because the false data injection attack has high concealment and strong relevance, which can cause great damage to the power system. It has aroused widespread concern in academic circles. At present, the research on constructing false data injection attack can be divided into two categories:

The attackers mastered the topology of power system and all kinds of important power data to construct the false data injection attack.

The attackers don't know the power grid topology in advance or can't obtain the important parameters, which they can only construct the attack according to the measurement matrix.

False data injection attack has a certain concealment, and has brought great harm to the safe and efficient operation of the power grid. So how to accurately identify the attack has become the focus of many scholars. In reference [3], considering the system state estimation module, an Euclidean algorithm is proposed to design the detection threshold of residual check in order to achieve the purpose of attack detection. Reference [4] proposes a bilateral hypothesis test attack, which assumes that the measured data collected by the control center follow the Gaussian distribution. It can help to detect and eliminate the measured values. In reference [5], a false data injection attack detection mechanism is designed with integrates multiple extreme learning institutions. These detection mechanisms for false data injection attacks can effectively detect false data in the power system, so as to enhance the anti-jamming ability of the power system. However, due to the noise interference of the system, only the construction of DC attack model can also brings great limitations to the above attack detection mechanism.

2 Related Work

As soon as false data injection attack is proposed, it has aroused much attention by scholars. Among them, the research around FDIA can be roughly divided into attack construction and defense construction. Whether the construction of FDIA is successful or not depends on the power grid information mastered by the attackers. References [6] and [7] introduce that the attacker has enough power grid topology information and electrical data to construct attack vectors. Literature [8] assumes that the attacker only knows part of the power grid parameters and build the attack vector. Because the important electrical parameters and topology information are strictly encrypted in the actual power grid. It is difficult for attackers to obtain them. Therefore, the reference [9] proposes a method to infer the power network topology parameters only from the observable measurement information and construct the FDIA. In order to improve the effectiveness of power information obtained from measurement matrix, a subspace transformation method is proposed to construct attack vector in references [10] and [11]. And an attack construction strategy based on robust principal component analysis is proposed in reference [12]. As a result, the concealment of the attack is significantly enhanced, and the feasibility of the attack is also greatly improved.

At present, the false data injection attack is one of the typical malicious attacks against the smart grid. The attacker injects false data into the important nodes of the power grid, and the uploaded data containing malicious information to the control center will cause some adverse effect. Therefore, the research on the detection and defense of FDIA is of great significance. Reference [13] proposes to select the important data of the power system, protect the key measurement data and then test its performance on the DC model. In reference [14], the selection of key measurement data in power system is regarded as a set of complex linear combinatorial problems. And a fast greedy algorithm is used to solve them. In reference [15], it is proposed that node voltage stability index and static reactive power compensation signal are used as parameters to define the importance of nodes, and clustering algorithm is used to locate high-risk and vulnerable nodes. In reference [16], the power load reduction is taken as the reporting function, and a game model is established for attackers and defenders.

Many researchers also add the principle of consistency test to the detection of FDIA which can improve the detection accuracy. In reference [17], an auto regressive model is proposed to establish a short-term state prediction model of power system. And the measurement data and prediction data are tested uniformly to improve the detection accuracy. Gu et al. [18] proposed real-time tracking of measurement data, and established a KLD model to find abnormal nodes. Ashok et al. [19] proposed a set of FDIA detection framework using synchronous phasor detection device, load forecasting and generation planning components. Aiming at the attack detection methods introduced above, this paper also proposes a FDIA detection model based on machine learning. At the same time, we have also learned from some methods of data poisoning to carry out false data injection attacks on the power grid [20].

3   Proposal AC Attack Model

3.1   State Estimation

In the power system, the SCADA system is responsible for collecting information from the power grid, and uploading the collected data to the energy management system to evaluate and analyze the security of equipment or line failures in the power system. Power system state estimation is the key point to ensure the real-time data quality of EMS system in smart grid. The main functions of state estimation include improving the accuracy of measurement data, calculating other important power data according to the data uploaded by SCADA system, and improving the reliability of data. It is the basis for EMS system to carry out power network load forecasting, optimal power flow analysis and transient stability analysis. We also found some inspiration from honeypot attacks. At the same time, we have also learned from the structure of some cloud system platforms (Fig. 1).

The SCADA system collects the measured values of the bus, including the active power injected by the bus, the reactive power injected by the bus and the active power and reactive power injected by the branch. Suppose that in a power system with N buses, m measurements are represented as $z = [z_1, z_2, \cdots, z_m]$. The state variable is generally taken as the complex voltage of the bus (including voltage amplitude and phase angle).

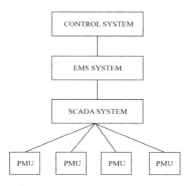

Fig. 1. Power data upload process

If the reference node is removed, there are $(2N - 1)$ state variables. The relationship between measurements and state variables can be expressed as follows:

$$z = h(x) + e \tag{1}$$

Where, h (x) represents the nonlinear relationship between the measured value and the state variable, $e = [e_1, e_2, \cdots e_m]^T$ is expressed as a measurement error that obeys a Gaussian distribution.

Assuming that the amplitude of all bus voltages in the power system is 1 and the line loss is ignored, there is no reactive power in the measurement. So there is a linear relationship between the measured value and the state variable, and the DC power flow equation is obtained as follows:

$$z = Hx + e \tag{2}$$

Where H represents the measurement Jacobian matrix, z represents the measurement value, x represents the state variable, and e represents the measurement error. Since the state variable can not be measured directly by the measuring instrument, its estimated value needs to be calculated by weighted least square method:

$$\hat{x} = (H^T W H)^{-1} H^T W z \tag{3}$$

3.2 Bad Data Detection Mechanism

The SCADA system uploads the collected measurements to the state estimation module for calculation and processing, and needs to check the residual error of the state estimation results, so as to eliminate the bad data or malicious data contained in the measurement matrix. At present, most power systems use residual check mechanism to detect bad data, and the residual expression is as follows:

$$r = z - H(\hat{x}) \tag{4}$$

Where r represents the difference between the real measured value and the estimated measured value calculated based on the estimated value of the state estimation, and the detection mechanism for detecting whether the measurement matrix contains bad data is:

$$\begin{cases} \|r\| \leq \tau, \ SE = True \\ \|r\| > \tau, \ SE = False \end{cases} \tag{5}$$

When the residual r is less than or equal to the threshold τ set by the system, it means that there is no bad data in the measurement matrix; when the residual r is greater than the threshold, it means that the measurement matrix z contains bad data and needs to be eliminated.

The false data injection attack based on DC attack model makes use of the loopholes in residual check, so that the constructed false data can successfully bypass the residual check module and achieve the purpose of attack. Suppose the attacker constructed a set of attack vectors $a = [a_1, a_2, \cdots a_m]^T$ and superimposed them on the original measurements to get the measurement matrix $z_{bad} = z + a$ with malicious data. At this time, the state variable obtained after state estimation is $x_{bad} = x + c$. c represents the estimation error caused by the false data injection measurement matrix. Therefore, the residual expression after the injection attack is:

$$\|r\| = \|z_{bad} - Hx_{bad}\| = \|z + a - H(\hat{x} + c)\| = \|z - H\hat{x} + a - Hc\| \tag{6}$$

When $a = Hc$, the $\|r\| = \|z_{bad} - Hx_{bad}\| = \|z - H\hat{x}\|$ is established, which means that the bad data detection mechanism based on residual check can not detect the malicious attack data injected into the measurement matrix, and the attacker can modify the measurements and state variables arbitrarily, so as to destroy the normal operation of the power system (Fig. 2).

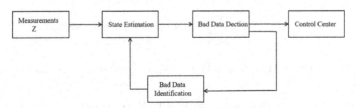

Fig. 2. State estimation module

3.3 FDIA AC Model

In the realistic power system operation, the resistance and reactance between the lines can not be easily ignored. So the measurement and state variables can not be simply assumed a linear relationship. In fact, the relationship between measurements and state variables is a nonlinear relationship determined by the line injected active power, reactive power, line admittance and so on. Therefore, the construction of AC FDIA model is more universal for the study of false data injection attacks.

The nonlinear difference relationship between the measurement matrix and the state variable matrix can be used to construct an AC model combined with the historical data of the power system and the snapshot of the current measuring instrument:

$$a = h(x + c) - h(x) \tag{7}$$

Where an and x represent the attack vector and the actual state variable respectively, and c represents any non-zero column vector, which $h(\cdot)$ represents the nonlinear relationship between the measurement and the state variable.

$$P_i = \sum_{j \in \Omega_B} V_i V_j \left(G_{ij} \cos \theta_{ij} + B_{ij} \sin \theta_{ij} \right) \tag{8}$$

$$Q_i = \sum_{j \in \Omega_B} V_i V_j \left(G_{ij} \sin \theta_{ij} - B_{ij} \cos \theta_{ij} \right) \tag{9}$$

$$P_{ij} = -(V_i)^2 G_{ij} + V_i V_j \left(G_{ij} \cos \theta_{ij} + B_{ij} \sin \theta_{ij} \right) \tag{10}$$

$$Q_{ij} = (V_i)^2 B_{ij} + V_i V_j \left(G_{ij} \sin \theta_{ij} - B_{ij} \cos \theta_{ij} \right) \tag{11}$$

Where P_i and Q_i represent the injected active power and reactive power of the I bus, Ω_B represents the set of all buses, V_i and V_j represent the voltage amplitudes of the i bus and j bus, G_{ij} and B_{ij} represent the real and imaginary parts of the system admittance matrix.

Objective: $\min \| z_a - h(x_a) \|_0$

$$P_i + \Delta P_{ia} = V_{ia} \sum_{j \in \Omega_B} V_{ja} \times \left(G_{ij} \cos \theta_{ija} + B_{ij} \sin \theta_{ija} \right) \tag{12}$$

$$Q_i + \Delta Q_{ia} = V_{ia} \sum_{j \in \Omega_B} V_{ja} \times \left(G_{ij} \sin \theta_{ija} - B_{ij} \cos \theta_{ija} \right) \tag{13}$$

$$P_{ij} + \Delta P_{ija} = (g_{sh,i} + g_{ij})(V_{ia})^2 - V_{ia} V_{ja} \left(g_{ij} \cos \theta_{ija} + b_{ij} \sin \theta_{ija} \right) \tag{14}$$

$$Q_{ij} + \Delta Q_{ija} = -(b_{sh,i} + b_{ij})(V_{ia})^2 - V_{ia} V_{ja} \left(g_{ij} \sin \theta_{ija} - b_{ij} \cos \theta_{ija} \right) \tag{15}$$

$$V_i + \Delta V_{ia} = V_{ia}, \theta_i + \Delta \theta_{ia} = \theta_{ia} \tag{16}$$

$$V_i^{\min} \leq V_{ia} \leq V_i^{\max} \tag{17}$$

$$P_{GK}^{\min} \leq P_k + \Delta P_{ka} \leq P_{GK}^{\max} \tag{18}$$

$$Q_{GK}^{\min} \leq Q_k + \Delta Q_{ka} \leq Q_{GK}^{\max} \tag{19}$$

Where z_a represents the measured value after the attack vector is superimposed, x_a represents the state variable after the attack, P_i and Q_i represent the injected active power and reactive power of the line I, ΔP_{ia} and ΔQ_{ia} represent the active power increment and reactive power increment caused by the attack vector, P_{ij} and Q_{ij} represent the active and reactive power increments of the ij branch, and ΔP_{ija} and ΔQ_{ija} represent the active and reactive power increments. V_i and θ_i represent the voltage amplitude and phase angle of line I, P_{GK} and Q_{GK} represent the active and reactive power output of the generator, G_{ij} and B_{ij} represent the real and imaginary parts of the bus admittance matrix, and $g_{sh,i}$ and $b_{sh,i}$ represent the real and imaginary parts of the branch admittance matrix. By using the above nonlinear conditions, the minimum 0 norm value of $(z_a - h(x_a))$ is solved, and the optimal attack vector an is found.

4   Detection of False Data Injection Attacks

4.1   Random Forest Algorithm for Ensemble Learning

In the supervised learning algorithm as machine learning, integrated learning mainly combines several weak supervised models to form a strong supervised model to learn the data, so as to reduce variance, deviation or improve prediction. The underlying idea of ensemble learning is that even if one weak supervision model gets the wrong prediction, other weak supervision models can correct the error. We also refer to the characteristics of some neural networks, but finally choose a decision tree as the recognition algorithm.

The attack detection mechanism also draws on offensive and defensive game theory. There are three methods of integrated learning: Bagging, Boosting and Stacking. As one of the typical applications of bagging method, random forest is an integrated learning model composed of multiple decision trees, which can be used for regression or classification. When random forest is used for classification problems, multiple classification models are generated to learn and predict the samples, and finally these prediction results are combined to generate the final prediction results. The performance of random forest is better than the single decision tree, because its result is determined by the voting of multiple decision trees, and the generalization performance of the model is better (Fig. 3).

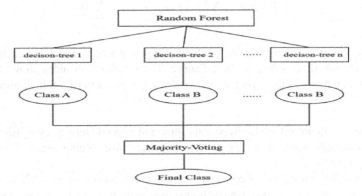

Fig. 3. Random forest structure

4.2 Principle of FDIA Detection

From the perspective of machine learning, detection of false data injection attacks can be regarded as a two-classification problem. We should select suitable classifier to detect classify and filter state variables containing false data for achieving detection purpose. The adaptive alarm classifier reduces the false alarm rate and also gives this article some inspiration (Fig. 4).

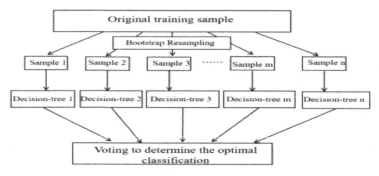

Fig. 4. FDIA detection model

The principle of detecting false data injection attacks can be divided into four steps:

1. Random sampling: Suppose that there are altogether 3 samples collected from the node training dataset. Samples are randomly sampled from this dataset by using Boostrap (return) method. Each sample is different. These samples constitute training data sets of decision tree.
2. Feature selection: Suppose each sample has K characters in this sample, and calculates each feature using Gini index, thus judging the important characteristic that determines the classification result.

$$Gini(p) = \sum_{k=1}^{K} p_k(1 - p_k) = 1 - \sum_{k=1}^{K} p_k^2 \tag{20}$$

Among them, p_k represents sample feature types, which indicate that samples are correctly classified according to the k feature. The smaller Gini index shows that the smaller probability of classifying samples selected in collections is, the higher purity samples are.

3. Generating random forests: Repeat the first and second steps to establish M tree, which should ensure complete growth without excessive pruning resulting in random forest formation.
4. Classification prediction: According to prediction results of every decision tree in random forest, voting mechanism is that few suits from majority (assuming that more than half decision tree considers node as contaminated node) and determine its contamination and the final prediction category of sample data.

4.3   Detection Process for FDIA

The proposed method can be divided into three steps: firstly establishing an AC attack model and generating attack test samples for different IEEE power systems. secondly collecting test samples from different IEEE nodes systems and selecting important node parameters from each node system test sample. Thirdly node parameters are used as sample training sets and random forest algorithms are used to classify them thus detecting contaminated nodes exposed to false data injection. The followings are details about each step:

Based on the nonlinear relationship between measurement matrix Z and state variable X in power system, attack vectors are solved in power system. Then we add the constructed attack vectors into some important nodes randomly selected and generate test samples.

$$a = h(x + c) - h(x) \tag{21}$$

$$\min \|z_a - h(x_a)\|_0 \tag{22}$$

1. After generating test samples by using the attack model, test samples of each IEEE node system are arranged into sample data sets which contain voltage amplitude phase angle input active power and reactive power input. According to whether nodes inject false data distinguish normal nodes and abnormal nodes (i.e. polluted nodes) according to whether nodes inject false data.
2. Aiming at false data injection attack detection adopting supervised learning method, this paper divides sample training sets generated by test samples of each node system. And label normal nodes 0 and anomaly nodes 1. Secondly, random forest algorithm is used to divide and train sample training sets, thus detecting abnormal nodes.

5   Experimental Analysis

Simulation experiments can be divided into two parts: firstly, attack vectors are designed according to established AC attack model, and false data injection attacks are carried out under power information of system, which makes measurement value information of nodes in power system is obtained. Secondly, we sort out state variables information generated by different nodes into sample training sets and classify samples by random forest algorithm. The algorithm can identify the normal nodes and abnormal nodes, which means achieving the attack detection purposes.

According to Tian et al. using Matpower and python simulation system, we convert IEEE 14 node system, IEEE 57 node system and IEEE 118 node system configuration files into text files on Matpower, then utilize simulation system to obtain power data of each node system (Figs. 5 and 6).

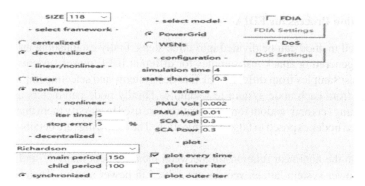

Fig. 5. Attack model GUI

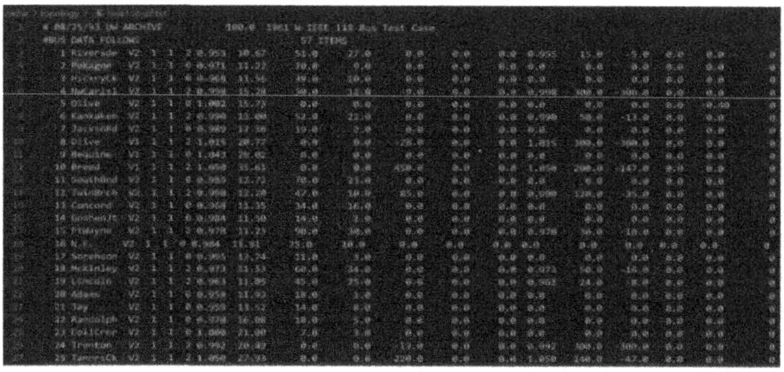

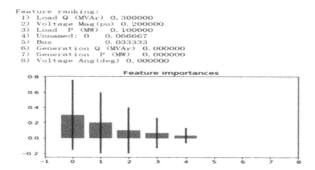

Fig. 6. IEEE 118 node system parameters

After obtaining node parameters of each IEEE node system after attacking simulation system. We use the random forest algorithm to identify IEEE 14 node system data, IEEE 57 node system data and IEEE 118 node system data, and then detect abnormal node (Figs. 7 and 8).

Feature ranking:
1) Load Q (MVAr)   0.300000
2) Voltage Mag(pu) 0.200000
3) Load   P (MW)   0.100000
4) Unnamed: 0   0.066667
5) Bus   0.033333
6) Generation Q (MVAr) 0.000000
7) Generation P (MW) 0.000000
8) Voltage Ang(deg)   0.000000

Fig. 7. IEEE 118 nodes feature importance

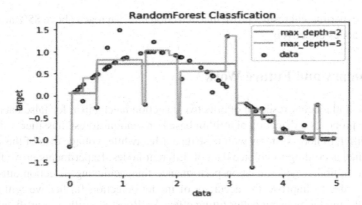

Fig. 8. Stochastic Forest Classification model tuning

Taking IEEE 118 node system as example, random forest algorithm is used to select node-state data such as voltage amplitude, voltage phase angle, node input active power and reactive power etc. Then supervised learning is used to train random forest model (Figs. 9 and 10).

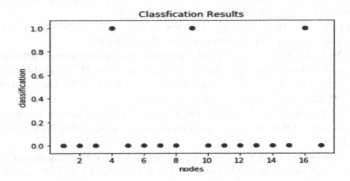

Fig. 9. Classification result of IEEE 118 node system

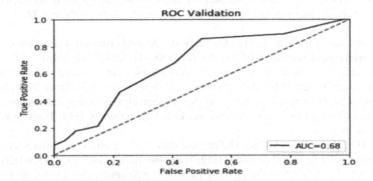

Fig. 10. IEEE 118 node Prediction ROC Curve

Many experimental results prove that detection rate can reach above 85% and detect abnormal nodes effectively.

6 Summary and Future Work

In order to find a better research of effective detection mechanism for false data attack, this paper proposes a detection algorithm based on random forest classifier, which can classify different node systems with false data. Meanwhile, voltage data of these nodes are classified according to voltage data of different nodes. Experiments prove that this model shows higher generalization performance thus achieving detection attack purposes. In order to improve the accuracy of model detection further we will plan to optimize the model by using better fitting effect XGBoost algorithm or artificial neural network.

References

1. Tian, J.W., Wang, B.H.: TFalse data injection attacks based on robust principal component analysis in smart grid. J. Comput. Appl. 1943–2947 (2017)
2. Weller, L.Y.N.P., Re. M.K., et al.: On the stability of cyber-physical systems under false data injection attacks. Acta Automatica Sinica 196–205 (2019)
3. Wang, Q., Tai, W., Tang, Y., et al.: A review on false data injection attack toward cyber physical power system. Acta Automatica Sinica 72–83 (2019)
4. Tong, X.Y., Wang, X.R.: Inferrence and countermeasure presuppostion of network attack in incdient on Ukrainian Power grid. Autom. Electr. Power Syst. **40**(7), 144–148 (2016)
5. Liu, Y., Peng, Q.N.: False data injection attacks against state estimation in electric power grids. ACM Trans. Inf. Syst. Secur. **14**(1), 1–34 (2011)
6. Ahn, C.H., Kim, B., Lim, Y., Lee, B., Oh, K.: Distributed coordination for optimal energy generation and distribution in cyber-physical energy networks. IEEE Trans. Cybern. **48**(3), 941–954 (2018)
7. Hong, Y., Liu, W.M., Wang, L.: Privacy preserving smart meter streaming against information leakage of appliance status. IEEE Trans. Inf. Forensics Secur. **12**(9), 2227–2241 (2017)
8. Wu, G., Sun, J., Chen, J.: optimal data injection attacks in cyber-physical systems. IEEE Trans. Cybern. **48**(12), 3302–3312 (2018)
9. An, H.L., Yang, G.: Decentralized adaptive fuzzy secure control for nonlinear uncertain interconnected systems against intermittent DoS attacks. IEEE Trans. Cybern. **49**(3), 827–838 (2019)
10. Mousavinejad, X.E., Yang, F., Han, Q., Vlacic, L.: A novel cyber attack detection method in networked control systems. IEEE Trans. Cybern. **48**(11), 3254–3264 (2018)
11. Sedjelmaci, J.H., Senouci, S.M., Ansari, N.: A hierarchical detection and response system to enhance security against lethal cyber-attacks in UAV networks. IEEE Trans. Syst. (2018)
12. Sedjelmaci, E.H., Senouci, S.M., Ansari, N.: A hierarchical detection and response system to enhance security against lethal cyber-attacks in UAV networks. IEEE Trans. Syst. **48**(9), 1594–1606 (2018)
13. Yu, J.J.Q., Hou, Y., Li, V.O.K.: Online false data injection attack detection with wavelet transform and deep neural networks. IEEE Trans. Ind. Inform. **14**(7), 3271–3280 (2018)
14. Lin, J.Y., Abur, A.: Highly efficient implementation for parameter error identification method exploiting sparsity. IEEE Trans. Power Syst. **32**(1), 734–742 (2017)

15. Wu, T., Chung, C.Y., Kamwa, I.: A fast state estimator for systems including limited number of PMUs. IEEE Trans. Power Syst. **32**(6), 4329–4339 (2017)
16. Singh, S.K., Khanna, K., Bose, R., Panigrahi, B.K., Joshi, A.: Joint-transformation-based detection of false data injection attacks in smart grid. IEEE Trans. Ind. Inform. **14**(1), 89–97 (2018)
17. Li, Z., Shahidehpour, M., Aminifar, F.: Cybersecurity in distributed power systems. In: Proceedings of the IEEE, vol. 105, no. 7, pp. 1367–1388 (2017)
18. Wang, J., Yang, G.: Data-driven methods for stealthy attacks on TCP/IP-based networked control systems equipped with attack detectors. IEEE Trans. Cybern. **49**(8), 3020–3031 (2019)
19. Kurt, M.N., Yılmaz, Y., Wang, X.: Real-time detection of hybrid and stealthy cyber-attacks in smart grid. IEEE Trans. Inf. Forensics Secur. **14**(2), 498–513 (2019)
20. Li, M., Sun, Y., Lu, H., Maharjan, S., Tian, Z.: Deep reinforcement learning for partially observable data poisoning attack in crowdsensing systems. IEEE Internet Things J. **7**(7), 6266–6278 (2020)

An Adversarial Examples Defense Method Based on Image Low-Frequency Information

ZiAn Song[1,2] and ZhengJie Deng[1,2(✉)]

[1] Hainan Normal University, Haikou 571158, China
[2] Guangxi Key Laboratory of Image and Graphic Intelligent Processing, Guilin 541004, China

Abstract. Convolutional neural networks have been applied in image recognition widely, and acquired well-known results. However, the discovery of adversarial examples in recent years has attracted many researcher's attention on the safety and reliability of convolutional neural networks. Adversarial examples are small perturbations added only to the clean image data, which could cause the trained model makes wrong identifications, while people could still recognize. In this paper, we propose a new convolutional neural network to defense the adversarial examples. It breaks into two branches after inputting an image. One branch likes a normal image recognition model, while another branch distills the low-frequency information of the image firstly, and then uses the low-frequency image to train. The two branches combine to make the output of the model. The presented model uses the image's low-frequency information, through which people often recognizes an object. The experiments show that the presented model suppresses the success rate of the attack in the face of the adversarial examples, and improves the model's recognition success rate, comparing to some other methods.

Keywords: Adversarial examples · Defense method · Image low-frequency information

1 Introduction

Deep neural networks are now widely used in life, and the application of convolutional neural networks in the direction of computer vision is considered one of the most successful applications of neural networks. Convolutional neural networks are currently used in face recognition, target detection, and automated driving; however, these areas have high requirements for the safety and robustness of the model. After the discovery of adversarial examples where only adding small perturbations can make the model wrong, researchers realized that enhancing the robustness of deep neural network models based on convolutional neural networks and increasing their prediction accuracy in the face of adversarial examples is important for the safety of artificial intelligence. This paper is also focused on improving the robustness of the model.

Current approaches to defending against examples fall into three main directions:

(1) The training part: adjust the model weights by modifying or adding training examples to the data set to reduce the influence of perturbation in the prediction process,

X. Sun et al. (Eds.): ICAIS 2021, CCIS 1424, pp. 204–213, 2021.
https://doi.org/10.1007/978-3-030-78621-2_16

in order to improve the robustness of the model. For example, adding adversarial examples to the training set.

(2) The model part: By modifying the neural network model to make the extracted features change or affect the weights of the extracted features, the influence of perturbation on the prediction results can be reduced, in order to improve the robustness of the model.

(3) Data part: data processing is used to enhance the part of the data that can improve the robustness of the model by highlighting the importance of this part of the data in the prediction of the model.

Methods 1 and 2 above both hope that the model will reduce the weights of the pixels that may be perturbed during prediction, so that the added perturbations have as small an impact as possible on the prediction results, thus improving the model robustness. Method 3 is to reduce or filter out as many perturbations as possible through data preprocessing before prediction, to complete the correct prediction without affecting the model weights.

Inspired by the above methods, the method mentioned in this paper will first extract the low-frequency information from the image information by image compression, then use the prediction of the clean image by the model and the prediction of the extracted low-frequency information by the model trained on the low-frequency information, and combine the prediction results of both to obtain the final prediction results. This method adds a new model to make predictions on low-frequency information without changing the parameters of the original model, which is equivalent to increasing the weight of the low-frequency information in the prediction results and obtaining better results.

2 Related Work

With the breakthroughs in computer vision have come some new security challenges [1]. Adversarial example, first discovered by Szegedy et al. [2], interfere with the clean example by adding slight perturbations to the dataset, causing the deep neural net to give erroneous output with high confidence. In many cases, humans do not perceive the difference between the clean example and the adversarial example, but the neural network makes false predictions with great variability.

Following this, many methods for generating adversarial examples have been proposed, such as FGSM (Fast Gradient Sign Method) [3], DeepFool [4], PGD (Project Gradient Descent) [5].

Goodfellow et al. [3] proposed to train a mixed team model with adversarial examples and clean examples, which greatly improves the generalization ability of the model, allowing the model to obtain better robustness. Papernot et al. [6] experimented with defensive distillation, replacing the dataset labels with the output of the teacher network, and using this to train a new network, resulting in an improvement in model robustness.

Guo et al. [7] experimentally verified that denoising and randomness methods such as JPEG compression and total variation minimization have excellent performance on adversarial example defense. After that, Xie et al. [8] proposed randomly varying the image size and filling, and experimentally verified the importance of randomness.

GridMask [9] wants to enhance the data by pre-processing for the purpose of data augmentation by data pre-processing, computationally generating multiple mask blocks for data augmentation. This kind of data augmentation scheme helps to improve the generalization ability of the model, but it does not achieve the purpose of eliminating additional interference. Goodman et al. [10] use a method called extbf{Attention and Adversarial Logit Pairing (AT+ALP)} to defend against adversarial attacks and improve the robustness of the model.

3   Image Low-Frequency Information Extraction

Adversarial example is defined as the addition of a perturbation to an image that cannot be perceived by humans or that can be perceived by humans but does not affect recognition. For human vision, image information is two-dimensional information, and humans can recognize the general shape when they see it, without the need to carefully distinguish the specific numerical information in the image. For this reason, humans are much less sensitive to high-frequency information than low-frequency information in images. For a model, the dimensionality of an image is determined by the number of pixels, and each pixel is a dimensional piece of information, which also makes it sensitive to high-frequency information. If only the low-frequency information in the image is recognized, the recognition accuracy of the model will be greatly reduced.

Compression is a commonly used method to reduce the effects of perturbations, in which JPEG compression scheme is proven to be an effective way to reduce the image high-frequency signal. The method proposed in this paper also uses compression, but there and JPEG compression scheme is not the same. The method used in this paper is the clean image of four pixels compressed into one pixel, that is, the image will be compressed to a quarter of the size of the clean image. After that, the pixels of the compressed image will be filled to the size of the clean image according to the ratio of one to four. This method of compressing the image and the clean image there are perceptible differences, but can retain a greater degree of low-frequency information in the clean image, including contours and shapes.

Two implementations of the compression method exist, and both methods have some filtering ability against perturbations in the example. The two implementations include the fixed pixel position approach and the average compression approach.

3.1   Compression Method for Fixed Pixel Positions

The method selects the value of a pixel at a fixed position in the 4 pixels immediately next to each other (shape 2·2) as the compressed value, which will be filled to the corresponding positions of these 4 pixels when filling later. As shown in Fig. 1.

In some special cases, the perturbations in these 4 pixels will be filtered out or their effect on the results reduced:

(1)   if the selected pixel does not have an added perturbation or the added perturbation is cropped because it exceeds the range 0 to 255, and the added perturbation of the remaining three pixels will be filtered at this time.

(2) If the selected pixel has perturbations added, and the unselected pixel is not perturbed or the direction of the added perturbation is inconsistent. It is possible for the selected pixel to fill the remaining pixel positions without filtering the perturbation so that the loss decreases to reduce the effect of the perturbation.

For the low-frequency information image generated using this method, it is noted as X_1to4 when a distinction is needed.

3.2 Average Compression Method

This method takes the average of the pixel values as the compressed value in the 4 pixels immediately next to each other (shape 2·2), like going through an average pooling layer of shape 2-2. On subsequent fills, this value is filled to the position corresponding to these 4 pixels. As shown in Fig. 1.

This approach also makes the loss due to perturbations less severe under certain circumstances, allowing for some reduction in losses in predicting the adversarial example:

(1) If the added perturbations on the four pixels are in different directions, they will all be reduced when averaged, and in some more special cases the added perturbations may even be restored.

For the expected information image generated using this method, it is noted as X_4av4 when a distinction is needed.

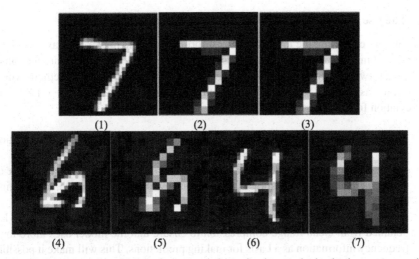

Fig. 1. (1) clean examples; (2) Low-frequency information image obtained using a compression method with fixed pixel positions; (3) Low-frequency information image obtained using average compression. (4) Adversarial examples at $\varepsilon = 0.1$; (2) Low-frequency information image obtained using a compression method with fixed pixel positions; (3) Adversarial examples at $\varepsilon = 0.1$; (4) Low-frequency information image obtained using average compression.

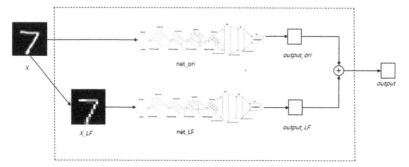

Fig. 2. Flow of model recognition using low-frequency information image aids.

4   Use of Low-Frequency Information

The method used in this paper is intended to use the low-frequency information extracted by the methods mentioned above to aid in model prediction. Since the compressed images are compressed in order to substantially retain the low-frequency information, this also leads to a substantial loss of their high-frequency information. If only the compressed images are used for training and prediction, the prediction accuracy of the model for clean images will be compromised. This defeats the purpose of this paper, which is to make the model more robust without affecting the model accuracy. So, we have made special settings.

4.1   The Use of Low-Frequency Information in Training

Since we are extracting the low-frequency information of the image, we have filled the compressed image so that the dimensions of the shape of the two images are the same. So I set up two identical convolutional neural network models in this method, which are denoted as net_ori ("ori" is an abbreviation for "original") and net_LF ("LF" is an abbreviation for Low-frequency.).

(1)   The clean image X is first compressed to generate the low-frequency information image X_LF.
(2)   During training, net_ori uses a clean image X to ensure that the model makes use of the high-frequency information in it when faced with a clean example, maintaining the model's accuracy in the final prediction.
(3)   At the same time, net_LF is trained using low-frequency information images X_LF obtained from clean image compression to ensure that the model uses more low-frequency information as a basis for making predictions. This will make it possible to increase the accuracy of the model's predictions when defending against attacks against the example.

4.2   The Use of Low-Frequency Information in the Defense Adversarial Attacks

The two models, trained with clean images, will work simultaneously in prediction. As shown in Fig. 2.

(1) Adversarial example X' will initially undergo an image compression operation to generate a low-frequency information image X'_LF of the Adversarial example.

(2) The identification of the adversarial example X' using a model net_ori trained on clean image X' to obtain the identification result output_ori. ensure that the high frequency information in the image still has an impact on the final prediction, but this will preserve the effect of the perturbation on the result, which also makes the result output_ori is not highly plausible.

(3) Identify the low-frequency information image X'_LF obtained by compression of the adversarial example using the model net_LF trained on the low-frequency information image X_LF obtained by clean image compression, and obtain the identification result output_LF. For the reasons I mentioned in Part 3, X'_LF filters out some of the perturbations and reduces some of the perturbations compared to X'. It filters out most of the high-frequency information in X' and retains the low-frequency information, which makes the result output_LF more reliable than output_ori.

(4) The net_ori is more sensitive to high frequency information and less affected by perturbations in clean examples and less perturbed adversarial examples, so output_ori is more reliable in this case. In the case of high perturbations in the adversarial example, net_LF is not sensitive to high-frequency perturbations and is less affected by them, and some of them are filtered out in the compression, so output_LF is more reliable. The result is better than output_LF when the image is clean or the perturbation is low, and better than output_ori when the perturbation is high, combining the advantages of both results.

5 Implementation of the Method

5.1 Data Sets

The experiments in this paper will use the MNIST dataset as the training and attack dataset. The MNIST dataset contains 60,000 examples for training and 10,000 examples for testing. The numbers have been size-standardized and are in the center of the image, which is a fixed size (28*28 pixels) and has a value of 0 to 1.

5.2 Network Model

In this paper we will use a classical convolutional neural network, LeNet, which in its early days achieved the most advanced results in handwriting recognition at the time.

The name comes from Yann LeCun, the first author of the LeNet paper, and it was again afterwards that convolutional neural networks became well known and sought after by researchers, making them one of the most widely used deep neural networks. The model is shown in Fig. 3.

5.3 Methods for Generating Adversarial Examples

The adversarial examples in this experiment will all be generated by the FGSM (Fast Gradient Sign Method). The Fast Gradient Sign Method, one of the earliest and most

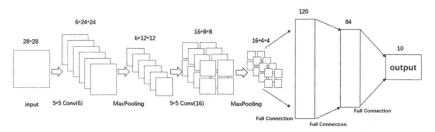

Fig. 3. Diagram of the modified LeNet model used in this experiment.

popular adversarial attacks to date, was proposed by Goodfellow et al. in [3] as a simple but effective algorithm for generating adversarial examples like the formula (1). It aims to attack neural networks by exploiting model learning methods and gradients. The idea is simple: the attack adjusts the input data to maximize loss based on the same back propagation gradient. In other words, the attack exploits the gradient of the loss function and then adjusts the input data to maximize the loss.

$$X' = X + \varepsilon sign(\nabla xJ(\theta, X, y)) \tag{1}$$

$$sign(x) = \begin{cases} 1, x > 0 \\ 0, x = 0 \\ -1, x < 0 \end{cases}$$

The formula θ represents the parameters of the model. X is the clean image. X' is the adversarial example obtained after adding perturbations by the FGSM. y is the label corresponding to X. J() is the loss function. ∇X represents the gradient over X for the loss function. ε is the value of the limit on the perturbation, like the learning rate.

Table 1. The variation in correctness in the face of adversarial examples under three model settings.

Models	Clean examples accuracy	Adversarial examples accuracy						
	$\varepsilon = 0$	$\varepsilon = 0.05$	$\varepsilon = 0.10$	$\varepsilon = 0.15$	$\varepsilon = 0.20$	$\varepsilon = 0.25$	$\varepsilon = 0.30$
LeNet(X)	0.9878	0.9277	0.7005	0.4112	0.2296	0.1153	0.0577
+ LeNet (X_1to4)	0.9899	0.9355	0.7376	0.472	0.2973	0.1957	0.1358
+ LeNet (X_4av4)	0.9881	0.9536	0.8078	0.5551	0.3376	0.191	0.0992

6   Experiments

As shown in Table 1 and Fig. 4, we can see that the use of low-frequency information extracted from the images using both compression methods to aid in prediction has led to an improvement in the robustness of the model when defending against an adversarial attack. When using X_1to4 and clean image co-identification, the model identification accuracy gradually improves with the increase of perturbation, up to about 8%.

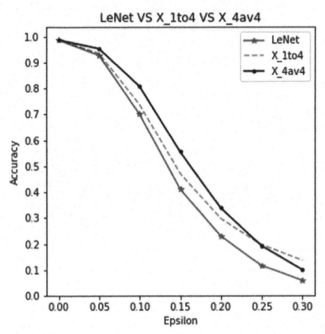

Fig. 4. Line graph of the change in correctness in the face of an adversarial example for the three model settings.

When using X_4av4 and the clean image together, the recognition accuracy of the model improves by more than 10% when the perturbation is $0.10 < \varepsilon < 0.20$, and reaches the highest when $\varepsilon = 0.15$, which improves by about 14%.

As shown in Fig. 5, the trained model works very accurately in classifying clean examples. The level of confidence in the correct classification is significantly different from that of the other classifications. However, when classifying adversarial examples, the confidence level of the results is very confusing and the classification is no longer possible. When predicted using the method proposed in this paper, the perceived confusion of the results is restored and some of the examples can already be correctly classified.

When the perturbation is low, i.e., the human eye cannot detect the perturbation, the decrease in the accuracy of the model is very small. When the perturbation is large, the human eye can tell that it has added the perturbation, and part of it is already a problem for the human eye to recognize, and the part that can be recognized successfully is

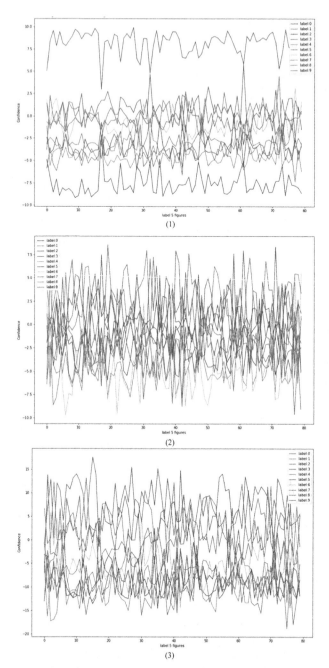

Fig. 5. (1) Output of the trained LeNet model when predicting 80 examples with a label of 5. (2) The output of the trained LeNet model when predicting 80 adversarial examples with label 5 and $\varepsilon = 0.15$. (3) Output of the trained LeNet+LeNet(X_4av4) when predicting 80 adversarial examples with labels of 5 and $\varepsilon = 0.15$.

starting to become difficult. Perturbations can also be difficult to filter out in the process of compression.

7 Conclusion

From the experimental results, the accuracy of the modified model is significantly improved in the face of adversarial examples, according to the adversarial example defense method based on low-frequency information proposed in this paper. Although the effect is not particularly significantly improved when the perturbation is large, some of the images are so destructive that they can affect the human eye's judgment because of the perturbation. This already deviates somewhat from the definition of an adversarial example. Therefore, the method proposed in this paper achieves the desired results.

Acknowledgement. This work was financially supported by the National Natural Science Foundation (61502127, 61562023), Hainan Natural Science Foundation (620RC604), the Open Funds from Guilin University of Electronic Technology, Guangxi Key Laboratory of Image and Graphic Intelligent Processing (GIIP2012), Scientific Research Projects in Universities of Hainan Province (Hnky2017-17), and Key R&D Projects in Hainan Province (ZDYF2019010).

References

1. Akhtar, N., Mian, A.: Threat of adversarial attacks on deep learning in computer vision: a survey. IEEE Access **6**, 14410–14430 (2018)
2. Szegedy, C., Zaremba, W., Sutskever, I., et al.: Intriguing properties of neural networks. arXiv.preprint. arXiv:1312.6199 (2014)
3. Goodfellow, I.J., Shlens, J., Szegedy, C.: Explaining and harnessing adversarial examples. In: ICML (2015)
4. Moosavi-Dezfooli, S.M., Fawzi, A., Frossard, P.: Deepfool: a simple and accurate method to fool deep neural networks. In: Computer Vision and Pattern Recognition (CVPR) (2016)
5. Madry, A., Makelov, A., Schmidt, L., et al.: Towards deep learning models resistant to adversarial attacks. In: International Conference on Learning Representations (2018)
6. Papernot, N., McDaniel, P.D., Wu, X., et al.: Distillation as a defense to adversarial perturbations against deep neural networks. In: IEEE Symposium on Security and Privacy (SP) (2016)
7. Guo, C., Rana, M., Cisse, M., van der Maaten, L.: Countering adversarial images using input transformations. In: International Conference on Learning Representations (2018)
8. Xie, C., Wang, J., Zhang, Z., et al.: Mitigating adversarial effects through randomization. In: International Conference on Learning Representations (2018)
9. Chen, P., Liu, S., Zhao, H., Jia, J.: GridMask Data Augmentation. arXiv.preprint. arXiv:2001.04086 (2020)
10. Goodman, D., Li, X., Huan, J., et al.: Improving Adversarial Robustness via Attention and Adversarial Logit Pairing. arXiv.preprint. arXiv:1908.11435 (2020)

Information Hiding

A Robust Watermarking Algorithm for Video Game Artwork Based on Pose Estimation Neural Network

Li Li$^{(\boxtimes)}$, Rui Bai, Shanqing Zhang, and Qili Zhou

Department of Computer Science, Hangzhou Dianzi University, Hangzhou 310018, China
lili2008@hdu.edu.cn

Abstract. Video game artworks serve a crucial role in video game development, the associated copyright protection remain largely unsolved. We propose a robust watermarking for protecting the copyright of video game artwork. Specifically, the watermarking algorithm uses pose estimation neural network to select pose joint points, and construct feature areas with the pose joint points as the center. Compared with existing local feature watermarking methods, the pose joint points are selected by the pose estimation neural network are much more evenly distributed, stable and orderly. Next non-maximum suppression (NMS) is used to select non-overlapping feature areas. Then discrete Wavelet transformation (DWT) performs on each feature area, and then dividing each sub-band into blocks. Finally, each block is decomposed by QR decomposition and select R matrix to embed watermarks. In the extraction procedure, the video game artwork is corrected using affine transformation before extraction. Experimental results indicate that the proposed algorithm outperforms the state-of-the-art methods in terms of imperceptiblity, robustness and computational cost. The algorithm is robust to common image attacks and geometric attacks, can effectively resist special attacks including text addition, tampering weapon, and cutting body parts of video game artwork.

Keywords: Video game artwork · Pose estimation neural network · Discrete wavelet transformation · QR · Robustness

1 Introduction

With the development of the video game industry, video games attract players of different age groups with their interesting and affluent presentation. Video game artwork is an important part for the video game, which are images refer to characters, equipment, accessories or monsters, etc. Some video game companies plagiarize the video game artworks of other companies to ensure that they keep costs down and save time. Even worse, current copyright laws for video game artwork plagiarism are ambiguous and imperfect, causing a tremendous numbers of forgery cases that seriously infringe the interests of copyright owners [1, 2]. Therefore, the copyright protection of video game artworks have become an urgent problem to be solved.

X. Sun et al. (Eds.): ICAIS 2021, CCIS 1424, pp. 217–229, 2021.
https://doi.org/10.1007/978-3-030-78621-2_17

Image watermarking techniques are used for copyright protection. A good image watermarking algorithm must be able to resist various attacks, mainly including image processing and geometric attacks. There are some specific image watermarking methods that resist various attacks in the frequency domain. Wang and Zhao [3] proposed an adaptive image watermarking method combining singular value decomposition and wang-landau sampling. Jayashree and Bhuvaneswaran [4] presented a new watermarking scheme that combining discrete wavelet transform, Z-transform and bidiagonal diagonal singular value decomposition. Li and Yuan [5] proposed a new digital image watermarking algorithm, which applied QDFT and Quaternion QR decomposition in color image. Mansi et al. [6] demonstrated image steganography scheme that using redundant discrete wavelet transform (RDWT) and QR factorization. In [7, 8], QR decomposition is less computation than SVD and avoids false positive problem of SVD. Su et al. [9] proposed a blind image watermarking scheme, the cover image is divided non-overlapping pixel blocks, each block is performed QR decomposition, and the triangle matrix R is used for embedding watermark.

Local features watermarking algorithms generally perform well in resisting attacks, there are several methods. Pan et al. [10] introduced a identification algorithm based on gradient vector flow, Harris detection, and scale invariant feature transform to extract features. Tang and Hang [11] proposed a robust image watermarking algorithm, that used Mexican-Hat wavelet scale interaction to detect feature points and the points were used for both watermark embedding and detection. Pham et al. [12] presented a geometrically invariant watermarking, which used scale invariant feature transformation to obtain feature points. Then these feature points are performed with the object matching operation. Lee et al. [13] put forward a blind watermarking scheme, that used SIFT to generate circular patches and embed the circular shape watermark repeatedly in all patches. Seo and Yoo [14] developed a synchronization method, and this method used Harris-Laplacian method to set up a scale space to embed watermark. Han Fang et al. [15] proposed an intensity-based scale-invariant feature transform (I-SIFT) algorithm, which can accurately locate the embedding regions.

The above methods are traditional feature detection methods, and these methods are rarely applied to protecting the copyright of video game artworks. The traditional feature detection methods detect a large number of feature points, the points are unevenly distributed and unstable. Harris corner detection method is one of the most widely used in traditional local feature point detection methods. Harris feature points are denser and uneven distribution, and more likely to prone overlapping when structure embedding areas, the watermarking information extraction might incomplete. However, pose joint points can alleviate the problems. Cao et al. [16] introduced a concept refer to pose joint points, there are some traits for the pose feature points, one is the distribution of the character's pose joint points is relatively even, the other is the character's torso area is relatively stable, such as the relative position of the pose joint points remain unchanged regardless of the attacks.

Based on [16], this paper proposes a robust watermarking algorithm for video game artwork based on pose estimation neural network. The algorithm effectively resists various conventional attacks and special attacks for video game artworks. The special attacks, including tampering clothing, tampering hairstyle, tampering weapon, and cutting body parts of video game artwork. The pose estimation neural network is more suitable for video game artworks and is used to select pose joint points with evenly distributed, stable and orderly.

2 Relevant Techniques

2.1 Pose Estimation

Human pose joint points are composed of human body frame, including wrists, elbows, shoulders, hip, knees, and ankles. Human pose estimation is defined as the localization of the key points of human body. Pose estimation is a basic task in computer vision, as well as the pre-tasks of human action recognition, behavior analysis, and human-computer interaction. Nie et al. [17] indicated two ways to design the human body pose estimation network. One is top-down way, which first performs target detection, and then performs single-person key points estimation for each detected person; the other is bottom-up that first detects all the key points, and then associates the key points. Generally speaking, bottom-up is faster than top-down method. So we choose the bottom-up method to detect pose of video game artwork.

2.2 Caffe Model

Caffe model is a deep learning network framework. Zhang et al. [18] presented Caffe neural networks with multiple hidden layers between the input and output layers, the main advantage of Caffe is the high speed of operation. Caffe is widely used in industrial applications and solve a lot of problems in many fields, such as visual, audio, and multimedia. This paper uses Caffe model to perform human pose estimation. Caffe model is trained on COCO dataset and generates pose joint points training model. The pose estimation model has 18 pose joint points including: {0,'Nose'}, {1,'Neck'}, {2,'RShoulder'}, {3,'RElbow'}, {4,'RWrist'}, {5,'LShoulder'},{6,'LElbow'}, {7,'LWrist'}, {8,'RHip'}, {9,'RKnee'}, {10,'RAnkle'}, {11,'LHip'},{12,'LKnee'}, {13,'LAnkle'}, {14,'REye'}, {15,'LEye'}, {16,'REar'}, {17,'LEar'}, the sequence is shown in Fig. 1.

3   Watermarking Scheme

This paper proposes a robust image watermarking algorithm for video game artworks based on pose estimation in the frequency domain, the flow diagram is shown in Fig. 2. To improve the robustness of algorithm, the repeated embedding strategy is used to embed watermarks. When some areas are attacked and watermark cannot be extracted, the watermarks in the rest areas can extract completely.

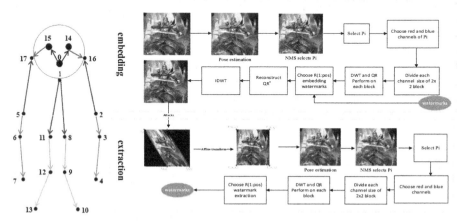

Fig. 1. Pose pairs   **Fig. 2.** Flow diagram

3.1   Human Pose Estimation Neural Network

The pose joint points are detected using popular machine learning network are highly accurate, it is generally applied to real person. There will be inadaptability to the exaggerated shape of a video game artwork, such as disordered connection sequence, wrong detection and missed detection of pose joint points. We improve human pose estimation model based on the method [18], the above problems can be avoided. The pose estimation neural network is shown in Fig. 3.

Pose estimation model has stage layers, the stage layer contains L_1 and L_2 branches, L_1 predicts the confidence map **F** of the pose joint points and L_2 predicts the pose points relation vector **G**, the original image features ζ are generated by Relu5. The inputs of each stage are $\mathbf{F^{s-1}}$, $\mathbf{G^{s-1}}$ and ζ, $\mathbf{F^{s-1}}$ and $\mathbf{G^{s-1}}$ are the output of the first branch and the second branch of the previous stage, respectively. Finally, pose points **F** and pose relation vector **G** are combined to obtain the human pose skeleton. f_1 and f_2 are the output functions, and s is the stage series. The functions are shown in Formula (1):

$$\begin{cases} F^s = f_1(\zeta, F^{s-1}, G^{s-1}) & \forall s \geq 2 \\ G^s = f_2(\zeta, F^{s-1}, G^{s-1}) & \forall s \geq 2 \end{cases} \tag{1}$$

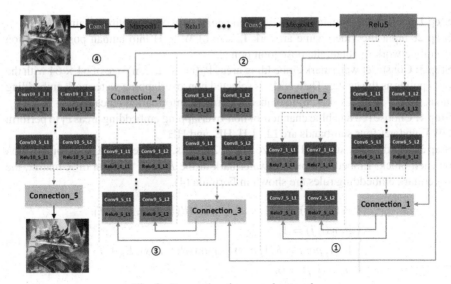

Fig. 3. Pose estimation neural network

For the network iteratively predict confidence maps of body parts in the first branch and part affinity fields in the second branch, we apply two loss functions C_F^s and C_G^s at the branches respectively.

$$\begin{cases} C_F^s = \sum_{i=1}^{m} \sum_d Q(d) \bullet \left\| F_i^s(d) - F_i^{s*}(d) \right\|_2^2 \\ C_G^s = \sum_{i=1}^{n} \sum_d Q(d) \bullet \left\| G_i^s(d) - G_i^{s*}(d) \right\|_2^2 \end{cases} \tag{2}$$

F* and G* are the pose joint points and the connected group-truth generated by the known data label, respectively. $Q(d) \in [0,1]$ indicates whether the joint point is detected. If $Q(d) = 0$, there is no joint point detected and vice versa. Where d is joint point, $d \in [0, 1, 2,..., 17]$. '$\bullet$' is dot product symbol. The cost function L consists of two parts, as shown in Formula (3):

$$L = \sum_{s=1}^{S} (C_F^s + C_G^s) \tag{3}$$

3.2 Watermark Embedding

The flow diagram of embedding watermark is shown in Fig. 2. We choose red and blue channels of a feature area to embed different watermarks, respectively. The red channel is embedded in watermark M_1 size of 32×32, and the blue channel is embedded in video game artwork skeleton M_2 with 32×32. The digital watermark embedding process is divided into six steps and is briefly described as follows:

Step 1: Generate a human pose estimation neural network by training sample.

Step 2: Input the video game artwork I_o size of W × H into human pose estimation neural network to abtain the pose joint points.

Step 3: Construct watermark embedding areas P_i (i = 1, 2,... n) size of 64 × 64 with the joint points as the center. Then NMS is selected non-overlapping watermark embedding areas P_i (i = 1, 2,... k, k < n) to embed watermark information repeatedly.

Step 4: Choose red and blue channels of non-overlapping embedding areas P_i to perform DWT, and get four sub-bands are LL, LH, HL, and HH.

Step 5: Divide each sub-band into size of 2 × 2 blocks, then perform QR decomposition on each block. Embedding one bit watermark at the $R(1, 2)$ position of R matrix, the watermark embedding rules are shown in Formula (4):

$$
\begin{cases}
R'(1, pos) = R(1, pos) - \mod(R(1, pos), E) + T_1 \\
if \ w(i, j) = 1; \\
R'(1, pos) = R(1, pos) - \mod(R(1, pos), E) + T_2 \\
if \ w(i, j) = 0.
\end{cases}
\tag{4}
$$

where mod(*) is the modulo operation. $w(i, j) \in [0, 1]$ is the watermark information, E is the watermark embedding strength, and *pos* is the length value of R(1,:). Tsai et al. [19] showed that selecting $T_1 = 3E/4$ and $T_2 = E/4$ provides good robustness against attacks, so we use the rule for watermark.

Step 6: Reconstruct QR' and perform IDWT to obtain watermarked video game artwork I_o'.

3.3 Watermark Extraction

The process of watermark extraction is shown in Fig. 2. First, the affine transformation is applied to geometric correction of artwork on the detecting. Katayama et al. [20] added a framwork with four points (x_1, y_1), (x_2, y_2), (x_3, y_3) and (x_4, y_4) to correct image under geometric attack. And then generating a mapping from the distorted artwork to the corrected artwork. We use the method to correct the watermarked video game artwork under the geometric attacks.

The steps of watermark extraction are as follows:

Step 1: Perform affine transformation on watermarked video game artwork I_m size of $W_m \times H_m$, and obtain the corrected video game artwork I_m'.

Step 2: Use the pose estimation neural network to detect the pose feature points of the video game artwork I_m'.

Step 3: Construct the watermark extraction areas P_i' (i = 1, 2,... n) with size of 64 × 64 centered on the pose joint points, then NMS selects non-overlapping extraction areas P_i' (i = 1, 2,... k, k < n).

Step 4: Choose red and blue channels of non-overlapping extraction areas P_i to perform DWT and get four sub-bands are LL, LH, HL and HH.

Step 5: Divide each sub-band into blocks size of 2 × 2, and then perform QR decomposition on each block.

Step 6: Extract the watermark information using the watermark extraction rules in the first row and second column of the upper triangular matrix R. The watermark extraction rule is shown in Formula **(5)**:

$$\begin{cases} if \quad \mod\ (R(1, pos), E) > (T_1 + T_2)/2 \quad w(i,j) = 1 \\ if \quad \mod\ (R(1, pos), E) \leq (T_1 + T_2)/2 \quad w(i,j) = 0 \end{cases} \tag{5}$$

Step 7: Obtain watermarks M_1 and M_2 using the watermark extraction rule.

4   Experimental Results and Analysis

In this paper, we use peak signal to noise ratio (PSNR) and structural similarity (SSIM) to evaluate image quality, normalized correlation (NC) and bit error ratio (BER) is used to evaluate watermark extraction quality.

The test image library **T** is the video game artwork library, and consists of 1,000 color images in JPEG format download from the game castle library and CG model king library. Female warrior, male wizard and female wizard are selected from **T** for the attack experiment. The experimental data is shown in Fig. 4. Two different watermarks are selected to be embedded in the red and blue channels of each feature area, respectively. The red channel embeds watermark M_1, and the blue channel embeds the skeleton thumbnail M_2, as shown in Fig. 5. The overall embedding capacity of a video game artwork reaches $1024 \times 2 \times k$ bits.

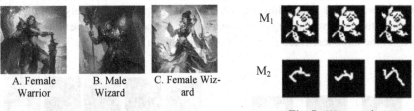

| A. Female Warrior | B. Male Wizard | C. Female Wizard | M_1 | M_2 |

Fig. 4. Video game artworks   **Fig. 5.** Watermarks

4.1   Embedding Strength Analysis

To achieve a perfect balance between the imperceptibility and robustness, we select a appropriate watermark embedding strength. The watermark strength range is between 10 and 200, when the strength is gradually increasing, NC gradually increases, and PSNR decreasing. However, when E is too large, NC and PSNR, meawhile, are gradually decreasing. Because of E is too large, the coefficients of the R triangular matrix changes too large, that in turn affects the DWT coefficients, causing a large destruction for image quality. The quality of image is too poor, watermarks can not be completely extracted. After experiment analysing, the appropriate E values are shown in Table 1, the PSNR and SSIM of three video game artworks are shown in Table 2, the PSNR for various watermarking methods are shown in Table 3.

Table 1. The E of LL, HL, LH, HH.

E	LL	HL	LH	HH
Red	41	14	16	16
Blue	44	20	20	20

Table 2. PSNR and SSIM of three video game artworks.

	Female warrior	Male wizard	Female wizard
PSNR	54.7507	54.3540	55.2195
SSIM	0.9992	0.9989	0.9992

Table 3. The PSNR for various watermarking methods.

Methods	Li and Yuan [12]	Mansi et al. [13]	Su et al. [16]	The proposed method
Average PSNR	40 (dB)	48.1535 (dB)	36.4548 (dB)	54.7747 (dB)

4.2 Local Feature Areas Selection

For tampering and plagiarism of the video game artworks, cropping and replacement parts of the video game artwork's character are two common attacks, including cropping legs, replacing the weapon, and replacing headgear. And we found that the upper body area of a character is generally not cropped or replaced. To this end, we embed the watermarks in the upper body of video game artwork's character. The first row in Fig. 6 shows the watermark embedding areas constructed by pose joint points, and the second row shows the non-overlapping embedding areas selected by NMS. The non-overlapping blocks of the three test video game artworks are shown in Fig. 7.

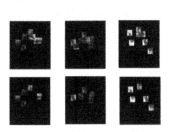

Fig. 6. Embedding areas

Fig. 7. Non-overlapping embedding areas

4.3 The Performance of Our Proposed Algorithm

Table 4 and Table 5 show NC under common attacks and special attacks. It is easily to discern from the tables, the proposed algorithm has good robustness to various attacks. And the best watermarks are extracted from blue channels of the three images are display in the last column of Table 5.

Table 4. NC under different common attacks.

NC (red channel)	Female warrior	Male wizard	Female wizard	NC (blue channel)	Female warrior	Male wizard	Female wizard
Gussian blur	0.9852	0.9927	0.9900	Gussian blur	0.9497	0.9820	0.9075
Median filter	0.9660	0.9711	0.9953	Median filter	0.9564	0.9219	0.9721
Salt& pepper	0.9679	0.9785	0.9547	Salt& pepper	0.9825	0.9487	0.9133
Guassian noise	0.8135	0.7882	0.7833	Guassian noise	0.7998	0.8273	0.7914
Sharpen attack	0.9491	0.9556	0.9242	Sharpen attack	0.9437	0.9567	0.9018
Scaling (2)	0.7395	0.8703	0.7518	Scaling (2)	0.8287	0.7439	0.7610
Scaling (0.5)	0.8622	0.8962	0.8369	Scaling (0.5)	0.9364	0.8273	0.8669
Cropping 128 × 128	0.9926	0.9945	0.9724	Cropping 128 × 128	0.9825	0.9909	0.8828
Cropping 256 × 256	0.9483	0.9601	0.9533	Cropping 256 × 256	0.9497	0.9820	0.9075

To show the performance of our algorithm, we compare the proposed algorithm with three state-of-art existing methods [13, 14], and [17]. The NC and BER comparison are shown in Table 6 and Table 7, respectively.

From Table 6 and Table 7, we found that the performance of our algorithm overall better than the existing three methods [13, 14, 17]. Except for above experiments, we also compare algorithm's time. The comparison of algorithm's time is shown in Table 8.

The embedding time of the proposed algorithm is 0.671677, the extraction time is 0.575088, and the overall time is 1.246765. It is longer than Su et al. [17] and Mansi et al. [14], but shorter than the rest 4 papers. Su et al. [17] only performed QR decomposition, while we performed both DWT and QR decomposition, so the overall time of our algorithm will be longer. Mansi et al. [14] only embedded watermark information in the HH sub-band, while this paper embeds watermarks into all four sub-bands, so the time of our algorithm is longer.

Table 5. Average NC under different special attacks.

Average NC value	Female warrior	Male wizard	Female wizard	Watermark (red)	Watermark (blue)
1. Replacement weapon	1	0.9996	1		
2. Addition text	1	1	1		
3. Scaling (2)	0.8125	0.7369	0.7784		
4. Scaling (0.5)	0.9102	0.8205	0.8559		
5. Tampering with color	0.9987	1	0.9989		
6. Rotation (20)	0.8622	0.8513	0.9115		
7. Cropping legs	1	1	1		
8. Cropping weapon	0.9977	0.9999	1		
9. Tampering with head	0.9995	1	0.9978		
10. Complex tampering	0.7833	0.7675	0.7995		

Table 6. NC of the proposed algorithm and the methods in [13, 14, 17] under common attacks.

Average NC	Salt &peppers	Sharpening	Gaussian noise	Blurring	Median filter	Cropping	Jpeg
The proposed method	**(0.01)** **0.9670**	0.9430	**(0.1)** **0.995**	**0.9893**	**(3 × 3)** **0.9808**	**(25%)** **0.9539**	**(90)** **0.9969**
Su et al. [16]	(0.02) 0.9373	(0.2) 0.9785	(0.1) 0.9420	(0.2) 0.9858	(3 × 1) 0.9076	(25%) 0.7589	(90) 0.9672
Mansi et al. [13]	(0.01) 0.8981	0.8988	(0.001) 0.9463	0.9835	(3 × 3) 0.9783	0.9439	(75) 0.9729

Table 7. BER of the proposed algorithm and the methods in [13, 14, 17] under common attacks

Average BER	Salt &peppers	Sharpening	Gaussian noise	Rotation	Median filter	Cropping	Jpeg
The proposed method	**(0.01) 0.0095**	**0.0102**	(0.001) 0.0365	**(20) 0.0010**	**(3 × 3) 0**	**(25%) 0.0112**	(90) 0.022
Mansi et al. [13]	(0.01) 0.01776	0.01858	(0.001) 0.015425	(45) 0.0156	(3 × 3) 0.013	0.01563	(75) 0.0134
Li and Yuan [12]	(0.01) 0.0107	0.3229	(0.001) 0.0120	(10) 0.0011	(3 × 3) 0	(20%) 0.1654	(90) 0.0067

Table 8. The comparison of algorithms time.

	Embedding time	Extraction time	Total time
The proposed method	**0.671677**	**0.575088**	**1.246765**
Su et al. [16]	0.686992	0.427003	1.113998
Mansi et al. [13]	0.654402	0.12340	0.777542
Chou et al. [21]	1.406568	1.105751	2.512319
Golea et al. [22]	1.909066	0.905950	2.815017
Yashar et al. [23]	0.913247	0.455445	1.368692
Su et al. [24]	1.263168	0.591873	1.855041

5   Conclusions

In this paper, we use human pose estimation neural network to detect pose joint points as local feature points. The proposed method combines local feature with frequency domain has good robustness. DWT-QR double transform and the repeated embedding strategy are used to enhance the robustness. DWT-QR double transform aggregate image energy that helps to choose appropriate embedding position against attacks. The repeated embedding strategy can extract watermarks completely when some embedding areas are attacked. Our algorithm performs well in terms of imperceptibility. According to human visual characteristic, we select red and blue channels to embed watermarks and select appropriate embedding strength to embed watermarks. The proposed algorithm well resistant to common attacks, as well as resistant special attacks for video game artworks. Moreover, the proposed method works with blind detection, which is important in the real applications. In the future, we hope to improve the time efficiency of the proposed algorithm and make our algorithm application to more video game artwork's scenes.

Funding Statement. This work was partially supported by National Natural Science Foundation of China (No. 61370218, No. 61971247), Public Welfare Technology and Industry Project of Zhejiang Provincial Science Technology Department (No. LGG19F0-2016).

References

1. Tan, W., Wu, Y., Wu, P., Chen, B.: A survey on digital image copy-move forgery localization using passive techniques.J. New Med. **1**(1), 11–25 (2019)
2. Binti, N., Ahmad, M., Mahmoud, Z., Mehmood, R.M.: A pursuit of sustainable privacy protection in big data environment by an optimized clustered-purpose based algorithm. Intell. Autom. Soft Comput. **26**(6), 1217–1231 (2020)
3. Wang, B., Zhao, P.: An adaptive image watermarking method combining SVD and Wang-Landau sampling in DWT domain. Mathematics **8**, 691 (2020)
4. Jayashree, N., Bhuvaneswaran, R.S.: A robust image watermarking scheme using z-transform, discrete wavelet transform and bidiagonal singular value decomposition. Comput. Mater. Continua **58**(1), 263–285 (2019)
5. Li, M., Yuan, X.: Quaternion discrete fourier transform-based color image watermarking method using quaternion QR decomposition. IEEE Access **8**, 72308-72315 (2020)
6. Subhedar, M.S., Mankar, V.H.: Image steganography using redundant discrete wavelet transform and QR factorization. Comput. Electr. Eng. **54**, 406–422 (2016)
7. Li, X., Fan, H.: QR factorization based blind channel identification with second-order statistics. IEEE Trans. Signal Process. **48**(1), 60–69 (2000)
8. De Moor, B., Van Dooren, P.: Generalizations of the singular value and QR decompositions. SIAM J. Matrix Anal. Appl. **13**(4), 993–1014 (1992)
9. Su, Q., Niu, Y., Wang, G., Jia, S., Yue, J.: Color image blind watermarking scheme based on QR decomposition. Signal Process. **94**, 219–235 (2014)
10. Pan, N., Pan, D., Liu, Y.: The crime scene tools identification algorithm based on GVF-Harris-Sift and KNN. Intell. Autom. Soft Comput. **25**(2), 413–419 (2019)
11. Tang, C.-W., Hang, H.-M.: A feature-based robust digital image watermarking scheme. IEEE Trans. Signal Process. **51**(4), 950–959 (2003)
12. Pham, V.Q., Miyaki, T., Yamasaki, T., Aizawa, K.: Geometrically invariant object-based watermarking using SIFT feature. In: Proceedings of IEEE International Conference on Image Process, vol. 5, pp. 473–476 (2007)
13. Lee, H.-Y., Kim, H., Lee, H.-K.: Robust image watermarking using local invariant features. Opt. Eng. **45**(3), p. 037002(1)–11 (2006)
14. Jin, S., Seo, C., Yoo, D.: Localized image watermarking based on feature points of scale-space representation. Pattern Recognit. **37**(7), 1365–1375 (2004)
15. Fang, H., Zhang, W., Zhou, H., Cui, H., Yu, N.: Screen-shooting resilient watermarking. IEEE Trans. Inf. Forensics Secur. **14**(6), 1403–1418 (2019)
16. Cao, Z., Hidalgo Martinez, G., Simon, T., Wei, S., Sheikh, Y.A.: OpenPose: realtime multi-person 2d pose estimation using part affinity fields. IEEE Trans. Pattern Anal. Mach. Intell. **43**(1), 172-186 (2019)
17. Nie, X., Feng, J., Xing, J., et al.: Pose partition networks for multiperson pose estimation. In: ECCV, Proceedings of the 2018 European Conference on Computer Vision, pp. 705–720 (2018)
18. Zhang, C., Sun, G., Fang, Z., Zhou, P., Pan, P., Cong, J.: Caffeine: toward uniformed representation and acceleration for deep convolutional neural network. IEEE Trans. Comput. Aided Des. Integr. Circuits Syst. **38**(11), 2072–2085 (2019)
19. Tsai, M.J., Yu, K.Y., Chen, Y.Z.: Joint wavelet and spatial transformation for digital watermarking. IEEE Trans. Consumer Electron. **46**(1), 241–245 (2000)

20. Katayama, A., Nakamura, T., Yamamuro, M., Sonehara, N.: New high-speed frame detection method: Side trace algorithm (STA) for i-appli on cellular phones to detect watermarks. Mobile Ubiquit. Multimed. **83**, 109–116 (2004)
21. Chou, C.H., Wu, T.L.: Embedding color watermarks in color images.: EURASIP J. Adv. Signal Process. 32–40 (2003). https://doi.org/10.1155/S1110865703211227
22. Golea, N.E.H., Seghir, R., Benzid, R.: A bind RGB color image watermarking based on singular value decomposition. In: Proceedings of the 2010 IEEE/ACS International conference on Computer Systems and Applications, pp. 1–5 (2010)
23. Yashar, N., Saied, H.K.: Fast watermarking based on QR decomposition in wavelet domain. In: Proceedings of the 2010 Sixth International Conference on Intelligent Information Hiding and Multimedia Signal Processing, pp. 127–130 (2010)
24. Su, Q., Niu, Y., Liu, X., Zhu, Y.: Embedding color watermarks in color images based on Schur decompositon. Opt. Commun. **285**(7), 1792–1802 (2012)

Research on Content Authentication Technology of Electronic Bills Based on Text Watermarking Algorithm

Dan Liu[1], Yajun Chen[2], Shaokang Wang[1(✉)], Yinping Bai[1], and Zhaofeng Zhou[1]

[1] Beijing Suwell Technology Co., LTD., Beijing 100089, China
newdan@suwell.cn
[2] China Electronics Standardization Institute, Beijing 100007, China

Abstract. To solve the problems of electronic bills being easy to forge, easy to steal, difficult to verify and difficult to locate the position in the process of network transmission, an electronic bill generation method based on format documents is proposed. Combining with traditional electronic seal, digital signature and text watermarking technology, it verifies the integrity of the content of electronic bills and locates the specific tampering location by judging whether the watermark information is complete, thus providing a comprehensive security authentication solution for electronic bill. The experimental results show that the proposed electronic bill generation method is very simple with higher security. It can not only verify the integrity and authenticity of the electronic bill content, but also can support the content authentication in the offline state after being output as a paper-based document, and accurately obtain the specific tampering location information.

Keywords: Format document · Electronic invoice · Content tampering · Digital watermarking

1 Introduction

At present, with the rapid development of computer science and Internet technology, all kinds of traditional business activities have realized electronization, networking and informatization. For example, the electronic bills rely on the Internet technology platform to realize electronization of physical bills, and replace paper bills for transfer, discount, pledge, collection and other commercial transactions [2]. However, electronic bills often encounter a variety of destruction attacks in the process of network transmission, such as being easily tampered with, intercepted or disseminated, which makes the protection of Internet financial information and personal privacy data face huge challenges [3]. Therefore, it is an urgent problem to ensure the security of electronic bill.

In order to ensure the consistency and stability of the typesetting, preview and output of electronic bills, people often choose layout documents as the information carrier, such as PDF (Portable Document Format) files [4–7]. The electronic bill document based on PDF file has the advantages of fixed format, good compression performance and beautiful

© Springer Nature Switzerland AG 2021
X. Sun et al. (Eds.): ICAIS 2021, CCIS 1424, pp. 230–243, 2021.
https://doi.org/10.1007/978-3-030-78621-2_18

layout [4]. At the same time, the integrity and authenticity of the electronic bill content can be verified through traditional digital signature technology, thereby ensuring the security of the electronic bill file [5]. However, this method mainly has two shortcomings: 1) The digital signature requires that the data information of the file and the signature information are stored separately. If the signature information is damaged or lost, the electronic bill content authentication cannot be completed. 2) The digital signature can verify the integrity of the electronic bill, but cannot obtain the specific tampering location information. Ma [7] proposed a method to generate electronic receipt files after encapsulating the content data in XML file format. The electronic bills generated in this way can adapt to the upgrading and changes of various technological environments, and it is easy for retrieval and archive storage of the electronic bills content. Fang et al. [8] proposed an electronic invoice generation method based on SVG (Scalable Vector Graphic) file format, designed and implemented a fragile digital watermarking algorithm based on XML/HTML file to conduct content authentication and tamper location of electronic bills. At present, XML Signature technology [9, 10] or XML/HTML-based digital watermark technology [11–14] determines the security performance of the above two electronic receipt files with the help of XML format encapsulation. However, the digital watermarking algorithm based on XML/HTML has many limitations for the protection of electronic bill content. That is, the protected information easily affects the block size and structure division of the XML/HTML content, and when the block order and number of the XML/HTML contents change before and after the watermark information is embedded, the results of watermark information extraction, integrity verification and tampering location of electronic bill content will have a large deviation. There are also some scholars who convert electronic bill files into digital image files as a whole, and use fragile or semi-fragile digital image watermarking algorithms to verify the integrity and authenticity of electronic bill content [15, 16]. The digital image watermarking algorithm can be used for anti-counterfeiting and tampering positioning of electronic bills, but the converted electronic bill files are too large and the network transmission efficiency is low. In addition, digital image files are extremely susceptible to interference and damage from external factors, which affects the final authentication result of the electronic bill content.

Aiming at the problems of the above methods, this paper proposes a method to generate electronic bill documents based on OFD (Open fixed-layout document) file. The OFD uses XML technology to describe the content data of document, and maintains the layout information of all objects in the file with high precision, including text, graphics, images, formulas, etc. This feature has good compatibility with the system platform, which can be stored for a long time, prevent leakage, prevent tampering, anti-repudiation and support metadata semantic embedding. In addition, the OFD file is relatively independent. It supports metadata addition and semantic embedding integration, and also can provide flexible electronic bill template customization related functions. The combination of OFD file and digital signature technology can effectively prevent file tampering, thereby ensuring the integrity and credibility of the electronic bill. At the same time, two-dimensional code, watermark and other processing can also be performed to further expand the security mechanism of the format document.

2 Text Digital Watermarking Algorithm

Let M be the set of all watermarking information m, X be the set of all information carriers x to be protected, W be the set of the initial watermark signal w, K be the set of watermark embedding and extraction keys k, and G be the watermark generation algorithm, namely:

$$G : M * X * K \rightarrow W, w = G(m, x, k) \tag{1}$$

The algorithm for embedding the watermark information into the information carrier is represented by E_m, namely:

$$E_m = X * W \rightarrow X, x^w = E_m(x, w) \tag{2}$$

Where, x is the original carrier and x^w is the watermarked carrier. The security performance of the watermark algorithm can be improved by hiding the information key in the watermark embedding process.

2.1 Watermark Embedding

In this paper, it uses a text watermarking algorithm based on character structure modification [17] to embed watermark into the content of electronic bill file. Firstly, a special watermark font file is designed, that is, by changing the topological structure of the character contour curve appropriately, and a variety of transformations with the same semantic and different character contour curves are designed. Each deformation is assigned a different character code to represent different watermark information bit string, and all the character structure data are saved to a new watermarked font file. The watermark information bit string is embedded in real-time by selecting corresponding characters from different watermarked font files. The design method of watermark character structure is shown in Fig. 1. And Fig. 1(a) is the font structure diagram of the original standard Chinese character "数", and Fig. 1(b) shows the display effect of the modified watermarked characters.

The above modification method is to map each character structure into four different variants, and each watermark character can represent 2-bits information. For example, the structures of four watermarked characters as shown in Fig. 1(b) represent "00", "01", "10" and "11", respectively. What needs to be explained here is that in the actual design process of watermarked font file, each character can be mapped to more kinds of different glyph structures to represent more watermark information.

2.2 Watermark Extraction

Firstly, the watermarked character image is obtained and regarded as the template image A sized of $M_A * N_A$ pixels. The standard character images are generated from stand font file and watermarked font file respectively, and each watermarked character image is regarded as image B to be matched with the size of $M_B * N_B$ pixels, where $M_A \leq M_B$ and $N_A \leq N_B$. Through the method of normalized cross correlation (NCC), it calculates the difference between images A and B to determine whether the character image contains watermark information or not.

(a)

(b)

Fig. 1. A diagram of the design of the character structure, (a) is the original standard Chinese character "数"; (b) are four deformed watermarking characters.

NCC-Based Template Matching. Character image matching is performed by calculating the similarity between very two character images, that is, the autocorrelation coefficients of the template image A and the image B to be matched at different positions are calculated. The maximum of all coefficients is the similarity of two images.

When the template image A slides to (u, v) on the image B to be matched, the normalized correlation coefficient $r(u, v)$ between two images is calculated as follows [18]:

$$r(u, v) = \frac{\sum_{i,j} [f(u+i, v+j) - \overline{f}_{u,v}][t(i,j) - \overline{t}]}{\sqrt{(\sum_{i,j} [f(u+i, v+j) - \overline{f}_{u,v}]^2)(\sum_{i,j} [t(i,j) - \overline{t}]^2)}} \tag{3}$$

where $f(i, j)$ is the pixel value of character image B to be matched at position (i, j), $t(i, j)$ is the pixel value of template character image A at position (i, j), $\overline{t}$ is the pixel average value of template image A, and $\overline{f}$ is the average pixel value of corresponding character image B under the current position of image A.

Due to the high computational complexity of the above Eq. (3), the following accelerated calculation methods can be adopted in practical applications:

First, let $t'(i, j) = t(i, j) - \overline{t}$, and the numerator of Eq. (3) can be written as follows:

$$\sum_{i,j} f(u+i, v+j)t'(i,j) - \overline{f} \sum_{i,j} t'(i,j) \tag{4}$$

Apparently, the latter part of Eq. (4) is always equal to zero, and the former part of Eq. (4) can be rewritten as follows:

$$\sum_{i,j} f(u+i, v+j)t(i,j) - \overline{t} \sum_{i,j} f(u+i, v+j) \tag{5}$$

The former part of the Eq. (5) can be regarded as the convolution of two signals in spatial domain, and the convolution in spatial domain is equivalent to the coefficient multiplication operation based on frequency domain. Accordingly, the former part of Eq. (5) is be equal to the following calculation:

$$F^{-1}[F(f)F^*(t)] \tag{6}$$

Where, F is the Fourier transform of the original signal, F^* is the conjugate complex operation of the transformed result, and F^{-1} is the inverse Fourier transform for the frequency domain signal.

Next, for the denominator of Eq. (3), the later term is the pixel value variance of image A. After simplifying the former item, the result is as shown in Eq. (7):

$$\sum_{i,j} [f(u+i, v+j)]^2 - \frac{[\sum_{i,j} f(u+i, v+j)]^2}{M_A * N_A} \tag{7}$$

If Eq. (7) is calculated, it is necessary to calculate the cumulative sum of all the pixel values in the sliding window of the image B at (u, v), and calculate the corresponding cumulative sum of squares.

The Calculation of Accumulation Matrix. In image matching process, it is necessary to calculate the cumulative sum of pixel values and the cumulative sum of squares of any sub-matrix of the image B in real-time. Therefore, in order to improve the matching efficiency, the idea of dynamic programming is used. It saves the cumulative sum and sum of squares of the sub-matrix in the cache data table for subsequent calculation process, so as to avoid repeated calculation. Next, we take the cumulative sum matrix of image B as an example to describe its accelerated calculation method.

The size of the image B is scaled to the same size as the template character image A, and the width and height are M_B and N_B, respectively. The current image matrix is K, $K[i, j] = K_{ij}$, $0 < i < M_B$, $0 < j < N_B$. The cumulative sum of pixel values can be obtained by the following methods.

1) Extend the current matrix K to K' with the size of $3M_B*3N_B$, the expansion method is to set the matrix K to the center position of K', and all the positions of the surrounding 8 neighborhoods are set to 0, as shown in Fig. 2:

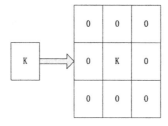

Fig. 2. The extension of matrix K.

2) Do the following operations on K' to obtain $K1$, that is, each element of $K1$ is the original matrix, and K' is summed up in turn for row elements (Fig. 3):

$$K1 = \begin{pmatrix} k11 & k12 & ... & k1n \\ k11 + k21 & k12 + k22 & ... & k1n + k2n \\ ... & ... & ... & ... \\ k11 + k21 + ... + kn1 & k12 + k22 + ... + kn2 & ... & k1n + k2n + ... + knn \end{pmatrix} \tag{8}$$

where $m = 3M_B, n = 3N_B$, the matrix $K1$ is obtained after the above transformation as shown in Fig. 4, where $KA[i, j] = s(i, j), KB[i, j] = s(M_B, j), s(i, j) = K[1, j] + ... + K[i, j]$.

0	0	0
0	KA	0
0	KB	0

0	KA	0
0	KC	0
0	KB	0

Fig. 3. The composition of matrix $K1$.   **Fig. 4.** The composition of matrix $K2$.

5) For matrix $K1$, from the first row to the $2M_B$ row, the elements of each row are calculated to get $K2$ as follows:

$$K2[i, j] = K1[i + N_B, j] - K1[i, j] \tag{9}$$

where $KC[i, j] = s(M_B, j) - s(i, j)$.

4) For matrix $K2$, each element is summed up based on column element values to obtain matrix $K3$:

$$K3 = \begin{pmatrix} k11 & k11 + k12 & ... & k11 + k12 + ... + k1n \\ k21 & k21 + k22 & ... & k21 + k22 + ... + k2n \\ ... & ... & ... & ... \\ km1 & km1 + km2 & ... & km1 + km2 + ... + kmn \end{pmatrix} \tag{10}$$

The matrix $K3$ is obtained, and its composition is shown in Fig. 5.
Let $t(K)(i, j) = K[i, 1] + ... + K[i, j]$, then

$$KD[i, j] = t(KA)(i, j) = KA[i, 1] + ... + KA[i, j] = s(i, 1) + ... + s(i, j) \tag{11}$$

$$KG[i, j] = t(KA)(i, N_B) = s(i, 1) + ... + s(i, N_B) \tag{12}$$

$$KF[i, j] = t(KC)(i, j) = KC[i, 1] + ... + KC[i, j] \\ = s(M_B, 1) - s(i, 1) + ... + s(M_B, j) - s(i, j) \tag{13}$$

Fig. 5. The composition of matrix *K3*.   **Fig. 6.** Cumulative sum matrix SB.

$$KT[i.j] = t(KC)(i, N_B) = KC[i, 1] + \ldots + KC[i, N_B]$$
$$= s(M_B, 1) - s(i, 1) + \ldots + s(M_B, N_B) - s(i, N_B) \tag{14}$$

$$KE[i, j] = t(KB)(i, j) = KB[i, 1] + \ldots + KB[i, j] = s(M_B, 1) + \ldots + s(M_b, j) \tag{15}$$

$$KH[i, j] = t(KB)(i, N_B) = KB[i, 1] + \ldots + KB[i, N_B] = s(M_B, 1) + \ldots + s(M_B, N_B) \tag{16}$$

1) For matrix *K3*, from column one to column $2N_B$, the elements of each column are calculated as follows to obtain matrix *K4*:

$$K4[i, j] = K3[i, j + N_B] - K3[i, j] \tag{17}$$

Take the first $2M_B$ rows and $2N_B$ column elements of matrix *K4* to form the final accumulation sum matrix SB, as shown in Fig. 6.

The Calculation of Matching Correlation. For the image *B* to be matched, all the elements in *B* are multiplied, and then the cumulative sum of squares matrix S2B is obtained in the same way as above mentioned, then the calculation method of image matching similarity is as follows:

1) Calculate the correlation coefficient *demon_T* as follows:

$$demon\_T = \sqrt{(M_A * N_A - 1)} * std(A) \tag{18}$$

   where $std(A)$ is the variance of template image *A*.
2) Calculate the denominator of the correlation measure Eq. (3)

$$demon\_B[i, j] = demon\_T * \sqrt{\max(S2B[i, j] - \frac{SB[i, j]^2}{M_B * N_B}, 0)} \tag{19}$$

3) The molecular part of the correlation measurement Eq. (3) can be obtained:

$$numerator[i, j] = r[i, j] - \frac{SB[i, j] * sum(A)}{M_B * N_B} \tag{20}$$

Where $sum(A)$ is the sum of pixel values of template image *A*, and *r* is the convolution matrix of the template image *A* and the matching image *B*.

4) The template matching similarity matrix C with the size of $2M_B*2N_B$ is generated, and all elements are set as 0, and the following calculation is performed:

When it satisfied the condition $demon\_B[i,j] > 0$, then

$$C[i,j] = \frac{numerator[i,j]}{demon\_B[i,j]} \tag{21}$$

The correlation between A and B is the maximum element value of matrix C, which is the similarity between two images.

Judgment of Watermark Information. According to the above method, the template character image A is matched with the character image B of standard font file and watermarked file respectively, and the corresponding template matching similarities value are obtained.

1) If the template character image A has the highest similarity with the standard character image B, it means that the template character image A is normal character and does not contain any watermark information.
2) If the similarity between the template character image A and one of the watermarked character images B is the highest, the character image A is a watermarked character image, and the corresponding watermark information is obtained.

3 Generation of Electronic Bill File

3.1 Authentication Watermark Information Embedding

The tampered content is located by verifying the missing position of the watermark information.

1) First, read all the text information bound to the data field in the template document of electronic bill, and get the character sequence $T = \{T_1, T_2, ..., T_n\}$, where n is the length of the string T.
2) The MD5 message digest algorithm is used to calculate 128-bits hash value of sequence T.
3) Using the text watermarking algorithm proposed in this paper, the hash value D is embedded into the content of electronic bill as watermark information in the following way:

- The 0/1 bit information in D is grouped in sequence, and each group contains 2-bits continuous information.
- All the text information is imported into the electronic bill file through the data field.
- According to the different watermark information, the specific font structure data is dynamically selected to imported into OFD file, and each character is embedded with 2-bits information.

When the number of characters bound in the data field of electronic bill file is large, the watermark information D will be repeatedly and redundantly embedded into the document content, and the final embedded watermark information bit string is marked as C, and the corresponding length is P.

3.2 Digital Signature and Encapsulation

For all the information mentioned above, such as hash value D of the string sequence T, watermark bit string length P, font type, watermark key parameter k and other relevant parameters information, a two-dimensional barcode image is generated and inserted into the OFD file.

To ensure the authenticity, integrity, security and availability of the electronic bill, the electronic signature seal technology is used to process and encapsulate the electronic bill in OFD format.

3.3 Verification of Electronic Bill

Firstly, the electronic seal is used to verify the validity of electronic bill documents. If the verification is passed, the content of the electronic bill is complete. If the verification fails, the content of the electronic bill may be tampered with, and the specific tamper location information is obtained.

Then, all the information hidden in the two-dimensional barcode is extracted, and it verifies whether the key content of the data field binding in the electronic bill have changed as follows:

Step 1: Recalculate the MD5 hash value D' of all text information bound to the data field and determine whether D and D' are the same. If they are same, the text content of the electronic bill has not changed, otherwise the operation of step 2 is performed.

Step 2: All character images are read from the content of OFD file and watermark information is extracted in turn. If there are standard characters that do not contain watermark information, these characters will be directly identified as tampering content, and the tampering methods are "character addition" or "character modification", and the corresponding tampering position will be recorded.

Step 3: Extract all watermark information bit string C', and the length is P'.

Step 4: The original watermark information bit string D is spliced into the information bit string C with the length of P according to the redundancy embedding method of watermark information.

Step 5: Since any kind of tampering method will reduce the number of watermark information bit strings, there will be $(P - P')$ bit watermark information lost. The longest common substring of the two signal sequences C and C' is calculated according to the string minimum edit distance algorithm, and the positions of the characters corresponding to the other different watermark information bit strings are regarded as suspicious tampering positions.

4 Experimental Results and Analysis

4.1 Robustness Verification of Text Watermarking Algorithm

First, the text sample is generated as shown in Fig. 7, in which the font type is Fangsong in Chinese and the font size is 40 pt. This image contains 113 characters, in which 97 Chinese characters are embedded with 194 bits information except for punctuations, English word "OFD" and simple character "一". Each character corresponds to four different variants, and 2-bits watermark information are embedded respectively. The visual effect of the watermarked text image is shown as Fig. 8. In order to more clearly explain the visual effect of the text watermarking algorithm described in this paper, we enlarge the four characters " 数科网维". The original text image is shown as Fig. 9(a), and the Fig. 9(b) shows the image after watermark embedding in the Fig. 9(a). It can be seen from Fig. 9 that the text watermarking algorithm based on the modification of character glyph structure has good visual concealment, and it is difficult for human eyes to find the modification, which does not affect the normal reading effect of documents. Next, the robustness of the text watermarking algorithm against various attacks is further verified.

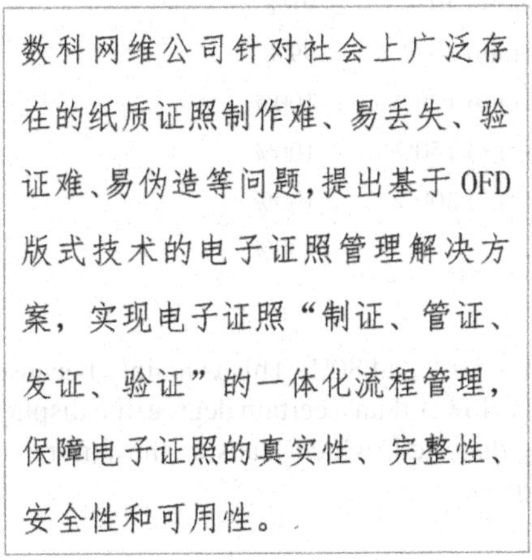

数科网维公司针对社会上广泛存在的纸质证照制作难、易丢失、验证难、易伪造等问题,提出基于 OFD 版式技术的电子证照管理解决方案,实现电子证照"制证、管证、发证、验证"的一体化流程管理,保障电子证照的真实性、完整性、安全性和可用性。

Fig. 7. The original text image.

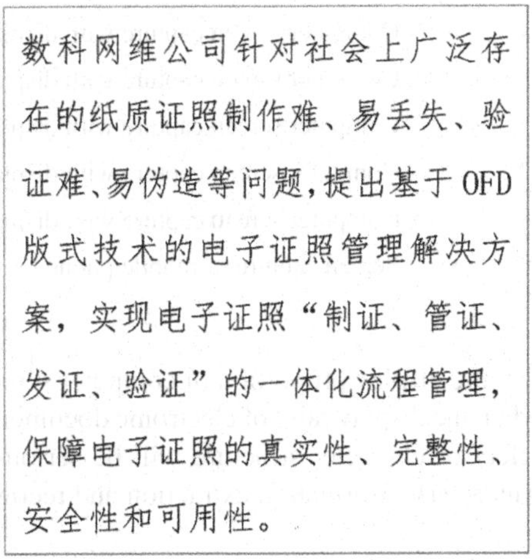

数科网维公司针对社会上广泛存在的纸质证照制作难、易丢失、验证难、易伪造等问题,提出基于 OFD 版式技术的电子证照管理解决方案,实现电子证照"制证、管证、发证、验证"的一体化流程管理,保障电子证照的真实性、完整性、安全性和可用性。

Fig. 8. The watermarked text image.

The image with watermark information embedded in Fig. 8 is print out and displayed on the screen, respectively. Next, we will verify the extraction efficiency of the text watermark algorithm. The printed paper document is digitized to get watermarked images through the scanner (Epson ds-570w, resolution 600dpi), high-resolution camera (Liangtian BS2000p, 18 million pixels) and mobile phone (OPPO K5, 64 million pixels), respectively. The screenshot images are obtained through computer and mobile phone screen, and the corresponding display ratios of computer screen are set to 50%, 80%, 100%, 150% and 200%, respectively. The watermark information is extracted from above images by our proposed method as shown in Table 1.

It can be seen from Table 1 that our proposed text watermark algorithm has strong robustness. The correct extraction rate of watermark information can reach 100%, except

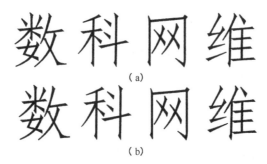

Fig. 9. Comparison of visual effect before and after watermark information embedding.

Table 1. Watermark information extraction results.

Index	Image acquisition method	Correct extraction rate
1	Scanner	100%
2	High-resolution camera	100%
3	Mobile phone	100%
4	Computer screen capture with display ratio 50%	91%
5	Computer screen capture with display ratio 80%	99%
6	Computer screen capture with display ratio 100%	100%
7	Computer screen capture with display ratio 150%	100%
8	Computer screen capture with display ratio 200%	100%
9	Screen capture of mobile phone	100%

that the display proportion of computer screen is 50% and 80%. This is mainly because when the display ratio of electronic documents is lower than a certain degree, the display effect of character structure will be seriously distorted, which leads to the failure of watermark information extraction and recognition.

4.2 Content Authentication of Electronic Bill

First of all, we use the OFD format electronic receipt support platform named Suwell, which developed by Beijing Suwell Technology Co., LTD., to complete the production and generation of electronic invoice documents, reading of credentials, printing output, and verification of secure electronic invoice. The template file only contains the public part of electronic bill content, and the key data is bound by variable data field and automatically imported into the layout document.

Then, the key data of electronic invoice is read from the variable database, cleaned and integrated to form the data information of electronic invoice file.

Next, the authentication watermark information of the content of the electronic invoice document is calculated and embedded by the text watermarking method in Sect. 4.2.

Finally, the electronic invoice file embedded with watermark is signed with electronic seal, and encapsulated in XML format to get the final file as shown in Fig. 10.

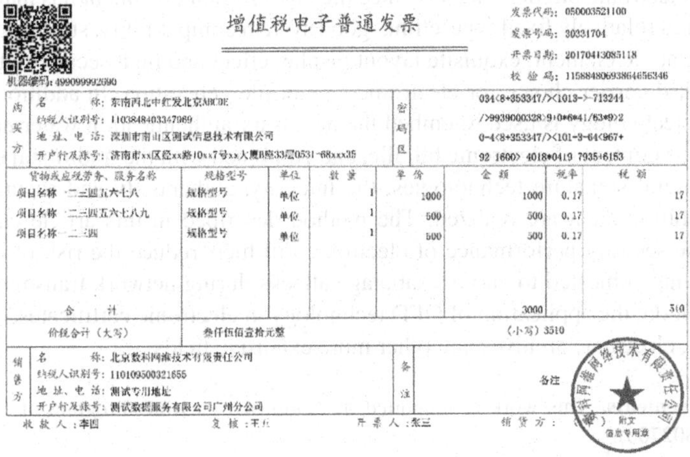

Fig. 10. The OFD format based electronic bill file with watermark information embedded.

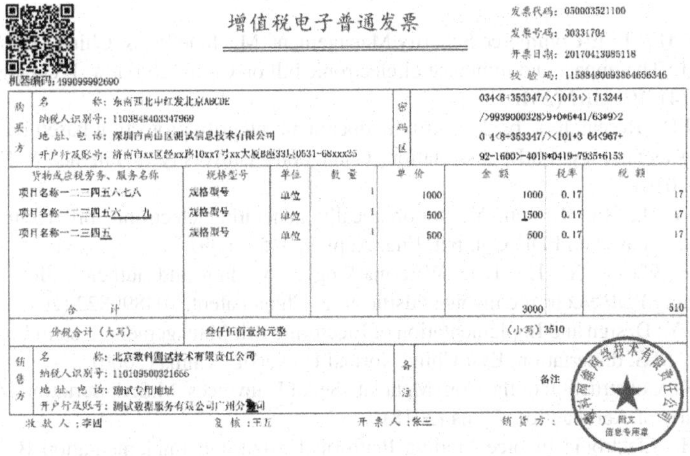

Fig. 11. The OFD electronic invoice file after tampering.

After performing content tampering on the electronic invoice file as shown in Fig. 10, it verifies the integrity and authenticity of the content of the electronic invoice file by our method described in Sect. 3.4, and the corresponding specific tampered positions are located as shown in Fig. 11. It can be seen that any tampering operations can be detected, such as adding, deleting, and replacing operations.

5 Conclusion

Based on OFD format, this paper proposes a method of generating and security authentication of electronic bill documents. Since the OFD format document has many advantages, such as relatively fixed typesetting, good system compatibility, strong description ability of graphic element, exquisite layout display effect and high security, etc., it provides an ideal carrier choice for electronic receipt file generation. In addition, the text watermark technology is used to embed the necessary authentication watermark information in the content of electronic bill file, and combined with the traditional electronic seal and digital signature technologies, the integrity, authenticity and security of the electronic bill content are realized. The method described in this article can greatly improve the security performance of electronic bill files, reduce the risk of electronic bill files being subjected to various sabotage attacks during network transmission, and further promote the application of OFD technology in electronic certificates, electronic documents, electronic archives and other more extensive fields.

Acknowledgements. This work is supported by National Key R&D Program of China (No. 2017YFB0802700).

References

1. Yan, Q., Hu, T.: E-Commerce Security Management. Machine Press, China (2007)
2. Chen, H.: The impact and influence of electronic bill on China's bill law. J. Guangdong Inst. Soc. **41**(4), 101–107 (2010)
3. Hung, J.H.: Research on bank electronic document integrity protection based on the watermarking technology. Ph.D. dissertation, Guangdong University of Finance & Economics, China (2010)
4. Zhang, G.H., Xu, P., Sun, Y.: Automatically generating electronic bill technology and application based on PDF. Comput. Eng. Appl. **9**, 3–5 (1999)
5. Chen, F., Zhang, X., He, H.J.: Watermarking embedding and authentication method of positioning PDF electronic invoice falsification. China patent, 104899822 (2015)
6. Ding, T.Y.: Design and Implementation of Electronic Bill Management System Based on List manage. M.S. dissertation, East China Normal University, China (2006)
7. Ma, Z.K.: Construction of the Core Metadata Set of E-invoices. M.S. dissertation, Zhengzhou University of Aeronautics, China (2018)
8. Fang, H.: Electronic Invoice Trading Platform Design and Implementation Based on the Digital Watermarking Technology. Ph.D. dissertation, Southwest Jiaotong University, China (2016)
9. Yon, D.C., Jong, W.K., Myyong, H.K.: Efficient preprocessing of XML queries using structured signatures. Inf. Process. Lett. **87**(5), 257–264 (2003)
10. Eric, L.J.L., Chen, R.F.: An XML multi-signature scheme. Appl. Math. Comput. **149**(1), 1–14 (2004)
11. Romaric, T., Stelvio, C., Nadia, B.: Ensuring XML integrity using watermarking techniques. In: Proceedings 2012 Eighth International Conference on Signal Image Technology and Internet Based Systems, pp. 668–674 (2012)
12. Li, B., Li, W., Chen, Y.Y.: HTML integrity authentication based on fragile digital watermarking. In: Proceedings of ICGC, pp. 322–325 (2009)

13. Zhang, Z.L., Peng, H., Long, X.Z.: A fragile watermarking scheme based on hash function for web pages. In: Proceedings of 2011 International Conference on Network Computing and Information Security, pp. 417–420 (2011)
14. Long, X.Z., Peng, H., Zhang, C.L.: A fragile watermarking scheme for tamper-proof of web pages. In: Proceedings of 2009 WASE International Conference on Information Engineering, pp. 155–158 (2009)
15. Fridrich, J.: Security of fragile authentication watermarks with localization. In: Proceeding of SPIE, Security and Watermarking of Multimedia Contents IV, SanJose, Allfornia, pp. 691–700 (2002)
16. Ullah, R., Khan, A., Malik, A.S.: Dual-purpose semi-fragile watermark: authentication and recovery of digital images. Comput. Electr. Eng. **39**(7), 2019–2030 (2013)
17. Qi, W.F., Guo, W., Zhang, T.: Robust authentication for paper-based text documents based on text watermarking technology. Math. Biosci. Eng. **16**(4), 2233–2249 (2019)
18. Jae, C.Y., Tae, H.H.: Fast normalized cross-correlation. Circ. Syst. Signal Process **28**, 819–843 (2008)

Finding the Better Distortion Function from Prior Scheme for Image Steganography

Lin Li$^{(\boxtimes)}$ and Mingyu Fan

School of Computer Science and Engineering, University of Electronic Science and Technology of China (UESTC), Chengdu 611731, China

Abstract. Steganography is the science and art of concealing the presence of potential communication. However, due to the intricate high dimensional distribution of covers, it is challenging to design more secure schemes in traditional steganography. In this paper, we propose a scheme to find a better steganographic distortion function via a hitting model combined with the prior scheme and an adversarial game. Hitting model is to measure the complexity of the cover elements from the costs given by prior scheme. The adversarial game between steganographic scheme and analyser is implemented as a stackelberg game. The pure and mixed strategies obtained from the hitting model and this game to adjust the costs provide the novel distortion functions. Experiments show that our scheme could find steganographic distortion function with a better security performance compared with the traditional steganographic algorithm against the targeted adversaries.

Keywords: Steganography · Steganalysis · Deep learning · Distortion function · Security game

1 Introduction

Steganography is the art and science of hiding the secret communication process under strict surveillance by a warden. The hiding process is commonly achieved by spreading messages into the elements of covers, e.g. pixels or DCT coefficients of the image. On the contrary, a steganalyser struggles to capture the possible evidence to infer the potential steganographic activity. Intuitively, there exists a trade-off for performing better steganography while defending against the appropriate steganalysis.

The commonly used steganographic schemes in practical are designed in the framework of distortion minimization, such as HUGO [17], WOW [10], and S-UNIWARD [11], which try the best to utilize higher dimensional statistical features. However, the distortion function is usually heuristic designed and the relationship between distortion minimization and security of steganography is also ambiguous. Undoubtedly, steganalysis methods with much higher dimensional(thousands or ten thousand) features, such as spatial rich model (SRM) [6],

© Springer Nature Switzerland AG 2021
X. Sun et al. (Eds.): ICAIS 2021, CCIS 1424, pp. 244–253, 2021.
https://doi.org/10.1007/978-3-030-78621-2_19

were proposed to defeat the state-of-the-art steganographic algorithms. Moreover, deep learning has been incorporated into steganalysis and related tasks [5,12] and achieves an outstanding performance [4]. The deep models, such as XuNet [21], YeNet [22] and SRNET [2] are the state-of-the-art steganalysis deep models. The progress in steganalysis throws a great challenge for steganography.

There have some works to incorporate machine learning/deep learning trying to perform better steganography to evade the detection by the newly steganalysers. They are mainly inspired by GANs [7] and adversarial attack. After incorporating the traditional steganographic method into GANs model, Tang et al. proposed a framework (ASDL-GAN) [20] to learn the embedding change probabilities for the cover images. Through playing 3 player game, the steganographic scheme could be learned in an unsupervised manner [9,23,24,26]. ADV-EMB [19] adjusts the costs of DCT coefficients via attacking the targeted steganalysis model. Zhang et al. [25] find a suitable version of cover images iteratively to embed message bits by attacking the targeted steganalysis model. These steganography schemes via attacking the steganalysers could achieve better security performance compared to state-of-the-art hand-crafted steganographic algorithms, such as J-UNIWARD [11]. However, the problem of unexpected artefacts is still a critical issue. Moreover, the adjustment rule in ADV-EMB is heuristic.

Although these steganographic schemes based on adversarial attack could learn to perform more secure steganography, they strongly rely on the target steganalyser. This might be dangerous because the possible overtraining might lead to exposing detectable artefacts to other unknown classifiers. Moreover, there exists a margin for security between the schemes based on GANs and the hand-crafted algorithms.

The distortion function proposed by the schemes in hand-crafted algorithms such as S-UNIWARD might not capture the adequate complexity of cover elements [3,18]. To design a better distortion function is still a difficult problem.

In this paper, we propose to find novel distortion functions via a hitting model and security game. Hitting model could be utilised to evaluate the complexity of the cover elements and provide the information to adjust costs by learning and cooperating with the prior scheme. The adversarial game between steganographic scheme and analyser is realised as a strong stackelberg game. Randomising the strategies makes steganographic schemes difficult to be predicted by steganalysers. The pure and mixed strategies obtained from this game provide new adjustment rules for costs thus providing the novel distortion functions. Experiments show that our scheme could achieve better performance compared to the state-of-the-art hand-crafted steganographic algorithm against the targeted adversaries.

Our contributions are listed as follows.

1. We propose a hitting model to model the complexity of cover elements. The modelling deviation between two cost functions, i.e. the prior and learned versions, is utilised to perform the hitting strategy.
2. We propose novel distortion functions based on hitting model and security game. The threshold set in hitting model is utilised as the pure strategy

for steganographic schemes. The mixed strategy are solved from the strong stackelberg game provides the better solution. We could obtain new distortion functions from these pure and mixed strategies. These distortion functions have better security performance.

The rest of this paper is structured as follows. Section 2 introduces the related work. Section 3 describes the basic concepts, notations. Section 4 describes our models. Section 5 details the experiments and the results. Section 6 concludes this paper and introduces our future work.

2   Related Work

2.1   Traditional Schemes in Image Steganography

The practical and common used modern steganographic algorithms are working in distortion minimization framework, such as HUGO [17], WOW [10], and S-UNIWARD [11]. However, due to the difficulty of designing the distortion function, the distortion function is usually designed in the additive form with the independent hypothesis of cover elements, but it is usually too simplified. JSteg algorithm modifies the least significant bits of the DCT coefficients, which is designed specifically for JPEG images [16].

2.2   Deep Learning for Steganography

Jamie Hayes et al. proposed an adversarial training method learning to generate steganographic images in an unsupervised manner (StegGAN) [9]. As indicated in [8] and [15], machine learning or deep learning classifiers could be fooled by adversarial examples. By constructing some intentional adversarial perturbations of the inputs (adversarial example), the behaviour of trained classifier will deviate from the original. Zhang et al. [25] tried to iteratively add adversarial perturbations on cover images first, and then embed messages into the "enhanced" cover images. The stego images generated in this way are robust against the detection of the target steganalyser. However, the perturbations may introduce unexpected artifacts detectable by other non-target steganalyzers. Similar to the ASO(Adaptive Steganography by Oracle) scheme [14], ADV-EMB [19] adjusts the costs of DCT coefficients via fooling the steganalysis model and minimise the ratio of the adjusted elements to diminish the influence of the unexpected artefacts. The experiment evidence indicates that it is beneficial to promote the security performance. However, the adjust rule is heuristic and it also faces the risk of unexpected artefacts.

3   Preliminary

In this section, we introduce some notations and basic concepts.

3.1   Notations

Let message be represented as $\mathbf{m} \in \mathcal{M} = \{0,1\}^m$. Let secret key $\mathbf{k} \in \mathcal{K} = \{0,1\}^k$. Let cover and stego objects be represented as $\mathbf{x} \in \mathcal{X} \subseteq \Sigma^n$, $\mathbf{y} \in \mathcal{Y} \subseteq \Sigma^n$ respectively, with $\Sigma = \{0,1,2,...,q-1\}$ being the alphabet and n being the number of elements. The sets $\mathcal{X}$, $\mathcal{Y}$, $\mathcal{M}$ and $\mathcal{K}$ correspond to the spaces of cover objects, stego objects, messages and keys respectively. In this paper, we focus on image cover of grayscale format, where $q = 256$ and $n = W \times H$, where H and W are the height and width of the image.

In steganography, the embedding function

$$f_{emb} : \mathcal{X} \times \mathcal{M} \times \mathcal{K} \mapsto \mathcal{Y} \tag{1}$$

accepts the cover $\mathbf{x}$, messge $\mathbf{m}$ and secret key $\mathbf{k}$, then samples a stego object $\mathbf{y}$. Provided with the correct key k, the extracting function

$$f_{ext} : \mathcal{Y} \times \mathcal{K} \mapsto \mathcal{M} \tag{2}$$

can restore the message.

Let $P_{\mathcal{X}}$ be the unknown distribution of cover objects, and $P_{\mathcal{Y}}$ be the distribution of stego objects. The steganography scheme tries to minimize the distance function between $P_{\mathcal{X}}$ and $P_{\mathcal{Y}}$

$$f_{dis} : P_{\mathcal{X}} \times P_{\mathcal{Y}} \mapsto \mathbb{R}_0^+. \tag{3}$$

The covert communication process in steganography tries to solve the optimization problem

$$\arg\min f_{dis}(P_{\mathcal{X}}, P_{\mathcal{Y}}), subject\ to\ f_{ext}(\mathbf{y}, \mathbf{k}) = \mathbf{m}. \tag{4}$$

3.2   Distortion Minimization Principle

The popular steganographic schemes are based on the distortion minimization principle, where a change of cover object's each element is assigned a cost. The modification of a cover object is to communicate a message while minimizing a distortion function $D(x,y)$ as for the implementation of f_{dis}, specifically,

$$D(x,y) = \sum_{i=1}^{H \times W} \rho^+ \sigma_1(y_i - x_i) + \rho^- \sigma_{-1}(y_i - x_i) \tag{5}$$

There are some works focusing on adjusting the assigned costs. Adaptive Steganography by Oracle(ASO) [14] derives embedding costs from an ensemble of Fisher Linear Discriminants(FLD). Adv-Emb [19] modifies costs ρ_i^+ and ρ_i^- for increasing and decreasing the (i)-pixel obtained by some prior function to evade detection by classifier f. However, there is no single strategy to decide how to assign costs ρ_i. And in the classical methods such as S-UNIWARD, the costs may be assigned inadequately [18].

4   Novel Distortion Function

In this paper, we propose novel distortion functions which focus on cost adjustment strategy utilizing the knowledge about the costs from multiple sources, i.e.
costs from prior scheme and the learned ones. To adjust the costs from prior
scheme, we measure the complexity through a *Hitting* model. When hitted, it
means that the corresponding cover elements might be of lower complexity, and
the corresponding costs from prior scheme might be increased via a threshold
and vice-versa. There exists an adversarial game between steganographic scheme
and analyser. The threshold is utilized as the pure strategy of steganographic
scheme. The analyser also utilizes some strategies. Thus, the novel distortion
functions are obtained represented as the pure and mixed strategy based on hitting model derived from this game, to provide better performance against the
targeted adversaries.

4.1   Hitting Model

Hitting model is to measure the complexity of the cover elements from the costs
from prior scheme and the learned ones. Let $f_{prior}(X)$ be the function to provide
the costs from prior scheme. Let $f_{cost}(X; \theta)$ be the function to learn the costs
from $f_{prior}(X)$. Let *thres* be the threshold to decide the adjustment scale. After
the training process, $f_{cost}(X; \theta)$ has learned the costs from $f_{prior}(X)$. However,
there have some modelling error between $f_{prior}(X)$ and $f_{cost}(X; \theta)$. This information could be utilised to perform the hitting strategy to explore the possible
complexity of the cover elements. The hitting information is to adjust the costs
through *thres*. Formally,

$$\arg \min_{\theta} = \mathbb{E}_{X \sim P_X} \frac{1}{W \times H} ||f_{prior}(X) - f_{cost}(X; \theta)||_2 \tag{6}$$

$$sgncost(X) = sgn(f_{cost}(X; \theta) - \frac{f_{prior}(X)}{2}) \tag{7}$$

$$f_{prior}^+ = f_{prior}^+(sgncost(X) * thres + 1) \tag{8}$$

$$f_{prior}^- = f_{prior}^-(sgncost(X) * thres + 1) \tag{9}$$

$$sgn(x) = \begin{cases} +1 \ , x > 0 \\ \ \ 0 \ \ , x = 0 \\ -1 \ , x < 0 \end{cases} \tag{10}$$

where f_{prior}^+ is the corresponding costs of prior scheme where $sgncost(X)$ is
positive, and f_{prior}^- is the corresponding costs of prior scheme where $sgncost(X)$
is negative. We train the $f_{cost}(X; \theta)$ to obtain the parameter θ. $f_{prior}(X)$ is
implemented by the *Suniward* scheme, and $f_{cost}(X; \theta)$ is implemented by neural
network.

Algorithm 1. Distortion Function Finding Algorithm

$f_{prior}(X)$ is the cost function obtained from prior scheme.
$f_{cost}(X; \theta)$ is the function to learn the costs from $f_{prior}(X)$.
Initialize the θ by learn the costs from $f_{prior}(X)$.
Adjust $f_{prior}(X)$ according to the threshold.
Solve the mixed strategy from the game.
Derive distortion functions from these pure and mixed strategies.

4.2 Strong Stackelberg Game Model

There exists an adversarial game between steganographic scheme and analyser. The threshold *thres* is utilized as the pure strategy of steganographic scheme. Randomization makes steganographic scheme unpredictable. Thus the steganographic scheme utilizes the mixed strategy based on hitting model to play the role of distortion function in steganography.

Let P_{s_i} be the probability of *ith* strategy $thres_i$ exploited by steganographic scheme. Let P_{adv_j} be the probability of j_{th} strategy exploited by the adversary or analyser. The mixed strategy P_{mix} of steganographic scheme is the solution of the strong stackelberg game to provide better performance. The payoff is the corresponding undetectability probability $P_e(k, i)$, where k is the k_{th} strategy of adversary and i is the *ith* strategy of steganographic scheme. Let $payoff_{adv}(\cdot)$ is the payoff of adversary or analyser. The mixed strategy is solved to make the adversary aiming at $payoff_{adv}$ indistinguishable between these pure strategies. In this paper, we utilize two types pure strategies for adversary, i.e. trained on dataset produced by prior scheme($adv - 0$) and trained on dataset produced directly by the new steganographic scheme($adv - 15$). And we utilize the pure and mixed strategies to obtain novel distortion functions to assign cost for each element for steganographic schemes. Formally,

$$payoff_{adv}(k, i) = P_e(k, i) \tag{11}$$

$$\underset{P_{mix}}{\arg\min}\{|\mathbb{E}_{P_{s_i}} payoff_{adv}(k, i) - \mathbb{E}_{P_{s_i}} payoff_{adv}(t, i)|\} \tag{12}$$

where $P_{s_i} = P_{mix}(i)$.

The overall of the process to find distortion function from prior scheme is as shown in Algorithm 1.

5 Experiments

In this section, we conducted experiments to evaluate the performance for security. The settings and notations in the experiments are described in Sect. 5.1. The experimental results and discussions are present in Sect. 5.2.

5.1 Settings

Dataset. All the experiments were performed on image dataset: Bossbase1.01 [1]. We exploited the random splitting strategy to generate corresponding disjoint training, validating, and testing datasets. The Bossbase1.01 dataset was split randomly into 80%, 5%,15% to obtain TRN, VAL and TST respectively. Then we resized them with a Bicubic kernel to obtain a smaller dimension which is 128 because of memory limitation.

XuNet [21] were used for the security performance metric in testing datasets. The *thres* utilized for steganographic schemes was 0, 0.15, 0.2 and the mixed one respectively(i.e. $s - 0$, $s - 15$, $s - 2$, and $s - mix$). When $thres = 0$(s-0), it implies that the steganographic scheme is S-UNIWARD algorithm. TRN and its stego counterparts generated by the steganographic schemes of $s - 0$ and $s - 15$ were used for training the steganalysers. TST and its stego counterparts were used for testing. The trained XuNets are in the setting of $adv - 0$ and $adv - 15$. The message payload is 0.4 bpp. XuNet was trained in the setting of 0.4 bpp.

Implementation Details. We adopted Adam optimizer [13] with learning rate at 2×10^{-4}, $\beta_1 = 0.1$, $\beta_2 = 0.9$, and batch size of 16. The parameters β_1 and β_2 are selected by experience. All weights were initialized from a zero-centered normal distribution with standard deviation 0.02. $f_{cost}(X; \theta)$ was trained with iteration steps before the overfitting occurs. Our proposed scheme and steganalyser were implemented using Tensorflow with Python interface. The experiments were run on an NVIDIA Geforce GTX 1080Ti GPU platform.

5.2 Evaluation Results

In this section, we measure the performance and show the results.

Security Performance. The error rate of missed detection P_{md} and the error rate of false alarm P_{fa} are the two error probabilities measured by steganalyser. We use the average error rate P_e, which is the average of P_{md} and P_{fa} under equal Bayesian prior for cover and steganographic images, to measure the schemes' behaviour against steganalyser. P_{md}, P_{fa}, and P_e are defined as:

$$P_{md} = Pr\{\psi(\mathbf{y}) = 0\} \tag{13}$$

$$P_{fa} = Pr\{\psi(\mathbf{x}) = 1\} \tag{14}$$

$$P_e = \frac{P_{md} + P_{fa}}{2} \tag{15}$$

where ψ is the classifier.

The security performance of schemes is as shown in Table 1. From the results, we can conclude that the security performance of our schemes is promising close to and even surpasses $S - UNIWARD$ against the target steganalysers. The strategy $s - 15$ behaves best when attacking the steganalyser $adv - 0$ through increasing the P_{md}. Although the strategy $s - 2$ has lower P_e than $s - 15$, it still surpass the original prior strategy $s - 0$. These results indicate that the hitting model could find the better assignment for costs by hiding more bits in the complex place and hiding less bits in the clean place. When attacking the steganalyser $adv - 15$, The strategies $s - 0$ and $s - 2$ perform better than $s - 15$, but still worse than the scenario $adv - 0$. This might contribute to the possible advance of $s - 15$ to capture the better complexity of cover's elements.

To satisfy the condition for Eq. 12, we search the mixed strategy s_{mix} of steganographic schemes. In this experiment, the s_{mix} is the strategy with equal probability. The security performance of strategy $s - mix$ is outperformed from these schemes. This indicates that the strong stackelberg game model is beneficial to promoting the security against many adversaries. The possible reason is that the mixed strategy produces less artefacts thus leading to leak less information to adversaries. Thus the decision boundary provided by the mixed strategy is more smooth.

Table 1. The security performance of schemes in the setting of 0.4 bpp

Schemes	adv-0			adv-15		
	P_{fa}	P_{md}	P_e	P_{fa}	P_{md}	P_e
$s - 0$	0.37	0.25	0.31	0.32	0.38	0.35
$s - 15$	0.37	0.39	0.38	0.32	0.34	0.33
$s - 2$	0.37	0.30	0.34	0.32	0.37	0.35
$s - mix$	0.37	0.43	0.40	0.32	0.40	0.36

6 Conclusions and Future Work

We proposed to find better steganographic distortion functions via a hitting model combined with the prior scheme and stackelberg game. The experimental results show that the proposed scheme could find a distortion function which achieves better security performance compared to the human-crafted stegano-graphic algorithm against the target adversary. There are many directions to extend this work, for example, exploring more details of the hitting model; the better game model and architecture of neural network; working on frequency domain. In the future, we plan to expand this work to advance the steganogra-phy from the view of deep learning and security game.

References

1. Bas, P., Filler, T., Pevný, T.: "Break our steganographic system": the ins and outs of organizing BOSS. In: Filler, T., Pevný, T., Craver, S., Ker, A. (eds.) IH 2011. LNCS, vol. 6958, pp. 59–70. Springer, Heidelberg (2011). https://doi.org/10.1007/978-3-642-24178-9_5

2. Boroumand, M., Chen, M., Fridrich, J.: Deep residual network for steganalysis of digital images. IEEE Trans. Inf. Forensics Secur. **14**(5), 1181–1193 (2018)
3. Butora, J., Yousfi, Y., Fridrich, J.: Turning cost-based steganography into model-based. In: Proceedings of the 2020 ACM Workshop on Information Hiding and Multimedia Security, pp. 151–159 (2020)
4. Chaumont, M.: Deep learning in steganography and steganalysis from 2015 to 2018. arXiv preprint arXiv:1904.01444 (2019)
5. Chen, X., Zhang, Z., Qiu, A., Xia, Z., Xiong, N.: A novel coverless steganography method based on image selection and StarGan. IEEE Trans. Netw. Sci. Eng. (2020)
6. Fridrich, J., Kodovsky, J.: Rich models for steganalysis of digital images. IEEE Trans. Inf. Forensics Secur. **7**(3), 868–882 (2012)
7. Goodfellow, I., et al.: Generative adversarial nets. In: Advances in Neural Information Processing Systems, pp. 2672–2680 (2014)
8. Goodfellow, I.J., Shlens, J., Szegedy, C.: Explaining and harnessing adversarial examples. arXiv preprint arXiv:1412.6572 (2014)
9. Hayes, J., Danezis, G.: Generating steganographic images via adversarial training. In: Advances in Neural Information Processing Systems, pp. 1954–1963 (2017)
10. Holub, V., Fridrich, J.: Designing steganographic distortion using directional filters. In: 2012 IEEE International Workshop on Information Forensics and Security (WIFS), pp. 234–239. IEEE (2012)
11. Holub, V., Fridrich, J., Denemark, T.: Universal distortion function for steganography in an arbitrary domain. EURASIP J. Inf. Secur. **2014**(1), 1–13 (2014). https://doi.org/10.1186/1687-417X-2014-1
12. Hu, B., Wang, J.: Deep learning for distinguishing computer generated images and natural images: a survey. J. Inf. Hiding Priv. Protect. **2**(2), 95 (2020)
13. Kingma, D.P., Ba, J.: Adam: a method for stochastic optimization. arXiv preprint arXiv:1412.6980 (2014)
14. Kouider, S., Chaumont, M., Puech, W.: Adaptive steganography by oracle (ASO). In: 2013 IEEE International Conference on Multimedia and Expo (ICME), pp. 1–6. IEEE (2013)
15. Kurakin, A., Goodfellow, I., Bengio, S.: Adversarial examples in the physical world. arXiv preprint arXiv:1607.02533 (2016)
16. Li, B., He, J., Huang, J., Shi, Y.Q.: A survey on image steganography and steganalysis. J. Inf. Hiding Multimed. Sig. Process. **2**(2), 142–172 (2011)
17. Pevný, T., Filler, T., Bas, P.: Using high-dimensional image models to perform highly undetectable steganography. In: Böhme, R., Fong, P.W.L., Safavi-Naini, R. (eds.) IH 2010. LNCS, vol. 6387, pp. 161–177. Springer, Heidelberg (2010). https://doi.org/10.1007/978-3-642-16435-4_13
18. Pevny, T., Ker, A.D.: Exploring non-additive distortion in steganography. In: Proceedings of the 6th ACM Workshop on Information Hiding and Multimedia Security, pp. 109–114 (2018)
19. Tang, W., Li, B., Tan, S., Barni, M., Huang, J.: CNN-based adversarial embedding for image steganography. IEEE Trans. Inf. Forensics Secur. **14**(8), 2074–2087 (2019)
20. Tang, W., Tan, S., Li, B., Huang, J.: Automatic steganographic distortion learning using a generative adversarial network. IEEE Signal Process. Lett. **24**(10), 1547–1551 (2017)
21. Xu, G., Wu, H.Z., Shi, Y.Q.: Structural design of convolutional neural networks for steganalysis. IEEE Signal Process. Lett. **23**(5), 708–712 (2016)
22. Ye, J., Ni, J., Yi, Y.: Deep learning hierarchical representations for image steganalysis. IEEE Trans. Inf. Forensics Secur. **12**(11), 2545–2557 (2017)

23. Yedroudj, M., Comby, F., Chaumont, M.: Steganography using a 3 player game. arXiv preprint arXiv:1907.06956 (2019)
24. Zhang, K.A., Cuesta-Infante, A., Xu, L., Veeramachaneni, K.: SteganoGAN: high capacity image steganography with GANs. arXiv preprint arXiv:1901.03892 (2019)
25. Zhang, Y., Zhang, W., Chen, K., Liu, J., Liu, Y., Yu, N.: Adversarial examples against deep neural network based steganalysis. In: Proceedings of the 6th ACM Workshop on Information Hiding and Multimedia Security, pp. 67–72 (2018)
26. Zhu, J., Kaplan, R., Johnson, J., Fei-Fei, L.: HiDDeN: hiding data with deep networks. In: Ferrari, V., Hebert, M., Sminchisescu, C., Weiss, Y. (eds.) ECCV 2018. LNCS, vol. 11219, pp. 682–697. Springer, Cham (2018). https://doi.org/10.1007/978-3-030-01267-0_40

Application in Aviation Customer Churn Prediction Using Classification Algorithm Based on Machine Learning

Yuming Ling[1], Zhixi Wang[1(✉)], and Che Wu[2]

[1] Hunan University of Science and Technology, Xiangtan 411201, China
[2] Air Co., Ltd., Guangzhou 510000, China

Abstract. According to the traditional machine learning model as a learner, customer loss prediction model is implemented by Logistic Regression, Decision Tree, Random Forest, Support Vector Machine, Gradient Boosting Decision Tree, Multi-Layer Perceptron algorithm and Long Short-term Memory Neutral Network in deep learning, and experiments used the real sample data set of about 30,000 customers of an airline. The results show that the Gradient Boosting Decision Tree model is the most accurate prediction model among the seven prediction models, and has the best prediction effect, which can accurately predict customers who will be lost.

Keywords: Customer churn · Prediction model · Machine learning · Gradient lifting tree model

1 Introduction

Customer churn means that the original customers of the company stop buying the products of the company or refuse to accept the services of the company1. With the rapid development of all walks of life, the competition among companies is becoming more and more fierce. Therefore, how to develop new customers and prevent the loss of customers are two major problems faced by companies. Research shows that the cost of developing a new customer is 5–6 times that of maintaining an old customer, so preventing customer churn is the most important problem for the company1. Accurately predicting the customers who are about to lose will help the company to adjust its strategy effectively in advance to retain customers. Because the cost of retaining customers is limited, the model should be able to predict the customers who intend to lose more accurately, so as to prevent excessive costs from being invested in the wrong predicted customers. For these customers who are about to lose, the relevant departments of the company can formulate specific plans and adjust marketing strategies, so as to retain customers.

In recent years, there have been a lot of researches on the analysis of customer churn in various industries, especially in the communication industry. For example, J. M. Ding et al. [2] proposed an improved random forest algorithm to solve the problem of data

© Springer Nature Switzerland AG 2021
X. Sun et al. (Eds.): ICAIS 2021, CCIS 1424, pp. 254–264, 2021.
https://doi.org/10.1007/978-3-030-78621-2_20

imbalance when predicting customer churn. Aiming at the division method of each tree branch node generated in random forest: information gain, this algorithm adds the information of customer life value to the information gain division method, and then applied the improved random forest algorithm to the customer churn prediction of a telecom company. The results show that the improved algorithm not only effectively solves the problem of data imbalance, but also has better accuracy in the prediction of high-value customer churn; Z. Y. Zhu et al. [3] put forward two improved Bayesian network models: tree enhanced naive Bayesian network and Markov blanket Bayesian network model, and made an experimental analysis of losing customers in the mobile field. Compared with the basic neural network model, it is proved that the Markov blanket Bayesian network model proposed by him has better performance; Y. Zhang et al. [4] applied the C5.0 algorithm to predict customer churn in postal short message service; G. E. Xia et al. [5] put forward two improved multi-layer perceptron models. The main improvement methods are to use stacking self-encoder and entity embedding respectively. By mapping the high-dimensional coded data of discrete attributes to low-dimensional space, the sparse data generated by one-hot coding is reduced, and the correlation between discrete attribute values is increased. And experiment on two published telecommunication user data sets prove the effectiveness of the proposed improved algorithm; In the field of electronic commerce, C. H. Ju et al. [6] integrated individual activity into the prediction model of electronic commerce customer churn, and compared with other methods on a B2C e-commerce customer data set, the experiment verified that this model has higher accuracy and efficiency; In the medical field, Min X, Yu B et al. [7] used traditional machine learning algorithms: logistic regression, random forest, support vector machine, gradient boosting decision tree, multi-layer perceptron and neural network to predict whether patients will lose after 30 days. The prediction accuracy is about 70%, and the experimental results show that the prediction effect of neural network is not as good as some traditional machine learning methods.

In the field of aviation customer churn prediction, there are few researches and applications at present, and most of them use a single method to build a churn prediction model for prediction. For example, Y. Q. Cui [8] used the C5.0 algorithm to predict aviation customer churn, and the accuracy reached 88.3%. W. T. Yang et al. [9] used logistic regression algorithm and C5.0 algorithm to predict the loss of aviation customers, which proved that C5.0 algorithm has higher accuracy. Reference [7] shows the effect of various methods on patient churn prediction, and we apply these methods to airline customer churn prediction Experiments show that the traditional machine learning method is more suitable for aviation customer churn prediction than the patient churn prediction in the medical field, but the same thing is that the prediction effect of the deep learning model is not better than that of some traditional machine learning methods.

2   Machine Learning Model and Customer Churn Prediction

Customer churn prediction can be regarded as a binary classification problem. Different algorithms can be used to build prediction models. Some samples are selected from the data set to train the models, and then the trained models are obtained. Through the trained models, the test samples are predicted, and the customers who are about to lose are discovered. In the face of customer churn in different fields, the prediction effects of various models are different. Only by comparative analysis under specific conditions can we identify the better model. In this paper, six traditional machine learning models and a deep neural network are used to analyze and compare the prediction of aviation customer churn.

2.1 Logistic Regression (LR) [10]

Logistic regression is a commonly used machine learning method to estimate the probability of something happening. The form of logistic regression is basically the same as that of linear regression. A sigmod function is added to logistic regression based on linear regression. The function of sigmod function is to substitute the output value of linear regression into sigmod function, and then a final output value above the interval [0, 1] can be obtained. The value range is [0, 1], so the output value at this time is equivalent to a probability. Those with probability greater than 0.5 are classified as one class, and those with probability less than 0.5 are classified as another class. On this basis, the construction of binary classification logistic regression model is completed. The logistic regression model is robust to the small noise in the data, but if the feature space in the data is large, the performance of the logistic regression model is not very good, and there is a high probability of over-fitting, so the regularization process needs to be added.

2.2 Support Vector Machine (SVM) [11]

SVM algorithm is a machine learning algorithm based on statistical learning theory. SVM maps vectors to a higher dimensional space. In this space, hyperplane with good classification ability can be found by learning. The function of this hyperplane is to separate different kinds of data in the dataset as much as possible, and to maximize the interval between data near the hyperplane and hyperplane. The classifier constructed on this basis can maximize the interval between different classes. The larger the interval, the better the classifier effect. Compared with other algorithms, SVM is more effective when dealing with small samples and high-dimensional data, and SVM has good generalization ability. However, when dealing with large sample data sets, SVM runs much longer than LR, and is sensitive to the problem of missing data.

2.3 Decision Tree (DT) [12]

Decision Tree algorithm is an inductive learning method, which can train a tree-like model similar to flow chart from a given disordered training sample. Each non-leaf node in the decision tree uses Gini coefficient or information entropy method to record which feature is used to judge the category, and each leaf node represents the final judged category. The separate path is formed from the root node to each leaf node. Whenever a new sample is tested, it is only necessary to start from the root node, make feature judgment at each branch node, and continue to enter the subtree along the corresponding branch for retest until it reaches the leaf node. The category represented by the leaf node is the prediction category of the current test sample. Compared with other models, the data preparation of Decision Tree model is simpler, which can process numerical data and category data at the same time without removing redundant or blank attributes. Moreover, it is easy to realize, and the meaning expressed by the results of decision tree can be better explained. But the decision tree model is suitable for large sample sets and few features. When the sample set is small, the decision tree model is unstable, and when the number of features is too large, the accuracy of the decision tree model is not high enough.

2.4 Random Forest (RF) [13]

Random Forest algorithm is an integrated learning algorithm, which trains several weak learners and then combines them to form the final strong learner. The weak learner used in Random Forest algorithm is CART Decision Tree, and the results of several CART Decision Trees are used for simple voting to make the final decision. The biggest characteristic of random forest is that randomness is introduced in two places: the first randomness is to extract a certain amount of training samples from the total training set as the training set of a decision tree in random forest; The second randomness is that in the process of decision tree splitting, m feature subsets (m << M) are randomly selected from the total feature dimension M, and a certain feature is selected from the extracted m features as the best splitting feature of the decision tree. The decision tree will continue to split every time according to this process and grow to the maximum extent until it reaches the specified depth or can no longer split.

2.5 Gradient Boosting Decision Tree (GBDT) [14]

The decision tree used by GBDT is CART Regression Tree. Every iteration of the weak learner fits the negative gradient of the loss function, which can be simply understood as the error between the real value and the prediction of the weak learner, and then the results of each weak learner are added to get the final decision. When constructing decision tree, the left and right subtrees of decision tree are roughly the same as those of Random Forest algorithm, which is divided by information entropy, mutual information and Gini coefficient according to different situations. In total, GBDT improves the overall performance by reducing the model deviation.

2.6 Multi-layer Perceptron (MLP) [15]

Multi-Layer Perceptron is also called artificial neural network. Besides the input and output layer, it can have multiple hidden layers. The simplest MLP contains only one hidden layer, that is, three-layer structure. Multilayer perceptron is a kind of artificial neural network with forward structure, which maps a set of input vectors to a set of output vectors. Each layer in MLP is fully connected to the next layer. Except the input layer node and the output node, each node is a neuron with activation function, which is trained by back propagation algorithm. However, in the hidden layer of MLP, the number of nodes contained in each hidden layer is not easy to determine, and when the input scale is large, the learning speed is slow, and it is easy to fall into local extremum, so the potential meaning of data cannot be fully mined.

2.7 Long Short-Term Memory Neural Network (LSTM) [16]

LSTM is a variant of Recurrent Neural Network, and its basic units include output gate, input gate, forgetting gate and cell state, in which cell state can save long-term historical information and ensure the effective flow of information during model training, and the gate mechanism can limit the amount of information. Recurrent Neural Network can only have short-term memory because of gradient disappearance, while LSTM combines short-term memory with long-term memory through subtle gate control, which can solve the problem of gradient disappearance to a certain extent.

2.8 Customer Churn Forecast

In this paper, we choose Logistic Regression, Decision Tree, Random Forest, Support Vector Machine, Gradient Boosting Decision Tree, Multi-Layer Perceptron and Long Short-term Memory Neutral Network in deep learning to build customer churn prediction model by using the machine learning tool scikit-learn and deep learning toolkit torch in Anaconda 3.0 software version published by Anaconda company. The flow chart of prediction model is shown in Fig. 1.

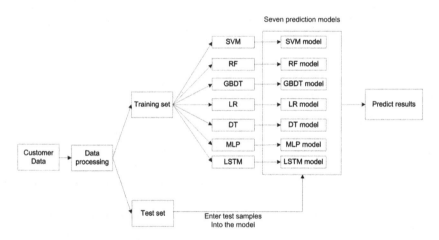

Fig. 1. Flow chart of prediction model

Firstly, carry out data processing on customer data, and then the data set is divided into training set and test set. The training set is used to train the model, and the test set is input into the trained model to get the prediction result finally.

3 Experimental Process and Result Analysis

3.1 Data Statistics

The experimental data set of this paper comes from the real database of an airline, and the data of 30,038 users from January 2017 to December 2017 are selected. The data set includes the following categories: customer membership number; customer's gender, customer's age, total number of tickets purchased, total amount of tickets purchased, last purchase time, registration time, cabin class, purchase method, baggage weight, and whether the seat is near the window.

3.2 Data Processing

The lost customers have the characteristic of not buying airline products any more. Based on this characteristic, we define the customers who no longer have the airline ticket purchase record from November 1st as lost customers, and those who still have the ticket purchase record after November 1st as non-lost customers. In this paper, the time interval is set to 1 month, and the user data from January 1, 2017 to September 31, 2017 is used to analyze and predict the customer churn state one month later. In the experiment, the positive sample is the undiluted user data from January to September, and the label is 1; The negative sample is the lost user data from January to September, and the label is 0. Finally, the number pairs of lost customers and non-lost customers are shown in Table 1.

Table 1. Lost customers and Non-lost customers

Customers	Numbers
Non-lost customers	27415
Lost customers	2623

Among 30038 customers, 27,415 customers were not lost and 2,623 customers were lost.

The characteristics of 30038 customers were processed in the following ways: customer gender: 1- female, 2- male; Whether it is by the window: 1- near the window, 2- not near the window; Because different customers may have multiple ticket purchase records, select the item with the most frequent occurrence of cabin class and purchase method for one-hot processing; The customer's age, total number of tickets purchased, total amount of tickets purchased, last purchase time, registration time and baggage weight all adopt actual values, and all attribute features are standardized by 0–1, so that data of different scales are scaled to the same data interval and range, and reduced the influence of data differences on the model.

References [17–19] introduce a variety of feature selection methods, and we choose the sequence backward selection algorithm (SBS) 18 to select experimental features. The algorithm is described as follows: First, the feature set M starts, and one feature X is removed from the feature set M, so that the prediction accuracy reaches the highest after the remaining M-1 features are input into the model, and then the remaining M-2 features are input. Because the number of output features of each model is different through SBS, five customer features with the most frequent occurrences are selected as model input features. Ten characteristics are: customer gender, customer age, total number of tickets purchased, total amount of tickets purchased, last time of purchase, length of registration, cabin class, purchase method, baggage weight, and whether the seat is by the window. The features selected by the final sequence backward selection algorithm are shown in Table 2.

Table 2. Features selected by SBS

Experimental characteristics
registration time (days)
total purchase amount
purchase times
last purchase time (days)
cabin class

Finally, we use five features: registration time (days), total purchase amount, purchase times, last purchase time (days), and cabin class as input features when training the model.

3.3 Evaluation Methods

For the two classification problems of customer churn, the *accuracy*, *recall* and *F1* are usually used to evaluate the model [1]. In this paper, we take the average of *accuracy*, *recall* and *F1* sum as the final evaluation index of the models. Understanding the *recall*, *accuracy* and *F1* requires confusion matrix, which is shown in Table 3.

Table 3. Confusion matrix

True	Predict	
	1	0
Non-lost customers (1)	TP	FN
Lost customers (0)	FP	TN

In the confusion matrix, a positive example is represented by 1: Non-lost customers; Use 0 as a counter example: Lost customers. TP represents the number of positive cases with correct prediction, FP represents the number of positive cases with wrong prediction, FN represents the number of counter-examples with wrong prediction, and TN represents the number of counter-examples with correct prediction. Formulas 1–5 respectively give the calculation formulas of *accuracy*, *precision*, *recall*, *F1* and the final evaluation index of the models (A*verage*).

$$Accuracy = \frac{TP + TN}{TP + TN + FP + FN} \tag{1}$$

Accuracy means the ability of classifier system to judge the whole sample.

$$Precision = \frac{TP}{TP + FP} \tag{2}$$

Precision means the ratio of correctly predicted positive cases to the total predicted positive cases.

$$Recall = \frac{TP}{TP + FN} \tag{3}$$

Recall means the ratio of the positive cases of the prediction pair to the real positive cases.

$$F1 = \frac{2 * R * P}{R + P} \tag{4}$$

F1 means that weighted harmonic means of Precision and Recall.

$$Average = \frac{A + R + F1}{3} \tag{5}$$

Average indicates the final evaluation index of the models.

3.4 Experimental Results

In this paper, by 5-cross validation, 80% of the experimental data set is selected randomly as the training set, and the remaining 20% is used as the test set. Support Vector Machine Model, Logistic Regression Model, Random Forest Model, Gradient Boosting Decision Tree Model, Decision Tree Model, Multi-Layer Perceptron Model and Long Short-term Memory Neutral Network are used to study on the training set, and the trained model is used to predict on the test set. Though five experiments, the average values of *accuracy, recall* and *F1* of the seven prediction models, and the average values of the three evaluation indexes after addition are shown in Table 4. In order to see the prediction effect of each model more intuitively, the final evaluation results are displayed in the form of a column chart, as shown in Fig. 2.

It can be concluded from Table 4 that the LR prediction model has the lowest *accuracy* among the seven prediction models. The GBDT model has the highest *accuracy* and *F1* value in the prediction of aviation customer churn, and its prediction *accuracy* reaches 95.8% and *F1* value reaches 97.7%. SVM model has the highest *recall* score; The *accuracy* index of RF model is only about 0.4% lower than that of GBDT model; The *accuracy* of LSTM prediction model reaches 93%, but its *recall* and *F1* value are the worst among the seven models.

In reference [7], the *accuracy* of traditional machine learning methods: LR, SVM, RF, GBDT and MLP in predicting patient readmission is about 75%; The prediction *accuracy* of deep learning model is about 65%, and the effect is still inferior to the traditional machine learning method. In this paper, the traditional machine learning methods: LR, SVM, DT, RF, GBDT and MLP all have an *accuracy* rate of over 90%. Although the prediction model using the popular LSTM method is not as effective as

Table 4. Model prediction results

Model	Accuracy	Recall	F1	Average
SVM	0.9129	0.9997	0.9545	0.9557
RF	0.9541	0.9751	0.9749	0.9680
GBDT	0.9586	0.9774	0.9773	0.9711
LR	0.9126	0.9956	0.9543	0.9542
DT	0.9396	0.9635	0.9663	0.9565
MLP	0.9401	0.9492	0.9678	0.9524
LSTM	0.9305	0.7434	0.7636	0.8215

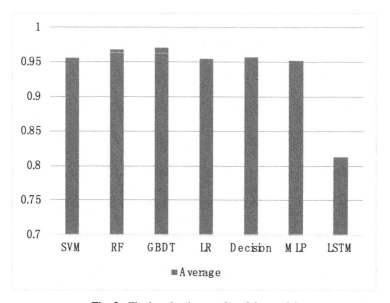

Fig. 2. Final evaluation results of the model

the traditional GBDT, RF, DT and MLP method, its *accuracy* is also over 90%, which proves that these traditional machine learning methods and LSTM are effective in the field of aviation customer churn prediction. It can be seen from Fig. 2 that the GBDT model has the highest evaluation index among all models, and the GBDT model can more accurately identify the customers who are about to be lost and the customers who are not lost, save the energy that airlines spend on the customers who are not lost, and put limited energy into the customers who are about to be lost.

4   Conclusion and Prospect

The phenomenon of customer churn widely exists in various industries, which makes it difficult to use the forecasting method to a certain extent. In this paper, aiming at the phenomenon of customer churn in aviation field, seven forecasting models of customer churn in aviation field are trained and tested on existing real data sets. Experimental results show that although LSTM is a popular deep learning method, its prediction accuracy is not the highest. As a traditional machine learning method, the GBDT model has the highest prediction accuracy, while the prediction accuracy of LR and SVM are relatively low. Airlines can adopt different forecasting models on different data sets, and take corresponding measures to reduce the losses caused by customer churn according to the forecasting results obtained by the models. In view of the problem that the specific definition of airline customer churn is not accurate enough, in the future work, we will consider how to take into account the characteristics of airline customers' ticket purchasing habits and seasonal factors, such as customers who have continuously reduced their monthly consumption times, do not buy tickets during holidays or have no consumption record within three months are defined as lost customers. Aiming at the problem that the data scale is not large enough and the accuracy of the model is not high enough, we will consider how to improve the accuracy of the model by improving the algorithm or combining models on larger data sets.

Funding Statement. Thanks for the support of 9 Air Co., Ltd.

Conflicts of Interest. We have no conflicts of interest to report regarding the present study.

References

1. Yu, X.B., Cao, J., Gong, Z.W.: Review on customer churn issue. Comput. Integr. Manuf. Syst. **18**(10), 2253–2263 (2012)
2. Ding, J.M., Liu, G.Q., Li, H., et al.: The application of improved random forest in the telecom customer churn prediction. PR & AI **28**(11), 1041–1049 (2015)
3. Zhu, Z.Y., Xu, C.M., Liu, Z.B., et al.: Research of customer churn analysis based on the Bayesian network. Comput. Eng. Sci. **35**(3), 155–158 (2013)
4. Zhang, Y., Zhang, Z.M.: A customer churn alarm model based on the C5.0 decision tree-taking the postal short message as an example. Stat. Inf. Forum **30**(1), 89–94 (2015)
5. Xia, G.E., Tang, Q., Zhang, X.Q.: Research of customer churn analysis based on the Bayesian network. Comput. Eng. Appl. **56**(14), 257–263 (2020)
6. Ju, C.H., Lu, Q.B., Guo, F.P.: E-commerce customer churn prediction model combined with individual activity. Syst. Eng.-Theory Pract. **33**(1), 141–150 (2013)
7. Min, X., Yu, B., Wang, F.: E-commerce customer churn prediction model combined with individual activity. Sci. Rep. **9**(1), 2362–2371 (2019)
8. Cui, Y.Q.: Analysis of the airline customer churn based on C5.0 algorithm. J. Xi'an Aeronaut. Univ. **36**(1), 72–77 (2018)
9. Yang, W.T.: Research on the Loss of Customers Based on Logistic Regression and Decision Tree Algorithm, M.S. dissertation, Dalian University of Technology, China (2019)
10. Lee, S.I., Lee, H., Abbeel, P., Ng, A.Y.: Efficient l~1 regularized logistic regression. In: AAAI, Boston, USA, pp. 401–408 (2006)
11. Cortes, C.: Support-vector networks. Mach. Learn. **20**(3), 273–297 (1995)
12. Salzberg, S.L.: C4.5: programs for machine learning. Mach. Learn. **16**(3), 235–240 (1994)
13. Breiman, L.: Random forests. Mach. Learn. **45**(1), 5–32 (2001)
14. Friedman, J.H.: Greedy function approximation: a gradient boosting machine. Ann. Stat. **29**(5), 1189–1232 (2001)

15. Rumelhart, D.E., Hinton, G.E., Williams, R.J.: Learning representations by back-propagating errors. Nature **323**(9), 533–536 (1986)

16. Hochreiter, S., Schmidhuber, J.: Long short-term memory. Neural Comput. **9**(8), 1735–1780 (1997)

17. Xiao, J., Xiao, Y., Huang, A., Liu, D., Wang, S.: Feature-selection-based dynamic transfer ensemble model for customer churn prediction. Knowl. Inf. Syst. **43**(1), 29–51 (2014). https://doi.org/10.1007/s10115-013-0722-y

18. Song, F.X., Gao, X.M., et al.: Dimensionality reduction in statistical pattern recognition and low loss dimensionality reduction. Chin. J. Comput. **28**(11), 1915–1922 (2005)

19. Liu, Y., Cao, J.J., et al.: Survey on stability of feature selection. J. Softw. **29**(9), 2559–2579 (2018)

Color Image Steganography Scheme Based on Convolutional Neural Network

Cheng Zeng[1], Jingbing Li[1,2(✉)], Jingjun Zhou[1], and Saqib Ali Nawaz[1]

[1] College of Information and Communication Engineering, Hainan University, Haikou, Hainan, People's Republic of China
[2] State Key Laboratory of Marine Resource Utilization in the South China Sea, Hainan University, Haikou, Hainan, People's Republic of China

Abstract. Image steganography has always an important part in the field of information security. In this paper, we propose a new color image steganography scheme base on convolutional neural network, which can hide the secret image into the cover image of the same size. The steganography scheme consists of two parts, the hiding network and the reveal network. Hiding network uses the skip connection, the low-level features of the image can be transmitted to each subsequent layer, which helps to hide the details of the secret image. Experimental results show that this scheme can not only achieve the steganography of color images, but also maintain a high embedding ability. Compared with other methods, the PSNR and SSIM mean values of our steganography image reach 43.6 dB and 0.987, the secret images extracted through the extracting network have also achieved good results.

Keywords: Information hiding · Color image steganography · Skip connection · Convolutional neural network

1 Introduction

With the rapid development of networks and smart devices, digital media has become an important carrier of communication. At the same time, with the rapid development of cloud computing, people store more and more data on cloud platforms. The Internet generates hundreds of millions of images, texts, videos and other data every day [1, 2]. How to protect information security has become a new challenge in the era of big data. Steganography is an effective way. Steganography is different from traditional encryption technology, the encryption technology mainly converts secret content into ciphertext to protect the integrity and security of secret content [3]. Steganography can be regarded as disguised encryption technology. Steganography embeds the message into the carrier without changing its perception characteristics, ensure that the carrier with embedded secret information looks very similar to the original carrier visually, thus avoid being intercept and attack. Steganography can be divided into two basic parts, the information to be hidden and the carrier. Because the image has rich texture characteristics, the image is usually the carrier, and the hidden information can be text, image, and audio. The main evaluation criteria for image steganography include steganography capacity,

© Springer Nature Switzerland AG 2021
X. Sun et al. (Eds.): ICAIS 2021, CCIS 1424, pp. 265–277, 2021.
https://doi.org/10.1007/978-3-030-78621-2_21

imperceptibility and security, these three indicators always restrict each other. Image steganography algorithms can be divided into traditional steganography algorithms and deep learning-based steganography algorithms.

According to different steganography methods, traditional image steganography algorithms can be divided into spatial domain-based image steganography and transform domain-based image steganography. Image steganography based on spatial domain mainly realizes the embedding of information by directly modifying pixel values. The representative algorithm is the LSB algorithm [4]. The LSB algorithm embeds information into the cover image by modifying the lowest bit of the pixel value. The transform domain algorithm first transforms the image and then embeds the information into the cover image by modifying the transform domain coefficients. The representative algorithm is the steganography algorithm based on JPEG in the DCT domain as the carrier [5–7]. Deep learning has excellent feature extraction and feature representation capabilities, have been widely used in tasks such as computer vision and natural language processing, and have achieved remarkable results [8, 9]. Many researchers are committed to applying deep learning to image steganography to obtain better steganography results. The application of deep learning enables image steganography to abandon part of the professional domain knowledge and achieve image steganography through large-scale sample training. The SGAN [10] model is composed of generator G, discriminator D and analyzer S, this is the first image steganography model based on deep learning. The generator G generates image samples, the discriminator D judges whether the generated samples are real samples, the analyzer S judges the security of the stego-image, and the three models alternately update the parameters during training. SGAN improves the security of image steganography, but the steganography part still uses traditional algorithms. SSGAN [11] proposed a method base on SGAN, improve stego-image security, but the stego-image generated by SGAN and SSGAN has the problem of semantic distortion. Baluja et al. [12] proposed a deep steganography model based on a self-encoder, which can embed a color image into another color image, and this model can generate a high-quality stego-image. However, when the attacker obtains the cover image, the secret image can be discovered by calculating and enlarging the residual image between the cover image and the stego-image. Rehaan et al. [13] proposed an image steganography model based on encoder-decoder, which can embed a gray-scale image into another color image. The model is composed of an encoder and a decoder. The hiding capacity of the model is high, but the stego-image has serious color distortion problems, which leads to poor concealment of the secret image. Zhang et al. [14] proposed the ISGAN model, which embeds the grayscale image in the Y channel of the cover image. The Y channel does not contain color difference information, so it will not cause color distortion problems, but the value of the Y channel will become larger, resulting in brighter images. Zhang et al. [15] proposed a new image steganography method based on convolutional neural network, which can support images of different sizes and arbitrary binary data, and embed it in the cover image. Wang et al. [16] proposed an image steganography model based on generative adversarial networks and perceptual loss. The model maintains the same statistical characteristics of the cover image and the stego-image in the high-dimensional feature space, and improve the security of the stego-image. Zhang [15] and Wang [16] have improved in security, but the capacity is still very limited. Li et al. [17] proposed a grayscale image steganography scheme, which can embed grayscale images into grayscale images of the same size. The scheme also encrypts the secret image before embedding to improve the security of the secret image.

Our solution uses CNN to embed the encrypted color image into the same size color image. The major contributions of our work can be summarized as follows:

a) Before inputting to the hidden network, input the cover image and the secret image to the convolutional neural network to obtain high-dimensional features, which can improve the security of image steganography.
b) The hiding network uses skip connections to connect low-level features and high-level features, which helps to hide the secret image.
c) Achieve the steganography of color images, with high steganography capacity, and the stego-image generated without distortion.

2   Related Work

2.1   Traditional Image Steganography Algorithm

The LSB [4] algorithm embeds information into the cover image by modifying the lowest bit of the pixel value. This algorithm has a small impact on the perception of the cover image and the algorithm complexity is low. However, the LSB algorithm makes the stego-image have obvious statistical characteristics, which does not exist in the cover image. Therefore, adaptive image steganography has been proposed in the field of spatial image steganography [18–20]. The neighborhood correlation of pixels in the region with rich image texture is complicated, and the pixel value is difficult to predict based on its neighborhood pixels, so it is difficult to be detected after modification. Therefore, the cost of modifying the complex texture area is small, and it should be modified first. For texture smooth areas, the pixel value can be predicted through the neighborhood, and it is easy to detect the change of the pixel value after modification, so a larger modification cost is given to prevent it from being easily modified. Then the hidden information is embedded into the cover image through STC or other encoding methods. The main representative algorithms are Hugo [18], UNIWARD [19] and WOW [20]. The steganography algorithm in the transform domain is mainly based on the JPEG in the DCT domain as the carrier. The main algorithms are F5 [5], MME [6] and J-UNIWARD [7]. The core of these algorithms is the LSB algorithm Extend to the DCT domain, the approximate flow of this type of algorithm as shown in Fig. 1.

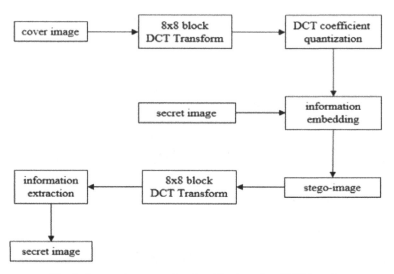

Fig. 1. Image steganography algorithm based on DCT domain

2.2 Image Steganography Based on Deep Learning

The development of deep learning provides an effective way for image steganography. Currently, the models proposed by many researchers are based on generative adversarial networks and use steganalysis to improve security, but the steganography capacity of many models are still very limited. The model proposed by Baluja [12] is based on a deep convolutional neural network, which can embed color images into color images of the same size. The model as shown in Fig. 2. The network is composed of three parts: pre network, hidden network and reveal Network. The pre network has two functions: If the size of the image to be hidden is smaller than the cover image, it will be enlarged so that it has the same size as the cover image; the second function is to convert the pixel features of the secret image into more useful ones. The hidden network takes the cover image and the image of pre network output as input, and output stego-image. The network has multiple convolution kernels of different sizes and can obtain features of different scales of the image. The reveal network takes the stego-image as input, and outputs the secret image through the deep convolutional neural network. Unlike the traditional method, this solution can embed the secret image into all available bits of the cover image through convolutional neural network, and has high steganography capacity. Rehaan et al. [13] proposed an image steganography model based on convolutional neural network and encoder-decoder, the network can embed grayscale images in color images, the model structure as shown in Fig. 3. The encoder part of the model has two branches: host branch and guest branch. The guest branch input the secret image, and through a series of convolutional layer, a series of low-level (color, texture, etc.) and high-level features are extracted. Input cover image to host branch, decompose the cover image into feature representation and hierarchical structure through a series of convolutional layer, and merge the information extracted by the guest branch into the host branch. Finally, the stego-image is obtained through a series of convolutional layers. The decoder network takes the stego-image as input and obtains the secret image through a series of convolutional layers. The model has achieved good results in many data sets, such as MNIST, CIFAR10, PASCAL-VOC12, ImageNet, etc. However, when the attacker obtains the cover image, If we use the model of [12, 13] to generate the stego-image, the attacker can find the secret image by calculating and enlarging the residual image of the stego-image and the cover image. The model in [12, 13] provides ideas for our image steganography, and we will design an image steganography network based on [12, 13].

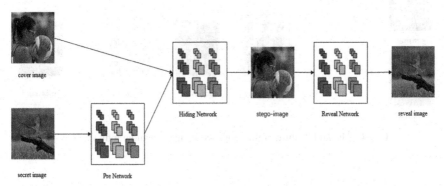

Fig. 2. The image steganography model proposed in the paper [12]

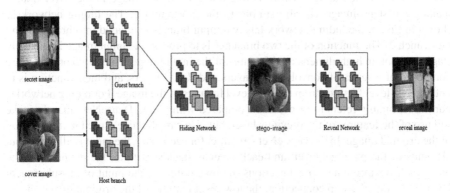

Fig. 3. The image steganography model proposed in the paper [13]

3 Proposed Scheme

Our method based on the paper [12, 13] and optimized base on them. Our image steganography model as shown in Fig. 4, the model is mainly composed of two parts: hiding network and reveal network. The hiding network has two input channels and one output channel. The cover image and secret image to be hidden are input from channel 1 and channel 2 respectively. Channel 1 and Channel 2 are composed of convolutional neural networks, and their main function is to obtain the high-dimensional features of the cover image and the secret image. Then connect the two channels and input them into the hiding network to get the stego-image. The stego-image is similar to the cover image in visual perception. When the recipient gets the stego-image, it is input into the reveal network, which is composed of a convolutional neural network, which can extract the secret image from the stego-image.

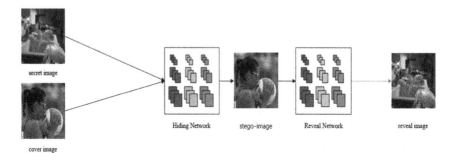

Fig. 4. The architecture of the proposed image steganography scheme

3.1 Hiding Network

The function of the hiding network is to embed the secret image in the cover image, making the stego-image visually similar to the cover image. The hiding network as shown in Fig. 5, the hiding network has two input branches, divided into branch 1 and the branch 2. The function of the two branches is to process the input image in the early stage, and obtain high-dimensional features of the input image. These two branches are composed of a series of convolutional layers and ReLU layers, and their function is to obtain high-level features from the low-level features of the image. For hiding networks, our model mainly refers to DenseNet. Compared with U-net, DenseNet not only make full use of the features of the previous layer, but also can effectively use the information of the original image. In the DenseNet structure, for each layer, the input is all the output elements of the previous layer, and each layer is stacked with all the elements of the previous layer through skip connections, Its own output is the input of all subsequent layers. Through the skip connection, the low-level features of the original image can be transmitted to each subsequent layer, and then the original information and the high-level features of each subsequent layer can be merged.

3.2 Reveal Network

The reveal network model as shown in Fig. 6, the input of the reveal network is a 3-channel tensor, and the output is a 3-channel tensor. The reveal network is mainly composed of convolutional layer, ReLU layer and Tanh layer. The main purpose of the reveal network is to extract the secret image from the stego-image, and the extracted secret image should be as similar to the original secret image as possible. What we need to explain is that the extracted secret image does not require the best image quality, as long as it does not affect the recipient's understanding.

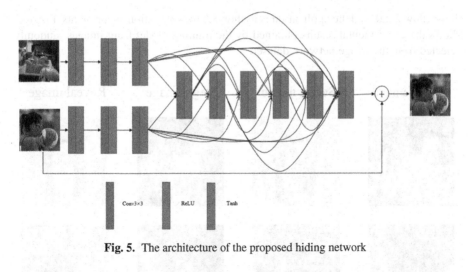

Fig. 5. The architecture of the proposed hiding network

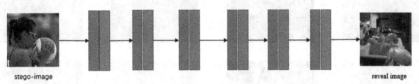

stego-image   reveal image

Fig. 6. The architecture of the proposed reveal network

3.3 Loss Function

In our work, the hiding network is to reduce the loss between the stego-image and the cover image. The function of the reveal network is to extract the image from the stego-image to make it as similar to the secret image as possible and reduce the loss between the extracted secret image and the original secret image, the loss function as shown in Eq. (1).

$$\zeta = \alpha(c - c') - \beta(s - s') \tag{1}$$

Where, α and β is weight, c and c' represent the cover image and stego-image, s and s' represent original secret image and the extracted secret image.

4 Experimental Results and Analysis

In this work, 8,000 training images and 2,000 test images were collected from the ImageNet dataset to train the network model. In order to optimize the model parameters, the Adam optimization method is used to automatically adjust the learning rate during the training process. The initial learning rate is set to 0.001, then the gradient drops, and the parameters α and β are set to 1.00 and 0.60, respectively. The number of images in each batch is set to 32. The GPU is NVIDIA GeForce 1080Ti, the experimental environment is

Tensorflow 2.2.0, and the application is Python 3.6 for simulation experiments. Figure 7 shows the experimental results obtained by the training model from images randomly selected from the image network dataset.

Cover image	Secret image	Stego-image	Reveal image

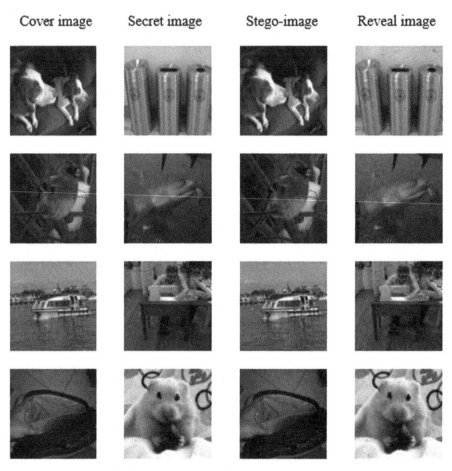

Fig. 7. Steganography effect on ImageNet dataset

The first column in Fig. 7 represents the cover images, which are color images with a size of 256 × 256. The second column represents the secret image to be hidden, which are color images with a size of 256 × 256. The third column represents the stego-image , which is obtained by inputting the images in the first and second columns to the hiding network. From the visual effect, there is almost no difference between the pictures in the first column and the pictures in the third column. The fourth column is obtained by inputting the stego-image to the reveal network, from the visual effect, there is almost no difference in semantic content between the second and fourth column, which shows that our model can achieve better results.

In order to verify the excellent performance of our proposed model, we will compare from two aspects: subjective visual effects and objective evaluation indicators. The comparison result with [12] and [17] as shown in Fig. 9. The first column in Fig. 9 represents the cover image, the second column represents the stego-image, the third column represents the secret image to be hidden, and the fourth column represents the residual image between the cover image and the stego-image, which has been enlarged by 20 times. The first two rows of Fig. 9 represent the result of [12]. We can find that there is a lot of semantic information about the secret image in the residual image. The middle two rows of Fig. 9 show the results of [17]. It is difficult to find semantic information in the residual image, but [17] uses grayscale images. Compared with grayscale images, color images are used more. The last two lines of Fig. 9 are the solutions proposed in this article, using color image steganography, and you can see that there is no semantic information about the secret image in the residual image (Fig. 8).

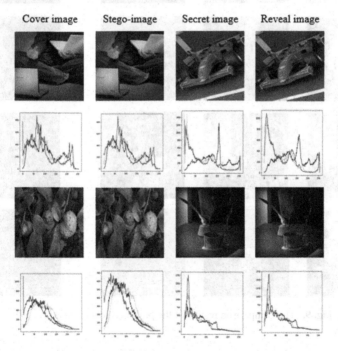

Fig. 8. Histograms, the 2th and 4th line histograms correspond to lines 1th and 3th, respectively

In order to evaluate the effect and performance of the model, not only the payload size of the stego-image and the visual effect of the stego-image need to be considered, but also need a quantitative measure to evaluate the quality of the stego-image. In previous

Cover image   Stego-image   Secret image   Residual Image(×20)

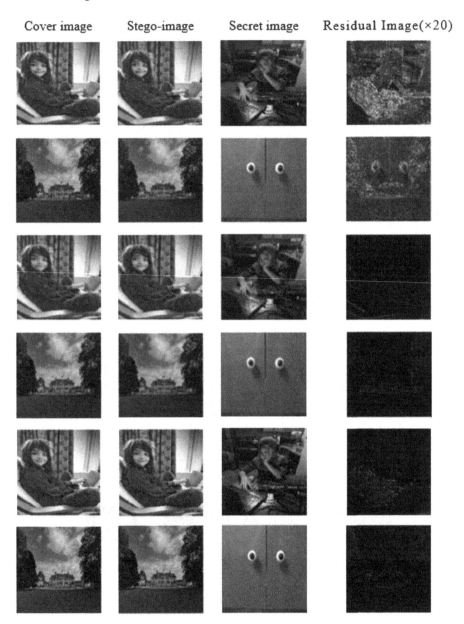

Fig. 9. The comparison results of the proposed scheme and [12, 17].

studies, the main evaluation indicators were PSNR (peak signal-to-noise ratio) and SSIM (structural similarity). PSNR evaluates the image quality by calculating the error between the corresponding pixels. The larger the PSNR value, the better the image quality. The general evaluation criterion is 30 dB, if the PSNR value is less than 30 dB, the quality of the generated image is poor. PSNR calculation formula as shown in Eq. (2).

$$PSNR = 10 log_{10} \frac{(2^n - 1)^2}{MSE} \qquad (2)$$

Where, MSE represents the mean square error between the original image and the evaluated image, $2^n - 1$ represents the maximum pixel value of the image, and n is the number of bits in each sample value. SSIM evaluates the processed image quality by comparing the brightness, contrast, and structural similarity of the original image. The calculation formula of SSIM as shown in Eq. (3).

$$SSIM(x, y) = \frac{(2\mu_x\mu_y + c_1)(2\sigma_{xy} + c_2)}{\left(\mu_x^2 + \mu_y^2 + c_1\right)\left(\sigma_x^2 + \sigma_y^2 + c_2\right)} \qquad (3)$$

Where, x represent a cover image or secret image, y represent stego-image or the reveal secret image, μ_x and μ_y represent pixel average, σ_x^2 and σ_y^2 represent the variance of pixel values, σ_{xy} represent the covariance of x and y, c_1 and c_2 are constant sets (Table 1).

Table 1. SSIM and PSNR comparison for different steganography schemes

Scheme	PSNR (dB) (c, c')	SSIM (c, c')	PSNR (dB) (s, s')	SSIM (s, s')
[12]	41.2	0.98	37.6	0.97
[13]	32.5	0.937	34.76	0.93
[17]	42.3	0.987	38.45	0.953
[21]	40.45	0.985	37.32	0.981
[22]	40.47	0.97	36.92	0.984
Ours	43.57	0.987	38.14	0.967

Steganography capacity is also one of the important evaluation criteria for image steganography. Traditional algorithms have lower steganography capacity. Compared with current algorithms, the results as shown in Table 2. We can clearly see that our solution is superior to other solutions.

$$Relative\ capatity = \frac{Absolute\ capatity}{The\ size\ of\ the\ image} \qquad (4)$$

Table 2. Steganographic capacity comparison for different steganography schemes

Scheme	Absolute capacity (bytes/image)	image size	Relative capacity (bytes/pixel)
[23]	1.725	512×512	4.29e−6
[24]	2.25	512×512	8.58e−6
[25]	6.5	16×16	2.5e−2
Ours	256×256	256×256	1

5 Conclusions

This paper proposes an image steganography scheme based on convolutional networks, through the end-to-end training model, which can embed color images into color images of the same size. The hidden network uses skip connections to connect low-level features and high-level features, which helps to hide the details of the secret image. Experiments show that the steganography scheme in this paper can embed the secret image into the cover image, and our method has advanced visual effects and high steganographic capacity. In future research, we will try to embed text information and audio information into images, while optimizing the model to improve steganography performance.

Acknowledgement. This work was supported in part by the Natural Science Foundation of China under Grant 62063004 and 61762033, and by the Hainan Provincial Natural Science Foundation of China under Grant 2019RC018, in part by the Hainan Provincial Higher Education Research Project under Grant Hnky2019-73, in part by the Key Research Project of Haikou College of Economics under Grant HJKZ18-01, in part by the Innovative Research Projects for Graduate Students in Ordinary Universities of Hainan Province under Grant Hys2020-222.

References

1. Qin, C., Zhang, W., Cao, F., Zhang, X., Chang, C.-C.: Separable reversible data hiding in encrypted images via adaptive embedding strategy with block selection. Signal Process. **153**, 109–122 (2018)
2. Carpentieri, B., Castiglione, A., De. Santis, A., Palmieri, F., Pizzolante, R.: One-pass lossless data hiding and compression of remote sensing data. Futur. Gener. Comput. Syst. **90**, 222–239 (2019)
3. Hussain, I., Zeng, J., Xinhong, X., Tan, S.: A survey on deep convolutional neural networks for image steganography and steganalysis. KSII Trans. Internet Inf. Syst. (TIIS) **14**, 1228–1248 (2020)
4. Mielikainen, J.: LSB matching revisited. IEEE Signal Process. Lett. **13**, 285–287 (2006)
5. Westfeld, A.J.L.: F5-A steganographic algorithm : high capacity despite better steganalysis **2137**, 289–302 (2001)
6. Kim, Y., Duric, Z., Richards, D.: Modified matrix encoding technique for minimal distortion steganography. In: Proceedings of the 8th International Conference on Information Hiding (2006)
7. Holub, V., Fridrich, J., Denemark, T.: Universal distortion function for steganography in an arbitrary domain. EURASIP J. Inf. Secur. **2014**, 1 (2014)

8. Strobelt, H., et al.: Seq2Seq-Vis: a visual debugging tool for sequence-to-sequence models. IEEE Trans. Vis. Comput. Graphics **25**, 353–363 (2019)

9. Huang, C., Loy, C.C., Tang, X.: Unsupervised learning of discriminative attributes and visual representations. In: Computer Vision & Pattern Recognition (2016)

10. Volkhonskiy, D., Borisenko, B., Burnaev, E.: Generative adversarial networks for image steganography (2016)

11. Shi, H., Dong, J., Wang, W., Qian, Y., Zhang, X.: SSGAN: secure steganography based on generative adversarial networks. In: Zeng, B., Huang, Q., El Saddik, A., Li, H., Jiang, S., Fan, X. (eds.) PCM 2017. LNCS, vol. 10735, pp. 534–544. Springer, Cham (2018). https://doi.org/10.1007/978-3-319-77380-3_51

12. Baluja, S.: Hiding images in plain sight: Deep steganography. In: Advances in Neural Information Processing Systems, pp. 2069–2079 (2017)

13. Rahim, R., Nadeem, S.: End-to-end trained CNN encoder-decoder networks for image steganography. In: Proceedings of the European Conference on Computer Vision (ECCV) (2018)

14. Zhang, R., Dong, S., Liu, J.: Invisible steganography via generative adversarial networks. Multimed. Tools Appl. **78**(7), 8559–8575 (2018). https://doi.org/10.1007/s11042-018-6951-z

15. Zhang, K.A., Cuesta-Infante, A., Xu, L., Veeramachaneni, K.J.A.P.A.: SteganoGAN: high capacity image steganography with GANs (2019)

16. Wang, Z., Gao, N., Wang, X., Xiang, J., Zha, D., Li, L.: HidingGAN: high capacity information hiding with generative adversarial network. Comput. Graph. Forum **38**, 393–401 (2019)

17. Li, Q., et al.: A novel grayscale image steganography scheme based on chaos encryption and generative adversarial networks. IEEE Access **8**, 168166–168176 (2020)

18. Pevný, T., Filler, T., Bas, P.: Using high-dimensional image models to perform highly undetectable steganography. In: International Workshop on Information Hiding, pp. 161–177. Springer (2010)

19. Holub, V., Fridrich, J.: Digital image steganography using universal distortion. In: ACM Workshop on Information Hiding and Multimedia Security, p. 59 (2013)

20. Holub, V., Fridrich, J.: Designing steganographic distortion using directional filters. In: 2012 IEEE International Workshop on Information Forensics and Security (WIFS), pp. 234–239. IEEE (2012)

21. Duan, X., Jia, K., Li, B., Guo, D., Zhang, E., Qin, C.: Reversible image steganography scheme based on a u-net structure. IEEE Access **7**, 9314–9323 (2019)

22. Xintao, D., Nao, L.J.A.P.A.: Hide the image in FC-DenseNets to another image (2019)

23. Zheng, S., Wang, L., Ling, B., Hu, D.: Coverless Information hiding based on robust image hashing. In: Huang, D.-S., Hussain, A., Han, K., Gromiha, M.M. (eds.) ICIC 2017. LNCS (LNAI), vol. 10363, pp. 536–547. Springer, Cham (2017). https://doi.org/10.1007/978-3-319-63315-2_47

24. Zhou, Z.L., Cao, Y., Sun, X.M.: Coverless information hiding based on bag-of-words model of image. J. Appl. Sci. **34**, 527–536 (2016)

25. Zhu, J., Kaplan, R., Johnson, J., Fei-Fei, L.: HiDDeN: hiding data with deep networks. In: Ferrari, V., Hebert, M., Sminchisescu, C., Weiss, Y. (eds.) ECCV 2018. LNCS, vol. 11219, pp. 682–697. Springer, Cham (2018). https://doi.org/10.1007/978-3-030-01267-0_40

Robust JPEG Steganography Using Singular Value Decomposition in DCT Domain

Xiaofeng Song[1(✉)], Yi Zhang[2], and Jia Du[1]

[1] National University of Defense Technology, Xi'an 710106, China
[2] Special Police College, Beijing 102211, China

Abstract. Image steganography is an important technology for convert communication. When the stego images are transmitted through lossy network channel, the robustness of steganography algorithm is very crucial. Based on singular value decomposition in DCT domain, a robust JPEG steganography algorithm is proposed, which can resist image compression and correctly extract the embedded secret message from the compressed stego image. First, the robust embedding domain is constructed by exploiting the correlation of the maximum singular values got from two adjacent 8×8 DCT blocks. Then, the framework of the proposed JPEG steganography algorithm is given and the key steps are described in details. The experimental results show that the proposed JPEG steganography algorithm can achieve competitive robustness in contrast to the state-of-the-art robust steganography algorithms. Moreover, it can extract the secret messages correctly even if the stego image is compressed by WeChat.

Keywords: JPEG steganography · Robustness · DCT domain · Singular value · Correlation

1 Introduction

Digital steganography is a kind of covert communication technique that embeds secret messages in multimedia objects such as images, audio, video, text and so on [1]. It can realize the transmission of secret messages through the innocuous-looking stego objects. Due to the wide application of JPEG images on the Internet, JPEG image steganography has received extensive attentions. In recent years, many JPEG steganography algorithms have been proposed, such as Uniform embedding Distortion (UED) [2] steganography, JPEG UNIversal WAvelet Relative Distortion (J-UNIWARD) steganography [3], and so on. They usually constrain the embedding changes to the complex texture regions difficult to model and then achieve the good anti-detection ability. In other words, the primary goal of these content-adaptive steganography algorithm is the strong resistance ability to steganalysis technique. However, they are not robust to the lossy image processing such as image compression, Image resizing, etc. For example, in recent years, the instant communication tools, social platforms, and multimedia sharing websites are becoming more and more popular. These tools, platforms, and websites transmit and exchange massive amounts of digital images every day. With these massive images as cover, more

© Springer Nature Switzerland AG 2021
X. Sun et al. (Eds.): ICAIS 2021, CCIS 1424, pp. 278–290, 2021.
https://doi.org/10.1007/978-3-030-78621-2_22

secure covert communication can be achieved. However, in order to save transmission and storage costs, the images are often compressed during the process of transmission and sharing, which makes the extraction error rate of secret messages is very high when the message embedding is performed by non-robust steganography algorithms such as J-UNIWARD. Therefore, robust JPEG steganography against lossy image processing is becoming a research hotspot in field of information hiding.

For the design of robust JPEG steganographic schemes, Zhang et al. [4] constructed the robust embedding domain based on the relative relationship of inter-block DCT coefficients, and proposed a robust and adaptive JPEG steganography algorithm against JPEG compression; Qian et al. [5] proposed a robust steganography algorithm using texture synthesis, however, the extraction error rate of secret messages is relatively high; Zhang et al. [6] also proposed a JPEG compression and detection resistant steganography algorithm based on dither modulation when the quantization table of JPEG compression is assumed to be known; Zhao et al. [7] proposed a robust and adaptive JPEG image steganography algorithm based on transmission channel matching, however, the behavior of repeatedly uploading images for re-compression is very suspicious; Tao et al. [8] proposed a robust JPEG steganography by generating the "intermediate image" that is just the stego image after JPEG compression with special quality factor, however, the quality factor of JPEG compression must to be known previously; Yu et al. [9] proposed a robust image steganography algorithm based on generalized dither modulation and embedding domain expansion, which can achieve better robustness and anti-detection ability, however, the quantization table of JPEG compression is assumed to be known. Recently, Zhang et al. [10] proposed a robust steganography algorithm with multiple robustness enhancements, however, the anti-detection ability is quite weak.

In this paper, a robust JPEG steganography algorithm is proposed based on inter-block singular value correlation in DCT domain. As we know, the inter-block DCT coefficients of JPEG image have strong correlation. Moreover, the correlations are relatively stable even though some lossy processing are performed for the image. Furthermore, considering the stability of singular values [11], we construct the robust embedding domain by exploiting this correlation of the maximum singular values of the two matrixes generated using the DCT coefficients in middle frequency bands of two adjacent 8×8 DCT blocks. The binary cover elements can be got using the correlation of the maximum singular values of the generated matrixes. In addition, based on the embedding distortion function of J-UNIWARD, the embedding distortion of the proposed steganography algorithm is defined according to the embedding changes of DCT coefficients caused by modifying the maximum singular values of the generated matrixes. To reduce message extraction errors, the secret messages are encoded by Reed-Solomon (RS) error correcting code, and the encoded messages are embedded using STCs [12] which is widely used for minimal distortion steganography. Finally, the stego elements are embedded by modifying the maximum singular values of the corresponding matrixes and the stego image is generated using the modified DCT coefficients.

The rest of the paper is organized as follows: Sect. 2 introduces the construction of robust embedding domain; Section 3 proposes a robust JPEG steganography algorithm and the implementation details are described in details; Section 4 verifies the effectiveness of the proposed steganography algorithm by comparing it with the state-of-the-art robust image steganography algorithms; Section 5 is the conclusion.

2 Robust Embedding Domain Construction Using SVD

2.1 Singular Value Decomposition

SVD is a kind of orthogonal transforms used for matrix diagonalization. Let $\mathbf{A} \in \mathbf{R}^{m \times n}$ be a $m \times n$ matrix. Then, the matrix $\mathbf{A}$ can be represented by its SVD in the following form,

$$\mathbf{A} = \mathbf{U} \mathbf{S} \mathbf{V}^T = (\mathbf{u}_1, \mathbf{u}_2, \cdots, \mathbf{u}_N) \begin{pmatrix} \lambda_1 & & \\ & \ddots & \\ & & \lambda_r \\ & & & 0 \end{pmatrix} \begin{pmatrix} \mathbf{v}_1^T \\ \mathbf{v}_2^T \\ \vdots \\ \mathbf{v}_N^T \end{pmatrix} = \sum_{i=1}^r \lambda_i \mathbf{u}_i \mathbf{v}_i^T \qquad (1)$$

where $\mathbf{U}$ and $\mathbf{V}$ are orthogonal $M \times N$ and $N \times M$ matrices, respectively, and $\mathbf{S}$ is a diagonal matrix with nonnegative elements. Diagonal terms $\lambda_1, \lambda_2, \cdots, \lambda_r$ of matrix $\mathbf{S}$ are singular values of matrix $\mathbf{A}$ in a descending order and r is the rank of matrix $\mathbf{A}$.

There are many attractive mathematical properties of SVD, such as the singular values $\lambda_1, \lambda_2, \cdots, \lambda_r$ are unique and have good stability. In other words, when a small perturbation is added to a matrix, in contrast to the changes of matrix element values, the changes of singular values are very small.

2.2 DCT Coefficient Properties of JPEG Image

JPEG is one of the most popular image formats on the Internet because it can achieve good tradeoff between storage size and image quality. The basis for JPEG is the DCT (Discrete Cosine Transform) which is a lossy image compression technique. For JPEG compression, the image is performed two-dimensional (2D) DCT on 8×8 blocks, and then the DCT coefficients are quantized according to the quality factor or JPEG quantization table, finally, the DCT blocks are encoded using Huffman encoding.

As we know, a DCT block of JPEG image can be separated into low, middle, and high frequency bands as shown in Fig. 1. The DCT coefficients in low frequency band is most important for image quality and the small changes to the DCT coefficients will change the image quality significantly. On the other hand, although the changes of DCT coefficients in the high frequency band will no significantly degrade image quality, the DCT coefficients or their statistics are not robust for lossy image processing. Therefore, to get a high quality and robust stego image, middle frequency band is suitable for message embedding.

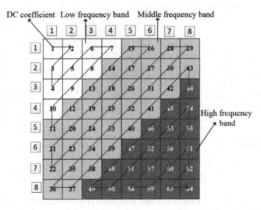

Fig. 1. Zig-zag ordering and frequency bands for DCT coefficients.

2.3 Robust Embedding Domain Construction

For JPEG image, it is generally known that the inter-block DCT coefficients have strong correlation. That is to say, the DCT coefficients at the same positions in two adjacent DCT blocks have close values. Moreover, the correlations between them are relatively stable against lossy image processing. Unlike [4], we do not directly use the coefficient correlation to extract the cover elements. Considering the stability of singular values, we extract the cover elements by exploiting this correlation of the maximum singular value of the matrixes generated using the DCT coefficients in middle frequency bands of two adjacent 8 × 8 DCT blocks. Therefore, A binary cover element can be extracted based on two adjacent DCT blocks.

In Fig. 2, the adjacent relations of DCT blocks and the construction of matrix for SVD are both shown. To get the adjacent relations, all the DCT blocks are scanned in a snake-like order, and then each DCT block has an adjacent DCT block according to the scan order. To extract a binary cover element, two matrixes should be respectively constructed using the DCT coefficients in middle frequency band of two adjacent DCT blocks such as $B_{(i,j)}$ and $B_{(i,j+1)}$. Specially, to ensure the reference DCT coefficients are not altered during embedding process, the matrixes of two adjacent DCT blocks are constructed using the DCT coefficients at different positions. As shown in Fig. 2, if the traversing order of $B_{(i,j)}$ is an odd number, the matrixes of two adjacent blocks for SVD is $\mathbf{M}_{i,j}^{odd}$ and $\mathbf{M}_{i,j+1}^{odd}$. On the contrary; if the traversing order of $B_{(i,j)}$ is an even number, the matrixes of two adjacent blocks for SVD is $\mathbf{M}_{i,j}^{even}$ and $\mathbf{M}_{i,j+1}^{even}$.

After all the matrixes for SVD are constructed, SVD is performed for each matrix and the maximum singular value is got. Supposed the matrixes of two adjacent DCT blocks $B_{(i,j)}$ and $B_{(i,j+1)}$ are $\mathbf{M}_{i,j}^{odd}$ and $\mathbf{M}_{i,j+1}^{odd}$ respectively, the corresponding maximum singular values are $\lambda_{i,j}$ and $\lambda_{i,j+1}$. Then, a binary cover element can be extracted according to Eq. (2),

$$c_{i,j} = \begin{cases} 1, & \text{if } \lambda_{i,j} \geq \lambda_{i,j+1} \\ 0, & \text{if } \lambda_{i,j} < \lambda_{i,j+1} \end{cases}. \tag{2}$$

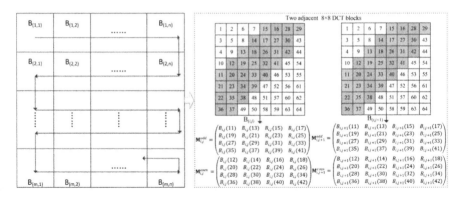

Fig. 2. DCT blocks scan order and matrix construction for SVD.

Therefore, for each DCT block, we can extract a binary cover element and all the cover elements are used as the cover object. For example, suppose the size of cover image is 512×512, and then the number of 8×8 DCT blocks and the cover elements are both 4096. Finally, the extracted cover object is used for robust message embedding.

3   Proposed Robust JPEG Steganography Algorithm

3.1   Framework of Proposed JPEG Steganography Algorithm

In Fig. 3, the whole framework of the proposed robust JPEG steganography algorithm is shown, which includes the message embedding procedure and extracting procedure.

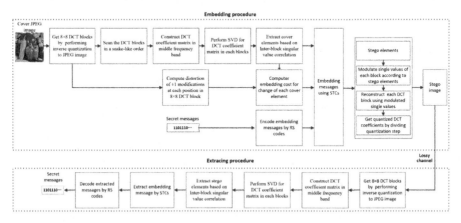

Fig. 3. Framework of proposed robust and adaptive JPEG steganography algorithm.

As shown in Fig. 3, the embedding procedure gives the execution steps for message embedding. The inverse quantization operation is performed by multiplying the DCT coefficients by the corresponding quantization step, then all the 8×8 DCT blocks are scanned in a snake-like order shown in Fig. 2 and the adjacent relations of DCT blocks are determined according to the scan order. For each DCT block, a DCT coefficient matrix is constructed in middle frequency band and SVD is performed for the constructed DCT coefficient matrix, and then the cover elements are extracted according to the inter-block maximum singular value correlation. For embedding cost of each cover element, the distortion of ±1 modification at each position in 8 × 8 DCT block is firstly computed, and then the embedding cost is measured according to the changes caused by the modification of maximum singular value. In addition, to improve the robustness, the secret messages are encoded by RS codes which can correct some error bits. Then, based on the cover elements and the corresponding embedding costs, the encoded secret messages are embedded using STCs and the corresponding stego elements are generated. Finally, the maximum singular values of the constructed DCT coefficient matrixes are modified according to the stego elements, and then all the 8 × 8 DCT blocks are reconstructed and the stego image is generated.

For message extraction, as shown in Fig. 3, the stego image is performed inverse quantization operation and then the corresponding 8×8 DCT blocks are got. For each DCT block, the DCT coefficient matrix is constructed in middle frequency band and SVD is performed for the constructed DCT coefficient matrix. Then, the stego elements can be extracted according to the inter-block maximum singular value correlation. Finally, the encoded messages are extracted by STCs and then the secret messages are obtained using RS decoder.

3.2 Extract Cover Elements

Let $\mathbf{X}$ denotes the cover JPEG image of size $M \times N$ and $B_{(i,j)}$ denotes the (i, j)-th 8 × 8 DCT blocks. According to the steganography framework shown in Fig. 3, the DCT blocks are scanned in snake-like order and a binary cover element can be extracted using two adjacent DCT blocks such as $B_{(i,j)}$ and $B_{(i,j+1)}$.

For ease of description, according to the block scanning order, we denote the B_k as the k-th DCT block and its adjacent DCT block is B_{k+1}. The number of DCT blocks is $\lfloor M/8 \rfloor \times \lfloor N/8 \rfloor$ where $\lfloor \cdot \rfloor$ denotes the floor function. Then, matrix $\mathbf{M}_k$ and $\mathbf{M}_{k+1}$ are respectively constructed using the DCT coefficients in middle frequency band of DCT blocks B_k and B_{k+1}. Next, SVD is performed for $\mathbf{M}_k$ and $\mathbf{M}_{k+1}$, the corresponding maximum singular values are λ_k and λ_{k+1}. Finally, the cover element c_k can be extracted according to Eq. (3),

$$c_k = \begin{cases} 1, & \text{if } \lambda_k \geq \lambda_{k+1} \\ 0, & \text{if } \lambda_k < \lambda_{k+1} \end{cases}. \tag{3}$$

According to Eq. (3), we know that the cover element c_k equals 0 or 1. For each block can generate a cover element, L cover elements $c_1, c_2, \cdots, c_L$ are generated in total and L equals $\lfloor M/8 \rfloor \times \lfloor N/8 \rfloor$. These cover elements construct the cover object which is a binary sequence.

3.3 Define Embedding Costs of Cover Elements

As shown in Fig. 3, the cover object is constructed based on the maximum singular value correlation in DCT domain and then the secret messages are embedded by STCs.

Therefore, an embedding cost need to be defined for each cover element. We know that J-UNIWARD is one of the most powerful JPEG steganography algorithms and it has good anti-detection ability against the state-of-the-art steganalysis techniques. Therefore, we use the embedding distortion function of J-UNIWARD to measure the cost of ± 1 modification for DCT coefficient.

The embedding distortion function of J-UNIWARD is defined in Eq. (4),

$$D(X, Y) = \sum_{k=1}^{3} \sum_{i,j} \frac{\left| W_{ij}^{(k)}(X) - W_{ij}^{(k)}(Y) \right|}{\varepsilon + \left| W_{ij}^{(k)}(X) \right|}, \tag{4}$$

where X,Y denote the cover image and stego image respectively, $W_{ij}^{(k)}(X)$ and $W_{ij}^{(k)}(Y)$ denote the (i, j)-th wavelet coefficient got using k-th wavelet filter, ε is a stabilizing constant to avoid dividing by zero.

Furthermore, $D(X, Y)$ can be denoted as additive form as follows,

$$D(X, Y) = \sum_{i,j} \rho_{ij}(X, Y_{ij}), \tag{5}$$

where $\rho_{ij}(X, Y_{ij})$ denotes the embedding distortion with only (i,j)-th element changed. In other words, $\rho_{ij}(X, Y_{ij})$ is the cost of ± 1 modification for (i,j)-th DCT coefficient.

For the proposed robust and adaptive JPEG steganography algorithm, the cover element is extracted by modifying the maximum singular values of the matrix $\mathbf{M}_k$ and $\mathbf{M}_{k+1}$ constructed using the DCT coefficients in middle frequency bands of two adjacent DCT blocks. Therefore, the modification of a cover element will cause the changes of multiple elements. Then, the embedding cost of the cover element is measured by summing all the embedding costs of the corresponding DCT coefficients. The specific form is shown in Eq. (6),

$$\rho(c_k) = \sum_{Y_{i,j} \in \mathbf{M}_k} d_{ij}(X, Y_{ij}) \times \rho_{ij}(X, Y_{ij}) + \sum_{Y_{i,j} \in \mathbf{M}_{k+1}} d_{ij}(X, Y_{ij}) \times \rho_{ij}(X, Y_{ij}), \tag{6}$$

where $d_{ij}(X, Y_{ij})$ denotes the modifications of (i,j)-th DCT coefficients that are caused by modification to the cover element c_k.

3.4 Embed Stego Elements by Modifying Maximum Singular Values

Based on the cover object and the corresponding embedding cost, the encoded secret messages can be embedded by STCs. Then, the stego object is generated and it includes L binary stego elements. According to the steganography framework shown in Fig. 3, the stego elements need to be embedded by modifying the maximum singular value correlation.

Suppose the maximum singular values of matrixes $\mathbf{M}_k$ and $\mathbf{M}_{k+1}$ are λ_k and λ_{k+1} respectively, and s_k denote the k-th stego element. Then, the stego element s_k can be embedded by modifying λ_k and λ_{k+1} according to Eq. (7) and Eq. (8),

$$\lambda'_k = \begin{cases} E + \alpha \\ E - \alpha \end{cases}, \ if \ s_k = 1 \tag{7}$$

$$\lambda'_{k+1} = \begin{cases} E - \alpha \\ E + \alpha \end{cases}, \ if \ s_k = 0 \tag{8}$$

where λ'_k and λ'_{k+1} denotes the modified maximum singular values, $E = (\lambda_k + \lambda_{k+1})/2$ and α is the embedding strength factor. After the modification for λ_k and λ_{k+1}, the new matrixes $\mathbf{M}'_k$ and $\mathbf{M}'_{k+1}$ are reconstructed using λ'_k and λ'_{k+1}, and the corresponding DCT coefficients are also modified.

In Eq. (7) and Eq. (8), it can be seen that the parameter α is the key factor for the robustness of stego elements against lossy image processing. The large α means strong robustness whereas the corresponding modifications are large which led to the weak anti-detection ability. Therefore, a suitable parameter α should be selected which can achieve good tradeoff between steganography robustness and anti-detection ability.

3.5 Extract Stego Elements

As shown in Fig. 3, for message extraction, the stego object $S = (s_1, s_2, \cdots, s_L)$ should be firstly extracted and then the embedded messages are extracted by STCs and RS decoder.

According to the embedding rule of stego elements in Eq. (7) and (8), the stego elements can be extracted using Eq. (9),

$$s_k = \begin{cases} 1, \ if \ \lambda'_k \geq \lambda'_{k+1} \\ 0, \ if \ \lambda'_k < \lambda'_{k+1} \end{cases}. \tag{9}$$

where λ'_k and λ'_{k+1} respectively denote the maximum singular values of two matrixes constructed using two adjacent DCT blocks of stego image.

To summarize, the embedding procedure and extraction procedure of the proposed robust and adaptive JPEG steganography can be respectively described in Algorithm 1 and 2.

Algorithm 1 Embedding algorithm	
Input:	Cover image **X**, message **m**, embedding strength factor α
Output:	Stego image **Y**
Step1:	The inverse quantization operation is performed for cover JPEG image by multiplying the DCT coefficients with the corresponding quantization step.
Step2:	All DCT blocks are scanned in a snake-like order from the upper left to the lower right and the adjacent relations of DCT blocks are determined.
Step3:	For each DCT block, a matrix $\mathbf{M}_k$ is constructed using the DCT coefficients in middle frequency band and the corresponding matrix $\mathbf{M}_{k+1}$ is constructed using its adjacent block.
Step4:	SVD is performed for matrixes $\mathbf{M}_k$ and $\mathbf{M}_{k+1}$, a cover element c_k can be extracted according to Eq.(3), and the other cover elements are extracted in the same way.
Step5:	The embedding costs of the cover elements are computed according to Eq.(4), Eq.(5) and Eq.(6).
Step6:	The secret messages are encoded by RS code.
Step7:	The stego elements are generated by embedding the encoded secret messages based on cover elements, embedding costs and STCs.
Step8:	The stego elements are embedded according to Eq.(7) and Eq.(8).
Step9:	The corresponding DCT coefficients of each DCT block are modified according to the modified maximum singular values.
Step10:	The stego image is got by quantizing the DCT coefficients.

Algorithm 2 Extracting algorithm	
Input:	Stego image **Y**, embedding strength factor α
Output:	message **m**
Step1:	The inverse quantization operation is performed for stego JPEG image
Step2:	All DCT blocks are scanned in a snake-like order and the adjacent relations of DCT blocks are determined.
Step3:	For each DCT block, a matrix $\mathbf{M}_k$ is constructed using the DCT coefficients in middle frequency band and the corresponding matrix $\mathbf{M}_{k+1}$ is constructed for its adjacent block.
Step4:	SVD is performed for matrixes $\mathbf{M}_k$ and $\mathbf{M}_{k+1}$, a stego element s_k can be extracted according to Eq.(9), and the other stego elements are extracted in the same way.
Step5:	The encoded secret messages are extracted using STCs.
Step6:	The secret messages are got by RS decoder.

4   Experimental Results and Analyses

In the experiments, the robustness against JPEG compression attack and the anti-detection ability of the proposed steganography algorithm are compared with the other robust JPEG steganography algorithms. Moreover, the proposed steganography algorithm is used in WeChat platform and the corresponding experiment results are shown. For the robustness and anti-detection experiments, the 10000 grayscale images from

BOSSbase1.01 [13] are used as sample images. The size of sample images is 512×512 and all the sample images with PGM format are converted to JPEG image with quality factor (QF) 85. The parameter of RS code is (31, 19).

4.1 Robustness Against JPEG Compression Attack

As we know, the complex image has strong resistance to the detection. Therefore, we should select some images with complex texture for messages embedding. Here, one-level wavelet transform is performed for the image and the energy of wavelet coefficients of the three high-pass subbands is used to measure the complexity of the image.

To evaluate the robustness against JPEG compression attack of the proposed steganography algorithm, the most complex 2000 images from BOSSbase1.01 are used to generate the stego images. The robust steganography algorithms used for comparison are MREAS-P$_S$ and MREAS-P$_J$ [10]. For the proposed steganography algorithm, the number of cover elements is 4096 because the image size is 512×512 and DCT block size is 8×8. Therefore, the length of the embedded message bits cannot exceed 4096. The payload is set to 0.001, 0.002, 0.003, 0.004, 0.005 bpnzAC (bit per non-zero AC DCT coefficient) respectively. Then, for each robust steganography algorithm, we have one group of cover images and five groups of stego images.

Table 1. Average extraction error rates of three robust steganography algorithms for the 2000 complex images in BOSSbase1.01. ($\times 10^{-3}$)

QF	Algorithm	Payload (bpnzAC)				
		0.001	0.002	0.003	0.004	0.005
65	Proposed	0.74	0.71	0.72	0.63	0.68
	MREAS-P$_S$	248	249	251	253	255
	MREAS-P$_J$	245	248	247	250	249
75	Proposed	3.7	3.6	3.7	3.9	3.7
	MREAS-P$_S$	12.3	12.5	13.1	13.3	13.0
	MREAS-P$_J$	0.92	1.00	1.20	1.50	1.50
85	Proposed	0.50	0.40	0.44	0.43	0.51
	MREAS-P$_S$	0.88	1.00	1.10	1.30	1.30
	MREAS-P$_J$	0.13	0.12	0.28	0.36	0.44
95	Proposed	0.51	0.42	0.45	0.44	0.52
	MREAS-P$_S$	0.60	0.56	0.75	0.91	0.88
	MREAS-P$_J$	0.13	0.12	0.25	0.42	0.47

According to the average extraction error rates shown in Table 1, the proposed robust and adaptive JPEG steganography algorithm has achieved the competitive robustness.

As shown in Table 1, for MREAS-P$_J$, the average extraction error rates are low when the QFs of JPEG compression attack are 85 and 95. However, the extraction error rates become very high when the QF of JPEG compression attack is 65 which means strong attack.

4.2 Detection Resistance for Typical Steganalysis Features

The anti-detection ability is important for robust image steganography. Here, the proposed steganography algorithm is compared with MREAS-P_S and MREAS-P_J using CC-PEV [14] and DCTR [15] which are the typical steganalysis features.

Same with Sect. 4.1, the most complex 2000 images from BOSSbase1.01 are used to generate stego images. The payloads are from 0.001 to 0.050 bpnzAC. The ensemble classifier [16] is trained by the steganalysis feature and used as the final detector. The ratio of training and test images is 0.5:0.5. The detection accuracy is quantified using the minimal total error probability under equal priors $P_E = min_{P_{FA}}(P_{FA} + P_{MD})/2$, where P_{FA} denotes the false-alarm probabilities and P_{MD} denotes the missed-detection probabilities. The value of $\bar{P}_E$ is averaged over ten random image database splits.

According to the detection performances, we find that the detection resistance of the proposed steganography algorithm is relatively weak in contrast to MREAS-P_S and MREAS-P_J. It is possible that the embedding changes of the proposed algorithm is larger.

4.3 Application in WeChat Platform

WeChat is the most popular chat app in China and it provide a good public channel for covert communication by image steganography. However, the compression algorithm of WeChat is unknown. Therefore, UEDR-P cannot realize robust steganography by WeChat channel. Therefore, only the robustness of MREAS-P_J and the proposed steganography is evaluated for WeChat channel.

(a)   (b)

Fig. 4. Cover image for covert communication by WeChat. (a) '8.jpg' in BOSSbase1.01 and (a) '4226.jpg' in BOSSbase1.01.

The two cover images are shown in Fig.4 and the image sizes are both 512×512. The left cover image is '8.jpg' in BOSSbase1.01 with 157 KB and the right cover image is '4226.jpg' with 258 KB. First, the stego images are generated by MREAS-P$_J$ and the proposed steganography algorithm with (31,19) RS codes and the payload is 0.01 bpnzAC. Next, the stego images are posted on the moment of WeChat. Then, the stego images are downloaded from the moment of WeChat and the file size of the downloaded WeChat images are 54 KB and 105 KB respectively. Finally, the embedded messages are extracted from the downloaded WeChat image and the extraction error rates are calculated. The experimental results are shown in Table 2.

Table 2. Comparisons of robustness of MREAS-P$_J$ and the proposed steganography algorithm against WeChat compression.

Image	Algorithm	Error rate	Communication
8.jpg	Proposed	0	Success
	MREAS-P$_J$	0	Success
4226.jpg	Proposed	0	Success
	MREAS-P$_J$	0	Success

Table 2 shows that MREAS-P$_J$ and the proposed algorithm both can realize the correct message transmission under lossy WeChat channel.

5   Conclusions

Robust image steganography techniques are important for covert communication under lossy transmission channels. Based on the singular value decomposition in DCT domain, a robust JPEG steganography algorithm is proposed. Considering the inter-block DCT coefficient correlation and the stability of singular value, the robust embedding domain is constructed using the correlation of the maximum singular values generated from two adjacent DCT blocks. Then, the whole frame of the proposed steganography algorithm is given and the procedure of message embedding and extraction are described in details. The experimental results show the proposed JPEG steganography is effective against JPEG compression and WeChat channel compression.

Furthermore, we also notice that the anti-detection ability of the current robust image steganography techniques is all weak when the detection is performed by the classifier trained using the cover images and the corresponding stego images. This is because that the embedding changes of the robust JPEG steganography scheme are much larger than the non-robust JPEG steganography scheme such as J-UNWARD. In other words, to achieve the robustness, the embedding changes will be large. In the future, the robust embedding domain which can led to the stronger robustness and anti-detection ability should be studied.

Acknowledgements. This research was supported by National Natural Science Foundation of China (Grant Nos 61872448, U1804263).

References

1. Fridrich, J.: Steganography in Digital Media: Principles, Algorithms, and Applications. Cambridge University Press, Cambridge (2010)
2. Guo, L., Ni, J., Shi, Y.: Uniform embedding for efficient JPEG steganography. IEEE Trans. Inf. Forensics Secur. 9(5), 814–825 (2014)
3. Holub, V., Fridrich, J.: Digital image steganography using universal distortion. In: 1st Workshop on ACM Information Hiding and Multimedia Security, Montpellier, France, pp.59–68. ACM (2013)
4. Zhang, Y., Luo, X., Yang, C., Ye, D., Liu, F.: A JPEG-compression resistant adaptive steganography based on relative relationship between DCT coefficients. In: Proc. of the 10th International Conference on Availability, Reliability and Security, Toulouse, France, pp. 461–66. IEEE (2015)
5. Qian, Z., Zhou, H., Zhang, W., Zhang, X.: Robust steganography using texture synthesis. In: Pan, J.S., Tsai, P.W., Huang, H.C. (eds.) Intelligent Information Hiding and Multimedia Signal Processing, vol. 63, pp. 25–33. Springer, Cham (2016). https://doi.org/10.1007/978-3-319-50209-0_4
6. Zhang, Y., Zhu, X., Yang, C., Luo, X., Qin, C.: Dither modulation based adaptive steganography resisting JPEG compression and statistic detection. Multimed. Tools Appl. 77(14), 17913–17935 (2018)
7. Zhao, Z., Guan, Q., Zhang, H., Zhao, X.: Improving the robustness of adaptive steganographic algorithms based on transport channel matching. IEEE Trans. Inf. Forensics Secur. 14(7), 1843–1856 (2018)
8. Tao, J., Li, S., Zhang, X., Wang, Z.: Towards robust image steganography. IEEE Trans. Circ. Syst. Video Technol. 29(2), 594–600 (2018)
9. Yu, X., Chen, K., Wang, Y., Li, W., Zhang, W., Yu, N.: Robust adaptive steganography based on generalized dither modulation and expanded embedding domain. Signal Process. 168, 1–12 (2019)
10. Zhang, Y., Luo, X., Guo, Y., Qin, C., Liu, F.: Multiple robustness enhancements for image adaptive steganography in lossy channels. IEEE Trans. Circ. Syst. Video Technol. 1–13 (2019)
11. Bao, P., Ma, X.: Image adaptive watermarking using wavelet domain singular value decomposition. IEEE Trans. Circ. Syst. Video Technol. 15(1), 96–102 (2005)
12. Filler, T., Judas, J., Fridrich, J.: Minimizing additive distortion in steganography using syndrome-trellis codes. IEEE Trans. Inf. Forensics Secur. 6(3), 920–935 (2011)
13. Bas, P., Filler, T., Pevný, T.: Break our steganographic system: the ins and outs of organizing BOSS. In: Filler, T., Pevný, T., Craver, S., Ker, A. (eds.) IH 2011. LNCS, vol. 6958, pp. 59–70. Springer, Heidelberg (2011). https://doi.org/10.1007/978-3-642-24178-9_5
14. Pevny, T., Fridrich, J.: Multiclass detector of current steganographic methods for JPEG format. IEEE Trans. Inf. Forensics Secur. 3(4), 635–650 (2008)
15. Holub, V., Fridrich, J.: Low-complexity features for JPEG steganalysis using undecimated DCT. IEEE Trans. Inf. Forensics Secur. 10(2), 219–228 (2015)
16. Kodovský, J., Fridrich, J., Holub, V.: Ensemble classifiers for steganalysis of digital media. IEEE Trans. Inf. Forensics Secur. 7(2), 432–444 (2012)

3D Coverless Image Steganography Scheme Based on 3D Slice Technology

Xuyu Xiang[1,2] ⓘ, Qiang Liu[2] ⓘ, Jiaohua Qin[2(✉)] ⓘ, and Yun Tan[2] ⓘ

[1] Hunan Applied Technology University, Changde 415000, Hunan, China
[2] College of Computer Science and Information Technology, Central South University of Forestry and Technology, Changsha 410004, China

Abstract. Due to the property that coverless image steganography can hide secret information without modifying the carrier, it has the ability to resist the existing steganalysis tools effectively. However, with the continuous development of new media and the increasing complexity of application scenarios, finding a more secure means of covert communication has become an urgent problem. In this paper, we propose a 3D coverless image steganography (3D-CIS) method. Based on the properties of 3D image and the relationship between 2D image and 3D image, the 2D-CIS method is applied to 3D image. Using 3D image as the carrier not only enriches the data types of steganography, but also provides a more secure means of steganography communication. Specifically, this paper combined 3D image slice technology with the existing 2D-CIS scheme to achieve 3D image steganography, which is beneficial to improve the capacity and security performance of CIS technology and promote the development of coverless image steganography.

Keywords: 3D image · 3D slice · Coverless image steganography

1 Introduction

With the development of information technology and the Internet, a large number of sensitive data, including military, political, financial, commercial and other countries, enterprises or personal information flow on the network of a large range of transmission, the security of digital information has been unprecedented attention. As an effective means of information security, Information hiding is to hide the secret message in the carrier and transmit the secret message in an unobserved way. Information hiding technology makes use of the redundancy of digital carrier and human sensory characteristics, and embeds the secret message into the redundant space of carrier without affecting the perception, so as to avoid the attack of the third party. Information hiding includes dig-

© Springer Nature Switzerland AG 2021
X. Sun et al. (Eds.): ICAIS 2021, CCIS 1424, pp. 291–300, 2021.
https://doi.org/10.1007/978-3-030-78621-2_23

ital steganography and digital watermarking. Watermarking is the process of marking digital media to realize copyright protection [1], while steganography is mainly used for covert communication [2–6]. Traditional image steganography is to make tiny changes in the space domain or transform domain to embed the secret information. However, these modification traces will cause some distortion in the cover images, which makes the steganographic analysis [7] possible.

Aiming at the shortcomings of traditional steganography, a coverless information hiding method without modifying the carrier is proposed. Coverless information hiding is achieved by establishing the mapping relationship between the secret information and the carrier rather than absence of carrier. Instead, the hiding process is implemented by an image [8], text [9] or video [10].

The concept of coverless image stegography was proposed by Zhou et al. [8] in 2015, it divided the image into 9 blocks and generated an 8-bit robust hash sequence using adjacent coefficients, thus proposing a robust hash algorithm. Subsequently, combining SIFT feature with CIS, Zheng et al. [11] proposed a robust hash algorithm based on SIFT feature. In order to optimize the above method, Yuan et al. [12] uses SIFT and bag-of-features (BOF) to replace SIFT, which effectively improves the robustness of the scheme. Due to previous methods that do not consider the security of carrier selection, and the robustness of the existing schemes still needs to be further improved. Zhang et al. proposed a CIS technology based on DCT and LDA topic classification [13]. Inspired by the former scheme, Liu et al. [14] used the supervised learning retrieval scheme to filter carrier images, and used DWT to further improve the robustness of the scheme. In addition, a coverless steganography framework for secret image transmission is proposed by Zhou et al. [15], it used a set of appropriate similar blocks of a given secret image as steganographic images to transmit the hidden image. Based on the above steganography framework, a real-time steganography scheme based on image block matching and Dense Convolutional Network is proposed by Luo et al. [16]. In 2019, Qin et al. [17] summarized the above CIS scheme. In addition to the traditional CIS methods, several new approaches have emerged in recent years. Qin et al. [18] proposed a CIS method based on generative adversarial network, which encode secret information into carrier image for information hiding. Luo et al. [19] use Faster RCNN to detect multi-object of image and establish mapping rules between them and secret information. The field of CIS has been fully developed in recent years.

Compared with 2D image steganography, the research of 3D steganography is still in the preliminary stage and still has great research value. With the development of virtual reality, real-time simulation and cross-3D design technology. 3D model data generated as the underlying support technology for many important applications, this new 3D model is a basic research subject of computer graphics itself. With the development of computer graphics and the improvement of computing performance in the era of big data, 3D models have been widely applied, including 3D rendering, 3D computing and virtual reality, etc. The research on steganography and steganography analysis of 3D models is also increasing day by day, which has attracted more and more attention in recent years. The research of 3D model steganography meets the urgent need for multimedia data steganography security in complex and diverse social environments.

In the early research phase of 3D information hiding, researchers regarded water-marking and steganography as the same technology, and proposed a batch of algorithms for embedding secret messages. Since the spatial description of 3D mesh model, shown in Fig. 1, includes important attributes such as geometric characteristics and connection structure, 3D mesh steganography is one of the mainstream directions of 3D steganography at present. It can be divided into four categories according to the position of message embedding: two-state modulated steganography, least-bit steganography, permutation steganography and transform domain steganography.

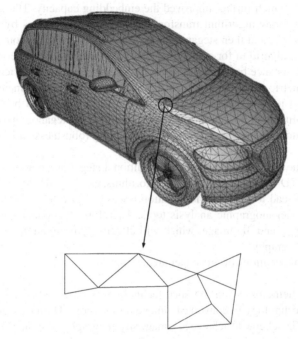

Fig. 1. 3D mesh and its local shapes.

Two-state modulation steganography usually bisects the line segment between two adjacent coordinate points, marked as states 0 and 1. It modifies the coordinate of the third point according to the state corresponding to the value of the secret message. Fran-goiset al. [20] uses quantized index modulation, which uses vertex coordinate value modulation to embed secret information. Wang et al. [21] proposed a fast path search method based on hierar-chical k-dimensional tree and advanced jumping strategy, and a multi-level segmented embedding strategy is also designed, which embeds the secret information in the embedded region aims to improve the capacity of stegography. In order to improve the ability of steganalysis resistance, Li et al. [22] proposed a method which embedding secret messages only in the distance component. Least-significant steganography is a method of hiding information in the least significant bit. Yang et al. [23] proposed a method to estimate the curvature of coordinate points and adaptively modify the least significant bits of some coordinate points according to the magnitude of curvature to embed secret messages. Li et al. [24] proposed a 3D grid steganography algorithm based on key modulation under distortion constraints. Permutation steganography embeds secret messages by perturbing the order of the elements in the set. Bogomjakov et al. [25] proposed an improved permutation steganography algorithm, which encodes the permutation values through secret messages piecemeal, and predates the coordinate elements of the corresponding positions of the permutation values to embed the secret messages. Huang et al. [26] improved the encoding method and increased the embedding capacity with the same embedding efficiency. Tu et al. [27–29] proposed the encoding method based on binary tree, left oblique binary tree and maximum expectation tree respectively, which further improved the embedding capacity. The transformation domain steganography algorithm transforms the vertex coordinates by some kind of mapping in advance, and then steganography in the transformation domain. Cho et al. [30] proposed an algorithm for embedding secret messages in the spherical coordinate system with the distance between the vertex coordinates and the spherical center coordinates as the metric value, and then clustering into segments with mean modulation. Kanai et al. [31] proposed a secret message embedding algorithm based on wavelet transform domain and multi-resolution representation. The steganography algorithm in transformation domain has the characteristics of strong robustness and low embedding capacity.

However, due to the characteristics of traditional steganographic modification carriers, similar to 2D image steganographic algorithms, existing 3D steganographic algorithms will also lead to obvious modification traces of 3D models, which are easy to be detected by steganographic analysis tools. Therefore, this paper combines coverless steganography and 3D image, which will effectively promote the development of coverless steganography.

The main contributions of this paper are as follows:

- A 3D-CIS scheme based on 3D slice technology is proposed. Creative use of 3D image slice technology to convert 3D image into several 2D images, combined with the existing CIS scheme to achieve 3D image steganography. The capacity and security of steganography algorithm can be effectively guaranteed by designing 3D image slice rules.

The organization of the remaining part is given as follows. Section 2 introduces the proposed method. Section 3 analysis the application scenarios. Section 4 concludes this article.

2 The Proposed 3D-CIS Scheme Based on 3D Slice Technology

Figure 2 shows the framework of the proposed scheme 1, which is composed of sender and receiver and can be roughly divided into four modules: 3D slice, the process of establishing 3D-2D index, information hiding and secret information extraction.

First, we need to slice the 3D image to get a 2D image set. In this scheme, the 3D model can act as a small independent 2D image database. We sliced the 3D image with a dimension step of t from the X, Y and Z directions respectively. Taking 3D image as an

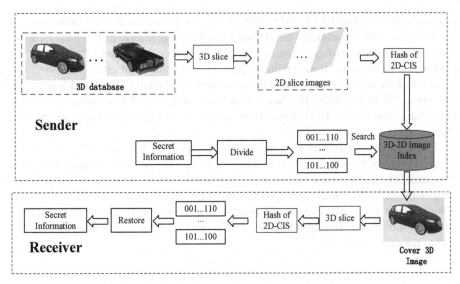

Fig. 2. The framework of the proposed scheme.

example, $(1, 1 + t), (2, 1 + t)$ and $(3, 1 + t)$ respectively represent the slice image of 3D image with a dimension of $1 + t$ in the X, Y and Z directions, and all this information is recorded as position information. The process of 3D slice is shown in Fig. 3, we can control the steganographic capacity by adjusting t according to the requirement of the 3D-CIS scheme.

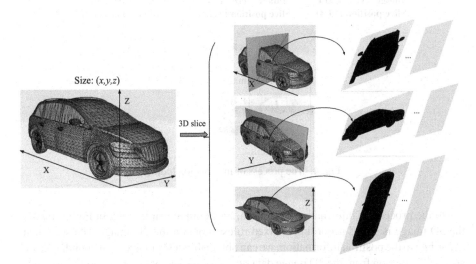

Fig. 3. The process of 3D slice.

Then, with the completion of the slicing process, we realized the conversion from 3D image to 2D image. Therefore, we can directly apply the CIS algorithm to 2D images. Taking the DWT-CIS [14] with the strongest robustness as an example, we can use this algorithm to transform all 2D images into different hash codes. That is, a 3D image uses multiple hash sequences, and we can control the steganography of secret information through the aforementioned position information. In order to improve the matching efficiency of secret information, we need to establish a 3D-2D index structure containing 3D image path, 2D slice position information and hash sequence, which is similar to the DWT-CIS [14] structure and we use Mysql performance to improve efficiency.

In the process of information hiding, an example can be seen in Fig. 4. Firstly, the secret information is converted to binary sequence by the corresponding transform algorithm. Then, the binary sequence segment needs to search for the corresponding hash sequence, which may correspond to different slices of the same 3D image and corresponding slices of different 3D images. Finally, we will get the corresponding cover 3D image and corresponding cover slice position information, which should be sent to the receiver in turn.

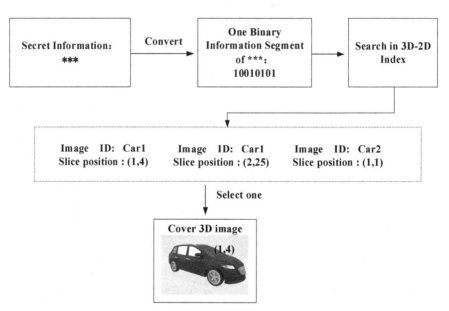

Fig. 4. The process of information hiding.

In the process of information extraction, an example can be seen in Fig. 5. Firstly, the 3D image is sliced according to fixed rules to obtain the 2D image data set. Then, according to the position information, we can obtain the stego-image corresponding to the secret information from the 2D image data set. Next, the secret binary information can be obtained by using the same 2D-CIS hash rule for stego-image. Finally, the secret binary is extracted by the corresponding extraction algorithm of the steganography algorithm.

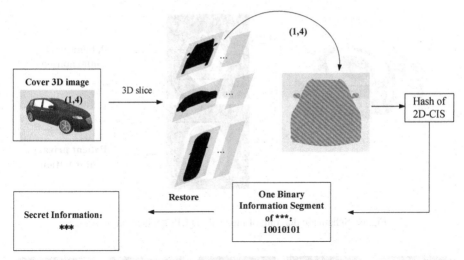

Fig. 5. The process of information extraction.

3 Application Scenarios Analysis

With the progress of software and hardware conditions, especially the emergence of new equipment such as high-resolution computed tomography (CT) and magnetic resonance imaging (MRI) and medical 3D imaging technology, the effect of medical images has made a qualitative leap. Three-dimensional medical images can obtain the spatial relative position relationship between organs. It is easy to establish three-dimensional spatial structure in people's minds. However, the details of the local surface of the lesion may remain unclear from the 3D image alone. Generally, the combination of three-dimensional medical stereoscopic images and two-dimensional CT sections will enable doctors and patients to observe more intuitively whether there are lesions in the tissues or organs represented by the images, or the location and size of lesions. For visualization of 3d medical volume data based on network transmission, the patient's personal information is still facing a steal at any time, tamper with the information security problems. We can hide patient information in slice CT images, such as not only solving the problem in transmission of steal, can effectively control medical re-port in the medical record management is separated from medical image storage disorder phenomenon occurs.

In essence, 3D images can be regarded as a collection of 2D images. It is of great significance to combine coverless image steganography with 3D images. Therefore, from a medical point of view, the slice of 3D medical image reflects the detailed information of the local lesion of the patient, if we can hide the patient's private information in the slice CT image and decrypt the private information during visualization. It can not only assist medical diagnosis but also ensure the security of patient privacy. The schematic diagram of medical 3D CIS application scene is shown as Fig. 6. Some commonly medical slice images are shown in Fig. 7. According to the above analysis and Fig. 6 and Fig. 7, the combination of 3D image and 2D slice image will be helpful for doctors to diagnose and prevent the disclosure of patient information.

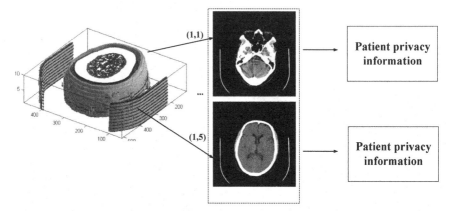

Fig. 6. Schematic diagram of medical 3D CIS application scene.

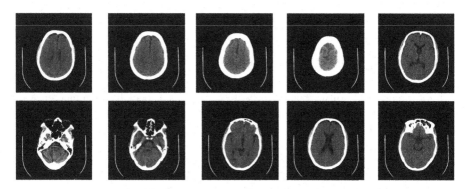

Fig. 7. Common medical slice images.

4   Conclusion and Future Work

This paper proposes a 3D-CIS method based on 3D slice technology. In this paper, we use the3D image (new media data) as the steganography carrier, since the projection of 3D image (slice image), can directly apply 2D image method, the steganography method combining 3D image and 2D image can be realized by setting projection rules. Therefore, new type of carrier data can not only effectively enrich the steganography data types but also be expected to provide more abundant steganography methods. At the same time, the proposed scheme can not only increase the capacity of steganography, but also ensure a certain security performance. In the future, we will provide enough experiment data to illustrate the steganography ability of the method. In addition, we will try to draw lessons from the existing 2D-CIS scheme to design a more direct 3D-CIS method.

Acknowledgments. This work was supported in part by the National Natural Science Foundation of China under Grant 61772561; in part by the Key Research and Development Plan of Hunan Province under Grant 2019SK2022; in part by the Science Research Projects of Hunan

Provincial Education Department under Grant 18A174; in part by the Degree & Postgraduate Education Reform Project of Hunan Province under Grant 2019JGYB154; in part by the Postgraduate Education and Teaching Reform Project of Central South University of Forestry & Technology under Grant 2019JG013; in part by the National Natural Science Foundation of China under Grant 62002392; in part by the Natural Science Foundation of Hunan Province under Grant 2020JJ4141; in part by The Natural Science Foundation of Hunan Province under Grant 2020JJ4140 and in part by the Postgraduate Excellent teaching team Project of Hunan Province under Grant [2019]370-133.

References

1. Tan, Y., Qin, J., Xiang, X., et al.: A robust watermarking scheme in YCbCr color space based on channel coding. IEEE Access **7**(1), 25026–25036 (2019)
2. Yang, C., Weng, C., Wang, S., et al.: Adaptive data hiding in edge areas of images with spatial LSB domain systems. IEEE Trans. Inf. Forensics Secur. **3**(3), 488–497 (2008)
3. Luo, W., Huang, F., Huang, J.: Edge adaptive image steganography based on LSB matching revisited. IEEE Trans. Inf. Forensics Secur. **5**(2), 1448–1458 (2010)
4. Zhang, X., Wang, S.: Steganography using multiple-base notational system and human vision sensitivity. IEEE Signal Process. **12**(1), 67–70 (2005)
5. Holub, V., Fridrich, J.: Designing steganographic distortion using directional filters. In: IEEE International Workshop on Information Forensics and Security, pp. 234–239 (2012)
6. Pevný, T., Filler, T., Bas, P.: Using high-dimensional image models to perform highly undetectable steganography. In: Böhme, R., Fong, P.W.L., Safavi-Naini, R. (eds.) IH 2010. LNCS, vol. 6387, pp. 161–177. Springer, Heidelberg (2010). https://doi.org/10.1007/978-3-642-16435-4_13
7. Qin, J., Sun, X., Xiang, X., et al.: Principal feature selection and fusion method for image steganalysis. J. Electron. Imaging **18**(3), 1–14 (2009)
8. Zhou, Z., Sun, H., Harit, R., Chen, X., Sun, X.: Coverless image steganography without embedding. In: Huang, Z., Sun, X., Luo, J., Wang, J. (eds.) ICCCS 2015. LNCS, vol. 9483, pp. 123–132. Springer, Cham (2015). https://doi.org/10.1007/978-3-319-27051-7_11
9. Zhou, Z., Qin, J., Xiang, X., et al.: News text topic clustering optimized method based on TF-IDF algorithm on spark. Comput. Mater. Continua **62**(1), 217–231 (2020)
10. Pan, N., Qin, J., Tan, Y., Xiang, X., Hou, G.: A video coverless information hiding algorithm based on semantic segmentation. EURASIP J. Image Video Process. **2020**(1), 1–18 (2020). https://doi.org/10.1186/s13640-020-00512-8
11. Zheng, S., Wang, L., Ling, B., Hu, D.: Coverless information hiding based on robust image hashing. In: Huang, D.-S., Hussain, A., Han, K., Gromiha, M.M. (eds.) ICIC 2017. LNCS (LNAI), vol. 10363, pp. 536–547. Springer, Cham (2017). https://doi.org/10.1007/978-3-319-63315-2_47
12. Yuan, C., Xia, Z., Sun, X.: Coverless image steganography based on SIFT and BOF. J. Int. Technol. **18**(2), 435–442 (2017)
13. Zhang, X., Peng, F., Long, M.: Robust coverless image steganography based on DCT and LDA topic classification. IEEE Trans. Multimed. **99**, 3223–3238 (2018)
14. Liu, Q., Xiang, X., Qin, J., et al.: Coverless steganography based on image retrieval of DenseNet features and DWT sequence mapping. Knowl.-Based Syst. **192**(2020), 105375–105389 (2020)
15. Zhou, Z., Mu, Y., Wu, Q.M.J.: Coverless image steganography using partial-duplicate image retrieval. Soft. Comput. **23**(13), 4927–4938 (2018). https://doi.org/10.1007/s00500-018-3151-8

16. Luo, Y., Qin, J., Xiang, X., et al.: Coverless real-time image information hiding based on image block matching and dense convolutional network. J. Real-Time Image Process. **17**(1), 125–135 (2020)
17. Qin, J., Luo, Y., Xiang, X., et al.: Coverless image steganography: a survey. IEEE Access **7**, 171372–171394 (2019)
18. Qin, J., Wang, J., Tan, Y., et al.: Coverless image steganography based on generative adversarial network. Mathematics **8**(9), 1394 (2020)
19. Luo, Y., Qin, J., Xiang, X., et al.: Coverless image steganography based on multi-object recognition. IEEE Trans. Circ. Syst. Video Technol. (2021). https://doi.org/10.1109/TCSVT.2020.3033945
20. Cayre, F., Macq, B.: Data hiding on 3-D triangle meshes. IEEE Trans. Signal Process **51**(4), 939–949 (2003)
21. Wang, C., Cheng, Y.: An efficient information hiding algorithm for polygon models. Comput. Graph. Forum **24**(3), 591–600 (2005)
22. Li, Z., Beugnon, S., Puech, W., et al.: Rethinking the high capacity 3D steganography: increasing its resistance to steganalysis. In: Proceedings of 2017 IEEE International Conference on Image Processing (ICIP), pp. 510–414. IEEE (2017)
23. Yang, Y., Peyerimhoff, N., Ivrissimtzis, I.: Linear correlations between spatial and normal noise in triangle meshes. IEEE Trans. Vis. Comput. Graph. **19**(1), 45–55 (2012)
24. Li, N., Hu, J., Sun, R., et al.: A high-capacity 3D steganography algorithm with adjustable distortion. IEEE Access **5**, 24457–24466 (2017)
25. Bogomjakov, A., Gotsman, C., Isenburg, M.: Distortion-free steganography for polygonal meshes. In: Computer Graphics Forum, vol. 27, no. 2, pp. 637–642. Blackwell Publishing Ltd., Oxford (2008)
26. Huang, N., Li, M., Wang, C.: Toward optimal embedding capacity for permutation steganography. IEEE Signal Process. Lett. **16**(9), 802–805 (2009)
27. Tu, S., Tai, W., Isenburg, M., et al.: An improved data hiding approach for polygon meshes. Vis. Comput. **26**(9), 1177–1181 (2010)
28. Tu, S., Hsu, H., Tai, W.: Permutation steganography for polygonal meshes based on coding tree. Int. J. Virtual Reality **9**(4), 55–60 (2010)
29. Tu, S., Tai, W.: A high-capacity data-hiding approach for polygonal meshes using maximum expected level tree. Comput. Graph. **36**(6), 767–775 (2012)
30. Cho, J., Prost, R., Jung, H.: An oblivious watermarking for 3-D polygonal meshes using distribution of vertex norms. IEEE Trans. Signal Process. **55**(1), 142–155 (2006)
31. Kanai, S., Date, H., Kishinami, T.: Digital watermarking for 3D polygons using multiresolution wavelet decomposition. In: Proceedings of Sixth IFIP WG, vol. 5, pp. 296–307 (1998)

Software Information Hiding Algorithm Based on Import Table of Portable Executable File

Zuwei Tian$^{(\boxtimes)}$ and Hengfu Yang

Hunan First Normal University, Changsha 410205, China

Abstract. Import table is a very important data structure in PE file, and it is the basis of dynamic link and code reuse. The import address table (IAT) is a collection of all the JMP instruction operands in the PE file. The user program can call a specific import function by jumping to virtual address (VA) of an import function through unconditional transfer instruction. This paper proposes an information hiding algorithm based on IAT table. The algorithm makes use of the feature that the IAT table of PE file will be rewritten by the actual function entry address after loading into memory to hide information. Obviously, it will not increase the length of the file. At the same time, because all the hidden information will be rewritten after loading into memory, the PE image file loaded into memory is analyzed and dynamically tracked. Theoretical analysis and experimental results show that the algorithm can overcome the shortcomings of traditional PE file information hiding algorithm, such as too centralized hidden information, and improve the concealment and anti-attack ability.

Keywords: Information hiding · Portable executable file · Import table · Windows loader · Import address table

1 Introduction

Import function (input function) is a function that is called by the program, whose execution code is located in the dynamic link library (DLL). Import table is a very important data structure in PE file, and it is the basis of dynamic link and code reuse. The calling program only retains some basic information of the function, including the function name and the DLL file name, which are saved in the import table of PE file. When the PE file is not loaded, the actual address of the import function in memory is uncertain. When the program is executed, windows loader loads all the import DLL files and associates the instructions calling the import function with the real address of the function in memory through the PE file import table.

The effect of import table is that PE file can call functions exported by other modules, so as to achieve code reuse. PE files need to call the system functions provided by the core DLL through the import table to complete the functions of the software itself in the windows platform [1, 2]. Windows applications will call three important DLL functions: kernel32.dll, user32.dll, gdi32.dll. The kernel32.dll is a kernel level file, which provides

© Springer Nature Switzerland AG 2021
X. Sun et al. (Eds.): ICAIS 2021, CCIS 1424, pp. 301–311, 2021.
https://doi.org/10.1007/978-3-030-78621-2_24

system storage management, I/O management, interrupt management and other functions. The user32.dll is a windows user interface related application program interface, which provides windows processing and basic functions. The gdi32.dll is a Windows GDI graphical user interface related program, which provides functions such as drawing images and displaying text.

Import functions are functions introduced from dynamic link libraries. The import table stores the relevant information of all import functions called by PE file. When loading PE file, windows loader will read the related DLL file into memory, and fill the actual address of the import function in memory into the related structure of the import table to prepare for calling the import function. Import function, also known as import function or input function, is called by program but its execution code is located in dynamic link library (DLL). The calling program only keeps some basic information of function, including function name and DLL file name, which are saved in the import table of PE file. When the PE file is not loaded, the actual address of the import function in memory is uncertain. When the program is executed, the windows loader loads all the imported DLL files and associates the instruction calling the import function with the real address of the function in memory through the PE file import table.

Long Feiyu et al. [3] proposed an information hiding algorithm by introducing table data structure transformation into PE file. This method embeds the secret information into the table structure of PE file and the order of import function by analyzing the characteristics of introducing table data structure of PE file and calling method of import function. Experimental results show that the first mock exam is better than the PE file redundancy space and resource structure watermarking algorithm, and provides a more secure software copyright protection mode. However, the PE file import table structure has its default order. The alignment of the entry function in the same module is arranged in ascending order according to the string of the function name, and the structure and function of the import table are changed. The permutation order will cause the attacker's suspicion, and the security is not high. At the same time, rearranging the structure of the import table and the order of functions will destroy the hidden information, and the robustness is not good.

Duanmu Qingfeng et al. [4] Based on the working principle of spread spectrum communication, a new spread spectrum software watermarking scheme is proposed, in which the calling times of different import functions in PE file are taken as the feature vector of the program, and the watermark signal is dispersed and embedded into the code section of the PE file by modifying the component values of the eigenvector. Experiments show that, compared with the existing software watermarking, the scheme has high concealment, simple implementation, and can effectively resist a variety of attacks. However, the algorithm is implemented by changing the number of references of the import function. It needs to add redundant import function call code in the code. On the one hand, the addition of redundant import function call code will reduce the performance of the program, on the other hand, by modifying the It is very difficult to increase the number of calls to import function by compiled binary code. This algorithm is only applicable to the program with active code. Adding calls to the import function in the source code file will change the feature vector of the program.

Zhang zhong [5] proposed the use of windows to load the import table of the PE File and shell. Based on the import table structure of the PE file and the principle of system loading the import table, it is defined in the shell. the import table of the shell and that of the PE file are combined in one by using Win32 assembly program. Which is initialized while windows load PE file, so as to realize normal calling API functions in the PE file and shell.

2 Structure of PE File Import Table

Import table is one of the data types registered in the data directory, and its description information is located in the second directory of the data directory [6–9]. IMAGE_ IMPORT_DESCRIPTOR is defined in winnt.h. The descriptor structure is used to describe the import table. The import table adopts a two-level index structure, and the first level is a module directory IMAGE_IMPORT_DESCRIPTOR array (IID array for short), each element of which describes a DLL dynamic link library file, with all 0 bytes as the end mark of the array; the second level is two similar import name table INT or import address table IAT, each element of INT or IAT points to an IMAGE_IMPORT_NAME structure (including a function sequence number and a function name string).

2.1 Definition of IMAGE_IMPORT_DESCRIPTOR

Import table is defined by using IMAGE_IMPORT_DESCRIPTOR (IID)structure array in PE file. Each IID structure array element describes the relevant information of a dynamic link library DLL referenced by the PE file. There are 5 domain members, accounting for 20 bytes in total. All members of the last IID structure are 0, indicating the end of the import table descriptor structure. That is, the import can be calculated by the starting address of the import table and the all-0 element The number of dynamic link libraries referenced in the table. The structure is defined as follows:

```
typedef struct _IMAGE_IMPORT_DESCRIPTOR
{ union
    {  DWORD   Characteristics;
       DWORD   OriginalFirstThunk;
    };
    DWORD   TimeDateStamp;
    DWORD   ForwarderChain;
    DWORD   Name;
    DWORD   FirstThunk;
} IMAGE_IMPORT_DESCRIPTOR;
```

The structure member OriginalFirstThunk is a double word data type, and its value is the relative virtual address of the import name table (INT). The import name table is an IMAGE_THUNK_DATA structure array, an array element describes the information of an import function, the array element value of all 0 means IMAGE_THUNK_DATA structure end. There are two cases of this structure member: one is that when the highest bit is 0, it means that the import symbol is a value and the value is an RVA; the other is when the highest bit is 1, it means that the import symbol is a name.

Structure member TimeDateStamp is double word data type (DWORD type). If the value of the field is 0, it means that the current PE file does not perform import binding. When bound in the old way, this field is set to the timestamp of the corresponding DLL file. When bound in a new way, the value of this field is - 1. When the windows operating system loads the DLL file, it is through this timestamp to judge whether the binding information is out of date.

The structure member ForwarderChain is a double word data type. It is used when a program refers to an API in a DLL, which in turn refers to the API of other DLLs. Its value is usually 0.

Structure member Name is double word data type (DWORD type), pointing to RVA of DLL file name string to be imported, which is an ASCII string ending with 0. Such as user32. DLL file.

Structure member FirstThunk points to the RVA of the import address table (IAT). IAT is an IMAGE_THUNK_DATA array in which the data members First-Thunk and OriginalFirsThunk point to two images that are essentially the same IMAGE_THUNK_DATA structure.

2.2   Definition of IMAGE_THUNK_DATA

IMAGE_ THUNK_ DATA is used to define information about the import function of the import table. IMAGE_ THUNK_ DATA detailed definition is as follows:

> *typedef struct _IMAGE_THUNK_DATA32*
> *{   union*
> *{ DWORD ForwarderString;*
> *DWORD Function;*
> *DWORD Ordinal;*
> *DWORD AddressOfData;*
> *} u1;*
> *} IMAGE_THUNK_DATA32;*

This is a double word common body data structure. When the highest bit is 1, it means that the function is imported by serial number; the lower 31 bits of the common body member ordinal indicate the serial number of the import function; when the highest bit is 0, it means that the function is imported as a string. The AddressOfData value of the community member is the relative virtual address pointing to the name of the import function.

2.3   Definition of IMAGE_IMPORT_BY_NAME

IMAGE_IMPORT_BY_NAME structure is used to store information about an import function. It is defined as follows:

> *typedef struct _IMAGE_IMPORT_BY_NAME {*
> *WORD   Hint;*
> *BYTE   Name[1];*
> *} IMAGE_IMPORT_BY_NAME;*

The member hint identifies the index number of the import function in the DLL. The PE loader can use the hint field to speed up the query function in the DLL export table. The value of the member is generally assigned to 0. The name field identifies the function name of the import function, i.e., an ASCII string with a zero end flag (Fig. 1).

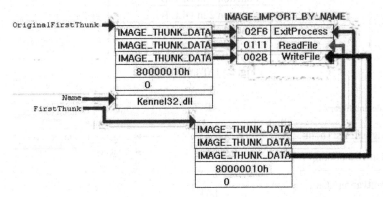

Fig. 1. Structure of PE file import table

2.4 2Import Address Table

The import address table (IAT) is a collection of JMP instruction operands of all import functions in the PE file. It is a double word array. Each double word stores a virtual address of the import function, that is, the import function address. The user program can call a specific import function by jumping to virtual address of an import function through unconditional transfer instruction. Because there may be multiple DLL functions defined in IAT, in order to distinguish the functions imported from different DLL, it is stipulated that all imported functions are classified according to DLL: the function addresses of the same DLL are arranged together, and finally end with a double word 0.

There is a close relationship between import table and IAT. IAT can be located through FirstThunk. At the same time, IAT is also the 13th directory item in the data directory of the PE file. You can also locate IAT by accessing the 13th directory item. When the PE file is loaded into memory, the content of IAT will be modified by the operating system to import the real VA of the function in memory. In this way, in memory, the name or index number of the imported function can be found through OriginalFirstThunk, and the starting address of the instruction code of the imported function in memory space can be found through FirstThunk (Fig. 2).

When the PE file is loaded into the virtual address space, the loader first searches for the OriginalFirstThunk. After reading successfully, the loader circularly reads the values of each element in the array to find the actual addresses of all the import functions. Then the content of IAT will be modified by the operating system to the true entry address of the function. In this way, there is no way to find out which address is called through the FirstThunk. This is the main reason why the import table needs to save both original first chunk and first chunk at the same time (Fig. 3).

Function 1 in DLL A
Function 2 in DLL A
......
0x0000 0000
Function 1 in DLL B
Function 2 in DLL B
0x0000 0000
......

Fig. 2. IAT table structure

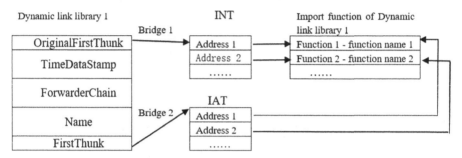

Fig. 3. Relationship between import table in disk file and IAT

3   Information Hiding Scheme Based on IAT Table

Through the analysis of PE file import table structure, we know that there are two identical data structures INT and IAT in PE file, namely two identical IMAGE_THUNK_DATA array type. When the PE file is loaded into memory, the loader will find the function name according to the value of OrignalFirstThunk, call the system function GetProcAddress according to the function name to get the actual entry address of the import function in memory, and rewrite the corresponding value in the IAT table with the actual entry address of the function. In other words, the content of IAT in PE disk file can be rewritten, because it will be rewritten completely after being loaded into memory (except for the implementation of binding import mechanism, but binding import mechanism is a technology to improve the loading speed of PE file, which can only play an auxiliary role. Whether it is accessed or not will only affect the program loading process, but will not affect the PE file loading result and running result. In this way, the information can be hidden in the IAT table in the PE file. This scheme does not increase the file length, only affects the start-up speed of the PE file of the import table binding, and does not affect the start-up speed of the program that does not perform the import table binding.

3.1   Information Embedding

This algorithm makes use of the feature that the IAT table of PE file will be rewritten by the operating system loader after loading into memory, and hides the information directly into the IAT table of PE file after encryption.

The detailed algorithm is as follows:

Input: secret information M, PE file P, key k.

Output: the watermarked PE file P'.

Step 1: Analyze the original carrier PE file, judge IMAGE_DATA_DIRECTORY, the size attribute of the seventh object in the directory array. The value is 0xFFFFFF indicates that the information has been hidden and exit. Otherwise, go to step 2.

Step 2: Analyze the original carrier PE file, read the address ADDR and SIZE of the IAT table of the PE file from the data directory, and calculate the hidden capacity C of the IAT table of the PE file.

Step 3: Key and asymmetric encryption algorithm RSA are used to encrypt the hidden information and get the encrypted information.

Step 4: Traverse the IID array, and write the encrypted information into the IAT structure of the PE file import table in turn.

Step 5: Write the hidden flag 0xFFFFFFFF in its size attribute.

Step 6: Output a steganographic PE file embedded with hidden information.

3.2 Extracting Information

Firstly, the PE file is analyzed to find the first address of the original IID array, and then the information hidden in the original IID array and the original INT table is read and assembled according to the convention, and finally decrypted. The main steps are listed as following:

Input: the watermarked PE file P', key k.

Output: secret information M.

Step 1: analyze the steganography PE file with hidden information, judge whether the information has been hidden, and view the size of the seventh object of IMAGE_DATA_DIRECTORY array attribute. 0xFFFFFFFF indicates that the information has been hidden. Go to step 2. Otherwise, exit.

Step 2: Read the address ADDR and SIZE of the IAT table of the PE file from the data directory, and calculate the hidden capacity C of the IAT table of the PE file.

Step 3: Traverse IID array, read out IAT data of each DLL file in PE file import table in turn, and assemble to get secret information.

Step 4: use the private key and asymmetric encryption algorithm RSA to decrypt the watermark information and get the decrypted information.

3.3 Algorithm Improvement

Because IAT table is one of the data types registered in PE file, its description information is located in the data directory table IMAGE_DATA_DIRECTORY of the 12th element of directory. In this element, the relative virtual address RVA of IAT table and the size of import table are stored. Visit IMAGE_DATA_DIRECTORY of the 12th element in the directory table can get the starting position and size of the IAT table in the file. According to the RVA, the data related to the IAT table can be found. The concealment is relatively poor. In order to further improve the concealment and anti-attack, we propose a method to migrate the IAT table, hide the information in the original IAT table, and modify the RVA value of the 12th element in the data directory to point to the new IAT.

The call to import function in PE file is realized by IAT table. In order to move IAT table, we must modify all the call instructions to import function in PE file. The specific algorithm of moving IAT table is described as follows.

Step 1: use the disassembly engine to disassemble the code section of PE file.

Step 2: traverse the indirect jump instruction of the code section, and judge whether its reference address is in the range of IAT table, if so, record the jump instruction.

Step 3: move the original IAT table to the free area of the PE file, and record the address of the new IAT table.

Step 4: according to the address of the new IAT table, modify the jump instruction recorded in step 2 to point to a unit in the new IAT table.

Step 5: modify the address of IAT table in the data directory to point to the new IAT table.

After moving IAT, it is very convenient to realize information hiding. It can hide information in both the original IAT table and the moved IAT table. To address the original IAT table, the first address of the original IAT table is stored in the last item of the new IAT table. In this way, the hiding capacity is almost doubled. At the same time, the original IAT table can't be located through the 12th element of the data directory table. As a result, the concealment and anti-attack ability of the information hidden in the original IAT table are improved significantly.

4   Experimental Results

PE files used in the experiment come from windows system folder and Internet. In order to accurately calculate the embedded capacity of the proposed method, we selected 200 PE files from the windows system folder, and selected common software installed in the system, such as QQ.exe, thunder.exe More than 100 PE files are used as test files.

4.1   Capacity

In the test set, we embed the watermark information into IAT table. The embedded capacity is related to the size of IAT table in PE file, that is, to the number of DLL files and functions imported by PE file. Generally speaking, the more complex the program function is, the more import functions are called, and the larger the IAT table is, the larger its hidden capacity is.

Compared with other methods, this scheme uses the feature that the IAT table of PE file will be rewritten by the actual function entry address after loading into memory to hide information. Obviously, this scheme will not increase the length of the file. At the same time, because all the hidden information will be rewritten after loading into memory, the PE image file loaded into memory is analyzed and dynamically tracked, therefore, it has high security (Table 1).

Table 1. Analysis of hiding capacity of algorithm based on IAT table

Filename	Size of file(byte)	Number of DLL files referenced	Number of import function	Capacity(bytes)
write.exe	5,632	3	19	88
notepad.exe	66,560	9	201	900
tenet.exe	85,504	9	185	776
acrord32.exe	1,498,552	9	544	2212
qq.exe	99,744	7	93	400
360sd.exe	1,697,400	14	845	3436
thunder.exe	1,808,176	29	1194	4892

4.2 Impact on the Speed of Program Starting

In order to reduce the IAT table that PE loader needs to modify every time when loading PE files, most windows system files adopt binding import technology. The so-called binding import technology is to advance the IAT address correction work in the charge of windows loader to loading. This work can be done by the programmer manually or by a special program, and then declare binding import in the PE file to tell the operating system loader that it does not need to do this work again. In this scheme, the information is hidden in the IAT table of the PE file, and the contents of the IAT table have been destroyed in the disk file. If these PE files have been bound and imported, this scheme will destroy this binding, and the operating system loader will revise the IAT table again when loading, thus affecting the loading speed of the file. However, the binding import technology is only a kind of auxiliary work, the DLL base address is usually different in different operating systems, which will lead to different entry addresses of the same import function in different operating systems. When this happens, PE will start the error detection mechanism. If the address detection error occurs, PE will load the controller will take over this work again, and the IAT will be corrected again when loading.

In the windows operating system, most of the PE files in the system use the binding import table technology, such as write.exe, notepad.exe, winmine.exe For applications, most of them do not use the binding import table technology, QQ.exe, thunder.exe, 360sd.exe, and so on. Through the experimental analysis, we can see that rewriting the IAT table has little effect on the startup speed of PE files using the binding import table technology, and has no effect on the startup speed of PE files not using the binding import table technology (Table 2).

The embedding capacity of the proposed method is related to the number of import functions called by the program. The more import functions called, the larger the IAT table and the larger the hidden capacity. For the program without binding import table, its program performance will not be affected. For the program bound to import table, it only affects the startup speed of the program, and the impact is very small, and it does not affect the performance of the program execution.

Table 2. Program start time analysis table after rewriting IAT table

Filename	Normal start time (ms)	Start time after rewriting IAT table (ms)	Performance loss (%)
write.exe	15.4	15.8	2.5974
notepad.exe	20.3	20.9	2.9557
telnet.exe	64.2	64.2	0.0
winmine.exe	70.8	71.6	1.1299
winrar.exe	39.4	39.4	0.0
qq.exe	27.3	27.3	0.0
360sd.exe	113.7	113.7	0.0
thunder.exe	83.8	83.8	0.0

5   Conclusion

PE file is the standard format of executable file on Windows platform. It is widely used and is very suitable for information hiding. Based on the analysis of the structure of PE file import table and the working principle of windows loader, this paper proposes a PE file information hiding algorithm based on import address table (IAT). The algorithm overcomes the problems of the traditional PE file information hiding algorithm, such as too concentrated hidden information, the exchange of PE file import table data structure elements will destroy the hidden information, and enhance the concealment and anti-attack.

References

1. Petzold, A., Fang, C., Zhang, S., Liang, L.P., et al.: Windows Programming. 5th edn. Beijing: Tsinghua University Press, Beijing (2010)
2. Zaidan, A.A., Zaidan, B.B., Alanazi, O.H., et al.: Novel approach for high (secure and rate) data hidden within triplex space for executable file. Sci. Res. Essays **5**(15), 1965–1977 (2010)
3. Long, F.Y., Liu, J.Y., Yuan, X.: A software watermark for transforming PE file into table structure. Comput. Appl. **30**(1), 217–219 (2010)
4. Duanmu, Q.F., Wang, Y.B., Zhang, X.W., Zhang, K.Z.: Spread spectrum software watermarking scheme based on the number of references of import function. Comput. Res. Dev. **46**(supply.) 88–92 (2009)
5. Zhang, Z.: The use of windows to load the import table of the PE file and shell. Comput. Knowl. Technol. **11**(03), 117–120 (2015)
6. Zhou, Q.L., Li, B.: Dual software watermarking scheme based on tamper proof. Comput. Eng. **39**(7), 185–188 (2013)
7. Zhang, M.: Chen J X, Zhang P C : Efficient backdoor steganography algorithm for executable files. Comput. Appl. Res. **30**(4), 1198–1120 (2013)

8. Jang, J., Ji, H., Hong, J.M., et al.: Protecting android applications with steganography-based software watermarking. In: Proceedings of the 28th Annual ACM Symposium on Applied Computing, Coimbra, pp.1657–1658 (2013)
9. Liu, J.C.: Research on Unknown PE Virus Detection Technology Based on Behavior Analysis. Beijing University of Posts and telecommunications, Beijing (2014)

A Novel Robust Reversible Watermarking Method Against JPEG Compression

Hongya Wang[1,2], Xiaolong Li[1,2(✉)], Mengyao Xiao[1,2], and Yao Zhao[1,2]

[1] Institute of Information Science, Beijing Jiaotong University, Beijing 100044, China
lixl@bjtu.edu.cn
[2] Beijing Key Laboratory of Advanced Information Science
and Network Technology, Beijing 100044, China

Abstract. Robustness limits the application of reversible watermarking. To overcome this weakness, several robust reversible watermarking (RRW) techniques have been proposed so far. However, most existing RRW methods are unstable in terms of robustness and reversibility. Then, in this paper, to ameliorate these disadvantages, a new RRW algorithm is presented. A cover image is first divided into non-overlapping blocks, and a high pass filter is applied to each block to generate a histogram which is a Laplacien-like distribution. Then, the watermark is embedded into the blocks by shifting the generated histogram. Specifically, the histogram shifting is conducted by modifying each pixel in the block, and the embedding distortion is minimized based on a new modification mechanism. Moreover, for blind data extraction and image recovery, a strategy for determining the parameters used in histogram shifting is also proposed. In this way, more than 4,096 bits can be reversibly embedded into a cover image with a good visual quality and sufficient robustness against JPEG compression. The superiority of the proposed method is verified through extensive experiments.

Keywords: Robust reversible watermarking · Histogram shifting · JPEG compression · Blind extraction and recovery · Embedding distortion

1 Introduction

Reversible watermarking [1] is a special type of digital watermarking where both the watermark extraction and the host content recovery can be accomplished without loss at the decoder side. In the past two decades, many reversible watermarking methods have been proposed for digital images [2–9]. However, the transmission channel is supposed to be lossless in these methods, and the watermark extraction becomes a challenge in case of attack. To overcome this weakness, a new type of reversible watermarking, namely, robust reversible watermarking (RRW) is proposed [10]. By RRW, not only the embedded watermark but also the original host image can be restored without distortion in a lossless environment. Moreover, if the marked image is lossily compressed, although the host image may not be restored exactly, the embedded watermark should be recovered in this case. Existing RRW methods can be classified into two categories: redundant histogram

© Springer Nature Switzerland AG 2021
X. Sun et al. (Eds.): ICAIS 2021, CCIS 1424, pp. 312–322, 2021.
https://doi.org/10.1007/978-3-030-78621-2_25

shifting (RHS) based methods and multi-layer watermarking (MLW) based methods, and representative achievements of RHS techniques mainly include histogram rotation (HR) and generalized histogram shifting (GHS).

In [10], Vleeschouwer *et al.* first proposed the HR technique, in which each embedding block is randomly divided into two groups with equal number of pixels, and the watermark is embedded by modifying the centroid vectors of the two groups, while the salt and pepper noise is introduced. To deal with this issue, Zou *et al.* [11] proposed to modify the average values of the intermediate frequency sub-band in integer wavelet domain. In [12], Ni *et al.* improved the method [10] and avoided the salt and pepper distortion of HR while error bits are introduced for the blocks with extreme values 0 or 255. And thus, the error correction coding has been exploited in this work. Later on, Zeng *et al.* [13] proposed to divide the cover image into blocks to calculate the arithmetic difference of each block, and introduced two thresholds to embed the watermark by shifting the arithmetic differences. The performance of this method is better than some previous works, but the side information for data extraction and image recovery should be send to the receiver by using an additional communication channel, and thus this method is not blind. Then, in [14–17], An and Gao proposed several RRW methods to improve the robustness performance. Especially, in [15], they proposed a new robust reversible embedding framework based on clustering and wavelet transformation. However, this method is not blind as well, and the side information is still necessary for the decoder. In [18] and [19], Coltuc *et al.* first proposed the MLW technique, and there are two layers of watermark to be embedded into the cover image: a robust watermark is first embedded into the cover image to derive an intermediate image, and then a reversible watermark is embedded into the intermediate image. Most traditional reversible watermarking and robust watermarking techniques are available for this framework. However, for MLW, the noise is inevitably introduced to the intermediate image because both the robust and reversible embedding are applied on the same embedding domain. Then, in [20], Wang *et al.* proposed a new RRW technique to separately embed the robust and reversible watermark into the independent embedding domains to avoid the noise.

Existing RRW methods, including Zeng *et al.*'s work [13], have the disadvantages of insufficient embedding capacity and weak robustness due to the large embedding distortion. Based on this consideration, to improve the previous work [13], we propose a new RRW method in this paper. First, the cover image is divided into non-overlapping blocks and a histogram is generated by applying a high pass filter to each block. The generated histogram follows a Laplacien-like distribution. Then, the watermark is embedded into the blocks by shifting this histogram. Specifically, the method [13] is improved by minimizing the embedding distortion using a new modification mechanism. In addition, for blind data extraction and image recovery, a strategy for determining the parameters used in histogram shifting is also proposed. In this way, the proposed method is reversible without side information at the decoder side, and it provides a significant performance improvement in terms of both visual quality and embedding capacity. Experimental results show that the proposed scheme has sufficient robustness against JPEG compression compared with Zeng *et al.*'s method [13].

The rest of the paper is organized as follows. In Sect. 2, Zeng *et al.*'s RRW algorithm [13] is briefly introduced, and followed by the proposed scheme described in detail in

Sect. 3. Then, the experimental results and the comparison with Zeng *et al.*'s method [13] are reported in Sect. 4. Finally, the conclusions are presented in Sect. 5.

2 Related Work

In [13], Zeng *et al.* proposed a new RRW method by using two thresholds. The watermark is embedded by shifting the arithmetic differences of the divided image blocks.

First, the cover image is divided into non-overlapping blocks of size $m \times n$. Then, a matrix M sized $m \times n$ is introduced to calculate the arithmetic difference of each block. Specifically, the matrix M is given by

$$
M(i,j) = \begin{cases} 1, & \text{if } i \text{ and } j \text{ have the same parity} \\ -1, & \text{otherwise} \end{cases}.
\tag{1}
$$

As an example, a matrix sized 8×8 is shown in Fig. 1. After that, the arithmetic difference of each block, is given by

$$
\alpha = \sum_{i=1}^{m} \sum_{j=1}^{n} C(i,j)M(i,j),
\tag{2}
$$

where $C(i,j)$ means the pixel value of a given block C in the location (i,j). For example, the distribution of α for the Barbara image with block size of 8×8 is shown in Fig. 2, where the vertical axis represents the values of α and the horizontal axis is the occurrence of α.

1	-1	1	-1	1	-1	1	-1
-1	1	-1	1	-1	1	-1	1
1	-1	1	-1	1	-1	1	-1
-1	1	-1	1	-1	1	-1	1
1	-1	1	-1	1	-1	1	-1
-1	1	-1	1	-1	1	-1	1
1	-1	1	-1	1	-1	1	-1
-1	1	-1	1	-1	1	-1	1

Fig. 1. Matrix M sized 8×8.

For the data embedding of a given block C, two thresholds $T, G > 0$ are utilized to shift the value of α. If $\alpha > T$, it is shifted to the right side by $2G + T$ to create vacancy. Specifically, the cover pixel $C(i,j)$ is modified as

$$
C^*(i,j) = \begin{cases} C(i,j) + \beta_1, & \text{if } M(i,j) = 1 \\ C(i,j), & \text{otherwise} \end{cases},
\tag{3}
$$

where

$$
\beta_1 = \left\lceil \frac{4G + 2T}{mn} \right\rceil.
\tag{4}
$$

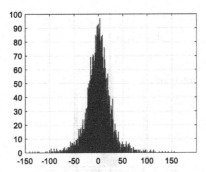

Fig. 2. The distribution of α of the Barbara image with the 8×8 matrix shown in Fig. 1.

In this way, one can verify that the value of α will be changed as

$$\sum_{i=1}^{m} \sum_{j=1}^{n} C^*(i,j)M(i,j) = \alpha + \frac{mn}{2}\beta_1 > 2(G+T). \tag{5}$$

That is to say, there is no value inside the range of $(T, 2(G+T)]$ after shifting. Similarly, if $\alpha < -T$, it is shifted to the left side by modifying the cover pixel $C(i,j)$ as

$$C^*(i,j) = \begin{cases} C(i,j) + \beta_1, & \text{if } M(i,j) = -1 \\ C(i,j), & \text{otherwise} \end{cases}. \tag{6}$$

If $\alpha \in [0, T]$, the cover pixel $C(i,j)$ is modified as

$$C^*(i,j) = \begin{cases} C(i,j) + \omega\beta_2, & \text{if } M(i,j) = 1 \\ C(i,j), & \text{otherwise} \end{cases}, \tag{7}$$

where $\omega \in \{0, 1\}$, represents the watermark bit to be embedded and

$$\beta_2 = \left\lceil \frac{2G + 2T}{mn} \right\rceil. \tag{8}$$

Similarly, if $\alpha \in [-T, 0)$, the cover pixel $C(i,j)$ is modified as

$$C^*(i,j) = \begin{cases} C(i,j) + \omega\beta_2, & \text{if } M(i,j) = -1 \\ C(i,j), & \text{otherwise} \end{cases}. \tag{9}$$

As shown in Fig. 3, the value of α falls into the range of $[-T,T]$ due to the embedding bit '0', called bit-0-zone. And the value of α is within the range of $[T + G, 2T + G]$ or $[-(2T + G), -(T + G))$ due to the embedding bit '1', called bit-1-zone.

In case of no attack, the extraction is a reverse process, where a bit '0' is extracted when $\alpha \in [-T,T]$, and a bit '1' is extracted when $\alpha \in (T, 2T + G]$ or $\alpha \in [-(2T + G), -T)$. Moreover, the cover image can be recovered completely. If $\alpha \in (T, 2T + G]$, the original pixel $C(i,j)$ can be recovered by

$$C(i,j) = \begin{cases} C^*(i,j) - \omega\beta_2, & \text{if } M(i,j) = 1 \\ C^*(i,j), & \text{otherwise} \end{cases}, \tag{10}$$

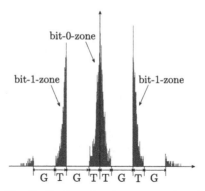

Fig. 3. The distribution of α after watermark embedding.

where $\omega \in \{0, 1\}$, represents the extracted watermark bit. Similarly, if $\alpha \in [-(2T + G), - T)$, the original pixel $C(i, j)$ can be recovered and the details are omitted. If $\alpha > 2T + G$ or $\alpha < -(2T + G)$, the original pixel $C(i, j)$ can be recovered as well according to Eq. (3) and Eq. (6).

As shown in Fig. 4, when the marked image has been attacked by JPEG compression, Zeng *et al.* [13] first find two ranges of $[-Adj\_0, Adj\_0]$ and $[-Adj\_1, Adj\_1]$. Then, the values of T and G can be calculated by Eq. (11). Finally, the watermark can be extracted correctly even if the marked image has been attacked by JPEG compression to some extent.

$$\begin{cases} T = Adj\_0 \\ G = Adj\_1 - 2Adj\_0 \end{cases} \tag{11}$$

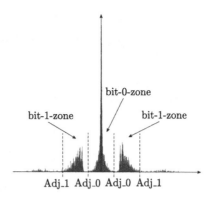

Fig. 4. The distribution of α after JPEG compression.

In general, since the value of T is supposed to be sufficiently large to ensure the robustness. In the experiments of [13], all the pixels are just expanded. Clearly, for this method, the MSE is about $\frac{2(T+G)^2}{mn}$. Moreover, in terms of reversibility, the values of T and G are necessary for the decoder to correctly extract the watermark.

3   Proposed Method

In this section, our proposed method is introduced in detail, which is an improvement of Zeng *et al.*'s work [13]. Here, we adopt the notations used in Sect. 2. We first introduce the proposed data embedding process. The cover image C is firstly divided into a number of non-overlapping blocks sized $m \times n$. Then, as shown in Eq. (1) and Eq. (2), the arithmetic difference α of each block is calculated using the matrix M. Next, two thresholds $T > 0$ and $G > 0$ are selected as parameters for data embedding. Notice that, in our method, the threshold T is selected such that it is exactly larger than the maximum of α for all divided image blocks. Finally, the watermark is embedded by shifting the histogram of α. Specifically, if $\alpha \geq 0$, the marked pixel $C^*(i, j)$ is modified as

$$C^*(i,j) = \begin{cases} C(i,j) + \omega\beta, & \text{if } M(i,j) = 1 \\ C(i,j) - \omega\beta, & \text{if } M(i,j) = -1 \end{cases}, \tag{12}$$

where $\omega \in \{0, 1\}$, represents the watermark bit to be embedded and

$$\beta = \left\lceil \frac{G + T}{mn} \right\rceil. \tag{13}$$

And if $\alpha < 0$, the marked pixel $C^*(i, j)$ is modified as

$$C^*(i,j) = \begin{cases} C(i,j) - \omega\beta, & \text{if } M(i,j) = 1 \\ C(i,j) + \omega\beta, & \text{if } M(i,j) = -1 \end{cases}. \tag{14}$$

Figure 5 shows the distribution histogram after embedding the watermark. The value of α falls into the range of $[-T, T]$ due to the embedding bit '0', called bit-0-zone. While the value of α is within the range of $[T + G, 2T + G]$ or $[-(2T + G), -(T + G))$ due to the embedding bit '1', called bit-1-zone. Bit-0-zone and bit-1-zone are separated by the length G. In this way, after a non-malicious attack such as JPEG compression, the two areas will not overlap each other so that the watermark can be correctly extracted. In other words, the proposed algorithm is robust against non-malicious attacks.

Here, by minimizing the embedding distortion, we optimize Zeng *et al.*'s embedding method [13] and then propose the embedding algorithm as described above. For $T > 0$ and $G > 0$, the two methods both shift α by $T + G$ to embed bit '1' into a divided image block. In [13], only half of the pixels in the block have changed by $\left\lceil \frac{2(T+G)}{mn} \right\rceil$. After calculation, the mean square error (MSE) is about $\frac{2(T+G)^2}{mn}$. While in this paper, we have modified all pixels in the block by $\left\lceil \frac{(T+G)}{mn} \right\rceil$, and then conclude that the MSE is approximate to $\frac{(T+G)^2}{mn}$, only half of the MSE in [13]. In other words, our proposed algorithm has superior performance in terms of visual quality.

If the marked image C^* is not distorted, as shown in Fig. 5, we can find two ranges of $[-Lim\_0, Lim\_0]$ and $[-Lim\_1, Lim\_1]$ to get the values of T and G. In particular, T and G are initialized to the integer multiple of $m \times n/2$ in our proposed algorithm. According to that, we can first calculate the value of Lim_1 using the maximum of α for all blocks. Then, we can obtain the value of Lim_0 according to the number of bits '1' embedded

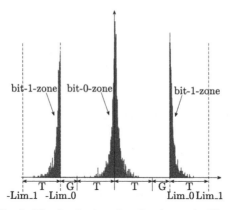

Fig. 5. The distribution of α after data embedding.

into the image. Finally, the values of T and G can be calculated by Eq. (15). Similarly, when the watermarked image C^* is attacked by JPEG compression, we can also find two ranges and calculate T and G according to Eq. (11). In this case, although the cover image cannot be restored completely, the watermark can be extracted using T and G. In particular, if $\alpha \in [-T, T]$, a bit '0' is extracted. If $\alpha \in [-(2T + G), -T) \cup (T, 2T + G]$, a bit '1' is extracted.

$$\begin{cases} T = Lim\_1 - Lim\_0 \\ G = 2Lim\_0 - Lim\_1 \end{cases} \tag{15}$$

Now consider the case that the marked image C^* is not distorted. Not only we can extract watermark correctly, but also the original cover image C can be recovered without loss. Specifically, if $\alpha \in (T, 2T + G]$, the original pixel $C(i, j)$ is given by

$$C(i, j) = \begin{cases} C^*(i, j) - \omega\beta, & \text{if } M(i, j) = 1 \\ C^*(i, j) + \omega\beta, & \text{if } M(i, j) = -1 \end{cases}, \tag{16}$$

where $\omega \in \{0, 1\}$, represents the extracted watermark bit. And if $\alpha \in [-(2T + G), -T)$, the original pixel $C(i, j)$ is given by

$$C(i, j) = \begin{cases} C^*(i, j) + \omega\beta, & \text{if } M(i, j) = 1 \\ C^*(i, j) - \omega\beta, & \text{if } (i, j) = -1 \end{cases}. \tag{17}$$

4   Experimental Results

In this section, three commonly used images including Lena, Airplane and Barbara are utilized to evaluate the robustness of our algorithm compared with Zeng *et al.*'s method [13]. For each image, 100 groups of watermarks are embedded to calculate PSNR and bit error rate (BER). The BER is given by

$$BER = \frac{\omega_e}{\omega_b}. \tag{18}$$

where ω_e indicates the number of bits extracted incorrectly, and ω_b denotes the number of bits embedded into the image.

Figure 6 shows the relationship between PSNR and embedding level β, where $\beta = \left\lceil \frac{T+G}{mn} \right\rceil$. To ensure the watermark invisible to human eyes, PSNR should be greater than 38 dB [21], i.e., $\beta < 5$. Here, the threshold T is decided such that it is exactly larger than the maximum of α for all divided image blocks, where T and G are integer multiples of $m \times n/2$. For the Lena image with the block sized 8×8, we decide that $T = 128$ and $G = 64$ such that β is equal to 6, not less than 5. In the same way, thresholds T and G are selected for the Airplane image with the block of size 8×8, i.e. $T = 160, G = 32$.

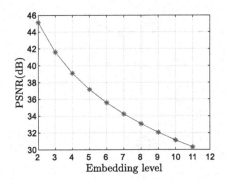

Fig. 6. The relationship between β and PSNR.

Specifically, we evaluate the robustness according to the relationship between BER and q with the same value of PSNR, and the relationship between 1-BER and PSNR with the same compression strength. With the same value of q and PSNR, the lower the BER, the stronger the robustness against JPEG compression.

Table 1 shows the BER with compression quality factors of 90, 85 and 80 respectively. Meanwhile, the PSNR of our algorithm is slightly higher than that of Zeng *et al.* [13]. Moreover, the values of BER are obviously lower under the same compression quality factor. That is to say, the proposed algorithm is more robust to JPEG compression than Zeng *et al.*'s method [13].

Table 1. Comparison for block size 8×8.

Method	Zeng *et al.* PSNR = 38.59 dB			Proposed PSNR = 39.10 dB		
q	90	85	80	90	85	80
Lena	0.05	0.13	19.65	0	0	0.01
Airplane	0	0.05	24.94	0	0	0.03
Barbara	0.23	0.62	19.89	0	0	0.16

As shown in Fig. 7, we initialize the JPEG quality to 90%, 80% and 70%. Notice that when the PSNR value is less than a certain value, the BER is quite low. While the PSNR becomes lager than this value, the BER increases sharply. Obviously, if the PSNR value is the same, the 1-BER of the proposed algorithm is smaller. That is to say, our proposed algorithm outperforms [13] in terms of the robustness.

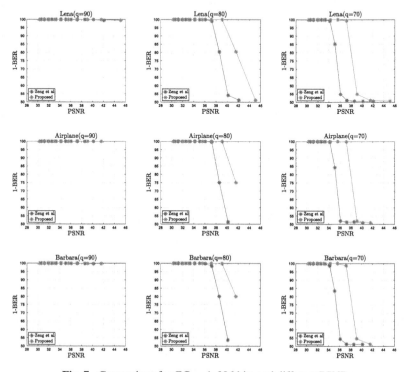

Fig. 7. Comparison for $EC = 4,096$ bits and different PSNRs.

Figure 8 shows the relationship between BER and q with the same value of PSNR. In [13], the BER increases sharply in case of $q < 85\%$. The proposed algorithm has the same phenomenon in case of $q < 80\%$. Therefore, the proposed algorithm is more robust to JPEG compression.

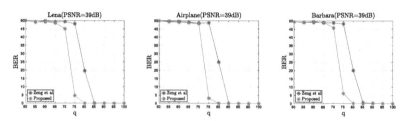

Fig. 8. Comparison for $EC = 4,096$ bits and quality factors.

5 Conclusions

To overcome the disadvantages of insufficient embedding capacity and weak robustness of the previous RRW methods, in this paper, a new embedding mechanism for RRW is proposed. First, the cover image is divided into non-overlapping blocks and a histogram is generated by applying a high pass filter to each block. Then, the watermark is embedded into the blocks by shifting this histogram. Specifically, instead of using half pixels in the block, each pixel is modified to minimize the embedding distortion. Moreover, a strategy for determining the parameters is proposed to make the method reversible without side information. Experimental results show that compared with the previous methods, the proposed scheme has sufficient robustness against JPEG compression.

Acknowledgements. This work was supported by the National Natural Science Foundation of China (Nos. 61972031 and U1736213).

References

1. Barton, J. M.: Method and apparatus for embedding authentication information within digital data. U.S.Patent 5646997 (1997)
2. Fridrich, J., Goljan, M., Du, R.: Lossless data embedding new paradigm in digital watermarking. EURASIP J. Appl. Signal Process. **2002**(2), 185–196 (2002)
3. Tian, J.: Reversible data embedding using a difference expansion. IEEE Trans. Circ. Syst. Video Technol. **13**(8), 890–896 (2003)
4. Ni, Z., Shi, Y.-Q., Ansari, N., Su, W.: Reversible data hiding. IEEE Trans. Circ. Syst. Video Technol. **16**(3), 354–362 (2006)
5. Sachnev, V., Kim, H.J., Nam, J., Suresh, S., Shi, Y.-Q.: Reversible watermarking algorithm using sorting and prediction. IEEE Trans. Circ. Syst. Video Technol. **19**(7), 989–999 (2009)
6. Shi, Y.-Q., Li, X., Zhang, X., Wu, H.-T., Ma, B.: Reversible data hiding: advances in the past two decades. IEEE Access **4**, 3210–3237 (2016)
7. Xiang, L., Yang, S., Liu, Y., Li, Q., Zhu, C.: Novel linguistic steganography based on character-level text generation. Mathematics **8**, 1558 (2020)
8. Xiang, L., Guo, G., Li, Q., Zhu, C., Chen, J.: Spam detection in reviews using lstm-based multi-entity temporal features. Intell. Autom. Soft Comput. **26**(6), 1375–1390 (2020)
9. Yang, Z., Zhang, S., Hu, Y., Hu, Z., Huang, Y.: VAE-stega: linguistic steganography based on variational auto-encoder. IEEE Trans. Inf. Forensics Secur.ity **16**, 880–895 (2021)
10. De Vleeschouwer, C., Delaigle, J.F., Macq, B.: Circular interpretation of bijective transformations in lossless watermarking for media asset management. IEEE Trans. Multimed. **5**(1), 97–105 (2003)
11. Zou, D., Shi, Y., Ni, Z., Su, W.: A semi-fragile lossless digital watermarking scheme based on integer wavelet transform. IEEE Trans. Circ. Syst. Video Technol. **16**(10), 1294–1300 (2006)
12. Ni, Z., Shi, Y., Ansari, N., Su, W., Sun, Q., Lin, X.: Robust lossless image data hiding designed for semi-fragile image authentication. IEEE Trans. Circ. Syst. Video Technol. **18**(4), 497–509 (2008)
13. Zeng, X.-T., Ping, L.-D., Pan, X.-Z.: A lossless robust data hiding scheme. Pattern Recogn. **43**(4), 1656–1667 (2010)
14. Gao, X., An, L., Yuan, Y., Tao, D., Li, X.: Lossless data embedding using generalized statistical quantity histogram. IEEE Trans. Circ. Syst. Video Technol. **21**(8), 1061–1070 (2011)

15. An, L., Gao, X., Li, X., Tao, D., Deng, C., Li, J.: Robust reversible watermarking via clustering and enhanced pixel-wise masking. IEEE Trans. Image Process. **21**(8), 3598–3611 (2012)
16. An, L., Gao, X., Yuan, Y., Tao, D.: Robust lossless data hiding using clustering and statistical quantity histogram. Neurocomputing **77**(1), 1–11 (2012)
17. An, L., Gao, X., Yuan, Y., Tao, D., Deng, C., Ji, F.: Content-adaptive reliable robust lossless data embedding. Neurocomputing **79**, 1–11 (2012)
18. Coltuc, D.: Towards distortion-free robust image authentication. J. Phys.: Conf. Ser. **77**(1), 012005 (2007)
19. Coltuc, D., Chassery, J.: Distortion-free robust watermarking: a case study, vol. 6505. International Society for Optics and Photonics (2007).
20. Wang, X., Li, X., Pei, Q.: Independent embedding domain based two-stage robust reversible watermarking. IEEE Trans. Circ. Syst. Video Technol. **PP**(99), 1 (2019)
21. Katzenbeisser, S., Petitcolas, A.P.: Information hiding techniques for stegano-graphy and digital watermarking. Artech House Inc. **28**(6), 1–2 (1999)

A Common Steganalysis Method of Low Embedding Rate Steganography in Compressed Speech Based on Hierarchy Feature Extraction and Fusion

Songbin Li[(⊠)], Jingang Wang, Qiandong Yan, Peng Liu, and Miao Wei

Institute of Acoustics, Chinese Academy of Sciences, Beijing 100190, China
lisongbin@mail.ioa.ac.cn

Abstract. The current steganalysis researches have not specifically explored the compressed speech stream with 1%–9% embedding rates. In this paper, we propose a common steganalysis method of low embedding rate steganography based on hierarchy feature extraction and fusion. Firstly, codewords in each frame are converted to a multi-hot vector. And each multi-hot vector will be mapped into a fixed length embedding vector to get a more compact representation by utilizing the pre-trained dictionaries. Then, a hierarchy feature extraction and fusion framework is employed to perform the extraction and fusion of different levels of correlation features. Specifically, a 5-layer convolutional neural network is used to extract correlation feature information from local to global. The features of different local scales are restored to the same size by the transposed convolution. In addition, the attention mechanism is introduced in different layers of the network to assign different importance weights to the output feature within each layer. Finally, the prediction results can be generated by the fully connected layer. Experimental results show that our method performs better than the existing steganalysis methods for detecting multiple steganographies in the low bit-rate compressed speech streams. On the mixed dataset of multiple steganography methods, the proposed method can reach 73.56% on the speech stream under 5% embedding rate. And the accuracy can exceed 83% on the dataset under 9% embedding rate.

Keywords: Low embedding rate · Steganalysis · Codeword embedding · Hierarchy feature extraction and fusion

This work was supported in part by the Important Science and Technology Project of Hainan Province under Grant ZDKJ201807, in part by the Hainan Provincial Natural Science Foundation of China under Grant 618QN309, in part by the Scientific Research Foundation Project of Haikou Laboratory, Institute of Acoustics, Chinese Academy of Sciences, and in part by the IACAS Young Elite Researcher Project under GrantQNYC201829 and Grant QNYC201747.

© Springer Nature Switzerland AG 2021
X. Sun et al. (Eds.): ICAIS 2021, CCIS 1424, pp. 323–334, 2021.
https://doi.org/10.1007/978-3-030-78621-2_26

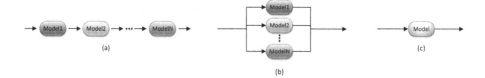

Fig. 1. Steganalysis strategy of compressed speech streams facing unknown steganographies methods. (a) Different detection methods are used in turn. (b) Multiple detection methods are used simultaneously. (c) There is only one model to detect multiple steganographies simultaneously.

1 Introduction

Steganography is a technique of embedding secret information into digital carriers without perception. There are many varieties of carriers, such as texts [1,2], images [3,4], audios [5,6], videos [7,8], etc. In recent years, with the increase of bandwidth requirements and network convergence, network streaming media services for communication has developed a lot. Among them, Voice over Internet Protocol (VoIP) is widely used in real-time communication. Thus, it has become a suitable steganographic carrier. However, VoIP-based steganography brings serious safety issues from another perspective. People with ulterior motives may use steganography techniques to transmit some illegal information. Hence, it is important to develop the steganalysis method to effectively detect VoIP-based steganography.

The existing steganalysis methods have the problems of two respects. The first problem is the lack of generality for multiple steganography methods. Most of the current steganalysis methods are designed for a specific steganography algorithm. Normally, specific features are extracted from the compressed stream and then fed to a machine learning model to detect whether there is a hidden message. However, in practice, it is impossible to learn in advance about which steganography method is used. Facing unknown steganography methods, there are mainly three detection strategies as shown in Fig. 1. In Fig. 1(a), different steganalysis methods are used in order. In Fig. 1(b), multiple steganalysis models are used simultaneously to detect whether hidden message exists. Both the two strategies are time-consuming and laborious. There is a pressing need to develop a common detection method like Fig. 1(c), which can detect multiple steganographies by one model.

The second problem is the poor detection performance under the condition of low embedding rate. Theoretically, the VoIP streams have an infinite length. The attacker can improve the concealment by increasing the length of the carrier and reducing the embedding rate. The existing steganalysis methods have been able to achieve satisfactory detection results when the steganography embedding rate is high. When the embedding rate is greatly reduced, the detection accuracy will drop significantly. This is because the reduction of the embedding rate makes the steganographic speech streams less different from the cover ones.

Current methods are difficult to accurately capture these small changes, resulting in their performance degradation. For example, the detection accuracies of some representative steganalysis methods IDC [9], QCCN [10], RNN-SM [11] are 52.75%, 57.35% and 59.64% respectively under an embedding rate of 10%. It is not satisfactory and still needs to be improved. Therefore, there is an urgent need to propose a more effective and stable steganalysis method targeting low-embedding-rate speech streams.

Our research aims to resolve the above two issues. In this paper, we present a common steganalysis method of low embedding rate steganography in compressed speech streams based on hierarchy feature extraction and fusion. Since all above mentioned steganography methods will eventually modify the codewords in the compressed speech stream, our proposed method takes into account all the codewords for obtaining more general representations for codewords. In addition, we build a hierarchy feature extraction network to capture tiny changes caused by the embedding of a small amount of hidden information. This hierarchy framework employs convolutional neural network to extract correlation features of different scales layer by layer. The output feature maps of each branch are combined into a new feature representation by the attention mechanism and transposed convolution.

2   Related Works

Information hiding methods based on low-bit-rate compressed speech streams can be divided into three categories according to the embedding position. The first category is to use the pitch synthesis filter for information hiding [12–14]. Embedding is conducted by modulating the search strategy of fixed codebooks or adaptive codebooks. The second category uses the LPC synthesis filter to hide information [15–17]. The basic idea of these methods is derived from the Quantization Index Modulation (QIM) [18] information hiding method. The third category embeds information by directly modifying the value of some codewords in the compressed speech stream [19–21].

For detecting the above steganography methods, researchers have proposed many corresponding steganalysis methods. In the work of Ding et al. [22,23], different categories of histogram features related to the pulse position distribution are extracted to train SVM classifiers. Li et al. [20] focus their research on the quantization index modulation steganography. Combined with SVM classifiers, they employ independent and joint vector quantization codebooks respectively. Yang et al. [24] propose a novel model based on a codeword Bayesian network (CBN). The CBN is built by the steganography-sensitive transition relationships and the probability distribution of codewords. Utilizing regression and second statistical detection, the model proposed by Huang et al. [25] can detect whether least significant bits (LSBs) substitution exists in the compressed speech stream.

As far as we know, there is no strictly general method designed for the detection of the steganography in compressed speech streams. However, The MFCC-based steganalysis method [26] can detect any type of steganographies based on the decoded audio/speech data in theory. In this sense, we think this method is a general method. Moreover, Hu et al. [27] fuse features extracted from different codewords to detect heterogeneous parallel steganography (HPS). This is a successful attempt from specific steganalysis to common steganalysis in recent years.

In addition, the embedding rates of the speech samples studied by the existing steganalysis methods are all higher than 10%. It can be seen from the existing research that the changes caused by steganography gradually become less as the embedding rate decreases. It becomes more difficult for the steganalysis models to capture such minor changes, and the performance of the existing steganalysis models are significantly reduced. To our best knowledge, there is no related research on low embedding rate (1%–9%) steganalysis in compressed speech streams. Therefore, a steganalysis method for low embedding rates needs to be studied urgently. In the proposed method, we take into account the generality and the robustness at low embedding rates.

3   Method

There exists strong correlations between codewords in VoIP streams [11]. These correlations can be divided into two types: intra-frame correlation and inter-frame correlation. Intra-frame correlation represents the correlation between different codewords in the same frame, and inter-frame correlation represents the correlation between codewords in different frames. Both of them may be weakened when original codewords are embedded with hidden data. Thus, these correlations can be utilized for steganalysis. In this paper, we use convolutional neural network (CNN) to extract the local characteristics of speech signals [28]. In the rest of this section, we will first give an overall description of the proposed method and then describe each part in detail.

3.1   Overview

The architecture of the proposed steganalysis method is illustrated in Fig. 2. It can be divided into three parts: codeword embedding, hierarchy feature extraction and feature fusion and classification.

Codewords are converted into their corresponding codeword embeddings before they are input into the network. For each frame, we concatenate the one-hot vectors of all codewords and then get a multi-hot vector. Then, by the pre-trained dictionaries, we map the multi-hot vector to an embedding vector.

To extract the hierarchy feature of different local scales for these embeddings, we construct a 5-layer CNN. The output feature maps of some certain layers of the network will be concatenated. In this process, the attention mechanism is employed to assigns different weights to different parts of the feature map to determine which part gets more attention. In addition, we utilize transposed convolution to keep different levels of features the same size.

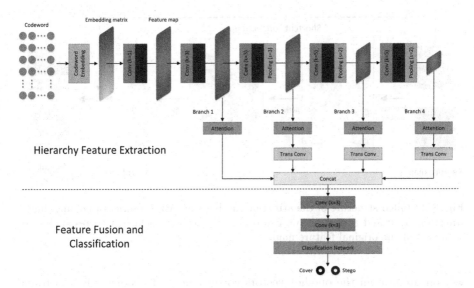

Fig. 2. The architecture of the proposed steganalysis method. Our overall framework is mainly composed of three parts: codeword embedding, hierarchy feature extraction and feature fusion and classification.

The part of feature fusion and classification mainly consists of convolution layers, a fully connected layer, a batch normalization layer and a softmax activation layer. We finally get two probability values to determine whether hidden messages exist in a current examined speech segment.

3.2 Codeword Embedding

Human speech is normally continuous in daily life, and there is a certain correlation between the sentences. Hence, there are local characteristics in the speech stream. Before designing a model to take advantage of these correlations, we first need to convert the values of codewords into a form that is easy to use by the subsequent convolutional neural network. We try to build the mapping from the codewords to more powerful feature representations.

One-hot coding is utilized to map each codeword into a feature vector. For a codeword that occupies a bits, its coded value range is $0\sim2^{a-1}$. In one-hot encoding, a vector with a length of 2^a is used to represent this codeword. If the coded value of this codeword is b, the one-hot representation can be denoted by:

$$F_{one-hot}(x) = \left\{ h_0, h_1, \cdots, h_{2^{a-1}} \right\} \tag{1}$$

where

$$h_i = \begin{cases} 1, & if\ i = b \\ 0, & else \end{cases} \tag{2}$$

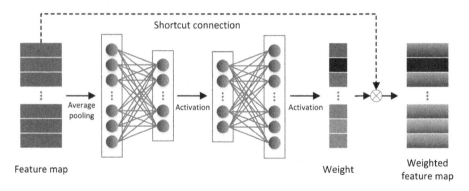

Fig. 3. Detailed structure of the attention mechanism. After a series of pooling, linear transformation and activation, we can obtain the weight coefficient corresponding to each part of the original feature map.

we concatenate all the one-hot vectors corresponding to codewords in a frame to form a multi-hot vector.

Before multi-hot encoding, we use encoding method based on frequency count to reduce the dimensionality of data. For each codeword that occupies more than 8 bits, we count the occurrence frequency of its every coded value. Then we arrange them in order of frequency and select the first 255 values. These values are encoded as 0~254. The other coded values are encoded as 255. By this way we can map the coded value of all codewords into 0~255.

We build a dictionary for each codeword to convert the multi-hot vectors to more compact representations. Codewords of each frame are mapped to an embedding vector with k-dimensional dictionaries. The dictionaries are trained by a training network consisting of a two-layer bidirectional long short time memory (Bi-LSTM) layer and a fully connected layer. In this way, we get a more compact representation for codewords in the compressed speech stream.

3.3   Hierarchy Feature Extraction Network

We utilize one dimensional (1D) convolution to extract the local characteristics of codewords hierarchically. The hierarchy feature extraction network consists of five convolution layers, each with 256 convolution kernels. The convolution filter kernels slide between frames. In different CNN layers, is equal to 1, 3, 3, 5 and 5 respectively. The increasing size of the kernel enhance the network's ability to capture global information. For a pooling layer, the outputs of max pooling and average pooling will be added to contain more information. The pooling strides are 3, 2 and 2 respectively. From bottom to top, the output of each layer of CNN represents the correlation information on different local scales.

The attention mechanism is used to assign weights to the output feature map in each branch. By attention mechanism, we can make the neural network pay more attention to the important part of output features of each layer. The brief process of the attention mechanism [29] is shown in Fig. 3. The feature map output by the previous layer is performed average pooling, and then converted into a vector. After going through the linear layer and the activation layer twice, we obtain the weight that characterizes the importance of the feature part of each codeword. Multiplying these weights with the original feature map, we can get the weighted feature map.

We use the transposed convolution to restore the feature map of different layers to the original size. Mathematically the mapping between the output size and the input size of the transposed convolution operation can be defined as follows:

$$o = (i - 1)s - 2p + k + u \qquad (3)$$

where o and i refer to size of output and input. The stride, kernel size, padding and output padding are represented by s, k, p and u respectively. By this learnable upsampling process, the output size generated for each 1D transposed convolution layer used in the proposed network is equal to the original size. The parameters of the transposed convolution on different branches are shown in Table 1.

Table 1. The parameters of the introduced transposed convolution

	Kernel size	Number of kernels	Stride	Padding	Output padding
Branch 2	3	128	3	0	0
Branch 3	5	64	6	0	4
Branch 4	5	64	13	5	0

3.4 Feature Fusion and Classification Network

In our method, we utilize a 2-layer CNN to fuse the feature maps of different levels. The first layer has 128 convolution kernels with a size of 3, and the last layer has 32 filter kernels with the same size. In order to maintain the integrity of the information at this stage, we did not introduce any pooling operations. The output size of the feature fusion network is $(32, T)$. To facilitate subsequent processing, we turn it into a vector with a length of $32T$. We build a classification network for predicting whether hidden messages exist from the feature vector calculated by the feature fusion network. The classification network consist of a fully connected layer, a batch normalization layer and a softmax activation layer. Finally, we get two probability values p_1 and p_2. The prediction result can be obtained by:

$$Detection \quad Result = \begin{cases} cover, & p_1 < 0.5 \\ stego, & p_2 \geq 0.5 \end{cases} \qquad (4)$$

4 Experiments and Discussion

4.1 Datasets

We collect speech segments of seven categories from the Internet: Chinese man, Chinese Woman, English man, English woman, Japanese, German and French. Each category contains 1000 10-s segments, for a total of 7000 speech segments. The G.723.1 (6.3 kbit/s) codec is used as the low-bit-rate speech codec. Thus, there are 24 codewords in a frame. These 7000 coded samples constitute the dataset of cover speech. The speech segments in each category are divided into a training set, a validation set and a testing set at a 3:1:1 ratio. The training dataset is used to conduct parameters adjustment of the model, and the testing dataset is used to evaluate the model performance.

There are mainly three categories of steganography methods for AbS-LPC low-bit-rate compressed speech. In order to comprehensively test the performance of our proposed model, we choose a representative literature [14,15,19] for each steganography category. For simplicity, they are denoted by ACL [14], CNV [15] and HYF [19] respectively. Embedding hidden information in cover dataset by these three steganographies respectively, we get three different stego datasets. In addition, we take a third of each of these three datasets and obtain a mixed dataset for common steganalysis.

4.2 Experiments Setup

Both the training and testing stages were executed on GeForce GTX 2080 GPU with 11G Graphics Memory. The proposed network has been developed using the PyTorch framework. In addition, in the process of training the neural network, we choose Adam [30] as the optimizer with a learning rate of $1e-4$ and the binary cross entropy as loss function. The model has been trained for 200 epochs for all the datasets. The batch size for every epoch was set to be 32.

We use classification accuracy to evaluate the effectiveness of each method. Classification accuracy is the fraction of the correctly classified samples among all the testing samples. Higher classification accuracy denotes better effectiveness.

4.3 Performance Analysis for the Specific Steganography Method

The embedding rate is defined as the ratio of the number of embedded bits to the whole embedding capacity. A higher embedding rate means that more codewords are modified. Hence, there is a greater impact on the correlations between codewords. We conduct experiments for the three general steganography methods under the conditions of 9 different embedding rates (1%–9%) and 10-s clip length. The experiment results are shown in Table 2. As can been seen in the table, the classification accuracies of SFFN and ours increase with an increasing embedding rate.

To be specific, for the steganography method ACL, when the embedding rate is 5% or above, the accuracies of both SFFN and Ours exceed 80%, and when

Table 2. The detection accuracies (%) of SFFN and Ours for the three steganography methods at different embedding rates

Steganography method	Detection method	Embedding rate								
		1%	2%	3%	4%	5%	6%	7%	8%	9%
ACL	SFFN	64.58	73.42	78.99	81.65	84.89	88.22	89.69	92.03	93.57
	Ours	50.29	66.99	73.21	78.60	81.76	85.49	88.58	90.52	92.21
CNV	SFFN	50.14	50.32	50.18	51.49	53.81	55.04	54.71	57.62	60.13
	Ours	50.25	59.91	64.48	67.42	70.69	73.33	77.66	80.04	83.94
HYF	SFFN	50.09	50.36	50.22	52.33	53.68	54.38	56.57	57.61	59.45
	Ours	50.53	58.46	64.15	68.96	72.56	75.50	79.53	82.54	85.02

the embedding rate is 8% or above, the accuracies exceed 90%, which reflects a good performance. At a lower embedding rate, SFFN shows advantages. In particular, when the embedding rate is 1%, the accuracy of our method is only 50.29%, while the accuracy of SFFN reaches 64.58%, which is 14.29% higher than ours. This may be because SFFN focuses on strengthening the codeword part related to the ACL steganography method when selecting the input. By contrast, our method focuses on a more general situation, treating all codewords equally at the input. Subsequent paragraphs, however, are indented.

For the steganography methods HYF and CNV, when the embedding rate is 9%, the SFFN method can only achieve an accuracy of about 60%, while the accuracy of our method can reach more than 83.94%. When the embedding rate is 3%, the accuracy of the SFFN method is only 50.22%, while our method can achieve an accuracy of more than 64%. These results demonstrate the superiority of our proposed method. However, when the embedding rate drops to 1%, the classification accuracies of both methods are only about 50%, which is slightly better than random guessing.

4.4 Performance Analysis on the Mixed Dataset of Multiple Steganography Methods

In this section, we conduct experiments for the common steganalysis performance on the mixed dataset. The experiment results are shown in Table 3. As can been seen in the table, the classification accuracies of SFFN and ours increase with an increasing embedding rate.

At an embedding rate of 9%, the accuracy of our method is nearly 18% higher than that of SFFN. Our method can still achieve an accuracy of over 80% when the embedding rate is 7%. Compared with that, SFFN can only correctly distinguish 63.01% of the samples to be tested. These show the great advantage of our method in common detection performance. When the embedding rate drops to 1%, the accuracy of both methods drops to about 50%. Undoubtedly, general steganography detection under 1% embedding rate is extremely difficult, which also leaves room for our follow-up work.

Table 3. The detection accuracies (%) of SFFN and Ours for the mixed steganography methods at different embedding rates

Detection method	Embedding rate								
	1%	2%	3%	4%	5%	6%	7%	8%	9%
SFFN	50.11	54.71	58.76	60.02	62.75	62.28	63.01	63.09	66.34
Ours	50.35	60.42	65.16	70.98	73.56	75.72	80.60	79.63	83.91

5   Conclusion and Future Work

In this paper, we propose a novel hierarchy feature extraction and fusion framework for common steganalysis of low bedding rate steganography. In practical, no matter what steganography method is employed, the codeword correlations are changed. Therefore, our proposed method focuses on the utilization of the change of codeword correlation features before and after steganography. Experimental results demonstrate that the proposed method performs better than the existing steganalysis method for detecting multiple steganographies in compressed speech streams.

In the future, we will aim to implement a more general detection method for multiple steganography methods and improve the classification accuracies at low embedding rates further.

References

1. Satir, E., Isik, H.: A Huffman compression based text steganography method. Multimed. Tools Appl. **70**(3), 2085–2110 (2014)
2. Chang, C.-Y., Clark, S.: Practical linguistic steganography using contextual synonym substitution and vertex colour coding. In: Proceedings of the 2010 Conference on Empirical Methods in Natural Language Processing, ser. EMNLP 2010, pp. 1194–1203. Association for Computational Linguistics, USA (2010)
3. Pevny, T., Filler, T., Bas, P.: Using high-dimensional image models to perform highly undetectable steganography. In: Proceedings of the 12th International Conference on Information Hiding, ser. IH-10, pp. 161–177. Berlin (2010)
4. Holub, V., Fridrich, J., Denemark, T.: Universal distortion function for steganography in an arbitrary domain. EURASIP J. Inf. Secur. **2014**(1), 1–13 (2014). https://doi.org/10.1186/1687-417X-2014-1
5. Djebbar, F., Ayad, B., Meraim, K.A., Hamam, H.: Comparative study of digital audio steganography techniques. EURASIP J. Audio Speech Music Process. **2012**, 1–16 (2012)
6. Hua, G., Huang, J., Shi, Y.Q., Goh, J., Thing, V.L.: Twenty years of digital audio watermarking-a comprehensive review. Signal Process. **128**(C), 222–224 (2016)
7. Sadek, M.M., Khalifa, A.S., Mostafa, M.G.M.: Video steganography: a comprehensive review. Multimed. Tools Appl. **74**(17), 7063–7094 (2014). https://doi.org/10.1007/s11042-014-1952-z
8. Yang, J., Li, S.: An efficient information hiding method based on motion vector space encoding for HEVC. Multimed. Tools Appl. **77**(10), 11979–12001 (2017). https://doi.org/10.1007/s11042-017-4844-1

9. Li, S.B., Tao, H.Z., Huang, Y.F.: Detection of quantization index modulation steganography in G.723.1 bit stream based on quantization index sequence analysis. J. Zhejiang Univ.: Sci. C **13**(8), 624–634 (2012)

10. Li, S., Jia, Y., Kuo, C.C.J.: Steganalysis of QIM steganography in low-bit-rate speech signals. IEEE/ACM Trans. Audio Speech Lang. Process. **25**(5), 1011–1022 (2017)

11. Lin, Z., Huang, Y., Wang, J.: RNN-SM: fast steganalysis of VoIP streams using recurrent neural network. IEEE Trans. Inf. Forensics Secur. **13**(7), 1854–1868 (2018)

12. Yan, S., Tang, G., Chen, Y.: Incorporating data hiding into G.729 speech codec. Multimed. Tools Appl. **75**(18), 11493–11512 (2015). https://doi.org/10.1007/s11042-015-2865-1

13. Ren, Y., Wu, H., Wang, L.: An AMR adaptive steganography algorithm based on minimizing distortion. Multimed. Tools Appl. **77**(10), 12095–12110 (2017). https://doi.org/10.1007/s11042-017-4860-1

14. Huang, Y., Liu, C., Tang, S., Bai, S.: Steganography integration into a low-bit rate speech codec. IEEE Trans. Inf. Forensics Secur. **7**(6), 1865–1875 (2012)

15. Xiao, B., Huang, Y., Tang, S.: An approach to information hiding in low bit-rate speech stream. In: IEEE GLOBECOM 2008–2008 IEEE Global Telecommunications Conference, pp. 1–5 (2008)

16. Huang, Y.F., Tao, H.Z., Xiao, B., Chang, C.C.: Steganography in low bit-rate speech streams based on quantization index modulation controlled by keys. Sci. China Technol. Sci. **60**(10), 1585–1596 (2017). https://doi.org/10.1007/s11431-016-0707-3

17. Liu, P., Li, S., Wang, H.: Steganography integrated into linear predictive coding for low bit-rate speech codec. Multimed. Tools Appl **76**(2), 2837–2859 (2016). https://doi.org/10.1007/s11042-016-3257-x

18. Chen, B., Wornell, G.W.: Quantization index modulation: a class of provably good methods for digital watermarking and information embedding. IEEE Trans. Inf. Theory **47**(4), 1423–1443 (2001)

19. Huang, Y.F., Tang, S., Yuan, J.: Steganography in inactive frames of VoIP streams encoded by source codec. IEEE Trans. Inf. Forensics Secur. **6**(2), 296–306 (2011)

20. Liu, J., Zhou, K., Tian, H.: Least-significant-digit steganography in low bitrate speech. In: 2012 IEEE International Conference on Communications (ICC), pp. 1133–1137 (2012)

21. Lin, R.S.: An imperceptible information hiding in encoded bits of speech signal. In: 2015 International Conference on Intelligent Information Hiding and Multimedia Signal Processing (IIHMSP), pp. 37–40 (2015)

22. Ding, Q., Ping, X.: Steganalysis of compressed speech based on histogram features. In: 2010 6th International Conference on Wireless Communications Networking and Mobile Computing (WiCOM), pp. 1–4 (2010)

23. Ding, Q., Ping, X.: Steganalysis of analysis-by-synthesis compressed speech. In: 2010 International Conference on Multimedia Information Networking and Security, pp. 681–685 (2010)

24. Yang, J., Li, S.: Steganalysis of joint codeword quantization index modulation steganography based on codeword Bayesian network. Neurocomputing **313**, 316–323 (2018)

25. Huang, Y., Tang, S., Bao, C., Yip, Y.J.: Steganalysis of compressed speech to detect covert voice over internet protocol channels. IET Inf. Secur. **5**(1), 26–32 (2011)

26. Liu, Q., Sung, A.H., Qiao, M.: Temporal derivative based spectrum and mel-cepstrum audio steganalysis. IEEE Trans. Inf. Forensics Secur. **4**(3), 359–368 (2009)
27. Hu, Y., Huang, Y., Yang, Z., Huang, Y.: Detection of heterogeneous parallel steganography for low bit-rate VoIP speech streams. Neurocomputing **419**, 70–79 (2021)
28. Nidadavolu, P.S., Iglesias, V., Villalba, J., Dehak, N.: Investigation on neural bandwidth extension of telephone speech for improved speaker recognition. In: ICASSP 2019–2019 IEEE International Conference on Acoustics, Speech and Signal Processing (ICASSP), pp. 6111–6115 (2019)
29. Hu, J., Shen, L., Albanie, S., Sun, G., Wu, E.: Squeeze-and-excitation networks. IEEE Trans. Pattern Anal. Mach. Intell. **42**(8), 2011–2023 (2020)
30. Kingma, D., Ba, J.: Adam: a method for stochastic optimization. In: International Conference on Learning Representations (2014)

TStego-THU: Large-Scale Text Steganalysis Dataset

Zhongliang Yang, Jin He, Siyu Zhang, Jinshuai Yang, and Yongfeng Huang[(✉)]

Department of Electronic Engineering, Tsinghua University, Beijing 100084, China
yfhuang@tsinghua.edu.cn

Abstract. In recent years, with the development of natural language processing (NLP) technology, linguistic steganography has developed rapidly. However, to the best of our knowledge, currently there is no public dataset for text steganalysis, which makes it difficult for linguistic steganalysis methods to get a fair comparison. Therefore, in this paper, we construct and release a large-scale linguistic steganalysis dataset called TStego-THU, which we hope to provide a fair enough platform for comparison of linguistic steganalysis algorithms and further promote the development of linguistic steganalysis. TStego-THU includes two kinds of text steganography modes, namely, text modification-based and text generation-based modes, each of which provides two latest or classical text steganography algorithms. All texts in TStego-THU come from three common transmitted text medias in cyberspace: News, Twitter and commentary text. Finally, TStego-THU contains 240,000 sentences (120,000 cover-stego text pairs), each steganographic sentence is generated by randomly choosing one of these four steganographic algorithms and embedding random bitstream into randomly extracted normal texts. At the same time, we also evaluate some latest text steganalysis algorithms as benchmarks on TStego-THU, the detail results can be found in the experiment part. We hope that TStego-THU will further promote the development of universal text steganalysis technology. The description of TStego-THU and instructions will be released here: https://github.com/YangzlTHU/Linguistic-Steganography-and-Steganalysis.

Keywords: TStego-THU · Text steganalysis · Dataset

1 Introduction

According to Shannon's summary in his monograph on information theory [1], security systems in cyberspace can be divided into three categories: encryption system, privacy system and concealment system. Among them, encryption system and privacy system mainly encrypt important information or control the access rights to ensure the security of information content. Concealment system mainly protects the information from the perspective of communication behavior security, which hides the existence of important information to ensure the security of it. However, the convert communication system's powerful information concealing ability may also be used by criminals to transmit some dangerous information, thus endangering cyberspace security and public safety [2].

© Springer Nature Switzerland AG 2021
X. Sun et al. (Eds.): ICAIS 2021, CCIS 1424, pp. 335–344, 2021.
https://doi.org/10.1007/978-3-030-78621-2_27

Therefore, making in-depth researches in steganalysis and detecting the potential harmful information in the network information flow is of great significance for maintaining cyberspace security.

In theory, any information carrier can serve as a medium for covert communication. In cyberspace, the most common information carriers for covert communication are image [3], audio [4], and text [5–7]. For different periods of historical development (whether in the paper-media age or the electronic-media age), text is one of the most important information carriers, playing a very important role in human lives. Therefore, in recent years, there has appeared more and more information hiding methods based on texts [5–7]. These text steganographic methods, embedding some secret information into common texts, pretending as normal texts and disseminating widely in public networks, pose a great threat and challenge to the security of cyberspace [2]. Currently, the main text steganography algorithms can be divided into two categories: steganography based on text modification [8–10] and steganography based on text generation [5–7]. Steganography based on carrier modification is mainly used to embed covert information by modifying the original texts, such as synonym substitution and syntactic structure substitution. This kind of methods can only make very little affect on the semantic expression of the texts to achieve a very high concealment, which makes it very difficult to be detected. However, usually, such methods are difficult to achieve a higher embedding rate.

Another kind of methods is information hiding based on text automatic generation [5–7]. The most important characteristic of this kind of methods is that they do not need to be given the specify texts beforehand, but can automatically generate steganographic texts according to the convert information that need to be transmitted. They usually implement secret information hiding by encoding words during the automatic text generation process. Especially with the rapid development of natural language processing technologies in recent years, text automatic generation technology based on neural networks has made rapid development, and has made great progress in the fields of human-computer dialogue [7], automatic translation [11] and image captioning [12]. With the help of these technologies, researchers can generate high quality natural steganographic texts according to the secret information and ensure reliable concealment [5, 6]. At the same time, since almost every word in the generated texts can be embedded with secret information, this kind of methods can usually achieve a high information hiding capacity [5, 7]. However, it is worth noting that although information hiding technology plays an important role in protecting the privacy of users in cyberspace. But this technology may also be used by criminals and even terrorists to build covert communication systems and transmit dangerous information, endangering public safety and cyberspace security [2]. Therefore, we also need to conduct deeply research on text steganalysis to detect whether the texts transmitted in the cyberspace contains dangerous information.

Current steganalysis methods basically adopt the same framework, that is, by constructing specific statistical features or analytical methods, to find the differences in statistical distribution in a certain dimension between the covertext and the stegotext to conduct steganalysis [13–19]. Traditional text steganalysis methods usually firstly construct a series of text statistical features manually, then analyze the changes of these features before and after steganography, and finally design the corresponding discriminators [17–19]. However, most of the statistical features utilized by these methods are simple, such as word frequency distribution [17], transition probability distribution between words [18], and so on [19]. However, with the development of artificial neural network technology and natural language processing technology, more and more neural network-based text steganalysis models have emerged in recent years [13–16]. Such models usually need a large number of labeled texts to train the corresponding neural network model, and then judge whether the input text is normal text or steganographic text according to the extracted features.

However, as far as we know, currently there is no public dataset for text steganalysis. In order to provide an open test platform for researchers in the field of text steganography and steganalysis, and to promote the development of text steganography and steganalysis technology, in this paper, we construct and release a large-scale universal text steganalysis dataset, called TStego-THU. This dataset contains 240,000 sentences that may contain hidden information. The original sentences in TStego-THU comes from some widely used network platforms. And in order to make the dataset more universal, we use different steganography methods, including two modification-based and two generation-based steganography algorithms, to embed random bit streams into sentences.

In the remainder of this paper, Sect. 2 introduces the details of the construction process of TStego-THU, including data collection and preprocessing, information embedding algorithms. The following part, Sect. 3, describes the steganalysis benchmarks we used and their performance on TStego-THU dataset. Finally, conclusions are drawn in Sect. 4.

2 The Construction of TStego-THU

In this section, we will introduce the details of the construction procedure of TStego-THU, including source text collection, text preprocessing and information hiding methods. Finally, we give the overall distribution characteristics of TStego-THU.

2.1 Source Text Collection

In order to ensure that the samples in the constructed dataset are close enough to the real scene, in the process of constructing TStego-THU, we mainly used three common transmitted text medias in cyberspace, namely Twitter, movie reviews and News. For Twitter, we chose the sentiment140 dataset published by Alec Go et al. [20]. It contains 1,600,000 tweets extracted using the Twitter API. For the movie review dataset, we chose the widely used IMDB dataset published by Maas et al. [21], which contains 25,000 movie reviews from IMDB. The texts of the two datasets above are of the social media type. In addition, we also chose a news dataset [22] containing relatively more standard texts. It contains 143,000 articles from 15 American publications, including the New York Times, Breitbart, CNN, etc. The topics of the dataset are mainly politically related and the published time is mainly between 2016 and July 2017.

2.2 Text Preprocessing

Before steganography, we need to pre-process the collected original texts. Firstly, we unified all the texts in TStego-THU into lowercase. Secondly, we divided all the collected text into single sentences, that is, each sample in TStego-THU contains only one sentence. Then, we removed special symbols from the texts, such as emoticons, web links, special formatted text, etc. Finally, we built a dictionary of all the text in TStego-THU and filtered out words whose word frequency is below a certain threshold (usually between 5–10), mainly to avoid some misspellings and low-frequency words. After pre-processing, the text details of each source are shown in Table 1.

Table 1. The details of each text source.

Dataset	Twitter	IMDB	News
Average length	9.68	19.94	22.24
Sentence number	2,639,290	1,283,813	1,962,040
Words number	25,551,044	25,601,794	43,626,829
Unique number	46,341	48,342	42,745

2.3 Information Hiding

Since currently text steganography algorithms mainly include two types: text modification based and text generation based. Steganographic samples in TStego-THU mainly used these two kinds of algorithms for random bits stream embedding. The general framework of these two algorithms is shown in Fig. 1. For each type of steganographic methods, we chose two steganographic algorithms for embedding. For modification based methods, one of them we choose T-Lex, which is a very classic and widely used text steganographic model proposed by K. Winstein et al. [23], and the other one we chose the latest algorithm proposed by H. Hu et al. [24]. Both of these two algorithms are based on synonym substitution (SS), which embeds secret information by changing cover words for their synonyms. In the process of building TStego-THU, we first used WordNet [25] to build a synonym list of different data sources. Then we randomly selected 10,000 sentences from each data source, for each of which, we randomly used one of the two text steganography algorithms to embed the random bit stream into the text to form 10,000 cover-stego sentence pairs. It is worth noting that in some cases, even if no words are replaced in the whole sentence, it may also carry hidden information (e.g. "0").

For generation based steganographic methods, we mainly used the two steganographic models proposed by Yang et al. [5, 26]. These two models first learn the statistical language model of a large number of normal texts and then encode the conditional probabilities of each word in the generation process to achieve the hiding of secret information. The difference lies in the generation model used by both: the model proposed in [26] uses the Markov chain model and the model in [5] uses the recurrent neural network (RNN) model. In the process of constructing TStego-THU, we first trained these two models with all the texts from different sources to learn the overall statistical language model. Then, in the process of text generation, the conditional probability space is dynamically encoded by the Huffman tree. And finally the steganographic texts are generated according to the random bits stream. Both methods can adjust the overall embedding rate by adjusting the number of bits embedded in each word. To ensure high concealment, we embeded only one bit per word (bpw = 1) when constructing TStego-THU. It is also worth noting that, considering the text generation models can also generate texts without hidden information, and in fact many texts on the network are automatically generated by computers, such as some man-machine dialogues, news summaries and so on. Therefore, in order to be more consistent with the real scene, when constructing the cover set of TStego-THU, we also incorporated some texts that are automatically generated by the models without covert information.

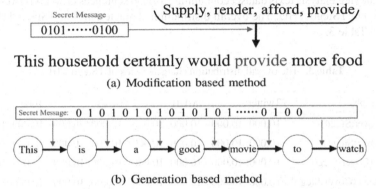

(a) Modification based method

(b) Generation based method

Fig. 1. The general frameworks of two types text steganographic algorithms: text modification based and text generation based.

2.4 Embedding Rate

After completing the information embedding, we calculated the actual embedding rate of different embedding algorithms. The embedding rate is calculated as the ratio of the number of bits actually embedded in all texts and the number of bits occupied by the texts stored in the computer. Through the actual test, the embedding rate of each steganography algorithms on different source of texts is shown in Table 2. As can be seen from Table 2, the modification-based steganography algorithm usually has an embedding rate of less than 1%. The generated steganographic model, even if each word is only embedded in 1 bit, greatly exceeds the modification-based steganography algorithms. Finally, the average embedding rate of the TStego-THU is 1.543%.

Table 2. The embedding rate of each steganography algorithms on different sources of texts.

Stegnography	Twitter	IMDB	News	Average
T-lex [23]	0.773%	0.689%	0.539%	0.667%
STC [24]	0.584%	0.476%	0.364%	0.475%
Markov [26]	2.424%	2.182%	2.087%	2.231%
RNN-Stega [5]	3.060%	2.814%	2.763%	2.879%
Average	1.710%	1.540%	1.438%	1.563%

2.5 Overall Details of TStego-THU

After all these operations, we obtained 10,000 cover-stego text pairs by using different steganography algorithms for different source of texts. We mixed them together to form a large-scale steganalysis texts dataset containing 240,000 sentences (120,000 cover-stego text pairs) in TStego-THU. The overall distribution characteristics of TStego-THU are shown in Table 3.

Table 3. The overall distribution characteristics of TStego-THU.

Stegnography	Twitter	IMDB	News	Total
T-lex (Cover:Stego)	10,000: 10,000	10,000: 10,000	10,000: 10,000	10,000: 10,000
STC (Cover:Stego)	10,000: 10,000	10,000: 10,000	10,000: 10,000	10,000: 10,000
Markov (Cover:Stego)	10,000: 10,000	10,000: 10,000	10,000: 10,000	10,000: 10,000
RNN-Stega (Cover:Stego)	10,000: 10,000	10,000: 10,000	10,000: 10,000	10,000: 10,000
Total (Cover:Stego)	40,000: 40,000	40,000: 40,000	40,000: 40,000	40,000: 40,000

3   Experiment

In order to evaluate the difficulty of TStego-THU and also to provide benchmark results for subsequent researchers, in this section, we will evaluate some latest text steganalysis algorithms on TStego-THU.

3.1 Benchmark Methods and Evaluation Metrics

We choose three latest text steganalysis models as the benchmark models of TStego-THU, which are proposed in [13, 14, 16]. These three text steganalysis models are all based on neural networks. Among them, the authors in [13] described the semantic correlations between words in texts, which has been explained in Fig. 3. They analyzed that once the covert information was embedded in the text, it may destroy the semantic correlations between words. So they mainly use word vector and fasttext model to extract the semantic correlations of words and conduct text steganalysis. The authors in [14] further refined the correlations of words into successive word correlation, cross word correlation and cross sentence correlation, and used multi-channel convolution kernels to extract these words correlations for text steganalysis.

words correlation

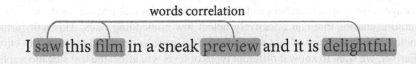

The authors in [16] analysised that the conditional probability distribution of words in the sentence may be effected once the covert information was embedded. Therefore, they use bidirectional Long Short-Term Memory (Bi-LSTM) model [27] model to extract the conditional probability distribution features in texts, and then conduct text steganalysis according to the distribution differences. The experimental results show that they can even estimate the amount of covert information that may be contained in steganographic sentence based on the distribution of text features [16].

3.2 Detection Results of Benchmark Methods

We randomly selected 80% sentences from TStego-THU as the training samples to train each steganalysis model, and the remaining 20% used as the test samples to evaluate model's steganalysis ability. The final test results are shown in Table 4.

Table 4. The overall performance of each benchmark methods.

Methods	Accuracy	Precision	Recall	F1
Fasttext [13]	0.593	0.593	0.593	0.593
CNN [14]	0.584	0.584	0.584	0.584
LSTM [16]	0.591	0.591	0.591	0.591
Bi-LSTM [16]	0.578	0.578	0.578	0.578

From the results in Table 4, the first thing worth noting is that the detection performance of these three models are very close, and their detection accuracy are all less than 60%. This shows that TStego-THU dataset is very difficult and very challenging for steganalysis. We think there are several reasons. The first and most important reason is that we used a very low embedding rate when building the dataset, as shown in Table 2. Secondly, most of the previous text steganalysis algorithms were aimed at one single steganographic algorithm. In order to encourage researchers to explore more general text steganalysis algorithms, TStego-THU contains four different text steganography algorithms, which is more challenging. Thirdly, for the same purpose, in order to encourage the study of text steganalysis algorithms in more general scenarios, texts in TStego-THU comes from three different sources and is ultimately mixed together. Since the statistical distribution patterns of each different type of text have certain differences, mixing them together further increases the versatility of the dataset, but at the same time further increases the difficulty.

Based on the above analysis, we can see that TStego-THU has the characteristics of low embedding rate, multiple steganography algorithms, and multiple text types. We encourage follow-up researchers to further develop universal text steganalysis models for multi scenarios that can effectively detect low embedding rates. This will further promote the development of text steganalysis in a more general and practical direction.

Further, we want to know if different types of texts will affect the text steganographic detection performance. Therefore, according to the detection results in Table 4, we further counted the detecting accuracy of texts from different sources in the test samples. The results are shown in Table 5. From Table 5, it seems that Twitter text is relatively easier to detect, while the accuracy of other two types of text detection is relatively close. This also reflects that the statistical characteristics of various source texts are indeed different.

Table 5. The detection results of texts from different sources in the test samples.

Steganalysis	Dataset	Accuracy	Precision	Recall	F1
Fasttext [13]	IMDB	0.560	0.560	0.560	0.560
	News	0.586	0.586	0.586	0.586
	Twitter	0.633	0.633	0.633	0.633
CNN [14]	IMDB	0.575	0.575	0.575	0.575
	News	0.595	0.595	0.595	0.595
	Twitter	0.581	0.581	0.581	0.581
LSTM [16]	IMDB	0.565	0.565	0.565	0.565
	News	0.597	0.597	0.597	0.597
	Twitter	0.610	0.610	0.610	0.610
Bi-LSTM [16]	IMDB	0.551	0.551	0.551	0.551
	News	0.567	0.567	0.567	0.567
	Twitter	0.616	0.616	0.616	0.616

4   Conclusion

In this paper, we construct and release a large-scale univeral text steganalysis dataset called TStego-THU. In TStego-THU, we used text from several different sources, used multiple steganographic algorithms, and kept the embedding rate low. We hope TStego-THU can provide a fair enough platform for comparison of text steganalysis algorithms and further promote the development of universal text steganalysis.

Acknowledgement. Authors are deeply indebted to anonymous reviewers for their constructive suggestions and helpful comments.

Funding Statement. This work was supported in part by the National Key Research and Development Program of China under Grant 2018YFB0804103 and the National Natural Science Foundation of China (No. U61972168, No. U1705261 and No. U1636113).

Conflicts of Interest. The authors declare that they have no conflicts of interest to report regarding the present study.

References

1. Shannon, C.E.: Communication theory of secrecy systems. Bell Syst. Tech. J. **28**(4), 656–715 (1949)
2. Theohary, C.A.: Terrorist Use of the Internet: Information Operations in Cyberspace. DIANE Publishing (2011)
3. Yang, Z., Wang, K., Ma, S., Huang, Y., Kang, X., Zhao, X.: Istego100k: Large-scale image steganalysis dataset. In: Wang, H., Zhao, X., Shi, Y., Kim, H.J., Piva, Alessandro (eds.) Digital Forensics and Watermarking. LNCS, vol. 12022, pp. 352–364. Springer, Cham (2020). https://doi.org/10.1007/978-3-030-43575-2_29
4. Yang, Z., Peng, X., Huang, Y.: A sudoku matrix-based method of pitch period steganography in low-rate speech coding. In: Lin, X., Ghorbani, A., Ren, K., Zhu, S., Zhang, A. (eds.) Security and Privacy in Communication Networks, vol. 238, pp. 752–762. Springer, Cham (2018). https://doi.org/10.1007/978-3-319-78813-5_40
5. Yang, Z.L., Guo, X.Q., Chen, Z.M., Huang, Y.F., Zhang, Y.J.: RNN-stega: linguistic steganography based on recurrent neural networks. IEEE Trans. Inf. Forensics Secur. **14**(5), 1280–1295 (2018)
6. Yang, Z.L., Zhang, S.Y., Hu, Y.T., Hu, Z.W., Huang, Y.F.: VAE-Stega: linguistic steganography based on variational auto-encoder. IEEE Trans. Inf. Forensics Secur. **16**, 880–895 (2020)
7. Yang, Z., Zhang, P., Jiang, M., Huang, Y., Zhang, Y.J.: Rits: real-time interactive text steganography based on automatic dialogue model. In: Sun, X., Pan, Z., Bertino, E. (eds.) ICCCS 2018. LNCS, vol. 11065, pp. 253–264. Springer, Cham (2018). https://doi.org/10.1007/978-3-030-00012-7_24
8. Xiang, L., Luo, G., Xie, Y., Chen, W.: Research on the coding strategies for synonym substitution-based steganography. J. Comput. Inf. Syst. **10**(22), 9877–9888 (2014)
9. Xiang, L., Wu, W., Li, X., Yang, C.: A linguistic steganography based on word indexing compression and candidate selection. Multimed. Tools Appl. **77**(21), 28969–28989 (2018). https://doi.org/10.1007/s11042-018-6072-8
10. Xiang, L., Wang, X., Yang, C., Liu, P.: A novel linguistic steganography based on synonym run-length encoding. IEICE Trans. Inf. Syst. **100**(2), 313–322 (2017)
11. Bahdanau, D., Cho, K., Bengio, Y.: Neural machine translation by jointly learning to align and translate. arXiv preprint arXiv:1409.0473 (2014)
12. Yang, Z., Zhang, Y.J., Rehman, S., Huang, Y.: Image captioning with object detection and localization. In: Zhao, Y., Kong, X., Taubman, D. (eds.) ICIG 2017. LNCS, vol. 10667, pp. 109–118. Springer, Cham (2017). https://doi.org/10.1007/978-3-319-71589-6_10
13. Yang, Z., Huang, Y., Zhang, Y.J.: A fast and efficient text steganalysis method. IEEE Signal Process. Lett. **26**(4), 627–631 (2019)

14. Yang, Z., Huang, Y., Zhang, Y.-J.: TS-CSW: text steganalysis and hidden capacity estimation based on convolutional sliding windows. Multimed. Tools Appl. **79**(25–26), 18293–18316 (2020). https://doi.org/10.1007/s11042-020-08716-w
15. Wen, J., Zhou, X., Zhong, P., Xue, Y.: Convolutional neural network based text steganalysis. IEEE Signal Process. Lett. **26**(3), 460–464 (2019)
16. Yang, Z., Wang, K., Li, J., Huang, Y., Zhang, Y.J.: TS-RNN: text steganalysis based on recurrent neural networks. IEEE Signal Process. Lett. **26**(12), 1743–1747 (2019)
17. Yang, H., Cao, X.: Linguistic steganalysis based on meta features and immune mechanism. Chin. J. Electron. **19**(4), 661–666 (2010)
18. Meng, P., Hang, L., Yang, W., Chen, Z., Zheng, H.: Linguistic steganography detection algorithm using statistical language model. In: 2009 International Conference on Information Technology and Computer Science, vol. 2, pp. 540–543. IEEE, July 2009
19. Samanta, S., Dutta, S., Sanyal, G.: A real time text steganalysis by using statistical method. In: 2016 IEEE International Conference on Engineering and Technology (ICETECH), pp. 264–268. IEEE, March 2016
20. Go, A., Bhayani, R., Huang, L.: Twitter sentiment classification using distant supervision. CS224N project report, Stanford **1**(12), 2009 (2009)
21. Maas, A., Daly, R.E., Pham, P.T., Huang, D., Ng, A.Y., Potts, C.: Learning word vectors for sentiment analysis. In: Proceedings of the 49th Annual Meeting of the Association for Computational Linguistics: Human Language Technologies, pp. 142–150, June 2011
22. Thompson, A.: Kaggle. https://www.kaggle.com/snapcrack/all-the-news/data
23. Winstein, K.: Lexical steganography through adaptive modulation of the word choice hash (1998)
24. Huanhuan, H., Xin, Z., Weiming, Z., Nenghai, Y.: Adaptive text steganography by exploring statistical and linguistical distortion. In: 2017 IEEE Second International Conference on Data Science in Cyberspace (DSC), pp. 145–150. IEEE, June 2017
25. Miller, G.A.: WordNet: a lexical database for English. Commun. ACM **38**(11), 39–41 (1995)
26. Yang, Z., Jin, S., Huang, Y., Zhang, Y., Li, H.: Automatically generate steganographic text based on Markov model and Huffman coding. arXiv preprint arXiv:1811.04720 (2018)
27. Hochreiter, S., Schmidhuber, J.: Long short-term memory. Neural Comput. **9**(8), 1735–1780 (1997)

IoT Security

Integration Innovation of Competitive Intelligence, AI and Big Data Analysis

Wen Sun[1(✉)], Yan Nan[1], Tian Ze Yang[1], Xiao Yun Hu[1], and Yu Jiang[1,2]

[1] School of Cyber Science and Engineering, Southeast University,
No. 2, Southeast University Road, Nanjing 211189, China
101012533@seu.edu.cn
[2] Purple Mountain Laboratories, Nanjing, China

Abstract. With the rapid development of AI and big data analysis, competitive intelligence is facing unprecedented opportunities and challenges. This paper analyzes the changes of competitive intelligence in the new era and the applications of AI and data intelligence in the competitive intelligence system, deeply discusses the integration, innovation, and development of competitive intelligence, and establishes a closed loop of competitive intelligence analysis. Finally, future competitive-intelligence-related systems and work-flows are studied.

Keywords: Competitive intelligence · Data intelligence · AI · Analytical decision system

1 Introduction

Thanks to the rapid development of computer power and big data, intelligence collection and analysis methods are constantly changing with the environment. Gathering competitive intelligence is like a treasure hunt with hidden information everywhere, and our challenge is to go out and get it. However, if we want to develop a truly effective competitive intelligence system, we need to "hunt" with a purpose, with which we need to build an intelligence system that constantly improves and integrates new methods to ensure that we can be always ahead of the competitors [1].

The rest of the paper is organized as follows. Section 2 gives the basic definition of the Competitive intelligence. Section 3 presents the AI application in competitive intelligence. Section 4 shows the application of data analysis in competitive situation. Section 5 gives the novel construction of the competitive intelligence system. Section 6 analyzes the impacts of the proposed competitive intelligence system. Conclusions and future work are discussed in the last section.

2 Changes in Competitive Intelligence in the New Era

Competitive intelligence (CI) is defined as the collection and analysis of information about products, customers, competitors, and any aspect of an enterprise's competitive

© Springer Nature Switzerland AG 2021
X. Sun et al. (Eds.): ICAIS 2021, CCIS 1424, pp. 347–357, 2021.
https://doi.org/10.1007/978-3-030-78621-2_28

environment. It can conduct research and analysis according to the needs of decision-makers, and then draw satisfactory conclusions. Intelligence also needs to be delivered on a timely basis so it can be incorporated into the process of decision making. Effective competitive intelligence systems mainly include [2] (Table 1):

Table 1. Competitive intelligence systems

Competitive intelligence activity	Purpose
Strategy	Situation of market, reasonable arrangement
Collection	All organization activities associated with the market
Analysis	Market dynamics, turning raw data into real competitive intelligence
Publicity	Market services, competitive intelligence is transmitted to stakeholders and applied

Competitive intelligence reveals essentially what is happening so that you can compete effectively. Moreover, that's why it's not just about analyzing your competitors, but learning as much as you can about their industries, their consumers and your own strengths and weaknesses, and even broader trends that will drive decision-makers to make appropriate strategic decisions [3]. When competitive intelligence is used effectively, enterprises can quickly adapt to the changing market environment [4].

With the development of the market, AI and big data analysis tools can collect effective market and competitor intelligence from massive amounts of data to gain valuable business insights [5].

3 AI Application in Competitive Intelligence

3.1 Functional Framework of AI

The application of AI in competitive intelligence is manifested from the following aspects [6]:

First, AI can provide complete intelligence about competitors.

AI can be used to track the complete footprints of competitors, and this all-round intelligence enables enterprises to understand the market/competitors' strategies and plans. Main tracks include:

- Presentations of executive management that provides information about the company's future strategy.
- Annual reports and regulatory documents.
- News coverage and other feature communities created by people inside or outside the company.
- Product specifications and other company profiles distributed at conferences, trade shows, and other events.

- Practical observations of competitors' activities at trade shows or investor events.
- Specific research on the industry/company, research papers, and analysis reports.
- Interaction with customers, suppliers, and other industry participants.
- Industry-specific social networking sites.

Second, AI can identify the effective competitive environment changes, and distinguish the information about competitive intelligence from the interference items [7].

The ideal role for artificial intelligence in business is to supplement and enhance the information that humans ignore. AI can replace repetitive programmable tasks and automate corporate daily tasks so that marketers can focus their time and energy on data analysis with a higher value. AI can also identify subtle anomalies in large data sets.

Third, AI can make decision-making and implementation more effective by suggesting more likely strategies. For example, the content AI platform could suggest getting an above-average article topic or title [8].

3.2 Deficiencies of AI

Although the innovation-driven by artificial intelligence is fierce, the core of competitive intelligence analysis is still related to the writer's thought and analysis. While current AI narration can come up with simple and repeatable descriptions, it is relatively difficult to provide original narrative or commentaries [9]. The analysis and prediction of pre-competitive intelligence may not be fully automated, because the formulation and implementation of decisions and strategies involve interpersonal communication, decision-maker preferences and some unpredictable situation.

3.3 The Combination of AI and Competitive Intelligence

Can AI reshape the way that companies now focus on competitive intelligence? It depends on maintaining the balance between continuous innovation and disruptive innovation.

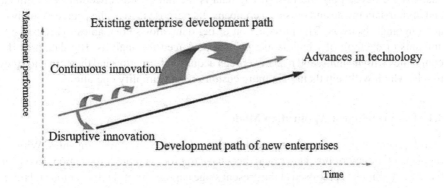

Fig. 1. Disruptive innovation is critical to the development of competitive intelligence

Figure 1 reveals the relationship between traditional enterprises and new technology companies. Traditional enterprises gain market share through continuous innovation, while new enterprises increase their market value through the application of new technologies. The "value-added part" in the development path of new enterprises is the market value brought by new technologies. New technologies cannot be separated from the accumulation of big data [10]. The application of AI will continue to optimize the products and services of new enterprises and make them occupy a place in the competitive market [10].

Faced with the tide of new technology, traditional enterprises need to reshape their value through competitive intelligence analysis, follow the development of technology, and explore sustainable and innovative business models to adapt to the rapid change of the future market [11]. This is the pressure brought by technological progress on traditional enterprises.

In the new system, the application of AI and big data analysis can help enterprises to solve the problems of current products/services. New enterprises combine disruptive innovative technologies to lead the construction of commercial innovation network and create higher commercial value and market competitive advantage. This is the opportunity given by technological change to new technology enterprises.

Data analysis has been widely applied in the intelligence analysis of enterprises [12]. AI is a disruptive innovation for competitive intelligence. However, the original competitive intelligence system has a deeper understanding of industry and market demand. Besides, due to the reliance on the data training set, the application of AI in competitive intelligence still has a long way to go.

Therefore, the most likely reconstruction of competitive intelligence analysis by AI and big data analysis is to form an intelligent competitive intelligence system through in-depth combination of data mining, analysis and prediction [13].

4   Application of Data Analysis in Competitive Intelligence - Data Intelligence

AI cannot be separated from data analysis. Nowadays, big data and its computational analysis are developing the fastest. Big data is the integrated collection of traditional and digital data inside and outside a company. Its purpose is to be the source of analysis and ongoing discovery. The introduction of big data allows companies to access large amounts of data, all of which is merged and packaged for analysis. Big data provides companies with insights, and researchers can acquire information and then use it to study trends, which will help them gain more customers and simplify operations.

4.1   Data Intelligent Application Mode

Development of data intelligence can keep the competitiveness of companies. With the rapid development of big data, researchers have to process more information. However, the data intelligence proposed at the present stage captures useful information and filters out invalid data.

First, data intelligence allows companies to combine all data during segmentations. It uses existing data and strategies, past performance, and external data on market conditions and requirements to gain a more comprehensive understanding of the market and competition.

Meanwhile, machine-learning and other technologies have eliminated much of the human bias in processes. Smart industry and data segmentation start with no assumptions, and then find market characteristics and analyze them. Market or industry's profiles based on such data are analyzed based on realistic conditions to identify and improve the conversion and utilization of competitive intelligence.

Second, real-time data analysis is where data science really comes into play. These programs combine data from a variety of sources and analyze them as they are collected to provide immediate, timely insights based on what is collected [14].

Finally, good data planning depends on a timely flow of information, which is provided by data intelligence methods such as data analysis. Analyzing multiple data streams creates real-time, evolving competitive intelligence. Processing data and presenting it in a dynamic visual format often show unexpected patterns. Some inefficiencies and redundancies in processes are difficult to detect in the raw data. For example, information that is naturally generated in one department may not be passed on, forcing other departments to recreate it [15]. There may also be a staffing imbalance relative to the number of customers at certain times of a day, which can be avoided with advance warning. Whatever forms these problems take, data intelligence can help to find solutions.

4.2 Shortcomings of Data Intelligence

While understanding the benefits of data intelligence, it should be clear that data intelligence should not be seen as a panacea for all corporate woes. Unrealistic expectations can end data science projects as easily as a lack of underlying support. If you surround yourself with new analysis tools, and expect an immediate return on investment, it is equally undesirable for companies to be disappointed when expected results do not materialize and to take the data science as a failure [16].

Treat data intelligence as decision supports, not decision-makers. Data analysis is not magic, but it provides targeted insights and advice to help executives develop corporate strategies. Maintaining realistic expectations of its potential is a key step towards realizing the data competitive intelligence program.

5 Construction of a Competitive Intelligence System

5.1 Establish a Closed Loop of a Competitive Intelligence System

The development of competitive intelligence is an eternal process that can never be described as an end. Data is always changing, incomplete, and requiring further validation. A closed-loop management and control mechanism is required to ensure that a rigorous and reliable conclusion is reached in intelligence analysis [17, 18].

The system shown below is used to periodically identify changes in target intelligence, collect data to fill in these changes, and then update the analysis and report it to

Fig. 2. Competitive intelligence system

decision-makers. Routine checks are also inserted into this procedure to ensure that the system is working properly (Fig. 2).

First, the system identifies the changes and fills in the gaps by specifying a list of gaps and assigning responsible stakeholders to look for specific information. When the data collection is completed, aggregation and analysis are performed, and then recommendations can be made based on the analysis and checked afterward.

Periodic inspection is an effective supplement to competitive intelligence closed loop which is necessary because there is no deadline for competitive intelligence analysis.

5.2   Innovate and Improve the Intelligence System – Intelligent System

The methods to measure and collect data increase with the development of technology. Even a strong competitive intelligence system still has loopholes that are hard to fill, which typically require detailed data to fully establish the right value proposition and ensure effective market positioning [19].

Intelligent intelligence system should have the following functions: based on existing resources and technologies, intelligent perception of intelligence needs, intelligent acquisition of massive information, dynamic fusion of multi-source information, comprehensive analysis of multi-dimensional correlation, intelligent interpretation of analysis results, automatic generation of intelligence reports, and timely service-oriented to the scene.

Intelligent intelligence analysis system subdivides decision objectives, optimizes decision schemes, solves professional problems supplemented by other disciplines, and guides the planning and design of information system based on the management science theory. The artificial intelligence realizes in the information system the auxiliary computation of decision simulation and analysis forecast domain, and promotes the unceasing consummation of the system research with practice (Fig. 3).

Because of different requirements generated by different scenarios, an intelligence analyst needs to collect and integrate data information through the intelligence analysis system to analyze from different perspectives and methods. Competitive intelligence is dynamic, which means it needs timely adjustment and reform according to policies, market conditions and other dimensions.

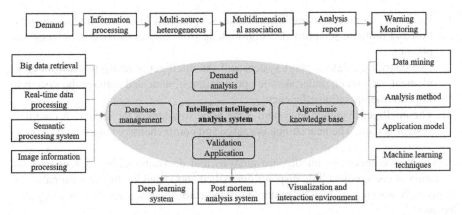

Fig. 3. Intelligent intelligence analysis system

With the development of AI and big data analysis, continuous innovation and improvement of intelligent decision-making system can adapt to the demands of the time [20].

6   Analysis on the Structure of New Competitive Intelligence System

6.1   Construction of a New Competitive Intelligence System

New competitive intelligence analysis architecture based on big data and artificial intelligence is as below:

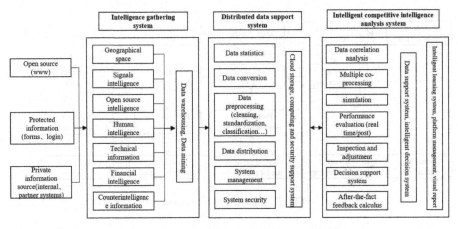

Fig. 4. Intelligent intelligence system architecture

As can be seen from the Fig. 4, the construction of a new competitive intelligence analysis and decision-making system requires the establishment of a good ecological environment in which privilege selection can be open, shared and evolved.

(1) Establish a competitive intelligence analysis platform to control the overall situation and promote scientific decision-making from the perspective of strategy and planning;

(2) The distributed data support system and the intelligence analysis platform complement each other, undertake the optimization of data, and manage the system to improve the operation efficiency;

(3) The intelligence gathering system is the basic structure of the system. A complete system is built. The nearest one is a large and comprehensive data source.

The new competitive intelligence analysis and decision-making system tests the operation of each project link, displays diversified and visual intelligent terminals, performs early warning analysis on multiple key indicators, and verifies the efficiency after the event.

As can be seen from the description of the above system, the system is further upgraded and improved on the big data analysis system. Combined with AI technology, big data analysis system is able to simplify and optimize the composition of the system. The adoption of AI technology can also combine data management and security management, and integrate analysis and decision support system into a visual system.

The key technologies of intelligent competitive intelligence analysis system are data model and intelligence model. The main task of the data model layer is to transform the data collected by intelligence into identifiable semantics according to specific requirements, which is essentially a process of information extraction. The data model layer uses natural language processing technology, knowledge mining algorithm, neural network model and other data processing methods to solve the problem of insufficient data analysis ability of the traditional competitive intelligence systems (Fig. 5).

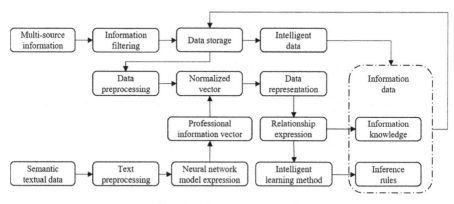

Fig. 5. Data model framework

The intelligence model layer is a competitive intelligence analysis model based on information knowledge. The advantage of competitive intelligence is to capture the truth behind the market competition in the case of information asymmetry. However, the accumulation of data and the analysis of the system of learning and training are crucial.

Only through accuracy verification can the intelligence model layer be used for analysis such as research and prediction (Fig. 6).

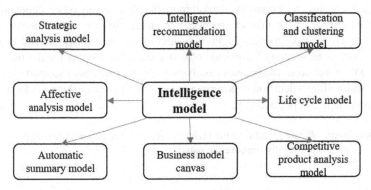

Fig. 6. Intelligence model framework

Intelligence information is transformed into identifiable and diversified professional information on the data model layer to provide data support for the intelligence model layer. The intelligence model layer provides visual and intelligent intelligence according to the information transformed by the data model for decision-makers' reference and monitors the market public opinion to timely adjust the strategy.

6.2 Challenges

In the new system, the artificial intelligence calculation method can deal with imperfect data, continuously study and summarize in the process of data processing, learn knowledge and discover rules from massive data.

Data in the big data intelligence analysis are characterized by complex relationship, data drift, super-high dimension, noise and sparse attributes, which makes it difficult for traditional data mining and machine learning algorithms to effectively conduct data processing and intelligence analysis. Therefore, new machine learning theories and methods need to be studied to solve these problems [21].

In addition, it is necessary to study the data mining programming model and distributed parallel execution mechanism suitable for big data distributed processing, which supports the programming of complex algorithms such as iteration, recursion, aggregation, integration and merge in data mining algorithms, and designs and implements distributed parallel machine learning and data mining algorithms with low complexity and high parallelism on existing parallel computing platforms.

7   Conclusion

The development of technology brings about the change of demand and working mode and therefore requires the competitive intelligence and analysis system to provide new services. With the rapid development of AI and big data analysis technology, China's competitive intelligence system is also undergoing rapid reform [10].

Schemes combined with big data and streaming technologies can improve operational efficiency and understand the market more deeply than any other algorithm. With the constant change of the market, the needs of enterprises are getting more complex and diverse. The competitive intelligence system makes more effective use of AI and big data analysis technology to provide effective decision support for the market and industry. Moreover, from the business analysis tools and intelligent support system, AI and big data intelligent decision making can fundamentally reduce the cost of enterprises and improve their competitiveness.

Acknowledgment. We are grateful to the reviewers for their useful comments and suggestions which helped us to significantly improve the paper.

Funding Statement. Support from the Natural Science Foundation Program of Jiangsu Province [Grant No. BK20200352] for the first author is also acknowledged.

Conflicts of Interest. The authors declare that they have no known competing interests that could have appeared to influence the work reported in this paper.

References

1. Bulger, N.J.: The evolving role of intelligence: migrating from traditional competitive intelligence to integrated intelligence. Int. J. Intell. Secur. Public Aff. **18**(1), 57–84 (2016)
2. White, C.: How to start a competitive analysis: 57 questions you need to ask. HubSpot (2018)
3. Bohrer, C.: 5 Ways big data and analytics will impact e-commerce. In 2018. Data Economy (2018)
4. Bao, C., Xie, X.: Introduction to Competitive Intelligence, pp. 4–176. Tsinghua University Press (2011)
5. Liebowitz, J: Strategic Intelligence: Business Intelligence, Competitive Intelligence, and Knowledge Management. Auerbach Publications (2006)
6. Guan, S., Li, Z.: The development status of American competitive intelligence system and its enlightenment to China. Book Intelligence Work, pp. 83–92 (2015)
7. Prescott, J.: The evolution of competitive intelligence. Int. Rev. Strategic Manage. **6**, 71–90 (1995)
8. Huang, X.: Build enterprise competitive intelligence system model based on big data. J. Intell. (2013)
9. Sun, Z., Wang, P.P.: Big data, analytics and intelligence: an editorial perspective. J. New Math. Nat. Comput. **13**(2), 75–81 (2017)
10. Wang, F.-Y.: A big-data perspective on AI: Newton, Merton, and analytics intelligence. IEEE Intell. Syst. **27**(5), 2–4 (2012)
11. Lichtenthaler, U.: Beyond artificial intelligence: why companies need to go the extra step. J. Bus. Strategy (2018)
12. Sun, L., Wang, Y.-Z.: Identifying the core competitive intelligence based on enterprise strategic factors. J. Shanghai Jiaotong Univ. (Sci.) **20**(1), 118–123 (2015). https://doi.org/10.1007/s12204-015-1598-7
13. Farias, H.: How will data intelligence transform the enterprise? InfoWorld (2018)

14. Huixin, H.X.Z.: Build enterprise competitive intelligence system model based on big data. J. Intell. (2013)

15. Li, M., He, W., Ding, B.: Research on multiple cooperative supply mechanism of competitive intelligence for micro enterprises based on S2B model. Inf. Sci. 52–56 (2018)

16. Huang, H., Cao, C., Feng, C.: The opportunities of development and challenges of big data intelligence analysis. J. Intell. Syst. 720–727 (2016).

17. Tang, X., Zheng, D., Zhai, S.: Research on competitive intelligence system model based on big data intelligence. Inf. Theory Pract. **133–137**, 160 (2018)

18. Gan, Y., Wang, L., Huang, J., Chen, L.: Intelligence analysis and technology exploration in the era of big data and artificial intelligence. Telecommun. Technol. 506–513 (2018)

19. Garca, S., Luengo, J., Herrera, F.: Data preprocessing in data mining. Comput. Sci. **72** (2000)

20. Liang, B., Guo, J.L., Lao, S.Y.: Cross-media intelligence processing based on deep cognition neural networks. J. Command Control (2016)

21. Porter, M., Kramer, M.: The big idea: creating shared value. How to reinvent capitalism unleash a wave of innovation and growth. Harv. Bus. Rev. **89**, 62–77 (2011)

22. Hua, B., Li, G.: Architecture design and key technology research of intelligent intelligence analysis system. Books Inf. 74–83 (2017)

23. Zhang, Y., Guo, Q., Wang, J.: Neural network method for big data analysis. J. Sichuan Univ. (Eng. Sci. Edn.). 9–18 (2017)

24. Vassakis, K., Petrakis, E., Kopanakis, I.: Big data analytics: applications, prospects and challenges. In: Skourletopoulos, G., Mastorakis, G., Mavromoustakis, C., Dobre, C., Pallis, E. (eds.) Mobile Big Data, vol. 10, pp. 3–20. Springer, Cham (2018). https://doi.org/10.1007/978-3-319-67925-9_1

A Comprehensive Review of IoT Technologies and Applications for Healthcare

Shiqi Chen, Xuran Jin, Lulu Zhang, and Jie Wan$^{(\boxtimes)}$

Nantong University China, Nantong, China
jiewan@ntu.edu.cn

Abstract. With the recent technological advancements, The Internet of Things offers numerous and potentially revolutionary benefits to all aspects of today's digital world. Personalised and connected healthcare is one of the most promising areas. IoT is multidiscipline research area, which envisages a number of technologies, such as sensing, networking, data management, artificial intelligence and so on. Sensors and smart devices are the fundamental elements for observing the participants and their surrounding environment. In terms of networking and communications, several techniques have been widely adopted, for example, NB-IoT, ZigBee, Wi-Fi, 4G/5G etc. In addition, Big Data, Cloud computing are often embedded for data storage and analysing. Here as, this paper surveys the emerging IoT technologies and typical applications in healthcare.

Keywords: Narrow-band IoT · Healthcare · Ambient assisted living

1 Introduction

With the demographic changes in the last few decades, population ageing has become problematic worldwide. Therefore, ambient pervasive healthcare has been playing a significant role in the economy. In the developed countries, an average of approximately 10% of Gross Domestic Product (GDP) are spent in healthcare by 2020. However, besides the advancement of the healthcare technologies, ICT (Information and Communication Technologies) are the promising solutions for dramatically reduce the healthcare cost. In particular, with the recent advancement of IoT, a diverse range of healthcare related applications and services have been developed and deployed, which including smart medication, ambient assisted living, health monitoring and so on. With the recent advancement, IoT has been embedded in a diverse of areas, such as healthcare, energy control, entertainments and so on. In healthcare, a wide range of scenarios have

This work is supported by NanTong Science and Technology Bureau under grant JC2018132 and National Natural Science Foundation of China under grant 62002179 within Nantong University China.

been investigated, which include biomedical monitoring and disease diagnoses, emotion or facial expression monitoring, emergency monitoring, intelligent assistance, location-based services, activity and exercise monitoring, diet monitoring, etc. as is illustrated in Fig. 1. Therefore, in the healthcare domain, IoT mainly promises intelligent, reliable and comprehensive monitoring and health related parameters as well as further classification and recognition of various situations.

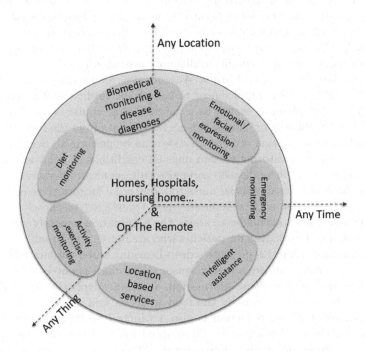

Fig. 1. IoT for healthcare: applications and scenarios

2   IoT for Healthcare Monitoring and Classification

IoT emphasise the connection and communication among heterogeneous physical and cyber devices and components over the Internet. Hence, IoT often envisages a number of techniques with a four layers framework, which includes Sensing, Networking, Data Management, and Intelligent Applications and Services. In healthcare, sensors and smart devices are often adopted for observing the information of the individuals (often patients, elderly, or people unable to maintain independent lives), such as their locations, biomedical parameters, behaviours and activities, emotions and so on. Sensors often with limited memory and computing capacity, thereby, the sensed information is often transmitted to a central server for further processing, via a number of transmission protocols, such as NB-IoT, 4G/5G, WiFi, ZigBee, 6LowPAN etc. Moreover, to provide intelligent services, machine learning based techniques and algorithms have been deeply investigated for data analysis, in order to retrieve more valuable information. Furthermore, cloud computing, artificial intelligence is often integrated to implement ambient, reliable and effective services.

Extensive research effort has been made in IoT enabled healthcare monitoring [1–7,16]. Existing health monitoring system can be organised into a number of categories: firstly, the biomedical parameter monitoring which commonly utilises wearable sensors or implantable sensors and medical devices to observing the vital signals [6] such as heartbeat, blood pressure etc. In this case, disease related parameter monitoring and condition diagnose are often involved. For example, some researchers [8] focus on Cardiac Auscultation monitoring, which adopts a Bluetooth enabled heart sound sensor to collect the cardiovascular parameters, and then a smart phone is served as a gateway that transfers the data to the cloud. Hence the doctors or clinical can access the data from the Internet, therefore, a further classification of heart diseases can be performed. Secondly, many researchers aim at monitoring certain unusual conditions or behaviours. For an instance, some researchers develop a remote pain monitoring system [4], which amounts a wearable sensing facial mask to monitor he facial surface electromyogram (sEMG) signals, such signals are then transferred to the cloud for the caregivers and other stakeholder to access the information remotely via the web. Such system may be adopted for patients who are not be able to self-report their feelings. The Smart-log [12] presents a deep-Learning based automated nutrition monitoring system, it utilises a weight sensor and a smart phone-based camera to collect the food and ingredient information, and then adopts the neural network and Bayesian network to classify the food items as well as predict next meal. Moreover, sleep disorder detection is also a widely investigated research area, especially for elderly. For example, [3] adopted IoT and Big Data technologies for sleep condition monitoring. Furthermore, others may concern on designing and developing a monitoring platform for general health related information collecting [5,7,20]. Researcher in [15] presented an IoT enabled smart medicine box to monitoring the medicine intakes of the subjects.

Thirdly, behaviour, activity, and motion monitoring, where wearable sensors, motion sensors, as well as ambient sensors are often embedded [10,11]. Behaviour and activity monitoring have been deeply investigated, for example, some researchers [12] utilising wearable sensors and combined with Improved Bayesian Convolution Network to recognise human activities [13,14]. In recent years, deep learning techniques and algorithms have also been widely embedded for behaviour monitoring or other health condition recognition and diagnose [17]. [23] presented a life-logging monitoring platform. Moreover, with the growing size of the sensor network or other data source, the oversized volume of data is generating every second, which results in several networking issues, such as latency, hence, recently, fog computing techniques are often embedded with the IoT platform [20–22]. Some researchers may focus on extending the battery life of the smart devices [18], while others may aim at designing a secure data transmission mechanism to protect the privacy and security of the subjects.

3 IoT for Healthcare: Technologies

3.1 Sensing Devices and Fog Devices

The introduction of IoT [27, 28] to healthcare is one of the major applications of IoT, and there have been massive projects, products, applications and services developed in the past decades. In general, IoT in healthcare is often developed for tracking the changes in their health parameters, such as vital signals, biomedical information, as well as behaviour and activity information, for better diagnosis and the higher quality of delivered healthcare services. Therefore, sensors and smart devices are the key enabler, which often include several categories: 1) wearable sensors for gathering vital signals, such as heartbeat sensor, blood pressure sensor etc.; 2) wearable sensors for collecting the body movement signal, such as accelerometer etc.; 3) ambient sensors for observing the environmental information and the interaction behaviours between the individual and other objects. Sensors are often designed with limited storage and computation capacity; hence sensor data are often transmitted to a centre sever or the Cloud for further processing. However, in many scenarios, large number of sensors are deployed, which generate massive amount of data that may lead to increased latency, heavy network traffic, and overload on the Cloud. Recently, many researchers introduced the fog computing to the IoT network, where sensor data can be processed immediately on the fog devices.

3.2 Communications

As mentioned above, sensor data are often transmitted to the Cloud or other processing unit, therefore, the wireless technologies are the fundamental, [26]. In the past few decades, a number of communication technologies have been developed and commonly embedded, depends on the various demand of different applications [16], as is depicted in Fig. 2. There are two categories of communication technologies, the licensed and unlicensed spectrums. On the other hands, the wireless technologies can often be divided as short-range (such as Bluetooth, ZigBee, Wi-Fi etc.) and wide-range (4G/5G, LoRa, NB-IoT etc.). ZigBee has been one of the most widely adopted short-range wireless technologies, with its low power consumption, lost cost, reliable connection, low data rate as well as massive connection. However, in many scenarios, a long-range connection is required, hence, 5G [25] and NB-IoT [29] have been extensively explored in recent few years.

5G [30] wireless communication technique is the next generation of cellular network, which has already been emerging from the previous 4G network, and it is expected to be deployed in the next decade worldwide. 5G technology promises a large number of existing features of which few of the key features are described below:

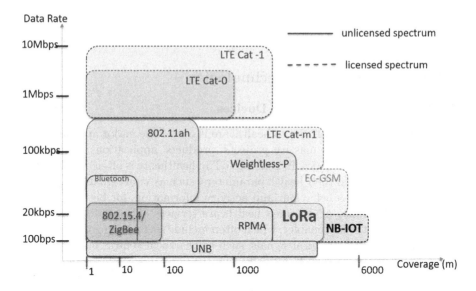

Fig. 2. Communication technologies for IoT

- the peak rate can reach up the 20 Gbit/s
- the user experienced date rate achieves up to 100 Mbit/s
- the Mobility can be improved to 500 km/h
- the user latency can be reduced to less than 1 ms
- the connection density can be increased to 106/km^2

In addition, 5G is also delivering a rich number of fundamental features such as machine type communication, device to device communication, smaller cells. Moreover, from the technology perspective, 5G implements massive MIMO advanced antenna techniques, adaptive beam-forming, flexible FDD/TDD sub-frame design, scalable OFDM numerology and modulation schemes and so on. Therefore, the deployment of 5G network enables many new use cases and applications that are not feasible to run over 4G network. In general, the 5G network enhances and expands three new scenarios, which are the enhances mobile broadband (eMBB), massive machine type communication (eMTC) and ultra-low latency and ultra-high reliability communication (URLLC). the 5G NB-IoT is officially introduced by 3GPP whilst is initialised from the NB-M2M techniques that developed by HuaWei in 2014. NB-IoT is designed as a low power wide-area network solution that operates in licensed spectrum bands as part of the LTE standards, thereby, it can be benefited from the ecosystem offered by traditional LTE technology and existing mobile operators. While on the other hands, data transmission fees must be paid to the corresponding operators. NB-IoT enables the connected devices communicate with each other through the cellular infrastructure, where 3GPP has allocated 180kHz bandwidth for NB-IoT. NB-IoT is designed to connect a massive number of devices in a wide range, with low power consumption and low data transmission rate. NB-IoT promising a number of key features as presented below:

- Massive Connection: NB-IoT enables massive connection about over 200k machines per cell.
- Low power consumption: NB-IoT is expected to prolong the battery life up to ten years with battery capacity of 5WH
- Extended coverage: NB-IoT targets to extends coverage of 20 dB compared to GPRS, which is expected to enable the advanced connection at underground or under water etc.
- Low data rate: NB-IoT covers 180 kHz bandwidth with the data rate can be range from 10 s of kbps to few hundreds of kbps.
- Low complexity: NB-IoT provides ultra-low complexity devices in many IoT scenarios to achieve ultra-low cost.

With the above-mentioned features, the NB-IoT devices can be heterogenous range from sensors, actuators, machines, vehicles and many other types. Therefore, NB-IoT promise a highly connected world which enables sensing, monitoring and controlling in many application scenarios in healthcare, agriculture, industry, environmental and so on.

3.3 Big Data

In many healthcare applications, the volume of data generated is astronomically high, Consequently, there is a requirement of massive data processing. Machine Learning (ML) is the most promising solution, where many of the ML algorithms have been implemented and evaluated.

4 IoT for Healthcare: A Case Study

In this case, we developed a smart home-based elderly health monitoring system as is illustrated in Fig. 3. It includes three main components, which are the sensor based smart home, the NB-IoT Cloud Server, and the Observer platform. Smart home is one of the most promising solution for remote health related monitoring, in particularly, for elderly and people with chronic disease, whilst be capable of maintaining a relatively independent life. One of the main goals of smart home solutions is to enable elderly or patients to stay in their own home for a longer period, rather than hospitals or nursing homes. Thereby, smart home based remote health monitoring solutions have been deeply investigated and widely deployed, to enable elderly and patients to maintain safer, healthier, and happier lives at their own homes, whilst to ensure their stakeholders.

In terms of remote monitoring, sensors are the core elements. A number of categories of sensors are commonly used in health monitoring, as is presented in Fig. 3, which is described below:

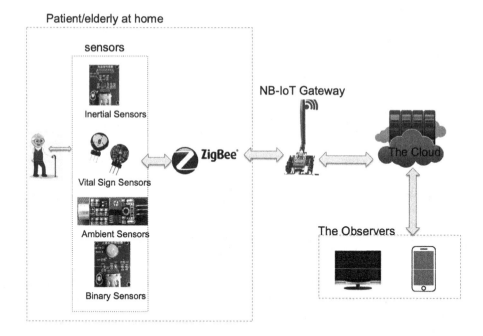

Fig. 3. The architecture of the NB-IoT based smart home monitoring platform

- Inertial Sensors: which often include the Accelerometers, gyroscope sensors and so on, in the healthcare domain, such sensors are often adopted for detecting body movements, for example, recognizing exercise levels, fall detection etc.
- Vital Sign Sensors, includes heart-beat sensors, blood pressure sensors, body temperature sensors and so on, which are utilised for measuring medical related parameters.
- Ambient Sensors, such as the temperature, humidity, smoke, light etc., which are often amounted for environmental monitoring, in assisted of further analysis.
- Binary Sensors, such as PIR sensors, magnetic contact sensors etc., which are often adopted for detecting interactions between the smart home residents and home appliances.

Sensors are often designed with limited computation capability and memory capacity, thereby, data generated by sensor are often transmitted to a data centre for further processing. In this case, data generated by the sensor nodes are transmitted to a NB-IoT gateway, and then transferred to a NB-IoT cloud server. NB-IoT offers the ability of low power consumption, long distance communication, which is one of the most favourable communication protocols for remote health monitoring.

5 Challenges and Future Works

IoT emphasises the connection of diverse physical and cyber devices and objects over the Internet, which enhances the communications and information sharing. In healthcare, various sensors, actuators, and other smart devices are commonly integrated. Such devices are responsible for gathering the health information of the subjects, their environment, as well as the interaction between them. With the networking and data processing advantages provided by the IoT framework, several benefits can be offered for healthcare applications, such as the reliable and scalable healthcare services, life time monitoring, efficient healthcare management, personalised recognition and prediction, international cooperation, as well as cost reduction. IoT technologies coordinate the patients, families, clinics, hospitals and various medical centres across various locations seamlessly, it promises intelligent and efficient healthcare services, whilst it is also presenting numbers of issues and challenges. A number of issues remains problematic, for example, within the IoT framework, heterogeneous devices with diverse platforms, communication protocols and data structures are often integrated, which may result in the compatibility issues. Secondly, IoT platforms are often deployed with dynamic environment, which requires the network topologies can be flexible, scalable and robust. Thirdly, a large IoT system may generate massive volume of data, thereby, massive data processing facilities must be provided. And Finally, the data security and privacy issue are also must be highlighted, a reliable encryption mechanism must be designed and adopted. A number of research avenue can be further explored. The commercial launch of 5G technology enables the fully, seamlessly connection of heterogeneous machines and devices, which will significantly empower the development and deployment of IoT- Healthcare applications. Secondly, machine learning techniques will also play an important role in massive data processing, as sensors and smart devices can generate massive volume of data every second. Big Data technology must be integrated with many IoT-healthcare applications. With the increasing size of the network with the growing number of sensing devices, the over-sized the data volume may lead to the heavy network traffic as well as delays and data loss, therefore, Fog computing could be a preferable solution to enable reliable and real-time services.

6 Conclusion

This paper presents a comprehensive review of IoT technologies in healthcare, mainly focused on the sensing and networking technologies. It discusses the advantages and disadvantages of few recent networking technologies. Moreover, the anthers develops a NB-IoT enabled healthcare framework, which allows real-time health monitoring of the subjects within the home context, meanwhile, established a Cloud based platform that allows other stakeholders to access related information.

Acknowledgement. This work is supported by NanTong Science and Technology Bureau under grant JC2018132 and National Natural Science Foundation of China under grant 62002179 within Nantong University China.

References

1. Firouzi, F., Farahani, B., Ibrahim, M., Chakrabarty, K.: Keynote paper: from EDA to IoT eHealth: promises, challenges, and solutions. IEEE Trans. Comput. Aided Des. Integr. Circuits Syst. **37**(12), 2965–2978 (2018)
2. Tokognon, C.A., Gao, B., Tian, G.Y., Yan, Y.: Structural health monitoring framework based on internet of things: a survey. IEEE Internet Things J. **4**(3), 619–635 (2017)
3. Yacchirema, D.C., Sarabia-JCome, D., Palau, C.E., Esteve, M.: A smart system for sleep monitoring by integrating IoT with big data analytics. IEEE Access **6**, 35988–36001 (2018)
4. Yang, G.: IoT-based remote pain monitoring system: from device to cloud platform. IEEE J. Biomed. Health Inform. **22**(6), 1711–1719 (2018)
5. Haghi, M.: A flexible and pervasive IoT-based healthcare platform for physiological and environmental parameters monitoring. IEEE Internet Things J. **7**(6), 5628–5647 (2020)
6. Xu, G.: IoT-assisted ECG monitoring framework with secure data transmission for health care applications. IEEE Access. **8**, 74586–74594 (2020)
7. Mostafa, H., Sebastian, N., Andre, G., Heidi, F., Norber, S., Kerstin, T.: A flexible and pervasive IOT-based healthcare platform for physiological and environmental parameters monitoring. IEEE Internet Things J. **7**(6), 5628–5647 (2020)
8. Ren, H., Jin, H., Chen, C., Ghayvat, H., Chen, W.: A novel cardiac auscultation monitoring system based on wireless sensing for healthcare. IEEE J. Transl. Eng. Health Med. **6**, 1–12 (2018)
9. Sundaravadivel, P., Kesavan, K., Kesavan, L., Mohanty, S.P., Kougianos, E.: Smart-log: a deep-learning based automated nutrition monitoring system in the IoT. IEEE Trans. Consum. Electron. **64**(3), 390–398 (2018)
10. Akay, B.: Human activity recognition based on parallel approximation kernel k-means algorithm. Comput. Syst. Sci. Eng. **35**(6), 441–456 (2020)
11. Kabir, M.H., Thapa, K., Yang, J., Yang, S.H.: State-space based linear modeling for human activity recognition in smart space. Intell. Autom. Soft Comput. **25**(4), 673–681 (2019)
12. Zhou, Z., Yu, H., Shi, H.: Human activity recognition based on improved Bayesian convolution network to analyze health care data using wearable IoT device. IEEE Access. **8**, 86411–86418 (2020)
13. Choe, S., Cho, W., Kim, J., Kim, A.K.: Reducing operational time complexity of k-NN algorithms using clustering in wrist-activity recognition. Intell. Autom. Soft Comput. **26**(4), 679–671 (2020)
14. Gumaei, A., Al-Rakhami, M., AlSalman, H.: DL-HAR: deep learning-based human activity recognition framework for edge computing. Comput. Mater. Continua **65**(2), 1033–1057 (2020)
15. Yang, G.: A health-IoT platform based on the integration of intelligent packaging, unobtrusive bio-sensor, and intelligent medicine box. IEEE Trans. Industr. Inf. **10**(4), 2180–2191 (2014)

16. Alam, M.M., Malik, H., Khan, M.I., Pardy, T., Kuusik, A., Moullec, Y.L.: A survey on the roles of communication technologies in IoT-based personalized healthcare applications. IEEE Access **6**, 36611–36631 (2018)

17. Ismail, W.N., Hassan, M.M., Alsalamah, H.A., Fortino, G.: CNN-based health model for regular health factors analysis in internet-of-medical things environment. IEEE Access **8**, 52541–52549 (2020)

18. Hooshmand, M., Zordan, D., Testa, D., Grisan, E., Rossi, M.: Boosting the battery life of wearables for health monitoring through the compression of biosignals. IEEE Internet Things J. **4**(5), 1647–1662 (2017)

19. Chen, Y., Sun, W., Zhang, N., Zheng, Q., Lou, W., Hou, Y.T.: Towards efficient fine-grained access control and trustworthy data processing for remote monitoring services in IoT. IEEE Trans. Inf. Forensics Secur. **14**(7), 1830–1842 (2019)

20. Verma, P., Sood, S.K.: Fog assisted-IoT enabled patient health monitoring in smart homes. IEEE Internet Things J. **5**(3), 1789–1796 (2018)

21. Kun, W., Yun, S., Lei, X., Jie, W., Song, G.: Adaptive and fault-tolerant data processing in healthcare IoT based on fog computing. IEEE Trans. Netw. Sci. Eng. **7**(1), 263–273 (2020)

22. Pathinarupothi, R.K., Durga, P., Rangan, E.S.: IoT-based smart edge for global health: remote monitoring with severity detection and alerts transmission. IEEE Internet Things J. **6**(2), 2449–2462 (2019)

23. Po, Y., et al.: Lifelogging data validation model for internet of things enabled personalized healthcare. IEEE Trans. Syst. Man Cybern. **48**(1), 50–64 (2018)

24. Kumar, A., Krishnamurthi, R., Nayyar, A., Sharma, K., Grover, V., Hossain, E.: A novel smart healthcare design, simulation, and implementation using healthcare 4.0 processes. IEEE Access. 1–39 (2020). (Online Access)

25. Abdul, A., Mohammad, T., Kok-lim, A.Y.: 5G-based smart healthcare network: architecture, taxonomy, challenges and future research directions. IEEE Access **7**, 100747–100762 (2019)

26. Yazdan, A.Q., Ali, N., Yousaf, B.Z., Athanasios, V.V., Sung, W.K.: The future of healthcare internet of things: a survey of emerging technologies. IEEE Commun. Surve. Tutor. **22**(2), 1121–1167 (2020)

27. Kumar, N.: IoT architecture and system design for healthcare systems. In: Smart-TechCon Proceedings, Bangalore, pp. 1118–1123 (2017)

28. Shaikh, Y. Parvati, V. K. Biradar, S. R.: Survey of smart healthcare systems using internet of things (IoT): (invited paper). In: IC3IoT Proceedings, Chennai, India, pp. 508–513 (2018)

29. Udhir, K.F., Sharath, A.: Narrowband IoT for healthcare. In: Proceedings of International Conference on Information Communication and Embedded Systems, pp. 1–4. IEEE, Chennai (2017)

30. Zhao, C., Wang, T., Yang, A.: A heterogeneous virtual machines resource allocation scheme in slices architecture of 5G edge datacenter. Comput. Mater. Continua **61**(1), 423–437 (2019)

A Pervasive Narrow-Band Internet of Things (NB-IoT) Based Health Monitoring Platform for Ambient Assisted Living

Xuran Jin, Shiqi Chen, Lulu Zhang, and Jie Wan$^{(\boxtimes)}$

Nantong University China, Nantong, China
jiewan@ntu.edu.cn

Abstract. The Internet of Things (IoT) has become a prominent technology is all aspects of human lives, especially in healthcare. As an assistive technology, IoT plays a crucial rule in medical, physical and environmental parameter monitoring, data transmitting and processing. IoT aims at integrate diverse and heterogeneous physical and cyber objects through the Internet, in order to enable the communication and data transmission among them. In terms of healthcare, a wide range of sensors, actuators, and smart devices are interconnected, which are either worn on or implanted in body, or distributed in the environment to collect rich information of the individual's physical or mental state. In addition, the wireless communication technologies are the key enablers, which allows reliable, secure, and efficient data transmission. Several wireless technologies have been widely adopted, such as Bluetooth, ZigBee, Wi-Fi etc. In this paper, a pervasive Narrow-Band Internet of Things (NB-IoT) enabled healthcare monitoring platform (NB-HIoT) is introduced.

Keywords: Narrow-band IoT · Healthcare · Ambient Assisted Living

1 Introduction

The Internet of Things (IoT) becomes a prominent technology that affect every artefacts of human's daily lives, in particularly, the healthcare [1,2]. IoT enables the immediate access to the information of the physical world and its objects, which in fact presents a network of almost every physical thing, such as the sensors, actuators, vehicles, and a diverse of devices. A typical Healthcare IoT (HIoT) solution may include several components, which are describe as follow:

- the IoT medical sensing devices such as sensors, actuators, and smart medical devices etc.

This work is supported by NanTong Science and Technology Bureau under grant JC2018132 and National Natural Science Foundation of China under grant 62002179 within Nantong University China.

X. Sun et al. (Eds.): ICAIS 2021, CCIS 1424, pp. 368–376, 2021.
https://doi.org/10.1007/978-3-030-78621-2_30

- the wireless communication network, where a number of communication standards may adopt such as WiFi, Bluetooth, 3G/4G/5G and so on. In many scenarios, it requires wide-area, low cost, low power consumption, massive connections, and low data rate communication technologies. The 3GPP 5G technologies introduced a new radio interface, which is the Narrow-band IoT (NB-IoT). NB-IoT is designed as low cost, low power consumption, low rate, wide area communication standards, which has been widely adopted for transmitting of small packet over the LTE network.
- the Cloud, where intelligent services may be implemented, such as situation recognition, emergency detection and notification and so on. Machine Learning, AI technologies are often adopted.

In this work, a Pervasive Narrow-band Internet of Things (NB-IoT) based health monitoring platform for Ambient Assisted Living (NB-HIoT) is introduced. The remaining of this paper is organised as follow:

Section 2 presented the related research in Healthcare IoT; Sect. 3 discusses the 5G Narrow Band Internet of Things Technologies in healthcare; whilst the design of NB-HIoT is illustrated in Sect. 4; then this paper is concluded in Sect. 5.

2   Related Research

Extensive efforts have been made to explore intelligent, accurate, reliable, secure healthcare services and products using the IoT technologies [3,5]. The existing works are mainly focused on monitoring and keep track of the elderly or patients in everyday lives. Several aspects have been widely investigated, such as medical or health parameter identification, behaviour and activity recognition [8,9], accidents and emergencies detection and prediction, emotion detection and so on [4]. The IoT technologies offers opportunities to monitoring life-logging data via a variety of assets, such as wearables, smart phones, as is presented in [6], the authors designed a rule based adoptive LPA validation model for eliminating irregular uncertainties and estimating data reliability in an IoT healthcare environment. Some researchers [7] aims at design a configurable and adaptable platform for comprehensive parameter monitoring, according to the convenient mode of wearability. In addition, some researchers implemented a IoT based healthcare platform, that supports decentralised and mobile monitoring of human's life style in either healthcare centre or the individual's home, which aims at identifying certain food and physical activity disorders [10].

However, the vast majority of the existing research works are based on standard IoT technologies, which demands the sensing and monitoring devices have relatively large processing and computation capacity. Recently, with the introduction of the NB-IoT techniques, the potential of adopting NB-IoT in healthcare has been emerging. Some researchers develop a NB-IoT enabled fall detection system based on wearable gyroscope sensor [11]. The work presented in [12] describes the general architecture of the NB-IoT enabled healthcare system. Compared to the standard IoT techniques, the main advantages of NB-IoT is its low power consumption, low complexity, and wide area communication. NB-IoT is designed for transmitting small data packages over the traditional LTE network, which is the ideal solution for transmitting sensor data in the healthcare domain. However, there has not been much work conducted and published in this area. Hence, in this paper, the NB-HIoT platform is illustrated.

3 5G Narrow-Band Internet of Things in Healthcare

5G wireless communication technique is the next generation of cellular network, which has already been emerging from the previous 4G network, and it is expected to be deployed worldwide in the next decade. 5G technology promises a large number of exciting features of which few key features include the peak rate reaches up to 20 Gbit/s, the mobility can be improved to 500 km/h, the connection density can be increased to 106/km^2, as well as the improved the user experience and shorter latency. A number of new techniques have been implemented in 5G network, such as massive MIMO advanced antenna techniques, adaptive beam-forming, flexible FDD/TDD subframe design, scalable OFDM numerology and modulation schemes and so on. Hence, 5G network enhances and expands three new scenarios, which are the enhanced mobile broadband (eMBB), massive machine type communication (eMTC) and ultra-low latency and ultra-high reliability communication (URLLC). Therefore, the deployment of 5G network enables many new use cases and applications that are not feasible to run over 4G network, such as auto-driven car, virtual reality etc., whereas healthcare is one of the typical scenarios [13].

NB-IoT [17] is officially introduced by 3GPP whilst is initialised from the NB-M2M techniques that developed by Huawei Ltd. in 2014. NB-IoT is designed as a low power wide-area network solution that operates in licensed spectrum bands as part of the LTE standards, thereby, it can be benefited from the ecosystem offered by traditional LTE technology and existing mobile operators. However, data transmission fees must be paid to the corresponding operators. NB-IoT enables the connected devices communicate with each other through the cellular infrastructure, where 3GPP has allocated 180 kHz bandwidth for NB-IoT. NB-IoT is designed to connect a massive number of devices in a wide range, with low power consumption and low data transmission rate [14,15]. NB-IoT promising a number of key features as presented below:

- Massive Connection: NB-IoT allows over 200k machines per cell.
- Low power Consumption: NB-IoT is expected to prolong the battery life up to ten years with battery capacity of 5 WH.
- Extended Coverage: NB-IoT targets to extends coverage of 20 dB compared to GPRS, which is expected to enable the advanced connection at underground or under water.
- Low Data Rate, NB-IoT covers 180 kHz bandwidth with the data rate can be range from 10 s of kbps to few hundreds of kbps.
- Low Complexity: NB-IoT provides ultra-low complexity devices in many IoT scenarios to achieve ultra-low cost and low power consumption.

With the above-mentioned features, the NB-IoT devices can be heterogenous range from sensors, actuators, machines, vehicles and many other types. Therefore, NB-IoT promise a highly connected world which enables sensing, monitoring and controlling in many application scenarios in healthcare, agriculture, industry, environmental and so on.

NB-IoT is an economical and simpler version of IoT, which emphasises the key feature of low power consumption, low complexity and wide area communication. Such features enable that NB-IoT can be embedded in many essential sectors of human lives, especially in healthcare. Several occasions can be explored, such as patients or elderly health monitoring, remote observation, emergency detection and so on. NB-IoT Sensors are often requisite to be deployed either on-body or in the immediate surroundings of the subjects.

4   The Design of NB-HIoT

In this paper, we presented a NB-IoT based pervasive health monitoring platform (NB-HIoT), as is illustrated in Fig. 1. The NB-HIoT is designed with four major components, which are the Ubiquitous Sensing module, the ZigBee &NB-IoT gateway, the Cloud Services, and the Internet Service.

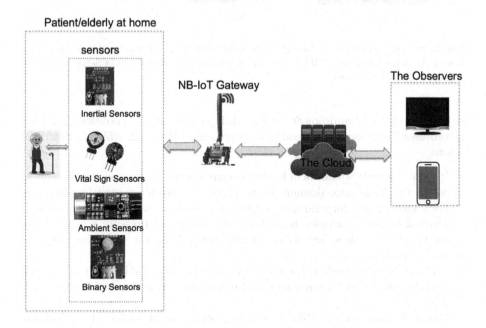

Fig. 1. The architecture of the NB-HIoT platform

4.1   NB-HIoT – Ubiquitous Sensing Module

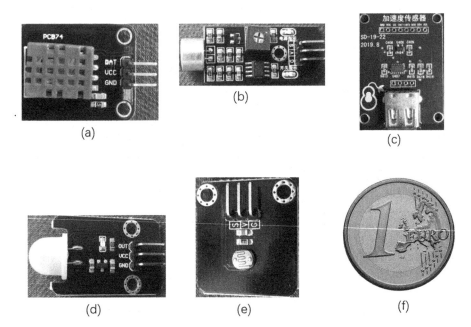

Fig. 2. Sensor Examples in NB-HIoT Sensing Module (a: Temperature & Humidity Sensor, b: Sound Sensor, c: 3D Accelerometer Sensor, d: PIR-Motion Sensor, e: Light Sensor, f: one Euro Corn)

In the NB-HIoT - Ubiquitous Sensing Module, sensors are the core elements. Four categories of sensors are embedded as is presented in Fig. 2, which is described below:

- Inertial Sensors: which include the accelerometers, gyroscope sensors and so on, in the healthcare domain, such sensors are often adopted for detecting body movements, for example, recognizing exercise levels, fall detection etc.
- Medical Sensors, includes heart-beat sensors, blood pressure sensors, body temperature sensors and so on, which are utilized for measuring medical related parameters.
- Ambient Sensors, such as the temperature, humidity, smoke, light etc., which are often deployed for environmental monitoring, in assisted of further analysis.
- Binary Sensors, such as PIR sensors, magnetic contact sensors etc., which are often adopted for detecting interactions between the elderly and other objects or devices.

A few sensor examples are illustrated in Fig. 2, which are described as below:

- a: Temperature & Humidity Sensor, which are adopted in each room to detect the temperature and humidity values.

- b: Sound Sensor, A number of sound sensors are deployed within the smart home to detect the noise level.
- c: 3D Accelerometer Sensor, such sensors are amounted on room and cabinet doors, windows etc. to recognizing the opening/closing status of the doors
- d: PIR-Motion Sensor, which are distributed within the smart home every few meters, to capture the motion and location information of the subjects.
- e: Light Sensor, which is installed in each room, to observing the light level.

4.2   NB-HIoT – Gateway

Sensors are often designed with limited computation capability and memory capacity, thereby, data generated by sensors will be transmitted to the Cloud server for further processing. For the communication technologies, two major protocols have been embedded in NB-HIoT platform, which are ZigBee and NB-IoT. As is illustrated in Fig. 3 where a is the NB-IoT module based on the Arduino platform, and b is the ZigBee module. The smart home sensor data can be transmitted to the gateway through ZigBee protocol, whilst the ZigBee module can be connected to the NB-IoT mote, therefor sensor data can be further transmitted to the Cloud Sever via NB-IoT techniques.

(b)

(a)

Fig. 3. NB-HIoT Gateway Modules (a: NB-IoT Communication Module, b: ZigBee Communication Module)

Both of them are low-cost, low power consumption, low-rate standards. The main advantages of ZigBee are that it supports diverse and flexible networking topologies, and it operates on the unlicensed frequencies, which is free of charge. However, ZigBee is a short-range communication protocol, due to its advantages of reliability, scalability and robust, ZigBee has been widely adopted in many scenarios and applications in Wireless Sensor Network (WSN), and recently, it is also been embedded in many IoT application. However, ZigBee is not compatible with the Internet protocol as well as not supporting the long-range communication, therefore, many wide-area communication techniques have been designed and integrated. NB-IoT is a recently emerging wide area communication standards, based upon the traditional LTE network, which is designed to transmit small packages over the network, however, a roaming fee must be paid to the network operators. Therefore, in NB-HIoT, both ZigBee and NB-IoT are embedded. Sensors in the Ubiquitous Sensing Module can transmit data to the ZigBee&NB-IoT gateway via ZigBee, and the gateway supports both ZigBee and NB-IoT, hence it will be able to collect all the sensor data and transmit data to the cloud server within one single frame.

4.3 NB-IoT – Cloud Service

The Cloud server plays several important roles, which are described below:

- a listening module, which is designed to collecting the data from the gateway.
- a SQL Server database is developed to store all the sensor data and the user profile data, which include the patient information, the doctors, and family members' information.
- an encryption mechanism is also developed and implemented to protect the sensor data and users privacy.

4.4 NB-IoT – Internet Services

This module is designed for a diverse of stakeholders such as the elderly themselves, the caretakers or family members and the doctors etc., to access the information in convenient means. Two main methods are developed. Authorised users can access the information either from the web services, or from the Android Applications.

5 Conclusion and Future Works

In this paper, we introduced a NB-IoT based pervasive healthcare monitoring platform for Ambient Assisted Living (NB-HIoT). A number of sensors are adopted for monitoring the physical and environmental information of the elderly, which include the wearable medical sensors, ambient environmental sensors and so on. Moreover, the low cost, low power consumption, reliable ZigBee standards is adopted and implemented to enhance a reliable and flexible sensor networks, whilst a NB-IoT standard is also embedded to transmit the sensor data to the Cloud. Furthermore, a Cloud based server is designed for data storage, management and further processing. In addition, an Internet service platform is integrated for authorised users to access the information. On the other hands, several aspects can be further explored. For example, adaptive and more flexible platform can be further developed, which allows self-configuration of the network. Secondly, more comprehensive and intelligent algorithms must be designed, which will be able to recognise the elderly's behaviours and emotions, detect accidents and emergency situation, diagnoses medical conditions and so on. Thirdly, along with the increasing number of embedded sensors or other smart devices, the fog computing technologies may be adopted to reduce the network traffic.

Acknowledgement. This work is supported by NanTong Science and Technology Bureau under grant JC2018132 and National Natural Science Foundation of China under grant 62002179 within Nantong University China.

References

1. Yazdan, A.Q., Ali, N., Yousaf, B.Z., Athanasios, V.V., Sung, W.K.: The future of healthcare internet of things: a survey of emerging technologies. IEEE Commun. Surv. Tutor. **22**(2), 1121–1167 (2020)
2. Naresh, V.S., Pericherla, S.S., Sita, P., Reddi, S.: Internet of things in healthcare: architecture, applications, challenges, and solutions. Comput. Syst. Sci. Eng. **35**(6), 411–421 (2020)
3. Kadhim, T.K., Ali, M.A., Salim, M.W., Hussein, T.K.: An overview of patient's healthcare status monitoring system based on Internet of Things. Wirel. Pers. Commun. (2020, early Access)
4. Vincent, S.A.: Effective and efficient ranking and re-ranking feature selector for healthcare analytics. Intell. Autom. Soft Comput. **26**(2), 261–268 (2020)
5. Mahntest, M.B., Savita, S.H.: Internet of Things based distributed healthcare systems: a review. J. Data Inf. Manag. (2020, Early Access)
6. Po, Y., et al.: Lifelogging data validation model for Internet of Things enabled personalized healthcare. IEEE Trans. Syst. Man Cybern. **48**(1), 50–64 (2018)
7. Mostafa, H., Sebastian, N., Andre, G., Heidi, F., Norber, S., Kerstin, T.: A flexible and pervasive IOT-based healthcare platform for physiological and environmental parameters monitoring. IEEE Internet Things J. **7**(6), 5628–5647 (2020)
8. Akay, B.: Human activity recognition based on parallel approximation kernel k-means algorithm. Comput. Syst. Sci. Eng. **35**(6), 441–456 (2020)
9. Kabir, M.H., Thapa, K., Yang, J., Yang, S.H.: State-space based linear modeling for human activity recognition in smart space. Intell. Autom. Soft Comput. **25**(4), 673–681 (2019)
10. Pace, P.: INTER-health: an interoperable IoT solution for active and assisted living healthcare services. In: 5th World Forum on Internet of Things (WF-IoT), Limerick, Ireland, pp. 81–86 (2019)
11. Wiraphon, M., Suvit, P., Panjai, T.: Narrowband-Internet of Things (NB-IoT) system for elderly healthcare services. In: 5th International Conference on Engineering. Applied Sciences and Technology (ICEAST), Luang Prabang, Laos, pp. 2–5 (2019)
12. Sudhir, K.R., Sharath, A.: Narrowband IoT for healthcare. In: International Conference on Information Communication and Embedded Systems (ICICES), Chennai, India, pp. 23–26 (2017)
13. Abdul, A., Mohammad, T., Kok-lim, A.Y.: 5G-based smart healthcare network: architecture, taxonomy, challenges and future research directions. IEEE Access **7**, 100747–100762 (2019)
14. Sung, M.O., Jaesheung, S.: An efficient small data transmission scheme in the 3GPP NB-IoT system. IEEE Commun. Lett. **21**(3), 660–663 (2017)

15. Pilar, A.M., Mads, L., Pablo, A., Juan, M.L.S.: Analytical modeling and experimental validation of NB-IoT device energy consumption. IEEE Internet Things J. **6**(3), 5691–5701 (2019)
16. Shaikh, Y., Parvati, V.K., Biradar, S.R.: Survey of smart healthcare systems using Internet of Things (IoT). In: IC3IoT, Chennai, India, pp. 508–513 (2018)
17. Udhir, K.F., Sharath, A.: Narrowband IoT for healthcare. In: International Conference on Information Communication and Embedded Systems, Chennai, India, pp. 1–4 (2017)

Design and Development of Mobile Monitoring System for Forest Fire Fighting

Minna Xia[1], Ying Wang[1]([✉]), and Kuan Wang[2]

[1] Hunan Automotive Engineering Vocational College, Zhuzhou 412000, China
[2] DHC Software Co., Ltd., Changsha 410000, China

Abstract. In the forest fire scene, the situation is complex and changeable, the front fireman and the rear command center will face the difficulties of field data delay, error transmission and so on, thus reducing the efficiency of fighting and fighting, endangering the life and safety of firefighters. It is necessary to design a device which can transmit the accurate data of the field environment to the rear command center in time, so as to provide the basis for the decision of fire fighting, and then shorten the time of fire fighting and improve the efficiency of fire fighting. According to the characteristics of forest fire, this paper analyzes the demand of information transmission before and after forest fire fighting, and puts forward the design plan. According to the demand analysis and the study of forest fire characteristics, the alternative hardware modules are compared and analyzed to determine the appropriate hardware, and the hardware of each sub-module is integrated and encapsulated to complete the physical design of mobile monitoring nodes. optimize the transmission mechanism in the process of fighting and fighting, so as to improve the efficiency and stability of communication transmission in the process of forest fire fighting and fighting. Based on the data fusion processing of temperature, humidity and smoke concentration, an early warning algorithm for mobile monitoring nodes is proposed. In the laboratory environment, suitable mobile communication technology, virtual simulation software and compilation environment were selected to simulate the monitoring and early warning of forest fire scene. The mobile monitoring device designed in this paper can effectively collect real-time data, including temperature, humidity and smoke concentration, and select the optimal base station and path.

Keywords: Forest fire · Rescue scene · Monitoring · Wireless sensor network

1 Introduction

Forest natural disasters are mainly pest, disease and fire, the destructive power and influence of forest fire in the first three disasters. Once a fire occurs, its wide coverage, destructive power, the difficulty of extinguishing are eye-popping.In the 1990s, the number of forest fires in the world increased by about 10% every five years, with an average of 70000 forest fires of different degrees every year; forest fire prevention is of great significance to the protection of existing forest resources [1]. Forest fire protection has always been a weak link in our country [2]. Forest fire is sudden, random and harmful. At

© Springer Nature Switzerland AG 2021
X. Sun et al. (Eds.): ICAIS 2021, CCIS 1424, pp. 377–390, 2021.
https://doi.org/10.1007/978-3-030-78621-2_31

the scene of forest fire, the life safety of front-line firefighters is seriously threatened, at the same time, the rear command personnel urgently need to understand the situation of the scene. Therefore, it is necessary to develop a new forest fire field monitoring system.

According to the characteristics of forest fire field, it has broad development prospect and unlimited research potential using wireless sensor module to monitor forest fire field [3–5].

Abroad, the forest fire risk prediction system (EFFRFS) based on satellite remote sensing and computer technology has covered the whole of Europe [6]. digital radio station and ground information transmission system transmit the image information of the fire scene back to the command center. the command center can project the forest fire situation to the large screen. The image and GIS analysis from the scene get the forest fire situation to switch, and provide the reasonable command and rescue decision to the command center [7]. Through the timely meteorological data collected by the forest land small weather station, combined with the climate and combustible characteristics of the forest area, and then according to the expert database model, the forest fire registration data of the corresponding area are estimated [8]. Wireless sensor network is a new generation of sensor networks, and has a very broad application prospects. Nowadays, countries all over the world attach great importance to the research of wireless sensor networks [9–11].

At home, the rapid development of science and technology has created the possibility for many high-tech applications in forest fire prevention research, such as aerospace technology, high elimination or technology, especially information technology has been widely used in the field of forest fire protection. The use of wireless sensor networks for forest fire prevention monitoring has broad development prospects and great research potential [4, 12, 13]. Nowadays, in the field of forest fire prevention technology research in the world, the prediction of forest fire, the regulation of stand fire resistance and other technologies are more in-depth [14].

With the increasing proportion of forest fire prevention plate in social disaster prevention and mitigation, forest fire prevention uses high and new technology to increase the comprehensive defense and control ability of forest fire, and to improve the information technology content of forest fire and the scientific, effective and timely command of fire fighting [15]. In the process of forest fire occurrence and rescue, through wireless monitoring nodes, the field environmental data are continuously detected and transmitted back to the command center in time, so as to effectively organize the rescue activities and improve the efficiency of rescue and rescue [16].

2 Analysis of Environmental Monitoring and Early Warning of Forest Fire Fighting and Its Overall Scheme

2.1 Requirements Analysis

Large-scale disasters such as forest fire, wind direction and wind speed change rapidly, fire point and fire unpredictable, each forest topography and existing resources are also different, the command center to formulate a rescue plan need to have objective data as the basis [17]. A mobile and wearable monitoring and warning transmission node is designed to grasp the danger situation of the fire scene so as to obtain the situation of the fire scene and ensure the personal safety of the firefighters, so that the data can be communicated in time, so that the command center can make the correct decision after effective data analysis, and finally reduce the cost of forest fire fighting and reduce the economic losses caused by the fire.

According to the above requirements, the scheme considers these three aspects: first, firefighters can wear and move the forest fire monitoring node; second, the transmission mechanism of forest fire fighting environment monitoring and early warning is optimized; third, the realization and application of forest fire fighting environment monitoring and early warning.

1. Design of Mobile Monitoring Node for 1. Forest Fire Fighting Environment

   For the monitoring of forest fire fighting environment, there are many kinds of hardware and technology that can be selected. the overall design scheme of the node should fully consider the working efficiency in the forest fire environment. the selected module hardware should be as simple and practical as possible and easy to implement. the selected hardware also needs to refer to the appropriate parameters, stable performance, low cost and better compatibility performance [18].

   According to the characteristics of monitoring nodes in this paper, the design requirements of mobile monitoring nodes are summarized as follows:

   (1) Small size. (2) High reliability. (3) Low cost. (4) Strong scalability.

2. Transmission mechanism of mobile monitoring nodes for forest fire fighting environment

   Forest fire, because of its wide spread, sudden strong, more on-site rescue personnel, complex situation, chaotic order, need stable and fast transmission speed, wide coverage of communication technology to achieve signal transmission.In fact, mobile communication technology is more suitable for mobile monitoring and early warning in forest fire fighting scene. Mobile communication technology includes data transmission technology such as wireless communication system GSM, GPRS and CDMA.

3. Realization and Application of 3. Forest Fire Environment Monitoring and Early Warning

   This paper is to monitor the environmental data of forest fire fighting scene by moving the monitoring node, which can directly and easily show the change of environmental indexes and transmit them back to the command center through the signal station in time. In order to meet the needs of mobile monitoring nodes for application software, and can coordinate between software and hardware to achieve the best results. The following principles should be followed in software design:

   (1) Real-time (2) Reliability (3) Flexibility.

2.2 Programme Design

The overall structure of environmental monitoring and early warning design for forest fire fighting is shown in Fig. 1.

In the case of complex forest fire, the information transmission between the front firefighters and the rear command center is not timely and accurate, which may cause

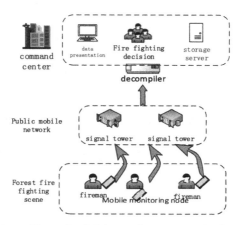

Fig. 1. Structure of forest fire fighting environment monitoring and warning.

great economic losses. Therefore, it is necessary to effectively monitor and warn the data of forest fire fighting scene, and use all kinds of sensors to collect the temperature and humidity of forest fire scene, harmful gas, fireman position and other information to transmit back to the command center in time and accurately, and form a complete monitoring and early warning system [19]. Real-time monitoring and early warning can not only realize the effective information transmission between the front and the command center, but also can monitor whether the warning is in a dangerous environment and protect the life safety of the firemen in front to a great extent.

3 Design of Mobile Monitoring Node for Forest Fire Fighting Environment

3.1 Hardware Selection of Forest Fire Mobile Monitoring Node

Before the real-time data monitoring and transmission in the forest by the mobile acquisition node network in the forest fire environment, the hardware and software basic configuration of the wireless sensor network should be completed first. After programming, the sensor nodes need to be encapsulated, and the nodes must meet certain requirements: first, the package must be waterproof and corrosion-proof, the environment in the forest is more complex, the wet environment or rainfall may cause damage to the nodes, so the waterproof package is necessary; secondly, the hardware of the node must be high-temperature resistant, able to work stably at higher temperature; Finally, the package of nodes must maintain good air flow, temperature and humidity sensor and smoke sensor perception data will not be distorted. Encapsulated sensor nodes are embedded into the firemen's clothing in a certain way, and self-organized network is carried out between each node, and then the real-time monitoring data is transmitted back to the base station.

This design selects C51 series AT89C51 model single chip microcomputer to carry on the integration. The A T89C51 chip developed by American A TMEL Company has 40 pins. For the screen display requirement in this paper, only a very few word banks are needed, and the 4 KB flash memory module in the A T89C51 can meet the requirements of word bank storage without adding external memory.

This design is selected DS18B20 digital temperature sensor, it is a single bus digital temperature sensor developed by DALLAS company. Compared with other temperature sensors, DS18B20 has the advantages of small size, small power consumption, strong anti-interference ability and strong compatibility performance. It is widely used in the field of high precision temperature measurement system and is suitable for such harsh environment as forest fire. DS18B20 temperature sensor works stably in forest environment and forest fire fighting environment.

A HS1101 humidity sensor is used in this design, which is equivalent to a variable capacitance in the circuit, and its capacitance increases with the increase of humidity in the measured environment. In general, there are two methods to accurately convert the change of capacitance into the digital signal acceptable to the main chip: one is to connect the wet-sensitive capacitance to the bridge oscillation circuit composed of the operational amplifier and the capacitance resistance, the sinusoidal voltage signal generated by DC amplification is converted into digital signal transmission through digital-analog conversion; the other is to connect the wet-sensitive capacitance into the 555 oscillation circuit, convert the change value of capacitance to the voltage frequency signal of inverse ratio, and then transmit it to the single chip microcomputer for data processing.

This design is MQ2 smoke sensor, is the lower conductivity in the air metal oxide tin dioxide ($SnO)2$) N semiconductor gas sensor. MQ-2 smoke sensor must convert the collected smoke concentration analog signal through the ADC0808 chip into an identifiable digital signal if it wants to transmit the collected smoke concentration analog signal to the main chip.

This design selected display module is mainly composed of 128 x6464 liquid crystal display screen and its driving circuit, through the main chip AT89C51 drive 12864 display Chinese characters and numbers, showing data including ambient temperature, humidity, smoke concentration and danger level.

This design selects the system is based on SIMCOM company's SIM800M2M wireless communication module project research and development. SIM800 is a four-frequency GSM/GPR module. The SIM800 frequency of wireless communication is GSM/GPRS 850/900/1800/1900MHz, can be used globally, and the transmission of voice, SMS and data information can be realized with low power consumption.

The SIM800 is mainly composed of six parts: digital baseband (DBB), analog baseband (ABB), RF transmission module (RF), power management (PMU), storage and interface. The DBB and peripherals mainly realize the functions of digital baseband signal processing, GSM/GPRS protocol stack, software platform, application sub-application and peripheral management. ABB and peripheral parts mainly realize analog and digital signal conversion and codec processing, charging, backlight, Audio and Voice codec functions; RF part mainly completes GSM signal up/down frequency conversion, filtering, power amplification, transceiver switching and other functions; PMU is mainly to provide the main chip required, all, multi-grade and different voltage supply, Like processors, RF devices, storage modules, (b) To enable the units to function properly; Storage mainly includes ROM and RAM, ROM for storing code and data, RAM is mainly used to store read and write data in operation. The interface part is mainly an analog and digital interface with different functions, The analog interface has audio input and output, ADC wait. The audio interface can be connected Speaker (speaker) and MIC (microphone). The digital interface has the GPIO, UART, SIM card, the USB, KEY, PCM, SPI, SD and so on interface, so that the module can be connected to various external devices.

3.2 Integration and Encapsulation of Mobile Monitoring Node for Forest Fire Fighting Environment

Monitoring Node Integration. According to the selection of main chips and sensors, a node design of forest fire environment monitoring based on AT89C51 control module can be obtained. The main control module is provided by the power supply module, which has the function of reading, writing and storing environmental data, clock timing function, environmental data display function and early warning function after abnormal environmental data. A wireless sensing module is composed of each sensor, and the data is transmitted through the serial port and the main control module. Finally, the main control module transmits the processed data through the GPRS communication module to the rear command center. The integrated construction of mobile monitoring nodes is shown in Fig. 2.

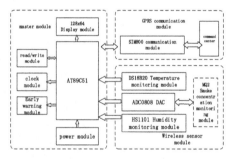

Fig. 2. Schematic diagram of mobile monitoring node integration.

Monitoring Node Encapsulation. When forest fire occurs, the site belongs to high temperature and high corrosive environment, and the field wind direction can not be predicted. In order to ensure the normal and stable operation of the monitoring node, the core circuit integrated board should be encapsulated with special high temperature and corrosion resistance material.

Nano-modified high-temperature, corrosion-resistant and energy-saving metal coating is a kind of modified inorganic binder polymerized with polymer. The coating film is formed on the metal matrix, solidified at room temperature, hard, dense and hydrophobic after curing, and insoluble in water. sintering to 200 °C can achieve ideal hardness, strength and density. A metal coated with MES-I, is used to resist high temperature and corrosion.

4   Realization and Application of Monitoring and Early Warning Function of Forest Fire Fighting Environment

4.1   Mobile Monitoring Node Development Environment

Keil C51 is the C language development system developed by American Keil Software Company for 51 single chip microcomputer, Unlike assembly languages, C language has the characteristics of simple structure, readability, maintainability, etc. and thus received more extensive applications. Keil comes with a complete development plan that includes C compiler, macro assembly, linker, library management, and a powerful simulation debugger. combine these parts through an integrated development environment (μVision). Keil current compatible system has NT, WINDOWS series etc.

Keil software companies release Keil μVision4,Keil μVision4 introduce flexible window management systems that allow programmers to perform multiple monitors, providing a neat, efficient platform to develop related programs.

Keil μVision4 generation target program high efficiency, generation code structure clear, easy to understand. In the development of large-scale software can reflect the advantages of high-level language.

4.2   Mobile Monitoring Node Simulation Operating Environment

Design and research of this paper will test the running effect by analog circuit on protues software. Proteus is an analog simulation software developed by the British Labcenter Electronics Company. The software comes with more than 30 model libraries. There are more than 8,000 analog components, which can simulate analog and digital circuits. Debugging tools inside the software are powerful, can debug Keil, MPLAB and other development source programs, can also observe the changes of registers and memory, the program in the simulation circuit real-time operation, but also the button, display screen, keyboard and other interactive visualization equipment simulation.

Proteus software is divided into two modules Proteus VSM (virtual system simulation software) and P roteus PCB Design (printed circuit board design software).

From the original principle circuit diagram design, to circuit analysis and simulation, circuit system module testing, to the final generation PCB design drawing folder, are implemented by two modules Proteus VSM (virtual system simulation software) and P roteus PCB Design (printed circuit board design software).P rotues are characterized by:

(1) Analog circuit simulation, digital circuit simulation and analog and digital circuit mixed simulation can be carried out.
(2) The simulation system also has the functions of full speed, single step, setting breakpoint and so on. It can observe the state of each variable and register.
(3) With a variety of virtual modules, such as oscilloscope, logic analysis module, signal generator.
(4) Has powerful schematic drawing function.

4.3   Research on Early Warning Algorithm of Mobile Monitoring Node

The accuracy of the early warning behavior of the monitoring node is of great significance to the firefighters in front, and the false warning will delay the normal development of the forest fire fighting work, and the delayed warning will bring hidden danger to the firefighters' personal safety. In this section, the monitoring temperature, humidity and smoke concentration of three groups of data are fused, and the environmental safety level in forest fire fighting is divided into three levels: safety, general and danger. Appropriate hazard environment judgment algorithm is used to achieve accurate hazard warning. Its implementation process is shown in Fig. 3.

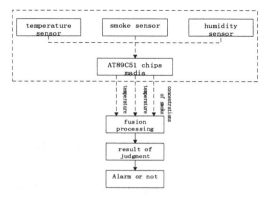

Fig. 3. Realization process of early warning algorithm.

The algorithm is judged according to three parameters: temperature value t (unit °C), humidity value h (unit%), smoke concentration g (unit%). Because MQ2 smoke concentration sensor monitors the data is analog information, it needs to be converted to digital signal for discrimination. VRL can be calculated from $logR = mlogC + n$ (m = 1/2, n constant) and $R = (Vc/VRL-1)$.

Criterion process of environmental safety rating:

After opening the mobile monitoring node, the current environment is "safe" when the following conditions are satisfied:

t < 40 °C;

2 h > 40%;

3 g < 0.4%;

When any of the following conditions is satisfied, the environment is judged to be "general":

°C1 40 °C ≤ t ≤ 50;

2 20 ≤ h ≤ 40%;

3.4% ≤ g ≤ 1%;

Firemen need to keep an eye on peripheral anomalies and notify their peers.

The environment is judged to be "dangerous" when any of the following conditions is satisfied:

t > 50°C;

2 h < 20%;
3 g > 1%;
This means that the environment is extremely dangerous, and the early warning module of the monitoring node begins to alert firefighters in front of the scene to need immediate evacuation and help.

4.4   Function Implementation of Mobile Monitoring Node

The mobile monitoring node is mainly composed of 6 parts. After the node is opened, the system is initialized, and then each function is started: temperature acquisition module, humidity acquisition module, smoke concentration acquisition module, early warning function module, data display module, data transmission module. The temperature acquisition module first collects the forest fire scene temperature data by the DS18B20 sensor and transmits back to the main chip to make the condition judgment, if beyond the pre-set warning range, the early warning module alerts the front firefighters; the humidity acquisition module first collects the forest fire scene humidity data through the HS1101 sensor and transmits back to the main chip to make the condition judgment, if beyond the pre-set warning range, the early warning module alerts the front firefighters; The smoke concentration acquisition module first collects the smoke concentration data in the forest fire scene through the MQ2 sensor, and converts the analog data into digital data through the ADC0808 chip to transmit back to the main chip for conditional judgment. If it exceeds the pre-set warning range, the warning module alerts the front firefighters. Each module stores the collected data through the main chip and transmits it to the wireless transmission module. At this time, the wireless receiving module of the command center receives the instant data and finally reaches the command center server storage. The flow chart of its main program is shown in Fig. 4 below:

Temperature Detection Module. The temperature detection module subroutine is mainly responsible for starting the temperature sensor DS18B20 to work, writing commands to the sensor through serial communication mode, and reading the temperature, storing the value to the P3.1 port. The flow chart of the temperature monitoring subroutine is shown in Fig. 5:

A schematic diagram of the circuit connections on the P rotues is shown below:

Humidity Sensing Module. The humidity sensor module subroutine is mainly responsible for starting the humidity sensor HS1101 to carry on the work, writes the command to the sensor through the serial port communication mode, reads the temperature, stores the value to the P2.7 port, the humidity detection subroutine flow chart is shown in Fig. 7 (Fig. 6):

A schematic diagram of the circuit connections on the P rotues is shown in Fig. 8:

Smoke Concentration Sensing Module

Smoke concentration sensor module subroutine is mainly responsible for starting smoke concentration sensor MQ2 to work, Write commands to the sensor via serial communication, And read the temperature, But because the data MQ2 read is analog, A digital-to-analog conversion chip is required ADC0808 perform a digital-to-analog conversion.

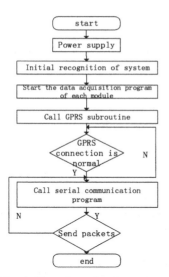

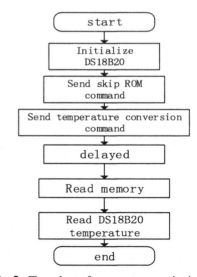

Fig. 4. Flow chart of main program.   **Fig. 5.** Flow chart of temperature monitoring subroutine.

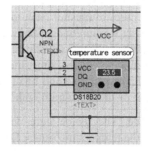

Fig. 6. DS18B20 temperature sensor simulation diagram.

Converting the detected analog signal to the extracted digital signal of the main chip, Then store the OUT1-OUT8 eight digits to the P 1.0-P1.7 port, Eight bits in order OUT8 the highest bit, OUT1 lowest, The flow chart of the smoke concentration.

Monitoring subroutine is shown in Fig. 9:

A schmatic diagram of the circuit connections on the P rotues is shown in Fig. 10:

Display Module. The display module subroutine is mainly responsible for starting 128 × 64 display screen to work, writing commands to the display screen through serial port communication mode, displaying the timely data of the forest fire fighting scene detected by the mobile monitoring node on the screen, and the schematic diagram of the circuit connection on the P rotues is shown in Fig. 11:

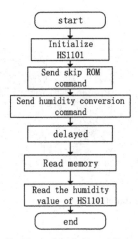

Fig. 7. Flow chart of humidity monitor.

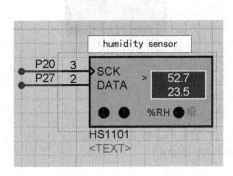

Fig. 8. HS1101 humidity sensor simulation diagram.

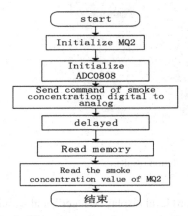

Fig. 9. Flow chart of smoke concentration monitor.

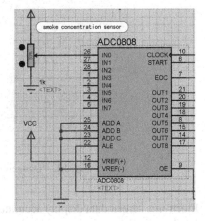

Fig. 10. HS1101 humidity sensor simulation diagram.

4.5 Simulation Operation and Results

Under the forest environment, when the mobile monitoring node is turned on, the circuit is turned on, and each sub-module starts to run. The current forest temperature is set to 23.5 °C, the humidity is set to 52.7 RH%, the smoke concentration is set to 0.3 ppm, then the simulation results are shown in Fig. 12 below:

The electronic screen shows normal, the danger level shows "safe", and the warning module does not alarm at this time.

Electronic screen data display accurate, hazard level display "general", and warning module at this time no alarm.

When the measured temperature is 62.4 °C, humidity is 19.5 RH%, smoke concentration is 1.1 ppm, the simulation results are shown in Fig. 13 below:

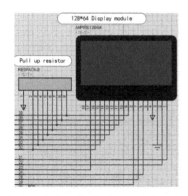

Fig. 11. 128×64 display module simulation diagram.

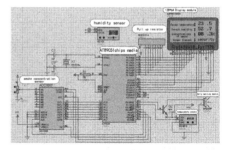

Fig. 12. Simulation results of safety.

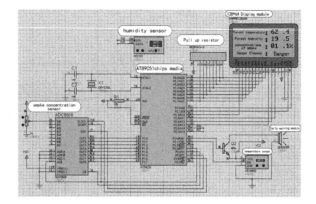

Fig. 13. "Dangerous" simulation results.

Electronic screen data display accurate, hazard level display "danger", and warning module began to alarm.

From this we can see that the monitoring and early warning of forest fire fighting environment is simulated on the protues software to achieve accurate data, and the function is basically realized.

5 Conclusions and Discussions

Based on the analysis of wireless sensor network technology, this paper analyzes and studies the development of current forest fire scene detection technology, and proposes a portable mobile wireless sensor node for detecting environmental data of forest fire scene. The current wireless sensor network technology is applied to the real-time monitoring and early warning of fire, and the four parameters of temperature, humidity, smoke concentration and fireman position are realized to monitor, warn and transmit. A forest fire monitoring and early warning system is set up by several mobile monitoring nodes. The system has the characteristics of fast transmission, accurate data and real-time.

Through these studies, the following theoretical and practical results are obtained:

(1) Reasonable design of mobile acquisition nodes in forest fire fighting environment by using the characteristics and principle of wireless sensor network. The wireless sensing network is established to meet the monitoring and early warning in forest fire fighting environment. To AT89C51 the wireless sensing network composed of main control chip, DS18B20 temperature sensor, HS1101 humidity sensor, MQ2 smoke concentration sensor and SIM800GPRS communication module, it can improve the monitoring accuracy, transmission efficiency and reduce hardware loss.

(2) According to the design requirements of forest fire environment monitoring and early warning system, the system function is developed by software, combined with the development environment and simulation tools, the system function is simulated and displayed, and finally the system simulation effect is evaluated.

However, from theory to practice, the following problems remain to be solved:

Portable mobile monitoring nodes;
Research on high power and low power modules;
Research on timely switching of multiple transmission modes.

With the development of technology, each functional module will be continuously improved and optimized, and it is believed that the monitoring and early warning system for forest fire fighting will be continuously upgraded, and the performance will be continuously improved, which will bring more far-reaching effects to the harmony between human beings and nature.

Funding Statement. This research is supported by Scientific research project of Hunan Education Department (20C0997).

References

1. Zhu, H., Zhu, J.: Research on auxiliary decision system of forest fire fighting based on GIS. J. Nat. Disast. **8**(1), 60–70 (1999)
2. Qiao, Q.: A study on the system of fire-fighting equipment in water-extinguishing forest. J. Beijing For. Univ. **Z1**, 191–195 (2002)
3. Hefeeda, M., Bagheri, M.: Forest fire modeling and early detection using wireless sensor networks. Ad Hoc Sens. Wirel. Netw. **7**(3), 169–224 (2009)
4. Lloret, J., Garcia, M., Bri, D., Sendra, S.: A wireless sensor network deployment for rural and forest fire detection and verification. Sensors **9**(11), 8722–8746 (2009)
5. Yu, L., Wang, N., Meng, X.: Real-time forest fire detection with wireless sensor networks. In: International Conference on Wireless Communications (2005)
6. Katie, A.H., Joseph, D., Clark, R., Dwayne, E., et al.: Direct and indirect effects of fire on eastern box turtles. Wildlife **84**(7), 1384–1395 (2020)
7. Casas, K.T., Arnulf, J.K.: Are Chinese teams like western teams? Indigenous management theory to leapfrog essentialist team myths. Front. Psychol. **11**, 1758 (2020)
8. Chuvieco, E., Congalton, R.G.: Application of remote sensing and geographic information systems to forest fire hazard mapping. Remote Sens. Environ. **29**(2), 147–159 (1989)

9. Banerjee, T., Sharma, P., Pradhan, S.: Consensus based data aggregation for energy conservation in wireless sensor network. Int. J. Distrib. Parallel Syst. **11**(5), 11–26 (2020)
10. Zhang, Z., Zhang, Y.: Application of wireless sensor network in dynamic linkage video surveillance system based on Kalman filtering algorithm. J. Supercomput. **75**(9), 6055–6069 (2019)
11. Zhou, X., Peng, T.: Application of multi-sensor fuzzy information fusion algorithm in industrial safety monitoring system. Saf. Sci. **122**, 256–264 (2020)
12. Sun, L., Li, J., Chen, Y., Zhu, H.: Wireless Sensor Network. Tsinghua University Press, Beijing (2005)
13. Jang, E., Kang, Y., Im, J., et al.: Detection and monitoring of forest fires using himawari-8 geostationary satellite data in South Korea. Remote Sens. **11**(3), 1694 (2019)
14. Yu, L., Wang, N., Meng, X.: Real-time Forst Fire Detection with Wireless Sensor Networks. In: International Conference, pp. 1214–1217 (2005)
15. Chen, S.: High efficient combination of fire extinguishing technologian forest fire fighting. J. Beijing For. Univ. **29**(Z2), 120–124 (2007)
16. Ma, H.: The construction of comprehensive command platform for fire prevention and fighting in forests and grasslands in the new era. For. Mach. Woodwork. Equip. **48**(7), 54–58 (2020)
17. Zhu, H., Gao, D., Zhang, S.: A perceptron algorithm for forest fire prediction based on wireless sensor networks. J. Internet Things **1**(1), 25–31 (2019)
18. Wang, J., Chen, W., Wang, L., Ren, Y., Sherratt, R.S.: Blockchain-based data storage mechanism for industrial internet of things. Intell. Autom. Soft Comput. **26**(5), 1157–1172 (2020)
19. Xu, Z., Zhou, Q.: Industrial informatics-based applications and techniques in intelligent automation. Intell. Autom. Soft Comput. **26**(5), 1005–1006 (2020)

ZigBee Wireless Network Attack and Detection

Taifeng Pan[✉] [ID]

Beijing University of Posts and Telecommunications, Beijing 100876, China
pantaifeng@bupt.edu.cn

Abstract. With the large-scale use of ZigBee technology in industry and smart home system, the security problems of ZigBee emerge gradually. And people pay more and more attention to ZigBee security. In view of the lack of a mature Zig-Bee attack detection product in the market, this paper will research on ZigBee and design a simple ZigBee attack detection system. First, according to some internal operation mechanisms of ZigBee protocol, we analyze the potential attack threats on ZigBee during its operation, and propose four specific attacks including association attack, replay attack, network PANID conflict attack and malicious orphan frame attack. Then we propose corresponding detection schemes for those four attacks. Besides, we point out two possible vulnerabilities in ZigBee Network: network short address conflict vulnerability and association table vulnerability. Finally, we design a ZigBee attack detection system which is divided into three parts: device scanning module, attack detection module and vulnerability detection module. The system has the characteristics of rapid deployment and rapid detection. It can meet some simple security requirements of a ZigBee application scene.

Keywords: IoT · Wireless network security · ZigBee · Attack detection

1 Introduction

ZigBee [1] is a wireless network protocol with low speed and short distance transmission. Its bottom layer is the media access layer and physical layer based on IEEE 802.15.4 standard. Its main features are low power consumption, low cost, supporting a large number of network nodes, supporting a variety of network topologies, low complexity, fast and reliable [1, 2]. Due to these advantages, ZigBee has become the primary technology implementation of sensor networks and smart home devices.

However, the large-scale use of ZigBee in industrial and smart home systems makes the security problems of ZigBee emerge gradually. Because of the particularity of ZigBee wireless sensor network, the traditional network security strategy is difficult to be directly applied to this type of network. In view of this situation, it is necessary to put forward the corresponding security protection scheme for ZigBee to resist the attack of ZigBee network.

In 2004, Yuan Yi and Su Honggen [3] discussed the characteristics and application fields of ZigBee technology, and proposed a method of device identity authentication using license technology in ZigBee wireless network. In 2009, Xu et al. [4]

© Springer Nature Switzerland AG 2021
X. Sun et al. (Eds.): ICAIS 2021, CCIS 1424, pp. 391–403, 2021.
https://doi.org/10.1007/978-3-030-78621-2_32

studied the security problems of data transmission in ZigBee wireless network based on IEEE802.15.4. and proposed the development of ZigBee wireless network in the future. At the information security conference in 2009, Joshua Wright [5] released a public tool KillerBee, to evaluate the security of ZigBee technology. In 2010, at the black hat conference in Barcelona, Spain, the wireless sensor network attack tool sensys [6] was released to study the security vulnerabilities of wireless sensor networks. In 2013, Xiao et al. [7] analyzed and summarized common interference attack detection methods for wireless sensor networks and proposed a consistency detection method combining signal strength and retransmission rate. In 2016, Huang et al. [8] studied the characteristics of Sybil attacks in ZigBee networks and proposed corresponding attack detection schemes. In 2016, Yue Quan [9] analyzed three traditional virus transmission models and random immunization, target immunization and acquaintance immunization strategies. Based on the traditional virus propagation model, a new Sid virus propagation model is proposed. In 2017, Shi Yanqing et al. [10] studied the anti wormhole attack method of ZigBee network, designed the defense and detection scheme, and finally implemented a Zigbee network anti wormhole attack prototype system. In 2017, Bi Ganbin [11] proposed an optimization scheme for AES algorithm according to the characteristics of ZigBee communication, that is, to speed up the encryption speed as much as possible when the security and storage resources meet the requirements of ZigBee confidential communication. In 2019, He Kuan and Yu Bin [12] proposed an "on-demand interference attack" detection scheme to solve the problem of disrupting normal network communication caused by "on-demand interference attack" in ZigBee network, which enhanced the security performance of ZigBee network.

The scholars above have invested a lot of effort and made great contributions to ZigBee security. However, many of the current research is inclined to the underlying problem or based on a specific type of ZigBee attack, they can achieve good detection results in a specific attack. But in a complex attack scene, attackers often implement not only one attack, but also multiple attacks in turn or even at the same time to destroy ZigBee network. There is no deep mechanism behind these attack methods. Attackers may just use several simple attack modes to attack. In fact, simple attacks account for a large proportion of all attack schemes, and they are also the main culprit of network security system damage. Therefore, we should not only study complex attack means, but also analyze and summarize the conventional attack methods, and give detection scheme for them. The main contributions of this articles are as follows.

Firstly, according to some internal operation mechanisms of ZigBee protocol, we analyze the potential attack threats on ZigBee during its operation, and propose four possible attacks specifically. Then we propose corresponding detection schemes for those four attacks. In addition, we point out two possible vulnerabilities in ZigBee Network: network short address conflict vulnerability and association table vulnerability. Finally, we design a ZigBee attack detection system which is divided into three parts: device scanning module, attack detection module and vulnerability detection module. The detailed function and implementation of each module will be introduced later. The system can be rapidly deployed and operate detection function in the production environment.

2 Basic Knowledge of ZigBee

ZigBee devices can be divided into full function device (FFD) and reduced function device devices(RFD) [13]. The full function device can be used as coordinator, router and terminal device, while the reduced function device can only be used for terminal device. ZigBee has defined a total of 27 physical channels, and the specific channel allocation is shown in Table 1 [4, 14].

Table 1. Frequency distribution of ZigBee channel

Channel	Frequency/MHz	Upper limit/MHz	Lower limit/MHz
k = 0	868.3	868.6	868.0
k = 1, 2, 3…10	906 + 2(k − 1)	928.0	902.0
k = 11, 12, 13…26	2401 + 5(k − 11)	2483.5	2400.0

ZigBee network topology mainly includes star network, tree network and mesh network [13]. Star topology is the simplest form of topology. Each end device node can only communicate with the coordinator node. If communication is needed between two end device nodes, the information must be transmitted through the coordinator node. The tree topology consists of a coordinator and a series of router and end device nodes. The coordinator connects a series of routers and end devices, and its child node router can also connect a series of routers and end devices. In this way, multiple levels can be repeated. The mesh topology consists of a coordinator and a series of routers and end devices. Mesh network topology has more flexible information routing rules, where possible, routing nodes can communicate directly.

In order to satisfy different security requirements of ZigBee devices, ZigBee specification defines two security modes [15]: Standard Security Mode and High Security Mode. The standard security mode uses a single shared key to provide authentication to ZigBee nodes, and ZigBee Trust Center uses access control list (ACL) to authenticate devices. High security mode requires a device in ZigBee network as ZigBee Trust Center to track all encryption algorithms and authentication keys used in the network, and enforce network authentication and key upgrade policies.

3 Analysis of ZigBee Attack Principle

While ZigBee network technology is convenient for our life, it also brings a lot of security risks. Therefore, it is necessary to analyze the security of ZigBee and put forward the corresponding solutions. The following will analyze several typical attacks that ZigBee may be subject to.

3.1 Association Attack

ZigBee protocol maintains an association table named AssociatedDevList internally. The association table of the parent node records all the child nodes associated with it.

The IEEE address of the information in the table is unique. When each device joins its parent node, a record will be added to the table. However, the record will not be deleted when the child node leaves the network after power failure. If there are multiple child nodes, frequent replacement of the parent node will cause the association table to be full or overflow, making other child nodes unable to join the parent node. According to this flaw, attackers often launch attacks on association table to destroy the expansion function of ZigBee network.

3.2 Replay Attack

ZigBee is not perfect in replay protection. ZigBee network is based on IEEE 802.15.4 protocol specification. IEEE 802.15.4 specification has limited replay protection mechanism, even encrypted messages can not completely defend against this attack. As a result, a crafty attacker can replay any traffic observed previously until key rotation (assuming IEEE 802.15.4 does not have authentication enabled). Replay attacks are usually accompanied by several other attacks, such as DDoS. Malicious users can receive packets at one point in the network, and then replay these packets in other areas to interfere with the overall network function (wormhole attack [10]). Over the years, researchers have also successfully implemented replay attacks using the "KillerBee" tool, and clearly explained the serious problems it may cause.

3.3 Network PANID Conflict Attack

The attacker sends the "Beacon Request" frame, and then waits for the victim coordinator to return the "Beacon" frame to obtain the current personal area network identifier (PANID) of the ZigBee network. Then the attacker sends a forged "Beacon" frame, which contains the same PANID as the current ZigBee network but different extended address (IEEE address) from real Coordinator. Coordinator will find a personal area network identifier conflict, which will change its personal area network identifier. The terminal device or router does not know that the personal area network identifier has changed. They still send packets with old personal area network identifier. If the attacker continues to send attacking packets, the terminal device or router will not be able to transmit the message to network with correct personal area network identifier. Users also have no control over terminal devices or routers. When the attacker stops the attack, the terminal device or router will not be able to obtain the current network identifier in a short time.

3.4 Malicious Orphan Frame Attack

Low power consumption is an advantage of ZigBee network, and it is one of the reasons for the promotion of ZigBee technology. ZigBee nodes can work under the support of ordinary batteries for a long time. Battery power supply can greatly simplify the complexity of ZigBee network deployment, but the battery power is limited after all. Under normal circumstances, batteries of ZigBee can last more than a month. However, if the ZigBee terminal enters an abnormal state due to external attacks, the terminal has to process some unnecessary data every time it wakes up, which will greatly reduce the endurance of the device. The attacker can disguise as a normal node, and then send the "Orphan Notification" frame to the coordinator, and change the source address of the frame to be same as a normal ZigBee terminal in the network. In this way, after receiving the "Orphan Notification" frame, the coordinator will mistakenly think that a device in the network is off the network, so he will reply a "Coordinator Realignment" frame. After the normal terminal gets this frame, it will make corresponding processing. The specific process is shown in Fig. 1. If the attacker sends fake "Orphan Notification" frames continuously, the coordinator will continue to send "Coordinator Realignment" frames to the normal node. The normal terminal node and coordinator will process a large number of useless command frames, resulting in extra power consumption. In addition, if the "Orphan Notification" frame is sent too fast, the coordinator will be too busy, thus causing the effect of a DoS attack on the coordinator.

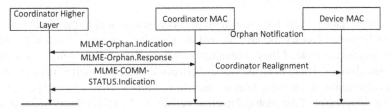

Fig. 1. Coordinator realignment process

3.5 Potential Vulnerability

Cve-2019-15914 [16] network short address conflict vulnerability refers to that when two devices with the same short address are mounted under the coordinator or router device, the coordinator will modify the conflicting short address. This is a reasonable operation mechanism, but if the attacker maliciously forges the same short address, and the coordinator and router modify the conflicting address blindly, it will make the address of the attacked device be changed frequently. In a short period of time, other devices connected in the network do not know the change of the short address, they will send the data packet to the old address, which will cause the data loss of the attacked equipment in the network communication process, and in serious cases, it will cause the denial of service.

Figure 2 shows the process of device interaction when network short address conflict occurs. From T_0 to T_1, device R and device E conduct normal data communication. At T_1 time, a large number of "Rejoin Request" frames with the same NWK address as R, but different IEEE address from R, lead to the NWK address of device R becoming 0x82cb at T_2. However, the device E connected to the coordinator does not know that the NWK address of device R has changed, At T_3 time, device E is still sending data to device R, but there is no response.

In addition, ZigBee may also fall into the threat of malicious filling of child device association table. A malicious device can constantly forge its own IEEE address, produce

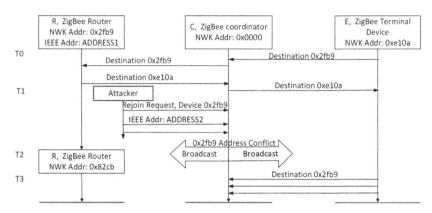

Fig. 2. Principle of network short address conflict vulnerability

a 16-bit short address, and then search all the coordinators and routers in the network. The coordinator and router will allocate association table space for the malicious device, and the association table of the coordinator or router will be full, causing it to be unable to add new devices. There is no difference between ZigBee association attack and association vulnerability in essence. They are just the conclusion from different perspectives. From the perspective of the protocol itself, it belongs to the vulnerability of ZigBee protocol, because the protocol does not do any security authentication for the association request, and directly puts it into its own association table, causing network paralysis. Therefore, we can take the initiative to test whether there is such a vulnerability in the ZigBee network before the real attack comes, and verify whether it has been repaired or compensated by other means.

4   Detection System

We design a ZigBee security detection system. The system mainly includes three modules: device scanning, attack detection and vulnerability detection. Attack detection includes association attack detection, replay attack detection, network PANID conflict detection and malicious orphan frame detection. Vulnerability detection includes NWK conflict vulnerability and association table vulnerability.

To test the detection system, we simulate a ZigBee attack scene. The equipment and software used in scene include: ZigBee module CC2530, TelosB rod, USB Dongle, KillerBee, Scapy. CC2530 simulates the normal devices in the environment, including coordinator, router and terminal. USB Dongle serves as a ZigBee wireless packet sniffing device, The TelosB bar can perform both capturing and sending functions. It can simulate ZigBee attack under the control of KillerBee. Scapy is used to parse the captured ZigBee packets. Figure 3 shows the module functions of the system and modules used in the test environment.

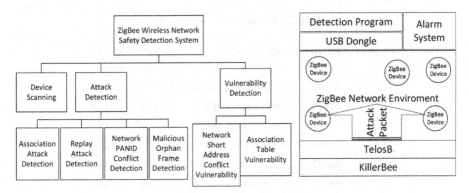

Fig. 3. System architecture and attack and detection system

4.1 Device Scanning

Before the attack detection, all the ZigBee devices in the network need to be identified. In the 2.4 GHz frequency band, the working channels of ZigBee are distributed from 11 to 26 channels, so it is necessary to scan the 16 channels and record all the devices in the 16 channels. Capture the ZigBee packets in each channel, and parse the PANID, NWK and IEEE addresses according to the ZigBee protocol, and finally get the online devices in each channel.

MAC layer:	Frame Control	Sequence Number	Dst PAN Identifier	Dst Address	Src PAN Identifier	Src Address	Auxiliary Security HDR	Frame Payload	FCS

NWK layer:	NWK Frame Control Field	NWK Dst Address	NWK Src Address	Broadcast Radius	Broadcast Seq.num	NWK Paylpad
	Dst IEEE Address	Src IEEE Address	Multicast Control	Src Route Subframe	Frame Payload	

Fig. 4. ZigBee MAC layer packet format and ZigBee NWK layer packet format

Device scanning involves ZigBee MAC layer and NWK layer, MAC layer contains PANID and short address, NWK layer contains IEEE address and NWK address (short address). Therefore, as long as the data frames of these two layers are correctly parsed, the required PANID, NWK address and IEEE address can be obtained. We use polling scanning method to scan in turn in 16 channels. In this round, the device which is scanned will be marked as on-line. When the next round of scanning does not find the device, it will be marked as off-line.

The MAC layer of ZigBee directly uses the IEEE 802.15.4 standard. Figure 4 shows ZigBee MAC layer packet format and ZigBee NWK layer packet format. Table 2 shows the devices scanned in channel 11 and channel 25.

Table 2. ZigBee device scan results

Channel	PANID	IEEE address	NWK address	STATE
11	0xfff1	0xf8301e442844e044	0x2c7b	on-line
11	0xfff1	0xf8109e4428441f44	0x0000	on-line
11	0xfff1	0xf830c844e1448344	0x11a6	on-line
11	0xfff1	0x00239448c0073372	0x2414	off-line
11	0xfff2	0xf810804480440044	0x0000	on-line
25	0xae36	0x00158d0001f36d4b	0x0000	on-line

4.2   Attack Detection

Association Attack Detection. The key point of association attack is to send a large number of frames with forged IEEE addresses in a short period of time, and try to establish association with the coordinator to fill the association table. Normally, only when ZigBee starts networking, a large number of devices will send out "Association Request" frames. However, when the networking process is completed, there is no "Association Request" frame in the network. Even if a new ZigBee node wants to join the network, it is an individual device, and the number of "Association Request" frames generated by it will not be too large. Therefore, the number of "Association Request" frames can be monitored to realize association attack detection. If a large number of "Association Request" frames are found in a certain period of time, excluding the initial networking stage, it indicates that the network may be suffering from the association attack at this time, and the alarm information can be sent appropriately. It is necessary to set a threshold here. If the number of frames is greater than this threshold, it will be judged as an attack. Otherwise, it is normal. The threshold needs to be evaluated according to the specific network environment to strike a balance between false alarms and missed alarms.

Association Attack Detection. The key point of association attack is to send a large number of frames with forged IEEE addresses in a short period of time, and try to establish association with the coordinator to fill the association table. Normally, only when ZigBee starts networking, a large number of devices will send out "Association Request" frames. However, when the networking process is completed, there is no "Association Request" frame in the network. Even if a new ZigBee node wants to join the network, it is an individual device, and the number of "Association Request" frames generated by it will not be too large. Therefore, the number of "Association Request" frames can be monitored to realize association attack detection. If a large number of "Association Request" frames are found in a certain period of time, excluding the initial networking stage, it indicates that the network may be suffering from the association attack at this time, and the alarm information can be sent appropriately. It is necessary to set a threshold here. If the number of frames is greater than this threshold, it will be judged as an attack. Otherwise, it is normal. The threshold needs to be evaluated according to the specific network environment to strike a balance between false alarms and missed alarms.

Fig. 5. Association attack packet data 1

Fig. 6. Association attack packet data 2

Fig. 7. Association attack detection

Figure 5 shows that when the coordinator's capacity is true and the association table is not full, the attacking device continuously sends "Association Request" frames, and the coordinator will reply "Association Response" when it receives them, indicating that association operation is allowed. Figure 6 shows that when the coordinator's association table is full, the coordinator's capacity is false, then the attack device and the coordinator cannot interact with each other in "Association Request" and "Association Response". The attack device cannot be connected to the network. At this point, if there is a normal device to join the network, it will also be unable to access the network. As shown in Fig. 7, a large number of Association Requests are found in a period of time, the detection system judged that the ZigBee network is under association attack and issue an alarm.

Replay Attack Detection. There are two detection strategies for replay attack. First, if the replay attack is a single replay attack, we can judge whether the device is attacked according to the "Sequence Number" of the same type frame. Normally, the frame "Sequence Number" is the continuous increase one by one in general, even if there is a mismatch, that is not too serious, but the replay attack frame "Sequence Number" may be very different from the data stream frame "Sequence Number". Thus, we can set a threshold m, when the frame "Sequence Number" is seriously out of order, beyond the threshold, then we can think that the network is being suffering from a replay attack. Second, a replay attack can be multiple replays over a short period of time, often accompanied by a DoS effect. At this point, we can judge it according to the content of the frames. If many data frames with the same content are detected within a short period of time and the number of them exceeds a specific threshold n, we can also consider that the network is under replay attack.

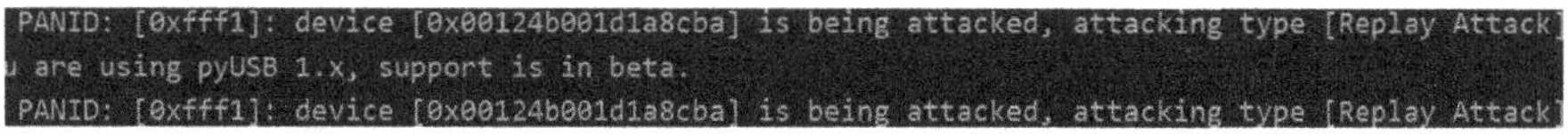

Fig. 8. Replay attack detection

During the experiment, we should grasp the data packet between Xiaomi ZigBee gateway and devices in advance, and extract one of the data packets to copy multiple copies, and then use KillerBee to replay. At the same time, we turn on the detection system to detect. Figure 8 shows that the detection system detected that the ZigBee network is under replay attack.

Network PANID Conflict Detection. The key point of network conflict attack is that the attacker forges a coordinator and makes the PANID of itself the same as that of the normal coordinator, thus causing network chaos. Although the PANID is the same, the IEEE address of the forged coordinator is generally different from that of the normal coordinator. Therefore, if the packets with the same PANID but different IEEE addresses are found under the same channel, and their src addresses are 0x0000 which represents they are sent out from coordinator, it indicates that there are two coordinators in the same network at this time, then we can also consider that the network falls into network PANID conflict.

Figure 9 shows that the PANID of the current ZigBee coordinator is 0xe9cb, and the IEEE address of the coordinator is 00:12:4b:00:1d:1A:98:0f. If there is a packet whose short address is 0x0000 (representing the coordinator), PANID is 0xe9CB and the IEEE address is not 00:12:4b:00:1d:1a:98:0f, it indicates that the illegal device is posing as the coordinator in the ZigBee network at this time. Figure 10 is the result detected by the system when the network PANID conflict attack is simulated.

Malicious Orphan Frame Attack Detection. In order to pose effective power consumption and DOS attacks, attackers must send a large number of "Orphan Notification" frames in a short period of time, causing the coordinator to repeatedly send the "Coordinator Realignment" frame to the normal node. Normally, these two kinds of frames are rare, even if they appear, the number is very small. Therefore, it is necessary to monitor the "Orphan Notification" and "Coordinator Realignment" frames in current

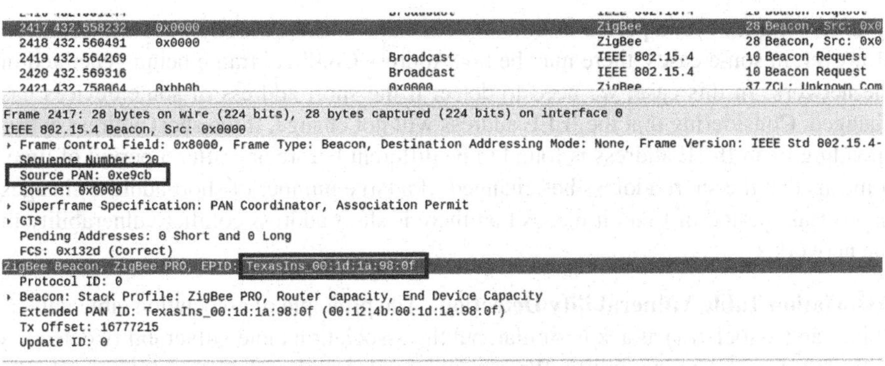

```
2417 432.558232    0x0000                                    ZigBee           28 Beacon, Src: 0x0
2418 432.560491    0x0000                                    ZigBee           28 Beacon, Src: 0x0
2419 432.564269                      Broadcast               IEEE 802.15.4    10 Beacon Request
2420 432.569316                      Broadcast               IEEE 802.15.4    10 Beacon Request
2421 432.758864    0xbb0b            0x0000                  ZigBee           37 ZCL: Unknown Com
```

```
Frame 2417: 28 bytes on wire (224 bits), 28 bytes captured (224 bits) on interface 0
IEEE 802.15.4 Beacon, Src: 0x0000
▶ Frame Control Field: 0x8000, Frame Type: Beacon, Destination Addressing Mode: None, Frame Version: IEEE Std 802.15.4-
  Sequence Number: 28
  Source PAN: 0xe9cb
  Source: 0x0000
▶ Superframe Specification: PAN Coordinator, Association Permit
▶ GTS
  Pending Addresses: 0 Short and 0 Long
  FCS: 0x132d (Correct)
ZigBee Beacon, ZigBee PRO, EPID: TexasIns_00:1d:1a:98:0f
  Protocol ID: 0
▶ Beacon: Stack Profile: ZigBee PRO, Router Capacity, End Device Capacity
  Extended PAN ID: TexasIns_00:1d:1a:98:0f (00:12:4b:00:1d:1a:98:0f)
  Tx Offset: 16777215
  Update ID: 0
```

Fig. 9. Network conflict packet data

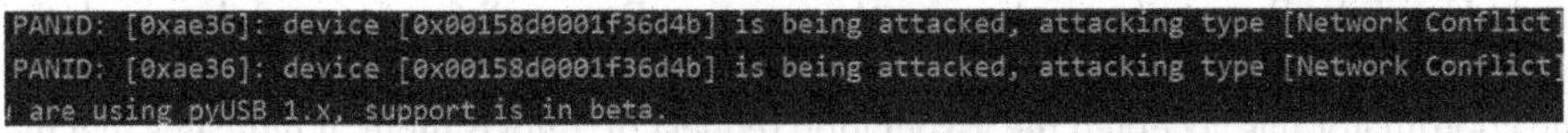

```
PANID: [0xae36]: device [0x00158d0001f36d4b] is being attacked, attacking type [Network Conflict]
PANID: [0xae36]: device [0x00158d0001f36d4b] is being attacked, attacking type [Network Conflict]
 are using pyUSB 1.x, support is in beta.
```

Fig. 10. Network conflict detection

environment. If a large number of these two frames appear in a short period of time, it indicates that the network may be under a malicious orphan frame attack. Figure 11 shows a large number of "Orphan Notification" frames appearing on the network.

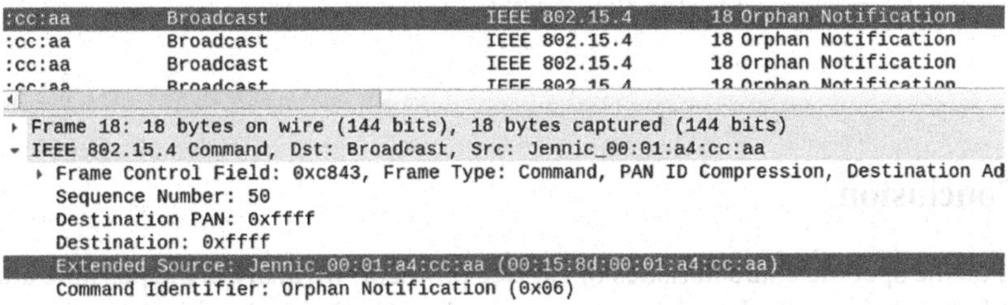

```
:cc:aa         Broadcast               IEEE 802.15.4      18 Orphan Notification
:cc:aa         Broadcast               IEEE 802.15.4      18 Orphan Notification
:cc:aa         Broadcast               IEEE 802.15.4      18 Orphan Notification
:cc:aa         Broadcast               IEEE 802.15.4      18 Orphan Notification
```

```
▶ Frame 18: 18 bytes on wire (144 bits), 18 bytes captured (144 bits)
▼ IEEE 802.15.4 Command, Dst: Broadcast, Src: Jennic_00:01:a4:cc:aa
  ▶ Frame Control Field: 0xc843, Frame Type: Command, PAN ID Compression, Destination Ad
    Sequence Number: 50
    Destination PAN: 0xffff
    Destination: 0xffff
    Extended Source: Jennic_00:01:a4:cc:aa (00:15:8d:00:01:a4:cc:aa)
    Command Identifier: Orphan Notification (0x06)
```

Fig. 11. Orphan notification packet

4.3 Vulnerability Detection

Network Short Address Conflict Vulnerability Detection. Network short address conflict vulnerability detection allows the vulnerability detection module to forge and send fake "Rejoin Request" frames, and set its own short address to be the same as Zig-Bee device R (shown in Fig. 2). In this way, the coordinator will find the short address conflict and modify the conflicting short address, that is, the address of R will change from A to B. For some devices, when a short address conflict occurs, the coordinator will send a network "Address Conflict" frame to inform the network that there is a network short address conflict. So by monitoring whether there are a lot of network "Address

Conflict" frames over a period of time, we can know if there are short address conflicts. However, in some cases, there may be no "Address Conflict" frame being generated in the network. In this case, we need to detect if the short address of some devices has changed. Considering that the IEEE address will not change, if the short address corresponding to an IEEE address is found to be different before and after a period of time, it means that the short address has changed. If a large number of short address changes in a certain period of time, it means that there is short address conflict vulnerability in the network.

Association Table Vulnerability Detection. The principle of association table vulnerability and association attack is similar, but the association table vulnerability detection is to detect it as a vulnerability. We can make vulnerability detection tool imitate the association attack and observe the effect of the attack to determine whether there is an associated table vulnerability. This process requires the support of TelosB mote memory stick. Use TelosB mote to send some "Association Request" frames, and then grab the packets with USB dongle. If the "Association Response" frame is found, which means the coordinator has accepted the association request of TelosB mote, it indicates that the ZigBee network coordinator has an association table vulnerability. Figure 12 shows the scanning results of the vulnerability detection module on the target network.

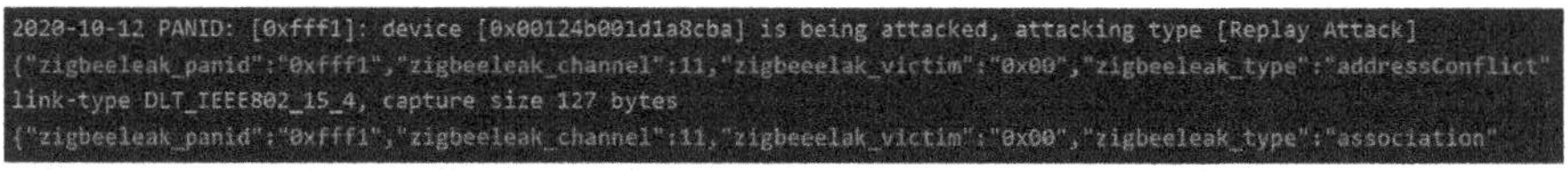

2020-10-12 PANID: [0xfff1]: device [0x00124b001d1a8cba] is being attacked, attacking type [Replay Attack]
{"zigbeeleak_panid":"0xfff1","zigbeeleak_channel":11,"zigbeeelak_victim":"0x00","zigbeeleak_type":"addressConflict"
link-type DLT_IEEE802_15_4, capture size 127 bytes
{"zigbeeleak_panid":"0xfff1","zigbeeleak_channel":11,"zigbeeelak_victim":"0x00","zigbeeleak_type":"association"

Fig. 12. Vulnerabilities detection result

5 Conclusion

Based on the specific characteristics of ZigBee protocol, we analyze the possible attacks and vulnerabilities of ZigBee devices in practical use, and give the corresponding detection schemes for these attacks and vulnerabilities. Finally, these detection schemes are implemented into a complete ZigBee security detection system, which has the following advantages.

The ZigBee security detection system is not limited to a specific attack, but focuses on four typical attacks and two potential vulnerability threats, which can satisfy the requirements of most scenarios.

The detection scheme in this paper will not affect the original ZigBee network, and does not need to change the original network structure. It can realize rapid deployment and rapid detection.

This detection system adopts modular design, it can easily add other ZigBee attack detection schemes, or combine with Bluetooth, WIFI and other near-field communication security detection modules to form a complete wireless network attack vulnerability detection system to protect the device security in a complex wireless network environment.

References

1. Wang, Q., Wang, L.: Analysis of ZigBee technology. Telecom World **101**(4), 41–43 (2003)
2. Mu, N.: Introduction to ZigBee technology. Telecommun. Technol. **53**(3), 84–86 (2006)
3. Yuan, Y., Su, H.: The study of wireless network applications based on ZigBee technology. Computer Applications and Software **21**(6), 89–91 (2004)
4. Xu, X., Gao, Y., Zhang, W.: Research on data transmission security tactics of ZigBee network based on IEEE 802.15.4. Netinfo Secur. **9**(6), 10–12 (2009)
5. Wright J.: KillerBee:practical zigbee exploitation framework. In: 11th ToorCon Conference, San Diego (2009)
6. Giannetsos, T., Dimitriou, T., Prasad, N.R.: Weaponizing wireless networks: an attak tool for launching attacks against sensor networks. In: Black Hat Technical Secirity Conference, Barcelona (2010)
7. Xiao, H., Zhang, D., Liu, L.: A detecion scheme of reactive jamming attack based on retransmission rate consistency in WS. In: 18th National Youth Communication Conference of China, Beijing, pp. 95–98 (2013)
8. Huang, M., Yu B., Kong, Z.: Sybil attack detection scheme design in ZigBee network. J. Syst. Simul. **28**(6), 1452–1460 (2016)
9. Yue, Q.: The research of attack and defense strategies of worm based on ZigBee network. MA thesis, Beijing Institute of Technology, China (2016)
10. Shi, Y., Chen, W., Yu, B.: The design and implimentation of schemes against wormhole attack in ZigBee networks. J. Syst. Simul. **29**(4), 853–858 (2017)
11. Bi, G.: The research and application of encryption algorithm based on ZigBee technology. MA thesis, Guizhou University, China (2017)
12. He, K., Yu, B.: Detection scheme of reactive jamming in ZigBee network. J. Electron. Meas. Instr. **33**(1), 128–134 (2019)
13. Guo, S., Ma, S., Wu, P.: Application of wireless sensor network based on ZigBee technology in remote home monitoring system. Appl. Electron. Tech. **32**(6), 28–31 (2006)
14. Geng, X., Sha, F., Li, Y.: Sensor application design of ISMLink production based on IEEE 802.15.4 standard. In: ICEMI, Beijing, pp. 243–247 (2005)
15. Wright, J.: ZigBee security design rules. In: Hacking Exposed Wireless, Wireless Security secrects & Solutions. 2nd edn. China Machine Press, Beijing (2012)
16. Github. https://github.com/chengcheng227/CVE-POC/blob/master/CVE-2019-15914_2.md. Accessed 1 Oct 2020

Joint ToF and Doppler Estimation for Reflection Path Under the Wi-Fi TTW Scenario

Z. Tian, X. Yuan, X. Yang[✉], and L. Xie

School of Communication and Information Engineering, Chongqing University of Posts and Telecommunications, Chongqing 400065, China
yangxiaolong@cqupt.edu.cn

Abstract. In recent years, with the popularity of Wi-Fi, the wireless sensing technology based on Wi-Fi channel state information (CSI) has become a research hotspot. The signal propagates through multiple paths, the signal of each path, especially generated by the reflection of reflector, will carry rich environmental information. The reflection path is used to obtain many parameters, such as time of flight (ToF) and Doppler shift, for purposes such as target positioning or gesture recognition. The core lies in the CSI based sensing technology is the signal parameter estimation, especially signal ToF, which describes the transmission distance of the signal. At present, many researchers have tried to use ToF to achieve detection and sensing of target under the line-of-sight (LoS) scenario, but no one tried to use ToF and Doppler to detect the target under the through-the-wall (TTW) scenario. In this paper, we propose a 2-dimensional matrix pencil algorithm, which jointly estimates the reflection's ToF and Doppler frequency shift, through leveraging the phase differences between subcarriers and CSI packets, respectively, under the TTW scenario. Our implementation and evaluation demonstrate that the proposed system provides the median reflection ToF estimation error of 1.36 ns, better than the state-of-the-art solutions, under the TTW scenario.

Keywords: CSI · TTW · Doppler · ToF

1 Introduction

The wireless technology plays an essential role in people's lives today. The conventional system mainly uses, such as accelerometers and infrared, to sense the surrounding environment or targets, so as to realize purpose such as behavior recognition. These systems usually require the target to wear sensor devices, which make it hard to deploy. Recently, the Wi-Fi-based wireless sensing becomes a hot issue, especially with the emergence and appliance of CSI [1]. The wireless sensing system based on Wi-Fi works in a passive manner, which means it doesn't hold requirement for carrying any equipment. Under the LoS scenario, Wi-Fi sensing technology can be used to develop systems such as gesture recognition and behavior recognition. Under the TTW scenario, this technology can be used to detect dynamic targets [2]. Limited by the signal bandwidth and the number of antennas, the performance of Wi-Fi sensing technology is relatively weaker than that of

© Springer Nature Switzerland AG 2021
X. Sun et al. (Eds.): ICAIS 2021, CCIS 1424, pp. 404–413, 2021.
https://doi.org/10.1007/978-3-030-78621-2_33

through-the-wall radar. But the cost of Wi-Fi based sensing is lower, so it has received extensive attention from industry and academia.

Compared with traditional sensing methods, the Wi-Fi signal based system have the following advantages:

Wider coverage: Wi-Fi signals are basically present in major shopping malls and private houses. So far, more than 13 billion Wi-Fi devices have been deployed around the world [3]. Such wide coverage provides a good environment for promoting such systems.

Lower cost: the Wi-Fi sensing can be realized via the existing Wi-Fi equipment, without changing the hardware, software or communication protocol. Meanwhile, it does not affect the communication of the system, which is affordable for most people.

In an indoor environment, the signal always reaches the receiver through multiple propagation paths. In addition to the LoS path from the transmitter to the receiver, multiple propagation paths carry rich environmental information once the signal is reflected by one or more objects before reaching the receiver. Thus, researchers convert Wi-Fi signals from communication medium to perception work, thus realize the perception of human behavior or movement. For instance, authors in [4] design a system which can detect the target under the TTW scenario. However, it can only detect the moving direction of the target, and the detection range of the system is limited to the LoS scenario.

In [5], the authors propose a commercial Wi-Fi based passive wireless radar system without any modification of firmware and hardware, under the TTW scenario. It uses the CLEAN algorithm [6] to eliminate the direct path and more accurately determine the signal from the human body, which can be used for breathing detection, human counting, etc.

So far, most Wi-Fi sense systems can only realize sensing under the LoS scenario as described above. Since when a signal penetrates an obstacle and reaches the receiving, its energy is heavily weakened by the obstacle, such as a wall, making the relevant signal features, such as the angle-of-arrival (AoA) parameters and the amplitude characteristics of the signal, difficult to be extracted accurately [7].

In response to the above-mentioned problem, in this paper, we propose a joint estimation algorithm based on matrix pencil (MP) algorithm, which extends the original one-dimensional matrix pencil algorithm to two-dimensional space and uses the phase difference between the data packets caused by the change of path length and subcarriers induced by the ToF of signal, to estimate the Doppler and ToF of reflected signal, under the TTW scenario. Compared with the traditional one-dimensional MP algorithm, the resolution of the algorithm is improved by increasing the dimension of the estimation. At the same time, the signal-to-noise ratio (SNR) is enhanced to a certain extent through the cumulative use of multiple data packets, so as to improve the parameter accuracy estimation.

The main contributions of this paper can be summarized as follows:

We propose a joint Doppler and ToF estimation algorithm, unlike the previous one-dimensional MP algorithm, it improves the resolution of algorithm and parameter estimation accuracy to a certain extent through dimension expansion and data packet accumulation.

Under the real-world TTW scenario, we built an experimental platform to evaluate the proposed algorithm. Experimental results show that the ToF of reflected signal can be estimated accurately, with a median ToF error of 1.26 ns.

2   Signal Model

For the 802.11ac protocol based Wi-Fi signals, the CSI, which is the sampled version of channel frequency response (CFR), describes the influence of the channel on the wireless signal in terms of delay and amplitude. To simplify the discussion, suppose there is only one signal propagation path, then the CSI of the signal at time t_0 can be expressed as:

$$x(f, t_0) = A_0 e^{-j2\pi f \tau_0} \tag{1}$$

where f represents the carrier of the signal, A_0 is the attenuation of signal and τ_0 is the propagation delay. As the target moves, the length of the signal reflected from the target changes accordingly [8]. Assuming that the path length of the signal reflected from the target changes at a constant speed v, then the Doppler shift can be expressed as $f' = f(v/c)$, where c is the speed of signal in the air. Ignoring the attenuation of the signal for a relatively short time period t, the velocity of propagation path change is $\Delta l = vt$ and the corresponding delay change is $\Delta \tau = vt/c$. Taking the Doppler frequency into consideration, thus, the CSI of the signal can be expressed as follow:

$$x(f, t_0 + t) = A_0 e^{-j2\pi f \tau_0 + f'} = x(f, t_0) e^{-j2\pi f \frac{vt}{c}} \tag{2}$$

Accurate Doppler shift estimation requires uniform sampling intervals, which can be obtained by means of multiple sample timestamps. Suppose M samples are received, $t_1 = 0$ is the time stamp of the first sample and the sampling interval is $\Delta \sigma$. So, the sampling interval of each subsequent sample relative to the first sample is $[\Delta t_2, \Delta t_3, ..., \Delta t_M]$ and the phase difference between the M samples and the first sample can be expressed as follows:

$$\mathbf{a}(v) = [1, e^{-j2\pi f \frac{v\Delta t_2}{c}}, e^{-j2\pi f \frac{v\Delta t_3}{c}}, ..., e^{-j2\pi f \frac{v\Delta t_M}{c}}]^T \tag{3}$$

The CSI with M samples can be expressed as:

$$\begin{aligned}
\mathbf{X}(f) &= [x(f, t_0), x(f, t_0 + \Delta t_2), ..., x(f, t_0 + \Delta t_M)]^T \\
&= [1, e^{-j2\pi f \frac{v\Delta t_2}{c}}, e^{-j2\pi f \frac{v\Delta t_3}{c}}, ..., e^{-j2\pi f \frac{v\Delta t_M}{c}}]^T x(f, t_0) + n \\
&= \mathbf{a}(v) x(f, t_0) + n
\end{aligned} \tag{4}$$

where n is the noise. The formula (4) is the CSI with Doppler frequency shift obtained from all samples when only one propagation path and one subcarrier are considered. However, according to the IEEE 802.11ac, the Wi-Fi signal with the bandwidth of 80 MHz has multiple subcarriers and the error caused by random noise can be greatly reduced if multiple subcarriers are used for calculation. So, we sample 256 subcarriers with equally spaced and accumulate M CSI packets. Then the frequency difference between each subcarrier is $\Delta\psi$. For signals with M samples and N CSI subcarriers, the formula (3) can be transformed into:

$$
\mathbf{A}(v) = \begin{pmatrix} 1 & e^{-j2\pi\Delta\psi\tau_0} & \cdots & e^{-j2\pi(N-1)\Delta\psi\tau_0} \\ e^{-j2\pi f\frac{v\Delta t_2}{c}} & e^{-j2\pi\left(f\frac{v\Delta t_2}{c}+\Delta\psi\tau_0\right)} & \cdots & e^{-j2\pi\left(f\frac{v\Delta t_2}{c}+(N-1)\Delta\psi\tau_0\right)} \\ \vdots & \vdots & \ddots & \vdots \\ e^{-j2\pi f\frac{v\Delta t_M}{c}} & e^{-j2\pi\left(f\frac{v\Delta t_M}{c}+\Delta\psi\tau_0\right)} & \cdots & e^{-j2\pi\left(f\frac{v\Delta t_M}{c}+(N-1)\Delta\psi\tau_0\right)} \end{pmatrix}_{M\times N}
\tag{5}
$$

Accordingly, formula (4) can be expressed as:

$$
\begin{aligned}
\mathbf{X}(f) &= \mathbf{A}(v)[\mathbf{x}(f_1,t_0),\mathbf{x}(f_2,t_0),...,\mathbf{x}(f_N,t_0)]^T + n \\
&= \mathbf{A}(v)\mathbf{S}(f) + n
\end{aligned}
\tag{6}
$$

where $\mathbf{A}(v)$ is an $M \times N$ matrix with all phase difference between carriers and packets, f_n is the carrier frequency of the n-th subcarrier, $\mathbf{x}(f_n, t_0)$ mean signal of the n-th subcarrier at the first sampling time t_0, $\mathbf{S}(f)$ is the signal matrix containing n snapshots. The above discussion assumes that there is only one propagation path. However, under the real-world scenario, signals usually travel through multipaths, thus, the received signal is a superposition of signal of all propagation paths. Therefore, the CSI for all propagation paths can be expressed as follow:

$$
\begin{aligned}
\mathbf{X}(f) &= \sum_l \mathbf{A}(v_l)\mathbf{S}_l(f) + n \\
&= [\mathbf{A}(v_1), \mathbf{A}(v_2),\ldots,\mathbf{A}(v_L)][\mathbf{S}_1(f),\mathbf{S}_2(f),\ldots,\mathbf{S}_L(f)]^T + n
\end{aligned}
\tag{7}
$$

Correspondingly, CSI of the m-th sample and the n-th subcarrier signals without noise can be expressed as:

$$
x_{m,n} = \sum_l^L A_{m,l,n} e^{-j2\pi\left(f\frac{v_l\Delta t_m}{c}+(n-1)\Delta\psi\tau_l\right)} e^{-j2\pi f\tau_l} = \sum_l^L B_{m,l,n} e^{-j2\pi\left(f\frac{v_l\Delta t_m}{c}+(n-1)\Delta\psi\tau_l\right)}
\tag{8}
$$

where $A_{m,l,n}$ is the attenuation of the signal, $B_{m,l,n}=A_{m,l,n}e^{-j2\pi f\tau_l}$.

3 Modified 2-dimensional (2-D) Matrix Pencil Algorithms

In this work, the 2-D MP algorithm is proposed to estimate the Doppler shift and the time delays, where the first dimension is the CSI packet in the time dimension, and the second dimension is the OFDM subcarriers, which are distributed equally in the frequency dimension. Based on the previous signal model, the CSI extracted from the IEEE 802.11ac based receiver can be denoted as:

$$
\mathbf{H} = \begin{pmatrix}
\sum\limits_{l}^{L} B_{1,l,1} & \sum\limits_{l}^{L} B_{1,l,2}e^{-j2\pi \Delta \psi \tau_l} & \cdots & \sum\limits_{l}^{L} B_{1,l,N}e^{-j2\pi(N-1)\Delta \psi \tau_l} \\
\sum\limits_{l}^{L} B_{2,l,1}e^{-j2\pi f \frac{v\Delta t_2}{c}} & \sum\limits_{l}^{L} B_{2,l,2}e^{-j2\pi (f\frac{v\Delta t_2}{c}+\Delta \psi \tau_l)} & \cdots & \sum\limits_{l}^{L} B_{2,l,N}e^{-j2\pi\left(f\frac{v\Delta t_2}{c}+(N-1)\Delta \psi \tau_l\right)} \\
\vdots & \vdots & \ddots & \vdots \\
\sum\limits_{l}^{L} B_{M,l,1}e^{-j2\pi f \frac{v\Delta t_M}{c}} & \sum\limits_{l}^{L} B_{M,l,2}e^{-j2\pi (f\frac{v\Delta t_M}{c}+\Delta \psi \tau_l)} & \cdots & \sum\limits_{l}^{L} B_{M,l,N}e^{-j2\pi\left(f\frac{v\Delta t_M}{c}+(N-1)\Delta \psi \tau_l\right)}
\end{pmatrix}_{M \times N}
\tag{9}
$$

As can be seen from formula (9), the phase difference between packets and subcarriers can be denoted as $\alpha_l = \exp(-j2\pi \left(v_l\Delta\sigma /c\right)$ and $\beta_l = \exp(-j2\pi \Delta \psi \tau_l)$, respectively. Since the rank of $\mathbf{H}$ is smaller than L, neither α_l nor β_l can be represented by a vector of $\mathbf{H}$ without a complete inner product space. Thus, it is necessary to enhance the dimension of the signal subspace by partitioning and stacking. Considering the formula (9), each row in formula (9) can be used to create the Hankel matrix for each Doppler shift as follows:

$$
\mathbf{Y}_m = \begin{pmatrix}
x_{m,0} & x_{m,1} & \cdots & x_{m,N-P} \\
x_{m,1} & x_{m,2} & \cdots & x_{m,N-P+1} \\
\vdots & \vdots & \ddots & \vdots \\
x_{m,P-1} & x_{m,P} & \cdots & x_{m,N-1}
\end{pmatrix}_{P \times (N-P+1)}
\tag{10}
$$

where P is a pencil parameter used to acquire the matrix $\mathbf{Y}_m$. Based on this, an enhanced Hankel matrix block can be constructed as follow:

$$
\mathbf{Y}_e = \begin{pmatrix}
\mathbf{Y}_0 & \mathbf{Y}_1 & \cdots & \mathbf{Y}_{M-K} \\
\mathbf{Y}_1 & \mathbf{Y}_2 & \cdots & \mathbf{Y}_{M-k+1} \\
\vdots & \vdots & \ddots & \vdots \\
\mathbf{Y}_{K-1} & \mathbf{Y}_K & \cdots & \mathbf{Y}_{M-1}
\end{pmatrix}_{KP \times (M-K+1)(N-P+1)}
\tag{11}
$$

where K is a pencil parameter used to acquire the matrix $\mathbf{Y}_e$. To achieve a better estimation accuracy, as investigated in [7], the pencil P and K should satisfied the constraints:

$$
\begin{cases}
(K-1)P \geq L \\
K(P-1) \geq L \\
(M-K+1)(N-P+1) \geq L
\end{cases}
\tag{12}
$$

After that, the singular value decomposition (SVD) of $\mathbf{Y}_e$ in (11) is carried out to reduce the influence of random noise as follows:

$$
\mathbf{Y}_e = \mathbf{U}\sum \mathbf{V}^H
\tag{13}
$$

where H is conjugate transpose, U and V are unitary matrices, and $\sum$ is a diagonal matrix, which can be decomposed into a diagonal matrix representing the maximum singular value of the signal and a diagonal matrix representing the minimum singular value of noise. So, the SVD of (13) can be decomposed as:

$$\mathbf{Y}_e = \mathbf{Y}_s + \mathbf{Y}_n = \mathbf{U}_s \sum{}_s \mathbf{V}_s^H + \mathbf{U}_n \sum{}_n \mathbf{V}_n^H \qquad (14)$$

where $\mathbf{U}_s$ and $\mathbf{V}_s$ are submatrices of $\mathbf{U}$ and $\mathbf{V}$ corresponding to SVs of $\sum_s$, $\mathbf{U}_n$ and $\mathbf{V}_n$ are submatrices of $\mathbf{U}$ and $\mathbf{V}$ corresponding to SVs of $\sum_n$. Next, matrices $\mathbf{U}_{s1}$ and $\mathbf{U}_{s2}$ can be obtained by deleting the last and the first P row of $\mathbf{U}_s$ respectively, and α_l is extracted as eigenvalues from $\mathbf{U}_{s1}^\dagger \mathbf{U}_{s2}$, where $\mathbf{U}_{s1}^\dagger$ is the Moore-Penrose pseudo-inverse of $\mathbf{U}_{s1}$. The l-th Doppler shift can then be calculated via:

$$\hat{v}_l = \arg(\alpha_l^*).c/2\pi \triangle \sigma \qquad (15)$$

where $l = 1, \ldots \widehat{L}$. Then, for extracting β_l, we use the shuffling matrix to introduce permutation matrix as $\mathbf{U}_{sp} = \mathbf{P}\mathbf{U}_s$, where the $\mathbf{P}$ can be expressed as follow:

$$P = [s(1), s(1+P), \cdots s(1+(K-1)P), s(2), s(2+P), \cdots ,$$
$$s(2+(K-1)P), \cdots s(P), s(P+P), \cdots , s(P+(K-1)P)]^T \qquad (16)$$

where $s(i)$ is a column vector of size KP, which has value only in i-th, matrices $\mathbf{U}_{sp1}$ and $\mathbf{U}_{sp2}$ can be obtained by deleting the last and the first K row of $\mathbf{U}_{sp}$, respectively, and then β_l is extracted as eigenvalues from $\mathbf{U}_{sp1}^\dagger \mathbf{U}_{sp2}$, where $\mathbf{U}_{sp1}^\dagger$ is the Moore-Penrose pseudo-inverse of $\mathbf{U}_{sp1}$. Fianlly, the l-th time delay can then be calculated from:

$$\hat{\tau}_l = \arg(\beta_l^*)/2\pi \triangle \psi \qquad (17)$$

where $l = 1, \ldots \widehat{L}$. So far, the proposed 2-D MP algorithm realizes the joint estimation of Doppler and ToF for human induced reflection.

4 Evolution

In this section, experiments are conducted to evaluate the performance of the proposed algorithm, under the TTW brick wall scenario. First, we present the joint estimated 2-D Doppler and ToF spectrum to verify that the algorithm can estimate reflection, under the TTW scenario. Second, we analyze the ToF estimation accuracy of the reflection at different test positions to analyze the influence of different spatial positions on the ToF estimation accuracy. The proposed algorithm is compared to those described in [9] and [10], which are labeled as MUSIC and cross-correlation here.

4.1 Implementation

A typical office room, which has furniture such as desks and chairs, iron bookcases, potted plants, and computer printers, as shown in Fig. 2, is selected for the experiment. For hardware configuration, we choose the Asus RT-AC86U as the receiver and an Honor-X1-Pro as the transmitter, to receive and transmit the signal, respectively. We replaced the original firmware with the tool provided by authors in [11], which enables the receiver to enter a monitoring mode similar to csitool [12, 13] to grab the signal of the specified commercial Wi-Fi and output CSI after parsing. We use a splitter to connect the transmitter and receiver, as shown in Fig. 1, to eliminate packet detection delay (PDD) and other phase errors. Another output of the splitter is externally connected with a 90-degree directional antenna with horizontal polarization and gain of 14 dB, to send the signal. The transmitter sends signals with the transmission rate of 100 Hz. The center frequency of the signal is 5.805 GHz and the bandwidth is 80 MHz (256 subcarriers in total and the subcarrier spacing is 0.3125 MHz). The transmitter and receiver are placed at the same the height of 1.8 m. At the same time, during the experiment, in order to accurately obtain the ground truth of the reflection, the tester was asked to stand at the pre-set test locations to generate the reflection.

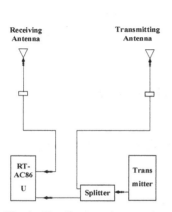

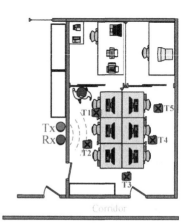

Fig. 1. The diagram of connection   **Fig. 2.** A typical TTW scenario

4.2 Performance

Spectrum Peak Experiment. Figure 3 shows the ability of three algorithms to identify reflection at test point 5. As can be seen, the parameter estimation resolution of the 2-D MP algorithm proposed in this paper is better than the other two algorithms. Compared with the cross-correlation algorithm, which cannot identify the reflection path, the 2-D MP algorithm and the MUSIC algorithm can accurately identify the path of the direct signal and the reflected signal and obtain the ToF according to the spectrum peak in the time dimension. Based on the location of the test point, we can see that the difference between the estimated ToF of the 2-D MP algorithm and the ground truth ToF is only 1.50 ns, which is smaller than that of MUSIC algorithm.

ToF Estimation at Different Locations. It can be seen from the Fig. 4 that the ToF estimation accuracy of the algorithm proposed in this paper is higher at different locations. For example, at the second test point, the ToF estimation error of the 2-D MP algorithm is only 1.61 ns, while the estimation error of the MUSIC and cross-correlation

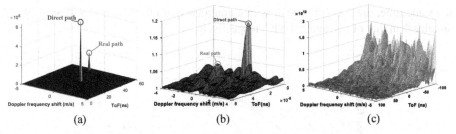

(a)   (b)   (c)

Fig. 3. (a) estimated spectrum of the proposed the algorithms at test point 5. (b) and (c) show the estimated spectrums of the MUSIC and the cross-correlation algorithm, respectively

algorithms are 3.16 ns and 6.47 ns, respectively. At the third test point, the estimation errors of the three algorithms are close, but the estimation error of the 2-D MP algorithm is 1.26 ns, which is still smaller than the 2.46 ns and 1.60 ns of the MUSIC and cross-correlation algorithms. The reason is that under the TTW scenario, the energy of the reflected signal is weak, which makes the reflection easy to be submerged in the strong direct path and the reflection path from the wall. Through the accumulation of data packets, the proposed algorithm improves the SNR of the reflection, thereby improving the ToF estimation accuracy of the reflection.

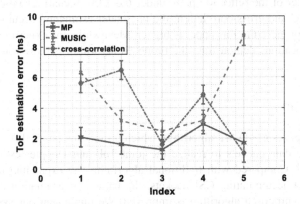

Fig. 4. The ToF estimation accuracy of the three algorithms at five test points

The Overall ToF Estimation Comparison. The statistical results of ToF estimation accuracy for all test points are shown in Fig. 5. It can be seen from Fig. 5, under the TTW brick wall, the accuracy of the algorithm proposed in this paper is higher than the other two algorithms. Specifically, for the 2-D MP algorithm, the median error and the error with a confidence of 66.7% are 1.36 ns and 2.10 ns, respectively. For the MUSIC algorithm, the median error and the error with a confidence of 66.7% are 3.16 ns and 4.81 ns, respectively. The accuracy of the cross-correlation algorithm is the lowest, and its value is higher than that of MP and MUSIC 2.46 ns and 0.66 ns, respectively. At the same time, the 2-D MP's error with a confidence of 66.7% is 2.71 ns and 3.29 ns, smaller than that of MP and MUSIC, respectively.

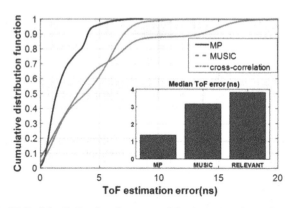

Fig. 5. The CDF of the ToF estimation error of the three algorithms for all test points

Overall, from the above experimental results, it can be seen that the algorithm proposed in this paper can effectively detect the target reflection signal and estimate the ToF and Doppler of the reflection path, under the TTW scenario. Compared with the existing MUSIC and cross-correlation, the parameter estimation accuracy of the 2-D MP algorithm proposed in this paper is higher. Meanwhile, the experimental results at different test locations demonstrate the proposed algorithm is more robust than other algorithms.

5 Conclusion

This paper proposes a 2-D MP algorithm, which utilizes the phase difference between subcarriers and data packets to realize the joint ToF and Doppler estimation of the reflected signal. Compared with traditional algorithms, by expanding the estimation dimensions and accumulating CSI packets, the parameter estimation resolution and accuracy of the proposed algorithm is improved. We implement our system on Asus RT-AC86U with NEXMON tool and conduct comprehensive experiments under TTW scenario to evaluate its performance. The experimental results show that the median error of the ToF estimation of the reflected path of the proposed algorithm can reach 1.36 ns, indicating the proposed algorithm can effectively detect the reflection path and estimate the signal parameters under the TTW scenario.

Acknowledgement. This work was supported in part by the Science and Technology Research Project of Chongqing Education Commission (KJQN201800625, KJZD-K202000605, KJQN202000630), the Chongqing Natural Science Foundation Project (cstc2019jcyj-msxmX0635, cstc2020jcyj-msxmX0842), and the National Natural Science Foundation of China (61771083, 61771209).

References

1. Yang, X., Wu, S., Zhou, M., et al.: Indoor Through-the-wall passive human target detection with WiFi. In: 2019 IEEE Globecom Workshops (GC Wkshps), pp. 1–6. IEEE, Waikoloa, HI, USA (2019)
2. Wang, J., Tian, Z., Yang, X., Zhou, M.: CSI component reconstruction-based AoA Estimation for subtle human-induced reflection under the TTW scenario. IEEE Commun. Lett. **23**(8), 1393–1396 (2019)
3. Wi-Fi Alliance 2017. https://www.wi-fi.org/news-events/newsroom/wi-fi-in-2019. Accessed 21 Feb 2019
4. Banerjee, A., Maas, D., Bocca, M., et al.: Violating privacy through walls by passive monitoring of radio windows. In: the 2014 ACM Conference on Security and Privacy in Wireless and Mobile Networks, pp. 69–80. ACM, New York, NY, USA (2014)
5. Li, W., Piechocki, R.J., Woodbridge, K., Tang, C., Chetty, K.: Passive WiFi radar for human sensing using a stand-alone access point. IEEE Trans. Geoence Remote Sens. **59**(3), 1986–1998 (2020)
6. Chetty, K., Smith, G.E., Woodbridge, K.: Through-the-wall sensing of personnel using passive bistatic WiFi radar at standoff distances. IEEE Trans. Geosci. Remote Sens. **50**(4), 1218–1226 (2012)
7. Wang, J., Tian, Z., Yang, X., Zhou, M.: TWPalo: Through-the-wall passive localization of moving human with Wi-Fi. In: 2019 IEEE Global Communications Conference (GLOBECOM), pp. 1–6. IEEE, Waikoloa, HI, USA (2019)
8. Li, X., et al.: IndoTrack: device-free indoor human tracking with commodity Wi-Fi. ACM Interact. Mobile Wearable and Ubiquit. Technol. **1**(3), 1–22 (2017)
9. Kotaru, M., Joshi, K., Bharadia, D., Kattim, S.: SpotFi: decimeter level localization using Wi-Fi. In: 2015 ACM Conference on Special Interest Group on Data Communication (SIGCOMM 2015), pp. 269–282. ACM, New York, NY, USA (2015)
10. Xie, Y., Xiong, J., Li, M., Jamieson, K.: MD-Track: leveraging multi-dimensionality for passive indoor Wi-Fi tracking. In: 25th Annual International Conference on Mobile Computing and Networking (MobiCom 2019), pp. 1–16. ACM, New York, NY, USA (2019)
11. Schulz, M., Link, J., Gringoli, F., Hollick, M.: Shadow Wi-Fi: teaching smartphones to transmit raw signals and to extract channel state information to implement practical covert channels over Wi-Fi. In: 16th Annual International Conference on Mobile Systems, Applications, and Services (MobiSys 2018), pp. 256–268. ACM, New York, NY, USA (2018)
12. Xi, W., Zhao, J., Li, X.Y., et al.: Electronic frog eye: counting crowd using WiFi. In: IEEE INFOCOM 2014 - IEEE Conference on Computer Communications, pp. 361–369. IEEE, Toronto, ON, Canada (2014)
13. Halperin, D., Hu, W., Sheth, A., Wetherall, D.: Predictable 802.11 packet delivery from wireless channel measurements. In: the 2010 ACM SIGCOMM Conference, pp. 159–170. ACM, New York, NY, USA (2010)

Securing Satellite Internet of Things by Perceiving Content Semantics

Zhiqiang Ruan[1](✉), Liuling Huang[2], and Haibo Luo[1,3]

[1] Minjiang University, Fuzhou 350108, China
[2] Fujian Chuanzheng Communications College, Fuzhou 350007, China
[3] Digital Fujian IoT Laboratory of Intelligent Production, Fuzhou 350108, China

Abstract. Satellite internet of things (S-IoT) is the combination of satellite mobile communication system and internet of things. It can provide vehicle and fleet management, container monitoring, oil and gas monitoring, meteorological data collection, emergency rescue and other related services. Despite the benefits, the communication pattern is built upon the traditional Internet architecture, which makes the information exchange and data protection nontrivial. This paper proposes an efficient and secure data communication paradigm for S-IoT by semantic-aware content perception. It incorporates a particular network model tailored for marine fishery application, and an efficient content encryption and retrieval strategy that achieves self-organized data access. The proposed scheme realizes different levels of data communication based on a set of combinatorial techniques, such as symmetric encryption, asymmetric encryption, content identification and caching. Unlike current data secure solutions that based on TCP/IP architecture, the proposed method does not involve online certificate distribution or complex key management, which especially facilities to implement in large-scale network scenarios. Simulations results demonstrate that our scheme provides a better flexibility for data access in S-IoT.

Keywords: Satellite internet of things · Security · Content-oriented · Self-organized

1 Introduction

The future Internet will be dominated by the big amount of Internet of Things (IoT) data traffic generated by billions of small and affordable embedded devices for sensing, processing, actuation, and communication for serving different applications, including patient monitoring, smart home, industry automation, disaster management, and satellite services [1].

The emerging of IoT faces two fundamental challenges: how to interconnect all different types of digital devices locally and globally that provide IoT functions, and how to realize the data communication associated with things in a consistent and friendly way. The former problem is normally addressed by using host-to-host communication patterns via the Internet Protocol (IP), while the latter is more complicated, to access the

© Springer Nature Switzerland AG 2021
X. Sun et al. (Eds.): ICAIS 2021, CCIS 1424, pp. 414–425, 2021.
https://doi.org/10.1007/978-3-030-78621-2_34

associated real-world data, the application routine must go through a series of mappings among subnetworks, channels, devices, and interface addresses [2, 3]. Although a recent trend is to shift data storage, computation, and communication from resource-constrained devices to the edge or cloud devices [4], it does not fundamentally change the working law of original devices.

In this paper, we aim to address the above two challenges by Named Data Networking (NDN), a promising future Internet architecture within the field of Information Centric Networking (ICN) [5]. Instead of sending packets between source and destination devices identified by numeric IP addresses, NDN disseminates named data at the network level, forwarding directly on names that carry application semantics. This provides a new perspective for IoT applications to name their things and forward related data directly by those names, which makes network infrastructure and IoT applications to operate with unified semantics, and also achieves higher security [2, 6].

The adoption of content-based communication model requires end-to-end data security rather than host-to-host IP-dependent solutions, it is reasonable to assume that only authorized users can access to certain contents, especially in some sensitive environments of IoT applications. Although a variety of access control mechanisms [7–11] have been proposed to provide different purposes of data confidentiality and access control, however, these solutions are implemented on TCP/IP protocol stack, and involve complex operations at the network layer for key distribution and content retrieval [12]. In addition, these schemes use third-party services such as DNS for key distribution and storage that also increases the risk of the whole system being attacked.

We propose an efficient and secure data communication paradigm by leveraging naming convention of NDN and combination of cryptography techniques. In particular, data is first encrypted by a symmetric key, which is then encrypted by the public parameter of the control center, only the expect receivers who occupy the access rights can decrypt the packet and grasp the data. Combined with the comprehensibility of hierarchical structured naming, it can achieve automated cryptographic key management, which overcomes many challenges in the application of typical technologies in current IP networks.

The contribution of this paper is summarized as two-fold:

On the one hand, we identify the challenges of IoT and explore NDN to improve and simplify the communication of IoT in a more straightforward and innovate manner. We argue that the security approaches used in current Internet applications are brittle in IoT environments, among which are the overlapping networks with different administrative domains, heterogeneous devices, and intermittent connectivity via multiple communication channels.

On the other hand, all the elements in IoT, such as data and cryptographic keys are named by leveraging the hierarchically structured naming convention of NDN, such that they can be retrieved automatically, e.g., securing a channel or session between devices by expressing identity of a thing without the addresses of devices, managing the provenance of data, scheming trust relationships among communicating elements, and handling key distribution directly.

2 Models and Design Goals

2.1 Network Model

We consider the scenarios of satellite Internet of things (S-IoT), i.e., china' Tiantong-1, as shown in the Fig. 1, which mainly provides voice and data communication coverage for various handheld and small mobile terminals in china and its surrounding waters. There are no restrictions on the covered terrain, and seamless coverage can be achieved for oceans, mountains, plains, forests, Gobi and desert. It covers all kinds of mobile users such as vehicles, aircraft, ships and individuals. It provides all-weather, all-time, stable and reliable mobile communication services for personal communication, marine transportation, ocean fishing, aviation rescue, tourism scientific research and other fields.

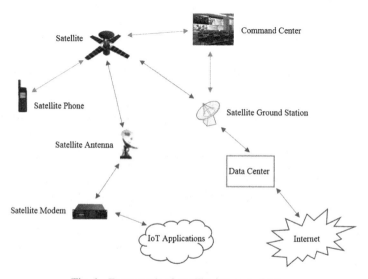

Fig. 1. Framework of satellite internet of things.

For simplicity, we consider the application of S-IoT to marine fishery systems. In particular, there are four types of entities in our network scenario: 1) entities, which including cyber-physical devices, people, and information resources, these entities can be named as "/Tiantong-1/ocean/boat (A/B/C)/..." and "/Tiantong-1/air/aircraft/(A/B/C)/...", they communicate with the earth stations, command center and other entities (i.e., radio buoys); 2) ground station, a dish antenna and accessory electronic engineering for receiving and transmitting satellite signals, it is named by "/Tiantong-1/communication"; 3) command center, which determines the participants' access privileges in S-IoT and represented by "/Tiantong-1/control"; 4) Forwarders, i.e., gateways, satellites, and other repeaters. These devices forward data among things, earth station and command center. For instance, patrol boat, aircraft gateway, and satellite help to forward packets through broadcast channel.

This S-IoT scenario indicates that only authorized entities can obtain specific parts of data and further verify its integrity. For example, when the command center sends an order only pointed to boat A, the devices on boat A return the required data (along with their signatures) toward to the civil earth station or the command center. However, during this process, all the other entities such as aircraft A and boat B cannot see the content even though they have helped to transmit the data packets. In what follows, we will use this scenario to illustrate how the presented method helps to provide effective communication confidentiality and access control.

Note that such network model is also applicable to the generic Internet of things scenarios, except that the functionality and performance of devices in this work could be several orders of magnitude higher than that of normal IoT nodes, e.g., satellite phone, which has much longer communication distance and larger computing power.

2.2 Design Goals

In a S-IoT system, the primary motive of the adversary is unauthorize access to the devices and to the intended data that they collect and store; the signature of a data packet can be forged with the designed access rules that do not assigned to the adversary; they can also reveal the privacy of specific individual by prying into data packets to get the key primitives or attributes. To address these problems, one should establish proper trust relationships among different parties in the system. In specifically, each member in the system has a pair of public key/private key, it can only access data content that authorized to itself, all the data packets in the system can be authenticated via signature verification. Take Fig. 1 as an example, a boat can check the data packets either from the command center or the aircraft that intend to it, and verse vice.

Different from traditional access control mechanisms that focus on media access on network layer, we aim to achieve data content control with additional objectives: 1) access control needs to be performed at a fine-grained level; 2) the execution of access control is automated as possible without continuous intervention; 3) the design approach is robust against the network intermittent connections.

3 The Proposed Scheme

3.1 Design Principle

There are four parties in the system corresponding to the referred four types of entities: the control center (e.g., command center), the data center (e.g., civil earth station), the data producer, and the data consumer. The control center makes access rules and publishes a list of named key pairs, which are called PKC (public key of control center) and SKC (Secret key of control center). We utilize structured semantic-aware named data to formulate access strategy and logical hierarchy (the conventional symmetric data encryption algorithm and public-based cryptography are also used in as a supplement), the name of a PKC means which name prefix of content (namespace hierarchy) can be encrypted with the key. Similarly, the name of a SKC defines the access granularity to whom the data can be authorized to decrypted.

The data producers are entities who generated data for S-IoT system, the data content is first encrypted by a data encryption key (DK), which is further encrypted by a PKC.

When a producer wants to encrypt the data, it retrieves the named PKC from the network or data center according to the content name prefix of the data. Since the required PKC has been published by the control center previously, any producers who have such same name prefix (located in the same group) can retrieval the PKC through sending an interest packet, after data encryption is completed ($E_{DK}(data)$), the shared key is encapsulated ($E_{PKC}(DK)$) into a separate data packet (in other cases, these two parts can be concatenated in the same packet). On the other hand, when a potential data receptor obtains the encrypted data, it sends an interest packet to get the named SKC. Note that the SKC is encrypted by the authorized entity's public key, and only the authorized consumers can decrypt SKC and recover SK ($D_{SKC}(E_{PKC}(DK))$) with which to further decrypting the data ($D_{DK}(data)$). Figure 2 shows the design principle of our work.

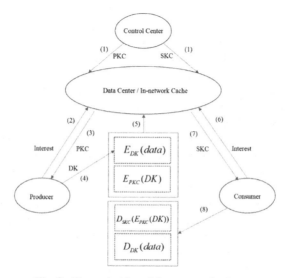

Fig. 2. The main idea of the proposed scheme.

The above scheme requires producers to encrypt data content according to the name prefix of PKC to achieve fine-grained access control. A more specific PKC name leads to the SKC decrypts less content packets. We also leverage the control center to restrict authorized parties through SKC distribution. The more SKCs a consumer has, the more data packets he can access. In order to achieve self-organized content access and data encryption and decryption, all key materials should be available from the network. Since PKCs (access rules), DKs and SKCs (decryption keys) are all released as NDN packets, each entity can directly retrieve them by names, as a result, the whole system is able to operate automatically after that. In addition, NDN's in-network cache ensure that as long as there is a replica of these keys on repository, they can be retrieved at any time even if the network suffers from intermittent connectivity, this is vital for many particular purposes, such as maritime search and rescue operations. Clearly, delay is the primary consideration for these applications.

3.2 Object Identification

A significant difference between the presented scheme and conventional IoT is whether the things have semantic meanings. All the things in S-IoT are identified by a specific name, such as data, keys, and entities. The entities and some important keys that used are named as follows.

1) *Entities*: Similar to DNS, each region in S-IoT is associated with the affiliation, for instance, "ocean" is named "Tiantong-1/ocean". Then, each entity can be uniquely identified by naming with "region name + entity id", e.g., boat A in the ocean is named "/Tiantong-1/ocean/boat A". In addition, sensors in the same entity are organized into the same group, e.g., sensor X in boat A is named "Tiantong-1/ocean/boat A/sensor X". Each node names the generated data by a unique name and an increasing integer, that is, "sensor id + serial number", e.g., "/Tiantong/ocean/boat A/sensor 1/30". One salient feature of such naming convention is that all objects as name prefixes regardless of node heterogeneity, enables the applications to IoT.

2) *DK*: The producers generate DKs to encrypt the data, it uses the naming convention for DK and DK data packet as:

DK Name = "/Tiantong-1/encryptor name identifier/DK/key-id".
DK Data Packet Name = "/Tiantong-1/name identifier of encryptor/DK/key-id/ENCRYPTED-BY/name identifier of data/PKC/ key-id".

where name identifier is the prefix of respective entity. PKC is the encryptor's ECC key, key-id is the identifier of the key, and the item "ENCRYPTED-BY" indicates that the SK data packet is encrypted by PKC.

3) *PKC*: A producer needs to retrieval the PKC from data center or in-network repository so as to encrypt DK. The name of PKC and the corresponding data packet are denoted by

PKC Name = "/Tiantong-1/name identifier of data/PKC/ key-id".

The PKC is published by the control center in a plaintext, to ensure the truthfulness of the released packets, the control center should append the signature on the packet.

4) *SKC*: The naming convention of SKC is similar to PKC expect that SKC is encrypted with the authorized entity's public key, so that only the intended entity can recover it and obtain the corresponding information.

SKC Name: "/Tiantong-1/ name identifier of data/ SKC/ key-id1".
SKC Data Packet: "/Tiantong-1/name identifier of data/SKC/key-id1/ENCRYPTED BY/name identifier of consumer/public-key of consumer/key-id2".

where key-id1 is the key identifier of PKC and key-id2 is the key identifier of the consumer that used to encrypt the SKC.

3.3 Data Access Control

Access control consists of five steps: key generation and setup, key distribution, encryption, decryption, access structure update.

1) Key Generation and Setup. The control center is associated with a dedicated NDN namespace, i.e., "/control center". In addition to the PKC and SKC mentioned above, the control center also generates signature keys, attributes and other necessary public parameters. Most of parameters can be preloaded on different devices, for example, a set of attributes and decryption key chain can be predefined on each node.

When the network is not stable or the control center is switch to the silent mode after the bootstrapping process, the system can still rely on in-network data storage to provide PKC and SKC to the requesters, such that producers and consumers can continue to work without passing through the control center.

2) Key Distribution. It is noted that conventional IoT usually takes great efforts in dealing with key distribution and management, either in a distributed or centralized manner, this may consume a lot of network resources, especially when the number of nodes reaches to a large scale (e.g., tens or hundreds of millions). In this work, both PKC and SKC are fetched through interest packet query, a query process delivers the name information of key, who can use the key and what kinds of data can be encrypted/decrypted with that key. Producers and consumers can generate interest packet automatically to fetch PKC and SKC by following the naming convention, interest packets are sent only if the required content is needed to retrieve, avoiding unnecessary waste of communication resources.

3) Data Encryption. For anyone in the network who wants to encrypt the data, it first generates DK locally, the data encryption algorithm can choose AES (Advanced Encryption Standard) with block cipher in CBC (Cipher Block Chaining) mode. Then it sends an interest packet that includes the corresponding PKC name from the network, the data name prefix decides which PKC should be used. When receiving the required PKC, the encryptor adds DK name to the encrypted data packet, and finally publishes the encrypted DK data packet to the network. Based on the application needs, the encrypted data packet and the encrypted DK packet can be wrapped together in one data packet. In addition, all data packets are signed by the encryptor's signature key. There are two ways of signing, one method is based on the conventional asymmetric cryptosystem, the encryptor signs the data packet with its own private key, and the verifier uses the public key to check its integrity, the public key of encryptor can also be released by the control center in advance.

4) Data Decryption. The consumer obtains the desired data through sending an interest packet to the network, any node who holds the required data can reply to it. Otherwise, the request will be directed to the data center, where the content data packet has earlier been published by the producer (see Sect. 3.1). After receiving the required data, the consumer checks the integrity of the data by signature verification, and then it learns the DK name from the encrypted content packet, if the DK data packet is not wrapped with the content packet, it will send an interest to fetch the DK packet separately. If the consumer is the potential decryptor, it can learn the PKC name from the DK packet and then send an interest packet to get the corresponding SKC from the network. For example, a consumer with name "Tiantong-1/air/aircraft B" wants to decrypt the data "/Tiantong-1/ocean/boat A/Content" from the producer "/Tiantong-1/ocean/boat A", the data access includes the following steps.

Step1: Aircraft B sends an interest to the network for a particular category of data, "/Tiantong-1/air/aircraft B/ocean/boat A/name identifier of data/TS1", where TS1 is a timestamp or random number that used to prevent replay attacks.
Step2: The network replies data packet to aircraft B, "/Tiantong-1/ocean/boat A/air/aircraft B/name identifier of data/TS2/ENCRYPTED BY/Tiantong-1/ocean/boat A/DK/DK-id", where the data content is encrypted by boat A's DK, and TS2 is another timestamp.
Step3: Aircraft B sends an interest to the network for DK data packet, "/Tiantong-1/air/aircraft B/ocean/boat A/DK/DK-id/TS3", aircraft B sets a timer or threshold for every interest packet until it receives the data or the timer times out.
Step4: Aircraft B receives DK packet and obtain PKC, "Tiantong-1/air/aircraft B/ocean/boat A/DK/DK-id/ENCRYPTED BY/Tiantong-1/ocean/boat A/PKC/key-id". Note that a data packet contains data name item and the content item, aircraft B can read the DK name easily from the received data packet, but the content item is encrypted by PKC. Similarly, aircraft B can extract the SKC name from PKC name and sends an interest to retrieve SKC.
Step5: Aircraft B sends an interest packet to fetch the SKC from the network, "/Tiantong-1/air/aircraft B/SKC/key-id1/TS4", here, aircraft B has learned SKC name from the obtained DK packet by replacing PKC to SKC.
Step6: The network replies SKC data packet to aircraft B, "Tiantong-1/air/aircraft B/SKC/key-id1/ENCRYPTED BY/Tiantong-1/control center/name identifier of data/Tiantong-1/ocean/boat A/ sensor X/ public key of aircraft B /key-id2", where key-id1 is the identifier of SKC and key-id2 is the public key of aircraft B. Later, aircraft B can use its private key to decrypt the packet for obtaining DK and to further decrypt the content data.

5) Access Structure Update. There are several reasons for the control center to renew the access rights of users (entities or nodes). First, a user withdraws normally from the network based on certain adjustment strategies; Second, a user is reported to be captured by the adversary, and once a user is compromised, all the key primitives and data are acquired by the adversary; Third, in most cases, PKC and SKC are short-term and need to be revoke periodically by the control center, especially in sensitive military exercises or real war environments. The granted access rights are canceled to avoid a user further acquiring network information, however, revocation operations are transparent to the remaining users, as they can automatically retrieve the newly key information from the network. In particular, the control center publishes a special broadcast packet to the data center or in-network like "/Tiantong-1/ control center/ update/ PKC/ < old key-id, new key-id > / name identifier of data", where a two tuple of old key-id and new key-id is used to notify a user of the change of the corresponding PKC according to the data name prefix. The user will generate a new DK and encrypt it with the new PKC. The update of

SKC is similar to PKC except that the data packet is encrypted by the consumer's public key: "/Tiantong-1/control center/update/ SKC/<old key-id, new key-id>/ENCRYPTED BY/name identifier of consumer/public-key of consumer/key-id".

4   Evaluation

We evaluate the performance of the proposed scheme in terms of cryptography operations and data retrieval efficiency, and compare it to conventional TCP/IP-based solutions RBAC [7] and TACIoT [11]. We choose 10 groups of sensors with each group member ranges from 6 to 20, sensors adopt IEEE 802.15.4 2.4 GHz to communication with each other. There is a gateway within each group (emulating each boat, aircraft, etc.), and several drones roaming between each group. The packet sizes of Interest and Data are 40 bytes and 132 bytes, respectively.

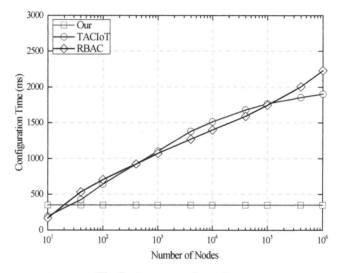

Fig. 3. Average configure time.

Figure 3 examines the configuration time of key distribution by three schemes under different number of nodes. In TCP/IP-based scheme, the key distribution might involve network setup and configuration (IP address, DNS resolution), service startup and invocation, and other necessary routines. Although TACIoT does not need to execute key assignment, but it has to calculate the trust values according to devices' social relationships, security considerations, reputation, and quality of service. We can see that the configuration time of the proposed scheme is independent of the number of nodes, while the configuration time of RBAC and TACIoT are both increase with the increasing number of nodes.

Figure 4 investigates the cache hit rate under different packet loss rate of all three schemes. Note that RBAC and TACIoT do not or rare to adopt in-network cache mechanism, thus, the request has to go through a much longer path, in most cases, the request needs to be directed to the data center, when the number of loss rate of packets increases, they have to retransmit the requests, which increases the entire response time. On the contrary, we can improve the query speed and recall rate within the network, for a particular of data, we allow to store multiple copies of the data on different nodes across the network, thus, it can hit the required data among the nodes.

Next, we compare the retrieval time of three schemes under different number of requests. As can be seen from Fig. 5, with the number of requests grows larger, all three schemes incur more time to obtain the data, however, TCP/IP-based solutions require the most time to deal with request, the reason is straightforward, it involves a lot of time to route the request across the various sub-networks with different kinds of interface and channels, and as well to transform rules to a comprehensible manner. What's more, the delay in TACIoT includes a series of operations, such as evaluate the authorization credential and the time to validate the token manager's signature, as a result, the retrieval time is rapidly increases as the number of requests increases.

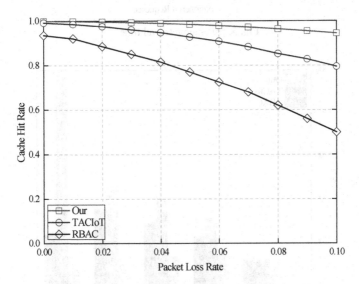

Fig. 4. Cache hit rate.

Finally, we investigate the cryptography operations incur by three schemes. Figure 6 shows that during the encryption stage, three schemes incur almost the same time, while in the decryption phase, TACIoT consumes the highest time, as it needs to collect trust values and perform a lot of calculations on the reputations and other parameters. The signing phase and verifying phase have the similar effect, while our method still incurs the less time, this is due to the fact that signing key can be retrieved before the system start or dynamically request by the users during system operation. In both cases, it only needs to obtain the required key from in-network data depository. The most difference lies in the revoking stage, where TACIoT consumes the highest time, and our scheme reacts the fastest one. This is because TACIoT needs to generate new access rights and then inform all remaining nodes through complex operations via broadcast or multicast.

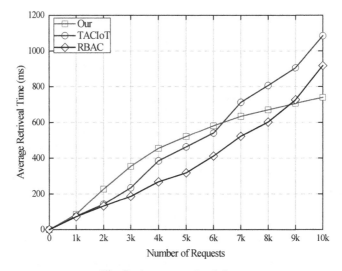

Fig. 5. Average retrieval time.

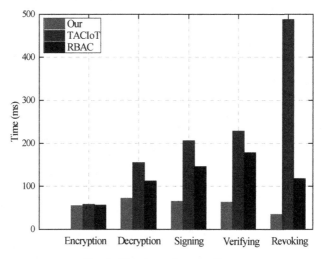

Fig. 6. Cryptography operations.

5 Conclusions

This paper provided a new data communication and access scheme with security in mind, which integrates content-aware identification, routing and caching. Data and cryptographic keys are named by hierarchical naming structure, such that they can be retrieved automatically. Experimental results show that the proposed scheme can greatly reduce the complexity of the network and improve the data retrieval time. As future work, we envisage to continue with further incorporates the attribute features of IoT, and employing attribute-based encryption and signature. We also expect to conduct more experiments in real IoT scenarios.

Acknowledgement. This work is supported by the National Nature Science Foundation of China (61871204, 61902167 and 61901207) and the Natural Science Foundation of Fujian Province (2018J01544). The authors declare that they have no conflicts of interest to report regarding the present study.

References

1. Al-Fuqaha, A., Guizani, M., Mohammadi, M., Aledhari, M., Ayyash, M.: Internet of things: a survey on enabling technologies, protocols, and applications. IEEE Commun. Surv. Tutor. **17**(4), 2347–2376 (2015)
2. Shang, W., et al.: Named data networking of things. In: Proceedings of 1st IEEE International Conference on Internet-of-Things Design and Implementation, Berlin, Germany, pp. 1–12 (2016)
3. Adat, V., Gupta, B.: Security in internet of things: issues, challenges, taxonomy, and architecture. Telecommun. Syst. **67**(3), 423–441 (2018)
4. Zhu, C., Leung, V.C.M., Wang, K., Zhang, Y., Yang, L.T.: Multi-method data delivery for sensor-cloud. IEEE Commun. Mag. **55**(5), 176–182 (2017)
5. Zhang, L., et al.: Named data networking. ACM SIGCOMM Comput. Commun. Rev. **44**(3), 66–73 (2014)
6. Ravidas, S., Lekidis, A., Paci, F., Zannone, N.: Access control in internet-of-things: a survey. J. Netw. Comput. Appl. **144**, 79–101 (2019)
7. Liu, Q., Tinghuai, M., Fan, X., Yuan, T., Abdullah, A.D., Mohammed, A.D.: Access control policy based on friend circle. Comput. Mater. Con. **62**(3), 1143–1159 (2020)
8. Liang, K., Shi, Y., Zhang, L., Liu, D., Yang, Q.: A lightweight three-factor user authentication protocol for the information perception of IoT. Comput. Mater. Con. **58**(2), 545–565 (2019)
9. Jahid, S., Mittal, P., Borisov, N.: Easier: encryption-based access control in social networks with efficient revocation. In: Proceedings of the 6th ACM Symposium on Information, Computer and Communications Security, Hong Kong, China, pp. 411–415 (2011)
10. Mahalle, P.N., Thakre, P.A., Prasad, N.R., Prasad, R.: A fuzzy approach to trust based access control in internet of things. In: Proceedings of IEEE International Conference on Wireless Communications, Atlantic, NJ, USA, pp. 212–221 (2013)
11. Bernal Bernabe, J., Hernandez Ramos, J.L., Skarmeta Gomez, A.F.: TACIoT: multidimensional trust-aware access control system for the Internet of Things. Soft. Comput. **20**(5), 1763–1779 (2015). https://doi.org/10.1007/s00500-015-1705-6
12. Hady, A.A.: Duty cycling centralized hierarchical routing protocol with content analysis duty cycling mechanism for wireless sensor networks. Comput. Syst. Sci. Eng. **35**(5), 347–355 (2020)

Research on Cultivating Senior Technical Talents Based on the Internet of Things Platform

Jian Zhao, Shengqian Ma$^{(\boxtimes)}$, Qiang Wei, Chao Zhang, Chunling Jiang, Shunwei Wu, Baitao Feng, Zhenyuan Han, Yi Liu, Le Chang, and Jingfang Tan$^{(\boxtimes)}$

School of Physics and Electronic Engineering, Taishan University,
Taian 271000, Shandong, People's Republic of China

Abstract. Based on the discussion of the perception layer, network layer and application layer of the Internet of Things (IOT), this paper constructs a platform for cultivating senior technical talents of the Internet of things, which takes the application layer as the core, radiates the perception layer and network layer, provides the comprehensive and high-quality characteristics of senior technical talents, and discusses the senior technical talents with advanced engineering technology background, and create senior technical personnel with high starting point, strong application ability and strong engineering adaptability.

Keywords: Internet of Things · Senior technical personnel · Sensors

1 Introduction

In 1998, Massachusetts Institute of Technology (MIT) put forward the idea of the Internet of Things (IOT) with EPC (Electronic Product Code) system. In 1999, the concept of internet of things was first put forward by auto - ID center in the United States. The internet of things uses sensor sensing technology to obtain various parameter information of objects and environment. Through various wireless communication technologies, the information is summarized to the information communication network, and transmitted to the back-end for data analysis and mining processing. Valuable information is extracted to the decision-making level. Through certain mechanisms and measures, the intelligent control of the real world is realized, and all items are passed through RFID information sensor equipment is connected with the internet to realize intelligent identification and management. IOT is a kind of network which uses radio frequency identification (RFID), sensors, infrared sensors, global positioning system, laser scanner and other information acquisition equipment, according to the agreed protocol, to connect any object with the Internet for information exchange and communication, so as to realize intelligent identification, positioning, tracking, monitoring and management. Thus, the core of the internet of things is to connect objects to the network, and the future of the internet of things will be the artificial intelligence life perception decision-making action system. The internet of things is a comprehensive technology system involving computers, communications, control, and electronics. In the future, it can also integrate

X. Sun et al. (Eds.): ICAIS 2021, CCIS 1424, pp. 426–439, 2021.
https://doi.org/10.1007/978-3-030-78621-2_35

blockchain, artificial intelligence, wearable devices, augmented reality (AR), robots, autonomous driving, drones and other technologies. Intelligent interaction, intelligent presentation of information, and action at any time to realize the internet of things +. At present, China has formed a certain market scale, and the internet of things technology has been applied in the fields of public safety, urban management, environmental monitoring, energy saving and emission reduction, and transportation supervision. Wuxi, Xiamen and other places have begun to deploy, actively promote industry applications, and build demonstration projects and demonstration zones. It is predicted that China's sensor network terminals will reach hundreds of billions around 2035, and sensors will be ubiquitous in life by 2050. The internet of things has a wide range of uses, involving all aspects of life, such as intelligent transportation, environmental protection, public safety, smart home, industrial monitoring, agricultural production, food traceability and many other fields. Although the internet of things has not yet been widely used, some successful cases have achieved substantial improvements in management efficiency, and the application of internet of things technology has a broad prospect. Compared with traditional IT applications for the management of people, equipment, things, operation mode, environment, etc., IOT applications have the following characteristics:

Real-time: The acquired information is the information that occurs in real time, while traditional IT applications often obtain the result information, which can only be processed after the event, and cannot be controlled in real time to change the result.

Refinement: IOT applications pay more attention to collecting process information that produces results, so that the accuracy of the information can be ensured, and accurate analysis and effective improvement can also be performed.

Intelligentization: IOT applications often have the characteristics of automatic collection, processing, and automatic control, especially the transfer of the original information processing functions in the terminal to the internet server, so that it can complete more complex information processing, and the learning function, the information processing rules can be adapted to the continuous changes of business.

2 Key Technologies of the Internet of Things

The IOT has three features: first, comprehensive perception, that is, the use of radio frequency identification, sensors, two-dimensional code and other objects to obtain information anytime and anywhere; Second, reliable transmission, through a variety of telecommunications network and the integration of the internet, the object information real-time and accurate transmission out; Third, intelligent processing, the use of cloud computing, fuzzy recognition and other intelligent computing technologies, massive data and information analysis and processing, intelligent control of objects. Therefore, the architecture of the IOT is divided into three layers: the bottom layer is the perception layer used to perceive data, the second layer is the network layer (transmission layer) for data transmission, and the top layer is the application layer. As can be seen from the three-layer structure of the IOT, the industry chain of the IOT can be subdivided into four links, namely object identification, perception, processing and information transmission. Key technologies include two-dimensional code, radio frequency identification, sensors, smart chips and wireless transmission network of telecom operators.

2.1 Item Identification Technology

Two-Dimensional Code. Two-dimensional code is also called two-digit barcode or two-dimensional barcode. It is an application technology that uses a certain geometric shape to be distributed on a plane (black and white) according to a certain rule to record information. From the perspective of technical principles, the two-dimensional code cleverly uses the concepts of "0" and "1" bit streams which constitute the internal logic basis of the computer, uses some geometric shapes corresponding to binary to represent the numerical information, and automatically reads the information through the image input device or photoelectric scanning equipment to realize the automatic processing of the information. At present, two-dimensional codes are mainly used in the field of information/value stream, that is, the field that needs to describe the characteristic attributes of the subject matter (that is, goods). In this field, the description of information and attributes cannot be achieved with simple codes (one-dimensional codes) function, therefore, two-dimensional code and radio frequency identification technology must be used. Two-dimensional code is widely used in customs/tax collection and management, document and book circulation management (China's State Council is implementing the official document management by agencies, using the two-dimensional code technology; at the same time, the state press has officially announced that it will replace the original one-dimensional book code with two-dimensional code), vehicle management, ticket management (including almost all industries), payment applications (such as electronic receipt) and asset management and industrial production process management, e-commerce and other fields.

RFID Technology. RFID is a kind of non-contact automatic identification technology. It can automatically identify the target object and obtain relevant data through radio frequency signal. The identification work can work in various harsh environments without manual intervention. A complete radio frequency identification system is composed of three parts: the reader, the electronic tag (TAG), the so-called transponder, and the application software system. Its working principle is that the reader transmits a specific frequency. The radio wave energy is given to the transponder to drive the transponder circuit to send out the internal data. At this time, the reader receives and interprets the data in sequence and sends them to the application for corresponding processing. Radio frequency identification technology can be applied to various fields of society, such as security, logistics, warehousing, traceability, anti-counterfeiting, tourism, medical treatment, education and other fields, mainly to realize product identification, tracking, and traceability and so on.

2.2 Sensor Technology

A sensor is a detection device that can feel the measured information, and can transform the monitored and fall information into electrical signals or other required forms of information output according to certain rules to meet the needs of information transmission, processing, storage, and reality, recording and control requirements. It is the primary link to realize automatic monitoring and automatic control. In the IOT system, equipment that collects information and simple processing of various parameters is called an IOT sensor. In the IOT system, the equipment for information collection and simple processing of various parameters is called the IOT sensor. The sensor can exist independently or present with other devices. However, it is the perception and input part of the IOT in either way. sensor is a device or device that senses and detects some parameter information of an object, such as temperature, humidity, pressure, size, composition, etc., and converts these parameter information into transmissible signals (such as voltage) according to the conversion rules. They are usually composed of a parameter sensitive component and a conversion component. At present, sensor technology has penetrated into various fields of science and national economy, and plays an increasingly important role in industrial and agricultural production, scientific research and improving people's lives.

2.3 Network Communication Technology

Network communication technology includes wired and wireless transmission technology, switching technology, gateway technology and so on. M2M communication technology refers To machine-to-machine communication To realize the connection and communication among people, machines and systems. M2M technology can combine WiMAX, WiFi, Bluetooth, ZigBee, LoRa, NB-IOT, RFID, UWB and other wireless connection technologies to provide communication services. Common wireless communication technologies include: mobile communication 2G, 3G, 4G, 5G technology, WiMAX, WiFi, Bluetooth, ZigBee, LoRa, NB- IOT, RFID, etc. Network communication technology refers to the collection, storage, processing and transmission of data in the form of graphics and text through computers and network communication equipment, so that information resources can be fully shared. Communication network is a communication system in which communication endpoints, nodes (junctions) and transmission links are organically connected to each other in order to provide connected or unconnected transmission between two or more specified communication endpoints. According to the function and purpose, communication network can be divided into physical network, business network and support management network. Physical network is an entity structure composed of user terminal, switching system, transmission system and other communication equipment. It is the material foundation of communication network, also known as equipment network. In the network, the information can be transmitted to the user's electromagnetic network, which can be transmitted to the user's electromagnetic network. According to their different functions, user terminals can be divided into telephone terminals, non telephone terminals and multimedia communication terminals. Telephone terminal refers to ordinary telephone, mobile telephone, etc.; A business network is a network that unblocks various communication services such as telephone, telegraph, fax, data, and images, and refers to the service function of the communication network. According to their business types, they can be divided into telephone networks, telegraph networks, and data networks. Support management network is a network formed to ensure the normal operation of the business network, enhance the network function and improve the service quality of the whole network. In the support management network transmission is the corresponding control, monitoring and signaling signals. According to their different functions, it can be divided into signaling network, synchronization network and management network [1].

2.4 Positioning Technology

At present, the positioning technology has four systems:

American global positioning system: in 1994, 24 GPS satellites were set up, 21 work, 3 spare; Russian "Glonas" system: in 2011, it was officially put into operation around the world, with 24 working, 3 maintenance, 3 spare and 1 test; European "Galileo" system: launched in 2002, the system plan by 30 satellites, only 4 satellites at present; China's "Beidou" system: In 2012, 12 satellites were in orbit, covering the Asia-Pacific region.

In the late 20th century, China began to explore the development path of satellite navigation systems suitable for national conditions and gradually formed a three-step development strategy: at the end of 2000, the Beidou No. 1 system was built to provide services to China; At the end of 2012, the Beidou No. 2 system was built to provide services to the Asia-Pacific region; On June 23, 2020, the last Beidou-3 global system (ie the fifty-fifth Beidou navigation satellite) networking satellite was successfully launched, marking the completion of the Beidou global constellation deployment six months in advance. This is a global satellite navigation system independently constructed and operated by China, which will provide global users with all-weather, all-day, high-precision positioning, navigation and timing services. Construction of Beidou-3 was launched in November 2009. For more than 10 years, the project construction has gone through five stages of key technology research, experimental satellite engineering, minimal system, basic system, and complete system. The global constellation deployment was completed six months in advance and the full system service was opened. Open as soon as it is built, and open as a service. The first is to conquer key core technologies and achieve autonomous control. More than 400 units and more than 300,000 scientific and technological personnel have gathered wisdom to tackle key problems, overcome more than 160 key core technologies such as inter-satellite links, high-precision atomic clocks, and break through the localization of more than 500 device components, and realize the domestic production of Beidou-3 satellite core components, which the conversion rate is 100%. The second is to give full play to the advantages of the nationwide system to efficiently complete networking. Strengthen centralized and unified leadership, build a strong project overall and two general research teams, and innovate research and development systems based on overall, technology, quality, and progress. The single-satellite development cycle is shortened by a quarter, and the carrier rocket assembly cycle is shortened by a third, The satellite network access cycle is shortened by three quarters. Build and form a risk analysis and control guarantee chain, launch without hidden dangers and go to heaven without doubts. Since November 2017, 18 arrows and 30 satellites have been launched with high-density in two and a half years, and more than 40 ground stations have been built, rapidly forming the satellite ground integrated operation capability.

The construction target is benchmarked with the international standard, iterative upgrading and incremental engineering are implemented, and the functional performance index reaches the world-class level. First, the system is powerful. Beidou-3 has two major functions of navigation, positioning and communication data transmission. It can provide seven kinds of services, including positioning and navigation time service, global short message communication, regional short message communication, international search and rescue, satellite based enhancement, ground-based enhancement and precise point positioning. It is a powerful global satellite navigation system. Second, the performance index is advanced. The global positioning accuracy is better than 10 m, the speed measurement accuracy is better than 0.2 m/s, the time service accuracy is better than 20 ns, and the service availability is better than 99%, and the performance in the Asia-Pacific region is better. After the completion of the beidou global system, the global service availability of the beidou system has exceeded 99%, and there are no areas that the system cannot cover; the sky map of the beidou satellites over typical areas in the world shows that the number of visible satellites in each area has increased significantly. The third is the positioning accuracy of the Beidou system. According to the calculation results of the global continuous monitoring and evaluation system in the latest week, the global measured positioning accuracy of the Beidou system is 2.34M. The short message communication service has been upgraded and expanded. The regional communication capacity has reached 14000 bits (1000 Chinese characters) each time. It can not only transmit text, but also voice and pictures, and support 560 bits (40 Chinese characters) global communication capability each time. Satellite-based enhanced services have a first-class approach vertical guidance (APV-I) capability, which fills the gap in my country's satellite-based enhanced services. The detection probability of the international search and rescue service is better than 99%, and it has the characteristic ability to confirm the return link, which significantly enhances the survival confidence of people in distress. In addition, enhanced ground and precise single-point positioning can provide the highest centimeter-level positioning service. It also includes interface control documents for five types of services including positioning and navigation timing (B2b), satellite-based enhancement (BDSBAS-B1C), ground-based enhancement, precision single-point positioning (PPP-B2b), and international search and rescue services. The Beidou official website is simultaneously online. The interface control documents for the two types of services of regional short message communication and global short message communication will be released directionally. So far, the interface control documents issued by Beidou system have covered all 7 types of services.

The Beidou system has fully served the transportation, public safety, disaster relief, agriculture, forestry, animal husbandry and fishery, urban governance and other industries, and has integrated into the construction of national core infrastructure such as electricity, finance, and communications. The 28 nm process chip has been mass-produced, and the 22nm process chip is about to be mass-produced. Most smartphones support the Beidou function, and mobile phones that support Beidou ground-enhanced high-precision applications are already on the market. A complete industrial chain integrating chips, modules, boards, terminals and operation services is built. In the past 10 years, the total output value of China's satellite navigation and location service industry has increased by more than 20% annually, reaching 345 billion yuan in 2019 and is expected to exceed 400 billion yuan in 2020. Beidou has been applied in China Europe train transportation, construction and operation of Beijing Zhangjiakou high-speed railway, civil aviation, etc. the high-precision service based on Beidou has played an active role in fighting against the new epidemic situation and flood in southern China. It is speeding up its entry into new infrastructure, and is deeply integrated with new technologies such as new generation communication, blockchain, Internet of things, artificial intelligence, and so on Come forth. Second, China's Beidou, the world's Beidou. Beidou is one of the four major global satellite navigation systems approved by the United Nations. The compatibility and interoperability of satellite navigation with the United States, Russia and the European Union, as well as the cooperation between the systems, have continued to deepen. It has successfully entered many international organizations such as civil aviation, maritime affairs, search and rescue satellite, mobile communication, etc., and a number of international standards supporting Beidou system have been released. China Arab Beidou Cooperation Forum and China Central Asia Beidou cooperation forum were successfully held. The first overseas Beidou center was built in Tunisia, and the Algerian foundation strengthening network project was awarded. At the 9th ministerial meeting of the China Arab Cooperation Forum, China and Argentina agreed to continue to promote in-depth cooperation. At present, Beidou related products have been exported to more than 120 countries and regions, providing services to users above 100 million. The land mapping, precision agriculture, digital construction and smart port based on Beidou have been successfully applied in ASEAN, South Asia, Eastern Europe, West Asia and Africa. So the main purpose of the positioning system.

(1) Land applications, mainly including vehicle navigation, emergency response, atmospheric physical observation, geophysical resource exploration, engineering measurement, deformation monitoring, crustal movement monitoring, municipal planning control, etc.

(2) Marine applications, including the determination of the best voyage route of ocean-going vessels, real-time ship scheduling and navigation, marine rescue, marine treasure hunting, hydrogeological survey and marine platform positioning, sea level rise and fall monitoring, etc.

(3) Aerospace applications, including aircraft navigation, aviation remote sensing attitude control, low-orbit satellite orbit determination, missile guidance, aviation rescue, and manned spacecraft protection and detection.

3 Internet of Things Management Platform

The Fig. 1 shows IOT management platform. As everyone knows, the IOT has perception layer, network layer and application layer. The IOT management platform is mainly established for the application layer. As can be seen from the figure, the platform covers smart industry (production process control, production environment monitoring, manufacturing supply chain tracking, product life cycle monitoring, promotion of safe production and energy saving and emission reduction), smart agriculture (agricultural resource utilization, agriculture Refined production management, production and breeding environment monitoring, agricultural product quality and safety management and product traceability), intelligent logistics (building inventory monitoring, distribution management, safety traceability and other modern circulation application systems, building a logistics public service platform across regions, industries, and departments, realize the

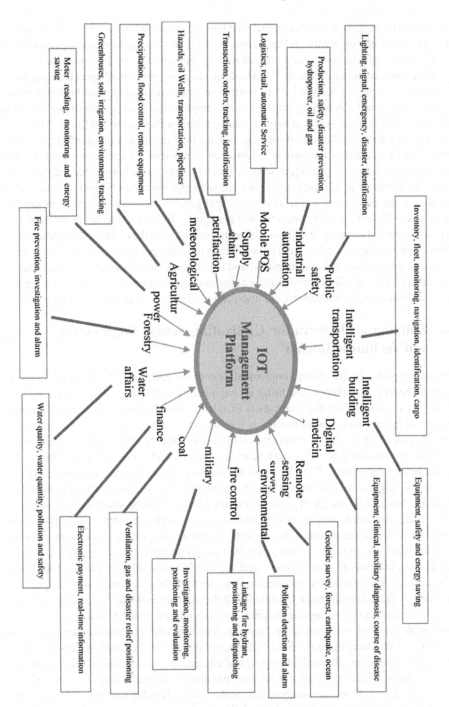

Fig. 1. Internet of Things management platform

integrated management of e-commerce and logistics distribution), intelligent transportation (traffic state perception and exchange, traffic guidance and intelligent management and control, vehicle positioning and scheduling, vehicle remote detection and service, vehicle-road collaborative control, and build an open integrated intelligent transportation platform), smart grid (power facility inspection, smart substation, distribution network automation, smart electricity, smart dispatch, remote meter reading, building a safe, stable, and reliable smart power network), smart environmental protection (pollution source monitoring, water quality monitoring, air monitoring), ecological monitoring, the establishment of intelligent environmental protection information collection network and information platform), intelligent security (social security monitoring, hazardous chemical transportation monitoring, food safety monitoring, important bridges, buildings, rail transit, water conservancy facilities, municipal pipeline network and other infrastructure safety Detection, early warning and emergency linkage), intelligent medical care (pharmaceutical circulation and hospital management, with the collection and analysis of human physiological and medical parameters as the entry point to carry out telemedicine services for families and communities) and smart home (home network, home security, home appliance intelligence) control, energy intelligent calculation, energy saving and low carbon, distance education), etc. each sub-project is a small management platform.

4 Building a Platform for Cultivating Senior Engineering and Technical Talents

In order to achieve the smooth implementation of the conversion between new and old kinetic energy, to cultivate and bring up engineering and technical personnel with the spirit of craftsmanship, the cultivation of talents must be first, especially innovative engineering and technical personnel is the top priority. The spirit of craftsmanship is the pursuit of excellence, the spirit of quality, the spirit of customer-oriented service. At present, universities and governments are only discrete, immature, or crossing the river byrubbing stones. They have not raised these to the height of science. Today's society is impetuous and pursues "short, flat and fast" (less investment, the immediate benefits brought by the short cycle and quick results. College students who adhere to the "craftsman spirit" rely on beliefs and beliefs to watch the continuous improvement and perfection of the products they design. Therefore, innovation and entrepreneurship are the main line in teaching and practice. Taking curriculum system reforms, training platforms, technology competitions, and school-enterprise alliances as the four horse-drawn carriages, gradually establish a more reasonable and more complete practical model [6]. Based on this model, through rich theoretical knowledge, create theoretically excellent engineering technology talents, use electronic engineer training and participate in various types of electronic design competitions to gradually cultivate the professional qualities of engineering and technical talents, through writing scientific papers, to achieve higher scientific and theoretical qualities of engineering and technical talents, through school-enterprise cooperation and internship training, the practical application ability to solve specific problems in work practice, and explore a feasible way for college students to cultivate in engineering technology [2–5].

Platform construction paradigm follows the result oriented, reverse design and continuous improvement (see Fig. 2).

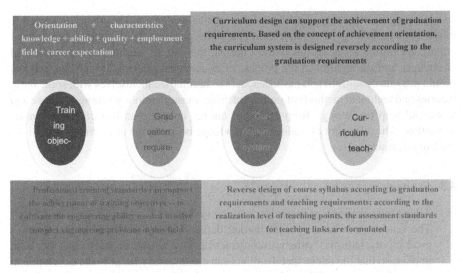

Fig. 2. Platform construction paradigm

4.1 Talent Demand Analysis

From the three levels of the IOT, senior engineering and technical personnel not only have the skills of the application layer, but also have rich knowledge and skills related to the perception layer, which is a dynamic and comprehensive senior talent with various skills. For product engineers only, including sensor equipment provider, chip provider, network equipment provider and software development supplier; For system engineer, including system integrator and solution provider.

4.2 Teaching Staff

Teachers are required to have a reasonable structure, meet the requirements of training objectives and good development trend from the perspective of professional title, education background and academic background. In terms of engineering experience and experience, he has a double-qualified type, and has the experience of instructing student competitions and the experience of completing collaborative education projects [7]. At the same time, it also has advanced concepts, appropriate methods and informational methods, with students as the main body, teachers as the leading, and insisting on the principle of output orientation.

In the traditional teaching process, "student-oriented + teacher-led" has always been the mainstream thinking. Many teachers are not yet psychologically prepared to adapt to new educational theories and educational technologies. There are not a few outdated thinking, but with the "student-centered" People began to pay more attention to students' active learning methods and learning experience. With the widespread application of computer networks and modern educational technology, the ways for students to acquire knowledge have appeared diversified, convenient, and fragmented. Teachers must comprehensively innovate educational concepts and improve their own networked and informatized teaching capabilities and application levels, The ability to integrate information technology and curriculum can better promote the in-depth integration of online and offline teaching links, and improve the overall teaching quality and level of colleges and universities in the process of educational information reform. Schools should provide conditions and guide teachers to familiarize themselves with some basic theories and technical methods of online teaching, master various teaching software and tools, and help teachers go from offline to online, or to a road that combines online and offline. The instructor of traditional knowledge becomes the mastermind behind the students' learning.

4.3 Strategy

(1) Adjust the vocational skill quality training system
The school must keep up with market demand, grasp the development level of productivity, industrial structure adjustment and the new characteristics of the talent market, so that the talent specifications can continuously adapt to the development needs of the new era. With reference to the national vocational standards, combined with the employment feedback of graduates, and with the assistance of enterprises and experts, construct a practical and unique "vocational skills quality structure system" and "vocational skills quality implementation standards" and other content.

(2) Innovative school-enterprise cooperation
The existing practice, experience and problems of school enterprise cooperation are summarized and studied, so as to form a more systematic and advanced theory of school enterprise cooperation mode, operation mechanism and guarantee mechanism. We should strengthen the initiative and sense of urgency of all teachers, expand cooperation ideas, take school enterprise cooperation as a strategy to improve teachers' quality, innovate school running ideas, and establish all-round close cooperative relationship with enterprises.

(3) Research on training base
In accordance with the requirements of professional construction and improving the quality of talent training, focusing on cultivating students' practical ability, the school interacts with enterprises, and building a batch of functions that integrate practical teaching, vocational skills training and appraisal assessment, vocational qualification certification and vocational quality training, etc. Practical teaching base inside and outside the school. Increase investment and build a high-level school practice training base to meet basic school practice teaching. Give full play to the role of off-campus practice training bases, and hire all kinds of high-quality and capable technical personnel as instructors for student internships to improve students' practical ability.

(4) Create training plan
Through the professional construction steering committee, industry and business leaders and experts are invited to participate in the formulation or revision of professional talent training programs, carefully listen to the opinions and suggestions of industry and business experts, and jointly formulate talent training plans with the company. In terms of talent training goals, it is negotiated by the school-enterprise

cooperation committee; in terms of talent training programs and curriculum settings, a professional steering committee participates; in professional theory teaching, enterprise technical backbones are hired as part-time teachers to participate in guidance; in skills training and practice In the link, the company's workshops, laboratories, R&D centers, and teaching factories are the bases; in the internship and job placement process, cooperative enterprises are the main body.

(5) Innovation and reform of curriculum teaching

The school closely focuses on the actual production of the enterprise and the standards of the enterprise's demand for talents. Using the professional school-enterprise cooperation committee as a platform, the school hires corporate leaders and technical backbones to participate in the curriculum reform, and both schools and enterprises set up courses in accordance with the needs of talents. A large number of part-time teachers with rich practical experience are hired from industries and companies to teach, give lectures, and make academic reports to students on a regular or irregular basis, and pass on the latest knowledge, latest technology, and latest experience from the front line of business management to students. The company provides a large number of off-campus practice bases for the school, and the company's business backbone, technical experts, and management elites serve as internship instructors to guide students. So as to form a mechanism for school-enterprise cooperation to build classrooms and jointly cultivate high-quality skilled talents.

According to different types of online teaching, university teaching managers, teachers, and students should jointly participate in the formulation of basic standards for online teaching under the new situation, taking into account science, rationality, fairness and justice. In terms of syllabus design, teaching resource construction, teaching progress control, online and offline time allocation, course evaluation, and even allowance allocation, a standardized and rigorous system should be formed, entry thresholds should be established, and quality control should be strictly controlled.

5 Expectation

The future prospects of the IOT industry are extremely broad and the market space is huge (far exceeding the scale of the existing IT industry). The current level of development in my country is basically synchronized with the world, and my country's huge domestic market is a favorable condition for winning in this global competition. The development of the IOT industry will recreate dozens of IBM, Microsoft, Alibaba, and Google. When conducting demonstration applications, we should continue to build and improve the city's shared standardized IOT core platform, which can not only reduce the waste of repeated construction by different departments, but also provide a shared platform for the whole society and reduce the cost of promoting the IOT. At the same time, we should make full use of and promote the relevant projects that have been built to give full play to their effects. All government departments should learn to understand the revolutionary impact of the IOT on social development, and actively develop innovative IOT applications, which can not only improve management efficiency, solve many unsolvable problems, but also quickly drive the IOT industry in our province. Development of. The size of the promotion of government departments determines the starting speed of the development of the regional IOT and promotes the formation of core competitiveness. Reasonably lay out the industrial chain, give full play to industry-university cooperation, Fujian-Taiwan cooperation, support, cultivate, and introduce leading enterprises in each link, and form a complete industrial chain as soon as possible. At the same time, we will continue to build the core industrial chain and standardization through applications. Develop the foundation for long-term advantages; give full play to the role of chambers of commerce, public platforms and industrial alliances to form a joint force to promote the development of the IOT in our province in the aspects of IOT application display, promotion, joint research and development, product matching, talent training, and standard formulation. Through policy propaganda, guidance, and promotion of the majority of enterprises to introduce IOT technology to achieve product upgrades, realize the integration of the two, improve the management level and product quality of enterprises, promote exports, and drive private investment. Through the publicity and training of IOT application for students in school, we will stimulate students' innovative ability of IOT application, provide more IOT talents, and form a talent advantage. The application of the IOT in the whole society is the long-term driving force for the application of the IOT to stay ahead.

Through this platform, university teaching managers can conduct data mining and analysis, and target online teaching activities, such as online records, platform visits, class opening conditions, online teaching resources construction, student learning details, teacher-student interaction, Data such as examination and evaluation is mined and utilized, and reports are formed through a visual interface. In this way, teaching administrators can not only report teaching quality-related issues to the college and teachers in a timely manner, but also can iteratively upgrade all aspects of the school's quality assurance based on data analysis, such as evaluation standard formulation, teaching monitoring mechanism, supervision and evaluation, and talent training result feedback, internship training and other links.

In the future, the mobile phone technology system will evolve to the super system, and many functions will be migrated to the super system. Especially with the help of the Internet of Things system, the future form of the mobile phone or the alternative technology system will be integrated with the Internet of Things +, based on the IOT, integrated blockchain, artificial intelligence, combined with augmented reality (AR), virtual reality (VR), wearable devices, 3D printing, robots, drones and other technologies and equipment for content presentation, interaction, and command control. [1] Adhering to the development concept of "China's Beidou, the world's Beidou, and the first-class Beidou", we vigorously promote the new era Beidou spirit of "independent innovation, open integration, unity, and pursuit of excellence". It will be built by 2035 to be more ubiquitous, more integrated, A smarter national integrated positioning and navigation timing system will provide core support for future intelligent and unmanned development, continue to promote system upgrades, integrate new-generation communications, low-orbit enhancements and other emerging technologies, and vigorously develop quantum navigation, all-source navigation, Micro-PNT and other new qualitative capabilities to build a spatiotemporal information service infrastructure that covers the sky, the earth and the sea, has unified benchmarks, high precision, high intelligence, high security, and high efficiency. The form of mobile phones in the future will no longer exist. The functions of mobile phones will be carried by the Internet of Things + various new technologies. The Internet of Things + will be the future form of mobile phones. The mobile phone-based alternative system Internet of Things + fusion of various new technologies will bring completely innovative business application forms, bringing earth-shaking changes to life, work and society. Serve the world and benefit mankind!

Conflicts of Interest. The authors declare that they have no conflicts of interest to report regarding the present study.

References

1. Gao, Z.H., Sun, W.S.: Internet of Things: Architecture, Protocol Standard and Wireless Communication, pp. 5–154. Tsinghua University Press, China (2020)
2. Li, B., Du, W., Sun, Y.F.: Research on the training model of school-enterprise collaborative innovation and entrepreneurship talents. Shanxi Agric. Econ. (3) (2018)
3. Zhao, W.Z.: Research on the construction of school-enterprise collaborative innovation and entrepreneurship talent training system and its guarantee mechanism. Educ. Modernization (54) (2019)
4. Qian, J.: Summary of research on innovation and entrepreneurship education in colleges and universities. J. Zhangjiakou Vocational Coll. Technol. (9) (2016)
5. Liu, M.: Explore the cultivation and practice of innovative and entrepreneurial talents from the perspective of entrepreneurship and employment. Theoret. Res. Practice Innov. Entrepreneurship (1) (2018)
6. Che, B., Liu, L., Zhang, H.: KNEMAG: key node estimation mechanism based on attack graph for IOT security. J. Internet Things 2(4), 145–162 (2020)
7. Tang, X., Sun, X., Wang, Z., Yu, P., Cao, N.: Research on the pedestrian re-identification method based on local features and gait energy images. Comput. Mater. Continua **64**(2), 1185–1198 (2020)

Liquid Metal Droplet Series Based Wire Oscillation

Bin Yuan[1,2(✉)], Sen Chen[3], Yang Wu[1,2], and Huixin Yuan[1,2]

[1] Jiangsu Key Lab of IoT Application Technology, Wuxi Taihu University, Wuxi 214064, China
[2] School of Intelligent Equipment Engineering, Wuxi Taihu University, Wuxi 214064, China
[3] Technical Institute of Physics and Chemistry, Beijing Key Laboratory of Cryo-Biomedical Engineering, Chinese Academy of Sciences, Beijing 100190, China

Abstract. Gallium based room temperature liquid metal alloy has attracted continuous attention due to it combined properties of both liquid and metal, such as low viscosity, high surface tension, great thermal and electrical conductivity. Besides, it has low toxicity compared to mercury. These properties enable liquid metal to be used in various fields, especially in the soft electronics and soft robotics domain. Liquid metal could transform and move under electrical field in alkaline solution. Besides, by adding aluminum to liquid metal, it can actuate itself for minutes. What's more, we have discovered that by inserting a thin copper wire into the self-actuated liquid metal, the copper wire could oscillate by itself. It is the first ever discovery of liquid metal and copper wire coupled oscillation phenomenon induced by chemical and mechanical principle. However, the oscillation period varies along time and the motion behavior of the copper wire is unstable, which limits its further application. Here, we propose several new ways to stabilize the oscillation process and extend the motion direction. By arranging the position of several separate liquid metal droplets, we manage to realize stable and continuous oscillation. Besides, bended copper wire could also oscillate in circular manner. Such findings enrich the liquid metal based soft robotics research and have potential applications in liquid metal-based sensors, actuators and counters.

Keywords: Liquid Metal Droplet Series · Oscillation · Copper wire · Wetting

1 Introduction

As a newly emerging material, gallium based room temperature liquid metal has drawn enormous attention in various fields, such as soft robotics [1, 2], microfluidics [3], dielectric and energy storage materials [4–6]. Different from conventional solid metals, gallium based liquid metal has a low melting point of about 20 °C, which enables it to be in liquid phase at room temperature. Compared with Hg, gallium based liquid metal has low toxicity due to its low vapor pressure and high boiling point. This advantage ensures its further application [7]. Besides, liquid metal has great electrical and thermal conductivity, which makes it possible to be used in flexible printing circuits [8–11] and heat dissipation [12–14]. In addition, the unique interfacial behavior between liquid metal and other materials makes it possible to fabricate thin films and other delicate

© Springer Nature Switzerland AG 2021
X. Sun et al. (Eds.): ICAIS 2021, CCIS 1424, pp. 440–447, 2021.
https://doi.org/10.1007/978-3-030-78621-2_36

structures on liquid metal surface [15, 16]. Recently, we found that liquid metal added with Al showed great self-actuation performance. Liquid metal droplets containing Al granules could move at the speed of centimeters per second in alkaline solution for minutes. These running droplets could speed up and change direction under electric and magnetic fields [1]. The driving mechanism is mainly due to the surface tension gradient induced surface flow. What's more, we found that liquid metal could wet copper wire and induce periodic motion of the wire across liquid metal droplet. This is the first ever discovery of liquid metal and solid wire coupling motion. Besides, the oscillation period could be shortened by steel needle manipulation [17]. However, the oscillation process is still quite random in both the speed and direction. Periodic motion direction of copper wire would change with time due to the force change in the vertical and circular direction. The pausing time also varies with time.

In this study, we disclose the liquid metal droplet series based copper wire oscillation. Compared with single droplet oscillation, droplet series based oscillation is more stable in both direction and period. The contact angle between copper wire and liquid metal droplet was measured to verify previous assumption. The number and position of liquid metal droplets could be arranged to achieve desired copper wire motion. Besides, linear copper wire could be bent into circular shape and realize circular motion across liquid metal droplets. The present findings enrich the liquid metal copper wire coupled motion behavior and might open new way for developing solid-liquid hybrid liquid robotics and devices.

2 Materials and Methods

Materials used in the experiment included liquid metal (LM) alloy $GaIn_{10}$ (10 wt % In), NaOH aqueous solution (0.5 mol/L), aluminum foil, rubber O-rings (diameter 10.6 mm), plastic Petri dish, beaker and copper wire (length 38.2 mm, diameter 0.19 mm). Liquid metal $GaIn_{10}$ was injected into a 10 ml beaker filled with NaOH aqueous solution (0.5 mol/L). A piece of Al foil was inserted into liquid metal. The mass ratio of $GaIn_{10}$ and Al foil was about 200:1. After about 10 min, Al foil was totally decomposed by liquid metal into small Al granules and distributed uniformly inside liquid metal. H_2 bubbles could be seen on the interface between liquid metal and NaOH aqueous solution due to the redox reaction between Al and NaOH aqueous solution. At the same time, rubber O-rings were placed in the Petri dish filled with NaOH aqueous solution (0.5 mol/L). Then, the prepared liquid metal (approximately 0.4 ml) was moved onto the O-rings to in the form of droplets. Copper wires were wetted by liquid metal in advance and then inserted into the liquid metal droplets horizontally. Copper wire Oscillation process happened stably after a while. Videos were taken from the front side and top side.

3 Results and Discussion

The oscillation process of the copper wire across two liquid metal droplets can be divided into four stages, as shown in Fig. 1. The copper wire moves back and forth across liquid metal droplets continuously for more than half an hour. On the two sides, it would pause for a while before moving to another side. Compared with copper wire oscillation across single liquid metal droplet [17], oscillation across two droplets is more stable in both the oscillation period and oscillation direction. During oscillation across one liquid metal droplet, the copper wire would swing in vertical direction due to gravity imbalance. During oscillation across two or more liquid metal droplets, the copper wire moves almost horizontally due to supports from droplets.

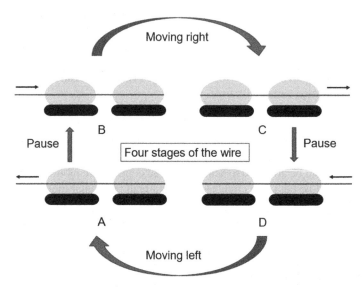

Fig. 1. Side view of four stages of the copper wire oscillation process across liquid metal droplets. The red line represents the copper wire. The grey ellipsoid represents the liquid metal droplet. The black bar represents the rubble O-ring. The copper wire moved to the left side (A), pausing for a period (B) before moving to the right side (C), pausing again (D) before moving to the left side. (Color figure online)

During the oscillation process, H_2 bubbles are generated on the surface of the copper wire continuously, as shown in Fig. 2 (a) (b), due to the redox reaction between Al granules attached to the copper wire surface and the surrounding NaOH aqueous solution ($2Al + 2OH^- + 2H_2O \longrightarrow 2AlO_2^- + 3H_2 \uparrow$). These H_2 bubbles reduce the friction force between the copper wire and the liquid metal droplets so that the oscillation could happen. The dragging force of the copper wire is related to the contact angle between copper wire and liquid metal droplet.

Previously, we suppose that the oscillation process is due to the drag force imbalance on the two sides of the copper wire. The contact angle between copper wire and liquid metal droplet can be described by the Cassie-Baxter equation [18], i.e. $\cos \theta_c = f_1 \cos \theta_1 + f_2 \cos \theta_2$, where θ_c represents the apparent contact angle, f_1 represents the total area of solid under the drop per unit projected area, with θ_1 as the contact angle on a smooth surface of material 1. Likewise, f_2 is defined in a similar way. H_2 bubbles generated on the surface of copper wire enlarge the apparent contact angle between copper wire and liquid metal droplet. However, it's hard to capture the contact

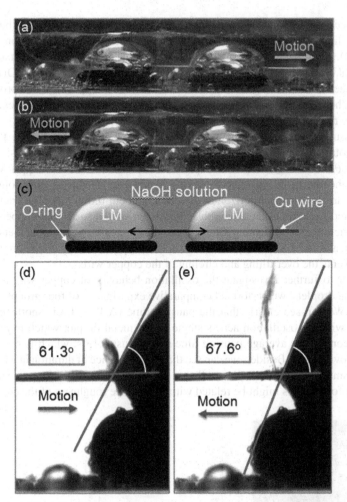

Fig. 2. Side view of copper wire oscillation across two liquid metal droplets: (a) The copper wire was moving right; (b) The copper wire was moving left. (c) Schematic of the copper wire motion; (d) The contact angle at the three phase region when the copper wire was moving inside liquid metal droplet was 61.3°; (e) The contact angle at the three phase region when the copper wire was moving outside liquid metal droplet was 67.6°.

angle region between copper wire and liquid metal droplet due to the vertical motion of copper wire.

In this experiment, we captured the side view pictures of the copper wire moving inside and outside the liquid metal droplet successfully, as shown in Fig. 2 (d) (e), due to the supporting of another liquid metal droplet. Two liquid metal droplets ensure almost horizontal motion direction of copper wire, as shown in Fig. 2 (c). It is obvious that the contact angle between copper wire and liquid metal droplet is larger when the copper wire moves outside the liquid metal droplet than inside the liquid metal droplet, which verifies our previous consumption. The black parts around the copper wire are the H_2 bubbles.

When the copper wire moves inside liquid metal droplets, most of the H_2 bubbles are rejected by liquid metal into surrounding solutions due to high surface tension, as shown in Fig. 2 (d). At the same time, small amounts of NaOH aqueous solution is taken inside liquid metal droplet due to the surface roughness of copper wire. These NaOH aqueous solution reacts with the Al granules on the surface of the copper wire and produces H_2 bubbles. When the copper wire moves outside liquid metal droplet, these generated H_2 bubbles are released into surrounding solution, as shown in Fig. 2 (e).

We assume that the diameter on the left and right are almost the same, then the total driving force acting on the copper wire is expressed as: $F_{drive} = \pi D \gamma_{LA}(cos\theta_{in} - cos\theta_{out})$, where D represents the diameter of the copper wire, γ_{LA} represents the interfacial tension between liquid metal and NaOH aqueous solution. The calculated driving force in horizontal direction is about 0.006 mN. The friction force is greatly reduced due to the H_2 bubbles generated on the surface of copper wire. H_2 bubbles function as a lubricating film between the copper wire and liquid metal droplet. In the vertical direction, two liquid metal droplets support the copper wire on both sides, which prevents the over tilting and circling of the copper wire.

In order to further investigate the oscillation behavior of copper wire across two liquid metal droplets, we performed comparative experiments of four groups, as shown in Fig. 3. We can see clearly that the pausing time (A-B, C-D) is shortened greatly compared with the oscillation across single liquid metal droplet which might last for several seconds. The average pausing time here is just 0.15 s, which is much shorter than the moving time. Besides, we can see that the difference of duration in each stage is also quite small, which means the oscillation process is quite stable. The time difference among the four groups might be related with the surface roughness of the copper wire.

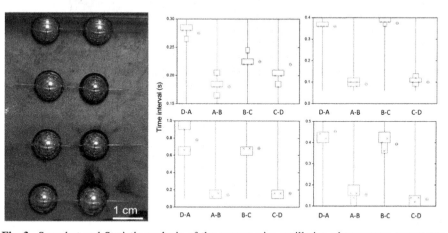

Fig. 3. Snapshot and Statistic analysis of the copper wire oscillation phenomenon across two liquid metal droplets. Time interval between the four stages during 4 period times is recorded. The box chart indicates the 25%, 50%, and 75% of the data (the crosses on the left represent the data). The circle indicates the mean of the data. The following box charts follow the same setting.

Apart from the copper wire oscillation across two liquid metal droplets, we also performed the experiment of oscillation across three liquid metal droplets, as shown in

Fig. 4. Compared with copper wire oscillation across two liquid metal droplets, oscillation across three liquid metal droplets is more stable in the oscillation direction due to the supporting of three droplets at the same time. However, the pausing time (A-B, C-D) varies more than that in oscillation process across two liquid metal droplets. This might be resulted from the reduced amount of H2 bubbles generated on copper wire surface. Since the length of the copper wire is fixed, the distance between liquid metal droplets is shortened. Thus, the moving time is also shorted (B-C, D-A). In this case, the reaction time for Al granules on the copper wire surface is also reduced, which results in the less difference of contact angle at two sides of the liquid metal droplet. According to the Cassie-Baxter equation mentioned above, the driving force is also reduced. Here, we can see that time interval of the moving time in oscillation process across three liquid metal droplets is about 0.25 s, which is shorter than that in oscillation process across two liquid metal droplets (about 0.4 s).

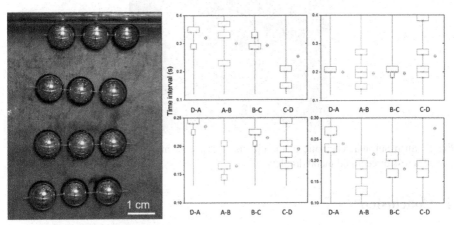

Fig. 4. Snapshot and Statistic analysis of the copper wire oscillation phenomenon across three liquid metal droplets. Time interval between the four stages during 4 period times is recorded.

During the experiment, we found that the straightness of the copper wire had almost no influence on the oscillation process. So we tried to bend the copper wire into a circular shape and rearranged the position of the liquid metal droplets, as shown in Fig. 5. Interesting, we found that the bent copper wire could also move back and forth across the liquid metal droplets in circular direction. Such kind of finding really refreshes our view towards the oscillation across liquid metal droplets. Compared with linear oscillation, circular oscillation is slower. However, the oscillation process is also quite stable and could last for about half an hour. We can also see H2 bubbles generated on the surface of copper wire continuously. The mechanism of the driving force is similar with that of linear oscillation. Although the copper wire is bended, the direction of the driving force is still along the copper wire according to previous analysis. The contact region of copper wire, liquid metal and surround solution determines the driving force of the oscillation process.

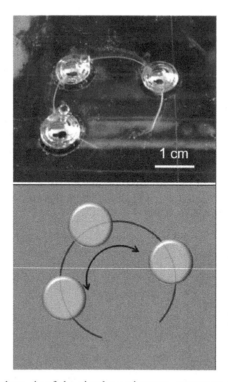

Fig. 5. Snapshot and schematic of the circular reciprocate movement of circular copper wire placed across three liquid metal droplets

4 Conclusion

In conclusion, we realize the copper wire oscillation across several liquid metal droplets. Compared with oscillation across single liquid metal droplet, oscillation across several liquid metal droplets is far more stable in both period and direction. The pausing time is related with the moving time. Less moving time allows less reaction time for Al granules and NaOH solution, thus results in less difference of contact angle on the two sides of the liquid metal droplet. Contact angle between liquid metal and copper wire is captured and measured. The contact angle at the three phase region when the copper wire is moving inside liquid metal droplet is 61.3° while the contact angle at the three phase region when the copper wire is moving outside liquid metal droplet is 67.6°. The contact angle difference offers the driving force of the oscillation process. Besides, we also find the circular oscillation mode of the bended copper wire across several liquid metal droplets. The present findings enrich the solid-liquid coupled motion phenomenon of liquid metal soft robotics, which might open new way of fabricating more complicated liquid metal machines.

References

1. Xu, S., Yuan, B., Hou, Y., Liu, T.Y., Fu, J.H., Liu, J.: Self-fueled liquid metal motors. J. Phys. D: Appl. Phys. **52**(35), 353002 (2019)
2. Wang, D., Gao, C., Wang, W., Sun, M., Guo, B.: Shape-transformable, fusible rod-like swimming liquid metal nanomachine. ACS Nano **12**(10), 10212–10220 (2018)
3. Khoshmanesh, K., Tang, S.Y., Zhu, J.Y., Schaefer, S., Mitchell, A., et al.: Liquid metal enabled microfluidics. Lab Chip **17**(6), 974–993 (2017)
4. Pan, C., Markvicka, E.J., Malakooti, M.H., Yan, J., Majidi, C.: A liquid-metal–elastomer nanocomposite for stretchable dielectric materials. Adv. Mater. **31**(23), 1900663 (2019)
5. Xie, H., Zhao, H., Wang, J., Chu, P., Zhang, Y.: High-performance bismuth-gallium positive electrode for liquid metal battery. J. Power Sources **472**(1), 228634 (2020)
6. Guo, X., Zhang, L., Ding, Y., Goodenough, J.B., Yu, G.: Room-temperature liquid metal and alloy systems for energy storage applications. Energy Environ. Sci. **12**, 2605–2619 (2019)
7. Chen, S., Wang, H.Z., Zhao, R.Q., Rao, W., Liu, J.: Liquid metal composites. Matter **2**(6), 1446–14803 (2020)
8. Yang, Y., et al.: Liquid-metal-based super-stretchable and structure-designable triboelectric nanogenerator for wearable electronics. ACS Nano **12**(2), 2027–2034 (2018)
9. Neumann, T.V., Dickey, M.D.: Liquid metal direct write and 3D printing: a review. Adv. Mater. Technol. **5**(9), 2000070 (2020)
10. Thrasher, C., Farrell, Z., Morris, N., Willey, C., Tabor, C.: Mechanoresponsive polymerized liquid metal networks. Adv. Mater. **31**(40), 1903864 (2019)
11. Gaillac, R., et al.: Liquid metal–organic frameworks. Nat. Mater. **16**, 1149–1154 (2017)
12. Yang, X.H., Tan, S.C., He, Z.Z., Zhou, Y.X., Liu, J.: Evaluation and optimization of low melting point metal PCM heat sink against ultra-high thermal shock. Appl. Therm. Eng. **119**(5), 34–41 (2017)
13. Zhang, X.D., et al.: Experimental investigation of galinstan based minichannel cooling for high heat flux and large heat power thermal management. Energy Convers. Manage. **185**(1), 248–258 (2019)
14. Malakooti, M.H., Kazem, N., Yan, J., Pan, C., Majidi, C.: Liquid metal supercooling for low-temperature thermoelectric wearables. Adv. Func. Mater. **29**(45), 1906098 (2019)
15. Zavabeti, A., et al.: A liquid metal reaction environment for the room-temperature synthesis of atomically thin metal oxides. Science **358**(6361), 332–335 (2017)
16. Ozutemiz, K.B., Wissman, J., Ozdoganlar, O.B., Majidi, C.: EGaln–metal interfacing for liquid metal circuitry and microelectronics integration. Adv. Mater. Interfaces **5**(10), 1701596 (2018)
17. Yuan, B., Wang, L., Yang, X.H., Ding, Y.J., Liu, J.: Liquid metal machine triggered violin-like wire oscillator. Adv. Sci. **3**(10), 1600212 (2016)
18. Milne, A.J.B., Amirfazli, A.: The cassie equation: how it is meant to be used. Adv. Coll. Interface. Sci. **170**(1–2), 48–55 (2012)

Linear Time-Invariant System Reduced-Order Finite-Time Observer

Yang Wu[1,2(✉)] [iD], Jiancheng Zhang[3], Yuexin Ye[3], and Bin Yuan[1,2]

[1] Jiangsu Key Lab of IoT Application Technology, Wuxi Taihu University, Wuxi 214064, China
001027@wxu.edu.cn
[2] School of Intelligent Equipment Engineering, Wuxi Taihu University, Wuxi 214064, China
[3] School of Science, Jiangnan University, Wuxi 214122, China

Abstract. Due to its excellent estimation performance and great application value, finite-time observers have attracted more and more scholars' attention in recent years. Compared with traditional asymptotic observers, finite-time observers not only have fast convergence speed, but also have high estimation accuracy. However, the classical method only discusses the full-order finite-time observer, and the research on the reduced-order finite-time observer has not been reported. To this end, this paper considers the design of a reduced-order finite-time observer for a class of linear time-invariant systems. First, a new state transformation method is proposed so that the transformed partial state can be represented by the measured output, and a finite-time observer is designed for another unmeasurable partial state to estimate it. According to this idea, it is proved that the observability condition required in the classical full-order finite-time observer design can also guarantee the existence of a reduced-order finite-time observer. Finally, a numerical example is given to verify the effectiveness of the proposed method.

Keywords: Finite-time observer · Reduced-order observer · Observability condition

1 Introduction

As we all know, with its unique advantages, state feedback plays an important role in pole configuration, stabilization design, dynamic decoupling control, static decoupling control, progressive tracking and disturbance suppression, and linear quadratic optimal control. However, in actual system, as the internal variables of the system, the state is often not directly measurable, or even if it can be measured, the cost is high [1]. This makes the physical realization of state feedback difficult. To solve this contradiction, state observer technology emerged [1]. In recent decades, scholars have continuously studies observers for various dynamic systems, and have proposed many new observer technologies and methods, such as unknown input observer [2–7], sliding mode observer [8, 9], functional observer [10] and interference observer [11, 12], etc.

It is noted that the above-mentioned classical observer design methods, whether for deterministic systems or systems with uncertainties, are all asymptotically convergent

© Springer Nature Switzerland AG 2021
X. Sun et al. (Eds.): ICAIS 2021, CCIS 1424, pp. 448–457, 2021.
https://doi.org/10.1007/978-3-030-78621-2_37

observers, that is, the estimated states obtained by the observer can realize the asymptotic tracking of the real state of the system. For the asymptotically convergent observer, its advantage is that the design method is simple and the system itself is not demanding. However, the convergence speed and accuracy of the asymptotic convergent observer are often difficult to control. This is because the convergence effect of the asymptotically convergent observer not only depends on the initial state error of the original system and the observer system, but also on the pole configuration of the observer. Since the initial value of the system is difficult to obtain, it is difficult to reduce the initial error and improve the convergence effect by setting the initial conditions of the observer. A feasible solution is to select the largest possible gain matrix for the observer system to make the poles of the system far away from the imaginary axis. However, this approach can only improve the convergence accuracy and speed of the observer to a certain extent (still cannot control the convergence of the observer time and accuracy). On the other hand, the introduction of a large gain matrix may make the observer system more sensitive to noise and reduce the estimation performance of the observer. In 2002, Engel et al. gave the design method of finite-time observer (FTO) for the first time in a paper published in "IEEE Transactions on Automatic Control" [13]. When the system has no unknown input and the observable condition is satisfied, the finite-time observer of the system exists. Due to its fast convergence speed and high estimation accuracy, the finite-time observer has been extended to some new systems. For example, Zhang et al. extended the finite-time observer method in literature [13] to systems with actuator and sensor faults, and designed a finite-time fault estimation observer [14].

It should be pointed out that the above finite-time observers proposed for linear time-invariant linear or nonlinear systems are all full-order observers. Compared with full-order observer, the reduced-order observer only needs to estimate part of the state of the system, so its dimension is lower. This means that fewer integrators are needed to estimate the state of the entire system when using reduced-order observers. It not only saves hardware costs, but also reduces the complexity of the closed-loop system to a large extent. However, the research on reduced-order finite-time observer design have not been reported in the published literature. Based on this, the design of reduced-order finite-time observer for a class of linear time-invariant systems is studied in this paper. The contributions and innovations of this paper are as follows:

1) A new state transformation method is proposed so that part of the state of the transformed system can be expressed by the measured output.
2) It is proved that the classical full-order finite-time observer satisfies the observability conditions which can also guarantee the existence of the reduced-order finite-time observer.
3) The design method of a reduced-order finite-time observer is presented, which can accurately estimate the state of the original system in any given time.

The rest of this article is organized as follows: Sect. 2 is the problem description. Section 3 gives the design method and proof of reduced-order finite-time observer. In Sect. 4, a simulation example is given to verify the effectiveness of the method. Finally, the conclusion is given in Sect. 5.

2 Problem Description

Consider one class of linear time-invariant systems

$$\begin{cases} \dot{x}(t) = Ax(t) + Bu(t) \\ \quad y(t) = Cx(t) \end{cases} \tag{1}$$

Where $x \in R^n$, $u \in R^m$, $y \in R^p (n > m, n > p)$ are the state, control input and measurable output vectors of the system respectively; A, B, C are known constant matrices respectively. Without loss of generality, assume that the matrix C are full rank.

The main purpose of this paper is to design a reduced-order finite-time observer for the system (1), so that it can achieve accurate estimation of the system state in any short time. First, assume hypothesis 1.

Hypothesis 1: The system (A, C) satisfies the observability condition.

Note 1. In literature [13], it has been proved that as long as the observability condition is satisfied, a full-order finite-time observer can be designed. In this paper, it is proved that a reduced-order observer can also be designed under the same conditions.

3 Reduced-Order FTO Design

For the measured output matrix C, according to the Schmidt orthogonalization process, the non-singular matrix $S \in R^{p \times n}$ and the matrix $C \in R^{p \times n}$ can be found to satisfy $\hat{C}\hat{C}^T = I_p$ and $C = S\,\hat{C}$. Then expand the matrix C to an orthogonal matrix $W = \begin{bmatrix} \hat{C} \\ M \end{bmatrix}$, so we have $W^{-1} = W^T$, $MM^T = I_{n-p}$ and $CW^{-1} = \begin{bmatrix} S & 0 \end{bmatrix}$.

For system (1), linear transformation $\bar{x} = Wx$ can be obtained as follows:

$$\begin{cases} \dot{\bar{x}}(t) = \overline{A}\bar{x}(t) + \overline{B}u(t) \\ \quad y(t) = \overline{C}\bar{x}(t) \end{cases} \tag{2}$$

where $\overline{A} = WAW^{-1}$, $\overline{B} = WB$ and $\overline{C} = CW^{-1} = \begin{bmatrix} S & 0 \end{bmatrix}$.

The component block matrix of system state $\bar{x}$ and matrix $\overline{A}, \overline{B}, \overline{C}$ is divided into:

$$\bar{x} = \begin{bmatrix} \bar{x}_1 \\ \bar{x}_2 \end{bmatrix}, \quad \overline{A} = \begin{bmatrix} \overline{A}_{11} & \overline{A}_{12} \\ \overline{A}_{21} & \overline{A}_{22} \end{bmatrix}, \quad \overline{B} = \begin{bmatrix} \overline{B}_1 \\ \overline{B}_2 \end{bmatrix}, \quad \overline{C} = \begin{bmatrix} S & 0 \end{bmatrix}$$

Then system (2) can be written

$$\dot{\bar{x}}_1(t) = \overline{A}_{11}\bar{x}_1(t) + \overline{A}_{12}\bar{x}_2(t) + \overline{B}_1 u(t) \tag{3}$$

$$\dot{\bar{x}}_2(t) = \overline{A}_{21}\bar{x}_1(t) + \overline{A}_{22}\bar{x}_2(t) + \overline{B}_2 u(t) \tag{4}$$

$$y(t) = S\bar{x}_1(t) \tag{5}$$

$\bar{x}_1(t) = S^{-1}y(t)$ is obtained from (5) and is substituted into (3) and (4)

$$S^{-1}\dot{y}(t) = \bar{A}_{11}S^{-1}y(t) + \bar{A}_{12}\bar{x}_2(t) + \bar{B}_1 u(t) \tag{6}$$

$$\dot{\bar{x}}_2(t) = \bar{A}_{21}S^{-1}y(t) + \bar{A}_{22}\bar{x}_2(t) + \bar{B}_2 u(t) \tag{7}$$

Since $\bar{x}_1$ can be represented directly by the output $y(t)$, we only need to design an observer to estimate the remaining state $\bar{x}_2$. By (6):

$$\bar{A}_{12}\bar{x}_2(t) = S^{-1}\dot{y}(t) - \bar{A}_{11}S^{-1}y(t) - \bar{B}_1 u(t) := \bar{y}(t).$$

In order to estimate state $\bar{x}_2$ in (7), a sub-observer with the following form is designed

$$\dot{z}_1(t) = \bar{A}_{22}z_1(t) + L_1\big(\bar{y}(t) - \bar{A}_{12}z_1(t)\big) + \bar{B}_2 u(t) + \bar{A}_{21}S^{-1}y(t) \tag{8}$$

$$\dot{z}_2(t) = \bar{A}_{22}z_2(t) + L_2\big(\bar{y}(t) - \bar{A}_{12}z_1(t)\big) + \bar{B}_2 u(t) + \bar{A}_{21}S^{-1}y(t) \tag{9}$$

Here, we want $N_i = \bar{A}_{22} - L_i\bar{A}_{12}(i = 1, 2)$ to be the Hurwitz stability matrix. Then

$$N = \begin{bmatrix} N_1 & 0 \\ 0 & N_2 \end{bmatrix}, L = \begin{bmatrix} L_1 \\ L_2 \end{bmatrix}, G = \begin{bmatrix} \bar{B}_2 \\ \bar{B}_2 \end{bmatrix}, H = \begin{bmatrix} \bar{A}_{21}S^{-1} \\ \bar{A}_{21}S^{-1} \end{bmatrix}, z = \begin{bmatrix} z_1 \\ z_2 \end{bmatrix}, T = \begin{bmatrix} I_{n-p} \\ I_{n-p} \end{bmatrix}.$$

So the reduced-order finite-time observer that we're going to design is

$$\dot{z}(t) = Nz(t) + L\bar{y}(t) + Gu(t) + Hy(t) \tag{10}$$

$$\hat{\bar{x}}_2(t) = K\Big[z(t) - e^{N\tau}z(t - \tau)\Big] \tag{11}$$

$$\hat{x}(t) = W^T \begin{bmatrix} S^{-1}y(t) \\ \hat{\bar{x}}_2(t) \end{bmatrix} \tag{12}$$

where $K = \begin{bmatrix} I_{n-p} & 0_{(n-p \times (n-p)} \end{bmatrix}[T \; e^{N\tau}T]^{-1}$, $\tau > 0$ is any given constant.

According to the finite-time observer theory, if (10)–(12) are the finite-time observer of system (1), it is required that $N_1 = \bar{A}_{22} - L_1\bar{A}_{12}$ and $N_2 = \bar{A}_{22} - L_2\bar{A}_{12}$ have completely different eigenvalues. In other words, we need $(\bar{A}_{22}, \bar{A}_{12})$ to satisfy the observability. So let me give you Lemma 1.

Lemma 1: (A, C) can be observed if and only if $(\bar{A}_{22}, \bar{A}_{12})$ can be observed.

Proof: According to the definition of the equivalence of the observables, the observables of (A, C) are for any complex number s, there are.

$$rank \begin{bmatrix} sI_n - A \\ C \end{bmatrix} = n \tag{13}$$

So, we have

$$n = rank \begin{bmatrix} sI_n - A \\ C \end{bmatrix} = rank \left(\begin{bmatrix} W & 0 \\ 0 & I_p \end{bmatrix} \begin{bmatrix} sI_n - A \\ C \end{bmatrix} W^{-1} \right)$$

$$= rank \begin{bmatrix} sI - \overline{A} \\ C \end{bmatrix} = rank \begin{bmatrix} sI_p - \overline{A}_n & -\overline{A}_{12} \\ -\overline{A}_{21} & sI_{n-p} - \overline{A}_{22} \\ S & 0 \end{bmatrix}$$

$$= rank \begin{bmatrix} 0 & -\overline{A}_{12} \\ 0 \ sI - \overline{A}_{22} \\ S & 0 \end{bmatrix} = rank(S) + rank \begin{bmatrix} sI - \overline{A}_{22} \\ -\overline{A}_{12} \end{bmatrix}$$

$$= p + rank \begin{bmatrix} sI - \overline{A}_{22} \\ -\overline{A}_{12} \end{bmatrix} \tag{14}$$

From (13)–(14), for any complex number s

$$rank \begin{bmatrix} sI_{n-p} - \overline{A}_{22} \\ \overline{A}_{12} \end{bmatrix} = n - p$$

So $(\overline{A}_{22}, \overline{A}_{12})$ can observe.

Note 2. Because $(\overline{A}_{22}, \overline{A}_{12})$ is observable, it can be seen that the gain matrix L can be selected to make $(\overline{A}_{22}, L\overline{A}_{12})$ have arbitrary eigenvalues, which makes it possible to select L_1 and L_2 to make $N_1 = \overline{A}_{22} - L_1\overline{A}_{12}$ and $N_2 = \overline{A}_{22} - L_2\overline{A}_{12}$ have completely different eigenvalues.

Note 3. From the above analysis, it can be seen that whether the reduced-order finite-time observer (10)–(12) exists depends on whether $(\overline{A}_{22}, \overline{A}_{12})$ satisfies the observability condition. And from Lemma 1, (A, C) can be observed is the same thing as $(\overline{A}_{22}, \overline{A}_{12})$ can be observed. Therefore, it can be concluded that the classical full-order finite-time observer satisfies the conditions of the observability which can also guarantee the existence of the reduced-order finite-time observer.

Theorem 1: Based on hypothesis 1 and Lemma 1, the gain matrices L_1 and L_2 are selected so that N_1 and N_2 are Hurwitz stable matrices, and for a given $\rho_1 > \rho_2 > 0$, it satisfy.

$$-\rho_2 < \lambda_i(N_1) < \lambda_j(N_2) < -\rho_1, \quad i, j = 1, 2, \ldots, n - p$$

is true, then (10)–(12) is the reduced-order finite-time observer of system (1), so $\forall t \geq \tau$, have $\hat{x}(t) \equiv x(t)$.

Proof: Due to $\overline{x}(t) = \begin{bmatrix} \overline{x}_1(t) \\ \overline{x}_2(t) \end{bmatrix} = \begin{bmatrix} S^{-1}y(t) \\ \overline{x}_2(t) \end{bmatrix} = Wx(t)$, we know.

$$x(t) = W^T \begin{bmatrix} S^{-1}y(t) \\ \overline{x}_2(t) \end{bmatrix}$$

So in order to prove that when $t \geq \tau$, $\hat{x}(t) \equiv x(t)$, you just have to prove that when $t \geq \tau, \hat{\overline{x}}_2(t) \equiv \overline{x}_2(t)$.

In fact,

$$\frac{d}{dt}[z(t) - T\bar{x}_2] = Nz(t) + L\bar{y}(t) + Gu(t) + Hy(t)$$

$$- \begin{bmatrix} I_{n-p} \\ I_{n-p} \end{bmatrix} \left(\bar{A}_{21}S^{-1}y(t) + \bar{A}_{22}\bar{x}_2(t) + \bar{B}_2u(t) \right)$$

$$= \begin{bmatrix} N_1 & 0 \\ 0 & N_2 \end{bmatrix} \begin{bmatrix} z_1(t) \\ z_2(t) \end{bmatrix} + L\bar{y} - \begin{bmatrix} \bar{A}_{22}\bar{x}_2(t) \\ \bar{A}_{22}\bar{x}_2(t) \end{bmatrix}$$

$$= \begin{bmatrix} N_1 & 0 \\ 0 & N_2 \end{bmatrix} \begin{bmatrix} z_1 \\ z_2 \end{bmatrix} + L\bar{A}_{12}\bar{x}_2(t) - \begin{bmatrix} \bar{A}_{22}\bar{x}_2(t) \\ \bar{A}_{22}\bar{x}_2(t) \end{bmatrix}$$

$$= Nz(t) - \begin{bmatrix} (\bar{A}_{22} - L_1\bar{A}_{12})\bar{x}_2(t) \\ (\bar{A}_{22} - L_2\bar{A}_{12})\bar{x}_2(t) \end{bmatrix}$$

$$= N(z(t) - T\bar{x}_2(t)) \tag{15}$$

It is known from (15) that for any $\tau > 0$, there is

$$z(t) - T\bar{x}_2(t) = e^{N\tau}[z(t - \tau) - T\bar{x}_2(t - \tau)]$$

On the other hand, if you can verify $KT = I_{n-p}$ and $Ke^{N\tau}T = 0$, then for any $t \geq \tau$

$$\bar{x}_2(t) = KT\bar{x}_2(t) = K\left[z(t) - e^{N\tau}z(t - \tau) + e^{N\tau}T\bar{x}_2(t) \right]$$

$$= K\left[z(t) - e^{N\tau}z(t - \tau) \right]$$

Therefore, for the state estimate $\hat{\bar{x}}_2(t)$ given by the observer, when $t \geq \tau$, we have $\hat{\bar{x}}_2(t) \equiv \bar{x}_2(t)$, it is proved.

4 Numerical Simulation

This section gives a numerical example and uses it to verify the effectiveness of the method. Consider a system with the following equation:

$$\begin{cases} \dot{x} = Ax + Bu \\ \quad y = Cx \end{cases} \tag{16}$$

Where $A = \begin{bmatrix} -1 & 0 & 0 \\ 0 & -2 & 0 \\ 0 & 0 & -2 \end{bmatrix}$, $B = \begin{bmatrix} 1 \\ -1 \\ 1 \end{bmatrix}$, $C = \begin{bmatrix} 0 & 1 & 0 \\ 1 & 0 & 1 \end{bmatrix}$, $u(t) = 6\sin(4t)$, the system is simulated with a reduced-order finite-time observer.

From the output matrix C, according to Schmidt's orthotropic method, we get:

$$S = \begin{bmatrix} 1.000000000000000 & 0 \\ 0 & 1.414213562373095 \end{bmatrix}$$

$$W = \begin{bmatrix} 0 & 1.000000000000000 & 0 \\ 0.707106781186547 & 0 & 0.707106781186547 \\ -0.707106781186547 & 0 & 0.707106781186548 \end{bmatrix}$$

and $\bar{A}_{11} = \begin{bmatrix} -1 & 0 \\ 0 & -2 \end{bmatrix}$, $\bar{A}_{12} = \begin{bmatrix} 0 \\ 0 \end{bmatrix}$, $\bar{A}_{21} = \begin{bmatrix} 0 & 0 \end{bmatrix}$, $\bar{A}_{22} = [-2]$.

Then the observer of residual state $\bar{x}_2$, namely reduced-order observer (10), is designed and the matrix is calculated

$$N = \begin{bmatrix} -2 & 0 \\ 0 & -2 \end{bmatrix}, L = \begin{bmatrix} 0 & 1 \\ 0 & -1 \end{bmatrix}, G = \begin{bmatrix} 1 \\ 1 \end{bmatrix}, H = \begin{bmatrix} 0 \\ 0 \end{bmatrix}, T = \begin{bmatrix} 1 \\ 1 \end{bmatrix}$$

The initial state of the system is set as $x(0) = \begin{bmatrix} -5 & -5 & 8 \end{bmatrix}^T$, the initial state of the observer is set as $z(0) = \begin{bmatrix} -3 & 10 \end{bmatrix}$, the value of τ is set as 0.5, and the time interval is set as (0s – 10s). With the help of MATLAB mathematical software, the state curve of the system and the state observed by the reduced-order finite-time observer are given by using the Longge-Kutta method, as shown in the Figs. 1, 2 and 3.

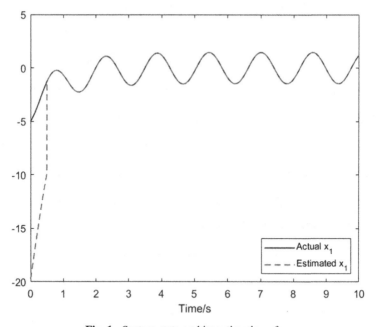

Fig. 1. System state and its estimation of x_1

It can be seen from the simulation results in Figs. 1, 2 and 3 that the state estimation can track its true value well within finite time $\tau = 0.5$ s, which shows that the reduced-order finite-time observer method proposed in this paper can well realize the accurate estimation of the system state.

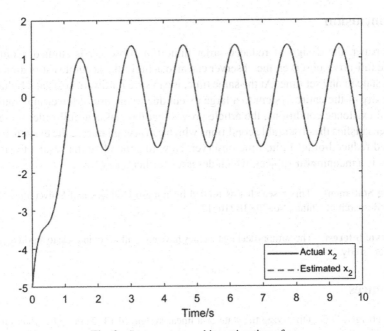

Fig. 2. System state and its estimation of x_2

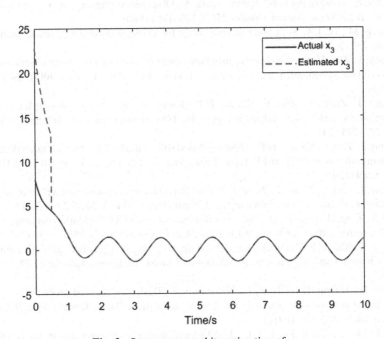

Fig. 3. System state and its estimation of x_3

5 Conclusion

In this paper, the design of reduced-order finite-time observer is studied. Compared with the full-order observer, the observer can also achieve the accurate estimation of the system state in any set time. At the same time, it can save hardware costs and reduce the complexity of the entire system to a large extent due to the use of fewer integrators. In terms of existence conditions, the article proves that the classical full-order finite-time observer satisfies the observable conditions which can also guarantee the existence of the designed reduced-order finite-time observer. How to generalize the results to singular systems is a meaningful subject, which deserves further study.

Funding Statement. This research was funded by Jiangsu Colleges and Universities Natural Science Research of China (No. 20KJB210012).

Conflicts of Interest. The authors declare that they have no conflicts of interest to report regarding the present study.

References

1. Luenberger, D.G.: Observing the state of a linear system. IEEE Trans. Mil. Electron. **8**(2), 74–80 (1964)
2. Kudva, P., Viswanadham, N., Ramakrishna, A.: Observers for linear systems with unknown inputs. IEEE Trans. Autom. Control **25**(1), 113–115 (1980)
3. Corless, M., Tu, J.A.: State and input estimation for a class of uncertain systems. Automatica **34**(6), 757–764 (1998)
4. Zhang, J., Zhu, F.: On the observer matching condition and unknown input observer design based on the system left-invertibility concept. Trans. Inst. Meas. Control. **40**(9), 2887–2900 (2018)
5. Zhang, J., Zhao, X., Zhu, F., Karimi, H.R.: Reduced-order observer design for switched descriptor systems with unknown inputs. In: IEEE Transactions on Automatic Control, pp. 287–294 (2019)
6. Zhang, J., Zhu, F., Karimi, H.R.: Observer-based sliding mode control for TS fuzzy descriptor systems with time-delay. IEEE Trans. Fuzzy Syst. (2019). https://doi.org/10.1109/TFUZZ.2019.2893220
7. Zhang, J., Zhu, F., Zhao, X., Wang, F.: Robust impulsive reset observers of a class of switched nonlinear systems with unknown inputs. J. Franklin Inst. **354**(7), 2924–2943 (2017)
8. Yin, S., Yang, H., Kaynak, O.: Sliding mode observer-based FTC for Markovian jump systems with actuator and sensor faults. IEEE Trans. Autom. Control **62**(7), 3551–3558 (2017)
9. Wang, X., Tan, C.P., Zhou, D.: A novel sliding mode observer for state and fault estimation in systems not satisfying matching and minimum phase conditions. Automatica **79**, 290–295 (2017)
10. Trinh, H., Huong, D.C., Hien, L., Nahavandi, S.: Design of reduced-order positive linear functional observers for positive time-delay systems. IEEE Trans. Circuits Syst. II Express Briefs **64**(5), 555–559 (2016)
11. Ni, J., Liu, L., Chen, M., Liu, C.: Fixed-time disturbance observer design for Brunovsky systems. IEEE Trans. Circuits Syst. II Express Briefs **65**(3), 341–345 (2017)
12. Chen, M., Shao, S.Y., Shi, P., Shi, Y.: Disturbance-observer-based robust synchronization control for a class of fractional-order chaotic systems. IEEE Trans. Circuits Syst. II Express Briefs **4**(64), 417–421 (2017)

13. Engel, R., Kreisselmeier, G.: A continuous-time observer which converges in finite time. IEEE Trans. Autom. Control **7**(47), 1202–1204 (2002)
14. Zhang, K., Jiang, B., Cocquempot, V.: Robust fault estimation observer design with finite-time convergence specification. IET Control Theory Appl. **11**(1), 1–9 (2016)

Research on Invulnerability of WSN Based on Small World Characteristics of Complex Networks

Gongxue Cheng[1,2,3], Qian Sun[1,2,3(✉)], Xiaoyi Wang[1,2,3], Jiping Xu[1,2,3], Li Wang[1,2,3], Huiyan Zhang[1,2,3], Jiabin Yu[1,2,3], and Ning Cao[4]

[1] School of Artificial Intelligence, Beijing Technology and Business University, Beijing 100048, China
[2] China Light Industry Laboratory of Industrial and Big Data, Beijing Technology and Business University, Beijing 100048, China
[3] Beijing Laboratory For Intelligent Environmental Protection, Beijing Technology and Business University, Beijing 100048, China
[4] Shandong Chengxiang Information Technology Co. Ltd., Dezhou 253000, China

Abstract. Network security is an important indicator of wireless sensor networks, so how to improve the security performance of the network is an important issue of wireless sensor networks. Because the number and location of heterogeneous nodes play a decisive role in the performance of the network, this paper focuses on the optimal number and the deployment of heterogeneous nodes. By studying the optimal number and deployment of heterogeneous nodes, the network performance can be improved. Moreover, the invulnerability of the sensor network is also discussed. The simulation results show that the network efficiency and maximum connectivity are improved after the optimization of heterogeneous nodes, which proves the effectiveness of the algorithm.

Keywords: Network security · Small world characteristics · Invulnerability · Wireless sensor network · Heterogeneous nodes

1 Introduction

Wireless sensor network (WSN) is a multi-hop distributed network system formed by a large number of micro sensor nodes through wireless communication. Wireless sensor network is also used in many fields. However, the limited computing capacity, storage capacity, energy and other constraints of nodes affect the development of wireless sensor networks [1, 2]. In particular, wireless sensor networks are deployed randomly in complex environments and are vulnerable to routing attacks from malicious nodes. Therefore, the design of secure routing protocol has become a hot topic in wireless sensor networks [3]. There are numerous studies on WSN secure routing protocols, and various experts and scholars try to extend the life cycle of the network and improve the security transmission of the network from various perspectives [3–9]. Network survivability refers to the ability of the network to maintain or restore its performance to an acceptable

© Springer Nature Switzerland AG 2021
X. Sun et al. (Eds.): ICAIS 2021, CCIS 1424, pp. 458–469, 2021.
https://doi.org/10.1007/978-3-030-78621-2_38

level when the network is attacked selectively or randomly. As an important character-istic of wireless sensor networks, its theoretical significance and application value have increasingly attracted people's attention. How to construct a directed scale-free network topology with good destruction resistance has become an important challenge faced by wireless sensor networks. At present, most of the research on WSNs destructibility topology is based on the classical scale-free BA model, and the purpose of improving network destructibility is achieved by introducing destructibility related parameters. In this paper, we consider how to improve the invulnerability of wireless sensor networks based on the small-world characteristics.

The theory of complex network has made rapid development in recent years, and has been widely used in biological network, social network, power network and communica-tion network. The research on the common features of these different networks provides an effective theoretical basis for solving the problems existing in these large-scale prac-tical networks. With the deepening of research, people gradually find that many actual networks are not regular networks or random networks, but complex networks with other obvious statistical characteristics [10]. Watts and Strogatz introduced the concept of small world network model in 1998, which is also called WS small world model. If a network has both smaller average path length and larger clustering coefficient, then the network is called small world network. Watts and Strogatz start from a regular nearest neighbor coupled network with n nodes, and construct WS small world network by ran-domly reconnecting each edge of the network with probability p. By adjusting the value of p, we can realize the transition from a completely regular network to a completely random network. The reconnection probability $p = 0$ corresponds to a completely regu-lar network, and, when $p = 1$, it corresponds to a completely random network, as shown in Fig. 1 [11].

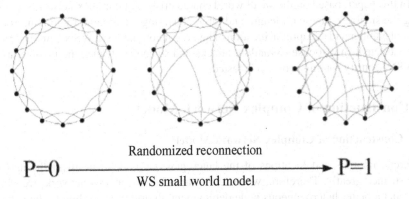

P=0   Randomized reconnection   P=1

WS small world model

Fig. 1. Small world network model with random reconnection

The survivability of wireless sensor network refers to the ability of network topology to maintain connectivity when the nodes or edges of the network fail or are attacked. In this section, we combined these two factors together, which are the intermediate centrality based on the shortest path number and the node access degree of the node's own characteristics. A survivability measurement model is built to measure the importance of nodes and the degree of influence on network survivability. Which is shown as Eq. (1):

$$D_i = \frac{BC_i}{\sum\limits_{j=1}^{n-1} BC_j} \cdot \frac{k_i}{\sum\limits_{j \in A} k_i} \tag{1}$$

Where, i is the node number, j is the transmission path. A is the set of neighbor nodes, and k is the global invulnerability factor, which is composed of the ratio of individual nodes to the overall betweenness centrality. Intermediary centrality is one of the indicators to measure the importance of nodes. It is defined as the proportion of the number of paths passing through a certain node in the total number of shortest paths in the network. It reflects the number of paths available for nodes when transmitting data.

For the invulnerability of wireless sensor networks, considering that the network failure caused by its own defects and the network paralysis caused by attacks may affect the normal operation of the network. Invulnerability of wireless sensor networks refers to the ability of network topology to maintain connectivity when nodes or edges in the network fail or are attacked [12]. There are two kinds of attacks to complex networks, random attack and selective attack. The random attack is mostly caused by energy consumption failure and fault failure. Selective attack is usually caused by attack failure. Common attack strategies include ID attack strategy, IB attack strategy, RD attack strategy and RB attack strategy.

In this paper, based on the small world characteristics of complex networks, considering the small average path length and large clustering coefficient, by looking for the optimal number and the optimal location of heterogeneous nodes, a WSN with super links is constructed. In response to random attacks and selective attacks, the invulnerability of WSN security routing protocol is tested.

2 Construction of Complex Network Model

2.1 Construction of Complex Network Model

Different amounts and locations of the heterogeneous nodes can affect the network performance greatly. Therefore, when setting up a heterogeneous network, we should construct a better heterogeneous node deployment algorithm according to the network distribution characteristics and topology.

In heterogeneous sensor networks, compared with ordinary nodes, heterogeneous nodes have obvious advantages in power energy, computing power, and communication capabilities. However, the cost of heterogeneous nodes is relatively expensive. Therefore, when setting up heterogeneous sensor networks, we must consider the network cost, and can not add heterogeneous nodes without restrictions. In the construction of heterogeneous network, we should select the appropriate number of heterogeneous nodes according to the distribution characteristics of the network, so that the network performance can be greatly improved with low network cost.

2.2 Determination of the Amounts and Locations of the Heterogeneous Nodes

In the construction of heterogeneous sensor network, it is necessary to consider how to minimize the cost of the network while improve the performance of the network to meet our needs [13]. In this case, the determination of the optimal amount of heterogeneous nodes is related to the specific requirements of sensor networks. In general, the average distance between ordinary nodes and sink is an important factor which affects the network performance. Therefore, the average distance between ordinary nodes and sink node can be taken as a standard. In this reference [11], the minimum number of heterogeneous nodes β_{min} is calculated according to the network size.

Research on network deployment [14–18], given the minimum number of heterogeneous nodes β_{min}, and the locations of heterogeneous nodes are h_k (u_k, v_k), $k = 1$, $2..., \beta_{min}$. The locations of ordinary node in the network are v_i (x_i, y_i), $i = 1, 2, ...,$ N. The location of sink node is (x_m, y_m). First of all, the data transmission mode of the ordinary node is judged according to the distance between the ordinary nodes and the heterogeneous nodes and the sink node. The ordinary node can directly transmit data to sink or transmit the data to sink through the hyperlink. The transmission path of the ordinary node v_1 is shown in Fig. 2. When the ordinary node directly transmits data to sink, the ordinary node v_i finds the shortest transmission path through the greedy algorithm. The distance that the ordinary node v_i transmits data to sink is $d_i{}^s$. When the ordinary node v_i transmits data to sink through the hyperlink, the ordinary node v_i also finds the shortest transmission path to the heterogeneous node through the greedy algorithm, and the transmission distance as $d_i{}^h$. Then the data is transmitted from the heterogeneous node to sink through the hyperlink. When $d_i{}^s \geq d_i{}^h$, ordinary nodes transmit through the hyperlink; When $d_i{}^s < d_i{}^h$, the ordinary node transmits directly to sink node.

Secondly, it is assumed that the number of the nodes which directly transmit data to sink is S and the number of the nodes which transmit data to sink through the hyperlink is H, satisfying $H + S = N$. When the nodes transmit data to sink through the hyperlink, the relay nodes in the transmission path are assigned IDs. Assume that there are l relay nodes; the relay node coordinates are (α_{id}, β_{id}), ($id = 1, 2, ..., l$), and the transmission distance is:

$$d_i^h = \frac{\sqrt{(x_i - \alpha_1)^2 + (y_i - \beta_1)^2} + \sqrt{(\alpha_1 - \alpha_2)^2 + (\beta_1 - \beta_2)^2} + \cdots}{+\sqrt{(\alpha_{l-1} - \alpha_l)^2 + (\beta_{l-1} - \beta_l)^2} + \sqrt{(\alpha_l - u_k)^2 + (\beta_l - v_k)^2}} \tag{2}$$

In addition, in the network model with small-world characteristics, a hyperlink is formed between heterogeneous nodes and sink, and the hyperlink carries out data transmission without considering energy consumption. Therefore, only the distance between ordinary nodes and heterogeneous nodes should be considered.

Similarly, when S nodes directly transmit data to sink, assign IDs to the relay nodes in the transmission path. Assuming that there are j relay nodes; the relay node coordinates

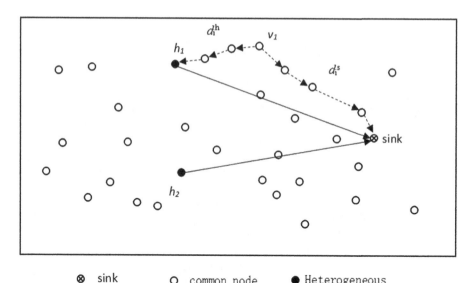

⊗ sink   ○ common node   ● Heterogeneous

Fig. 2. Data transmission mode of common nodes

are $(\gamma_{id}, \sigma_{id})$, $(id = 1, 2, ..., j)$. The transmission distances:

$$d_i^s = \frac{\sqrt{(x_i - \gamma_1)^2 + (y_i - \sigma_1)^2} + \sqrt{(\gamma_1 - \gamma_2)^2 + (\sigma_1 - \sigma_2)^2} + \cdots}{+\sqrt{(\gamma_{j-1} - \gamma_j)^2 + (\sigma_{j-1} - \sigma_j)^2} + \sqrt{(\gamma_j - x_m)^2 + (\sigma_j - y_m)^2}} \quad (3)$$

Finally, when the heterogeneous node h_k is at the position of (u_k, v_k), the total distance d_k that all nodes transmit data to sink node is calculated, and the distance d is:

$$d_k = \sum_{i=1}^{H} d_i^h + \sum_{i=H+1}^{N} d_i^s \quad (4)$$

The heterogeneous node h_k can be placed at M locations. At each location, we can calculate a distance d_k. The set of d_k. is $D = \{d_1, d_2, ..., d_M\}$. Then, calculate the minimum value of the set D, which indicates the optimal location of the first heterogeneous node.

$$d_{min} = \min D \quad (5)$$

There are β_{min} heterogeneous nodes in the network, we can find optimal locations of other heterogeneous nodes by the same way. The simplified diagram t is shown in Fig. 3. Heterogeneous nodes h_i and h_j are deployed. Heterogeneous nodes and sink node communicate by a hyperlink (the solid lines in the figure). In the process of data transmission, the node near the heterogeneous node transmits data to the heterogeneous node and then the heterogeneous node transmits data to sink through the hyperlink. Otherwise, the node near sink transmits data to sink directly (the dashed lines in the figure).

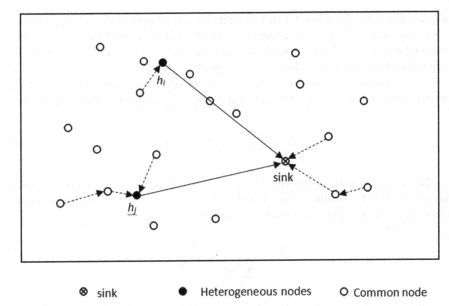

⊗ sink   ● Heterogeneous nodes   O Common node

Fig. 3. Deployment diagram of heterogeneous nodes in complex network

3   Invulnerability of Wireless Sensor Networks

The strategies for network invulnerability enhancement include routing control, network reconfiguration and topology evolution. Among them, routing control is soft optimization and does not need to change the hardware structure. Routing optimization improves the invulnerability of the network. Network reconfiguration and topology evolution are hardware optimization, which can improve the invulnerability of the network by improving the heterogeneity and scale of the network.

In order to obtain better invulnerability benefits, network reconfiguration is considered to enhance the heterogeneity of the network, so as to improve the invulnerability of the network. The main methods of network reconfiguration are the introduction of relay nodes and the construction of small world network. The introduction of relay node is to improve the heterogeneity of network by introducing heterogeneous nodes with large initial energy as the relay of data transmission [19]. To build a small world network is to build a communication link that is more reliable than the original link through the super links and heterogeneous nodes of the network [20].

In this paper, we introduce the small world network to improve the network invulnerability. Using the characteristics of small world network with large clustering coefficient and short average path, heterogeneous nodes are introduced to build super links between heterogeneous nodes, so that the network has better connectivity. Using the small world network to build a reliable super link, when the network suffers from random damage, it adopts compression, redundancy removal and other processing, as well as shortening the transmission path length of the network, which reduces the energy consumption of the network, thus weakening the risk of energy consumption failure. In view of the selective attack, the super link of the network has good reliability. If a limited number of super links are damaged, the network can still maintain normal operation, and only the data transmission rate and energy consumption rate of the network will be affected. Thus, when building a small world network, the network heterogeneity can be improved, and the invulnerability of network links can be improved.

In the network $G = (V, E)$, if the number of nodes in the network is N and the number of nodes with degree k is $n(k)$, then the degree distribution of the network is

$$P_K = \frac{n(k)}{N}, \sum_{k=1}^{k_{max}} P(k) = 1 \tag{6}$$

The degree of anode is reduced through the introduction of random edge, so as to improve the invulnerability of the constructed wireless sensor network to intentional attacks [21]. The invulnerability model of the network is [22]:

$$D_i = \frac{BC_i}{\sum_{j=1}^{n-1} BC_j} \cdot \frac{k_i}{\sum_{j\in A} k_j} \tag{7}$$

Where i and j are numbers, A is the set of neighbor nodes, BC is the betweenness of the attacked edge, k is the node degree. In small world networks, random edges are introduced to reduce the degree value k of the node, so that the degree value k_i of the ith node and the degree value $\sum_{j\in A} k_j$ of the set of neighbor nodes of the denominator are larger than that of the ith node of the numerator, i.e. $\frac{k_i}{\sum_{j\in A} k_j}$ increases. Furthermore, the invulnerability D_i and $\frac{k_i}{\sum_{j\in A} k_j}$ of the network are deduced proportional, that is, by building a small world network model, the invulnerability of the network is improved.

4 Simulation and Discussion

Firstly, the network degree distribution and destructiveness measurement of the model were simulated, and the experimental parameters were shown in Table 1. Secondly, the maximum connected branch ratio and network efficiency are compared among 3 algorithms. The IWSM (Invulnerability algorithm for Wireless sensor networks based on Small world Model) refers to the algorithm that we add heterogeneous nodes randomly to the network. The IEWSM (Invulnerability Enhancement algorithm for Wireless sensor networks based on Small world Model) refers to the algorithm that we add heterogeneous nodes optimally. BSL is the Best Sink Locations algorithm which optimized the location of the sink node. In order to study the performances of different algorithms, the same network size was set at the beginning, and the same initial node link was assumed. The data results were averaged over 50 experiments.

Table 1. Experimental parameters

Parameter (unit)	The values
Node number N(number)	100
Node distribution region A	500×500
Node maximum communication radius D_{max}(m)	150
The number of initial nodes in the network is M_0	3
Transmitting/receiving circuit loss EELEC (J/bit)	50×10^{-9}
Amplifier circuit loss ε(amp/J/bit/m^2)	100×10^{-12}

Figure 4 shows the comparison of the maximum connectivity between random attack and selective attack. Figure 5 shows the change of network benefit over node failure.

Also compare the invulnerability of wireless sensor network using different algorithms. The largest connected ratio is defined as when the dead nodes in the network have been removed, the ratio between the connected component of the remaining network and the total number of nodes in the network.Fig. 4 shows the comparison of random attack and selective attack. From Fig. 4 we can see that the maximum connectivity ratio decreases with the increase of random attack ratio, and the decrease trend of IEWSM algorithm is slower than that of BSL and IWSM algorithm, which means the IEWSM algorithm has a higher connectivity than the others. Figure 5 shows the variation diagram of network efficiency over node failure. With the increase of the proportion of random attack and selective attack, the network efficiency decreases. From Fig. 5, we can find that the decrease trend and range of IEWSM algorithm is slower than that of BSL algorithm and IWSM algorithm, which proves that IEWSM algorithm is superior to BSL algorithm and IWSM algorithm in terms of network efficiency. The simulation results show that the introduction of the small world can greatly improve the invulnerability of the network.

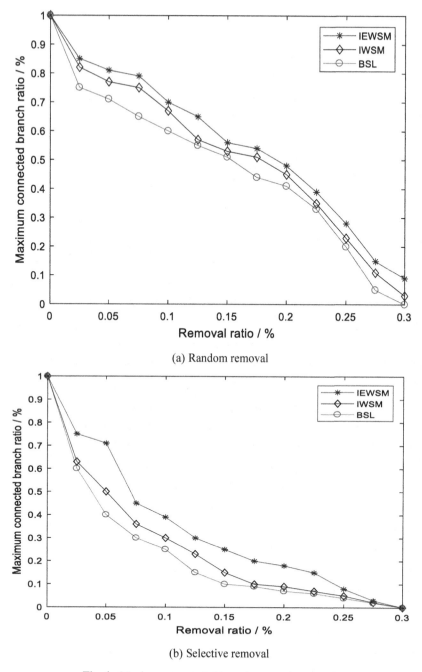

(a) Random removal

(b) Selective removal

Fig. 4. Maximum connected branch comparison graph

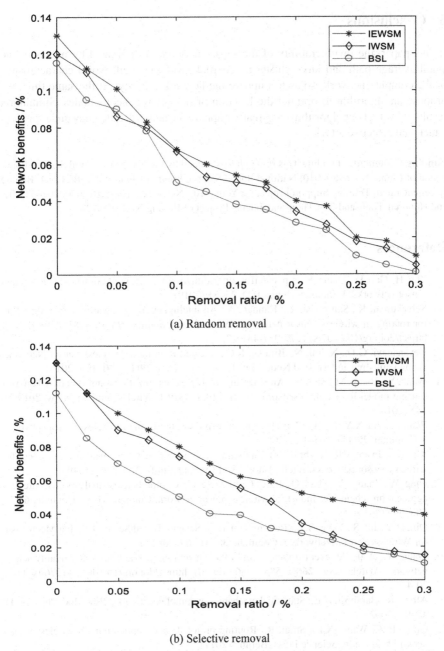

(a) Random removal

(b) Selective removal

Fig. 5. Network efficiency comparison graph

5   Conclusions

In this paper, the invulnerability of the sensor network is optimized by means of the small average path and large clustering coefficient of the small world characteristics of the complex network, so as to improve the network security. At the same time, we propose an algorithm to optimal the location of the heterogeneous nodes. Simulation results show that our algorithm can greatly improve the network efficiency under random attack and selective attack.

Funding Statement. Funding This research was funded by the National Natural Science Foundation of China, No. 61802010; National Social Science Fund of China, No.19BGL184; Beijing Excellent Talent Training Support Project for Young Top-Notch Team No. 2018000026833TD01; and Hundred-Thousand-Ten Thousand Talents Project of Beijing No. 2020A28.

References

1. Zhu, H., Gao, D., Zhang, S.: A perceptron algorithm for forest fire prediction based on wireless sensor networks. J. Internet Things 1(1), 25–31 (2019)
2. Selvakumar, K., Sairamesh, L., Kannan, A.: An intelligent energy aware secured algorithm for routing in wireless sensor networks. Wirel. Pers. Commun. 96(3), 4781–4798 (2017). https://doi.org/10.1007/s11277-017-4417-7
3. Devanagavi, G.D., Nalini, N., Biradar, R.C.: Secured Routing in Wireless Sensor Networks Using Fault-free and Trusted Nodes. Int. J. Commun. Syst. 29(1), 170–193 (2016)
4. Wang, Y., Zhang, M., Shu, W.: An emerging intelligent optimization algorithm based on trust sensing model for wireless sensor networks. EURASIP J. Wirel. Commun. Netw. 2018(1), 145 (2018)
5. Wang, C., Jia, X.Y., Lin, Q.: Trust based secure routing algorithm for wireless sensor networks. J. Commun. 29(11), 105–113 (2008)
6. Kaur, S., Joshi, V.K.: Hybrid soft computing technique based trust evaluation protocol for wireless sensor networks. Intell. Autom. Soft Comput. 26(2), 217–226 (2020)
7. Fang, W., Zhang, W., Zhao, Q., Ji, X., Chen, W., et al.: Comprehensive analysis of secure data aggregation scheme for industrial wireless sensor network. Comput. Mater. Continua 61(2), 583–599 (2019)
8. Qin, D.Y., Jia, S., Yang, S.X.: Research on Trust Sensing Based Secure Routing Mechanism for Wireless Sensor Network. J. Commun. 38(10), 60–70 (2017)
9. Wang, X., et al.: An event-driven energy-efficient routing protocol for water quality sensor networks. Wirel. Netw. 26(8), 5855–5866 (2020). https://doi.org/10.1007/s11276-020-023 20-4
10. Albert, R., Barabosi, A.L.: Statistical mechanics of complex networks. Rev. Mod. Phys. 74(1), 47–97 (2002)
11. Gong, B.Z., Wang, X.L., Shun, R.: Routing protocols and applications in wireless sensor networks. 2nd edn. Science Press, Beijing (2017)
12. Wu, J., Tan, Y.J.: Research on invulnerability measurement of complex networks. J. Syst. Eng. 20(2), 128–131 (2005)
13. Bayrakdar, M.E.: Cost effective smart system for water pollution control with underwater wireless sensor networks: a simulation study. Comput. Syst. Sci. Eng. 35(4), 283–292 (2020)
14. Sun, Z.W., Shen, D.: Optimal deployment of WSN nodes based on secure connection. J. Sens. Technol. 31(7), 1077–1084 (2005)

15. Chen, X., Ge, G.Y., Liu, Y.M., Cheng, A.M.: Deployment scheme of WSN coverage and connection nodes based on BBO algorithm. Comput. Appl. Res. **12**(10), 1–5 (2019)
16. Hao, Z.J., Hou, J., Dang, X.C., Qu, N.J.: A node optimal coverage method for strip WSN. Comput. Eng. **47**(6), 107–184 (2020)
17. Mu, C., Wang, M.: Deployment strategy of WSN along high-speed railway based on linear double sink nodes. J. Lanzhou Jiaotong Univ. **36**(6), 52–58 (2017)
18. Xie, H.: Research on DV hop positioning accuracy of anchor node deployment in WSN. Internet Things Technol. **7**(2), 34–36 (2017)
19. Sivakumar, N.R.: Stabilizing energy consumption in unequal clusters of wireless sensor networks. Comput. Mater. Continua **64**(1), 81–96 (2020)
20. Wang, J.L., Tan, X.B.: Research on invulnerability of WSN based on complex network theory. Commun. World **23**(20), 67–71 (2016)
21. Liu, H., Wang, X.Q.: A directed topology model for wireless sensor networks with destructiveness. Control Theory Appl. **6**(37), 1225–1231 (2020)
22. Li, W.F., Fu, X.W.: Invulnerability of wireless sensor networks. Acta Sin. **38**(3), 625–647 (2015)

Collaboration Energy Efficiency with Mobile Edge Computing for Target Tracking in IoT

Guobin Zou[1,2,5,6], Gang Yu[2,5,6], Jian Zhang[3(✉)], Jian Tang[4], and Junwu Zhou[1,2,5,6]

[1] College of Information Science and Engineering, Northeastern University,
Shenyang 110819, China
[2] State Key Laboratory of Process Automation in Mining and Metallurgy, Beijing 102600, China
[3] School of Computer and Software, Nanjing University of Information
Science and Technology, Nanjing 210044, China
[4] Faculty of Information Technology, Beijing University of Technology, Beijing 100024, China
[5] Beijing Key Laboratory of Process Automation in Mining
and Metallurgy, Beijing 102600, China
[6] BGRIMM Technology Group Co., Ltd., Beijing 102600, China

Abstract. In this paper, the target tracking problem is investigated with mobile edge computing (MEC) mechanism in internet of things (IoT), where the challenge of energy efficiency is a significant issue when the target tracking event is driven. In order to prolong the lifetime of IoT, we adopt dynamic clustering methods to improve energy efficiency while guaranteeing target tracking effects. We deign the sensor selection scheme for carrying out the tracking tasks according to energy distribution of the sensor node. Concretely, by considering the reality of random deployment and introducing the definition of node density for IoT, we develop a Pareto optimality for sensor nodes selection in terms of energy efficiency without reducing the accuracy of target tracking. Furthermore, we recruit voluntary mobile devices as mobile edge computing servers to offload the data from selected sensor nodes in the cluster and process them to the estimate the target state. Simulations demonstrate the efficiency for tracking performance on energy balance in terms of efficiently prolonging the IoT lifetime.

Keywords: IoT · Mobile edge computing · Pareto optimality · EKF · Target tracking

1 Introduction

With the development of the micro-electro-mechanical system (MEMS) technology, internet of things (IoT) have been widely applied to many applications, such as building structure monitoring and control, target tracking and localization, military defense and other fields [1–3], where a large number of low cost and spatially dispersed position sensors are densely deployed as a general paradigm for information collection, transmission and processing data. Target tracking in IoT is one of the most important applications and often needs coverage of broad areas. However, the resources like bandwidth and energy are actually restricted [4], which has been investigated via the scheduled schemes of

© Springer Nature Switzerland AG 2021
X. Sun et al. (Eds.): ICAIS 2021, CCIS 1424, pp. 470–480, 2021.
https://doi.org/10.1007/978-3-030-78621-2_39

sensors to realize the goal of the tracking task while satisfying advanced performance of IoT.

The sensor selection problem for target tracking has been developed to get the desired information gain or reduction in estimation error in [5–7]. Authors in [8] proposed distributed algorithms to select cluster members to gather data and formulated an optimization for target tracking to maximize utilization of data quality through a rendezvous-based data collection algorithm which not only integrates above positive factors to track a target but also maintains WSNs' functions. In [9], the sensor selection problem with and without sensing range is demonstrated by utilizing a fixed area and a circle drawn with the help of communication range to select sensor nodes for two cases, respectively. In order to improve the performance of energy efficiency, the quantization technique has been adopted to decrease the transmission rates for energy saving [10], which would lead to additional errors on the available measurements in terms of quantization effects [11], which may degrade the filtering/estimation performance.

The problem of collaborative tracking of mobile nodes in wireless sensor networks is studied in [12], where target tracking and node selection procedures are employed together to identify proper sensor locations and information route for an energy-efficient tracking strategy. Generally, mobility can improve the performance of IoT [13], which characterizes three node sets of the cluster as a theoretical foundation to enhance high performance of WSNs, and propose optimal solutions by introducing rendezvous and Mobile Elements (MEs) to optimize energy consumption for prolonging the lifetime of WSNs. Meanwhile, MEs can be used as mobile edge computing server to collect data from WSNs and process them for target tracking due to their capacity of computing, storage, rich energy and so on. Considering offloading this type of deep learning (DL) tasks to a mobile edge computing (MEC) server, Bo Yang [14] proposed an optimization problem to minimize the weighted-sum cost including the tracking delay and energy consumption introduced by communication and computing of the UAVs, while taking into account the quality of data input to the DL model and the inference errors.

The main contribution of this paper is that we proposed a Pareto optimality for sensor nodes selection in terms of energy efficiency without reducing the accuracy of target tracking. Furthermore, we recruit voluntary mobile devices as mobile edge computing servers to collect the data from selected sensor nodes in the cluster and process them to the estimate the target state. Unlike the most of previous target tracking method, it is shown that the proposed algorithm exhibits excellent performances in terms of energy efficiency.

The layout of the paper is as follows: in Sect. 2, problem statements are described, including motion model and clustering for target tracking. Section 3 is Energy statements. Quantization and sensor selection is demonstrated in Sect. 4 and Sect. 5. In Sect. 6, the tracking steps of algorithm is given. Simulation results are discussed. We conclude the paper in Sect. 8.

2 Problem Statements

A model-based wireless sensor network consists of the motion model and the observation model. In this paper, the single target tracking is addressed in the region monitored by wireless sensor networks.

2.1 Motion Model

For the convenience of description, the state equation of the target is introduced, and the nonlinear discrete dynamic model can be expressed as:

$$X(k + 1) = F(\Delta t_k)X(k) + \omega(k, \Delta t_k) \tag{1}$$

where $X(k)$ is the state variable of the moving target at time k, Δt_k is the sampling interval between two adjacent states, $F(\Delta t_k)$ is the state transition matrix, and $\omega(k, \Delta t_k)$ is the process noise. If the observation value of the node i at time k is $z_i(k)$, then the observation model can be expressed as

$$Z(k) = H(X(k)) + V(k) \tag{2}$$

where $Z(k) = (z_1(k), z_2(k), \cdots, z_N(k))^T$, $H(X(k)) = (h_1(X(k)), h_2(X(k)), \cdots, h_N(X(k)))^T$, $V(k) = (v_1(k), v_2(k), \cdots, v_N(k))^T$, $h_i(\cdot)$ And $v_i(k)$ respectively represent the observation equation and observation noise of the node i. In this paper, it is assumed that $\omega(k, \Delta t_k)$ and $v_i(k)$ are independent of each other, and their covariance matrices are $Q(k, \Delta t_k)$ and $R(k)$, respectively. According to EKF process,

① The prediction equation is shown as follows:

$$\hat{X}(k + 1/k) = F(\Delta t_k)\hat{X}(k/k) \tag{3}$$

where the covariance matrix is:

$$P(k + 1/k) = F(\Delta t_k)P(k/k)F^T(\Delta t_k) + Q(k, \Delta t_k) \tag{4}$$

② The forecasting process is given by:

$$\hat{Z}(k + 1/k) = h(\hat{X}(k + 1/k)) \tag{5}$$

③ The update process can be calculated by:

$$\delta(k + 1) = Z(k + 1) - \hat{Z}(k + 1/k) \tag{6}$$

where the covariance matrix is:

$$C(k + 1) = H(k + 1)P(k + 1/k)H^T(k + 1) + R(k + 1) \tag{7}$$

and $H(\cdot)$ denotes the Jacobian matrix of $h_j(\cdot)$, then the gain matrix is given by the following equation

$$K(k + 1) = P(k + 1/k)H^T(k + 1)C^{-1}(k + 1) \tag{8}$$

④ The estimation process:

$$\hat{X}(k + 1/k + 1) = \hat{X}(k + 1/k) + K(k + 1)\delta(k + 1) \tag{9}$$

where the covariance matrix is:

$$P(k + 1/k + 1) = P(k + 1/k) - K(k + 1)C(k + 1)K^T(k + 1) \tag{10}$$

2.2 Clustering for Target Tracking

In order to improve the energy efficiency, we configure the cluster in grid for state estimation of the target, which is shown in Fig. 1. However, due to random deployment of sensor nodes in WSNs, the node density of the cluster is a random variable that could effect the performance of target tracking. In order to balance the energy consumption of local or global WSNs, the sensor node selecting scheme is significant to improve the energy efficiency, which will be illustrated in the follow section.

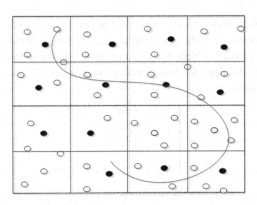

Fig. 1. Clustering for target tracking

3 Energy Statements

The tracking cost is expressed as energy consumption, and energy model in [13] is shown as follows. For the sake of convenience, we consider energy consumption at the cost of a b-bit message and a distance d between sensor s_i as a transmitter and sensor s_j as a receiver. The energy consumed in transmitting by the sensor s_i is

$$E_{Tx}(s_i, s_j) = b \cdot E_{Telec} + b \cdot \varepsilon_{amp} \cdot d_{i,j}^{\alpha} \tag{11}$$

and to receive this message, the radio expends:

$$E_{Rx}(s_j) = b \cdot E_{Relec} \tag{12}$$

In addition, the receiver s_j also spends energy in sensing or processing. The radio expends:

$$E_{Sx}(s_j) = b \cdot E_{Selec} \tag{13}$$

where E_{Telec} and ε_{amp} are determined by transmitter s_i, $d_{i,j}$ indicates the distance between sensor s_i and sensor s_j. E_{Relec} and E_{Selec} are decided by receiver s_j. α depends on the channel characteristics and is known as $\alpha = 2$.

Therefore, the total energy consumption between senor s_i and sensor s_j is demonstrated by

$$E(s_i, s_j) = E_{Tx}(s_i, s_j) + E_{Rx}(s_j) + E_{Sx}(s_j)r$$
$$= b \cdot E_{Relec} + b \cdot E_{Selec} + b \cdot E_{Telec} + b \cdot \varepsilon_{amp} \cdot d_{i,j}^2 \qquad (14)$$

where $E_0 = bE_{Telec} + bE_{Relec} + bE_{Selec}$, $e_0 = b\varepsilon_{amp}$.

4 Quantization

Considering the sensor node density, we deal with a more complicated scenario which includes redundant sensors. Although we introduce the wake-up mechanism, redundant information maybe produce which also consume more energy of WSNs. As a result, we adopt quantization technology for further energy saving, and the quantization for sensor node i is shown as follows

$$m_i = \begin{cases} 0 & -\infty < z_i < \gamma_1 \\ 1 & \gamma_1 < z_i < \gamma_2 \\ \vdots & \vdots \\ L-1 & \gamma_{(L-1)} < z_i < \infty \end{cases} \qquad (15)$$

where γ_i in Eq. (9) indicates the quantization thresholds and $L = 2^m$ is the number of quantization levels.

5 Collaboration of Sensor Node Selection and Data Quantization

In this section, we consider the optimality of sensor selection for energy efficiency in the process of target tracking.

5.1 Pareto Optimality

We utilize Pareto optimality to select sensor nodes for target tracking in terms of a given tracking accuracy. In the grid cluster including a sensor set $S = \{ s_1, s_2, \cdots, s_n \}$, we supposed that there exist a set $S' = \{ s_1', s_2', \cdots, s_r' \}$ to accomplish the tracking task, where $S' \subseteq S$ holds. However, this is a permutation and combination problem and it is hard to solve this problem when the sensors are densely deployed in the area. Naturally, the permutation and combination problem of sensor selection for target tracking can be evolved into the constraint optimization problem as follows.

$$\min \sum_{i=1}^{r} (E_{s_i'} - \overline{E})^2$$
$$s.t. \Phi_{S'} \leq \Phi_0 \qquad (16)$$

where $E_{s_i'}$ is the residual energy of sensor s_i' in set S', $\overline{E}$ denotes the average energy of the cluster, $\Phi_{S'}$ is the actual tracking accuracy obtained by the sensor combination of set S', and Φ_0 denotes the given target accuracy. According to expression (16), we design a Pareto optimality mechanism to get the approximate sensor combination set.

Step 1: arbitrarily select a sensor with a certain probability, and get $\{s_1'\}$;

Step 2: select another sensor in the set $S\backslash\{s_1'\}$ and get $\{s_1', s_2'\}$. According to the concept of Pareto optimality, increasing sensor s_2' is not reduce the revenues of s_1';

Step 3: continue to select a set $S' = \{s_1', s_2', \cdots, s_r'\}$ until expression (16) is satisfied.

5.2 Collaboration of Sensor Selection and Data Quantization

Considering the energy consumption of data transmission, we collaborate the sensor selection and data quantization for energy efficiency in the target tracking process. In this scenario, we deal with target data on the premise of sensors being randomly deploy in the interest area. Actually, due to the approximate solution in terms of Subsect. 5.1, we demonstrate four cases for collaboration of sensor selection and data quantization according to the density of the cluster, which are shown in the following table.

Table 1. Collaboration of sensor selection and data quantization

	Quantization	No quantization
Selection	(1,1)	(1,0)
No selection	(0,1)	(0,0)

Case 1: for energy efficiency, we not only select sensors but also quantize the data, that is (1,1) in Table 1. In this scenario, the density of the cluster is higher.

Case 2: (1,0) in Table 1, that is, we plan to select sensors while not quantize the data.

Case 3: (0,1) denotes we are about to quantize the data of sensing data while not select sensors for target tracking.

Case 4: (0,0) stands for neither selection nor quantization. In this scenario, the density of the cluster is lower.

6 MEC Server Placement

In the process of target tracking, MEC server play roles of collecting data, processing data and transmitting data.

6.1 MEC Server Placement

For further reducing the energy consumption of the cluster, we set the optimal position of MEC server according to Eq. (11). After selecting the sensing nodes, the position of each node is confirmed. Therefore, we can find a point to place the MEC server to minimize the expression (16).

6.2 MEC Server for Data Processing

In this subsection, we illustrate offloading the computation of sensor nodes to the MEC server in the cluster. According to (1), $F(\Delta t_k)$ and $Q(k, \Delta t_k)$ can be shown as follows, respectively.

$$
F(\Delta t_k) = \begin{bmatrix} 1 & \Delta t_k & 0 & 0 \\ 0 & 1 & 0 & 0 \\ 0 & 0 & 1 & \Delta t_k \\ 0 & 0 & 0 & 1 \end{bmatrix}
\tag{17}
$$

$$
Q(k, \Delta t_k) = q \begin{bmatrix} \frac{\Delta t_k^3}{3} & \frac{\Delta t_k^2}{2} & 0 & 0 \\ \frac{\Delta t_k^2}{2} & \Delta t_k & 0 & 0 \\ 0 & 0 & \frac{\Delta t_k^3}{3} & \frac{\Delta t_k^2}{2} \\ 0 & 0 & \frac{\Delta t_k^2}{2} & \Delta t_k \end{bmatrix}
\tag{18}
$$

If $P(k|k)$ is set by

$$
P(k|k) = \begin{bmatrix} \sigma_{11} & \sigma_{12} & \sigma_{13} & \sigma_{14} \\ \sigma_{21} & \sigma_{22} & \sigma_{23} & \sigma_{24} \\ \sigma_{31} & \sigma_{32} & \sigma_{33} & \sigma_{34} \\ \sigma_{41} & \sigma_{42} & \sigma_{43} & \sigma_{44} \end{bmatrix}
\tag{19}
$$

MEC server can calculate the covariance of the target prediction position error in terms of $P(k|k)$.

$$
P(k+1|k) = \begin{bmatrix} 1 & \Delta t_k & 0 & 0 \\ 0 & 1 & 0 & 0 \\ 0 & 0 & 1 & \Delta t_k \\ 0 & 0 & 0 & 1 \end{bmatrix} \cdot \begin{bmatrix} \sigma_{11} & \sigma_{12} & \sigma_{13} & \sigma_{14} \\ \sigma_{21} & \sigma_{22} & \sigma_{23} & \sigma_{24} \\ \sigma_{31} & \sigma_{32} & \sigma_{33} & \sigma_{34} \\ \sigma_{41} & \sigma_{42} & \sigma_{43} & \sigma_{44} \end{bmatrix} \begin{bmatrix} 1 & \Delta t_k & 0 & 0 \\ 0 & 1 & 0 & 0 \\ 0 & 0 & 1 & \Delta t_k \\ 0 & 0 & 0 & 1 \end{bmatrix}^T + q \begin{bmatrix} \frac{\Delta t_k^3}{3} & \frac{\Delta t_k^2}{2} & 0 & 0 \\ \frac{\Delta t_k^2}{2} & \Delta t_k & 0 & 0 \\ 0 & 0 & \frac{\Delta t_k^3}{3} & \frac{\Delta t_k^2}{2} \\ 0 & 0 & \frac{\Delta t_k^2}{2} & \Delta t_k \end{bmatrix}
\tag{20}
$$

furthermore,

$$
P(k+1|k) = \begin{pmatrix} \sigma_{11} + 2\sigma_{12}\Delta t_k + \sigma_{22}\Delta t_k^2 + q\frac{\Delta t_k^3}{3} & \sigma_{12} + \sigma_{22}\Delta t_k + \frac{\Delta t_k^2}{2} & \sigma_{13} + (\sigma_{23} + \sigma_{14})\Delta t_k + \sigma_{24}\Delta t_k^2 & \sigma_{14} + \sigma_{24}\Delta t_k \\ \sigma_{12} + \sigma_{22}\Delta t_k + \frac{\Delta t_k^2}{2} & \sigma_{22} + \Delta t_k & \sigma_{23} + \sigma_{24}\Delta t_k & \sigma_{24} \\ \sigma_{31} + (\sigma_{32} + \sigma_{41})\Delta t_k + \sigma_{42}\Delta t_k^2 & \sigma_{32} + \sigma_{42}\Delta t_k & \sigma_{33} + 2\sigma_{34}\Delta t_k + \sigma_{44}\Delta t_k^2 + q\frac{\Delta t_k^3}{3} & \sigma_{34} + \sigma_{44}\Delta t_k + \frac{\Delta t_k^2}{2} \\ \sigma_{41} + \sigma_{42}\Delta t_k & \sigma_{42} & \sigma_{43} + \sigma_{44}\Delta t_k + \frac{\Delta t_k^2}{2} & \sigma_{44} + \Delta t_k \end{pmatrix}
\tag{21}
$$

Therefore, MEC server calculate The error covariance of the target predicted position can be expressed as

$$
\sum(\Delta t_k) = \begin{bmatrix} \sigma_{11} + 2\sigma_{12}\Delta t_k + \sigma_{22}\Delta t_k^2 + q\frac{\Delta t_k^3}{3} & \sigma_{13} + (\sigma_{23} + \sigma_{14})\Delta t_k + \sigma_{24}\Delta t_k^2 \\ \sigma_{31} + (\sigma_{32} + \sigma_{41})\Delta t_k + \sigma_{42}\Delta t_k^2 & \sigma_{33} + 2\sigma_{34}\Delta t_k + \sigma_{44}\Delta t_k^2 + q\frac{\Delta t_k^3}{3} \end{bmatrix}
\tag{22}
$$

7 Simulation Results

To illustrate advantages of the new method, some simulation results are discussed and some assumptions for simulations here. In these simulations, the number of sensors N = 100, sensor radius R = 60 m and sampling interval T_s = 1 s. They are randomly deployed in a square field 300*300 m². The target tracking time continues for 50 s. Simulation parameters about energy consumption model are listed in Table 2.

Table 2. Simulation parameters

parameters	values	parameters	values
α	2	E_0	0.5 J
ε	10 J/bit/m²	N	100
d	60	Eelec	50 nJ/bit
E_{amp}	0.0013 PJ/bit m⁴		

Figure 2 illustrates energy consumption for different accuracy. According to the target tracking accuracy, Pareto optimality is employed to select sensing data, which is offloaded to mobile edge computing server for computation. Seen from the Figure, the energy consumption of IoT increases with the growth of accuracy. However, the energy consumption maintains balance for each accuracy. In this process, we design sensor selection scheme with optimality, place MEC server for data offloading, and quantize data for data transmission. Especially, our sensor selection scheme with Pareto optimality is utilized to schedule sensor in the premise of the given accuracy. MEC server not only collects data from cluster as the cluster head, but also relays the computation result to the Sink node for reducing the energy consumption of data route. Furthermore, data quantization is used for reducing the energy consumption of data collection in the cluster.

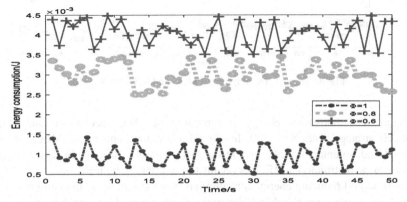

Fig. 2. Energy consumption for different accuracy with N = 100

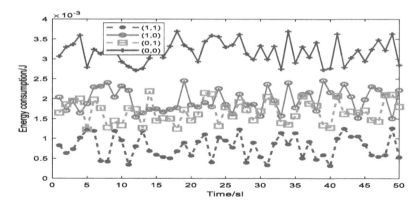

Fig. 3. 4 cases for energy consumption with N = 200

In Fig. 3, collaboration of sensor selection and data quantization as shown in Table 1 are considered with the number of sensors N = 200. Given a target tracking accuracy, energy consumption changes with different scenarios. It can be seen in Fig. 3, the scenario of (1,1) get the best performance of IoT according to the sensor density of each cluster. the scenario of (0,0) gets the worse performance of IoT when the sensor density of IoT become larger compared to N = 100. Although different collaboration of sensor selection and data quantization plays the role of reducing different energy consumption, they can keep the performance of energy balance for IoT.

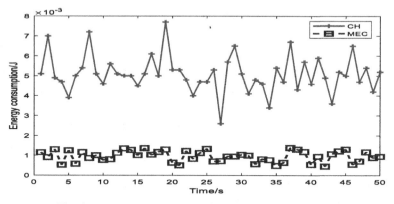

Fig. 4. Energy consumption of MEC and CH with N = 300

Figure 4 demonstrates energy consumption of MEC mechanism and cluster head(CH) strategy with N = 300. In our proposed mechanism, the MEC server is recruited and voluntary to take part in the task of target tracking. In this way, each cluster can be distributed a MEC server for target tracking with the goal of replacing cluster head and reducing energy consumption. Seen from Fig. 4, the employment of MEC server is more superior than CH strategy. Furthermore, MEC mechanism also gets more superior performance in terms of energy balance of IoT.

8 Conclusions

In this paper, dynamic clustering methods is adopted to improve energy efficiency while guaranteeing target tracking effects. We deign the sensor selection scheme for carrying out the tracking tasks according to energy distribution of the sensor node. Concretely, by considering the reality of random deployment and introducing the definition of node density for IoT, we develop a Pareto optimality for sensor nodes selection in terms of energy efficiency without reducing the accuracy of target tracking. Furthermore, we recruit voluntary mobile devices as mobile edge computing servers to collect the data from selected sensor nodes in the cluster and process them to the estimate the target state.

Acknowledgments. This work is supported by the State Key Laboratory of Process Automation in Mining & Metallurgy and Beijing Key Laboratory of Process Automation in Mining & Metallurgy (BGRIMM-KZSKL-2020–02), and National Key Research and Development Project (2020YFE0201100, 2019YFE0105000).

References

1. Akyildiz, F., Su, W., Sankarasubramaniam, Y., Cayirci, E.: Wireless sensor networks: a survey. Comput. Netw. **38**(4), 393–442 (2002)
2. Gezici, S., et al.: Localization via ultra-wideband radios: A look at positioning aspects for future sensor networks. IEEE Signal Process. Mag. **22**(4), 70–84 (2005)
3. Zhu, D., Sun, Y., Du, H., Cao, N., Baker, T., Srivastava, G.: HUNA: a method of hierarchical unsupervised network alignment for IoT. IEEE Internet Things J. **8**, 3201–3210 (2020) https://doi.org/10.1109/JIOT.2020.3020951
4. Wang, J., Qiu, X., Tu.: An improved mds-map localization algorithm based on weighted clustering and heuristic merging for anisotropic wireless networks with energy holes. Comput. Mater. Continua **60**(1), 227–244 (2019)
5. Liu, S., Kar, S., Fardad, M., Varshney, P.K.: Sparsity-aware sensor collaboration for linear coherent estimation. IEEE Trans. Signal Process. **63**(10), 2582–2596 (2015)
6. Liu, S., Kar, S., Fardad, M., Varshney, P.K.: Optimal periodic sensor scheduling in networks of dynamical systems. IEEE Trans. Signal Process. **62**(12), 3055–3068 (2014)
7. Cao, N., Sora, C., Engin, M., Pramod, K.V.: Sensor selection for target tracking in wireless sensor networks with uncertainty. IEEE Trans. Signal Process. **64**(20), 5191–5204 (2015)
8. Zhang, J., Wang, T., Tang, J.: Optimising rendezvous-based data collection for target tracking in WSNs with mobile elements. Int. J. Sens. Netw. **30**(4), 218–230 (2019)
9. Liu, H.Q., So, H.C., Lui, K.W.K., Chan, F.K.W.: Sensor selection for target tracking in sensor networks. Prog. Electromagnet. Res. **95**, 267–282 (2009)
10. Zhang, D., Yu, L., Zhang, W.A.: Energy efficient distributed filtering for a class of nonlinear systems in sensor networks. IEEE Sens. J. **15**(5), 3026–3036 (2015)
11. Hu, L., Wang, Z., Liu, X.: Dynamic state estimation of power system with quantization effects: Arecursive filter approach. IEEE Trans. Neural Netw. Learn. Syst. **27**(8), 1604–1614 (2016)

12. Hamid, M., Walid, M., Aghdam, A.G., Kamran, S.P.: An energy-efficient target-tracking strategy for mobile sensor networks. IEEE Trans. Cybern. **47**(2), 512–524 (2017)
13. Zhang, J., Tang, J., Wang, Z.H., Wang, F., Yu, G.: Load-balancing rendezvous approach for mobility-enabled adaptive energy-efficient data collection in WSNs. KSII Trans. Internet Inf. Syst. **14**(3), 1204–1227 (2020)
14. Yang, B., Cao, X., Yuen, C., Qian, L.: Offloading optimization in edge computing for deep learning enabled target tracking by internet-of-UAVs. In: IEEE Internet of Things Journal (2020). https://doi.org/10.1109/JIOT.2020.3016694

Realization of CSI-Based Human Behavior Recognition: A Survey

Xinxing Tang, Xiaolong Yang[✉], Mu Zhou, and Liangbo Xie

Chongqing University of Posts and Telecommunication, Chongqing 400065, China
yangxiaolong@cqupt.edu.cn

Abstract. With the rapid popularization and development of smart home and Internet of Things (IoT), wireless sensing technique has become more and more popular due to its better privacy protection, insensitivity to light and avoiding obstacles. As one of the most popular wireless sensing devices, Wi-Fi has the advantages of extensive deployment and low cost, which attracts a large number of interests. Thus, this survey mainly focuses on the Wi-Fi-based human behavior recognition systems in recent years, and analyzes its realization process. Concretely, we summary these process from four aspects. First, the collection tool and characteristic of channel state information (CSI) data are simply introduced. Second, the data pre-processing algorithms are described, such as phase correction, low-pass filter, outlier removal, principal component analysis, discrete wavelet transform, activity segmentation and extraction and so on. Third, the recognition modes are outlined, including CSI speed model, Fresnel Zone model, angle of arrival model, machine-learning based mode and deep-learning based model. Forth, applications of human behavior recognition are concluded according to recognition content. Finally, this survey summarizes current challenges and issues of behavior recognition systems, and gives some suggestions for future research.

Keywords: Channel state information · Human behavior recognition · Wi-Fi

1 Introduction

In recent years, with the rapid development of the Internet of Things (IoT), the perception of human activities has become an inevitable part of various fields such as entertainment and medical treatment. Therefore, a large number of researchers have begun to study human behavior recognition.

According to different auxiliary equipment, existing behavior recognition systems are mainly divided into three categories. The first category requires the target to wear special equipment such as sensors, and realizes behavior recognition through processing captured sensor data, which is not convenient for wearers. The second category is a camera-based behavior recognition system, which has perfect performance under the condition of line-of-sight (LoS) scenes. However, it is difficulty to realize human behavior recognition under the condition of non-line-of-sight (NLoS). What's worse, it is unable to guarantee people's privacy protection. The third category is behavior

© Springer Nature Switzerland AG 2021
X. Sun et al. (Eds.): ICAIS 2021, CCIS 1424, pp. 481–491, 2021.
https://doi.org/10.1007/978-3-030-78621-2_40

recognition system based on wireless sensing, which realizes the behavior recognition of human targets by extracting the characteristics of wireless channel variation caused by human activities and constructing a classifier. For the reason that wireless signal can be insensitive to light, avoid obstacle and take the air as the medium for propagation, it overcomes the shortcoming of the first two types of behavior recognition systems, making the wireless sensing technologies more and more popular.

As an important part of the wireless sensing-based behavior recognition system, Wi-Fi-based behavior recognition system has been the focus of attention. This system consists of Wi-Fi access points (AP) and several receiving devices. When the target moves in the detection area, its behavior will affect the Wi-Fi signal transmission environment.

This paper summarizes the related research of human behavior recognition based on commercial Wi-Fi devices. This section discusses the related work of human behavior recognition based on auxiliary equipment, camera and wireless signal. The rest of this paper is organized as follows. Section 2 introduces the basic concepts of CSI acquisition tools, orthogonal frequency division system and CSI. Section 3 mainly introduces the basic framework of CSI-based behavior sensing system. Section 4 introduces the applications of the behavioral perception system, and Sect. 5 summarizes and analyzes current challenges and issues and proposes some future research directions.

2 Preliminary

2.1 Collection Tool of CSI

At present, the commercial Network Interface Cards (NIC) that have been used to collect CSI data are Intel 5300 and Atheros NIC, as shown in Fig. 1(a) and (b) respectively. Xie *et al.* and Halperin et al. realized the collection of CSI data at the physical layer by modifying the firmware of the network card. CSI-tool and installation tutorials can be found on the open source website.

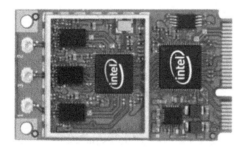

(a) Intel 5300 NIC	(b) Atheros NIC

Fig. 1. Collection tool of CSI

Table 1. Applications of CSI-based behavior recognition

Reference	Type	Signal	Preprocessing	Classifier	Performance
WiHACS [1]	Daily behavior recognition	CSI amplitude	Liner interpolation; Hampel;	SVM	LOS:97% NLOS:92%
TW-See [2]	Daily behavior recognition	CSI amplitude	Low-pass filter; PCA; RPCA	BP network	94.6%
Dong et al. [3]	Daily behavior recognition	CSI	Low-pass filter; Hampel	SVM; RNN	92%
WiFall [4]	Fall detection	CSI amplitude	LOF; Anomaly detection algorithm	SVM; RF	87%
RT-Fall [5]	Fall detection	CSI	Low-pass filter;	SVM	Batter than WiFall
FallDeFi [6]	Fall detection	CSI amplitude	Interpolation; DWT; PCA	SVM	93%
NotiFi [7]	Abnormal activity detection	CSI	PCA	Bayesian model	LOS:89.2% NLOS:85.6%
Smokey [8]	Smoking detection	CSI amplitude	Interpolation; PEM	Autocorrelation	92.8%
WiStep [9]	Step counting	CSI	PCA; DWT; Bandpass filter	Short-time energy	Lab:90.2%; Classroom:87.59%
WiFinger [10]	Gesture recognition	CSI	DWT; Butterworth;	MD-DTW	93%
PhaseBeat [11]	Breath detection	CSI phase	Subcarrier Selection; DWT	FFT-based peak detection	90% data: error under 0.5
R-TTWD [12]	Human detection	CSI amplitude	PCA; Hampel filter; DWT	SVM	Over 99%
CARM [13]	Daily behavior recognition	CSI	PCA	CSI-speed model; CSI-activity model	96%
TR-breath [14]	Breath detection	CSI phase	Data Calibration; Rott-Music	SVM	LOS:98.65%; NLOS:97.3%
WiFit [15]	Exercise type classification	CSI	Doppler effect	SVM	95.8%
BreathTrack [16]	Breath detection	CSI phase	Music	AOA model	99%

2.2 Orthogonal Frequency Division Multiplexing

OFDM is actually a type of multi-carrier modulation. The main idea is to divide the channel into several orthogonal sub-channels, and use the sub-channels to transmit the sub-data streams in the high-speed data signal. Orthogonal signals can be separated by using demodulation technology at the receiving end, which can reduce mutual interference between sub-channels. When the signal bandwidth on each sub-channel is smaller than the relevant bandwidth of the channel, the signal on each sub-channel can be regarded as flat fading.

Under the action of the OFDM system, the bandwidth of wireless devices will be divided into 30 groups. Each CSI measurement value is a matrix containing $30 \times Ntx \times Nrx$ dimensions, Ntx is the number of transmitting antennas, and Nrx is the number of receiving antennas.

2.3 Channel State Information

In the field of wireless communication, CSI is the channel attribute of the communication link. It describes the propagation process of wireless signals between transmitter and receiver, including the influence of distance, scattering, and fading on the signal. When the human body moves in the coverage of the Wi-Fi signal, the propagation channel of the Wi-Fi signal will also be affected, and the CSI will also change. Therefore, we can use CSI to evaluate the state of the communication link, so as to recognize human activities. We modified the firmware of the Intel 5300 network card to extract the CSI information from the physical layer.

In the frequency domain, the wireless channel can be modeled as:

$$\mathbf{Y} = \mathbf{H} \times \mathbf{X} + \mathbf{N} \tag{1}$$

where $\mathbf{Y}$ and $\mathbf{X}$ are the received signal matrix and the transmitted signal matrix respectively, $\mathbf{N}$ is additive white Gaussian noise; $\mathbf{H}$ is the matrix containing CSI information. In general, the dimension of matrix $\mathbf{H}$ is $n \times m$, where n is the number of subcarriers, and m is the number of sampling points. When the number of sampling points is 1, $\mathbf{H}$ represents the CSI value of a single received data packet, and the CSI of the kth subcarrier can be expressed as

$$H(k) = |H(k)|e^{j\angle H(k)} \tag{2}$$

where $|H(k)|$ and $\angle H(k)$ respectively represent the amplitude information and phase information of the CSI of the kth subcarrier.

3   CSI-Based Behavior Recognition

CSI-based behavior recognition system refers to the use of CSI to identify the behavior type of the detected target. CSI can sensitively reflect changes in the surrounding environment. The behavior recognition system mainly includes three parts: basic signal selection, signal processing and behavior recognition, as shown in the Fig. 2. Each part is described in detail as follows. Table 1 shows the research content and research methods of some human behavior recognition systems.

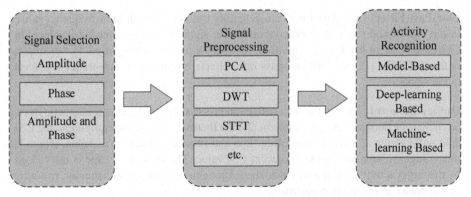

Fig. 2. Realization of human behavior recognition

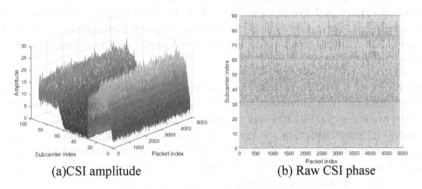

(a)CSI amplitude   (b) Raw CSI phase

Fig. 3. Raw CSI amplitude and phase

3.1 Basic Signal Selection

The CSI data collected by the receiver is in a complex form, including both CSI amplitude information and CSI phase information. Therefore, the basic signals used by the CSI-based behavior recognition system are divided into three types: amplitude, phase, combined signal of amplitude and phase. E-eye [17] uses the amplitude information of CSI to detect nine kinds of daily activities. Wu et al. [18] uses phase-corrected CSI phase information to achieve user authentication. NotiFi [7] uses CSI amplitude and phase information to automatically detect abnormal activities (Fig. 3).

3.2 Signal Processing

Phase Correction. In practical applications, limited by the hardware performance of commercial Wi-Fi network cards, the extracted CSI phase information has various errors, such as channel initial phase error, clock synchronization phase error, carrier frequency error, etc. Therefore, if the phase is used as the basic signal for behavior recognition, the phase needs to be corrected. Wu et al. [18] removed the phase deviation by linear elimination, thus realizing moving target detection.

Low-Pass Filter. Low-pass filters are generally used to filter out high-frequency noise in the signal, and retain the components of the signal below the cutoff frequency. In CSI-based human behavior recognition, low-pass filters are widely used. For example, in the R-TTWD [12] system, low-pass filter effectively filter out high-frequency noise in the signal.

Outlier Removal. During the data collection process, due to the electromagnetic interference in the surrounding environment and the thermal noise of the equipment, the CSI data will change at a certain sampling time and produce an abnormal value, which is much larger or smaller than the adjacent CSI value. The abnormal value is not caused by the target activity, and it may cause the misjudgment of the target behavior, resulting in a decrease in recognition accuracy.

In order to eliminate the influence of outliers, Hampel filters are often used to remove the outliers in the signal. For example, R-TTWD [12] uses Hampel filter to remove outliers and realizes human activity detection under non-line-of-sight conditions. Wi-HACS [1] uses Hampel filters to eliminate noise and recognizes activities such as walking, running, and falling.

Discrete Wavelet Transformation. In CSI-based behavior recognition, discrete wavelet transform (DWT) is usually used for denoising. Under normal circumstances, the energy of the useful signal is concentrated on one or two wavelet coefficients, while the energy of the noise exists on most of the wavelet coefficients, and the energy is relatively small. Therefore, a threshold is set, the wavelet coefficients larger than the threshold are regarded as useful signals, and the coefficients are shrunk through the threshold function to achieve denoising.

At present, many systems use wavelet transform to denoise in the data processing process, such as WiFinger [10], WiStep [9], PhaseBeat [11] etc.

Principal Component Analysis. Generally, CSI data is in the form of a matrix, and the dimension of the matrix is related to the number of subcarriers and the number of received data packets. In order to extract the signal that can characterize the target activity from the original CSI data, principal component analysis (PCA) is often used. PCA can reduce the dimension of data, improve the efficiency of data processing, and eliminate noise.

Activity Segmentation and Extraction. In CSI-based human behavior recognition, it is extremely important to extract the data during the action period from the original data. This can eliminate the data during the non-action period to improve the accuracy of action recognition, and provide a good precondition for subsequent research. Wu et al. [2] proposed a normalized variance sliding window algorithm, which uses the relationship between the set threshold and the sliding variance to determine the start and end time of the activity, thereby realizing activity segmentation.

3.3 Activity Recognition

Model-Based

CSI Speed Model. When the human body moves within the coverage area of the Wi-Fi signal, part of the propagation path of the Wi-Fi signal changes. Based on this, Wang *et al.* [13] believes that the total propagation path of Wi-Fi signals can be divided into two parts, a dynamic path and a static path. The two paths correspond to the static channel frequency response and the dynamic channel frequency response respectively. The researchers calculated the instantaneous power of the channel frequency response and found that the power of the signal frequency response was the sum of a constant offset and a series of sine waves, where the frequency of the sine wave was related to the speed of the changing path. By measuring the frequency of these sine waves, the speed change of the dynamic path can be obtained, and the CSI speed model can be established. CARM [13] can distinguish 8 different actions. For trained samples, the average accuracy is 96%. However, there are still some limitations in identifying fine-grained activities.

Fresnel Zone Model. In the field of radio propagation, the Fresnel zone is an ellipsoid region focusing on receiver and transmitter. When the human body passes through different Fresnel zones, the signal changes according to the different Fresnel zones. The Fresnel zone model describes the relationship between the target's position and the CSI amplitude or power. Wu *et al.* [17] uses the Fresnel zone model to detect the direction of the target's movement.

Angle of Arrival Model. The AOA model estimates the propagation direction of radio frequency waves in the antenna array. The principle is to calculate the direction by measuring the difference between the arrival time and the delay of each antenna. The more the number of antennas, the better the performance of AOA. Sun et al. [18] proposed a gesture tracking system based on the AOA model, which extracts the AOA value from the CSI, and the recognition accuracy of the system is 91%.

Machine-Learning Based. Behavior recognition based on machine learning generally includes two parts, feature extraction and behavior classification. Feature extraction refers to the use of data processing methods to extract features that can best characterize the original data and reduce redundant data. At present, researchers usually extract statistical features (TW-see [2], RT-Fall [5]), Doppler shift (WiSee [14], WiFit [15]), wavelet features and time-frequency information (E-eyes [17], WiStep [9]) from the data as features. Behavior classification is to use the classifier trained by feature data to discriminate behavior. Zhou et al. [19] realized gesture recognition using support vector machines, with an average recognition accuracy of 94%. Based on behavior detection using anomaly detection algorithms, Wang et al. [20] used support vector machines and random forest algorithms to classify different types of human activities.

Deep-Learning Based. In recent years, behavior recognition methods based on deep learning have received widespread attention. Compared with machine learning, this method does not need to manually extract features from the original data, and can achieve higher recognition accuracy. Deep learning algorithm has three layers and can handle large-scale data with complex characteristics.

In CSI-based behavior recognition systems, common deep learning models are autoencoders, convolutional neural networks (CNN), LSTM, BP-neural networks and so on. Jakkala et al. [21] used deep convolutional neural networks to study user's gait.

4 Application Based on CSI Behavior Recognition

Currently, thanks to the rapid development of the Internet of Things, human activity recognition has also received great attention. According to the intensity of the target movement, human activity perception can be divided into two categories, coarse-grained behavior and fine-grained behavior. The former mainly includes daily behavior activities (such as walking, running, sitting, lying down, etc.), fall detection, abnormal activity detection, smoking detection. The latter mainly includes keystroke detection, breathing and heartbeat detection, gesture recognition, sleep detection, etc.

4.1 Daily Behavior Recognition

In recent years, human activity recognition plays an important role. It can be used in smart home, augmented reality, human-computer interaction and other fields. Therefore, as the basic part of human activity recognition, daily behavior recognition has been widely studied. Wu et al. [2] Proposed a device free behavior recognition system TW-see, which can recognize seven different actions with an average accuracy of 94.46%. Firstly, the correlation between human activities and CSI changes caused by human activities is obtained by RPCA algorithm to eliminate the influence of background environment information. Then, the start time and end time of actions are extracted by normalized variance sliding window algorithm to realize the extraction of actions. Finally, the corresponding features of each action are put into BP-neural network to realize action recognition.

4.2 Fall Detection

For the elderly, falling is always one of the most important factors affecting physical health. Wang et al. [5] designed a real-time fall detection system RT-fall, which has the characteristics of low cost and high accuracy. Firstly, RT-fall system extracts the fall action from the original signal according to the change of the CSI phase difference on the two antennas. Then, it extracts the features of the fall action to achieve fall detection. Compared with WiFall [4], which is also used for fall detection, this system has a 14% higher sensitivity and an average 10% higher specificity.

4.3 Breath Detection

The behavior recognition system based on CSI can also be applied to the field of health monitoring. Zhang et al. [16] used existing Wi-Fi equipment to monitor the state of breathing and proposed a non-contact breathing tracking system, BreathTrack. The system uses the sparse recovery method to find the main path in the multipath, and derives the corresponding complex attenuation coefficient. Then, according to the phase change of the complex attenuation coefficient, it extracts the detailed breathing state and breathing rate. A large number of experiments have shown that BreathTrack can estimate the breathing rate with an average accuracy rate of over 99%. Chen et al. [14] proposed a non-contact respiratory monitoring system TR-breath, which can estimate the respiratory frequency of multiple persons. In the line-of-sight scene, the average accuracy rate of the respiratory frequency estimation of 12 people is 98.07%, and in the non-line-of-sight scene, the average accuracy rate of the respiratory frequency estimation of 9 people is 98.07%.

4.4 Intrusion Detection

With the improvement of people's security awareness, the research of intrusion detection has gradually become a hot spot. Liu et al. [22] used Wi-Fi equipment to implement an intrusion detection system EPID, which uses a low-pass filter and conjugate correction to eliminate the random phase shift of CSI. The intrusion detection accuracy rate of this system is 96.6%.

4.5 Smoking Detection

At present, smoking detection systems based on cameras or sensors are widely used in public places, but neither of them can provide ubiquitous smoking detection. Zheng et al. [8] proposed a smoking detection system Smokey based on commercial Wi-Fi equipment, which can identify smoking behavior in line-of-sight and non-line-of-sight environments. The experimental results show that the Smokey system has high accuracy and robustness in various scenarios.

5 Summary and Outlook

This article mainly discusses the basic framework and some applications of using commercial Wi-Fi devices for behavior recognition. Generally speaking, CSI-based behavior recognition is divided into four steps, collecting raw data, selecting basic signals, signal processing and action recognition. In the phase of signal processing, multiple data processing methods such as principal component analysis, filters, wavelet transform are used to achieve dimensionality reduction and denoising of the basic signal. In the action recognition stage, behavior recognition can be achieved through the CSI speed model, the angle of arrival model and other learning-based methods. The behavior recognition based on CSI has been extensively studied, and it can be roughly divided into coarse-grained behavior and fine-grained behavior according to recognition content. Coarse-grained behaviors include daily behavior, fall detection, and smoking monitoring, and fine-grained behaviors include heartbeat and breathing detection, keystroke recognition, mouth shape recognition, etc.

In addition, the behavior recognition method still faces many challenges in practical applications. First, the migration application of the action discrimination model. At present, most CSI-based behavior recognition systems realize action discrimination by machine learning or deep learning, and they all need to collect sample data to train an action classification model. If the surrounding environment changes or the location of the data collection device changes, the effectiveness of the original classification model will be greatly reduced. Second, multi-target behavior detection. Single-target behavior recognition has been widely studied, and each action has a high recognition accuracy, but the research on multi-target behavior recognition is still in its infancy. Third, the limitations of activity recognition method. The model-based behavior recognition method requires sample data to construct a classification model. If it is applied in practice, it will undoubtedly increase the user's usage cost. Fourth, segmentation and extraction of continuous actions. At present, some researchers can extract a single or a specific action through some specific methods. But for some continuous actions (such as falling down immediately after walking), they cannot be segmented and extracted. Fifth, electromagnetic interference. The massive deployment of Wi-Fi devices has brought us more convenient network connections, but it will cause serious electromagnetic interference and affect the accuracy of behavior recognition.

References

1. Chowdhury, T.Z., Leung, C., Miao, C.Y.: WiHACS: leveraging WiFi for human activity classification using OFDM subcarriers' correlation. In: IEEE Global Conference on Signal and Information Processing (GlobalSIP), Montreal, QC, pp. 338–342 (2017)
2. Wu, X., Chu, Z., Yang, P., Xiang, C., Zheng, X., et al.: TW-see: human activity recognition through the wall with commodity Wi-Fi devices. IEEE Trans. Veh. Technol. **68**(1), 306–319 (2019)
3. Dong, Z., Li, F., Ying, J., Pahlavan, K.: Indoor motion detection using Wi-Fi channel state information in flat floor environments versus in staircase environments. Sensors **18**(7), 2177 (2018)
4. Wang, Y., Wu, K., Ni, L.M.: WiFall: device-free fall detection by wireless networks. IEEE Trans. Mob. Comput. **16**(2), 581–594 (2017)
5. Wang, H., Zhang, D., Wang, Y., Ma, J., Wang, Y., et al.: RT-fall: a real-time and contactless fall detection system with commodity WiFi devices. IEEE Trans. Mob. Comput. **16**(2), 511–526 (2017)
6. Palipana, S., Rojas, D., Agrawal, P., Pesch, D.: FallDeFi: ubiquitous fall detection using commodity Wi-Fi devices. Proc. ACM Interact. Mobile Wearable Ubiquitous Technol. **1**(4), 1–25 (2018)
7. Zhu, D., Pang, N., Li, G., Liu, S.: NotiFi: a ubiquitous WiFi-based abnormal activity detection system. In: Proceedings of International Joint Conference on Neural Networks (IJCNN), Anchorage, AK, pp. 1766–1773 (2017)
8. Zheng, X., Wang, J., Shangguan, L., Zhou, Z., Liu, Y.: Smokey: ubiquitous smoking detection with commercial WiFi infrastructures. In: IEEE INFOCOM 2016 - The 35th Annual IEEE International Conference on Computer Communications, San Francisco, CA, pp. 1–9 (2016)
9. Xu, Y., Yang, W., Wang, J., Zhou, X., Li, H., et al.: WiStep: device-free step counting with WiFi signals. Proc. ACM Interact. Mobile Wearable Ubiquitous Technol. **1**(4), 1–23 (2018)
10. Li, H., Yang, W., Wang, J., Xu, Y., Huang, L.: WiFinger: talk to your smart devices with finger-grained gesture. In: Proceedings of ACM International Joint Conference on Pervasive Ubiquitous Computing, pp. 250–261 (2016)
11. Wang, X., Yang, C., Mao, S.: PhaseBeat: exploiting CSI phase data for vital sign monitoring with commodity WiFi devices. In: 2017 IEEE 37th International Conference on Distributed Computing Systems (ICDCS), Atlanta, GA, pp. 1230–1239 (2017)

12. Zhu, H., Xiao, F., Sun, L., Wang, R., Yang, P.: R-TTWD: robust device-free through-the-wall detection of moving human with WiFi. IEEE J. Sel. Areas Commun. **35**(5), 1090–1103 (2017)
13. Wang, W., Liu, A.X., Shahzad, M., Ling, K., Lu, S.: Device-free human activity recognition using commercial WiFi devices. IEEE J. Sel. Areas Commun. **35**(5), 1118–1131 (2017)
14. Chen, C., Han, Y., Chen, Y., Lai, H.Q., Zhang, F., et al.: TR-BREATH: time-reversal breathing rate estimation and detection. IEEE Trans. Biomed. Eng. **65**(3), 489–501 (2018)
15. Li, S., Li, X., Lv, Q., Tian, G., Zhang, D.: WiFit: ubiquitous bodyweight exercise monitoring with commodity Wi-Fi devices. In: 2018 IEEE SmartWorld, Ubiquitous Intelligence & Computing, Advanced & Trusted Computing, Scalable Computing & Communications, Cloud & Big Data Computing, Internet of People and Smart City Innovation (SmartWorld/SCALCOM/UIC/ATC/CBDCom/IOP/SCI), Guangzhou, pp. 530–537 (2018)
16. Zhang, D., Hu, Y., Chen, Y., Zeng, B.: BreathTrack: tracking indoor human breath status via commodity WiFi. IEEE Internet Things J. **6**(2), 3899–3911 (2019)
17. Wang, Y., Liu, J., Chen, Y., Gruteser, M., Yang, J., et al.: E-eyes: device-free location-oriented activity identification using fine-grained WiFi signatures. In: Proceedings of the 20th Annual International Conference on Mobile Computing and Networking, pp. 617–628 (2014)
18. Wu, C., Yang, Z., Zhou, Z., Liu, X., Liu, Y., et al.: Non-invasive detection of moving and stationary human with WiFi. IEEE J. Sel. Areas Commun. **33**(11), 2329–2342 (2015)
19. Zhou, Q., Xing, J., Li, J., Yang, Q.: A device-free number gesture recognition approach based on deep learning. In: 2016 12th International Conference on Computational Intelligence and Security (CIS), Wuxi, pp. 57–63 (2016)
20. Wang, W., Liu, A.X., Shahzad, M., Ling, K., Lu, S.: Understanding and modeling of WiFi signal based human activity recognition. In: Proceedings of the 21st Annual International Conference on Mobile Computing and Networking, pp. 65–76 (2015)
21. Jakkala, K., Bhuya, A., Sun, Z., Wang, P., Cheng, Z.: Deep CSI learning for gait biometric sensing and recognition, arXiv:1902.02300 (2019)
22. Liu, Y., Liao, Q., Zhao, J., Han, Z.: Deep learning based encryption policy intrusion detection using commodity WiFi. In: 2019 IEEE 5th International Conference on Computer and Communications (ICCC), Chengdu, China, pp. 2129–2135 (2019)

Security Analysis of Blockchain Smart Contract: Taking Reentrancy Vulnerability as an Example

Mingtao Ji[1], GuangJun Liang[1,2($\boxtimes$)], Meng Li[1], Haoyan Zhang[1], and Jiacheng He[1]

[1] Department of Computer Information and Cyberspace Security, Jiangsu Police Institute, Nanjing, China
[2] National and Local Joint Engineering Laboratory of Radio Frequency Integration and Micro Assembly Technology, Nanjing University of Posts and Telecommunications, Nanjing, China

Abstract. As the blockchain enters the 2.0 era, the smart contract which is based on the blockchain platform has gradually entered people's field of vision. By its transparency, non-tampering, independence from third-party arbitration, and trustlessness, it is widely applied in equity crowdfunding, games, insurance, particularly the Internet of Things. However, the attack on the TheDAO smart contract alert public awareness of the security of a smart contract. The essence of the smart contract is an electronic contract written in code. Due to reasons like lacking standard libraries for its programming language, several loopholes will inevitably appear in the code. Once they are found by attackers, the interests of the main body using smart contracts will be damaged. There are many types of vulnerabilities in smart contracts, such as reentrancy, short address attacks, and timestamp dependence. This article mainly focuses on re-entry vulnerabilities as the research object and analyzes the principle of re-entry vulnerabilities. Featuring immutable after being chained, the smart contract must be checked before it is chained to make up for the vulnerability. This paper provides a detection method based on symbolic execution to detect reentrancy vulnerabilities. We hope to strengthen people's security awareness of smart contracts and boost the research of smart contracts in terms of security by our study of the smart contract reentrancy vulnerability in this article. Promote the research and development of smart contracts.

Keywords: Smart contract · Blockchain · Reentrancy vulnerability · Fallback function · Symbolic execution

1 Introduction

The publishment of an article titled "Bitcoin: A Peer-to-Peer Electronic Cash System"[1] by a mysterious person named Satoshi Nakamoto as well as the open-source of the Bitcoin system [2] marked the great invention of blockchain. The advantages of blockchain, including tamper resistance, transparency and credibility, and protection of privacy, meet people's needs and attract people's attention. With the development of informatization, blockchain has broken through the limitations of digital currency applications, being utilized in digital assets and smart contracts [3]. Moreover, smart contracts which run on the

© Springer Nature Switzerland AG 2021
X. Sun et al. (Eds.): ICAIS 2021, CCIS 1424, pp. 492–501, 2021.
https://doi.org/10.1007/978-3-030-78621-2_41

blockchain are widely used in the fields of finance, energy system, deposit certificates, and digital copyrights.

However, every coin has two sides. Though the literature [4–6] all recognized the advantages of blockchain, they raised questions about the security of the blockchain. Literature [4] investigated the challenges faced by blockchain in terms of technology, risks, and security. Literature [5] pointed out that the attack on the blockchain is the vulnerability itself in the context of extensive application. Literature [6] proposed some vulnerabilities majorly consisting of design flaws, code-level implementation flaws, ecosystem problems (such as wallets), and 51% attacks. The following two cases sufficiently prove the existence of security problems.

Blockchain attacks are all exploiting code vulnerabilities in smart contracts on the blockchain. This triggered our thinking about the security of smart contracts. The literature [7–10] all analyzed the loopholes of smart contracts running on the blockchain. Literature [7] pointed out that because smart contracts cannot be modified or updated once they are on the chain, the best way to prevent vulnerabilities in a smart contract is to check the contract code before it is deployed on the blockchain. Literature [8] comprehensively categorizes smart contract security issues and uses secure code analysis tools that identify known vulnerabilities to thoroughly review known vulnerabilities. The literature [10] specifically introduces the loopholes of the Ethereum smart contract and the corresponding defense mechanism. Literature [9] introduced a general technique for building core functional models for model checking to help alleviate the security issues in smart contract development.

2 Smart Contract Introduction

2.1 What is a Smart Contract

The definition: "A smart contract is a set of commitments defined in digital form, including a contract that participants can perform these commitments on its agreement [11]," is the earliest concept of the smart contract which was proposed by scholar Nick Szabo in 1994. A smart contract is like a vending machine. Customers need to select a product and complete the payment. Afterward, the vending machine will automatically spit out the product.

Partially, smart contracts have the same attributes as real-life contracts that both parties need to sign a certain agreement in light of law whereas the difference lies in that there is no possibility of the bargain, discount, or something sophisticated during the transactions in the smart contract. After all, the only goal of codes is to execute themselves strictly under established rules and output.

2.2 Smart Contracts in Various Blockchain Platforms

The development of the blockchain can be divided into three stages, namely the 1.0, 2.0, and 3.0 era [12]. Each period has a distinctively typical blockchain platform on which smart contracts are not rare to be seen. Such as the Bitcoin system in the era of blockchain 1.0, Ethereum in the era of blockchain 2.0, Hyperledger in the era of blockchain 3.0. Scripts are simple, stack-based execution languages that are processed from left to right.

A blockchain-based smart contract is comprised of a transaction processing mechanism, a data storage mechanism, and a complete state machine for receiving and processing various conditions.

The principle of the smart contract running on the blockchain system is shown in Fig. 1. Each node has its smart contract that contains the balance of the account and the information of the blockchain where it is located. When the preset trigger conditions in the smart contract are met, the smart contract accesses the corresponding data for calculations according to the preset response rules. Then it saves up the results on the blockchain. In other words, after the smart contract runs, the smart contract account which contains account balance, storage, and other content is automatically generated and store up on the blockchain [13]. Subsequently, when executing the contract code (also called smart contract call) in the virtual machine, as soon as every node reaches a consensus on the ultimate execution result, the state of the smart contract on the blockchain will be updated accordingly or even create a new block (see the dotted box in Fig. 1).

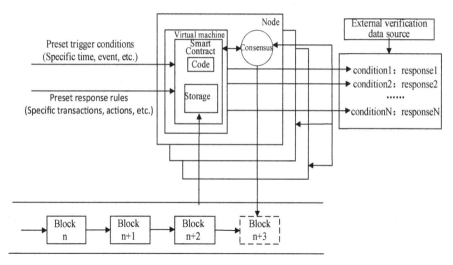

Fig. 1. The principle of running smart contracts on the blockchain system

3   Smart Contract Vulnerability Analysis: Reentrancy Vulnerability

The prosperity of smart contracts drives the increasing number of smart contracts. Additionally, the popularity of decentralized applications prompts digital assets involved in smart contracts to boom significantly. Due to the difficulty of patching smart contracts after they are on the chain and the lack of assessment standards for ensuring smart contract quality, they have become the target of hacker attacks [14]. This article mainly studies reentrancy vulnerabilities.

3.1 Overview of Reentrancy Vulnerabilities

Reentrancy vulnerability emerges in a virtual machine. One of the characteristics of Ethereum smart contracts is the ability to call and utilize the codes of other external contracts. Besides, it is normal for contracts to deal with Ether in the way that the Ether would be sent to various external user addresses when being processed. Both transfers and calls to external contracts require the contract to submit external calls. However, it is these external calls that are easily hijacked by attackers. These attacks and improper operations are carried out by attacking the contract itself through the fallback function or callback. Similar to the reentrant phenomenon that occurs when the operating system is interrupted during process scheduling, reentrancy is usually manifested as multiple calls to a function at the same time. The malicious contract calls the attacked function multiple times before calling other functions to complete. The code execution is re-entered in the attacked contract to realize the attack, which may result in huge damage [15].

In general, the key point of the attacker's reentrancy attack lies in the fallback function on account of the malicious exploitation of the fallback function of the smart contract for reentrancy vulnerabilities.

3.2 Functions Involved in Reentrancy Vulnerabilities

Fallback Function. The fallback function is a special function in a smart contract in that it has no name, no parameters, and no return value. Therefore, it frequently calls other functions. By and large, the fallback function will be called when there is no available function for the contract to call or the call does not contain any data.

Withdraw Function. To allow users to perform withdrawal operations(namely convert the tokens in the contract system into the ether and withdraw), withdraw function often exists in contracts such as wallets and decentralized transactions. As a result, this has become the focus of reentrancy vulnerability attacks [16].

Other Functions. In addition to the above two key functions that lead to reentrancy vulnerabilities in the smart contract code, other functions ensure the normal operation of the code. Such as call, transfer, send, and balance functions. The call function is also one of the reasons for the reentrancy vulnerability.When using $< address >$.gas().call.value()() to transfer, all available gas can be called, which cannot effectively prevent reentrancy.

3.3 Principles of Reentrancy Vulnerability Attack

When attackers attack smart contracts with reentrant vulnerabilities, they exploit the fallback function of the attacker's contract and the withdraw function of the attacked contract. During the transferring process, the attackers will use the reentrance vulnerability to "modify the Storage variable and transfer" the contract which is supposed to be an atomic [17] transaction. Use the sequence of a first transfer before modifying Storage variables. If the target of the transfer is a contract with a malicious fallback function, it may be called by the malicious contract to the victim contract, thereby destroying the atomicity of the operation and bypassing the check to repeatedly obtain the transfer revenue [18].

Take the Bank contract [19] as an example:

As is shown in Fig. 2 Bank contract part code, balances[msg. sender] represent the amount of Ether balances the user has. The purpose of the withdraw function is to allow users to withdraw assets through the receiver.call.value(amount). The call function is a function for sending ether in a smart contract. When the user calls this function, the contract first checks whether the user balance is bigger than the number of funds withdrawn. If the check is passed, the requested asset will be transferred to the user in the form of Ether, and the corresponding balance will be deducted from the user account.

Owing to the operating mechanism of the Ethereum smart contract that if the address receiving the transfer is a contract address, the fallback function of that address will be triggered, this mechanism may be utilized by malicious attackers to launch reentrancy attacks. An attack is an attack contract, and its code is shown in Fig. 3.

The attacker only needs to call the withdraw function of the victim contract through the step2(uint256 amount) public function. When the receiver. call.value(amount)() statement in the withdraw function of the victim contract is executed, it will trigger the fallback function in the attack contract. In this function, the call to the victim contract withdrawal is initiated again, and the recursive call will be repeatedly initiated before the user's balance is reduced until the Gas is exhausted, thereby continuously stealing the ether in the victim contract.

The entire attack process is shown in Fig. 4. The attacker triggers the fallback function when transferring money to the vulnerable contract through the attack function, and then uses the fallback function to repeatedly call the withdraw function to construct a loop between steps 2 and 3 to continuously steal the ether in the victim contract. In this process, the vulnerable contract continues to transfer money to the attacker contract until the end of the cycle.

```
contract Bank {
......
function withdraw(address receiver, uint256 amount) public{
require(balances[msg.sender] > amount);
require(address(this).balance > amount);
receiver.call.value(amount)();
    // When using call.value()() for ether transfer, there is no gas limit
balances[msg.sender] -= amount;
}
function balanceOf(address addr) public view returns (uint256) {
return balances[addr];
}
}
```

Fig. 2. Bank contract part code

```
contract Attack {
    ……
    function step2(uint256 amount) public{
        victim.call(bytes4(keccak256("withdraw(address,uint256)")),
this,amount);}
    ……
    function () public payable {
        if (msg.sender == victim) {
            victim.call(bytes4(keccak256("withdraw(address,uint256)")),
this,msg.value);}
    }
}
```

Fig. 3. Bank contract attack part of the code

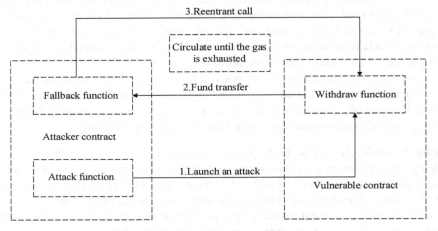

Fig. 4. Brief flowchart of reentrancy attack

Using reentrant vulnerabilities to attack contracts is mainly to fully call all available gas through the gas mechanism of the call instruction of the Ethereum virtual machine, as well as features such as the fallback function mechanism and recursive access that allows low-level calls.

4   Smart Contract Security Vulnerability Detection Method

In fact, by analyzing a large number of cases that smart contracts being attacked cases, we can easily conclude that the vulnerabilities of smart contracts are mainly in the code. Lacking standard libraries which could be commonly found in high-level programming languages, it is difficult for all developers to program smart contract, reducing the security of the code [20]. Furthermore, the code of the smart contract cannot be changed once it is on the chain. In this case, to prevent the smart contract from being attacked, we need to check the code before the contract code is on the chain.

At present, the main detection methods include five methods: formal verification, symbolic execution, static analysis, dynamic strain analysis, and fuzz testing [21]. This article centers on symbolic execution-based methods to detect code reentrancy vulnerabilities.

4.1 Symbolic Execution Principle

Symbolic execution is a promising technique adopted widely in smart contract analyzers. It abstracts variables into symbols, which are then used as program input. The symbolic execution method explores all possible program execution paths through the input of abstract symbols and uses a constraint solver to calculate a concrete input (test case) for each feasible path [22, 23].

Time witnessed the evolution of symbolic execution from static symbolic execution to dynamic symbolic execution. The core idea of static symbolic execution is to use abstract symbol values to replace the specific variable values of the program, and to represent the actual program input with symbolic input. However, this method is only suitable for relatively simple programs. Moreover, this execution method cannot obtain system calls or third-party library call functions [22].

Therefore, Godefroid [24, 25] proposed a dynamic symbolic execution method. Combining concrete execution with symbolic execution and using concrete values instead of symbolic values as the input of the program, the analysis accuracy has been widely applied in recent years for higher accuracy and plain feasibility.

Static Symbolic Execution. In the process of symbolic execution, each branch statement is searched when a program branch statement is encountered. At the same time, the symbolic execution analyzer will add the branch condition of the branch statement to the constraint condition set of the current path. To determine whether the target area code is reachable, a constraint solver [26] needs to be used to verify the solvability of all constraints. If the constraint solver successfully solves the value, the path is reachable; otherwise, the path is unreachable, thus ending the further analysis of the path [27].

Static symbol execution is similar to the select the statement in C language, but there are also differences. As shown in Fig. 5, when the C language program runs to the if statement, if the condition of the if statement is met, the else statement no longer runs . In static symbol execution, the if…else statement is regarded as two branches to analyze. As soon as the two variables reach the numerator along the established path of the program, we assign the value of A + 1 − B to A, namely the statement A = A + 1 − B. On condition that the eighth line of code is the correct code and both branches are executable, then at the if statement, A + 1 − B < 0; at the else statement A + 1 − B ≥ 0 [27, 28]. To execute the path of the error code after the else statement, it needs to conform to conditional statement A + 1 − B ≤ 0 [26].

Dynamic Symbolic Execution. Supposing that the code is replaced with x = x*x − 2 *y as others remaining unchanged. The execution steps are shown in Fig. 6. The actual value is randomly determined as the test seed input, and the path to execute the

```
int fun(int x,int y)
{
    x++;
    x=x-y;
    if(x<0)
        x++;
    else
        //some error
    return x;
}
```

Fig. 5. C language code example

target program is the path corresponding to the actual value. The execution path also maintains the symbolic execution information of the program, that is, the symbol status corresponding to the path and the constraint conditions representing the path, and the constraints are collected at the same time. In the execution process, the corresponding constraint conditions of the branch statement of the program that have not been explored are obtained by inverting the current branch condition. Then, determine the satisfiability of the branch. If it is unsatisfied, it cannot be executed, and if it is satisfied, the calculated value will be saved as the data for the subsequent generation of test cases [29]. Finally, the loop is repeated until the traversal is completed.

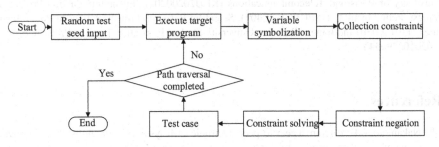

Fig. 6. Dynamic symbolic execution steps [29]

4.2 The Basic Process of Using Symbolic Execution to Detect Contract Vulnerabilities [29]

Using the principle of dynamic symbol detection to detect smart contract vulnerabilities, the specific steps are shown in Table 1.

Table 1. Basic steps to detect contract vulnerabilities using symbolic execution.

Basic steps to detect contract vulnerabilities using symbolic execution
1. Use the solc compiler to compile the contract source code to generate assembly code, which contains deployment code, runtime code, and aux data
2. Use the solc compiler to decompile the runtime code to generate the ethereum contract bytecode
3. Construct a control flow graph through the Ethereum contract bytecode
4. Generate test data randomly, traverse the reachable path of the control flow graph, and collect path constraints
5. Use the constraint solver to solve the path constraints and generate test cases

5 Conclusion

As a vital feature of the blockchain 2.0 era, smart contracts play an irreplaceable role on the Ethereum platform. Since the occurrence of the TheDAO incident, the security of smart contracts has attracted widespread attention. This article analyzes the reentrant vulnerability at the Ethereum virtual machine level and explains how TheDAO was attacked. At the end of this article, a detection method based on symbolic execution is proposed to detect the contract before the chain to avoid loopholes.

Acknowledgments. This work is supported by Open project of National and Local Joint Engineering Laboratory of Radio Frequency Integration and Micro-assembly Technology, Nanjing University of Posts and Telecommunications (KFJJ20200201), Talent Introduction Project of Jiangsu Police Institute (JSPI19GKZL407), Scientific Research Project of Jiangsu Police Institute (2110120030) and Jiangsu Province University Student Innovation Training Program Project (202010329034Y).

References

1. Nakamoto, S.F.: Bitcoin: a peer-to-peer electronic cash system (2008). https://bitcoin.org/bitcoin.pdf
2. Qing, B., et al.: Bitcoin and legal digital currency. J. Cryptologic Res. **4**(2), 176–186 (2017)
3. Zh, J.M., Yang, F., Fu, F.: Research progress of blockchain applications. Sci. Technol. Rev. **55**(9), 70–76 (2017)
4. Kadena, E., Holicza, P.:Security issues in the blockchain (ed) world. p. 216. In: CINTI (2018)
5. Jonathan, K., Sari, A.K.: Security issues and vulnerabilities on a blockchain system: a review. In: ISRITI, Yogyakarta, pp. 228–232, Indonesia (2019)
6. Keenan, T.P.: Alice in blockchains: surprising security pitfalls in PoW and PoS blockchain systems. In: PST, pp. 400–4002, Calgary, AB (2017)
7. Sayeed, S., Marco-Gisbert, H., Caira, T.: Smart contract: attacks and protections. In: IEEE Access **8**, 24416–24427 (2020)
8. Dika, A., Nowostawski, M.: Security vulnerabilities in ethereum smart contracts. In: 2018 IEEE International Conference on Internet of Things, Physical and Social Computing and IEEE Smart Data, pp. 955–962, Halifax, NS, Canada (2018)

9. Kongmanee, J., Kijsanayothin, P., Hewett, R.: Securing smart contracts in blockchain. In: ASEW, pp. 69–76, San Diego, CA, USA (2019)
10. He, D., Deng, Z., Zhang, Y., Chan, S., Cheng, Y., Guizani, N.: Smart contract vulnerability analysis and security audit. IEEE Netw. **34**(5), 276–282 (2020)
11. http://virtualschool.edu/mon/Economics/SmartContracts.html. Accessed 21 Nov 2020
12. Cao, B., Lin, L., Li, Y., Liu, Y.X., Xiong, W., Gao, F.F.: Overview of blockchain research. J. Chongqing Univ. Posts Telecommun. (Nat.Sci. Ed.) **6**, 1–14(2020)
13. Han, X., Liu, Y.M.: Research on consensus mechanism in blockchain technology. Netinfo Secur. **9**, 147–152 (2017)
14. Liao, J.W., Tsai, T.T., He, C.K., Tien, C.W.: SoliAudit: smart contract vulnerability assessment based on machine learning and fuzz testing. In: IOTSMS, pp. 1959–1966, Granada, Spain (2019)
15. Qiu, X.X., Ma, Z.F., Xu, M.K.: Analysis and countermeasures of security vulnerabilities of ethereum smart contract. In: Information Security and Communications Privacy, pp. 44–53 (2019)
16. Wang, Y.Z., Chen, J.L., Wang, X., He, Z.S.: Smart contract security analysis and audit guide. Publishing House of Electronics Industry, no. 11, p. 142 (2019)
17. Luu, L., Olickel, H., et al.: Making smart contracts smarter. In: SIGSAC, pp. 254–269, Vienna Austria (2016)
18. Ni, Y.D., Zhang, C., Yin, T.T.: A review of research on smart contract security vulnerabilities. J. Cyber Secur. **34**, 78–99 (2020)
19. CSDN Homepage. https://blog.csdn.net/weixin_43405220/article/details/100553931. 10 Nov 2020
20. Huawei Blockchain Technology Development Team.: Blockchain technology and application. Tsinghua University Press (2019)
21. Zhong, Z.B., Wang, C.D., Cai, J.H.: An overview of the research status and detection methods of smart contract security. In: Information Security and Communications Privacy, pp. 93–105 (2020)
22. Yang, K.: Automated security audit of smart contract based on symbolic execution. M.S. dissertation, University of Electronic Science and Technology (2020)
23. Zhang, W., Banescu, S., Pasos, L., Stewart, S., Ganesh, V.: MPro: combining static and symbolic analysis for scalable testing of smart contract. In: ISSRE, pp. 456–462, Berlin, Germany (2019)
24. Godefroid, P., Klarlund, N., Dart, K.: Directed automated random testing. In: ACM, pp. 213–223 New York, NY, USA (2005)
25. Sen, K., Marinov, D., Cute, G.: A concolic unit testing engine for. In: ACM, pp. 263–272, New York, NY, USA (2005)
26. de Moura, L., Nachmanson, L., Wintersteiger, C.M.: The Z3 Theorem Prover (2018). https://github.com/Z3Prover/z3
27. Zhang, Y.W.: Dynamic symbolic execution constraint solving optimization design and realization, M.S. dissertation, Chongqing Universit (2017)
28. Tan, C.: Security detection system for ethereum smart contract code. M.S. dissertation, University of Electronic Science and Technology (2019)
29. Zhao, W., et al.: Smart contract vulnerability detection scheme based on symbolic execution. J. Comput. Appli. **40**(4)947–953(2020)

Research on Data Security Protection System of Monitoring and Acquisition System Based on Block Chain Technology

Linjiang Xie$^{(\boxtimes)}$, Feilu Hang, Yao Lv, and Wei Guo

Information Center, Yunnan Power Grid Co., Ltd., Kunming 650217, China
xielinjiang@yn.csg.cn

Abstract. The monitoring collection system is a system that uses computer, control and other technologies to realize the data storage, collection and monitoring of the field environment. It is widely used in data collection and monitoring in various fields. It often collects data generated by various types of equipment during operation through various sensors and actuators, and these collected data are often the key to analyzing system failures and discovering that equipment is under network attack. In the current environment, attacks occur frequently, and how to protect and utilize these data is very important. Therefore, data security protection system of monitoring and acquisition system Based on blockchain is proposed. Its purpose is to improve data security and better use of data. By combining the blockchain technology, the collected data is stored on the blockchain, and the integrity check mechanism is used to ensure the integrity of the collected data and prevent the data from being tampered with. The association rule base is formed by establishing association rules, and the rule base is used to analyze data, detect data anomalies and feed back the analysis results to the administrator. The data security and system security of the monitoring acquisition system is improved, and the burden of manpower analysis of data is reduced.

Keywords: Monitoring collection system · Blockchain · Data security

1 Introduction

The monitoring collection system is a system that uses computer and control technologies to realize data storage, collection and monitoring of the field environment. It is widely used in the field of industrial control, but there are still many loopholes. If the protection measures are not appropriate, it is vulnerable to attacks from the network and insiders [1, 2]. In the past few years, the number of data security issues in the global industrial sector has gradually increased. The number of reports reached 329, covering multiple industries such as manufacturing, energy, communications and nuclear industries.

On December 23, 2015, 1.4 million residents of the Ukrainian capital Kiev and parts of western Ukraine suffered a massive power outage that lasted for several hours. At least three power districts were attacked, accounting for half of the country. After the attacker gained control of the system, he continued to download malicious components,

© Springer Nature Switzerland AG 2021
X. Sun et al. (Eds.): ICAIS 2021, CCIS 1424, pp. 502–513, 2021.
https://doi.org/10.1007/978-3-030-78621-2_42

causing the system to restart without a bootloader. The attacker also cleared the system log to increase the difficulty of post-analysis, and many important files and data were modified and deleted.

In March 2018, the Cisco Talos security research team pointed out that Allen-Bradley MicroLogix 1400 series programmable logic controllers have many serious vulnerabilities. Attackers can use these vulnerabilities to write or delete data in the memory. However, this series of programmable logic controllers are widely used in social production practices, and they are easy to be attacked and cause significant economic losses.

In December 2018, the servers of Italian oil and gas extraction companies in the Middle East and India were attacked by variants of the Shamoon malware, resulting in a large amount of data and infrastructure damage. Shamoon can activate the disk wiper at a predetermined time to achieve the purpose of clearing the host's data. Although data loss was avoided through data backup related technologies in the later stage, the loss caused is still immeasurable.

In addition, there are computer viruses that specifically attack data collection and monitoring systems, such as Stuxnet (Stuxnet). Stuxnet is the first "worm" virus that specifically targets real-world infrastructure, such as nuclear power plants, dams, and the national grid. After attacking the target, it can cover up the failure of the system and feed back the record of normal operation to the manager, which will cause serious consequences [3, 4]. The virus once infected and damaged Iran's nuclear facilities in Natanz, and eventually delayed the start of Iran's Bushehr nuclear power plant.

Reference [5] proposed a PKI-based identity authentication technology to improve system security. Reference [6] uses depth message analysis (Deep Packet Inspection,DPI) technology based on industrial control protocol. Check the abnormal communication data of industrial control protocol in real time and identify the abnormal data events in the system. Document [7] security protection for servers in the system. Deploy data anomaly detection equipment, monitor network traffic safely and isolate all illegal connections. However, this can not guarantee the security of the system data collection, nor does it manage the data well.

Reference [8] is the first attempt to apply block chain technology to data security in industrial control systems. proposed blockchain platform ict-blockops, improve the security of plant data. and deployed in a water treatment plant for experimental verification. Among the block chain schemes related to industrial system data security, the reference [9] proposed a decentralized, point-to-point industrial Internet of things platform based on block chain. Peer nodes in the network can interact with each other without trust mediation. A new distributed network construction scheme is introduced in reference [10]. A block chain architecture is used to reshape the traditional IIoT architecture. Better security and privacy protection than traditional architecture.

In the blockchain system, the entire network relies on the consensus mechanism and is maintained by all nodes (which can be any device). Under the consensus mechanism [11], even if a node fails, the remaining nodes can still maintain normal operation. It solves the shortcomings of traditional centralized models that are vulnerable to malicious attacks and tampering [12, 13]. Blockchain solves the problem of intermediary trust, so that both parties do not need to conduct transactions or other activities through a third-party intermediary. For example, Bitcoin transactions do not have a third party, even if the two parties do not know each other and there is no basis for trust, the transaction can proceed smoothly. Unless you master more than half of the data nodes in the blockchain, it is difficult to modify the data on the chain. Blockchain also embodies a large number of applications of cryptography, such as hash algorithms. The security of the blockchain is guaranteed.

The PBFT (Practical Byzantine Fault Tolerance) algorithm was proposed by Miguel Castro and Barbara Liskov in 1999. It solves the problem of low efficiency of the original Byzantine Fault Tolerance algorithm, making it applicable to actual social production scenarios. PBFT consensus algorithm can tolerate malicious nodes and invalid nodes less than one-third of the total nodes, can reach a consensus in a short time and is easy to implement, and the time to form a block is relatively short. The algorithm will not affect the normal operation of the monitoring and acquisition system, and does not need to consume a lot of computing energy to mine blocks.

The application of blockchain technology to data monitoring and collection improves the security of collected data and provides effective data protection measures. However, there are still some problems. Although the data security is guaranteed, the collected data is not analyzed and the data is not used well.

Therefore, a data security protection system based on the blockchain technology of the monitoring collection system is proposed. Through the introduction of blockchain related technologies, the problem of tampering of data received through sensors in specific scenarios is effectively solved, and the integrity of the data is guaranteed. In addition, the introduction of association rules related technologies to enhance the security of the system.

Association rules reflect the interdependence and association between one thing and other things. It is an important technology of data mining, which is used to mine the correlation between valuable data items from a large amount of data. The original motivation is to address the problem of shopping basket analysis. It can analyze from a certain connection relationship between data that certain events will lead to other events.

The formation of association rules needs to generate frequent itemsets first, and the algorithms for generating frequent itemsets include Apriori algorithm and FP-Growth algorithm. This article will use the former to generate frequent itemsets from the data set. The Apriori algorithm finds the largest frequent itemset through continuous iteration, so the algorithm process is easy to understand and the specific implementation is not complicated. In the iterative process, the non-conforming itemsets are continuously filtered through the minimum support established in advance, until the largest frequent itemsets are finally obtained. Then filter the strong association rules according to the confidence. The Apriori algorithm needs to scan the database multiple times and consumes certain computing resources. The calculation formula for confidence and support is as follows:

Support degree:

$$suppot(A \Rightarrow B) = (A \cup B)$$

It represents the probability of events A and B occurring together.

Confidence degree:

$$confidence(A \Rightarrow B) = suppot(A \cup B) \big/ suppot(A)$$

It represents the proportion of event A and event occurrence when event A occurs, similar to the calculation of conditional probability in probability theory.

Through the processing and filtering of data that has changed when the previous system is attacked, a specific algorithm is used to generate appropriate association rules. Based on this, an association rule library is formed, and the association rule library is used to analyze the collected data and detect whether there is any abnormality, and periodically feedback the analysis results to the manager. Designed to improve the security of the system and reduce the burden of data analysis for managers.

2 Security Protection System of Monitoring Acquisition System Based on Block Chain Technology

As shown in Fig. 1. This system is mainly composed of a three-tier structure. The sensors used to collect data, the database in the system, and the blockchain nodes and their constituent blockchain networks. Administrators can access blockchain data and add new association rules to the rule base. At the same time, the administrator will regularly receive the results of data analysis for system management, and the administrator's related permissions will also be written into the smart contract.

2.1 Deployment of Sensors for Real-Time Data Acquisition

The sensor is deployed at the bottom of the monitoring and acquisition system and is directly connected to various specific devices. The operation data of various equipments are obtained in real time, for example, the flow rate recorded by electromagnetic Flowmeter in water plant or the current and voltage measured by current transformer and voltage transformer in power station. The sensor will store the collected data in the system database to facilitate data storage and further processing. These data can be used to analyze system failures and detect whether equipment is under network attack, so it is often modified or deleted by attackers. In order to cover up the fact that the system has been attacked, the attacker will modify these data and feed back information that it is operating normally.

2.2 Create System Database and Store Collected Data

The system database will store the specific equipment operating data collected from the sensors in order to reduce the number of reading sensor data and system memory overhead. Every once in a while, the blockchain node reads the data collected during this period, further processes the data, and finally stores it on the blockchain through consensus. At the same time, the system database is also a backup of equipment operating data. If the content of the database is tampered with, it will be found in the detection link of the blockchain, and the data on the chain can be used to cover the modified part of the database.

2.3   Build Block Chain Network and Generate Block Chain Node

The node regularly collects the device running data and data log from the database, and the time interval is the time of consensus completion. The time when a consensus is completed is selected as the time point for data collection because the data processing efficiency is the highest at this time, which is the best choice.each node has a pair of keys (public key, private key), which are signed by asymmetric key system. Each node contains two modules: the data processing module and the inspection module.

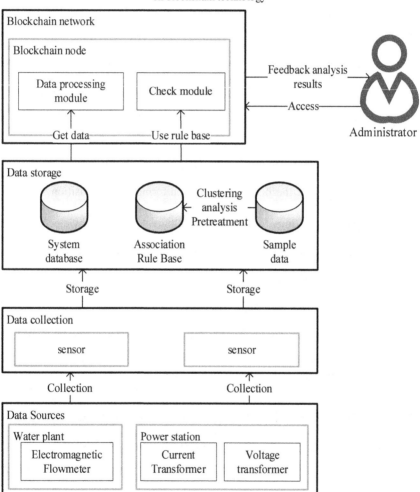

Architecture diagram of security protection system of monitoring acquisition system based on blockchain technology

Fig. 1. Architecture diagram of monitoring and acquisition system based on block chain technology Consensus uses the PBFT method.

Data Processing Module. After the node collects the data, it hashes the data to obtain the hash value of the data. Then use your own private key to encrypt the data and the hash value of the data and the current time, which is the digital signature. The verifier decrypts the received digital signature with the public key, and compares the decrypted result with the original text. If the original text is changed, it will be different from the decrypted result. It is verified whether the message and original text sent by the node have been tampered with. After the node initiates a consensus request, if the consensus is reached, the data collected by the sensor is stored on the blockchain. As shown in Fig. 2:

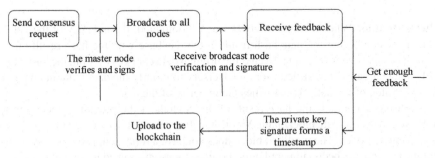

Fig. 2. The process of uploading data to the blockchain

a. The nodes in the blockchain take turns as the master node. The master node is responsible for receiving requests and broadcast messages from ordinary nodes. Every time the master node is replaced, a message will be broadcast, allowing all nodes to synchronize data.

b. When a certain node wants to store data on the chain, it sends a consensus request to the master node. The node will sign the requested content to prevent the master node from tampering with the content and also facilitate other nodes to verify the authenticity of the requested content. After the master node verifies that the request information is correct, it will broadcast the request message.

c. The node that receives the message verifies it, checks the authenticity of the request, and confirms whether the content of the request has been tampered with. After the node checks the request and determines that there is no problem with the request, it will send a confirmation message. If a node detects a problem, the primary node will be replaced. When more than a certain number of nodes confirm the request, they enter the commit phase and broadcast a commit message.

d. When the node receives enough commit messages, the receiver adds the hash value of the received content to the time of receiving the content, signs it with its own private key, and sends it to the requester. If the requesting node receives feedback information from f + 1 (f is the number of malicious nodes) nodes, it indicates that the consensus is completed correctly. The requester uses the received digital signature as a time stamp proof, adds it to the block, and uploads it to the blockchain together. At this point, one round of consensus has been completed and the next round of consensus has begun.

e. If no consensus is reached within the prescribed time, the requester will broadcast his request. If the master node does not broadcast the request message for a certain period of time, it will be discovered at this time, and a new master node will be generated. This effectively prevents the master node from maliciously concealing the message and causing the consensus to fail to complete. The content of the message is signed by the requester, and it is difficult for the master node to tamper with the content of the message. The receiver will check the authenticity of the message after receiving the message, and if the message is found to be modified, a new master node will be created. This effectively prevents the master node from tampering with the content of the message.

Check Module. When a round of consensus is completed, the integrity of the data is verified by comparing the data hash result in the database with the hash result on the chain. The hash result is unique. Even if the original data changes by 1 bit, the hash value will change greatly. It is difficult for an adversary to modify the data without changing the hash value of the data. This verifies the integrity of the data.

Each block contains the hash result of the content of the previous block, and all nodes store the complete blockchain. Modifying the content of one of the blocks requires modifying all nodes. The modified block does not have a timestamp, so it is easy to find that the content has been tampered with. Forging timestamps need to unite the nodes of the entire network, which is almost impossible, ensuring that the data cannot be tampered with. As shown in Fig. 3, as the length of the blockchain increases, the number of blocks continues to increase, and the block always contains the hash result and timestamp of the content of the previous block. Modifying the block content will become more difficult, and the blockchain will be more difficult to tamper with.

In addition, the inspection module will periodically analyze the collected data according to the established association rule library to detect whether there is abnormal data. If there is an abnormality, feedback information will be sent to the administrator, which reduces the workload of the administrator to analyze data and improves the security of the system.

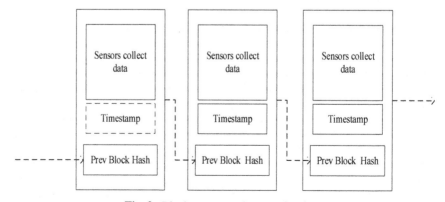

Fig. 3. Block storage and connection form

2.4 Establish an Association Rule Library

The data that has changed when the previous system is attacked is used as sample data, and the sample data is clustered and preprocessed to form some small subsets. (These subsets are represented by data) Set the minimum support threshold (min_sup) to 60%, and the minimum confidence threshold (min_conf) to 80%. Generate frequent itemsets S through Apriori algorithm.

The data is clustered to form a two-item table, the first column is the ID of the transaction, and the second column is the set of items contained in the transaction. As shown in Table 1.

1. Scan each transaction in the table, and calculate the support of item1, item2, ... itemn, and get the candidate item set C_1.
2. Filter each item in the candidate set C_1, and the filter condition is whether the support is greater than or equal to the preset min_sup. Thus, the frequent itemset L_1 is obtained. L1 is the frequent 1 item set.
3. The frequent item set L_1 is connected to itself and the corresponding support is calculated to obtain the candidate item set C_2, and the frequent item set L_2 is obtained by repeating the screening process. L_2 is the frequent 2 item set.
4. When the candidate item set C_{K+1} is generated from the frequent itemset L_K, a condition needs to be observed. The condition is that a subset of each item in the candidate item set should be a frequent item set. If you do not meet this condition, you need to delete this item.
5. Repeat the above steps until a larger set of frequent items cannot be generated. In the end, all frequent itemsets will be obtained, namely: $L_1 \cup L_2 \cup L_3 \ldots \cup L_k$.

Table 1. Binomial table

ID	Items
1	Item$_1$, Item$_2$, Item$_3$
2	Item$_1$, Item$_2$, Item$_4$,...,Item$_n$
3	Item$_1$, Item$_2$, Item$_3$, Item$_4$, Item$_5$
4	Item$_3$, Item$_4$
...	Item$_1$, Item$_4$

List all association rules in frequent itemset S that match the meta-rules below. (X represents the variable of the type of system being attacked, itemi represents the variable of the changed data. The right arrow is the previous item on the right, and the left is the next item)

$$\forall x \in data, (X, item_1) \wedge \cdots (X, item_{n-1}) \Rightarrow (X, item_n)$$

If:

$$count\{item_1, \ldots item_{n-1}\}/count\{item_1, \ldots item_n\} \geq \min\_conf$$

Established. Add this association rule to the association rule library. Count{$item_1$, ... $item_{n-1}$} and count{$item_1$, ... $item_n$} represent the number of {$item_1$, ... $item_{n-1}$} and {$item_1$, ... $item_n$} contained in the set. After screening, an association rule library is formed. The administrator can add new association rules to the rule base, or add new sample data for filtering. The check module of the blockchain node analyzes the collected data by comparing the association rule library, and feeds back the analysis result to the administrator. The minimum confidence threshold of the association rule library is adjusted by establishing a simulation scenario to find the optimal small confidence threshold. As shown in Table 2.

Table 2. The influence of the minimum confidence level on the false alarm rate and the missing report rate

Min_conf	False alarm rate	Missing report rate
20%	17.67%	5.35%
40%	10.14%	7.41%
60%	8.45%	10.68%
80%	5.79%	12.35%

It can be seen from the table that as the minimum confidence threshold increases, the false alarm rate decreases and the missing report rate increases. This is because as the minimum confidence threshold increases, the number of strong association rules generated will decrease. There are fewer strong association rules, and the probability of matching abnormal data is lower. As the probability of matching decreases, the number of false positives will naturally decrease, while the number of false negatives will increase. After repeated tests, the minimum confidence threshold between 60% and 80% works well. This article chooses 80% as the minimum confidence.

2.5 Create an Administrator Contract

The contract stores the administrator's account information and the device operating data they can access. The permissions can be modified, but only the owner of the contract can modify it. The creation of administrator contracts is also to control the access of administrators to data, reduce the probability of receiving attacks from insiders, and increase the security of the system.

Through the above method, the monitoring collection system and the blockchain technology are combined to establish a data security protection system based on the blockchain technology. By storing the collected data on the blockchain, data integrity check and tampering are realized, and data security is strengthened. Through the establishment of a rule base to analyze the collected data and send feedback information to the administrator regularly to improve the security of the system.

3 Security Analysis

This scheme is compared with other schemes in three aspects: anomaly detection, data integrity and data tamper-proof. As shown in Table 3.

The reference [5] constructs the identity authentication module on the basis of the PKI system, and divides the user's authority. Using the traditional data storage method, the data is easy to be tampered with, and there is no data integrity check. Reference [6] configures the access control strategy on the server, clearly allows access to the IP range, prohibits illegal access, deploys a firewall, and conducts unified management, analysis and display of the security data in the industrial control system. There is no data integrity check, nor can it be Prevent data from being tampered with. Reference [7] centralized account management, high-strength authentication reinforcement, encrypted audit and other functions make the operation of internal personnel and maintenance personnel under control. However, when the system is invaded, the data is easy to be tampered with. The proposed blockchain platform ICT-BlockOPS proposed in reference [8] can effectively protect the security of device operation data, but it requires personnel to check the data and passively detect whether there is abnormal behavior.

Table 3. Security performance analysis

Scheme	Anomaly detection	Data integrity	Tamper-proof
Reference [5]	×	×	×
Reference [6]	√	×	×
Reference [7]	–	×	×
Reference [8]	×	√	√
Proposed scheme	√	√	√

The above schemes all have certain shortcomings, but the scheme proposed in this article hashes the device operating data collected by the sensor and checks the data integrity by comparing the hash value. The hash result of the data is unique, even if the original data is changed by 1 bit, the hash value will change greatly. For example, the commonly used MD5 algorithm requires that when the original text changes by 1 bit, the result of the hash must change more than half of the information. It is difficult for an adversary to modify the data without changing the hash value of the data. By comparing the result of the hash of the data with the result of the hash stored on the chain, you can verify that the data is complete.

The content of each block mainly includes: the hash of the content of the previous block, the data collected by the sensor, and the data hash value. If an attacker modifies the content of any one of the blocks, the hash result of the content will change, which will be different from the hash value recorded in the next block. If an adversary modifies the content of a block, it must modify all the block contents. Moreover, all nodes in the entire network store a complete blockchain, which is very difficult to modify. Each block has a timestamp. The timestamp is the result of the digital signature of the entire network node, which proves the time when the block is formed. It is very difficult to forge the timestamp with the nodes of the whole network. The modified block content does not have a corresponding timestamp and is easy to find. This ensures that the data on the chain cannot be tampered with. As the length of the blockchain grows and the number of blocks continues to increase, it will become more difficult to modify the content of the block, and the content of the block will be more difficult to tamper with. So as the blockchain runs, the data stored on the blockchain will be more secure.

Every once in a while, the node's check module will check the most recently stored data on the blockchain. Start matching from the first rule in the association rule base. Look for the antecedent that meets the association rule, and if there is, then look for the subsequent item that meets the current rule. If the search is successful, it is deemed to have been attacked by the system, and feedback information is sent to the manager. If the match is not successful, the system is considered to be operating normally. This reduces the difficulty for administrators to analyze data and ensures data security in the monitoring collection system.

4 Summary

The importance of the monitoring collection system and its remaining problems are introduced in this paper, and the current security vulnerabilities in the monitoring collection system is analyzed. In response to these security vulnerabilities, a method of combining the monitoring collection system with blockchain technology is proposed, and a data security protection system based on the blockchain technology is established to solve the data security problem of the monitoring collection system. The solution combines blockchain technology to store the device operating data collected through sensors on the blockchain, ensuring the integrity of the data and preventing data from being tampered with. Form an association rule library by establishing appropriate association rules, analyze data and detect abnormalities, and send feedback to the administrator regularly. Reduce the burden of manpower analysis data and improve system security.

References

1. Peng, Y., Jiang, C.Q., Xie, F., Dai, Z.H., Xiong, Q., Gao, Y.: Advances in information security research on industrial control systems. J. Tsinghua Univ. (Nat. Sci. Ed.) **52**(10), 1396–1408 (2012)
2. Delgado, R., et al.: Safe and Policy Oriented Secure Android-Based Industrial Embedded Control System. Appl. Sci. **10**(8), 2796 (2020)
3. Luo, X.D.: Analysis for the security of industrial control system and coping strategies **3481**, 427–432 (2014)
4. Xia, Q., Sifah, E.B., Asamoah, K.O., Gao, J., Xiaojiang, D., Guizani, M.: MeDShare: trustless medical data sharing among cloud service providers via blockchain. IEEE Access **5**, 14757–14767 (2017). https://doi.org/10.1109/ACCESS.2017.2730843
5. Feng, L.C.: Security access technology of wind farm SCADA system based on identity authentication. Electron. Technol. Softw. Eng. **2020**(02) 256–258 (2020)

6. Zhang, S.B., Jia, L.D., Wei, Y.X., Shi, W., Wang, J.: "The Exploration and Realization of Network Security Strategy for SCADA System of Gas Transmission Pipeline—Taking the Natural Gas Pipeline Project of China-Russia East Line as an example." for example Oil and Gas Storage, 39(06), pp. 685–691 (2020)

7. Wang, Y.P.: Security protection plan for industrial control system centralized control center. Inf. Secur. Res. 5(08), 756–760 (2019)

8. Maw, A., Adepu, S., Mathur, A.: ICS-BlockOpS: blockchain for operational data security in industrial control system. Pervasive Mob. Comput. 59, 101048 (2019)

9. Bahga, A., Madisetti, V.: Blockchain platform for industrial internet of things. J. Softw. Eng. Appl. 9(10), 533–546 (2016)

10. Wan, J., Li, J., Imran, M., Li, D., et al.: A blockchain-based solution for enhancing security and privacy in smart factory. IEEE Trans. Ind. Inf. 15(6), 3652–3660 (2019)

11. Xu, L.D., Xu, E.L., Li, L.: Industry 4.0: state of the art and future trends. Int. J. Prod. Res. 56(7–8), 2941–2962 (2018)

12. Meng, W., Tischhauser, E., Wang, Q., et al.: When intrusion detection meets blockchain technology: a review. IEEE Access 6, 10179–10188 (2018)

13. Castro, M., Liskov, B.: Practical Byzantine fault tolerance, pp. 173–186 (1999)

Adaptive Active Immune Policy for Sensor Nodes in Internet of Things

Cheng Zhong[1], Pengcheng Lu[1(✉)], Shaoyong Guo[2], and Song Kang[2]

[1] State Grid Xiongan New Area Power Supply Company, Xiongan 071000, China
[2] Beijing University of Posts and Telecommunications, Beijing 100876, China

Abstract. The Internet of Things (IoT) is a ubiquitous network formed on the basis of the traditional Internet. The sensor layer of IoT is the bridge between the world of information and the real world. The security of the sensor network of IoT is the primary basis for the credibility of the IoT. Only when the security of the sensor network is guaranteed, the security of IoT can be guaranteed. However, the existing security mechanism is mainly based on passive defense and cannot actively respond to many unknown security threats. Therefore, it is necessary to study an active immunity mechanism suitable for IoT sensor nodes. This article will mainly design an active immune mechanism that can meet the security requirements of IoT sensor nodes for the sensor layer of IoT, and combine the relevant feedback mechanism to adjust the credibility measurement policy between nodes in real time, so that the mechanism can be adjusted in real time according to environmental changes. In this way, it is more proactive to ensure the security of the sensor network. Simulation results show that the security strategy in this paper can better deal with the security threats brought by malicious nodes than the traditional strategy, and the response time is reduced by about 50% .

Keywords: The Internet of Things (IoT) · Active immunity · Behavior measurement · Privacy protection

1 Introduction

From the perspective of technical architecture, IoT can be divided into a senor domain, network communication domain and application computing domain. Among them, the sensor domain is composed of a large number of heterogeneous sensor nodes, and its main task is to collect, process and forward data according to specific task requirements. Similar to the Internet, IoT is the inheritance and extension of the Internet. It also inherits the problem of Internet security immune deficiency. At the same time, due to the characteristics of IoT sensor node, the problem of security immune deficiency is further magnified. In addition, it also faces more complex security threats than the Internet.

Aiming at the security issues of IoT sensing computing environment. It is necessary to ensure that the sensor node can complete the expected computing tasks and data transmission tasks when dealing with multiple security threats. According to the security protection requirements of the sensor node, design an adaptive and self-adjusting active

© Springer Nature Switzerland AG 2021
X. Sun et al. (Eds.): ICAIS 2021, CCIS 1424, pp. 514–525, 2021.
https://doi.org/10.1007/978-3-030-78621-2_43

immune security policy, and at the same time realize the self-evolution of the security policy, ensure that the sensor node can deal with unknown security threats, and realize the trusted operation of the sensor network. The security architecture of the sensor network and the policies to deal with security threats are the main factors affecting the security and credibility of the sensor domain of IoT.

2 Current Research

In view of the actual application scenarios of the Internet of things, such as smart transportation, smart medical care, smart supermarkets and location services, the actual application scenarios are independent of each other and the differences are obvious. The security problems faced are also different, and the requirements for security mechanisms are also different. Literature [1] proposed a game theory-based intrusion detection mechanism for the Internet of Things, which activates anomaly detection based on the characteristics of different attacks, effectively reducing the false alarm rate, and fully considering the computing power and energy level of the sensor node, but this mechanism needs to collect the characteristics of different types of attacks, and it is not effective in dealing with unknown attacks. Literature [2] proposed a remote authentication mechanism suitable for sensor nodes in the Internet of Things, which can measure sensor nodes and monitor the sensitive data generated by sensor nodes, including the management of the full life cycle of keys, which provides better security guarantees for perceptual computing nodes, and lower requirements for node computing capabilities, but the mechanism is too dependent on specific hardware platforms, and its versatility and cross-platform are not good.

Due to the heterogeneity of nodes in the sensor computing layer, a general security mechanism suitable for different types of nodes is the focus of research in this field. Literature [3] discusses the general security mechanism of heterogeneous sensor nodes, with data protection as the core, enhancing the security of sensor nodes, but the protection mechanism is too single to deal with different types of security threats. Literature [4] studied the compressed perception mechanism applicable to sensor nodes, enhanced the security sensitivity of the compressed perception stage, and was able to effectively deal with plaintext attacks, and achieved a good balance between compression and security strength, but this mechanism could not deal with ciphertext attacks and has poor robustness. Literature [5] starts from the security risks faced by sensor nodes, evaluates the security risks faced by IoT sensor nodes in its application environment, and then issues security warnings. It fully considers the dynamics of the Internet of Things. The security risk assessment is rigorous, but it lacks the response mechanism for security risks, can only be used as reference information in the process of security protection. Literature [6] proposed an attack detection mechanism based on distributed deep learning, which has a low false alarm rate and good scalability. However, this method requires a large amount of attack data and powerful computing capabilities, which is a burden on sensor nodes.

At the same time, in the sensor computing layer of the Internet of Things, many heterogeneous and loosely coupled devices are everywhere. The traditional access control model is no longer suitable for nomadic, decentralized, and dynamic scenarios of the

Internet of Things environment. Therefore, the access control mechanism is very important to control the nodes in the sensor computing layer and ensure their security and credibility. Literature [7] proposes an access control mechanism based on identity and trust. This mechanism integrates trust fuzzy computing to achieve access control to sensor nodes on the basis of identity verification. It has the characteristics of good scalability and low energy consumption, but this mechanism has low abstraction of node attributes, cannot fully reflect the operating characteristics of nodes, and lacks the protection of key information. Because IPv6 can provide enough public addresses, its communication protocol with Machine-to-Machine (M2M) is considered to be the core protocol of the future Internet of Things [8]. Based on the integration of IPv6 and M2M communication, literature [9] proposes a distributed access control architecture, which improves the overall performance of the sensor network and realizes dynamic network management and load balancing. However, the architecture overemphasizes network performance, lacks a comprehensive assessment of the security situation of sensor nodes, and has insufficient ability to respond to security threats. Literature [10] refers to human relations in sociology and proposes an adaptive access control mechanism for sensor nodes. Through adaptive access control protocols, sensor nodes can adaptively select the best parameter settings to cope with changing application environments. But the mechanism is too subjective and fluctuates too much in actual operation.

The essence of trusted computing is that computing meets expectations. The development of trusted computing technology [11] has opened a new door for the study of access control in the perceptual computing layer. Literature [12] has constructed an access control model suitable for the sensor node based on trusted computing technology. This model is based on the trustworthiness of nodes, guarantees the trustworthiness of associated nodes through the chain of trust transfer mechanism, and integrates trustworthiness metrics to feedback control of sensor nodes. However, this model too much refers to the defense mechanism of Trusted Computing 2.0 and lacks active immunity and defense mechanisms. However, this model has too much reference to trusted computing 2.0 defense mechanism, lack of active immunity and defense mechanism. Distributed Internet of Things is emerging as a new paradigm of Internet of Things, in which smart objects can perceive/drive, store and interpret the information created by them or in the surrounding environment. According to the characteristics of distributed Internet of Things, literature [14] proposed an access control architecture driven by a smart community, which formulated a unified access control specification, which can effectively define the access rights of different nodes and determine the security boundary, but this architecture is only suitable for distributed Internet of Things and has poor versatility.

In summary, the access control mechanism in the sensing computing layer of the Internet of Things is mainly aimed at specific application scenarios and special protocols of the Internet of Things, and lacks universality. There are too few reference dimensions in the feedback control process of the sensor node, and the operation is not stable enough.

Therefore, according to the node credibility, computing power and energy characteristics of the sensor node, this paper combines the specific application and the characteristics of the sensor network in different regions to realize the adaptive adjustment of the sensor network and build a clear hierarchical sensor network as a whole. At the same time, this paper will start from the security threats faced by the existing sensor domain, and study the security threat response mechanisms applicable to different types of sensor nodes. On this basis, study general security policies that can achieve active immunity and realize automatic update mechanism of security policies to enable it to evolve simultaneously with security threats, and achieve security policy updates for different types of sensor nodes, so as to resist unknown security threats.

3 Active Immune Defense Policies Applicable to the Sensing Computing Domain

In the sensing network, the threats that a node may face are diverse, and the response of the node to each security threat should also be different. Since the nodes in the sensing computing network of the Internet of Things are different from traditional network nodes and have specificity, so it is unpredictable to upcoming security threats. Traditional passive defense mechanisms cannot effectively guarantee the security and credibility of the sensing network. Therefore, a security policy that can actively defend is needed to resist known and unknown security threats. The active immune policy should have the adaptive ability of the application environment and different types of nodes, which is the basis for ensuring the normal completion of the calculation and data transmission tasks of the sensing network. The active immune policy should have the calculation of the degree of unknown threats faced, the periodic detection of the node's own credibility, and the corresponding discrimination criteria.

In perceptual computing networks, the main security threats faced can be divided into the following categories: 1. Physical capture, 2. Brute force cracking, 3. Cloning nodes, 4. Identity forgery, 5. Routing attacks, 6. Denial of service attacks, 7. Node privacy leakage. The above security threats are represented by vectors $(st_1, st_2, \ldots, st_7)$.

The security policy of the sensor node is used to deal with the security threats it faces. The security policy can be described by a four-tuple (S, TR, U, Y). Among them, S represents the security threat index of the node, $S = fr(\Pr(st_1), \Pr(st_2), \ldots, \Pr(st_7), z)$, where $z = \{z_1, z_2, z_3, z_4\}$, the meaning is the same as in the previous section, indicating the computing power, energy level, channel status and trustworthiness of the node. $\Pr(st_i)$ represents the probability of a node facing each security threat, and the function fr is an exponential calculation function of the node facing security threats.

Definition: Node security threat index calculation function fr

$$fr = 1 - \left(\overline{\Pr(st_1)} \cup \overline{\Pr(st_2)} \cup \ldots \cup \overline{\Pr(st_7)} \right) \tag{1}$$

The response mechanism adopted by TR according to the security threat index includes the periodic trusted self-check rate $pt(SI)$ of the node, the measurement time window $\Delta t(SI)$ for the trusted behavior of the node, the trusted information t_p of the node's own platform, and the trusted node self-check function f_{tp}, so $TR = (pt, \Delta t, t_p, f_{tp})$. Among them, the values of the trusted self-check frequency $pt(SI)$ and the trusted measurement time window $\Delta t(SI)$ are related to the calculation result of the security threat index. When the security threat is high, the corresponding self-check frequency should be increased, the credibility measurement time window should also be reduced, vice versa. U represents the control policy input by the node. Y represents the description of the expected output of the node. Whether the node is credible should be judged based on the output result. The security and credibility of the sensor node is essentially that the calculation result meets the user's expectations. If the node output meets the expectation, it is deemed credible.

In the sensing network, the network environment is complex and changeable, the input of the sensor node is varied, and the operation of the sensor node is very uncertain. As a result, it is difficult to quantify and determine whether the output of the sensor node meets expectations at a certain moment. To solve this problem, we refer to predictive control theory to control the input and output of the sensor node. The process can be described as follows.

The input and output control process of the sensor node is described as follows:

$$A\left(z^{-1}\right)y(t) = B\left(z^{-1}\right)u(t-1) + D\left(z^{-1}\right)v(t-1) + C\left(z^{-1}\right)\omega(t)/\Delta \qquad (2)$$

$y(t)$, $u(t)$, $v(t)$ and $\omega(t)$ respectively represent the output, input, pre-feedback measurable interference and white noise interference of the controlled object at time t, The $y(t)$ and $u(t)$ of the sensor node are the realization of the output control policy and the input control policy in the security policy. The pre-feedback measurable interference and white noise interference can be considered as malicious attacks around the sensor node. $\Delta = 1 - z^{-1}$, indicating the difference operator.

The sensor node is a non-deterministic system. Therefore, it is difficult for the predictive control algorithm to obtain $A\left(z^{-1}\right)$, $B\left(z^{-1}\right)$, $C\left(z^{-1}\right)$, $D\left(z^{-1}\right)$ in the controlled equation when inputting and outputting the sensor node. At the same time, due to the uncertainty of user behavior parameters and behavior output, it is necessary to establish the user-controlled parameters during the operation of the system, and need to use the method of parameter estimation, online estimation $A\left(z^{-1}\right), B\left(z^{-1}\right), C\left(z^{-1}\right), D\left(z^{-1}\right)$. Therefore, when the parameters of the controlled virtual machine are unknown, the input and output-controlled process of the sensor node can be expressed as follows:

$$\hat{A}\left(z^{-1}\right)y(t) = \hat{B}\left(z^{-1}\right)\Delta u_f(t-1) + \hat{D}\left(z^{-1}\right)\Delta v_f(t-1) \qquad (3)$$

Among them, $\hat{A}\left(z^{-1}\right)$, $\hat{B}\left(z^{-1}\right)$, $\hat{D}\left(z^{-1}\right)$ need to be identified and acquired online.

4 Simulation Experiment

In this section, we use the Netlogo simulation environment to simulate the above active immune mechanism. Netlogo is a programmable modeling environment that can model complex environments based on time clues.

4.1 Active Immune Security Policy

Assuming that in this experiment, the number of network nodes is 100, and the initial number of attacked nodes is 5, which means that there are 100 sensor nodes in the entire sensing network simulation environment, and 5 of them have security threats. Next, we will verify the feasibility of the immune mechanism in this article through experimental simulation, observe whether malicious nodes in the sensing network can be found and resisted, and observe the time it takes to be discovered.

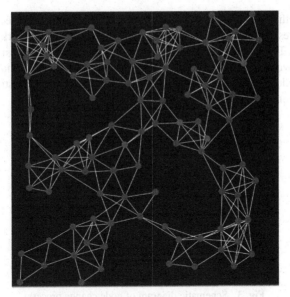

Fig. 1. Initial state of sensor network

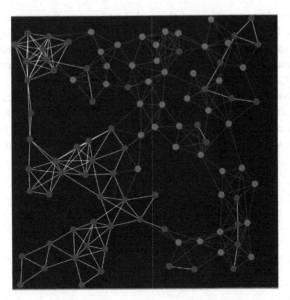

Fig. 2. State transition after simulation

First, assume that the threat propagation probability is 10%, and the credible self-check frequency is set to 5, that is, a self-check is performed every 5 units of time. The initial state of the simulated environment is shown in Fig. 1. Among them, the blue nodes indicate the normal nodes, the red nodes indicate the nodes under security threat, and the connection between nodes indicates that there is a communication connection between the two nodes, that is, security threats may spread through this connection. When the simulation process is finished, the schematic diagram of sensor network environment is shown in Fig. 2. The gray nodes in the Fig. 2 represent nodes that are resistant to security threats. As shown in the Fig. 1 and 2, the red nodes have been eliminated completely. Most of the nodes developed resistance to security threats by adjusting the security policy. The system is restored to a safe state.

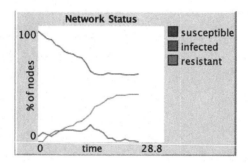

Fig. 3. Schematic diagram of node change process

The dynamic change process of the node status when the system faces threats is shown in Fig. 3. In the figure, the blue line represents the proportion of normal nodes, the red line represents the percentage of nodes infected by security threats, and the gray line represents the percentage of nodes that are resistant to security threats.

From Fig. 3, it can be concluded that in about 28 units of time, security threats are eliminated completely from the sensor network, there are no nodes facing security threats in the entire network, and the entire sensor network is restored to security. It can be shown that the proposed solution can make the nodes in the entire network respond to security threats as soon as the threat occurs, and can solve the threats faced in a short time.

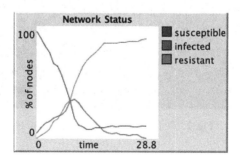

Fig. 4. Dynamic diagram of 30% threat propagation efficiency

The above experiments can show that this security mechanism can be more effective against security threats of the sensor network security threats, but the threat index and propagation efficiency of different security threats are different. Next, for different security threats, different propagation efficiencies are designed to compare how the security mechanism responds to threats with different propagation capabilities. It can be seen from the experimental results in Fig. 4 to 6 that as the probability of threat propagation increases, the time required for the system to return to normal after security defenses has no significant difference. Therefore, it shows that this mechanism can respond quickly and promptly to different security threats (Fig. 5).

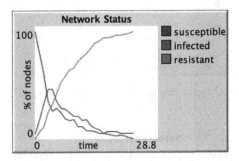

Fig. 5. Dynamic diagram of 50% threat propagation efficiency

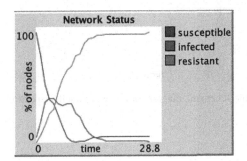

Fig. 6. Dynamic diagram of 70% threat propagation efficiency

As mentioned earlier that when we face different security threats, we should adjust the frequency of credible self-inspection according to different security threat indexes. In the case of high threats, increasing the frequency of credible self-inspection can effectively shorten the time need to respond to threats. Therefore, when the threat propagation probability is 70, we adjust the self- inspection frequency from 5 units of time to 1 units of time, which means that when the security threat level is high, the credible self- inspection frequency is increased to verify whether it can be quickly respond to security threats. The experimental results are shown in the Fig. 7 and 8, when the threat propagation frequency is 70% (higher threat level), and the self-inspection frequency is 5 units of time, it takes about 28 units to restore the network to a safe state, and after increasing the frequency of trusted self-inspection to 1 units of time, it only takes about 7 units of time to recover the network security. Therefore, it can be concluded that when the security threat level is high, increasing the credible self-inspection frequency can effectively shorten the response time to security threats and better protect the security of the sensor network.

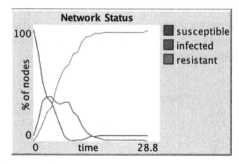

Fig. 7. Dynamic schematic diagram of nodes with self-inspection frequency of 5

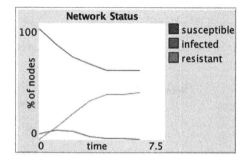

Fig. 8. Dynamic schematic diagram of nodes with self-inspection frequency of 1

4.2   Controlled Experiment

In this section, by changing the proportion of malicious nodes in the area and the propagation probability of security threats, the effectiveness of the proposed policy is verified by comparing the protection ability of the active immune security policy and the traditional security policy of the Internet of things sensor layer.

In the control experiment, the Netlogo simulation experiment environment is also used, and the initial number of nodes in the sensor network is set to 100, the credible self-inspection frequency is 5, the probability of security threat propagation is 30%, and the proportion of malicious nodes is 5%. 10%, 15%, 20%. Do four sets of control experiments to compare the time required for the sensor network to recover to a safe state. The specific results are shown in Fig. 9.

It can be seen from the above table that the defense time comparison experiment was conducted on the proportion of malicious nodes at 5%, 10%, 15%, and 20% respectively. The time required for the traditional policy is about twice that of the active immune security policy in this paper. In view of the same security threat, it can respond quickly

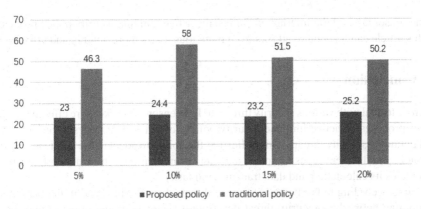

Fig. 9. Response time of security policy under different proportion of malicious nodes

and efficiently even with different proportions of malicious nodes, which greatly reduces the time of security threats in the sensor network.

When the proportion of malicious nodes is the same, change the transmission probability of security threats, set the proportion of malicious nodes to 5%, and control the transmission probability of security threats to 10%, 30%, 50%, and 70% respectively. The response time of sensor network is compared between the security policy described in this paper and the traditional policy, the comparison experiment results are shown in Fig. 10.

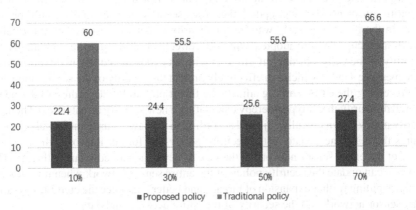

Fig. 10. Response time of security policy under different security threat propagation probability

As can be seen from the above table, under the same proportion of malicious nodes, the defense time of the two policies is compared for the propagation probability of different security threats. The security policy described in this article is lower in response time than the traditional policy. Based on the above two experimental results, under the same conditions, the security policy in this article can better deal with the security threats brought by malicious nodes. Compared with the traditional security policy, the response time is reduced by about 50%. In summary, compared with the traditional security policy at the sensor layer of the Internet of Things, the active immune security policy proposed in this article can respond to attacks from malicious nodes more quickly and effectively.

5 Conclusion

In order to deal with various security threats to IoT sensor networks more effectively, this paper proposes an active immune security policy for IoT sensor nodes to resist known and unknown security threats. This policy has the ability to adapt to the application environment and different types of nodes, and can ensure that the sensor network normally completes its calculation and data transmission tasks.

First, according to the types of security threats that may be faced in the perceptual computing network, a security threat description vector is proposed, and the existing security policy in the node is represented by the security policy quadruple. The description of the security policy includes the security threat index, the countermeasures taken, the control policy and the expected output result. Through these four aspects to describe the node security policy. At the same time, a trusted self-inspection policy for nodes is proposed, and the frequency of self-inspection is set according to the security threat index, so that nodes can perform periodic self-inspection to ensure the security and credibility of nodes.

In addition, in response to the endless attack methods of each type of security threat, an automatic update mechanism of security policies that evolves synchronously with security threats is designed. When a new security threat is discovered, the security threat warning is carried out between the node and the sensor network, so that the nodes in the entire sensor network can update their own security policies to deal with the new threat. In the process of early warning of security threats, necessary key information protection mechanisms are adopted, which can effectively guarantee the authenticity and reliability of the early warning information without exposing the key node information of the message sender, which can effectively protect the security of the sensor node. The node receiving the early warning adjusts the threat probability according to the newly generated security threat type, thereby calculating a new security threat index. Then, the security policy is dynamically adjusted according to the new security threat index, which ensures the real-time update of the security policy and further improves the response ability of the entire sensor network in the face of newly generated security threats. This enables it can update the security policy of the entire sensor network when it is attacked locally, avoiding further expansion of threats, and better guarantee the credible operation of the sensor network and the security of the entire network and data.

In the next research work, the focus should be on applying the mechanism to actual IoT devices and environments, and further optimizing the policy.

Acknowledgement. This work is supported by State Grid Technical Project "Research on key technologies of secure and reliable slice access for Energy Internet services" (5204XQ190001). The authors declare that they have no conflicts of interest to report regarding the present study.

References

1. Sedjelmaci, H., Senouci, S.M., Taleb, T.: An accurate security game for low-resource IoT devices. IEEE Trans. Veh. Technol. **66**(10), 9381–9393 (2017)
2. Wang, J., Hong, Z., Zhang, Y., Jin, Y.: Enabling security-enhanced attestation with Intel SGX for remote terminal and IoT. IEEE Trans. Comput. Aided Des. Integr. Circuits Syst. **37**(1), 88–96 (2018)
3. Kim, M., Lee, N., Park, J.: A security generic service interface of Internet of Things (IoT) platforms. Symmetry **9**(9), 171 (2017)
4. Mangia, M., Pareschi, F., Rovatti, R., Setti, G.: Low-cost security of IoT sensor nodes with rakeness-based Compressed sensing: statistical and known-plaintext attacks. IEEE Trans. Inf. Forensics Secur. **13**(2), 327–340 (2018)
5. Nurse, J.R.C., Creese, S., Roure, D.D.: Security risk assessment in internet of things systems. IT Professional **19**(5), 20–26 (2017)
6. Abeshu, A., Chilamkurti, N.: Deep learning: the frontier for distributed attack detection in fog-to-things computing. IEEE Commun. Mag. **10**(2), 169–175 (2018)
7. Mahalle, P.N., Thakre, P.A., Prasad, N.R., Prasad, R.: A fuzzy approach to trust based access control in Internet of Things. In: Proceedings of the Wireless VITAE 2013, pp. 1–5. IEEE, Atlantic City (2013)
8. Abbas, R., Shirvanimoghaddam, M., Li, Y., Vucetic, B.: Random access for M2M communications with QoS guarantees. IEEE Trans. Commun. **65**(7), 2889–2903 (2017)
9. Li, Y., Chai, K., Chen, Y., Loo, J.: Distributed access control framework for IPv6-based hierarchical Internet of Things. IEEE Wirel. Commun. **16**(10), 17–23 (2016)
10. Chen, I., Bao, F., Guo, J.: Trust-based service management for social Internet of Things systems. IEEE Trans. Dependable Secure Comput. **13**(6), 684–696 (2016)
11. Maene, P., Gotzfried, J., Clercq, R.D., Muller, T., Freiling, F.: Hardware-based trusted computing architectures for isolation and attestation. IEEE Trans. Comput. **99**(1), 1–14 (2017)
12. Margheri, A., Masi, M., Pugliese, R., Tiezzi, F., Rigorous, A.: Framework for specification, analysis and enforcement of access control policies. IEEE Trans. Software Eng. **99**(1), 1–58 (2016)
13. Hussein, D., Bertin, E., Frey, V.: A community-driven access control approach in distributed IoT environments. IEEE Commun. Mag. **50**(3), 146–153 (2017)
14. MeenaKowshalyal, A., Valarmathi, M.L.: Trust management for reliable decision making among social objects in the social Internet of Things. IET Networks **6**(4), 75–80 (2017)

ELM Forecasted Model of Ammonia Nitrogen in Lake Taihu Combined with Adaboost and Particle Swarm Optimization Algorithms

Sunli Cong[1], Aiyun Hu[1(✉)], Chen Liu[1], and Zheyu Jiang[2]

[1] Jiangsu Key Lab of IoT Application Technology, Wuxi Taihu University, Wuxi 214064, China
[2] Wuxi Water Group Co., Ltd, Wuxi 214000, China

Abstract. To understand the change trend of Lake Taihu's water quality indexes in advance and prevent the occurrence of pollution incidents such as blue algae, the ammonia nitrogen index forecasted model was studied by taking the water quality monitoring data of Nanquan in Wuxi City as an example. The chromaticity, odor and taste, pH, nitrite nitrogen, chloride, dissolved oxygen, and algae were determined as input variables by implementing linear regression analysis through SPSS software to establish the Extreme Learning Machine (ELM) model for forecasting ammonia nitrogen index. Aiming at the problem of ELM randomly generating weights and thresholds resulting in low forecast accuracy, the Particle Swarm Optimization (PSO) algorithm was adopted to optimize ELM parameters. In order to solve the situation that the PSO algorithm is easy to fall into local optimum, the Adaboost algorithm was introduced to train weak ELM predictors, which were later combined into a strong predictor for the forecast. The results represent that the Adaboost-PSO-ELM model's forecast coefficient of determination (R^2) and root mean square error ($RMSE$) for ammonia nitrogen are 0.955 mg/L and 0.023 mg/L, respectively. Compared with the two models of ELM and PSO-ELM, the forecast accuracy is significantly improved. Therefore, the ELM model based on Adaboost and PSO algorithms is feasible for forecasting water quality index of ammonia nitrogen in Lake Taihu, providing new ideas for accurate forecast in water quality aspect.

Keywords: Lake Taihu · Ammonia nitrogen · Adaboost-PSO-ELM

1 Introduction

As a multi-lake country, our country has as many as 2,759 lakes with an area greater than 1km^2, accounting for about 1% of the total area. The existence of lakes is closely related to human survival and social economic development. However, with the increasing development of environmental resources by humans, a large amount of industrial wastewater and domestic sewage are discharged into water bodies without proper treatment. Over time, the concentration of ammonia nitrogen, phosphorus and organic pollutants in the water will increase, leading to water eutrophication and so on [1]. Our country has promulgated the "Surface Water Environmental Quality Standard" (GB3838–2002)

© Springer Nature Switzerland AG 2021
X. Sun et al. (Eds.): ICAIS 2021, CCIS 1424, pp. 526–536, 2021.
https://doi.org/10.1007/978-3-030-78621-2_44

[2], which stipulates the concentration standard limits of water quality indexes at all levels. Exceeding the limits will inevitably bring threats to the health of water organisms and humans. Lake Taihu is the third largest freshwater lake in China. As early as 2007, cyanobacteria broke out in the Lake Taihu due to eutrophication, directly causing a serious nutritional crisis of drinking water safety for residents in Wuxi City, Jiangsu Province. Recently, due to the rapid increase in temperature, large areas of cyanobacteria have also appeared in some waters of Lake Taihu [3]. In this regard, if we can forecast the water quality of Lake Taihu and understand the changing trend of some indexes in advance, it can help prevent the occurrence of eutrophication in Lake Taihu.

In recent years, establishing a reliable water quality forecasted model has become one of the research hotspots in the field of water environment science. Researchers at home and abroad mainly utilize mathematical statistics, grey system theory, water quality simulation models, artificial neural networks and other methods for water quality prediction [4–7], but these methods are usually easy to fall into local minima, and parameters cannot be adjusted easily leading to over-learning and under-learning, dimensionality disaster, weak generalization ability and so on. Especially when predicting small sample data, the results of these methods are frequently not satisfactory [8]. ELM is a nonlinear modeling method with simple parameter setting and short learning time. Reference [9] presented a ELM-based forecasted model for total phosphorus and total nitrogen in a reservoir in Yunnan, finally the forecast coefficient of determination was 0.93, which was higher than the traditional Back Propagation (BP), Radial Basis Function (RBF) and even Genetic Algorithm optimized BP (GA-BP) models. Authors of reference [10] selected Chaohu Lake's water quality data from 2010 to 2015 as the research object, and optimized the weights and thresholds of ELM through the Fruit Fly Optimization Algorithm (FOA), which achieved high forecast accuracy of water quality. The above researches together indicate that it is feasible to employ ELM and its related optimization models for water quality forecast, but there are still few related studies, and the forecast accuracy needs to be improved currently.

The water quality monitoring data of Nanquan in Wuxi City was taken as the instance in the study to construct a forecasted model of water pollution index—ammonia nitrogen in Lake Taihu. Aiming at the problem of ELM's poor ability to recognize unknown input data due to randomly initialize parameters, the PSO algorithm was adopted to iteratively optimize the input layer weights and hidden layer thresholds of ELM. On this basis, a strong predictor was formed through the Adaboost algorithm's training to avoid PSO from falling into the local optimum, eventually improving the forecast accuracy of the ELM model. The purpose of this study is to obtain an effective and reliable forecasted model of water pollution indexes in Lake Taihu, and to provide a new method idea for other water quality forecast.

2 Materials and Methods

2.1 Data Source

The water data of Lake Taihu in this study came from the water quality monitoring center of Nanquan in Wuxi City, Jiangsu Province. The time span of data was from January 2011 to December 2019. The monitoring indexes contained water temperature

(°C), turbidity, chromaticity, odor and taste, pH, total coliforms (MPN/L), nitrite nitrogen (mg/L), ammonia nitrogen (mg/L), chloride (mg/L), oxygen consumption (mg/L), dissolved oxygen (mg/L), total iron (mg/L), total number of bacteria (CFU/mL), algae (10,000/L). To make the monitoring data representative, all monthly monitoring values of each index were taken averaged, then used as the current month's sample data.

2.2 Variable Selection

Ammonia nitrogen is one of the indexes of water body eutrophication, which is due to organic pollution caused by man-made sewage. Ammonia nitrogen, which generally exists in surface water and groundwater, refers to nitrogen in the form of free ammonia (NH_3) and ionic ammonium (NH_4^+), and mainly comes from the decomposition products of nitrogen-containing organic matter in domestic sewage by microorganisms and nitrogen-containing industrial wastewater. When ammonia nitrogen in the water body exceeds the standard, it will harm the health of organisms and even humans [11, 12]. According to the prior statistics of all indexes in this study, it is observed that the changes of various indexes are all non-linear, especially the ammonia nitrogen changes most significantly. Therefore, it is reasonable to utilize the ELM nonlinear analysis model in this study, and ammonia nitrogen can be selected as the output variable of the ELM model.

Table 1. The list of the significance value sig. of each index

Number	Indexes	Sig.
1	Water temperature	0.054
2	Turbidity	0.165
3	Chromaticity	0.000
4	Odor and taste	0.006
5	PH	0.046
6	Total coliforms	0.543
7	Nitrite nitrogen	0.000
8	Chloride	0.000
9	Oxygen consumption	0.300
10	Dissolved oxygen	0.005
11	Total iron	0.960
12	Total number of bacteria	0.351
13	Algae	0.040

Taking into account that all input indexes of the model will increase the model complexity and fail to achieve better forecast results [13], the SPSS software was adopted to perform linear regression analysis of all indexes [14]. According to the significance value (sig.) in the analysis results, it should be less than 0.05 (as shown in Table 1) to screen out indexes with strong forecast ability for ammonia nitrogen. According to Table 1, the sig. values of chromaticity, odor and taste, pH, nitrite nitrogen, chloride, dissolved oxygen, and algae are all less than 0.05, which meet the screening condition. Among them, chromaticity, nitrite nitrogen, chloride particularly have the greatest correlation with ammonia nitrogen. Hence, the 7 indexes selected above can be regarded as input variables of the ELM model.

2.3 Methods

The ELM algorithm is essentially a forward propagation neural network. Compared with the traditional neural network, its advantages are reflected in that the connection weight W between the input layer and the hidden layer, and the threshold B in the hidden layer can both be determined randomly, and there is no necessary to adjust them after setting again. Moreover, the connection weight β between the hidden layer and the output layer does not need to be adjusted iteratively, and it only demands to be certain once by solving the equation. The ELM algorithm has fast learning speed and good generalization ability, and has been widely applied in nonlinear function fitting, regression and pattern classification researches [15].

The ELM algorithm randomly generates W and B parameters prone to make hidden layer neurons redundant, which reduces the ability to recognize unknown input data [16]. The PSO is a swarm intelligence optimization algorithm generated by simulating the foraging behavior of a flock of birds. It has the odds of fast search speed, high efficiency, and simple structure [17]. The algorithm updates the speed and position of individual particles by constantly comparing fitness values, and eventually determines the individual optimal solution and the global optimal solution [18]. Hence, the PSO was adopted to optimize the ELM parameters of W and B in the study. In the PSO algorithm, the initial value of inertia weight ($wmax$) was set to 0.8; the final value of inertia weight ($wmin$) was set to 0.4; the number of particle populations (N) and the maximum number of iterations ($itmax$) were both set to 100; c_1, c_2 represents the cognitive coefficients, respectively set to 2.4 and 1.6; the mean square error (MSE) between the forecast value and the actual value is regarded as the fitness function of the PSO algorithm:

$$MSE = \frac{1}{N} \sum_{i=1}^{N} (\hat{y}_i - y_i)^2 \tag{1}$$

In the formula, N is the number of samples, $\hat{y}_i$ is the forecast value, and y_i represents the actual value [19].

In order to prevent PSO algorithm from falling into the local optimal solution when optimizing ELM parameters, the Adaboost algorithm was adopted to further improve the forecast accuracy of the ELM model. The core idea of Adaboost algorithm is to first train a base learner from the initial training set, and adjust the training samples according to the performance of the base learner, so that the training samples that the base learner did wrong would get more attention in the follow-up. Then the next base learner is trained based on the adjusted sample distribution, and repeated until the number of base learners reaches the specified value [20]. The algorithm has a simple structure, high integration, and is not tended to get over-fitting when combined with a regression model for forecasting [21].

Based on the above theoretical basis, the Adaboost-PSO-ELM algorithm was put forward to forecast the water pollution index — ammonia nitrogen. By initializing an ELM base learner and repeatedly training to obtain 10 weak ELM predictors, the Adaboost algorithm can be used to compose weak predictors into a strong predictor, and the forecast accuracy of the ELM model can be improved, also the risk of ELM falling into the local optimum can be reduced, thereby increasing ELM's generalization ability. Figure 1 depicts the forecast flow chart of the Adaboost-PSO-ELM algorithm.

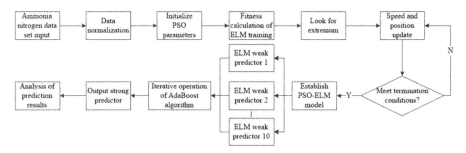

Fig. 1. The forecast flow chart of Adaboost-PSO-ELM algorithm

3 Results and Analysis

Based on the determined input and output variables, the first 75% of the sample data was selected as the training set of the ELM model, and the last 25% as the test set. Taking the coefficient of determination (R^2) and the root mean square error ($RMSE$) as performance evaluation indexes, the calculation formulas are represented in Eqs. (2) and (3) respectively:

$$R^2 = 1 - \sum_{i=1}^{N} (y_i - \hat{y}_i)^2 / \sum_{i=1}^{N} (y_i - \bar{y})^2 \tag{2}$$

In the formula, $\bar{y}$ is on behalf of the average actual value. Normally, the value of R^2 is from 0 to 1, and the higher the R^2 value is, the better the regression effect is, also the higher the matching degree between the forecast value and the actual value is.

$$RMSE = \sqrt{MSE} \tag{3}$$

Normally, the smaller the $RMSE$ value is, the higher the forecast accuracy of model is [22].

In the paper, in order to reduce the impact of the dimensions of different indexes on network training, the Min-Max normalization method was utilized to normalize the data to the (-1, 1) interval uniformly [23]. In the ELM training process, the activation function needs to be used to transform the input information to make the input and output respond. Its types involve Sigmoid, Sine, Hardlim, and RBF [24]. In this paper, the monotonically increasing and continuously derivable sigmoid function was selected as the activation function of the ELM model [25]. Then it was worth determining that the number of input and output layer nodes were 7 and 1, respectively. Considering that there is still no scientific guidance for defining the number of hidden layer nodes, the evaluation index changes of the ELM model under different hidden layer nodes were examined, as shown in Fig. 2. It should be noted that the number of hidden layer nodes was increased from 1 to 10, and then to 200 according to the interval of 10. Since randomly generating input weights of ELM, the average of 30 experiments was determined as the final forecast result of each point in Fig. 2. It can be seen from Fig. 2 that when the number of hidden layer nodes exceeds 10, R^2 shows a downward trend, and $RMSE$ gives an upward trend. On the whole, R^2 is the largest when the number of hidden layer nodes is 8, and $RMSE$ is the smallest when the number of hidden layer nodes reaches 9. Considering that when the number of hidden layer nodes is 9, R^2 is also very close to the maximum value, so the number of hidden layer nodes of 9 is the most appropriate and ideal for the ammonia nitrogen forecast.

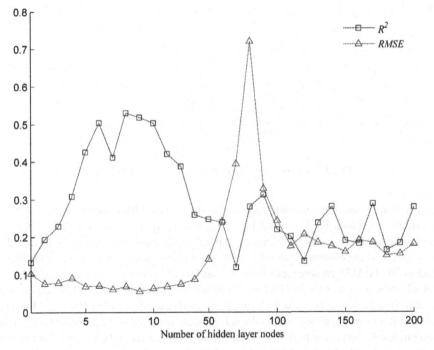

Fig. 2. ELM evaluation indexes under different hidden layer nodes

At this time, the forecast results comparison of the ELM model for ammonia nitrogen is shown in Fig. 3. It can be observed that the matching degree between the forecast value and the actual value is very low, and the regression effect is not good, with R^2 of only 0.773 and $RMSE$ of 0.073 mg/L for test set. It indicates that the ELM model can capture the non-linear change law of ammonia nitrogen better. However, the ELM algorithm has a relatively large randomness in the operation process, and its ability to forecast unknown sample data is not ideal, which contributes to the low forecast accuracy of ammonia nitrogen.

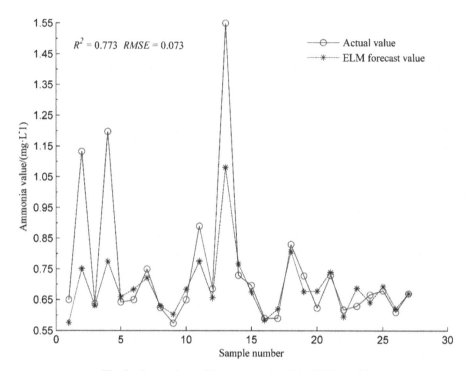

Fig. 3. Comparison of forecast results of the ELM model

The fitness function curve and forecast results of the ELM model optimized by PSO algorithm are shown in Fig. 4 and Fig. 5 separately. It is visible from Fig. 4 that as the number of PSO iterations increases, the value of fitness function (*MSE*) gradually decreases, and the downward trend is from fast to slow; when the number of iterations reaches 70, the *MSE* change tends to be flat, and finally converges to the lowest value of 0.0043, indicating that the PSO-ELM model training has reached the expected error at present. In addition, compared with Fig. 3, the forecast effect of the PSO-ELM model in Fig. 5 has been improved, that is the actual value is closer to the forecast value. This moment the R^2 increased to 0.899, and the *RMSE* decreased to 0.034 mg/L for test set. It illustrates that the PSO algorithm obtained the optimal weight and threshold for ELM parameters optimization, and improved the forecast effect of the ELM model to a certain extent.

Since the PSO algorithm will inevitably fall into the local optimal situation during parameter optimization, it will not be possible to search for the global optimal solution, which affects the forecast accuracy of the ELM model. Further on the basis of the ELM optimized by PSO, the Adaboost algorithm was applied to train 10 weak predictors, then composed into a strong predictor to re-forecast ammonia nitrogen. The forecast results are shown in Fig. 6. It is thus clear that the forecasted R^2 and *RMSE* of the new

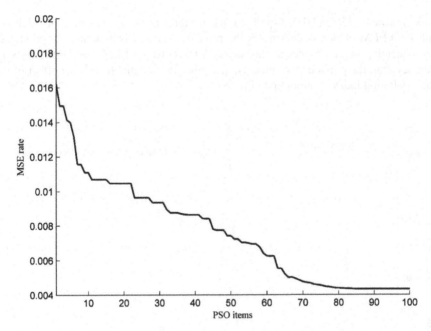

Fig. 4. The fitness iteration curve of PSO algorithm

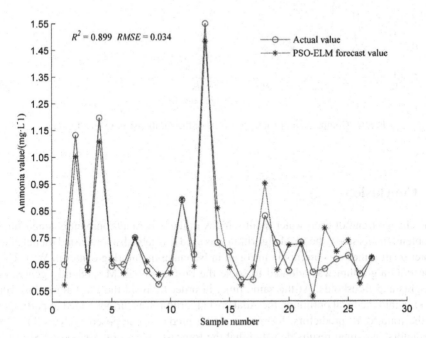

Fig. 5. Comparison of forecast results of the PSO-ELM model

model reaches 0.955 and 0.023 mg/L for test set through the combination of Adaboost with PSO-ELM, which demonstrates the forecast accuracy is dramatically promoted. Consequently, the end model in this study, Adaboost-PSO-ELM, has higher forecast accuracy than the previous two models, achieving the optimal forecasted effect of the water pollution index — ammonia nitrogen.

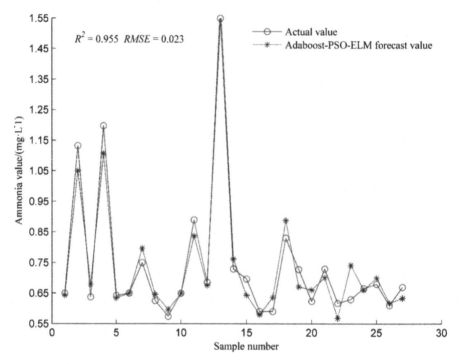

Fig. 6. Comparison of forecast results of the Adaboost-PSO-ELM model

4   Conclusion

The change trend of each water quality index in the water environment is a non-linear problem. In this study, the ELM algorithm was used to establish a forecasted model of the water quality index — ammonia nitrogen in Nanquan monitoring center in Wuxi City. The PSO algorithm was adopted to solve the problem of ELM randomly generating weights and thresholds. At the same time, in order to avoid the PSO algorithm from sinking into the local optimum, the Adaboost algorithm was further added to participate in the training of predictors, forming a strong predictor composed of 10 weak ELM predictors. The final results depicted that the forecast indexes of Adaboost-PSO-ELM model for ammonia nitrogen reached R^2 of 0.955 and $RMSE$ of 0.023 mg/L for test set, which was obviously improved when compared to the forecast accuracy of both the ELM and PSO-ELM models.

The experiment demonstrates that this method of Adaboost-PSO-ELM has high forecast accuracy. On the one hand, it solves the difficult problem of ELM weight and threshold setting. And on the other hand, it improves the situation that the PSO algorithm is easy to fall into local optimum when searching for optimum. It further explains the employment of Adaboost-PSO-ELM model can effectively forecast the water pollution index ammonia nitrogen in Lake Taihu, which can provide new ideas for accurate forecast of water quality and a scientific basis for water quality management in Lake Taihu.

Acknowledgement. We gratefully acknowledge the assistance of the Nanquan Water Quality Monitoring Center from Wuxi Water Group Co., Ltd.

Funding Statement. The paper was supported by Wuxi City Soft Science Project (201913571004Z) and Industry-University Cooperation Collaborative Education Project of the Ministry of Education (201902167006).

Conflicts of Interest. The authors declare that they have no conflicts of interest to report regarding the present study.

References

1. Han, P., Yang, P.: Research on water quality prediction method—Taihu Lake basin as an example. Agric. Sci.-Technol. Inf. **3**, 157–158 (2016)
2. GB3838–2002 Surface water environmental quality standards. http://www.biaozhun8.cn/bia ozhun8519/. Accessed 24 June 2005
3. Gu, G., Lu, G.: On the integrated control of water environment of wuli lake. Lake Taihu. J. Lake Sci. **16**(1), 56–60 (2004)
4. Oh, H., Ahn, C., Lee, J., Chon, T., Choi, K., et al.: Community patterning and identification of predominant factors in algal bloom in Daechung Reservoir (Korea) using artificial neural networks. Ecol. Model. **203**(1–2), 109–118 (2007)
5. Hu, Z., Pang, Y., Song, W., Shao, Y.: Application of grey system dynamic model group GM(1,1) in water quality prediction of qinghuai river. Sichuan Environ. **38**(1), 122–125 (2019)
6. Yi, Y., Tang, C., Zhang, S.: One-dimensional hydrodynamic simulation and water quality prediction of typical channel of the middle route of South-to-North water diversion project. Water Resour. Hydropower Eng. **50**(2), 14–20 (2019)
7. Khalil, B., Awadallah, A., Karaman, H.: Application of artificial neural networks for the prediction of water quality variables in the Nile Delta. J. Water Resour. Prot. **4**(6), 388–394 (2012)
8. Wang, J., Xiang, F., Qiu, F., Wang, H., Liu, H.: Research progress of water quality prediction model. Environ. Sci. Surv. **37**(4), 63–67 (2018)
9. Cui, D.: Application of extreme learning machine to total phosphorus and total nitrogen forecast in lakes and reservoirs. Water Resour. Prot. **29**(2), 61–66 (2013)
10. Krishna, B., Gnanasekaran, T.: Retinal vessel extraction framework using modified adaboost extreme learning machine. Comput., Mater. Continua **60**(3), 855–869 (2019)
11. Ahmed, A., Othman, F., Afan, H., Ibrahim, R., Elshafie, A., et al.: Machine learning methods for better water quality prediction. J. Hydrol. 578 (2019). https://doi.org/10.1016/j.jhydrol.2019.124084

12. Zhang, Q., Wang, X., Zhang, T., Yang, C., Lv, X.: Prediction of water quality index of Honghu Lake based on back proportion neural network model. Wetland Sci. **14**(2), 212–218 (2016)
13. Yu, J., Zheng, W., Xu, L., Zhang, L., Zhang, G., et al.: A PSO-XGBoost model for estimating daily reference evapotranspiration in the solar greenhouse. Intell. Autom. Soft Comput. **26**(5), 989–1003 (2020)
14. Ludbrook, J.: A primer for biomedical scientists on how to execute model II linear regression analysis. Clin. Exp. Pharmacol. Physiol. **39**(4), 329–335 (2012)
15. Sun, Y., Yuan, Y., Wang, Q., Sai, J., Wang, L., et al.: Impact damage identification for composite material based on transmissibility function and OS-ELM algorithm. J. Quantum Comput. **1**(1), 1–8 (2019)
16. Fan, C., Guo, Y., Cao, P., Yang, T.: Modeling of the grain yield prediction using extreme learning machine based on principal component analysis. Grain Proc. **42**(2), 1–5 (2017)
17. Alaviani, F., Sedghi, H., Asghari Moghaddam, A., Babazadeh, H.: Adopting GMS–PSO model to reduce groundwater withdrawal by integrated water resources management. Int. J. Environ. Res. **12**(5), 619–629 (2018). https://doi.org/10.1007/s41742-018-0115-x
18. Miao, J., Cheng, L., Lv, H.: Comprehensive charging demand of multi-type electric vehicles based on traffic information. Electr. Power Eng. Technol. **39**, 165–169 (2020)
19. Bay, H., Tuytelaars, T., Gool, L., Zurich, E.: Speeded-Up robust features. Comput. Vis. Image Underst. **110**(3), 404–417 (2008)
20. Wyner, A., Olson, M., Bleich, J., Mease, D.: Explaining the success of Adaboost and random forests as interpolating classifiers. J. Mach. Learn. Res. **18**, 1–33 (2015)
21. Wen, T., Yu, F.: Research on prediction of water inrush from coal seam floor based on PSO_SVM_AdaBoost. Appl. Res. Comput. **35**(12), 150–153+163 (2019)
22. Kumarasamy, M.: Deoxygenation and reaeration coupled hybrid mixing cells based pollutant transport model to assess water quality status of a river. Int. J. Environ. Res. **9**(1), 341–350 (2015)
23. Zhang, L., Nie, L., Bai, Q.: Rapid detection of piracetam content in piracetam injection with NIR spectroscopy. Chin. J. Pharm. Anal. **34**(8), 1465–1469 (2014)
24. Yu, T., Yang, S., Bai, Y., Gao, X.: Inlet water quality forecasting of wastewater treatment based on kernel principal component analysis and an extreme learning machine. Water **10**, 873 (2018)
25. Li, R., Liu, Y., Qiao, Y., Ma, T., Wang, B., et al.: Street-level landmarks acquisition based on svm classifiers. Comput., Mater. Continua **59**(2), 591–606 (2019)

Study on Identification of Multiple Pesticide Residues in Lettuce Leaves Based on Hyperspectral Technology

Sunli Cong[✉], Chen Liu, Zhi Zhu, and Aiyun Hu

Jiangsu Key Lab of IoT Application Technology, Wuxi Taihu University, Wuxi 214064, China

Abstract. With the long-term irrational use of pesticides, the resistance of diseases and insect pests to pesticides is increasing. The effect of relying solely on a single species of pesticide to control diseases and insect pests is no longer significant, which causes the phenomenon of mixed use of pesticides is becoming more and more common. To solve the problem that current nondestructive methods for detecting a single pesticide residue cannot meet simultaneous multiple pesticide residues, one method based on hyperspectral imaging technology for identifying multiple pesticide residues in lettuce leaves was investigated. In this paper, nondestructive and fast identification for multiple pesticide residues was performed from the angle of spectral analysis. Comprehensively considering the running time, the detection accuracy, the convergence iteration number and the particle number (N) of GSA algorithm, the support vector machine optimized by Gravitational search algorithm (GSA-SVM) model ($N = 40$) achieved the best performance, with the accuracies of 100% and 96.08% for training set and test set, respectively. The hyperspectral imaging technology combined with GSA-SVM model is feasible for identifying multiple pesticide residues in lettuce leaves, and so hopefully to provide a methodological basis for detecting multiple pesticide residues in other vegetables.

Keywords: Hyperspectra · Lettuce leaves · Multiple pesticide residues

1 Introduction

Vegetable planting area in China is large, and vegetables are various and account for over 40% of the proportion of dietary structure, which can provide the necessary vitamin and mineral for human body [1]. Vegetable growing time is short, and the vegetable growth is accompanied with many diseases and insect pests, which are often prevented by spraying pesticides. There are 150 to 160 kinds of pesticides commonly used in China, and most of these pesticides are toxic. Different kinds of pesticides show different toxicity and safety interval, and the phenomenon of misuse of pesticides or high toxic pesticides is also frequent because of the lack of common sense of pesticides. With the long-term irrational use of pesticides, the resistance of diseases and insect pests to pesticides is increasing. The effect of relying solely on a single species of pesticide to control diseases and insect pests is no longer significant, which causes that the phenomenon of mixed use

© Springer Nature Switzerland AG 2021
X. Sun et al. (Eds.): ICAIS 2021, CCIS 1424, pp. 537–550, 2021.
https://doi.org/10.1007/978-3-030-78621-2_45

of pesticides is becoming more and more common [2]. Hence, it is of great significance to explore the species of pesticide residues in vegetables.

Lettuce is one of the most popular leafy vegetables in China and is commonly known as leaf lettuce. Its stem and leaf contain vitamins, carotene and other nutrients, which can refresh heat, relieve pain, hypnosis and reduce cholesterol. Meanwhile, lettuce leaf can also be eaten raw and has the reputation of "slimming lettuce", so it is very popular with people [3, 4]. Traditional methods for detecting pesticide residues usually contain gas chromatography (GC) [5], high performance liquid chromatography (HPLC) [6], gas/liquid chromatography mass spectrometry (GC/LC-MS) [7, 8], immunoassay (IA) [9] and so on. These methods are destructive, complex for sample pretreatment, and are not suitable for on-site online detection. In recent years, spectral detection methods widely applied in pesticide residue detection (such as near infrared spectroscopy [10], Raman spectroscopy [11] and fluorescence spectroscopy [12]) although are no damage and no sample pretreatment, the point source sampling method restricts the comprehensiveness of the collected information, which is easy to result in the insufficient effect of pesticide residue detection; at the same time, the researches of this aspect are focused on the detection of a single species of pesticide residue in the sample, and the phenomenon of mixed use of pesticides in real life makes the nondestructive detection methods for a single species of pesticide residue difficult to meet the simultaneous detection of multiple pesticide residues. Therefore, it is particularly necessary to study a non-destructive and accurate method to identify multiple pesticide residues in lettuce leaves.

Hyperspectral imaging (HSI) technology is a fast developing nondestructive testing technology, which can obtain both spectral and image information of the sample simultaneously [13]. At present, the study on the quality detection of agricultural products by HSI technology has been relatively mature [14], but is still at development stage in the detection of pesticide residues. Xu et al. used ultraviolet light and halogen lamp as two kinds of light sources to discriminate the pesticide residues (fenvalerate and phoxim) on the surface of Hami melon by HSI technology, which achieve the accuracy of 100% with Bayesian model [15]. Zhao et al. used HSI technology to detect DuPont residue with different concentrations in Fragrant Pears and established MLR and PCR models, which show that the MLR model gets the correlation coefficient of 0.973 and root mean square error of 0.260 for calibration set [16]. The above researches present that HSI technology applied in the pesticide residues in agricultural products is feasible, but most of them are aimed at a single species of pesticide residue, and the researches on HSI technology used in multiple pesticide residues are rarely reported. In this paper, HSI technology was used to identify lettuce leaves with no pesticide residue, dimethoate residue, fenvalerate residue, Bacillus thuringiensis residue, dimethoate mixed with fenvalerate residue and fenvalerate mixed with Bacillus thuringiensis residue. And three algorithms of Artificial bee colony (ABC), Cuckoo search (CS) and Gravitational search algorithm (GSA) were given to compare the effect of SVM parameter optimization. This study provides a methodological basis for the detection of multiple pesticide residues in other vegetables, and also lays a foundation for the development of a detector for multiple pesticide residues in vegetables.

2 Materials and Methods

2.1 Sample Preparation

In the experiment, lettuce was cultivated in the Venlo greenhouse of Key Laboratory of Modern Agricultural Equipment and Technology, Jiangsu Province. The variety of lettuce was Italy's year-to-night pickled lettuce, which was experimented by perlite potted plant. During the growth period, daily and quantitative nutrient solution was guaranteed to irrigate. Until the lettuce grew to the rosette stage, pesticides were sprayed.

The pesticide varieties were dimethoate (40% of active component content, the dosage form of milk oil, Jiangsu Tenglong Bio Pharmaceutical Co., Ltd.), fenvalerate (20% of active component content, the dosage form of milk oil, Zhejiang Welda Chemical Co., Ltd.) and Bacillus thuringiensis (4000IU/μL of active component content, the dosage form of suspension agent, Bio pesticide factory of Ruicheng county, Shanxi province), respectively. Because Bacillus thuringiensis cannot be mixed with organophosphorus insecticides or fungicides of internal absorbability, the phenomenon of Bacillus thuringiensis mixed with dimethoate was not considered to study in the paper.

In the experiment, three kinds of pesticides were allocated to pesticide solutions mixed with clean water according to ratios of 1:1000, 1:1000 and 1:500, respectively. Furthermore, the dimethoate and fenvalerate 0.5 mL each were mixed fully, then 1000mL of clean water was poured in. The hybrid method of fenvalerate and Bacillus thuringiensis was also similar.

In order to identify that whether or not lettuce contains pesticide residues, a group of lettuce sprayed with clean water was selected to prepare reference group (group A). The remaining five groups (group B, C, D, E and F) of lettuce were respectively sprayed with five kinds of pesticide solutions, including dimethoate solution, fenvalerate solution, Bacillus thuringiensis solution, dimethoate mixed with fenvalerate solution and fenvalerate mixed with Bacillus thuringiensis solution. It is important to note that both sides of the lettuce leaf should be sprayed wet. Then, all the lettuce was placed in the cool and ventilated place for 48 h. After the new and old leaves were removed, 60 leaves with the same leaf position, little difference of leaf area and free of disease were picked from each group (a total of 360 leaves). After that, all lettuce leaves were put in plastic bags with numbered labels for seal storage, then sent to the laboratory for hyperspectral imaging acquisition immediately.

2.2 Hyperspectral Imaging Acquisition and Data Extraction

The hyperspectral image system [17] used is mainly composed of a hyperspectral camera (ImSpector, V10E, Finland), a group of 150W fiber halogen lamps (Fiber-Lite DC 950Illuminator, DolanJenner Industries Inc, MA, the United States), a precision electronic control translation table (Zolix, SC30021A, Beijing), a computer and so on, and the schematic diagram of system is shown in Fig. 1. Before the imaging acquisition, the system was fist preheated for half an hour. Then the exposure time of the camera was set to 50 ms and the speed of the conveying device set to 1.25 mm/s. It is known that the image resolution of the camera is 775 pixel $\times$ 1628 pixel, the spectral resolution is 2.9 nm, and the spectral range is 431$-$962 nm. In order to correct the phenomenon of image blur and distortion caused by dark current effect in camera, black and white calibration [18] was conducted for hyperspectral images. Finally, hyperspectral images of each sample at $431-962$ nm (618 wavelengths) were obtained.

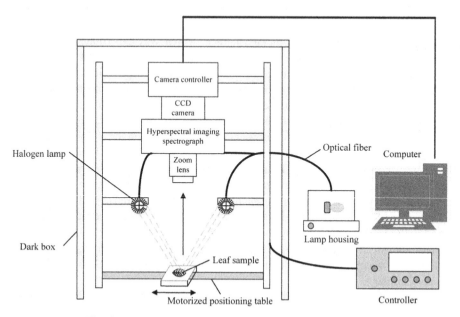

Fig. 1. The schematic diagram of hyperspectral image system

For reducing the influence of the inhomogeneity of chemical information in the sample on the modeling effect, the "rectangular area method" was adopted to uniformly select four 64×64 pixel regions as the region of interest (ROI) in the similar positions (avoid the main stem) of the leaf image. Then the reflectance spectra of four ROIs were extracted and the average spectra calculated as the original spectra of the sample. Ultimately, the original hyperspectral data of each sample at $431-962$ nm was acquired (a total of 360 spectra). Due to the noise and serious spectra overlapping existed in the range of $431-450$ nm and $897-962$ nm, the hyperspectral data of $451-896$ nm (a total of 518 wavelengths) were selected for the follow-up study. Figure 2 is the original spectral curves of all the samples.

2.3 Support Vector Machine Based on Gravitational Search Optimization

As a common qualitative modeling method, support vector machine (SVM) has been widely used in the research of pattern recognition and control [19]. In general, the radial basis kernel function (RBF) suitable for nonlinear sample data classification is often used as the kernel function of SVM. The two important parameters in RBF (penalty factor c and kernel parameter g) play a key role in the classification performance of SVM, so choosing a suitable intelligent algorithm is crucial to parameters' optimization [20].

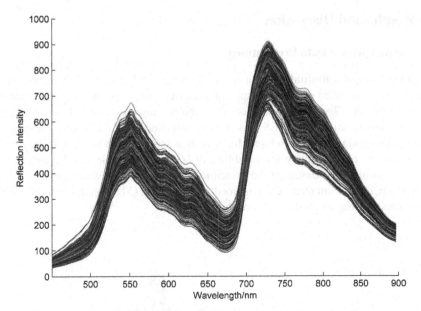

Fig. 2. The original spectral curves of all the samples

The gravitational search algorithm (GSA) [21] is a new intelligent optimization algorithm based on Newton's law of universal gravitation and the law of motion. In the GSA algorithm, each individual is a mass particle that operates in space and attracts each other through universal gravitation. The quality of particles depends on the mass of them. A large mass indicates that the particle has a low fitness value and is better. All particles in the space form a population, and gravity causes the particles of smaller masses to move toward larger masses of particles, prompting all particles to converge to the population of particles. In the study, the specific steps for optimizing parameters c and g in SVM using GSA algorithm are as follows.

1) The particle population size of N and the maximum iteration number of *max_it* in GSA are both initialized, where N also presents the number of randomly generated particle positions;

2) The search ranges of c and g (also the moving ranges of particles) are both set, and the position of each particle corresponds to a set of (c, g);

3) The number of cross-validation of training samples is set, and the optimal particle position is determined according to the fitness value of each particle;

4) The mass of each particle, the gravitational constant and the acceleration of each particle in each dimension are calculated in turn, and the position of the particle is continuously updated [22];

5) The optimal particle position is determined by returning to step 3, and the iteration is stopped until reaching *max_it*. The optimal particle position determined at the time corresponds to the selected best parameter (c, g);

6) The best parameter (c, g) is used to establish the SVM model to predict samples.

3   Results and Discussion

3.1   Hyperspectral Data Pretreatment

Singular Sample Elimination. During the hyperspectral imaging acquisition, some singular samples often exist in the spectral data due to factors such as the instrument environment, etc. To reduce the effect of singular samples on the effect of models, the descriptive statistics in SPSS was used to calculate the Z value of each sample's spectral data and import it into Excel for condition screening. In general, if the Z value of the sample cannot satisfy the condition of $|Z| \leq 2$, the sample will be judged as a singular sample [23]. Based on the principle, singular samples were eliminated from each group, and 52 samples were remained in each group (312 samples in total) finally. The corresponding spectral curves are shown in Fig. 3.

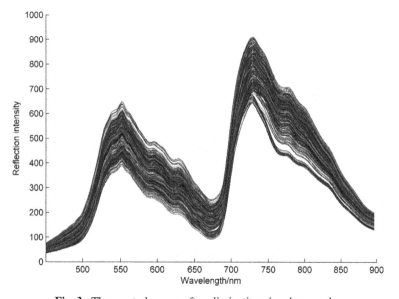

Fig. 3. The spectral curves after eliminating singular samples

As can be seen from Fig. 3, there are two prominent reflection peaks (at 552 nm and 728 nm) in the range of 451−780 nm, and the two peaks are in the green and red bands, respectively. In the blue band of 451 nm and the red band of 670 nm, there are two distinct absorption valleys because of the strong absorption of blue and red light by chlorophyll in the leaf. Therefore, the spectral curves of lettuce leaves extracted in the study was basically consistent with the law of spectral curves of green vegetation [24]. Figure 4 shows the average spectral curves of six groups of lettuce leaf samples. It is easy to find that the spectral curve differences of different groups are obvious, indicating that there is a certain degree of separability among six groups of samples in theory. It can also be observed that the reflection intensity of group A is higher than that of group B, C, D, E and F, indicating that the presence of pesticide residues in samples resulted in a decrease in reflectivity. In addition, the curve of group E is located between group B and C, and the curve of group F is located between group C and D, that is, the reflection intensity of samples containing mixed pesticide residues is between that of samples containing the two single pesticide residue. It further proves the correlation between the reflectance of leaf samples and the varieties of pesticide residues, which is enough to lay a theoretical foundation for the establishment of identification models for pesticide residues.

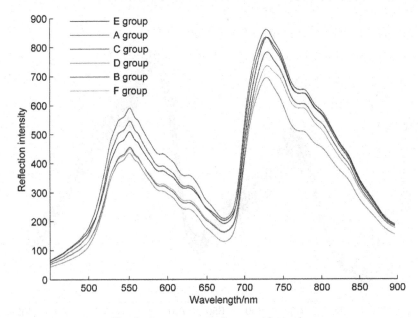

Fig. 4. Average spectral curves of samples

Note: A, B, C, D, E and F represent lettuce leaf samples containing no pesticide residue, dimethoate residue, fenvalerate residue, Bacillus thuringiensis residue, dimethoate mixed with fenvalerate residue and fenvalerate mixed with Bacillus thuringiensis residue, respectively.

SNV Pretreatment. To reduce the influence of factors unrelated to the sample properties generated during hyperspectral imaging acquisition on the effect of models, the standard normalized variable (SNV) algorithm was used to pretreat the spectral data after eliminating singular samples, and the spectral curves after SNV pretreatment is shown in Fig. 5. The difference among the spectral curves after SNV pretreatment was greatly reduced, indicating that the SNV achieved spectral correction caused by solid particle size, surface scattering and optical path change.

3.2 Characteristic Wavelength Selection

In the study, the successive projection algorithm (SPA) was used to select characteristic wavelengths based on the preprocessed spectral data. In the algorithm, the number of final selected wavelengths was set from 3 to 20. And the number of wavelengths was determined based on the root mean square error (*RMSE*) at different wavelength numbers. The characteristic wavelengths produced by 10 times running were compared, and the optimal wavelength combination was determined based on the principle of relatively low *RMSE* and fewer wavelengths. The optimal wavelengths selected is shown in Fig. 6. The circles represent the 15 characteristic wavelengths of 451, 492, 504, 505, 507, 514, 630, 666, 686, 692, 715, 722, 733, 744 and 811nm, respectively.

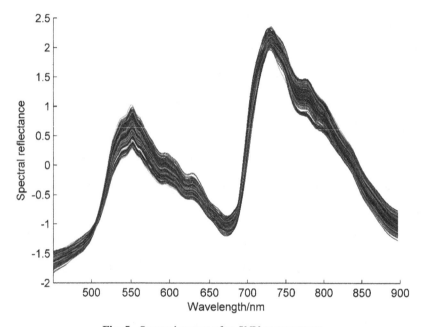

Fig. 5. Spectral curves after SNV pretreatment

3.3   Qualitative Model Establishment

Sample Set Division. There were five groups of leaf samples containing multiple pesticide residues and one group of leaf samples without pesticide residue in the study. For sample set division, 35 samples were randomly selected from each group of samples as the training set (210 samples in total), and the remaining samples were used as the test set (102 samples in total). Then the six groups (group A, B, C, D, E and F) were labeled as 1, 2, 3, 4, 5, and 6 in sequential order. And the full spectral data after pretreatment (namely spectral data under 518 wavelengths) and SPA spectral data (namely spectral data under 15 characteristic wavelengths) were respectively applied to establish SVM models, which enabled identification of multiple pesticide residues in lettuce leaf samples. Since randomly sampling would result in different sample sets for each division, multiple fittings were used to select the best results for comparative analysis of SVM models.

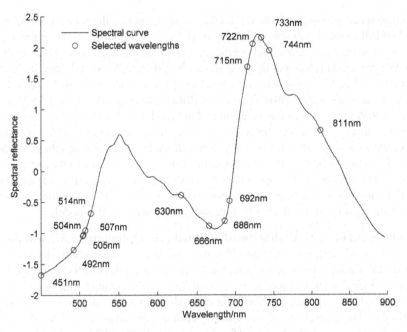

Fig. 6. Optimal wavelength combination by SPA

SVM Model Establishment. The full spectral data and SPA spectral data were respectively used as the input variables and the label of samples as the output variable of SVM models. Besides, RBF was selected as the kernel function of SVM, and parameters c and g were the default values of 1 and 0.1. Finally, the identification model with a better performance was determined according to the indicators (running time and identification accuracy of training set and test set) of SVM models. Table 1 shows the identification results of SVM models based on full spectral data and SPA spectral data.

Table 1. Identification results of SVM models based on full spectral data and SPA spectral data

Data	Wavelength number	Running time/s	Accuracy/%	
			Training set	Test set
Full spectral data	518	0.60	100 (210/210)	83.33 (85/102)
SPA spectral data	15	0.18	98.57 (207/210)	87.25 (89/102)

As shown in Table 1, the running time of SVM model based on SPA spectral data was less than that based on full spectral data, which was because the wavelength number used in the model was significantly reduced after SPA selection, further improving the operating speed of model. From the identification accuracy, the training set accuracy based on full spectral data was higher (up to 100%), but the identification effect on test set was not ideal due to the model overfitting. Although the training set accuracy based on SPA spectral data was not as good as that based on full spectral data, the test set accuracy reached 87.25% so that the test set samples were identified well. Considering the above factors comprehensively, it is not difficult to conclude that the SVM model based on SPA spectral data was better than that based on full spectral data. In addition, as seen from Fig. 6 that the characteristic wavelengths selected by SPA were mostly concentrated near the absorption valleys and reflection peaks of spectral curves. Most of the wavelengths in the range were significantly related to the varieties of pesticide residues. The reason for the superiority of the SVM model based on SPA spectral data was that more redundant wavelengths not related to the varieties of pesticide residues were eliminated by SPA, effectively improved the accuracy of the model.

Establishment of SVM Models Based on Intelligent Optimization Algorithms. In the study, ABC [25], CS [26] and GSA were selected respectively to determine the optimal SVM parameters c and g, which was then used to establish SVM models based on SPA spectral data. Comprehensively considering the running time, identification accuracy and convergence iterations, the optimal optimization algorithm of SVM was determined. Therefore, to more conveniently compare and analyze the three algorithms, the 10-fold cross-validation was used for three models (ABC-SVM, CS-SVM and GSA-SVM), and the other parameters in ABC, CS and GSA were set as follows: the colony size (SN) of ABC, the nest size (n) of CS and the particle number (N) of GSA were all set to 20; the maximum number of iterations ($MaxCycles$, N and max_it) of three algorithms were all 100; the search ranges for parameters c and g were all from 0.01 to 100. Table 2 shows the identification results of SVM models based on three optimization algorithms.

Table 2. Identification results of SVM models under three optimization algorithms

Models	Running time/s	c	g	Accuracy/%	
				Training set	Test set
ABC-SVM	27.53	91.1864	1.2984	100 (210/210)	89.22 (91/102)
CS-SVM	23.88	15.9424	2.5838	99.05 (208/210)	92.16 (94/102)
GSA-SVM	13.79	51.4909	0.9119	99.52 (209/210)	93.14 (95/102)

Comparing Table 1 and Table 2, the running time of three SVM models based on optimization algorithms was all higher than that of SVM models without optimization, which was because the optimization needed additional time. Meanwhile, among ABC-SVM, CS-SVM and GSA-SVM models, the GSA-SVM model took the shortest time

(13.79s) for running. From the identification accuracy, the accuracy of SVM models after optimization were all improved. The test set accuracy of three models were all above 89%, and the test set accuracy of GSA-SVM model was the highest (93.14%). At this point, the optimal parameters c and g optimized by GSA were 51.4909 and 0.9119, respectively. Figure 7 is an iterative graph of three optimization algorithms for SVM models.

From Fig. 7, it can be observed that three algorithms had an upward trend of the optimal fitness value (also the cross-validation accuracy) before 13th iteration. After that, the value of optimal fitness remained constant, and algorithms reached the convergence state. Among all the models, the GSA-SVM model converged when it reached the fourth time, which was faster than the other two models and the optimal fitness value higher. Considering the running time, identification accuracy and convergence iterations, GSA-SVM model had more obvious advantages than the other two models, which also validated the relevant research conclusion [27] that the GSA algorithm makes the established model have good generalization and identification capabilities.

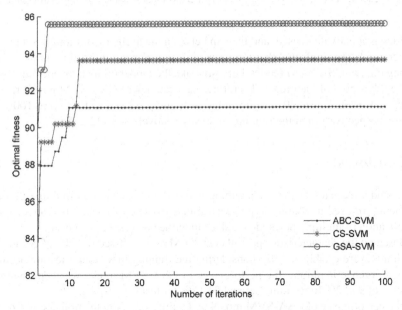

Fig. 7. Iteration figure of three optimization algorithms

Since the size of particle number (N) in GSA would affect the identification performance of SVM models, the particle number was increased from 20 to 80 (in steps of 10) to study the accuracy and running time of SVM models under different particle numbers in the study. The other parameters in GSA remained unchanged, and Fig. 8 shows the identification results of GSA-SVM models under different particle numbers (N).

As can be seen from Fig. 8, the running time of GSA-SVM model was also increasing, and the training set accuracy was basically stable at over 95%. When N was less than 40, the test set accuracy gradually increased; when greater than 40, the test set

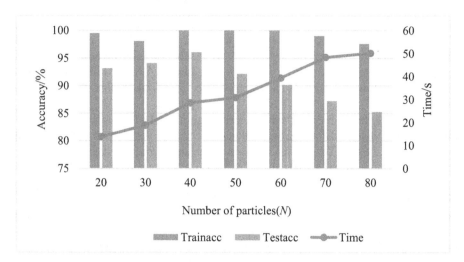

Fig. 8. Trend chart of accuracy and time of GSA-SVM models under different particle numbers

accuracy gradually decreased, and the gap between the accuracy of training set and test set increased. This indicated that too large of N would not only lead to an increase of running time of GSA-SVM model, but also make the model prone to overfitting, reducing the robustness of the model. Therefore, the accuracy of GSA-SVM model reached the highest when N was 40. The accuracy of training set and test set were 100% and 96.08%, respectively, and the running time was relatively short (28.55 s).

4   Conclusion

In the study, the lettuce leaves containing no pesticide residue and multiple pesticide residues were used to acquire hyperspectral images. The nondestructive and accurate identification of multiple pesticide residues in lettuce leaves was achieved.

Based on the characteristic spectral data, SVM models based on ABC, CS and GSA algorithms were established. By considering the running time, identification accuracy and convergence iterations, the performance of GSA-SVM model was better with the accuracy of 99.52% for training set and 93.14% for test set, respectively;

The performance of GSA-SVM model under different particle numbers (N) in GSA was studied, which showed that when N took 40, the accuracy of training set and test set were respectively 100% and 96.08%, and the running time was short (28.55s).

Therefore, the use of hyperspectral technology for identifying multiple pesticide residues in lettuce leaves is feasible, providing a methodological basis for the detection of multiple pesticide residues in other vegetables, and laying a foundation for the development of a detector for multiple pesticide residues in vegetables.

Funding Statement. The paper was supported by Wuxi City Soft Science Project (201913571004Z) and Industry-University Cooperation Collaborative Education Project of the Ministry of Education (201902167006).

Conflicts of Interest. The authors declare that they have no conflicts of interest to report regarding the present study.

References

1. Loha, K.M., Lamoree, M., de Boer, J.: Pesticide residue levels in vegetables and surface waters at the Central Rift Valley (CRV) of Ethiopia. Environ. Monit. Assess. **192**(8), 1–14 (2020). https://doi.org/10.1007/s10661-020-08452-6
2. Zhou, D., Zhang, D., Zhang, J., Liu, Y., Li, L., et al.: Cell-mediated immunotoxicity and mechanisms of mixed pesticides of organophosphate and pyrethroid to mice. J. Environ. Health **32**(9), 787–791 (2015)
3. Slavin, J., Lloyd, B.: Health benefits of fruits and vegetables. Adv. Nutr. **3**(4), 506–516 (2012)
4. Colonna, E., Rouphael, Y., Barbieri, G., De Pascale, S.: Nutritional quality of ten leafy vegetables harvested at two light intensities. Food Chem. **199**, 702–710 (2016)
5. Hakme, E., Lozano, A., Uclés, S., Gomez-Ramos, M., Fernández-Alba, A.: High-throughput gas chromatography-mass spectrometry analysis of pesticide residues in spices by using the enhanced matrix removal-lipid and the sample dilution approach. J. Chromatogr. A **1573**, 28–41 (2018)
6. Velkoska-Markovska, L., Petanovska-Ilievska, B., Markovski, A.: Application of high performance liquid chromatography to the analysis of pesticide residues in apple juice. Contemp. Agric. **67**(1), 93–102 (2018)
7. Hadiana, Z., Eslamizadb, S., Yazdanpanahb, H.: Pesticide residues analysis in iranian fruits and vegetables by gas chromatography-mass spectrometry. Iran. J. Pharm. Res. **18**(1), 275–285 (2019)
8. Turnipseed, S., Storey, J., Wu, I., Andersen, W., Madson, M.: Extended liquid chromatography high resolution mass spectrometry screening method for veterinary drug, pesticide and human pharmaceutical residues in aquaculture fish. Food Addit. Contam. **36**(10), 1501–1514 (2019)
9. Malarkodi, C., Rajeshkumar, S., Annadurai, G.: Detection of environmentally hazardous pesticide in fruit and vegetable samples using gold nanoparticles. Food Comtrol **80**, 11–18 (2017)
10. Yazici, A., Tiryaki, G., Ayvaz, H.: Determination of pesticide residual levels in strawberry (Fragaria) by near-infrared spectroscopy. J. Sci. Food Agric. **100**(5), 1980–1989 (2020)
11. Alsammarraie, F., Lin, M.: Using standing gold nanorod arrays as surface-enhanced raman spectroscopy (SERS) substrates for detection of carbaryl residues in fruit juice and milk. J. Agric. Food Chem. **65**, 666–674 (2017)
12. Zhou, X., Sun, J., Zhang, B., Wu, J.: Classification of different kinds of pesticide residues on lettuce based on fluorescence spectra and WT–BCC–SVM algorithm. Mod. Phys. Lett. B 31, 1740082–1–6 (2017)
13. Song, H., Yang, W., Yuan, H., Bufford, H.: Deep 3d-multiscale densenet for hyperspectral image classification based on spatial-spectral information. Intell. Autom. Soft Comput. **26**(6), 1441–1458 (2020)
14. Fu, P., Xu, Q., Zhang, J., Geng, L.: A noise-resistant superpixel segmentation algorithm for hyperspectral images". Comput., Mater. Continua **59**(2), 509–515 (2019)
15. Xu, J., Yang, J., Sun, J., Ye, J., Jiang, W., et al.: Discriminant analysis of pesticide residues on Hami melon surface based on hyperspectral technology. Jiangsu Agricultural Sciences **44**(12), 338–340 (2016)
16. Zhao, M., Li, B., Zhou, Y., Hou, B., Zhang, D.: Detection of low concentration pesticide residue on pears by hyperspectral image technology. Opt. Technol. **42**(5), 408–412 (2016)

17. Gabriele, C., Nicoletta, P., Loredana, P., Marcello, C.: Characterization of fine metal particles derived from shredded WEEE using a hyperspectral image system: preliminary results. Sensors **17**(5), 1117 (2017)
18. Isaza, C., Mosquera, J., Gómez-Méndez, G., Paz, J., Sandoval, O.: Development of an acousto-optic system for hyperspectral image segmentation. Metrol. Meas. Syst. **26**(3), 517–530 (2019)
19. Cong, S., Sun, J., Mao, H., Wu, X., Wang, P., et al.: Non-destructive detection for mold colonies in rice based on hyperspectra and GWO-SVR. J. Sci. Food Agric. **98**, 29–35 (2017)
20. Mazumder, A., Chatterjee, S., Chatterjee, S., Gonzalez, J., Bag, S., et al.: Spectropathology-corroborated multimodal quantitative imaging biomarkers for neuroretinal degeneration in diabetic retinopathy. Clin. Ophthalmol. **11**, 2073–2089 (2017)
21. Gang, J., Wang, J., Yang, G., Liu, H., Yang, L.: Gravitational search algorithm-least squares support vector machine model forecasting on hourly urban water demand. Control Theory Appl. **31**, 1377–1382 (2016)
22. Wang, H., Fan, Z., Xu, X., Li, X.: Prediction model of steam turbine exhaust based on grey correlation analysis method and GSA-LSSVM. Electr. Power Const. **37**(11), 115–122 (2016)
23. Steinley, D.: Categorical data analysis with SAS and SPSS applications, categorical data analysis using the SAS system. J. Am. Stat. Assoc. **101**(473), 400 (2006)
24. Sun, L., Chen, L.: Analysis of spectral response of vegetation leaf biochemical component. Spectrosc. Spectral Anal. **30**(11), 3031–3035 (2010)
25. Kharis, S., Hadi, I., Hasanah, K.: Multiclass Classification of Brain Cancer with Multiple Multiclass Artificial Bee Colony Feature Selection and Support Vector Machine. J. Phys: Conf. Ser. **1417**(1), 012015 (2019)
26. Karoum, B., Benani, Y.: Discrete cuckoo search algorithm for solving the cell formation problem. Int. J. Manuf. Res. **14**(3), 1 (2019)
27. Zhang, W., Niu, P., Li, G., Li, P.: Forecasting of turbine heat rate with online least squares support vector machine based on gravitational search algorithm. Knowl.-Based Syst. **39**, 34–44 (2013)

Robust JPEG Image Steganography Based on SVD and QIM in Stationary Wavelet Domain

Zhiguo Wang[1][(✉)], Zhiyuan Li[2], Xiaofeng Song[1], and Yi Zhang[3]

[1] National University of Defense Technology, Xi'an 710106, China
[2] Geely University, Chengdu 641423, China
[3] Special Police College, Beijing 102211, China

Abstract. Robust image steganography technology is important for covert communication under lossy network environment where the images are often compressed. To resist the lossy image compression, the robust embedding domain should be constructed firstly and then the secret messages are embedded by special steganography code. In this paper, by taking the advantages of stationary wavelet transform, SVD and QIM, a robust JPEG image steganography algorithm is proposed based on SVD and QIM in stationary wavelet domain. First, the framework of the proposed robust JPEG steganography algorithm is given. Then, the embedding distortion of cover element is defined. Finally, the message embedding and extraction procedure are described in the details. The experimental results show that the proposed robust steganography algorithm has competitive robustness and detection resistance.

Keywords: JPEG · Steganography · Robustness · Wavelet · QIM · SVD

1 Introduction

Digital steganography is a kind of covert communication technology in which secret messages are hidden in public digital carriers and transmitted through open channels [1]. For the behavior of covert communication is concealed, steganography is very deceptive and often used for the important message transmission in unsafe public network channel. Due to the extensive use of digital images, image is one of the most widely used carrier. Researchers have proposed many image steganography algorithms with high anti-detection ability [2, 3], which greatly improves the security of covert communication. In recent years, WeChat, microblog and other social media are rising rapidly. These social platforms transmit and share a large amount of image data every day, which provides a huge amount of cover images for covert communication by image steganography, which greatly increases the difficulty of communication behavior detection. However, in order to save bandwidth and processing costs, and speed up image loading speed, most social network channels will compress and scale image data, which makes the current image steganography algorithm for lossless processing difficult to apply. The design of image steganography algorithm with lossy processing resistance and anti-detection ability has become the research hotspot in the field of information hiding.

© Springer Nature Switzerland AG 2021
X. Sun et al. (Eds.): ICAIS 2021, CCIS 1424, pp. 551–560, 2021.
https://doi.org/10.1007/978-3-030-78621-2_46

Image steganography for lossy network channel requires steganography to be robust to lossy processing such as compression, cutting, scaling and so on, and at the same time, the anti-detection ability should be considered. Compared with adaptive steganography with high anti-detection ability, robust steganography has attracted less attention in the previous years. However, in the recent years, a series of robust image steganography algorithms have been proposed. In [4], a robust JPEG steganography algorithm is proposed based on DCT coefficient correlation. In [5], a robust image steganography algorithm is proposed based on dither modulation. In [6], a robust image steganography algorithm is proposed based on texture synthesis. In [7], Zhao et al. proposed a robust and adaptive JPEG image steganography algorithm based on transmission channel matching. In [8], Tao et al. proposed a robust JPEG steganography by generating the 'intermediate image' that is just the stego image after JPEG compression with special quality factor. In [9], Yu et al. proposed a robust image steganography algorithm based on generalized dither modulation and embedding domain expansion. In [10], Zhang et al. proposed an adaptive steganography algorithm with multiple robustness enhancements, which uses the difference of inter-block DCT coefficients to embed the secret messages. Although these algorithms can improve the extraction accuracy of the embedded secret messages to a certain extent. However, they are generally weak against detection, and how to improve the detection resistance of image robust steganography needs to be studied.

The wavelet transform has good time-frequency analysis characteristics and has a wide range of applications in image analysis, information hiding and other fields. In image steganography, wavelet transform is widely used, for example, in the design of adaptive steganography algorithms J-UNIWARD [2], the embedding distortion is defined according to the ratio between the amount of change of image wavelet coefficients and the image wavelet coefficients, which can limit the embedding change to the complex texture area of the image, and achieve good anti-detection ability. In terms of robust image watermarking, wavelet domain watermarking algorithm is usually more robust than spatial domain watermarking algorithm [11]. At the same time, the singular value of image has good characteristics in describing the distribution characteristics of image pixel matrix, which can better represent the important basic structure of image data. The singular value of image pixel matrix represents the relationship between pixels rather than visual features [12]. The change of singular value will not cause large image distortion. Moreover, the singular value of the matrix has good stability, and will not fluctuate with the disturbance of the matrix. Therefore, it has been widely used in robust image watermarking.

Considering the characteristics of image wavelet transform and SVD, the robust embedding domain is constructed by using SVD in image wavelet domain. Because the discrete orthogonal wavelet transform will be sampled after image filtering, and it does not have translation invariance. Here, the image is decomposed by using the translation invariant stationary wavelet transform. The size of the low frequency and high frequency subband is the same as the original image after the stationary wavelet transform. Because the lossy network channel is mainly used to change the high frequency information of the image when compressing the image, the low frequency subband after the image stationary wavelet transform is used to embed the message.

The procedure of the proposed robust JPEG steganography algorithm can be described briefly as follows. First, the image is transformed by stationary wavelet transform to get a low frequency subband and three high-frequency subbands. Since the lossy processing has a great influence on the high frequency subband, the low-frequency subband is divided into non overlapping 8×8 blocks, and the corresponding singular values are obtained by performing SVD for each block. Then, taking advantage of the good stability of the maximum singular value, the corresponding message embedding and extraction method are proposed. Second, the embedding distortion function is defined according to the texture complexity of blocks, and the secret message embedding is realized by STCs coding [13] and the stego elements are got. Finally, the QIM(quantization index modulation) method is used to embed the stego elements to obtain the final stego image.

2 Proposed Robust JPEG Steganography Algorithm

2.1 Overall Framework

The framework of the proposed robust JPEG steganography algorithm is shown in Fig. 1. According to Fig. 1, it can be seen that the proposed algorithm includes robust message embedding procedure and the corresponding message extraction procedure.

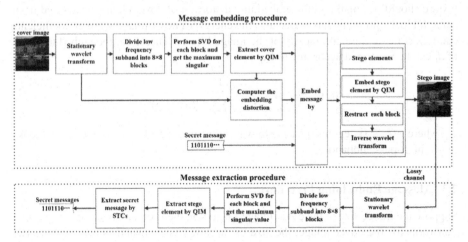

Fig. 1. Framework of the proposed steganography algorithm.

For secret message embedding, first, one-level stationary wavelet transform is performed for the cover image and the low-pass subband is used for embedding domain construction, and then the low-pass subband is divided into 8×8 blocks and the maximum singular value of each block is generated; secondly, the cover elements are extracted by performing QIM for the maximum singular values and the embedding distortion of each cover element is measured according to the embedding changes and texture complexity of block; thirdly, the secret messages are embedded by STCs and the correspond stego elements are obtained; finally, the stego elements are embedded by performing QIM for the maximum singular values of the 8 × 8 blocks, and then each block is reconstructed using the modified maximum singular values and the inverse stationary wavelet transform is performed to get the stego image.

For secret message extraction, firstly, the one-level stationary wavelet transform is also performed for the received stego image and the low-pass subband is divided into 8 × 8 blocks; secondly, the maximum singular values of all blocks are generated and the stego elements are extracted by performing QIM for the maximum singular values; finally, the secret messages are extracted by STCs.

According to the above descriptions, it can be seen that the definition of the embedding distortion function, the message embedding method and the message extraction method are crucial for the proposed robust image steganography algorithms. Therefore, they are introduced in details as follows.

2.2 Embedding Distortion Function

According to the framework shown in Fig. 1, it can be seen that one cover element can be extracted from one 8 × 8 block. And the embedding distortion of the cover element should be related with the anti-detection ability of stego image. As we know, the embedding changes occur in the complex texture region are difficult to be detected. Therefore, the embedding distortion of cover element extracted from the 8 × 8 block with complex texture should be small and the embedding distortion of cover element extracted from smooth block should be large. Because the energy value of image wavelet coefficients can reflect the texture complexity of the image blocks. Therefore, the embedding cost of d_i can be is defined according to Eq. (1),

$$d_k = \frac{1}{\sum_{l=1}^{3} \sum_{i=1}^{8} \sum_{j=1}^{8} |f_l(k, i, j)|} \tag{1}$$

where $f_l(k, i, j)$ denotes the (i, j)-th wavelet coefficient of the corresponding blocks in l-th high-pass subband.

2.3 Message Embedding Procedure

Suppose the image size of the cover image I is $m \times n$, therefore, after stationary wavelet transform for the cover image, the size of the low-pass subband is also $m \times n$. The detailed message embedding procedure can be described as follows:

(1) The stationary wavelet transform is performed for the cover image I and the low-pass subband L is got.
(2) The low-pass subband L is divided into 8 × 8 blocks $B_{i,j}$, $1 \le k \le u_B$, $1 \le l \le v_B$, $u_B = \lfloor m/8 \rfloor$, $v_B = \lfloor n/8 \rfloor$, $\lfloor \bullet \rfloor$ indicates the floor integer of $\bullet$.
(3) SVD is performed for each block $B_{i,j}$ and the corresponding maximum singular value set $S = \{s_i | 1 \le i \le u_B \times v_B\}$ are obtained.

(4) Suppose the secrete message sequence $\mathbf{m} = \{m_i | 1 \leq i \leq u_B \times v_B\}$, the quantization step is T, then the cover element set $\mathbf{X} = \{x_i | 1 \leq i \leq u_B \times v_B\}$ can be extracted according to Eq. (2),

$$x_i = mod(\lfloor s_i/T \rfloor, 2) \tag{2}$$

(5) The embedding distortion of each cover element x_i is computed according to Eq. (1).

(6) The secrete message sequence $\mathbf{m}$ is embedded using STCs and the corresponding stego element set $\mathbf{Y} = \{y_i | 1 \leq i \leq u_B \times v_B\}$ can be obtained.

(7) Each stego element y_i is embedded by perform QIM for maximum singular value s_i according to the Eq. (3),

$$s_i' = \begin{cases} \left(\lfloor \frac{s_i}{T} \rfloor + \frac{3}{2}\right) \times T, & if \ mod\left((\lfloor \frac{s_i}{T} \rfloor + y_i), 2\right) = 1 \\ \left(\lfloor \frac{s_i}{T} \rfloor + \frac{1}{2}\right) \times T, & else \qquad \quad otherwise \end{cases} \tag{3}$$

(8) Each block is reconstructed by performing inverse SVD based on the maximum singular value s_i'.

(9) Inverse stationary wavelet transform is performed based on the modified low-pass and the original three high-pass subbands, and then the stego image is generated.

2.4 Message Extracting

The receiver can get the stego image which may be applied the lossy operation by the public network channel. To extract the embedding secret messages, the following steps should be performed.

(1) Stationary wavelet transform is performed for the stego image and the low-pass subband is obtained.

(2) The low-pass subband is divided into 8×8 blocks and the SVD is performed for each block.

(3) According to Eq. (4), the stego elements are extracted by performing the QIM for all the maximum singular values extracted from the 8×8 blocks.

$$y_i' = mod(\lfloor s_i'/T \rfloor, 2) \tag{4}$$

where s_i' denotes the maximum singular value of i-th 8×8 block of the received stego image, and y_i' denotes the corresponding stego element.

(4) The secret messages are extracted by performing STCs for the extracted steg elements.

3 Experimental Results and Analysis

In the experiments, the robustness against JPEG compression attack and the anti-detection ability of the proposed steganography algorithm are compared with the other robust JPEG steganography algorithms. For the robustness and anti-detection experiments, the 10000 Gy-scale images from BOSSbase1.01 [14] are used as sample images. The size of sample images is 512×512 and all the sample images with PGM format are converted to JPEG image with quality factor(QF) 85. The parameter of RS code is (31, 19).

3.1 Robustness Experiment

As we know, the complex image has strong resistance to the detection. Therefore, we should select some images with complex texture for messages embedding. Here, one-level wavelet transform is performed for the image and the energy of wavelet coefficients of the three high-pass subbands is used to measure the complexity of the image.

To evaluate the robustness against JPEG compression attack of the proposed steganography algorithm, the most complex 2000 images from BOSSbase1.01 are used to generate the stego images. The robust steganography algorithms used for comparison are UEDR-P [8], MREAS-P_S [10] and MREAS-P_J [10] and. For the proposed steganography algorithm, the number of cover elements is 4096 because the image size is 512×512 and DCT block size is 8×8. Therefore, the length of the embedded message bits cannot exceed 4096. The payload is set to 0.001, 0.002, 0.003, 0.004, 0.005 bpnzAC ((bit per non-zero AC DCT coefficient) respectively.

After the stego images are generated, the JPEG recompression attack is applied to the steg images. The QF of JPEG recompression is 65, 75, 85 and 95 respectively. The parameter T in Eq. (2), (3) and (4) is set according to requirement for extraction error rate. In other words, the low extraction error rate means large T. For UEDR-P, the assumed QF of JPEG compression attack is 85. The other parameters of the robust steganography algorithms used for comparison are all set as the default values. The average extraction error rates of the compressed stego images are shown in Table 1.

According to the average extraction error rates shown in Table 1, the proposed robust and adaptive JPEG steganography algorithm has achieved the competitive robustness.

As shown in Table 1, for MREAS-P_J, the average extraction error rates are low when the QFs of JPEG compression attack are 85 and 95. However, the extraction error rates become very high when the QF of JPEG compression attack is 65 which means strong attack. For UEDR-P, the average extraction error rate is 0 only when the QF of JPEG compression is same to the assumed QF, and the extraction error rates are very high when the QFs are different with the assumed QF.

In Table 2, the average extraction error rates are given for all the 10000 images in BOSSbase1.01. According to the experimental results in Table 1, it can be seen that the extraction error rates decrease in contrast to the 2000 complex images. This is because that the JPEG compression has larger impact for complex images than for simple images. However, we should notice that the detect resistance of the simple images is often weak.

3.2 Detection Resistance Experiment

The detection resistance is important for robust image steganography. Although the UEDR-P has the strongest an-detection ability, it is robust only when the QF of JPEG

Table 1. Average extraction error rates of three robust steganography algorithms for the 2000 complex images in BOSSbase1.01. ($\times 10^{-3}$)

QF	Algorithm	Payload (bpnzAC)				
		0.001	0.002	0.003	0.004	0.005
65	Proposed	**0.25**	**0.26**	**0.41**	**0.75**	**0.93**
	MREAS-P_S	248	249	251	253	255
	MREAS-P_J	245	248	247	250	249
	UEDR-P	499	500	500	500	500
75	Proposed	**0.74**	**0.77**	**0.89**	**1.45**	**1.30**
	MREAS-P_S	12.3	12.5	13.1	13.3	13.0
	MREAS-P_J	0.92	1.00	1.20	1.50	1.50
	UEDR-P	500	499	499	499	500
85	Proposed	0.09	0.09	0.22	0.35	0.63
	MREAS-P_S	0.88	1.00	1.10	1.30	1.30
	MREAS-P_J	0.13	0.12	0.28	0.36	**0.44**
	UEDR-P	**0**	**0**	**0**	**0**	**0**
95	Proposed	**0.09**	**0.09**	**0.15**	**0.32**	**0.45**
	MREAS-P_S	0.60	0.56	0.75	0.91	0.88
	MREAS-P_J	0.13	0.12	0.25	0.42	0.47
	UEDR-P	499	500	500	499	499

compression attack is known. Therefore, the proposed steganography algorithm is compared with MREAS-P_s and MREAS-P_J using CC-PEV [15] and DCTR [16] which are the typical steganalysis features.

First, the most complex 2000 images from BOSSbase1.01 are used to generate stego images. The payloads are from 0.001 to 0.005 bpnzAC. The ensemble classifier [17] is trained by the steganalysis feature and used as the final detector. The ratio of training and test images is 0.5:0.5. The detection accuracy is quantified using the minimal total error probability under equal priors $P_E = min_{P_{FA}}(P_{FA} + P_{MD})/2$, where P_{FA} denotes the false-alarm probabilities and P_{MD} denotes the missed-detection probabilities. The value of $\overline{P}_E$ is averaged over ten random image database splits.

In Fig. 2, the detection error rate $\overline{P}_E$ of two steganalysis features are respectively shown for the three robust steganography algorithms when the stego images are generated by 2000 complex images from BOSSbase1.01. According to the detection performances, it can be seen that the proposed steganography has stronger detection resistance than MREAS-P_S and MREAS-P_J. This is because that the robust embedding domain is constructed in the low-frequency subband and the image high-frequency features such as texture, edge have been preserved. Therefore, the stego image has stronger detection resistance. In addition, we should notice that the high-dimensional feature DCTR has better detection performances.

Table 2. Average extraction error rates of three robust steganography algorithms for all images in BOSSbase1.01. ($\times 10^{-3}$)

QF	Algorithm	Payload (bpnzAC)				
		0.001	0.002	0.003	0.004	0.005
65	Proposed	**0.18**	**0.16**	**0.23**	**0.29**	**0.32**
	MREAS-P_S	185	186	186	187	188
	MREAS-P_J	180	180	181	181	181
	UEDR-P	500	500	499	500	500
75	Proposed	**0.28**	**0.30**	**0.32**	**0.37**	**0.39**
	MREAS-P_S	8.5	9.0	9.1	8.9	8.6
	MREAS-P_J	0.48	0.49	0.49	0.56	0.55
	UEDR-P	500	499	499	500	500
85	Proposed	0.04	0.04	0.07	0.10	0.16
	MREAS-P_S	0.40	0.38	0.37	0.42	0.37
	MREAS-P_J	0.05	0.06	0.10	0.12	**0.11**
	UEDR-P	**0**	**0**	**0**	**0**	**0**
95	Proposed	**0.03**	**0.05**	**0.05**	**0.06**	**0.10**
	MREAS-P_S	0.29	0.25	0.26	0.30	0.27
	MREAS-P_J	0.06	0.06	0.07	0.11	0.10
	UEDR-P	499	500	500	499	500

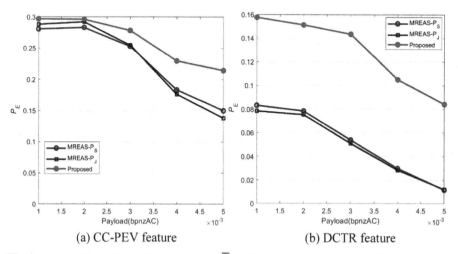

(a) CC-PEV feature   (b) DCTR feature

Fig. 2. Comparisons of detection error rates $\overline{P}_E$ of two steganalysis features for stego image generated from 2000 complex images in BOSSbase1.01.

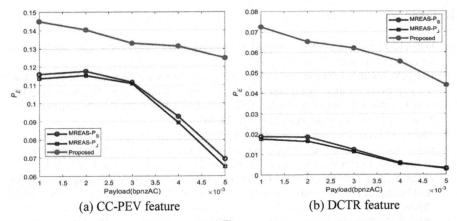

(a) CC-PEV feature   (b) DCTR feature

Fig. 3. Comparisons of detection error rates $\overline{P}_E$ of two steganalysis features for stego image generated from all the 10000 images in BOSSbase1.01.

In Fig. 3, the detected cover and stego images are all the 10000 images from BOSS-base1.01. Compared with the detection error rate $\overline{P}_E$ in Fig. 3, the detection error rates in Fig. 3 are relatively low. This is because that the detection for the complex images is more difficult.

4 Conclusion

Robust image steganography is an important technique for covert communication by lossy public channels. In this paper, a robust JPEG steganography algorithm is proposed based on SVD and QIM in wavelet domain. The experimental results show the proposed steganography algorithm can achieve competitive robustness and detection resistance in contrast to the stat-of-the-art techniques. This is because that the maximum singular values in wavelet domain have strong robustness. Moreover, QIM and embedding changes in low-pass subband can achieve stronger detection resistance because the texture and edge features of stego image can get better maintained.

In addition, we should notice that the detection resistance of the robust image steganography is relatively weak when the detection is performed by the classifier trained by the original cover image and the corresponding stego image. This is because that the embedding changes of robust steganography is larger than the non-robust steganography such as J-UNWARD. In other words, the large embedding changes is used to achieve the robustness. In the future, we will study the construction of robust embedding domain which can led to the stronger robustness and anti-detection ability.

Acknowledgements. This research was supported by National Natural Science Foundation of China (Grant Nos 61872448, U1804263).

References

1. Fridrich, J.: Steganography in Digital Media: Principles, Algorithms, and Applications. Cambridge University Press, UK (2009)
2. Holub, V., Fridrich, J.: Digital image steganography using universal distortion. In: Proceedings of 1st ACM Information Hiding and Multimedia Security Workshop, pp. 59–68. ACM (2013)
3. Guo, L.J., Ni, J.Q., Shi, Y.Q.: Uniform embedding for efficient JPEG steganography. IEEE Trans. Inf. Forensics Secur. **9**(5), 814–825 (2014)
4. Zhang, Y., Luo, X.Y., Yang, C.F., et al.: A JPEG-compression resistant adaptive steganography based on relative relationship between DCT coefficients. In: Proceeding of the 17th International Conference on Availability, Reliability and Security, pp. 461–466 (2015)
5. Zhang, Y., Zhu, X.D., Qin, C., et al.: Dither modulation based adaptive steganography resisting JPEG compression and statistic detection. Multimedia Tools Appl. **77**(14), 17913–17935 (2018)
6. Qian, Z.X., Zhou, H., Zhang, W.M., et al.: Robust steganography using texture synthesis. In: Proceeding of the 12th International Conference on Intelligent Information Hiding and Multimedia Signal Processing, pp. 25–33 (2016)
7. Zhao, Z.Z., Guan, Q.X., Zhang, H., Zhao, X.F.: Improving the robustness of adaptive steganographic algorithms based on transport channel matching. IEEE Trans. Inf. Forensics Secur. **14**(7), 1843–1856 (2018)
8. Tao, J.Y., Li, S., Zhang, X.P., Wang, Z.C.: Towards robust image steganography. IEEE Trans. Circuits Syst. Video Technol. **29**(2), 594–600 (2019)
9. Yu, X.Z., Chen, K.J., Yao, Y.F., et al.: Robust adaptive steganography based on generalized dither modulation and expanded embedding domain, 168, 107343 (2020)
10. Zhang, Y., Luo, X.Y., Guo, Y.Q., et al.: Multiple robustness enhancements for image adaptive steganography in lossy channels. IEEE Trans. Circuits Syst. Video Technol. **33**(8), 2750–2764 (2020)
11. Bao, P., Ma, X.H.: Image adaptive watermarking using wavelet domain singular value decomposition. IEEE Trans. Circuits Syst. Video Technol. **15**(1), 96–102 (2005)
12. Kang, X.-B., Zhao, F., Lin, G.-F., Chen, Y.-J.: A novel hybrid of DCT and SVD in DWT domain for robust and invisible blind image watermarking with optimal embedding strength. Multimedia Tools Appl. **77**(11), 13197–13224 (2017). https://doi.org/10.1007/s11042-017-4941-1
13. Filler, T., Judas, J., Fridrich, J.: Minimizing additive distortion in steganography using syndrome-trellis codes. IEEE Trans. Inf. Forensics Secur. **6**(3), 920–935 (2011)
14. Bas, P., Filler, T., Pevný, T.: Break Our steganographic system: the ins and outs of organizing BOSS. In: Proceeding of the 13th International Workshop on Information Hiding, pp. 59–70 (2011)
15. Pevny, T., Fridrich, J.: Multiclass detector of current steganographic methods for JPEG format. IEEE Trans. Inf. Forensics Secur. **3**(4), 635–650 (2008)
16. Holub, V., Fridrich, J.: Low-complexity features for JPEG steganalysis using undecimated DCT. IEEE Trans. Inf. Forensics Secur. **10**(2), 219–228 (2015)
17. Kodovský, J., Fridrich, J., Holub, V.: Ensemble classifiers for steganalysis of digital media. IEEE Trans. Inf. Forensics Secur. **7**(2), 432–444 (2012)

Raw Material Traceability of Industrial Control System Based on Blockchain

Jun Xu[1(✉)], Zheming Yang[1], and Hongbo Fang[2]

[1] Zhejiang Zheneng Natural Gas Operation Co., Ltd., Hangzhou 310052, China
xujung@zjenergy.com.cn
[2] Zhejiang Anke Network Technology Co., Ltd., Hangzhou 310012, China

Abstract. Industrial control system is widely used in industrial production with a complex industrial chain. With a large industrial chain, it is easy for some raw materials to be falsified, which will affect the quality of finished products. Therefore, it is particularly important to trace the source of raw materials needed in the process of commodity production. As a decentralized and distributed ledger of stored data, blockchain has the characteristics of decentralization, non-tampering and distribution. The blockchain is applied to the industrial control system to realize the traceability of raw materials. The supply of raw materials uses the block chain technology to accurately record the source information, logistics information and transaction status of raw materials. Raw material information can be checked accurately by this system, and meanwhile the source problem of inferior raw material can be found in time and solved quickly. Finally, the reliability of supply chain is improved and the traceability of raw materials is solved.

Keywords: Blockchain · Industrial control system · Traceability of raw materials

1 Introduction

Industrial Control System refers to a collection of various automatic Control components (including equipment, systems, networks and controllers) used for operation, Control, auxiliary automation of Industrial production and operation, process Control and monitoring. Industrial Control System mainly includes Supervisory Control and Data Acquisition System, Distributed Control System and Programmable Logic Controller [1].

With the development and spread of Internet + and the new generation of information technology, the industrial control system occupying the "control brain" of industrial Internet + is also developing towards the Internet. Industrial control system original relatively closed environment is broken, openness and a growing interconnectedness, make industrial control system possible to collaboration with various business systems, industrial equipment, people, information systems and data links more and more closely, system integration, intelligent equipment, business cooperation, information sharing, all process network become the developing trend of the industrial control system, etc.

© Springer Nature Switzerland AG 2021
X. Sun et al. (Eds.): ICAIS 2021, CCIS 1424, pp. 561–572, 2021.
https://doi.org/10.1007/978-3-030-78621-2_47

According to relevant survey data, hundreds of millions of industrial control systems have been connected with the Internet, including SCANA, PLC, RTU and its connected computers, servers, gateways and so on. Industrial control system is widely used in important industries and critical infrastructure. With the new round of industrial revolution, the Internet has been popularized and applied in various fields, but the penetration rate of industrial Internet is not high [2]. Industrial production industry has this strong closed characteristics, resulting in the industry-related network can't be integrated into the framework of the industrial Internet. Reference [2] points out that data collection is an important content in the development of industrial Internet, which realizes the effective connection between human and machine equipment and business system. However, equipment connection is not a major issue in the industrial site.

The industrial production chain is huge and involves many enterprises. Just the raw materials needed in the production process may reach dozens of kinds. As long as there is a problem with one raw material, the quality of finished products will be affected. There are a lot of raw material information in industrial production, and the mixed information is the problem faced by the traditional traceability system, which makes the traceability difficult to play a practical role. Monitoring the quality of materials from the source and preventing inferior raw materials from entering the production process is an important means to ensure the quality of finished products.

However, most of the traditional traceability systems establish centralized traceability platform, which has problems such as asymmetric information, untrue data, low traceability efficiency and narrow traceability coverage, etc., which makes the credibility of the traditional traceability system lower. Centralized systems lack transparency of information and are poorly regulated, motivated by the desire to tamper with data stored locally.

Blockchain is a decentralized, distributed storage of data books, transactions trusted technology. This technology USES every node in the P2P network to have the authority of data storage to realize the distributed sharing ledger, and USES consensus and signature to ensure that the data in the system cannot be tampered with.

The essence of a distributed storage system is to distribute transaction information and other information to multiple nodes to share the load of data storage. When the internal data of the blockchain changes, other nodes can quickly obtain and consult the changed information, which improves the availability of data and the storage efficiency of the system. Blockchain is not only a data structure, accounting system, but also a kind of value Internet protocol, technology.

In this paper, it is believed that blockchain is a chain database with value protocol formed after decentralized and tamper-free distributed processing of on-chain data through consensus mechanism, smart contract, encryption algorithm and other technologies. The blockchain industry chain system architecture consists of three layers, namely the upstream basic network layer, the midstream protocol layer and the downstream service layer. Among them, the upstream basic network layer is composed of network layer and data layer. The network layer is the decentralized point-to-point transmission of data after distributed processing. Data layer is to build blocks and chains through calculation and encryption of data blocks. The mid-stream protocol layer is based on the consensus layer maintenance record mechanism and forms the intelligent contract layer through the node incentive layer. The downstream application service layer is the landing scene and industrial application case of blockchain technology.

According to the principle of block chain technology and the analysis of block chain architecture, it is concluded that the block chain technology chain includes sending transactions, node broadcast, block calculation, generating parent hash, refreshing nodes, verifying transactions, creating blocks, calculating block header hash, building new blocks, writing block chain system and cycling. In the blockchain technology chain, the core technologies are mainly involved in: peer-to-peer processing technology (P2P), asymmetric encryption algorithm, distributed processing technology, consensus mechanism and smart contract. Peer-to-peer processing differs from "client-server" data processing in that it is peer-to-peer connection processing between nodes.

Asymmetric encryption algorithm mainly uses public key and private key for interactive encryption and decryption. The main function of distributed processing technology is to record each node generated chronologically in the blockchain system. Consensus mechanism is reached when each node generates the same consistent state.

Smart contracts are the key to connecting assets, and code executes the contracts. Smart contracts act as "legal agreements" defined in digital form within the blockchain. In other words, when a pre-set promise is triggered or a transaction is completed, the blockchain system must unconditionally execute the promise or record the transaction, so as to get rid of the dependence on third-party credit institutions. Consensus mechanism can be understood as the consistent certification of the same transaction by all nodes of the blockchain. Its advantage lies in that when one or a few nodes (<51%) fail in the blockchain system, the information integrity of other nodes in the supply chain will not be affected, which improves the fault tolerance of the blockchain technology.

Asymmetric encryption is refers to the block chain within the system to complete the work such as information, query to read and write all by a set of science complete cryptography theory to ensure the implementation, each node can be the data after the access to information for encryption and decryption, specific operation procedure for when a node can use the public key to encrypt data information, the other node must through the private key to decrypt the encrypted message, or when a node using the private key to encrypt data, other nodes must pass the public key to decrypt the encrypted message, the asymmetric encryption and decryption technology to enhance the security of a block chain internal data was significant.

Public chains, private chains, and federated chains are the three main types of blockchain. Different types of blockchain have different participants, characteristics, advantages and disadvantages. Public chain has the attributes of everyone participation, complete decentralization, multi-point collaboration, high energy consumption and low efficiency. Private chain has the characteristics of multi-centralization, single node control, low energy consumption and high efficiency. Alliance chain is the most widely used technology between private chain and public chain.

Blockchain technology features:

Prevent data tampering and falsification. Block chain technics of Pease and Lamport put forward in the 1980s of the Byzantine fault tolerance (Byzantine fault how BFT) the safety of the common mechanism for data storage and sharing, if when block a block in the chain of information has been modified, the block needs to be calculated and reasonable hash value, and then all the blocks are requires a lot of time and calculate the force to recalculate the hash value, unless you can master more than 51% of the data block chain nodes and tampering with data information, Otherwise, the information in the blockchain system, once confirmed, will not be subject to any intervention.With the increasing number of blockchain nodes, the possibility of internal information being tampered with will be lower and lower, which helps enterprises or regulatory authorities to identify abnormal transactions and prevent the occurrence of fraud.

Effectively trace and track data and information. Chain block by block distribution chain store the blocks after the creation of all the history data, therefore occurs in the chain of blocks in the system all trading activity records, including transaction object, way to trade, transaction amount, transaction amount, transaction time, etc., can all through the chain structure on the distributed books to carry on the track and trace, is convenient for regulators to track the cause and effect of trading information, improve the regulation efficiency.

Help the market distinguish the authenticity of goods. Block chain all the data in the system is open, anyone can access the node after check and verify the relevant data information, also can use asymmetric encryption mechanism of block chain store related data information, to use block chain technology can effectively verify the authenticity of a commodity, insight into the commodity production and processing, detailed information such as time, place, person, enhance market recognition of high quality commodities, to crack down on counterfeit goods circulation in the market, brand for the enterprise to set up a positive image.

From the perspective of data storage, blockchain is a unit of data storage. A blockchain has several blocks, and a block has several transactions or other information. Transaction information is stored in blocks with certain rules, and blocks are connected with certain rules to form a blockchain. The specific information stored in the block is transaction information or other information.

Due to the advantages of non-tamper and traceability of blockchain, researches on the application of blockchain technology to the source of traceability began in 2018. Reference [1] applied the blockchain technology to the industrial control system related to tobacco to prevent engineering files from being tampered with and identity authentication. Reference [4] mainly realizes the safety monitoring and protection of data by industrial control system. Reference [5] proposed a data security protection scheme for industrial Internet platform based on blockchain. No relevant literature has proposed to apply blockchain to the industrial control system to realize the traceability of raw materials, so as to ensure the authenticity of raw materials used in the production process. In this paper, a raw material traceability scheme based on the industrial control system based on blockchain will be proposed to realize the traceability of required raw materials in industrial production, so as to ensure the production quality.

2   Industrial Control System Traceability Scheme Based on Blockchain

2.1   Participate in Enterprise and Chain Information

Traditional traceability systems generally adopt centralized traceability information storage and collection. No matter who is the maintenance subject of information, they may tamper with the data due to various interests, resulting in questionable credibility of the traceability system.

   The raw material traceability system based on blockchain involves multiple enterprises and various information input, including raw material enterprise A, raw material enterprise B and logistics companies. Participating enterprises shall participate in the input and maintenance of traceability information. Once the input information is determined, it cannot be modified. Each paragraph should start with an indentation of 4 spaces or 0.20" (Table 1).

Table 1. Traceability system enterprise and chain information

	Raw material Enterprise A	Raw material Enterprise B	Logistics Company C	Manufacturer D
1	An enterprise name	An enterprise name	Company name	Manufacturer name
2	Enterprise business information	Enterprise business information	Company business information	Manufacturer business information
3	Name of raw material	Name of raw material	Transport license plate number	Transport license plate number
4	The raw material ID	The raw material ID	The time of departure	The goods time
5	Source of raw materials	Source of raw materials	Where and when to stop	ID of raw material received
6	Raw material roughing workshop	Raw material roughing workshop	Departure time after docking	Security seal number
	Raw material Enterprise A	Raw material Enterprise B	Logistics Company C	Manufacturer D
7	The raw material batch	The raw material batch	Time of arrival	–
8	Storage warehouse	Storage warehouse	Security seal number	–
9	Transport license plate number	Transport license plate number	–	–

2.2 Collection of Traceability Information

Based on the traceability of raw materials realized by blockchain technology, all parties and participants jointly maintain the traceability data and chain the product traceability information independently, which greatly expands the acquisition channels of traceability information and improves the authenticity of the traceability data. The traceability information of the collected raw materials is traced back to the chain. The traceability data on the chain USES the data chain structure to form the traceability data with time stamp. Through encryption algorithm and distributed storage, the traceability data is completely stored in the nodes on the chain, forming the traceability information chain that is Shared by multiple parties and cannot be tampered with.

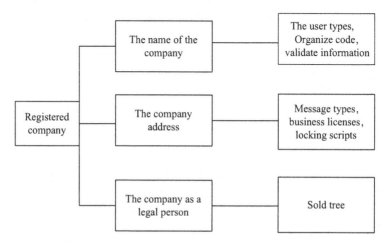

Fig. 1. The data structure of the registration information

The blockchain-based product information collection method requires each raw material manufacturer and finished product manufacturer to register an address before using the system. When the raw material manufacturer sells raw materials, the raw material manufacturer needs to provide the trading information to the system to ensure that the finished product manufacturer can query the relevant raw material information in the system when purchasing raw materials.

System initial stage: the merchants in the raw material supply link, circulation link and production link generate public-private key pair, and register and authenticate to the system with locking script and personal information, as shown in Fig. 1, where the registration information includes company name, company address, company legal person and so on. When registering, the node broadcasts the registration information, and other nodes put the registration information into the cache after receiving the message. The smart contract is then executed. If the message meets all the conditions in the smart contract, the registration information is packaged in a block and waits for consensus. If the message does not meet all the conditions in the smart contract, the message is removed from the cache.

The intelligent contract checks whether the information provided by the registrant is his/her own to prevent the attacker from maliciously registering the information of others. Verify that you are a person by checking the contents of the verifiable information field in the registration information. Registration information has three functions: first, to know whether the company is legal; Second, when a product accident occurs, it can be traced to the person responsible; Third, prevent raw material manufacturer counterfeit product. If all conditions are checked correctly, it returns pass; if one of them is checked incorrectly, it returns no pass.

The data structure field of registration information is resolved as follows:

Company name: represents company name.

User type: raw material manufacturer, transportation company, finished product manufacturer. Indicates the type of user the message belongs to.

Organization code: Company organization code.

Verifiable information: other information that can prove that the person who initiated the registration belongs to the same person as the registration information.

Company address: Hash combination of public and private keys and personal information generated during registration and then hash operation, uniquely identifying a registration information in the block chain.

Message types: There are registration messages, trading messages.

Business license: Business license and other certificates of the company.

Lock script: The lock script is used as a traceability query to verify that the owner of the product is actually pointing to the registration information. Use the unlock script to prove that some businesses own the registration information when transactions occur between individual businesses. It can also be used to verify that the trader has access to the information to prevent an attacker from selling fake goods using information from a manufacturer of raw materials.

Company Legal person: Name of company legal person.

Corporate ID card: Corporate ID card.

Sold tree: Each company has a sold tree that is used to counter - copy products. Each raw material sold links its number to the end of the sold tree. When querying, a binary tree is constructed with the raw material number as the node for querying.

2.3 Data Flow in the Traceability Scheme

The structure of traceability system based on blockchain technology is an architecture that can effectively trace the quality and safety of commodities, which is based on the development level of blockchain, the architectural level of existing blockchain technology and the way of commodity traceability. The traceability of industrial control system based on blockchain is not implemented by a single manufacturer, but by the traceability system jointly established by all the manufacturers involved in the production of finished products. Participating manufacturers have multiple raw material suppliers, manufacturers, distributors and transportation companies in the process of circulation and transportation. The data storage process of each participant in the traceability system is as follows:

Step1 Deploy the traceability system to each raw material supplier and a finished product manufacturer. All enterprises should be registered, fill in the basic information of enterprises: 1, 2 items.

Step2 Complete the registration after waiting for the administrator's approval. The administrator is usually assigned by the quality department of the finished product manufacturer, but each raw material supplier has the supervision function of the administrator.

Step3 Number the original material produced by the raw material supplier, assign a unique ID number to each batch of raw materials, and affix a qr code with anti-counterfeiting and uniqueness.

Step4 Then input the detailed information of raw materials: item A (3, 4, 5, 6, 7, 8) into the traceability system.

Step5 When raw materials are ready for transportation, record the vehicle information of the logistics company transporting raw materials: C (2, 3, 4, 5, 6, 7, 8) and other information into the system.

Step6 When the finished product manufacturer receives the goods, enter item D (4, 5, 6) information, and classify the received raw materials.

Step7 After input, the intelligent contract will automatically detect whether the raw material ID information entered by the raw material supplier is consistent. If the information is successfully matched, the transaction will be confirmed and the information entered by the manufacturer will also be written into the block.

Most of this information is filled out with the assistance of a scanner, reducing the rate of manual error. Once the information is verified, the uploaded information will be recorded in the blockchain and cannot be modified.

The steps involve the relevant blockchain information as follows: if the raw material vendor sells the material to the manufacturer, the vendor USES the public key hash value of the transporter or manufacturer, the registration address and the registration information unlock script to build the transaction information and broadcast the transaction information to other nodes. When other nodes receive the transaction information, they will first put the transaction information in their own cache queue, and then execute the intelligent contract. If the transaction information meets all the conditions in the intelligent contract, they will package the transaction information into the block chain and wait for consensus. If the transaction information does not satisfy all the conditions in the smart contract, wait for the next consensus. If all the conditions in the smart contract are not satisfied after n attempts at consensus, the node removes the transaction information from the cache queue. Adding a transaction information to the block also adds the corresponding raw material information to the raw material vendor's "sold tree" (Fig. 2).

Data structure field analysis of transaction information:

Previous hash: last traded public key address.
Output index: Last trade output index (array index).
Unlocking script: Private key signature, enterprise verification of ownership of transaction information.
Name of raw material: the name of the raw material used in the product.

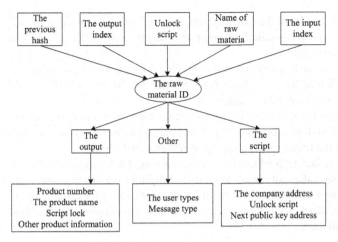

Fig. 2. Blockchain data structure

Input index: The index of the input array for this transaction.

Output: The output array index of this transaction.

Product number: The product number that the seller sells to the buyer.

Product name: The name of the product sold by the seller to the buyer.

Script lock: In combination with the unlock script entered for the next transaction, prove that the buyer owns the product this time.

Other Product information: Other information of the products sold by seller to buyer.

Others: subscript of this transaction type.

User type: Indicates the type of user the message belongs to.

Message type: Indicates the type of the message.

Traceability series: Reserved fields.

Script: An executable that is written according to certain requirements, during which the user can perform a series of actions.

Company address: Unique identification of the seller's registration information. Unlock script: The lock script with the registration information verifies that the registration information pointed to by the company address is valid and true.

The next public key address: the unique identity of the buyer's registration information. Next unlock script: Verify buyer ownership.

2.4 Traceability Process of Raw Materials

The important function of traceability system lies in the traceability process of raw materials. From the traceability, check and test the quality of raw materials, find out the reasons for poor quality of raw materials, and achieve the purpose of improving the production quality of finished products. The traceability process of raw materials is as follows:

Step1 When the manufacturer's supervision department tests the quality of raw materials, input the ID of raw materials to query the detailed information of raw materials.

According to the ID of the raw material, the detailed information of the raw material in the database and the detailed information of the transportation process is called up and displayed on the interface.

Step2 Perform hash operation on the detailed information of raw materials. If the hash value is different from the hash value written by the raw material supplier, the raw material information will be tampered.

Step3 Contact the raw material manufacturer for further communication, and the raw material will no longer be used for production, and then contact the raw material supplier to help find the reason for the supply of raw material fraud.

Step4 For raw materials whose hash values have not been tampered with, relevant inspectors shall also make spot checks to verify the eligibility of raw materials. For spot checks, the system will randomly select the ID of the spot checks for testing, and record the test report in the block, so as to prevent the raw material suppliers from colluding with the testers to fabricate.

In the traceability system, once the raw material information and finished product information are entered, they cannot be changed and cannot be deleted by the administrator. The data authenticity and non - tampering are guaranteed. Companies can only go to the blockchain to view production data.

2.5 Security Performance Analysis

Table 2. Performance analysis of each scheme

Plan	Security			The traceability
	Physical security	Tamper proof	Raw materials for anti-counterfeiting	
Reference [1]	√	√	–	×
Reference [3]	√	√	–	√
Reference [6]	√	√	–	√
Reference [7]	√	√	×	√
Method in this paper	√	√	√	√

From the point of view of security: Reference [1] solves the security problems in the industrial control system from the field control layer and the port and module of the layer where the field equipment is located, ensures the security of file compilation and input instructions, and improves the security of the industrial control system. Reference [3] USES hash value, time stamp, intelligent contract and so on to ensure data security and improve data authenticity. Reference [6] introduces the blockchain-based drug traceability system, which USES RFID, GPS and other Internet of things devices to collect traceability information, thus ensuring the safety and authenticity of information. Reference [7] elaborates on the application of blockchain technology in dairy product traceability in cross-border trade, which has the advantages of physical security and non-tampering (Table 2).

From the perspective of traceability: Reference [1] mainly elaborated the application scheme of blockchain technology in the tobacco system. It did not trace the source of tobacco raw materials and did not solve the problem of counterfeiting in the transportation of finished tobacco products. Literature [3] elaborated the shortcomings of the traditional commodity traceability system, and proposed a commodity traceability system based on blockchain, with the focus on the group of consumers, so as to facilitate consumers to check back the real situation of commodities. Reference [6] traceability process is divided into drug manufacturing, packaging, distribution and sales to achieve traceability. The fly in the ointment is that it has not realized the problem of "how to record the information of consumer purchase when the drug is sold to individual consumers", which remains to be solved in the last part. Reference [7] solves the problems of poor quality and difficult traceability in imported dairy products, facilitates the supervision and management of relevant departments, and opens the channel of consumer traceability. However, the paper does not mention the process of carrying out quality detection of raw milk and linking the detection data, and the lack of raw milk quality inspection information.

In the scheme proposed in this paper, a series of links of finished goods from raw materials to production and final sales are recorded in the blockchain, connecting the upstream and downstream manufacturers and enterprises such as raw material suppliers and manufacturers. In this system, each raw material merchant checks the transportation status of raw materials, and the downstream enterprises can timely improve the selection, design and transportation of relevant raw materials through feedbacks. Moreover, it can avoid the fake and shoddy raw materials, eliminate the appearance of defective products from the source, and create a healthy environment for the production of finished products.

Due to the decentralized and non-tamper able characteristics of blockchain, data input is not only subject to the supervision of relevant upstream and downstream enterprises, but also cannot be easily tampered after input, which ensures the authenticity of data of all enterprises in the process of finished product production. When the finished products form blocks from the relevant information of material selection, transportation and other processes, each block is interconnected to form a complete set of processes, and then Banks, venture capital and other financial enterprises can understand the industry information and enterprise development status through blockchain information, so as to solve the problem of loans for industrial enterprises.

3   Conclusion

To sum up, based on the study of blockchain, this paper explores the application of blockchain in industrial control system to realize the innovative application of raw material traceability. This paper gives full consideration to the difficulties of raw material traceability. The system realizes the combination of raw materials, commodity traceability and blockchain application in the field of industrial control. It solves the problems of material selection, data acquisition in transportation, slow efficiency in tracing the authenticity of materials, and inconvenience in finding relevant corporate responsibility.

It ensures the feasibility of raw material traceability scheme in industrial control system based on blockchain.

References

1. Xu, Y.Q., Zhuo, W.: Application of blockchain technology in industrial control safety of tobacco system. Microcomput. Appl. **35**(03), 113–116 (2019)
2. Tong, Q.: Development status and countermeasures of industrial internet. Equip. Manage. Maintenance **22**, 57–59 (2018)
3. Jiao, B., Zhang, J., Liang, Q.D.: Product traceability method based on blockchain. Modern information technology, **4**(12), 154–156+160 (2020)
4. Zhang, M., Zeng, B., Zhu, C.W.: Design and implementation of safety monitoring and traceability system for industrial control system. Inf. Technol. Network Secur. **38**(01), 14–19 (2019)
5. Cheng, G., Han, W.P., Zou, G.X., An, G.: Research on the application of blockchain in industrial Internet. Inf. Commun. Technol. **14**(03), 19–24 (2020)
6. Cao, Y.C., Li, T., Lin, H.N.: Research on the construction of drug traceability system based on blockchain technology. Sci. Technol. Manage. Res. **40**(16), 215–224 (2020)
7. Chen, L.L.: Research on the application of blockchain technology in the traceability of cross-border trade dairy products. Inf. Comput. (Theor. Ed.) **32**(14), 8–12 (2020)
8. Aitzhan, N.Z., Svetinovic, D.: Security and privacy in decentralized energy trading through multi-signatures. Blockchain Anonymous Messaging Streams **15**(5), 840–852 (2018)

Survey: Research on Blockchain Consensus Mechanism in IoT Security

Xiangyan Tang[1,2], Guangjing Hu[1,2(✉)], Yuming Yuan[3], Hui Li[3], Yuan Zhang[1,2],
Yifan Li[1], Mengyang Li[1,2], and Jieren Cheng[1,2]

[1] School of Computer Science and Cyberspace Security, Hainan University, Haikou 570228,
China
[2] Hainan Blockchain Technology Engineering Research Center, Hainan
University, Haikou 570228, China
[3] Hainan Huochain Tech Company Limited, Haikou 570100, China

Abstract. The Internet of Things (IoT) technology, as an important part of a new
generation of information technology, is beginning to be applied in more and more
fields. However, due to the lack of basic security technology, the Internet of Things
is facing a severe information security situation. Blockchain technology, as a new
solution that can realize decentralized collaboration in an untrusted network, has
a natural fit with IoT, which is inherently distributed. The performance of the
blockchain largely depends on the consensus mechanism, but the current research
rarely discusses IoT security from the perspective of the consensus mechanism.
In this article, we comprehensively analyzed the impact of the consensus mechanism on IoT security. First, we briefly explained the blockchain technology. Next,
we analyzed and discussed typical consensus mechanisms. Then, we proposed to
classify current IoT security issues from three perspectives: data security, communication security, and application security. Next, we discussed the consensus
mechanism of single-chain and multi-chain in IoT. Finally, we analyzed the problems of blockchain consensus in IoT security. In response to the security challenges
of IoT, it is proposed to look forward to the optimization of consensus from three
perspectives: the optimization of blockchain node evaluation, the optimization of
blockchain architecture, and the optimization of blockchain storage. We hope to
contribute to the future development and innovation of blockchain in IoT.

Keywords: Blockchain · Internet of Things · Security · Consensus mechanism ·
DAG

1 Introduction

1.1 Overview of IoT

IoT technology includes technologies such as wireless sensor networks (WSN) to radio
frequency identification (RFID). Based on the concept of the Internet, it extends from a
computer to all general physical devices that can be independently addressed on the basis
of the Internet concept, including sensors, mobile terminals, home smart facilities, and

© Springer Nature Switzerland AG 2021
X. Sun et al. (Eds.): ICAIS 2021, CCIS 1424, pp. 573–584, 2021.
https://doi.org/10.1007/978-3-030-78621-2_48

wearable devices, and gradually expanded to transportation, logistics, smart home, wearable devices, industry and agriculture and other fields [1]. Information sensing equipment is widely used in smart homes, smart logistics, smart cities, and sharing economy. People and devices exchange information and communicate through information media.

IoT has a large number of heterogeneous and uniquely identifiable terminals, which can sense and collect a huge amount of data, but at the same time, the memory computing power of IoT devices is very limited, which makes IoT have a great security risk.

1.2 Advantages of Blockchain in IoT

Different from the traditional centralized structure, the blockchain can realize decentralized peer-to-peer collaboration in an untrusted network. It uses a block-chain data structure to store distributed ledger databases, which is transparent and reliable, tamperproof, traceable, safe and reliable [2]. Generally speaking, blockchain can be divided into data layer, network layer, consensus layer, incentive layer, contract layer, and application layer. Its overall structure is shown in Fig. 1.

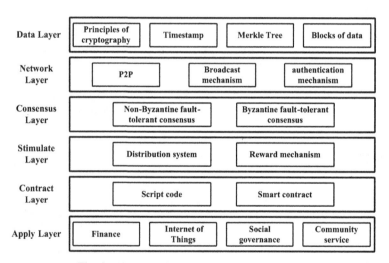

Fig. 1. The overall architecture of the blockchain

The characteristics of blockchain technology make it suitable for occasions where the cost of default is high and trust maintenance is difficult. Therefore, blockchain technology can be used to ensure data security and build a consensus system that can be shared. Nowadays, it has a wide range of applications in the Internet of Things (IoT) [3, 4], credit and ownership management [5], resource sharing [6], supply chain [7], data management [8, 9], energy [10, 11], medical care [12], and network security [13, 14]. Next, we analyze the advantages of blockchain in IoT from the perspective of decentralized architecture, security, and credibility.

Decentralized Architecture. Blockchain can provide a P2P distributed architecture to improve the opaque defects of centralized architecture, and all nodes are relatively independent. In this way, the anti-attack and fault tolerance capabilities of the system built by blockchain technology have also been improved.

Security. Smart contracts can optimize and upgrade IoT protocols to protect communications between devices. The code can also be transferred to the device in a safe way to complete remote upgrades and other operations [15].

Trustworthiness. Blockchain allows us to make secure payments in a trustless scenario, and also improves the interconnection of devices and access to data. For example, PoU consensus can be converted from different protocols, which requires less resources and is more suitable for IoT scenarios. Y B. Ren et al. studied the method of using blockchain to achieve trusted sharing of data in the IoT distributed environment [16]. Kataoka. K et al. provide automated doubt and verification on the edge network through software-defined networking (SDN) and blockchain to achieve automated traffic management [17].

1.3 Related Work

Atzori et al. made a preliminary analysis of the IoT platform, and also elaborated on the limitations and problems of the blockchain in the IoT [18]. In terms of IoT security, Kouicem [19] and Jesus [20] have also done corresponding research, and there are also preliminary discussions on corresponding methods.

In [21], the introduction of smart contracts into IoT to realize the verifiability of encryption is discussed. Chronicle uses a blockchain synchronization server to synchronize with Ethereum and Hyperledger, and has developed several encrypted IoT products [22]. In [23], the status of the goods is mainly recorded in the supply chain process to provide completeness certification for the goods. Riddle and Code proposed that Twin of Things generates hardware-based digital identities for connected physical objects. The device is equipped with a security encryption chip, which uses Android applications to operate. It can also work with BigchainDB blockchains and Ethereum. The Chain of Things puts forward a scheme of integrating blockchain and IoT hardware-Maru, and gives three schemes corresponding to security, solar energy, and logistics [24].

1.4 The Structure of Paper

The structure of this article is as follows: The first section briefly introduces IoT, blockchain architecture and characteristics, and the advantages of blockchain in IoT. Then, in the second section, we analyzed IoT security and challenges from the perspectives of data security, communication security, and application security. In the third part, we discuss the consensus in IoT from the perspective of classic consensus, single-chain structure and multi-chain structure. In the fourth quarter. We look forward to the optimization of consensus from the perspective of optimization of blockchain node evaluation, optimization of blockchain architecture, and optimization of blockchain storage. In the fifth part, we summarized the work done.

2 IoT Security and Challenges

IoT security is very different from traditional device security, traditional device security requires security software, firewall, etc. to protect the device and the data on the device. All this requires a large investment of computing power, and computing and storage capabilities on the IoT are limited, leaving very limited space for security software. In the next part, we classify the security and challenges in IoT into three categories: data security issues, communication security issues, and application security issues.

2.1 Data Security Issues

Data Privacy Level. Many IoT devices collect private information. Some information is closely related to personal privacy, and personal related information can be obtained directly or indirectly through devices such as cameras and smart bracelets, causing serious information leakage.

Data Integrity Level. Attackers can also tamper with data to destroy the integrity and authenticity of the data. An important role of IoT is to make decision support for users. When an attacker injects wrong information, it may cause serious consequences, especially in industrial systems that process real-time messages.

2.2 Communication Security Issues

Network Transmission Level. One-to-many information transmission is more prone to security issues than point-to-point transmission. When using public networks for one-to-many data transmission, if security issues are not discovered in time, this can easily cause large-scale leaks [25].

Data may pass through multiple nodes, and appropriate encryption methods are required to ensure security during transmission. Many devices have loopholes in encryption, authentication, and access. At the same time, early devices may not be able to remotely upgrade software in time, which also leaves a lot of hidden dangers. There are other devices involved in key areas such as energy and transportation. When these devices are controlled, attackers can use direct destruction or covertly forged data to cause catastrophic consequences.

Network Communication Level. Attackers can continue to send random electromagnetic signals that do not follow the protocol to disrupt the network, affecting the reception of legal signals and the stability of the system; Or use other interference methods to prevent legitimate nodes from accessing the channel to achieve the purpose of the attack. At the perception layer, authentication mechanisms should be used to avoid unauthorized access to information.

Network Architecture Level. Due to the deployment of IoT centralized architecture, IoT is also facing the threat of distributed denial of service (DDoS). DDoS attacks are easy to implement, difficult to track and defend, and are highly destructive, which may lead to a complete collapse [26, 27]. The KrebOnSecurity.com website was once launched by IoT botnets with a large-scale DDoS attack of up to 620Gbps attack traffic, causing great losses.

Network Communication Protocol Level. Attackers can adopt more covert and lower-cost interference methods. For example, it is more difficult to detect the channel monitoring and wait until there is data transmission before launching an attack. At the same time, the open sharing of wireless channels makes the communication protocol easy to attack. At the transport layer, it is necessary to study end-to-end confidentiality and authentication, and use key-related security protocols to safely transmit data.

2.3 Application Security Issues

At the application layer, technologies such as data encryption retrieval, security access control, information protection and forensics technology need to be studied. Using unsafe interfaces and software components, or when updating software and hardware, may introduce errors [28, 29].

Authentication Access Level. Both IoT devices and users need to verify and authenticate, and the encryption mechanism adopted needs to take into account resource consumption and efficiency. Friese. I et al. put forward the challenges faced by IoT authentication and authorization [30]; Bahga. A et al. proposed a framework in which devices in IoT can communicate with blockchain networks [31] and send data to the cloud for storage; Christidis. K and others described smart contracts to promote IoT service sharing, such as electronic transactions and supply chain management [21]; Xiaoyang. Zhu et al. mainly studied the identity management system in IoT and related solutions, and elaborated on the existing problems of IoT in the construction of identity management system [32].

Regulatory Level. Lijing. Z, Kolokotronis. N, Fabiano. N et al. considered the role of blockchain in the regulatory framework [33–35], such as the protection of data privacy and other regulatory aspects. Fatih proposed an unknown encryption attack detection method to deal with the detection of encryption attacks in IoT [36]. Li et al. proposed an abnormal attack detection method for the Industrial Internet that can protect IoT users from abnormal attacks [37].

Privacy Protection Level. Xu. F et al. combined the computing power of edge computing with the non-tamperable feature of blockchain to reach a consensus in IoT devices [38]. Halpin. H et al. proposed a blind signature privacy protection identity framework: NEXTLEAP, through which applications can be created [39].

3 Consensus Mechanism in IoT Blockchain

3.1 Overview of Blockchain Consensus Mechanism

Blockchain is composed of multiple technologies. The main technologies include consensus mechanism, cryptography principles, P2P network structure, smart contracts and time stamps. The design of the consensus mechanism is the key to determining performance. It can make honest nodes reach an agreement in distributed trustless or low-trust scenarios to ensure the credibility and security of the blockchain.

The main performance indicators of the consensus mechanism can be evaluated from the following perspectives: Transaction per second (measure the speed of reaching a consensus on the proposal), scalability (the ability to support the expansion of network nodes), robustness (the ability to maintain normal functions when errors occur), and security (prevent malicious nodes) The ability to attack and the ability to identify malicious nodes).

3.2   Consensus Mechanism in IoT

The Internet of Things collects data through a large number of terminals, and it is inherently distributed, which accord with the characteristics of the blockchain. However, the Internet of Things will access a huge number of heterogeneous devices, therefore the throughput and computing storage capabilities are limited. The transmission delay of heterogeneous data in low communication broadband affects the consensus. The device itself also has the characteristics of being easily hacked, which leads to the need of a lightweight blockchain architecture for the Internet of Things.

The current consensus mechanism has not yet emerged a mechanism that can achieve a perfect balance in terms of resource consumption, degree of decentralization, security, scalability, and efficiency. Due to the massive amount of data generated by heterogeneous devices in IoT and the limited processing capacity of a single device, the current blockchain cannot fully adapt to IoT. In the next part, we discuss the consensus mechanism in IoT in terms of the PoW mechanism and the PoS mechanism, the single-chain structure and the DAG structure.

Classic Consensus in IoT Blockchain. However, the simple PoW mechanism has a series of problems. The setting of PoW difficulty must be able to prevent frequent forking, the energy consumption required for calculation is large while the practical value is small [40]. However, due to some limitations, the available resources of IoT devices are very limited, and the high amount of calculation required by the pure PoW consensus mechanism does not meet the characteristics of IoT. At the same time, in order to ensure security, PoW has a very low TPS, requires hardware bandwidth, and has a long block creation time. It is not suitable for scenarios such as IoT with large transaction volume and high time response.

The PoW mechanism in the Internet of Things has been improved accordingly. For example, [41] uses the public key to record the identity and the private key to encrypt the PoW consensus IoT security blockchain solution [42]. Sagirlar. G et al. proposed a hybrid blockchain architecture for IoT -Hybrid-IoT, which treats IoT devices as peers on the Pow sub-chain, and uses BFT interconnectors between the sub-chains to improve performance [43].

Compared with the PoW mechanism, the PoS mechanism has shortened the consensus time a lot, and TPS is improved as well. Although the amount of calculation is significantly reduced, there is still considerable pressure for devices with low storage and energy consumption. At the same time, PoS may bring about oligopoly and monopoly, and it is easier to fork. In terms of security, there are also issues such as currency issuance, nothing at stake attack, and the age of coins can accumulate even when nodes are offline [44]. Therefore, a simple PoS consensus mechanism is not suitable to establish a distributed IoT system.

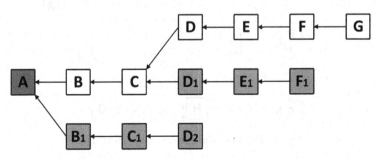

Fig. 2. The single-chain structure of blockchain

Single-chain and Multi-chain Structure in IoT Blockchain. Both PoW and PoS mechanisms are single-chain structures. In order to avoid the risks caused by frequent forks, the consensus mechanism has large restriction on the block generation speed, which will cause bottlenecks in the application of IoT. At the same time, because IoT has a large throughput, which presents a great test on the performance of TPS in the consensus mechanism and the design of transaction costs. The single-chain structure is as shown in Fig. 2, where the green block represents the creation block, the white block represents the verified block, and the gray block represents the discarded block.

In order to change the low TPS of the single-chain structure, the inability to parallelize the block generation and other shortcomings that are not suitable for IoT, someone proposed a new blockchain structure based on Directed Acyclic Graph (DAG). Through this data structure, the resources consumed by nodes to create new blocks can be reduced to adapt to the status quo of IoT. The multi-chain structure is shown in Fig. 3. The green blocks represent the creation blocks, the white blocks represent the verified blocks, and the gray blocks represent the blocks that have not yet passed verification.

In this data structure, there is no concept of blocks. The DAG component is a transaction of a single user, which saves the time of packaging and generating blocks compared to the blockchain. When making a transaction, you need to verify the previous transaction, which allows the DAG to write transactions asynchronously, and the expansion capability of its structure has been greatly enhanced. The structure of DAG includes Tangle [45] and Hashgraph [46].

IOTA adopts the "Tangle" DAG topology, which can achieve Blockless consensus. Based on the structure of DAG, Junqin Huang proposed a credit-based PoW mechanism based on the characteristics of the Industrial Internet of Things (IIoT), using the data authority management methods to regulate data access [47].

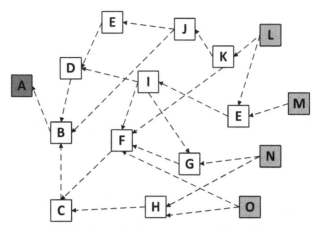

Fig. 3. The multi-chain structure of blockchain

4   IoT Security and Optimization of Blockchain Consensus

4.1   IoT Security and Blockchain

When the IoT uses public networks for one-to-many data transmission, this is likely to cause large-scale data leakage. Especially in devices that collect private information, such as surveillance cameras and smart bracelets. And other key fileds' equipments, such as energy, transportation, once invaded, may bring catastrophic consequences.

Some devices of IoT are old; Some use outdated software. These hidden dangers have caused a lot of resistance to remotely trusted updating and upgrading software. And due to the deployment of IoT centralized architecture, IoT faces the threat of distributed denial of service (DDoS) [48]. At the same time, there are security vulnerabilities in the communication hardware level, network transmission, IoT application layer, and identity verification.

Malviya. H et al. pointed out that blockchain technology is an important technology to solve IoT privacy protection issues and data credibility [49]; Sicari et al. discussed issues such as identity verification and data security [17]; Granjal et al. discussed security issues from the IoT protocol [50]; M. Ruta et al. proposed a new type of service-oriented architecture (SOA) based on semantic blockchain for registration selection and payment through smart contracts, which can alleviate the problem of scarcity of IoT computing resources [51]. In the following sections, we propose to look forward to consensus optimization from three perspectives: the optimization of blockchain node evaluation, the optimization of blockchain architecture, and the optimization of blockchain storage.

4.2   The Optimization Direction of the Blockchain Consensus Mechanism in IoT

Optimization of Blockchain Node Evaluation. The evaluation of nodes can also be regarded as the screening of honest nodes. Huang et al. introduced trust evaluation in the PoW mechanism. Through the evaluation of the positive and negative aspects of the node, the probability of the node that is evaluated as malicious will be lowered. The other is the lazy node, and the penalty coefficient will be dynamically adjusted to enhance the security of the network [47].

EricKe Wang et al. proposed a protocol (X-repute) based on reputation applications on the IoT, and designed reputation rewards and penalties to judge the reputation value of nodes. Nodes with high reputation are more likely to obtain accounting rights, and nodes with less computing resources participate in the accounting. The opportunity to account is also greater [52].

Optimization of Blockchain Architecture. The single-chain structure has a low TPS and cannot produce blocks in parallel, which is not suitable for IoT scenarios. Therefore, the DAG structure is introduced to reduce the resources consumed by creating new blocks. The DAG is composed of transactions of a single user, and the previous transaction needs to be verified when performing a transaction. Since the time of packaging and generating blocks is saved, transactions can be written asynchronously, which improves the scalability.

Optimization of Blockchain Storage. In the face of the current low TPS problem of blockchain, off-chain storage technology can be used to improve it. For example, Lightning Network and Raiden Network, users can adopt the method of paying a deposit in advance, using the huge throughput of the off-chain transaction server, and placing the result in the blockchain only after the transaction is over. In off-chain transaction disputes, community voting can also be used to determine the direction of development.

There are other ways to improve IoT. For example, Biswas. S et al. proposed the use of a local peer-to-peer network to reduce the workload and improve efficiency by stipulating the threshold for entering the global blockchain [53]. Q. Xu et al. proposed a smart contract method based on blockchain OSD: Sapphire storage system [54]. The combined use of this large-scale storage system can reduce the overhead required for data analysis.

5   Conclusion

In this article, we have made a comprehensive overview of the impact of the blockchain consensus mechanism on IoT security. Due to the lack of basic security technologies, the Internet of Things has privacy risks and security vulnerabilities. The IoT of distributed and blockchain of decentralized has a natural fit. The distributed IoT and decentralized blockchain have a natural fit, and the combination of the two may have a huge impact on the trusted access of heterogeneous terminal devices and data security management. First, we analyzed the current development status of IoT and introduced blockchain technology and typical consensus mechanisms. Then, we analyzed the current security and challenges of IoT from three perspectives: data security, communication security and application security. Next, we discussed the impact of blockchain consensus on IoT security. Finally, we also looked forward to the possible future optimization directions of blockchain consensus in IoT.

Acknowledgment. This work was supported by the Hainan Provincial Natural Science Foundation of China (Grant No. 2019RC041 and 2019RC098), Research and Application Project of Key Technologies for Blockchain Cross-chain Collaborative Monitoring and Traceability for Large-scale Distributed Denial of Service Attacks, National Natural Science Foundation of China (Grant No. 61762033), Opening Project of Shanghai Trusted Industrial Control Platform (Grant No. TICPSH202003005-ZC), Education and Teaching Reform Research Project of Hainan University (Grant No. hdjy1970) and Innovative Research Project for Postgraduates of Hainan Province (Grant. No. Hys2020–89).

References

1. Singh, G.S., Singh, S.: A review on the use of block chain for the Internet of Things. Int. J. Comput. Sci. Eng. **7**, 332–358 (2019)
2. Dinh, T.T.A., Liu, R., Zhang, M., Chen, G., Ooi, B.C., Wang, J.: Untangling blockchain: a data processing view of blockchain systems. IEEE Trans. Knowl. Data Eng. **30**, 1366–1385 (2018)
3. Kshetri, N.: Can blockchain strengthen the Internet of Things? It Professional **19**, 68–72 (2017)
4. Sharma, P.K., Chen, M.Y., Park, J.H.: A software defined fog node based distributed blockchain cloud architecture for IoT. IEEE Access **6**, 115–124 (2018)
5. Dunphy, P., Petitcolas, F.A.P.: A first look at identity management schemes on the blockchain. IEEE Secur. Priv. **16**, 20–29 (2018)
6. Sikorski, J.J., Haughton, J., Kraft, M.: Blockchain technology in the chemical industry: machine-to-machine electricity market. Appl. Energy **195**, 234–246 (2017)
7. Tian, F.: An agri-food supply chain traceability system for china based on RFID & blockchain technology. In: 2016 13th International Conference on Service Systems and Service Management (2016)
8. Karafiloski, E., Mishev, A.: Blockchain solutions for big data challenges: a literature review. In: IEEE EUROCON 2017 -17th International Conference on Smart Technologies (2017)
9. Dai, W., Dai, C., Choo, K.K.R., Cui, C., Zou, D., Jin, H.: SDTE: a secure blockchain-based data trading ecosystem. IEEE Trans. Inf. Forensics Secur. **15**, 725–737 (2020)
10. Chaudhary, R., Jindal, A., Aujla, G.S., Aggarwal, S., Kumar, N., Choo, K.-K.R.: BEST: blockchain-based secure energy trading in SDN-enabled intelligent transportation system. Comput. Secur. **85**, 288–299 (2019)
11. Bao, J., He, D., Luo, M., Choo, K.K.R.: A Survey of Blockchain Applications in the Energy Sector. IEEE Syst. J. 1–12 (2020)
12. Azaria, A., Ekblaw, A., Vieira, T., Lippman, A.: MedRec: Using Blockchain for Medical Data Access and Permission Management (2016)
13. Singh, A., Parizi, R.M., Zhang, Q., Choo, K.-K.R., Dehghantanha, A.: Blockchain smart contracts formalization: approaches and challenges to address vulnerabilities. Comput. Secur. **88**, 101654 (2020)
14. Singh, A., Click, K., Parizi, R.M., Zhang, Q., Dehghantanha, A., Choo, K.-K.R.: Sidechain technologies in blockchain networks: an examination and state-of-the-art review. J. Network Comput. Appl. **149**, 102471 (2020)
15. Veena, P., Panikkar, S., Nair, S., Brody, P.: Empowering the edge-practical insights on a decentralized Internet of Things. IBM Institute for Business Value (2015)
16. Yanbing, R., Xinghua, L., Hai, L., Qingfeng, C., Jianfeng, M.: Blockchain-based trust management framework for distributed internet of things. Compu. Res. Develop. **55**, 108–124 (2018)

17. Kataoka, K., Gangwar, S., Podili, P.: Trust list: internet-wide and distributed IoT traffic management using blockchain and SDN. In: 2018 IEEE 4th World Forum on Internet of Things (WF-IoT) (2018)
18. Atzori, M.: Blockchain-Based Architectures for the Internet of Things: A Survey. SSRN Electr. J. (2017)
19. Kouicem, D.E., Bouabdallah, A., Lakhlef, H.: Internet of things security: a top-down survey. Comput. Netw. **141**, 199–221 (2018)
20. Jesus, E.F., Chicarino, V.R.L., de Albuquerque, C.V.N., Rocha, A.A.d.A.: A survey of how to use blockchain to secure Internet of Things and the stalker attack. Secur. Commun. Networks (2018)
21. Christidis, K., Devetsikiotis, M.: Blockchains and smart contracts for the Internet of Things. IEEE Access **4**, 2292–2303 (2016)
22. Chronicled.https://chronicled.com/. Accessed 16 Dec 2020
23. Modum. https://modum.io/. Accessed 01 Feb 2018
24. Chain of things. https://www.chainofthings.com/. Accessed 01 Feb 2018
25. Wang, J., Chen, W., Wang, L., Sherratt, R.S., Tolba, A.: Data secure storage mechanism of sensor networks based on blockchain. Comput., Mater. Continua **65**, 2365–2384 (2020)
26. Abou, E.l., Houda, Z., Hafid, A., Khoukhi, L.: Co-IoT: a collaborative DDoS mitigation scheme in IoT environment based on blockchain using SDN. In: 2019 IEEE Global Communications Conference (2019)
27. Rodrigues, B., Stiller, B.: Acm: Cooperative Signaling of DDoS Attacks in a Blockchain-based Network (2019)
28. Brachmann, M., Keoh, S.L., Morchon, O.G., Kumar, S.S.: End-to-end transport security in the IP-based Internet of Things. In: International Conference on Computer Communications and Networks (2012)
29. Sethi, M., Arkko, J., Keränen, A.: End-to-end security for sleepy smart object networks. In: Local Computer Networks Workshops (2012)
30. Friese, I., Heuer, J., Kong, N.: Challenges from the Identities of Things: introduction of the Identities of Things discussion group within kantara initiative. China Pharm. **22**, 2708–2710 (2011)
31. Bahga, A., Madisetti, V.K.: Blockchain Platform for Industrial Internet of Things. J. Softw. Eng. Appl. **09**, 533–546 (2016)
32. Zhu, X., Badr, Y.: Identity management systems for the Internet of Things: a survey towards blockchain solutions. Sensors (Basel, Switzerland) (2018)
33. Zhou, L., Wang, L., Sun, Y., Lv, P.: BeeKeeper: a blockchain-based IoT system with secure storage and homomorphic computation. IEEE Access 1–1 (2018)
34. Kolokotronis, N., Limniotis, K., Shiaeles, S., Griffiths, R.: Secured by blockchain: safeguarding Internet of Things devices. Consumer Electronics Magazine, IEEE (2019)
35. Fabiano, N.: The Internet of Things ecosystem: The blockchain and privacy issues. The challenge for a global privacy standard. In: 2017 International Conference on Internet of Things for the Global Community (IoTGC) (2017)
36. Özkaynak, F.: Brief review on application of nonlinear dynamics in image encryption. Nonlinear Dyn. **92**(2), 305–313 (2018). https://doi.org/10.1007/s11071-018-4056-x
37. Li, X., Niu, J., Bhuiyan, M.Z.A., Wu, F., Karuppiah, M., Kumari, S.: A robust ECC-based provable secure authentication protocol with privacy preserving for industrial Internet of Things. IEEE Trans. Industr. Inf. **14**, 3599–3609 (2018)
38. Xu, F., Yang, F., Zhao, C., Fang, C.: Edge computing and caching based blockchain IoT network. In: 2018 1st IEEE International Conference on Hot Information-Centric Networking (HotICN) (2018)

39. Halpin, H.: NEXTLEAP: decentralizing identity with privacy for secure messaging. In: Proceedings of the International Conference on Availability, Reliability and Security (ARES2017) (2017)

40. BitFury, G.: Proof of Stake Versus Proof of Work. white paper. 19 Sep 2020

41. Miraz, M.H., Ali, M.: Blockchain Enabled Enhanced IoT ecosystem security. In: Miraz, M.H., Excell, P., Ware, A., Soomro, S., Ali, M. (eds.) iCETiC 2018. LNICSSITE, vol. 200, pp. 38–46. Springer, Cham (2018). https://doi.org/10.1007/978-3-319-95450-9_3

42. Singh, M., Singh, A., Kim, S.: Blockchain: A game changer for securing IoT data. In: 2018 IEEE 4th World Forum on Internet of Things (WF-IoT) (2018)

43. Sagirlar, G., Carminati, B., Ferrari, E., Sheehan, J.D., Ragnoli, E.: Hybrid-IoT: hybrid blockchain architecture for Internet of Things-PoW sub-blockchains. In: 11th IEEE International Congress on Conferences on Internet of Things, pp. 1007–1016. Institute of Electrical and Electronics Engineers Inc. (2018)

44. Song, R., Song, Y., Liu, Z., Tan, M., Zhou, K.: gaiaworld: a novel blockchain system based on competitive PoS consensus mechanism. Cmc-Comput. Mater. Continua 60, 973–987 (2019)

45. Popov, S.: The Tangle. https://www.iota.org/research/academic-papers.whitepaper. 08 Nov 2020

46. Baird, L.: The Swirlds Hashgraph Consensus Algorithm: Fair, Fast, Byzantine Fault Tolerance. http://www.swirlds.comd/developer-resources/whitepapers,whitepaper. 25 Oct 2020

47. Huang, J., Kong, L., Chen, G., Wu, M.Y., Liu, X., Zeng, P.: Towards secure industrial IoT: blockchain system with credit-based consensus mechanism. IEEE Trans. Ind. Inf. 1–1 (2019)

48. Cheng, J., Li, J., Tang, X., Sheng, V.S., Zhang, C., et al.: A novel DDOS attack detection method using optimized generalized multiple kernel learning. Comput., Mater. Continua 62(3), 1423–1443 (2020)

49. Malviya, H.: How Blockchain Will Defend IOT. Social Science Electronic Publishing (2016)

50. Granjal, J., Monteiro, E., Sa Silva, J.: Security for the Internet of Things: a survey of existing protocols and open research issues. IEEE Commun. Surv. Tutor. 17, 1294–1312 (2015)

51. Ruta, M., Scioscia, F., Ieva, S., Capurso, G., Di Sciascio, E.: Semantic blockchain to improve scalability in the Internet of Things. Open J. Internet Things. 3(1), 4661(2017)

52. Wang, E.K., Sun, R.P., Chen, C.M., Liang, Z., Khan, M.K.: Proof of X-repute blockchain consensus protocol for IoT systems. Comput. Secur. 95, 101871 (2020)

53. Biswas, S., Sharif, K., Li, F., Nour, B., Wang, Y.: A Scalable Blockchain Framework for Secure Transactions in IoT. IEEE Internet of Things J. (2018)

54. Xu, Q., Aung, K.M.M., Zhu, Y., Yong, K.L.: A blockchain-based storage system for data analytics in the Internet of Things. In: Yager, R.R., Pascual Espada, J. (eds.) New Advances in the Internet of Things. SCI, vol. 715, pp. 119–138. Springer, Cham (2018). https://doi.org/10.1007/978-3-319-58190-3_8

Research on Life Prediction Model of Field Seismic Equipment Based on IFA-RVM Algorithm

Xiaojun Li[1,3], Jincan Yin[2(✉)] ⓘ, Xiaogang Zhang[1,3], and Kangda Yin[1,3]

[1] Hebei Earthquake Agency, Shijiazhuang 050000, China
[2] School of Information Science and Engineering, Hebei University of Science and Technology, Shijiazhuang 050000, China
[3] Innocative Research Team of Hebei Earthquake Agency for Seismograghs Calibration, Valuation and Selection of Observation Sites, Shijiazhuang 050021, China

Abstract. Aiming at the problem of low prediction accuracy of FA-RVM model, a life prediction model of field seismic equipment based on IFA-RVM is proposed. Based on the standard firefly algorithm, the inertia weight is introduced to adjust the search step dynamically to improve the search ability and convergence speed of the algorithm in the later stage of iteration. The improved firefly algorithm is used to optimize the correlation vector machine, and the IFA-RVM prediction model is established. Simulation experiments show that the IFA-RVM model can effectively predict the remaining life of the equipment, which provides a theoretical basis for further improving the management of field seismic equipment.

Keywords: Firefly algorithm · Correlation vector machine · Inertia weight · Life prediction

1 Introduction

Field seismic equipment includes a large number of optical, mechanical, and electrical components combined. Due to the large number of components and they are usually in continuous operation, aging and life problems are inevitable. In order to improve the operation rate, the staff must understand the working principle and remaining life of the equipment in order to replace the new equipment in time. Therefore, predicting the remaining life of field seismic equipment has practical basis and theoretical value for improving the equipment operation rate [1].

Scholars at home and abroad have paid extensive attention to the research on the life prediction of field seismic equipment, and have made considerable progress in the past ten years. Autoregressive and exponential smoothing models have good predictive effects in traditional methods. In addition, support vector machines [2], Markov models [3], Bayesian principles [4] and other machine learning algorithms are also used for the remaining life of the equipment. Malun et al. explained that HMM must be forced to conform to the exponential distribution in time and cannot be directly used to predict

© Springer Nature Switzerland AG 2021
X. Sun et al. (Eds.): ICAIS 2021, CCIS 1424, pp. 585–596, 2021.
https://doi.org/10.1007/978-3-030-78621-2_49

the remaining life [5]. Dong Ming used the status of HSMM to diagnose the equipment and retrograde health and predict the remaining life [6]. Jun Zhu et al. put forward CNN-RUL prediction model [7]. They first perform temporal feature extraction, then use a convolutional network to reduce the dimensionality of high-dimensional features, and finally use a multi-scale convolutional neural network for RUL prediction. After the proposed method is verified on the gear life data set, it is shown Good forecast results.

Firefly algorithm is a swarm intelligence optimization algorithm, which has the advantages of simple algorithm model and easy implementation [8]. However, in the later stage of the parameter optimization of the standard FA algorithm, due to the increase in the number of iterations, the convergence speed of the algorithm decreases, and it is easy to fall into the local optimal solution. RVM is a highly sparse super-vised learning algorithm [9]. Its kernel function does not need to meet the Mercer condition. It can increase the flexibility of kernel function selection and is more suitable for function regression. It has received extensive attention in the field of model prediction. Based on the above problems, this paper proposes a power supply reliability prediction model (IFA-RVM) based on the improved firefly optimization relevance vector machine model. The inertia weight factor is introduced to improve the local search capability of the Firefly algorithm in the later iteration, and the search step is dynamically adjusted to improve the convergence speed of the algorithm. The improved firefly algorithm is used to optimize the correlation vector machine. Using the IFA-RVM model to predict the remaining life of field seismic equipment can speed up the convergence speed, effectively improve the prediction accuracy, and solve the problem of falling into the local optimum in the later iteration of the standard firefly algorithm.

2   IFA and RVM

2.1   Relevance Vector Machine Theory

On the basis of SVM [10, 11], RVM combines the results of Markov chain, Bayesian principle, automatic correlation decision prior and maximum likelihood theory [12]. Compared with the support vector machine (SVM), the correlation vector machine (RVM) only has the kernel function setting, which can save training time and has the advantage of high sparsity. The kernel function of RVM does not need to meet Mercer condition, which can increase the flexibility of kernel function selection.

Set the input set of the training sample to, and the corresponding output set to, the regression model of the correlation vector machine can be defined as:

$$y_i = \sum_{i=1}^{N} w_i K(z, z_i) + v_0 + \lambda \tag{1}$$

Among them, λ obeys $N(0, \sigma^2)$, $v_i(i = 0, 1, \ldots, N)$ is the weight coefficient, $K(z, z_i)$ is the kernel function, and N is the number of samples. For mutually independent output sets, the likelihood distribution of samples is:

$$p(y|v, \sigma^2) = (2\pi\sigma^2)^{-N/2} \exp\left\{-\frac{1}{2\sigma^2}||t - \Phi(z)v||^2\right\} \tag{2}$$

Among them, $y = (y_1, y_2, ..., y_N)$, $v = [v_0, v_1, ..., v_N]^T$, $\Phi = [\phi(z_1), \phi(z_2), ..., \phi(z_N)]^T$, $\phi(z_N) = [1, K(z_1, z_N), K(z_2, z_N), ..., K(z_n, z_N)]^T$. The maximum likelihood estimation of v and σ^2 will often cause serious over-adaptation, so the zero-mean Gaussian prior distribution of v is used to avoid this phenomenon:

$$p(v|\alpha) = \prod_{i=0}^{N} N(v_i|0, \alpha_i^{-1}) \tag{3}$$

α is a hyperparameter, w is a weight, and each weight w of C corresponds to a hyperparameter α, which reduces the influence of the prior distribution on the parameters and realizes the sparse characteristics of the correlation vector machine.

According to Bayesian principle, the posterior probability distribution of all unknown parameters can be obtained:

$$p(v|y, \alpha, \sigma^2) = (2\pi)^{-(N+1)/2} |\psi|^{-1/2} \exp\left\{ -\frac{1}{2}(v - \mu)^T \psi^T (v - \mu) \right\} \tag{4}$$

Among them, $\psi = (\sigma^{-2}\varphi^T \varphi + A)^{-1}$ is the posterior covariance moment; $\mu = \sigma^{-2}\psi\varphi^T t$, $A = diag(\alpha_0, \alpha_1, ..., N)$. The estimated hyperparameter α and variance σ^2 can be obtained by the maximum likelihood method. If a new input value z is given, the output probability distribution obtained is Gaussian distribution, and the predicted value is $t = \mu^T \varphi(z)$.

2.2 Improved Firefly Algorithm(IFA)

Firefly Algorithm (FA) is a swarm intelligence optimization algorithm proposed by Xin-She Yang in 2008 based on the activities of fireflies in nature [13]. The algorithm is based on the process of the low-brightness fireflies moving towards the high-brightness fireflies in nature, thereby simulating the optimization of parameters [14, 15]. Brightness and attractiveness are two important factors of the firefly algorithm. High-brightness fireflies are attractive to low-brightness fireflies, and low-brightness fireflies are attracted to move toward their location, and the brightness and attractiveness are proportional during the movement., The higher the brightness of the fireflies have a higher degree of attraction, which attracts the lower the brightness of the fireflies to move longer [16, 17].

However, in the later stage of parameter optimization, due to the increase in the number of iterations, fireflies mostly surround the fireflies with the highest brightness, and the convergence speed of the algorithm decreases, and it is easy to fall into a local optimal solution.

In order to solve the local optimization problem in the later stage of the FA algorithm, this article optimizes the FA algorithm. The specific steps are as follows:

(1) The relative fluorescence brightness of the fireflies and the relative attraction between the fireflies.

$$H = H_0 \times e^{-\gamma r_{ij}} \tag{5}$$

$$L = L_0 \times e^{-\gamma r_{ij}^2} \tag{6}$$

Among them, H_0 is the brightness of the firefly at $r = 0$; L_0 is the attraction of fireflies at $r = 0$; r_{ij} is the brightness absorption coefficient; ith is the distance between the first firefly and the jth firefly.

(2) Firefly mobile location update. During the optimization process, the location where Firefly A is attracted by Firefly B and moved to its location is updated to:

$$x_i = x_i + L \times (x_j - x_i) + \alpha \times (rand - \frac{1}{2}) \tag{7}$$

Among them, x_i is the position of the firefly i, x_j is the position of the firefly j; α is the step factor, [0, 1] is the upper constant, and $rand$ is the random factor, which satisfies $rand \in [0, 1]$.

(3) Introduce inertial weights. In the late iteration of the FA algorithm, the random movement of the fireflies causes local oscillations, slower convergence speed and lower accuracy. In order to improve the local search ability of the algorithm, the inertia weight is introduced and the update formula of the firefly moving position is optimized:

$$x_i = w(t)x_i + L \times (x_j - x_i) + \alpha \times (rand - \frac{1}{2}) \tag{8}$$

Among them, $w(t)$ is the inertia weight, which belongs to the constant on [0, 1]. The value of the inertia weight affects the update of the moving position of the firefly. In order to avoid blindly changing the value of the inertial weight, the inertial weight factor needs to be adaptively changed with the update of the position of the firefly. The calculation method is as follows:

$$w(t) = \exp(-\lambda(t)/\lambda(t-1)) \tag{9}$$

Among them, t is the number of location updates during the firefly iteration process, $\lambda(t)$ is the degree of smoothness of the inertia weight factor change, and $\lambda(t)$ and the degree of smoothness of the inertia weight factor are inversely proportional.

(4) Dynamically adjust the search step. In the classic FA algorithm, the step factor α cannot be changed, so that individuals with low brightness in the early FA algorithm cannot approach the individuals with high brightness as quickly as possible; in the later stage of the algorithm, the difference in brightness between individual fireflies is reduced, and the location is relatively close, which cannot be changed. α makes it impossible for the individual firefly to move to the position of the individual with the brightest brightness, resulting in shocks and reduced algorithm accuracy. In order to solve the above problems, a variable step factor α is used. In the early stage of the algorithm, a larger α is used to find a new search space, which improves the global search capability and accelerates the convergence speed; in the later stage, a smaller α is used for local exploration to avoid shocks.

The dynamic adjustment algorithm search step α can balance the global search capability of the FA algorithm. The adjustment formula for variable α is:

$$\alpha = 0.4/(1 + \exp(0.015 \times (p - maxN)/3)) \tag{10}$$

Among them, p is the number of iterations, and max N is the maximum number of iterations.

3 Life Prediction Model of Field Seismic Equipment Based on IFA-RVM

To establish a life prediction model for field seismic equipment based on IFA-RVM, the specific steps are as follows.

(1) Initialize training data. Determine the training data set and test data set corresponding to the field seismic equipment life prediction model, and normalize it.

(2) The IFA algorithm is used to optimize the parameters of the RVM model. Initialize the RVM model parameters and simulate the optimization process of the improved Firefly algorithm to iteratively optimize the RVM optional parameters.

(3) Calculate the objective function value of the firefly, and use the training data set as the objective function value of the RVM.

(4) The brightness of the firefly is optimized and the position is updated. The brightness of the firefly is determined according to the result of (3), and the reverse order is performed to obtain the optimal firefly, and the position is updated according to formula (7).

(5) It is judged whether the optimal objective function value is obtained, and the inertia weight is introduced to update the position according to formula (8).

(6) It is judged whether the number of iterations reaches or meets the conditions for stopping iteration, if it is satisfied, the optimized RVM parameters are output, otherwise, it returns to step (3) to continue iterative optimization.

(7) Obtain the optimal parameters of the RVM algorithm.

(8) Use the results obtained in (7) to predict the life of field seismic equipment, and denormalize the prediction results to obtain the actual field seismic equipment life prediction value.

The specific process is shown in Fig. 1:

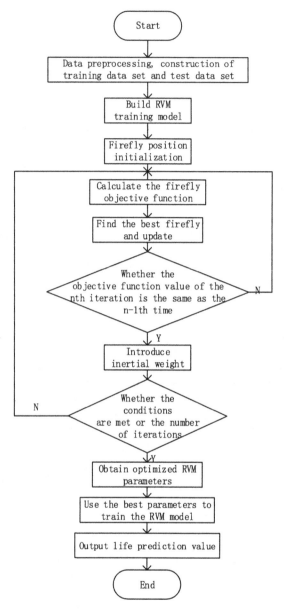

Fig. 1. IFA-RVM Flow chart

4 Simulation Analysis of IFA-RVM Instance

The lifetime prediction model of field seismic equipment based on IFA-RVM is established by selecting the historical data samples of field seismic equipment. The model is trained with the established training samples, and then the trained model is used to predict the equipment life. Simulation analysis is realized in MATLAB software environment. The mean absolute error (MAE) and root mean square error (RMSE) were used to evaluate the prediction results, and the calculation formula was as follows:

$$MAE = \frac{1}{N} \sum_{i=1}^{N} |Q_i - P_i| \tag{11}$$

$$RMSE = \sqrt{\frac{1}{N} \sum_{i=1}^{N} (Q_i - P_i)^2} \tag{12}$$

Where, Q_i is the actual value and P_i is the predicted value.

4.1 RVM Optional Parameters and Optimizations

The selection and optimization of kernel function can greatly improve the generalization ability of RVM. Radial basis kernel function (RBF) has good performance in nonlinear approximation, and RBF is used as the kernel function of correlation vector machine. IFA algorithm is used to find the optimal width solution of RBF kernel function satisfying RVM constraints. The calculation formula of RBF kernel function is shown in Eq. (17).

$$k(x, x_i) = \exp[-\frac{1}{2\delta^2} ||x - x_i||^2] \tag{13}$$

Where δ is the width of the nucleus. The optimization iteration diagram of IFA-RVM is shown in Fig. 2.

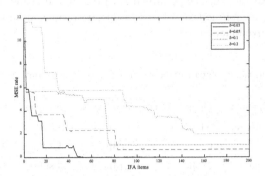

Fig. 2. IFA-RVM Optimized iteration diagram

As shown in Fig. 2, when $\delta = 0.03$, IFA-RVM converges faster and has higher accuracy.

In order to verify the effectiveness of IFA algorithm, four standard test functions with different complexity are used in this paper to carry out simulation experiments on IFA algorithm and FA algorithm, and the results are compared and analyzed.

(1) Sphere Model Function:

$$f(x) = \sum_{i=1}^{s} x_i^2 \tag{14}$$

(2) Rastrigin Function:

$$f(x) = \sum_{i=1}^{N} [x_i^2 - 10 \times \cos(2\pi x_i) + 10] \tag{15}$$

The specific parameter Settings of each test function are shown in Table 1:

Table 1. Parameter setting for the function

The name of the function	Dimension	Maximum iteration number	Optimization of space	Objective function value
Sphere Model	2	200	(−100, 100)	0
Rastrigin	2	200	(−30, 30)	0

In the comparison experiment, the basic parameters set by the algorithm are: population number $N = 50$, max $N = 200$, $\gamma = 1$, initial step size $\alpha = 0.2$, and maximum brightness $L_0 = 1$. FA algorithm and IFA algorithm were used to conduct 50 experiments on four standard test functions respectively, and the results were averaged. The statistical results are shown in Table 2. The performance of FA algorithm and IFA algorithm was evaluated by using the four indexes of worst value, best value, mean value and standard deviation of objective function.

Table 2. Performance comparison between standard FA algorithm and IFA algorithm

Algorithm	Test functions	Optimal value	Worst value	Average	Standard deviation
FA	Spher Model	3.04E−4	4.97E−4	4.01E−4	4.87E−5
IFA		0	5.43E−5	5.17E−5	9.32E−7
FA	Rastrigin	2.24E−3	2.14E−2	8.86E−3	5.47E−3
IFA		0	1.30E−3	1.05E−3	1.32E−4

It can be seen from Fig. 3 and Fig. 4 that the improved Firefly algorithm has faster convergence speed and higher accuracy for the Sphere function and Rastring function, which proves the effectiveness of the IFA algorithm.

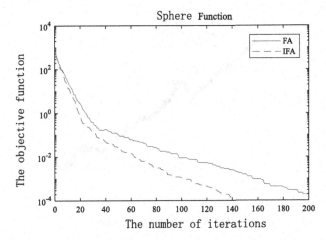

Fig. 3. FA and IFA algorithms compare the convergence curves of Sphere functions

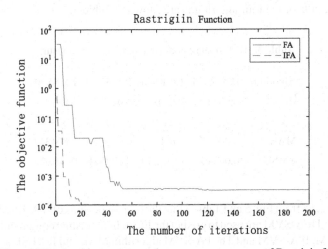

Fig. 4. FA and IFA algorithms compare the convergence curves of Rastrigin functions

4.2 Experimental Results and Analysis

Using the optimal IFA-RVM parameter A to predict the remaining life of the field seismic equipment, the comparison between the predicted result and the actual value is shown in Fig. 5.

In order to further verify the validity and reliability of the IFA-RVM prediction model in the reliability of the distribution network power supply, the IFA-RVM algorithm and the unimproved FA-RVM algorithm and the support vector machine (FA-SVM) algorithm optimized by the Firefly algorithm. The improved Firefly algorithm optimized support vector machine (IFA-SVM) algorithm to predict and analyze the life of field seismic equipment. Use correlation coefficient, algorithm prediction time T, mean absolute error (MAE) and root mean square error (RMSE) as evaluation indicators. The

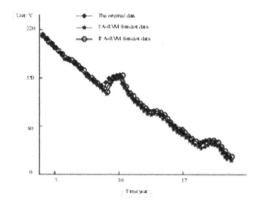

Fig. 5. Forecast result graph

optimal parameters of the four algorithms are used to predict the data. The simulation prediction results of the four algorithms are shown in Table 3.

Table 3. Performance comparison of prediction results

Algorithm	IFA-RVM	FA-RVM	IFA-SVM	FA-SVM
R	0.9999	0.9998	0.9916	0.9518
T(s)	1.4362	2.4460	2.6582	3.5237
MAE	0.00045	0.000833	0.000633	0.001317
RMSE	0.00046	0.000874	0.000794	0.001673

It can be seen from Fig. 5 and Table 3 that the four algorithms of IFA-RVM, FA-RVM, FA-SVM, and IFA-SVM are used to predict the life of field seismic equipment. Compared with FA-RVM, IFA-SVM and The FA-SVM algorithm MAE and RMESE are the lowest values. The improved firefly optimized correlation vector machine algorithm (IFA-RVM) has a lower MAE of 0.000383 and a lower RMSE of 0.000414 than the standard firefly optimized correlation vector machine algorithm (FA-RVM). The running time of the algorithm is 1.098 s faster, indicating the effectiveness of the improved Firefly algorithm. The improved Firefly algorithm optimized support vector machine algorithm (IFA-SVM) is 0.000684 lower than the standard Firefly optimized support vector machine algorithm (FA-SVM) in MAE and RMSE lower than 0.000879. The running time of the algorithm is 0.8655 s faster, which also shows improve the effectiveness of the Firefly algorithm. At the same time, compared with the IFA-SVM algorithm, the IFA-RVM algorithm has a higher correlation between the predicted value and the actual value, the iteration speed is 1.222 s faster, and the error is smaller. Compared with the IFA-SVM algorithm, the MAE is 0.000183 and the RMSE is 0.000334 lower, indicating the improvement. The firefly algorithm optimizes the correlation vector machine algorithm for better performance in predicting the life of seismic equipment in the field.

Probability corresponding to λ, and the probability is recorded as $P(o|\bar{\lambda})$, called likelihood logarithm. The probability value is normalized by the time sequence length to eliminate the influence of the time length on the probability, as shown in formula (16):

$$P\log(o|\bar{\lambda}) = \log P(o|\bar{\lambda})/n \tag{16}$$

The judging formula for user gesture authentication is shown in the following formula (17):

$$P\log(o|\bar{\lambda})\begin{cases} > \tau \ \textit{Legal gesture} \\ \leq \tau \ \textit{Illegal gesture} \end{cases} \tag{17}$$

It can be seen that the value of the threshold τ seriously affects the authentication result. In this paper, the threshold value of each user is determined through the user registration gesture sample, as shown in formula (18):

$$\tau = mean - \omega \times var \tag{18}$$

Where, *mean* and *var* respectively represents the mean and variance of the training user's registered gesture sample set, which is the threshold coefficient. For each user's test gesture set, ω has the same value.

5   Conclusion

The paper proposes a model based on IFA-RVM, and uses this model to predict the life of seismic equipment in the field. The model uses the RBF kernel function, and uses the improved firefly algorithm to optimize the parameters of the RBF kernel function to obtain the optimal parameters. Then the RVM model is trained to predict the life of field seismic equipment. The results show that compared with FA-RVM model, FA-SVM model and IFA-SVM model, the IFA-RVM model constructed in this paper has higher prediction accuracy and is a practical and effective method for predicting the life of field seismic equipment.

References

1. Xia, L., Cao, Y., Yan, Y.: Research on equipment remaining life prediction based on gray dynamic model. China Computer Automatic Measurement and Control Technology Association (2016)
2. Shah, M.S., Malik, T.A., Khatoon, R., Hassan, S.S., Shah, F.A.: Human behavior classification using geometrical features of skeleton and support vector machines. Comput. Mater. Continua **61**(2), 535–553 (2019)
3. Al-Wesabi, F.N.: A smart English text zero-watermarking approach based on third-level order and word mechanism of Markov model. Comput. Mater. Continua **65**(2), 1137–1156 (2020)
4. Maheswari, U., Umamaheswari, R.: Wind turbine drivetrain expert fault detection system: multivariate empirical mode decomposition based multi-sensor fusion with Bayesian learning classification. Intell. Autom. Soft Comput. **26**(3), 479–488 (2020)

5. Lun, M., Jianshe, K., Qiang, Z.: Implementation of equipment residual life prediction framework based on Hidden Markov model. Comput. Simul. **27**(5), 88–91 (2010)
6. Dong, M.: A new device health management method based on autoregressive implicit semi-Markov chain. Sci. China: Inf. Sci. 2185–2198 (2008)
7. Zhu, J., Chen, N., Peng, W.: Estimation of bearing remaining useful life based on multiscale convolutional neural network. IEEE Trans. Industr. Electron. **66**(4), 3208–3216 (2019)
8. Wang, X., Peng, H., Deng, C., Huang, H., Zhang, Y., Tan, X.: Firefly algorithm based on uniform local search and variable step size. Comput. Appl. **38**(3), 715–721+727 (2018)
9. Xie, K., Zhou, J., Billinton, R.: Reliability evaluation algorithm for complex medium voltage electrical distribution networks based on the shortest path. IEE Proc-Gener. Transm. Distrib. **150**(6), 686–690 (2003)
10. Bi, F., Fu, X., Chen, W., Fang, W., Miao, X., et al.: Fire detection method based on improved fruit fly optimization-based SVM. Comput. Mater. Continua **62**(1), 199–216 (2020)
11. El Mamoun, M., Mahmoud, Z., Kaddour, S.: SVM model selection using PSO for learning handwritten Arabic characters. Comput. Mater. Continua **61**(3), 995–1008 (2019)
12. Tipping, M.E.: Sparse Bayesian learning and the relevance vector machine. J. Mach. Learn. Res. **1**(3), 211–244 (2001)
13. Yang, X.-S.: Firefly algorithms for multimodal optimization. In: Watanabe, O., Zeugmann, T. (eds.) SAGA 2009. LNCS, vol. 5792, pp. 169–178. Springer, Heidelberg (2009). https://doi.org/10.1007/978-3-642-04944-6_14
14. Cheng, M., Ni, Z., Zhu, X.: Review of theoretical research on firefly optimization algorithm. Comput. Sci. **42**(4), 19–24 (2015)
15. Liu, C., Ye, C.: Firefly optimization algorithm with chaotic search strategy. J. Syst. Manag. **22**(4), 538–543 (2013)
16. Gao, W.: Research and Application of Firefly Algorithm. Lanzhou University, Lanzhou (2013)
17. Pati, J., Kumar, B., Manjhi, D., et al.: A comparison among ARIMA, BP-NN, and MOGA-NN for software clone evolution prediction. IEEE Access **5**, 11841–11851 (2017)

Optimization of Location Technology in Meteorological Wireless Sensor Network

Haichuan Li[1], Man Zhang[2]([⊠]), Xinli Shi[3], and Yanzhao Wang[1]

[1] Cangzhou Meteorological Bureau, Cangzhou 061000, China
[2] School of Information Science and Engineering, Hebei University of Science and Technology, Shijiazhuang 050000, China
[3] Botou City Meteorological Bureau in Hebei Province, Botou 062150, China

Abstract. With the continuous development of modern communication technology, China has made considerable achievements in the field of wireless communication technology. In the process of application of modern meteorological observation technology, the maximum level of automation and information technology has been improved. Through the analysis of RFID positioning technology, this paper proposes a positioning algorithm based on the phase difference and signal strength of radio frequency signal. Aiming at the problem of low positioning accuracy of RFID system, the signal strength received by the antenna is firstly processed by Gaussian filtering. The filtered signal strength is combined with KNN algorithm and Bayesian optimization estimation for the initial positioning of the positioning tag. Then the position of the reference tag is marked and its phase difference and signal strength are collected to form the feature vector. The feature vectors of reference tags were trained in BP neural network algorithm, and the hidden layer features were extracted and input into the SVR training model. In order to improve the training speed, SMO algorithm is combined in the process of training the model. Finally, by inputting the feature vector of the pending positioning tag into the model that has been trained in advance, the position coordinates of the pending positioning tag can be calculated more accurately.

Keywords: RFID · Gaussian filtering · KNN algorithm · SMO algorithm

1 Introduction

Wireless sensor network (WSN) is an integrated intelligent information system integrating information acquisition, information transmission and information processing [1]. At present, the related research is very active and has a broad application prospect. WSNs (Wireless Sensor Networks) has brought a revolution in the field of information perception [2]. In the process of application of modern meteorological observation technology, the maximum level of automation and information technology has been improved.

© Springer Nature Switzerland AG 2021
X. Sun et al. (Eds.): ICAIS 2021, CCIS 1424, pp. 597–608, 2021.
https://doi.org/10.1007/978-3-030-78621-2_50

The research on localization technology in foreign countries is relatively early. Jeffrey et al. designed the Spot ON system in 2000. This system is the earliest RFID [3] based positioning system. The distance between the base station and the target is estimated according to the wireless signal attenuation model [4], and the location of the target is calculated by triangulation method. In order to improve the accuracy of location, the hill-climbing algorithm [5] is also used in the calculation process. However, the use of Spot On system is limited by the high cost, short distance to be located, and the measurement value is easy to be interfered by the external environment. Until now, Spot On system has not been completely built. Ni et al. improved the LANDMARC indoor positioning system on the existing basis [6]. This system introduces the concept of reference tag. In the process of using this system for measurement, fewer readers are required, which not only reduces the cost of the system, but also improves the accuracy of system measurement [7]. Jin et al. proposed an improved RSSI value algorithm for the LANDMARC system [8]. The improved algorithm only needs to measure a few reference tags adjacent to the target tag to get the position coordinates. This algorithm not only reduces the complexity of calculation, but also improves the accuracy of positioning [9]. Cricket system [10] introduced ultrasonic signals into the indoor positioning system. The principle of ultrasonic positioning is similar to that of radar system, which is based on the method of reflected distance. The system will be RFID signal and ultrasonic signal joint analysis can get the specific location of the target positioning. Blue Bot system [11] combines Wi-Fi signal and RFID signal for analysis and then obtains the position. As can be seen from the above study, most researchers analyze the RSSI information of RFID signal to get the location of the positioning target. However, some RFID chips cannot obtain the RSSI value directly, which limits the development of RSSI-based positioning system.

The localization technology has also been studied deeply in China. Huang Yihua and Liu Zongyuan et al. from Sun Yat-sen University proposed an optimized topology deployment mode of reference tags. According to the prior positioning information and combined with the Bayesian algorithm, this optimization method is used to estimate the location points of the target through probability analysis. In the positioning process, the basic principles and characteristics of RFID technology are combined [12]. Deng Huifang, Ma Qiping, et al. from East China University of Science and Technology classified the RSSI value received by the reader to reduce the impact of the uncertainty during signal transmission [13]. In this method, the data read by the same reader is put into a collection, and the label that appears most frequently in the collection is taken as the nearest distance label. Ju Ying, Yan Ge et al. introduced the concept of virtual reference tag, which is used to locate the boundary position of an area. The RSSI value of boundary virtual reference tag was obtained by establishing regression equation. This method improves the accuracy of the signal received by the system at the positioning boundary [14]. Professor Liu Yunhao of Tsinghua University proposed an RFID indoor positioning algorithm based on phase difference method [15], aiming at the problem of using RSSI information for positioning. The measurement error caused by the multipath effect is greatly reduced by using the phase difference data [16]. By comparing and analyzing the phase difference values of RFID target tags and spatial position points, the specific position points of the positioning targets are obtained. The system reduces the interference of the external environment, improves the accuracy of the system positioning, and can be well applied in the indoor environment positioning.

The RFID positioning technology is studied in this paper. By analyzing the measurement parameters of the received RFID signal, the phase difference information and signal strength information of the signal are emphatically studied, and the two are combined to determine the location of the positioning target. Finally, this paper designs an RFID-based positioning system. Three localization algorithms are tested. Through the analysis of the test results, the comparison between the proposed algorithm and the other two algorithms is verified. It has a great advantage in positioning accuracy. The rest of this article is arranged as follows: Sect. 2 is to study the antenna structure and signal phase. In Sect. 3, an optimized positioning algorithm is proposed which combines the phase information and signal strength information of the tag. Section 4 designs the system architecture according to the requirement analysis of RFID-based positioning system. The superiority of the proposed localization algorithm is verified by a comparative test. Finally, Sect. 5 gives a brief summary of this article.

2 Antenna Structure and RFID Phase Analysis

2.1 Analysis of Antenna Structure

Phase is an important feature of RFID signal [17]. There is a certain relation between the structure and phase of the antenna. This chapter will first study the relationship between the two. The carrier frequency of the antenna was 920.875 MHz. Shift the label from the front antenna 50 cm along the X-axis to 120 cm. Measure the change in the phase value at every 2 cm shift, read the phase 300 times at each position point and average it out. The average value obtained and the position point are recorded for the convenience of later analysis and research. The relationship between distance change and phase can be obtained through graph analysis of the recorded data, as shown in Fig. 1. According to the data variation trend analysis in the figure, the phase of the tag received by the antenna will change periodically with the increase of distance. In a period, the phase decreases as the distance increases.

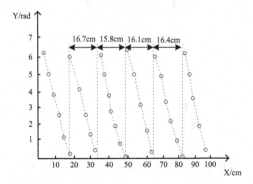

Fig. 1. Relationship between distance change and phase

When the carrier frequency of the antenna is 920.875 MHz, the distance variation when $\varphi = 2\pi$ can be calculated by formula $d = \frac{\varphi c}{4\pi f}$:

$$d = \frac{\varphi c}{4\pi f} = \frac{c}{2f} = \frac{\lambda}{2} \tag{1}$$

For each half-wavelength change of 16.3 cm, the phase changes by one period. So that's 360°. The measured distance change value in real life is 16.7 cm, 15.8 cm, 16.1 cm and 16.4 cm. The result is 16.25 cm by averaging several values. By observing the data changes in Fig. 1, we know that the measured data differs little from the theoretical value, and the error is maintained within 1 cm.

Because it is impossible to determine the position of the positioning target based on the phase received by one antenna, this paper uses two antennas to determine the position through the phase difference of the received label. The positioning geometric model of phase difference is shown in Fig. 2. From the analysis of geometric relations in the figure, it can be seen that:

$$R_1 - R_2 = -\frac{\lambda}{4\pi}(\Delta\varphi - \Delta\varphi_A) \approx -Dsin\theta \tag{2}$$

In this equation, $\Delta\varphi = \varphi_1 - \varphi_2$, $\Delta\varphi_A = \varphi_{A1} - \varphi_{A2}$. The geometric model of phase difference is shown in Fig. 2. The distance between the two antennas in the figure is represented by D. When distance D is less than half wavelength, since the difference between the two sides in the triangle is less than the third side, the distance difference between the two antennas is less than D. That is to say, the phase difference of these two antennas within a period, the arrival Angle θ is:

$$\theta = \sin^{-1}\left[\frac{\lambda}{4\pi D}(\Delta\varphi - \Delta\varphi_A)\right] \tag{3}$$

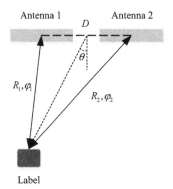

Fig. 2. Geometric model of phase difference

As can be seen from the phase difference geometric model, because there is a certain relationship between the position of the tag and the phase between the two antennas, the position of the target tag can be determined through the phase.

2.2 Processing of Dynamic Phase Sequences

The preprocessing of dynamic phase is mainly to solve the problem of hop "1". The purpose is to reduce the impact caused by external environment interference or the equipment itself. By analyzing the phase value of the target tag within the antenna recognition range of a single reader under the static condition, a small part of the measured phase value has the phenomenon of jumping, which leads to the unsmooth change process of the phase curve.

In theory it's only before and after the periodic transformation that you have a change of 2π. The rest of the static data transformation should be continuous. Changes in values between two adjacent measurements should not result in these excessive jumps. This is because the measured value changes by π units over the true phase value, requiring "hop π" processing of the data. If the previous measured value is the true value, calculate the difference between the next measured value and the last measured value, and then analyze the change of the value. The threshold range setting of this paper is shown in formula (4). When the change of the phase value is within the threshold range, it is necessary to "hop π" the phase value, that is, subtract π or add π to the current measured value.

$$\pi - \omega\pi \leq |\Delta\theta| \leq \pi + \omega\pi \tag{4}$$

ω is the difference coefficient of continuous phase, and its value range is [0, 1]. The smaller the value, the smaller the phase change. The phase curve after "jump π" processing is shown in Fig. 4. In the figure, it is easy to find that two points jump greatly. This is a normal phenomenon during the transformation period, resulting in a jump of "2π". This problem is known as the phase unwinding problem [18]. A $X = (\theta_1, \theta_2, \cdots, \theta_n)$ phase sequence is presented, and the phase sequence is processed simply according to the following phase unwrapping algorithm.

The phase sequence variation curve after unwinding is shown in Fig. 3. By observing the data in the graph, it is found that the data graph after the phase unwrapping process has good continuity and there is no point with great jump degree. The reliability of phase unwrapping is proved.

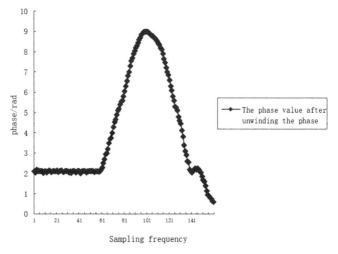

Sampling frequency

Fig. 3. Data graph after phase unwinding

The above data change curve is processed on the premise that the first phase initial value is correct. Therefore, the correct initial value should be ensured before the phase processing, so as to improve the accuracy of the system positioning. It is found that there are two initial values of phase: "θ" and "$\theta + \pi$", and the difference between these two initial values is compared. If the difference is greater than π, you need to take the remainder of π. If the difference is close to π, the subsequent phase initial value needs to be added by π. If the difference is small, there is no need to process the phase value, and the final real phase sequence is the phase sequence with fewer processing times. Through the research and analysis of experimental data, it can be concluded that the number of normal values in the dynamic sequence is much more than the data that needs to be processed. Through this analysis, the true and false of the sequence can be distinguished.

From the above study it is concluded that using an antenna cannot be positioned according to the phase. In this paper, the localization technology is studied on the two-dimensional level. Only when the target is matched with the antenna for two days at the same time at a certain time can the position be located successfully.

3 Research on Location Algorithm Optimization

3.1 Reference Tag Deployment

A certain number of reference tags are placed in the area to be located. The improved RSSI-based localization algorithm mainly estimates the approximate location based on the proximity between the RSSI value of the target tag and the reference tag. Figure 4 is the reference tag deployment diagram, the black star is the target tag location, and the light blue square is the reference tag location.

In the process of deploying tags, too sparse deployment of reference tags will lead to too large positioning data error, and too dense deployment of reference tags will affect

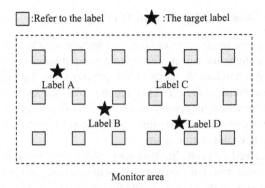

Fig. 4. Refers to the label deployment diagram

the reading of RSSI value. Therefore, the density of tag deployment has a great impact on the positioning accuracy of the system. In this paper, the influence of nearest neighbor reference tag number - K value on positioning accuracy is studied. It can be observed from Fig. 5 that the MSE when K values 1, 2, 3, 4, 5, 6 and 7 respectively.

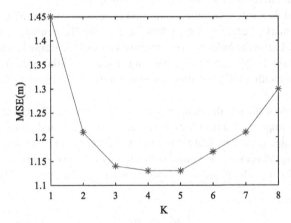

Fig. 5. The MSE of the system under different K values

When K is equal to 1, the MSE value is relatively large, with the value of 1.45 m. When the value of K changes from 1 to 3, the MSE value of the system shows K significant downward trend. When K is equal to 4, the MSE value measured is 1.13 m, at which time the positioning accuracy of the system is relatively good. When K value rises to between 3 and 5, the MSE of the system does not change significantly. The positioning accuracy of the system has reached the best effect and can meet the requirements of the system. However, with the increase of K value, the amount of calculation will also increase, so the maximum number of neighbors K will usually choose 3 or 4, and K value chosen in this paper is 4.

3.2 The Realization of the Algorithm in This Paper

First, in order to receive more accurate data, the antenna structure should be designed well. Design test locations for tags according to the requirements of the test scenario. Let's say I have L antenna, N target tag, T reference tag. Firstly, the signal value and phase difference value at the reference tag are collected and calculated. Then the processed data and the actual geographic location (x, y) of the reference tag are recorded to form the feature vector. In order to improve the accuracy of system data, 800 sets of data were collected at each location point.

Filtering the received data can eliminate some abnormal data values caused by external environment interference. It not only improves the accuracy of received data, but also reduces the computation of the system. In the filtering process, principle 3σ is adopted, which is expressed by the following formula:

$$\mu - 3\sigma \leq f(x) \leq \mu + 3\sigma \tag{5}$$

The received signal phase difference information and signal strength value are calculated to get the distance. Take the average of the data and get the mean μ. The standard deviation is σ. According to the above principle, the data that differs 3σ from the average is eliminated. Put the rest of the data into the training set.

The collected data information is composed of feature vectors. The position of the reference tag is marked and the data is first put into the BP neural network algorithm [19] for training. Using the hidden layer characteristics of the trained model and putting it into the SVR model can improve the operating efficiency of the system. The processed data are combined with SMO algorithm for fitting training to complete the final training stage.

In the process of data collection, 800 sets of data were collected at each location point in order to improve the accuracy of the data. The collected phase difference and signal strength value constitute feature vectors which are put into the database, as shown in Eq. (8). The signal vectors of group i measured by antenna m at position point (x, y) are represented by R_m^i. The phase difference between the j antenna and the n antenna is denoted by $P_{j,n}^i$.

$$R_{(x,y)} = \begin{bmatrix} R_1^1, R_2^1, P_{1,2}^1, x, y \\ R_1^2, R_2^2, P_{1,2}^2, x, y \\ \ldots\ldots \\ R_1^{800}, R_2^{800}, P_{1,2}^{800}, x, y \end{bmatrix} \tag{6}$$

In the process of filtering the data, the distance value is calculated according to the phase difference of the label and the signal strength value. Calculate the average value of the calculated data and get E_{avg}. The standard deviation is E_{std}. According to principle 3σ, 800 groups of data were selected, as shown in Eq. (7). After filtering, about 700 sets of data will be left, and the remaining data will be put into the training set for training.

$$E_{avg} - 3E_{std} \leq E_Q \leq E_{avg} + 3E_{std} \tag{7}$$

We received 800 sets of data from each location point, and sorted out the data to obtain the following formula.

$$U = \begin{bmatrix} R_1^1, R_2^1, P_{1,2}^1 \\ R_1^2, R_2^2, P_{1,2}^2 \\ \cdots \cdots \\ R_1^{800}, R_2^{800}, P_{1,2}^{800} \end{bmatrix} \tag{8}$$

In order to improve the accuracy of positioning data, it is necessary to filter the received data first and eliminate abnormal data caused by external environment interference and its own reasons. And then the data that's left is averaged and treated as eigenvalues. By putting the processed eigenvalues into the optimized model for calculation, the specific location points of the target to be determined can be obtained.

4 Algorithm Testing and Analysis

In this experiment, a 1.5 m × 3 m rectangular area was selected for testing. Each side was divided at an interval of 0.15 m, and the whole positioning area was divided into 200 parts. In the off-line stage, 800 times of label data were collected for each reference point of intersection. Then the collected data is filtered by Gaussian filter to remove the abnormal data. The average value of the processed data is taken as the reference value of the coordinate point, which reduces the error of the data collected in the measurement process. During the experiment, 5 locations to be fixed were selected, as shown in Fig. 6.

The location of the registration point is calculated by the two-frequency arrival phase difference ranging, KNN algorithm [20] and the optimization algorithm. Figure 7 shows the actual location point coordinates of the positioning target and the location point coordinates calculated by the three algorithms.

Put the statistical data results in Table 1. Among them, Algorithm 1 is the arrival phase difference ranging based on dual-frequency. Algorithm 2 is KNN algorithm. Algorithm 3 is the optimization algorithm proposed in this paper.

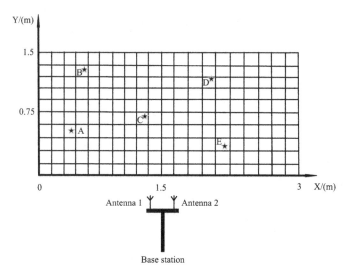

Fig. 6. Location diagram of selected test points

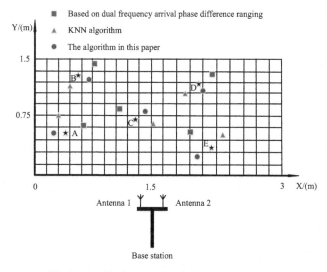

Fig. 7. Positioning results of different algorithms

The positioning errors of the three algorithms are shown visually through Fig. 8: From the data changes in the figure, it can be found that the positioning difference generated by the positioning results calculated by the proposed positioning algorithm is the smallest. The coordinate error range of the positioning position point is about 15 cm, and the positioning accuracy is higher than the other two algorithms. It can be seen that the localization algorithm in this paper has some advantages compared with the traditional localization algorithm.

Table 1. Algorithm positioning result table

Localization algorithm	The actual coordinates/m	Output the coordinates/m	Positioning difference/m
Algorithm 1	A(0.41, 0.51)	(0.61, 0.62)	0.23
	B(0.56, 1.31)	(0.78, 1.46)	0.27
	C(1.32, 0.71)	(1.10, 0.85)	0.26
	D(2.02, 1.17)	(2.20, 1.33)	0.25
	E(2.17, 0.36)	(1.95, 0.54)	0.28
Algorithm 2	A(0.41, 0.51)	(0.30, 0.69)	0.21
	B(0.56, 1.31)	(0.45, 1.15)	0.19
	C(1.32, 0.71)	(1.51, 0.61)	0.21
	D(2.02, 1.17)	(1.91, 1.04)	0.17
	E(2.17, 0.36)	(2.31, 0.49)	0.19
Algorithm 3	A(0.41, 0.51)	(0.28, 0.41)	0.16
	B(0.56, 1.31)	(0.71, 1.22)	0.17
	C(1.32, 0.71)	(1.42, 0.80)	0.13
	D(2.02, 1.17)	(2.11, 1.09)	0.12
	E(2.17, 0.36)	(2.05, 0.28)	0.14

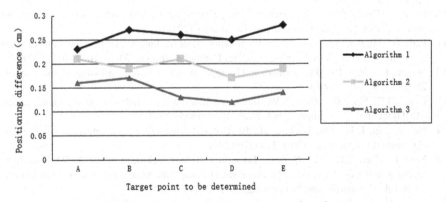

Fig. 8. Positioning algorithm error comparison figure

5 Conclusion

Aiming at the problem of low positioning accuracy of RFID system, the signal strength is combined with KNN algorithm and Bayesian optimization estimation for the initial positioning of the positioning tag. Then the position of the reference tag is marked, and its phase difference and signal strength are collected to form the feature vector input training model for training. Finally, the eigenvectors of the pending positioning tags are input into the model that has been trained in advance for positioning. Through experimental comparison, the algorithm proposed in this paper is superior to algorithms 1 and 2 in positioning accuracy.

References

1. Zhang, Z.L., Bao, R.G., Wang, X.F., et al.: Design of meteorological data acquisition system based on wireless sensor network. Shaanxi Meteorol. **2010**(6), 6–8 (2010)
2. Kienle, F.: Architectures for Baseband Signal Processing. Springer, New York (2014)
3. Wang, X., Zhang, M., Lu, Z.: A frame breaking based hybrid algorithm for UHF RFID anti-collision. Comput. Mater. Continua **59**(3), 873–883 (2019)
4. Han, Y., Zheng, W., Wen, G.C., et al.: Multi-rate polling: improve the performance of energy harvesting backscatter wireless networks. Comput. Mater. Continua **60**(2), 795–812 (2019)
5. Gong, J.J.: Research on THREE-DIMENSIONAL Positioning Method of Wireless Sensor Network Based on RSSI. Nanchang Aviation University (2011)
6. Ni, L.M., Liu, Y.H., Lau, C.L.: LANDMARC: indoor location sensing using active RFID. Wirel. Netw. **10**(6), 701–710 (2004)
7. Zou, X.Y., Han, F.W.: Recent neighbor improvement algorithm based on LANDMARC. J. Wuhan Univ. **59**(3), 255–259 (2013)
8. Jin, G.Y., Lu, X.Y., Park, M.S.: An indoor localization mechanism using active RFID tag. In: IEEE International Conference on Sensor Networks, Ubiquitous and Trustworthy Computing, vol. 1, no. 4 (2006)
9. Zhou, J.R., Zhang, H.J., Mo, L.F.: Two-dimension localization of passive RFID tags using AOA estimation. In: Instrumentation and Measurement Technology Conference (I2MTC), pp. 1–5 (2011)
10. Li, Z.Z.: Research on Autonomous Navigation System of Omnidirectional Four-Wheel Mobile Robot. Qingdao University of Technology (2018)
11. Patil, A., Munson, J., Wood, D., et al.: Bluebot: asset tracking via robotic location crawling asset tracking via robotic location crawling. Comput. Commun. **31**(6), 1067–1077 (2008)
12. Sun, Y., Fan, Z.P.: RFID technology and its application in Indoor positioning. Comput. Appl. **25**(5), 1205–1208 (2005)
13. Deng, H.F., Ma, Q.P., Zhou, S.W.: Indoor positioning using radio frequency identification (RFID) technology. Comput. Appl. **7**(28), 1858–1865 (2008)
14. Gu, Y., Liu, K.H., Shi, W.G., et al.: RFID-based boundary virtual reference tag location algorithm. Comput. Eng. **37**(6), 274–276 (2011)
15. Yang, L., Chen, Y.K., Li, X.Y., et al.: Tagoram: real-time tracking of mobile RFID tags to high precision using COTS devices. In: Proceedings of the 20th Annual International Conference on Mobile Computing and Networking, pp. 237–248 (2014)
16. Chen, N., Xialihaer, N., Kong, W., et al.: Research on prediction methods of energy consumption data. J. New Media **2**(3), 99–109 (2020)
17. Qiu, L.Q., Huang, Z.Q., Liang, X.X.: Overview of RFID tag location perception technology. Res. Comput. Appl. **34**(12), 3521–3526 (2017)
18. Hong, C.: Research on RFID Tag Positioning Algorithm Based on Unwrapping Phase. Wuhan Huazhong University of Science and Technology (2018)
19. Wang, Q., Wang, X.: Parameters optimization of the heating furnace control systems based on BP neural network improved by genetic algorithm. J. Internet of Things **2**(2), 75–80 (2020)
20. Pan, N., Pan, D., Liu, Y.: The crime scene tools identification algorithm based on GVF-Harris-SIFT and KNN. Intell. Autom. Soft Comput. **25**(2), 413–419 (2019)

A Survey on the Applications of Wi-Fi Sensing

Fan Li, Chao Li$^{(\boxtimes)}$, Yang Lv, Haoshan Xu, Xinhao Wang, and Zhenlei Yu

Guangzhou University, Guangzhou 510700, China
lichao@gzhu.edu.cn

Abstract. With the increasing demand for wireless data, more and more Wi-Fi devices are being constructed. Recently, people are not satisfied that Wi-Fi is only used for data exchange. Wi-Fi starts to be used for sensing in various scenarios. To understand the fundamental technology and the development trends of Wi-Fi sensing, this paper provides a comprehensive survey of resent application and performance of Wi-Fi sensing to describe the fundamental technology. Based on the sensing objects, this paper divides Wi-Fi sensing into two categories: dynamic sensing and static sensing. With the emergence of new Wi-Fi technology, Wi-Fi sensing will be developed. This paper also analyses two research trends of Wi-Fi sensing including multi-antenna fusion and multi-sensor fusion, three research challenges: limitation, robustness, and practicality, promising research directions in applications of Wi-Fi sensing.

Keywords: Wi-Fi sensing · Dynamic sensing · Static sensing

1 Introduction

With the popularity of wireless networks, Wi-Fi develops very rapidly. Multi-Input Multi-Output (MIMO) technology improves the reliability, transmission range and throughput of Wi-Fi. Orthogonal Frequency Division Multiplexing (OFDM) technology improves the spectral efficiency of Wi-Fi and reduces the influence of multipath [1]. MIMO-OFDM technology provides a description of channel state information (CSI) for each carrier frequency between each transmit/receive antenna pair of Wi-Fi. Recently, more and more people are paying attention to Wi-Fi sensing technology based on CSI. Based on a large number of deployed wireless systems, the Wi-Fi system is inexpensive and easy to promote. The Wi-Fi signal is different from the camera-based solution, which is so vulnerable when the privacy issues come, and usually used with privacy protection [2, 3] or intrusion detection [4]. Wi-Fi is not restricted by ambient light, which can protect the privacy of users to the greatest extent.

CSI can provide the amplitude attenuation and phase shift of electromagnetic waves, which is convenient for us to study the behavior of electromagnetic waves in space. We can quantify the changes of Wi-Fi signals in space so that Wi-Fi signals can be used for sensing. When electromagnetic waves spread in the environment, they will be affected by everything in the environment, and the impact will be reflected on the changes in the CSI, so that the CSI can be applied to various wireless sensing scenarios. For example, changes in the amplitude and phase obtained from CSI have different responses to

© Springer Nature Switzerland AG 2021
X. Sun et al. (Eds.): ICAIS 2021, CCIS 1424, pp. 609–618, 2021.
https://doi.org/10.1007/978-3-030-78621-2_51

different motions produced by different objects in space, which is the fundamental of dynamic sensing of Wi-Fi. This feature is mainly used in human activity detection. The amplitude change of CSI can be used for human presence detection [5–7], smoking detection [8], fall detection [9–11], gesture recognition [12–14], people counting [15–18], etc. The phase shift and signal transmission delay of CSI can also be used for human localization and tracking [19–22]. Different main frequency components in the CSI phase can be extracted to estimate breathing rate [23–25] and sleep detection [26–28], etc. For static sensing, it is used to extract the stable CSI amplitude or phase value in the environment for liquid identification [29, 30] and object imaging [29, 31]. According to the difference of application, the signal processing methods, and learning algorithms used by Wi-Fi sensing are also different. To understand the current situation of Wi-Fi perception, this paper reviews the application scenarios, performance, challenges and future trends of Wi-Fi sensing.

The main contributions of this paper are:

- The paper analyze the application domains of Wi-Fi sensing, including the comparison of basic principles and performance, which can be divided into two categories: dynamic perception and static perception.
- The paper identifies challenges and future trends, including multi-antenna fusion and multi-sensor fusion, to enhance existing Wi-Fi sensing capabilities and promote applications of Wi-Fi sensing.

2 Background and Related Work

We will introduce the background and related work of Wi-Fi perception technology in this section.

2.1 Background of CSI

CSI can characterize the behavior of the electromagnetic wave used by Wi-Fi signals, which is affected by multipath effects. CSI can be expressed as [32]:

$$H(f;t) = \sum_{i=1}^{n} a_i(f,t) \cdot e^{-j\psi(f,t)} \qquad (1)$$

where f represents the frequency, t represents the time, n is the number of multipath, $|a_i(f,t)|$ and $\psi(f,t)$ are the absolute value of the amplitude and the absolute value of the phase respectively. It means that we can extract the amplitude and phase information of electromagnetic waves from CSI with simple calculations.

For a Wi-Fi system with MIMO-OFDM, its CSI can be represented as a matrix, which can be expressed as [33]:

$$H_{i,j,k} = (\sum_{n}^{N} a_n e^{-j2\pi d_{i,j,n} f_k / c}) \cdot e^{-j2\pi \tau_i f_k} \cdot e^{-j2\pi \rho f_k} \cdot e^{-j2\pi \eta (\frac{f_k'}{f_k} - 1) f_k} \qquad (2)$$

where i is the serial number of the transmitting antennas, j is the serial number of receiving antennas, and k is the serial number of subcarriers. Each data packet can be parsed into an i * j * k three-dimensional matrix. The main part of CSI is Multi-Path Channel, which means the true CSI value under n-th multipath. It is also what we want to get. The CSI matrix also contains many noises. These noises will be superimposed on the true value of the received CSI, so that the amplitude and phase values of CSI will shift and fluctuate, and noise will be generated. Therefore, in many application scenarios, noise reduction processing of the raw CSI is required to obtain the true value as much as possible before it can be used for sensing. For the real measurement situation, we can adjust the sending rate of data packets used by Wi-Fi signals to obtain a series of CSI containing time information, so that we can construct a CSI information matrix in the time domain. It is a four-dimensional matrix containing a lot of information, and it can meet the sensing demand in many scenarios.

The IEEE 802.11n describes that Wi-Fi includes CSI. But almost all existing NIC drivers do not support the CSI extraction function. We need to use the corresponding network card and the changed driver to extract the CSI easily. Currently, CSI tools can be divided into two categories according to the different network cards used. The 802.11n CSI tool [34] appeared earlier and is the tool of most research. It uses Intel 5300 NIC to report compressed CSI. The Atheros CSI tool [35] can also provide CSI. It uses Qualcomm Atheros NIC, and it can extract 56 CSI subcarriers from a 20 MHz Wi-Fi channel, while the 802.11n CSI tool can extract 30 subcarriers from the same bandwidth. The more subcarriers can be provided, the more information of frequency can be obtained. Both tools can run at a frequency of 2.4 GHz or 5 GHz.

2.2 Related Work

In previous researches, there are some surveys based on specific Wi-Fi sensing scenarios, such as human localization [36–38], gesture recognition [36] and activity recognition [39–42]. The focus is to sort out the models, basic principles, noise reduction methods and algorithms established by Wi-Fi sensing in specific scenarios. Another survey [33] summarizes and sorts out the algorithms, signal processing methods and performance results used in Wi-Fi sensing using CSI. The difference between this paper and other surveys is that it is not limited to only discussing Wi-Fi sensing applications related to motions. From the perspective of whether the object is moving or not, Wi-Fi sensing is divided into dynamic sensing and static sensing. The survey also summarizes the signal processing methods and results of researches in various scenarios. Finally, this paper puts forward the challenges and development directions of Wi-Fi sensing. The structure of the Wi-Fi sensing scene division in this paper is shown in Table 1.

3 Wi-Fi Dynamic Sensing

Wi-Fi dynamic sensing is using Wi-Fi to perceive the environment based on the movement of objects. Based on this, many Wi-Fi sensing application scenarios were born. This section divides these application scenarios into three categories based on the fundamental principles: regularity sensing, motion sensing, localization and tracking. We will introduce Wi-Fi dynamic sensing from these three levels.

Table 1. Overview of Wi-Fi sensing scene divided by this paper.

Wi-Fi Dynamic Sensing	Regularity Sensing	Smoking Detection [8], Fall Detection [9–11], People Counting [15–18], Breathing Rate Sensing [23–25], Sleep Detection [26–28]
	Action Sensing	Gesture Recognition [12–14, 44], Human activity recognition [42]
	Localization and Tracking	Human Presence Detection [5–7], Human Localization and Tracking [19–22, 45]
Wi-Fi Static Sensing	Imaging	Object Imaging [29, 31]
	Material Identification	Liquid Identification [29, 30]

3.1 Regularity Sensing

For the regularity sensing, the influence of the movement regularity in some special scenes on CSI is usually used in Wi-Fi sensing. Regular and continuous actions that occur in space will continue to interfere with the stability of Wi-Fi signals, causing Wi-Fi signals to change regularly at similar frequencies. One intuition is to use the regularity of CSI changes to perceive the occurrence of such actions. The sensing targets in such scenarios can often be accomplished by methods that do not rely on training sets, but there are high requirements for signal processing methods, and the restrictions on the scenarios are relatively strict.

The typical application of regularity sensing is Wi-count [15]. Wi-count detects the direction of people passing between antenna arrays by detecting the changing trend of the CSI phase difference. At the same time, because the shape and walking habits of each person are different, Independent Components Analysis (ICA) is used for the phase difference sequence of all subcarriers to obtain the number of noise sources to realize the detection of the number of people and the direction of travel between the antenna arrays. In order to eliminate the ambiguity of the phase difference, a clustering algorithm is used for the phase difference sequence to restore the initial phase difference information. The Savitzky-Golay filter is used for the phase difference sequence to eliminate random noise. In order to eliminate the independent phase difference sequence between each subcarrier, Wi-count uses Principal Component Analysis (PCA) to make the counting results more accurate. To test the results of the experiment, the accuracy of Wi-count exceeds 92%.

Smoking detection is another application of regularity. Smokey [8] uses the features left on the CSI to test smoking. Because human actions during smoking are very similar, including a series of sequential movements of the chest and hands, it will leave regular features in the amplitude of CSI. Based on the foreground detection in image processing community, Smokey eliminates the noise in CSI, extracts smoking features, and detect smoking without relying on the training set. Experiments have shown that in a relatively stable environment, Smokey's TPR for smoking activity is 0.976. When there are four non-smokers around the target, the accuracy can also reach 70%.

We can also use regularity sensing in sleep detection. Wi-Sleep [26] extracts regular changes caused by breathing and sudden changes from CSI. Since people almost only have regular breathing during sleep, this will cause the human chest to move between the line-of-sight (LOS) and NLOS, leading to regular fluctuations. After Wi-Sleep performs outlier removal, noise removal, and subcarrier selection on the value of CSI collected, the breath rate is extracted. In addition, Wi-Sleep studied the performance of breath rate extraction in different sleeping positions and tried to detect the sleeping position through the various effects of breathing in different sleeping positions on CSI.

3.2 Action Sensing

Different from regularity sensing, the object of action sensing is irregular actions, which greatly broadens the application of action sensing. Action sensing focuses on identifying a specific single action without repetition and often relies on training samples and machine learning methods to get results. It is comparing the measured real features with the sample features to get the result.

Human activity recognition is a typical application of action sensing. Wi-Chase [42] extracts the CSI of the Wi-Fi channel from continuous data packets, analyzes its changes over time and recognizes human activities. It uses all the subcarriers that can be extracted from the Wi-Fi signal, combines the changes in amplitude and phase information, and proposes an adaptive Activity Detection Algorithm (ADA) to capture changes. Wi-Chase uses a majority voting system to select subcarriers for activity classification, and experiments on multiple receiving/transmitting antenna pairs have achieved an average accuracy of 97%.

Gesture recognition is a prevalent application scenario in action sensing. Traditional method [43] uses sEMG or other features combined with CNN for gesture recognition. WIMU [44] uses the basic method of Wi-Fi gesture recognition. When there are actions in the Wi-Fi environment, the CSI and RSSI of Wi-Fi will change. The change patterns are positively related to different postures. Wi-Fi-based gesture recognition uses machine learning to train a model for each predefined gesture and recognizes it when the user performs the same motion. Different from similar research, WIMU proposes a method to generate virtual samples of any multi-gesture data samples by using multiple single-gesture data samples, with the help of which, it is no longer necessary to collect data sets of almost infinite combinations when multi-gesture recognition, and we can realize multi-gesture recognition easily. When WIMU recognizes six gestures at the same time, the accuracy rate is still above 90%.

3.3 Localization and Tracking

Most of the current localization technologies can only obtain satisfactory positioning accuracy under outdoor conditions, and indoor localization and tracking technologies have always been problems that people want to solve. The emergence of Wi-Fi sensing makes indoor positioning and tracking possible. Wi-Fi-based localization and tracking can perceive people or objects. Due to the limitation of Wi-Fi wavelength and bandwidth, it is difficult for Wi-Fi-based positioning to obtain position information through Angle of Arrival (AoA) and Time of Arrival (ToA), so we need other methods. At the same time, in such scenarios, only a single target can be located and tracked. In a multi-target system, the disturbance will be excessive and dramatically reduces accuracy.

Indo Track [19] uses Doppler information to locate humans. When a person moves between the receiving and transmitting antenna, the path length reflection will change, which causes Doppler shift. The amplitude and direction can be estimated from the phase information extracted from the CSI. The Doppler frequency shift is related to the target's speed and position. The AoA spectrum obtained from CSI is associated with the target's angular probability. Indo Track combines the above to determine the rate, the location and absolute trajectory of the target. The tracking accuracy of Indo Track is about 35 cm.

WiTraffic [45] extracts the impact of passing vehicles on the CSI as a training set to train the vehicle classification model and proposes a vehicle speed estimation and lane estimation algorithm based on Earth Mover's Distance (EMD). WiTraffic can get 96% average classification accuracy and 95% lane detection accuracy, and the estimation of speed can get an average root-mean-square error of 5mph.

4   Wi-Fi Static Sensing

Wi-Fi perception can not only be applied to the perception of movement in space but also has a good perception effect for stationary objects. Wi-Fi static sensing is to perceive stationary objects with Wi-Fi. Compared with the rich application scenarios of Wi-Fi dynamic sensing, the system of Wi-Fi static sensing needs to be developed. For Wi-Fi static sensing, the goal is to obtain a sufficiently stable CSI and to achieve the sensing target based on modelling or machine learning methods.

4.1   Imaging

Current imaging technologies are mostly based on cameras, but this is not conducive to the protection of user privacy. It brings additional security risks to users' personal information. There are some new imaging technologies. For example, we can image with Wi-Fi [31]. Wi-Fi signals transmitted by independent Wi-Fi transmitters have separate modes and can be used for frequency sampling in space. The work does not require extensive bandwidth or high gain. It only needs to use standard commercial Wi-Fi routers with sparse antenna arrays, which can perform two-dimensional imaging to the metal balls and X-shaped target within 25 MHz bandwidth and 10 s integration time.

However, it should be noted that due to the characteristics of electromagnetic wave, imaging technologies using Wi-Fi signals has great limitations. Since electromagnetic waves have a huge attenuation when penetrating metals and liquids, their attenuation will be much smaller when they penetrate clothing, thin bred and other objects. It leads to Wi-Fi signal imaging objects can only be based on liquid, metalwork or human body (mostly composed of water).

4.2   Material Identification

Material identification rarely appears in our lives because its cost is too expensive. But based on Wi-Fi signals, we can achieve a certain degree of material identification. WiMi

[30] proposes a new CSI pre-processing scheme to solve the problems of multipath noise and hardware noise, to obtain a stable CSI amplitude ratio and phase difference, and calculate it into a new material feature. This feature is independent of size. WiMi can realize the identification of the liquid type on the LOS link.

5   Challenges and Prospects

This paper lists many examples of Wi-Fi sensing. At present, Wi-Fi sensing can be used in a lot of scenarios, but there are some problems.

Limitations: Compared with other higher frequency RF technologies, such as UWB, the frequency and bandwidth of Wi-Fi make it difficult for Wi-Fi to produce sufficient response to objects below 6cm scale (which is the electromagnetic wave wavelength at 5GHz frequency). Wi-Fi signals tend to bypass these objects.

Robustness: Wi-Fi single has noises that are difficult to eliminate, which severely limits the direct use of CSI, and additional noise reduction measures are required. Movement in the environment will seriously affect the stability of the CSI, which causes Wi-Fi sensing is challenging to be used in complex environments. Many application scenarios are often limited to relatively unique experimental settings.

Practicality: For Wi-Fi sensing applications that rely on the training set, a large number of dataset need to be collected in advance, which dramatically limits the scope of application of Wi-Fi sensing. When the environment changes, the training often set at risk of failure and need to be recollected.

To the future development trends of Wi-Fi sensing, this paper proposes two points:

Multi-antenna fusion: The NIC used by Wi-Fi sensing supports MIMO and often has three transmitting antennas and three receiving antennas. In fact, many applications only use two or three of them. It is a waste of basic resources. Suppose we can use the extra antennas to form a more ingenious antenna array. In that case, it is not only hopeful to expand the spatial sensing range of Wi-Fi sensing, but also to provide more labels for various learning-based methods. It is hopeful of achieving greater accuracy. There are many methods to extract high-quality and low-cost data sources from sensor-cloud systems [46], which will be more conducive to the use of multi-device antennas.

Multi-sensor fusion: Although the UWB-based sensing solutions have been commercially available, solutions that use Wi-Fi for sensing have not yet appeared on the market. On the one hand, due to the short time of it has occurred, on the other hand, due to the many limitations of Wi-Fi sensing, it is difficult to be directly used in people's lives. Wi-Fi sensing has meager hardware cost and good portability. In the future, it can even make existing devices have Wi-Fi sensing capabilities by updating firmware. Therefore, if the limitations are difficult to resolve, Wi-Fi sensing is expected to be a cheap and effective non-contact solution integrating into the existing IoT sensor network and becomes a sensor node to work with other sensors to complete more fine-grained sensing work.

6   Conclusion

Based on the current researches of Wi-Fi sensing, this paper summarizes the existing application scenarios of it. It divides its application scenarios into dynamic sensing and static sensing according to different perception objects. The basic principles and performance results are concluded. This article proposes three challenges faced by Wi-Fi sensing, including limitations, robustness and practicality. We believe that multi-antenna fusion and multi-sensor fusion will be the future development trends of Wi-Fi sensing, which will enhance the existing Wi-Fi sensing capabilities and promote Wi-Fi sensing on a large scale.

Funding Statement. This work supports in part by National Key R&D Program of China (No. 2018YFB2004200), Industrial Internet Innovation and Development Project of China (2019), National Science Foundation of China (No. 61872100).

References

1. Nee, R., Prasad, R.: OFDM for Wireless Multimedia Communications. Artech House, Fitchburg (2000)
2. Jiang, W.: Optimal network security strengthening using attack-defense game model. In: 2009 Sixth International Conference on Information Technology: New Generations, pp. 475–480. IEEE, Piscataway (2009)
3. Sun, Z.: The QoS and privacy trade-off of adversarial deep learning: an evolutionary game approach. Comput. Secur. **96**, 101876 (2020)
4. Tian, Z.H.: An architecture for intrusion detection using honey pot. In: Proceedings of the 2003 International Conference on Machine Learning and Cybernetics (IEEE Cat. No. 03EX693), vol. 4, pp. 2096–2100. IEEE, Piscataway (2003)
5. Adib, F.: See through walls with WiFi! In: Proceedings of the ACM SIGCOMM 2013 conference on SIGCOMM, pp. 75–86. Association for Computing Machinery, New York (2013)
6. Qian, K.: Enabling contactless detection of moving humans with dynamic speeds using CSI. ACM Trans. Embed. Comput. Syst. (TECS) **17**(2), 1–18 (2018)
7. Soltanaghaei, E.: Peripheral WiFi vision: exploiting multipath reflections for more sensitive human sensing. In: Proceedings of the 4th International on Workshop on Physical Analytics, pp. 13–18. Association for Computing Machinery, New York (2017)
8. Zheng, X.: Smokey: ubiquitous smoking detection with commercial WiFi infrastructures. In: IEEE INFOCOM 2016-The 35th Annual IEEE International Conference on Computer Communications, pp. 1–9. IEEE, Piscataway (2016)
9. Wang, Y.: Wifall: device-free fall detection by wireless networks. IEEE Trans. Mob. Comput. **16**(2), 581–594 (2016)
10. Palipana, S.: FallDeFi: ubiquitous fall detection using commodity Wi-Fi devices. Proc. ACM Interact. Mobile Wearable Ubiquit. Technol. **1**(4), 1–25 (2018)
11. Zhang, F.: WiSpeed: a statistical electromagnetic approach for device-free indoor speed estimation. IEEE Internet Things J. **5**(3), 2163–2177 (2018)
12. Abdelnasser, H.: Wigest: a ubiquitous WiFi-based gesture recognition system. In: 2015 IEEE Conference on Computer Communications (INFOCOM), pp. 1472–1480. IEEE, Piscataway (2015)
13. Ali, K.: Keystroke recognition using WiFi signals. In: Proceedings of the 21st Annual International Conference on Mobile Computing and Networking, pp. 99–102. Association for Computing Machinery, New York (2015)
14. Ali, K.: Recognizing keystrokes using WiFi devices. IEEE J. Sel. Areas Commun. **35**(5), 1175–1190 (2017)

15. Yang, Y.: Wi-count: passing people counting with COTS WiFi devices. In: 2018 27th International Conference on Computer Communication and Networks (ICCCN), pp. 1–9. IEEE, Piscataway (2018)
16. Reichl, P.: Using WiFi technologies to count passengers in real-time around rail infrastructure. In: 2018 International Conference on Intelligent Rail Transportation (ICIRT), pp. 1–5. IEEE, Piscataway (2018)
17. Oshiga, O.: Human detection for crowd count estimation using CSI of WiFi signals. In: 2019 15th International Conference on Electronics, Computer and Computation (ICECCO), pp. 1–6. IEEE, Piscataway (2019)
18. Ibrahim, O.T.: CrossCount: a deep learning system for device-free human counting using WiFi. IEEE Sens. J. **19**(21), 9921–9928 (2019)
19. Li, X.: IndoTrack: device-free indoor human tracking with commodity Wi-Fi. Proc. ACM Interact. Mobile Wearable Ubiquit. Technol. **1**(3), 1–22 (2017)
20. Qian, K.: Widar: decimeter-level passive tracking via velocity monitoring with commodity Wi-Fi. In: Proceedings of the 18th ACM International Symposium on Mobile Ad Hoc Networking and Computing, pp. 1–10. Association for Computing Machinery, New York (2017)
21. Virmani, A.: Position and orientation agnostic gesture recognition using WiFi. In: Proceedings of the 15th Annual International Conference on Mobile Systems, Applications, and Services, pp. 252–164. Association for Computing Machinery, New York (2017)
22. Winter, E.: Measuring human values in software engineering. In: Proceedings of the 12th ACM/IEEE International Symposium on Empirical Software Engineering and Measurement, pp. 1–4. Association for Computing Machinery, New York (2018)
23. Liu, X.: Contactless respiration monitoring via off-the-shelf WiFi devices. IEEE Trans. Mob. Comput. **15**(10), 2466–2479 (2015)
24. Ma, J.: When can we detect human respiration with commodity WiFi devices? In: Proceedings of the 2016 ACM International Joint Conference on Pervasive and Ubiquitous Computing: Adjunct, pp. 325–328. Association for Computing Machinery, New York (2016)
25. Niu, K.: A fresnel diffraction model based human respiration detection system using COTS Wi-Fi devices. In: Proceedings of the 2018 ACM International Joint Conference and 2018 International Symposium on Pervasive and Ubiquitous Computing and Wearable Computers, pp. 416–419. Association for Computing Machinery, New York (2018)
26. Liu, X.: Wi-Sleep: contactless sleep monitoring via WiFi signals. In: 2014 IEEE Real-Time Systems Symposium, pp. 346–355. IEEE, Piscataway (2014)
27. Gu, Y.: Sleepy: Wireless channel data driven sleep monitoring via commodity WiFi devices. IEEE, Piscataway (2018)
28. Liu, J.: Tracking vital signs during sleep leveraging off-the-shelf WiFi. In: Proceedings of the 16th ACM International Symposium on Mobile Ad Hoc Networking and Computing, pp. 267–276. Association for Computing Machinery, New York (2015)
29. Wang, C.: Towards in-baggage suspicious object detection using commodity WiFi. In: 2018 IEEE Conference on Communications and Network Security (CNS), pp. 1–9. IEEE, Piscataway (2018)
30. Feng, C.: WiMi: target material identification with commodity Wi-Fi devices. In: 2019 IEEE 39th International Conference on Distributed Computing Systems (ICDCS), pp. 700–710. IEEE, Piscataway (2019)
31. Vakalis, S.: Imaging with WiFi. IEEE Access **7**, 28616–28624 (2019)
32. Wang, W.: Understanding and modeling of WiFi signal based human activity recognition. In: Proceedings of the 21st Annual International Conference on Mobile Computing and Networking, pp. 65–76. Association for Computing Machinery, New York (2015)
33. Ma, Y.: WiFi sensing with channel state information: a survey. ACM Comput. Surv. (CSUR) **52**(3), 1–36 (2019)

34. Halperin, D.: Tool release: gathering 802.11 n traces with channel state information. ACM SIGCOMM Comput. Commun. Rev. **41**(1), 53–53 (2011)
35. Zhang, T.: The design and implementation of a wireless video surveillance system. In: Proceedings of the 21st Annual International Conference on Mobile Computing and Networking, pp. 426–438. Association for Computing Machinery, New York (2015)
36. Wengrowski, E.: A survey on device-free passive localization and gesture recognition via body wave reflections. ACM Trans. Auton. Adapt. Syst. **5**, 1–15 (2014)
37. Xiao, J.: A survey on wireless indoor localization from the device perspective. ACM Comput. Surv. (CSUR) **49**(2), 1–31 (2016)
38. Yang, Z.: From RSSI to CSI: indoor localization via channel response. ACM Comput. Surv. (CSUR) **46**(2), 1–32 (2013)
39. Wang, Z.: Wi-Fi CSI-based behavior recognition: from signals and actions to activities. IEEE Commun. Mag. **56**(5), 109–115 (2018)
40. Wu, D.: Device-free WiFi human sensing: from pattern-based to model-based approaches. IEEE Commun. Mag. **55**(10), 91–97 (2017)
41. Zou, Y.: Wi-Fi radar: recognizing human behavior with commodity Wi-Fi. IEEE Commun. Mag. **55**(10), 105–111 (2017)
42. Arshad, S.: Wi-chase: a WiFi based human activity recognition system for sensorless environments. In: 2017 IEEE 18th International Symposium on A World of Wireless, Mobile and Multimedia Networks (WoWMoM), pp. 1–6. IEEE, Piscataway (2017)
43. Ding, Z.: sEMG-based gesture recognition with convolution neural networks. Sustainability **10**(6), 1865 (2018)
44. Venkatnarayan, R.H.: Multi-user gesture recognition using WiFi. In: Proceedings of the 16th Annual International Conference on Mobile Systems, Applications, and Services, pp. 401–413. Association for Computing Machinery, New York (2018)
45. Won, M.: WiTraffic: low-cost and non-intrusive traffic monitoring system using WiFi. In: 2017 26th International Conference on Computer Communication and Networks (ICCCN), pp. 1–9. IEEE, Piscataway (2017)
46. Li, M.: Answering the min-cost quality-aware query on multi-sources in sensor-cloud systems. Sensors **18**(12), 4486 (2018)

Efficient Partially Policy-Hidden CP-ABE for IoT Assisted Smart Health

Zhishuo Zhang[1], Wei Zhang[1], Hanxiang Zhuang[1], Yu Sun[2], and Zhiguang Qin[1]($\boxtimes$)

[1] School of Information and Software Engineering, University of Electronic Science and Technology of China (UESTC), Chengdu 610054, China
qinzg@uestc.edu.cn
[2] Fujian Normal University, Fuzhou, Fujian, China

Abstract. With the rapid advancements of Internet of Things (IoT) technologies, wearable devices assisted cloud-based smart health (s-health) has become the promising solution to improve the quality and convenience of healthcare. However, the privacy preserving and data security has not been perfectly addressed. In past few years, ciphertext-policy attribute-based encryption (CP-ABE) proposed as a flexible and powerful cryptographic primitive to realize one-to-many encryption and fine-grained access control has been regarded as a promising solution to the security problem in cloud. But in traditional CP-ABE, the attribute values in access policy are presented in cleartext. This will easily divulge the privacy of the data owners (patients). So in this paper, we propose a efficient partially policy-hidden CP-ABE scheme (PPH-CP-ABE), which can effectively hide the attribute values in ciphertext to protect the sensitive information in access policy. Our access policy in our PPH-CP-ABE scheme can supports both AND and OR gates which is based on the Linear Secret Sharing Scheme (LSSS). And our PPH-CP-ABE scheme is more efficient and lightweight than the other CP-ABE schemes with hidden policies. Furthermore, we give a rigorous security proof and analysis to state that our scheme is selectively indistinguishable secure under chosen plaintext attacks (selectively IND-CPA secure) and resistant to the off-line dictionary attacks. Through comparison with the state-of-art schemes from the perspective of functionality and efficiency, it is easily to observe that our scheme is more practical, secure and efficient in the real s-health scenarios.

Keywords: Internet of Things (IoT) · Smart health (s-health) · ciphertext-policy attribute-based encryption (CP-ABE) · Policy-hidden · Linear Secret Sharing Scheme (LSSS)

This work was supported in part by NSFC with No. 61520106007, the Natural Science Foundation of China under Grant U1936101 and the 13th Five-Year Plan of National Cryptography Development Fund for Cryptographic Theory of China under Grant MMJJ20170204.

X. Sun et al. (Eds.): ICAIS 2021, CCIS 1424, pp. 619–636, 2021.
https://doi.org/10.1007/978-3-030-78621-2_52

1   Introduction

With the wide adoption of cloud computing [1,2,21] and rapid development of Internet of Things (IoT) [16,17], the mobile health has been ushereded in as a new way to monitor human health in real-time. The smart health (s-health) is a new context-aware health paradigm of mobile health in smart cities [24]. S-health has extraordinary potential since it delivers the healthcare services via the ubiquitous smartphones. Although s-health mitigates many health-related issues, security and privacy are still the two inescapably struggling challenges in s-health to be addressed. Because of the fact that s-health will gather unprecedented amounts of the highly personal information, the privacy and security issues in s-health are more apparent than in other contexts. To solve the security and privacy problem in IoT environment, many works design some authentication protocols [5,9,32], signature schemes and keyword search encryption mechanisms [29] for Industrial Internet of Things (IIoT) [25,31,33,34], Internet of Vehicles (IoV) [15], mobile Internet, 5G networks [30] and RFID networks [26]. But how to design a one-to-many encryption mechanism with fine-grained access control for the s-health has still been a open issue.

The traditional access control can only provide the coarse-grained access policies and can not protect the privacy and security adequately. Ciphertext-policy attribute-based encryption (CP-ABE) is a new versatile and flexible cryptographic primitive proposed in recent years [4,22,27], as a type of attribute-based encryption (ABE) [23], which refines the access control to the attribute level. In CP-ABE, the user's attributes are embedded in the user's private key and each plaintext is encrypted using an attribute-based access policy over a attribute set. If and only if the user's attributes meet the attribute-based access policy, the user can decrypt the ciphertext successfully. CP-ABE is envisioned as a more suitable access control scheme in s-health owe to its capability of allowing the patients to customize a access policy for each health record or disease data. As Fig. 1, a cloud-based s-health system uses traditional CP-ABE as its access control architecture. If a patient wishes his health records such as blood pressure and blood oxygen concentrate only be accessed by the designated attending physician whose "DoctorNum" is "13568" and "Department" is "Orthopedics department", the patient will encrypt his health data using the access formula as "DoctorNum=13568 AND Department=Orthopedics department". Then the patient uploads the encrypted health data as well as the access formula (access policy) to the s-health cloud. So the designated physician can track changes of the patient's condition in realtime according to the patient's health data. But in traditional CP-ABE, the attribute values embedded in access policies are in cleartext form. This will reveal the privacy of the patients and the doctors. Consider the access policy "DoctorNum=13568 AND Department=Orthopedics department" in Fig. 1. An adversary or the untrusted third party cloud server (CS) can not only detect the patient is suffering from musculoskeletal problems but also can know the doctor who can decrypt the encrypted health data is an orthopedic surgeon with the "DoctorNum:13568". Obviously, the sensitive information in the access policy can be easily divulged to the unauthorized users. And in s-health, users and data owners use the IoT resource-constrained devices to enjoy the healthcare services. So how to design a lightweight policy-hidden CP-ABE scheme is also a non-negligible challenge for conventional CP-ABE.

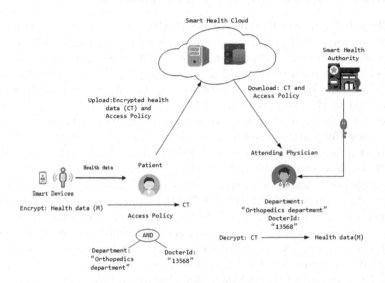

Fig. 1. Smart Health System with traditional CP-ABE

So in this paper, we propose the PPH-CP-ABE scheme which fullfils the following noteworthy points.

- Real-Anonymity Partially Policy-hidden (PPH): To address the defect that the explicitness of the attribute values in access policy will divulge the privacy, we construct the CP-ABE scheme with the partially hidden policy. An adversary only can extract the attribute categories from the access structures and the attribute values are hidden in ciphertext. What's more, our hidden policy can resist the off-line dictionary attacks to realize real anonymity.
- Fine-grained Access Control: The access structure of our PPH-CP-ABE scheme can support any AND and OR gates which is based on LSSS.
- Scalable and Efficient: Our PPH-CP-ABE supports large universe attribute values that any users can customize his own attribute values to the corresponding attribute categories. And our PPH-CP-ABE scheme is built from the efficient prime-order bilinear pairing groups. Comparison with other CP-ABE schemes with hidden policies, our scheme is more efficient and lightweight.

2 Related Works

The policy-hidden CP-ABE (PH-CP-ABE) can be classified into two types. The one is the fully policy-hidden CP-ABE (FPH-CP-ABE), which hides the entire attributes in ciphertext. And the other is the partially policy-hidden CP-ABE (PPH-CP-ABE), which divides one attribute into category domain and value domain and only hides the attribute values in the ciphertext. An attacker only can extract the attribute categories from the access policy.

1) Fully policy-hidden CP-ABE (FPH-CP-ABE): Kate et al. [8] first proposed Inner-product Predicate Encryption (IPE) for implementing fully attribute-hiding. Phuong et al. [19] propose a new algorithm which is used to transform the Viete's formula to the hidden vector to apply the IPE for achieving the fully attribute-hiding. But as mentioned in [11], the attribute-hiding IPE [8] may lead to the "superpolynomial blowup" problem. Recently, the work in [36] first introduced a creative structure——Attribute Bloom Filter (ABF) to achieve fully attribute-hiding. And the schemes in [7,20,28] use the same ABF structure as [36] to construct FPH-CP-ABE. These ABF based schemes [7,20,28,36] cannot withstand the off-line dictionary attacks.

2) Partially policy-hidden CP-ABE (PPH-CP-ABE): Without exposing the privacy, some works build the PHP-CP-ABE to make a tradeoff between efficiency and FPH-CP-ABE. The PPH-CP-ABE schemes in [13,18,37] only supports the And-gates in access policy, and the second scheme in [18] as well as the schemes in [13,37] cannot withstand the off-line dictionary attacks. To improve the flexibility of the access structure, Lai et al.[10] use the expressive LSSS to build their hidden policy. And the scheme [38] expands [10] to large attribute universe and optimizes the decryption testing algorithm for [10]. But the schemes in [10,38] are built from the much more inefficient composite order bilinear pairing, which will aggravate the computing burden of users. Cui et al. [6] construct a prime order PPH-CP-ABE scheme which is also using expressive LSSS. But there are too many exponential operations and bilinear pairing operations in encryption and decryption phase. This leads to a high time complexity.

3   Preliminaries

3.1   Linear Secret Sharing Scheme (LSSS)[3,22]

Let p be a prime and $\mathcal{U}$ be a attribute set. For each monotone access structure over $\mathcal{U}$, there can be found a matrix $M_{l \times n}$ which has l rows and n columns called the share-generating matrix. In matrix $M_{l \times n}$, there is a map function ρ which maps one row to a attribute $Attr$ in $\mathcal{U}$, that is $\rho(i) \rightarrow Attr_i$, where $i \in \{1, 2, \ldots, l\}$ and $Attr_i \in \mathcal{U}$. During generating the share vector of secret $s \in \mathbb{Z}_p$, considering a column vector $\vec{v} = (s, r_2, r_3, \ldots, r_n)^\mathsf{T}$, where $\{r_2, \ldots, r_l\} \xleftarrow{R} \mathbb{Z}_p^*$. Then $\vec{\lambda} = M_{l \times n}\vec{v}$ is the share vector of the secret s. The element λ_i in $\vec{\lambda}$ corresponds to the attribute $\rho(i)$. We commonly called $(M_{l \times n}, \rho)$ as the access policy.

According to [3], LSSSs must satisfy the linear reconstruction requirement. For each authorized attributes set S, define a set I as $I = \{i|\rho(i) \in S\}$ where I is a subset of $\{1, 2, \ldots, l\}$. Then the row $(1, 0, 0, \ldots)$ is in the rows of matrix M_I

or matrix $(M_I)_{re}$, where $(M_I)_{re}$ denotes the result of linear transformation of matrix M_I. What's more, we can find some constants $\{\omega_i\}_{i \in I}$ in $\mathbb{Z}_p$ in polynomial time which can make the equation $\sum_{i \in I} \omega_i \lambda_i = s$ be true. In addition, we can use the technique in [12] to convert any monotonic access tree which contains any AND and OR gates to the corresponding LSSS matrix.

The access structure of our basic decentralized ABE scheme [12] is using the LSSS.

3.2 Symmetric Bilinear Pairings

G is a group with prime order p, g is a generator of G. $\hat{e} : G \times G \to G_T$ is called symmetric bilinear pairing if

- For any $a, b \in \mathbb{Z}_p^*$, $\hat{e}(g^a, g^b) = \hat{e}(g, g)^{ab} = \hat{e}(g^b, g^a)$;
- $\hat{e}(g, g) \neq 1$.
- Group operation in G and $\hat{e} : G \times G \to G_T$ are both efficiently computable.

$\{G, G_T, \hat{e}, p, g\}$ is called a symmetric bilinear pairing tuple.

3.3 Decisional q-Parallel Bilinear Diffie-Hellman Exponent (Decisional q-PBDHE) Assumption [27]

$b, s, \{o_j\}_{j=1}^{q} \xleftarrow{R} \mathbb{Z}_p^*$ where "$\xleftarrow{R}$" means "randomly choose from". Give $T, \vec{p} =$

$$G, p, \hat{e}, g,$$
$$\{g^{b^i}\}_{1 \le i \le 2q, i \neq q+1}, \{g^{so_j}\}_{1 \le j \le q},$$
$$\{g^{b^i/o_j}\}_{1 \le i \le 2q, i \neq q+1, 1 \le j \le q},$$
$$\{g^{b^i s o_k / o_j}\}_{1 \le i,j,k \le q, k \neq j}.$$

to any probabilistic polynomial-time (PPT) adversaries. Then no one can distinguish $T = \hat{e}(g, g)^{b^{q+1}s}$ or $T = R \in G_T$ where R is a random element.

4 Our Highly Efficient PPH-CP-ABE Scheme

4.1 Our Partially Hidden Policy (PHP) Based on LSSS

We split one attribute into two parts $attr \to \{c = v\}$. One part is attribute category c which is defined by AA and the other is attribute value v which supports large universe through hash function. Our access structure are monotonous based on linear secret sharing schemes (LSSS). The detailed structures and features of LSSS can be found in [3,22]. In access matrix $M_{l \times n}$, each row i is mapped to an attribute $\Upsilon(i) = \{c(i) = v(i)\}$. We will hide the attribute values $\{v(i)\}_{i=1}^{l}$ in ciphertext. And the attribute categories $\{c(i)\}_{i=1}^{l}$ in access policy are in cleartext for facilitating matching. Then our PHP denotes as $\{M_{l \times n}, \{c(i) = * * *\}_{i=1}^{l}\}$.

4.2   Our Security Model

Our scheme needs to achieve two security goals: selectively IND-CPA secure and really anonymous under off-line dictionary attacks. Here we define two security games for our scheme. The "$\xleftarrow{R}$" means "randomly choose".

Selective IND-CPA Security Game. A challenge algorithm $\mathcal{C}$ and an adversary algorithm $\mathcal{A}$ play this game. Through this security game, we will prove that our scheme is selectively secure against CPA.

- **Initialization** $\mathcal{A}$ sends a challenge access policy $\{M_{l \times n}, \{c_i : v_i\}_{i=1}^l\}$ to $\mathcal{C}$.
- **Setup** $\mathcal{C}$ runs **Setup** to output master private key MK and public key PK and then sends PK to $\mathcal{A}$.
- **Key Query 1** $\mathcal{C}$ runs $AttrKeyGen$ to response $\mathcal{A}$ the key requests. All the key in key queries cannot satisfy the $\{M_{l \times n}, \{c_i : v_i\}_{i=1}^l\}$.
- **Challenge** $\mathcal{A}$ submits two same length messages m_0, m_1 to $\mathcal{C}$. $\mathcal{C}$ $b \xleftarrow{R} \{0, 1\}$ and encrypts $m_b \to CT$, then $\mathcal{C}$ sends CT to $\mathcal{A}$.
- **Key Query 2** Same as **Key Query 1**.
- **Guess** $\mathcal{A}$ outputs a guess $b' \to b$.

$Adv_{\mathcal{A}} = Pr[b' = b] - \frac{1}{2}$. The $\mathcal{A}$ wins this security game if $Adv_{\mathcal{A}}$ is non-negligible.

Anonymity Security Game. A challenge algorithm $\mathcal{C}$ and an adversary algorithm $\mathcal{A}$ are invovled in this game. Through this game, we will prove our hidden policy can achieve fully anonymous under the off-line dictionary attacks.

- **Initialization** $\mathcal{A}$ submits two challenge access structures $\{M_{l \times n}, \{c_i : v_{0,i}\}_{i=1}^l\}$ and $\{M_{l \times n}, \{c_i : v_{1,i}\}_{i=1}^l\}$ to $\mathcal{C}$ where only the attribute value sets $\{v_{0,i}\}_{i=1}^l$, $\{v_{1,i}\}_{i=1}^l$ are different.
- **Setup** $\mathcal{C}$ runs **Setup** to output master private key MK and public key PK and then sends PK to $\mathcal{A}$.
- **Key Query** $\mathcal{A}$ queries $\mathcal{C}$ about the keys of a series of attribute sets. Notice that the attribute values in challenge attribute value sets $(\{\{v_{j,i}\}_{i=1}^l\}_{j=0}^1)$ can not in the key queries. $\mathcal{C}$ generates the attribute-based keys for $\mathcal{A}$.
- **Challenge** $\mathcal{A}$ submits a message m to $\mathcal{C}$. $\mathcal{C}$ $b \xleftarrow{R} \{0, 1\}$ and encrypts $m \to CT$ using the access structure $\{M_{l \times n}, \{c_i : v_{b,i}\}_{i=1}^l\}$, then sends CT to $\mathcal{A}$.
- **Guess** $\mathcal{A}$ outputs a guess $b' \to b$.

$Adv_{\mathcal{A}} = Pr[b' = b] - \frac{1}{2}$. The $\mathcal{A}$ wins this game if $Adv_{\mathcal{A}}$ is non-negligible. If any PPT adversary can not win this game, we say the hidden policy can achieve real anonymous against off-line dictionary attacks.

4.3   Our System Framework

The framework of our IoT assisted s-health system is shown in Fig. 2. There are four entities involved in our system which are stated below.

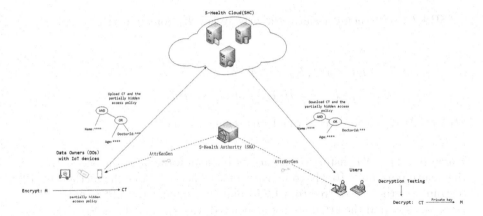

Fig. 2. Our system framework

- **S-Health Authority (SHA)** SHA is the fully trusted entity and in charge of generating the private keys for users.
- **S-Health Cloud(SHC)** The SHC is responsible for storing the ciphertexts for DOs.
- **Data Owner (DO)** DOs encrypt the data to ciphertexts and upload the ciphertexts to the CS.
- **User** Users get the ciphertexts from the cloud and retrieve the plaintext by running the decryption algorithm.

4.4 Our Constructure

Setup. The SHA derives a symmetric bilinear pairing tuple $\{G, G_T, \hat{e}, p, g\}$ by using the security parameter κ. And the SHA defines collision resistent hash function as $H : \{0,1\}^* \to G$, $H' : G_T \to \{0,1\}^*$. SHA chooses a symmetric encryption scheme as $SE = (CT = SE.Enc(\mathcal{K}, M), M = SE.Dec(\mathcal{K}, CT))$. $CT = SE.Enc(\mathcal{K}, M)$ is the encryption algorithm of SE and $M = SE.Dec(\mathcal{K}, CT)$ is the decryption algorithm of SE. $\mathcal{K} \in \{0,1\}^*$ is the key, $M \in \{0,1\}^*$ is the plaintext and $CT \in \{0,1\}^*$ is the ciphertext. SHA $\{\alpha, b, d, k, \gamma\} \xleftarrow{R} \mathbb{Z}_p^*$. The master private key (MK) and the public parameters (PK) are set as:

$$MK = g^\alpha, b, d, k, \gamma$$

$$PK = g, \hat{e}(g,g)^\alpha, g^b, g^d, g^\gamma, H, H', SE$$

AttrKeyGen. The user can form all his/her attributes into a attribute set which consists of the attributes in equivalent form as $S_u = \{\Upsilon_{c_i} = \{c_i = v_i\}\}_{i=1}^\varphi$. Then the user sends the well-formed attributes set S_u to SHA over a secure channel.

SHA $t \xleftarrow{R} \mathbb{Z}_p^*$ then computes the private key K_u for the user as

$$K_u = \{$$
$$K_1 = g^{kdt}, K_2 = g^\alpha g^{bkdt},$$
$$\{c_i : K_{c_i,1} = H(\Upsilon_{c_i})^{kt}, K_{c_i,2} = H(\Upsilon_{c_i})^\gamma\}_{i=1}^\varphi\}$$

SHA sends K_u to the user through the secure channel.

Encrypt. The DO customizes an access boolean formula as the access tree for the health data $hd \in \{0,1\}^*$ to be encrypted. Then DO uses the method in [12] to tranform the access tree to a LSSS matrix. Suppose the LSSS matrix has l rows as $M_{l \times n}$ and the attribute set associated with the matrix as $S_M = \{\Upsilon(i) = \{c(i) = v(i)\}\}_{i=1}^l$. The DO $Z \xleftarrow{R} G_T, \{s, v_2, v_3, \cdots, v_n\} \xleftarrow{R} \mathbb{Z}_p^*$ and creates a random vector $\vec{v}$ as

$$\vec{v} = (s, v_2, v_3, \ldots, v_n)^\mathsf{T}$$

And computes the share vector $\vec{\lambda}$ as

$$\vec{\lambda} = M_{l \times n}\vec{v} = (\lambda_1, \lambda_2, \ldots, \lambda_l)^\mathsf{T}$$

Then the DO $r', r_1, r_2, \ldots, r_l \xleftarrow{R} \mathbb{Z}_p^*$ and generates the ciphertext CT for hd as

$$CT = \{$$
$$\tilde{C} = SE.Enc(H'(Z), hd)$$
$$C_1 = Z \cdot \hat{e}(g,g)^{\alpha s}, C_2 = g^s, C_3 = g^{r'}$$
$$\{c(i) : C_{i,1} = (g^d)^{r_i},$$
$$C_{i,2} = (g^b)^{\lambda_i} \cdot H(\Upsilon(i))^{-r_i}$$
$$C_{i,3} = \hat{e}((g^\gamma)^{r'}, H(\Upsilon(i)))\}_{i=1}^l$$
$$\}$$

Then DO uploads the ciphertext CT to the SHC.

Decrypt. The user uses his private key K_u by running the decryption algorithm to restore the health data hd from CT. The decryption algorithm has two phase: testing phase and decryption phase. Because the user also can not know the attribute values in the hidden access policy, the user need the testing phase to ascertain whether he/she can decrypt the ciphertext. The testing phase and the decryption phase are as following.

– **Testing Phase** The user first computes the matching set $\mathcal{I}$ as

$$\mathcal{I} = \{i|\hat{e}(K_{c(i),2}, C_3) = C_{i,3}, 1 \le i \le l\}$$

where $C_3 = g^{r'}$, $K_{c(i),2} = H(\Upsilon_{c(i)})^\gamma$ and $C_{i,3} = \hat{e}((g^\gamma)^{r'}, H(\Upsilon(i)))$. Then if and only if user can find a constant vector $\vec{\omega}$ in polynomial time which can satisfy the equation as $\sum_{i \in \mathcal{I}} \omega_i M_i = \overbrace{(1, 0, \ldots, 0)}^{n}$ where ω_i is an element in $\vec{\omega}$ and M_i denotes the i-th row in $M_{l \times n}$, this means the attribute set of $\mathcal{I}$ can meet the access policy then the user can use his/her private key to decrypt the ciphertext. And the equation $\sum_{i \in \mathcal{I}} \omega_i \lambda_i = s$ is held.

- **Decryption Phase** The user uses the rows of $M_{l \times n}$ in $\mathcal{I}$ and the constant vector $\vec{\omega}$ to decrypt the ciphertext as

$$
D = \frac{\hat{e}(C_2, K_2)}{\prod_{i \in \mathcal{I}}(\hat{e}(C_{i,2}, K_1)\hat{e}(C_{i,1}, K_{c(i),1}))^{\omega_i}}
$$

$$
= \frac{\hat{e}(g^s, g^\alpha g^{kbdt})}{\prod_{i \in \mathcal{I}}(\hat{e}((g^b)^{\lambda_i} H(\Upsilon(i))^{-r_i}, g^{kdt})\hat{e}((g^d)^{r_i}, H(\Upsilon_{c(i)})^{kt}))^{\omega_i}}
$$

$$
= \frac{\hat{e}(g,g)^{s\alpha}\hat{e}(g,g)^{skbdt}}{\hat{e}(g,g)^{kbdt \sum_{i \in \mathcal{I}} \omega_i \lambda_i}}
$$

$$
= \hat{e}(g,g)^{\alpha s}
$$

$$
Z = \frac{C_1}{D} = \frac{Z \cdot \hat{e}(g,g)^{s\alpha}}{\hat{e}(g,g)^{s\alpha}}
$$

$$
hd = SE.Dec(H'(Z), \hat{C})
$$

4.5 Security Proof and Analysis

Theorem 1. *If the decisional q-parallel BDHE assumption holds. Then any PPT adversaries can't selectively break our scheme.*

Proof. Suppose there is a PPT attacker $\mathcal{A}$ with non-negligible advantage $Adv_{\mathcal{A}}$ against our PHP-OPPDT-CP-ABE scheme. With the decisional q-PBDHE assumption terms $\{\vec{p}, T\}$, we will build a PPT simulator $\mathcal{C}$ to simulate our scheme. The simulator $\mathcal{C}$ interacts with the attacker $\mathcal{A}$ during the security game. With the attacker $\mathcal{A}$, we will prove the simulator $\mathcal{C}$ has the non-negligible advantage $Adv_{\mathcal{A}}$ to break the decisional q-PBDHE assumption.

Initialization. The simulator $\mathcal{C}$ initializes with a set of attribute categories $\{c_i\}_{i=1}^m$. And the simulator $\mathcal{C}$ receives the terms $\{\vec{p}, T\}$ from the decisional q-PBDHE assumption, one challenge policy $\{M_{l \times n}, \{\Upsilon_i = \{c_i = v_i\}\}_{i=1}^l\}$ $(l, n \leq q)$ from attacker $\mathcal{A}$.

Setup. The simulator $\mathcal{C}$ $\{k, d, \gamma, \alpha'\} \xleftarrow{R} \mathbb{Z}_p^*$. $\mathcal{C}$ computes $\hat{e}(g^b, g^{b^q}) \cdot \hat{e}(g,g)^{\alpha'} = \hat{e}(g,g)^\alpha$ to implicitly set $\alpha = \alpha' + b^{q+1}$. $\mathcal{C}$ sets $\{g^b, g^d, g^\gamma, \hat{e}(g,g)^\alpha\}, \{c_i\}_{i=1}^m\}$ as the public parameters.

H Oracle Query. H function takes a attribute set $\Upsilon = \{c = v\}$ as input. I denotes a set that consists of some row indexes i in $M_{l' \times n}$ which has $\Upsilon_i = \{c_i = v_i\} = \Upsilon$. So $I = \{i | \Upsilon_i = \Upsilon\}_{1 \leq i \leq l}$. If Υ is not in hash table, the simulator $\tilde{v} \xleftarrow{R} \mathbb{Z}_p^*$

and records $\{\Upsilon : \tilde{v}\}$ in the hash table. Otherwise, the simulator takes $\tilde{v}$ out from the hash table.

- If $I \neq \emptyset$. The simulator returns

$$H(\Upsilon) = g^{\tilde{v}} \prod_{i \in I} (g^{b/o_i})^{M_{i,1}} \cdot (g^{b^2/o_i})^{M_{i,2}} \cdots (g^{b^n/o_i})^{M_{i,n}}$$

$M_{i,j}$ denotes the (i,j) element in $M_{l \times n}$.
- If $I = \emptyset$ The simulator returns $H(\Upsilon) = g^{\tilde{v}}$.

Key Query Phase 1. Attacker $\mathcal{A}$ submits a series of attributes sets to simulator $\mathcal{C}$ for key querying. All the attributes sets for the key querying can not satisfy $\{M_{l \times n}, \{\Upsilon_i = \{c_i = v_i\}\}_{i=1}^l\}$. Take one queried attribute set $S_u = \{\Upsilon_{c_i} = \{c_i = v_i\}\}_{i=1}^m$ for instance. We denote I' as a row indexes set that contains row index i in $M_{l \times n}$ which has $\Upsilon_i = \{c_i = v_i\} \in S_u$, so $I' = \{i | \Upsilon_i = \{c_i = v_i\} \in S_u\}_{1 \leq i \leq l}$. The simulator $\mathcal{C}$ can find a vector $\vec{\theta} = (\theta_1, \theta_2, \ldots, \theta_n)^{\mathsf{T}}$ which $\theta_1 = -(dk)^{-1}$ and $M_{\{i\}} \vec{\theta} = 0, \forall i \in I'$ in probabilistic polynomial time (PPT) according to the LSSS properties.

The simulator $\tilde{t} \xleftarrow{R} \mathbb{Z}_p^*$ and computes $g^t = g^{\tilde{t}} \prod_{i=1}^n (g^{b^{q-i+1}})^{\theta_i}$ to implicitly set $t = \tilde{t} + \theta_1 b^q + \theta_2 b^{q-1} + \cdots + \theta_n b^{q-n+1}$. So the simulator can compute

$$K_1 = (g^t)^{kd};$$
$$K_2 = g^{\alpha} g^{bdkt}$$
$$= g^{\alpha'} g^{b^{q+1}} (g^b)^{\tilde{t} dk} (\prod_{i=1}^n (g^{b^{q-i+2}})^{\theta_i})^{dk}$$
$$= g^{\alpha'} g^{b^{q+1}} (g^b)^{\tilde{t} dk} g^{-b^{q+1}} (\prod_{i=2}^n (g^{b^{q-i+2}})^{\theta_i})^{dk}$$
$$= g^{\alpha'} (g^b)^{\tilde{t} dk} (\prod_{i=2}^n (g^{b^{q-i+2}})^{\theta_i})^{dk}$$

We consider one attribute $\Upsilon_\eta = \{c_\eta : v_\eta\}$ in S_u. And $I_{x,\eta} = \{i | \Upsilon_i = \Upsilon_\eta\}_{1 \leq i \leq l} \subseteq I'$. Then

$$K_{c_\eta,2} = (H(\Upsilon))^{\gamma};$$
$$K_{c_\eta,1} = H(\Upsilon_\eta)^{kt}$$
$$= (g^t)^{k\tilde{v}_\eta} \prod_{i \in I_{x,\eta}} \prod_{j=1}^n (g^{b^j/o_i})^{M_{i,j} \tilde{t} k}$$
$$\cdot (\prod_{i \in I_{x,\eta}} \prod_{j=1}^n \prod_{\xi=1}^n (g^{b^{q-\xi+1+j}/o_i})^{\theta_\xi M_{i,j}})^k$$

when $\xi = j$, we have

$$\prod_{i \in I_{x,\eta}} \prod_{j=1,\xi=j}^{n} (g^{b^{q+1}/o_i})^{\theta_\xi M_{i,j}} = \prod_{i \in I_{x,\eta}} (g^{b^{q+1}/o_i})^{\sum_{j=1}^{n} \theta_j M_{i,j}} = 1$$

So the simulator computes $K_{c_\eta,1}$ as

$$K_{c_\eta,1} = (g^t)^{k\tilde{v}_{x,\eta}} \prod_{i \in I_{x,\eta}} \prod_{j=1}^{n} (g^{b^j/o_i})^{M_{i,j}\tilde{t}k}$$

$$\cdot \left(\prod_{i \in I_{x,\eta}} \prod_{j=1}^{n} \prod_{\xi=1,\xi\neq j}^{n} (g^{b^{q-\xi+1+j}/o_i})^{\theta_\xi M_{i,j}} \right)^k$$

Challenge Phase. The attacker $\mathcal{A}$ chooses two same length elements $m_0, m_1 \in G_T$ to simulator $\mathcal{C}$ as the challenge messages. Then simulator $\mathcal{C}$ $b \xleftarrow{R} \{0,1\}$ to choose m_b for encryption. Then the simulator $r' \xleftarrow{R} \mathbb{Z}_p^*$ and computes CT as

$$C_1 = m_b \cdot T \cdot \hat{e}(g^s, g^{\alpha'}); C_2 = g^s; C_3 = g^{r'};$$

For each $\xi \in [1, l]$, the simulator $\tilde{r}_\xi \xleftarrow{R} \mathbb{Z}_p^*$ and computes

$$C_{\xi,1} = (g^{-\tilde{r}_\xi} g^{so_\xi})^d = (g^d)^{r_\xi}; C_{\xi,3} = \hat{e}(H(\Upsilon_\xi), g^\gamma)^{r'}$$

So r_ξ is implicitly set as $r_\xi = -\tilde{r}_\xi + so_\xi$.

The simulator $\mathcal{C}$ sets $\gamma_1 = 0$ and $\gamma_2, \gamma_3, \ldots \gamma_n \xleftarrow{R} \mathbb{Z}_p^*$. The simulator implicitly sets

$$\vec{v} = (s, sb + \gamma_2, \ldots, sb^{n-1} + \gamma_n)^{\mathsf{T}}$$

$$\lambda_\xi = M_{\{\xi\}}\vec{v} = M_{\xi,1}s + M_{\xi,2}(sb + \gamma_2) + \cdots + M_{\xi,n}(sb^{n-1} + \gamma_n) = \sum_{j=1}^{n} M_{\xi,j}(sb^{j-1} + \gamma_j)$$

by computing

$$C_{\xi,2} = g^{b\lambda_\xi} H(\Upsilon_\xi)^{-r_\xi}$$

$$= g^{b\sum_{j=1}^{n} M_{\xi,j}\gamma_j} g^{\sum_{j=1}^{n} M_{\xi,j}sb^j} \cdot H(\Upsilon_\xi)^{\tilde{r}_\xi} \cdot (g^{-so_\xi})^{\tilde{v}_\xi} \cdot \prod_{i \in I_\xi} \prod_{j=1}^{n} g^{-sb^j M_{i,j}o_\xi/o_i}$$

$$(I_\xi = \{i | \Upsilon_i = \Upsilon_\xi\}_{1 \le i \le l})$$

when $i = \xi$,

$$\prod_{i \in I_\xi} \prod_{j=1}^{n} g^{-sb^j M_{i,j}o_\xi/o_i} = \prod_{j=1}^{n} g^{-sb^j M_{\xi,j}}$$

So

$$C_{\xi,2} = g^{b\lambda_\xi} H(\Upsilon_\xi)^{-r_\xi}$$

$$= g^{b\sum_{j=1}^n M_{\xi,j}\gamma_j} g^{\sum_{j=1}^n M_{\xi,j} s b^j} \cdot H(\Upsilon_\xi)^{\tilde{r}_\xi} \cdot (g^{-s o_\xi})^{\tilde{v}_\xi} \cdot \prod_{i \in I_\xi, i \neq \xi} \prod_{j=1}^n g^{-s b^j M_{i,j} o_\xi / o_i} \prod_{j=1}^n g^{-s b^j M_{\xi,j}}$$

$$= g^{b\sum_{j=1}^n M_{\xi,j}\gamma_j} \cdot H(\Upsilon_\xi)^{\tilde{r}_\xi} \cdot (g^{-s o_\xi})^{\tilde{v}_\xi} \cdot \prod_{i \in I_\xi, i \neq \xi} \prod_{j=1}^n g^{-s b^j M_{i,j} o_\xi / o_i}$$

$$(I_\xi = \{i | \Upsilon_i = \Upsilon_\xi\}_{1 \leq i \leq l})$$

The simulator sends the challenge ciphertext CT to the attacker $\mathcal{A}$.

Key Query Phase 2. Same as Key Query Phase 1.

Guess Phase. Eventually, the attacker $\mathcal{A}$ gives the guess b' of b to the simulator $\mathcal{C}$.

If $b' = b$, the simulator $\mathcal{C}$ outputs 0 and guesses $T = \hat{e}(g,g)^{s b^{q+1}}$; Otherwise, $\mathcal{C}$ outputs 1 and guesses $T = R$.

If the decisional q-parallel BDHE assumption sends $T = \hat{e}(g,g)^{s b^{q+1}}$ to the simulator $\mathcal{C}$. The attacker $\mathcal{A}$ plays the real security game as our actual scheme. Referring to our supposition, the attacker has $Adv_{\mathcal{A}}$ selectively breaking our actual scheme. So

$$Pr[b' = b | T = \hat{e}(g,g)^{s b^{q+1}}] = \frac{1}{2} + Adv_{\mathcal{A}}$$

$$Pr[\mathcal{C}(\vec{p}, T = \hat{e}(g,g)^{s b^{q+1}}) = 0] = \frac{1}{2} + Adv_{\mathcal{A}}$$

If the decisional q-parallel BDHE assumption sends $T = R$ to $\mathcal{C}$, $C_{1,1} = m_b \cdot R \cdot \hat{e}(g^s, g^{\alpha'})$, all the bits in m_b is hidden due to the R. So

$$Pr[b' = b | T = R] = \frac{1}{2}$$

$$Pr[\mathcal{C}(\vec{p}, T = R) = 0] = \frac{1}{2}$$

So

$$Pr[\mathcal{C}(\vec{p}, T = \hat{e}(g,g)^{s b^{q+1}}) = 0] - Pr[\mathcal{C}(\vec{p}, T = R) = 0] = Adv_{\mathcal{A}}$$

So the simulator can distinguish $\hat{e}(g,g)^{s b^{q+1}}$ and $R \in G_T$.

Theorem 2. *If the Computational Diffie-Hellman Problem (CDHP) and discrete logarithm Problem (DLP) holds in G, our scheme is real anonymity under the off-line dictionary attacks.*

Proof. The g^b, g^d are known to the attacker. Due to CDHP, the attacker cannot compute the term g^{bd}. So the attacker cannot launch the off-line dictionary attacks by the following discriminant

$$\hat{e}(C_2, g^{bd}) \overset{?}{=} \prod_{i \in \mathcal{I}} (\hat{e}(H(\Upsilon_i'), C_{i,1}) \hat{e}(g^d, C_{i,2}))^{\omega_i}$$

where $\{\Upsilon_i'\}_{i \in \mathcal{I}}$ is the attributes in the attribute dictionary. $C_2 = g^s$, $C_{i,1} = (g^d)^{r_i}$, $C_{i,2} = (g^b)^{\lambda_i} \cdot H(\Upsilon(i))^{-r_i}$.

And due to the DLP, the attacker cannot compute the $\gamma \in \mathbb{Z}_p^*$ from the g^γ and $H(\Upsilon)^\gamma$, so the attacker cannot forge the $H(\Upsilon)^\gamma$ by using the attribute dictionary.

5 Evaluation and Implementation

5.1 Theoretical Analysis

In this subsection, we compare our scheme with the two prime order LSSS based PPH-CP-ABE schemes [6,35] in terms of transmission overhead, storage costs, computational complexity. Tabel 1 shows the definitions of the notations. The comparison of the transmission overhead (ciphertext length) and storage costs (private key length) is shown in Table 2. The algorithm complexity is compared in Table 3.

Table 1. Notations for comparsion

Notations	Meaning
$\lvert \mathbb{Z}_p^* \rvert$ /$\lvert G \rvert$/ $\lvert G_T \rvert$	Size of one element in the group $\mathbb{Z}_p^*/G/G_T$. $e : G \times G \to G_T$ mod p is a symmetric bilinear pairing
T_e^G/ $T_e^{G_T}$	Time for one group exponential operation in G/G_T
T_p	Time for the a symmetric bilinear pairing $e : G \times G \to G_T$ mod p
l	The number of rows of the LSSS matrix
$\lvert S \rvert$	The number of the attributes in the user's attribute set
W	A set that contains the minimum rowsets which satisfy the LSSS matrix $M_{l \times n}$
κ_0	The size of W. So $W = \{\vec{w}_1, \vec{w}_2, \ldots, \vec{w}_{\kappa_0}\}$
$\lvert \vec{w}_i \rvert, 1 \le i \le \kappa_0$	The number of rows in the rowset $\vec{w}_i$
κ_1	The number of rows as $\kappa_1 = \sum_{i=1}^{\kappa_0} \lvert \vec{w}_i \rvert$

5.2 Implementation

We use the **PBC** library[14] to simulate our scheme as well as the schemes in [6,35]. The hardware environment of the experiment is intel i5-1135G7 2.40 Ghz with 16.0GB LPDDR4 4266MHz RAM, OS is Windows 10 1903. To realize the symmetric bilinear pairing $\hat{e} : G \times G \to G_T$ with the security level of 80 bits,

Table 2. Comparison of the transmission overhead and storage costs

Scheme	Private key length	Ciphertext length
[6]	$(2 + 5 S|)|G|$	$(6l + 2)|G| + |\mathbb{Z}_p^*|$
[35]	$(2 + 5 S|)|G|$	$(6l + 3)|G| + |\mathbb{Z}_p^*|$
Ours	$2|G| + 2 S||G|$	$|G_T| + 2|G| + 2l|G| + l|G_T|$

Table 3. Comparison of Algorithm Complexity

Scheme	AttrKeyGen	Encrypt	Decrypt
[6]	$(8 S| + 4)T_e^G$	$(8l + 3)T_e^G$	$\leq ((1 + 6\kappa_1)T_p + 2\kappa_0 T_e^G + \kappa_1 T_e^{G_T})$
[35]	$(8 S| + 5)T_e^G$	$(4 + 8l)T_e^G + T_p$	$\leq ((3 + 6\kappa_1)T_p + 2\kappa_0 T_e^G + \kappa_1 T_e^{G_T})$
Ours	$2T_e^G + 2 S|T_e^G$	$T_e^{G_T} + 3T_e^G + 3l T_e^G + l T_p$	$\leq (l T_p + T_p + 2l T_p + l T_e^{G_T})$

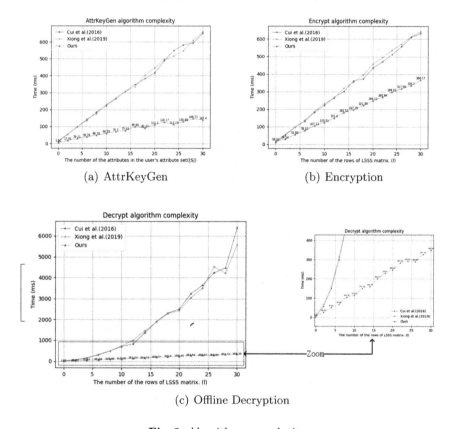

(a) AttrKeyGen   (b) Encryption

(c) Offline Decryption

Fig. 3. Algorithms complexity

we adopt the super-singular (symmetric) curve $E(\mathbb{F}_q) : y^2 = x^3 + x \bmod q$ with embedding degree $k = 2$ in the field $\mathbb{F}_q$ with the prime q of 512 bits. And the G is an additive subgroup in the $E(\mathbb{F}_q)$ with the prime order r of

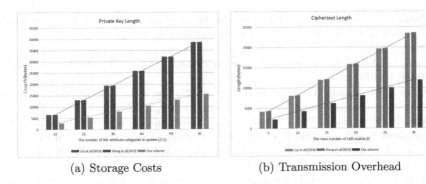

(a) Storage Costs   (b) Transmission Overhead

Fig. 4. Comparison of occupied storage space (private key length) and transmission overhead (ciphertext length)

160 bits. In this case, $|G| = |G_T| = 512(bits) \times 2 = 1024(bits) = 128(bytes)$, $|\mathbb{Z}_p^*| = 160(bits) = 20(bytes)$, $T_e^G = 3.379\,ms$, $T_e^{G_T} = 0.538\,ms$, $T_p = 5.869\,ms$. To make the experimential results clear, we simplify set $\kappa_1 = (\kappa_1)_{max} = (\frac{l}{2}+1)\frac{l}{2}$. (In this case $\kappa_0 = \frac{l}{2}$, $|\vec{w}_1| = \cdots = |\vec{w}_{\kappa_0}| = \frac{l}{2}+1$). From the Fig. 4, we can observe that our scheme is superior to others in terms of the transmission overhead and storage costs. The Fig. 3 presents the time complexity of the three schemes and we can easily infer that our scheme has the highest efficiency. From the Fig. 3, we can detect that the complexity of **AttrKeyGen, Encryption** algorithms in the three works are Linear complexity, but time growth rate of the two algorithms in our work is much smaller than the other two works. What's more, from the Fig. 3(c), we can know that the complexity of the **Decryption** algorithms in the other two works are Quadratic complexity and our is only linear complexity. This means in the other two works, the user will take quadratic time to retrieve the plaintext by running the **Decryption**(offline) algorithm.

6   Conclusion

In this paper, we propose a large universe prime-order LSSS based PPH-CP-ABE scheme with high efficiency. By using our PPH-CP-ABE scheme in s-health, the patients can enjoy the high quality healthcare services and protect their privacy from divulging to the corrupted users at the same time. And the sensitive data in access policies also can be held. And our scheme is more efficient and lightweight, this makes our scheme is more suitable and practical for the IoT assisted s-health.

References

1. A Vouk, M.: Cloud computing-issues, research and implementations. J. Comput. Inf. Technol. **16**(4), 235–246 (2008)
2. Armbrust, M., et al.: A view of cloud computing. Commun. ACM **53**(4), 50–58 (2010)

3. Beimel, A.: Secure schemes for secret sharing and key distribution. Technion-Israel Institute of technology, Faculty of computer science (1996)
4. Bethencourt, J., Sahai, A., Waters, B.: Ciphertext-policy attribute-based encryption. In: 2007 IEEE Symposium on Security and Privacy (SP 2007), pp. 321–334. IEEE (2007)
5. Chen, C.M., Huang, Y., Wang, K.H., Kumari, S., Wu, M.E.: A secure authenticated and key exchange scheme for fog computing. Enterprise Inf. Syst. 1–16 (2020)
6. Cui, H., Deng, R.H., Wu, G., Lai, J.: An efficient and expressive ciphertext-policy attribute-based encryption scheme with partially hidden access structures. In: Chen, L., Han, J. (eds.) ProvSec 2016. LNCS, vol. 10005, pp. 19–38. Springer, Cham (2016). https://doi.org/10.1007/978-3-319-47422-9_2
7. Hao, J., Huang, C., Ni, J., Rong, H., Xian, M., Shen, X.S.: Fine-grained data access control with attribute-hiding policy for cloud-based IoT. Comput. Netw. **153**, 1–10 (2019)
8. Katz, J., Sahai, A., Waters, B.: Predicate encryption supporting disjunctions, polynomial equations, and inner products. In: Smart, N. (ed.) EUROCRYPT 2008. LNCS, vol. 4965, pp. 146–162. Springer, Heidelberg (2008). https://doi.org/10.1007/978-3-540-78967-3_9
9. Kumari, S., Chaudhary, P., Chen, C.M., Khan, M.K.: Questioning key compromise attack on Ostad-Sharif et al'.s authentication and session key generation scheme for healthcare applications. IEEE Access **7**, 39717–39720 (2019)
10. Lai, J., Deng, R.H., Li, Y.: Expressive CP-ABE with partially hidden access structures. In: 7th ACM Symposium on Information, Computer and Communications Security, ASIACCS 2012, pp. 18–19 (2012)
11. Lewko, A., Okamoto, T., Sahai, A., Takashima, K., Waters, B.: Fully secure functional encryption: attribute-based encryption and (hierarchical) inner product encryption. In: Gilbert, H. (ed.) EUROCRYPT 2010. LNCS, vol. 6110, pp. 62–91. Springer, Heidelberg (2010). https://doi.org/10.1007/978-3-642-13190-5_4
12. Lewko, A., Waters, B.: Decentralizing attribute-based encryption. In: Paterson, K.G. (ed.) EUROCRYPT 2011. LNCS, vol. 6632, pp. 568–588. Springer, Heidelberg (2011). https://doi.org/10.1007/978-3-642-20465-4_31
13. Li, J., Ren, K., Zhu, B., Wan, Z.: Privacy-aware attribute-based encryption with user accountability. In: Samarati, P., Yung, M., Martinelli, F., Ardagna, C.A. (eds.) ISC 2009. LNCS, vol. 5735, pp. 347–362. Springer, Heidelberg (2009). https://doi.org/10.1007/978-3-642-04474-8_28
14. Lynn, B., et al.: The pairing-based cryptography library. Internet: crypto. stanford. edu/pbc/[Mar. 27, 2013] (2006)
15. Mei, Q., Xiong, H., Chen, J., Yang, M., Kumari, S., Khan, M.K.: Efficient certificateless aggregate signature with conditional privacy preservation in IoV. IEEE Syst. J. (2020)
16. Miorandi, D., Sicari, S., De Pellegrini, F., Chlamtac, I.: Internet of things: vision, applications and research challenges. Ad Hoc Netw. **10**(7), 1497–1516 (2012)
17. Mishra, D., Gunasekaran, A., Childe, S.J., Papadopoulos, T., Dubey, R., Wamba, S.: Vision, applications and future challenges of internet of things. Ind. Manag. Data Syst. **116**(7), 1331–1355 (2016)
18. Nishide, T., Yoneyama, K., Ohta, K.: Attribute-based encryption with partially hidden encryptor-specified access structures. In: Bellovin, S.M., Gennaro, R., Keromytis, A., Yung, M. (eds.) ACNS 2008. LNCS, vol. 5037, pp. 111–129. Springer, Heidelberg (2008). https://doi.org/10.1007/978-3-540-68914-0_7

19. Phuong, T.V.X., Yang, G., Susilo, W.: Hidden ciphertext policy attribute-based encryption under standard assumptions. IEEE Trans. Inf. Forensics Secur. **11**(1), 35–45 (2015)
20. Ramu, G.: A secure cloud framework to share EHRs using modified CP-ABE and the attribute bloom filter. Educ. Inf. Technol. **23**(5), 2213–2233 (2018)
21. Rittinghouse, J.W., Ransome, J.F.: Cloud Computing: Implementation, Management, and Security. CRC Press (2016)
22. Rouselakis, Y., Waters, B.: New constructions and proof methods for large universe attribute-based encryption. IACR Cryptology EPrint Archive **2012**, 583 (2012)
23. Sahai, A., Waters, B.: Fuzzy identity-based encryption. In: Annual International Conference on the Theory and Applications of Cryptographic Techniques. pp. 457–473. Springer (2005)
24. Solanas, A., et al.: Smart health: a context-aware health paradigm within smart cities. IEEE Commun. Mag. **52**(8), 74–81 (2014)
25. Wang, E.K., Liang, Z., Chen, C.M., Kumari, S., Khan, M.K.: PoRX: A reputation incentive scheme for blockchain consensus of IIoT. Futur. Gener. Comput. Syst. **102**, 140–151 (2020)
26. Wang, K.H., Chen, C.M., Fang, W., Wu, T.Y.: On the security of a new ultra-lightweight authentication protocol in IoT environment for RFID tags. J. Supercomput. **74**(1), 65–70 (2018)
27. Waters, B.: Ciphertext-policy attribute-based encryption: an expressive, efficient, and provably secure realization. In: Catalano, D., Fazio, N., Gennaro, R., Nicolosi, A. (eds.) PKC 2011. LNCS, vol. 6571, pp. 53–70. Springer, Heidelberg (2011). https://doi.org/10.1007/978-3-642-19379-8_4
28. Wu, A., Zhang, Y., Zheng, X., Guo, R., Zhao, Q., Zheng, D.: Efficient and privacy-preserving traceable attribute-based encryption in blockchain. Ann. Telecommun. **74**(7–8), 401–411 (2019)
29. Wu, T.Y., Chen, C.M., Wang, K.H., Meng, C., Wang, E.K.: A provably secure certificateless public key encryption with keyword search. J. Chin. Inst. Eng. **42**(1), 20–28 (2019)
30. Wu, T.Y., Lee, Z., Obaidat, M.S., Kumari, S., Kumar, S., Chen, C.M.: An authenticated key exchange protocol for multi-server architecture in 5G networks. IEEE Access **8**, 28096–28108 (2020)
31. Xiong, H., Bao, Y., Nie, X., Asoor, Y.I.: Server-aided attribute-based signature supporting expressive access structures for industrial internet of things. IEEE Trans. Industr. Inf. **16**(2), 1013–1023 (2019)
32. Xiong, H., Kang, Z., Chen, J., Tao, J., Yuan, C., Kumari, S.: A novel multiserver authentication scheme using proxy resignature with scalability and strong user anonymity. IEEE Systems Journal (2020)
33. Xiong, H., Wu, Y., Jin, C., Kumari, S.: Efficient and privacy-preserving authentication protocol for heterogeneous systems in IIoT. IEEE Internet Things J. (2020)
34. Xiong, H., et al.: Heterogeneous signcryption with equality test for IIoT environment. IEEE Internet Things J. (2020)
35. Xiong, H., Zhao, Y., Peng, L., Zhang, H., Yeh, K.H.: Partially policy-hidden attribute-based broadcast encryption with secure delegation in edge computing. Futur. Gener. Comput. Syst. **97**, 453–461 (2019)
36. Yang, K., Han, Q., Li, H., Zheng, K., Su, Z., Shen, X.: An efficient and fine-grained big data access control scheme with privacy-preserving policy. IEEE Internet Things J. **4**(2), 563–571 (2016)

37. Zhang, Y., Chen, X., Li, J., Wong, D.S., Li, H.: Anonymous attribute-based encryption supporting efficient decryption test. In: Proceedings of the 8th ACM SIGSAC Symposium on Information, Computer and Communications Security, pp. 511–516 (2013)
38. Zhang, Y., Zheng, D., Deng, R.H.: Security and privacy in smart health: efficient policy-hiding attribute-based access control. IEEE Internet Things J. 5(3), 2130–2145 (2018)

A Novel Hand Gesture Recognition Method for FMCW Radar

Yuzhu Shui, Yong Wang[(✉)], Zhaoyu Li, and Mu Zhou

Chongqing University of Posts and Telecommunications, Chongqing 40065, China
yongwang@cqupt.edu.cn

Abstract. This paper focuses on the hand gesture recognition method based on interference suppression and fusion neural networks using a frequency modulated continuous wave (FMCW) radar. Firstly, the range and Doppler information of the target is obtained by estimating the parameters of the collected radar data. We apply a non-extreme interference suppression (NEIS) method to remove the static and dynamic interference. Then, a hand gesture extraction method based on multi-feature fusion neural network is proposed. Finally, experiments are carried to verify the effectiveness of the proposed algorithm and the results show that the proposed algorithm not only effectively suppresses the interference, but also achieves the hand gesture recognition accuracy as high as 97.26% .

Keywords: FMCW radar · Hand gesture recognition · NEIS · Multi-feature fusion network

1 Introduction

With the continuous development of artificial intelligence technology [1, 2], Human Computer Interaction (HCI) has become an indispensable part of our daily life. Hand Gesture Recognition (HGR), as an important expression of HCI, has become a hot research topic [3, 4]. According to the adopted devices, the traditional hand gesture recognition methods contain the wearable-based [3] and optical-based ones [4]. These methods classify the hand gestures using the motion trajectory according to the motion amplitudes of hand gestures. For the wearable-based HGR, the users need to wear gloves, helmets or other sensor devices. Due to the high cost and inconvenience, the application of this method is limited. The optical-based HGR method collects hand gesture signals using cameras, and then extracts and classifies the hand gestures. Although it has a very high recognition accuracy, the accuracy can be easily affected by light [5]. Compared with the mentioned two HGR methods, the radar-based HGR has the advantages of high frequency band, large bandwidth and high resolution [6], which can realize non-contact detection and has inherent advantages in protecting users' privacy. Therefore, the radar-based HGR technology has broad application prospects.

Due to the instability of the radar equipment itself, the clutter disturbance and the existence of other targets, the collected radar data contains interferences from other targets. The Constant False Alarm Rate (CFAR) [7] is usually adopted to suppress the

© Springer Nature Switzerland AG 2021
X. Sun et al. (Eds.): ICAIS 2021, CCIS 1424, pp. 637–649, 2021.
https://doi.org/10.1007/978-3-030-78621-2_53

interference signals. Unfortunately, this method can only eliminate the impact of class targets from the perspective of power, which greatly limits the practical application. On the other hand, Convolutional Neural Network (CNN) is one of the most classic methods to extract image features. The deep image information of hand gesture is sent to the CNN network for extraction and classification [8]. However, CNN can only extract one image feature at a time. Then, A. Karpathy et al. [9] extract and fuse the features of each frame image through CNN that effectively resolve the limitation of single image extraction. In 2015, D. Tran et al. [10] propose 3D-CNN to simultaneously extract multiple frames of continuous image features. The 3D-CNN method replaces the original two-dimensional convolution by three-dimensional convolution, so that the network can effectively solve the problem of continuous feature extraction of multi-frame images. In Google's soli project [11], range Doppler map (RDM) data are sent to the 3D CNN network to extract the range and Doppler features of the micro-motion hand gestures. However, the traditional 3D-CNN network cannot extract the image features completely because of the single size and few layers of convolution kernel, as well as the temporal relevance of hand gesture actions. In addition, after obtaining the range, Doppler features and the corresponding time features, the traditional 3D-CNN network structure cannot process the two features synchronously. More importantly, the angle information of the hand gestures is usually not mentioned in the above studies.

Based on the above analysis, this paper adopts a 77 GHz FMCW radar with a sweep bandwidth of 4 GHz to collect the hand gesture data. According to the different motion characteristics of the dynamic hand gestures between static and dynamic target, a non-extreme interference suppression (NEIS) algorithm [12] is used to effectively suppress the interference caused by human body. Since the traditional feature extraction methods cannot process parameter and time features synchronously, we propose a hand gesture extraction method based on multi-feature fusion network to fuse the range, Doppler and angle information, which makes the final hand gesture recognition accuracy rate as high as 97.26%.

The remainder of this paper is structured as follows: In Sect. 2, the mechanism of FMCW radar and parameter estimation method are introduced. In Sect. 3, we introduce the target detection interference suppression method, and then propose a multi-feature fusion hand gesture extraction method. In Sect. 4, we verify the performance of the proposed algorithm by experiments. Finally, conclusions are given in Sect. 5.

2   Radar Principle and Parameter Estimation

2.1   FMCW Radar

In this paper, the FMCW radar is a linear FMCW radar with sawtooth modulation mode. The signal is transmitted and then received after a time delay τ. The specific form is shown in Fig. 1:

In FMCW radar, the transmitted signal in one cycle can be expressed as:

$$s_t = A_0 \exp[j2\pi (f_0 t + \theta)] = A_0 \exp\left[j2\pi \left(f_0 t + \frac{1}{2}kt^2\right)\right] \tag{1}$$

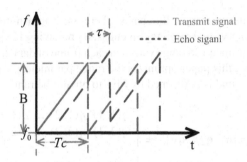

Fig. 1. FMCW radar antenna model

where A_0 is the amplitude of the transmitted signal, B is the bandwidth of the linear frequency modulation signal, f_0 is the signal carrier frequency, K is the frequency modulation slope and t (the fast time) is the time variable in the frequency modulation period. In general, the Radar Cross Section (RCS) fluctuations of hand gesture targets or other moving targets in one cycle is very small, so that the amplitude of echo signal A_0 is basically unchanged. Therefore, A_0 will be regarded as a constant in this paper. Thus, the echo signal of the target point can be written as:

$$s_r = A_0 \exp\left\{ j2\pi \left[f_0 \left(t - \frac{2R_t}{c} \right) + \frac{1}{2}k \left(t - \frac{2R_t}{c} \right)^2 \right] \right\} \tag{2}$$

where R_t denotes the distance between the target and the radar, $\frac{2R_t}{c} = \tau$ denotes the target echo delay.

Assume that the amplitude of the intermediate frequency (IF) signal is A_{IF}. Then the transmitted signal s_t and the received signal s_r are mixed and passed through a low-pass filter to obtain the IF signal:

$$\begin{aligned} S_{IF} &= A_{IF} \exp\left[j2\pi \left(f_0 t + \tfrac{1}{2}kt^2 \right) \right] \exp\left\{ j2\pi \left[f_0(t - \tau) + \tfrac{1}{2}k(t - \tau)^2 \right] \right\} \\ &= A_{IF} \exp\left[j2\pi \left(2f_0 t + kt^2 + \tfrac{1}{2}k\tau^2 - kt\tau - f_0\tau \right) \right] \end{aligned} \tag{3}$$

In practical, the value of fast time t is very small, and t^2 can be ignored. Similarly, τ represents the delay of the target echo signal, which is actually smaller than t, so $t\tau$ and τ^2 are ignored. Then, the frequency of the IF signal can be written as:

$$f_{IF} = 2f_0 t - f_0 \tau \tag{4}$$

where $\Delta\phi = f_0\tau$ is the phase change of the received signal relative to the transmitted Signal.

2.2 Parameter Estimation

Range-Doppler Estimation. According to the range estimation principle of FMCW radar, the range parameters can be extracted on every FM wave period. The experimental results show that using multiple sweep range spectrum achieves better signal-to-noise ratio and lower clutter power. In this paper, there are 2 transmitting and 4 receiving antennas, which form 8 virtual receiving antennas. By receiving 128 sweep cycles signals in a frame, we can estimate 128 range values in each frame of data. In order to effectively use the sweep period, this paper optimizes the range parameters. The sweep frequency in the time domain signal is performed by FFT to obtain the range spectrum matrix.

$$
\mathbf{q}_r = [\mathbf{q}_1, \mathbf{q}_2, ... \mathbf{q}_N]^T = \begin{bmatrix} q(1,1) & q(1,2) & ... & q(1,n) \\ q(2,1) & q(2,2) & ... & q(2,n) \\ ... & ... & ... & ... \\ q(N,1) & q(N,2) & ... & q(N,n) \end{bmatrix}
\tag{5}
$$

where n denotes the number of sampling points, N represents the number of frequency sweeps, $q_1, q_2 ...... q_N$ represents the range parameters of the N sweep. First, we perform FFT on each sampling point to get the range vector. Then, the range spectrum matrix is multiplied by points $Q = q_r \cdot q_r$. Finally, in order to reduce the influence of noise components on the target signal, we obtain the average value $\overline{Q} = Q/N$ of N frequency sweeps.

In order to make better use of the velocity information in radar signals, this paper uses 2D Fast Fourier Transform (2D-FFT) algorithm to estimate range and Doppler parameters of the hand gestures. Specifically, it is necessary to carry out FFT on each swept signal to obtain the range information of each fast time domain. The Doppler information of the hand gesture is obtained by performing a second FFT on all the frequency sweeps in a frame signal. Then, by coupling the range and Doppler information of hand gesture, the final RDM is obtained.

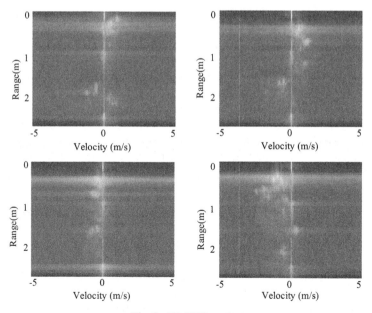

Fig. 2. 2D-FFT results

The RDM results of the push-pull hand gesture after the 2D-FFT are given as an example in Fig. 2. As can be seen in Fig. 2, the hand gesture velocity first becomes smaller, and the hand gesture movement direction is away from the radar direction. Then, the hand gesture velocity gradually becomes larger, and the motion direction is gradually closer to the radar direction.

Angle Estimation. In this paper, the angle parameters of hand gestures are also extracted to increase the information of the hand gestures. Therefore, this paper uses the Multiple Signal Classification (MUSIC) algorithm [13] to estimate the angle of hand gesture signals. The principle of MUSIC algorithm is to calculate the phase difference according to the time difference of echo signals received by different receiving antennas, and then determine the angle parameters of the target according to the phase difference of multiple antennas. The angle changes of the two hand gestures of left-right and push-pull are respectively given in Fig. 3.

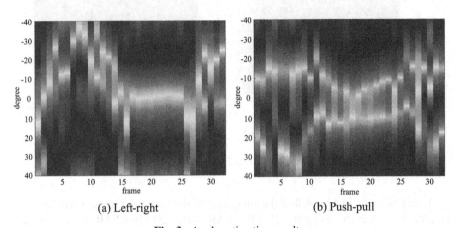

(a) Left-right   (b) Push-pull

Fig. 3. Angle estimation results

The abscissa represents the number of frames, the ordinate represents the angle of incidence. The angle range is from -40 degrees to 40 degrees, and the yellow bright spot in the figure represents the target peak. In the left-right sliding angle diagram, the angle change of the hand gesture can be clearly seen as a process of changing from a positive angle to a negative angle and then to a positive angle. However, the angle of push-pull hand gesture changes slowly, the range of change is basically from -10 degrees to 10 degrees. As a result, we can clearly distinguish the two angle changes.

3 Proposed Algorithm

3.1 Target Detection and Interference Suppression

When collecting the hand gestures, the noises with randomly characteristics are introduced in the collected radar signals. If the magnitude of the noise is too high, the peak value of the hand gesture signal is similar to the noise or even be covered. In this paper, the background noises in RDM and Angle-Time Map (ATM) are eliminated by inserting the background frames. The principle of background elimination is to find the differences between the current frame and the background frame, so as to reduce the background power in the parameter estimation.

Since the background frame subtraction method cannot effectively solve the problem of background noise fluctuation, according to the principle of 2D-OS-CFAR, this paper sets an appropriate detection threshold [14] to solve the problem of noise power fluctuation. The comparison results before and after 2D-OS-CFAR processing are shown in Fig. 4.

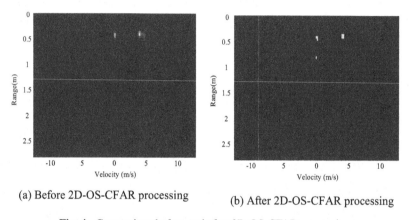

(a) Before 2D-OS-CFAR processing

(b) After 2D-OS-CFAR processing

Fig. 4. Comparison before and after 2D-OS-CFAR processing

It can be seen in Fig. 4 that the influence of the side lobe around the target can be greatly reduced by using the 2D-OS-CFAR. After 2D-OS-CFAR processing, multiple targets will be presented on RDM, including the hand gesture targets and other objects. Finally, the delay cancellation method [15] is used to suppress static and dynamic interference targets.

3.2   Hand Gesture Feature Extraction

According to the different characteristics of RDM and ATM, different neural networks are used for feature extraction. Due to the single frame characteristics of RDM, it is suitable to use a three-dimensional network for feature extraction [16]. Since Inflated 3D (I3D) network can avoid the occurrence of network overload and gradient disappearance, as well as retain the spatiotemporal characteristics of the input data, this paper applies the I3D network for feature extraction. For ATM parameters, this paper uses the general end-to-end network for feature extraction. The flow chart of the specific HGR framework is shown in Fig. 5.

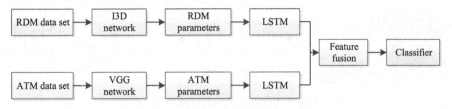

Fig. 5. Feature extraction of the proposed HGR framework

RDM Parameter Feature Extraction Based on I3D Network. The I3D network adopts the GoogleNet [17] structure, which stacks common convolution and pooling operations together. Then, we use the activation function to map the convolution output and sort according to the convolution result. Finally, different kinds of nonlinear features are obtained. Multiple Inception modules are used to increase the depth and width of the network while controlling the amount of calculation to prevent over-fitting and gradient disappearance. In each Inception module, four convolution kernels with different sizes are used for convolution, and then the convolution results are connected together to obtain the sub-feature set. The sub-features processed by multiple Inception modules are aggregated to strengthen the common features of the image while weakening the irrelevant features of the image. The I3D network structure diagram of this paper is given in Fig. 6.

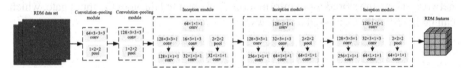

Fig. 6. I3D network structure

The I3D network uses a two-layer convolutional pooling module to simply extract RDM features, and uses 3 Inception modules to analyze and filter shallow features to obtain higher purity RDM features. Convolution and pooling operations are performed simultaneously in each Inception module to minimize unnecessary feature waste. To better extract hand gesture parameter features, this paper modifies the size of convolution kernel and reduces unnecessary parameters in the network. Moreover, since the RDM map is a single-frame distance-Doppler coupled parameter map, this paper changes the single-frame convolution size from 3×3 to 3×1 and 1×3.

ATM Parameter Feature Extraction Based on VGG-16 Network. The ATM diagram is obtained by arranging the angle information of 32 frames of hand gesture data. This paper improves the VGG-16 network [18] to extract ATM parameter features. The specific network structure is shown in Fig. 7.

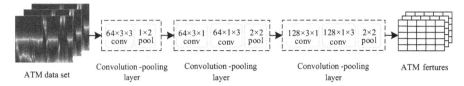

Fig. 7. Improved structure of VGG-16

We can see from Fig. 7 that the improved VGG-16 network has 3 layers. Firstly, 64 convolution kernels with 3 × 3 dimensions are used to extract the preliminary features and adjust the data size. Then, 64 convolution kernels with 1 × 3 and 3 × 1 sizes are used to process the preliminary features. Finally, 128 convolution kernels with 1 × 3 and 3 × 1 sizes are used to obtain the shallow features of ATM parameters.

Time Series Feature Extraction. The I3D network can extract the parameter features of a single frame picture, but it cannot extract the associated features of consecutive multiple frames. The gesture behavior is a continuous action with a certain correlation between frames. Therefore, if only the I3D network is used for hand gesture feature extraction, the coherence feature of hand gestures will be lost. To overcome these shortcomings, Long Short-Term Memory (LSTM) network is applied to extract the time features of the input sequence through each hidden layer. In order to extract the time series features, both RDM and ATM features are sent to the LSTM network for training. Thus, the useless information of C_{t-1} is removed by using the forgetting gate of LSTM network. Then, the stored input information $\tilde{C}_t$ is obtained through the input gate, which can be specifically expressed as follows:

$$\begin{cases} f_t = \sigma\left(W_f \cdot [h_{t-1}, x_t] + b_f\right) \\ i_t = \sigma(W_i \cdot [h_{t-1}, x_t] + b_i) \\ \tilde{C}_t = \tanh(W_C \cdot [h_{t-1}, x_t] + b_C) \\ C_t = f_t \cdot C_{t-1} + i_t \cdot \tilde{C}_t \end{cases} \tag{6}$$

where $\sigma(t)$ denotes the sigmoid function, $\sigma(\mathrm{t}) = \frac{1}{1+e^{-t}}$, W_f, W_i and W_c are the weights in the LSTM unit, b_f, b_i and b_C are the corresponding offsets.

Finally, the hidden layer state h_t and output information o_t are given through the output gate:

$$\begin{cases} o_t = \sigma(W_o[h_{t-1}, x_t] + b_o) \\ h_t = o_t \cdot \tanh(C_t) \end{cases} \tag{7}$$

Feature Fusion and Classification. After extracting the time sequence features for RDM and ATM, the feature results include parameter features and time sequence features. Therefore, this paper selects the corresponding features for fusion based on the difference between the parameter feature and the timing feature. The specific integration process is shown in Fig. 8.

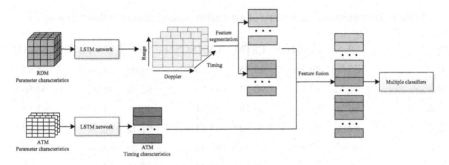

Fig. 8. Dual stream convergence network convergence

In Fig. 8, the normalized exponential function in the multi-classifier can be expressed as:

$$softmax(z) = \frac{\exp(\theta_i^T z_i)}{\sum\limits_{j=1}^{k} \exp(\theta_j^T z_j)} \tag{8}$$

where i represents the hand gesture category, and k represents the number of types of hand gestures. z_i is the i-th element of the feature vector and θ_i is the weight corresponding to z_i.

4 Experiment and Analysis

4.1 Experiment Platform

The FMCW radar platform used in this paper is the AWR1642 radar board of Texas Instruments, which is equipped with DCA1000 high-speed data acquisition card. The working frequency of the radar is 77–81 GHz, the bandwidth is 4 GHz, the sweep slope is 105.202 MHz/us, the sampling rate is 2000 kbps, and the number of sweep frequencies is 128. The FMCW radar has 2 transmitting and 4 receiving antennas that form 8 virtual antennas. Firstly, the FMCW modulated signals are generated by waveform generator, and echo signals are received. Then, the generated intermediate frequency signals are transmitted to PC through DCA1000 data acquisition card, and processed by software. Finally, the hand gesture category result is obtained by training in the Tensorflow deep learning framework.

4.2 Experimental Results

Different Network Hand Gesture Recognition Rate Based on RDM Data Set. To improve the recognition performance of the proposed I3D network, this paper chooses the learning rate as 0.00009.RDM data sets are sent to different neural networks for training and testing. The recognition accuracy of each type of hand gesture is shown in Table 1: CNN.

Table 1. Recognition accuracy rate of each network hand gesture in RDM data set (%)

Network model	CNN	3D-CNN	LSTM	LS3D-CNN	I3D	I3D-LSTM	SM-I3D
L	86.63	89.36	90.75	92.10	91.03	92.39	94.87
R	87.52	90.16	90.53	92.63	92.76	92.02	94.56
L-R	86.36	91.02	90.36	92.41	90.39	91.87	93.54
R-L	87.05	91.19	89.69	92.13	91.42	92.54	94.02
PS	80.17	83.62	88.63	91.84	89.25	93.64	95.24
PL	79.13	84.26	87.09	90.33	87.17	92.24	95.37
PS-PL	77.31	85.69	90.21	93.26	86.36	92.86	94.32
PL-PS	79.98	87.35	90.69	92.67	89.94	92.06	94.03
PS-L	80.03	84.16	90.03	91.69	86.69	92.87	93.28
PS-R	78.97	83.69	89.53	91.30	85.87	93.65	92.41
Average	82.31	87.05	89.75	92.03	89.08	92.61	94.16

In Table 1, when the I3D network is used with LSTM, the recognition accuracy of each type of hand gesture can reach over 90%. Because the Sequential Memory Inflated 3D (SM-I3D) network will carry out feature segmentation and reorganization according to the current parameter features, which will further improve its recognition accuracy. Therefore, the average recognition accuracy is significantly improved.

Different Network Hand Gesture Recognition Rate Based on ATM Data Set. Similarly, we also give the relevant experimental results on the ATM data set, and the results are shown in Fig. 9.

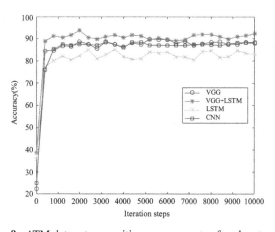

Fig. 9. ATM data set recognition accuracy rate of each network

It can be concluded in Fig. 9 that the VGG + LSTM network can fully extract the parameters and time characteristics of the hand gesture. Therefore, its recognition accuracy is 93.20%.

Hand Gesture Recognition Accuracy Rate Under Converged Network.
If the RDM features or ATM features are used alone, the accuracy of hand gesture recognition will be affected. Thus, we present the hand gesture recognition results under LS-I3D network and compares it with TS-I3D [19] network, as shown in Fig. 10.

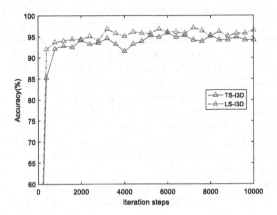

Fig. 10. Comparison of recognition accuracy under different networks

It can be seen from Fig. 10 that after combining RDM and ATM data sets, the accuracy of hand gesture recognition will be significantly improved. The TS-I3D network extracts time series features after fusing RDM and ATM parameter features. The accuracy rate of TS-I3D network is 94.71%. Compared with the TS-I3D network, the recognition accuracy of the proposed LS-I3D network used can reach 97.26%.

5 Conclusion

In this paper, we proposed a novel hand gesture recognition method for FMCW radar. Firstly, the FM signal was transmitted through the FMCW radar, and then the range, Doppler and angle information of the target were estimated. We adopted static and dynamic interference suppression methods to extract hand gestures. Then, the improved I3D network was applied to extract the features in RDM, and the VGG neural network was adopted to extract ATM features. The range, Doppler and angle features are sent to the LSTM network to extract the time-series features of hand gesture signals. The fused hand gesture features were input into the support vector machine classifier for classification. The experimental results showed that the accuracy rate of hand gesture recognition was 97.26%.

References

1. Song, J., Sörös, G., Pece, F., Fanello, S.R., Hilliges, O.: In-air gestures around unmodified mobile devices. In: Proceedings of the 27th Annual ACM Symposium on User Interface Software and Technology, pp. 319–329 (2014)
2. Dong, S.-L.: Analysis on the application of artificial intelligence technology in the construction of the internet interactive platform of inquiry curriculum. In: Mizera-Pietraszko, J., Pichappan, P. (eds.) RTIS 2016. AISC, vol. 613, pp. 24–32. Springer, Cham (2018). https://doi.org/10.1007/978-3-319-60744-3_3
3. Yang, X.D., Chen, Y.Q., Yu, H.C., Liu, J.F., Li, Z.G.: Ultrasonic waves based gesture recognition method for wearable equipment. Comput. Sci. **42**(10), 26–30 (2015)
4. Pigou, L., Oord, A., Dieleman, S., Herreweghe, M., Dambre, J.: Beyond temporal pooling: Recurrence and temporal convolutions for gesture recognition in video. Int. J. Comput. Vis. **126**(2–4), 430–439 (2016). https://doi.org/10.1007/s11263-016-0957-7
5. Nandwana, B., Tazi, S., Trivedi, S., Kumar, D., Vipparthi, S.K.: A survey paper on hand gesture recognition. In: 2017 7th International Conference on Communication Systems and Network Technologies (CSNT), Maharashtra, India (2017)
6. Chimeh, J.D., Parapari, S.B., Mousavinejad, S.M.: Millimetric waves technologies: Opportunities and challenges. Trans Tech Publications, vol. 500, pp. 263–268 (2011)
7. Abbadi, A., Abbane, A., Bencheikh, M.L., Soltani, F.: A new adaptive CFAR processor in multiple target situations. In: 2017 Seminar on Detection Systems Architectures and Technologies (DAT), pp. 1–5. IEEE, Algiers (2017)
8. Luduvico Coelho, Y., Marques Salomao, J., Rolf Kulitz, H.: Intelligent hand posture recognition system integrated to process control. IEEE Latin Am. Trans. **15**(6), 1144–1153 (2017)
9. Karpathy, A., Toderici, G., Shetty, S., Leung, T., Fei-Fei, L.: Large-scale video classification with convolutional neural networks. In: Proceedings of the IEEE Conference on Computer Vision and Pattern Recognition, pp. 1725–1732 (2014)
10. Tran, D., Bourdev, L.D., Fergus, R., Torresani, L., Paluri, M.: C3D: generic features for video analysis. CORR, abs/1412.0767, vol. 2, no. 7, p. 8 (2014)
11. Wang, S., Song, J., Lien, J., Poupyrev, I., Hilliges, O.: Interacting with soli: exploring finegrained dynamic gesture recognition in the radio-frequency spectrum. In: Proceedings of the 29th Annual Symposium on User Interface Software and Technology, pp. 851–860 (2016)
12. Zhao, Z., Wang, Y., Zhou, M., Yang, X., Xie, L.: Interference suppression based gesture recognition Method with FMCW radar. In: 2019 11th International Conference on Wireless Communications and Signal Processing (WCSP), pp. 1–6 (2019)
13. Schmidt, R.: Multiple emitter location and signal parameter estimation. IEEE Trans. Antennas Propag. **34**(3), 276–280 (1986)
14. Sor, R., Sathone, J.S., Deoghare, S.U., Sutaone, M.S.: OS-CFAR based on thresholding approaches for target detection. In: 2018 Fourth International Conference on Computing Communication Control and Automation (ICCUBEA), pp. 1–6 (2018)
15. Helkey, R.: Intensity noise suppression using differential delay cancellation in external modulation links. U.S. Patent No. 6,441,932. 27 Aug 2002
16. Zhu, G., Zhang, L., Shen, P., Song, J., Shah, S.A.A., Bennamoun, M.: Continuous gesture segmentation and recognition using 3DCNN and convolutional LSTM. IEEE Trans. Multimed. **21**(4), 1011–1021 (2018)
17. Wang, X., Miao, Z., Zhang, R., Hao, S.: I3D-LSTM: a new model for human action recognition. In: IOP Conference Series: Materials Science and Engineering, vol. 569, no. 3, pp. 032–035 (2019)

18. Simonyan, K., Zisserman, A.: Very deep convolutional networks for large-scale image recognition. Computer Vision and Pattern Recognition (2014). https://arxiv.org/abs/1409.1556
19. Wang, Y., Wang, S., Zhou, M., Jiang, Q., Tian, Z.: TS-I3D based hand gesture recognition method with radar sensor. IEEE Access 7, 22902–22913 (2019)

A Novel Blockchain-Based Revocable Permission Management on CP-ABE Scheme

Qianchuan Xv[1,2], Yubo Song[1,2(✉)], Xuan Li[1,2], Aiqun Hu[2,3], and Junbo Wang[3,4]

[1] Key Laboratory of Computer Networking Technology of Jiangsu Province, Nanjing 211189, China
songyubo@seu.edu.cn
[2] Purple Mountain Laboratory of Network Communication and Security, Nanjing 211189, China
[3] School of Information Science and Engineering, Nanjing 211189, China
[4] National Mobile Communications Research Laboratory, Nanjing 211189, China

Abstract. Relying on the characteristics of decentralized, tamper-proof, and traceable, blockchain technology has begun to be widely used in permission management. It can be used for access control by using smart contracts to distribute tokens. But also because of the immutability of the blockchain, it cannot dynamically revoke permission. This paper proposed an on-chain user permission management mechanism that could support automatic and active permission revocation. This model proposed an extended CP-ABE chain user permission management model, which realized the permission grant based on user attributes by smart contracts. Furthermore, on this basis, an extended CP-ABE permission revocation mechanism was proposed. The timestamp technology was used to realize the automatic revocation of permission, and the subset coverage algorithm was used to realize the active revocation of permission. A blockchain-based permission distribution model was built, and the permission revocation scheme was introduced into it to conduct experiments. Its performance was tested and analyzed. The experimental results showed that when the number of permission distributions is 1000, the delay is about 5 s. At the same time, the permission change is above 130TPS, which met actual application requirements.

Keywords: Blockchain · Permission management · Data security

1 Introduction

A distributed ledger is a database that is shared, replicated, and synchronized between network members. Participants can get a unique trustworthy ledger. Any legal modification to the ledger will be reflected in the ledger held by all other participants at the same time. The blockchain is one of the distributed ledger technologies. The difference is that the blockchain is a data structure in which each block connects all blocks into a chain by contacting the hash value of the previous block. Each block may store a series of transaction information. Since the advent of Bitcoin in 2008, blockchain as the core supporting technology of digital currency has also received great attention and has quickly become a new technology hotspot in Internet finance. Not only that, in the past

© Springer Nature Switzerland AG 2021
X. Sun et al. (Eds.): ICAIS 2021, CCIS 1424, pp. 650–663, 2021.
https://doi.org/10.1007/978-3-030-78621-2_54

few years, with its decentralized characteristics, the blockchain has rapidly developed from financial applications and distributed storage to the field of personally controllable data access permission management without a trusted third party.

The hash value of each block in the blockchain is related to the hash value of the previous block (parent block), especially the header hash value of the transaction data in the parent block. This encryption method is implemented by a Merkle tree. Each block in the blockchain will have a Merkle tree. It starts from a leaf node (the bottom of the tree). A leaf node is a transaction hash. When the leaf node represents When the content of the transaction changes, the Merkle hash value changes accordingly, and the block hash value also changes. As mentioned earlier, each block saves the hash value of the previous block. After the block hash value is changed, the hash value of all blocks will change afterward. Merkle hash and block hash together to ensure that the block content cannot be tampered with.

Yu [1] et al. used proxy re-encryption technology to realize user permission revocation, but this scheme only supports permission revocation with AND policies in the access control structure. At the same time, when revoking user permission, it is necessary to regenerate the proxy key. All keys were included. Liu et al. [2] proposed a proxy re-encryption scheme based on timestamp, which can revoke user access permission after a predefined period of time. Yanfeng Shi et al. [4] proposed a permission revocation scheme under the KP-ABE environment. The user ciphertext is divided into two parts. One part is related to the policy, and the other part is related to the user identity. Correspondingly, the decryption key is also divided into two parts, one part is related to user attributes, the other part is related to user identity. G. Ateniese et al. [5] proposed the use of variable blockchain technology-the chameleon hash function (chameleon hash) is similar to a public key encryption system, and its main idea is to artificially set a trapdoor, although It can be considered safe for most people, it destroys the two collision resistance of the hash function, and the purpose of revoking permission can be achieved by adjusting the random number. These schemes add additional computational overhead based on the basic attribute-based encryption scheme, increase the complexity of the algorithm, and even destroy the decentralized nature of the blockchain, and even threaten the data security of the entire chain.

In response to the above problems, this paper proposes a timestamp-based automatic permission revocation and a binary tree-based active permission revocation scheme. Realize coarse-grained automatic cancellation through time stamp, which can revoke the access permission of multiple data users at the same time. By organizing data users into a binary tree to achieve more fine-grained active revocation, it can be accurate to the permission revocation of a single data user, thus solving the problem of blockchain in permission management.

2 Blockchain-Based Permission Distribution Model

2.1 Overall Structure

The overall architecture of the chain permission distribution model proposed in this paper is shown in Fig. 1. The entire model is mainly divided into five layers: data storage layer, blockchain service layer, access control layer, chaincode layer, and the functional layer.

The data storage layer mainly includes three parts: blockchain storage, state database storage, and cloud database storage. In the on-chain permission distribution model, the private data of the data owner is symmetrically encrypted and uploaded to the cloud database to achieve data persistence. Then the symmetric key is encrypted and uploaded to the blockchain, reducing the storage pressure on the chain. The blockchain service layer mainly includes P2P transmission services and data broadcasting services, consensus reaching and query services supported by blockchain. The access control layer mainly realizes the distribution of permission on the chain. In this model, there are mainly three parties: data owners, data users, and attribute management institutions.

The data owner uploads his data to the cloud database storage after being encrypted by a symmetric key to achieve data persistence. The encrypted data is stored in the cloud database securely and cannot be decrypted without the symmetric key. Data users can apply to the attribute management agency for roles and attributes based on their own information, and the attribute management agency assigns corresponding roles and attributes to them. After the data user obtains the roles and attributes, they can apply to the data owner for a decryption key. The data owner generates the data user's decryption key based on the data user's own role and attributes and distributes it to the data user through the blockchain. The data owner can generate the key ciphertext by encrypting the symmetric key and upload the key ciphertext to realize the distribution of permission. The chaincode layer mainly includes the editing, deployment, execution, and update of the on-chain code. After the smart contract is written, it needs to be packaged by the chain code and deployed to the blockchain. The chain code generally runs in a secure Docker container independent of the consensus node on the chain, which initializes and manages the state database through transactions initiated by the application.

Finally, the functional layer indicates the functions implemented by the on-chain permission management model.

2.2 CP-ABE Encryption Algorithm

CP-ABE (cipher text policy attribute-based encryption) uses a specific access control structure to encrypt data, and the decryption key is generated based on a set of attributes. When the decryptor's attributes meet the access control structure, the ciphertext can be decrypted correctly. The biggest advantage of CP-ABE is that after the key is generated, the encryption party can flexibly change the access control structure during encryption to control which users can decrypt data.

When CP-ABE is initialized, it first selects a bilinear group G_0 of prime order p and generator g. Then, choose two random exponents α and β, and $\alpha, \in \beta Z_p$. The generated public key $PK = G_0, g, h = g^{\beta}, e(g, g)^{\alpha}$, the master key MK is (β, g^{α}). After public key PK and master key MK are generated, decryption key generation and data encryption can be realized based on PK and MK. The decryption key takes a set of attributes S of the decrypting party as input, and the decryption key generated according to this set of attributes is shown in Eq. 1.

$$SK = \left(D = g^{\frac{\alpha+r}{\beta}}, \forall j \in S : D_j = g^r H(j)^{r_j}, D_j^{'} = g^{r_j} \right) \tag{1}$$

When using CP-ABE for data encryption, the encrypting party needs to specify an access control tree, and the leaf nodes of the access control tree are all related to

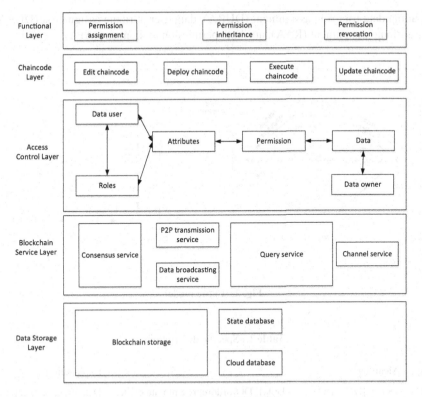

Fig. 1. Overall architecture

the attributes of the decrypting party. The encryption party controls which attributes the decryption party possesses by controlling the structure of the access control tree to decrypt the data, as shown in Eq. 2.

$$CT = (T, \tilde{C} = Me(g, g)^{\alpha s}, C = h^s, \forall y \in Y : C_y = g^{q_y(0)},$$

$$C_y' = H(att(y)^{q_y(0)}) \tag{2}$$

Permission allocation process based on smart contract.

1) Model description
The description of the entire model is shown in Fig. 2. The permission distribution process is completed in the blockchain. This process mainly has three parties: data owners, data users, and attribute management agencies. Among them, the attribute management organization is responsible for the assignment of data user roles and attributes. The model is mainly composed of two parts: 1. Seven entities and attribute management agencies, blockchain, cloud database, of which seven entities include data owner (DO), data user (DU), data set (D), role (R), attributes (A), permission (P), and sessions (S), the specific descriptions are shown in Table 1; 2. The relationship between the six entities, mainly

including data user role assignment (DURA), data user attribute assignment (DUAA), role attribute assignment (RAA), attribute permission assignment (APA).

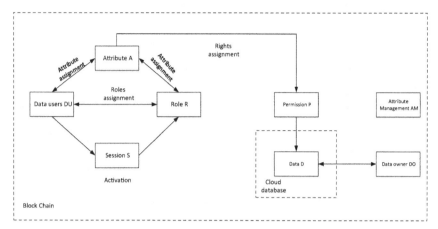

Fig. 2. Entire model

Table 1. Specific descriptions

Sign	Meaning	Explanation
DO	$DO = \{DO_1, DO_2, \ldots, DO_n\}$, DO_i ordorepresent data owner	Data owner collection
DU	$DU = \{DU_1, DU_2, \ldots, DU_n\}$, DU_i ordurepresent data user	Data users collection
D	$D = \{D_1, D_2, \ldots, D_n\}$, D_i ordrepresentone data	Data collection
R	$R = \{R, R_2, \ldots, R_n\}$, Rorrrepresentone role	Roles collection
A	$A = \{A_1, A_2, \ldots, A_n\}$, A_i orattrrepresentone attribute	Attributes collection
P	$P = \{P, P_2, \ldots, P_n\}$, P_i orp representone permission	Permission collection
S	$S = \{S_1, S_2, \ldots, S_n\}$, S_i orsrepresentone session	Session collection

2) Smart contract process
When using smart contracts to implement permission distribution, the process is shown in Fig. 3. The entire process has five main steps: blockchain system initialization, role and attribute assignment transactions, session transactions, on-chain data storage, and on-chain data acquisition. The blockchain system's initialization mainly includes the initialization of the entire blockchain network and the initialization of the entity state data. AM, DO, and DU joins the blockchain network with different identities. Each entity initiates state data initialization transactions and generates initial state data in the state database. Role and attribute assignment transactions mainly include data users requesting roles and attributes from the attribute management agency, and the attribute management agency assigns different roles and attributes to the data user based on their

identity, credentials, and other information. Conversation transactions mainly include the activation of roles and the acquisition of decryption keys. Data users can have multiple roles at the same time, and they determine their current roles in the conversation. The role activation is completed by the attribute management organization. When the role is activated, the available attributes of the data user will be activated at the same time, and the role attributes will be assigned to it. After the data user activates the role and attributes, it requests a decryption key from the data owner, and the data owner generates a decryption key for him according to his role and attributes. Data storage on the chain is completed by the data owner, who first uploads the private data to the cloud database after symmetric encryption and then uploads the symmetric key to the blockchain after being encrypted by the CP-ABE algorithm. Data acquisition of the chain is completed by the data user. It first requests data from the data owner. After the data owner agrees to the request, the data user obtains the key ciphertext from the chain and decrypts it with its own decryption key to obtain the symmetric key. The key, in turn, gains access to related private data.

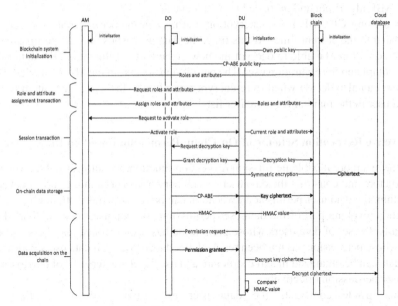

Fig. 3. Smart contract process

3 Permission Revocation Schemes

3.1 A Time Stamp-Based On-Chain Permission Automatic Revocation Scheme

The basic idea of using time stamps to revoke data user permission is to specify the effective time of data access for each data user who has been granted data access permission. In this solution, when the data owner agrees to the data user's data request, each data user specifies the time when the data can be accessed, which is stored in the data requester list maintained by the data owner.

The data users in the data users list all correspond to a valid time expire time, which is the same as the expiration time of the data user's decryption key. Only when the time is greater than the current time, the data user can access the data correctly. The specific steps are as follows:

- When the data owner is encrypting the symmetric key, in addition to specifying the conditions that the data user's attributes should meet in the access control structure, expireTime > now should also be specified, where now represents the current time when the symmetric key is encrypted;
- When the data user's permission to access the data expires, its access permission needs to be revoked. Since it already has the original symmetric decryption key, it needs to use the new symmetric key to re-enable the data owner's private data encrypt and upload to the cloud database;
- At the same time, the new symmetric encryption key needs to be encrypted by the CP-ABE algorithm and uploaded to the blockchain.
- When using CP-ABE for re-encryption, the now in the access control structure is updated to the current time. At this time, the data user whose access permission has expired will not be able to decrypt the new ciphertext. At this point, the data owner has completed the expiration user. The permission are automatically revoked; the data owner can also decide when to re-encrypt according to the expire time item of each data user in the maintained data user list.

3.2   Active Revocation Scheme of On-Chain Permission Based on Binary Tree

To achieve a more flexible permission revocation function, we introduce the revocation list structure and construct the data users as a binary tree. Through the subset coverage algorithm, the data user permission revocation can be realized more efficiently.

When revoking part of the data user permission, all data users can be divided into two parts: the set of data users whose permission has been revoked and the set of data users whose permission has not been revoked. For data owners, all data users who access their data can be organized in a tree structure and use the characteristics of that to revoke data user permission effectively.

This article constructs the data user as a binary tree T_{du}, T_{du} $=<$ $root_{du}$, V_{du}, V_{in}, V, $E>$. Among them, $root_{du}$ represents the root node, V_{du} represents the leaf node, each leaf node corresponds to a data user, V_{in} represents a non-leaf node, $root_{du} \in V_{in}$, V represents all nodes, $V = V_{du} \cup V_{in}$, E represents the edge in the tree.

If there are N data users, then $|V_{du}| = N$, we assume that the binary tree is a full binary tree and N is a power of 2, such a binary tree has $2N - 1$ nodes in total. For $1 \leq i \leq n$, let v_i denote a certain node in the tree, $v_i \in V$. Let R denote a group of leaf nodes, then R represents a group of data users. We stipulate that $ST(R)$ represents R and the smallest subtree introduced by $root_{du}$, and $ST(R)$ is unique. v_i is the node that is connected to all the nodes with out-degree 1 in $ST(R)$ but not in $ST(R)$. We use S_i to denote all leaf nodes on the subtree with v_i as the root node, that is, all data user. Given a list of data users whose permission has been revoked, the leaf nodes corresponding to these data users whose permission has been revoked form R, then the union of the leaf node sets S_i of these subtrees $S_1 \cup S_2 \cup \cdots S_i$ is all data users whose permission has not been revoked.

Consider a full binary tree as shown in Fig. 4. Its leaf nodes are $x_1, x_2, x_3, \cdots x_8$, these leaf nodes represent data users $DU_1, DU_2, DU_3, \cdots DU_8$. If we revoke the access permission of x_1 and x_4, x_1 and x_4 constitute a node set R, that is, $R = \{x_1, x_4\}$, then the minimum revocation subtree composed of x_1, x_4 and the root node x_{15} is shown in Fig. 5.

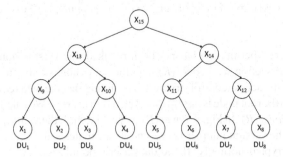

Fig. 4. Data users tree

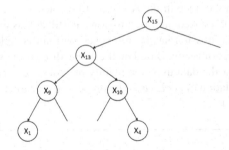

Fig. 5. Minimum revocation subtree

From the previous definition, x_2, x_3, x_{14} are v_i, and the data users represented by all leaf nodes of the subtree with it as the root node are all data users whose access permission has not been revoked, that is, $x_2, x_3, x_5, x_6, x_7, x_8$. We denote the set of nodes formed by nodes x_2, x_3 and x_{14} as $cover(R)$, namely $cover(R) = \{x_2, x_3, x_{14}\}$. Using each node in $cover(R)$ corresponds to a subset of data users who have not revoked permission, and a smaller number of nodes means more data users who have not revoked permission. This algorithm can be called. It is a subset coverage algorithm, which optimizes the efficiency of permission revocation.

The use of the data user tree to revoke permission described in this section requires improvements in the decryption key generation and data encryption phases:

- In the decryption key generation phase, each node x_i in the data user tree stores a random Version number ver_i, the version number saved in each node is different and not related. Each data user corresponds to a leaf node, which has all the version numbers of the nodes passing through the path from the leaf node to the root node.

• In the data encryption stage, when the data owner wants to revoke the access permission of some data users, it first calculates the $cover(R)$ based on the data users whose permission has been revoked, and then the nodes contained in the $cover(R)$ The version number inside is added to the access control tree with an "or" logical access strategy. For example, in Fig. 4, if the access permission of x_1, x_4 are revoked, it can be seen from the above that the nodes contained in $cover(R)$ are $\{x_2, x_3, x_{14}\}$, and the version numbers saved in these nodes are $\{ver_2, ver_3, ver_{14}\}$, the data owner will add the access control logic of $ver_2 \vee ver_3 \vee ver_{14}$ in the access control tree when encrypting data.

If the data user's permission has not been revoked, the version number set it owns must have an intersection with $cover(R)$, and the set contains only one element whose attributes satisfy the access control structure. Assuming that the data requester is DU_5 in Fig. 4, the path to the root node is $path_{DU_5} = \{x_5, x_{11}, x_{14}, x_{15}\}$. We calculate intersection of $path_{DU_5}$ and $cover(R)$. In Fig. 4, $cover(R) = \{x_2, x_3, x_{14}\}$, then $path_{DU_5} \cap cover(R) = \{x_{14}\}$. DU_5 has the version number ver_{14}, and its attributes satisfy $ver_2 \vee ver_3 \vee ver_{14}$, so it can be decrypted normally. If the data user's permission has been revoked, the intersection of its own version number set and $cover(R)$ must be an empty set, and its attributes do not satisfy the access control structure. Adding the logic of the version number and the OR in the node in the $cover(R)$ to the access strategy ensures that all data users who have not revoked their permission can still access the data normally, and the data users whose permission has been revoked will not be able to access the data. Active cancellation of permission. Based on the above discussion, we can know that the operation algorithm for the data user tree mainly includes the construction of the data user tree and the calculation of $cover(R)$. The process of constructing a data user tree is shown in Algorithm 3.1.

Algorithm 3.1

Input: Data users node set $duNodes$,   version set ver

output: Null

1: If the number of nodes in $duNodes$ is 0, 1 or 2, directly construct a binary tree of data users, specify the root node of the tree, and the algorithm ends.

2: Take every two adjacent nodes in $duNodes$ as the left and permission child nodes to construct its parent node $parentNode$, and these parent nodes form the parent node set $parentNodes$. If there are remaining nodes in $duNodes$, add them to $parentNodes$.

3: Take $parentNodes$ and ver as parameters, continue to run the $construTree$ algorithm.

The binary tree is constructed in an iterative manner. Iteration is to obtain the final result from the initial value by repeating a certain process. In the process of constructing the binary tree, it is to repeat a certain process, and the root node is obtained from the leaf nodes. The data user ID in the node only has a value in the leaf node, indicating the data user represented by the leaf node, and the internal node is not assigned a value. Given the revoked data user, the process of calculating cover(R) based on the data user tree is shown in Algorithm 3.2.

Algorithm 3.2

Input: Data user revocation list R

Output: Null

1: Get the revoke node list $revokeNodes$ of the data user through R.

2: For each node $revokeNode$ in $revokeNodes$, repeat step 3 to get the revoke subtree $revokeNode$.

3: Check each node from $revokeNode$ to the root node. If it is not included in the set of revoked permission nodes, add it, otherwise, the step ends.

4: Breadth-first traversal of the binary tree of data users. If a node is included in the set of revoked permission, check whether it has a node with default usage permission. If so, add the node to the cover. At the same time, it is unnecessary to traverse the sub If there is no subtree whose node is the root, continue to traverse.

5: Return $cover(R)$。

Given a data user revocation list, we need to be able to get $cover(R)$ from the data user revocation list. We obtain the corresponding leaf node in the data user tree from the given data user ID in the data user revocation list. Before revoking the data user, the color of all nodes in the data user tree is the default state of permission. When the permission of some data users are revoked, all the leaf nodes corresponding to the revoked data user will pass through the path to the root node. All nodes are classified into the revoked permission set, and the subtree formed by it is the revoked subtree. Each node that violates the revoked permission connected to the revoked subtree is the node in cover(R). When the data owner revokes the permission of some data users, he first uses the new symmetric key to encrypt related private data. Then, the new access control tree is used to encrypt the symmetric key. The access control tree contains the same structure as the previous encryption except for the version number information contained therein. The new access control tree includes the version number in cover(R) in the form of OR, realizing the cancellation of permission.

4 Testing and Analysis

4.1 System Architecture Design

The architecture of the on-chain permission revocation system is shown in Fig. 6. There are three parties to the system: data owners, data users, and attribute management agencies. The data owner stores his own private data in the cloud database after symmetric encryption, and at the same time, encrypts the symmetric key to generate the key cipher-text and saves it in the blockchain. The data user applies to the attribute management agency for roles and attributes through the blockchain, and the attribute management agency assigns roles and attributes to the data user through the blockchain based on the data user's identity and credentials. The data user requests a key from the data owner through the blockchain according to the obtained role and attributes. The data owner uses the role and attributes of the data user to generate a corresponding decryption key and distribute it to the data user through the blockchain. The data user can obtain the key ciphertext through the blockchain and decrypt it with its own decryption key. If it has the permission, it will decrypt it correctly, and then obtain the data owner's private data from the cloud database. If the permission is revoked, it cannot be decrypted, and thus cannot obtain the private data of the data owner.

4.2 Performance Testing

This section mainly tests the system from two aspects: latency and throughput. The latency refers to the time from the initiation of permission change to the time the blockchain system responds to the operation. The throughput is defined as per second the number of successfully completed operations can be expressed in units of TPS (Transactions Per Second).

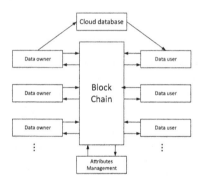

Fig. 6. Permission revocation system

The prototype implementation of the on-chain permission management system is completed by calling smart contracts. In this process, two types of functions are mainly involved: query and invoke. Query is used to read the current status of the data owner, data user, and attribute management organization in the current status database. It is not in the strict sense and does not require the consensus of each node. It is just a pure permission acquisition process and will not change participation the status data of the parties, but the throughput can still be used to express its performance. All other functions belong to invoke.

The relationship between the delay of permission acquisition and the number of con-current queries is shown in Fig. 7(a), where the unit of delay is milliseconds. The relationship between throughput and the number of concurrent queries is shown in Fig. 7(b),

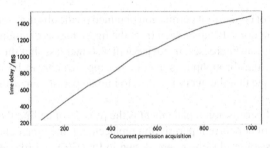

(a) Concurrent permission acquisition delay

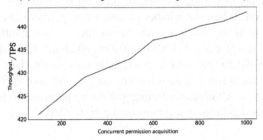

(b) Concurrent permission to obtain throughput

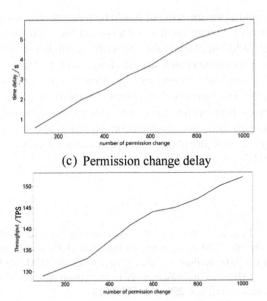

(c) Permission change delay

(d) Permission replacement throughput

Fig. 7. Performance graph

where the number of concurrent permission obtained on the abscissa represents the number of concurrent queries. It can be seen from the figure that as the number of concurrent permission acquisitions increases, the delay will also increase, but the growth is slower. At the same time, the throughput is also increasing, which can be maintained above 400TPS. You can see that the query is called to initiate permission acquisition with high efficiency.

The process of permission replacement is the process of calling the invoke function. With the increase of concurrent permission replacement, the time delay and throughput changes of permission replacement are shown in Fig. 7(c) and (d), respectively. It can be seen that the delay of calling the invoke function is significantly higher than that of the query function. When the number of concurrent permission changes is 1000, it is already about 5 s. At the same time, the throughput is significantly smaller than the query function, but it is also above 130TPS, and the efficiency is also high. Whether it is calling query or invoke, the reason why throughput is increasing here is the preliminary analysis is that the blockchain system has not yet reached saturation, and there is still room for improvement. Although the throughput during permission change is lower than that of permission acquisition, it also maintains a higher level.

5 Conclusion

This article mainly addresses the issue of blockchain permission management and proposes a user permission management mechanism on the chain that supports revocable permission: this solution extends the CP-ABE model and uses smart contracts to achieve data owners based on user attribute matching. Grant permission to data users; use timestamp technology and subset coverage algorithm to achieve permission revocation. Through the above two mechanisms, the flexibility is improved while reducing the complexity of the permission revocation operation. This paper implements and verifies the prototype system of permission management on the chain. The data user's autonomous and controllable permission distribution and permission cancellation function can be realized on the blockchain.

References

1. Yu, S., Wang, C., Ren, K., et al.: Attribute based data sharing with attribute revocation. In: Proceedings of the 5th ACM Symposium on Information, Computer and Communications Security, ASIACCS 2010, Beijing, China, 13–16 April 2010. ACM (2010)
2. Liu, Q., Wang, G., Wu, J.: Time-based proxy re-encryption scheme for secure data sharing in a cloud environment. Inf. Sci. **258**, 355–370 (2014)
3. Zhang, P., Chen, Z., Liang, K., et al.: A Cloud-Based Access Control Scheme with User Revocation and Attribute Update (2016)
4. Shi, Y., Zheng, Q., Liu, J., et al.: Directly revocable key-policy attribute-based encryption with verifiable ciphertext delegation. Inf. Sci. **295**, 221–231 (2015)
5. Ateniese, G., Magri, B., Venturi, D., Andrade, E.: Redactableblockchain–or–rewriting history in bitcoin and friends. In: IEEE European Symposium on Security and Privacy (EuroS&P), pp. 111–126. IEEE (2018)

6. Dorri, A., Kanhere, S.S., Jurdak, R.: MOF-BC: a memoryoptimized and flexible blockchain for large scale networks. Future Gen. Comput. Syst. **92**, 357–373 (2019)
7. Goyal, V.: Attribte-based encryption for fine-grained access control of encrypted data. Acm Ccs (2006)
8. Nakamoto, S., et al.: A peer-to-peer electronic cash system. Bitcoin (2018). https://bitcoin.org/bitcoin.pdf
9. ConsenSys, "Deloitte: 95% of Companies Surveyed Are Investingin Blockchain Tech" (2019). https://media.consensys.net/deloitte-95-ofcompanies-surveyed-are-investing-in-blockchain-tech-5566f4942b5d
10. Air France-KLM partners with Winding Tree to strengtheninnovation in the travel industry using Blockchain technology (2018). https://www.airfranceklm.com/en/news/air-france-klm-partnerswinding-tree-strengthen-innovation-travel-industry-using-blockchain
11. Bradbury, D.: Hyperledger 3 years later: That's the sound of the devs...working on the chain ga-a-ang. But is anyone actually using it?" (2018). https://www.theregister.co.uk/2018/01/02/hyperledger_at_three/
12. Panetta, K.: 5 Trends Emerge in the Gartner Hype Cycle for EmergingTechnologies (2018). https://www.gartner.com/smarterwithgartner/5-trends-emerge-in-gartner-hype-cycle-for-emerging-technologies-2018/
13. Dasaklis, T.K., Casino, F., Patsakis, C.: Blockchain meets smart health: towards next generation healthcare services. In: 2018 9th International Conference on Information, Intelligence, Systems and Applications (IISA). IEEE (2019)
14. Iqbal, M., Matulevicius, R.: Blockchain-Based Application Security Risks: A Systematic Literature Review (2019)
15. Deuber, D., Magri, B., Thyagarajan, S.A.K.: Redactable Blockchain in the Permissionless Setting (2019)
16. Puddu, I., Dmitrienko, A., Capkun, S.: μchain: How to forget without hard forks. IACR Cryptology ePrint Archive **2017**, 106 (2017)

Automated Authentication of Large-Scale IoT Devices with Hybrid Feature Selection

Qi Chen[1,2], Yubo Song[1,2(✉)], Aiqun Hu[3,4], and Junbo Wang[3,4]

[1] Key Laboratory of Computer Network Technology of Jiangsu Province,
School of Cyber Science and Engineering, Southeast University,
Nanjing 211189, China
songyubo@seu.edu.cn
[2] Purple Mountain Laboratories, Nanjing 211189, China
[3] National Mobile Communications Research Laboratory, Nanjing 211189, China
[4] School of Information Science and Engineering, Southeast University,
Nanjing 211189, China

Abstract. Nowadays, large-scale IoT (Internet of Things) devices are connected to the network. However, due to the simplicity, limited memory and poor computing power of most IoT devices, it is difficult to apply complex security authentication protocols to these devices. Many attackers use this loophole, impersonating legitimate devices to launch malicious attacks on the network, threatening the security of other legitimate devices. Therefore, in order to strengthen the identification and management of devices, the existing device fingerprint identification technology based on machine learning is to extract device traffic at the access gateway and generate device fingerprinting to realize the identification of IoT devices. However, to achieve high recognition accuracy, existing device fingerprint algorithms need to extract a large number of fingerprint features from network traffic for machine learning, which increases the complexity of implementation and delay of device identification. Also, it is not suitable for the current large-scale access environment. Therefore, this paper proposes a hybrid feature selection method to preprocess features for the optimal feature subset, which can not only reduce the feature dimension, but also improve the accuracy of device recognition. Firstly, the method filters the irrelevant features according to the characteristic fluctuation and the entropy of correlation information between the feature and the target. Then, based on the classification accuracy of the learning algorithm, a random search method—forest optimization algorithm is used to further optimize the filtered feature subsets under the evaluation criteria. Experiments show that this method can reduce feature dimension by 81.0% and improve classification accuracy from 86.4% to 93.1%.

Keywords: Iot device identification · Second keyword · Feature selection · Feature selection · Machine learning · Iot security

© Springer Nature Switzerland AG 2021
X. Sun et al. (Eds.): ICAIS 2021, CCIS 1424, pp. 664–676, 2021.
https://doi.org/10.1007/978-3-030-78621-2_55

1   Introduction

With the popularization of IoT devices, more and more devices are connected to the Internet. According to Gartner [1], the number of IoT devices in the network can reach nearly 15.9 billion in 2019, which was an increase of 31% compared with that in 2018. The number of IoT devices in the network will reach 113.4 billion in 2025. The number of IoT devices is growing on a larger scale, which would bring huge challenges to cyberspace security. For example, some hackers will enter the network with fake devices to obtain the control authority of the network, and then carry out offensive actions such as virus destruction, network control and information theft [2]. Furthermore, IoT devices are susceptible to be compromised because of the lack of reliable access authentication. In Maria attack [3], compromised cameras were linked to form "botnets3" to attack DNS service provider under the external control of attackers, which disabled websites with a flood of bogus requests. Due to the traditional identity recognition technology depends on the complex encryption protocol and client authentication mechanism. Meanwhile, most network intelligent terminals are hardware devices. They cannot install the client software for identities. Due to their limited computing and storage resources [4], devices fail to perform complex cryptographic protocol despite the installation of the client software. On the other hand, due to the complex and large number of devices in the network space, the current identity identification technology cannot be applied to all IoT devices. So, the unified security management of IoT devices cannot be realized. Therefore, it's crucial for researchers to pay attention to the problem of IoT devices identification.

Because traffic varies from device to device. The researchers propose using the traffic generated by device interactions to identify devices. Meidan et al. [5] is the first to apply machine learning technology to network traffic classification and identification, and this method can be used to identify unauthorized IoT devices in the network. The proposed method is aimed at two kinds of attacks: non-directed devices, that is, devices are infected by malware due to interaction; targeted devices, in which an attacker intentionally implants malware or viruses into a legitimate device. Shahid et al. [6] took IAT (Inter-Arrival-Time) of packets as the function of analyzing IoT devices. They use a fixed parameter N to indicate the number of packages from which to extract features. They used random forest, decision tree and other classification algorithms to improve the accuracy of equipment identification to 90%. However, because IAT is a controllable parameter, this method is vulnerable to the manipulation of attackers. Kai Yang et al. [7] collected 96 million IPv4 packets and stored them in a format (IP, protocol, port, packet). Different features are extracted at the network layer, transport layer and application layer. The data set reached 690,000, and more than 30,000 feature vectors were extracted from each packet. Finally, neural network is used to train the classifier to generate the final recognition model. This method is innovative in information collection and feature labeling, and contains devices that almost cover this network.

However, existing device fingerprint recognition needs to extract a large number of features from traffic for machine learning classification, which increases the complexity of the machine learning algorithm in the training stage, and may even lead to non-convergence of the algorithm. At the same time, in the actual identification process, too many device features need to be extracted. However, with the increase of the number of devices, the difficulty of information collection increases. If the collection is not timely, the device identification at the gateway will be delayed, and even lead to data congestion. Therefore, the current flow-based device fingerprint identification should not only improve the accuracy of device identification, but also enhance the timeliness and efficiency of device identification. Aiming at the problem of accuracy and efficiency, this paper proposes a hybrid feature selection method from the perspective of reducing feature dimensions, preprocessing feature subsets before training classifiers to reduce feature dimensions and reduce the complexity of training classifiers. Since the optimal feature subset can not only improve the accuracy of device setting, but also reduce the feature dimension, the time of feature extraction and device recognition will be reduced, so as to achieve the goal of improving efficiency.

The main research work of this paper is as follows:

1) Conduct a hybrid feature selection which mixes the FFS (Filter Feature Selection) with WFS (Wrapper Feature Selection) to preprocess the feature before training the classifier. In FFS, according to the variance, the irrelevant features are filtered out, and then the correlation information entropy between the features and the target is used. Then, WFS is used to select the remaining features, and FOA (Forest Optimization Algorithm), a random search method, is used to further subset the selected features according to the classification accuracy of the learning algorithm.

2) In order to verify the applicability of the hybrid feature selection, four machine learning algorithms—SVM (Support Vector Machine), KNN (K-Nearest Neighbor), LR (Logistic Regression) and DT (Decision Tree), were respectively trained for classifier training, and different fine-grained device types were identified, and the identification results were compared and analyzed.

3) We used the data from Miettinen [8]. Each device extracted 517 dimensional features, and the simulation results showed that after the hybrid feature selection, the number of dimensions was reduced to 101, reducing the dimension by 81%. The accuracy of device identification increased from 86.4%to 93.1%. The validity of the proposed method is verified.

2   Hybrid Feature Selection

2.1   Structure

As shown in Fig. 1, the hybrid feature selection in this paper is divided into two steps. In the first step, irrelevant features are deleted by FFS, and the information gain rate of each feature and target is given at the same time. In WFS, FOA generates the initial forest based on the gain rate. The initial forest of forest optimization algorithm has a great influence on the result. Because the subsequent tree seeding depends on the initial forest. Therefore, in order to generate a high-quality population, we first select features by FFS to remove irrelevant features. Then the advantages and disadvantages of each feature are correlated with the target. The FOA is used to generate the optimal feature subset for the specific classifier. This hybrid feature selection method is more efficient than using a single method to find the optimal feature subset and get higher accuracy of classification.

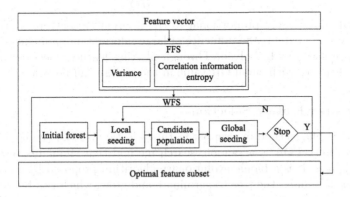

Fig. 1. Structure of hybrid feature selection

2.2   Filter Feature Selection

Firstly, the feature is selected by the variance of features. If the variance value of the feature is too small, it indicates that the performance of different types of devices is almost the same in terms of features, that is, the device cannot be effectively identified by the feature. Then the information gain rate is used to measure the correlation between features and the target, and the features that are not relevant to the target are deleted through the metric—information gain rate [9].

Let the feature attribute sequence be $X = \{x_1, x_2, \cdots x_m\}$, and target classification tag sequence be $Y = \{y_1, y_2, \cdots y_m\}$. The probability density function is $p(x_i), p(y_i)$. The entropy formula is as follows:

$$H(x) = -\sum_{i=1}^{m} p(x_i) \log(p(x_i)) \tag{1}$$

$$H(X \mid Y) = \sum_{i=1}^{m} p(y_i) H(X \mid Y = y_i) \tag{2}$$

$$IG(X \mid Y) = H(X) - H(X \mid Y) \tag{3}$$

According to Eq. (3), when the information gain is large, the correlation between features and targets is strong. Using the information gain can effectively reduce the noise sensitivity of the feature. However, because the calculation of information entropy is related to the probability of the occurrence of the eigenvalue, the feature with more occurrences will be deviated. Therefore, the penalty factor is introduced to reduce the influence of the probability density function, and the information gain rate—GR:

$$GR(X \mid Y) = \frac{IG(X \mid Y)}{H(Y)} \tag{4}$$

The GR is inversely proportional to the information entropy of the target tag. To a certain extent, the influence of large information gain caused by multiple occurrences can be solved. Through filtering feature selection algorithm, irrelevant features with small GR value in the feature can be deleted.

2.3   Wrapper Feature Selection

In this paper, the method in wrapper feature selection is FOA (Forest Optimization Algorithm). FOA is a random search method that simulates the planting process of trees. It is a bionic evolutionary algorithm proposed by Ghaemi [10]. Some seeds fall under the tree to germinate and grow, which can be called local sowing, which helps the tree to grow locally under better conditions; Other seeds spread over a wide area through natural processes and by animals that eat seeds or fruits, effectively avoiding local optimality.

The FSFOA (Feature Selection using Forest Optimization Algorithm) takes the initial forest as the starting point, produces new trees and updates the forest through the three main steps of local seeding, forming candidate areas, and global seeding. After multiple iterations of the FSFOA, the tree with the best performance of the classifier can be found. The specific process is as follows:

1) Initial forest stage: The classic binary method is used to encode features. Suppose the dimension of the feature is L, then the feature is represented as a binary string of 0,1. The string can be expressed as $(x_1, x_2, \cdots x_L)$, if $x_i = 1$ means the feature subset contains the i -th feature, otherwise not. Since the results of local seeding and global seeding depend on the selection of initial points, it is blind to select some features in a random way to complete the initialization. Therefore, the initialization strategy in this paper is to initialize the features based on the correlation between the features in the previous section and the target. The features were ranked according to the GR value from highest to lowest. The top 15% of the features were taken as 1 at the time of encoding, and the remaining 85% of the features were then selected through a bidirectional selection strategy combining forward selection and backward selection. In a bidirectional selection strategy, most tree initializations use a small number of features (forward selection) while the rest of the tree initializations use more features (backward selection) [11,12]. The forest initialized by the new strategy selects the feature subset with

the best performance through the interaction with local seeding and global seeding. This not only increases the intensity of dimension reduction, but also ensures the correctness of initialization forest. In addition to having the corresponding variable value represented by 0, 1, there is also an attribute "Age" that sets the age of all the trees just generated to 0. Each tree is this $(L + 1)$ dimensional binary string that represents a feature set. The age will be increased by 1 for each local seeding.

2) Local seeding stage: FSFOA sets up a random variables LSC (Local Seeding Changes) to simulate the seed falls on the land and then sprout. LSC is used to determine the number of selected features in the seeding. The value of the selected features changes from 0 to 1, and vice versa. After local seeding, the age of the newly generated trees is set to 0, the age of the remaining old trees is added to 1, and the new trees are added to the forest. The seeding process is shown in Fig. 2.

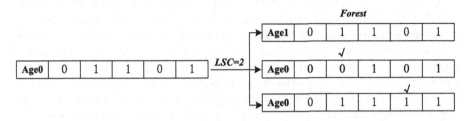

Fig. 2. An example of local seeding operation on one tree with LSC = 2

3) Candidate area generation stage: In the local seeding stage, forest trees grow continuously. In nature, an increase in the number of trees leads to a decrease in soil security density, which in turn leads to a decrease in survival rates. This essentially controls the number of trees in the forest. To avoid infinite forest expansion, the FSFOA algorithm sets two parameters: life span and area limit. Through natural selection, it was found that the ones that survived were the seedlings that started competing earlier than the others, the older trees. Therefore, first of all, trees whose age is greater than the upper age limit—life time are transferred from the forest to the candidate forest. If the remaining trees still exceeds the area limit, the excess trees will be removed from the top to the bottom according to the fitness value of the tree (classification accuracy), and the removed trees will be placed in the candidate forest.

4) Global seeding stage: a number of trees are randomly selected from the candidate areas according to certain probability—transfer rate. Then according to GSC (Global Seeding Changes) parameters decided to choose the number of features, then the value of the variable is selected from 0 to 1, and vice versa. But this stage is about changing the selected features simultaneously, rather than changing one feature at a time. As shown in Fig. 3, the FSFOA algorithm simulates the global seeding process and provides a global search method for the algorithm, which to some extent overcomes the shortcoming that local seeding may fall into the local optimal solution.

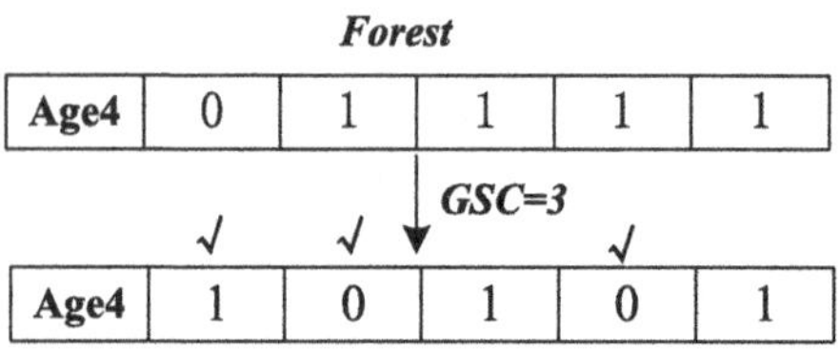

Forest

Age4	0	1	1	1	1

GSC=3

Age4	1	0	1	0	1

Fig. 3. An example of global seeding operation on one tree with GSC = 3

5) Update stage: At last, FSFOA only selects the tree with the highest fitness value as the best tree, sets age 0, and puts it back into the forest. The update phase iterates for several times until the stop condition is met the fitness value difference for five consecutive times does not exceed 0.05. Otherwise return local seeding stage.

Obviously, the updating strategy has the potential limitation of the traditional updating mechanism, that is, only the classification accuracy is considered in the updating process, but the dimension reduction is not considered. Therefore, in order to solve this problem, in addition to classification performance, dimension reduction is also taken into consideration. The specific update strategy is as follows: First, if the classification performance of the new tree is better than that of the old tree, the dimension problem is ignored and the new tree is updated to replace the old tree; Secondly, if the classification performance of the new tree is the same as that of the original tree, compare the dimensions. If the dimension of the new tree is smaller, update the new tree to replace the old tree. Otherwise, it will not be updated.

3   Experimental Results

3.1   Experimental Data

The data set in the experiment was derived from Miettinen [8]. Its application scenario is the smart home. The bypass monitoring traffic method is adopted to implement network data traffic through bypass monitoring: bypass detection, data acquisition, network analysis and information extraction. Specific scheme of data acquisition based on bypass detection: set up bypass monitoring on the data switch, regularly collect data traffic packets of devices accessing network services and internal resources, and extract network protocol and business information related to terminal devices [13]. Its architecture diagram is shown in Fig. 4.

Even if the bypass monitoring equipment fails or stops running, the existing network will not be affected. The data set used was from 27 different types of IoT devices, as shown in Table 1 which is a summary and description of the device in the experiment. It contains HomeMaticPlug, MAXGateway, TP Linkplughs100, TP Linkghs110, and so on. The researchers listened for traffic at the gateway through tcpdump, then filtered it through MAC addresses and stored it in PCAP file format.

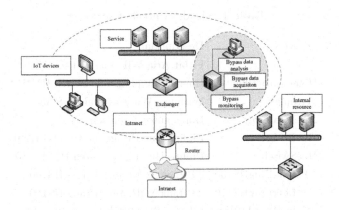

Fig. 4. Collect data architecture diagram

3.2 Feature Extraction

The experimental method in this paper is applicable to all kinds of features, but in order to facilitate the test and verification effect, we choose the features provided by Y. Song [14]. To build device fingerprinting related to IoT devices, we extract features from three dimensions, which include device network protocol stack fingerprint features, device network data sequence features, and device network data protocol features. The specific extracted features are shown in Table 1.

Extract device fingerprinting from the TCP/IP protocol stack, including a timestamp field, MSS (Maximum Segment Size), WS (Window Scale), TCP flags, SYN (Synchronous), FIN (Finish), ACK (Acknowledgement), PSH (Push), URG (Urgent), RST (Reset); Version, IHL (IP Head Length), TTL (Time-To-Live), DF (Don't Fragment), protocol field value, option value and port number in header of IP packet.The number of features of each packet is 12, and a 12*n dimension feature vector can be constructed from n network traffic data packets.

Extract features of the device traffic sequence. The length of each IP packet is regarded as a sequence to extract statistical features. Regard n network traffic data packets as a time-related sequence set. We extract statistical features and 5 highest magnitudes of FFT of IAT (Inter-Arrival-Time). Forward time means time interval sent by terminal equipment and backward time means received message time interval. They are also concluded.

Statistical characteristics include maximum, minimum, mean, variance, standard deviation, first quartile and third quartile. These statistical features constitute a 33-dimensional eigenvector.

Extract protocol features based on the application layer. There are HTTP protocol, HTTPS protocol, FTP protocol, Tel- net protocol based on TCP and onvif protocol, DNS protocol, NFS protocol, DHCP protocol, TFTP protocol based on UDP, a total of 14 characteristic values. We count times of applied

Table 1. The description of devices

NO.	Device	Description
1	Aria	Fitbit Aria WiFi-enabled scale
2	HomeMaticPlug	Homematic pluggable switch HMIP-PS
3	Withings	Withings Wireless Scale WS-30
4	MAXGateway	Home automation sensors
5	HueBridge	Philips Hue Bridge model 3241312018
6	HueSwitch	Philips Hue Light Switch PTM 215Z
7	TP-LinkPlugHS100	TP-Link WiFi Smart plug HS100
8	TP-LinkPlugHS110	TP-Link WiFi Smart plug HS110
9	EdimaxPlug1101W	Edimax SP-1101W Smart Plug Switch
10	EdimaxPlug2101W	Edimax SP-2101W Smart Plug Switch
11	EdnetGateway	Ednet.living Starter kit power Gateway
12	EdnetCam	Ednet Wireless indoor IP camera Cube
13	EdimaxCam	WiFi Network Camera
14	Lightify	Osram Lightify Gateway
15	WeMoInsightSwitch	WeMo Insight Switch model F7C029de
16	WeMoLink	WeMo Link Lighting Bridge model
17	WeMoSwitch	WeMo Switch model F7C027de
18	D-LinkHomeHub	D-Link Home Hub DCH-G020
19	D-LinkDoorSensor	D-Link Door & Window sensor
20	D-LinkDayCam	D-Link WiFi Day Camera DCS-930L
21	D-LinkCam	D-Link HD IP Camera DCH-935L
22	D-LinkSwitch	D-Link Smart plug DSP-W215
23	D-LinkWaterSensor	D-Link Water sensor DCH-S160
24	D-LinkSiren	D-Link Siren DCH-S220
25	D-LinkSensor	D-Link WiFi Motion sensor DCH-S150
26	SmarterCoffee	Coffee machine SMC10-EU
27	iKettle2	Smarter iKettle 2.0 SMK20-EU

protocols were used. Then a 14-dimensional eigenvector can be constructed from network traffic data packets.

A device is a sample. Suppose there are n packets in the sample, then the final generated feature dimension is $12 * n + 47$.

3.3   Feature Extraction

The optimal feature subset is generated by feature selection in the feature set of the previous section.

The Results of Filter Feature Selection. The length of the vector is 517-dimension. Figure 5 shows a total of 59 features. The abscissa is the correlation between the features and the target. The most important field value in the IP header is TTL. Nearly all kinds of statistical characteristics also have a significant impact on the classification of the target, such as maximum, the average value, the square deviation and so on. Delete the feature vectors whose correlation estimation is nearly zero, such as the protocol features—smtp, ssh, ftp, raw,lpd, onvif, snmp, rstp, nfs, and the minimum value of the time interval between sending and receiving packets. After the FFS, the number of the feature become 48, and the dimension become 506.

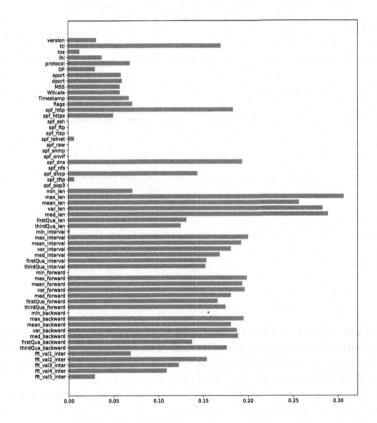

Fig. 5. The GA between feature and target

The Results of Wrapper Feature Selection. Forest Optimization Algorithm is used for feature selection. Among the parameters, the values of "life time", "area limit", "transfer rate" are not dependent on the size of the data set and set to constant, "rife Time" = 10, "area limit" = 100, "transfer rate" = 20%, LSC and GSC are dependent on the characteristic number of each data set, "LSC = 108 ", "GSC = 258". The fewest dimension of feature vector was reduced to 19%. In this experiment, in order to avoid the FOA getting trapped in an infinite loop, it is assumed that when the fitness value difference for five consecutive times does not exceed 0.05, the feature subset is considered to be optimal.

For different classification algorithms, the optimal feature subset is different. The result is shown in Table 2. The number of features obtained by SVM algorithm is 26. The number of features obtained by LR is 24. The minimum is KNN of 20, and the maximum is DT of 28.

Table 2. The results of hybrid feature selection

Feature	Version	TTL	TOS	IHL	Protocol	DF	sport	dport	MSS	Wscale
SVM	✓	✓	✓		✓	✓			✓	
LR	✓	✓	✓		✓	✓	✓			✓
KNN			✓		✓	✓			✓	
DT		✓	✓		✓	✓			✓	✓

Feature	Timestamp	Flags	spf_http	spf_https	spf_telnet	spf_tftp	spf_dns	spf_dhcp	fft1_inter	fft2_inter
SVM	✓	✓		✓			✓			✓
LR	✓	✓	✓	✓				✓		
KNN					✓	✓			✓	
DT	✓	✓					✓		✓	

Feature	fft3_inter	fft4_inter	min_len	max_len	mean_len	var_len	med_len	fq_len	tq_len	min_inter
SVM			✓	✓	✓	✓	✓			
LR	✓	✓		✓	✓		✓		✓	
KNN					✓	✓	✓	✓	✓	
DT	✓	✓	✓	✓	✓	✓				

Feature	max_inter	mean_inter	var_inter	med_inter	fq_inter	tq_inter	max_for	mean_for	var_for	med_for
SVM	✓	✓			✓	✓	✓	✓		✓
LR		✓		✓		✓	✓		✓	
KNN	✓	✓					✓	✓	✓	
DT	✓	✓	✓	✓			✓			✓

Feature	fq_for	tq_for	max_back	mean_back	var_back	med_back	fq_back	tq_back		total
SVM	✓		✓		✓		✓			26
LR					✓					24
KNN			✓	✓	✓		✓	✓		20
DT	✓	✓			✓		✓	✓		28

Device Type Identification. The problem of device identification in machine learning corresponds to multi-classification. The realization of the classification algorithm is based on the model in the scikit-learn python library. Use a 10-fold cross validation to generalize the validation results.

After the feature selection, the results are shown in Fig. 6, the feature dimension was reduced by nearly 80% on average.

The SVM algorithm improved the most, from 86.4% to 92.5%, which was increased by 6.1%. Taking SVM as an example, Fig. 7 shows a device comparison diagram with obvious increase in accuracy before and after feature selection. TP-LinkPlugHS100, TP-LinkPlugHS110, EdimaxPlug110 and EdimaxPlug2101W, among which the most obvious changes were TP-LinkPlugHS110 and Edimax-Plug2101W. The accuracy was increased by 35% and 37% respectively. The second largest increase of 22% was in WeMoInsightSwitch.

Compared with the work that used the same data, we can see that, Miettinen [8] extracted 23 features from the header of each packet, and its accuracy reached 81%. Also, S.A. Hamad [15] extracted 67 features, which were similar to the

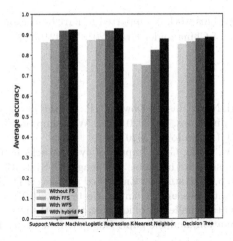

Fig. 6. The comparison of different algorithms

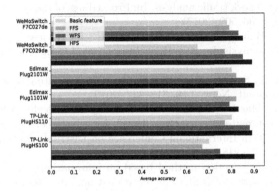

Fig. 7. The partial contrast before and after FS

features that we use. And the average accuracy was 90.3%. Therefore, when there are too few or too many features, the best recognition effect cannot be got. And feature selection can improve the accuracy of identification while reducing the dimension.

4   Conclusion

In this paper, hybrid feature selection is applied to IoT device identification which is based on machine learning. We combined the FFS and WFS—the first round of selection is made according to the information gain rate of features and targets, and then the remaining features are selected by forest optimization algorithm. Finally, the optimal feature subset which is adaptive to different classification algorithms can be obtained. Experimental results show that this hybrid feature selection reduces the dimension of feature to 19%. Meanwhile, the complexity of the classifier is reduced. The method not only speeds up the convergence and efficiency but also increases accuracy from 86.4% to 93.1%.

Funding Statement. This work is supported in part by National Key Research and Development Program of China under Grant 2018YFB2100400.

References

1. Karie, N.M., Sahri, N.M., Haskell-Dowland, P.: Iot threat detection advances, challenges and future directions. In: 2020 IEEE Workshop on Emerging Technologies for Security in IoT (ETSecIoT) (2020)
2. Sen, R., Verma, A., Heim, G.R.: Impact of cyberattacks by malicious hackers on the competition in software markets. J. Manag. Inf. Syst. **37**(1), 191–216 (2020)
3. Patsakis, C., Casino, F., Katos, V.: Encrypted and covert DNS queries for botnets: challenges and countermeasures. Comput. Secur. **88**, 101614 (2020)
4. Wachter, S.: Normative challenges of identification in the internet of things: privacy, profiling, discrimination, and the gdpr. Comput. Law Secur. Rev. **34**(3), 436–449 (2018)
5. Meidan, Y., et al.: Profiliot: a machine learning approach for iot device identification based on network traffic analysis. In: Proceedings of the symposium on applied computing, pp. 506–509 (2017)
6. Shahid, M.R., Blanc, G., Zhang, Z., Debar, H.: Iot devices recognition through network traffic analysis. In: 2018 IEEE International Conference on Big Data (Big Data) (2018)
7. Yang, K., Li, Q., Sun, L.: Towards automatic fingerprinting of iot devices in the cyberspace. Comput. Netw. **148**, 318–327 (2019)
8. Miettinen, M., Marchal, S., Hafeez, I., Asokan, N., Sadeghi, A.R., Tarkoma, S.: Iot sentinel: Automated device-type identification for security enforcement in iot. In: 2017 IEEE 37th International Conference on Distributed Computing Systems (ICDCS), pp. 2177–2184. IEEE (2017)
9. Lei, S.: A feature selection method based on information gain and genetic algorithm. In: 2012 International Conference on Computer Science and Electronics Engineering. vol. 2, pp. 355–358. IEEE (2012)
10. Ghaemi, M., Feizi-Derakhshi, M.R.: Feature selection using forest optimization algorithm. Pattern Recognit. **60**, 121–129 (2016)
11. Xue, B., Zhang, M., Browne, W.N.: Novel initialisation and updating mechanisms in pso for feature selection in classification. In: European Conference on Applications of Evolutionary Computation (2013)
12. Xu, Y.: Research and implementation of improved random forest algorithm based on spark. In: 2017 IEEE 2nd International Conference on Big Data Analysis (ICBDA), pp. 499–503. IEEE (2017)
13. Aksoy, A., Gunes, M.H.: Automated iot device identification using network traffic. In: ICC 2019–2019 IEEE International Conference on Communications (ICC) (2019)
14. Song, Y., Huang, Q., Yang, J., Fan, M., Hu, A., Jiang, Y.: Iot device fingerprinting for relieving pressure in the access control. In: Proceedings of the ACM Turing Celebration Conference-China, pp. 1–8 (2019)
15. Hamad, S.A., Zhang, W.E., Sheng, Q.Z., Nepal, S.: Iot device identification via network-flow based fingerprinting and learning. In: 2019 18th IEEE International Conference On Trust, Security And Privacy In Computing And Communications/13th IEEE International Conference On Big Data Science And Engineering (TrustCom/BigDataSE) (2019)

A Practical Blockchain Framework for Securing IoT Applications

Jizhou Chen[1,2]([⊠]), Jieren Cheng[2]([⊠]), Wenbao Han[2]([⊠]), and Xianghui Liu[3]([⊠])

[1] Guangdong Provincial Administration of Government Service and Data, Guangzhou, China
[2] School of Computer and Cyberspace Security, Hainan University, Haikou, China
[3] Telecommunications Planning and Design Institute Co., Ltd., Changsha, China
LiuXianghui@yeah.net

Abstract. The Internet of things (IoT) has become a guiding technology behind automation and intelligent computing. One of the main problems of Internet of things system is the lack of privacy and security protection scheme to control access and ensure data security. Most of the security problems are caused by the centralized architecture of the Internet of things system. Another problem is the lack of appropriate authentication and access control schemes to restrict access to information generated by IOT devices. The IoT applications face many security challenges, which can be solved by blockchain. We have initially designed a general system model, which can gradually refine and form a secure IOT solution based on blockchain.

Keywords: Blockchain · Security · IoT

1 Introduction

The rapid advancements in networking technologies have led to an increased number of devices or things being able to connect to the Internet, which forms the Internet of things, commonly known as IoT. Some leading applications of IoT include smart grid, smart home, industrial IoT, intelligent medical and so on. At a high level, a typical IoT ecosystem consists of sensors, actuators and other devices that perform application specific control and monitoring, network guided communication infrastructure and other devices. Protocols and local or centralized storage (cloud) are used to collect data from different devices and process them for further analysis. The data generated by various IoT devices are massive, heterogeneous and dynamic. Each device in the IoT environment has a unique identifier associated with it. Colakovic and hadialic (2018) described the IoT and its enabling technologies in detail. It is a challenging task to build a sustainable IoT ecosystem, which can adapt to specific application areas and play a good performance. With a variety of intelligent solutions using a large number of devices, maintaining the security of private or user data in centralized cloud storage is a very cumbersome task, which needs great attention. If private data falls into the hands of malicious entities, the risk is great. Another concern is the resource and energy constraints of devices, which makes it challenging to run large-scale encryption algorithms to enhance the security of

© Springer Nature Switzerland AG 2021
X. Sun et al. (Eds.): ICAIS 2021, CCIS 1424, pp. 677–686, 2021.
https://doi.org/10.1007/978-3-030-78621-2_56

generated data. Other challenges that need to be addressed in specific situations such as disasters are fault tolerance and recovery of remote devices. In addition, the diversity of IoT applications and the uncertainty of the technologies and solutions provided result in the lack of trust in these solutions. Therefore, a decentralized solution is needed to ensure the security of the IoT ecosystem, which is a basic requirement of any IoT application.

Since the blockchain concept was revealed in 2008, it has been very active in the field of cryptography and security. Significant progress in blockchain research has made cryptocurrency using bitcoin a reality. The circulation value of bitcoin is US $5431.43, and it has about 5.7 million blocks. With the help of more hashing capacity and mining pools, bitcoin is growing rapidly and continuously. Software giants such as the Linux foundation have been studying applications such as hyperledger to crack the potential of blockchain (Blummer et al. 2018). With the prediction of blockchain technology in the software industry, it is necessary to study the applicability of blockchain in the IoT in detail to solve the main security problems and the extent to which blockchain can successfully solve these problems.

When the blockchain and the IoT meet, some of the expected benefits brought by this integration are the establishment of trust between entities, the integrity, consistency and integrity of stored data, the invariance or tamper proof protection of private data, the reduction of cost, the enhancement of security and the acceleration of big data processing. The major objectives of the review work presented in this paper are:

- To investigate the security issues and challenges currently present in IoT applications.
- To highlight the decision criteria for applying Blockchain in IoT.
- To survey the scope of solutions that can be achieved through the convergence of Blockchain with IoT.
- To demarcate what IoT applications need and what distributed ledger technology (DLT) can offer.
- To present the state of the art in the integration of Blockchain with IoT.
- To identify and categorize IoT applications based on the issues addressed by Blockchain in the particular application area.

The rest of this paper is organized as follows: Sect. 2 discusses the concept of the IoT and analyzes its security challenges; Sect. 3 introduces the concept and functions of blockchain; Sect. 4 designs the framework of the IoT based on blockchain on the basis of analyzing the necessity of using blockchain in IoT. Finally, it comes to the conclusion that blockchain technology can bring trust and security to IoT applications.

2   Blockchain Concepts

Although many papers have expounded the technology and concept of blockchain and smart contract, we must emphasize the basic knowledge. Fernandez caramez and Fraga lamas (2018) well describe the function of blockchain. Blockchain is a distributed ledger of immutable records managed in peer-to-peer networks. All nodes in the network ensure the integrity and correctness of the blockchain through consistency algorithm. This method of building trust in node network enhances the security of blockchain.

Blockchain can be divided into public, private or consortium according to whether its membership is allowed or not. In a public blockchain, any user can be a member. There are no membership restrictions, they are only pseudo anonymous. Bitcoin and Ethereum are good examples of public blockchains. However, private blockchain is owned and operated by a company or organization, and any user who wants to join the network must apply to join through relevant personnel.

Thus there is only partial immutability offered. Private and consortium blockchains are faster in transaction processing compared to the public counterparts, due to the restricted number of members. Examples of some permissioned blockchains are Hyper-Ledger (Fabric Blummer et al. 2018, Hyperledger 2017) and R3 Corda (Brown et al. 2016). Some private blockchains impose read restrictions on the data within the blocks. Consortium blockchains are owned and operated by a group of organizations or a private community. Blockchain users use asymmetric key cryptography to sign on transactions. The trust factor maintenance within a distributed ledger technology (DLT), can be attributed to the consensus algorithms and the key desirable properties achieved thenceforth. Wüst and Gervais (2018) gives a good description of these properties. Some of them are Public Verifiability, Transparency, Integrity.

The main blockchain terms are discussed below:

1. Blocks: The transactions that occur in a peer-to-peer network associated with a blockchain are picked up from a pool of transactions and grouped in a block. Once a transaction has been validated, it cannot be reverted back. Transactions are pseudonymous as they are linked only to the user's public key and not to the real identity of the user. A block may contain several hundreds of transactions. The block-size limits the number of transactions that can be included in a block. The general structure of a block in a blockchain. A block consists of the version no., hash of the previous block, the Merkle root tree to trace the transactions in the block, hash of the current block, timestamp and nonce value. A blockchain starts with a genesis block.

2. Mining: Mining is a process in which the designated nodes in the blockchain network called miners collect transactions from a pool of unprocessed transactions and combine them in a block. In mining, each miner competes to solve an equally difficult computational problem of finding a valid hash value with a particular no. of zeroes that is below a specific target. In Bitcoin mining, the number of zeroes indicates the difficulty of the computation. Many nonce values are tried to arrive at the golden nonce that hashes to a valid hash with the current difficulty level. When a miner arrives at this nonce value, we can say that he has successfully mined a block. This block then gets updated to the chain.

3. Consensus: The consensus mechanism serves two main purposes, as given in Jesus et al. (2018): block validation and the most extensive chain selection. Proof-of-Work is the consensus algorithm used in Bitcoin Blockchain. The proof-of-stake algorithm is much faster than Proof-of-Work and demands less computational resources. The Ethereum blockchains use a pure proof-of-stake algorithm to ensure consensus. Besides Proof-of-Work, there are other consensus algorithms such as Proof of Byzantine Fault Tolerance (PBFT), proof- of activity, etc. Anwar (2018) presents a consolidated view of the different consensus algorithms. Proof-of-Work is a kind of

a signature which indicates that the block has been mined after performing computation with the required difficulty level. This signature can be easily verified by the peers in the network to ensure a block's validity. The longest chain is always selected as the consistent one for appending the new block.

4. Smart Contracts: They are predefined rules deployed in the Blockchain network that two parties involved in a settlement must agree to priorly. Smart contracts were designed to avoid disagreement, denial, or violation of rules by the parties involved. They are triggered automatically in the Blockchain, on the occurrence of specific events mentioned in the rules.

5. Overall functioning: Users connect to the Blockchain and initiate a transaction signed with their private key. This transaction is sent to a pool of transactions where it resides until it is fetched into a block by a miner. The miner then generates a new block after gathering transactions from the pool and computing the valid hash of the block. When a miner succeeds in generating a new block, the new block is broadcast to the nodes in the P2P network. All nodes in the network verify the block using a consensus algorithm, and upon successful validation, update it to their copy of the chain, and the transaction attains completion.

3 IoT Framework Overview

The traditional IoT business platform as a connection and service center, it connects and manages the IoT applications, IoT business, IoT equipment, IoT data. In the traditional IoT business platform, IoT applications and IoT services can access IoT equipment and IoT data only through IoT business platform.

According to the deployment and cooperation mechanism of IoT business platform, IoT business platform can be divided into three working modes: centralized working mode, distributed working mode and decentralized working mode.

In the centralized working mode, the IoT business platform is deployed in a single location on the system side (for example, a data center), managed by a single platform provider, and provides centralized services to IoT devices, IoT applications and IoT businesses.

In the distributed working mode, the IoT business platform can be deployed in multiple locations on the system side (for example, multiple data centers), and is usually managed by a single platform provider, and provides distributed services to IoT devices, IoT applications and IoT businesses.

In the "decentralized" working mode, the IoT business platform is established and maintained by a group of independent participants. These participants may not be related to each other, they can be mutual trust or not. In this working mode, IoT application, IoT business and IoT equipment can become part of IoT business platform and provide IoT services together. In addition, in the "decentralized" mode, whether the participants are on the system side or the terminal side is no longer considered.

Different types of IoT business platforms can be built on the same or different communication infrastructure,and the technical architecture of IoT is generally divided into three layers: perception layer, network layer and application layer.

- Perception layer: mainly refers to the acquisition of front-end data, such as the use of RFID to obtain electronic tags, the use of latitude and longitude, and environmental monitoring sensor activity information;
- Network layer: refers to the background server that transmits information through telecommunication network and Internet;
- Application layer: process the information from the front-end perception layer, and realize specific applications, such as automatic driving, environmental monitoring, health management and other practical applications.

Blockchain's natural decentralized and trusted feature provides a new idea for the design of the framework and architecture of the integration of blockchain and Internet of things. In the intelligent Internet of things (IOT) computing, multiple IOT devices running intelligent algorithms are scattered in the edge network. In order to cooperate to complete the task of artificial intelligence computing or to make joint intelligent group decision, these devices need to communicate frequently. However, both the device itself and the communication between devices are faced with a variety of network security threats, such as device failure or malicious, in this case, the information transmitted may be leaked or tampered. As a verifiable and tamper proof ledger supported by cryptography, blockchain can ensure secure interaction in decentralized and untrusted environment through transaction records and distributed consensus on the effectiveness of transaction records, and can play a role in the scenario of intelligent Internet of things computing. At the same time, the consensus mechanism and incentive mechanism of blockchain combined with smart contract are naturally suitable for building an economic market, which can effectively stimulate the sharing and interaction of information in IOT computing.

The Internet of things architecture built by integrating blockchain technology is a "decentralized" business architecture. This architecture can be divided into device awareness layer, network public chain layer, service and support layer and user oriented application layer. Among them, the device perception layer is connected with the physical object, which supports the Internet of things entities (such as Internet of things devices, Internet of things servers, Internet of things gateways, service gateways and end-user devices) to cooperate with each other in the "decentralized" mode, and can collect information through sensors. The collected information and data are stored on the network public chain, and the whole process can be traced, and the information can not be tampered with. The information is transmitted through the point-to-point distributed connection. Most of the new capabilities of IOT architecture based on blockchain are concentrated in the service and application support layer, including access control, consensus mechanism, encryption support, contract management, storage and computing, etc. At the same time, the application layer is customer-oriented, which requires IOT applications, IOT devices and IOT gateways to communicate and cooperate with each other through the capabilities provided by the service and application support layer, so as to further process information and provide intelligent services.

4   IoT Framework Based on Blockchain

According to the characteristics of IoT business, IoT business can be deployed on or outside the IoT blockchain.

The IoT blockchain supports smart contracts. If the IoT business can be presented and implemented through smart contracts, and the IoT business can also be deployed publicly, then this kind of IoT business can be directly deployed on the IoT blockchain in the form of smart contracts; for example, the identification of IoT devices, online processing of IoT data and other IoT services.

If the IoT business is complex and cannot be presented and implemented through smart contracts, or the IoT business cannot be deployed publicly, then such IoT services can be deployed outside the IoT blockchain, and smart contracts can also be deployed on the IoT blockchain to provide ancillary services, such as business diversion, device identity authentication, and so on Data storage, etc.

When the IoT business is deployed on the IoT blockchain in the form of smart contract, IoT devices can access the corresponding IoT business by searching and executing relevant smart contracts on the IoT blockchain. When the IoT business is deployed outside the IoT blockchain, IoT devices can search and execute relevant auxiliary smart contracts through the IoT blockchain to obtain the access permission to access IoT business, and then directly interact with the corresponding IoT business; meanwhile, according to the needs of IoT business, IoT devices can obtain access permission to access IoT business, IoT services and IoT devices can store the interactive result data on the IoT blockchain.

According to the data processing ability and network access ability of IoT equipment, the IoT equipment can be roughly divided into full-function IoT equipment and ability limited IoT equipment. Full functional IoT devices can be directly connected to the IoT blockchain, and can directly participate in the interaction and cooperation on the IoT blockchain. Capacity limited IoT devices can be indirectly connected to the IoT blockchain through the IoT gateway, and indirectly participate in the interaction and cooperation on the IoT blockchain.

When the IoT device is started or the state changes, it can register with the IoT blockchain or update the information on the IoT blockchain. The IoT devices can deploy smart contracts on the IoT blockchain, or the operators or managers of IoT devices can deploy smart contracts on the IoT blockchain, such as registration, update, authentication, access, data processing and other smart contracts of IoT devices.

Through the IoT blockchain, IoT business can find the registered IoT device information, such as registration information, access information, etc. For full-featured IoT devices, as part of the IoT blockchain, IoT businesses can directly interact with such IoT devices by executing relevant smart contracts. For capacity limited IoT devices, they are indirectly connected with IoT blockchain through IoT gateway. At this time, IoT business can interact with IoT devices indirectly through corresponding IoT gateway.

Both IoT services and IoT devices can store and access IoT data through smart contracts. The IoT blockchain can set data security and privacy protection policies, so that only the IoT devices and IoT businesses with agreed permission can access and process the agreed IoT data; at the same time, for the unlicensed IoT devices and IoT businesses, according to the IoT blockchain strategy, all (or part) of the IoT data can be accessed and processed Encrypted IoT data can be stored, but it is not authorized to decrypt and use encrypted IoT data. IoT blockchain has the data management characteristics of blockchain, which is conducive to the collection, storage and management of IoT data.

As a kind of "decentralized" IoT business platform, IoT blockchain is suitable for IoT reference model defined by ITU-T y.4000 standard. Considering the "decentralization" characteristics and trust cooperation mechanism of the IoT blockchain, some corresponding capability requirements need to be added in the IoT reference model.

Most of the new capacity requirements of IoT blockchain are focused on the service and application support layer of IoT reference model, including access control, consensus management, encryption support, data management, node control, contract management, peer-to-peer (P2P) communication, storage and computing. At the same time, in the application layer and the device layer, the IoT applications (services), IoT devices and IoT gateway should be able to communicate and cooperate with each other through the capabilities provided by the service and application support layer. In order to ensure the security and reliability of the blockchain, the newly added nodes of the IoT and the IoT can also guarantee the security and reliability of the blockchain.

4.1 Frame Description

The traditional centralized management mode is very fragile. As long as the central node is destroyed, the whole IOT service will be paralyzed. Therefore, we build a framework of IOT based on blockchain, which has the characteristics of decentralization and decentralized supervision. We divide the framework of IOT based on blockchain into perception layer, edge layer, data storage layer and application layer.

1. **Perception layer**
   The sensing layer contains all kinds of sensor nodes of the Internet of things. Through these sensors, we can obtain the information of temperature, humidity, air pressure, light, pressure and so on. These sensors are limited in resources and can only complete simple data processing tasks. So we transfer the complex computing tasks to the edge devices, request the edge devices to complete the processing, and receive the processing results to complete all kinds of responses. It should be noted that agents are devices with strong communication and computing ability, and their task is to help nodes with weak communication ability communicate with edge devices. The framework can also be compatible, and sensor nodes with strong communication ability can directly communicate with edge devices without agents.

2. **Edge layer**
   Edge layer the edge layer is composed of edge devices, which act as the edge node to run the smart contract of the blockchain. The smart contract is a pre written and deployed electronic contract, which contains two parts One function module is responsible for the management of Internet of things devices and user credibility scoring system, the other function module is responsible for analyzing the behavior of Internet of things devices and giving the processing rules.

3. **Data storage layer**
   When the data storage layer needs to store data, the smart contract will be executed automatically First, the smart contract will use elliptic curve cryptography algorithm to encrypt the data. The encryption algorithm and the corresponding decryption private key are selected by the smart contract and will not be disclosed to other devices or users. Then the smart contract will record the executed storage events

to the blocks in the block chain. Finally, all kinds of data of the Internet of things devices will be stored in the Storage hardware for edge devices.

4. **Application layer**

Application layer is a platform that provides various services for users, and it is also an interface to access Internet of things data. Users send service requests to the platform, and the platform verifies the user's identity. The platform sends the verified user requests to the smart contract of the edge layer. After receiving the user's request, the smart contract first queries the user's credibility score, and then Judge the rationality of the request, then decide whether to provide services, and feed back to the application layer (Fig. 1).

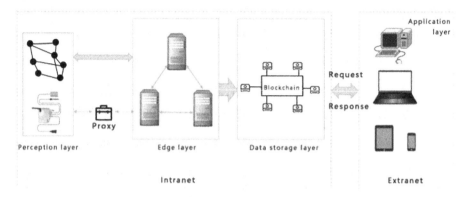

Fig. 1. Blockchain based IoT Framework

4.2 Framework Assessment

This scheme is different from the cloud based IOT scheme. The following table gives some performance evaluations. This scheme is superior to the cloud based IOT scheme in terms of access control and real-time performance, and this advantage is realized through the application of blockchain based on edge devices (Table 1).

Therefore, we use the blockchain based IOT framework to record the operation, user and device behavior in the system, and control the user and IOT device behavior with a unique binding trusted branch to ensure the system security. At the same time, the introduction of edge devices provides a reliable platform for us to process IOT data and deploy blockchain A large number of computing resources will cause short-term resource shortage, so there are certain restrictions on the scale and timeliness of the application, which is also the focus of future research on the application of the Internet of things based on blockchain.

Confidentiality, integrity and availability are the most basic requirements of a system framework. That is to say, only authenticated and authorized users can access the system information. The information received and sent by the system cannot be tampered with and guaranteed to be complete. The data and services provided by the system can be accessed and used by legitimate users.

Table 1. Comparison of IoT frameworks

Comparison of framework between traditional IoT and blockchain based IoT		
Properties	Traditional IoT	Blockchain based IoT
Access control mode	Static password	Dynamic password, trusted password
Storage mode	Plaintext	Ciphertext
Security mechanism	Static trusted password	Dynamic password, workload proof
Number of resources	Large	Medium
Real time	General	Strong
Scale	Medium	Large

5 Conclusions

The IoT applications face many security challenges, which can be solved by blockchain. We discussed the main security issues in the Internet of things, and analyzed the application of blockchain can help solve these problems. At present, a lot of research work has applied blockchain to the Internet of things, but the actual application effect and efficiency still need to be evaluated scientifically. We have initially designed a general system model, which can gradually refine and form a secure IOT solution based on blockchain.

References

Huggahalli, R., Iyer, R., Tetrick, S.: Direct cache access for high bandwidth network I/O. In: ISCA (2005)

Tang, D., Bao, Y., Hu, W., et al.: DMA cache: using on-chip storage to architecturally separate I/O data from CPU data for improving I/O performance. In: HPCA (2010)

Liao, G., Zhu, X., Bhuyan, L.: A new server I/O architecture for high speed networks. In: HPCA (2011)

León, E.A., Ferreira, K.B., Maccabe, A.B.: Reducing the impact of the MemoryWall for I/O using cache injection. In: 15th IEEE Symposium on High-Performance Interconnects (HOTI 2007), August 2007

Kumar, A., Huggahalli, R., Makineni, S.: Characterization of direct cache access on multi-core systems and 10 GbE. HPCA (2009)

Sun Niagara 2. http://www.sun.com/processors/niagara/index.jsp

PowerPC

Liao, G., Bhuyan, L.: Performance measurement of an integrated NIC architecture with 10 GbE. In: 17th IEEE Symposium on High Performance Interconnects (2009)

Foong, A., et al.: TCP performance revisited. In: IEEE International Symposium on Performance Analysis of Software and Systems, March 2003

Clark, D., Jacobson, V., Romkey, J., Saalwen, H.: An analysis of TCP processing overhead. IEEE Commun. **27**, 23–29 (1989)

Doweck, J.: Inside Intel Core microarchitecture and smart memory access. Intel White Paper (2006)

Kumar, A., Ram, H.: Impact of Cache Coherence Protocols on the Processing of Network Traffic

Wenji, W., Crawford, M.: Potential performance bottleneck in Linux TCP. Int. J. Commun. Syst. **20**(11), 1263–1283 (2007)

Weiwu, H., Wang, J., Gao, X., et al.: Godson-3: a scalable multicore RISC processor with x86 emulation. IEEE Micro **29**(2), 17–29 (2009)

Cadence Incisive Xtreme Series. http://www.cadence.com/products/sd/xtreme_series

Synopsys GMAC IP. http://www.synopsys.com/dw/dwtb.php?a=ethernet_mac

Miller, D.J., Watts, P.M., Moore, A.W.: Motivating future interconnects: a differential measurement analysis of PCI latency. ANCS (2009)

Binkert, N.L., Saidi, A.G., Reinhardt, S.K.: Integrated network interfaces for high-bandwidth TCP/IP. In: Proceedings of the 12th International Conference on Architectural Support for Programming Languages and Operating Systems (ASPLOS) (2006)

Liao, G., Bhuyan, L.: Performance Measurement of an Integrated NIC Architecture with 10GbE. HotI (2009)

Intel Server Network I/O Acceleration. http://download.intel.com/technology/comms/perfnet/download/ServerNetworkIOAccel.pdf

A Blockchain-Based Internet of Things Forensics Model

Guangjun Liang[1,2], Jianfang Xin[3(✉)], Qun Wang[1], Xueli Ni[1],
and Xiangmin Guo[1]

[1] Department of Computer Information and Cyber Security,
Jiangsu Police Institute, Nanjing, China
[2] National and Local Joint Engineering Laboratory of Radio Frequency Integration
and Micro Assembly Technology, Nanjing University of Posts
and Telecommunications, Nanjing, China
[3] School of Electrical Engineering, Anhui Polytechnic University, Wuhu, China

Abstract. The Internet of Things has been proposed for nearly 20 years.
Its rich digital trace repository provides insight into people's daily activities at home and elsewhere. On the other hand, IoT devices can become
targets of attacks, or even tools for a crime. The number of civil and
criminal cases involving IoT devices or services is increasing year by
year. IoT forensics refers to the process of collecting, analyzing, storing and providing digital evidence in IoT devices in a legally binding
manner. In particular, the traceability, integrity and tamper resistance
of the evidence should be maintained. However, traditional IoT forensics
architecture may be difficult to achieve these goals. This article aims
to explore the combination of blockchain technology and IoT forensics
which can make full use of the natural advantages of traceability and
tamper resistance. A forensic architecture of the Internet of Things based
on blockchain evidence is proposed, including an applications layer and
data layer. The applications layer includes various APP applications, and
the data layer includes the evidence analysis platform and the blockchain
platform. Furthermore, an IoT forensics model including blockchain storage and supervision is proposed which can ensure the traceability and
tamper-proof of forensic data.

Keywords: Internet of Things · Evidence · Forensic · Blockchain

1 Introduction

As the Internet of Things (IoT) penetrates our daily lives, people are increasingly
relying on various smart IoT services which leave digital traces on various IoT
devices. The rich digital trace repository in the IoT environment can provide
insight into people's daily activities at home and elsewhere for digital forensics [1]. On the other hand, the number of civil and criminal cases involving
IoT devices or services is increasing. IoT devices can not only become targets
of attacks, but also tools for a crime. Security vulnerabilities in the IoT system

© Springer Nature Switzerland AG 2021
X. Sun et al. (Eds.): ICAIS 2021, CCIS 1424, pp. 687–696, 2021.
https://doi.org/10.1007/978-3-030-78621-2_57

can be used for remote control systems, such as the zombie car battle in the 2017 Hollywood blockbuster "Fast and Furious 8". Therefore, there is an urgent need for IoT forensic research to help determine the person, location, time and method of the case.

In the current decade, the IoT market has and will continue to grow exponentially. Starting from USD 157 billion in 2016, the market value of the Internet of Things is expected to reach the market value of 2026, expanding to USD 771 billion [2,3]. Cisco predicts that by 2030, there will be 500 billion objects connected and linked to the Internet [4]. IoT devices exchange data with millions of other devices around the world. This type of open large-scale communication makes users especially those with illegal intentions invited. Only in 2017, attacks on IoT devices increased by 600% [5]. In many cases, intruders do not directly target IoT devices, but use them as weapons to attack other websites [6]. As a result, cybercrime has become the second most reported crime in the world [7]. IoT systems seem to be easily targeted by attackers. This is mainly due to the fact that when manufacturing IoT devices, manufacturers usually focus on cost, size and availability, while security and forensics are often overlooked.

According to the "Summary of my country's Internet Network Security Situation in 2019" issued by the National Internet Emergency Response Center, DDoS attacks still show a high frequency in 2019, and a large number of Internet of Things devices are still used to launch DDoS attacks after being invaded and controlled. There are about 220 high-traffic attacks with peak attack traffic exceeding 10Gbps in my country, an increase of 40.0% year-on-year. Although the activity of IoT devices participating in DDoS attacks showed a downward trend in late 2019. However, among the botnet control terminals discovered through monitoring, the number of IoT botnet control terminals still accounts for more than 54.0%, and the number of DDoS attacks initiated by them also accounts for more than 50.0%. In the future, more IoT devices will be connected to the network. If its security cannot be improved, it will inevitably bring more difficulties to network security defense and governance [8].

There are many security risks in the Internet of Things. Take the Industrial Internet of Things as an example. In 2019, there was 7,325 industrial equipment exposed to the Internet, an increase of 21.7% compared to 2018. It involves 50 equipment types including PLC equipment, intelligent buildings, and data acquisition from 39 well-known domestic and foreign manufacturers such as Siemens, Weike Automation, Rockwell, etc., and the equipment with high-risk vulnerabilities accounted for about 35%. There are 2,249 networked monitoring and management systems exposed in key industries such as electricity, oil and gas, medical and health, coal, urban rail transit, an increase of 21.9% compared to 2018, including 709 in the medical and health industry, 653 in electricity, and 584 in oil and gas. 203 sets of coal and 100 sets of urban rail transit. The types involved include government supervision, enterprise management, enterprise production management, industrial cloud platforms, etc., among which there are systems with high-risk vulnerabilities such as information leakage, improper configuration, and cross-site request forgery It accounts for about 46.1%. The continuous expansion of exposure has caused the safe operation of IoT-based industrial control systems to face greater risks.

This article compares the concepts of IoT forensics and digital forensics, and summarizes the research status of IoT forensics. Through exploring the combination of blockchain technology and Internet of Things forensics, an Internet of Things forensics architecture based on blockchain evidence is proposed. The framework includes an open interface layer such as APP interaction and a data layer. The APP open interface includes various APP applications. The data layer includes an evidence analysis platform and a blockchain storage platform. Furthermore, an IoT forensics model including blockchain storage and supervision is proposed, which can ensure the traceability and tamper-proof of forensic data.

The rest of this article is organized as follows. The second part is the description of IoT forensics and digital forensics. The third section is the research status of IoT forensics. Section 3 is blockchain infrastructure and data structure. Section 4 proposes a blockchain-based IoT forensics model. Section 5 presents the conclusion of this study.

2   IoT Forensics and Digital Forensics

2.1   The Impact of IoT on Digital Forensics

The Internet of Things makes more and more devices "online", providing various smart services closely related to people's lives (such as smart cities, healthcare, and smart homes). Considering the influence of the basic characteristics of the Internet of Things on digital forensics, as shown in Fig. 1.

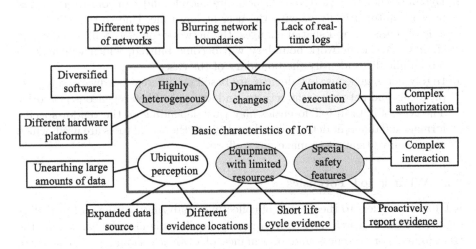

Fig. 1. The Impact of the Internet of Things on digital forensics.

1) Ubiquitous perception: With the help of massive sensors with various performances, the Internet of Things has universal ubiquitous perception capabilities, and people will leave traces on various IoT devices. On the other hand, the Internet of Things has produced more sources of evidence and subtle perceptions, which helps to reconstruct the background of the case, resulting in a large amount of forensic data that needs to be processed.

2) Devices with limited resources: Due to the low cost of most IoT devices and limited storage and computing resources, the data retained on the device has a short life cycle and is usually sent to the cloud or other data centers. Therefore, it is difficult to find a server or cloud to transfer evidence. On the other hand, these resource-constrained devices have greater security risks, and malicious users may easily modify or destroy logs and related data on the devices.

3) Special security features: The Internet of Things bridges the gap between the cyber world and the physical world, so security threats in the cyber world can bring security threats to the real world, and vice versa, which will shift or expand the impact and increase forensics complexity. In addition, due to the integration of the cyber world and the physical world, unsafe and unsafe operations on IoT devices may result in a real loss of services, or even loss of life, requiring forensics to reshape things and investigate security risks.

4) Automatic execution: There are real-time and automated interactions between IoT devices to promote collaboration between different IoT devices. The device can operate automatically based on information from the surrounding environment or other entities, thereby reducing human intervention. This series of interactive actions will make device traceability events extremely complicated.

5) Dynamic changes: Most IoT devices are mobile and can join or leave the network automatically or with the user at any time. Due to this characteristic of temporal and spatial changes, the network topology will dynamically change and the network boundary will become blurred, which will make it more difficult to identify the boundary of the case.

6) Highly heterogeneous: IoT devices are based on different hardware, software, protocols and network architectures, and are typical heterogeneous networks. The type of data in IoT forensics may vary depending on the vendor-specific format, and different detection and analysis methods and tools are used, which requires investigators to make more efforts.

2.2   What is IoT Forensics

IoT forensics refers to the process of collecting, analyzing, storing and providing digital evidence in IoT devices in a legally binding manner. In particular, the traceability, completeness and provenance of evidence should be maintained. However, resource-constrained IoT devices may struggle to achieve these goals. For example, insufficient memory may cause frequent data changes or overwrite. In addition, some devices may only be connected locally and lack the ability to quickly transfer evidence to researchers. Finally, although devices such as computers or servers can be confiscated by law enforcement agencies, it may not be that simple to identify all relevant IoT devices that are involved in the investigation of a particular case.

The rapid adoption of IoT has expanded the scope of digital evidence from PCs or laptops to a wide range of IoT devices (such as wearables and cars) and various cloud-based IoT services, which poses many challenges for researchers. Although the current forensic methods and tools are still proven to be useful in certain forensic stages of the Internet of Things, there is still an urgent need to update the current tools, procedures and regulations to deal with the unique characteristics of the Internet of Things [9]. However, protecting the entire IoT network is not easy. Unlike traditional computing devices that rely on traditional network security suites such as endpoint protection and firewalls, IoT communication is composed of countless protocols, device functions, and standards. Therefore, there is a high demand for IoT security and forensic tools [10].

In 2015, Shams Zawoad and Ragib Hasan formally gave the definition of IoT forensics for the first time [11], and improved Edewede Oriwoh's 1–2–3 regional method model, and for the first time proposed that IoT forensics are three digital forensics solutions A combination of: device-level forensics, network forensics, and cloud forensics [9] (see Fig. 2).

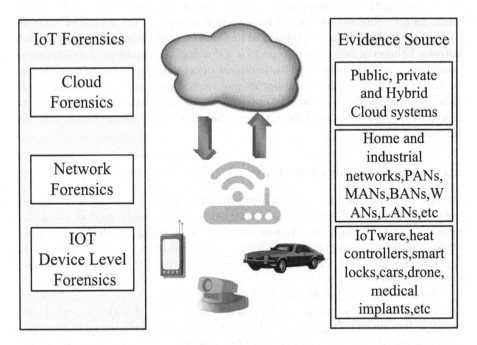

Fig. 2. Three-tier IoT forensics model.

3   Blockchain Infrastructure and Data Structure

3.1   The Birth and Development of Blockchain

In 2008, Satoshi Nakamoto first proposed a Bitcoin digital currency with blockchain as the underlying technology in his paper "Bitcoin: a peer-to-peer electronic cash system" [12]. The "mining" process was run to prove the Bitcoin theoretical system proposed in the paper. Bitcoin created a precedent for decentralized digital currency, which is a special type of distributed database. Through the association between the mining incentive mechanism and currency issuance, the consensus mechanism is then used to realize the confirmation of transactions and the safe transfer of Bitcoin on the database. Without the support of any third-party trusted organization, the exchange of currency between people who do not need to trust each other is realized. After the blockchain technology achieved great success in Bitcoin, Buterin proposed the concept of Ethereum on the basis of Bitcoin in December 2013 [13]. The author defines it as a program that not only inherits the digital currency function of Bitcoin, but also provides a Turing complete programming language to apply smart contracts to the blockchain system. The combination of smart contracts and blockchains, on the one hand, enables blockchains to use the programmability of smart contracts to simplify the complexity of distributed node operations. On the other hand, smart contracts can be effectively implemented in an untrusted environment with the help of the decentralized mechanism of blockchain. Compared with Bitcoin, Ethereum is designed to provide a development platform for distributed applications and decentralized autonomous organizations by introducing smart contracts in the blockchain and optimizing related protocols. The emergence of Ethereum has enabled blockchain applications to move from a single finance to a wider range of fields such as e-government, education, medical care, and the Internet of Things.

3.2   Blockchain Infrastructure

Architecture and implementation protocols are the two core elements of the network. The layered structure is a relational model widely used in computer networks, and the blockchain system also adopts a layered architecture. Figure 3 shows the 6-layer structure [14] adopted by Blockchain 2.0. From bottom to top, they are data layer, network layer, consensus layer, incentive layer, contract layer, and application layer.

The data layer is located at the lowest layer of the entire system structure and is responsible for storing the transaction data received within a period time into the data block being created. Then, the transaction data stored in the block is encapsulated through a specific hash function and Merkle tree data structure. And with the assistance of the upper-layer protocol, a new block with a timestamp conforming to the algorithm agreement is generated. Finally, it is linked to the main chain through the corresponding consensus mechanism. Blockchain is

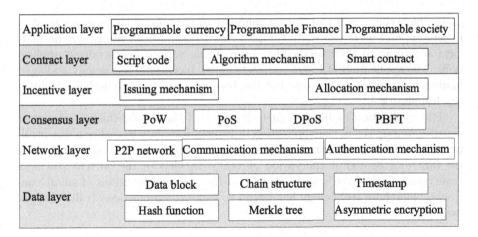

Fig. 3. Blockchain infrastructure.

an innovative application based on the Internet, and the organization of different nodes plays a key role in the overall performance of the blockchain system. The blockchain network layer adopts a completely decentralized P2P networking method that is not controlled by any authoritative node or restricted by a hierarchical model. In this way, the interconnection between various nodes in the blockchain system is realized. It provides a communication guarantee for the fast transmission and correctness verification of transaction data and new block creation information between nodes. It also provides a fair network environment for each node to participate in the competition for the accounting rights of the new block.

With the help of related consensus mechanisms, the consensus layer quickly reaches a consensus on the validity of transactions and data in a decentralized system involving highly dispersed nodes. Ensure the consistency and validity of the accounting of all nodes in the entire system. Among them, consistency means that the confirmed blocks in the main chain of the block saved in all nodes are the same, and validity means that the transaction data sent by each node can be stored in the new block. At the same time, the block data newly generated by the node can also be linked to the blockchain.

The incentive layer mainly stimulates each node in the network to participate in the generation and verification of new blocks in the blockchain by providing an incentive mechanism. It ensures the safe, effective and stable operation of the decentralized blockchain system. The operation of the incentive layer and the consensus layer have the same mechanism. Taking Bitcoin as an example, the consensus process is profitable. The purpose of each node participating in the consensus is to maximize its interests. The incentive is a currency issuance and distribution mechanism that has reached a consensus.

A smart contract is an agreement that uses a computer program to implement the content and execution process of the daily contract clauses deployed on the blockchain. A set of Turing complete programming languages is built in Ethereum, and users can write complex smart contracts on the Ethereum platform according to their needs, thereby realizing various decentralized applications. The application of smart contracts makes blockchain technology no longer limited to Bitcoin applications, but has become a universal underlying technology framework.

The application of blockchain technology in the public chain is the most mature. Among them, the application in Bitcoin is mainly to realize a decentralized digital encryption currency system. In Ethereum, in addition to inheriting the functions of digital encryption currency. In view of the current status of "everything is the Web", with the help of the powerful functions of smart contracts, blockchain technology has begun to support various decentralized applications [15].

3.3   Blockchain Data Block Structure

Although the data structures of different blockchain platforms are different in some details, the main framework is the same. Taking Bitcoin as an example, each block is composed of two parts, a block header and a block body [16]. Among them, the block header encapsulates the current version number, the hash of the previous block, the target difficulty value for the proof of the current block's workload, the random number used for the proof-of-work algorithm, and the transaction hash used to verify the block body. Information such as the Merkle root and the generation timestamp of the current block.

4   IoT Forensics Architecture Design

We propose a blockchain-based IoT forensics overall architecture which is divided into an application layer and a data layer, as shown in Fig. 4.

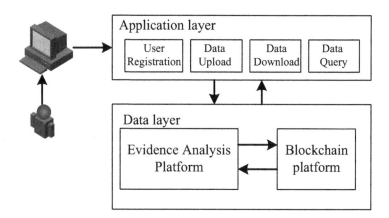

Fig. 4. Blockchain-based IoT Forensics overall Architecture.

The application layer includes modules such as user registration, data upload, data download, and data query which provides a friendly interface for the interaction between users and the system. This layer completes the data conversion between the blockchain and the user, and stores the digital assets submitted by the user on the blockchain after verification by the node, which is convenient for future users to query and use.

The data layer consists of two parts, a forensic analysis platform and a blockchain storage platform. After extracting the required data or real-time data, the forensic analysis platform selects specific equipment from the selected area, and the entire forensic process is restored to a more general digital forensic procedure. The procedure includes a chain of custody, laboratory analysis, results, certification, and filing and storage. The forensic analysis platform is compatible with payment, not only for traditional forensics models, but also for digital and application-specific forensics processes. It can be used for forensics for specific applications to ensure the importance of collecting evidence in the context of specific IoT applications.

The other part is the blockchain certification platform, which includes modules such as hash calculation, digital signature, blockchain storage, and supervision. The blockchain network of the data storage system is generated by the peer-to-peer network, and blocks are generated and verified. From the creation block of the evidence block chain to the newly generated block, the data storage system block chain contains all transaction data in the system.

5   Conclusions

This paper introduces the concept of IoT forensics by comparing the impact of IoT on digital forensics. It introduces the research results and trends of IoT forensics in recent years. The concept of blockchain is further introduced, and the basic framework and data structure of blockchain is introduced. Through exploring the combination of blockchain technology and Internet of Things forensics, an Internet of Things forensics architecture based on blockchain evidence is proposed. Furthermore, an IoT forensics model including blockchain storage and supervision is proposed, which can ensure the traceability and tamper-proof of forensic data.

Acknowledgments. This work is supported by open project of National and Local Joint Engineering Laboratory of Radio Frequency Integration and Micro-assembly Technology, Nanjing University of Posts and Telecommunications (KFJJ20200201), Talent Introduction Project of Jiangsu Police Institute (JSPI19GKZL407), Scientific Research Project of Jiangsu Police Institute (2110120030) and Jiangsu Province University Student Innovation Training Program Project (202010329034Y).

References

1. Zia, T.A., Liu, P., Han, W.: Application-specific digital forensics investigative model in Internet of Things (IoT). In: 12th International Conference on Availability. Reliability and Security, pp. 1–7. ACM, Reggio Calabria, Italy (2017)

2. Enabler, G.: Discover key trends and insights on disruptive technologies and IoT innovations. Market Pulse Report (2017)
3. Sharma, A.: Industrial dust collector market size, analysis and forecast to 2026. Market Study Report (2020)
4. Abie, H.: Cognitive cybersecurity for CPS-IoT enabled healthcare ecosystems. In: 13th International Symposium on Medical Information and Communication Technology (ISMICT), pp. 1–6. IEEE, Oslo, Norway (2019)
5. Internet Security Threat Report (ISTR). https://www.symantec.com/content/dam/symantec/docs/reports/istr-23-2018-en.pdf
6. Alabdulsalam, S., Schaefer, K., Kechadi, T., Le-Khac, N.A.: Internet of things forensics - challenges and a case study. IFIP Adv. Inf. Commun. Technol. **532**, 35–48 (2018). https://doi.org/10.1007/978-3-319-99277-8_3
7. Global Economic Crime and Fraud Survey (2018). https://www.pwc.com/gx/en/forensics/globaleconomic-crime-and-fraud-survey-2018.pdf
8. National Internet Emergency Center, Overview of my country's Internet network security situation in (2019)
9. Oriwoh, E., Jazani, D., Epiphaniou, G., Sant, P.: Internet of Things forensics: challenges and approaches. In: 9th IEEE International Conference on Collaborative Computing: Networking. Applications and Worksharing, pp. 608–615. IEEE, Austin, TX, USA (2013)
10. Chi, H., Aderibigbe, T., Granville, B.C.: A framework for IoT Data acquisition and forensics analysis. In: 2018 IEEE International Conference on Big Data, pp. 5142–5146. IEEE, Seattle, WA, USA (2019)
11. Zawoad, S., Hasan, R.: FAIoT: towards building a forensics aware eco system for the internet of things. IEEE International Conference on Services Computing. SCC, pp. 279–284. IEEE, NW Washington, DC, USA (2015)
12. Nakamoto, S.: Bitcoin: A peer-to-peer electronic cash system. https://bitcoin.org/bitcoin.pdf
13. Buterin, V.: next-generation smart contract and decentralized application platform (white paper). https://github.com/ethereum/wiki/wiki/White-Paper
14. Wang, S., Yuan, Y., Member, S.: An overview of smart contract: architecture, applications, and future trends. In: 2018 IEEE Intelligent Vehicles Symposium, pp. 108–113. IEEE, Changshu (2018)
15. Cai, W., Wang, Z., Ernst, J.: Decentralized applications: the blockchain-empowered software system. IEEE Access **6**, 53019–53033 (2018)
16. Zheng, Z., Xie, S., Dai, H.: An overview of blockchain technology:architecture, consensus, and future trends. In: 6th IEEE International Congress on Big Data, pp. 557–564. IEEE, Honolulu (2017)

Network Device Identification Based on MAC Boundary Inference

Xinmiao Guo, Xiangnan Li, Ruixiang Li, Xiuting Wang, and Xiangyang Luo[✉]

State Key Laboratory of Mathematical Engineering and Advanced Computing,
Zhengzhou 450000, China
luoxy_ieu@sina.com

Abstract. Network device is an important part of cyberspace, and accurate identification of network device is the basis of network management and security analysis. The current identification method based on MAC address is rely on converting MAC address and other information into fingerprints and MAC address distance to identify network device eventually. However, this identification method based on MAC address distance has high false alarm rate. A method for network device identification based on MAC boundary inference is proposed. Considering the device manufacturers' strategies of allocating MAC addresses in sequence for devices with same type, the relationship between the type and MAC address is built according known devices firstly. Then, MAC address aggregation rule is built to infer the MAC prefix for those known type, and the MAC boundary is obtained. Finally, the type of target network device is identified by matching target MAC with MAC prefix, or calculating the distance between target MAC with the MAC boundary. The experimental result in simulation dataset show that the identification method proposed in this paper is better than the identification method based on MAC address distance significantly, and then been less affected by the distribution of MACs of known devices. And the experimental result in Cisco device dataset show that our method increases the identification accuracy rate of the identification method based on MAC address distance by 11.9%.

Keywords: Network device identification · MAC boundary · Security assessment · Cyberspace situational awareness

1 Introduction

More and more devices around the world are connected to the Internet. According to IDC (Internet Data Center) estimates that by 2023 the global networking devices will reach 48.9 billion units [1]. The rapid increase in the number and types of devices in the network has led to the continuous expansion of the Internet, which has brought many security and management issues to the Internet and provided attackers with a wider range of attack surfaces. At present, many network devices in a low level of security protection. It is easy for attackers to obtain users' private information through some means, which may cause serious consequences. For example, starting in the evening of March 7, 2019 (local time), most areas including Caracas, the capital of Venezuela, were

© Springer Nature Switzerland AG 2021
X. Sun et al. (Eds.): ICAIS 2021, CCIS 1424, pp. 697–712, 2021.
https://doi.org/10.1007/978-3-030-78621-2_58

out of power for more than 24 h [2]. The power outage affected 20 states in Venezuela. Transportation, schools, hospitals, factories, airports, etc. have all been severely affected. This power outage was the longest and most widely affected area in Venezuela since 2012. The continuous occurrence of network security incidents has prompted us to think more deeply about maintaining and using network infrastructure.

However, the increasingly complex network devices and massive network devices have also brought more security challenges. Such as device vulnerabilities and configuration errors. Network devices identification uses network detection technology to obtain multiple types of data of devices in the target network, and realize the identification of physical devices and logical devices in the network through methods such as data fusion and data analysis. From a security perspective, the identification of massive devices in cyberspace is a prerequisite for risk assessment [3, 4] and vulnerability discovery [5], and it is important part of realize network asset assessment, network situation awareness [6, 7], network security assessment, and anomaly detection. At the same time, the identification of network devices can also reveal whether these devices have security threats, assess their security status, and security personnel can formulate more effective security strategies based on this. However, it is extremely important and challenging to determine the reliability of networked devices and devices type information.

Early research mainly focused on the identification of the operating system. Due to the differences in the internal implementation of different operating systems, the identification of the operating system was realized based on this difference. Some institutions have researched and launched several identification tools for operating systems, including Nmap [8], Xprobe [9], and P0f [10]. Z. Shamsi et al. [11] proposed to use the retransmission timeout delay of TCP packets as a characteristic value to realize the identification of operating system version information. T. Matsunaka et al. [12] studied the identification of operating systems from the unique domain name and the transmission cycle of Domain Name System (DNS) queries. S. V. Radhakrishnan [13] found that device hardware clock deviation caused differences in network behavior, and identified the device brand and model by analyzing the arrival interval of data packets sent by target traffic. T. Kohno et al. [14] proposed a network device identification method based on TCP protocol stack timestamp to estimate clock deviation. A. Cui et al. [15] proposed to use artificially extracted application layer protocol feature fields as fingerprints to identify embedded devices. Q. Li et al. [16] found that the monitoring device can be identified through the Graphic User Interface (GUI) of the monitoring device. At present, lots of industrial control systems are also connected to the Internet, and the core programmable logic controller is also exposed on the Internet. X. Pan et al. [17] analyzed the basic principles of PLC and summarized the current research on PLC protection.

The goal of this paper is to accurately identify the types of devices which connected to the Internet. Behind the work of this paper, there is an intuitive point of view, MAC address can uniquely identify a device. Therefore, MAC addresses can be used to identify devices. When manufacturers assign MAC addresses to each device, they usually allocate MAC addresses in a predictable manner, that is assign MAC addresses to each device in sequence within a certain range [18]. As we all know, the MAC address of a device is composed of 6 bytes. The first three bytes are codes assigned by the IEEE registry to different manufacturers to distinguish different manufacturers. The last three bytes are allocated to the devices by the manufacturer.

The main feature of the method in this paper is to judge the type of device based on the inferred MAC address boundary. However, there are two challenges in practice. One is that the standard document provided by IEEE shows the fuzzy mapping between each manufacturer and the OUI (Organizationally unique identifier), but this fuzzy mapping cannot be used as the basis for device identification, because only rough information about the device manufacturer can be obtained in OUI. The second is that under non-cooperative conditions, it is difficult to obtain the MAC address allocation strategy and address utilization of the manufacturers.

For these challenges, this paper proposes a feasible device type identification method, which realizes device type identification by studying the relationship between MAC address structure and device type. Manufacturers usually assign MAC addresses to devices in the order in the 2^{24} space [18]. This paper infers the MAC address boundary of a certain type of device from a large amount of data and uses this boundary as the basis for identifying the type of online network devices. This paper first studies the MAC address structure, and explores the abstract mapping relationship between the MAC address and the network device type, and realizes that the target device type can be determined by the distance between the MAC address to be identified and the boundary MAC address of the known type. This method can identify the type of network devices with high accuracy.

The main contributions of this work:

According to the decomposition of the MAC address structure, this paper discusses the relationship between the type of network device and the structure of the MAC address and proposes an identification method for inferring the type of network devices based on the MAC address boundary. This method can quickly infer the type of network devices based on the MAC address.

The experimental results in this paper show that when MAC addresses are not evenly distributed in a fixed interval, this method can effectively improve the accuracy of device identification, and the accuracy of network device type identification reaches 71.42%.

The rest of this paper is organized as follows: Sect. 2 introduces the related work of network device identification, Sect. 3 details the method of this paper, Sect. 4 provides the experiment and result from analysis of this paper, and finally the summary of Sect. 5 and the Prospects for future work.

2 Related Work

In recent years, network device identification has gradually become a research hotspot. Research methods often rely on scanning, detecting and other methods to obtain device data such as data packets [15], web page information [16] and physical identification [18, 19] of the device in the network, through the analysis of this data realize the identification of network device. N. Matthias et al. [19] captured the MAC address through MAC address broadcasting, and calculated the distance between the captured MAC address and the MAC address to be identified to realize device type identification. This method first builds a database of known device MAC addresses and device types based on known devices, and fuzzy matches the MAC address of the target device with the MAC address in the database, and then calculates the difference between the addresses to guess the correct device type and supplier information. The identification accuracy of this method depends on the type and number of known devices in the database. It may have a good identification effect when the amount of data is abundant. However, it is difficult to construct a database covering all devices and device types in practical applications.

In the literature [19], the author shows a possible MAC address allocation strategy. The allocation strategy shown in Fig. 1 is to allocate the address space under an OUI to three types. This distribution method is rare in actual production, because the address space that can be allocated in this case is 2^{24}. Because the address space that can be allocated in this case is 2^{24}, the number of devices of the same type produced by manufacturers rarely reaches this number.

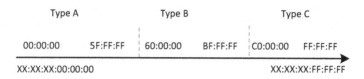

Fig. 1. A possible address block allocation strategy

J. Martin et al. [18] characterized the overall number and density of devices, the supplier's MAC address allocation strategy and utilization from the rich data set, and showed in the paper that the manufacturer assigns MAC addresses to devices according to certain strategies instead of randomly assigned. However, this also shows that the distribution strategy of the manufacturer is not single, but complex and diverse. A larger address block is allocated to a larger number of devices, and a smaller address block is allocated to a smaller number of devices, the same OUI may contain more types of device.

Based on the MAC address allocation strategy obtained in literature [18], this paper proposes a device type identification method based on MAC address boundary inference. First, the MAC address boundary of each type is inferred based on the relationship between the MAC address structure and the device type. Then, determine the device type by calculating and comparing the distance between the MAC address of the target device and the MAC address of the boundary. When the size of the data set is the same and the MAC addresses in the data set are not evenly distributed, the identification method based on MAC address boundary inference has better performance.

3   Proposed Method

In this section, this paper explains how to determine the MAC address boundary of the network devices type through the Classless Inter-Domain Routing, and realize the type inference of the target devices. This paper proposes a device type identification method based on MAC address boundary inference. Realizes the mapping from MAC address boundary to known device types and solves the problem of low identification accuracy in the existing MAC address-based identification methods.

3.1   Framework of Device Type Identification Principle

Figure 2 shows the overall architecture of network device type identification based on the minimum boundary MAC distance. The network device type identification method consists of two parts: the address superclass composition module and the device type determination module. This paper analyzes the MAC address allocation strategy of the manufacturers and maps the type information of known devices to the MAC address to form a data table with a mapping relationship. In the address superclass building block, this paper searches the MAC address boundary of the same device type from the data table. This paper first selects the same type of MAC address in the data table, and then automatically selects the same type of MAC address in the address set through the superclass algorithm, and forms the superclass of the device type, and finally obtains the MAC address prefix of the same type of device. In the device type discrimination module, this paper sets the boundary MAC address of each type as the standard value, and the distance between the MAC address of the target device and the boundary MAC address (the absolute value of the MAC address value subtracted) is used as the basis for the discrimination of the target device type.

This paper proposes a method to determine the target device type based on MAC boundary inference. This method has two advantages. First, the method in this paper can realize the inference of the target device type under non-cooperative conditions, manufacturers customize the MAC address allocation strategy and usage rate, though it is difficult to obtain MAC address allocation strategies under non-cooperative conditions. Secondly, the method in this paper can be extended to other devices (printers, cameras, etc.). At present, these devices are increasingly appearing in the network, bringing more threats to the network. But it is not realistic to cover all networked devices with training data. Therefore, this paper proposes a two-layer identification mechanism to make the method more scalable.

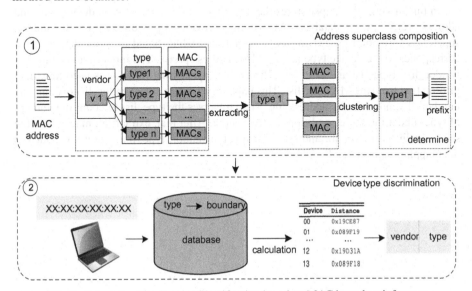

Fig. 2. Principle of device type identification based on MAC boundary inference

3.2 Address Superclass Composition

The paper [18] pointed out that the MAC address allocation strategy of the device is non-random, and the manufacturer will allocate consecutive address blocks under its OUI to each device model. In this module, according to the allocation strategy, this paper expresses the 48bit MAC address as (OUI, address prefix, address suffix) and formalized as { $<$OUI$>$, $<P>$, $<H>$ }. Among them, OUI is a 24bit organization unique identifier assigned to an organization or institution by the IEEE registry. This paper uses the address prefix to identify the device type, and OUI, address prefix, and address suffix form a 48bit MAC address.

This paper uses the principle of unclassified addressing to gather MAC address so that a network prefix represents multiple MAC addresses in a device type. This paper describes the process of forming a MAC address block consisting of OUI and contiguous MAC addresses with the same address prefix as constituting an address superclass, and an address block identifies a device type. The number of device types extracted in this paper is i, the number of MAC addresses in each type is n, and denote it as $type_i = [m_1, m_2, \ldots, m_n]$, where $i \in \{1, 2, \ldots, n\}$. First, set a threshold ϕ to determine whether two MAC addresses are of one type. As we all know, manufacturers produce device in batches, the number of devices of one type is generally not less than 2^{10}. That is the distance between MAC addresses is no more than 2^{10}, so the threshold is set to $\phi = 2^{10}$. If $|m_{n-1} - m_n| \leq \phi$, then the MAC addresses in each type are merged, merging rules is $S_c = m_{n-1} \oplus m_n$, where $c \in \{1, 2, \ldots, n\}$. Then, merge S_{c-1} and S_c. Since the length of the first merge result S_c is less than 24bit, first compare the sizes of S_{c-1} and S_c. If $S_{c-1} < S_c$, with 0 to complement S_{c-1} to 24bit, with 1 to complement S_c to 24 bit. Then according to the rule $Supernet = S_{c-1} \oplus S_c, c \in \{1, 2, \ldots, n\}$ to get the prefix length LL and the network prefix P, and finally get the address superclass composed of addresses with the same OUI and the same P.

In this module, this paper stores the mapping relationship between device type and address prefix into the database. Algorithm 1 provides a pseudo-code for the address superclass formation process to build a relational table (based on prior devices) that corresponds to the device type and its MAC address prefix. The input of algorithm 1 is vendor_list, type_list and mac_list. The database_construct function is used to extract information from the MAC file list. This paper first traverses the vendor_list to count the number of vendors in the address file. Then traverses the type_list to count the number of types under the same conditions as the vendor. After that, extracts all macs under the same conditions of vendor and type. Finally, the vendor: type: mac_ prefix is added to the mapping table at 1:1:1.

Algorithm 1: Address superclass composition strategy

Input: vendor_list, type_list, mac_list

Output: database

1: $\phi = 2^{10}$

2: **function** merge (n, m)

3: **if** $|m_{n-1} - m_n| \leq \phi$ **then**   /*Determine whether two addresses can be merged */

4:    $S_c = m_{n-1} \oplus m_n$

5: **else** no operation

6: **end if**

7: **return** S_c

8: **end function**

9: **function** merge_s (s, u)

10: **if** s, u $\neq$ 24bit **then**

11:    use 0 to complement u, s to 24bit

12:    supernet= $S_{c-1} \oplus S_c$

13: **else**

14:    supernet $= S_{c-1} \oplus S_c$

15: **end if**

16: **end function**

17: **function** database_construct (vendor, type_list, mac_list)

18: **for** each vendor $\in$ vendor_list **do**

19:    **for** each type $\in$ type_list **do**

20:       **for** n $\leq$ length (mac_list) **do**

21:          merge (mac[n-1], mac[n])   /* Call merge function */

22:          insert_into_list(S)

23:          merge_s (S [c-1], S [c])   /* Call merge_s function */

24:          insert_into_list (supernet)

25:       **end for**

26:       length $\leftarrow L$ /* Address prefix length */

27:       length = length (P)   /* Determine the prefix based on the prefix length*/

28:       vendor, type, P $\rightarrow$ database

29:    **end for**

30: **end for**

31: **end function**

3.3 Network Device Type Discrimination

In order to adapt the method in this paper to large-scale device type data sets and have better scalability. This paper proposes a two-layer identification mechanism. As shown in Fig. 3, in the first layer, if the MAC address to be identified matches the address prefix in the local database, the device type corresponding to the MAC address to be identified is output. If there is no match, it will be sent to the next layer, and the device type corresponding to the MAC address of the target device is determined by calculating and comparing the address distance with the device type boundary. When the MAC address of the target device does not match the device type prefix in the database, this paper uses the size of the MAC address distance as a measure to realize the type of the target device. The accuracy and scalability of the method are ensured through a two-layer recognition mechanism.

In the prefix matching layer, some device types can be easily and quickly determined by matching the MAC address of the target device with the type network prefix in the local database. For the MAC address of the target device that does not match the prefix, this paper determines the type by calculating and comparing the MAC address. In the address distance calculation layer. First, according to the network prefix P obtained in Sect. 3.2. The number of bit of P is less than 24bit at this time, so P is complemented by 0 to 24bit as the lower boundary B of the device type, and P is complemented by 1 to 24bit as the upper boundary B' of the device type. Based on the boundary B and B' of device type, this paper uses the address distance between the MAC address value of the target device and the boundary MAC address value to determine the device type. In this paper, the address distance D refers to the absolute value of the difference between the address values. The distance from the lower boundary is expressed as $D_i = |m_s - B_i|$, and the distance from the upper boundary is expressed as $D'_i = |m_s - B'_i|$, where D'_i represents the distance value calculated from the MAC address of the target device and the upper boundary of the type i, m_s refers to the MAC address value to be identified, then $D = \{D_1, D'_1, D_2, D'_2, \ldots, D_i, D'_i\}$. Manufacturers assign MAC addresses to various types of devices in consecutive blocks. This paper infers that adjacent MAC addresses have the same characteristic attributes. Therefore, this paper uses address distance D as the standard for judging device types and obtains the minimum $D_{\min}$ of address distance by comparing elements in D, the device type corresponding to $D_{\min}$ is the type of the target device.

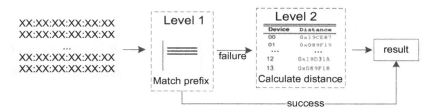

Fig. 3. Device type discrimination process

3.4 Method Performance Analysis

This section will mainly analyze the performance of the device type idesntification method based on MAC address boundary inference proposed in this paper. In Sect. 3.2, the format of the MAC address is specified as { <OUI>, <P>, <H> }. This section analyzes that under the same OUI and network prefix P, the impact on identification performance when the network suffix H of the MAC address is symmetrically distributed or non-symmetrically distributed on $[0, 2^H]$.

This paper first assumes that the sample is distributed symmetrically on $[0, 2^H]$. This paper takes the normal distribution as an example to analyze the identification performance of this method. Suppose that the MAC address X in the sample obeys a normal distribution with mean μ and variance σ^2, that is $X, \sim N(\mu, \sigma^2)$, and its probability density function is:

$$f(x) = \frac{1}{\sigma\sqrt{2\pi}} e^{\frac{-(x-\mu)^2}{2\sigma^2}}, \quad -\infty < x < +\infty \tag{1}$$

According to Eq. (1), the normal distribution diagram shown in Fig. 4(a) is obtained.

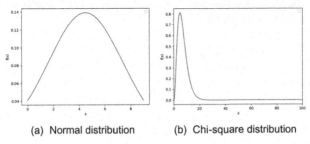

(a) Normal distribution   (b) Chi-square distribution

Fig. 4. Probability density function distribution diagram of two distributions

Figure 5(a)shows a schematic diagram of the address distance between the MAC of the target device and the smallest MAC when a sample of the two device types is symmetrically distributed in the sample interval. In this distribution, the average value represents the MAC address. In Fig. 5(a), R represents a MAC address in type a, d represents the distance between R and a point e in one type, and d' represents the distance between R and f. It can be seen from Fig. 5(a), that $d < d'$ is based on the MAC address distance identification method to judge R as type a. The method in this paper is to calculate the distance between R and the device type boundary L. It can be seen from Fig. 5(a) that the address distance calculated by our method is smaller. But the identification effects of the two methods are similar.

Secondly, suppose the sample is distributed asymmetrically on $[0, 2^H]$. Take the chi-square distribution as an example to analyze the performance of this method and the identification method based on MAC address distance. Suppose the MAC address suffix in the sample has n mutually independent random variables $m_1, m_2, \ldots, m_n$ in $[B, B']$, all of which obey the standard normal distribution. The MAC address X of a superclass is called obedience free Chi-square distribution with n degrees of freedom, where

$$X = \sum_{i=1}^{n} m_i^2 \tag{2}$$

The probability density function is:

$$f(x) = \frac{1}{2^{n/2}\Gamma(n/2)} e^{-x/2} x^{n/2-1}, x > 0 \tag{3}$$

According to Eq. (3), get the probability density map of Chi-square distribution shown in FIg. 4(b). Figure 5(b) shows a schematic diagram of the address distance between the MAC address of the target device and the MAC address in the database and the type boundary MAC address when the MAC address suffix of the two types are distributed asymmetrically. In Fig. 5(b), R represents a MAC address in type a, d and d' respectively represent the address distance between R and a point e in type a and a point f in type b. The identification method based on the MAC address distance judges R as type b. Figure 5(b) shows that R is inside the boundary of type a. Through the first-level identification mechanism of the method in this paper, it is very convenient to correctly determine the type of device corresponding to R.

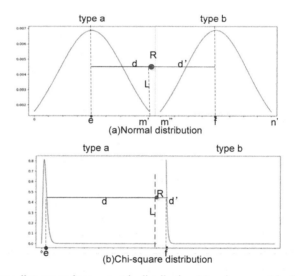

Fig. 5. Address distance under symmetric distribution (a) and asymmetric distribution (b)

From the above analysis, the identification method based on MAC address boundary inference proposed in this paper has the main advantage of higher identification accuracy when the MAC address is distributed asymmetrically in the address range compared to the identification method based on MAC address distance. The identification method based on the MAC address distance is to calculate the distance between the MAC address of the target device and the known device MAC address in the local database and compares the size of the distance value to realize the judgment of the target device type. However, it is difficult to cover all devices and device types in the local database, so the false alarm rate is high when the MAC addresses are unevenly distributed in the address range. The identification method proposed in this paper is to infer the type boundary based on the MAC address of the known device in the data set and then determine the target device type. In this method, firstly, calculates the distance between the MAC address of the target device and the MAC address of the type boundary, and then determines the minimum distance value through comparison, and finally, determines the type of the device. Compared with the identification method based on the MAC address distance, the identification accuracy can be effectively improved when the number of MAC addresses is relatively small.

4   Experiment

In order to evaluate the performance of the device type identification method proposed in Sect. 3, this section carries out simulation experiments and real data verification experiments. In the simulation experiment, the MAC address data set obtained by the MAC address generator is used, and the real data verification experiment is carried out on the MAC address data set of the Cisco device. The specific experimental process is detailed in Sect. 4.1 and 4.2.

4.1   Simulation Experiment

This section carries out simulation experiments to verify the performance of the method in this paper, and compares the identification method based on MAC address boundary inference proposed in this paper with the existing identification method based on MAC address distance.

Experimental Setup. This experiment measures the performance of this method based on the accuracy of device type identification. In this experiment, the address prefix length is set to 8. The MAC address generator is used to generate 3 sets of MAC addresses with normal distribution and chi-square distribution in the address range. Every group of data includes type a, type b, type c, type d and type e. Based on this data set, compared the identification effects of this method and the existing methods on different distributions. This experiment verifies the performance of this method on 3 data sets. In this experiment, 5% of the total number of MAC addresses in each type of address space is used for the experiment.

In order to ensure that the accuracy of the identification method based on the MAC address distance is similar to that in the literature [19], the test data of this experiment contains 7 types of device, of which 5 types of MAC address prefixes are related to type a, type b, and type c, type d and type e have the same address prefix, and the other two are unknown device types. A set of data in the data set is shown in Table 1.

Experimental Process and Result Analysis. In this paper, one of the 3 sets of normally distributed data is used for the experiment. The network prefixes P_a, P_b, P_c, P_d, P_e of type a, type b, type c, type d, type e, P_a, P_b, P_c, P_d, P_e and the number of network prefix bit l_a, l_b, l_c, l_d, l_e is obtained through the method of forming the address superclass in Sect. 3.2. Then add $24-l_i$ bit 0 after P_a, P_b, P_c, P_d, P_e to obtain the lower boundary B_i, complement $24-l_i$ bit 1 gets the upper boundary B_i', where $i \in \{a, b, c, d, e\}$. After that, determine whether the OUI of the target device's MAC address matches the OUI of known type. If the OUI matches, continues to determine whether the MAC address

Table 1. The composition of a set of data in the data set.

Set	Type	Scale
Set1	Type a	$2^{24-8} \times 5\% = 3276$
	Type b	$2^{24-8} \times 5\% = 3276$
	Type c	$2^{24-8} \times 5\% = 3276$
	Type d	$2^{24-8} \times 5\% = 3276$
	Type e	$2^{24-8} \times 5\% = 3276$

prefix matches P_a, P_b, P_c, P_d, P_e. If the target device MAC address prefix matches one of the known prefixes, the type of the target device can be inferred. If the OUI does not match, the second layer of device type discrimination is performed. At this layer, the address distance between the MAC address of the target device and the upper and lower boundaries of each type is calculated and compare the size of the obtained address distance value D_{min}. The device type corresponding to the minimum address distance value is the target device type.

In order to compare the performance of the method in this paper with the identification method based on MAC address distance. This paper conducts an experiment on the identification method based on the MAC address distance on the same data. Repeat the above experimental process for the other two data sets to obtain the comparison results shown in Table 2.

Table 2. Identification accuracy rate of 3 sets of data under symmetrical distribution.

Set	Set1	Set2	Set3
Our method	71.42%	71.42%	71.42%
Calculate MAC address distance	70.53%	71.27%	71.14%

Repeat the above experimental process under the Chi-square distribution data set and the identification accuracy of the three data sets is shown in Table 3.

Table 3. Identification accuracy rate of 3 sets of data under asymmetric distribution.

Method	Set1	Set2	Set3
Our method	71.42%	71.42%	71.42%
Calculate MAC address distance	66.74%	68.08%	67.66%

This paper has conducted experiments on the method in this paper and the method based on MAC address distance under two different distributions. The comparison results of the average accuracy rate are shown in Table 4.

Table 4. Identification accuracy rate under two different distributions.

Method	Normal	Chi-square
Our method	71.42%	71.42%
Calculate MAC address distance	70.98	67.49%

It can be seen from Table 2 that when the MAC address suffix is normally distributed in the sample interval, the identification accuracy of the method in this paper and the method based on the MAC address distance are not much different. However, it can be seen from Table 3 that when the MAC address suffix is Chi-squared in the sample interval, the method in this paper is significantly better than the identification method based on the MAC address distance. This is because when the MAC address suffix is Chi-squared in the sample interval, the MAC addresses in the sample are mainly concentrated at one end of the sample interval. Through the method in this paper, a relatively accurate address prefix and type boundary can be inferred according to the end with less MAC address distribution, and then a better identification effect can be achieved. However, the method based on the MAC address distance needs to infer the type of the MAC address in the sample, which is likely to cause misjudgment of the device type. Because the method in this paper realizes the identification of the device type by determining the MAC address prefix and the MAC address boundary. Determining the address prefix can determine the type boundary, so the recognition accuracy of the method in this experiment is the same.

Table 4 shows the average identification accuracy of the three sets of data under the two distributions of the method in this paper and the identification method based on MAC address distance. It can be seen from Table 4 that under the normal distribution, the method in this paper and the method based on MAC address distance have similar identification effects. However, under the Chi-square distribution, the identification accuracy of this method is much higher than the method based on MAC address distance.

4.2 Real Data Verification

This experiment uses Cisco devices to verify the method in this paper. They are Cisco servers and Cisco routers. This experiment selects two Cisco servers and four Cisco routers.

Experimental Setup. In order to verify the effectiveness of the method proposed in this paper, this experiment obtains the device type and its corresponding MAC address from the Cisco simulator. In this experiment, two types of devices are collected, server and router, and from the Cisco simulator The Server-PT and Meraki-Server under the server category, and Router-1941, ISR4321, Router-2620XM and Router-2901 under the router category are obtained on the page. The total number of MAC addresses in this experiment data set is 6000. In this experiment, the sample is divided into two parts of 9:1. The first part is used to infer the MAC address boundary corresponding to the device type, and the second part is used to test the identification performance of the method in this paper. The data set used in this experiment is shown in Table 5.

Table 5. Experimental data set.

	Server-PT	Meraki-Server	Router-1941	Router-ISR4321	Router-2620XM	Router-2901
train	900	900	900	900	900	900
test	100	100	100	100	100	100

Experimental Process and Result Analysis. In this experiment, first extract the device type and its MAC address from 6000 pieces of data, then determine the boundaries B_i and B'_i, in $i = \{SP, SM, R1940, RISR, R2620, R2901\}$, and address prefix $P_{SP}, P_{SM}, P_{R1941}, P_{RISR}, P_{R2620}, P_{R2901}$ of Route-2620XM, ISR4321, Router-620XM, Router-2901 server-PT and Meraki-server according to the method of forming the address superclass in Sect. 3.2. First, determine whether the MAC address prefix in the test sample matches the OUI of the MAC address in the database. If it matches, it matches with $P_{SP}, P_{SM}, P_{R1941}, P_{RISR}, P_{R2620}, P_{R2901}$. If it matches a certain type of address prefix, the device type of the target device is inferred. If the OUI does not match or the address prefix fails to match, then use the second layer to judgment the device type. At the second layer, calculate and compare the address distance between the MAC address of the target device and the upper and lower boundaries of each type, and compare the calculated address distance. If the address distance from a certain type boundary MAC is the smallest, the device type is inferred based on the minimum distance. Table 6 shows the comparison value of the identification accuracy between the method in this paper and the method based on MAC address distance. It can be seen form Table 6 that the method in this paper improves the recognition accuracy of existing methods by 11.9% on the same data set. Due to the MAC addresses obtained in the Cisco simulator are scattered on $[0, 2^{24}]$, the identification accuracy of the two methods is reduced compared to the simulation experiment.

Table. 6. Identification accuracy rate under two methods.

Method	Accuracy
Our method	19.04%
Calculate MAC address distance	17.01%

The above experimental results show that the method still has good identification performance in the actual environment. Through the evaluation of this method on two data sets, the identification performance of this method is better than the existing method based on MAC address distance.

5 Conclusion

Aiming at the problem of high false alarm rate in existing network device identification methods based on MAC address distance. This paper proposes a method to identify the device type by inferring the MAC address boundary corresponding to the device type and proves the effectiveness of the method through experiments. Through the identification experiment of two kinds of servers and four kinds of routers, the correlation between the device type and the MAC address structure is revealed, and the effectiveness of the method in this paper is proved. In addition, simulation experiments show that the accuracy of device identification is related to the distribution of MAC addresses suffix in the address range. When the MAC address suffix of a certain type of device are distributed symmetrically in the address range, the method in this paper and the existing identification methods based on MAC address distance have similar effects. However, under asymmetric distribution, the method in this paper has a higher identification accuracy rate.

In the future work we will focus on the large-scale identification method of network devices, realize the accurate identification of network devices and improve the security of the devices.

Acknowledgments. This work was supported by the National Natural Science Foundation of China (No. U1636219).

References

1. Gillivray, C.M., Reinsel, D.: IDC worldwide global data sphere IoT device and data forecast. IDC (2019)
2. Antiy Research Institute: Preliminary analysis and thinking enlightenment of Venezuela's massive blackout. Inf. Secur. Commun. Priv. (005), 28–39 (2019)
3. Feng, G.D., Zhang, Y., Zhang, Y.Q.: Overview of information security risk assessment. China Inst. Commun. **25**(7), 10–18 (2004)
4. Baig, Z., Zeadally, S.: Cyber-security risk assessment framework for critical infrastructures. Intell. Autom. Soft Comput. **25**(1), 121–129 (2019)
5. Antunes, J., Neves, N., Correia, M., Verissimo, P., Neves, R.: Vulnerability discovery with attack injection. IEEE Trans. Softw. Eng. **36**(3), 357–370 (2010)
6. Xi, R.R., Yun, X.C., Jin, S.Y., Zhang, Y.Z.: Research survey of network security situation awareness. Comput. Appl. **32**(01), 1–4 (2012)
7. Han, W., Tian, Z., Huang, Z., Zhong, L., Jia, Y.: System architecture and key technologies of network security situation awareness system YHSAS. Comput. Mater. Continua **59**(1), 167–180 (2019)
8. Medeiros, J.P.S.L., Brito, A.M., Pires, P.S.M.: A data mining based analysis of nmap operating system fingerprint database. In: Herrero, Á., Gastaldo, P., Zunino, R., Corchado, E. (eds.) Computational Intelligence in Security for Information Systems, vol. 63, pp. 1–8. Springer, Heidelberg (2009). https://doi.org/10.1007/978-3-642-04091-7_1
9. Yarochkin, F.V., Arkin, O., Kydyraliev, M.: Xprobe2++: low volume remote network information gathering tool. In: 2009 IEEE/IFIP International Conference on Dependable Systems & Networks, Lisbon, Portugal, pp. 205–210 (2009)
10. Beverly, R.: A robust classifier for passive TCP/IP fingerprinting. In: Barakat, C., Pratt, I. (eds.) PAM 2004. LNCS, vol. 3015, pp. 158–167. Springer, Heidelberg (2004). https://doi.org/10.1007/978-3-540-24668-8_16
11. Shamsi, Z., Nandwani, A., Leonard, D.: Hershel: single-packet OS fingerprinting. ACM SIGMETRICS Perform. Eval. Rev. **24**(4), 195–206 (2016)

12. Matsunaka, T., Yamada, A., Kubota, A.: Passive OS fingerprinting by DNS traffic analysis. In: 2013 IEEE Workshops of 27th International Conference on Advanced Information Networking and Applications, Barcelona, Spain, pp. 243–250 (2013)
13. Radhakrishnan, S.V., Uluagac, A.S., Beyah, R.: GTID: A technique for physical device and device type fingerprinting. IEEE Trans. Dependable Secure Comput. 12(5), 519–532 (2015)
14. Kohno, T., Broido, A., Claffy, K.C.: Remote physical device fingerprinting. IEEE Trans. Dependable Secure Comput. 2(2), 93–108 (2005)
15. Cui, A., Stolfo, S.J.: A quantitative analysis of the insecurity of embedded network devices: results of a wide-area scan. In: the 26th Annual Computer Security Applications Conference, Austin Texas, AT, USA, pp. 97–106 (2010)
16. Li, Q., Feng, X., Wang, H.: Automatically discovering surveillance devices in the cyberspace. In: the 8th ACM on Multimedia Systems Conference, New York, NY, USA, pp. 331–342 (2017)
17. Pan, X., Wang, Z., Sun, Y.: Review of plc security issues in industrial control system. J. Cyber Secur. 2(2), 69–83 (2020)
18. Martin, J., Rye, E., Beverly, R.: Decomposition of MAC address structure for granular device inference. In: Annual Computer Security Applications Conference, Los Angeles California, USA, pp. 78–88 (2016)
19. Niedermaier, M., Hanka, T., Plaga, S., von Bodisco, A., Merli, D.: Efficient passive ICS device discovery and identification by MAC address correlation. In: International Symposium for ICS & SCADA Cyber Security, Hamburg, Germany, pp. 21–30 (2018)

Providing Network-Based Datasets and Multi-dimensional Features for IoT Botnet Detection Research

Jie Yin[1,2], Xianda Wu[1,2(✉)], Junnan Wang[1,2], Kun Jia[1,2], Chaoge Liu[1,2], Yue Shi[4], and Xiang Cui[3]

[1] Institute of Information Engineering, Chinese Academy of Sciences, Beijing, China
wuxianda@iie.ac.cn
[2] School of Cyber Security, University of Chinese Academy of Sciences, Beijing, China
[3] Cyberspace Institute of Advanced Technology, Guangzhou University, Guangzhou, China
[4] China Academy of Information and Communications Technology, Beijing, China

Abstract. The vulnerabilities found in Internet of Things (IoT) devices have caused a large number of IoT devices being compromised and used as botnet platforms, which imposes a serious threat to the cyber security. In order to mitigate this threat, several network-based intrusion detection methods are proposed. While models and algorithms are important, so are the representative datasets and comprehensive feature vectors. In this paper, we firstly construct a botnet network traffic dataset by automatically monitoring some latest IoT botnet samples in our self-built experimental system. The dataset contains 17.5 GB network traffic which generated by 257 samples from 10 families. We can see the samples' entire lifecycle, including installation, propagation, scanning, DDoS attacks, C&C and other typical botnet behaviors. Then, through an in-depth analysis of the collected dataset, we propose a set of feature vectors for detecting. Since we are from the perspective of samples' entire lifecycle, our feature vectors provide more dimensions and is more expressive than existing works. To evaluate the effect of these feature vectors, we design a classification model based on machine learning, and run it on the constructed dataset and another public dataset. The experiment results demonstrate that the proposed feature vectors perform better on our dataset than on others, showing that the future IoT botnet detection model needs to face a longer botnet lifecycle and adopt more comprehensive feature vectors.

Keywords: Internet of Things · Botnet · Dataset · Feature vectors

1 Introduction

With the rapid development of the Internet, Internet of Things (IoT) plays an increasingly significant role in our daily activities. Unfortunately, IoT devices have traditionally lacked of proper control measures and proactive security management (e.g., usage of default passwords, no firmware updates, no access control policy), featuring them as high vulnerable and prone to be compromised devices. These features have been exploited to

© Springer Nature Switzerland AG 2021
X. Sun et al. (Eds.): ICAIS 2021, CCIS 1424, pp. 713–725, 2021.
https://doi.org/10.1007/978-3-030-78621-2_59

create large and powerful botnets by attackers, such as Mirai [1], Haijme [2], VPNFliter [3]. An IoT botnet [4] is a group of compromised IoT devices that can be controlled remotely by a botmaster to execute coordinated attacks. The lifecycle of a botnet such as Mirai are typically constructed in several distinct operational stages, namely propagation, C&C (Command and Control) communication and attack. By using the power of compromised IoT devices, IoT botnets can perpetrate a wide range of malicious attacks, from massive SPAM and phishing campaigns to distributed denial-of-service (DDoS). Most famously, the Mirai botnet [5] was used to launch a 623 Gbps DDoS attack [4] against krebsonsecurity.com, and a 1.2 Tbps attack [6] against Dyn DNS provider in 2016.

To mitigate the threats caused by IoT botnets, the most common countermeasures for defenders is to deploy network-based intrusion detection systems. Detection systems are built and trained using legitimate and malicious data to establish the normality or abnormality behavior patterns, then using machine learning algorithms to identify potential infected devices. The performance of detection systems based on machine learning algorithms heavily rely on data quality and extracted feature vectors. Therefore, a complete dataset and comprehensive feature vectors are key components for a high-performance effective IoT botnet detection system. While there have been in-depth studies into IoT botnet datasets [7, 11], as well as the features used by the detection models [12–14], there remain some drawbacks. First, most existing detection research only focus on some stage of a botnet lifecycle, making the datasets and the feature vectors incomplete, which not only can not accurately de-scribe the behavior pattern of botnets, but also affect the results of the detection model to some degree. Second, as malwares are constantly being updated, the datasets need to be continuously supplemented and improved.

To overcome limitations of existing studies, we focus on detecting botnets during its entire lifecycle, and present an in-depth analysis of IoT botnet traffic. In the dataset aspect, we construct an experimental environment that automatically captures botnet sample's traffic. By running more than 300 latest botnet samples, we construct a new realistic dataset including 257 botnets from 10 families which can truly reflect the behavior of IoT botnet in the wild. In the feature vectors aspect, we propose a new set of features which depict the traffic characteristics of the entire lifecycle of IoT botnets, including the propagation stage, the C&C stage and the attack stage. Our work is aimed at providing representative dataset and comprehensive features that could be useful for researchers to develop the detection model for IoT botnets. The main contributions of this paper are as follows:

- We collect some latest botnet samples, and construct a new realistic IoT botnet traffic dataset by running samples in a self-built lab environment.
- We propose a set of features including three dimensions that cover the network behavior characteristics of a botnet lifecycle.
- We evaluate the detection effect of the proposed features on our dataset by deploying machine learning algorithms, and it performs better than on some existing datasets, demonstrating that both representative datasets and comprehensive feature vectors are important to botnet detection models.

2 Related Work

In recent years, research on detection methods for IoT botnets has gradually studied. Some IoT botnet datasets and detection methods with different feature vectors were proposed.

Koroniotis et al. [7] deployed a testbed relying on some simulated IoT services and network platforms include normal and attacking virtual machines (VMs) with additional network devices such as a firewall, to generate a new realistic Bot-IoT dataset. By implementing different botnet scenarios, the dataset covers various types of attack traffic commonly used by botnets. To evaluate the reliability of the dataset and the performance of detection methods, authors proposed 45 features which indicated an attack flow, the attacks category and subcategory. This work focus on collecting IoT botnet traffic on diverse attack scenarios, and provides the baseline for allowing botnet identification across IoT-specific networks.

Alejandro et al. [8] provided a novel dataset with network data collected from a medium-sized IoT network architecture. To generate legitimate and malicious traffic, some virtual IoT devices were deployed using a Raspberry Pi which allows to emulate the behavior of an IoT device, and three IoT botnet malware were deployed in the IoT devices. The generated dataset focus on the first stages of a botnet deployment, including infection, propagation and C&C communication. Based on this dataset, a total of 100 network traffic statistical features were calculated within different time windows, and used as predictors/input for the machine learning models. Similarly, Bezerra et al. [9] also built an IoT experimental environment using a Raspberry Pi to generate a labelled dataset, but the dataset only covers the infection stage, including the device was not infected, and other ones when multiple botnet malware infected the device.

Meidan et al. [10] proposed and evaluated a novel IoT botnet detection method which extracts behavior snapshots of the network traffic and uses deep autoencoders to detect botnet attacks. The dataset used in this paper gathered from nine commercial IoT devices infected by authentic botnets from two families. To train the detection model, 115 traffic statistics features which capture behavioral snapshots are extracted from the packets' context. Different from [8, 9], this work focus on the attack stage, the propose is to detect compromised IoT devices which have been added to a botnet and have been used to launch attacks.

Different from these studies that only focus on a specific stage of the botnet lifecycle, we propose a set of new features which can cover the nearly all network characteristics of a botnet lifecycle, based on a new generated dataset. Our goal is to address the shortcomings by constructing a new botnet traffic dataset and extracting new detection feature vectors, thus providing a support for developing a high-performance IoT botnet detection model.

3 Experimental Environment and Dataset

This section presents the experimental environment developed to build a dataset, and the detail steps carried out to generate the dataset. The constructed dataset in this paper will be publicly available for the research community, and can be accessed at here [15].

Existing researches usually create a scenario to simulate the IoT botnet activities in local network. For that purpose, it is necessary to set up an isolated network, including the infected devices, C&C servers, real or virtual IoT devices and other network configurations, then capture the traffic generated by the bot. These requirements rely on very time-consuming tasks, multiple device components and complex network structure. Besides, to eliminate the risk of running the botnet sample, the source code is often modified to connect with the specific C&C server which is controlled by re-searchers. However, the C&C server and attack activities are often changed by the botmaster, so the captured traffic in this kind of experimental environment can only represent the behavior of the botnet during a certain period.

To construct datasets that can expose sample's actual behaviors in the wild, we design a real experimental environment allowing botnet samples to connect to real C&C servers. Because the architectures of IoT devices are various, such as MIPS, MIPSEL, ARM, we use QEMU [16] to deploy virtual hosting of several virtual computers on a single computer. QEMU is a free and open-source emulator that performs hardware virtualization, and it can provide a set of different hardware and device models for the machine, enabling it to run a variety of guest operating systems [17]. QEMU can also do CPU emulation for user-level processes, allowing applications compiled for one architecture to run on another.

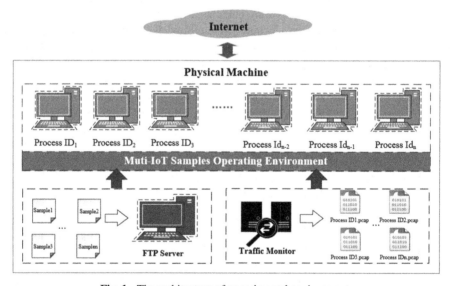

Fig. 1. The architecture of experimental environment.

The architecture of experimental environment is shown in Fig. 1. It consists of three components, namely multi-IoT samples operating environment, traffic monitor and FTP server. The multi-IoT samples operating environment is responsible for running IoT botnet samples. It can support the emulation of various architectures, including MIPS, PowerPC, ARM, RISC-V. The traffic monitor is responsible for capturing the traffic generated by the samples. In this paper, we use the QPA [18] tool as the traffic monitor.

QPA is an open source, real-time traffic analysis software which could capture network traffic generate by specific process. Based on the advantages of process capture, it can accurately determine the process of each package in real time. The FTP server is used to store malware samples. To improve the efficiency of the experiment, we develop a script automatically launch QEMU virtual machine, run botnet samples and capture network traffic.

We collected a set of fresh botnet samples which are captured from honeypots on March 2020. The total number of samples is more than 300, and shown as Table 1, 257 samples from 10 families exhibit network behavior. We executed these samples in the experimental environment and generated 17.5 GB pcap files containing only malicious traffic generated by them. This traffic became an important source for us to analyze IoT botnet network behaviors. Considering that training effective IoT anomaly detection methods rely on the acquisition of both malicious and normal behavioral traffic, we mixed the normal traffic comes from several popular public datasets, including Bot-IoT dataset [7], CTU-IoT-23 dataset [19].

Table 1. The malware families.

Family	Number of samples	Family	Number of samples
Agent	2	Generic	8
CoinMiner	1	Mayday	2
Ddostf	1	Mirai	131
Gafgyt	109	Xarcen	1
Ganiw	1	Xorddos	1

4 Feature Extraction

This section present the feature vectors extracted from the collected network traffic. Bots within a botnet typically exhibit the uniformity of traffic behavior and unique communication patterns. These botnet characteristics are well known and have been exploited by various researchers towards the development of detection systems. Based on the observation, most researches focus on analyzing the botnet network behavior at a certain stage. For example, [13] focus on detecting malicious activities, in particular attacks against DNS, HTTP, and MQTT protocols utilized in IoT networks, so the proposed statistical features are established from aggregating network flows with the potential analysis of MQTT, HTTP, and DNS protocols. In this case, the features are difficult to accurately describe the network behavior characteristics of the complete life cycle of a botnet, the proposed detection model can only be applied to datasets and scenarios containing some specific attacks.

To comprehensively depict the characteristics of botnet networks behavior, we propose a set of features from an in-depth analysis of the raw traffic, which covers the C&C

communication and attack activities of a botnet. The proposed features are based on the flows which are extracted from the captured pcap files, namely our constructed dataset. Flows contain header information about network connections between two endpoint devices. Typically, all transmitted network packets with the same source IP address, source port, destination IP address, destination port and transport protocol within a time window are aggregated into one flow. We divide these features into three groups: basic feature, time-based feature, and service-based feature.

Basic Feature: The basic feature contains flow statistics, packet statistics and the header information of raw packets. The group 'srcip', 'sport', 'dstip', 'dsport', 'proto' are considered network flow identifiers, as this information is capable of uniquely identifying a flow and assisting in the labeling process. The packet statistics assist the examination of the payload beside the headers of the packets. As a supplement of network behavior, we also extract some features of the TCP protocol, mainly containing TCP flags (e.g. SYN flag, ACK flag, etc.).

Time-based Feature: The time-based feature characterizes the regularity of flow behavior over time. The features contain a timestamp attribute like record start time, record last time, a continuous attribute like record total duration and numeric attributes like bytes per second.

Service-based Feature: The service-based feature comprises intrinsic information of the DNS and HTTP protocols which are acquired from the application layer of the TCP/IP model. These two protocols are often used in the C&C communication. Traditionally, malware finds the C&C server through querying the domain, and after establishing contact with C&C server, it begins to download the payload through the HTTP protocol. Therefore, we extract the DNS features from the common DNS queries and responses. The statistical features include the length and mean of the query and answer attributes. Similarly, the HTTP features are created from analyzing the HTTP requests and responses, and generating statistical features.

The detailed feature description is shown in Table 2, Table 3 and Table 4. These features are proposed based on the dataset which are generated in our experimental environment. They depict the botnet network behavior from multiple dimensions, and can be applied to detection models based on machine learning at various scenarios.

Table 2. Basic features.

#	Feature	Description
1	srcip	Source IP address
2	sport	Source port number
3	dstip	Destination IP address
4	dsport	Destination port number
5	proto	Transaction protocol
6	pktcount	Total count of packets
7	spkts	Source to destination packet count
8	dpkts	Destination to source packet count
9	sloss	Source packets retransmitted or dropped
10	dloss	Destination packets retransmitted or dropped
11–16	spktlength	Statistics on the packet size transmitted from source to destination packet (sum, max, min, avg, std and var)
17–22	dpktlength	Statistics on the packet size transmitted from destination to source packet (sum, max, min, mean, avg, std and var)
23–28	pktlength	Statistics on the packet size (sum, max, min, avg, std and var)
29–34	pktheader_length	Statistics on the packet header size (sum, max, min, avg, std and var)
35–40	spktheader_length	Statistics on the packet header size transmitted from source to destination packet (sum, max, min, avg, std and var)
41–46	dpktheader_length	Statistics on the packet header size transmitted from destination to source packet (sum, max, min, avg, std and var)
47	pktratio	The value of spkts divided by dpkts
48	pktlength_entropy	Entropy of packet length
49	spktlength_entropy	Entropy of source to destination packet length
50	dpktlength_entropy	Entropy of destination to source packet length
51	pktheader_entropy	Entropy of packet header length
52	spktheader_entropy	Entropy of the packet header size transmitted from source to destination packet
53	dpktheader_entropy	Entropy of the packet header size transmitted from destination to source packet
54–61	tcp_flag	TCP flags (FIN,SYN,RES,PSH,ACK,URG,ECE,CWR)
62–69	stcp_flag	TCP flags from source to destination (FIN, SYN, RES, PSH, ACK, URG, ECE, CWR)
70–77	dtcp_flag	TCP flags from destination to source (FIN, SYN, RES, PSH, ACK, URG, ECE, CWR)
79–81	swin	Source TCP window advertisement value(max, avg, std)
82–84	dwin	Destination TCP window advertisement value (max, avg, std)

Table 3. Time-based features.

#	Feature	Description
85	duration	Record total duration
86	bytes_second	Bytes per second
87	sbytes_second	Frequency of bytes transmitted from source to destination
88	dbytes_second	Frequency of bytes transmitted from destination to source
89	pkts_second	Packets per second
90	sbytes_second	Frequency of Packets transmitted from source to destination
91	dbytes_second	Frequency of Packets transmitted from destination to source
92–96	pkttimedistance	Statistics on time interval of all packets (sum, max, min, avg, std)
97–101	spkttimedistance	Statistics on time interval of source to destination packets (sum, max, min, avg, std)
102–106	dpkttimedistance	Statistics on time interval of destination to source packets (sum, max, min, avg, std)
107	sttl	The TTL of source to destination packets
108	dttl	The TTL of destination to source packets
109–111	sjitter	Statistics on jitter time from source to destination (max, min, avg)
111–113	djitter	Statistics on jitter time from destination to source (max, min, avg)

Table 4. Service-based features.

#	Feature	Description
114	Domain_count	Number of domain names requested
115	q_type	DNS Query type
116–118	len_qry	Length of DNS query packets (max, avg, std)
119–121	len_asn	Length of DNS response packets (max, avg, std)
122–123	ttls	Statistics on DNS query packet buffer time (max, std)
124	host_count	Total number of HTTP request hosts
125	len_host	Average length of the HTTP host header
126	url_count	The total number of HTTP request URLs
127	len_url	Average length of URL length

5 Evaluation

In this section, we present the design and results of several experiments conducted to evaluate the proposed features and generated dataset.

5.1 Detection Model

To distinguish botnet and benign traffic effectively, we design a detection model based on the proposed features, as shown in Fig. 2. The detection model consists of three classifiers, and each classifier is used to process the network flow data of the TCP/UDP, HTTP, DNS protocol, respectively. We first extract all flow information from the given pcap files, then parse the flows into relevant attribute vectors based on different protocols, and use corresponding classifier to identify malicious and benign traffic. As shown in Table 5, there are a total of 106,827 malicious flows in our test set. Of these flows, 76,315 are DNS flow, 512 are HTTP flow, and 30,000 are TCP/UDP flow. A total of 8,963 non-malicious flows are extracted from Bot-IoT dataset and CTU-IoT-23 dataset, including 4,509 DNS flows, 336 HTTP flows and 4,118 TCP/UDP flows.

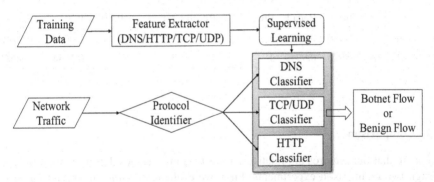

Fig. 2. Detection model.

We investigated different machine learning based classification techniques, finally selected the random forest classification algorithm for our classifiers. For each classifier, two performance metrics are reported: Precision and Recall. Precision (Pre) refer to the fraction of positive instances correctly classified among all the positive classified instances. Recall refer to the fraction of positive instances correctly classified among all the actual positive instances. All the performance metrics are bounded on the interval [0, 1]. If the classifiers show a performance close to 1 in both metrics it may be inferred that the data is suitable for machine learning-based IoT botnet detection, and can effectively distinguish between malicious traffic and legitimate traffic. To evaluate detection accuracy, we used the 5-fold cross validation. The results are listed in Table 6. As we can see, the detection model produce a very high precision and recall, 0.9996 and 0.9998 respectively in malicious flows, 0.9978 and 0.9949 respectively in non-malicious flows. We also observe that the results of the TCP/UDP classifier and the HTTP classifier both achieve a perfect value 1. On the one hand, it may be because the amount of HTTP traffic is too small, the difference between benign traffic and malicious traffic is obvious, so that it is easy to be detected; on the other hand, for the TCP/UDP classifier, it shows that the basic feature can well distinguish malicious traffic patterns from benign ones. Overall, these results indicate that the proposed feature vectors are effective in detecting IoT botnets.

Table 5. The number of flows in dataset.

Categories	DNS	HTTP	TCP/UDP	Total
Malicious flow	76,315	512	30,000	106,827
Non-malicious flow	4,509	336	4,118	4,509

Table 6. Classification results.

Categories	Total		TCP/UDP classifier		HTTP classifier		DNS classifier	
	Pre	Recall	Pre	Recall	Pre	Recall	Pre	Recall
Malicious	0.9996	0.9998	1	1	1	1	0.9994	0.9997
Non-malicious	0.9978	0.9949	1	1	1	1	0.9954	0.9897

5.2 Comparison

To prove that our features are relatively robust against various detection scenarios, we design two comparison experiments. First, we evaluate classification result based on Bot-IoT dataset using Bot-IoT features compare with ours. Bot-IoT dataset incorporates both normal IoT-related and other network traffic, along with various types of attack traffic commonly used by botnets. To enhance the predictive capabilities of classifiers, authors proposed 45 features which describe the patterns of several attacks. Based on the Bot-IoT dataset, we trained two classification models using our features and theirs, Table 7 lists the results of classification. We can see that the precision and recall using our features is higher than using theirs, which shows that the proposed features can more comprehensively represent the botnet network behavior pattern, effectively improve the predictive capabilities of classifiers. Second, we evaluate classification result using the Bot-IoT features on our dataset. As shown in Table 8, the result also achieves a very high precision and recall.

Both comparison results show that the proposed features can be applied to various datasets and detection scenarios, and achieve better performance. Moreover, our dataset is updated and more abundant, so we believe that the detection model trained with our feature vectors and dataset may be more powerful.

Table 7. Classification based on Bot-IoT dataset using different features.

Categories	Our features		Bot-IoT features	
	Pre	Recall	Pre	Recall
Malicious	0.9937	0.9951	0.9936	0.9941
Non-malicious	0.9768	0.9702	0.9718	0.9697

Table 8. Classification based on the proposed dataset using Bot-IoT features.

Categories	Total		TCP/UDP classifier		HTTP classifier		DNS classifier	
	Pre	Recall	Pre	Recall	Pre	Recall	Pre	Recall
Malicious	0.9933	0.9994	1	0.9962	1	0.9701	0.9995	0.9942
Non-malicious	0.9996	0.9950	0.9995	1	0.9806	1	0.9956	0.9920

5.3 Feature Importance

We also evaluated the feature importance on three classifiers based on the Random Forest algorithm. Feature importance gives a score for each feature of the dataset, the higher the score more important or relevant is the feature towards results. The TCP/UDP classifier used the basic feature and time-based feature, except the five tuple features, there are 108 features. The HTTP classifier used the basic feature, time-based feature, and HTTP feature, a total of 112 features, and the DNS classifier used 118 features. The sum of the scores of these features used by each classifier is 1. According to the algorithm, we got the top 10 features in each classifier as shown in Fig. 3, Fig. 4(a) and Fig. 4(b). For TCP/UDP classifier, we identified toe following best 10 features: sum_spktlength, avg_swin, max_swin, sum_pktlength, sum_spktheaderlen, sum_spktlength, pktcount, bytes_second, fwdpkts, slos. We can notice that the basic feature has higher weight than other features, a similar situation occurs in the HTTP classifier and the DNS classifier. In particular, the statistics features of packet header are more important in HTTP classifier. For DNS classifier, there are three features related to DNS protocol in top 10 features: the type of query, the max length of query and the average length of query. It shows that the domain query in IoT botnets is quite different from the normal domain query.

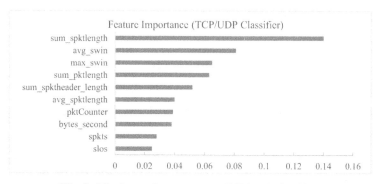

Fig. 3. The feature importance on TCP/UDP classifier.

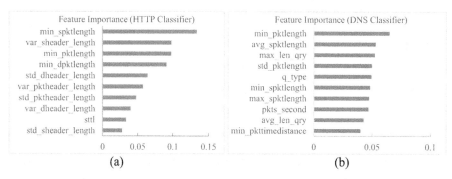

Fig. 4. The feature importance on HTTP classifier (a) and DNS classifier (b).

6   Conclusion

In this paper, we present an experimental environment based on QUME to automatically capture botnet samples' network traffic. By running 257 samples from 10 families, we construct an IoT botnet network traffic dataset, which covers all samples' network behaviors during their entire lifecycles, including propagate, C&C communication and attack stage. Through in-depth analysis of the botnet network behavior, a set of features are proposed. We divide these features into three groups, basic feature, time-based feature, and service-based feature which related to DNS and HTTP protocol. To measure the effect of these features, we design a detection model based on Random Forest algorithm. The results show that the proposed detection model using our extracted features perform well on both benign flows and malicious flows based on our dataset, with the precision and recall being above 99%. Besides, our features perform also well on both our and the other's dataset, especially in detecting malicious traffic. It is demonstrated that the proposed features have the potential to be applied to various detection scenarios. Finally, we compute feature importance on the generated dataset, and get the top 10 features. Although algorithms are the core of botnet detection model, the updated datasets and comprehensive feature vectors used for training and evaluation are important as well.

We hope that the dataset and the features provided in this paper can benefit researchers to develop and compare their detection methods.

Acknowledgement. This work is supported by the National Natural Science Foundation of China (No. 61902396), the Youth Innovation Promotion Association CAS (No. 2019163), the Strategic Priority Research Program of Chinese Academy of Sciences (No. XDC02040100), the Key Laboratory of Network Assessment Technology at Chinese Academy of Sciences and Beijing Key Laboratory of Network security and Protection Technology.

References

1. Antonakakis, M., April, T., Bailey, M., et al.: Understanding the mirai botnet. In: Proceedings of USENIX, USA, pp. 093–1110 (2017). Author, F.: Article title. Journal **2**(5), 99–110 (2016)
2. Herwig, S., Harvey, K., Hughey, G., et al.: Measurement and analysis of Hajime, a peer-to-peer IoT botnet. In: Proceedings of NDSS (2019)
3. Sicato, J.C.S., Sharma, P.K., Loia, V., et al.: VPNFilter malware analysis on cyber threat in smart home Network. Appl. Sci. **9**(13), 2763 (2019)
4. Bertino, E., Islam, N.: Botnets and internet of things security. Computer **50**(2), 76–79 (2017)
5. Akamai: Akamai's State of the Internet/Security, Q3 2016 Report (2016). https://www.aka mai.com/us/en/multimedia/documents/state-of-the-internet/q3-2016-state-of-the-internet-security-report.pdf
6. Dyn: Dyn analysis summary of Friday October 21 attack (2016). https://dyn.com/blog/dyn-analysis-summary-of-friday-october-21-attack/
7. Koroniotis, N., Moustafa, N., Sitnikova, E., et al.: Towards the development of realistic botnet dataset in the internet of things for network forensic analytics: bot-IoT dataset. Futur. Gener. Comput. Syst. **100**, 779–796 (2019)
8. Guerra-Manzanares, A., Medina-Galindo, J., Bahsi, H., et al.: MedBIoT: generation of an IoT botnet dataset in a medium-sized IoT network. In: Proceedings of ICISSP, pp. 207–218 (2020)
9. Bezerra, V.H., da Costa, V.G.T., Martins, R.A., et al.: Providing IoT host-based datasets for in-trusion detection research. In: Proceedings of SBC, pp.15–28 (2018)
10. Meidan, Y., Bohadana, M., Mathov, Y., et al.: N-baiot—network-based detection of iot botnet attacks using deep autoencoders. IEEE Pervasive Comput. **17**(3), 12–22 (2018)
11. Moustafa, N., Slay, J.: UNSW-NB15: a comprehensive data set for network intrusion detection systems (UNSW-NB15 network data set). In: Proceedings of MilCIS, pp. 1–6 (2015)
12. Sagirlar, G., Carminati, B., Ferrari, E.: AutoBotCatcher: blockchain-based P2P botnet detection for the Internet of things. In: Proceedings of 2018 IEEE 4th International Conference on Collaboration and Internet Computing (CIC), pp. 1–8 (2018)
13. Moustafa, N., Turnbull, B., Choo, K.K.R.: An ensemble intrusion detection technique based on proposed statistical flow features for protecting network traffic of internet of things. IEEE Internet Things J. **6**(3), 4815–4830 (2018)
14. McDermot, C.D., Majdani, F., Petrovski, A.V.: Botnet detection in the internet of things using deep learning approaches. In: Proceedings of 2018 International Joint Conference on Neural Networks (IJCNN), pp. 1–8 (2018)
15. Our Dataset. https://pan.baidu.com/s/19gR-lqT6kGy1iKYqxo0Rrw. code:zr2t
16. QUME. https://www.qemu.org/
17. QUME Wiki. https://en.wikipedia.org/wiki/QEMU
18. QPA. http://www.l7dpi.com/
19. CTU-IoT-23 Dataset. https://www.stratosphereips.org/blog/2020/1/22/aposemat-iot-23-a-lab eled-dataset-with-malicious-and-benign-iot-network-traffic

The Cross-Domain Identity Authentication Scheme Has no Trusted Authentication Center in the Cloud Environment

Mingming Zhang[1], Jiaming Mao[1(✉)], Zaojian Dai[2], Yong Li[2], Mingxuan Zhang[1], Lei Fan[1], Liangjie Xu[1,2], Jun Hu[1,2], and Anqi Wang[1,2]

[1] Information and Telecommunication Branch, State Grid Jiangsu Electric Power Co. Ltd., Nanjing 210008, Jiangsu, China
[2] State Grid Key Laboratory of Information and Network Security, Institute of Information and Communication, Global Energy Interconnection Research Institute, Nanjing 210003, Jiangsu, China

Abstract. This paper analyzes the existing problems of cross-domain authentication models and proposes a new cross-domain authentication model because there is no trusted authentication center in the cloud environment. The model is based on the certificateless public-key cryptosystem. It takes advantage of the transformability of heavy signature; A resigned proxy is introduced between two different domains for identity transformation. The authentication work is mainly concentrated in the key generation center KA and Proxy in different domains to reduce information interaction and computation between users and cloud service providers. At the same time, this message's identity information is added to each request message of the user, and check the identification information in the received reply message to confirm whether it is a reply to the application message. This method can prevent malicious attacks and improve security. The results show that the scheme satisfies key security, message unforgeability, and communication information confidentiality.

Keywords: Cloud computing · Cross-domain authentication model · Proxy re-signature · Identity authentication · Information identifier first section

1 Introduction

With the popularization of cloud applications, more and more application services are built on the cloud. Various enterprises and users upload data files to the cloud server [1]. At present, various cloud services have shown a trend of integration. More and more cloud services are interconnected with cloud services in other domains, but cloud servers are not fully trusted [2–4]. There is an urgent need to study cross-domain identity authentication technology in the cloud environment given the flexible and diverse, complex deployment, and open characteristics of cloud computing. Cross-domain authentication theory involves the unified authentication mechanism, framework, security model,

© Springer Nature Switzerland AG 2021
X. Sun et al. (Eds.): ICAIS 2021, CCIS 1424, pp. 726–738, 2021.
https://doi.org/10.1007/978-3-030-78621-2_60

and protocol design [5]. Currently, the most widely used is the introduction of a cross-domain authentication intermediary as a trusted third party in the cross-domain access of the cloud environment. There is no need to establish a direct trust relationship between the inter-cloud applications that access each other. They establish indirect trust through a common authentication intermediary. Cloud application domains that support cross-domain access need to establish a trust relationship with the authentication intermediary in advance. Users who need cross-domain access must also register with the authentication intermediary in advance and obtain identity credentials the authentication intermediary can recognize [6]. When the user cross-domain access, the authentication intermediary will authenticate the cross-domain user and send the identity authentication information and resource access request information to the cloud application service provider. In this way, the user's cross-domain access authentication is realized, and the efficiency and flexibility of establishing cross-domain trust in the cloud environment are improved.

Among the mainstream identity authentication technologies, user name/password, one-time password, token and digital signature all provide limited flexibility for its identity verification system [7]. Binu et al. [8] proposed a cloud identity authentication based on digital certificates. It used multiple factors to strengthen user identity security in the authentication process. But multiple certificate verifications are required, which is cumbersome to calculate. Based on cloud cross-domain identity authentication, Literature [9] completed a two-way identity authentication between the user and the cloud service provider, but cannot perform cross-domain authentication between heterogeneous domains. Literature [10] designed an anonymous cross-domain authentication with high execution efficiency. Literature [11] proposed a cross-domain identity authentication based on proxy re-signature in the cloud environment. The user and the cloud service provider provide authenticity authentication based on the validity of the digital certificate and the authentication message's validity. However, the authentication process needs to store many certificates and perform multiple verifications, which is complicated to calculate. The application of blockchain technology in the field of identity authentication is gradually paid attention to. Its core advantage is decentralization, which overturns the traditional centralized system architecture [12, 13]. Literature [14] proposed a cross-domain authentication model based on blockchain, which used joint blockchain technology to build a decentralized network, used the root certificate authority as the verification node, and omitd the encryption and decryption process; Literature [15] proposed a key exchange protocol for certificateless cross-domain authentication in the cloud environment, which satisfies authentication between different clouds. The user's private key in the cloud is composed of a secret value selected by the user and part of the private key generated by the authentication server in the cloud, which completely guarantees the security of the user's private key. Cloud authentication server completes the user authentication computation, improves the protocol execution efficiency. Literature [16] designed an efficient heterogeneous cross-domain authentication based on proxy blind signatures in a cloud environment, and introduced a trusted certification center CA between clouds to give third-party agents proxy authority to perform blind signature operations. It improved authentication security, and completed efficient and secure cross-domain authentication between heterogeneous domains. However, the security of inter-cloud authentication centers cannot be guaranteed.

Based on the existing cross-domain security authentication model, this paper provides a cross-domain identity authentication scheme with no trusted authentication center in the cloud environment, aiming at the threats to the authentication center of cross-domain authentication under the cloud environment. Due to the widespread use of mobile communication devices, the massive computing resources and storage and software resource links in the cloud lead to network complexity; cross-domain authentication centers will face network attacks from all sides, resulting in user data leakage and privacy protection. According to the improved cross-domain authentication model, the signature of a message in one domain can be transformed into that of another domain by using the transformability of proxy re-signature, avoids complex certificate authentication process, increases identity security, real integrity, reduces the communication load of cloud authentication, and improves the operational efficiency of the system [17].

2 Technological Base

Certificateless public key cryptography [18, 19] was developed to overcome private key hosting in identity-based systems. Al-Riyami and Patersonin in 2003 proposed the concept. Compared with PKI based public-key cryptosystem, certificateless public-key cryptosystem and identity-based system do not need the public-key certificate. Simultaneously, the certificateless cryptography system eliminates the problem of private key hosting in identity-based systems. It can be said that certificateless public key cryptosystem combines the advantages of the above two cryptosystems and overcomes their disadvantages to some extent. It is a public-key cryptosystem with excellent performance and convenient application. In a certificateless public key cryptography system, there is still a trusted third party key generation center (KGC), which owns the master key of the system. The role of KGC is to compute part of the user's private key based on the user's identity and the system master key and securely transmit to the user. After receiving part of his private key securely, the user then generates his complete private key using part of his private key and a secret value of his random choice. Public keys are calculated from their own secret values, identities, and system parameters and are released reliably. It can be decrypted and signed with its own private key. In such a system, KGC cannot know the private key of any user. Thus, the certificateless public key cryptography overcomes the problem of private key hosting in the identity-based system.

The proxy re-signature [20–22] was proposed by Blaze at the 1998 European Cryptography Conference. It was given a formalized security definition of its specification by Ateniese et al. The proxy uses the re-signature key to convert the proxy's signature into the proxy's signature for the same message, strong non-forgery proxy re-signature can effectively prevent the tampering of digital certificates. And it is convenient for cross-domain identity authentication.

3   Cross-Domain Identity Authentication Scheme

3.1   Cross-Domain Identity Authentication Trust Model

The scheme recreates the cross-domain authentication trust model shown in Fig. 1. Cross-domain authentication occurs between two different trust domains, each of which has a key issuing center KA. The key issuing center, trusted by all users in the domain, is responsible for completing identity authentication for users in the local region, legally saving user identity information, generating and issuing part of the private keys, and solving the key escrowing problem. The interdomain resigning agent, the key transformation center, is responsible for transforming the signature of a message from one domain to another's signature, ensuring the information transfer while reducing the computation time and computation burden between domains. This model sets up two agents. P_1 is mainly used for the key conversion from trust domain 1 to trust domain 2, and P_2 is mainly used for the signature conversion from trust domain 2 to trust domain 1. When there are multiple user requests in trust domain 1, the ISP trust Domain 2 can complete the signature conversion through P_2. This model is mainly based on four participating entities (1) Key issuing Center KA: responsible for the identity authentication of all users in this domain (2) Proxy, the agent of inter-domain re-signature, by using the re-signature key between domains, the valid signature of one domain is transformed into the valid signature of another domain to realize cross-domain authentication and establish the trust relationship between different domains. (3) User U completes the local authentication through KA1 and realizes the cross-domain authentication through the key conversion to the proxy re-signature. (4) Through key issuing center KA2, information service provider ISP completes the identity authentication in this domain and provides reliable cloud resource information service for users.

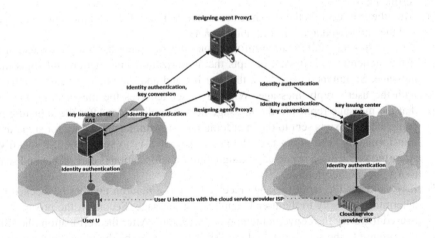

Fig. 1. Cross-domain identity authentication model

3.2   Basic Flow Chart of Cross-Domain Identity Authentication

To realize the authentication of cross-domain resource access for users in different domains without a trusted authentication center, this scheme restructures the basic flowchart of cross-domain authentication with re-signature, as shown in Fig. 2. The authentication of bi-directional cross-domain entity identity transfer is completed through the third-party trusted re-signature operation between clouds.

This model mainly takes user U cross-domain access information service provider ISP as an example to describe the authentication process.

(1)   The users in trust domains 1 and 2 have completed the identity authentication of their domains, respectively.

(2)   User U in trust domain 1 sends an access resource request to the key generation center KA_1 in this domain and sends proxy authorization information. KA_1 checks the servers' list for receipt of an application message to see if it is the first application. KA verifies the Proxy authorization information. After the verification, add a signature to the application access information through the private key and send it to the Proxy of re-signing between the clouds.

(3)   Proxy verifies the received application access message and uses the public key KA_1 to verify the identity of KA_1. After the verification, the interdomain re-signature key was used to convert the signature of KA_1 into KA_2's temporary signature of KA_2^* and sent it to KA_2 for verification.

(4)   After KA_2 receives the application access message, it uses its private key to decrypt the converted re-signature to verify the user's identity and check whether access is the resource access information. If all the verifications pass, the user U who made the request for the resource for the first time is put into the user list. The ISP is notified to send the request-reply message to the user U and the authorization certificate to KA_2.

(5)   After the ISP receives the resource access request, it will resend the reply message and the authorized agent information to KA_2.

(6) KA_2 verifies the authorization information after receiving the reply message, and if the authentication passes, accepts the authorization information and signs the message. Simultaneously, check the user list and add the random number agreed with the user's reply message. When the user receives the message, he knows that the message replies to the message he has applied for. After the signature is completed, Proxy is sent to the interdomain re-signature agent Proxy for signature transformation. The proxy uses the public key of KA_2 to verify the ISP identity. After the verification is passed, the signature transformation is carried out and sent to KA_1 in another domain.

(7) KA_1 validates the reply message received. First, a random number is checked to determine the reply to the user U application message. Secondly, the private key is used to verify the converted temporary signature. After the verification, the ISP is written into the server list, and the ISP is believed to be the trusted information provider. The reply message is sent to the user U.

(8)   Finally, cross-domain authentication of different domain entities is completed, session keys are calculated, and trust relationships are established.

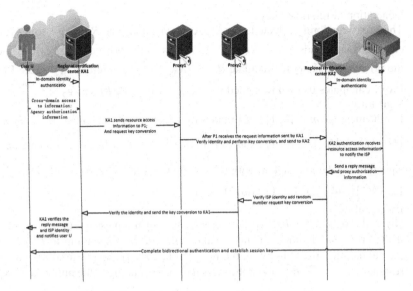

Fig. 2. Cross-domain identity authentication process

3.3 Scheme Described

For the convenience of description, two trusted domains are proposed in this paper: trusted domain 1 and trusted domain 2. KA_1 is the key issuing center in Trusted field 1, KA_2 is the key issuing center in trusted field 2, Proxy is a re-signed key agent responsible for key conversion between two domains, $Proxy_1$ is responsible for key conversion and identity authentication from trust domain 1 to trust domain 2. $Proxy_2$ is responsible for key conversion and identity authentication from trust domain 2 to trust domain 1. U is any user in trust domain 1, and ISP is any cloud service provider in trust domain 2. Take U cross-domain access ISP as an example. Two-way authentication between the two identities is completed through proxy re-signature technology, and an independent CLC system is established for each trust domain.

System Set Up

(1) System parameter generation

Let G_1 and G_2 are prime number p-order cyclic groups, g is a generator of G_1, bilinear mapping e: $G_1 * G_2 \rightarrow G_2$, the symbol $\|$ identifies the join operation for the string, n_m and n_c represent the fixed length of the string, choose two hash functions that carry the collision $H_1 : \{0, 1\}^* \rightarrow \{0, 1\}^{n_m}$ and $H_2 : \{0, 1\}^* \rightarrow \{0, 1\}^{n_c}$, among them $n_m < P$, $n_c < P$, so that the output value of the hash function is a member of Z_P, choose three elements at random $g_2, g_3, g_4 \in G_1$, and randomly select n_m elements in G_1, $(u_1, u_2 \dots u_m)$ exposed system parameters $cp = (G_1, G_2, p, e, g, g_2, g_3, g_4, u, u_1, u_2 \dots u_m, H_1, H_2)$.

(2) Key generation

$a \in Z_p^*$ was randomly selected as the private key sk, and calculate the corresponding public key $pk = g^a$.

(3) Generation of re-signed key

The Proxy randomly selected $r_K \in Z_p^*$, calculate and send $R_K = g^{r_k}$ to KA_1; KA_1 calculates and sends $R_{k1} = R_K g_2^{sk_{KA1}}$ to KA_2 with the private key sk_{KA1}; KA_2 uses the private key sk_{KA2} to calculate $R_{k2} = R_K g_2^{sk_{KA2}}/R_{K1}$, return R_{k2} to the Proxy; Proxy calculates its own re-signed key $rk_{KA1 \to KA2} = R_K R_{K2} = g_2^{SK_{KA1} - SK_{KA2}}$.

(4) Signature

For the message $m \in \{0, 1\}^*$, KA randomly selects $s \in Z_p$, calculate $M = H_2(m) = (M_1, M_2 \ldots M_{n_m}) \in \{0, 1\}^{n_m}$, $\omega = u \prod_{i=1}^{n_m}(u_i)^{M_i}$ and $h = H_1(m||g^s)$, generates the signature for the message m with the private key $sk_{KA} = \alpha$, $\sigma_{KA} = \left(\sigma_{KA}', \sigma_{KA}'\right) = \left((g_2^{sk_{KA}})(\omega g_3^h)^s, g^s\right) = \left(g_2^\alpha(\omega g_3^h)^s, g^s\right)$.

(5) Re-signature

Given the public key PK_{KA1} and the signature of the message m, $\sigma_A = \sigma_A^1, \sigma_A^2$, if the proxy validation σ_A is not a valid signature corresponding to PK_{KA1}, then the validation fails; Otherwise, the resigned key $rk_{KA1 \to KA2}$ is used to generate a resigned $\sigma_B = \left(\sigma_B^1, \sigma_B^2\right)$ about the message corresponding to the public key PK_{KA2}.

Domain User Registration. User U randomly selects a secret value $r_u \in Z_q$, calculate the temporary identity of U, $TID_U = H_1(ID_U||r_U P)$, where ID_U is U's real identity, U sends an encrypted registration application message $\{ID_U, TID_U, P_U, r_U P\}_{P_{KA}}$ to the key generation center KA. KA decrypts the message with her private key X_K, verifies U's temporary identity TID_U in the security domain CLC, and determines the temporary identity's validity, $TID_U = ?H_1(ID_U||r_U P)$. If the verification is successful, the key generation center KA selects a random number $r_U \in Z_q$, calculates $R = r_{KA}P$, and reads the local timestamp T_{KA}, and the signature calculation is performed for U's temporary identity $\theta_U = X_K H_1(TID_U||T_U)$, KA computes part of the key $D = r_{KA} + \theta_U$, and save the message $\{ID_U, TID_U, P_U, r_U P, T_{KA}\}$ to the user registration list, also return message $\{D, R, P_{KA}\}$ to U. After user U receives the return message, verify the correctness of $DP = ?R + H_1(TID_U||T_{KA})P_{KA}$, partial key D is accepted if the authentication is successful, U computes the private key $xk_U = D + r_U$ and public keys $pk_U = x_U P$. The same ISP applies to the KA registration process in this domain as above.

Cross-Domain Identity Trust Authentication. According to the cross-domain proxy re-signed trust model, cross-domain identity authentication mainly realizes the efficient and secure authentication between different domain bidirectional entities through five stages: resource request, proxy key generation, proxy re-signature, proxy re-signature key conversion, and transformed identity authentication. Finally, the session key is calculated, and the trust chain of two-way entity information interaction is established.

(1) The information service provider verifies the identity of user U

① The first phase resource request

According to user registration, known user U to the real identity ID_U temporary identity TID_U and public-private key pair (xk_U, pk_U); User randomly selects parameters $a_U \in Z_q^*$, calculates session negotiation parameters $Y_U = a_U P$, also gets the local timestamp T_U, identification of this request π_1, π_2. The user sends cross-domain resource application access message $\{Y_U, T_U, Access, H_1(TID_U), pk_U, \pi_1, \pi_2\}_{P_{ISP}}$ to KA_1 and notifies KA_1 for cross-domain identity authentication.

② The second phase authorizes the agent operation

The key generation center KA_1 shall authorize the Proxy operation of the third-party re-signed Proxy to perform the legitimate Proxy resigning operation to increase the privacy of identity. After KA_1 receives the application access request from local user U, it first checks the server registration list to see if it is the first session application, or performs the re-cross domain operation. If it is the first time application, the user U will send the agent authorization information to the key generation center in this domain KA_1, KA_1 calculates the proxy authorization certificate $O_\omega = x_U H_2(\omega)$, ω is a public authorization document. Meanwhile, KA_1 signs the application message, use σ_{KA1} and pick a random number s, $t \in Z_P$, resign the message and update the timestamp to $T_{U2}:\{Y_U, T_{U2}, Access, H_1(TID_U), pk_U, \pi_1, \pi_2, O_\omega, \omega\}_{\sigma_{KA1}}$. Encryption is sent to the Proxy Proxy. Proxy decrypts this message using its own key to obtain the public authorization file, verify that equation $O_\omega P = x_U H_2(\omega)P = P_U H_2(\omega)$ is true. If the equation is true, it is verified. After verification, the agent authorization certificate is accepted, and the agent authorization is completed.

③ The third stage is the key conversion stage

After Proxy validation, it first checks the timestamp $T'_{U2}s$ fresh row, then uses the public key of KA_1 to check the legitimacy of the identity of KA_1. If the validation does not pass, the transformation process is terminated; otherwise, use the re-signed key $rk_{KA1 \to KA2} = R_K R_{K2} = g_2^{SK_{KA1} - SK_{KA2}}$ between KA_1 and KA_2 to convert the key from KA_1 in σ_{KA1} to KA_2 temporarily authenticated key KA_2^*, since the key distribution center of any domain is a trusted and reliable third-party authentication agency, the agent is not subject to a conspiratorial attack by the key distribution center. The proxy converted temporary key has certain timeliness and a concise period of validity, ensuring credibility and authority.

④ Resigning and validation phase

KA_2 received a cross-domain resource request for access: $\{Y_U, T_{U2}, Access, H_1(TID_U), pk_U, \pi_1, \pi_2\}_{KA_2^*}$. Firstly, the freshness of the T_{U2} the timestamp is checked, and the validity of the re-signed key is verified by using its own private key through the verification algorithm, that is, verify that the equation $\sigma_{KA2}^* = \left(\sigma_{KA2}^1, \sigma_{KA2}^2\right) = e(g_2, pk_{KA2})e\left(\omega g_3^h, \sigma_{KA1}\right)$ is true. If the equation is true, then accept U as a legitimate user. Then, judge whether access is resource access information; If valid, user U is added to the user registration list, and π_1, π_2 are added to the list together with the access request session identification. The resource access information is then sent to the ISP. The ISP is notified to send the resource request response information to user U, and KA_2 in this domain is requested for cross-domain authentication.

(2) User U verifies the identity of the information service provider ISP.

In the reply message from the ISP to the user, KA_2, after receiving the authentication, add the session request id with the user request message to the reply message. During the verification process, KA_1 can determine whether the reply message replies to its own request message based on the identification, preventing malicious tampering and identity attack. The rest of the validation process is similar to the user U validation process and is not repeated.

4 Correctness and Safety Performance Analysis

Based on the mathematical difficulty and the trusted authentication center, this scheme introduces a trusted agent to operate the re-signature by taking advantage of the re-signature characteristics. It completes the cross-domain identity authentication without the trusted authentication center in the cloud environment by implementing the signature transformation between two domains. The security analysis mainly illustrates the scheme's security by taking user U's access to the cloud service provider ISP as an example. The security analysis of the cloud service provider ISP's return visit to user U can also prove the security.

4.1 Correctness Analysis

KA_1's signature for the message is $\sigma_{KA1} = (\sigma_{KA1}^1, \sigma_{KA1}^2) = (g_2^\alpha (\omega g_3^h)^s, g_s)$, use the resigned key $rk_{KA1 \to KA2} = R_K R_{K2} = g_2^{SK_{KA1} - SK_{KA2}} = g_2^{\alpha - \beta}$, among them $SK_{KA_1} = \alpha$, $SK_{KA_2} = \beta$, the re-signature for the message is:

$$\sigma_{KA2}^* = \left(\sigma_{KA2}^1, \sigma_{KA2}^2\right) = \left(rk_{KA1 \to KA2}\sigma_{KA1}^1, \sigma_{KA2}^2\right) \tag{1}$$

$$= \left(g_2^{\beta - \alpha}\left(g_2^\alpha \left(\omega g_3^h\right)^s\right), g^s\right) \tag{2}$$

$$= \left(g_2^\beta \left(\omega g_3^h\right)^s, g^s\right) \tag{3}$$

From this equation, we get $e\big((\sigma_{KA2}^1), g\big) = e\left(g_2^{KA2}(\omega g_3^h)^s, g\right)$. By bilinear mapping, we can get:

$$\sigma_{KA2}^* = e\left(g_2, g^{KA2}\right)e\left(\omega g_3^h, g^s\right) \tag{4}$$

$$= e(g_2, PK_{KA2})e\left(\omega g_3^h, \sigma_{KA1}\right) \tag{5}$$

An equation was set up.

4.2 Safety Analysis

Unforgeability. Since the previous scheme has proposed the re-signature algorithm of certificateless proxy, it can not be forged under the standard model. The signature of this scheme is based on this algorithm so that the signature of this scheme can not be forged.

Key Security. Calculating the user's private key according to the user's public key $pk_U = \left(g^{x_U}, g_1^{x_U}\right)$ is equivalent to solving the discrete logarithm problem, so we know that $g, g^{x_U} \in G_1$ solves for $x_U \in Z_q$. Because the discrete logarithm problem is difficult in mathematics, the new scheme satisfies the communication key's security.

Confidentiality of Communication Messages. *KA* uses its own private key to encrypt the application message and adds the session random number. Proxy and *KA* in the two trusted domains have established trust relationships before the session. Therefore, the proxy center decrypts the information through the public key and sends it to the *KA* in another domain. *KA* ensures the confidentiality of the message while verifying the key's correctness, and verifies the correctness of the message by verifying the random number.

4.3 Performance Analysis

Based on the mathematical difficulty, this scheme introduces the trusted agent to operate the agent re-signature by taking advantage of the feature of re-signature to realize the user interactive identity authentication in the cloud environment of different CLC domains securely. As shown in Table 1, compared with the literature [11], this scheme adopts the re-signing agent to convert the signature. The literature [11] is mainly based on the PKI domain. Users and servers use the legitimacy of digital certificates and the validity of authentication messages to complete the authentication of both parties' identities. Authentication paths are complex, and institutions that require specialized certificate storage are vulnerable to attacks. As shown in Table 1, in the message application stage, the user of this scheme and ISP have completed the identity authentication in this domain first. The request information can be directly sent to KA in this domain, KA authentication request message and authorization certificate. Do two cross-domain certifications. In the cross-domain authentication stage, KA and Proxy have generated the re-signature key, so only the authenticity of the application message and user identity must be verified twice. After verification, the signature is converted to generate computation. Where E_t stands for run the exponential algorithm once, P_t stands for running a linear operation, E_{nc} stands for run encryption algorithm once, D_{nc} stands for running one decryption algorithm, V_{er} represents the verification of a signature algorithm. The same computational overhead and the number of validations are incurred in the reply phase of the message in the application phase, which is not repeated.

As shown in Table 2, compared with the efficient heterogeneous cross-domain authentication scheme based on blind signature in literature [14], this scheme has the blindness of identity. In the literature scheme[14], the signer in the cross-domain proxy blind signature cannot get any signer information through the blind factor. In this scheme, users' real information is hidden by a temporary identity before establishing an information relationship. The temporary identity timestamp is set short to meet certain security.

Table 1. Computational overhead comparison

Program	Application Message phase		Cross-domain certification phase		Message reply phase	
	Computational overhead	Number of verifications	Computational overhead	Number of verifications	Computational overhead	Number of verifications
Literature [11]	$Et+Enc+2Ver$	3	$6Et + Ver$	4	$Et+Enc+2Ver$	2
Literature [14]	$3Et+Enc+Ver$	3	$Enc + 2Dnc + Pa$	3	$3Et+Enc+Ver$	3
This paper	$Enc + Dnc + Ver$	2	$2Et + D_{nc} + 2Ver + Pa$	2	$Enc + Dnc + Ver$	2

In literature [14], cross-domain information interaction mainly focuses on users in different domains, bringing a certain amount of computation to users and servers and affecting the normal cross-domain information interaction. In this scheme, the establishment of a cross-domain trust relationship is mainly focused on KA between different domains, which reduces the amount of information interaction between users and servers.

Table 2. Safety performance comparison

Program	Identity blindness	Certification Center security	Trust relationship credibility
Literature [11]	NO	NO	LOW
Literature [14]	YES	NO	LOW
This paper	YES	YES	HIGH

5 Conclusion and Next Work

In this paper, a cross-domain authentication technology without a trusted authentication center is proposed in the cloud environment. The new scheme introduces a re-signature agent to carry out cross-domain authentication. The two domains that need to generate information interaction establish a trust relationship with the resigning agent to generate the resigning key before interaction, which saves the time generated in the user session and reduces the process of authentication between users. The analysis shows that this scheme can resist anonymous attacks and substitution attacks. Compared with the traditional CLC trust system, the new cross-domain identity authentication scheme presented in this paper retains the traditional CLC technology, and has higher computing performance and security, which is more suitable for the security requirements in the cloud environment. Next, we will examine cross-domain identity authentication in heterogeneous domains without a trusted authentication center.

Acknowledgment. This work is supported by the Science and Technology Project of State Grid Jiangsu Electric Power Co., Ltd. under Grant No. J2020068.

References

1. Jo, B., Piran, M.J., Lee, D., Suh, D.Y.: Efficient computation offloading in mobile cloud computing for video streaming over 5G. Comput. Mater. Continua **61**(2), 439–463 (2019)
2. Dizdarević, J., Carpio, F., Jukan, A.: A survey of communication protocols for internet of things and related challenges of fog and cloud computing integration. ACM Comput. Surv. (CSUR) **51**(6), 1–29 (2019)
3. Tran, H.Y., Hu, J.: Privacy-preserving big data analytics a comprehensive survey. J. Parallel Distrib. Comput. **134**, 207–218 (2019)
4. Alsmadi, D., Prybutok, V.: Sharing and storage behavior via cloud computing: Security and privacy in research and practice. Comput. Hum. Behav. **85**, 218–226 (2018)
5. Zhang, Y.Q., Li, X.F., Liu, X.F.: Overview of cloud computing environment security. J. Softw. **27**(6), 1328–1348 (2016)
6. Liu, Q., Gong, B., Ning, Z.H.: Research on CLPKC-IDPKC cross-domain identity authentication for IoT environment. Comput. Commun. **157**, 410–416 (2020)
7. Castiglione, A.: A blind signature-based approach for cross-domain authentication in the cloud environment. Int. J. Data Warehous. Min. (IJDWM) **12**(1), 34–48 (2017)
8. Binu, S., Misbahuddin, M., Raj, P.: A mobile based remote user authentication scheme without verifier table for cloud based services. In: Proceedings of the Third International Symposium on Women in Computing and Informatics, pp. 502–509. ACM, New York (2015)
9. Yang, X.D., An, F.I., Yang, P.: Cross-domain identity authentication scheme in cloud based on certificateless signature. Comput. Eng. **43**(11), 128–133 (2017)
10. Dong, Z., Zhang, L., Li, J.: Security enhanced anonymous remote user authentication and key agreement for cloud computing. In: Proceedings of the 17th International Conference on Computational Science and Engineering, pp. 1746–1751. IEEE, Chengdu (2014)
11. Yang, X.D., An, F.Y., Yang, P.: Cross-domain authentication scheme based on proxy re-signature in cloud environment. Chin. J. Comput. **42**(4), 756–771 (2019)
12. Bordel, B., Alcarria, R., Martín, D., Sánchez-Picot, Á.: Trust provision in the internet of things using transversal blockchain networks. Intell. Autom. Soft Comput. **25**(1), 155–170 (2019)
13. Nguyen, B.L., Lydia, E.L., Elhoseny, M., Pustokhina, I.V., Pustokhin, D.A.: Privacy preserving blockchain technique to achieve secure and reliable sharing of IoT data. Comput. Mater. Continua **65**(1), 87–107 (2020)
14. Wang, W., Hu, N., Liu, X.: BlockCAM: a blockchain-based cross-domain authentication model. In: 2018 IEEE Third International Conference on Data Science in Cyberspace (DSC), pp. 896–901. IEEE, Guangzhou (2018)
15. Zhang, X.L., Li, D.L.: Cross-domain authentication key exchange protocol based on certificateless in cloud computing environment. Comput. Sci. Appl. **8**(5), 591–600 (2018)
16. Jiang, Z.T., Xu, J.J.: Efficient heterogeneous cross-domain authentication scheme based on proxy blind signature in cloud environment. Comput. Sci. 1–16 (2020)
17. Che, B., Liu, L., Zhang, H.: KNEMAG: key node estimation mechanism based on attack graph for IOT security. J. Internet Things **2**(4), 145–162 (2020)
18. Lin, X.J., Sun, L., Qu, H.P.: An efficient RSA-based certificateless public key encryption scheme. Discrete Appl. Math. **241**, 39–47 (2018)
19. Jun, Z., Lin, C.L., Xian, Z., Ling, X., Wei, W.: Certificateless proxy re-encryption scheme for cloud computing security. Comput. Eng. **43**(8), 8–14 (2017)

20. Yang, X.D., Yang, P., Li, Y., Liu, T.T., Wang, C.F.: A message authentication scheme for VANET based on certificateless proxy re-signature. Comput. Eng. Sci. **40**(1), 40–44 (2018)
21. Fan, Z., Ou, H.W., Pei, T.: A certificateless proxy re-signature scheme based on lattice. J. Cryptol. Res. **7**(1), 15–25 (2020)
22. Ge, C., Xia, J., Fang, L.: Key-private identity-based proxy re-encryption. Comput. Mater. Continua **63**(2), 633–647 (2020)

A Caching Strategy Based on Content Popularity Level for NDN

Min Feng[1], Ru Li[1], Yong Hu[2], and Meiju Yu[1(✉)]

[1] College of Computer Science, Inner Mongolia University, Hohhot, China
csymj@imu.edu.cn
[2] North United Powerd CO. LTD, Fuzhou, China

Abstract. Named data network (NDN) replaces the original IP address with the content name, which solves the security, mobility and other problems exposed by the current TCP/IP network, and becomes a typical representative of the future network. All routers in NDN support the caching function, which can cache the passing content and provide content services for users. Users can obtain the content from the router nearby without going to the remote content server. The current default caching strategy of NDN is Leave Copy Everywhere (LCE) strategy. This strategy does not distinguish the popularity of contents and the importance of nodes, and caches all contents on all nodes without difference, resulting in a high content redundant data that wastes cache resources and causes the cache hit rate to be unsatisfactory. In response to above problems, this paper proposes an improved cache strategy, which fully considers the popularity of the content, divides the content into different popularity levels, and divides the router nodes according to the distance from the user, and proposes a cache matching algorithm, which matches the two levels and combines the degree of the node to determine the cache nodes to place the content on. A large number of simulation experiments show that compared with LCE strategy, the strategy improves the content hit rate, reduces the average hit hop, cache replacement frequency and throughput.

Keywords: NDN · Content popularity level · Content node level · Node centrality

1 Introduction

In recent years, with the rapid increase in the number of internet users, the requirement for the speed and ability of information transmission within the network have also become stricter. At present, the TCP/IP network bases on "host-to-host" transfers information through addressing, so there are many problems in security, mobility and multicast transmission [1, 2], and it doesn't satisfy the present situation. In response to these problems in TCP/IP network, the experts and scholars have proposed various solutions to develop a brand-new network to replace the existing network. Among them, Named Data Network (NDN) [3, 4] uses content itself as the dominant entity in the network, completely subvert the TCP/IP network structure and become a typical representative of future network.

© Springer Nature Switzerland AG 2021
X. Sun et al. (Eds.): ICAIS 2021, CCIS 1424, pp. 739–750, 2021.
https://doi.org/10.1007/978-3-030-78621-2_61

One of the great advantages of the NDN is that the content cached at a certain node can be requested by other nodes, so it is very important for the content of the network to determine which node to cache on. However, the existing caching strategies rarely consider the popularity of the content. The content is cached on a large number of nodes, which causes a large amount of information redundancy in the network. At the same time, due to the limited cache space, the content of a large number of nodes is constantly replaced, which affects the hit rate and replacement frequency of the content. Hence the quality of the caching strategy directly affects the performance of the network. And it is of great significance to research an effective caching strategy that can increase the cache hit rate in the network, reduce the replacement frequency and the content redundancy rate.

This paper mainly studies the caching strategy in NDN, and proposes a caching strategy based on content popularity. This strategy not only considers the distance between the routing node and the user in cache selection, but also considers the influence degree of the node in the network. Through the simulation experiment, it is proved that the strategy proposed in this paper can effectively increase the cache hit rate, reduce the average hit hop, the cache replacement frequency and the throughput.

The main contributions of this paper are as follows:

- To put forward the content popularity level algorithm. According to the number of requests for content to calculate the popularity level.
- To propose a caching strategy based on content popularity level. According to the matching of content popularity level and router importance level, and combining the degree of the node to determine where to cache the content.

The rest of this paper is structured as follows. The second part introduces the existing work on the NDN caching strategy. The third section introduces the proposed caching strategy. The fourth section describes the simulation model used for the evaluation and the evaluation results. The fifth section is devoted to the conclusion.

2   Related Work

In [5], the LCE strategy is the default caching strategy in NDN. When a user requests a content, and the requested content hits, the data packet carrying the content will be returned to the user along the interest packet forwarding path, and the content is cached on all routing nodes that it passes through. So there are many redundant copies of content in the network. When the size of the cache space is limited, a large number of contents in the cache space can be replaced multiple times. In [6], the LCD strategy is called the reserve and copy strategy. When a user requests content hits at a node, only the first routing node of the node downstream caches the content, and other routing nodes only forward the content without caching it. Compared with the LCE strategy, this strategy effectively reduces the existence of a large number of copies. If the user make multiple requests for the content, it will be cached at the downstream node each time to achieve the final cache close to the user. In [7], the MCD strategy is called delete and copy strategy, which is similar to the LCD strategy. When a user requests content hits at a node, the first routing node of the node downstream caches the content and the hit node will delete the cache record. Compared with the LCD strategy, the MCD strategy further reduces the redundant copies.

In [8], the author studied the large streaming media content in the network. Due to the large file size, most users only request the first part of the content. This article discusses the size of the content in the network and proposes a streaming media caching method based on the popularity of content block, which defines a content naming granularity for comparison, if the content size is larger than the content naming granularity, the content needs to be segmented into blocks, but if it is less than, it does not need to be segmented. Through the method based on the popularity of content block, it can be found that different blocks of a content have different popularity, so they are cached on different nodes. This method can effectively increase the cache hit rate, reduce request delay, and improve user experience. In [9], the author puts forward the GFcache strategy, which adapts to the situation of data corruption by considering the failure rate and failure frequency, realizes the fault information sharing among users, and reduces unnecessary data duplicate cache, so as to have a good hit rate. In [10], the author proposes a block-level popularity prediction caching strategy (PPC), which divides video files into blocks with fine-grained granularity, and analyzes the relationship between video blocks through user requests for video access. Using historical requests to predict the future popularity of blocks, and replacing the block with the lowest future popularity with the predicted block with the highest future popularity, this strategy effectively reduces user perception delay.

3 Method

3.1 Content Router Level

In this paper, the classification method of router level is with the help of the classification method in [11]. When a user requests content, the router node on the request path calculates the level according to the number of hops from the user. So, the level of the router closest to the user is 1, and the levels of other routers are 2, 3, 4, ..., N. The lower the level, the greater the number, 1 is the highest level, N is the lowest level. This method only classifies the nodes on the request path, and other nodes do not participate in the classification. So router levels can be recorded using hop-counts. When the routing nodes increase or decrease in the network, because this dynamic method does not need to know the routing node information in advance, compared with the static rank assignment method, this method will not be affected by the change of routing nodes.

3.2 Content Popularity Level

In this paper, the content popularity is divided into five levels, as shown in Table 1 below:

According to the content request table, sort the H contents into 1, 2, 3, ..., h, ..., H by the number of requests. The popularity level j of the content can be calculated by formula (1).

$$j = \lceil h * 5/H \rceil \quad (j = 1, 2, 3, 4, 5) \tag{1}$$

Table 1. Description of content popularity level

Number of levels	1	2	3	4	5
Level description	Most popular	Popular	General popular	Not popular	Least popular

3.3 Caching Strategy Based on Content Popularity in NDN

According to the introduction of the previous two sections, the content router level and the content popularity level can be obtained. In order to connect the two, we will introduce cache matching value and degree centrality to implement the mapping between content router level and content popularity level in this section.

Match Cache Content By Level of Node. According to Sect. 3.1 and 3.2, the content popularity level is $j = \{1, 2, 3, 4, 5\}$, add a variable i to the interest packet to record the router level. To achieve an approximate match between the popularity level of the requested content and the router level, formula (2) and formula (3) are proposed to respectively indicate the position of the requested content popularity j in the entire content popularity level and the content router level i in the entire content router level. And to obtain the deviation between the two, it is calculated by the formula (4).

$$P_j = j/M \quad (j \in \{1, 2, 3, 4, 5\}) \tag{2}$$

$$R_i = i/N \quad (i \in \{1, 2, 3, ..., n\}) \tag{3}$$

$$a_i = \left| 1 - R_i/P_j \right| = |1 - (i * M)/(j * N)| \quad (j \in \{1, 2, 3, 4, 5\}, i \in \{1, 2, 3, ..., n\}) \tag{4}$$

Where M is the total number of content popularity levels, $M = 5$, N is the total number of router levels, it is equal to the total number of hops from the user to the hit node.

In order to measure whether the content popularity level matches the router level, we propose an threshold value as shown in formula (5):

$$\varepsilon = M/(j * N) \tag{5}$$

The threshold value is calculated at the hit node and a variable ε is added to the data packet to record the threshold value. During the return process, the path node calculates its own a_i and compares it with the threshold value ε. If it is less than or equal to the threshold value ε, the content is cached, otherwise it is not cached.

According to the above content description, when the user requests content a, the interest packet process of the content the user requests is shown in Fig. 1:

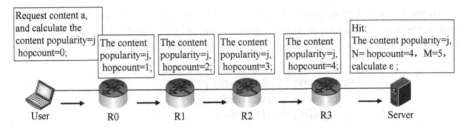

Fig. 1. The interest packet process

After hitting the content on the server side, the server calculates the threshold value ε and returns it through the data packet as shown in Fig. 2. When the data packet reaches a certain router, it judges whether its matching value is within the threshold range. If it is less than or equal to ε, the content is cached, otherwise, do not cache content.

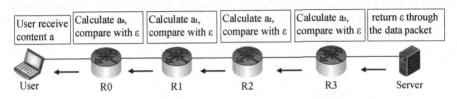

Fig. 2. The data packet process

Match Cache Content by Degree Centrality. The most influential nodes in the network are the network nodes with greater centrality. In terms of measuring the influence of nodes, there are traditional degree centrality (DC) [12], betweenness centrality (BC) [13] and closeness centrality (CC) [14]. This article will use the degree centrality (DC) method to measure the importance of node.

In order to reduce the distance and time of content hits, we choose to place content with a relatively high popularity level (popularity level ≤3) on the router with a high centrality. Here, we use node degree centrality to reflect the importance of the router. Degree centrality [12] is defined as the number of connections a node owns. Degree centrality measures the degree to which a node is connected to all other nodes in the network. The greater the degree of a node means the higher degree centrality of the node, and the more important the node is in the network.

For an undirected graph with n nodes, the degree centrality of node i is the total number of direct connections between i and other $n - 1$ nodes. In the interest packet of request content, add a variable DC to record the maximum degree centrality on the request path. When the user requests content, arrive at each router and judge whether its degree centrality is greater than the value DC in the interest packet. If it is greater than the value DC, replace it, otherwise do not replace.

$$if\,(DC_i > DC)$$
$$DC = DC_i;$$

In the data packet returning process, if the content requested by the user is relatively high-popularity content, each router compares the DC value in the data packet, and if it is equal, the content is cached, otherwise it is not cached.

Pseudo code 1：Data reply phase
1: for each (received data packet)
2:      if ($DC_i == DC$) then
3:          store content into CS
4:      else
5:          drop the data packet
6:      end if
7: end for

Hybrid Caching Method Based on Level Matching and Degree Centrality Matching. The above is a description of the two caching methods. In order to increase the hit rate and reduce the hit distance of the requested content in the network, we use the two caching methods in combination. The steps are shown in Fig. 3 and Fig. 4:

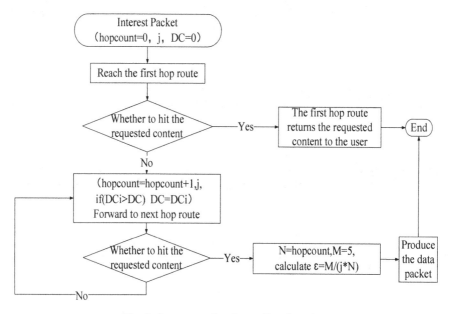

Fig. 3. Interest packet forwarding flowchart

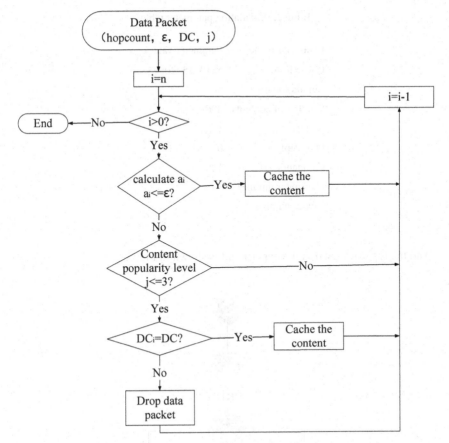

Fig. 4. Data packet return flow chart

4 Simulation

In the section, the ndnSIM [15] simulator in the NS-3 is used for experimental simulation to implement the caching strategy proposed in this article, and compare with the default LCE caching strategy in the NDN to observe the effect of the strategy.

4.1 Simulation Parameter Settings

The frequency of content request in the experiment follows a Zipf distribution, other experimental parameters are shown in Table 2:

Table 2. Simulation parameter table

Parameter name	Parameter values
Cache limit	5, 10, 15, 20, 25, 30
Simulation time	50
Number of contents	300
S of Zipf	1
Q of Zipf	0
Frequency	100
Consumer number	1
Router number	4

And the topology used in the experiment is shown in Fig. 5:

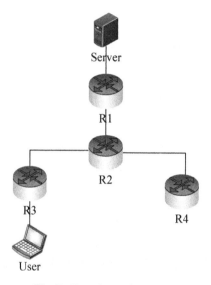

Fig. 5. Experimental topology

4.2   Simulation Comparison Index

In this experiment, we compare the following four indicators to analyze the performance of the strategy proposed in this paper:

(1)   Cache hit rate: When a user requests content, search for the content at all routing nodes on the path from the user to the content producer, and if found, it is called

hit. Cache hit rate is the ratio of the number of hit content to the total number of content requests.

(2) Average hop count: After the user request content is hit, it needs to go through a certain hop count to return to the user. This hop count is the response hop count. Average hop count is the ratio of the total number of response hops for all hit contents to the number of requested contents.

(3) Replacement frequency: When a node chooses to cache new content, and the node's cache space is full, the node swaps out the old content through the replacement strategy, and this behavior is replacement. Replacement frequency is the ratio of the total number of replacements of all routing nodes to the total number of routing nodes.

(4) Throughput: Throughput represents the amount of data passing through the network in a unit time. Throughput is the ratio of the total number of data packets that is transmitted to the running time.

4.3   Simulation Results and Analysis

In this simulation experiment, we set up 6 groups of comparative experiments. Because the cache size of the routing node has a great impact on the cache strategy, the larger the cache size of the routing node, the more cached content, and the higher the cache hit rate. Therefore, the independent variable of this experiment is selected as the cache size of the routing node, and its changes are 5, 10, 15, 20, 25, 30. Record the experiment results, and count the cache hit rate, average hop count, cache replacement frequency and throughput of this experiment. The results are displayed in a line chart or a histogram, and analyze the performance of the caching strategy proposed in this article.

Cache Hit Rate. As shown in Fig. 6, it shows the comparison of the performance of the cache hit rate between the strategy in this paper (CPL) and the LCE strategy when the cache size of the routing node changes. It can be seen from the figure that the cache hit rate of CPL strategy and the LCE strategy increases as the cache size increases. However, as shown in the figure, the cache hit rate of the CPL strategy has always been greater than that of the LCE. This shows that the CPL caching strategy proposed in this paper is

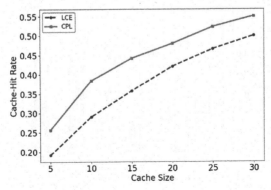

Fig. 6. Comparison of CPL and LCE cache hit rate with changes in cache size

effective in improving the cache hit rate in the NDN network, and satisfies the purpose of our design strategy.

Average Hop Count. As shown in Fig. 7, it shows the comparison of the performance of the average hop count between the strategy in this paper (CPL) and the LCE strategy when the cache size of the routing node changes. Because the energy consumption of content delivery is related to the average response hop count, the smaller the average response hop count, the lower the energy consumption. It can be seen from the figure that the average hop count of the CPL strategy has been lower than that of the LCE. This shows that the CPL caching strategy proposed in this paper can reduce network energy consumption compared with the LCE strategy.

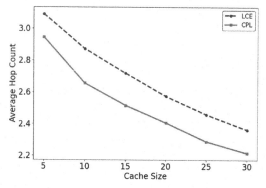

Fig. 7. Comparison of CPL and LCE average hop count with changes in cache size

Replacement Frequency. As shown in Fig. 8, it shows the comparison of the performance of replacement frequency between the strategy in this paper (CPL) and the LCE strategy when the cache size of the routing node changes. It can be seen from the figure that the replacement frequency of CPL strategy has been much lower than that of the

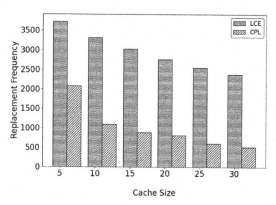

Fig. 8. Comparison of CPL and LCE replacement frequency with changes in cache size

LCE. This shows that the CPL strategy proposed in this paper can greatly reduce the energy consumption of network nodes.

Throughput. As shown in Fig. 9, it shows the comparison of the performance of throughput between the strategy in this paper (CPL) and the LCE strategy when the cache size of the routing node changes. It can be seen from the figure that the throughput of the CPL strategy has been lower than that of the LCE. This indicates that the CPL strategy proposed in this paper occupies a small network throughput, which effectively improves the performance of the network.

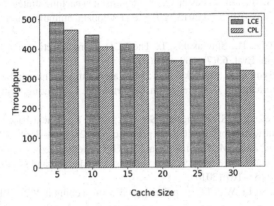

Fig. 9. Comparison of CPL and LCE throughput with changes in cache size

5 Conclusion

This paper considers the popularity of content, the level of routing node and the degree centrality of routing node, and proposed a caching strategy based on the matching of content popularity level, routing node level and degree centrality. Through the above simulation and comparison experiments with the LCE, it is proved that the caching strategy proposed in this paper (CPL) can effectively improve the cache hit rate, reduce the average hop count, the replacement frequency and the throughput. And it can be obtained that this strategy can improve the utilization of cache space resources and improve network performance.

Acknowledgment. This work is supported by the Inner Mongolia Natural Science Foundation of China under Grant No. 2018MS06024, the Research Project of Higher Education School of Inner Mongolia Autonomous Region under Grant NJZY18010, the National Natural Science Foundation of China under Grant No. 61862046 and the CERNET Innovation Project under Grant No. NGII20180626.

References

1. Xie, G., Zhang, Y., Li, Z., Sun, Y., Liu, Y.: A survey on future internet architecture. Chin. J. Comput. **35**(6), 1109 (2012)
2. Feldmann, A.: Internet clean-slate design: what and why? ACM SIGCOMM Comput. Commun. Rev. **37**(3), 59–64 (2007)
3. Zhang, L., et al.: Named data networking. ACM Sigcomm Comput. Commun. Rev. **44**(3), 66–73 (2014)
4. Ge, L., Peng, L., Xu, R.: Application and development of named data network architecture. Telecommun. Technol. **04**, 483–488 (2020)
5. Bernardini, C., Silverston, T., Festor, O.: A comparison of caching strategies for content centric networking. In: GLOBECOM 2015 - 2015 IEEE Global Communications Conference. IEEE (2015)
6. Laoutaris, N., Che, H., Stavrakakis, I.: The LCD interconnection of LRU caches and its analysis. Perform. Eval. **63**(7), 609–634 (2006)
7. Laoutaris, N., Syntila, S., Stavrakakis, I.: Meta algorithms for hierarchical Web caches. In: 2004 IEEE International Conference on Performance, Computing, and Communications. IEEE (2005)
8. Zeng, Y., Zhu, S., Gao, S., Zhang, H., Shen, S.: CSG: a segment-based network model in information centric networking. ICIC Express Lett. **7**(12), 3361–3368 (2013)
9. Deng, M., Liu, F., Zhao, M., Chen, Z., Xiao, N.: GFCache: a greedy failure cache considering failure recency and failure frequency for an erasure-coded storage system. Comput. Mater. Continua **58**(1), 153–167 (2019)
10. Zhang, Y., Tan, X., Li, W.: PPC: popularity prediction caching in ICN. IEEE Commun. Lett. 1 (2017)
11. Yu, M., Li, R., Liu, Y., Li, Y.: A caching strategy based on content popularity and router level for NDN. In: 2017 7th IEEE International Conference on Electronics Information and Emergency Communication (ICEIEC). IEEE (2017)
12. Sharma, D., Surolia, A.: Degree Centrality. Springer, New York (2013). https://doi.org/10.1007/978-1-4419-9863-7
13. Barthélemy, M.: Betweenness centrality in large complex networks. Eur. Phys. J. B **38**(2), 163–168 (2004)
14. Du, Y., Gao, C., Chen, X., Hu, Y., Sadiq, R., Deng, Y.: A new closeness centrality measure via effective distance in complex networks. Chaos **25**(3), 440–442 (2015)
15. Mastorakis, S., Afanasyev, A., Zhang, L.: On the evolution of ndnSIM: an open-source simulator for NDN experimentation. ACM SIGCOMM Comput. Commun. Rev. **47**(3), 19–33 (2017)

Author Index

Printed in the United States
by Baker & Taylor Publisher Services